TRAVEL COMPANION
ARGENTINA

TRAVEL COMPANION
ARGENTINA

GERRY LEITNER

© 1990 Gerry Leitner

First published in 1990 by by Travel Companion, PO Box 456, Mudgeeraba, Qld 4213, Australia

ISBN 0 9587498 0 9

The information in this book is as up-to-date as possible, but no responsibility for any loss, injury, or inconvenience sustained by the user of this book is accepted by the author or publisher.

This book is copyright. Apart from any fair dealing for the purpose of research or study, criticism, or review, no part may be reproduced by any process without written permission of Red White Red Publishing.

Edited by Michael Wyatt, Keyword Editorial Services, Studio 9, 426 Cleveland Street, Surry Hills, NSW 2010, Australia
Designed by U-Do Graphix, 4th floor, 197 Clarence Street, Sydney, NSW 2000, Australia
Photographs by the author
Maps drawn by Graham Keane, Cartodraft, 21/2 Freeman Place, Carlingford, NSW 2118, Australia
Cover design by Kathleen Phelps
Printed by Colorcraft Ltd, Room 502-3 Citicorp Centre, 18 Whitfield Road, Causeway Bay, Hong Kong

CONTENTS

Introduction
1 Introduction
16 How to use the *Travel Companion*
23 Color maps
24 Symbols
26 Glossary

City of Buenos Aires
31 City of Buenos Aires

Pampa Provinces
66 Buenos Aires
140 Córdoba
237 La Pampa
248 Santa Fé

Patagonia
270 Neuquén
317 Río Negro
357 Chubut
402 Santa Cruz
434 Tierra del Fuego

Cuyo Provinces
450 Mendoza
492 San Juan
509 San Luis

Contents

North-Western Provinces
- 528 Catamarca
- 559 La Rioja
- 583 Tucumán
- 610 Salta
- 644 Jujuy

Chaco Provinces
- 672 Formosa
- 683 Chaco
- 696 Santiago del Estero

Mesopotamia
- 722 Corrientes
- 751 Entre Ríos
- 787 Misiones

Index
- 823 Index

Acknowledgments

You will appreciate that a book of this scope could not have been written without the assistance of others.

I gratefully acknowledge the assistance afforded me during my researches in Argentina by the Provincial Tourist Offices and their *Casas de Turismo* in Buenos Aires.

In particular I wish to thank the Director and staff of Emitur in Posadas—Señora María Ema R de Lopez and Lic. Luis Spasiuk, also Señorita María Veronica Iglesias (Dirección de Turismo Territorial de Tierra de Fuego), and Señor Rolando Siluz, (Dirección de Turismo Chilecito). My thanks also to the Director and staff of the Dirección de Turismo de Neuquén for their detailed resumé of that province, the Director and staff of the Dirección de Turismo de Catamarca (in particular Señora Esther de Cuneo de Aguero and her husband Lic. Francisco Ramon de Aguero), and the Director and staff of the Consejo Provincial de Turismo de Jujuy (in particular Ingeniero Julio Ladislao Samoluk, Delegado Alterno, and Señor Luis E Basso).

Señor Sixto Vazquez Zuleta of the Museo Folklórico Regional de Humahuaca was a fount of knowledge on the cultural heritage of Jujuy and the Andean provinces of Argentina.

The Director and staff of the Secretaría de Desarrollo Subsecretaría de Turismo, Provincia de Santa Cruz (in particular Señor Eduardo Gabriel Aguirre; Señora Lucia E del Valle de Lombardich, Jefa División of the Turismo Municipalidad Puerto San Julián), and the Director and staff of the Dirección Provincial de Turismo de Salta, also provided me with valuable assistance.

The staff of the Asociación de Hoteles, Restauranes, y Afines in Salta helped me greatly with information about accommodation and restaurants. My thanks also go to Señorita Adriana Díaz Gomez of Salta, for her help in updating details about Jujuy's tourist facilities up to the last minute.

On the home front in Australia, I am indebted to Grahame Keane who revised and produced the maps for this book. My special thanks to Michael Wyatt who gently prodded and directed me into making a readable book from my original "ugly duckling".

Finally, I shall not forget the support and encouragement of my family who patiently awaited the completion of the *Travel Companion: Argentina*. My special thanks to daughter Gabriella who helped type the first draft.

Acknowledgments

You will appreciate that a book of this scope could not have been written without the assistance of others.

I gratefully acknowledge the assistance afforded me during my researches in Argentina by the Provincial Tourist Offices and their Crafts & Tourism in Buenos Aires.

Important I wish to thank the Director and staff of Boletín in Posadas – Señora María Luisa R de López Lindeke, Sra. Beaufil; also Señora María Verón Klekaila, Directora de Turismo Terrestre de Tierra de Fuego, and Señor Rolando Silva, Dirección de Turismo Chaco), Mujilants, also to the Director and staff of the Dirección de Turismo de Neuquén for their detailed resume of that province. The Director and staff of the Dirección de Turismo de Catamarca (in particular Señora Esther de Cuneo de Acuña and her husband Sr. Francisco Ramón de Agüero), and the Director and staff of the Consejo Provincial de Turismo de Jujuy (in particular Ingeniero Jubel Acosta Saroiuk, Pelegaud Alermo, an Señora Luisa Basso).

Señor Sixto Vazquez Zuleta of the Museo Folklórico Regional de Humahuaca was a fount of knowledge on the cultural heritage of Jujuy and the Andean provinces of Argentina.

The Director and staff of the Secretaría del Desarrollo Subsecretaría de Turismo, Provincia de Santa Cruz (in particular Señor Eduardo Gabriel Aguirre, Señor Luis T. del Valle de Lombardich, Jefa División of the Turismo Municipalidad Puerto San Julián) and the Director and Jefe of the Dirección Provincial de Turismo de Salta, also provided me with valuable assistance.

The staff of the Asociación del Hotel S. R. Betanzos y Asesor Sylla helped me greatly with information about accommodation and restaurants. My thanks also go to Señorita Adriana Díaz Gómez of Salta for her help in updating details about Jujuy - tourist facilities up to the last minute.

On the home front in Australia, I am indebted to Catherine Keane who revised and produced the maps for this book. My special thanks to Michael Wyatt who greatly produced and directed me into many a read, his book from my original "ugly duckling".

Finally, I shall not forget the support and encouragement of my family, who patiently awaited the completion of the Two Companion Journals. A special thanks to daughter Gabrielle who helped type the first draft.

viii

INTRODUCTION

Buenos Aires seemed a city of French architecture, full of Italians who spoke Spanish and thought they were English.

From *"Sweat of the Sun, Tears of the Moon"* by Jack Pizzey, published by the Australian Broadacasting Corporation

There is much, much more to Argentina than the urbane sophistication of Buenos Aires, the eighth largest city in the western world. Argentina includes a rich and varied culture, and a wealth of natural beauty which overseas visitors are just beginning to discover and appreciate.

For visitors to Buenos Aires with little time at their disposal, a trip further afield to the Cataratas del Iguazú (known in English as Iguazú Falls) or the Perito Moreno glacier is a must. For those tourists with more time, visits to the north-western provinces of Salta, Jujuy, Catamarca, and Tucumán are highly recommended.

For skiers, Mendoza, Neuquén, and Río Negro provinces contain many alpine resorts of world standard, such as Las Leñas, San Carlos de Bariloche (usually called just "Bariloche"), and Cerro Chapelco.

Nature lovers will find that Argentina has some of the best national parks in South America. Hikers will find many interesting trails in the lake districts around Bariloche, or on the Fitz Roy massif in Santa Cruz province, or around mighty Cerro Aconcagua in Mendoza. Visits to the provincial parks of Talampaya in La Rioja and Igualasto in San Juan are very worthwhile.

The old mission churches of the north-west are attracting growing numbers of tourists. The Jesuit remains of Misiones province (such as San Ignacio Miní near Posadas) are particularly awe-inspiring, and other ruins have still to be reclaimed from the dense undergrowth of the subtropical rain forests near the Brazilian border. Argentina is worth at least one visit ...

The country and its people

Modern Argentina is the child of Spain and Italy. Almost one-third of all Argentinians claim Italian descent. This Latin influence has found its way into every aspect of the country's lifestyle, including the cuisine. Only 15 per cent of

INTRODUCTION

the present population is from Indian stock, and this is mostly scattered through the provinces of Salta, Jujuy, Misiones, and Corrientes. Small pockets of Chaco Indians may still be found in Formosa and Chaco.

At present, Argentina's economy is deteriorating because most of its export earnings must be used to service foreign debts. For travelers with hard currency, traveling in Argentina today is like traveling in Italy or Spain in the 1950s.

Argentina has a good tourist infrastructure of roads, hotels, and bus services, and in contrast to other South American countries it is fairly safe for travelers. Some parts of Argentina such as Catamarca, La Rioja, San Juan, and Jujuy are almost unknown to overseas tourists.

Argentina is about one-third the size of the United States (2 777 000 sq km), and the second largest country in South America after Brazil. Situated in the southeast of the continent, Argentina shares its western border (the Andes) with Chile, and its northern borders with Bolivia and Paraguay, while Brazil and Uruguay are situated to the north-east. The eastern side, from the Río de la Plata to Tierra del Fuego in the south, fronts the South Atlantic Ocean.

In 1988, Argentina's population of 32 000 000 was concentrated in the larger urban centeres. Buenos Aires proper, which contains some 4 000 000 inhabitants (and greater Buenos Aires 8 000 000), is the largest city. This is still the official capital, although a new capital is planned on the Río Negro where Viedma and Carmen del Patagonés face each other. The next largest cities are Córdoba (1 000 000), Rosario (960 000), Mendoza (620 000), La Plata (580 000), and San Miguel de Tucumán (500 000).

Argentina includes a very wide range of climatic zones, from the tropical to the subantarctic. In the far north there are tropical regions in the provinces of Jujuy and Salta, while Misiones, Chaco, and Formosa are subtropical. The provinces between Córdoba and Río Negro are temperate, and Tierra del Fuego is subarctic.

The snowy peaks of the Andes extend from the equator to Antarctica, creating their own series of microclimates along the way. Argentina includes the highest mountain in South America (Cerro Aconcagua at 7 000 m), and this means that you can find cool regions in even the most northerly provinces of Argentina up next to the Bolivian border. Further south, montane glaciers are a striking natural feature of Santa Cruz province and Tierra del Fuego.

Spanish is the official language, but English, German, and Italian are widely spoken or understood. Argentine Spanish has been strongly influenced by Italian. Other languages preserved by ethnic communities include German, English, and

INTRODUCTION

Welsh (in some parts of Chubut). The Inca language Quechua is still spoken in some parts of Jujuy, Salta, Catamarca, Tucumán, and Santiago del Estero. The Guaraní language is still widely used in Misiones and Corrientes.

Major rivers of Argentina include the Río de la Plata, with its two large tributaries the Río Uruguay and Río Paraná, and the Río Negro further south which is used extensively for irrigation throughout its course.

The Río Paraná is navigable by large ships for most of the year as far as Corrientes. North of Corrientes it meets the Río Paraguay which is navigable for part of the year up to Asunción in Paraguay, and Puerto Suárez in Bolivia.

Major hydroelectric dams being built on the Alto Río Paraná include the huge Complejo Hidroeléctrico Yacyreta-Apipé near Ituzaingó. This project will create a 1600 sq km lake extending back to Posadas in Misiones province.

Perhaps the best-known natural feature in Argentina is the *pampas*. These are the large, flat grasslands extending east to west from the Atlantic Ocean to the Andean foothills, and from Córdoba and Santa Fé in the north down to the Río Negro. This region includes large *haciendas* and towns steeped in the *gaucho* tradition, reminiscent of the cowboys of North America. *Gauchos* have mixed Indian and Spanish ancestry and are noted for their free, gypsy–cowboy lifestyle. Argentines still have the romantic notion that the *gaucho* typifies the true Argentine lifestyle.

Cattle were initially brought to Argentina when the Spaniards first attempted to found Buenos Aires in 1536. After the Spanish retreated back to Asunción, the cattle they left behind proliferated in the lush *pampas* and grew into large herds. Cattle and wheat from the *pampas* became the basis of Argentina's wealth until the early 1950s.

Argentina's population is 85 per cent Caucasian and 15 per cent Indian or mixed Indian-Spanish, known as *mestizo*. The largest source for European migration has been Italy. Next come migrants of Spanish, German, and French origin.

Of the original Indian population, only three significant groups remain. The largest group is the Guaraní, found mostly in Corrientes and Misiones, then the Diaguitas of the north-west Andean *altiplano* in Catamarca, Jujuy, and Salta, followed by small groups of Pehuenches who live in reservations in Neuquén province. The *pampas* Indians were conquered during the Desert Campaign (*Campaña del Desierto*) of 1880. This campaign preceded the large-scale settlement of "pacified" areas by European migrants, in a process identical to the bloody demise of the north American plains Indian.

INTRODUCTION

Economic conditions

The unit of currency is the Austral (A). After the downfall of the Generals' junta in 1983, President Alfonsin's civilian administration created the "Austral" from a heavily-devalued Argentine Peso in an attempt to bring the economy back onto an even keel. However, further economic reforms have not been fully pursued, and recent rampant inflation has severely impoverished the Argentine middle class. The monthly inflation rate for July 1989 was 196%! The average per capita income for 1988 was US$1500, compared with US$2020 for Brazil and US$3230 for Venezuela.

History

Pre-Columbian (to 1492)

Traces of early settlement in Argentina have been found going back some 10 000 years. Rock paintings in Patagonia and other parts of the republic bear witness to the artistry of these aboriginal peoples, who were nomadic hunters and gatherers.

The first beginnings of permanent human settlements are found in the *chaco* region, and indicate that a lively interchange of ideas and goods took place between mountain tribes to the west and the local Indians. Cultural centers did develop in Catamarca and Tucumán, and many archeological sites here show that local Indians built complex agricultural communities. South American copper and bronze-age metallurgy may well have begun in northwestern Argentina.

However, the relative cultural development of the Argentine Indian tribes still varied greatly in the seventeenth century, and depended largely on a southward diffusion of ideas and techniques from the Tiahuanacan empire of Bolivia, and the Incan empire of Peru. It should be remembered that hunter-gatherers were still being systematically exterminated by European settlers in Tierra del Fuego around the turn of this century.

From around 1450 AD, the Peruvian Incas gradually moved southward into Argentina, subduing those mountain tribes they encountered, but never gaining complete control of the region.

Traces of Incan occupation may still be found along the Royal Road of the Incas which starts in southern Bolivia, traverses the province of Jujuy, and continues southwards along the *altiplano* through Salta, Catamarca, Tucumán, San Juan, and Mendoza. As a result, pockets of Quechua-speaking Indians are still found in the mountainous areas of northern Argentina.

Introduction

European discovery and conquest

The Spanish first set foot on Argentine soil in 1536 when Pedro de Mendoza arrived with a massive force of 1600 men and 14 ships to found the city of Buenos Aires on the banks of the Río de la Plata. After incessant attacks from the local Puelche Indians the settlement of the *pampas* was abandoned. Most settlers sailed back to Spain, but some marched north and founded the city of Asunción, the present-day capital of Paraguay. Argentina's first permanent European cities were founded from the north by Spanish settlers coming down from Alto Perú—Tucumán in 1565—and from Chile—Mendoza in 1561.

Buenos Aires was refounded from Asunción in 1580 by Juan de Garay. On his way down the Río Paraná he also founded Santa Fé, now Santa Fé La Vieja (Old Santa Fé).

Until the eighteenth century, Argentina remained little more than a backwater of the Spanish colonial empire. All trading goods had to be imported and exported through Lima in Peru and Panama. It was not until the Bourbons ruled Spain that Buenos Aires was made the capital of the Vice-Royalty of Río de la Plata, and allowed to develop into a major commercial and administrative centre, covering Paraguay, Uruguay, and parts of what is now southern Brazil.

During the Napoleonic wars in Europe, Spain's American colonies became independent for a brief period when they refused to recognize Napoleon's brother as the new king of Spain. The colonies had become more Spanish than Spain itself, and when the Bourbons were returned to the Spanish throne after Napoleon's defeat, a constitutional conference was held in Cadiz in Spain. This conference gave increased home rule to Spain's American colonies, but once Ferdinand was safely installed as king of Spain he unilaterally rescinded all constitutional reform.

The newly-liberated American colonies openly rebelled against Spain. They were helped by the British, Dutch, and French who hoped to gain territories of their own in South America. Argentina officially broke away from Spain on May 25, 1810, when a popularly-backed military junta took over from the Spanish viceroy. To this day May 25 is commemorated all over Argentina as Independence Day.

It took 16 more years to completely shake off Spanish rule. Some of the bloodiest battles for independence were fought in north-western Argentina near Tilcara in Jujuy, where royalist troops from Bolivia tried repeatedly to defeat the local armies.

The war produced such nationalist generals and heroes as Güemes, Peñalosa (who be-

Introduction

came known as "El Chacho"), and General Belgrano (who designed the Argentine flag), and international fighters such as General San Martín. San Martín later crossed the Andes into Chile with 16 000 men to defeat royalist troops at the Battle of Maipú. He also sailed with his troops to Peru where he defeated a royalist army outside Ayacucho. A magnificent memorial has been erected at Ayacucho listing the names of the opposing Generals and their high-ranking officers.

After independence had been achieved, there was little real social change at first. *Criollos*, Spanish settlers born in Argentinea, replaced civil servants from Spain, but life changed little for the local peoples who had helped overthrow the Spanish. Without the disciplined Spanish bureacracy, the newly independent states of South America fell into anarchy. The only centralized authority remained with the local army, and a series of army generals took control of Argentina as dictators. This period became known as the time of the *caudillos*, or strong leaders, and established the tradition whereby the Argentine army now believes it can intercede in national politics any time it perceives there is some internal or external security threat.

One of the first *caudillos* was the infamous dictator Manuel de Rosas who gained control in 1830 and ruled until 1851. Rosas was deposed by J J de Urquiza, the leading cattle baron of Entre Ríos and a former army general under Rosas. (It is said that Urquiza fathered over a hundred children—in some towns in Entre Ríos the predominant name of most of the population is Urquiza!)

By the late nineteenth century, the Argentine army's war against the Puelche Indians of the *pampas* and Patagonia had removed all resistance and opened these vast areas to a flood of migrants from Italy, Germany, Switzerland, and France. This period saw a great expansion of Argentina's agricultural economy. Argentina depended on the export of meat, wool, and hides to Europe (particularly England) until after World War I and imported most of its manufactured goods.

During World War II, Argentina began to develop its own manufacturing industry. In 1943 army officers staged a coup which was intended to break foreign domination of Argentina's emergent industries. This eventually brought Juan Perón and his charismatic first wife Evita to power. Until his death in 1974, Perón dominated Argentine politics, even during a period of exile in Spain. After Perón's death, Argentina plunged back into anarchy as the right-wing military took power and began waging an internal struggle against many left-wing orientated leaders. This so-called "Dirty War" only ended when General Gualtieri resigned after waging an unsuccessful war

Introduction

against Britain for control of the Falkland Islands (known in Argentina as the Islas Malvinas).

Raul Alfonsín became the first new civilian president and tried to stop Argentina's economic decline by instituting monetary reform. However, Alfonsin's reforms were frustrated by powerful groups within the army and wealthier classes, and he was replaced after the 1989 election by Carlos Menem, the leader of the opposition Justicialista party, which has developed from the popular Peronist movement.

Jesuit missions

During the seventeenth century, a network of Jesuit missions was set up throughout southern Brazil, Paraguay, and the northern Argentine provinces of Corrientes and Misiones, as a social experiment to civilize the Guaraní Indians.

The original purpose of the missions was to convert the Guaraní to Christianity, improve their lifestyle, and counter the infamous *encomienda* social system instituted by the Spanish in the Americas whereby all Indians within a conquered territory became the serfs of their Spanish landholders.

In 1609 the first Jesuits arrived in Paraná in the Guaraní homeland. Others were sent to the Río Guayra area inhabited by the Tapes people, and soon the first mission settlements were built in what became known as the "Misiones" region.

The indigenous population readily accepted the Jesuits and their work. However these missions were continually harassed by Portuguese *paulistas* (also called *mamelucos*) who captured the Indians to work as slaves in the Brazilian plantations (*fazendas*) to the north.

Between 1627 and 1631, nine mission settlements were destroyed and some 60 000 Indians enslaved or killed. The 11 000 remaining Guaraní abandoned their homelands in one great exodus to seek safety downriver. They trekked from central Brazil through the dense and difficult forest of the Río Paraná to found new settlements in southern Brazil and Paraguay, and at Corpus Christi, San Ignacio Miní, Loreto, and Itapua in Argentina. About 4000 Indians survived the trek.

The missions were self-governed under the guidance of Jesuit *padres* who encouraged those Guaraní traditions which did not conflict with their Christian teachings. The Guaraní were taught agricultural methods, and became skilled blacksmiths, musicians, administrators, and artists.

The Guaraní language was kept alive and encouraged. The Bible was translated into Guaraní and books such as a Guaraní–Spanish dictionary were written and printed in the missions. As Argentina's first printed books, these are now valuable library

Introduction

items and historically important reference works.

The success and prosperity of the mission settlements attracted the envy of nearby Spanish and Portuguese settlers. The *paulista* raids restarted and increased, so the non-violent Guaraní enlisted Spanish mercenaries to teach them how to use firearms. They successfully fought off all incursions after 1641, and in 1719 500 Guaraní laid siege to Montevideo, then the Portuguese town of Colonia del Sarmiento.

In 1767 King Carlos III of Spain signed a decree expelling the Jesuits from all Spanish territories. His decision was influenced by settlers who opposed the mission system because it restricted European exploitation of the region, and those who were alarmed at the military strength and independence of the Guaraní and Jesuits. The missions became part of the Spanish crown and soon disintegrated without the patronage of the Jesuits. Thus ended one of the most enlightened periods of South American colonization.

Today, Guaraní survives as a written and spoken language in Paraguay, and in parts of Corrientes and Misiones. The mission of San Ignacio Miní, north of Posadas, has now been restored for tourists and no visit to Misiones is complete without visiting this magnificent remnant of the great Jesuit experiment.

The Indians today

The great majority of Argentines are of European descent.

The only full-blooded Indian populations are found in the north-eastern provinces of Catamarca, Salta, and Jujuy. These peoples are mostly descendants of Diaguita tribes from the Andean *altiplano*.

Descendants of the Guaraní peoples live in the Mesopotamia area (the north-east provinces of Misiones, Corrientes, and Entre Rios, between the Paraná and Uraguay rivers). Today Guaraní is taught at Corrientes university, and Misiones still contains isolated Guaraní communities. When General San Martín called on Argentines to free themselves from Spanish rule in 1810, his call to arms was also written and distributed in the Guaraní language—the General himself probably spoke a smattering of Guaraní as he grew up in an ex-Jesuit mission amongst the Guaraní.

Isolated communities of Toba Indians exist in such northern provinces as Chaco, Formosa, and Salta. For example, in San Francisco de Laishi in Formosa province the Franciscans have a Toba mission.

Plate 1

Top: Parque Nacional Los Glaciares—Lago Argentina with Glaciar Perito Moreno
Bottom left: Valle de las Cuevas
Bottom right: Menhir park, near Tafí del Valle

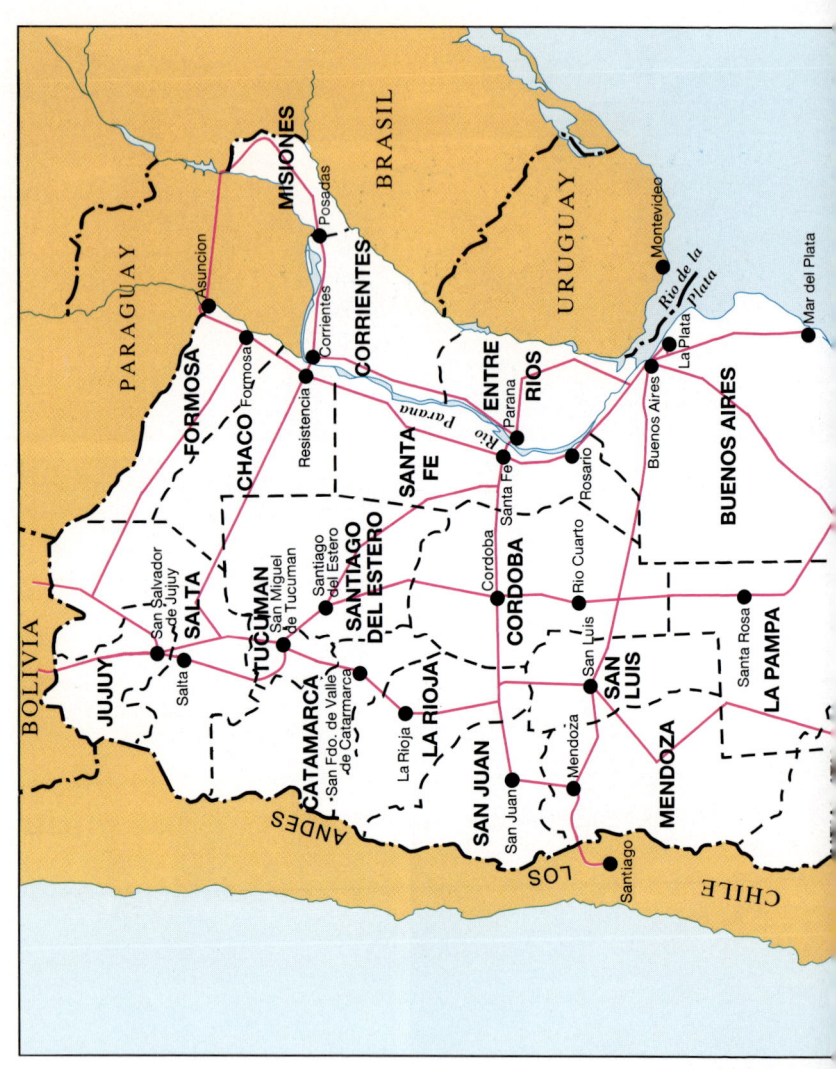

Plate 2

Map of Argentina

Plate 4

Top: Patagonia, near Sarmiento
Bottom: Cataratas del Iguazú

INTRODUCTION

Administration and government

Like most Western democracies, Argentina is essentially a two-party country.

In 1989 the Partido Justicialista government led by Carlos Menem replaced the Unión Cívica Radical (UCR) party of Raul Alfonsin. The new party is the re-formed Peronist movement. Menem himself comes from a Muslim family in La Rioja province, and changed his religion as the Argentine constitution only permits Catholics to become president.

Religion

The Catholic church is the dominant faith for some 95 per cent of the population, but religious freedom is enshrined in the Argentine constitution. Significant pockets of Protestantism occur in the larger cities, especially Buenos Aires, and include Anglican, Lutheran, some Greek Orthodox, and Armenian Catholic churches.

The Church of Latter Day Saints is very active, and you will find a Mormon temple in virtually every large town.

The climate

The Argentine mainland stretches from the Tropic of Capricorn in the north, to 55° latitude in the south. Therefore, while the northern lowlands of Salta province are tropical, most of Argentina is temperate. In the Andes, climate and temperatures are dictated by altitude rather than latitude. It can be bitterly cold up in the *cordillera*, while cities like like Salta and Jujuy a few kilometers away may be baking under a tropical sun. There is always a season for tourists somewhere in Argentina.

However, tourist visits to southern Patagonian provinces to see the spectacular scenery of Santa Cruz and Tierra del Fuego are limited to the summer months.

One effect of the climate is the *siesta*. This is a northern tradition, where the heat and Spanish influence are more noticeable. Further south in the *pampas* or Patagonia there is no such tradition. The *siesta* is described more fully in the introductions to the provinces where it is observed.

Argentina can be visited all year round, because its climate ranges from the tropical to the antarctic. However, southern Patagonia has a harsh winter climate, and is only accessible to tourists in the summer months. Northern Patagonia, including San Carlos de Bariloche, and the provinces of Neuquén and Chubut, offer some of the best skiing conditions in the world. These areas have good tourist facilities and attract growing numbers of winter sport enthusiasts.

INTRODUCTION

Getting to and from Argentina

Visa requirements

Visitors from the following countries can get a 90-day tourist visa stamped into their passport at the point of entry into Argentina:
- Austria
- Belgium
- Brazil
- Canada
- Colombia
- Denmark
- Finland
- Greece
- Holland
- Ireland
- Israel
- Italy
- Japan
- Luxembourg
- Morocco
- Norway
- Peru
- Portugal
- Spain
- Sweden
- Switzerland
- West Germany
- Uruguay
- Yugoslavia

Passport holders from the following countries must apply for a visa **in advance** from an Argentine consulate, preferably in their country of origin:
- Australia
- Great Britain
- New Zealand
- South Africa
- United States of America

Visas are normally valid for 90 days. Extensions on these 90-day visas can be obtained from *Migraciones* in major cities, such as Córdoba, Mendoza, and Salta; this is listed in the *Travel Companion* under "Visas, passports" in the appropirate cities. Alternatively, you may find it easier to cross the border into a neighboring country and obtain a new stamp, which lets you stay another 90 days.

Border crossings into Uruguay

Hovercraft and passenger ferries travel from Buenos Aires to Colonia, and there is a vehicle ferry to Montevideo which crosses in about four hours. The ferry terminal provides passport control.

From Tigre, a passenger ferry crosses the Paraná–Uruguay delta to Carmelo.

Bridges across the Río Uruguay, open 24 hours, include a link between Gualeguaychú in Entre Ríos and Fray Bentos, and the General Artigas bridge between Colón and Paysandú.

You can cross from Concordia to Salto in Uruguay either by passenger ferry—the passport control at the ferry terminal operates only while there are ferries running—or by bus over the Salto Grande bridge, which is open 24 hours a day.

Border crossings into Brazil

Day excursions from the Brazilian side of the Iguazú Falls to Puerto Iguazú in Argentina do not require a visa.

Paso de los Libres in Corrientes is linked to Uruguaiana by a modern bridge, open 24 hours.

INTRODUCTION

✈ Flights to Argentina

Aerolineas Argentina offers overseas tourists a special discount on flights booked within Argentina—"Conozca Argentina". This airline may also offer an internal air travel pass, effective for one month or 14 days. A variation on this is a selected destination pass over a set time period. All these options are good value, and may be available in Argentina, provided you can pay in US dollars.

If you arrive by air in Buenos Aires with no firm itinerary you can obtain good travel information about each region from the various *Casas de Provincias*. Many tour operators offer interesting tours in and around Buenos Aires, and most major travel agencies have staff who speak English, German, French, and Italian. The banks and *Casas de Cambio* usually have multilingual staff.

From	Airline	Services
Europe		
• Amsterdam	KLM	2 per week
	Aerolineas Argentinas	1 per week
• Budapest	Aeroflot	1 per week
• Copenhagen	SAS	1 per week
• Frankfurt	Aerolineas Argentinas	3 per week
	Lufthansa	3 per week
	Varig	Daily, but change in Rio de Janeiro
• London	Varig	Daily, but change in Rio de Janeiro
• Madrid	Iberia	4 per week
	Aerolineas Argentinas	3 per week
• Milan	Alitalia	2 per week
• Oslo	SAS	1 per week
• Paris	Aerolineas Argentinas	3 per week
	Air France	3 per week
• Rome	Alitalia	3 per week
	Aerolineas Argentinas	3 per week
• Stockholm	SAS	1 per week
• Zurich	Swissair	3 per week
	Aerolineas Argentinas	2 per week
North America		
• Los Angeles	Avianca	1 per week
	Ecuatoriana	2 per week
• Miami	Aerolineas Argentinas	5 per week
	Eastern	6 per week
• Montreal	Aerolineas Argentinas	2 per week
• New York	Aerolineas Argentinas	5 per week
	Pan Am	7 per week
	Aerolineas Argentinas	2 per week
• Toronto	Canadian Pacific	2 per week
• Vancouver	Canadian Pacific	2 per week
Australia and New Zealand		
• Auckland	Aerolineas Argentinas	1 per week
• Sydney	Aerolineas Argentinas	1 per week

Introduction

In Corrientes there are passenger ferry links from Santo Tomé to São Borja, and from Alvear to Itaquí over the Río Uruguay.

In Misiones there are passenger ferry links from San Javier to Porto Lucenas, from Alba Posse to Porto Magua, and a land crossing from Bernardo de Irigoyen to Dionisio Cerqueira.

At Puerto Iguazú you may cross the Río Iguazú to Foz do Iguaçu by the new Presidente Tancred Neve bridge.

Border crossings into Paraguay

To get from Puerto Iguazú to Puerto Presidente Stroessner, you must first cross over the Tancred Neve bridge to Foz do Iguaçu in Brazil, and cross the Ponte de Amistad from there to Puerto Presidente Stroessner. There are no direct ferry connections over the Río Alto Paraná between Puerto Iguazú and Paraguay.

From Misiones there is a new bridge over the Río Paraná from Posadas to Encarnación.

In Corrientes, a passenger ferry runs between Paso de la Patria in Argentina and Paso de la Patria in Paraguay over the Río Paraná.

In Formosa you can get from Clorinda to Asunción by the Puente Internacional Ignacio Loyola bridge over the Río Pilcomayo, or travel by passenger ferry from Puerto Pilcomayo to Ita Enramada across the Río Paraguay. From the city of Formosa itself, a passenger ferry runs to Isla Alberdí across the Río Paraguay.

The marshy border between Argentina and Paraguay along the Río Pilcomayo is not well-defined, because the river here is ever-shifting. There are no border crossings in this area.

Border crossings into Bolivia

From Salvador Mazza in Salta there is a land crossing to Yacuiba, and from Agua Blanca a passenger ferry crosses the Río Bermejo to Pozos Bermejo.

In Jujuy there is a bridge from La Quiaca across the Río La Quiaca to Villazon.

Border crossings into Chile

If you are entering from Chile you will find Argentine consulates in Santiago, Puntas Arenas, Arica, and Antofagasta.

A series of high mountain passes cross the Andes between Argentina and Chile. These may be closed by bad weather, and you should check with the Automóvil Club Argentina (ACA).

In Salta, cross from Paso Huaytiquina to San Pedro de Atacama. The pass is at an altitude of 4275 m.

In Catamarca, cross from Paso de San Francisco to Copiapó. The pass is at an altitude of 4720 m.

In San Juan, cross from Paso del Agua Negra to La Serena. The pass is at an altitude of 4770 m.

Introduction

In Mendoza, cross from Punta de Vacas to Caracoles over the Uspallata pass. This is the major link between Mendoza and Santiago de Chile and is kept open 24 hours, all year round.

The Maule pass between Bardas Blancas and Talca is closed indefinitely.

In Neuquén, cross to Temuco either from Zapala through the Paso Pino Hachado (altitude 1884 m), or from Junín de los Andes through the Paso de Mamuil Malal. From San Martín de los Andes you can make an excursion to Puerto Fuy through the Paso Río Hua-Hum.

In Río Negro, cross from San Carlos de Bariloche to Osorno and Puerto Montt through the Paso Puyehue (altitude 1308 m), which is open all year round. You can make an excursion to Puella from San Carlos de Bariloche through the Paso Perez Rosales (altitude 1022 m).

In Chubut, cross from Esquel to Futaleufú. This involves a passenger ferry journey along the Argentine Río Futaleufú. Alternatively, drive from Esquel to Palena via Carrenleufú, or from Río Mayo to Coihayque through the Paso Coyhaique.

In Santa Cruz, cross from Perito Moreno to Chile Chico. This trip requires fording a river some 400 m wide, not very deep but extremely cold. From Cancha Carrera there is a land crossing to Cerro Castillo, through the Torres del Paine national park in Chile. From Río Turbio, cross to Puerto Natales using the Paso Mina Uno.

Railroads

An extensive railroad system is provided by six major passenger-carrying lines in the north of Argentina, but there is no railway network for Patagonia. The southern-most point you can travel to by rail is Esquel in Chubut. All lines terminate in Buenos Aires.

Argentina's rail systems were mostly developed as part of Britain's economic expansion into Argentina, around the turn of this century, and used to open up the country for agricultural expansion once local Indian tribes had been exterminated.

Further information can be found under "Trains" on page 20.

Some trains will transport your car for long distances.

Tourism

Argentina has only recently been "discovered" by tourists. It is very popular with visitors from Europe, and especially those from Italy or those German-speaking countries which have provided Argentina with migrants in the past.

Argentina is the ideal summertime destination for vacationers fleeing from winters in the northern hemisphere. Overseas visitors should include on their itinerary the Cataratas del Iguazú and the Jesuit mission ruins in Misiones, and the Península Valdés in Chubut with its sea-lion, whale, and seal colonies. The Glaciar Perito Moreno in Santa Cruz, and the Calchaquies areas of Tucumán, Catamarca, and Salta with the pre-Hispanic ruins of Tafí del Valle are other tourist "musts".

Hitch-hiking

Argentina is an excellent place for hitch-hiking. It is reasonably safe, but women should not go on their own and should travel in pairs. In some cases the driver may ask for contributions and petrol, especially in the northern provinces.

What to take

Argentina is a modern country with ready access to most items found in North America or Europe—but at a price. All imported goods are expensive—films, cameras, pharmaceuticals, cosmetics, tape cassettes for mini-recorders, and so on. As a rule it can be said that if an item is available in Frankfurt, London, or New York, then you will find it in Buenos Aires. When traveling into the interior, most basic travelers' needs can be purchased in the provincial capitals. Further out from Buenos Aires, such as in Patagonia south of Comodoro Rivadavia, or in the north-west, local lifestyles become more basic still, and you should pre-purchase any special travel commodities you require to allow for this.

Getting around the cities and towns

Street names and city blocks

Most Argentine cities have been established on the traditional Spanish rectangular grid pattern, centred on a Plaza, usually named after San Martín. From the central plaza, main roads radiate to outer suburbs.

Street intersections create city blocks or *cuadras*. Each block out from the center starts numbering in divisions of a hundred, though some towns in Entre Ríos province start each block in divisions of fifty. Hence the first block of any street radiating from the central plaza is block zero with numbers from 1 to 100; the second block until the next cross street is block 100, with numbers running from 101 to 200; and so on.

Wherever you are in the suburbs, you can work out exactly how many blocks you are away from the center, and accordingly decide whether to walk, hail a taxi, or take a bus.

Argentines adore their heroes, and you will find the same street names used repeatedly. For example, the name of San Martín, who brought independence to Argentina, Chile, and Peru, is often used to name the main street, but can appear in the form of El

Introduction

Libertador or General José de San Martín. Other favorites include Belgrano, Urquiza, Sarmiento, Yrigoyen, and Roca.

The spelling of names on street signs can vary in the same street—many a street in a northern town is undecided between "Yrigoyen" (Hipólito) and "Irigoyen" (Bernardo de)!

Addresses

An address may include "Km" in the title following the highway number. In the case of "RP" (for "Ruta Provincial") this indicates the distance of an address from the provincial capital; and in the case of "RN" (for "Ruta Nacional") the distance from the national capital of Buenos Aires.

It is common for hotels in isolated areas to use "Km" as part of their address.

Future editions

Update material for this guide arrives constantly from local correspondents in Argentina. However, we welcome your suggestions for revisions, so please let us know of any changes required. The *Travel Companion* is intended as a source book for travelers, and your contributions will help others to make the best of their stay in Argentina.

Please write to us:

Travel Companion

PO Box 456

Mudgeeraba Qld 4213

Australia

How to Use the *Travel Companion*

As a convenient reference point, we have assumed that most tourists will enter Argentina by air, through Buenos Aires. The *Travel Companion* starts with Buenos Aires and is then subdivided into six sections, for each of the six main regions, moving counter-clockwise from Buenos Aires down the South Atlantic coast, back up the Andes, and then eastwards across to Buenos Aires again.

Each of the seven main subdivisions used here corresponds to some geographical, historical, or cultural region:
- Buenos Aires city and environs (the province of Capital)
- The Pampa provinces, which include Argentina's major agricultural hinterland, made up of the vast plains or *pampas* of Buenos Aires and La Pampa provinces
- Patagonia—Argentina south of the Río Negro, including the territory of Tierra del Fuego
- The Chaco provinces—Those provinces of Argentina in the *chaco*, the tropical and subtropical rainforests and the savannas of the central northern region which extend northwards into Bolivia and Paraguay
- The Cuyo provinces—The mid-continental desert regions, east of the Andes (originally part of the Vice-Royalty of Chile)
- Mesopotamia—The isolated north-eastern provinces between the Río Paraná and the Río Uruguay
- The north-western provinces—The area first permanently settled by Indians and the Spanish

Provinces

All provinces within each region are described separately. Each province begins with a table of cities and towns, each with a series of symbols indicating the facilities and attractions available.

Towns are listed in the order of the English alphabet—that is to say, "Ch" and "Ll" are treated as they are in English, not as in Spanish. Following the practise of the maps issued by the

How to Use

Automóvil Club Argentina, a space within a name files before the letter "A", so that "La Población" **precedes** "Laboulaye".

The table is followed by a general introduction to the province. An explanation of the symbols used in the *Travel Companion* is given on page 22, and is summarized on the accompanying bookmark.

The name of each province is given at the **head** of every page; and on every page opening the first and last town name is given at the **foot** of the page.

Cities and towns

Cities and towns listed in this *Travel Companion* provide a wide range of attractions for the visitor, such as cultural, historical, and sporting facilities.

All times are given according to the 24-hour clock.

Important towns may be known by two names, especially where that town is also a provincial capital, for example
- San Miguel de Tucumán is also known as "Tucumán"
- San Fernando del Valle de Catamarca is also known as "Catamarca"
- San Salvador de Jujuy is also known as "Jujuy"
- San Carlos de Bariloche is also known as "Bariloche"

Many smaller towns have been included for completeness—these contain facilities such as hotels, restaurants, and service stations, which are essential for long-distance travelers visiting the *pampas* or Patagonia, for example. With this *Travel Companion*, you should not feel stranded anywhere in Argentina.

Where possible, bureaux de change (*cambios*) are listed so you can cash travelers' checks as you proceed around Argentina. At the time of going to print, the Austral appeared to have stabilized at around 670 Australs (A670) to the US dollar. Prices quoted throughout this guide are in US dollar equivalents, as these should not vary much.

As a general rule, carry about two-thirds of your money as travelers' checks, and one-third as US dollars. Changing checks is always difficult, even in the bigger cities.

The information for each town has been itemized under up to 23 sections; not all sections appear under all towns. To facilitate scanning, each section heading has an identifying symbol; these symbols are listed on page 22 and on the bookmark.

To help you find your way around the major towns or tourist centers, 85 street maps are included. These street maps show the main points of interest, which are numbered and explained in accompanying keys. Numbers 1 to 6 on each map show the *Municipalidad* or Town Hall, *Casa de Gobierno* or provincial House of Assembly, main cathedral or church, post office, telephone, and tourist information bureau. These are then fol-

How to Use

lowed by indicators for airlines, currency exchange facilities, accommodation, and points of interest such as museums and monuments.

☞ When I have stayed at a hotel, eaten at a restaurant, or used some facility, and particularly enjoyed it or found it excellent value or the staff exceptionally helpful, I have marked the entry with a pointing hand ☞ to indicate a personal recommendation.

Index

At the end of the *Travel Companion* is an Index to all the places mentioned in the *Companion*. Each placename referred to in the Index appears in the text in **bold type**. To get the most out of the Index, read the "Introduction" to the Index carefully.

Sample entry

An example of the layout of entries for cities and towns follows.

Town or City Name

Postal code • Telephone area code • Population • Altitude

Distances to other major centers: The distance is given in kilometers (km), together with the highway numbers of the recommended routes from other major centers: "RN" for "Ruta Nacional" (or "National Highway"), and "RP" for "Ruta Provincial" (or "Provincial Highway"). Because of the state of some highways, the most direct route is not always a straight line!

☒ Festivals

Local *fiestas* are listed, together with the dates when they are held. Some people like fiestas; others prefer to avoid them as hotels may be full and the banks closed.

ⓘ Tourist information

Official city and provincial tourist information centers and offices (or *Casas de Turismo* are listed, together with any useful unofficial sources.

🛏 Accommodation

Listings for each city include those hotels recommended by their respective provincial tourist offices. The accommodation section for large towns is further divided into geographical areas. Each listing is graded by type of accommodation: Hotels, *Hosterías*, *Residenciales*, *Hospedajes*, Motels, *Cabañas*, and private accommodation.

Hotels have been assigned a star rating by appropriate local authorities, and are arranged here in decreasing star number order. In addition, *Residenciales* have been assigned an alphabetical rating from **A** through **C**.

Ratings can vary between provinces, so it is best to check in the tourist office in the provincial capital. As a guide, five stars in Argentina is about the same as four stars in the US or Europe.

Classifications used for accommodation include:
- Hostería—A smaller version of an hotel, with up to 20 bedrooms. Coded by up to three stars
- Residencial—Officially-recognized cheap accommodation. It is coded A, B, or C, A being the best
- Hospedaje—Cheaper lodgings, usually a type of *residencial*, but not officially recognized

How to Use

An address is given for each hotel, followed by symbols showing facilities available:
- ⑪ restaurant
- ⊡ cafeteria
- ⓑ bar
- ⓔ English-speaking staff
- ⓐ casino
- ⓣ disco or nightclub
- ⊕ excursion buses provided
- ⓢ bureau de change
- ⊠ swimming pool
- ⓙ golf course
- ⓟ tennis courts
- ⓞ bowling green
- ⓤ sauna
- ⓣ thermal pool

Telephone numbers, and rates for double rooms ⅱ and single rooms ⅰ are listed where known. Where appropriate, separate rates are given for full board (all meals) and half board (breakfast only). When a hotel's normal rate includes breakfast, this is indicated.

For budget-minded travelers and young people, we have listed the budget accommodation (private accommodation and *residenciales*) which is normally situated near bus terminals and train stations. Those which only have basic facilities have been specifically noted as being suitable for backpackers or budget travelers.

For smaller outlying towns all available accommodation has been listed.

⑪ Eating out

Restaurant listings for the larger cities may seem comprehensive, but are not exhaustive—they are intended to show you the range of eating facilities available to travelers. In larger cities this section is divided into districts to help you locate nearby eating places. Where known, eateries are further classified into restaurants (including *parrillas* or steakhouses), pizzerias, cafeterias, and coffee shops. Where a restaurant specializes in a particular cuisine, this is indicated, for example "Steakhouse, "Seafood, "Italian cuisine", "Vegetarian". Meal prices are not listed in this edition. However, breakfast should cost between $0.80 and $2.50, lunch between $3.50 and $12.00, and a full dinner between $5.00 and $20.00. A main meal in a fancy restaurant should cost about $25.00.

The main meal of the day in Argentina is supper, and usually starts from 2100 and goes until the early hours of the following morning. It is not unusual to order a full dinner at 1 am.

Cheap meals are usually available from cafeterias, bars, and pizzerias, as well as from kiosks in bus terminals and train stations.

✉ Post and telegraph

Post offices

Post and telegraph services are provided by the state-owned company Encotel.

Telephones

Public telephones are run by the state-owned company Entel. Different tokens (*fichas*) are required for local and long-distance calls—tokens may be purchased from newsagents, tobacconists, some bars, and from hotel cashiers. Calls from hotels are usually more expensive and it is better to use a telephone exchange, even if the wait is longer.

$ Financial

Here are listed facilities where money and travelers' checks can be exchanged. *Casas de cambio* usually give you a better exchange rate than the banks. Some institutions do not accept travelers' checks, and others may accept a particular type only. When planning your trip, it is a good precaution to refer to the "Financial" section in each town you plan to visit, so you know where money exchange facilities are available. This is particularly important on trips to Patagonia and to the northwestern provinces.

Banks and *casas de cambio* usually have multilingual staff.

It is important to note that the northwestern provinces of Tucumán, Salta, Jujuy, and Catamarca have their own provincial currencies, known as *bonos*, which are only valid in the province where they are issued. If you get stuck with provincial Australs, try exchanging

How to Use

them at bus companies serving that particular province.

Those banks in provincial capitals which give cash against a Visa card are indicated.

🗏 Services

Here are listed addresses for laundromats, equipment hire, supermarkets, and other services and facilities. Hospital and medical facilities are listed for major towns.

C Clubs

National clubs are listed by nationality. Many of these clubs serve meals.

✝ Churches

Every town has one or more Catholic churches, invariably in a central location. For this reason under "churches" the *Travel Companion* lists Protestant or Orthodox churches only.

The major Catholic church in a town is often listed under "Sightseeing": in larger cities this is usually a cathedral dating back to the city's foundation. Cathedrals are usually an historical feature, particularly for cities such as Córdoba, San Miguel de Tucumán, and Santiago del Estero.

🏳 Visas, passports

Provincial capitals often have consulates for other countries, particularly for those states neighboring Argentina. Capitals in border provinces have a *Migración* office where visa renewal applications may be lodged.

⊗ Border crossing

For border towns, the nature of the crossing is described, and any restrictions peculiar to each crossing are noted.

✈ Air services

Where known, the distance to the airport from the town center is provided, together with bus and taxi services to and from the airport and their approximate fares.

Offices and addresses are given for Argentine airlines only: Aerolineas Argentinas, Austral, LADE, LAPA, and ALFA. LADE is run by the Argentine Air Force, and serves isolated communities in Patagonia. Their aircraft are usually small so that they can land on short airstrips. The shuttle service they provide is generally cheaper than that of Aerolineas Argentinas or Austral, but flights take longer because of stops along the route in remote areas. All remote areas in Patagonia served by LADE are indicated in the *Travel Companion*. One drawback to the adventurous traveler is that these flights are usually heavily booked, so you should always confirm your travel arrangements beforehand.

Tables of airline destinations indicate the airfare, the time of departure of the first or only flight, days on which the services are provided, the duration of the flight, and the servicing airline. Destinations are listed in alphabetical order, except that the name of the applicable provincial capital heads the list. You must be aware that timetables are subject to at least two changes per year (summer and winter schedules), so you should always double-check. Night flights on domestic services are substantially cheaper than daylight flights. However it helps if you arrive as early as possible at your next destination as hotels in some locations may be booked out from late afternoon onwards, especially during the holiday season from December to early March. You can avoid disappointment by making a phone booking before leaving.

🚍 Buses

Tables indicate destinations, fares, the first (or only) bus, days on which services are provided, duration of journey, and servicing companies. Destinations are given in the same order as for "Air services—see above.

🚗 Motoring

The condition of principal roads to the town is given where this is significant.

How to Use

Service stations

A service station is given for every town; these are usually run by the Automóvil Club Argentino (ACA), and may have a good cafeteria or restaurant attached. They also sell provincial maps and *hojas de ruta* (or "road guide sheets"), which have important information required when traveling between two cities, such as from Buenos Aires to Córdoba, or from San Miguel de Tucumán to La Quiaca. The best place to buy any of these is the ACA center at Avenida del Libertador 1850, Buenos Aires, but all provincial towns have a major ACA center. If you are entering Argenitna from Bolivia at La Quiaca, there is an ACA service station a few hundred meters from the border with a good supply of most Argentine roadmaps.

Car rental

For those who prefer hiring cars, rental firms are indicated. All major car rental firms (Avis, Hertz, Budget) operate throughout Argentina. If you are a cardholder with any of these companies, charges incurred in Argentina can be paid in your home country.
Rates are fairly standard thoughout Argentina—for a guide to rates see "Motoring" in Buenos Aires on page 51.
You will be charged about $35 extra for crossing a border in a hire car.

Automóvil Club Argentina (ACA)

Members of foreign automobile clubs get the same service as ACA members on production of their membership card, or you can join up there. The joining fee is very cheap, and ACA hotels and some restaurants offer a 10–15% discount. ACA is a good source for road maps whether you are driving, busing, or hiking. Membership is recommended if your visit lasts three months or more.

Trains

Train services are quite good in Argentina for some sections, and are usually cheaper than bus travel, but will be slower. Most trains are known by names, such as "El Aconcagua", which travels from Buenos Aires to Mendoza and San Juan. The fares for the different classes are indicated: Sleeper ("*Cochecama*"), Pullman, First class ("*Primera*") and Tourist class ("*Turista*"). Tourist class is usually quite acceptable, but make sure you have a seat reservation. Also given is the time of departure, days on which the service is provided, and the duration of the journey. Railroad lines are usually named after famous generals or statesmen. The name of each line begins with the term "Ferro Carril Nacional" (meaning "National Railroad Line"), which is normally abbreviated to "F C" in Argentina, and this practice is used throughout the *Travel Companion*.

All railroad lines begin in Buenos Aires. The table below shows the name of the station in Buenos Aires from where the services start, and the names of principal cities served.

Train lines from Buenos Aires

Name of line	Station	Cities served
• F C General B Mitre	Retiro	Santa Fé, Rosario (Santa Fé province)
• F C General M Belgrano	Retiro	Córdoba, Santa Fé, San Miguel de Tucumán
• F C General San Martín	Retiro	San Luis, Mendoza, San Juan
• F C General Urquiza	Lacroze	Paraná (Entre Ríos province), Posadas (Misiones province), Corrientes
• F C D F Sarmiento	Once	Santa Rosa (La Pampa province)
• F C General Roca	Constitución	Neuquén, San Carlos de Bariloche (Río Negro province), Mar del Plata (Buenos Aires province)

How to Use

⚓ Water transport
Regular ferry services are tabulated, and pleasure craft excursions described.

⊞ Tours
Tour operators offering excursions to surrounding districts are listed, including departure time, duration of the excursion, and fare.

If you arrive in Buenos Aires without a firm travel plan, the *Casas de Provincias* can provide you with information to help you develop one.

Many tour operators offer interesting day trips in and around Buenos Aires, and most major travel agencies have staff who speak English, German, French, and Italian.

⊞ Shopping
Here are listed shops selling specialties of the district. Such special items include date liqueur (only available in La Rioja), gemstones (Misiones), and green onyx (San Luis). In the north-western provinces you can buy alpaca wool clothing.

🞴 Sport
Under this heading, you will find sporting facilities, starting with golf courses, fishing, waterskiing, skin diving, hiking, and so on. Addresses for mountaineering and ski clubs are given where applicable.

🍸 Entertainment
Includes lists of discos, night clubs, and casinos. For larger towns discos are grouped by district.

A form of entertainment unique to Argentina is the *tanguerías*, which specialize in tango music and dancing. The Boca district of Buenos Aires is full of them, but *tanguerías* are found all over Argentina.

📷 Sightseeing
Here are listed all museums and art galleries, major churches, convents, monuments, and public buildings of interest.

✦ Excursions
Here are summarized nearby sightseeing opportunities which are readily accessible as day tours from tour operators, or do-it-yourself tours by local bus routes. Cross-references are provided to fuller information found elsewhere in the *Travel Companion*.

Color Maps

Plate

2	Argentina	Between pages 8 and 9
5	Buenos Aires Province	Opposite page 120
6	Delta	Opposite page 121
7	Córdoba Province	Opposite page 152
9	La Pampa Province	Opposite page 216
11	Santa Fé Province	Opposite page 248
13	Neuquén Province	Opposite page 312
15	Río Negro Province	Opposite page 344
18	Chubut Province	Between pages 392 and 393
20	Santa Cruz Province	Opposite page 393
21	Tierra del Fuego	Opposite page 440
23	Mendoza Province	Opposite page 472
25	San Juan Province	Opposite page 504
27	San Luis Province	Opposite page 536
29	Catamarca Province	Opposite page 568
31	La Rioja Province	Opposite page 600
33	Tucumán Province	Opposite page 648
34	Salta and Jujuy Provinces	Between pages 648 and 649
37	Formosa Province	Opposite page 680
38	Chaco Province	Between pages 680 and 681
41	Santiago del Estero Province	Opposite page 696
43	Corrientes Province	Opposite page 728
45	Entre Ríos Province	Opposite page 760
47	Misiones Province	Opposite page 792

SYMBOLS

Symbols in the order in which they appear in the text

- Festivals
- Tourist information
- Accommodation
- Camping
- Restaurants
- Cafeterias
- Bars
- English spoken
- Post and telegraph
- Post office
- Telephone
- Banks
- Services
- Clubs
- Churches
- Passports
- Border crossing
- Air services
- Buses
- Trains
- Water transport
- Motoring services
- Car rentals
- Service stations
- Tours
- Shopping
- Wineries
- Sport
- Hiking
- Skiing
- Mountaineering
- Caving
- Beaches
- Fishing
- Water sports
- Sailing
- Swimming
- Golf
- Tennis
- Bowling green
- Horse riding
- Sauna
- Entertainment; Nightlife
- Casino
- Sightseeing
- Museums and galleries
- Colonial buildings
- Excursions
- Archeology
- Thermal springs
- Wildlife
- Electricity
- Hot water
- Toilets
- Laundry
- Kiosk

- (Telephone number
- i Single room
- ii Double room
- ☞ Recommended

Symbols

Symbols in alphabetical order

- Accommodation
- Air services
- Archeological sites
- Art galleries
- Auto rental
- Auto services
- Banks
- Bar(s)
- Beaches
- Bilingual staff
- *Bodegas*
- Border crossing
- Bowling green
- Buses
- Cafeteria(s)
- Camping
- Car rental
- Casino(s)
- Caving
- Churches
- Clubs
- Colonial buildings
- Consulates
- Disco(s)
- Double rooms
- Eating out
- Electricity
- English spoken
- Entertainment
- Excursions
- Facilities and services
- Ferries
- Festivals
- Financial
- Fishing
- Galleries
- Gas stations
- Golf
- Hiking
- Historic buildings
- Horse riding
- Hot springs
- Hot water
- Hotels
- Kiosks(s)
- Laundry
- Money
- Motoring services
- Mountaineering
- Museums
- Nightclub(s)
- Passports
- Pool
- Post and telegraph
- Post office
- Public phones
- Rail
- Recommended
- Restaurants
- Sailing
- Sauna(s)
- Service stations
- Services
- Ships
- Shopping
- Sightseeing
- Single rooms(s)
- Skiing
- Sport
- Swimming
- Telephones
- Tennis
- Thermal springs
- Toilets
- Tourist information
- Tours
- Trains
- Visas
- Water sports
- Water transport
- Wildlife
- Wine shops

GLOSSARY

A

ACA	Automóvil Club Argentino (Argentine Automobile Club)
Adobe	sunbaked bricks made of clay or mud with straw added
Aeroparque Jorge Newbery	airport in Buenos Aires for internal flights and some flights to Uruguay and Paraguay
Aeropuerto	airport
Alameda	wide avenue; mall
Albergue	hostel; lodging
Al diente	"eat as much as you like"
Alfajores	sweets; candy
Algorrobo	a tree in the *chaco*
Almirante	admiral
Alojamiento	accommodation
Alpaca	a relative of the llama, domesticated by the Indians
Altiplano	tableland above 3000 m
Andinista	mountaineer in the Andes
Apart Hotel	suite of apartments available for hire
Arco iris (as in "trucha arco iris")	rainbow trout
Arroyo	stream
Artesanías	handicrafts
Automotor	motor coach on the railroad; railcar
Autopista	motorway; freeway

B

Bagre	South American catfish
Bahía	bay
Balneario	beach resort; spa
Baño	toilet; bathroom
Bar	bar where both food and drink are available
Bis	where streets have numbers instead of names, "bis" is part of the name of a lane parallel to a neighboring larger street of the same name; for example "Calle 23 Bis" is a lane next to and parallel with "Calle 23"
Barrio	quarter; district
Boca	mouth (of a river)
Bodega	wine shop; wine cellar
Bosque	forest
Brazo	arm (of a lake)
Bulevar	boulevard

C

Cabaña	cabin
Cabildo	colonial town council
Cabina publica	public telephone booth
Cacique	Indian chief
Cafetería	coffee shop
Calle	street
Cambio	money exhange
Cañada	glen
Cañadon	large glen
Cañon	canyon
Capilla	chapel
Capitán	captain
Caranday	a type of palm growing in inland provinces
Carpincho	capybara, a type of native pig
Casa	house; home
Casa de té	tearoom
Casa de Gobierno	house of the Legislative Assembly
Castillo	castle
Catarata	large waterfall
Catedral	cathedral
Caverna	cavern
Ceiba	silk cotton tree
Centolla	spider crab

GLOSSARY

Cerro	hill; mountain
Cervecería	beer saloon
Chaco	savanna
Cherimoya	a tropical fruit; custard apple
Chico	small
Cholga	giant mussel
Chopería	beer garden
Chullpa	Indian burial ground in the Andes
Churrería	place where *churros* are served
Churrasquerria	restaurant serving barbecued meat
Churro	a type of sweet fritter
Ciudad	city
Coati	a tropical American raccoon
Coihue	a tree growing in the Andes
Colectivo	a type of municipal bus
Colegio	college
Colla	Indian inhabitant of the *altiplano*
Comandante	commandant
Comedor	eating place; dining room
Complejo	complex; compound
Confitería	confectionary shop cum coffee shop
Cordillera	mountain range
Cornisa	a narrow winding road, often through mountain scenery
Coronel	colonel
Costanera	wide pleasant road beside a river, lake, or sea
Cuadra	city block
Cuesta	moutain pass road
Cueva	cave
Cumbre	summit, mountain top

D

Delegación	branch office
Departamento	division of a province
Desagüe	outflow of water from a lake
Dique	dam
Dirección	government department
Dorado	a giant edible golden carp

E

Embalse	dam
Empresa	enterprise; equivalent of "Co."
Encotel	the name of the Argentine post office
Entel	the name of the Argentine telephone company
Estancia	cattle ranch
Este	east
Estero	swamp where a river finishes

F

Falda	the lower part of a hillside
F C	"Ferro Carril"–railroad
Feria	fair
Ferro Carril	railroad
Fray	Brother (religious)
Fuerte	fort

G

Galería	arcade
Gaucho	Argentine cowboy
Glaciar	glacier
Golfo	gulf
Grande	big
Guanaco	a relative of the llama living in the *pampa*
Guardaparque	ranger in a national park

H

Hacienda	farm
Heladería	icecream parlor
Hnos	"Hermanos"—equivalent of "Bros."
Hospedaje	cheap lodgings
Hostería	hostelry; inn
Huemul	an American deer

Glossary

I

Iglesia	church
Ingeniero	engineer
Intendencia	national park headquarters
Intendente	the chief officer of a *departamento*
Isla	island

J

Jefatura	local police station

L

Lago	lake
Laguna	small lake
Lavandería	laundry
Linea	train or bus line
Loberia	seal colony
Local	shop, as in *Local 12* (Shop number 12)
Locro	a meat and vegetable stew, popular in the north-west
Lomitería	a type of small restaurant serving meat dishes
Loro	parrot
Loro barranquero	a type of *loro*

M

Mandioca	manioc
Mara	Patagonian hare
Maté	Paraguayan herb tea
Mayor	bigger; older
Meseta	plateau
Mesón	restaurant serving Spanish-style meals
Micro	a type of municipal bus, synonymous with *colectivo*
Municipalidad	town hall
Museo	museum

N

Nación	nation
Nacional	national
Ñandú	rhea or South American ostrich
Norte	north

O

Oeste	west

P

Pacú	an Argentine river fish
Palo barroso, Palo borracho	trees growing in the *chaco*
Palometa	a carnivorous fish
Pampa	the huge grassy plains east of the Andes
Pampero	a cold southerly blowing across the *pampa*
Panadería	bakery
Parque	park
Parrilla	grill; grilled meat
Pasaje	passage; lane
Paseo	promenade
Paso	mountain pass
Pejerrey	atherine, an Argentine freshwater fish
Peña	informal folk concert, usually with both singing and dancing
Pescadería	fish market
Pico	mountain peak
Pizzería	literally a pizza shop, but also sells light meals
Plaza	place; town square
Plazoleta	small *plaza*
Portazuelo	highest point of a *cornisa*, often a pass
Posada	inn

GLOSSARY

Precordillera	foothills of the Andes
Propina	tip; gratuity
Provincia	province, the chief political and administrative division of Argentina
Pub	English-style "pub"
Pucará	pre-Hispanic fortifications
Puchero	a dish containing meat and vegetables
Pudu	a rare dwarf deer
Puerto	port
Puna	arid tableland in the Andes
Punilla	semi-arid tableland in the Sierras de Córdoba
Punta	point

Q

Quebracho blanco	a hardwood tree found mostly in the *chaco* region. *Quebracho* means "axe-breaker"
Quebrada	gorge; ravine
Quechua	the Inca language, still spoken widely in the north-west

R

Recreo	amusement place, usually with a dance floor
Reducción	settlement of Indians converted to Christianity; reservation
Refugio	mountain hut
Regionales	shop specializing in local handicrafts
Reserva Nacional	national nature reserve
Residencial	cheap lodgings
Río	river
RN	"Ruta Nacional"—national highway
Robalo	sea bass
RP	"Ruta Provincial"—provincial highway
Ruta	highway

S

S A	"Sociedad Anónima"—equivalent of "Ltd."
Salar	salt lake, usually dry, in the *altiplano*
Salina	salt pan
Salto	waterfall; rapids
Selva	jungle
Sierra	short mountain chain
Subte	the underground rail system in Buenos Aires
Sur	south
Surubí	an edible fish in the Río Paraná and Río Uruguay

T

Tambería, Tambo	staging post on a former Inca road
Tanguería	a place where tango music is played and danced to

T

Teatro	theatre
Teniente	lieutenant
Termas	hot springs
Trucha	trout

U

Unidad Turistica	a tourist complex owned by the Automóvil Club Argentino, usually consisting of good-quality cabins

GLOSSARY

V

Valle	valley
Ventisquero	glacier
Vicuña	a rare South American relative of the llama with particularly fine wool
Vizcacha	a South Amercian rodent living at high altitude

W

Whiskería	literally, a place for drinking whisky; bar

Y

Yacaré	cayman, a small alligator
Yaguarete	jaguar
YPF	the state-owned petrol company

City of Buenos Aires

City of Buenos Aires

City of Buenos Aires

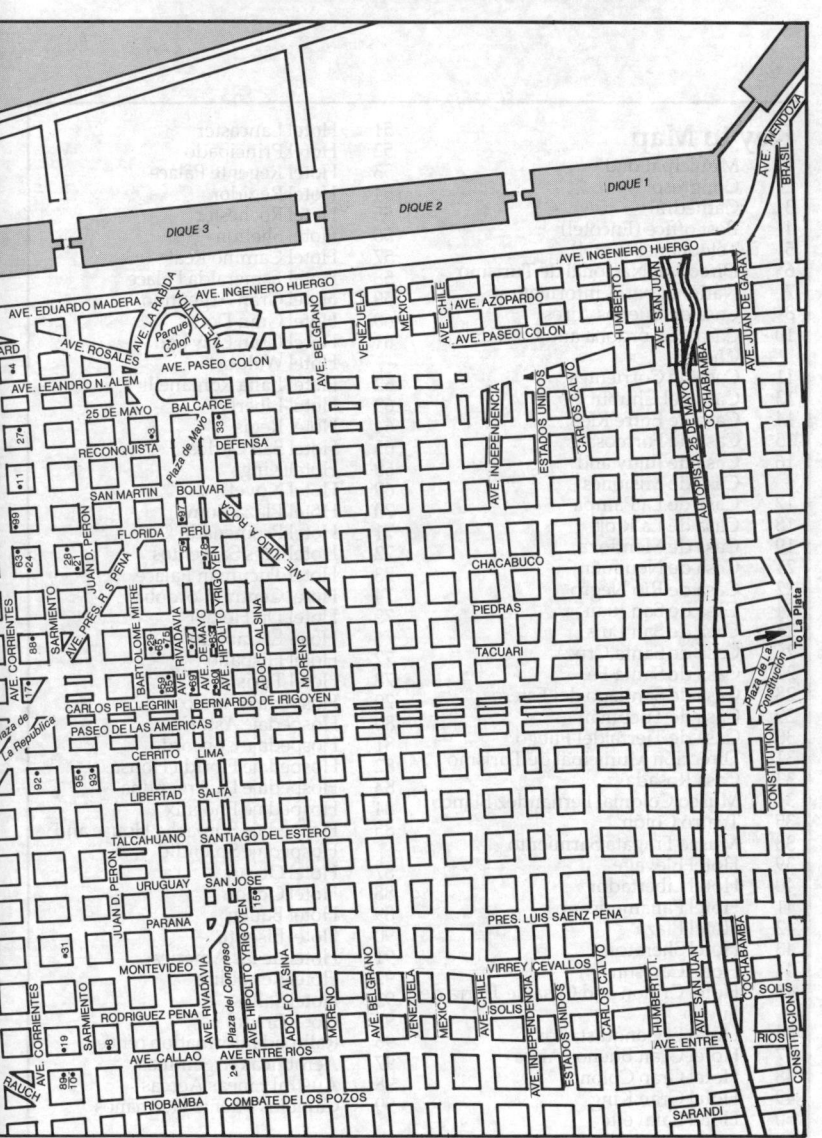

CITY OF BUENOS AIRES

Key to Map

1. Municipalidad
2. Congreso
3. Cathedral
4. Post office (Encotel)
5. Telephones (Entel)
6. Dirección Nacional de Turismo
7. National parks information
8. Casa de Buenos Aires
10. Casa de Córdoba and Casa del Chaco
11. Casa de Corrientes
13. Casa del Chubut
14. Casa de Entre Ríos
15. Casa de Formosa
16. Casa de Jujuy and Casa de Misiones
17. Casa de La Pampa
18. Casa de La Rioja
19. Casa de Mendoza
21. Casa de Neuquén
22. Casa de Río Negro
24. Casa de San Juan
25. Casa de San Luis
26. Casa de Santa Cruz
27. Casa de Santa Fé
28. Casa de Santiago del Estero
29. Casa de Tucumán
30. Casa de Tierra del Fuego
31. Dirección Municipal de Turismo
33. Casa Rosada
34. Museo Colonial Fernandez Blanco
35. Teatro Colón
38. Museo Fragata Sarmiento
39. Hotel Elevage
40. Hotel Libertador
41. Hotel Panamericano
42. Hotel Plaza
43. Hotel Sheraton
44. Hotel Carsson
45. Hotel Crillon and Casa de Tierra del Fuego
46. Hotel El Conquistador
47. Hotel Gran Buenos Aires
48. Hotel Gran Colón
49. Hotel Gran King
50. Hotel Lafayette
51. Hotel Lancaster
52. Hotel Principado
53. Hotel Regente Palace
54. Hotel Regidor
55. Hotel Rochester
56. Hotel Shelton
57. Hotel Camino Real
58. Hotel Esmeralda Palace
59. Hotel Gran Argentino
60. Hotel Gran Dora
61. Hotel Gran Orly and Hotel Waldorf
62. Hotel Italia Romanelli
63. Hotel Liberty
64. Hotel Regis
65. Hotel San Carlos
68. Hotel Kings
69. Hotel Novel
70. Hotel Plaza Roma
71. Hotel Promenade
72. Hotel Tres Sargentos
73. Hotel Tucumán Palace
74. Hotel Central Córdoba
75. Hotel Du Helder
76. Hotel El Cabildo
77. Hotel Hispano
78. Hotel Turista
79. Hospedaje Apolo
80. Hospedaje Astoria
81. Hospedaje Concorde
82. Hospedaje Florida House
83. Hospedaje La Argentina
84. Hospedaje Phoenix
85. Hospedaje Suipacha House and Hospedaje Splendid
87. Hotel Ocean
88. Hotel Odeon
89. Hotel Bauen
90. Hotel Bisonte
91. Hotel de las Américas
92. Hotel Republica
93. Hotel Salles
95. Hotel Bristol
96. Railroad information office
97. Aerolineas Argentinas
98. Austral Lineas Aereas
99. Cambios Puente Hermanos

City of Buenos Aires

City of Buenos Aires

Population: 8 000 000 • Altitude: Sea level

The city of Buenos Aires is located on the **Río de la Plata** (known in English as the River Plate), east of the **Río Paraná** and Uruguay delta. It covers an area of approximately 220 square kilometers, and has been virtually rebuilt since the beginning of this century. The city center has retained its original layout with its narrow streets, but none of the colonial buildings are left. Most of the streets are one-way.

[i] Tourist information

Buenos Aires is the best place to obtain up-to-date information on all parts of Argentina. All of the provincial tourist agencies have offices here, and it is a good idea—and easier—to take advantage of this and obtain information about the places you plan to visit while still in the capital, rather than count on being able to find the information once you are in the provinces.

National tourist offices
- Dirección Nacional de Turismo, Suipacha 1111 ℂ 3125611 and 3125621. The Dirección also organizes tours of the city; information about these is available at the kiosks in Calle Florida
- National Parks Information Service, Santa Fé 680

Provincial tourist offices
- Casa de Buenos Aires, Avenida Callao 235 ℂ 407045
- Casa de Catamarca, Avenida Cordoba 2080 ℂ 466891
- Casa de Córdoba, Avenida Callao 332 ℂ 456566
- Casa de Corrientes, San Martín 333, 4th floor ℂ 3947432
- Casa del Chaco, Avenida Callao 322, 1st floor ℂ 450961
- Casa del Chubut, Paraguay 876 ℂ 3122340
- Casa de Entre Ríos, Carlos Pellegrini 547 ℂ 3944010
- Casa de Formosa, H Yrigoyen 1429 ℂ 373699
- Casa de Jujuy, Avenida Santa Fé 967 ℂ 3931295
- Casa de La Pampa, Suipacha 346 ℂ 350511
- Casa de La Rioja, Avenida Callao 745 ℂ 441662
- Casa de Mendoza, Avenida Callao 445 ℂ 406683

Tourist information

CITY OF BUENOS AIRES

- Casa de Misiones, Avenida Santa Fé 9809 (3931615 and 3931211
- Casa de Neuquén, Perón (formerly called Cangallo) 687 (496385
- Casa de Río Negro, Tucumán 1916 (459931
- Casa de Salta, Diagonal Norte 933 (3928074
- Casa de San Juan, Maipú 331 (461698
- Casa de San Luis, Azcuenaga 1083 (833641
- Casa de Santa Cruz, Avenida Córdoba 1345, 14th floor (420381
- Casa de Santa Fé, 25 de Mayo 358 (3124620. Open Mon–Fri 0930–1730
- Casa de Santiago del Estero, Florida 274 (469398
- Casa de Tucumán, B Mitre 836, 1st floor (402214
- Casa de Tierra de Fuego, Santa Fé 790

City tourist information

- Dirección Municipal de Turismo, Sarmiento 1551, 5th floor.
- Airport information service for Ezeiza airport is open Mon–Fri 0830–2200
- Airport information service for Aeroparque Jorje Newbery is open Mon–Fri 0830–2000 and Sat 0900–1900
- Tourist information kiosks are located at each end of Calle Florida. The staff speak at least German, French, and English

Guides

- *Where* is a monthly English-language guide to social and cultural activities, and also contains listings of hotels, restaurants, and shops; it is free from information kiosks and large hotels
- *Salimos* is a useful booklet, printed in Spanish, containing information on local festivals
- *Guía Peuser* ($0.90) is the best street directory and includes a map of "Gran Buenos Aires" as well as *colectivo* routes
- Instituto Geográfico Militar (Military Geographic Institute), Cabildo 301. Open 0800–1300 take bus 152 from Retiro station. Provides maps
- *Guía de Turismo y Aventuras de la Argentina Desconocida, Arqueológica y Misteriosa* ("Tourism and Adventure Guide to Unknown, Archeological and Mysterious Argentina") by Federico Kirbus is available from bookshops
- Fundación Vida Silvestre, L N Alem 968, has information and books on Argentine flora and fauna

Booking for hotels in the provinces

- Casamerlo, Guemes 4182 (715591
- Calafate: Bookings for Motel La Loma, Callao 433 (near Refugio). Bookings for car campers at Lago Viedma: Turismo Argos, Maipú 812, 13th floor (3925460
- Mendoza: Bookings for Hotel Aconcagua, Florida 656, 2nd floor (3925004
- San Carlos de Bariloche: Accommodation service, Florida 520, room 116
- Termas de Río Hondo: Bookings for Hotel Casino Center (509861. Bookings for Hotel America, Corrientes 818, 4th floor (3131437. To book hotel apartments at La Recova and Hotel Río Dulce, contact A Ferreyra, 2539 Caseros (7508175
- Las Leñas ski resort in Mendoza province: Skileñas, Reconquista 385 (3121065

Transport in Buenos Aires

The Subte

The best and fastest way to travel in the city is on the *Subte*, the underground rail system. It is well signposted and connects with all the main rail stations. Routes and connections are displayed inside the carriages. Tokens ($0.15) are used instead of tickets and a single token entitles you to use any route or combination of routes. Linea "C" (from Retiro station to Constitución station) crosses the city center and connects with all other branch lines (at Calle Pellegrini station with Linea "B" and "D", and at Avenida de Mayo with Linea "A"). Five lines link the outer parts of the city to the center.
Stations are closed between 0100 and 0500. Backpacks and luggage are allowed on trains. Rail maps and timetables can be bought from station platforms.

- Linea "A" runs under Calle Rivadavia, from Plaza de Mayo up to Primera Junta. Change at Lima station for Linea "C"
- Linea "B" runs from the central post office, in Avenida L N Alem, under

Tourist information

CITY OF BUENOS AIRES

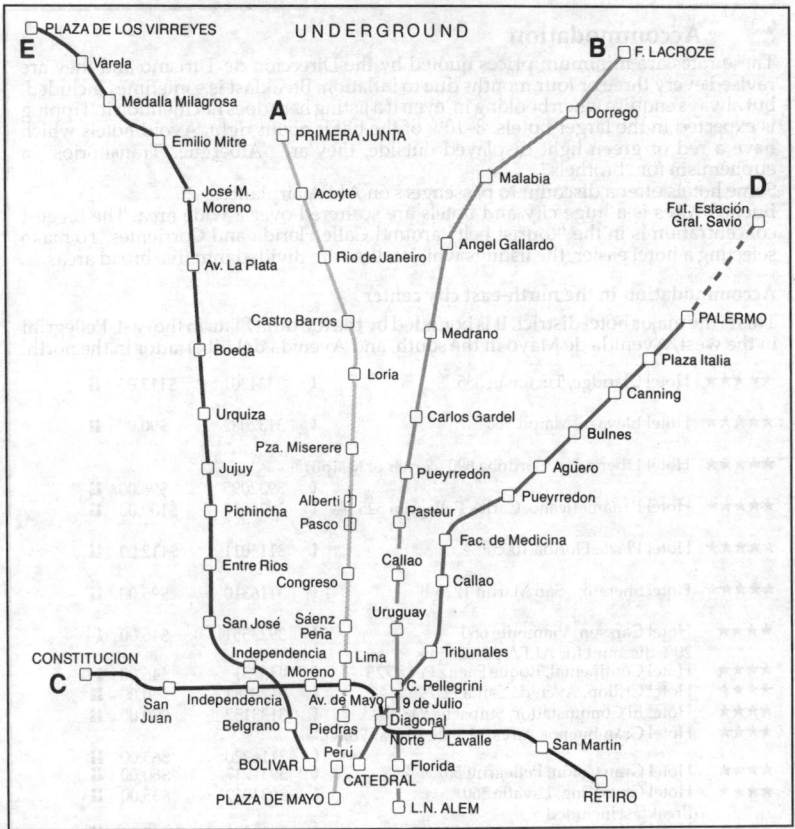

Avenida Corrientes, to Federico Lacroze station. Change at Pellegrini station for Linea "C"
- Linea "C" links Plaza Constitución with the Retiro station and provides connections with all the other lines
- Linea "D" runs from Plaza de Mayo under Diagonal Norte, Córdoba, and Santa Fé to the Palermo district, and is to be extended further. Change at 9 de Julio station for Linea "C"
- Linea "E" runs from Plaza de Mayo through San Juan to Avenida José María Moreno. Change at Independencia station for Linea "C"

Taxis

Taxis are easily recognizable by their yellow and black colours. Fares are apporoximately $1.00 per km, but meters are not always reliable, and traveling outside the city limits, and at night, is expensive. No tipping is required, but there is a charge for luggage. Taxi fares to Ezeiza airport range between $25.00 and $35.00.

Continued on page 41

Tourist information

City of Buenos Aires

Accommodation

These rates are minimum prices quoted by the Dirección de Turismo and they are revised every three or four months due to inflation. Breakfast is sometimes included, but always enquire when booking in, even if a listing here does not mention it. Tipping is expected in the larger hotels; 8–10% of the bill is about right. Avoid hotels which have a red or green light displayed outside; they are "Albergues Transitorios", a euphemism for "brothels".

Some hotels offer a discount to passengers on ALFA airplanes.

Buenos Aires is a huge city and hotels are scattered over a wide area. The biggest concentration is in the "tourist belt" around Calle Florida and Corrientes. To make selecting a hotel easier, the listings which follow are divided into five broad areas.

Accommodation in the north-east city center

This is the major hotel district. It is bounded by the Río de la Plata in the east, Pellegrini in the west, Avenida de Mayo in the south, and Avenida del Libertador in the north.

★★★★★	Hotel Claridge, Tucumán 535	3934301	$112.00	
★★★★★	Hotel Elevage, Maipú 960	3132082	$90.00	
★★★★★	Hotel Libertador, Córdoba 690 (corner of Maipú)	3932095	$96.00	
★★★★★	Hotel Panamericano, Carlos Pellegrini 525	3936017	$100.00	
★★★★★	Hotel Plaza, Florida 1005	3115011	$112.00	
★★★★★	Hotel Sheraton, San Martín 1225	3116310	$95.00	
★★★★	Hotel Carsson, Viamonte 650 *20% discount for ALFA passengers*	3923551	$46.00	
★★★★	Hotel Continental, Roque Saenz Peña 725	443251	$46.00	
★★★★	Hotel Crillon, Avenida Santa Fé 796	3128181	$50.00	
★★★★	Hotel El Conquistador, Suipacha 948	3133152	$70.00	
★★★★	Hotel Gran Buenos Aires, M T de Alvear 767	3116220	$65.00	
★★★★	Hotel Gran Colón, Pellegrini 507	3931717	$60.00	
★★★★	Hotel Gran King, Lavalle 560 *Breakfast included*	3934012	$35.00	
★★★★	Hotel Lafayette, Reconquista 546 *Breakfast included*	3939081	$45.00	
★★★★	Hotel Lancaster, Córdoba 405	3124061	$50.00	
★★★★	Hotel Principado, Paraguay 481	3133022	$60.00	
★★★★	Hotel Regente Palace, Suipacha 964 *Breakfast included*	3136628	$52.00	
★★★★	Hotel Regidor, Tucumán 451	3939615	$25.00	
★★★★	Hotel Rochester, Esmeralda 542	3939589	$45.00	
★★★★	Hotel Sheltown, M T de Alvear 742	3125070	$46.00	
★★★	Hotel Camino Real, Maipú 572	3923162	$28.00	
★★★	Hotel Esmeralda Palace, Esmeralda 527	3931085	$28.00	
★★★	Hotel Embajador, Carlos Pellegrini 1181	3939485	$28.00	
★★★	Hotel Gran Argentino, Carlos Pellegrini 37 *20% discount for ALFA passengers*	353071	$28.00	
★★★	Hotel Gran Dora, Maipú 963 *Breakfast included*	3127391	$45.00	
★★★	Hotel Gran Orly, Paraguay 474 *10% discount for ALFA passengers*	3125344	$20.00	

Accommodation

CITY OF BUENOS AIRES

Accommodation—continued

Accommodation in the north-east city center—continued

★★★	Hotel Italia Romanelli, Reconquista 647 20% discount for ALFA passengers	(3126361	$28.00	ii
★★★	Hotel Liberty, Corrientes 628 Breakfast included	(460261	$24.00	ii
★★★	Hotel Regis, Lavalle 813	(3935131	$21.00	i
★★★	Hotel San Carlos, Suipacha 39	(407021	$28.00	ii
★★★	Hotel San Antonio, Paraguay 372	(3125381	$15.00	i
★★★	Hotel Waldorf, Paraguay 450	(3122071	$28.00	ii
★★	Hotel Diplomat, San Martín 918	(3112708	$16.00	
★★	Hotel Eibar, Florida 334	(450969	$17.00	
★★	Hotel King's, Corrientes 623	(3928161	$22.00	ii
★★	Hotel Novel, Avenida de Mayo 915	(389176	$14.00	ii
★★	Hotel Plaza Roma, Lavalle 110 15% discount for ALFA pasengers	(3110839	$16.00	ii
★★	Hotel Promenade, M T de Alvear 444	(3125681	$22.00	ii
★★	Hotel Tres Sargentos, Tres Sargentos 345	(3126081	$22.00	ii
★★	Hotel Tucumán Palace, Tucumán 380	(3113555	$22.00	ii
★	Hotel Central Córdoba, San Martín 1021	(311175	$9.00	i
★	Hotel Du Helder, Rivadavia 857	(403404	$13.00	i
★	Hotel El Cabildo, Lavalle 748	(3926745	$13.00	i
★	Hotel Hispano, Avenida de Mayo 861	(344431	$12.00	i
★	Hotel Turista, Avenida de Mayo 686	(3312281	$13.00	i
A	Hospedaje Apolo, Tucumán 951 Credit cards accepted	(3936970	$7.00	i
A	Hospedaje Astoria, Avenida de Mayo 916	(379061	$9.00	i
A	Hospedaje Concorde, 25 de Mayo 630	(3132018	$9.00	i
A	Hospedaje Florida House, Florida 527	(3933791	$9.00	i
A	Hospedaje La Argentina, Avenida de Mayo 860	(349002	$8.00	i
A	Hospedaje Phoenix, San Martín 780	(3124845	$6.00	i
A	Hospedaje San Luis, Avenida de Mayo	(386398	$9.00	i
A	Hospedaje Suipacha Palace, Suipacha 18	(355001	$9.00	i
B	Hospedaje O'Rei, Lavalle 733	(3937186	$4.00	i
B	Hospedaje Splendid, Rivadavia 950	(372804	$5.00	i

- Hotel Ocean, Maipú 907
- Hotel Odeon, Esmeralda 368 and Corrientes
  Hotel Petit Goya, Suipacha 748

Accommodation in the south-west city center

This is the area bounded by Cerrito in the east, Avenida de Mayo in the south, Santa Fé in the north, and Callao in the west.

★★★★★	Hotel Bauen, Avenida Callao 346 Breakfast included	(8041600	$90.00	ii
★★★★	Hotel Bisonte, Paraguay 1207	(3948041	$46.00	i
★★★★	Hotel Bristol, Cerrito 286	(35401	$35.00	i
★★★★	Hotel de las Américas, Libertad 1020			
★★★★	Hotel Republica, Cerrito 370	(355058	$46.00	ii
★★★★	Hotel Salles, Cerrito 208 Breakfast included	(350091	$46.00	ii
★★★	Hotel Carlton, Libertad 1180	(440080	$28.00	ii
★★★	Hotel Columbia Palace, Corrientes 1533	(492123	$16.00	i

Accommodation

City of Buenos Aires

Accommodation—continued

Accommodation in the south-west city center—continued

★★★	Hotel Presidente, Cerrito 846	(	497671	$36.00	⁂
★★★	Hotel Savoy, Callao 181	(	400151	$28.00	⁂
★★	Hotel de la Paix, Rivadavia 1115	(	377140	$22.00	⁂
★★	Hotel Napoleon, Rivadavia 1364	(	372031	$22.00	⁂
★	Hotel Avenida Petit, Avenida de Mayo 1347	(	387831	$10.00	i
★	Hotel Chile, Avenida de Mayo 1297	(	377877	$13.00	i
★	Hotel Gran Vedra, Avenida de Mayo 1350	(	370584	$13.00	i
★	Hotel Majestic, Libertad 121	(	351949	$10.00	i
★	Hotel Marbella, Avenida de Mayo 1261	(	372338	$9.00	i
★	Hotel Milan, Montevideo 337	(	461906	$13.00	i
A	Hospedaje Callao, Callao 292	(	453534	$9.00	i
A	Hospedaje Europa, Mitre 1294	(	389629	$9.00	i
A	Hospedaje Gran Via, Sarmiento 1450	(	405763	$8.00	i
A	Hospedaje Lourdes, Callao 44	(	453080	$8.00	i
A	Hospedaje Orleans, Callao 680	(	419544	$9.00	i
A	Hospedaje Orense, Mitre 1359	(	453173	$9.00	i
A	Hospedaje Piramides, Peron 1473	(	404849	$9.00	i
A	Hospedaje Reyna, Avenida De Mayo 1120	(	372264	$6.00	i
B	Hospedaje Mediterraneo, Rodriguez Peá 149	(	452852	$8.00	⁂

Accommodation in the south city center

This is the area bounded by Avenida de Mayo in the north, Avenida Entre Ríos in the west, and Avenida Pedro de Mendoza in the east.

★★★★	Hotel City, Bolívar 160	(	346481	$30.00	i
★★★★	Hotel Los Dos Chinos, Brazil 780	(	232021	$46.00	⁂
	Near Constitución station				
★★★	Hotel Constitución Palace, Lima 1697	(	269011	$28.00	⁂
★★★	Hotel Nogaro, Diagonal J A Roca 562	(	3310091	$28.00	⁂
★	Hotel Solis Palace, Solis 352	(	407426	$13.00	i
A	Hospedaje Alba, Avenida Garay 1381	(	274303	$6.00	i
A	Hospedaje Carlos I, Carlos Calvo 1463	(	263700	$9.00	i
A	Hospedaje Cyrus, Humberto I 1162	(	231463	$6.00	i
A	Hospedaje Gran España, Tacuari 80	(	305541	$12.00	⁂
A	Hospedaje Gran Prince, Humberto I 1189	(	261154	$9.00	i
A	Hospedaje Nivi, Estados Unidos 827	(	272096	$9.00	i
A	Hospedaje 9 de Julio, Lima 1417	(	263967	$9.00	i
	Breakfast included				
A	Hospedaje Uruguay, Tacuari 83	(	372788	$9.00	i
B	Hospedaje Central, Alsina 1693	(	498785	$5.00	i

Accommodation in the north city center

This is the area bounded by Santa Fé in the south and Cerrito in the east.

★★★	Hotel Wilton Palace, Callao 1162	(	411818	$28.00	⁂
★	Hotel Prince, Arenales 1627	(	418004	$10.00	i

CITY OF BUENOS AIRES

Accommodation—continued

Accommodation in the north city cneter—continued

A	Hospedaje Central Argentina, Avenida Libertador 174	(3126742	$13.00	♦
	Near train station			
B	Hospedaje Versalles, Arenales 1394	(415214	$9.00	♦

Accommodation west of Callao and Avenida Entre Ríos

★★★	Hotel Sarmiento Palace, Sarmiento 1953	(453401	$28.00	♦♦
★★	Hotel N'Ontue, Corrientes 3321	(884098	$18.00	♦♦
★★	Hotel Alfa, Riobamba 1046	(442889	$13.00	♦♦
★	Hotel Castelli, Castelli 75	(489003	$10.00	♦
★	Hotel Condor, La Rioja 258	(937626	$17.00	♦♦
★	Hotel Rich, Bulnes 1247	(867732	$13.00	♦
A	Hospedaje Bahía, H Yrigoyen 3062	(977198	$9.00	♦
A	Hospedaje Florentino, General Urquiza 187	(939641	$9.00	♦
A	Hospedaje Gran Real, Riobamba 231	(459500	$9.00	♦
A	Hospedaje Gran Sarmiento, Sarmiento 1892	(452764	$9.00	♦
A	Hospedaje Hispano Argentino, Catamarca 167	(975543	$9.00	♦
A	Hospedaje Marfil, Ecuador 282	(871570	$8.00	♦
A	Hospedaje Miki, La Rioja 271	(931614	$7.00	♦
A	Hospedaje San Agustín, Avenida Pueyrredón 121	(882131	$12.00	♦♦

Accommodation in youth hostels

- José Marmol, 1555 (near Avenida la Plata), Barrio de Bodeo district
  (920774
  Take *Subte* Linea "E", fare $1.50 with Youth Hostels Association card
- YMCA, Reconquista 439. Central
- YWCA, Tucumán 884

Accommodation in apartments

If you intend to stay longer than a week or two renting an apartment may be a better choice. Check the tourist office for details.
- Aspen Building, Esmeralda 933 (3139011
  Kitchen, room service

Colectivos

These small buses cover a very wide area and are clean, frequent, and very fast. The basic fare is about $0.15. When taking a bus, look for little signs in the driver's window, as all bus numbers represent several routes.

Camping

- Villa Albertina, Lomas de Zamora, 15 km from city center

Eating out

Cafeterias, bars, and *choperías* are good for quick, inexpensive meals, but gourmets are also well catered for in Buenos Aires. One speciality worth trying is a meat dish called a *parrilla*. Check the *Buenos Aires Herald* for information about places that are currently in favor. The *Herald*, an English-language newspaper, is available at major hotels and airports, and from the tourist kiosks on Calle Florida. Away from the city center, good restaurants can

CITY OF BUENOS AIRES

be found on the Costanera Norte (which specializes in *parrillas*) and in the Boca district (which specializes in Italian cuisine). In the better restaurants dinner is served from 2100 until the early hours of the morning. The restaurants at Retiro and Constitución railway stations are open 24 hours. Most *Subte* stations also have cafeterias.

Eating out in the north-east city center

Argentine cuisine

- Restaurant Antigua Posada, Viamonte 966
- Restaurant El Quebracho, Avenida Córdoba 823. Credit cards accepted
- Restaurant La Chacra, Córdoba 941. Credit cards accepted
- ☞ Restaurant La Veda, Florida 1. Credit cards accepted
- Restaurant Paparazzi, corner of Avenida Córdoba Block 500 and San Martín. Credit cards accepted
- ☞ Restaurant Yapeyu, Maipú 383. Credit cards accepted

Chinese cuisine

- Restaurant Asia, Esmeralda 768
- Restaurant Chung King, Paraguay 725 (near Maipú)
- Restaurant Fortuna, Tucumán 912
- Restaurant Gran Victoria, Suipacha 783. Credit cards accepted
- Restaurant La Cantina China, Maipú 967
- Restaurant Nuevo Kowloon, Maipú 495
- Restaurant Oriente, Maipú 512

English cuisine

- Restaurant The Alexandra, San Martín 774. Credit cards accepted
- Restaurant The London Grill, Reconquista 455. Credit cards accepted

French cuisine

- Restaurant Catalinas, Reconquista 875. Credit cards accepted
- Restaurant Friday's, San Martín 961. Credit cards accepted
- La Casserolle, Carlos Calvo 2000
- Restaurant La Pergola, Hotel Libertador, corner of Córdoba and Maipú
- Restaurant Pinet, Alvear 2019

German cuisine

- Restaurant ABC, Lavalle 545
- Restaurant Club Alemán (German Club Restaurant), Corrientes 337
- Munich, Avenida D E Mayo 965
- Otto, Lavalle 895
- Zeppelin, Cabildo 3500
- Zur Eiche, San Martín 1537

Hungarian cuisine

- ☞ Restaurant Hostería del Caballito Blanco, Alvear 479

International cuisine

- Restaurant Blab, Florida 325. Credit cards accepted
- Restaurant Camara de las Sociedades Anonimas, Florida 1, 3rd floor
- City Hotel, Bolívar 160
- Restaurant Claridge, Tucumán 535
- Restaurant Clarke's II, Sarmiento 646. Credit cards accepted
- Restaurant El Recodo, Lavalle 130. Credit cards accepted
- Restaurant El Solar, Suipacha 1224
- Restaurant Gran Jorge, Maipú 924
- Restaurant La Pampa, Hotel Sheraton, San Martín 1225
- Restaurant La Mosca Blanca, opposite Hotel Sheraton in Retiro
- Restaurant Lois, Paraguay 487 across from Hotel Orly. Credit cards accepted
- Restaurant Pedemonte, Avenida de Mayo 676. Credit cards accepted
- Restaurant Rocinante, Pellegrini 715

Italian cuisine

- Restaurant A'Mamma Liberata, Medrano 974. Credit cards accepted
- Restaurant Aranjuez, Suipacha 1039. Credit cards accepted
- Restaurant Las Deliciosas Papas Fritas, Maipú 529
- El Palacio de la Pizza, Corrientes 750. Pizza
- Pizza Hut, Lavalle 876
- Pizzería Iguazú, Esmeralda 428
- Pizzería Los Inmortales, M T de Alvear 1234
- Pizzería Pampita, Esmeralda 517
- Pizzería Roma, Lavalle 888

Seafood

- Restaurant El Mundo, Maipú 550

Eating out

CITY OF BUENOS AIRES

- Restaurant El Salmon, Reconquista 968

Spanish cuisine

- Restaurant Chiquín, Perón (formerly called Cangallo) 920. Credit cards accepted
- Restaurant El Pulpo, corner of Reconquista and Tucumán
- Lo Prete, R S Peña 749
- Restaurant Tasca Tancat, Paraguay 645. Credit cards accepted

Steakhouses

- City Grill, corner of San Martín and Córdoba
- Restaurant El Palacio de la Papa Frita, Lavalle 735 Credit cards accepted
- Restaurant El Palacio de la Papa Frita, Lavalle 954. Credit cards accepted
- Restaurant Florida Grill, Florida 122. Counter service only
- Restaurant Hotel Navigante, Viamonte 100 (corner of Bouchard). Popular with the locals
- La Estancia, Lavalle 941
- Restaurant La Chacra, Córdoba 941
- Restaurant La Chacrita, Córdoba 972
- Restaurant La Rural, Suipacha 453. Open Sundays
- Restaurant Nazarenas, Reconquista 1132. Credit cards accepted
- Restaurant Paso El Abero, Avenida Córdoba Block 800 (corner of Esmeralda)

Vegetarian

- Restaurant Cavallo Blanco, Florida 245
- Restaurant El Jardin, Supacha block 400 (corner of Corrientes)
- Restaurant Grannix, Florida 126. Open for lunch Mon–Fri
- Restaurant Nueva Era, Maipú 650, 2nd floor
- Restaurant Yin Yang, Paraguay 868. Lunch only; closed Sun

Other restaurants

- Corrientes 11, Corrientes 135
- Don Luis, Viamonte 1169
- El Quijote, Pellegrini 663
- El Tronio, Reconquista 918
- Hunter's Place, Lavalle 445
- La Blanca, corner of Tucumán and Florida
- Restaurant La Cautiva, Sucre 1546, Belgrano district. Game
- La Escalerita, Lavalle 717. For snacks
- La Fonda, Lavalle 542
- La Pipeta, corner of San Martín and Lavalle
- Maxim's, on Paraguay between Florida and Esmeralda
- Oriente, corner of Avenida de Mayo and Avenida 9 de Julio
- Santa Generosa on Florida
- Smorgasbord, corner of Paraguay and Florida. Scandinavian cuisine
- Vasijas, Tres Sargentos 496 (corner of San Martín)

Cafeterias

- Cafetería Bar Etre, Avenida Córdoba 896
- Cafetería Cafe de L'Alliance, Córdoba 945. Closed Sun
- Cafetería Córdoba, Avenida Córdoba 853
- Cafetería Danny's, Viamonte 635. Closed weekends
- Cafetería El Castellar, Avenida Córdoba block 700 (corner of Esmeralda)
- Cafetería Exedra, Avenida Córdoba 999
- Cafetería Florida, Maipú 912
- Cafetería Holding Bar, Avenida Córdoba 829
- Cafetería La Bara, Avenida Córdoba 466
- Cafetería Lord Jim, Avenida Córdoba 628
- Cafetería San Mateo, Viamonte 699
- Cafetería Scorpio, Avenida Córdoba 802
- Cafetería Young Men's Bar, Avenida Córdoba 784
- Fast Food Pumper-nic, Suipacha 435
- Fast Food Pumper-nic, Florida 530
- Fast Food Kentucky Fried Chicken, Ortiz 1815. *Recoleta*
- Snack Bar St George, Viamonte 660
- Snack Bar Zakate, Tucumán 975

Eating out in the south-east city center

- Restaurant Anos Verdes, Corrientes 1219. Vegetarian
- Restaurant Arturito, Corrientes 1124. International cuisine; credit cards accepted
- Au Bec Fin, Arenales 1223. French cuisine
- Restaurant Cantabria, Callao 1235. Spanish cuisine; credit cards accepted

City of Buenos Aires

- Restaurant Casa China, Viamonte 1476. Chinese cuisine
- ☞ Corneta del Cazador, Cerrito Block 300
- Restaurant Edelweiss, Libertad 432. German cuisine; credit cards accepted
- El Ciervo, corner of Corrientes and Callao. German cuisine
- El Colonial, Alvear 1202. Steakhouse
- ☞ El Jocoso, corner of Corrientes and Callao
- ☞ Hispano, Rivadavia 1200. Seafood
- Hotel Español, Avenida de Mayo 1202
- ☞ Restaurant La Cabaña, Entre Ríos 436. Argentine cuisine
- La Churrasquita, Corrientes 1220. Steakhouse
- La Emiliana, Corrientes 1431
- Restaurant La Esquina de las Flores, Córdoba 1599. Vegetarian
- Restaurant Manantial, Montevideo 560. Vegetarian; closed Sun
- Pepito, Uruguay (between Corrientes and Sarmiento). Chicken dishes
- Pichin No 1, Paraná
- ☞ Pippo's, Paraná 356. Pasta and meat dishes
- Un Lugar, Avenida Corrientes block 1200. Steakhouse
- Pizzería Los Inmortales, Suipacha 429

Eating out in the south city center

French cuisine

- Au Coin de Marseille, Defensa 714. French cuisine
- Chez Louis, Alsina 541
- Restaurant Chez Moi, San Juan 1223. Credit cards accepted
- Restaurant Estragon, Defensa 855. Credit cards accepted
- Restaurant Flo, Reconquista 878. Credit cards accepted
- Restaurant La Crevette, San Juan 639 (in the tennis club rooms). Seafood; credit cards accepted
- Restaurant Tarrascon, Carlos Calvo 547, San Telmo district

German cuisine

- Restaurant Adam, Chile 274
- Restaurant El Jabali, Belgrano 538
- Munich Constitución, Lima 1589

International cuisine

- Restaurant El Repecho de San Telmo, Calvo 242. Credit cards accepted
- Restaurant La Autentica Banderita, Moreno 1127. Credit cards accepted

Spanish cuisine

- Restaurant Antigua Tasca de Cuchilleros, Calvo 319. Floor shows; credit cards accepted
- Restaurant Club Español, B de Irigoyen 180. Credit cards accepted
- Restaurant El Imparcial, H Irigoyen 1201
- Restaurant El Hispano Bar, Salta 26
- Restaurant Laurak-Bat, Belgrano 1144.
- Meson Español, Caseros 1750
- Restaurant Taberna Baska, Chile 980, seafood. Credit cards accepted
- Vasco Joxe Txiki, Belgrano 1211
- Restaurant Villarosa, H Yrigoyen 1389. Seafood; credit cards accepted

Other restaurants

- Barcito, Piedras 54
- Don Carlos, Balcarce 605. Hungarian cuisine
- El Pescadito, Mendoza 1483. Seafood
- Manolito's, Piedras 566
- Parrilla, Piedras 542
- Tres Coronas, Independencia 371. Scandinavian cuisine

Eating out in Costanera Norte

Argentine cuisine

- Restaurant A Los Amigos. Credit cards accepted
- Restaurant Los Años Locos. Credit cards accepted
- Restaurant El Fogón
- Restaurant Negro el 11. Credit cards accepted
- Restaurant Nicolás. Credit cards accepted
- Restaurant Los Platitos. Credit cards accepted
- Restaurant Yo y El. Credit cards accepted

Italian cusine

- Restaurant A'Nonna Immacolata. Credit cards accepted

CITY OF BUENOS AIRES

Other restaurants

- El Jacaranda
- El Timón
- Happening
- La Cabaña de Lano
- Las Tullas
- La Vaca Crie
- María Belén
- Rancho Inn

Eating out in La Boca

See "Entertainment in La Boca" on page 27.

Eating out in the suburbs

- Restaurant El Fogón de Martín Fierro, F Alcorta 7202. Credit cards accepted
- Restaurant La Tranquera, F Alcorta 6464

Tearooms and bars

Tearooms and bars in the north-east city center

The many bars and coffee shops on Avenida Corrientes (between Cerrito and Calleo) are a popular meeting place for the city's bohemians and intellectuals. On Lavalle there are *whiskerías* and *cervecerías* which serve coffee and drinks.

- Alekhine, Paraguay 860. For chess enthusiasts. It also has a moderately priced restaurant
- Alvear Palace, Alvear 189
- Arroyo, Arroyo 872
- Augustus, Florida 895
- Blue Horse, Suipacha 1082
- Cafetería Del Molino, Rivadavia 1801 (corner of Callao)
- ☞ Cafetería El Reloj, Lavalle 701 (corner of Maipú)
- Confetería Suiza, Tucumán 753
- En El Patio, Paraguay 886
- Cafetería Florida Garden, Florida 899 (corner of Paraguay)
- Cafetería Gran Rex, Maipú 501 (corner of Lavalle)
- Ideal, Suipacha 834
- La Estrella, corner of Maipú and Lavalle
- McGregor, Santa Fé 840
- Cafetería Richmond, Florida 468 between Lavalle and Corrientes. Chess tournaments in downstairs lounge
- Saint James, Córdoba 699

Tearooms and bars in the south-east city center

- Freddo, Callao 1400. Ice-cream parlor
- Cafetería La Paz, Corrientes 1599. Open very late
- Old Vic, Santa Fé 1102
- Cafetería Politeama, Corrientes 1496

Tearooms and bars in the Palermo area

- Cafetería Round Point, Figueroa Alcorta 3009 (corner of Tagle)

Whiskerías and cervecerías

Whiskerías and cervecerías in the city

- Arrayanes, corner of Córdoba and San Martín. Open Sunday
- Ascot, Libertador 3782
- Whiskería Bar-Baro, corner of Tres Sargentos and San Martín. Cosmopolitan atmosphere
- Bar Rua Nova, corner of Chacabuco and de Mayo. Cheap snacks
- ☞ Barila, Santa Fé 2375. Excellent confectionery
- Cafe Tabac, Libertador 2300 (corner of Díaz)
- Cafe Tortoni, Avenida de Mayo 829. *Peña* evenings, jazz music on weekends, and tango evenings
- Pub Down-Town Matias, San Martín 979. Irish–English style; lunch only
- Handicap Bar, Paraguay, near Hotel Orly. Has good cheap breakfasts
- Lepanto, Libertador 2814
- Rousillon, Montevideo 1151
- Ser, Libertador 2196
- Tip Tips, Santa Fé 1284
- Top Secret, corner of Libertador and Olleros
- Young Man's Bar, corner of Córdoba and Esmeralda

Whiskerías and cervecerías in La Boca

- Bar Verona

🕮 Post and telegraph

Overseas calls are a lot cheaper from Entel offices than from hotels, although they do take longer. The central telephone office on the corner of Maipú and Corrientes charges about $1.00 a minute for long-distance calls. All public telephones use

CITY OF BUENOS AIRES

tokens; there are different tokens for local calls and long-distance calls.

Post

- Central post office: Correo Central (Encotel), Sarmiento 189 (corner of L N Alem). Open Mon–Sat 0800–2000. There is a small charge for post restante letters. Parcels over 1 kg must be sent from the international parcels post office in Antartida Argentina, near Retiro station, which is open 0900–1500

Telephones

- Entel, Corrientes 707 (corner of Maipú). Open 24 hours every day; public telex in basement
- Entel, Retiro rail station and Once rail station. For international calls and cables. Open 7 days from 0700–2400

Financial

From time to time the government imposes restrictions on the activities of exchange houses. Banks charge about 5% commission on travelers checks'. Exchange houses ("Casas de Cambio") are open daily 0830–1630, and some also open on Saturdays 0900–1200. Most of the exchange houses are on Corrientes and San Martin.

- American Express, Calle Florida. This office will not give cash advances on the American Express card on Saturdays
- Baires, San Martín 215 ℂ 466851
- Banco de la Nación, Plaza de Mayo. Good rates, but only for Citicorp checks
- Banco de la Provincia de Buenos Aires. Agent for Visa card. You can get a cash advance at any branch of this bank upon presentation of your Visa card
- Banco Hollandes Unido, Florida 359
- Bank of America, corner of Perón (formerly called Cangallo) and San Martín. Exchanges only Bank of America travelers' checks
- Bank of London and South America Limited, corner of Reconquista and Mitre
- Cambio America, San Martín 312 ℂ 493676
- Cambio Baldino, Corrientes 328 ℂ 313295
- Cambio Baupesa, San Martín 363
- Cambio Calcos, Tucumán 994
- Cambio Intercam S A, San Martín 318
- Cambio Lancaster, San Martín 205
- Cambio Mercurio, San Martín 229 ℂ 453474
- Cambio Olimpic, Córdoba 433 ℂ 321844
- Cambio Piano, San Martín 347. Travelers checks
- Cambio Provincia, San Martín 120
- Cambio Puente Hnos, Lavalle 445 ℂ 320409. Possibly the best exchange house in Buenos Aires
- Cambio Vaccaro, Corrientes 489
- Cambio Veiga, Reconquista 379
- Cambio Velay José y Cia, San Martín 343
- Cambio Velox, San Martín 298
- Cambio Viatur, Reconquista 511
- Cambios Norte, Sarmiento 525 ℂ 3935959. Also travelers checks
- Cambios Norte, Santa Fé 1735 ℂ 411552
- Citibank, Mitre 502
- Citibank, Florida 746
- Columbus, San Martín 501
- Deutsche Bank, Mitre and Reconquista. Exchange open 1000–1300
- Exprinter, San Martín 176 ℂ 303324
- First National Bank of Boston, Florida 99. Will exchange travelers' checks for dollars for a small commission
- Royal Bank of Canada, corner of Florida and Perón (formerly called Cangallo)

Financial in Avellaneda

- Bank of London and South America, Mitre 553
- First National Bank of Boston. Open 1000–1600

Financial in San Isidro

- Bank of London and South America, Chacabuco 328. Open 1000–1600

Services and facilities

Medical services

- British hospital, Perdriel 74 ℂ 231081
- French hospital, Rioja 951 ℂ 971031
- German hospital, Pueyrredón 1650 ℂ 8214085
- Italian hospital, Gascon 450 ℂ 8115010
- Dental hospital, Pueyrredón 1940 ℂ 9415555

Innoculations

- Centro Medico Rivadavia, Bustamente 2531. Mon–Fri 0700–1900

CITY OF BUENOS AIRES

- Sanidad de Puerto, Ingeniero Huergo 1497, opposite Dique 1. Free. Take bus 20 from Retiro

Libraries

- Biblioteca Nacional (National Library), México 566. It has a collection of about 500 000 volumes and 12 000 manuscripts
- Biblioteca Lincoln, Florida 935. Open 0900–1745 weekdays. Membership $10.00 per month
- Harrods on Florida, 2nd floor. Membership $6.00 per month
- Cultura Inglesa, Suipacha 1333. Members only

Saunas

- Athenee, Paraguay 459
- Colmegna, Sarmiento 839
- Finlander, Cerrito 364

Laundry service

- Laundry and ironing: Viamonte 926
- M T Del Alvear 2018
- Junín 15 (corner of Rivadavia). Mon–Sat 0800–2100
- Junín 529 (corner of Lavalle)
- Tintoreria Constitución, Santiago del Estero 1572

Clubs

- Centro Cultural General San Martín, Sarmiento 1551. Free concerts and plays
- British: British Community Council, 25 de Mayo 444
- French: Alliance Française, Avenida Córdoba 946
- German: Goethe Institut, Corrientes 327 (310716. Movies, library and reading room (with latest German newspapers), concerts, theater, exhibitions, and restaurant

American

- American Club, Viamonte 1133, facing Teatro Colón. Restaurant
- American Women's Club, Córdoba 632, 11th floor

Churches

- Anglican: St John's Cathedral, 25 de Mayo 282. Half of the cost of building this church was met by the British government. It was consecrated in 1831. There is a Sunday service at 10.00
- Armenian: Iglesia Apostólica Armenia Basilica San Gregorio El Iluminador, Acevedo 1352
- German Evangelical Church: Iglesia Evangelica Alemana, Esmeralda 162 (454326
- Presbyterian: St Andrew's, Belgrano 579
- Russian Orthodox: Iglesia Ortodoxa Rusa, Brasil 315

Visas, passports

Authorities

- Policia de Turismo (Tourist Police) are policewomen who patrol the downtown district near the main tourist hotels from 0800–2200. They speak English, French, German and Portugese, and their function is specifically to help tourists
- Migraciones, Antartida Argentina 1365
- Central police station, Moreno 1550 (388041

Consulates

- Australia: Santa Fé 846 (3126841. Open Mon–Thurs 0830–1230
- Austria: French 3671 (8021400. Open Mon–Fri 0900–1200
- Belgium: Defensa 113, 8th floor (330066. Open Mon–Thurs 0900–1300
- Bolivia: 25 de Mayo 611, 2nd floor (3117365. Open Mon–Fri 0900–1400
- Brazil: Pellegrini 1363, 5th floor (3945260. Open Mon–Fri 1000–1800
- Canada: Suipacha 1111, 25th floor (3129081. Open Mon–Fri 0900–1200
- Chile: San Martín 439, 9th floor (3946582. Open Mon–Fri 0900–1400
- Denmark: L N Alem 1074, 9th floor (3126901. Open Mon–Fri 0930–1300
- France: Santa Fé 846, 4th floor (3122425. Open Mon–Fri 0900–1200
- Germany (West): Villanueva 1055 (7812002, 7715054, 7715059. Open Mon–Fri 0900–1200
- Israel: Arroyo 916 (3924481. Open Mon–Fri 0900–1100
- Italy: M T de Alvear 1149 (3939329. Open Mon–Fri 0830–1130. Closed Thurs
- Japan: Paseo Colón 275, 11th floor (302563. Mon–Fri 1000–1200 and 1500–1700

CITY OF BUENOS AIRES

✈ Air services

Buses 51 and 86 run the 1½-hour trip to Ezeiza airport from Plaza de Mayo (marked "Aeropuerto"); fare $2.20. The airport bus for Ezeiza airport leaves from outside the Hotel Gran Colón in Pellegrini; the fare is $5.50, and the trip takes an hour. A taxi to Ezeiza airport costs $25.00–$35.00.

- Aerolineas Argentinas (AA), Perú 2 ℡ 7732061
- Aerolineas Federal Argentinas (ALFA), C Pellegrini 738, 4th floor
- Austral, Corrientes 487 ℡ 499011
- Lineas Aereas del Estado (LADE), Perú 710 ℡ 3617071. LADE specializes in flights to Patagonia. They use small airplanes which can land on short airstrips in the Patagonian outback. Their fares are cheaper than Aerolineas Argentinas or Austral, but flights take longer. They are usually heavily booked, especially flights in and out of Ushuaia and El Calafate
- Lineas Aereas Privadas Argentinas (LAPA), Reconquista 1056

Destination	Fare	Depart	Services	Hours	Airlines
• Bahía Blanca	$56.00	0630	5–7 services daily	1	AA, Austral
	$46.00	0800	Tues, Thurs	3	LADE
• Chapelco	$57.00	0830	Mon, Wed	7	LADE
	$95.00	0915	Tues, Wed, Sat, Sun	3	AA
• Comodoro Rivadavia					
	$77.00	0625	3–7 services daily	2	AA, Austral
	$73.00	0800	Tues–Fri	9	LADE
• Córdoba	$55.00	0630	8–13 services daily	1	AA, Austral
• Corrientes	$58.00	0725	1–2 services daily	2	AA, Austral
• Esquel	$77.00	0800	Tues, Fri	7	LADE
	$95.00	0945	1–2 services daily	4	AA
• Formosa	$66.00	0725	daily except Sun	2	AA
• Goya	$56.00	1050	Mon, Wed, Sat	2	Austral
• La Rioja	$69.00	0640	1–2 services daily	3	AA
• Mar del Plata	$43.00	0710	6–9 services daily	1	AA, Austral
	$36.00	0800	Mon–Wed, Fri, Sat	2	LADE
• Mendoza	$72.00	0645	5–7 services daily	2	AA, Austral
• Necochea	$56.00	0920	Mon, Wed, Fri	2	LAPA
• Neuquén	$72.00	0650	4–6 services daily	2	AA, Austral
	$58.00	0800	Mon, Tues, Wed, Fri	5	LADE
• Paraná	$37.00	1510	daily except Sun	2	Austral
• Paso de los Libres	$45.00	0945	daily	2	Austral
• Posadas	$62.00	1430	2–4 services daily	2	AA, Austral
• Puerto Deseado	$79.00	0800	Tues, Fri	9	LADE
• Puerto Iguazú	$69.00	0750	3–5 services daily	2	AA, Austral
• Puerto San Julián	$80.00	0800	Tues, Fri	10	LADE
• Reconquista	$56.00	1050	Mon, Wed, Sat	3	Austral
• Resistencia	$58.00	0715	2–3 services daily	2	AA, Austral
• Río Cuarto	$49.00	1245	daily	2	AA
• Río Gallegos	$83.00	0610	5–7 services daily	4	AA, Austral
	$81.00	0800	Tues, Fri	9	LADE
• Río Grande	$90.00	0630	4 services daily	5	AA, Austral
	$81.00	0800	Tues, Fri	13	LADE
• Rosario	$32.00	0700	7–9 services daily	1	AA, Austral
• Salta	$83.00	0630	3–4 services daily	3	AA, Austral
• San Antonio Oeste					
	$37.00	0830	Mon, Thurs	4	LADE

CITY OF BUENOS AIRES

Air services—continued

Destination	Fare	Depart	Services	Hours	Airlines
• San Carlos de Bariloche					
	$95.00	0705	3–5 services daily	3	AA, Austral
	$76.00	0800	Mon, Tues, Wed, Fri	8	LADE
• San Fernando del Valle de Catamarca					
	$69.00	0640	daily	3	AA
• San Juan	$72.00	0645	2 services daily	2	AA, Austral
• San Luis	$63.00	0820	daily	2	AA
• San Miguel de Tucumán					
	$70.00	0630	4–7 services daily	2	AA, Austral
• San Rafael	$71.00	1245	daily	2	AA
• San Salvador de Jujuy					
	$85.00	0605	2–3 services daily	3	AA
• Santa Cruz	$80.00	0800	Tues, Fri	11	LADE
• Santa Fé	$37.00	0645	3–4 services daily	1	AA, Austral
• Santa Rosa	$52.00	1315	2–3 services daily	2	AA
• Santiago del Estero					
	$71.00	1030	daily	2	AA
• Trelew	$69.00	0710	3–6 services daily	3	AA, Austral
	$78.00	0800	Tues, Thurs, Fri	7	LADE
• Termas de Río Hondo			0820	2 services daily	3Austral
• Ushuaia	$96.00	0630	2 services daily	6	AA
• Viedma	$50.00	0800	Mon, Thurs, Fri	3	LADE
	$61.00	0920	daily	2	AA
• Villa Mercedes	$63.00	0645	daily except Sun	2	Austral
• Zapala	$47.00	0900	Wed	6	LADE

- Netherlands: Maipú 66, 2nd floor ℂ 333749. Open Mon–Fri 0900–1230
- New Zealand: New Zealand is at present represented by the Swiss consulate: see Switzerland below
- Paraguay: Maipú 464, 3rd floor ℂ 3926536. Open Mon–Fri 0930–1300
- Peru: Tucumán 637, 9th floor ℂ 3921344. Open Mon–Fri 0900–1400
- South Africa: M T de Alvear 590, 7th floor ℂ 3118991. Open Mon–Fri 0900–1100
- Spain: Guido 1760 ℂ 410078. Open Mon–Fri 0900–1400
- Sweden: Corrientes 330, 3rd floor ℂ 3113089. Open Mon–Fri 1000–1200
- Switzerland, Santa Fé 846, 12th floor ℂ 3116491. Open Mon–Fri 0900–1200. Switzerland at present also represents the UK and New Zealand from the office of the former British embassy in Luis Agote 2412 ℂ 8037070)
- United Kingdom: The UK is at present represented by the Swiss consultate: see Switzerland above
- Uruguay: Las Heras 1907 ℂ 8036032. Open Mon–Fri 1000–1800
- USA: Colombia 4300, Palermo district ℂ 7748811. Open Mon–Fri 0815–1100

Motoring

Clubs

- Automovil Club Argentino (ACA), Libertador 1850 ℂ 8026061. The ACA provides a range of services to members upon presentation of their membership card: a travel document service, road charts ("*Hojas de Ruta*", $1.00 each) and maps, vacation guides, and camping information. Tourist guides are available for sale. The club has its own service stations and accommodation facilities, which are of four kinds: motels,

City of Buenos Aires

🚌 Buses

The Buenos Aires bus terminal, Mejia 1680 (corner of Antartida), is next to Retiro rail station. It is a 400 m walk from the subway (*Subte* Linea "C") to the bus terminal. Facilities in the bus terminal include travel information, toilets, a restaurant, and a luggage office. All bus companies operating outside a radius of 200 km must use this terminal.

Destination	Fare	Depart	Services	Hours	Company
• Asunción	$34.00		2 services daily	28	Brújula, La Internacional
• Bahía Blanca	$15.30				
• Chilecito		1600	daily	19	ABLO
• Claromecó	$16.00				
• Clorinda	$29.00		daily	20	Godoy
• Comodoro Rivadavia	$35.00			32	
• Córdoba	$16.00	1600	2 services daily	10	ABLO
	$16.00	1200	10 services daily	13	TA Chevallier
	$14.80		daily		Cacorba, Urquiza
• Cosquín	$21.50				
• Curuzu Cuatia				9	
• Formosa	$27.00		daily	17	Godoy
• Gualeguaychú	$4.30		daily		
• Junín de los Andes	$40.20	1430	daily	22	TA Chevallier
• La Plata	$1.00			2	
• La Rioja		1600	daily	18	ABLO
• Mar del Plata	$11.80			6	TA Chevallier
• Mendoza	$26.50	1615	3 services daily	13	TA Chevallier
	$23.00			13	TAC
• Miramar	$7.00				
• Necochea	$8.50				
• Neuquén	$24.50	1315	1–2 services daily	16	La Estrella
	$24.00	2030	daily	18	El Valle
	$26.00	1235	3 services daily	16	TA Chevallier
• Obera	$26.00	1600	2 services daily	17	Singer
• Paraná	$8.50	daily			
• Paso de los Libres		1130	3 services daily	10	Singer
• Pergamino				1	
• Posadas	$24.00	1130	4 services daily	15	Singer
• Puerto Iguazú	$31.00	1130	daily	22	Singer
• Puerto Madryn	$27.00		3 services daily	24	
• Reconquista	$15.00		11 services daily	13	Brújula, La Internacional
• Resistencia	$18.00		daily	16	Brújula, La Internacional
• Roque Sáenz Peña	$23.50	2000	daily	18	La Internacional
• Rosario	$7.00		over 50 services daily	4	ABLO, General Urquiza, TA Chevallier
• San Antonio Oeste	$18.00				
• San Carlos de Bariloche	$44.20	1235	daily	22	TA Chevallier
	$41.00	2030	daily	24	El Valle
	$41.00	1315	daily	22	La Estrella

Buses

CITY OF BUENOS AIRES

Buses—continued

Destination	Fare	Depart	Services	Hours	Company
• San Fernando de Catamarca					
	$28.00	1200	2 services daily	17	TA Chevallier
	$28.00			19	Cacorba
• San Juan	$20.00	1830	daily		Rojas
• San Luis	$20.20	1615	3 services daily	14	TA Chevallier
• San Martín de los Andes					
	$40.00	1340	Fri	23	La Estrella
	$40.00	2000	Tues	26	El Valle
• San Miguel de Tucumán					
	$28.50	1600	daily	16	TA Chevallier
• San Rafael	$22.60	2200	daily		Rojas
• Santa Fé	$11.00	15 services daily		7	Brújula, La Internacional
• Santa Rosa	$14.00	0800	4 services daily	12	TA Chevallier
• Santiago del Estero					
	$22.30	1600	daily	14	TA Chevallier
• Termas de Río Hondo					
	$22.50	1600	daily	17	TA Chevallier
	$19.00	1830	daily	18	La Unión
• Trelew	$25.00			25	
• Viedma	$21.50	2030	daily		El Condor
• Villa Carlos Paz	$21.00	12	TA Chevallier		
• Villa Gesell	$9.40				
• Villa Mercedes	$20.00				
• Zapala	$37.00	1430	daily	19	TA Chevallier

hosterías, hotels, and *unidades turísticas*. Motel accommodation is limited to overnight stays. *Hosterías* are pleasant places and very friendly. Meals of some sort are available at all four types of accommodation.

• Touring Club Argentino, Esmeralda 605 (corner of Tucumán 781), 3rd floor ℂ 3926742

Car rental

Crossing the border to another country requires written authorization from the car hire company.

• A1 International, M T de Alvear 680 ℂ 329475 and 329476. Branches in all main cities
• Agencia Amorin, de Mayo 878 ℂ 303318
• Alquila Coches Hertz, Corrientes 6122 ℂ 553569. Hire within Buenos Aires only
• Avis Rent-a-Car, at five locations:
  Maipú 940 ℂ 3111008
  M T de Alvear 629 ℂ 318563
  Ezeiza airport
  Aeroparque Jorje Newbery
  Hotel Sheraton, San Martín 1225.
  Available for hire are: Fiat 147, Renault 12, Renault 11/18, Fiat 128 Super Europa, Ford Falcon, VW Kombi, VW Gacel, Fiat Regata 85, Fiat Super Europa, Ford Taunus, and Ford Sierra. You can have your bill sent to your home address if you wish
• Budget Rent-a-Car. Buenos Aires only
• Cars Express, M T de Alvear 680 ℂ 329475
• Cocha, Lavalle 547 ℂ 324104
• Delfino Autos, Laprida 1129 ℂ 843158
• Liprandi Rent-a-Car, Esmeralda 1065 ℂ 3118081

Continued on page 54

Motoring

CITY OF BUENOS AIRES

🚆 Trains

The railroad information office is at Florida 729, and is open Mon–Sat 0700–2100, Sun 0700–1300. The long-distance rail stations are:
- Constitución: southern and south-western lines
- Lacroze: north-eastern lines
- Once: western lines
- Retiro: northern, western, and north-western lines

As a rough guide to fares, first class is 33% more than tourist class, and Pullman is double tourist class.

Destination	Fare	Services	Hours	Station
• Bahía Blanca		2 services daily	10	Constitución
Sleeper	$26.00			
Pullman	$17.00			
First class	$11.00			
Tourist class	$8.50			
• Concordia		2–3 services daily	8	Lacroze
Sleeper	$22.60			
Pullman	$13.70			
First class	$9.20			
Tourist class	$6.70			
• Córdoba		2–3 services daily	12	Retiro
Sleeper	$27.80			
Pullman	$19.00			
First class	$12.50			
Tourist class	$9.50			
• Corrientes		daily	20	Lacroze
Sleeper	$35.50			
First class	$13.00			
Tourist class	$13.00			
• Esquel (via Ingeniero Jacobacci)		Wed, Sat	2 days	Constitución
Sleeper	$55.50			
Pullman	$46.50			
First class	$33.50			
Tourist class	$25.00			
• La Plata		16 services daily	1	Constitución
Tourist class	$1.00			
• Mar del Plata		2–3 services daily	5	Constitución
Pullman	$11.00			
First class	$7.50			
Tourist class	$5.50			
• Mendoza		1–2 services daily	14	Retiro
Sleeper	$36.00			
Pullman	$27.20			
First class	$17.00			
Tourist class	$13.50			
• Miramar		daily	6	Constitución
Tourist class	$8.00			
• Neuquén		daily	21	Constitución
Sleeper	$39.50			
Pullman	$30.50			
First class	$20.00			
Tourist class	$15.00			

City of Buenos Aires

Trains—continued

Destination	Fare	Services	Hours	Station
• Olavarría		2 services daily	5	Constitución
Sleeper	$18.50			
Pullman	$9.50			
First class	$6.30			
Tourist class	$4.80			
• Paraná		Sun, Fri	11	Lacroze
Sleeper	$23.70			
First class	$9.80			
Tourist class	$7.20			
• Paso de los Libres		1–2 services daily	12	Lacroze
Sleeper	$28.70			
Pullman	$19.80			
First class	$13.00			
Tourist class	$9.80			
• Posadas		1—2 services daily	19	Lacroze
Sleeper	$37.50			
Pullman	$28.50			
First class	$19.00			
Tourist class	$14.20			
• Quequén		Mon, Wed, Fri	10	Constitución
Pullman	$13.50			
First class	$9.00			
Tourist class	$6.70			
• Rosario		15 services daily	4	Retiro
Pullman	$12.00			
First class	$6.50			
Tourist class	$4.80			
• San Antonio Oeste		Wed, Sat	21	Constitución
Sleeper	$37.50			
Pullman	$28.50			
First class	$19.00			
Tourist class	$14.50			
• San Carlos de Bariloche		Wed, Sat, Sun	32	Constitución
Sleeper	$52.80			
First class	$29.00			
Tourist class	$21.50			
• San Juan		daily	20	Retiro
Sleeper	$39.80			
Pullman	$31.00			
First class	$20.50			
Tourist class	$15.20			
• San Luis		1–2 services daily	11	Retiro
Sleeper	$29.80			
Pullman	$21.00			
First class	$13.70			
Tourist class	$15.20			
• San Miguel de Tucumán		3–5 services daily	17	Retiro
Sleeper	$48.00			
Pullman	$37.50			
First class	$20.00			
Tourist class	$14.80			

Trains

City of Buenos Aires

Trains—continued

• San Rafael		Tues, Fri	18	Retiro
Pullman	$26.00			
First class	$17.20			
Tourist class	$12.80			
• Santa Fé		4–6 services daily	8	Retiro
Pullman	$14.50			
First class	$9.50			
Tourist class	$7.50			
• Santiago del Estero (La Banda station)		3–5 services daily	15	Retiro
Sleeper	$43.50			
Pullman	$32.50			
First class	$32.50			
Tourist class	$12.80			
• Villa Dolores		Mon, Wed, Fri	15	Retiro
Change at Villa Mercedes				
• Villa Mercedes		Mon, Wed, Fri	10	Retiro
Sleeper	$27.20			
Pullman	$18.20			
First class	$12.20			
Tourist class	$9.20			
• Zapala		daily	25	Constitución
Sleeper	$44.50			
Pullman	$35.50			
First class	$35.50			
Tourist class	$17.50			

- Serra Lima Alquila, Córdoba 3121 ℂ 805983 or 821661
- Turismo Autos, Florida 716 ℂ 3927330

Water transport

The *Buenos Aires Herald*, an English-language newspaper, lists all shipping schedules.

- Corrientes, up the Río Paraná and Río Paraguay: Flota Fluvial del Estado boats leave twice a week from the south basin
- Rosario, up the Río Paraná: Flota Fluvial del Estado boats leave twice a week from the Dársena Sur (South Basin)
- Antarctica: Two ships sail once a year in February for 30 days; each has are two four-berth cabins which cost $2200, including meals. Check with the tourist office

Hovercraft services

Aliscafos Alimar, Córdoba 1801 ℂ 415914. Hovercraft depart from Dársena Sur, Mendoza 443 (corner of Brazil).

- Montevideo (Uruguay): daily 0700, 0900, 1200, 1500, 1800; return daily 0430, 0630, 0930, 1130, 1330. Aliscafos Belt, Avenida Córdoba 787 ℂ 3824691. Departures and tickets at the corner of Pedro de Mendoza and J M Blanes.
- Colonia: $20.00; 0800; 6 services daily; 3 hours
- Montevideo (Uruguay): $25.00; 4 hours; first return journey 0510
- Punta del Este: $30.00. By hovercraft to Montevideo and bus to Punte del Este

Tours

See also the list of tour operators under "Sightseeing" on page 59.

Tour operators

- Antartur, Uruguay 485, 8th floor ℂ 493162. Bookings for Antarctic trips on MV *Bahía Pariso* from Ushuaia
- City Bus, Rodríguez Peña 431 ℂ 493298. Tours in the city and suburbs
- City Service Travel Agency, Florida 890 ℂ 328416. American Express agent

CITY OF BUENOS AIRES

⊕ Tours

All prices include half board and bus travel.

Destination	Cost	Length	Tour operator
• Asunción, Puerto Iguazú, and Posadas			
	$150.00	8 days	Estrella Condor
• Esquel	$260.00	4 days	Passing Tours
• Jujuy	$230.00	4 days	Passing Tours
• Lago Argentino	$210.00	4 days	Passing Tours
• Lago Argentino and Ushuaia			
	$420.00	8 days	Passing Tours
Air travel included			
• Peninsula Valdez	$240.00	4 days	Passing Tours
• Salta	$230.00	4 days	Passing Tours
• San Carlos de Bariloche			
	$190.00	4 days	Passing Tours
	$110.00	8 days	Estrella Condor
	$260.00	8 days	Passing Tours
• San Miguel de Tucumán			
	$200.00	4 days	Passing Tours
• Ushuaia	$210.00	4 days	Passing Tours
• Villa Carlos Paz	$90.00	7 days	Estrella Condor

- Diners Travel, Sarmiento. Diners Club card accepted
- Exprinter, Galería Güemes, San Martín 176 (corner of Santa Fé)
- Gleizer Travel, ground floor, Hotel Sheraton, San Martín 1225
- Lihue Expeditions, suite 104, Belgrano 262, San Isidro 1642 ((0541) 7477689. This company specializes in tours off the beaten track. English-speaking guides
- Oficina Flyer, Reconquista 617, 8th floor (3138165. ● English, Dutch and German spoken; credit cards accepted
- Passing Tours, Pellegrini 1057 (3116759
- Star Travel Service, Florida 556 (3922744
- Thomas Cook and Son, Córdoba 746
- Tennant's, Mitre 559 (337645 ●
- Turismo Estrella Condor, Avenida Córdoba 917

⊞ Shopping

Good streets for shopping are Calle Florida, in the main business district, and Avenida Santa Fé, which crosses Florida at Plaza San Martín. Avenida Santa Fé is less touristy and less expensive than Florida.

The Mercado de Abasto built in 1893 between Corrientes, Anchorena, Lavalle, and Agüero has been redeveloped as a cultural and entertainment center.

Books

- ABC, Córdoba 685
- Acme Agency, Suipacha 245
- ☞ El Ateneo, Florida 340. Stocks books in seventeen languages
- Librería Goethe, Corrientes 366. Good selection of German books, both new and secondhand
- Librería Hachette, Avenida Córdoba 936
- Librería Leonardo, Córdoba 335. Italian books
- Plazoleta Primera Junta. Books and magazines on Saturdays 1200–2000 and Sundays 1000–2000
- Plazoleta Santa Fé, corner of Santa Fé and Uriarte, Palermo district. Old books and magazines, Saturdays 1200–2000, Sundays 1000–2000
- There is a well-stocked secondhand bookshop inside the shopping arcade in front of Once station. Books can be exchanged and the prices are reasonable

City of Buenos Aires

Clothes
- Florida and Santa Fé for menswear
- Avenida Corrientes has a lot of menswear shops between blocks 600 and 1000
- There is also good shopping in Avenida Cabildo in the Belgrano district. To reach it take bus 152 from Retiro station
- For casual clothes try the boutiques in the suburb of Martínez

Jewelry
- Antoniazza-Chiappe, Avenida Alvear 1895. Jewelry and precious stones
- Art Petrus, shop 32, Florida 971. Precious stones
- Enne-A, Maipú 833. Precious stones
- Ricardo Saul, Avenida Quintana 450. Precious stones
- H Stern, at major five-star hotels. Jewelry and semi-precious stones

Photographic equipment
- Casa del Flash, Florida 37. Sales only
- Expofot, Suipacha 597 (agent for Fuji). One-hour hour service
- Laboclick, Esmeralda 444. Same-day service for prints, 24 hours for slides
- Le Lab, Viamonte 612 (corner of Florida)

Souvenirs and antiques
The best buys are found in the San Telmo district, particularly on Defensa, Carlos Calvo, and Humberto.
There is a antiques market in the Plaza Dorrego, in San Telmo. Catch a 29 bus from the Boca area or the end of Calle Florida.

Antiques
- Plaza Dorrego, San Telmo. Sunday market for souvenirs and antiques from 1000–1700; very touristy
- Sunday market on the corner of Humberto 1st and Defensa

Handicrafts
- Feria de Las Artes, corner of Defensa and Alsina. Fridays 1400–1700
- Craft and jewelry market on Saturdays 1000–1800 at corner of Avendia Santa Fé and Plaza Italia. Take *Subte* line "D"
- Kelly's at Paraguay 431 has a very large selection of Argentine handicrafts

- Plastic arts in the Caminito section of the Boca district

Stamps and coins
- Rivadavia 4900 (corner of Parque Rivadavia). Vendors congregate around the *ombú* tree. Sundays from 0900–1300

Sport

Boating
- The Tigre boat club, founded in 1888, is open for limited periods to British or American visitors for a small fee

Bowling
- Snack Bar Bowling, Pellegrini 157. Open Sundays

Golf
- Argentine golf association, Avenida Corrientes (3943743
- Municipal golf course, corner of Tornquist and Olleros, Palermo (7727576
- Golf driving range, Avenida Salguero, Costanera Norte. Open 0800–2000
- There are also golf courses at Hurlingham, Ranelagh, Ituzaingó, Lomas, San Andres, San Isidro, Saenz Peña, Olivos, Jockey, Campo Argentinos, and Hindu Country Club

Hang gliding
- Hang gliding club, Club Argentino Planeadores Albatross, Avenida de Mayo 1370, 6th floor (375504

Racing
- The Hipodromo Argentino (Argentine Racecourse), is next to Parques Palermo and seats about 45 000
- There is another excellent racecourse with a grass track at San Isidro, 25 minutes from the city center by train or car. The meetings alternate with those at Palermo. There are Saturday and Sunday races throughout the year, and on all holidays except May 25 and July 9. Betting is by totalizator

Shopping

City of Buenos Aires

Squash
- Embassy squash court, Suipacha 751 ℂ 3923350. Closed Sundays
- Olimpia Cancilleria squash court, Esmeralda 1042 ℂ 3118687. Sauna

Swimming
The water in the Río de la Plata is highly contaminated and swimming is prohibited.

🛛 Entertainment

Entertainment in the city center
Avenida Corrientes is the place to go for a night out; it is lined with dozens of restaurants, cafes, night clubs, and theaters. Close by is Calle Lavalle; here, and in streets nearby, are numerous cinemas and good restaurants. Calle Lavalle is for pedestrians only.

Bars, cabarets, discos
- Bar Atalaya, Hotel Sheraton, San Martín 1225, 23rd floor.
- Bar Claridge Hotel, Tucumán 535
- Bar Italia Romanelli, Reconquista 645
- Bar Lancaster Hotel, Córdoba 405
- Bar La Posta del Yatasto, Córdoba 698
- Bar Plaza Hotel, Florida 1005. Formal
- ☞ Cabaret Karim Club, Pellegrini 1143. Floor shows, dancing
- Cabaret Karina, Corrientes 636. Tango and strip show at 0100
- Cabaret King's Club, Córdoba 937. Dancing and strip shows
- Cabaret Maison Doree, Viamonte 458. Strip show
- Disco Atalaya, Hotel Sheraton, San Martín 1225. For adults; formal
- Disco Elevage Hotel, Maipú 960. Ladies' night Sundays; formal
- Disco Mau Mau, Arroyo 866. Formal

Nightclubs
- Achallay Huasi, Esmeralda 1040. Tango music; cover charge $10.00
- Arnaldo, Paraná 340
- Gong, Córdoba 630. Very fashionable
- Jamaica Club, San Martín 927
- La Querencia, de Mayo 870
- Queen Club, Esmeralda 565

Entertainment in the center west
- Bar Bauen Hotel, Avenida Callao 360. Piano bar
- Bar Bristol Hotel, Cerrito 285
- Bar Harry's, Quintana 134. Light snacks
- Bar Periplo, M T de Alvear 555. Maritime decor
- Bar Pink Gin, Riobamba 1173. Most patrons over 30; soft music
- Bar Queen Bess, Santa Fé 868
- Cabaret Vibroll, Alvear 628
- Disco Contramano, Rodríguez Peña 1082. Gay disco
- Disco Le Club, Avenida Quintana 111. Adults and teens; formal
- Disco Snob, Ayacucho 2038. All ages
- Disco Puerto Pirata, Libertad 1163. Adults and teens
- Tanguería Cano 14, Talcahuano 975. Floor shows and dancing
- Tanguería Sur, Belgrano 1178. Dancing
- Cambalache, Libertad 832
- La Ciudad, Talcahuano 1034
- Mi Rincón, Cerrito 1050
- Patio de Tango, Corrientes 1162. Dancing

Entertainment in La Boca
- Show Il Castello, Pedro de Mendoza 1455. Italian cuisine, dancing; credit cards accepted
- Show Spadavecchia, Necochea 1180. Italian cuisine, fixed price menu. A meal from the set menu with wine costs $10.00. Very popular. There's dancing, and the band is loud. Seats some 500 people. There are several other similar places also on Necochea. They all serve antipasta and chicken, and they all have loud bands. Be warned!
- Torna Sorrento, Lamadrid 709/109. Run by Italians and has live Chilean folk music
- ☞ Restaurant Napolitano, near Torna Sorrento. A set seafood lunch costs $10.00 for two here, and it has a good atmosphere. Wine list
- ☞ Tanguería Il Castello, Pedro de Mendoza 1455. Floor shows, dancing, restaurant

Entertainment in San Telmo
Bands usually start playing at about 2330. Most places open Fri, Sat, and Sun, and have a cover charge ($2.00 and up)

City of Buenos Aires

- Show El Cerrojo del Juglar, Peru 555. International cuisine, fixed menu; credit cards accepted
- Tanguería Bar Sur, Estados Unidos 299. Tango shows and dancing
- Tanguería Casa Rosada, Chile 318. Tango shows and dancing; young patrons
- La Tanguería de Don Emilio, Defensa 760. Dancing
- Tanguería El Viejo Almacen, corner of Independencia and Balcarce. Dancing
- Tanguería Los Dos Pianitos, J M Giuffra 305. Tango shows, dancing, informal
- Tanguería Michelangelo, Balcarce 433. Shows, dancing, Spanish cuisine
- Tanguería Taconeango, Balcarce 725. Shows, dancing
- El Candil, Chile 318
- Jazz Cafe, Chile 400
- Jazz y Pop, corner of Venezuela and Chacabuco
- La Yumba, corner of Chile and Bolívar. Dancing
- Malena Al Sur, Balcarce 854. Dancing
- Players, Humberto 1 528. Piano bar
- Vieja Recova, Paseo Colón 1381. Dancing
- La Peluqueria, Bolívar near Calvo. Samba

Entertainment in Palermo

- Disco San Francisco Tramway, Araoz 2424. All ages
- Show El Caldero, Gorriti 3972. Fixed menu; credit cards accepted
- Cantina Tango, Santa Fé 4673. Dancing
- Mi Cotorro, Libertador 3883. Dancing

Tango bars and dancing

- Disco Africa, Avenida Alvear 1885. Floor shows, adults
- Disco Cemento, Estados Unidos 1238. Open Thurs, Fri, Sat
- Disco Hippopotamus, Junín 1787. All ages; French cuisine; formal; credit cards accepted
- Disco New York City, Avenida Alvarez Thomas 1391. Young patrons
- Tanguería La Casa de Carlos Gardel, Jean Jaures 735. Tango show and dancing
- Tanguería La Casona de Maria Bullrich, Otamendi 365. Open Fri and Sat; restaurant
- Tanguería Corrientes Angosta, Lavalle 750. Over-30s
- Tanguería Tiempo Tango, Carlos Calvo 2282. Shows, dancing
- Athos, Diaz 1571
- El Boliche Rotondo, Humahuaca 4073. Dancing
- Mon Bijou, Alvear 965
- Once Al Sur, Mexico 2936. Dancing
- Tap Room, Agüero 726

Cinemas

Cinemas are concentrated on Lavalle. The choice of films is world-class, and films are shown uncensored, except for explicit sex. Films are shown with subtitles but dubbing is being used with increasing frequency.

Performing arts

Theater is very popular in Buenos Aires, and about 20 commercial theaters put on productions all year round. The Teatro Liceo is recommended. There are also many amateur theater companies. Book early for concerts, ballet, and opera. The opera season at the Teatro Colón (April to early December) is without doubt the finest in Latin America.

- Teatro Colón: One of the world's great opera houses overlooks Avenida 9 de Julio. The main entrance is on Libertad, between Tucumán and Viamonte. The Colón's interior is resplendent with red plush and gilt, and its vast stage is almost a block wide. The various salons, dressing-rooms, and banquet halls are all sumptuously decorated. Free guided tours run every day at half-hour intervals, but book in advance ℂ 355414, 355415, and 355416. The theater is closed Jan–Feb. Formal wear is expected at gala performances. Tickets are available three days before performances on the Calle Tucumán side of the theater. Prices range from $4.00 to $8.00
- Luna Park Stadium: Pop and jazz concerts are held here
- Teatro Alvear has free concerts Tuesday afternoons, usually the Orchestra de Tango de Buenos Aires

Entertainment

City of Buenos Aires

Sightseeing

Tour operators
- Autobuses Sudamericanos, Neuquén 1155, 1st floor ℡4311679
- City Tours, Lavalle 1444 ℡ 402304 and 402390. A three-hour tour of Buenos Aires costs $9.00
- Buenos Aires Tur, Lavalle 1440 ℡ 402304
- City Service, Florida 840, 4th floor ℡ 328416
- City Tur, Corrientes 1319 ℡ 456977

Sightseeing in Buenos Aires
- **Paseo Colón**: A broad avenue which runs south-east along the waterfront and on to the picturesque Boca district. Here the **Río Riachuelo** flows into the Río de la Plata. You can get here on the 152 bus, from Avenida L N Alem in the center
- **La Boca**: Most of the people living in the Boca are of Italian descent, and the place has its own distinctive traditions and restaurants. With its gardens, restaurants, and public concerts this is a pleasant place on a hot summer day, but it gets crowded on Sundays and public holidays. To get to the Boca district take a 33 bus from Retiro station
- **San Telmo** is located south of Plaza de Mayo. There are still a few late colonial buildings and *Rosista* buildings (that is, built during the office of Presidente Rosas). The area is centered around Calle Independencia, along the slope which leads down to the old beach of the Río de la Plata. It is an established artistic center and a charming area with plenty of cafes and *tanguerías*

Public buildings
- Casa de Gobierno, on the east side of the Plaza Mayo. Popularly known as the Casa Rosada (Pink House) because of its color, this building contains the offices of the President. The Casa Rosada is notable for its statues, lavish decoration, and libraries, but unfortunately it is not at present open to the public
- The Cabildo (Council Chambers), on the west side of the Plaza Mayo. The town hall was first built in 1711, but has been added to several times since. It was restored to its original state in 1940, and declared a national monument. It is guarded by soldiers in the picturesque red and blue uniforms of the San Martín grenadiers; the changing of the guard takes place at 1200
- The old Congreso (House of Assembly) on the south side of the Plaza Mayo, built in 1863, is a national monument
- Palacio del Congreso (the present House of Assembly) at the far end of Avenida de Mayo, is Argentina's legislature. Greco-Roman in style and monumental in size, it contains the Senate and the Chamber of Deputies. There is a public gallery but seating is limited. It opens at 1700 and you must present your passport at the desk which checks in small groups. They will give you a pink slip as a receipt, and a ticket for your seat. You can stay as long as you like but must remain seated

Sightseeing

- Bolsa de Comercio (Stock Exchange), built in 1916, is a handsome building in Calle 25 de Mayo, on the corner of Sarmiento. It contains the stock exchange and grain and produce markets

Churches

All historic churches are open 1700–2000.
- Cathedral, Rivadavia 437, on the north of Plaza de Mayo, flanked by the former residence of the archbishop. It occupies the site of the first church in Buenos Aires. Reconstruction of the cathedral begun in 1677; it collapsed in 1753, and the rebuilding was not completed until 1823. The eighteenth-century towers were never completed. The imposing tomb of General José de San Martín, known as the Liberator, is within the cathedral also; it was built in 1878
- Iglesia San Ignacio de Loyola (Church of St Ignatius of Loyola), Bolívar 225 (corner of Calles Alsina), was founded in 1710 and is one of the oldest colonial building in Buenos Aires. You can recognize it by its two high towers
- Iglesia San Francisco (St Francis' Church), on the corner of Calles Alsina and Defensa, is controlled by the Franciscan order. It was inaugurated in 1754 and given a new façade in 1808
- Iglesia La Merced (Mercy Church), at Reconquista 207 (corner of Perón, formerly called Cangallo), was founded in 1604 and rebuilt in 1732. The wooden figure of Christ was carved by an Indian in Misiones province during the eighteenth century
- Iglesia Santo Domingo (Dominican Church), corner of Defensa and Avenida Belgrano, was founded in 1756. In 1806 the towers were damaged during a British attempt to seize Buenos Aires. The British commando surrendered, and its regimental colors are still preserved in the church. The Salón Belgraniano (Belgrano Hall) contains many personal effects of this great General of the wars of independence, and much colonial furniture. Concerts are held here in on summer evenings
- Iglesia El Pilar (Church of the Pillar), built in a delightful garden setting on Calle Junín 1904, is a jewel of colonial architecture dating from 1717. In the side chapel to the left is the image of San Pedro de Alcantara

Art galleries, museums, libraries

Check the tourist office for opening hours.

Sightseeing

CITY OF BUENOS AIRES

Art galleries
- Museo de Arte Español "Enrique Larreta" (Enrique Larreta Museum of Spanish Art), Juramento 2291. Open 1500–1945; closed Thurs. The building dates from 1870. The exhibits here were once the personal collection of Enrique Larreta, a renowned Argentine writer. They comprise artefacts from the Spanish colonial era
- Museo de Arte Hispanoamericano "Isaac Fernandez Blanco" (Isaac Fernandez Blanco Museum of Spanish-American Art), Suipacha 1422. Open Tues–Sun 1500–2000. Large collection of colonial art, including some very fine silverware. Small admission fee; Thurs free
- Museo de Motivos Populares Argentinos José Hernandez (José Hernandez Museum of Argentine Popular Motifs), Avenida de Libertador 2373. *Gaucho* collection. Open Tues–Sun 1400–1800
- Museo Municipal de Arte Moderno (Municipal Modern Art Museum), Avenida Corrientes 1530, 9th floor. Open Tues–Sun 1600–2200. On display are paintings by Utrillo, Matisse, Dali, Picasso, and Renoir
- Museo Municipal de Artes Plasticas "Eduardo Sivori" (Eduardo Sivori Municipal Plastic Arts Museum), Junín 1930. Open Tues–Sun 1600–2000). The Teatro Municipal San Martín (San Martín Municipal Theatre) gives free perfomances here
- Museo Nacional de Arte Decorativo y Oriental (National Museum of Decorative and Oriental Art), Avenida del Libertador 1902. Open Wed–Mon 1500–1900
- Museo Nacional de Bellas Artes (National Fine Arts Mueseum), Avenida Libertador 1473. Open Tues–Sun 0900–1245 and 1500–1900. There are over 300 works on view, including a collection of Argentine painters of the nineteenth and twentieth centuries, as well as paintings by Van Gogh, Picasso, Manet, Monet, and Renoir

Historical museums
- Museo del Instituto Nacional Sanmartino (Museum of the National San Martín Institute), corner of Sanchez de Bustamente and Avenida A M de Aguardo. Open Mon–Fri 0900–1200 and 1400–1700, Sat and Sun 1400–1700
- Museo Histórico Nacional (National History Museum), Defensa 1600, in San Telmo district. Open Thurs–Sun 1400–1800. The rooms are divided into periods of Argentine history: discovery, conquest, Jesuit missions, the colonial era, the wars of independence, and national heros. The memorabilia of San Martín include some of his furniture from his house-in-exile in Boulogne sur Mer in France
- Museo Histórico Saavedra (Saavedra Historical Museum), Crisologo Larralde (formerly called Republiquetas) 6309.

Sightseeing

Open Wed–Fri 1400–1800, Sat 1800–2200, Sun 1500–1900. Covers the development of Buenos Aires from the eighteenth century onwards. Free on Wednesdays

Colonial buildings
- Museo de Cabildo y Revolucion de Mayo (Museum of the Council Chambers and the May Revolution), Bolívar 65 is the old Cabildo (Council Chambers) building. It was converted into a museum in 1940, and now contains memorabilia of the May 1810 revolution and of the British attack of 1806. Admission $0.50
- Museo y Biblioteca Mitre (Mitre Museum and Library), San Martín 336. This was the residence of President Bartolomé Mitre. Open Wed–Sun 1500–1900
- Museo y Biblioteca Ricardo Rojas (Ricardo Rojas Museum and Library), Charcas 2837. The writer Rojas lived in this beautiful colonial house for several decades. It contains his library, souvenirs of his travels, and many intriguing historical curios. Open Wed and Fri 1500–1800; small admission fee

Science museums
- Museo Argentino de Ciencias Naturales "Bernardino Rivadavia" (Bernardino Rivadavia Argentine Natural Sciences Museum), Avenida Angel Gallardo 470, in the Parque Centenario. A museum of natural history and science. Open Tues, Thurs, and Sun 1400–1800
- Museo Botánico (Botanical Museum), Las Heras 4102 and Malabia 2690. Open Mon–Fri 0880–1200 and 1400–1800. The herbarium is pleasant. About a thousand cats live here
- Museo de la Dirección Nacional del Antartico (Museum of the Federal Department of the Antarctic), Angel Gallardo 470. Open Tues, Thurs, and Sun 1400–1800

Social sciences museums
- Museo de Armas (Weapons Museum), Maipú and Santa Fé. Open 1500–1900 daily; small admission fee
- Museo del Teatro Colón (Museum of the Colón Theater), Tucumán 1161. Mon–Fri 1200–1800. History of the Teatro Colón
- Museo de la Ciudad (Museum of the City), Alsina 412, 1st floor. Open Sun–Fri 1100–1900. Exhibits on the past and future of Buenos Aires
- Museo Internacional de Caricatura y Humorismo (International Caricature and Humour Museum), Lima 1037. Open Fri only 1700–1800; small admission fee. Original twentieth-century cartoons and caricatures
- Museo Nacional de Aeronáutica (National Aeronautics Museum), Avenida Costanera Rafael Obligado, next to Aeroparque

Sightseeing

CITY OF BUENOS AIRES

Jorge Newbery. Open Thurs, Sat and Sun 1600–1900
- Museo Nacional Ferroviario (National Rail Museum), Avenida Libertador 405, in Retiro station. Mon–Fri 0900–1800. Free
- Museo Numismático (Numismatics Museum), Banco Central in San Martín
- Federal police museum, San Martín 353 on 7th floor
- Yuchan Centro de Artesanía Aborigen (Yuchan Center for Aboriginal Crafts), Defensa 788. Native artefacts on display and for sale

Ships
- *Presidente Sarmiento*, Darsena Norte. This sailing ship was used as a naval training ship before it was made into a museum. Open on weekend afternoons. Small admission fee

Libraries
- Biblioteca Nacional (National Library), México 566. The library was founded in 1810. It has a collection of about 500 000 volumes and 12 000 manuscripts, including publications of the Jesuit missions, many in the Guaraní language

Parks and squares

Parks
- Parque Lezama, corner of Calles Defensa and Brazil. Once one of the most beautiful in the city, this park is now somewhat run-down. It has an imposing statue of Pedro de Mendoza, the founder of the original city in 1535. Tradition has it is that the first founding took place on this very spot. The Museo Historico Nacional is also in the park
- Parque Tres de Febrero, popularly known as the Parques Palermo (Palermo Parks), features magnificent avenues. It is renowned for its rose gardens, Andalusian patios, and Japanese garden. The Palermo race course, called the Hipodromo Argentino, is also here. Opposite the park are the botanical gardens and the zoo. In the park are the the municipal golf club, Buenos Aires lawn tennis club, riding clubs, a polo field, and some popular athletic and fencing clubs. The planetarium, near the park exit, is open Sat and Sun only; from March to November there are shows at 1630, 1800, and 1930, and from December to February at 1800, 1930, and 2100; small admission fee
- Showgrounds, next to the Parques Palermo, where the Argentine rural society holds livestock and agriculture exhibitions each July
- Jardín Botánico Municipal (Municipal Botanical Gardens), Santa Fé 2951. Enter from Plaza Italia (*Subte* Line "D" from Palermo station). Contains specimens from all over the world. Trees native to Argentina form one section of the gar-

Sightseeing

CITY OF BUENOS AIRES

dens, which are also full of well-fed stray cats
- The Jardín Zoologico (Zoo) is next to the botanical gardens and it's worth seeing. The enclosures for animals like the Patagonian *mara* (a short-eared hare) are designed to allow them to roam freely

Squares
- Plaza de Congreso is the largest plaza in the city. It has a waterfall, and is floodlit in the evening
- Plaza de la Fuerza Aera, formerly Plaza Britanica, in front of Retiro station, features a clock modeled on the tower of Westminster presented by the British community
- Plaza de la Republica has a 67-meter obelisk at the junction of Diagonal Norte and the Avenida Corrientes
- Plaza de Mayo is the city's oldest square and is surrounded by many public buildings. It was here on May 20, 1810 that a huge gathering rallied to support Argentina's declaration of independence
- Plaza Lavalle has second-hand book stalls at the Calle Lavalle end
- Plaza San Martín contains, not surprisingly, a monument to San Martín in the center

Excursions
- **Isla Martín García**: Situated about 45 km from Buenos Aires in the **Río Uruguay** delta. Juan de Solis was the first European to make landfall here in 1516. For many centuries this island was the staging point for expeditions of conquest. In its time the island has been occupied by the Portuguese, Spanish, Uruguayans, Brazilians, and English. The last invasion was by Anglo-French troops in 1845 under the command of Giuseppe Garibaldi, as a starting point for his proposed invasion of Argentina. When the island returned to Argentine hands it was used as a military prison where several of Argentina's presidents have been incarcerated. Now it is a wildlife sanctuary. A small town has sprung up around the fortifications. There is a small hotel, and an air service. One-day excursions are organized by La Vallette Turismo, Carlos Calvo 4229 (9212050. The boat trip from Tigre takes two hours through the islands of the delta
- Montevideo in Uruguay: By hovercraft. See "Water transport" on page 24.
- **Tigre** and the **Río Paraná** delta, known as **Delta**: The delta is 14 000 square kilometers. By F C General Bartolomé Mitre train from Belgrano station, or by bus 60. Tour operators also run excursions to Delta. For a map of Delta see Plate 6.

Sightseeing

Pampa
Provinces

Buenos Aires Province

Plate 5 Map of Buenos Aires province
- **68** Azul
- **70** Bahía Blanca
- **71** Map
- **76** Bahía San Blas
- **77** Balcarce
- **77** Baradero
- **78** Campana
- **79** Carhué
- **80** Carmen de Patagonés
- **81** Chascomús
- **84** Claromecó
- **85** Dolores
- **85** Guaminí
- **85** Junín
- **86** La Plata
- **87** Map
- **90** Lobos
- **90** Luján
- **92** Mar del Plata
- **93** Map

Buenos Aires Province

- 99 Mar del Tuyú
- 100 Mercedes
- 100 Miramar
- 101   Map
- 105 Monte Hermoso
- 107 Necochea
- 108   Map
- 112 Olavarría
- 114 Pinamar
- 115   Map
- 118 Quequén
- 119 San Antonio de Areco
- 120   Map
- 121 San Clemente del Tuyú
- 122 San Miguel del Monte
- 122 San Nicolás de los Arroyos
- 123 San Pedro
- 124 Sierra de la Ventana
- 125 Tandil
- 126   Map
- 128 Tres Arroyos
- 128 Villa Gesell
- 138 Zárate

Buenos Aires is the largest and most populous province of Argentina. The provincial capital is **La Plata**, 56 km west of the city of Buenos Aires, the federal capital. Buenos Aires province forms part of the *pampa*, and is therefore mainly flat country. The exceptions are two small mountain ranges: the **Sierra de Tandil** near the town of the same name and the **Sierra de la Ventana** near the town of Tornquist, the highest elevation being 1136 m. Most of the Sierra de la Ventana is incorporated in the **Parque Provincial Ernesto Tornquist**.

During the 1860s railroad lines were built from Buenos Aires city, opening up the newly pacified regions to the south. European settlement followed closely.

Most of Argentina's world-renowned seaside resorts are located in Buenos Aires province. The most famous is **Mar del**

Buenos Aires Province

BUENOS AIRES PROVINCE

Plata, closely followed by **Necochea** 125 km further south.

In Buenos Aires province the *gauchos* cling to their traditions more than in any other province. Nearly every week a fiesta is held somewhere in the province, to which the *gauchos* on their horses congregate from far and near.

Buenos Aires shares borders with Río Negro to the south, La Pampa, San Luis, Córdoba and Santa Fé to the west, and Entre Ríos to the north. To the east it is bounded by the Atlantic Ocean.

In a number of towns, the streets have numbers instead of names, such as "Calle 33" (Thirty-Third Street). In these cases, the building numbers are separated from the number of the street by a dash, as in "Calle 33–312" (312 Thirty-Third Street).

AZUL

Postal code: 7300 • Altitude: 137 m • (area code: (0281) • Population: 55 000
Distances from Buenos Aires: 287 km southwards on RN 3

Azul is a thriving agricultural center with a few low hills to the south-west. Founded in 1832 as an outpost against Indians it was initially known as Fuerte San Serapio Martir del Arroyo Azul. The **Arroyo Azul**, which flows through the city center, marked until 1829 the western limit of Argentine expansion into the *pampas*. The riverside has been developed into a waterfront recreation area where swimming is popular. The wide streets and many plazas, such as Plaza San Martín, make Azul quite distinctive. The Nuestra Señora del Santo Rosario cathedral is worth visiting.

ⓘ Tourist information
- Dirección Municipal de Turismo, San Martín 612 (25163

Ⓐ Camping
- Camping Municipal, in the Balneario Municipal, corner of Avenida Pellegrini and Urioste

🍴 Eating out
- Restaurant Alumni, San Martín 333

🛏 Accommodation in Azul

★★★ Hotel Gran Azul, Colón 626	(22011	$23.50	⋕
★ Hotel Argentino, Yrigoyen 378	(25953	$13.50	⋕
★ Hotel Dior, Avenida Mitre 950	(23172	$13.50	⋕
★ Hospedaje Blue, Avenida Mitre 883	(22742	$12.50	⋕
A Hospedaje Cervantes, Caneva 586	(22581	$12.50	⋕
A Hospedaje Grand's, Necochea 674	(25151	$12.50	⋕
A Hospedaje Torino, San Martín 1000	(22749	$12.50	⋕
A Hospedaje Victoria, San Martín 983	(22301	$12.50	⋕

Accommodation outside Azul

★ Hotel La Estrella, RN 3 Km 299	(23999	$17.50	⋕

Buenos Aires Province

- Restaurant Cacique Catriel, corner of Pellegrini and Urioste
- Restaurant Dime, corner of Uriburu and Humberto
- Restaurant El Boliche de Oscar, Darhampe 432
- Restaurant Gran Hotel Azul, Colón 626
- Restaurant Guito, corner of Uriburu and Roca
- Restaurant Jockey Club, corner of 25 de Mayo and Belgrano
- Restaurant La Marca de Burgos, Maipú 663
- Restaurant La Recova, Yrigoyen 380
- Restaurant Majo, Yrigoyen 370
- Restaurant Sancho, Colón 1039
- Restaurant Terminal, in the bus terminal, corner of Avenida Mitre and Caneva
- Restaurant Torino, San Martín 1000
- Cafetería El Escote, corner of Belgrano and Colón
- Pizzería Rocinante, Uriburu 577
- Take-away: El Infierno de Los Pollos, corner of Avenida Humberto and Arenales
- Take-away: Rotisería Centro, San Martín 621
- Take-away: Rotisería Mary, Avenida Humberto 627
- Take-away: La Familia Azulena, Rivadavia 208
- Take-away: La Gruta, Amado Diab 424
- La Herencia del Nono, corner of Avenida Mitre and Alvear
- Take-away: La Nona Vicenta, Moreno 420

Eating out outside Azul

- Restaurant Bar Americano, RN 3, Km 299
- Restaurant Brescia, RN 3 where it enters the outskirts of Azul
- Restaurant Isaura, attached to the service station, RN 3 Km 298
- Restaurant La Estrella, RN 3 Km 299

Post and telegraph

- Post office: Encotel, corner of Yrigoyen and Uriburu
- Telephone: Entel, corner of Yrigoyen and Uriburu

Services and facilities

- Laundromat: Laverap, 25 de Mayo 683

Buses

The bus terminal is on the corner of Avenida Mitre and Caneva.

- Bahía Blanca: 8 services daily; 12 hours; Empresa El Condor
- Buenos Aires: 20 services daily; 4 hours; Empresa El Condor, Empresa La Estrella, Empresa Liniers
- Mar del Plata: 18 services daily; 6 hours; Empresa El Condor

Motoring

- Service station: ACA, RN 3
- Service station: Esso, corner of 9 de Julio and 25 de Mayo

Trains

The F C General Roca station is in the San Martín extension.

Tours

- Azul Turismo, Moreno 647 (22016
- Azul Mundus, Yrigoyen 526 (23054
- Virotour, San Martín 743 (25027

Shopping

The main shopping street is Calle Yrigoyen.

Entertainment

- Disco Cronopio, corner of Avenida Humberto and Colón
- Disco Gato Pardo, corner of Avenida Pellegrini and Chubut
- Disco Pitao, corner of Belgrano and Moreno
- Disco Torras, corner of 25 de Mayo and Yrigoyen
- Whiskería Isidoro, San Martín 500
- Whiskería Tío Beto, San Martín 477

Sightseeing

- Casa del Cacique Catriel, corner of Colón and Corrientes. The Indian Cacique Catriel was the advancing Argentine army's

main adversary during the Desert Campaign. After his defeat he settled in Azul
- Museo Etnográfico (Ethnographic Museum), corner of B J Ronco and San Martín. The museum also houses the province's historical archives
- Museo de Ciencias Naturales CITAC (CITAC Natural Science Museum), Parque Municipal D F Sarmiento
- Parque Municipal D F Sarmiento, corner of Colón and Guaminí: 22 ha of parkland planted with different varieties of trees and plants

Excursions
- **Boca de las Sierras**: Rolling hills 30 km to the south on RP 80, on the road to Pablo Acosta. Another 12 km further on is the Monasterio Cisterciense Nuestra Señora de Los Angeles (Our Lady of the Angels Cistercian Monastery)

Bahía Blanca

Postal code: 8000 • area code: (091) • Population: 240 000
Distances
- From Buenos Aires: 657 km south-west on RN 3
- From Viedma: 286 km northwards on RN 3
- From Santa Rosa: 326 km eastwards on RN 33

Bahía Blanca is located on the **Río Naposta**, which flows into the Bahía Blanca ("White Bay") nearby. The city's origin goes back to the foundation of Fortaleza Protectora Argentina in 1828 as a fort protecting the border against the Indians.

Key to Map
1	Municipalidad (Tourist information)	21	Hospedaje Argentino
2	Catedral	22	Hospedaje Bayon
3	Post office	23	Hospedaje Canciller
4	Telephone	24	Hospedaje Chiclana
5	Banco de la Nación	25	Hospedaje Los Vascos
6	Citibank	26	Hospedaje Molinari
7	Cambio Pullman	27	Hospedaje Roma
8	Aerolineas Argentinas	28	Hospedaje Moreno
9	Austral Lineas Aereas	29	Hospedaje Brandsen
10	LADE airline	30	Hotel Bahía Blanca
11	LAPA airline	31	Hotel Castilla
12	Hotel Argos	32	Hotel Danny
13	Hotel Austral	33	Hotel Milano
14	Hotel City Hotel	34	Hospedaje Andrea
15	Hotel Italia	35	Hospedaje El Trebol
16	Hotel Central Muñiz	36	Hospedaje Hogar
17	Hotel Atlantico	37	Hotel Belgrano
18	Hotel Barne	38	Hospedaje Soler
19	Hotel Caronti	39	Hospedaje Tizon
20	Hostería Santa Rosa	40	Hotel Victoria
		41	Residencial del Sur

BUENOS AIRES PROVINCE

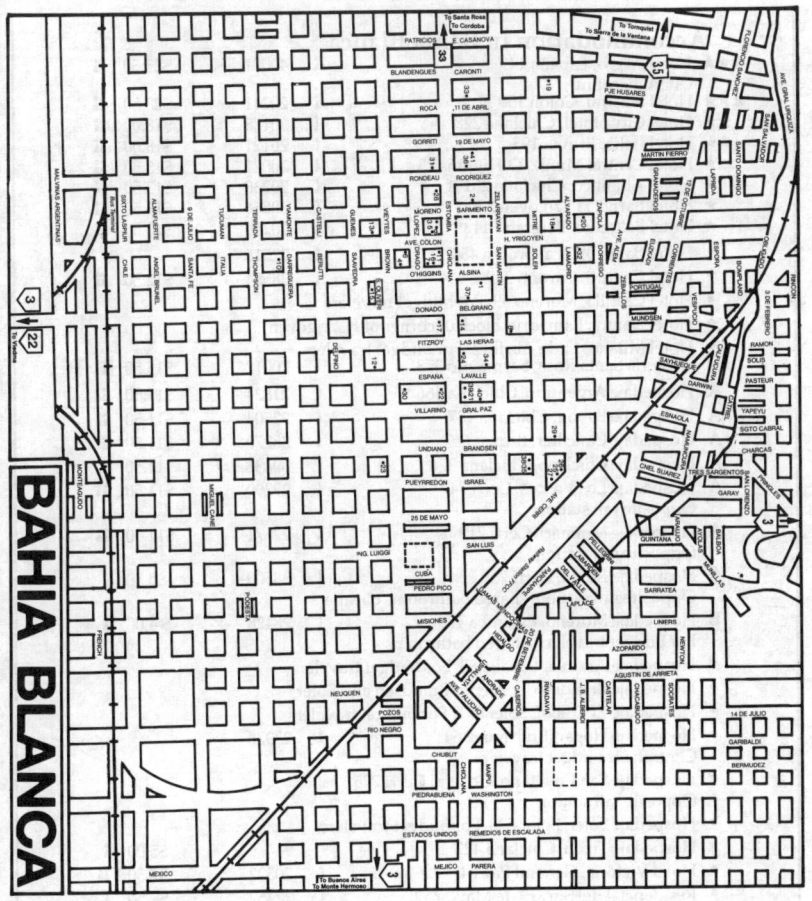

Bahía Blanca is the third largest city in Buenos Aires province. The city itself is some distance from the bay, and its five ports are strung out along the bay's northern side, **Puerto Galván**, **Puerto Belgrano**, and **Puerto Ingeniero White** being the most important. There is a important petrochemical complex fed by the Negro pipeline.

Owing to its importance and strategic location, Bahía Blanca is well served by frequent bus and air services, and by the General Roca railroad. It is laid out in the normal checkerboard fashion, with Parque Rivadavia as its center. There are lakes in Parque de

BUENOS AIRES PROVINCE

Accommodation in Bahía Blanca

★★★	Hotel Argos, España 149 (ACA discount)	(40001	$23.50	ii
★★★	Hotel Austral, Colon 159	(20241	$23.50	ii
★★	Hotel City Hotel, Chiclana 228	(30178	$18.00	ii
★★	Hotel Italia, Brown 195	(20121	$18.00	ii
★	Hotel Central Muñiz, O'Higgins 23	(20021	$13.50	ii
★	Hotel Atlantico, Chiclana 251	(20230	$13.50	ii
★	Hotel Barne, H Yrigoyen 270	(30864	$13.50	ii
★	Hotel Belgrano, Belgrano 44	(20240	$13.50	ii
•	Hotel Bahía Blanca, Brown 480	(22516		
•	Hotel Caronti, Caronti 369	(38584	$12.50	ii
•	Hotel Castilla, Moreno 39. For budget travelers			
•	Hotel Danny, Lamadrid block 0 (corner of H Yrigoyen)			
•	Hotel Milano, 11 de Abril 12. For budget travelers			
★★	Hostería Santa Rosa, Sarmiento 373	(20012	$15.50	ii
A	Hospedaje Argentino, Chiclana 466	(21824	$11.50	ii
A	Hospedaje Bayon, Chiclana 487	(22504	$11.50	ii
A	Hospedaje Canciller, Brown 667	(38270	$11.50	ii
A	Hospedaje Chiclana, Chiclana 376	(30436	$11.50	ii
A	Hospedaje Los Vascos, Cerri 747 Opposite rail station	(29290	$11.50	ii
A	Hospedaje Molinari, Cerri 719 Opposite rail station	(22871	$11.50	ii
A	Hospedaje Roma, Cerri 759 Opposite rail station; shared bathrooms cheaper	(38500	$5.50	i
B	Hospedaje Moreno, Estomba 170 For budget travelers; shared bathrooms	(28428	$4.00	i
•	Hospedaje Andrea, Lavalle 88. For budget travelers			
•	Hospedaje Brandsen, corner of Brandsen and Soler			
•	Hospedaje El Trebol, Soler 671. For budget travelers			
•	Hospedaje Hogar, Rodriguez 64 Central; for budget travelers	(23376		
•	Hospedaje San Cayetano, General Cerri 775 Opposite rail station			
•	Hospedaje Soler, Soler 638. For budget travelers			
•	Hospedaje Tizon, Chiclana 422		$5.00	i
•	Hotel Victoria, General Paz 84	(20522	$7.50	ii
•	Residencial del Sur, 19 de Mayo 75 For budget travelers	(22452	$7.50	i

Mayo, and a zoo in Parque Independencia.

Between Punta Alta and Pehuen-Có, and even beyond, are extensive unspoilt beaches.

Festivals

- Nuestra Señora de la Merced (Our Lady of Mercy): September 24
- Día de la Tradición (Day of Tradition): Nov 10

BUENOS AIRES PROVINCE

ℹ️ Tourist information
- Direccion de Turismo Municipal, Alsina 65 (Plaza Rivadavia) ✆ 25397

🍴 Eating out
- Cafetería Guard un Po', Chiclana 264
- Cafetería Las Cibeles, Alsina block 300 (corner of Lamadrid)
- Pizzería El Gran Caruso, Rodríguez 130
- ☞ Pizzería El Pirata, Lamadrid 360
- Restaurant Biscaya, Soler block 700 (corner of Israel)
- Restaurant La Cigala, Cerri, opposite rail station
- Restaurant Atlántico, Hotel Atlántico, Chiclana 251
- Restaurant El Sergio, Gorriti 61
- Restaurant Facon Pastas, Alsina 350. Jazz band on Saturdays
- Restaurant La Pirámide, Avenida Colón 59. English pub style
- ☞ Restaurant Lavalle, Lavalle 62
- Restaurant Los Camioneros, Rodríguez block 0 (corner of Estomba). For budget travelers
- Restaurant Lyon d'Or, corner of R de Escalada and L M Drago. Pizzas
- ☞ Restaurant Parrilla Kuntt, General Cerri 773

✈️ Air services from Bahía Blanca

Aeropuerto Comandante Espora is 16 km from the city center. Taxi fare $6.00.
- Aerolineas Argentinas, San Martín 298 ✆ 22257. The terminal is at Gorriti 50
- Austral Airlines, Avenida Colón 59 ✆ 26931
- LADE, Darregueira 21 ✆ 21063. Runs a shuttle service to country towns
- LAPA, Avenida Colón 24 ✆ 20346

Destination	Fare	Depart	Services	Hours	Airline
• La Plata	$38.00	1615	Wed, Fri	2	LADE
• Buenos Aires (Aeropuerto Jorje Newbery)					
	$56.00	0840	2–8 services daily	1	Aerolineas, Austral
	$46.00	1910	Wed	3	LADE
• Comodoro Rivadavia					
	$52.00	0845	Mon–Wed, Fri, Sat	2	Aerolineas, Austral
	$49.00	1045	Tues, Thurs	6	LADE
• Córdoba	$59.00	1815	Fri	2	Aerolineas
• Esquel	$47.00	1045	Tues	3	LADE
• Mar del Plata	$34.00	1910	Wed	1	LADE
• Neuquén	$35.00	1045	Tues	1	LADE
	$41.00	1830	daily	1	Austral
• Puerto Deseado	$50.00	1045	Tues	7	LADE
• Puerto San Julián	$50.00	1045	Tues	8	LADE
• Río Gallegos	$67.00	0800	2–3 services daily	3	Aerolineas, Austral
	$53.00	1045	Tues	9	LADE
• Río Grande	$77.00	0805	1–2 services daily	4	Aerolineas, Austral
	$58.00	1045	Tues	10	LADE
• San Antonio Oeste					
	$20.00	1140	Thurs	2	LADE
• San Carlos de Bariloche					
	$47.00	1040	Tues	2	LADE
	$63.00	1155	Sat	2	Austral
• Santa Cruz	$51.00	1045	Tues	8	LADE
• Trelew	$41.00	0845	1–3 services Mon–Sat	1	Aerolineas, Austral
	$48.00	1045	Tues, Thurs	5	LADE
• Ushuaia	$83.00	0805	2 services daily	5	Aerolineas
• Viedma	$20.00	1140	Thurs	1	LADE

Bahía Blanca

BUENOS AIRES PROVINCE

- ☞ • Restaurant Parrilla La Vieja Esquina, Moreno 202
- Restaurant Parrilla Petit Colón, Avenida Colón 72
- Restaurant Parrilla Tío Nico, Lavalle block 100 (corner of San Martín)
- Restaurant Suizo, Avenida Colón 234
- Restaurant Taberna Baska, Lavalle 284
- Restaurant Vegetariano, corner of Lavalle and Chiclana
- Pizzería Il Vesuvio, Hotel Atlantico, Chiclana 231
- Pizzería Plaza, Chiclana block 0 (corner of O'Higgins)

Post and telegraph
- Post office: Encotel, Moreno 34
- Telephone: Entel, O'Higgins 213

Financial
- Banco de Credito, Donado 14. Cash advances on Visa card

Buses from Bahía Blanca

The bus terminal (once a rail station) is at Brown block 1700 (corner of Estados Unidos, 2½ km from the city center). There are no hotels nearby. Take bus 515 to the city center and rail station ($0.20). The bus stop for local buses 515 and 517 is on the corner of Brown and Remedios de Escalada. A taxi from the terminal to the city center costs $2.00.

Destination	Fare	Depart	Services	Hours	Company
• Buenos Aires				9	La Puntual
• Comodoro Rivadavia			1–2 services daily	15	Don Otto, La Puntual
• Córdoba	$18.00	1610	3 services daily	15	TUP
• Guaminí	$4.50			4	Empresa Colón
• Mar del Plata	$11.50	0630	6 services daily		Pampas
• Mendoza		1700	daily		Andesmar
• Necochea	$8.00			5/2	Pampas
• Neuquén	$12.50	0630	6–7 services daily	9–10	El Valle, La Estrella, La Puntual
• Paraná		1715	2 services daily		Central Argentino, Nandu del Sur
• Puerto Madryn	$15.00			10	Don Otto
• Rawson	$13.50	2100	Mon, Wed, Fri, Sun		Don Otto, La Puntual
• Río Colorado	$2.70				Don Otto
	$4.00				El Valle
• Río Gallegos	$46.00	0800	Mon, Wed, Fri	30	Don Otto
Change in Comodoro Rivadavia					
• Rosario		1715	2 services daily		Central Argentino, Nandu del Sur
• San Antonio Oeste	$11.00			8	Don Otto, La Puntual
• San Carlos de Bariloche	$25.50	2130	daily	14	El Valle
• San Juan		1600	daily		Ticsa
• San Luis		1600	daily		Ticsa
• Santa Fé		1715	2 services daily		Central Argentino, Nandu del Sur
• Santa Rosa		0800	4–5 services daily		Andesmar, T U P
• Trelew	$16.50			11	Don Otto, La Puntual
• Viedma	$6.50	0700	4 services	5	La Puntual
• Zapala	$15.50	1600	2 services daily	12	El Valle

Bahía Blanca

Buenos Aires Province

🚆 Trains from Bahía Blanca

The F C General Roca station is at Cerri 750, six blocks from the city center. The line divides here into two branch lines: to Zapala via Neuquén, and to San Carlos de Bariloche via San Antonio Oeste.

Destination	Fare	Depart	Services
• Buenos Aires		0645	2 services daily
First	$11.00		
Tourist	$8.00		
• Esquel		1600	Sun, Thurs
Two-hour wait in Ingeniero Jacobacci			
• Ingeniero Jacobacci		0815	Thurs, Sun
First	$15.00		
Tourist	$11.20		
• Neuquén		2126	2 services daily
First	$9.50		
Tourist	$7.00		
• San Antonio Oeste			
First	$8.50		
Tourist	$6.50		
• San Carlos de Bariloche		1900	Wed, Sat, Sun
First	$18.00		
Tourist	$13.50		
• Viedma			
First	$5.50		
Tourist	$4.20		

☞ • Casa de Cambio Pullman, O'Higgins 23 (in Galería next to Hotel Muñiz). Takes all travelers' checks; good rates
• Casa de Cambio Pullman, San Martín 171. Takes all travelers' checks

🗄 Services and facilities

- Dry-cleaner: Espinoza, Soler 215
- Supermarket: Modelo, H Yrigoyen block 100 (corner of Mitre)

Laundromats

- Laverap, Soler 45. Open Mon–Sat 0800–2100, Sun 0900–1300; $2.00
- Marva, Belgrano block 200 (corner of Lamadrid); $2.00

Ⓒ Clubs

- English: Asociación Bahiense de Cultura Inglesa (Bahía Association for English Culture), Zelarrain 245
- French: Alliance Française, Las Heras 51
- Spanish: Asociación Española, Moreno 132

📰 Visas, passports

- French consulate, Alliance Française, Las Heras 51
- German consulate, Alsina 535

🚗 Motoring

RN 3 south to Viedma is a first-class sealed highway.
- Service station: ACA, Chiclana 305

Car rental

- A1 Rent a Car, ACA service station, Avenida Colón
- Liprandi Rent-A-Car, Colón 159 ✆ 439444

🎭 Entertainment

- Bar Karamba, Sarmiento block 100 (corner of Zelarrayan). Bands
- Bowling Palo 10, San Martín 453
- Night Club Toplay, Soler 693. Shows
- Tanguería Colonial, Soler 785

Bahía Blanca

BUENOS AIRES PROVINCE

◉ Excursions

- **Sierra de la Ventana**: 100 km north. The range is partly within the **Parque Provincial Ernesto Tornquist**. Its highest point is **Cerro de la Ventana** at 1136 m, in sharp contrast with the green farmlands below. Near the peak is a rock opening (*ventana* or "window"), to which wind erosion has given a freakish appearance. A scenic drive runs from **Tornquist** along RP 176 beside the **Río de la Ventana** through the Ventana gorge. There are frequent bus and train services. Fishing and golf are popular. Empresa El Condor runs buses to Tornquist for $1.80 and to Sierra de la Ventana for $2.50. See also Sierra de la Ventana on page 124
- **Monte Hermoso**: 106 km west. A beach resort; take RN 3 then turn onto RN 78. During the vacation season, which runs from December to February, buses run there frequently. Outside the vacation season most establishments are closed. Empresa La Acción company runs regular buses between 0500 and 1800; the two-hour trip costs $2.40. For accommodation see "Accommodation" in Monte Hermoso on page 124
- **Pehuen-Có**: A beach resort 84 km westwards on RN 3. It closes down during the off-season

BAHÍA SAN BLAS

Postal code: 8506
Distance from Viedma: 90 km north-east

Bahía San Blas is the southernmost seaside resort in the Buenos Aires province, and is popular during the summer months. It has good fishing. The hub of the town is the Avenida Costanera, where there are hotels, restaurants, post office, and public telephones. Bahía San Blas comes to life at the beginning of December for about four months. Most hotels are shut during the off-season.

Tourist facilities are located on Isla Jabalí, where there are several small hotels, private accommodation, and restaurants.

❂ Festivals
- Las 24 Horas de San Blas: A fishing competition held on the third Saturday in January
- Fiesta de la Corvina Rubia: February 3. Fishing competition

▭ Accommodation
- Hostería ACA, Avenida Comandante Luis Piedra Buena ⑪
- Residencial Mike
- Residencial Werneke
- Residencial Stangen

⑪ Eating out
- Restaurant Mike

🚌 Buses
Buses run regularly between Bahía Blanca, Viedma, and Carmen de Patagonés.

Bahía Blanca

BUENOS AIRES PROVINCE

🚗 Motoring
- Service station: ACA, corner of Calle 28 and Avenida 4

BALCARCE

Postal code: 7620 • Altitude: 108 m • (area code: (0266)
Distance from Mar del Plata: 64 km westwards on RN 226

Balcarce is located in a hilly area with many streams. Nearby is a satellite tracking station. Juan Fangio the great racing driver was born here.

Services and facilities
- Laundromat: Laverap, Calle 19 579

Buses
- Buenos Aires: 2 services daily; 6 hours: Empresa Costera Criolla, Empresa Micro Mar
- Mar del Plata: Regular buses

Excursions
- **Cinco Dedos hills**: Not very high, but the rock outcrops are peculiarly shaped

BARADERO

Postal code: 2942 • (area code: (0329)
Distance from Buenos Aires: 142 km north-west on RN 9

Baradero is located on the **Río Baradero** not far from the junction with the **Río Paraná**. It was founded in 1615 by Hernando Arias de Saavedra (known as "Hernandarias") and is thus the oldest settlement in Buenos Aires province. There are many clubs dedicated to water sports, such as sailing and fishing, many with private beaches along the river front.

Accommodation
- ★ Hotel Bariloche, Darregueira 448 (80921 $13.50
- ★ Hotel Edelweiss, San Martín 392 (80900 $13.50
- ★ Hotel Jacaranda, Boedo 1352 (81293 $13.50
- A Hospedaje Italia, Santa María de Oro 525 (80109 $11.50
- A Hospedaje Lourdes, Darregueira 648 (80351 $11.50

Camping
- Municipal camping ground, located on the right bank of the Río Baradero

Accommodation in Balcarce

★★★	Hotel Gran Balcarce, corner of Calle 17 and Calle 16 (2055, 2056	$23.50	
A	Hospedaje Cervantes, Calle 14–521 (between Calle 13 and Calle 15)	$11.50	
A	Hospedaje San José, Avenida Gonzalez Chavez 485	$11.50	
B	Hospedaje Moreno, Kelly 762	$8.50	
B	Hospedaje Su Hotel, Calle 15–527	$8.50	
B	Hospedaje Victoria, Calle 19–538 (between Calle 14 and Calle 16)	$8.50	

BUENOS AIRES PROVINCE

✉ Post and telegraph
- Post office: Encotel, corner of Araoz and Santa María de Oro
- Telephone: Entel, corner of Anchorena and Bulnes

🚌 Buses
T A Chevallier runs regular buses to Buenos Aires (2 hours) and Rosario (4 hours).

🚙 Motoring
- Service station: ACA, corner of Avenida Libertador General San Martín and E Genaud

🚆 Trains
Baradero is served by the F C General B Mitre railroad.

📷 Sightseeing
- Museo Histórico Municipal "Juan Lavalle" (Juan Lavalle Municipal Historical Museum)

CAMPANA

Postal code: 2804 • ☏ area code: (0315)

Campana is located on the **Río Paraná de las Palmas**. No official founding date has been recorded, but it is known that Juan Garay, a *conquistador* with a royal mandate, granted land to Don Pedro Franco who built a small *estancia*, which then passed on to Don Francisco Alvarez de Campana. The actual town was founded by Luis Costa in 1875. The Costa family's house is now a national monument.

Although Campana is an industrial center, the nearby river has attracted many tourists for water-skiing, fishing, and sailing. In 1907 the Spanish immigrant Manuel Iglesias built the first Argentine automobile here in Campana.

🍴 Eating out
- Restaurant Dalmine, corner of Balcarce and Güemes
- Restaurant Campana Boat Club, on the banks of the Río Paraná
- Restaurant Club Social, corner of Avenida Rocca and 25 de Mayo
- Restaurant Tobago, San Martín 389

✉ Post and telegraph
- Post office: Encotel, Avenida Rocca 273

🚌 Buses
The bus terminal for T A Chevallier and Expreso Paraná is on the corner of San Martín and Lavalle.

🛏 Accommodation in Campana

★ Hotel City, Belgrano 540	☏ 82536	$13.50
★ Hotel Plaza, San Martín 387	☏ 81072	$13.50
★ Hostería Alem, Alem 868		$12.50
★ Hostería El Talar, Colón 106	☏ 81074	$12.50
A Hospedaje Nuevo Palacio, Rocca 46	☏ 82932	$11.50
A Hospedaje Rex, Rivadavia 640	☏ 81062	$11.50
A Hospedaje Waldorf, corner of Rivadavia and Ameghino		$11.50

Baradero

BUENOS AIRES PROVINCE

Trains
The station for the F C General B Mitre line to Retiro station in Buenos Aires is on the corner of Avenedia Rocca and Alem.

CARHUÉ

Postal code: 6430 • Population: 18 000 • area code: (0936)
Distances
- From Buenos Aires: 603 km south-west
- From Bahía Blanca: 196 km northwards on RN 33

Carhué is located 5 km from **Lago Epecuen**. This lake's heavy salt content is said to render its waters beneficial to sufferers of rheumatism and skin diseases, but because of the saltiness the lake has no fish. During 1987 heavy rainfall caused damage to this tourist resort, and diluted the lake water. There are scores of hotels and restaurants. Public transport connections to Bahía Blanca and Buenos Aires are good.

Last century Carhué was an outpost of European culture against the Indians.

Tourist information
- Palacio Municipal, Pellegrini 361

Buses
Direct services run to Buenos Aires and Bahía Blanca.

Motoring
- Service station: ACA, corner of Avenida San Martín and Colón

Accommodation in Carhué

	Hotel	Phone	Price	
★	Hotel Apolo, Avenida Mayo	12	$13.50	
★	Hotel Consoll, Rivadavia	19	$13.50	
★	Hotel Elkie, Guatemala 50	48	$13.50	
★	Hotel Gran Azul, Avenida Mayo	21	$13.50	
★	Hotel Gran Hotel El Lago, Rivadavia		$13.50	
★	Hotel Gran Parque Patera, Mitre	3	$13.50	
★	Hotel Hispano Argentino, Avenida Mayo		$13.50	
★	Hotel Las Familias, Rivadavia	7	$13.50	
★	Hotel Los Cuatro Hermanos, Rivadavia	18	$13.50	
★	Hotel Mayo, Mitre	35	$13.50	
★	Hotel Plage, Avenida Costanera	10	$13.50	
★	Hotel Rambla, corner of Cerrito and Mitre	25	$13.50	
★	Hotel Rambla Anexo, Mitre		$13.50	
★	Hotel Victoria, Mitre	13	$13.50	
A	Hospedaje Adriativo, Rivadavia		$11.50	
A	Hospedaje Allende, Rivadavia		$11.50	
A	Hospedaje Altieri, Avenida Mayo		$11.50	
A	Hospedaje Aurora, corner of Mitre and Pellegrini		$11.50	
A	Hospedaje Avenida, Cangallo		$11.50	
A	Hospedaje Azul, Avenida Mayo	2	$11.50	
A	Hospedaje Besagonill (formerly called Brisas del Lago), Talcahuano	67	$11.50	
A	Hospedaje Buenos Aires, Urquiza 307	312	$11.50	

BUENOS AIRES PROVINCE

Accommodation in Carhué—continued

A	Hospedaje Casa Jamed, corner of Victoria and Avenida de Mayo	☎ 26	$11.50	♁♁
A	Hospedaje Coradini, Avenida Mayo	☎ 59	$11.50	♁♁
A	Hospedaje Dany, Mitre		$11.50	♁♁
A	Hospedaje El Ancia, Avenida Mayo		$11.50	♁♁
A	Hospedaje El Español, Vatteone		$11.50	♁♁
A	Hospedaje Gadalen, Avenida Mayo		$11.50	♁♁
A	Hospedaje Italia, corner of Vatteone and Mitre		$11.50	♁♁
A	Hospedaje Karina, Mitre		$11.50	♁♁
A	Hospedaje La Carioca, Mitre		$11.50	♁♁
A	Hospedaje La Española, corner of Vatteone and Cangallo		$11.50	♁♁
A	Hospedaje La Ideal, Vatteone		$11.50	♁♁
A	Hospedaje La Pauline, corner of Cangallo and Talcahuano		$11.50	♁♁
A	Hospedaje Lisboa, Mitre		$11.50	♁♁
A	Hospedaje Marconi, Irigoyen 991 🅣	☎ 277	$11.50	♁♁
A	Hospedaje Marsico, Cangallo		$11.50	♁♁
A	Hospedaje Mi Nena, Rivadavia		$11.50	♁♁
A	Hospedaje Monte Real, Avenida Mayo		$11.50	♁♁
A	Hospedaje Nicanora, Florida		$11.50	♁♁
A	Hospedaje Noemi, Mitre		$11.50	♁♁
A	Hospedaje 9 de Julio, Mitre		$11.50	♁♁
A	Hospedaje Pascual Niro, corner of Vatteone and Cangallo		$11.50	♁♁
A	Hospedaje Oscarcito, Mitre		$11.50	♁♁
A	Hospedaje Roma, Pellegrini		$11.50	♁♁
A	Hospedaje San Cristobal, Florida		$11.50	♁♁
A	Hospedaje Villa del Lago, Avenida Mayo		$11.50	♁♁
A	Hospedaje Tesorini, Avenida Mayo		$11.50	♁♁
A	Hospedaje Villa Graciela, Vatteone		$11.50	♁♁
A	Hospedaje Villa Marta, Suipacha		$11.50	♁♁
A	Hospedaje Violini, Sarmiento		$11.50	♁♁
A	Hospedaje Volpe, corner of Saenz Peña and 25 de Mayo	☎ 286	$11.50	♁♁

CARMEN DE PATAGONÉS

Postal code: 8504 • ☎ area code: (0920) •
Altitude: 44 m
Distance from Bahía Blanca: 276 km southwards on RN 3

Carmen de Patagonés is located on the northern bank of the **Río Negro** some 30 km from the river mouth, opposite **Viedma**. The two cities are linked by a bridge and a ferry service.

Carmen de Patagonés is often referred to simply as "Patagonés".

🅘 Tourist information

• Palacio Municipal, Rivadavia 191
☎ 61780 or 61783

Carhué

BUENOS AIRES PROVINCE

Accommodation

For accommodation outside Carmén de Patagones, see "Accommodation" in Viedma on page 354.
- ★ Hotel Percaz, Rivadavia 348 ☏ (61495 $13.50
- Hotel Argentino, Bynon 259 (61595
- A Hospedaje Reggiani, Bynon 420 (61389 $11.50
- Residencial La Normita, Suipacha 169 (61390
- Residencial Arizcurren, corner of Rivadavia and Yrigoyen (61495

Eating out

- Restaurant Hotel Percaz, Rivadavia 348
- Restaurant Reggiani, corner of Barbieri and Villegas
- Cafetería Sabatella, Rivadavia 218
- Cafetería Ghimel, Olivera 15

Services and facilities

- Laundromat: Laverap, España 242

Air services

See "Air services" in Viedma in Río Negro Province.

Buses

The bus terminal is on the corner of A Barbieri and Mejico. However, most bus companies stop only in Viedma, just across the river.
- Buenos Aires: 2 services daily: 15 hours: Empresa El Condor, Empresa El Valle, Empresa La Puntual

Motoring

- Service station: YPF, corner of Bynon and Alsina

Entertainment

- Disco Erika, San Juan 176

Sightseeing

- Museo Histórico Regional Municipal (Municipal Regional Historical Museum), ground floor of Municipalidad, Plaza 7 de Marzo. The museum provides an overview of the town's earliest colonial days and of historical events that took place in the vicinity, such as fierce resistance to an invading Brazilian squadron in 1827; and archeological findings from the pre-Hispanic era
- Tower of the old fort, built around 1780. Situated between the parish church and the school

Excursions

- **Cerro de la Caballada**: The battlefield where the Brazilian invasion in 1827 was repelled by the 200-odd defenders of the city. Located 1 km from the town center
- **Cuevas Maragatas**: A cave located on private property in the lower part of Calle Rivadavia. It served as the initial shelter for some Spanish families when they first arrived here
- **Bahía San Blas**: 100 km northeast. See Bahía San Blas on page 76

CHASCOMÚS

Postal code: 7130 • Population: 20 000 • (area code: (0241) • Altitude: 11m
Distance from Buenos Aires: 123 km southwards on RN 2

Chascomús, meaning "very salty water" in the Araucanian language, is located in the *pampa* on the shallow **Laguna Chascomús**, whose average depth is only

BUENOS AIRES PROVINCE

1.5 m. The *laguna* forms part of the chained lakes system, the other *lagunas* being **Chis-Chis**, **Vitel**, **Yalca**, and **Adela**. Laguna Chascomús is fed by the **Río Salado**; its size varies with the rainfall, but most of the time it averages 15 km long and 5 km wide.

The town grew up around Fuerte San Juan Bautista, founded in 1779 by Pedro Nicolas Escribano to contain the marauding Indians. In 1839 a rebellion known as "Los Libres del Sur" broke out against the tyranny of the dictator Rosas, but was crushed by Rosas' troops on the shores of the *laguna*. The first railroad arrived in 1865.

Avenida Costanera is the town's focal point, where most of the hotels and cafeterias are situated.

ℹ Tourist information
- Dirección Municipal de Turismo, Edificio del Turista, corner of Avenida Costanera and España (22470

▲ Camping
- Casa Amarilla, Camino Circunvalación
- Monte Brown, Camino Costanero
- Monte Corti, corner of Avenida Costanera and Mario L Osornio

🛏 Accommodation in Chascomús

★★	Hotel Santa María (formerly called Laguna), corner of Libres del Sur and Maipú	(22808	$17.50
★	Hotel Los Vascos, corner of España and Castelli 🔟	(22856	$13.50
★	Hotel Nuevo Colón, Libres del Sur 70	(22054	$13.50
•	Hotel Municipal, corner of Avenida Costanera and Santa Fé	(22328	
★	Hostería Veracruz, Belgrano 175	(22971	$12.50
A	Hospedaje Aguila Negra, RN2 Km 121	(23281	
A	Hospedaje Bosnia, corner of Córdoba and Lamadrid	(23337	$12.50
A	Hospedaje Costanera, corner of Castelli and Avenida Costanera	(22080	$12.50
A	Hospedaje La Madrileña, Lamadrid 39	(22141	$12.50
A	Hospedaje La Toja, Libres del Sur 102 (corner of Soler) 🔟	(22268	$12.50
A	Hospedaje Levuco, Bolivar 571		$12.50
A	Hospedaje Los Vascos, corner of España and Castelli An annex of the Hotel Los Vascos	(22856	$12.50
A	Hospedaje Nuevo El Lago, corner of Dolores and Sarmiento		$12.50
B	Hospedaje Alvear, Alvear 289	(22357	$8.50
B	Hospedaje Chascomus, Lastra 367	(22968	$8.50
B	Hospedaje Familiar, Mitre 202	(22328	$8.50
B	Hospedaje Ferrocarril, Belgrano 400	(22847	$8.50
B	Hospedaje San José, corner of Mazzini and Washington	(23276	$8.50
B	Hospedaje San Juan, corner of Franklin and Avenida Costanera		$8.50
B	Hospedaje Ugarte, Libres del Sur 400 (corner of Maipú)	(22567	$8.50

BUENOS AIRES PROVINCE

- San Luis, on the road to Ranchos

🍴 Eating out

- Restaurant Belgrano, Belgrano 82
- Restaurant Costanera, corner of Avenida Costanera and Castelli
- Restaurant Club de Regatas, corner of Avenida Costanera and Moreno
- Restaurant Club Pesca y Nautica, Avenida Costanera
- Restaurant Edificio del Turista, Avenida Costanera (upstairs)
- Restaurant Ferrocarril, corner of Belgrano and Caseros
- Restaurant Fire, Libres del Sur 142
- Restaurant La Taba, corner of Belgrano and Bolivar
- Restaurant La Toja, Hospedaje La Toja, Libres del Sur 102 (corner of Soler)
- Restaurant La Farola, corner of Costanera and Lamadrid
- Restaurant Los Vascos, Hotel Los Vascos, corner of Avenida Costanera and Castelli
- Cafetería Atletico, Alvear 31
- Cafetería El Soberano, corner of Mitre and Dolores
- Cafetería La Veneciana, Libres del Sur 255
- Cafetería La Casa de Candida, corner of Alvear and Arenales
- Cafetería Le Marok, Libres del Sur 8
- Cafetería Libertad, corner of Arenales and Alvear
- Cafetería Siboney, Avenida Lastra 194
- Cafetería Sky, Libres del Sur 86
- Cafetería Texas, Belgrano 112

Eating out outside Chascomús

- Restaurant ACA, RN 2 Km 121
- Restaurant Anahi, RN 2 Km 121
- Restaurant Atalaya, RN 2 Km 113
- Restaurant Caballito Blanco, RN 2 Km 121
- Restaurant Hoyo 19, in the golf clubhouse, RN 2 north
- Restaurant Pedro Chico, RN 2 Km 123
- Restaurant Tome y Traiga, RN 2 Km 119

🏨 Services and facilities

- Laundromat: Laverap, Alvear 72

🚌 Buses

Bus terminal ℂ 22524.
There are 17 daily services for the two-hour trip to Buenos Aires, run by Anton, Río de la Plata, Costera Criolla, and El Condor.

🎭 Entertainment

- Disco Burbujas, corner of Belgrano and Lastra
- Disco Laser, corner of Avenida Costanera and Colón
- Disco La Terraza, corner of RN 2 and Lastra

📷 Sightseeing

- Museo Pampeana (Pampas Museum), Parque de Los Libres Sur. Also known as the "gaucho museum", it is built in the style of a nineteenth-century stage-coach relay-dispatch house. There are displays of archeological artefacts, antique furniture, and leather clothing worn by gauchos
- Negro chapel, corner of Lamadrid and Venezuela. Built in 1862 by the Negro Brotherhood, a fraternity of freed Negro slaves, it served as a hospital during the cholera epidemic in 1866 and during the yellow fever outbreak in 1871
- Cathedral, Plaza Independencia. Built in 1832
- Hydrobiological experimental station, corner of Avenida Lastra and Juarez. The fertilization of *pejerrey* eggs for export can be observed

♦ Excursions

- **Villa del Sur**: 11 km north. The bottling plant of "Villa del Sur" mineral water

Chascomús

BUENOS AIRES PROVINCE

CLAROMECÓ

Postal code: 7505
Distances
- From Necochea: 193 km eastwards on RN 228
- From Bahía Blanca: 260 km eastwards on RN 3 then RN 228

Claromecó is a newly-developing seaside resort at the mouth of the **Arroyo Claromecó**. It can be reached by bus via Tres Arroyos 65 km inland. High dunes run along behind the beach. Because of a warm current coming down from Brazil, the water is considerably warmer than that quite a distance further north. A fishing contest is held during the second half of February.

Festivals
- Concurso de la Corvina Negra: A fishing competition held February 24

Tourist information
- Municipal tourist information office, Calle 28 (between Calle 9 and Calle 11) (0983) 26099

Camping
- ACA camp-site

Buses
- Buenos Aires: Departs 2245 Sun; 7 hours; Empresa La Estrella
- Tres Arroyos: 3 services daily. At least 2 additional services daily during the vacation season

Accommodation in Claromecó

Most hotels are closed during the off season, from April to November.

★★	Hotel La Perla, corner of Calle 9 and Calle 28	14	$18.00	
★	Hotel Claromec, corner of Calle 7 and Calle 26	7	$13.50	
★	Hostería Boston, corner of Calle 26 and Calle 13	114	$12.50	
★	Motel Rigel, corner of Calle 43 and Calle 10	26	$13.50	
A	Hospedaje Antartida, corner of Calle 15 and Calle 30	69	$12.50	
A	Hospedaje Beto, corner of Calle 26 and Calle 7	52	$12.50	
A	Hospedaje La Reserva, corner of Calle 7 and Calle 24	111	$12.50	
A	Hospedaje Luarca, corner of Calle 7 and Calle 20	179	$12.50	
A	Hospedaje Mar, corner of Calle 15 and Calle 26	20	$12.50	
A	Hospedaje Pablito, corner of Calle 26 and Calle 9	52	$12.50	
A	Hospedaje Suyai, corner of Calle 11 and Calle 28		$12.50	

Accommodation outside Claromecó

B	Hospedaje Doña Olga, Dunamar de Claromec (across the river)	$8.50	

BUENOS AIRES PROVINCE

DOLORES

Postal code: 7100 • Population: 10 000 • (area code: (0245)
Distance from Buenos Aires: 204 km southwards on RN 2

Founded in 1818, Dolores was destroyed by Indians in 1821 and later rebuilt. It is a grain-growing and cattle- farming center, subject to flooding during prolonged wet weather.

Accommodation
- Hotel Argentina

Services and facilities
- Laundromat: Laverap, Marquez 170

Buses
- Buenos Aires: 15 services daily; 4 hours; Empresa Anton, Empresa Río de la Plata, Empresa Costera Criolla

Motoring
- Service station: ACA, RN 2 Km 210

GUAMINÍ

Postal code: 6435 • Population: 4 000 • (area code: (0929) • Altitude: 110 m
Distances
- From Carhué: 38 km north-east
- From Bahía Blanca: 197 km northwards on Ruta 33

Guaminí is a summer resort located on **Laguna del Monte**, which has several islands. It is accessible by road and rail from Buenos Aires and Bahía Blanca. The heavy rains of 1987 have done some damage. Although the *laguna* is very salty, it contains *pejerrey*; fishing is one of the town's attractions.

Accommodation
A Hospedaje Avenida, H Yrigoyen 98 $8.50
A Hospedaje El Descanso, H Yrigoyen 138 $8.50

Accommodation outside Guaminí

A Hospedaje Motel Cochico, Laguna Cochico, 11 km from town $8.50

Buses
- Bahía Blanca: $4.50; 4 hours; Empresa Colón
- Buenos Aires: 3 services daily; 7 hours; Empresa Liniers, Empresa T A Chevallier

Trains
F C General Roca runs services from Buenos Aires, departing from Constitución station.

JUNÍN

Postal code: 6000 • Population: 60 000 • (area code: (O362) • Altitude: 81 m
Distance from Buenos Aires: 265 km westwards on RN 7

Junín is located near **Laguna de Gómez** and **Laguna Mar Chiquita** (not to be confused with Mar Chiquita in Córdoba province and Laguna Mar Chiquita north of Mar del Plata). The town is served by F C General Bartolomé Mitre railroad, and there are important rail workshops. It is an industrial town and the center of a rich agricultural region.

BUENOS AIRES PROVINCE

✷ Festivals
- Fiesta Patronal San Ignacio (Festival of the Patron Saint Ignatius): July 31
- Foundation day: December 27
- Fiesta Mayor del Pejerrey in April attracts many anglers

ⓘ Tourist information
- Oficina de Turismo, R S Peña 145 ✆ 21273

▲ Camping
- Chimihuin municipal camp site
- Pescadores

✉ Post and telegraph
- Post office: Encotel, Rivadavia 5
- Telephone: *Cabina publica*, General Paz 140

🗎 Services and facilities
- Laundromat: Laverap, R S Pena 310

🚍 Buses
- Buenos Aires: 16 services daily; 5 hours; Empresa Rojas

🚗 Motoring
- Service station: ACA, corner of C Saavedra and M Levenson

🚆 Trains
Trains run frequently to Buenos Aires.

◉ Excursions
- **Laguna Mar Chiquita**: *Pejerrey* fishing, boat hire
- **Laguna de Gómez**: 9 km west. Fishing

LA PLATA

Postal code: 1900 • ✆ area code: (021) • Population: 480 000
Distance from Buenos Aires: 56 km southeast on RN 2

La Plata was founded in 1882 by Dr Dardo Rocha as the capital of Buenos Aires province. It is located on the **Río de la Plata** (commonly known in English as the River Plate). Until federation the capital of Buenos Aires province was the city of Buenos Aires. When Buenos Aires became the federal capital, the province lost its seat of government, and it was decided to create a new provincial capital—La Plata.

The climate of La Plata is temperate, with a mean annual temperature of 16°C. Rain is evenly distributed over the year with about 90 wet days. The highest rainfall is during March–April and October.

La Plata is a modern city, and its busy port is an important outlet for the products of the Pampa provinces. The YPF oil refinery is the city's largest industrial complex, and is connected by a 72 km pipeline to Buenos Aires. In addition La Plata is an administrative and university center.

The city was completely planned on the drawing board. The streets have no names, but bear numbers instead.

✷ Festivals
- Fiesta de la Raza (Festival of the Race): October 12. This anniversary of Columbus' landing in the Americas in 1492 is a fiesta which bonds all the Spanish-speaking countries of South America
- Foundation of the city: November 19

ⓘ Tourist information
- Subsecretaria de Turismo, Calle 49–588 ✆ 219760

Junín

Buenos Aires Province

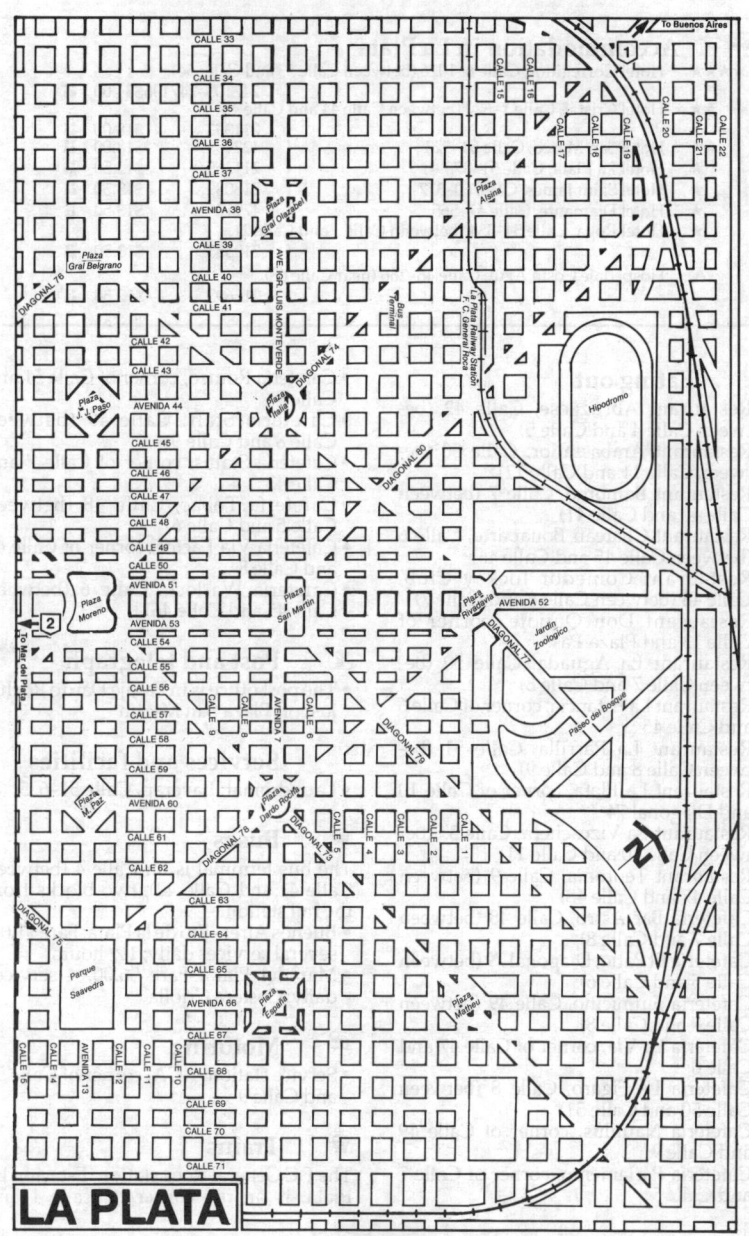

LA PLATA

BUENOS AIRES PROVINCE

🛏 Accommodation in La Plata

★★★★	Hotel Corregidor, Calle 6–1026 (between Calle 53 and Calle 54)	✆ 247103–247106	$34.00	👥
★★	Hotel Cristal, Calle 1–620 (between Calle 44 and Calle 45)	✆ 211393	$18.00	👥
★★	Hotel San Marco, Calle 54–523	✆ 42249	$18.00	👥
★	Hotel La Plata, Calle 51–873	✆ 211365	$13.50	👥
★	Hotel Saint James, Calle 60–377	✆ 218089	$13.50	👥
★	Hotel Diamante, Calle 41–565	✆ 47912	$13.50	👥
★	Hotel Roga, Calle 54–334 (betwenn Calle 1 and Calle 2)	✆ 219553	$13.50	👥
A	Hospedaje Costa Azul, Calle 46–266 (near Calle 68)	✆ 218693	$12.50	👥

🍴 Eating out

- Restaurant Abruzzese, Calle 42 (between Calle 4 and Calle 5)
- Restaurant Ambassador, Calle 50 (between Calle 11 and Calle 12)
- Restaurant Bambino, Calle 7 (between Calle 40 and Calle 41)
- Restaurant Chateau Bonaparte, Calle 6 (between Calle 45 and Calle 46)
- Restaurant Comedor Jockey Club, Calle 48 (between Calle 6 and Calle 7)
- Restaurant Don Quijote, corner of Calle 13 and Plaza Paso
- Restaurant La Aguada, Calle 50 (between Calle 7 and Calle 8)
- Restaurant La Estancia, corner of Calle 6 and Calle 45
- Restaurant La Parrilla, Calle 51 (between Calle 8 and Calle 9)
- Restaurant La Plata, corner of Calle 10 and Diagonal 74
- Restaurant La Vizcachera, Calle 37 (between Calle 10 and Calle 11)
- Restaurant Teutonia, Calle 9 (between Calle 47 and Calle 48)
- Cafetería Bar Astro, Calle 48 (between Calle 7 and Calle 8)
- Cafetería El Patio, Diagonal 79 (between Calle 5 and Calle 6)
- Cafetería Fiumicino, Calle 49 (between Calle 7 and Calle 8)
- Cafetería La Via, corner of Calle 47 and Calle 6
- Cafetería Le Figaro, Calle 8 (between Calle 50 and Calle 51)
- Cafetería Nautilus, corner of Calle 49 and Calle 9
- Cafetería Parlamento, corner of Calle 7 and Calle 51
- Cafetería Romeo, corner of Calle 51 and Calle 9
- Cafetería Staff, Calle 49 (between Calle 8 and Calle 9)
- Cafetería Status, corner of Calle 7 and Calle 43
- Cafetería Tobac, Calle 48 (between Calle 5 and Calle 6)
- Cafetería Via Lactea, corner of Calle 49 and Calle 8
- Cafetería Warlock, Calle 6 (between Calle 45 and Calle 46)

✉ Post and telegraph

- The post office is in Pasaje Dardo Rocha, just off Plaza San Martín

🛎 Services and facilities

- Laundromat: Laverap, Calle 51–625

🚌 Buses

The bus terminal is on Calle 4 (between Calle 41 and Calle 42), two blocks from the rail station.

- Buenos Aires–Río de la Plata: Fare $1.00; several services daily; 1½ hours
- Mar del Plata: Fare $6.00; 4 services daily; Costera Criolla

🚗 Motoring

- Service station: ACA, corner of Calle 51 and Calle 9

🚆 Trains

The F C General Roca station, Estación La Plata, is on the corner of Calle 1 and

La Plata

BUENOS AIRES PROVINCE

Calle 41. There are at least 10 trains daily between La Plata and Buenos Aires.

🍸 Entertainment
- Disco Barravento, Calle 50 (between Calle 9 and Calle 10)
- Disco Camel, Calle 7 (between Calle 39 and Calle 40)
- Disco Chatarra, Calle 7 (between Calle 42 and Calle 43)
- Disco Chihuahua, Calle 5 (between Calle 53 and Calle 54)
- Disco Juana, Calle 44 (between Calle 10 and Calle 11)
- Disco Macondo, Calle 45 (between Calle 8 and Calle 9)
- Disco Metropolis, corner of Calle 47 and Diagonal 74
- Disco Siddharta, Calle 46 (between Calle 13 and Calle 14)
- Disco Tizziano, Calle 34 (between Calle 7 and Calle 8)
- Teatro del Bosque, Avenida 1 (between Calle 60 and Calle 61)
- Teatro Opera, Calle 58 (between Calle 10 and Calle 11)

📷 Sightseeing
- Paseo del Bosque. Part of the Estancia Iraola, most of the trees were planted last century
- Teatro Martin Fierro, Paseo del Bosque. There are open-air performances of ballet and opera on the island in the center of the artificial lake during summer
- Jardín Zoológico (Zoo), Paseo del Bosque
- Museo Histórico Natural (Museum of Natural History). Open daily from 1300–1800; admission $0.40. The collection of extinct animals is one of the most complete in the world, and is most interesting. The 22 halls open to the public display zoological, botanical, ethnological, archeological, geological, and mineralogical exhibits, including mummies, prehistoric implements, and human skulls
- Observatorio Astronómico (Astronomical Observatory), Paseo del Bosque. Built in 1884
- Jardín de la Paz (Garden of Peace), Paseo del Bosque. All the countries in the world are represented by their national flower. During the Fiesta de la Raza, national flags are raised in the garden
- Plaza Moreno, intersected by Diagonal 73 and Diagonal 74, is the city's geographical center. It has many trees and four fountains. In the center of the park is a small structure depicting the spot where the city's foundation stone was laid
- The Municipalidad (Town Hall), built in 1886 by the German Hubert Stier, and the uncompleted cathedral are in the Plaza Moreno. Concerts are held in the Municipalidad's *Salón Dorado* ("Golden Hall"
- Museo Dardo Rocha, Calle 50 (between Calle 13 and Calle 14), home of the city's founder, built in 1885

♣ Excursions
- **Isla Paulina**: 9 km. A regular launch service runs to the beaches on the island
- **Punta Lara**: 14 km north on RP 13. A 20 km beach with many trees on the **Río de la Plata**. The road there is the continuation of Diagonal 74
- **Enseñada**: 18km north on RP 13, continuing on the Cos-

tanera from Punta Lara. Some of the walls have been preserved of the Museo Fuerte de Barragan, founded in 1781. There is also a naval museum
• Republica de los Niños (Children's Republic), located in the suburb of Manuel B Gonnet. Miniature houses and miniature trains, an artificial lake, and an aquarium are attractions for young and old

LOBOS

Postal code: 7240 • (area code: (0227) • Altitude: 29 m
Distance from Buenos Aires: 102 km south-west on RN 203 then RN 205

Lobos is located in the *pampa* on the **Laguna Lobos**. Its origins go back to Fuerte Lobos, a fort founded in 1779. The actual foundation of the township took place in 1803. Lobos is the birthplace of Juan Domingo Perón.

Laguna Lobos is 8 square km and 1.6–1.9 m deep, depending on the rainfall.

Tourist information
• Oficina de Turismo, Salgado (21414

Eating out
• Cafetería Venecia, 9 de Julio 57

Services and facilities
• Laundromat: Laverap, 9 de Julio 226

Buses
• Buenos Aires: 17 services daily; 2 hours; Empresa Liniers

LUJÁN

Postal code: 6700 • (area code: (0323) • Population: 35 000
Distance from Buenos Aires: 70 km eastwards on RN 7

Luján is located on the **Río Luján**. It is the major Catholic shrine in Argentina, and a place of worship for many pilgrims all year round, not only from Argentina but also from Uruguay, Paraguay, and Chile. The shrine's origin goes back to 1630, when an image of the Virgin Mary was carried around the district from church to church in an oxcart. At the spot where the

Accommodation in Lobos

★★	Hotel Country Club, Ruta 41 Km 172		(2189	$17.50	⋕
★	Hostería El Pescador II, Costanera			$12.50	⋕
	Hospedaje El Pescador I, Costanera			$12.50	⋕
A	Hospedaje 9 de Julio, 9 de Julio 263		(21328	$12.50	⋕
	ACA discount; credit cards accepted				
B	Hospedaje Muníz, corner of Buenos Aires and Rauch				
			(2151	$8.50	⋕
B	Hospedaje San Martín, San Martín 170		(21188	$8.50	⋕
B	Hospedaje "46", San Martín 46			$8.50	⋮

La Plata

BUENOS AIRES PROVINCE

◭ Accommodation in Luján

During religious celebrations, such as Easter, accommodation is scarce and prices tend to rise.

★	Hotel Biarritz, Torrezuri 717 (corner of Lezica)	ℂ 21230	$13.50	♙♙
★	Hotel de la Paz, 9 de Julio 1054	ℂ 24034	$13.50	♙♙
★	Hotel Real Luján, Avenida Luján 816	ℂ 20054, 20055	$13.50	♙♙
★	Hotel Royal, 9 de Julio 696	ℂ 21295	$13.50	♙♙
★	Hostería City Hotel, Torrezuri 631 (corner of Lezica)	ℂ 21546	$12.50	♙♙
A	Hospedaje Brown, Almirante Brown 10		$11.50	♙♙
A	Hospedaje Carena, Lavalle 114	ℂ 21287	$11.50	
A	Hospedaje Gran Venecia, Brown 100		$11.50	♙♙
A	Hospedaje Terminal, Torrezuri 601 (corner of Lezica)	ℂ 20671, 20692	$11.50	♙♙

church now stands the cart became stuck, and this was seen as a sign that the Virgin wanted to remain on this spot. The first building on the site was only a small chapel, but now a magnificent neo-Gothic basilica has been built and the Virgin has found her place on the high Altar. The individual arches and two of the transepts are dedicated to the Argentine provinces and to Uruguay and Paraguay, the countries linked to Argentina by special bonds.

❂ Festivals
- Fiesta de la Virgen de Luján: May 8
- Horse pilgrimage: last Sunday in September
- Fiesta Provincial de la Tradición: November 10. *Gaucho* festival

ⓘ Tourist information
- Edificio La Cúpula, opposite Parque Ameghino ℂ 20453

🚌 Buses
Compañía de Automotores de Luján runs regular bus services to and from Buenos Aires. It is a one-hour trip from the Once rail station in Buenos Aires.

🚗 Motoring
- Service station: ACA, RN 7 Km 62

🚆 Trains
- Buenos Aires: Fare $2.00; 2 hours. Change at Moreno to the F C General Sarmiento line to get to Once station in Buenos Aires

📷 Sightseeing
- Wax museum of the Virgen de Luján. Religious exhibits
- Basilica Nuestra Señora de Luján (Our Lady of Luján Basilica)
- Museo Colonial e Histórico (Colonial and Historical Museum). Located in the old Cabildo building. A good display of the historical and political development of Argentina. Open Wed–Sun 1200–1800

BUENOS AIRES PROVINCE

MAR DEL PLATA

Postal code: 7600 • (area code: (023) • Population: 450 000
Distance from Buenos Aires: 400 km southwards on RN 2

Mar del Plata may well be called South America's summer playground. It is very crowded between late December and mid-March, but fairly quiet for the rest of the year.

Festivals
- Foundation day: February 10
- Día de la Tradición (Day of Tradition): November 10
- St Cecilia's day: November 22

Eating out

International cuisine
- Restaurant a los Marineros de Cichilo, Bulevar Marítimo 177
- Hermitage Hotel, Bulevar Marítimo 2557
- Restaurant Tempone's, Alem 4661 Santiago del Estero 1330

Key to Map

1. Municipalidad
2. Basilica San Pedro
3. Post office (Encotel)
4. Telephone (Entel)
5. Tourist information
6. Banco de la Nación
7. Cambio La Moneda
8. Cambio Mar del Plata
9. Cambio Jonestur
10. Aerolineas Argentinas
11. Austral Lineas Aereas
12. Casino
13. Museo Municipal de Ciencias Naturales
16. Hotel Dos Reyes
17. Hotel Hermitage
18. Hotel Republica
19. Hotel Benedetti
20. Hotel Bizonte
21. Hotel Condesa del Mar
22. Hotel Gran Casino
23. Hotel Gran Opera
24. Hotel Gran Continental
25. Hotel Rivoli
26. Hotel Valles
27. Hotel Versalles
28. Hotel Antranik
29. Hotel Armida
30. Hotel Bertiani
31. Hotel Biarritz
32. Hotel Bologna
33. Hotel Castelmar
34. Hotel Cheyenne
35. Hotel Colonial
36. Hotel Corcel
37. Hotel Dunas
38. Hotel Esmeralda Select
39. Hotel Iercomar
41. Hotel Mediterraneo
42. Hotel Neptuno
43. Hotel Nueva América
44. Residencial Nueva Ostende
45. Hotel Nuevo Horizonte
46. Hotel Park Hotel
47. Hotel Skorpios
48. Hotel Traful
49. Hotel APA
50. Hotel Chila
52. Hotel Ideal
53. Hotel Indian Palace
54. Hotel Ipanema
55. Hotel King's
56. Hotel Las Heras
57. Hotel Lebet
58. Hotel Manila II
59. Hotel Mar
60. Hotel Antartida Argentina
61. Hotel Moli-Mar
62. Hotel Naval
63. Hotel Ocean Nelson
64. Hotel Pernas
65. Hotel Plaza España
66. Hotel San Carlos
67. Hotel Storni
68. Hotel Litre
69. Residencial Monterey
70. Hotel Paraná

Mar del Plata

BUENOS AIRES PROVINCE

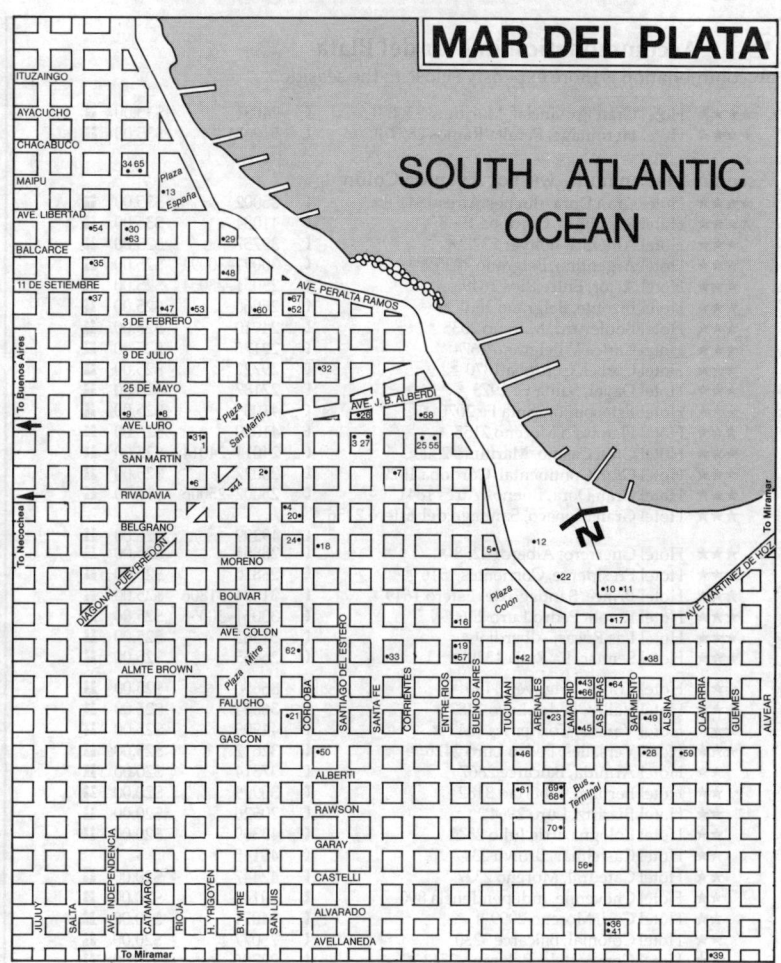

Seafood

- Restaurant Cantabrico, Justo 1800
- Club Aldosivi, Bermejo 271

Cafeterias

- Cafe Señor Gonzalez, Alem 3738

Eating out north-west of Avenida Colón

International cuisine

- Restaurant Angus, Constitución 4487
- Restaurant Antartida, Pedro Luro 2156
- Club Español, Yrigoyen 1653

Continued on page 96

Mar del Plata

BUENOS AIRES PROVINCE

🛏 Accommodation in Mar del Plata

Accommodation is more expensive close to the seaside.

★★★★	Hotel Gran Provincial, Marítimo 2500 🛉	(	24081	$35.00 👥
★★★★	Hotel Hermitage, Peralta Ramos 2657 🛉	(	519081	$35.00 👥

Accommodation north-west of Avenida Colón

★★★★	Hotel Gran Dora, Buenos Aires 1841 🛉	(	25002	$35.00 👥
★★★★	Hotel Republica, Córdoba 1968	(	41084	$35.00 👥
★★★	Hotel América, Bolívar 2322	(	39757	$25.00 👥
★★★	Hotel Argentino, Belgrano 2225	(	30091–30094	$25.00 👥
★★★	Hotel Astor, Entre Ríos 1649	(	23051–23054	$25.00 👥
★★★	Hotel Bizonte, Belgrano 2601	(	26060	$25.00 👥
★★★	Hotel Boulevard, Moreno 2035	(	24910	$25.00 👥
★★★	Hotel Carlos V Belgrano 2674	(	22175	$25.00 👥
★★★	Hotel Corbel, Córdoba 1870	(	29722	$25.00 👥
★★★	Hotel Daver, Santa Fé 1973	(	27187	$25.00 👥
★★★	Hotel Estocolmo, Santa Fé 2070	(	41009	$25.00 👥
★★★	Hotel Flamingo, Moreno 2155	(	41080	$25.00 👥
★★★	Hotel Gran Casino, Marítimo 2300	(	24011–24014	$25.00 👥
★★★	Hotel Gran Continental, Córdoba 1929	(	23027	$25.00 👥
★★★	Hotel Gran Dora, Buenos Aires 1841 🛉	(	25002–25006	$17.00 👥
★★★	Hotel Gran Monaco, Santiago del Estero 2156	(	49299	$25.00 👥
★★★	Hotel Guerrero, Alberdí 2288	(	28851	$25.00 👥
★★★	Hotel Presidente, Corrientes 1516	(	28810	$25.00 👥
★★★	Hotel Prince, Santiago del Estero 1649	(	31804–31806	$25.00 👥
★★★	Hotel Rivoli, Pedro Luro 2260	(	30051–30058	$25.00 👥
★★★	Hotel Las Rocas, Alberdí 9	(	51362	$25.00 👥
★★★	Hotel Sennac, La Rioja 1339	(	26465	$25.00 👥
★★★	Hotel Traful, Yrigoyen 1190	(	36650	$25.00 👥
★★★	Hotel Valles, Pedro Luro 2487	(	36604	$25.00 👥
★★★	Hotel Vaness, Corrientes 1842	(	44909	$25.00 👥
★★★	Hotel Versalles, Pedro Luro 2426	(	32612	$25.00 👥
★★	Hotel Armida, Balcarce 2867	(	37814	$20.00 👥
★★	Hotel Bertiani, Libertad 3182	(	30999	$20.00 👥
★★	Hotel Biarritz, Luro 2964	(	20526	$20.00 👥
★★	Hotel Bologna, 9 de Julio 2542	(	43369	$20.00 👥
★★	Hotel Castelmar, Brown 2347	(	45115	
★★	Hotel Catedral, Moreno 2327	(	42447	$20.00 👥
★★	Hotel Cheyenne, Independencia 890	(	30149	$20.00 👥
★★	Hotel Cini, Moreno 2099 🛉	(	24071	$20.00 👥
★★	Hotel Colónial, Balcarce 3230	(	25077	$20.00 👥
★★	Hotel Compestela, Belgrano 2561	(	22796	$20.00 👥
★★	Hotel Dallas Centre, Belgrano 2368	(	22937	
★★	Hotel Delfin, Rivadavia 2556	(	28571	$20.00 👥
★★	Hotel Dunas, Balcarce 3285	(	23777	$20.00 👥
★★	Hotel Gran Tronador, Moreno 2541	(	21798	$20.00 👥
★★	Hotel Litoria, Buenos Aires 1928 🛉	(	26050	$20.00 👥
★★	Hotel Manila I, Entre Ríos 1648 🛉	(	26018	$20.00 👥
★★	Hotel Miglierina, Belgrano 2367 🛉	(	27021	$20.00 👥
★★	Hotel Minerva, Bolívar 2535	(	24001	$20.00 👥
★★	Hotel Montreal, Corrientes 1886	(	45984	$20.00 👥
★★	Hotel Napoleon, Santa Fé 1913	(	410006	$20.00 👥
★★	Hotel Punta del Este, B Moreno 2563	(	48500	$20.00 👥

Mar del Plata

BUENOS AIRES PROVINCE

Accommodation in Mar del Plata, north-west of Avenida Colón—continued

★★ Hotel Roland, Corrientes 1965	ℂ	42488	$20.00
★★ Hotel Select, Corrientes 1956	ℂ	44170	$20.00
★★ Hotel Skorpios, 3 de Febrero 3071	ℂ	35758	$20.00
★★ Hotel Traful, Yrigoyen 1190	ℂ	36650	$20.00
★★ Hotel Winter, Belgrano 2338	ℂ	36608	$20.00
★ Hotel Alhambra, Corrientes 2131	ℂ	26232	$15.00
★ Hotel Alpe's, Moreno 2445	ℂ	48497	
★ Hotel Antartida Argentina, 3 de Febrero 2851	ℂ	21389	$15.00
★ Hotel Aragon, Buenos Aires 1933	ℂ	23064	$15.00
★ Hotel Arcos, Entre Ríos 1975	ℂ	23771	$15.00
★ Hotel Berry, Belgrano 2164	ℂ	21551	$15.00
★ Hotel Castelar, Yrigoyen 1154	ℂ	24040	$15.00
★ Hotel Center, Belgrano 2187	ℂ	24066–24068	$15.00
★ Hotel Cervantes, Santiago del Estero 2181	ℂ	21049	$15.00
★ Hotel del Paseo, Rivadavia 2569	ℂ	20416	$15.00
★ Hotel Frandor's, Belgrano 2243	ℂ	34423	$15.00
★ Hotel Garden, Moreno 2393	ℂ	27091	$15.00
★ Hotel Ideal, 3 de Febrero 2663	ℂ	31470	$15.00
Open during summer only			
★ Hotel Indian Palace, 3 de Febrero 2957	ℂ	27624	$15.00
★ Hotel Ipanema, Libertad 3222	ℂ	24723	$15.00
★ Hotel King's, Pedro Luro 2220	ℂ	30081	$15.00
★ Hotel K'Sinos, Belgrano 2163	ℂ	23733	$15.00
★ Hotel Luso Argentino, Santa Fé 2075	ℂ	34859–27184	$15.00
★ Hotel Manila II, Luro 2286	ℂ	28211–3	$15.00
★ Hotel Moli-Mar, Alberdí 1956			
★ Hotel Noro, Corrientes 2171	ℂ	22322	$15.00
★ Hotel N Raglan, Bolívar 2556	ℂ	33730	$15.00
★ Hotel Ocean Nelson, Balcarce 3101	ℂ	29392	$15.00
★ Hotel Ortegal, Moreno 2476	ℂ	28011	$15.00
★ Hotel Osorno, Moreno 2559	ℂ	28174	$15.00
★ Hotel Plaza España, Maipú 3155	ℂ	736912	$15.00
★ Hotel Po, Entre Ríos 1989	ℂ	20068	$15.00
★ Hotel Ramos Mejia, Entre Ríos 1961	ℂ	25949	$15.00
★ Hotel Rex, San Martín 2430	ℂ	28861–28863	$15.00
★ Hotel Rutibell, Bolívar 2456	ℂ	23397	$15.00
★ Hotel San Carlos, Corrientes 1939	ℂ	24384	$15.00
★ Hotel Sky, Corrientes 1862	ℂ	39068	$15.00
★ Hotel Storni, 11 De Setiembre 2642	ℂ	41444	$15.00

B Hospedaje Misiones, Misiones 69
  Near rail station

• Residencial Nueva Ostende, H Yrigoyen 1739

Accommodation south-east of Avenida Colón

★★★★ Hotel Chateau Frontenac, Alvear 2010	ℂ	519443	$35.00
★★★★ Hotel Dos Reyes, Colón 2129	ℂ	28694	$35.00
★★★★ Hotel Sasso, M de Hoz 3545	ℂ	840031	$35.00
★★★ Hotel Benedetti, Colón 2198	ℂ	30031–30033	$25.00
★★★ Hotel Condesa del Mar, Falucho 2652	ℂ	25420	$25.00
★★★ Hotel Cosmos, Buenos Aires 2481	ℂ	33544	$25.00
★★★ Hotel Gran Iruna, Alberti 2270	ℂ	24037	$25.00
★★★ Hotel Gran Opera, Falucho 1938	ℂ	21795	$25.00
★★ Hotel Antranik Gascon 1524	ℂ	516203	$20.00
★★ Hotel Corcel, Las Heras 2920	ℂ	513033	

Mar del Plata

BUENOS AIRES PROVINCE

	Accommodation in Mar del Plata, south-east of Avenida Colón—Continued			
★★	Hotel Esmeralda Select, Brown 1553	(23395		
★★	Hotel Iercomar, Güemes 3174	(515898		
★★	Hotel Lasalle, Entre Ríos 2262 🅣	(28416	$20.00	♀♀
★★	Hotel Mediterraneo, Las Heras 2136	(516189		
★★	Hotel Neptuno, Brown 1959	(25439		
★★	Hotel Nueva América, Brown 762	(21998		
★★	Hotel Nuevo Horizonte, Lamadrid 2506	(42355	$20.00	♀♀
★★	Hotel Park Hotel, Gascon 1970	(42582	$20.00	♀♀
★★	Hotel Waldorf, Buenos Aires 2389 🅔	(31825	$20.00	♀♀
★	Hotel APA, Falucho 1548	(514704	$15.00	♀♀
★	Hotel Chila, Gascon 2536	(35710	$15.00	♀♀
★	Hotel Las Heras, Las Heras 2849	(37841		
★	Hotel Lebet, Entre Ríos 2282	(28593	$15.00	♀♀
★	Hotel Mar, Gascon 1410	(511769	$15.00	♀♀
★	Hotel Naval, Córdoba 2229	(28839	$15.00	♀♀
★	Hotel Pernas, Brown 1628	(519223		

- Hotel Litre, corner of Lamadrid and Rawson, opposite bus terminal
- Hotel Paraná, corner of Lamadrid and Rawson, opposite bus terminal
- Residencial Monterrey, Lamadrid 2627

- Restaurant El Palacio del Bife, Córdoba 1857
- Restaurant La Paella, Entre Ríos 2025
- Restaurant Los Cercos, Belgrano 2220
- Restaurant Mustang, Constitución 5001
- Restaurant Sorento, 25 de Mayo 3005
- Restaurant Verdi, San Luis 1954

Seafood

- Restaurant Atalaya del Mar, Club de Pesca, corner of Bulevar Marítimo and Alberdí
- Restaurant El Palacio de la Cerveza, Hotel Gran Provincial, Marítimo 2500
- Restaurant La Cacerola, Martinez de Hoz 1799
- Restaurant La Caracola, corner of Martinez de Hoz and 12 de Octubre
- Restaurant La Casa de C Spadavecchia, Martinez de Hoz 343

Parrillas

A *parrilla* is a type of grill.
- Restaurant Clear, Santa Fé 1865
- Restaurant El Brasero, Rivadavia 2168
- Restaurant El Carbon, Moreno 2132
- Restaurant El Coyunco, Santiago del Estero 1962
- Restaurant La Achurita, Moreno 2132
- Restaurant La Estancia de Don Pepito, Peralta Ramos, opposite casino
- Restaurant La Hamburguesa, Moreno 2445
- Restaurant La Rueda, Corrientes 1829
- Restaurant La Tablita, Rivadavia 2479
- Restaurant Los Nogales, Santa Fé 1865
- Restaurant Miguel Angel, Bolívar 2380
- Restaurant Picacho, Entre Ríos 1930
- Restaurant Plaza, Moreno 2089
- Restaurant Tío Otto, Belgrano 2454

Italian cuisine

- Restaurant El Nilo, Pedro Luro 5614
- Restaurant El Rincón de Carlitos, 25 de Mayo 3992
- Restaurant Il Vero Napoli, Belgrano 3408
- Restaurant La Herradura, Camet 335
- Restaurant Los Amigos de Lanus, Constitución 4166
- ☞ Restaurant Mamma Mia, San Martín 2547
- Restaurant Renacimiento, Belgrano 2178
- Trattoria Napolitana, 3 de Febrero 3158

Vegetarian

- Restaurant El Jardin II, San Martín 2463 (upstairs)
- Restaurant La Huerta, San Martín 2300

Mar del Plata

BUENOS AIRES PROVINCE

Cafeterias

- Cafetería Pumpernic, San Martín 2339. Self-serve
- Cafetería Colonial, Entre Ríos 1950
- Cafetería Concert Colonial, corner of Dorrego and Moreno
- Cafetería Cultur Aqui Vivieron, Alberdí 2599
- Cafetería Del Teatro, Santiago del Estero 1750
- Cafetería El Fulerin, España 1940
- Cafetería La Forteresse, Independencia 895
- Cafetería La Mona, Hotel Gran Provincial, Marítimo 2500
- Cafetería Lar, Entre Ríos 1525
- Cafetería Medieval, corner of Salta and Bolivar
- Cafetería Melody, Santa Fé 1825
- Cafetería Orion, Bulevar Marítimo 1900
- Cafetería Romulo y Remo, San Luis 1203

Eating out south-east of Avenida Colón

International cuisine

- Restaurant Chateau Frontenac, Alvear 2010
- Restaurant El Almirante, Brown 1625
- Restaurant El Viejo Pop, corner of M de Hoz and 12 de Octubre
- Restaurant La Casa del Ruso, Roca 944
- Restaurant Monterrey, Saavedra 2307

✈ Air services from Mar del Plata

Aeropuerto Camet is 10 km from the city center.
- Aerolineas Argentinas, corner of Peralta Ramos and Moreno
- Lineas Aereas Austral, corner of Peralta Ramos and Moreno

Destination	Fare	Depart	Services	Hours	Airline
• Bahía Blanca	$34.00	0940	Tues	1	LADE
• Buenos Aires (Aeroparque Jorje Newbery)					
	$43.00	0915	6–10 services daily	1–2	Aerolineas, Austral, LADE, LAPA
• Chapelco	$49.00	1000	Mon, Wed	8	LADE
• Comodoro Rivadavia					
	$71.00	0820	Tues, Thurs, Sat, Sun	3	Aerolineas, Austral
	$58.00	0940	Tues, Wed, Fri	7	LADE
• Córdoba	$71.00	1100	Mon–Sat		Austral
• Esquel	$57.00	0940	Tues, Fri	4	LADE
• Mendoza	$74.00	1100	Mon–Sat	4½	Austral
• Neuquén	$46.00	0940	Tues, Wed, Fri	2–7	LADE
	$64.00	1000	Sun	½	Aerolineas
• Puerto Deseado	$58.00	0940	Tues, Fri	8	LADE
• Puerto San Julián	$61.00	0940	Tues, Fri	9	LADE
• Río Gallegos	$77.00	0820	Sun	4	Aerolineas
	$62.00	0940	Tues, Fri	10	LADE
• Río Grande	$67.00	0940	Tues, Fri	11	LADE
• San Antonio Oeste					
	$37.00	1000	Mon	3	LADE
• San Carlos de Bariloche					
	$80.00	1000	Sun	3	Aerolineas
	$57.00	1105	Mon–Wed, Fri, Sun	6	LADE
• Santa Cruz	$61.00	0940	Tues, Fri	9	LADE
• Trelew	$61.00	0820	2 services daily	1–2	Aerolineas, Austral
	$58.00	0940	Tues, Fri	6	LADE
• Ushuaia	$87.00	0820	Sun	6	Aerolineas
• Viedma	$38.00	0940	Mon, Fri	1	LADE
• Zapala	$40.00	1105	Wed	4	LADE

Mar del Plata

BUENOS AIRES PROVINCE

🚌 Buses from Mar del Plata

The bus terminal is on Alberti block 1600 (corner of Sarmiento).

Destination	Fare	Depart	Services	Hours	Company
• Bahía Blanca	$10.00	0800	5 services daily	9	El Pampa
• Buenos Aires	$11.80			6	TA Chevallier
• Córdoba	$22.50	1315	2 services daily	15	Expreso Córdoba
• La Plata	$6.50		4 services daily		Costera Criolla
• Mendoza	$11.50	1000	Thurs, Sun		TAC
• Paraná		1930	daily		Zenit Turismo
• Rosario		1930	4 services daily		Empresa Argentina, Zenit Turismo
• San Carlos de Bariloche	$31.00				Costera Criolla, El Cóndor, Micro Mar
• San Juan		2130	Thurs, Sun		Automotores San Juan
• San Luis		2130	Thurs, Sun		Automotores San Juan
• San Miguel de Tucumán	$37.50	1130	daily	26	La Estrella
• Santa Fé	$22.60	1930	daily		Zenit Turismo
• Santa Rosa		2030	daily		El Rapido
• Santiago del Estero		1130	daily	23	La Estrella
• Termas de Río Hondo		1130	daily	24	La Estrella

- Petit Restaurant, Del Valle 3940
- Restaurant Tío Curzio, Colón 846
- Restaurant Zabalita's, Córdoba 4508

Seafood

- Restaurant Chichilo, Martinez de Hoz 277
- Restaurant El Taburete, Pescadores 498
- Restaurant El Timon, corner of Martinez de Hoz and 12 de Octubre
- Restaurant Ismael Marisqueria, Alcorta 320
- Restaurant La Banquina del Puerto, Alvarado 2763
- Restaurant Rincón Gallego, Martinez de Hoz 201

Italian cuisine

- Restaurant Bona II Catina, Colón 2901
- Restaurant City, Castelli 3200
- Restaurant Il Vero Mangiare, Tucumán 2699
- Restaurant La Amistad, Alsina 2333
- Restaurant La Plata, Champagnat 2286

Cafeterias

- Cafetería Boliche de Chapa, corner of Catamarca and San Lorenzo
- Cafetería Zaratustra, corner of Entre Ríos and Falucho

📮 Post and telegraph

- Post office: Encotel, corner of Santiago del Estero and Pedro Luro
- Telephones: Entel, corner of Gascon and Alsina

💲 Financial

- Banco Alas, Belgrano 2140. Cash advances on Visa card
- Cambios Mar del Plata, Pedro Luro 3021
- Cambios Jonestur, Pedro Luro 3191
- Cambios La Moneta, San Martín 2314

🛎 Services and facilities

- Laundromat: Laverap, Alsina 2221

🚗 Motoring

- Car rentals: Avis Rent-a-Car, Bulevar Marítimo 2451, ℂ 37850

🚆 Trains

The F C General Roca station (Estación Norte) is on the corner of Avenida Luro

BUENOS AIRES PROVINCE

and Chaco. There is a booking office in J de San Martín block 2300 (corner of Santa Fé).

- Buenos Aires: "Golondrina" departs 0845. "El Atlantico" departs daily 1545. "Cruz del Sur" departs daily 2330. "Neptuno" departs Sun 1645. "El Marplatense" departs Sun, Tues, Thurs 1900. Fares: Pullman $11.00; first class $7.50; Tourist class $5.50

Sport

- Golf course
- Polo grounds: Parque Camet 8 km to the north of the city center
- Sailing club: Club Náutico, Bulevar Marítimo
- Yacht club: Bulevar Marítimo

Entertainment

- Disco Angie, corner of Alsina and Bulevar Marítimo
- Disco Eiffel Club, Constitución 4478. Fri–Sun, all ages
- Disco Enterprise, Constitución 6000. All ages
- Disco Ipanema, Constitución 5850. Fri–Sun; young people
- Disco Kiwi, Constitución 4830. Young couples only
- Disco Latex, Bulevar Marítimo 3200
- Disco Le Mirage, Almafuerte 235
- Disco Los Aromos, Constitución 5900. Adults
- Disco María Lopez, corner of Bulevar Marítimo and Rivas. Young people
- Disco Pacha Boite, Constitución 5330. Adults, couples only
- Disco Puerto Banus, Constitución 5800
- Disco Puerto Mara, Constitución 4545. Fri–Sun; all ages
- Disco Ritz, corner of Viamonte and Bulevar Marítimo
- Disco Sandbar, Rawson 18. Open every night
- Disco Sobremonte, Constitución 6690. Fri–Sun; all ages, couples only
- Disco Summertime, Constitución 6416. Fri–Sun; all ages
- Disco Sunset, Constitución 5096. All ages, couples only
- Disco Symbiosis, Constitución 5825. All ages
- Disco Xanadú, Constitución 6700. All ages, couples only
- Disco Ydolem, Constitución 5268
- Disco Zeus, Constitución 4854
- Tanguería del 40, Constitución 5203. Tango dancing; adults

Sightseeing

- Museo Municipal de Ciencias (Municipal Science Museum), Plaza España. Has exhibits of fossils from the tertiary and quaternary periods, and an aquarium

MAR DEL TUYÚ

Postal code: 7107
Distance from Mar del Plata: 213 km northwards on RP 11

Mar del Tuyú is one of the newer seaside resorts which have sprung up in this area. The beach extends for miles in both directions. The tourist season runs from mid-December to mid-March. Outside these months Mar del Tuyú is quiet, and much of the accommodation and other services close down. The streets have no names, but bear numbers instead.

Tourist information

- Oficina de Turismo, corner of Calle 80 and Calle 1

Post and telegraph

- Post office: Encotel, between Calle 72 and Calle 73
- Long distance telephone: Entel, Calle 73 (between Calle 1 and Calle 2)

Mar del Tuyú

Buenos Aires Province

🚌 Buses

Bus companies for buses to Buenos Aires, La Plata, and Mar del Plata are located on Calle 2 (between Calle 74 and Calle 75) and on Calle 1 (between Calle 72 and Calle 73).
- Buenos Aires: 4 services daily; 5 hours; Empresa La Estrella

MERCEDES

Postal code: 6600 • Population: 40,000 • ☎ area code: (0324) • Altitude: 37 m
Distance from Buenos Aires: 97 km westwards on RN 7

Services and facilities
- Laundromat: Laverap, Calle 25–285

🚌 Buses
- Buenos Aires: 8 services daily ; 3 hours; Empresa Liniers

🚗 Motoring
- Service station: ACA service station, corner of Calle 29 and Calle 16

MIRAMAR

Postal code: 7607 • ☎ area code: (0291)
Distances
- From Buenos Aires: 450 km southwards on RN 2
- From Mar del Plata: 45 km southwards on RP 11
- From Necochea 102 km eastwards on RP 88 then south-east on RN 77

Miramar is a major seaside vacation resort with good tourist facilities and lovely beaches. The town is laid out in the familiar chess-board fashion and the streets are numbered as in La Plata. Although prices rise during the summer months it is still cheaper than other seaside resorts. Paseo Costanero is a wide *avenida* with the beach on one side and high-rise apartment blocks and hotels on the other. The beachfront is set against a backdrop of cliffs.

ℹ️ Tourist information
- Dirección de Turismo, Avenida 26 1065 ☎ 611216

⛺ Camping
- Balneario Las Brusquitas. Run by the ACA

🍽️ Eating out
- Restaurant Atahualpa, Calle 19–1601
- Restaurant Cantina Italiana, corner of 9 de Julio and Calle 32
- Restaurant Circolo Italiano, corner of Avenida 9 and Calle 28
- Restaurant Costa Brava, Avenida 23–799
- Restaurant El Aguila, corner of Calle 19 and Calle 32
- Restaurant El Ciervo, Calle 16–1135
- Restaurant El Fogon, Calle 19–1181
- Restaurant El Palacio de la Papa Frita, Avenida 23–743
- Restaurant El Spiedo, Calle 30–1126
- Restaurant El Muelle, corner of Avenida Costanera and Calle 37
- Restaurant El Rodeo, corner of Calle 21 and Calle 14
- Restaurant Gran Hotel, Calle 29–586
- Restaurant Jet-Set, Avenida Costanera 1629
- Restaurant Jockey Club, corner of Calle 21 and Avenida 26
- Restaurant La Cautiva, corner of Calle 19 and Calle 24
- Restaurant La Costa, corner of Avenida 9 and Calle 12
- Restaurant La Estrella, Avenida 40–860
- Restaurant Lisandro, corner of Calle 21 and Calle 28
- Restaurant Lisboa, Avenida 40–830
- Restaurant Mavi, Avenida 9–1232

Mar del Tuyú

Buenos Aires Province

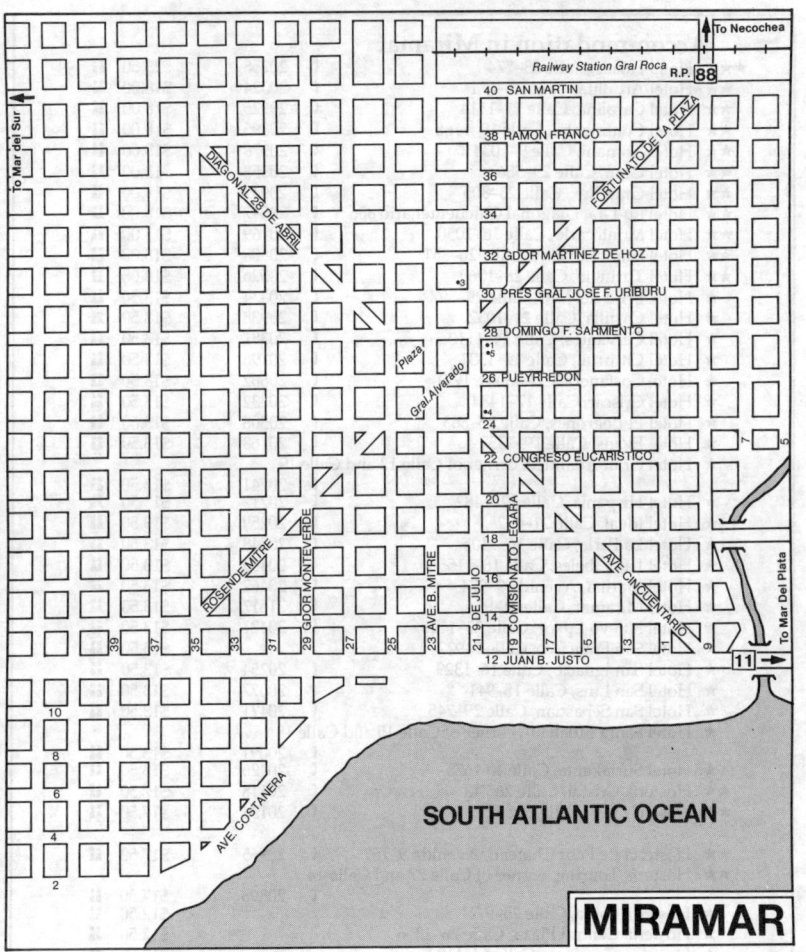

Key to Map
1 Municipalidad
2 Iglesia
3 Post office (Encotel)
4 Banco de la Nación
5 Casino

Miramar

BUENOS AIRES PROVINCE

Accommodation in Miramar

★★★	Hotel Palace, Calle 23–774	ℓ 20258	$23.50	ii
★★	Hotel Ardillita, Calle 28–671	ℓ 20024	$18.00	ii
★★	Hotel Carolina, Calle 11–1114	ℓ 20925	$18.00	ii
★★	Hotel Continental, Calle 19–1168	ℓ 20895	$18.00	ii
★★	Hotel Domani, Calle 9–1034	ℓ 20978	$18.00	ii
★★	Hotel Gran, Calle 29–586	ℓ 20358	$18.00	ii
★★	Hotel Gran Rex, Calle 23–805	ℓ 20942	$18.00	ii
★★	Hotel Lu-Gra, Diagonal Cincuentenario 856	ℓ 20547	$18.00	ii
★★	Hotel Montecarlo, Calle 16–1050	ℓ 20469	$18.00	ii
★★	Hotel Santa Eulalia I, Calle 26–851	ℓ 20808	$18.00	ii
★★	Hotel Turingia, Calle 28–1060	ℓ 20526	$18.00	ii
★	Hotel Brisa del Mar, Calle 29–597	ℓ 20334	$13.50	ii
★	Hotel Castilla, Calle 21–1032	ℓ 20938	$13.50	ii
★	Hotel Cervantes, Calle 24–1110	ℓ 20387	$13.50	ii
★	Hotel Citturini, Calle 12–1331	ℓ 20796	$13.50	ii
★	Hotel Costanera, Costanera 1771	ℓ 20662	$13.50	ii
★	Hotel Criscar, Calle 17–1434	ℓ 20232	$13.50	ii
★	Hotel El Logrones, Calle 25–863	ℓ 20508	$13.50	ii
★	Hotel Evans, Calle 19–1353	ℓ 20168	$13.50	ii
★	Hotel Gran Atlantico, corner of Calle 12 and Calle 19	ℓ 20741	$13.50	ii
★	Hotel Hispania, Calle 12–1482	ℓ 20217	$13.50	ii
★	Hotel Ideal, Calle 21–632	ℓ 20259	$13.50	ii
★	Hotel La Perla, Calle 16–1105	ℓ 20848	$13.50	ii
★	Hotel Las Cibeles, Calle 18–1155	ℓ 20489	$13.50	ii
★	Hotel Marina, Avenida 9–974	ℓ 20462	$13.50	ii
★	Hotel Miramar, Calle 21–954	ℓ 21617	$13.50	ii
★	Hotel Nuevo Luxor, Calle 23–1126	ℓ 20421	$13.50	ii
★	Hotel San Francisco, Calle 9–922		$13.50	ii
★	Hotel San Ignacio, Calle 16–1329	ℓ 20254	$13.50	ii
★	Hotel San Luis, Calle 15–941	ℓ 20077	$13.50	ii
★	Hotel San Sebastian, Calle 29–745	ℓ 20471	$13.50	ii
★	Hotel Santa Eulalia II, corner of Calle 15 and Calle 18	ℓ 20091	$13.50	ii
★	Hotel Suriakanta, Calle 10 1675	ℓ 20426	$13.50	ii
★★	Hostería Cristal, Calle 26 743	ℓ 20118	$17.50	ii
★★	Hostería Leli, Calle 26 881	ℓ 20134	$17.50	ii
★★	Hostería Le Petit Chateau, Avenida 9–752	ℓ 20965	$17.50	ii
★★	Hostería Touring, corner of Calle 27 and Calle 14	ℓ 20898	$17.50	ii
★	Hostería Bahía, Calle 25–971		$12.50	ii
★	Hostería Central Plaza, Calle 26–1356		$12.50	ii
★	Hostería Flamingo, Calle 16–1133		$12.50	ii
★	Hostería Lisboa, Calle 40–830	ℓ 20746	$12.50	ii
★	Hostería Los Copihues, Avenida Ruiz Quiñazu 169	ℓ 20723	$12.50	ii
★	Hostería Riviera, Calle 22–853		$12.50	ii
★	Hostería Santa Rita, Calle 25–1051		$12.50	ii
A	Hospedaje America, Diagonal B Mitre 1114	ℓ 20847	$12.50	ii
A	Hospedaje Aymara, Calle 23–1002	ℓ 20787	$12.50	ii
A	Hospedaje Bella Vista, Costanera 1433		$12.50	ii
A	Hospedaje España, Calle 14–1046		$12.50	ii
A	Hospedaje Filadelfia, Calle 9–1185		$12.50	ii

Miramar

BUENOS AIRES PROVINCE

Accommodation in Miramar—continued

A	Hospedaje Ivamca, corner of Calle 101 and Calle 23		$12.50	♔
A	Hospedaje La Gran Via, Calle 15–1138		$12.50	♔
A	Hospedaje La Ramie, Calle 28–783		$12.50	♔
A	Hospedaje Las Nenas, Calle 19–1656		$12.50	♔
A	Hospedaje Laurana, Calle 11–1728		$12.50	♔
A	Hospedaje Maricel, Calle 19–1405	✆ 20641	$12.50	♔
A	Hospedaje Mendez, Calle 23–1507		$12.50	♔
A	Hospedaje Platamar, Calle 36–926	✆ 21186	$12.50	♔
B	Hospedaje Arostegui, Calle 18–933		$8.50	♔
B	Hospedaje Cervantes, Calle 30–907		$8.50	♔
B	Hospedaje Colonial, Calle 19–1165	✆ 20365	$8.50	♔
B	Hospedaje Costa Azul, Calle 21–1684		$8.50	♔
B	Hospedaje Dorimar, Calle 24–839		$8.50	♔
B	Hospedaje Embassy, Calle 26–913	✆ 20788	$8.50	♔
B	Hospedaje Familia, Calle 23–1701	✆ 20671	$8.50	♔
B	Hospedaje Las Brusquitas, Calle 26–1431	✆ 20444	$8.50	♔
B	Hospedaje Namuncura, Calle 40–860	✆ 20672	$8.50	♔
B	Hospedaje Ocean, 9 de Julio 967	✆ 20783	$8.50	♔
B	Hospedaje San Miguel, Calle 22–1146	✆ 20894	$8.50	♔
B	Hospedaje Select, Calle 23–1031	✆ 20310	$8.50	♔
B	Hospedaje Victoria, Calle 26–1150	✆ 20603	$8.50	♔
B	Hospedaje "23", Calle 23–1728	✆ 20937	$8.50	♔
B	Hospedaje Villa Cruz, Calle 19–864		$8.50	♔

Accommodation outside Miramar

★★	Motel Copacabana, RP 11, northern exit		
A	Hospedaje Villa del Mar, Mar del Sud, 16 km south	$12.50	♔
B	Hospedaje Boulevard Atlantico, Boulevard Atlantico, 14 km south	$8.50	♔

- Restaurant Meson Espanól, Avenida 26–1351
- Restaurant Nito, Calle 21–602
- Restaurant Punto y Banca, Diagonal Fortunato de la Plaza 1426
- Restaurant Quinta La Azuzena, corner of Avenida Mitre and Calle 52
- Restaurant San Ignacio, Calle 30–1045
- Restaurant Santa Eulalia, Avenida 26–851
- Restaurant Sarmiento, Calle 28–1145
- Pizzería Aristegui, Calle 21–1186
- Pizzería Astral, corner of Calle 21 and Calle 30
- Pizzería Pizza a la Piedra, corner of Calle 22 and Calle 21
- Pizzería Pizzilandia, corner of Calle 21 and Calle 14
- Pizzería Stop, corner of Calle 21 and Calle 28
- Pizzería Teijeiro, corner of Avenida 23 and Calle 44
- Cafetería Charly, corner of 9 de Julio and Calle 18
- Cafetería Cita Club, corner of 9 de Julio and Calle 28
- Cafetería La Pergola, corner of Avenida Mitre and Calle 18
- Cafetería Las Gaviotas, corner of 9 de Julio and Calle 22
- Cafetería Mi Refugio, corner of 9 de Julio and Calle 28
- Cafetería Mingo's, corner of Calle 19 and Calle 18
- Cafetería Morgan, corner of 9 de Julio and Calle 22

Buenos Aires Province

- Cafetería Petit Cafe, corner of Avenida Costanera and Calle 21
- Cafetería Sitges, corner of 9 de Julio and Calle 22
- Cafetería Tabac, corner of 9 de Julio and Calle 26
- Cafetería Talamanca, corner of 9 de Julio and Calle 20
- Cafetería Un Rincon Suizo, corner of Calle 11 and Calle 46
- Cafetería Via Veneto, corner of 9 de Julio and Calle 28
- Beergarden: Bier Palast, corner of Avenida 26 and Calle 25

Eating out outside Miramar

- Restaurant ACA, corner of RP 11 and Las Brusquitas

Post and telegraph

- Post office: Encotel, corner of Calle 17 and Calle 32
- Telephone: Entel, Diagonal Fortunato de La Plaza 1451

Financial

- Banco de La Provincia, corner of Calle 21 and Calle 24, 610829. Cash advances on Visa card

Services and facilities

- Laundromat: Lavandería Laverap, Calle 16–1143
- Pharmacy: Farmacia del Pueblo, Calle 21–1598
- Hospital Municipal

Bicycle hire

- Acha, Avenida 2–973
- Prieto, corner of Calle 18 and Calle 19

Clubs

- German: Humboldt Institut, Calle 68 2994
- Italian: corner of Avenida 9 and Calle 28

Buses

Bus companies

- El Rápido del Sud, corner of Avenida 23 and Calle 34, runs buses between Miramar–Mar del Plata and the coast
- El Cóndor, Diagonal Fortunato de la Plaza 1678
- Costera Criolla, Diagonal Fortunato de la Plaza 1598
- Micro Mar, corner of Avenida 23 and Calle 34
- CAT, corner of Calle 23 and Calle 34

Services

- Buenos Aires: 11 services daily; 6–7 hours; Empresa Costera Criolla, Empresa El Cóndor, Empresa Micro Mar

Motoring

- Service station: ACA, Diagonal Fortunato de la Plaza 1733

Trains

The F C General Roca station is on the corner of Avenida San Martín and Calle 13. A daily *automotor* service connects with "El Atlántico" in Mar del Plata.

- Buenos Aires (Constitución station): "Cruz del Sur" departs 2220 daily; 7 hours

Sport

- Boat hire: Club Náutico Miramar, Espigon 1
- Golf: Golf Club Miramar, RP 11, corner of Calle 37 and Calle 20, 5 km north of the city center
- Squash: Padle Miramar, corner of Calle 30 and Calle 19

Fishing

- Muelle de Pescadores Deportivos, a jetty for anglers on the corner of Avenida Costanera and Avenida 37
- Laguna La Ballena, on the road to Mar del Sud

Entertainment

- Bowling: Caribe, corner of Calle 21 and Calle 28
- Bowling: Cita Club, corner of Calle 21 and Calle 28
- Bowling: Droppy, corner of Calle 24 and Calle 21
- Casino Miramar, corner of Calle 21 and Avenida 26

Miramar

BUENOS AIRES PROVINCE

- Disco Casablanca, corner of Avenida Costanera and Calle 35
- Disco Noa-Noa, corner of Calle 24 and Calle 19
- Disco Opus, corner of Avenida 9 and Calle 24
- Disco Pacha's, corner of Avenida Costanera and Calle 35
- Disco Symton, corner of Avenida 23 and Calle 12
- Disco Torremolinos, corner of Avenida Costanera and Calle 37
- Disco Yato's, corner of Calle 19 and Calle 16

Sightseeing

- Parque Dunícola Florentino Ameghino (Florentina Ameghino Dune Park), situated on Avenida 37. This partially-forested 50-ha portion of land previously consisted solely of dunes. Now it almost looks like a natural forest, harbouring many species of birds. It is popular with cyclists
- Museo Municipal Prehistórico (Municipal Prehistoric Museum), in the Vivero Dunícola Florentino Ameghino (Florentina Ameghino Dune Nursery). On display are early inhabitants' stone tools, and fossilised bones of prehistoric animals found in the area

Excursions

- **Mar del Sud**: 16 km south. Mar del Sud is still a quiet summer resort with clean beaches for those who seek tranquillity rather than excitement. There are several hotels. Fishing is good at **El Remanso** and **Rocas Negras**. There is also a camping ground
- **Laguna La Ballena**: Halfway between Miramar and Mar del Sud is a coastal lake of 36 ha, a little less than 1 km from the beach.

MONTE HERMOSO

Postal code: 8153
Distance from Bahía Blanca: 108 km eastwards on RP 78

Monte Hermoso is the southernmost highly developed beach resort in Buenos Aires province. It has only become popular in the last ten years or so. After the summer vacation it is fairly quiet. There are miles of quiet, unspoilt beaches and good facilities. The water is supposed to be warmer than the beaches further north due to a warm current coming down from Brazil. It attracts many campers.

Festivals

- Fiesta de la Cerveza (Beer Festival): December

Tourist information

- Bus terminal (8223

Camping

- Americano, Acceso Oeste (8249

Post and telegraph

- Post office: Encotel, Valle Encantado 55
- Telephone: *Cabina publica*, Casa de Buenos Aires

Buses

Services run daily from Bahía Blanca, less frequently in winter.

🛏 Accommodation in Monte Hermoso

Year-round accommodation

★	Hotel Florida, corner of Bahía Blanca and Río Colorado		$13.50	🛏
★	Hotel Hermitage, Faro Recalada 800		$13.50	🛏
	Hotel Otto Kundt, Faro Recalada 401		$13.50	
★	Hostería Monte Hermoso, Faro Recalada 1087	ℓ 8333	$12.50	🛏
★	Hostería Noryal, San Lorenzo 336		$12.50	🛏
★	Hostería Polo, Pedro de Mendoza 62	ℓ 8157	$12.50	🛏
A	Hospedaje Acaurium, corner of Chile and Tucumán		$11.50	🛏
A	Hospedaje Ambar, corner of Dufour and Faro Encalada		$11.50	🛏
A	Hospedaje Americano, corner of Faro Encalada and Patagonia			
		ℓ 8106	$11.50	🛏
A	Hospedaje Arismer, Sauce Grande		$11.50	🛏
A	Hospedaje Atlas, San Lorenzo 393	ℓ 8273	$11.50	🛏
A	Hospedaje Bahía Blanca, Bahía Blanca 767		$11.50	🛏
A	Hospedaje Comahue, corner of Valle Encantado and Avenida de Los Pinos			
		ℓ 8334	$11.50	🛏
A	Hospedaje Costa Azul, Chacabuco		$11.50	🛏
A	Hospedaje Galeon, Dufour 514	ℓ 8382	$11.50	🛏
A	Hospedaje El Pescador, corner of Calle 20 and 27		$11.50	🛏
A	Hospedaje Gabi, Sauce Grande		$11.50	🛏
A	Hospedaje Lega, Lega II 256	ℓ 8383	$11.50	🛏
A	Hospedaje Mary-Car, Antonio Costa 58	ℓ 8323	$11.50	🛏
A	Hospedaje Paco's, Valle Encantado 69	ℓ 8103	$11.50	🛏
A	Hospedaje Pecmar, Río Colorado 445		$11.50	🛏
A	Hospedaje Pedro, Avenida Traful 355	ℓ 8330	$11.50	🛏
A	Hospedaje Pi-Hue, corner of Costanera and Calle 11		$11.50	🛏
A	Hospedaje Rambla, Dufour 67	ℓ 8115	$11.50	🛏
A	Hospedaje Repetti, Faro Recalada 632		$11.50	🛏
A	Hospedaje San Francisco, Río Asunción 129		$11.50	🛏
A	Hospedaje Santa Ines, Avenida Traful 690	ℓ 8114	$11.50	🛏
A	Hospedaje Tino, Río Diamante 358	ℓ 8386	$11.50	🛏

Summer only

These hotels close after the summer holidays.

★★	Hotel España, corner of P de Mendoza and España			
		ℓ 8126	$18.00	🛏
★★	Hotel Maga, Chascomus	ℓ 8228	$18.00	🛏
★★	Hotel Savoy, Los Pinos 42	ℓ 8152	$18.00	🛏
★	Hotel Ameghino, Valle Encantado 60	ℓ 8198	$13.50	🛏
★	Hotel America, Valle Encantado 91	ℓ 8105	$13.50	🛏
★	Hotel Americano, Faro Recalada 341 🅰	ℓ 8107	$13.50	🛏
	Right on the beach			
★	Hotel Barrio, corner of Dufour and Neuquén	ℓ 8175	$13.50	🛏
★	Hotel Capri, Faro Recalada 599	ℓ 8229	$13.50	🛏
★	Hotel Cavismar, Avenida Costanera	ℓ 8172	$13.50	🛏
★	Hotel Erice, corner of Dufour and Neuquén	ℓ 8243	$13.50	🛏
★	Hotel Las Dunas, Las Dunas 531	ℓ 8171	$13.50	🛏
★	Hotel Lidel, Antonio Acosta	ℓ 8109	$13.50	🛏
★	Hotel Petit Hotel, Calle 1 244	ℓ 8108	$13.50	🛏
★	Hotel Prince, Los Pinos 70	ℓ 8141	$13.50	🛏

BUENOS AIRES PROVINCE

Accommodation in Monte Hermoso—Continued			
★ Hotel Romanos, Ave Argentina 350	(8222	$13.50	⋮⋮
★ Hotel Santa Isabel, Bahía Blanca 55	(8130	$13.50	⋮⋮
★ Hotel Saul, corner of Antonio Acosta and Bahía Blanca			
	(8230	$13.50	⋮⋮
★ Hotel Tirol, Pedro de Mendoza 144	(8133	$13.50	⋮⋮
★ Hotel Traful, Avenida Traful 343	(8163	$13.50	⋮⋮
★★★ Hostería La Goleta, corner of Costanera and Calle 10			
	(8242	$18.50	⋮⋮
★★★ Hostería Nauta Motel, Dufour 635	(8283	$18.50	⋮⋮
★★ Hostería Altea, Avenida Argentina 830	(8413	$15.50	⋮⋮
★★ Hostería Eventyr, Avenida Argentina 659	(8238	$15.50	⋮⋮
★★ Hostería San Jorge, B Juarez 60	(8206	$15.50	⋮⋮

- Buenos Aires: departs 2130 daily; 9 hours; Empresa La Estrella

Excursions
- **Laguna Sauce Grande**: 8 km. Good *pejerrey* fishing
- Faro Recalada (Recalada Lighthouse), with a beam reaching a distance of 30 km

NECOCHEA

Postal code: 7630 • (area code: (0262) • Population: 50 000
Distances
- From Buenos Aires: 490 km southwards on RN 3 then RN 86
- From Bahía Blanca: 336 km north-east on RN 223 then RN 228

Necochea is located on the coast on a 72 km beach. For 24 km this beach comes under the city's direct jurisdiction, before it continues northwards across the river into Necochea's sister city **Quequén**.

Founded in 1881, Necochea had a troubled early history, and Indian raids led by Chief Calfucura delayed its advance considerably.

Over the last 20 years or so it has attracted a steadily-growing number of tourists, and now over 100 000 vacationers visit Necochea each summer. It is probably the largest seaside resort after Mar del Plata. Necochea can be reached from Buenos Aires by road, rail, and air. It virtually closes during in the off-season, but comes to life from December to early March.

The city consists of two main parts: the civic center with its *Municipalidad*, and the beach front (Villa Díaz Velez), where most of the tourist facilities are concentrated. The newly-built tourist complex with a casino, swimming pools, cafeterias, night club, and sport facilities is located here. Necochea has excellent hotels and restaurants, as well as many large parks and recreational areas. The hub of the beach front is the mall on Calle 83, which is lined with cafeterias and shops.

Continued on page 111

BUENOS AIRES PROVINCE

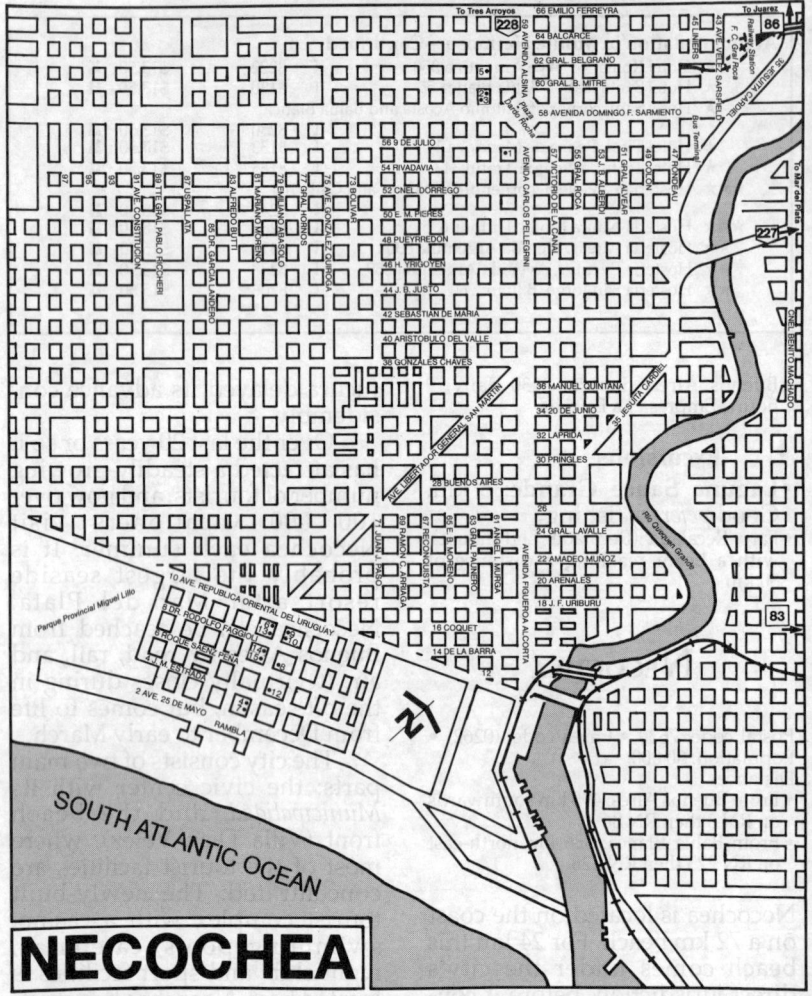

Key to Map
1. Municipalidad
2. Iglesia
3. Post office (Encotel)
4. Hotel León
5. Banco de la Nación
6. Hotel Milesi
7. Hotel Necochea
8. Hotel Alvarez Palace
9. Hotel Avenida
10. Hotel Bell Mar
11. Hotel Las Vegas
12. Hotel Real
13. Hotel Zure-Echea
14. Hostería Las Olas
15. Hotel Moderno

Necochea

BUENOS AIRES PROVINCE

🛏 Accommodation in Necochea

For further accommodation, see "Accommodation" in Quequén on page 118.

Town center

★★	Hotel Acapulco, Calle 52–2950 Near railway station	(23939	$18.00
A	Hospedaje Colón, Calle 62 3034 Near bus terminal	(24825	$11.50
A	Hospedaje Solchaga, Calle 62 2822 Near bus terminal	(25584	$11.50

Beach front

Only a handful of hotels are open outside the tourist season. The distance of each hotel from the beach is given in meters after the address.

★★★	Hotel Presidente, Calle 4–4040, 100 m	(23800	$23.50
★★★	Hotel San Martín, corner of Calle 85 and Calle 6, 200 m	(22042	$23.50
★★★	Hotel San Miguel, corner of Calle 85 and Calle 6, 200 m	(25155	$23.50
★★	Hotel Celeste, Avenida San Martín 696, 450 m	(25206	$18.00
★★	Hotel Corona, Calle 75–371, 350 m	(22646	$18.00
★★	Hotel Deruha, Calle 79–821, 600 m		$18.00
★★	Hotel Emperador, Calle 6–4052, 200 m	(22421	$18.00
★★	Hotel Horizonte, Calle 85–375, 350 m	(23344	$18.00
★★	Hotel Internacional, Calle 81–232, 50 m	(24587	$18.00
★★	Hotel León, Calle 79–229, 50 m	(24800	$18.00
★★	Hotel Marino, corner of Calle 79 and Calle 4, 100 m	(22140	$18.00
★★	Hotel Milesi, Calle 79–373, 350 m	(25387	$18.00
★★	Hotel Miami, Calle 85–233, 50 m	(23275	$18.00
★★	Hotel Necochea, Calle 79–217, 30 m	(22062	$18.00
★★	Hotel Perugia, Calle 81–288, 150 m	(22020	$18.00
★★	Hotel Tres Reyes, Calle 4 bis 4112, 150 m	(22011	$18.00
★★	Hotel Trocadero, Calle 81–275, 150 m	(22589	$18.00
★	Hotel Almirante, Calle 85–236, 50 m	(25151	$13.50
★	Hotel Alvarez Palace, corner of Calle 79 and Calle 6, 200 m	(23667	$13.50
★	Hotel Aniter, Calle 77–314, 200 m	(25560	$13.50
★	Hotel Argentino, corner of Calle 87 and Calle 6, 200 m	(23661	$13.50
★	Hotel Asturias, Avenida San Martín 842, 500 m	(24524	$13.50
★	Hotel Avenida, Calle 79–386, 350 m	(23718	$13.50
★	Hotel Bahía, Avenida San Martín 731, 450 m	(23353	$13.50
★	Hotel Bambi, Calle 83–323, 250 m	(24979	$13.50
★	Hotel Bell Mar, Calle 79–368, 300 m	(23673	$13.50
★	Hotel Bibbione, Calle 89–376, 350 m	(24678	$13.50
★	Hotel Campomar, Calle 81–385, 350 m	(23915	$13.50
★	Hotel Ca-Ra-Ma, Calle 77–237, 50 m	(25540	$13.59
★	Hotel Castilla, Calle 4–3727, 100 m		$13.50
★	Hotel Compostela, Calle 75–374, 350 m	(23924	$13.50
★	Hotel Continental, corner of Avenida 10 and 85, 500 m	(23394	$13.50
★	Hotel El Molino, Calle 22–4222, 500 m	(22536	$13.50
★	Hotel Epaña, Calle 89–217, 50 m	(22896	$13.50

Necochea

Accommodation in Necochea—continued

Beach front—contiunued

★ Hotel Esthor, Calle 87–383, 350 m	(	25338	$13.50 ♁
★ Hotel Hermitage, Calle 8–3815, 300 m	(	23925	$13.50 ♁
★ Hotel Hostal del Rey, Calle 81–335, 250 m	(	25170	$13.50 ♁
★ Hotel Infriccioli, Calle 4–4335, 100 m	(	25563	$13.50 ♁
★ Hotel Italia, Calle 20–4050, 450 m	(	25660	$13.50 ♁
★ Hotel Las Nieves, Avenida San Martín 1096, 700 m	(	23696	$13.50 ♁
★ Hotel Las Vegas, Calle 79–287, 70 m	(	28285	$13.50 ♁
★ Hotel Libertador, Calle 8–3850, 300 m	(	23918	$13.50 ♁
★ Hotel Lido, Calle 81–328, 250 m	(	23508	$13.50 ♁
★ Hotel Mar y Cielo, Calle 8–4366, 300 m	(	23338	$13.50 ♁
★ Hotel María Paula, Calle 4–3927, 100 m	(	23903	$13.50 ♁
★ Hotel Monte Carlo, Calle 85–335, 300 m	(	25959	$13.50 ♁
★ Hotel Monte Polino, Calle 6–3963, 200 m	(	25928	$13.50 ♁
★ Hotel Neptuno, Calle 81–212, 30 m	(	22653	$13.50 ♁
★ Hotel Plaza, Calle 85–261, 150 m	(	27295	$13.50 ♁
★ Hotel Real, Calle 79–264, 150 m	(	22656	$13.50 ♁
★ Hotel Riviera, Calle 8–3935, 300 m	(	25596	$13.50 ♁
★ Hotel Sandra, Avenida San Martín 1115, 700 m	(	22584	$13.50 ♁
★ Hotel Sarimar, Calle 8–4351, 300 m	(	24381	$13.50 ♁
★ Hotel Mi Valle, Calle 81–241, 70 m	(	25562	$13.50 ♁
★ Hotel Santander, Calle 83–877, 500 m	(	27090	$13.50 ♁
★ Hotel Suizo, Calle 22–4235, 500 m	(	24008	$13.50 ♁
★ Hotel Windsor, Calle 4–3957, 100 m	(	23171	$13.50 ♁
★ Hotel Zure-Echea, Calle 79–355, 300 m	(	22167	$13.50 ♁
• Hotel Ambassador, Avenida San Martín 722, 450 m			
• Hotel Moderno, Avenida 79–311, near the beach			
★★★ Hostería Posta Carreta, Calle 73 bis 319, 100 m	(	24499	$18.50 ♁
★★ Hostería Río Colorado, Calle 4–3855, 100 m	(	25514	$15.50 ♁
★★ Hostería Ruca-Lauquen, Calle 8–4271, 300 m	(	26413	$15.50 ♁
★★ Hostería San Javier, Calle 75–262, 100 m	(	24358	$15.50 ♁
★ Hostería Gabriele, Calle 71 bis 373, 250 m	(	24737	$12.50 ♁
★ Hostería Gaitero, Calle 8–4365, 400 m	(	23247	$12.50 ♁
★ Hostería Hawai, Calle 75–100, 50 m			$12.50 ♁
★ Hostería Ingo, Calle 79–698, 450 m			$12.50 ♁
★ Hostería Las Olas, Calle 79–333, 250 m	(	25197	$12.50 ♁
★ Hostería Nancy, Calle 75–368, 330 m	(	24731	$12.50 ♁
★ Hostería Nuevo Casino, Calle 87–375, 350 m	(	23846	$12.50 ♁
★ Hostería Pichi Mar, Calle 81–230, 50 m	(	23424	$12.50 ♁
★ Hostería Tobago, Calle 79–720, 450 m	(	23084	$12.50 ♁
★ Hostería Zulma, Calle 75–252, 100 m	(	25922	$12.50 ♁
A Hospedaje Astoria, Calle 4–4131, 100 m	(	25112	$11.50 ♁
A Hospedaje Bayo, Calle 87–388, 350 m	(	23334	$11.50 ♁
A Hospedaje Brisamar, Calle 83–336, 280 m	(	24909	$11.50 ♁
A Hospedaje City, Calle 81–237, 50 m	(	23768	$11.50 ♁
A Hospedaje Doramar, Calle 83–357, 270 m	(	25815	$11.50 ♁
A Hospedaje Flamingo, Calle 83–333, 270 m			$11.50 ♁
A Hospedaje Firenze, Calle 4–4356, 100 m			$11.50 ♁
A Hospedaje Gavin, Avenida San Martín 789, 470 m	(	27120	$11.50 ♁

Necochea

BUENOS AIRES PROVINCE

Accommodation in Necochea—continued

Beach front—continued

A	Hospedaje Gran Avenida, Avenida 10–4146, 400 m			
		(23390	$11.50	♁
A	Hospedaje Gran Splendid, Calle 2–4022	(23303	$11.50	♁
	On the beach			
A	Hospedaje Las Malvinas, Avenida San Martín 1141, 700 m			
		(24035		
A	Hospedaje Mar Azul, Calle 6–3762, 200 m	(25284	$11.50	♁
A	Hospedaje Montreal, Calle 85–384, 80 m	(22057	$11.50	♁
A	Hostería Necomar, corner of Calle 20 and Calle 79 bis, 450 m			
		(22689	$11.50	
A	Hostería Palermo Chico, Avenida San Martín 1313, 700 m			
		(25215	$11.50	♁
A	Hostería Pleno Mar, Calle 87–250, 50 m	(22674	$11.50	♁
A	Hostería Regis, Avenida San Martín 726, 450 m	(25870	$11.50	♁
A	Hostería Santa Clara, Calle 8–4329	(23850	$11.50	♁
A	Hostería Torremolinos, Calle 81–336, 300 m		$11.50	♁
A	Hostería Venus, Calle 71 bis 268, 100 m	(22875	$11.50	♁
A	Hostería Verona, Calle 83–767, 600 m		$11.50	♁

Only a few kilometers north across the **Río Quequén Grande** (which in spite of its name is rather small) is another beach resort, **Quequén**.

✴ Festivals
- Virgen del Carmen: July 16
- Fishermen's week: February

ℹ Tourist information
- Comisión Municipal de Turismo, Calle 56 2969 (22182 and 23706

🍴 Eating out
Most of the hotels have restaurants; most tourists eat there.
- Restaurant Viejo Contrabandista, central beach front. International cuisine

Services and facilities
- Laundromat: Lavandería Laverap, Calle 87 381

✈ Air services
The airport is located 12 km north on RP 86. LAPA runs services to and from Buenos Aires.

🚗 Motoring
- Service station: ACA, corner of Avenida C Pellegrini and Pueyrredon

🚆 Trains
The F C General Roca station is on the corner of Calle 62 and Calle 43.

Sport
- Canoeing: Río Quequén Grande. Boat hire
- Fishing: From promontories and in Río Quequén Grande

🎭 Entertainment
- Casino, in the tourist complex, corner of Avenida 2 and Calle 89, next to Parque Miguel Lillo
- Night club, in the tourist complex

Necochea

BUENOS AIRES PROVINCE

🚌 Buses from Necochea

The bus terminal is on the corner of Calle 58 and Calle 35, seven blocks from the city center. It has clean rest rooms, a cloakroom, and a cafeteria. A taxi from the terminal to the town center costs $1.50. Bus 502 takes about 20 minutes from the terminal to the beach; fare $0.20

Destination	Fare	Services	Hours	Company
• Azul	$6.50		4	La Estrella
• Bahía Blanca	$7.60		5½	Pampas SA
• Balcarce	$3.00		2	Rápido Argentina
• Buenos Aires	$13.50	8 services daily	9	La Estrella
• Mar del Plata	$3.50		2½	Pampas SA
• Tandil	$4.40		3	Pampas SA

🍎 Excursions

Miles of beaches extend north and south from Necochea and **Quequén**, interrupted by rocky seafronts where wind and water erosion have formed caves in the rocks. For those seeking quieter beaches go to **Balneario Los Angeles**, 30 km south of Necochea.

- **Parque Provincial Dunícola Miguel Lillo** (Miguel Lillo Provincial Dune Park): Past the tourist complex on Avenida 2 is an area of some 500 ha which was once sand dunes but has now been planted with trees, mostly conifers. There is a camping spot and an amphitheatre seating 8000
- **Los Manantiales**: 5 km upstream. Good camping spots and fishing
- **Río Quequén Grande**: 13 km upstream small islands in the river force the water to form little waterfalls. An idyllic place. Both sides of the river are lined with trees
- **Balneario Costa Bonita**: 14 km north. A small beach resort in Quequén, less crowded than Necochea. Fishing. Take bus 515 from the corner of Avenida 2 and Calle 85, on the beach front. There are six services a day during summer
- Fish hatchery: 12 km upstream on **Río Quequén Grande**, near **Puente Ardanaz**, the hatchery breeds *arco iris* trout and *pejerrey*. Opposite is Parque Cura-Meuco with kiosks serving hot meals

OLAVARRÍA

Postal code: 7400 • Population: 70 000 • area code: (0284) • Altitude: 310 m
Distances
- From Buenos Aires: 350 km southwards on RN 3
- From Bahía Blanca: 338 km north-east on RP 51 then RP 76

The terrain around Olavarría is predominantly flat *pampa*, with few hills breaking the monotony.

The first Spaniard to reach this region was Cristobal Cabral who signed peace treaties with the local Indians in 1741. In 1770

BUENOS AIRES PROVINCE

Accommodation in Olavarría

★★ Hotel Santa Rosa, Lopez 2956 ⑪	(	20772, 21521	$17.50 ♂♂
★★ Hotel Savoy, Moreno 2882 (corner of Belgrano) ⑪	(	21854, 21855	$17.50 ♂♂
★ Hotel Gran Olavarría, Necochea 3050	(	24016	$13.50 ♂♂
★ Hotel Residencial Centenario, General Paz 3009	(	21860	$13.50 ♂♂
★ Hotel Rohes, Alsina 3235	(	24232	$13.50 ♂♂
A Hospedaje El Jardín, Necochea 3298	(	20162	$12.50 ♂♂
A Hospedaje Hotel Cedro, Pringles 3247	(	21304	$12.50 ♂♂
A Hospedaje Nuevo Hotel Argentino, Pringles 3001 (corner of Dorrego)	(	20729	$12.50 ♂♂
A Hospedaje Rex, corner of Pringles and Cabral	(	22281	$12.50 ♂♂

Manuel Pinazzo reconnoitered the area in the company of a friendly Indian chief, Cacique Lincon. In 1828 Fuerte Laguna Blanca was founded and the tribe of Cacique Juan Manuel Catriel settled here. The fort remained the tribe's property for 50 years. In 1867 Olavarría was founded and for some time was the southernmost outpost of white Argentina. In 1872 the Argentine army, with the help of Indian chief Cipriano Catriel, defeated Calfucura ("Emperor of the Pampas") at the battle of San Carlos de Bolívar. Once peace was established many immigrants, particularly Wolga Germans, moved here and began to farm the area. They founded the agricultural settlement of **Hinojo** 6 km from Olavarría. The descendants of Cacique Manuel Catriel still live in the district.

ⓘ Tourist information

- Dirección Municipal de Turismo, Rivadavia 2836 (20535

⑪ Eating out

- Restaurant La Cabeza, General Paz 3038
- Restaurant La Casona de Alonso, corner of Colonel Suárez and Cerrito
- Restaurant La Fusta, corner of Necochea and España
- Restaurant La Marca, Necochea. Grill
- Restaurant Nuevo Alonso, Colonel Suarez 2639
- Restaurant Santa Rosa, Hotel Santa Rosa, V López 2956
- Restaurant San Telmo, corner of Coronel Suárez and R Barba. Grill
- Restaurant Savoy, Hotel Savoy, corner of Moreno and Belgrano
- Pizzería Kapicua, corner of San Martín and Moreno
- Pizzería Kenyo, Rivadavia
- Pizzería La Vicente, V López 2311
- Pizzería Munich, corner of V López and S Cabral
- Pizzería Olavarría, corner of Rivadavia and Bolívar
- Pizzería Pepito, V López 2665
- Pizzería Tropicana, Rivadavia 2764
- Cafetería Achaval, corner of Necochea and Rivadavia
- Cafetería Americano, V López 3169
- Cafetería Barril 17, Rivadavia 2617
- Cafetería Bianca, V López 2941
- Cafetería Boston, General Paz 2758
- Cafetería Carriego, corner of Coronel Suárez and R Bamba
- Cafetería Cero-Cero, Rivadavia 2912
- Cafetería La Farola, corner of V López and Belgrano
- Cafetería Paris, V López 2700

Eating out outside Olavarría

- Restaurant San Jacinto, RP 76. Grill

BUENOS AIRES PROVINCE

Post and telegraph
- Post office: Encotel, Belgrano 2439
- Telephone: *Cabina publica*, España 2965

Services and facilities
- Laundromat: Laverap, Belgrano 2825

Buses
Buses run regularly to Bahía Blanca.
- Buenos Aires: 16 services daily; 8 hours; Empresa Liniers, Empresa La Estrella

Motoring
- Service station: ACA, Villa Alfredo Fortabat, on RN 76 Km 19.5, just outside Olavarría

Entertainment
- Disco Floyd, corner of Rivadavia and San Martín
- Disco Las Vegas, Villa Alfredo Fortabat
- Disco Nivel 1, corner of A Del Valle and Pellegrini
- Disco Rodríguez, corner of Belgrano and Rivadavia
- Disco Wacadu, Sierras Bayas
- Disco Yamo, V López 2956

Excursions
- **Sierra Chica**: In 1855 a battle took place here between the troops of General Bartolomé Mitre and the Indians under the chiefs Catriel and Cachul. A granite monolith bearing a plaque has been erected as a memorial of the battle

PINAMAR

Postal code: 7167 • (area code: (0254)
Distance from Villa Gesell: 22 km southwest on RP 11

Pinamar has nearly 30 km of beaches and good surf. The tourist season runs from December to March; during this time prices tend to rise. Outside the season it is rather quiet. Further to the south are **Ostende** and **Valeria del Mar**, whose facilities are listed here.

Tourist information
- Dirección de Turismo, corner of Bunge and Libertador (82796. Open 0900–1900

Eating out

International cuisine
- Restaurant Berrizbeitia, corner of Avenida Bunge and Simbad
- Restaurant Crazy Cheese, corner of Avenida Bunge and Simbad
- Restaurant Golf Club, corner of Avenida del Mar and Tobias
- Restaurant Hotel del Bosque
- Restaurant Hotel Playas
- Restaurant Las Marías, corner of Robinson Crusoe and Rivadavia
- Restaurant La Galeana, Avenida del Tuyú between Serina and Libertador
- Restaurant La Posta De Ramallo, corner of Azopardo and Jorge
- Restaurant La Ventola, corner of Del Mar and Rivadavia

Steakhouses
- Restaurant Los Troncos, corner of Avenida Bunge and Shaw
- Restaurant La Casona del Tío, corner of Libertador and Avenida Bunge
- Restaurant Tío Enrique, corner of Jupiter and Rivadavia
- Restaurant Farita, corner of Avenida Bunge and Libertador
- Restaurant La Escondida, Constitución 948
- Restaurant El Encuentro, corner of Jason and Eneas

Italian cuisine
- Restaurant Il Garda, corner of de las Artes and Las Toninas
- Restaurant Cantina Don Pepone, corner of Del Mar and Avenida Bunge

Buenos Aires Province

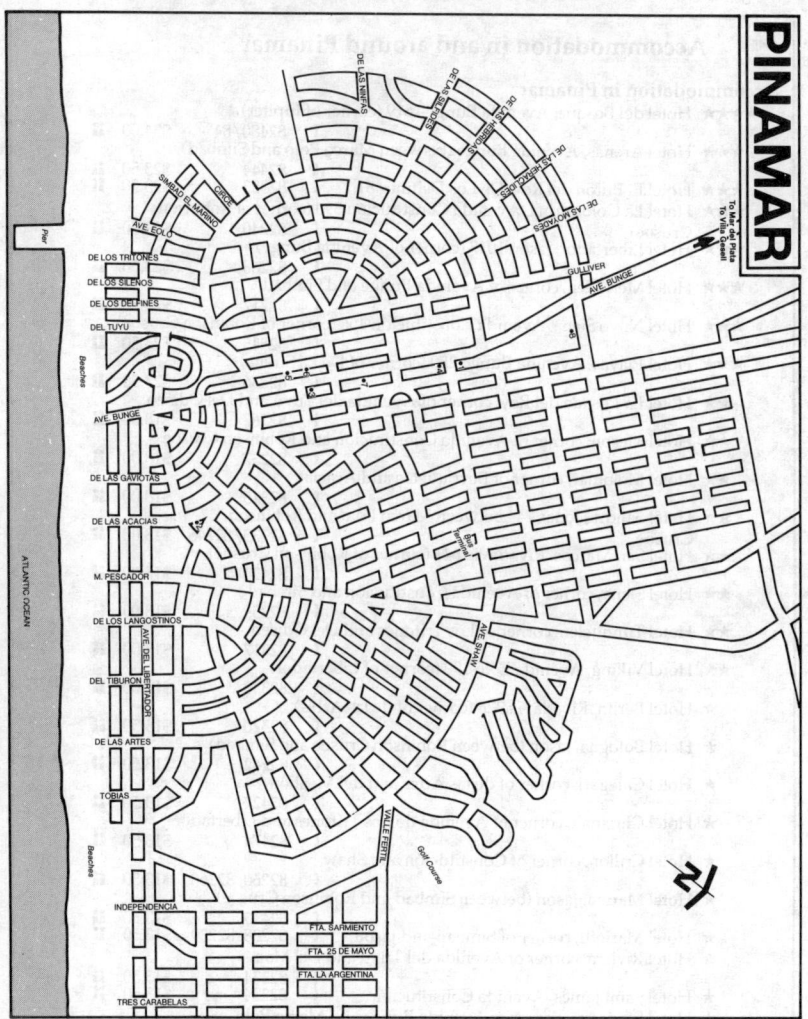

Key to Map

1. Municipalidad
2. Iglesia
3. Post office (Encotel)
4. Telephone (Entel)
5. Tourist information
6. Aerolineas Argentinas
7. Lineas Aereas Privadas Argentinas

Pinamar

Buenos Aires Province

📖 Accommodation in and around Pinamar

Accommodation in Pinamar

★★★★	Hotel del Bosque, Avenida Bunge 1619 (corner of Jupiter) ✆ 82480/84	$34.00	👥
★★★	Hotel Arenas, Avenida Bunge (between Marco Polo and Simbad) ✆ 82444	$23.50	👥
★★★	Hotel El Bufon del Rey, De Los Delfines 81 ✆ 82323	$23.50	👥
★★★	Hotel La Golondrina, Avenida Constitución 590 (corner of Robinson Crusoe) ✆ 82240	$23.50	👥
★★★	Hotel Libertador, Jason 1017 (corner of Avenida Bunge) ✆ 82268	$23.50	👥
★★★	Hotel Meri Plen, corner of Avenida Bunge and Simbad ✆ 82717	$23.50	👥
★★★	Hotel Novo Siena, Avenida Constitución 456 (corner of Robinson Crusoe) ✆ 82545	$23.50	👥
★★★	Hotel Playas, Avenida Bunge 250 (corner of De La Sirena) ✆ 82236	$23.50	👥
★★	Hotel La Posada del Rey, corner of Avenida del Tuyú and Del Odiseo ✆ 82267	$18.00	👥
★★	Hotel Meson, corner of Avenida Constitución and Robinson Crusoe ✆ 82237	$18.00	👥
★★	Hotel Mojomar, corner of Burriquetas and Acacias ✆ 82345	$18.00	👥
★★	Hotel Sandra, Jonas 744 between Marco Polo and Robinson Crusoe ✆ 82235/82245	$18.00	👥
★★	Hotel San Marcos, Rivadavia 641 (corner of Robinson Crusoe) ✆ 82424	$18.00	👥
★★	Hotel Siena, corner of Avenida Constitución and Simbad ✆ 82239	$18.00	👥
★★	Hotel Tunquelen, corner of Los Tritones and Del Odiseo ✆ 82317	$18.00	👥
★★	Hotel Viking, Avenida Eolo 199 (corner of Libertador) ✆ 82330	$18.00	👥
★	Hotel Berlin, Rivadavia 326 (corner of de las Artes) ✆ 82320	$13.50	👥
★	Hotel Bologna, Jason (between Robinson Crusoe and Simbad) ✆ 82242	$13.50	👥
★	Hotel Calegari, corner of de las Artes and del Mejillon ✆ 82427	$13.50	👥
★	Hotel Christian, corner of Avenida de Los Tritones and Libertador ✆ 82474	$13.50	👥
★	Hotel Crillon, corner of Constitución and Shaw ✆ 82260, 82260	$13.50	👥
★	Hotel Marina, Jason (between Simbad and Robinson Crusoe) ✆ 82413	$13.50	👥
★	Hotel Mariotti, corner of Simbad and Jason ✆ 82238, 82239	$13.50	👥
★	Hotel Riviera, corner of Avenida del Tuyú and Del Mar ✆ 82334	$13.50	👥
★	Hotel Saint James, Avenida Constitución ✆ 82234	$13.50	👥
★	Hotel Sardegna, corner of Avenida Bunge and Marco Polo ✆ 82334	$13.50	👥
★	Hotel Yacanto, corner of Rivadavia and Simbad ✆ 82367	$13.50	👥
★	Hotel Zita, Avenida Constitución (between Robinson Crusoe and Simbad) ✆ 82241	$13.50	👥
★★★	Hostería Bora Bora, corner of Avenida del Tuyú and Libertador ✆ 82394	$18.50	👥
★★	Hostería María Fernanda, corner of Eolo and Ondinas (near Avenida Constitución) ✆ 82483, 82682	$15.50	👥

Pinamar

BUENOS AIRES PROVINCE

Accommodation in and around Pinamar—continued

Acoommodation in Pinamar—continued

★ Hostería Cundari, Avenida Constitución	✆ 8246	$12.50	♙
★ Hostería La Gaviota, corner of Del Cangrejo and Shaw	✆ 82079	$12.50	♙
★ Hostería Pinamar, corner of Avenida del Tuyú and De Las Sirenas	✆ 82236	$12.50	♙
A Hospedaje Acacia, corner of Del Cangrejo and Shaw		$12.50	♙
A Hospedaje Rosemarie, corner of De Las Medusas and Inea	✆ 82522	$12.50	♙
A Hospedaje Valle Fertil, corner of Del Cangrejo and Valle Fertil		$12.50	♙

Accommodation in Ostende

★★ Hotel Blue, corner of Biarritz and Defensa	✆ 82253	$18.00	♙
★★ Hotel Dubrava, corner of Yrigoyen and San Martín	✆ 82556	$18.00	♙
★ Hotel de Palma, corner of Sarmiento and Brown	✆ 82259	$13.50	♙
★ Hotel Rambla, corner of Biarritz and P Florida	✆ 82428	$13.50	♙
★★ Hostería Olimpia, corner of Avenida del Valle and San Martín	✆ 82888	$15.50	♙
A Hospedaje El Dorado, corner of Avellaneda and Moreno	✆ 82544	$12.50	♙
A Hospedaje Ostende, corner of Biarritz and Cairo		$12.50	♙

Accommodation in Valeria del Mar

★★★ Hostería Gran Valeria, corner of Robinson and Azopardo	✆ 86083	$18.50	♙
★ Hostería Din Don, corner of Azopardo and Costanera	✆ 86106	$12.50	♙
A Hospedaje La Farola, Jorge		$12.50	♙
A Hospedaje Los Lagartos, corner of Azopardo and Costanera	✆ 82364	$12.50	♙

- Restaurant La Mamma Liberata, corner of Avenida Bunge and Simbad
- Pizzería Carlos V, corner of Libertador and De Las Artes
- Pizzería del Sol, corner of Avenida Bunge and Paseo Colon
- Pizzería Don Nicola, corner of Avenida Bunge and Marco Polo
- Pizzería Pucará, corner of Avenida Bunge and Paseo Colón
- Pizzería Pizuela, corner of Constitución and Shaw
- Pizzería Tío Arturo, corner of Shaw and del Lenguado

Seafood

- Restaurant El Vasco, corner of De Las Artes and Las Toninas
- Restaurant Paxapoga, corner of Libertador and Avenida Bunge.
- Restaurant Club de Pesca Hugo's, corner of Avenida Bunge and Del Mar
- Restaurant La Posada, corner of Shaw and Del Lenguado
- Restaurant El Gato que Pesca En La Playa, corner of Avenida Bunge and Del Mar
- Restaurant Status Playa, corner of Del Mar and De Las Acacias
- Restaurant El Dorado, corner of Del Mar and De Las Gaviotas
- Restaurant El Pájaro, corner of Del Mar and Pescador
- Restaurant Morgan, corner of Del Mar and De Las Artes

Pinamar

BUENOS AIRES PROVINCE

Cafeterías
- Cafetería Cafe Green, corner of Avenida Bunge and Shaw
- Cafetería Cabaña Innsbruck, corner of Avenida Bunge and Jupiter
- Cafetería Centro, corner of Libertador and Constitución

Eating out in Valeria del Mar
- Restaurant de María del Mar, Halcon. International cuisine

Post and telegraph
- Post office: Encotel, Edificio Marinas II, Avenida Bunge
- Telephone office: Telpin, Rivadavia 1183 (corner of Shaw). Open 0630–0200

Services and facilities
- Laundromat: Laverap, Constitución 555

Air services
- Aerolineas Argentinas, corner of Avenida Bunge and Libertador

Buses
The bus terminal is in Shaw between Del Lenguado and Pejerrey.
- Buenos Aires: 14 services daily; 6 hours; Empresa Anton, Empresa Río de la Plata

Sport
- Swimming: Complejo Balneario Integral C R features a series of connected swimming pools surrounded by palms and flowers. There is a bar in the pool which serves swimmers and sunbathers alike. The complex also has a sauna, rest rooms, volley-ball fields, a camp site, and a gymnasium. All buildings are set a meter above the beach, so that you have an unobstructed view of the sea. There is an indoor/outdoor restaurant next to the swimming pool. Tents can be hired by the month
- Golf: Organised by Pinamar SA at Links Pinamar. Most tournaments are held here in January and February

Entertainment
There are plenty of discotheques and pool rooms. The main entertainment center is near the corner of Libertador and Avenida Bunge.

Pinamar has clamped down on pinball parlours and no new licences are being issued.
- Casino, Valeria del Mar
- Disco Bunker, corner of Libertador and Avenida Bunge
- Disco Buzios, corner of Shaw and Avenida Bunge
- Disco Dallas, corner of Avenida Bunge and De La Sirena
- Disco Innsbruck, Avenida Bunge (between Shaw and Jupiter)
- Disco Liber Pool, corner of Avenida Bunge and De Las Gaviotas
- Disco Piu Cafe, corner of Avenida Bunge and Paseo Colón
- Disco Status, corner of Libertador and Avenida Bunge
- Disco Studios, corner of Lenguado and Shaw
- Long Time Pub, corner of Libertador and Avenida Bunge. English-style pub
- Night Club Hotel Arenas, Avenida Bunge (between Marco Polo and Simbad)

QUEQUÉN

Postal code: 7631

Quequén is separated from Necochea by the **Río Quequén Grande**. An excellent beach stretches along the coast for several kilometers. The harbor is silting up and requires frequent dredging. See also Necochea on page 107.

Accommodation
See also "Accommodation" in Necochea, on page 109.
- ★ Hotel Continental, Calle 512–924 ℂ 26056 $13.50

BUENOS AIRES PROVINCE

★ Hotel Mauna Loa, Almirante Brown (26023 $13.50 ⋕

🚌 Buses
See "Buses" in Necochea, on page 112.

🚆 Trains
The "Brisas del Mar" departs for Constitución station in Buenos Aires on Tues, Thurs, and Sun at 2100, and takes 11 hours. Fares: Pullman $13.50, First class $9.00, Tourist class $6.00.

SAN ANTONIO DE ARECO

Postal code: 2760 • (area code: (0326) • Altitude: 34 m
Distance from Buenos Aires: 113 km westwards on RN 8

San Antonio de Areco is located in the *pampa* on the **Río Areco**. It It was founded in 1730 on the farm of Don Ruiz de Arellano. The chapel, which was built in 1728 and dedicated to San Antonio de Padua, became the hub of the new town. It was an important place during the colonial era because of its location on the junction of the Camino Real to Asunción in Paraguay and Santiago in Chile. The fort erected nearby was called Carmen de Areco. The town's name is a combination of the names of the San Antonio de Padua chapel and the Carmen de Areco fort.

San Antonio de Areco is still very much a rural community steeped in the *gaucho* tradition. Many buildings and streets from the colonial era are still intact. Forests line the banks of the river; fishing is not permitted.

🏃 Festivals
- Día de la Tradición (Day of Tradition): November 11. Traditional *gaucho* festival with horse parades in remembrance of the days when Indians still attacked the settlements. Plenty of music, dancing, and songs

ℹ️ Tourist information
- Sub-Dirección de Turismo, corner of Alsina and Lavalle (2102

🛏️ Accommodation
- ★ Hotel Fuaz, corner of Smith and Azcuenaga (22487 $13.50 ⋕
- ★ Hotel San Carlos, corner of Zapiola and Zerbione (22401 $13.50 ⋕
- ★★ Hostería El Hornero, corner of Moreno 250 and San Martin (22733 $15.50 ⋕
- A Hospedaje Areco, corner of Segundo Sombra and Rivadavia (22166 $12.50 ⋕

Accommodation outside San Antonio
- ★ Motel Km 13, corner of RN 8 and Segundo Sombra $13.50 ⋕

🏕️ Camping
Camping is permitted on the northern river bank. Access is from the corner of J A Guiraldes and RN 8.

🛎️ Services and facilities
- Bicycle hire: corner of Zerboni and Alsina
- Laundromat: Laverap, corner of Alsina and Yrigoyen

🅒 Clubs
- Italian: corner of Alsina and Alvear

🚌 Buses
- Buenos Aires: 8 services daily; 2 hours; TAC, Empresa T A Chevallier

BUENOS AIRES PROVINCE

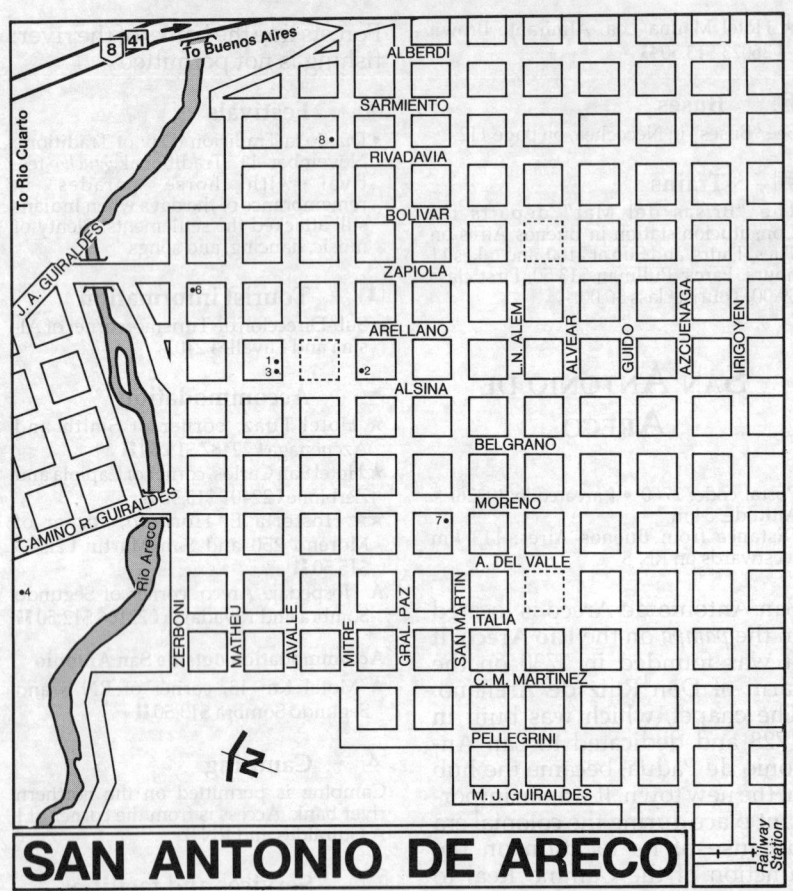

Key to Map
1. Municipalidad
2. Catedral
3. Tourist information
4. Museo Gauchesco Ricardo Guiraldes
6. Hotel San Carlos
7. Hostería El Hornero
8. Hospedaje Areco

🚆 Trains
The F C General Bartolomé Mitre station is on the corner of M J Guiraldes and Irigoyen.

🛍 Shopping
Beautiful handicrafts are available here and include silverware and leather goods, mostly in the *gaucho* style.

San Antonio de Areco

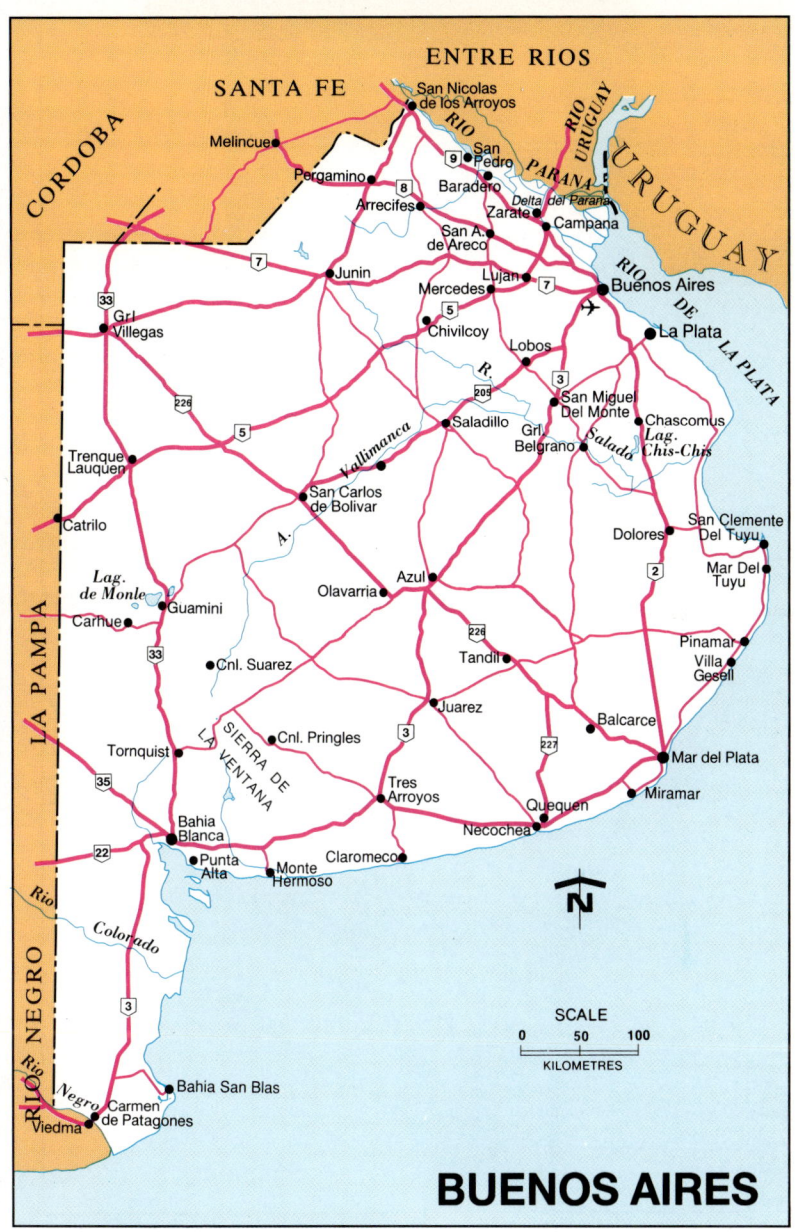

Plate 5

Map of Buenos Aires Province

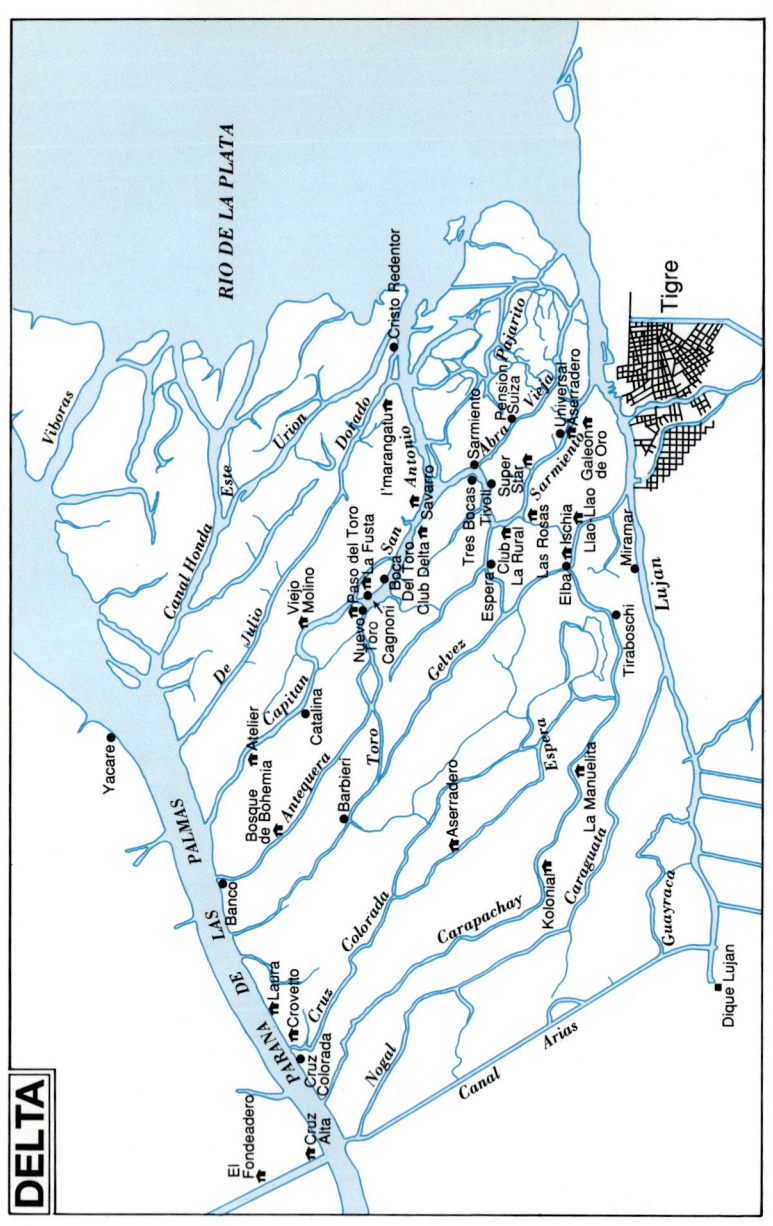

Plate 6

Map of the Río Paraná Delta

BUENOS AIRES PROVINCE

Sightseeing

- Museo Gauchesco Ricardo Guiraldes (Ricardo Guiraldes Gaucho Museum), corner of Camino R Guiraldes and Aurelino. Follow Calle Moreno to Río Areco and cross the Puente Viejo over the Río Areco, built in 1852. Named after a writer who described *gaucho* life, the museum is a splendid example of a late-nineteenth-century *estancia* and is surrounded by a park. Open Wed to Sun 1000–1200 and 1500–1800
- La Bamba Estancia, a *gaucho* ranch which has been made into a tourist attraction. There are facilities here for swimming, tennis, and golf. The ranch belongs to the Aldao family, and tours and short stays are arranged by Aldao Viajes, Maipú 872, Capital (3929707

SAN CLEMENTE DEL TUYÚ

Postal code: 7105 • (area code: (0252)
Distance from Buenos Aires: 320 km south-east on RN 2 then RP 63 and RP 11

Argentina's northernmost beach resort, located south of **Punta Norte del Cabo de San Antonio**, San Clemente del Tuyú bustles with life in the tourist season but is almost deserted in the winter months. All of the streets bear numbers instead of names.

Festivals

- Fiesta de la Corvina Negra: Fishing competition in December

Camping

- ACA camping ground, corner of access road and Calle 1

Accommodation in San Clemente del Tuyú

★★★★ Hotel Fontainbleau, Calle 3–2294	(187	$33.50	ii
★★★ Hotel Altair, corner of Calle 3 and Avenida Costanera	(429	$23.50	ii
★★★ Hotel Mareno, Calle 16–125		$23.50	ii
★★ Hotel Casino, Calle 2–2067	(315	$18.00	ii
★★ Hotel La Argentina, San Martín 270		$18.00	ii
★★ Hotel Savoia, San Martín (between Calle 3 and Calle 4)	(107	$18.00	ii
★★ Hotel Sol Mar, corner of Calle 50 and Costanera	(438	$18.00	ii
★ Hotel Aguila, Avenida Costanera (between Calle 3 and Calle 4)	(171	$13.50	ii
★ Hotel Amalfi, corner of Calle 4 and Calle 30		$13.50	ii
★ Hotel Capri, corner of Calle 31 bis and Calle 5	(159	$13.50	ii
★ Hotel Correa, corner of Ruta Acceso and Avenida 1	(212	$13.50	ii
★ Hotel del Mar, Calle 27–57	(356	$13.50	ii
★ Hotel Don Severo, Calle 2–2056	(217	$13.50	ii
★ Hotel Frasi's, Calle 16–145		$13.50	ii
★ Hotel Los Picapiedras, Avenida San Martín 243	(179	$13.50	ii

BUENOS AIRES PROVINCE

Accommodation in San Clemente del Tuyú—continued			
★ Hotel Melani, Calle 1–2325	(257	$13.50	⚑
★ Hotel Morales, corner of Calle 1 and Calle 22	(150	$13.50	⚑
★ Hotel Playa, corner of Calle 1 and Calle 18	(362	$13.50	⚑
★ Hotel Riviera, Calle 21–312		$13.50	⚑
★ Hotel Royal, Calle 30 (between Calle 3 and Calle 4)			
	(431	$13.50	⚑
★ Hotel San Jorge, corner of Avenida Costanera and Avenida 63		$13.50	⚑
★ Hotel Stella Marina, Avenida Costanera (between Calle 2 and Calle 3)			
	(453	$13.50	⚑
★★ Hostería Acuario, Avenida San Martín 144	(357	$15.50	⚑
★ Hostería Frente al Muelle, corner of Calle 16 and Calle 27			
	(218	$12.50	⚑
A Hospedaje Arco Iris, Calle 3–1835	(372	$11.50	⚑

🍴 Eating out
- Restaurant El Cangrejo Rojo. Seafood

🚌 Buses
Buses run regularly to Mar del Plata.
- Buenos Aires: 16 services daily; 6 hours; Empresa La Estrella, Empresa Río de la Plata

🚗 Motoring
- Service station: ACA, corner of Calle 18 and Calle 19

🛏 Accommodation
- ★ Hotel Laguna del Monte, corner of Costanera and J Sarden (20465 $13.50 ⚑
- ★ Hostería El Parque, RN 3 Km 112 $12.50 ⚑
- A Hospedaje La Chona, RN 3 Km 111 $11.50 ⚑

🚌 Buses
- Buenos Aires: 8 services daily; 3 hours; Empresa La Estrella

SAN MIGUEL DEL MONTE

Postal code: 7220 • (area code: (0271)
Distance from Buenos Aires: 110 km southwards on RN 3

Located in the *pampa*, the town of San Miguel del Monte town grew around the Fuerte San Miguel del Monte Gargano.

ℹ Tourist information
- Oficina de Turismo, Mitre 636 (20162

SAN NICOLÁS DE LOS ARROYOS

Postal code: 2900 • Population: 60 000 • (area code: (0461)
Distance from Buenos Aires: 206 km north-west on RN 9

Located on the **Río Paraná**, San Nicolas de los Arroyos, the northernmost town in Buenos Aires province, is an industrial town and a major port for the export of grain. It is served by the F C General B Mitre railroad.

BUENOS AIRES PROVINCE

Accommodation in San Nicolás de los Arroyos

★★★	Hotel Colonial, Avenida General Savio	(22031–22035	$23.50	⋮⋮
★★★	Hotel El Acuerdo, Francia 7	(28917, 27727	$23.50	⋮⋮
★★	Hotel San Martín, corner of Italia and Garibaldi	(22868, 22869	$18.00	⋮⋮
★★	Hotel Yaguaron, Mitre 409	(24549	$18.00	⋮⋮
★	Hotel San Nicolás, Savio 236	(25892	$13.50	⋮⋮
★	Hotel Tony, Nación 627	(22571	$13.50	⋮⋮
A	Hospedaje Belgrano, Belgrano 87	(23497	$11.50	⋮⋮
A	Hospedaje Citex, corner of Savio and Moreno	(22316	$11.50	⋮⋮
A	Hospedaje Igueldo, Mitre 321	(23633	$11.50	⋮⋮
A	Hospedaje Lovisolo, Urquiza 130	(24413	$11.50	⋮⋮
A	Hospedaje Rivadavia, Rivadavia 72	(25872	$11.50	⋮⋮
A	Hospedaje Torino, Savio 279		$11.50	⋮⋮

Tourist information
- Oficina de Turismo, España 23 (in the Parque General San Martín)

Services and facilities
- Laundromat: Laverap, Pellegrini 277

Buses
- Buenos Aires: 8 services daily; 3 hours; Empresa Argentina, Empresa T A Chevallier

Motoring
- Service station: ACA, RN 9 Km 242

Sightseeing
- Museum and archives of the first Argentine naval engagement, enacted against the Brazilians
- Museo y Bibliotheca Casa del Acuerdo (Acuerdo House Museum and Library)
- San Nicolás column, an historical monument

SAN PEDRO

Postal code: 2930 • (area code: (0329)

Distance from Buenos Aires: 159 km north-west on RN 9

San Pedro is an important overseas shipping terminal and has a paper-manufacturing plant.

Festivals
- Fiesta de la Rosa y del Durazno (Rose and Apricot Festival): December

Tourist information
- Dirección de Turismo, corner of Ituzaingo and Ayacucho (25232

Services and facilities
- Laundromat: Laverap, Obligado 141

Buses
- Buenos Aires: daily; 3 hours; Empresa T A Chevallier

Motoring
- Service station: ACA, corner of 3 de Febrero and Dr D Pellegrini

Sightseeing
- Museo Histórico Regional Municipal "Fray Juan María Bottaro" (Brother Juan María

BUENOS AIRES PROVINCE

	Accommodation in San Pedro			
★★★	Hotel Obligado, corner of Mitre and Liniers	(25334, 25364, 25330	$23.50	♊
★★	Hotel de Turismo, Bulevar Paraná 450	(25459	$18.00	♊
★★	Hotel Esser, Mitre 1335	(26214	$18.00	♊
★	Hotel Costa Azul, Dr D Pellegrini 55	(26297	$13.50	♊
A	Hospedaje Armengol, Belgrano 1310	(26167	$11.50	♊
A	Hospedaje Belgrano, Belgrano 1370	(26146	$11.50	♊
A	Hospedaje Marconi, Mitre 1199		$11.50	♊
A	Hospedaje Riviera, M A de Gomendio 620	(26675	$11.50	♊
A	Hospedaje San Pedro, Ruiz Moreno 174	(26249	$11.50	♊

Accommodation outside San Pedro
| ★ | Motel La Serena, RN 9 Km 162 | (26097 | $13.50 | ♊ |

Bottaro Municipal Regional History Museum)

SIERRA DE LA VENTANA AND VILLA ARCADIA

Postal code: 8168
Distance from Bahía Blanca: 124 km northwards on RN 33 then RP 76

Sierra de la Ventana and Villa Arcadia are neighboring towns located on the eastern side of the **Sierra de la Ventana** on the **Río Sauce Grande**. Together they constitute a favorite tourist resort, and their mountainous location gives them a temperate climate with cool summer nights. Vast pine forests have been planted in the area.

Accommodation is also available in **Villa Ventana**, about 40 km north.

Tourist information
- Dirección de Turismo, Avenida Roca (37

Post and telegraph
There is a post office and public telephones in Centro Urbano.

Buses
- Bahía Blanca: $2.50; Empresa El Condor
- Buenos Aires: 2330 daily; 8 hours; Empresa La Estrella
- Tornquist: $1.00; Empresa El Condor

Sport
- Fishing: *Pejerrey* fishing in the Río Sauce Grande
- Golf: Nine-hole golf course

Excursions
- **Parque Provincial Ernesto Tornquist** (Ernesto Tornquist Provincial Park): 22 km. Inside the park is the **Cueva del Toro**, a cave 30 m deep. You can climb to the summit and see the 8.5 m wide opening in the rock which gave the whole *sierra* its name— *ventana* means "window". During World War II part of the crew of the German warship *Graf Spee* was interned in the nearby hotel, then called the Club Hotel. See also "Excursions" in Bahía Blanca on page

San Pedro

BUENOS AIRES PROVINCE

🛏 Accommodation in Sierra de la Ventana and Villa Arcadia

Accommodation in Sierra de la Ventana

★★	Hotel Provincial, Drago	(23, 24	$18.00	♝
★	Hotel Atero, corner of San Martín and Güemes 🛉 ACA discount 10%	(2	$13.50	♝
★★	Hostería Malte, corner of Iguazú and San Martín		$15.50	♝
★	Hostería Carlitos, Colonel Suarez		$12.50	♝
★	Hostería Costanera, Pringles		$12.50	♝
★	Hostería Argentino, Avenida Roca		$12.50	♝
★	Hostería Silver Golf, Barrio Parque Golf 🅐 ACA discount 10%		$12.50	♝

Accommodation in Villa Arcadia

★	Hostería Pilla-huinco, corner of Pilla-huinco and Raiz	$12.50	♝

Accommodation in Villa Ventana

★★	Motel El Pinar, Ruta 76 Km 217	$17.50	♝
★★	Hostería La Espadana, Ruta 76, 13 km north of Villa Ventana	$15.50	♝
A	Hospedaje La Península	$11.50	♝

76. There is also a trout hatchery in the park

TANDIL

Postal code: 7000 • Population: 70 000 • (area code: (0293) • Altitude: 178 m
Distances
- From Buenos Aires: 390 km southwards on RN 3 then RP 30
- From Mar del Plata: 178 km north-west on RP 226

Tandil is located some 170 km inland in the **Sierra de Tandil**, a pre-Cambrian granite ridge whose highest point is **Cerro La Blanca** at 500 m.

🎭 Festivals
- Colorful Holy Week ceremonies attract many visitors

ℹ Tourist information
- Dirección Municipal de Turismo, 9 de Julio 555 (25661

⛺ Camping
- Camping Municipal Pinar de la Sierra: On the road to the Dique del Fuerte. Take yellow bus 500

💲 Financial
- Banco Comercial Del Tandil, corner of General Pinto 602 and Avenida Buzon. Cash advances on Visa card

🛠 Services and facilities

Laundromats
- Laverap, Pinto 980
- Laverap, Santamaría 326

🚌 Buses

The bus terminal is on Avenida Buzón block 400.
- Buenos Aires: 7 services daily; 6 hours; Empresa Costera Criolla, Empresa La Estrella

Tandil

BUENOS AIRES PROVINCE

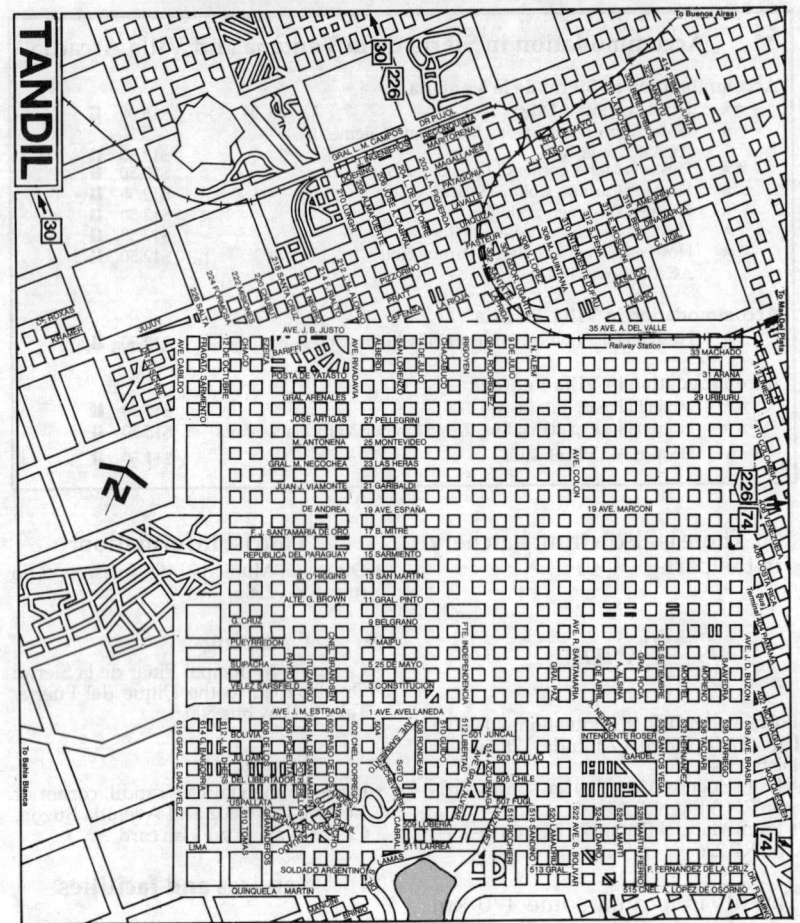

🚗 Motoring
- Service station: ACA, corner of General Rodríguez Belgrano

🏌 Sport
- Golf: Follow Avenida Avellaneda as far as Avenida Brazil. The golf club is on block 15 on the right. Or take blue bus 503 and ask the driver

🍸 Entertainment
- Casino, Avenida Buzón block 400, above the bus terminal. Open Wed–Mon 2100–0200

📷 Sightseeing
- Museo Tradicionalista, 4 de Abril 845. The museum complex used to be the Fuerte Inde-

Tandil

126

Buenos Aires Province

🛏 Accommodation in Tandil

★★★	Hotel Libertador, Mitre 545	(22127	$23.50	👥
★★★	Hotel Plaza, Pinto 438	(27160, 27180, 27190	$23.50	👥
★★	Hotel Austral, 9 de Julio 725	(25606	$18.00	👥
★★	Hotel Grand Hotel, España 545	(24002	$18.00	👥
★★	Hotel Italy, corner of Espora and Venezuela	(29923	$18.00	👥
★	Hotel Centro, Sarmiento 591	(24123	$13.50	👥
★	Hotel Crillon, San Martín 455	(24159	$13.50	👥
★	Hotel Cristal, General Rodríguez 871	(25951	$13.50	👥
★	Hotel Francia, Colón 1600	(23240	$13.50	👥
★	Hotel Hermitage, Avellaneda 300	(23987	$13.50	👥
★	Hotel Ro Che Hil, General Rodríguez 1100	(26135	$13.50	👥
★	Hotel Roma, L N Alem 474	(25217	$13.50	👥
★	Hotel Turista, 14 de Julio 60	(22626	$13.50	👥
★★★	Hostería Hostal de la Sierra, Avellaneda 931	(22330	$18.50	👥
A	Hospedaje Almar, Marconi 1048	(23995	$12.50	👥
A	Hospedaje Alvear, Alvear 55		$12.50	👥
A	Hospedaje Americano, Sarmiento 795	(23778	$12.50	👥
A	Hospedaje Elios, General Rodríguez 783	(25823	$12.50	👥
A	Hospedaje Graciela, Avellaneda 734	(27847	$12.50	👥
A	Hospedaje Iraéta, Maipu 522	(25424	$12.50	👥
A	Hospedaje Kaiku, Mitre 902	(23114	$12.50	👥
A	Hospedaje Loge, Montevideo 740	(24408	$12.50	👥
A	Hospedaje Rivadavia, Rivadavia 179	(27792	$12.50	👥
A	Hospedaje Regina, Sarmiento 968	(23311	$12.50	👥
A	Hospedaje Rub-Wal, Colón 974	(26220, 24220	$12.50	👥
A	Hospedaje Savoy, corner of LN Alem and Mitre	(25602	$12.50	👥
A	Hospedaje Torino, Sarmiento 502	(23454	$12.50	👥
A	Hospedaje Victoria, Machado 1061	(23397	$12.50	👥
B	Hospedaje Belgrano, Belgrano 745	(25353	$8.50	👥
B	Hospedaje El Rolo, Pinto 728		$8.50	👥
B	Hospedaje Las Delicias, Maipú 335		$8.50	👥
B	Hospedaje Nuevo Rumbo, Constitución 271	(24745	$8.50	👥
B	Hospedaje Rex, Paz 1279	(23824	$8.50	👥
B	Hospedaje San Carlos Paz 955		$8.50	👥
B	Hospedaje Yatay, Belgrano 785	(26457	$8.50	👥
A	Residencial Ramirez, San Martín 740	(23111	$12.50	👥

pendencia, and exhibits show what it was like when it was operating as a fort. Open Tues–Sun 1430–1830. Take yellow bus 500

- Museo Municipal de Bellas Artes (Municipal Fine Arts Museum), Chacabuco 367. Open Tues–Sun 1700–2000

🅟 Excursions

- **Dique del Fuerte**: Artificial lake and fishing club, Club Náutico. Take yellow bus 500
- **Cerro El Calvario**: Lourdes Grotto and Santa Gemma chapel. Take white bus 502
- **Reserva Natural Sierra del Tigre**: Follow Avenida Don

BUENOS AIRES PROVINCE

Bosco and turn right into Calle Suiza
- **Cerro La Movediza** ("Moving Stone Hill")

TRES ARROYOS

Postal code: 7500 • ℂ area code: (0983) • Population: 40 000
Distances
- From Buenos Aires: 500 km southwards on RN 3
- From Bahía Blanca: 195 km eastwards on RN 3

Located inland on the **Río Claromecó**, Tres Arroyos was founded in 1884. Many of the townsfolk are of Dutch descent. Cattle and wheat are the backbone of the district's economy.

Post and telegraph
- Post office: Encotel, Maipú 276
- Telephone: *Cabina publica*, Maipú 274

Services and facilities
- Laundromat: Laverap, Bertolaza 70

Buses
There is a modern bus terminal just outside town with clean rest rooms.
Empresa Pampas runs regular bus services to Bahía Blanca and Mar del Plata.

- Buenos Aires: 7 services daily; 9 hours; Empresa El Condor, Empresa La Estrella

Motoring
- Service station: ACA, corner of Colón and Lavalle

Excursions
- **Claromecó**: Beach, 65 km south on RP 73. See Claromecó on page 84

VILLA ARCADIA

See Sierra de la Ventana on page 184.

VILLA GESELL

Postal code: 7165 • ℂ area code: (0255) • Population: 14 000
Distances
- From Buenos Aires: 410 km southwards on RN 1 then Ruta 2 and RN 74
- From Mar Del Plata: 130 km northwards on RP 11

Villa Gesell is comparatively new. It owes its existence to the doggedness of a German immigrant who from 1931 onwards

Accommodation in Tres Arroyos

★★	Hotel Alfil, Rivadavia 142		$18.00
★★	Hotel Parque, Pellegrini 23		$18.00
A	Hostería Andrea, Istilart 228		$11.50
	Hostería City Hotel, corner of Lavalle and 28 de Mayo		$11.50
A	Hostería Comercio, corner of 25 de Mayo and Pedro Carrera		$11.50
A	Hostería Paris, Bertolaza 242		$11.50
B	Hostería Plaza, Chacabuco 443	ℂ 7083	$8.50
A	Hospedaje La Catalana, Maipú 187		$11.50

Tandil

BUENOS AIRES PROVINCE

planted thousands of pine and eucalyptus trees in the area to stabilize the shifting sand dunes. After many setbacks he succeeded, and Villa Gesell is now a very popular beach resort. The dunes to the north and south have partially given way to pine forests now, and there are some camping facilities. The sandy beach extends for 10 km.

Festivals
- Pineapple festival: July

Tourist information
- Dirección de Turismo, corner of Avenida Buenos Aires and Circunvalación (68596
- Tourist information kiosk in bus terminal, corner of Avenida 3 and Paseo 140

Camping
The distance of each camping ground to the beach is given in meters after the address.
- Africa, corner of Avenida Buenos Aires and Circunvalación, 1700 m (68507
- Autocamping Mar Azul, Ruta Interbalnearia Km 11, just off the roundabout outside Villa Gesell
- California, corner of Avenida Buenos Aires and Avenida Circunvalación, 1700 m (68346
- Campamento del Sol, corner of Bulevar S Gesell and Paseo 102, 1100 m (68207. Open all year round
- Caravan, corner of Avenida Circunvalacion and Paseo 101, 1400 m (68259
- Casablanca, Avenida 3, south of the town center, 100 m
- Coyote, corner of Alameda 212 and Calle 306), 1200 m (68448
- Duve Camping, corner of Paseo 117 and Avenida 14, 1400 m (62892
- El Faro, corner of Boulevard S Gesell and Paseo 101, 1200 m
- El Pinar, corner of Alameda 214 and Avenida Buenos Aires, 1400 m (68219
- Europa, corner of Alameda 214 and Calle 304, 1400 m (68292
- Mar Dorado, Avenida 3, south of the town center, 100 m
- Monte Bubi, Avenida 3, south of the town center, 100 m

Eating out

International cuisine
- Restaurant C'Aan Joan, corner of Paseo 109 and Avenida 4
- Restaurant Cabaña, Avenida 3 (between Paseo 104 and Paseo 105)
- Restaurant Don Diego, corner of Avenida 3 and Paseo 102
- Restaurant El Candil, Avenida 3 (between Paseo 123 and Paseo 124)
- Restaurant El Ciervo Dorado, corner of Paseo 105 and Avenida 4
- Restaurant La Canasta, Avenida 3 (between Paseo 102 and Paseo 104)
- Restaurant La Casona del Conde de Palermo, corner of Buenos Aires and Costanera
- Restaurant Samoana, corner of Avenida 3 and Paseo 102
- Restaurant Tirol, corner of Avenida 2 and Paseo 110

Steakhouses
- Restaurant Al Natural, corner of Avenida 3 and Paseo 102
- Restaurant Arturito, Avenida 3 (between Paseo 126 and Paseo 127)
- Restaurant Automovil Club Argentino, Avenida 1 (between and Paseo 112 and Paseo 113)
- Restaurant C Caravan, corner of Avenida Buenos Aires and Circunvalación
- Restaurant Club Español, Avenida Buenos (between Avenida 3 and Avenida 4)
- Restaurant Doña Julia, Avenida 5 (between Avenida 105 and Avenida 106)
- Restaurant Doña María, Paseo 109 (between Avenida 3 and Avenida 4)
- Restaurant El Caballito Blanco, Paseo 105 (between Avenida 3 and Avenida 3 bis)

Continued on page 136

Villa Gesell

Buenos Aires Province

Accommodation in Villa Gesell

The distance of each hotel to the beach is given in meters after the address.

★★★	Hotel Austral, Calle 306, on beach front	68050	$23.00	
★★★	Hotel Cap Arcona, Avenida 1 (between Paseo 117 and Paseo 118)	62209	$23.50	
★★★	Hotel Merimar, Paseo 104, on beach front	62243	$23.50	
★★★	Hotel Palace, Alameda 203 (near Avenida Buenos Aires), 400 m	68369	$23.50	
★★★	Hotel Reymar, Paseo 111 (on beach front)	62579	$23.50	
★★★	Hotel Topaco, Paseo 104 (near Avenida 1 bis)	62020	$23.50	
★★	Hotel Abetaia, Avenida 5 (between Paseo 104 and Paseo 105)	62454	$18.00	
★★	Hotel Apolo, Paseo 104 (near Avenida 2), 200 m	62451	$18.00	
★★	Hotel Augusta, Avenida 2 (between Paseo 108 and Paseo 109), 250 m	62366	$18.00	
★★	Hotel Capri, Paseo 108 (between Avenida 1 and Avenida 2), 150 m	62234	$18.00	
★★	Hotel Cervantes, corner of Avenida 3 and Paseo 120, 300 m	62435	$18.00	
★★	Hotel Delfin Azul, Paseo 104 (between Avenida 4 and Avenida 5), 450 m	62521	$18.00	
★★	Hotel Don Carlos, Avenida 3 (near Paseo 102), 300 m	62398	$18.00	
★★	Hotel El Loco Chavez, Avenida 3 (near Paseo 125), 300 m	62452	$18.00	
★★	Hotel Horizonte, Avenida 1 (near Paseo 103), facing beach front	62294	$18.00	
★★	Hotel Internacional, Paseo 103, on beach front	62317	$18.00	
★★	Hotel Lincoln, corner of Avenida 1 and Paseo 119, 150 m	62269	$18.00	
★★	Hotel Mallorca, Paseo 134 (between Avenida 2 and Avenida 3), 250 m	66163	$18.00	
★★	Hotel Mamajuma, corner of Paseo 111 and beach front	63106	$18.00	
★★	Hotel Marina, corner of Avenida 2 and Paseo 108, 200 m	62228	$18.00	
★★	Hotel Norte, corner of Alameda 205 and Calle 305, 300 m	68041	$18.00	
★★	Hotel Playa, corner of Alameda 205 and Calle 303, 200 m	68027	$18.00	
★★	Hotel Rideamus, Avenida 2 (between Paseo 107 and Paseo 108), 200 m	62307	$18.00	
★★	Hotel Riviera, corner of Avenida 1 and Paseo 107, 150 m	62217	$18.00	
★★	Hotel Romadrid, corner of Avenida 1 and Avenida Buenos Aires, 150 m	68368	$18.00	
★★	Hotel San Remo, corner of Avenida 1 and Paseo 107, 100 m	62221	$18.00	
★★	Hotel Sayonara, corner of Avenida 2 and Paseo 119, 200 m	62619	$18.00	
★★	Hotel Silvana, Avenida 3 (between Paseo 111 and Paseo 112), 300m	62597	$18.00	
★★	Hotel Tamanacos, Paseo 103 bis (between Avenida 1 and the beach front)	62453	$18.00	

Villa Gesell

BUENOS AIRES PROVINCE

Accommodation in Villa Gesell—continued

- ★★ Hotel Tejas Rojas, corner of Paseo 108 and Avenida 1
  ℂ 62274 $18.00
- ★★ Hotel Tiburones Club, Paseo 129 (between Avenida 1 and Avenida 2), 200 m
  ℂ 66342 $18.00
- ★★ Hotel Venezia, corner of Avenida 1 and 107/108, 150 m
  ℂ 62231 $18.00
- ★★ Hotel Verona, corner of Avenida 1 and Paseo 105, 100 m
  ℂ 62465 $18.00
- ★★ Hotel Waldeck, corner of Avenida 7 and Paseo 102, 700 m
  ℂ 62585 $18.00
- ★ Hotel Actinia, Avenida 3 (between Paseo 120 and Paseo 121), 300m
  ℂ 63103 $13.50
- ★ Hotel Acuarium, Paseo 139 (between Avenida 2 and Avenida 3), 300 m
  ℂ 66071 $13.50
- ★ Hotel Adriatico, corner of Alameda 202 and Avenida Buenos Aires, 300 m
  ℂ 68358 $13.50
- ★ Hotel Adrimar, corner of Avenida 2 and Paseo 118, 250 m
  ℂ 62613 $13.50
- ★ Hotel Aguila Blanca, Paseo 137 (between Avenida 2 and Avenida 3), 200 m
  ℂ 66132 $13.50
- ★ Hotel Albatros, Paseo 141 bis (between Avenida 3 and Avenida 4), 300m
  ℂ 66179 $13.50
- ★ Hotel Alfa, corner of Paseo 106 and Avenida 3, 300 m
  ℂ 62601 $13.50
- ★ Hotel Arco Iris, corner of Paseo 107 and Avenida 2, 200 m
  ℂ 62445 $13.50
- ★ Hotel Atlántico, corner of Avenida 1 and Paseo 105, on beach front
  ℂ 62253 $13.50
- ★ Hotel Bamba, Paseo 108 (between Avenida 1 and Avenida 2), 150 m
  ℂ 62681 $13.50
- ★ Hotel Bariloche, Pasaje Costanero (between Pasaje 201 and Avenida Buenos Aires), 150 m
  ℂ 68366 $13.50
- ★ Hotel Barracuda, Paseo 121, on beach front
  ℂ 63260 $13.50
- ★ Hotel Bavaria, Avenida 3 (between Paseo 126 and Paseo 127), 300 m
  ℂ 62361 $13.50
- ★ Hotel Bero, corner of Avenida 4 and Paseo 141, 400 m
  ℂ 66077 $13.50
- ★ Hotel Belverde, Avenida Buenos Aires (between and Paseo 105 and Paseo 106), 150 m
  ℂ 68399 $13.50
- ★ Hotel Biondi, Avenida 3 (between Paseo 105 and Paseo 106), 300 m
  ℂ 62311 $13.50
- ★ Hotel Bismarck, Avenida 1 (between Paseo 141 and Paseo 142), 100 m
  ℂ 66078 $13.50
- ★ Hotel Bonifati, corner of Avenida 2 and Paseo 104, 250 m
  ℂ 62493 $13.50
- ★ Hotel Cabanás, Paseo 125 (between Avenida 1 and Avenida 2), 150 m
  ℂ 62409 $13.50
- ★ Hotel Cantabrico, corner of Paseo 102 and Avenida 2, 300 m
  ℂ 62835 $13.50
- ★ Hotel Cocco's, Avenida 1 (between Paseo 110 and Paseo 111), 150 m
  ℂ 62580 $13.50
- ★ Hotel Colón, corner of Avenida 4 and Paseo 104, 400 m
  ℂ 62310 $13.50
- ★ Hotel Danubio, Paseo 105 (near Avenida 2), 200 m
  ℂ 62328 $13.50
- ★ Hotel Demi, corner of Avenida 3 and Paseo 111, 300 m
  ℂ 62658 $13.50

BUENOS AIRES PROVINCE

Accommodation in Villa Gesell—continued

- ★ Hotel de Poi, Paseo 142 (between Avenida 3 and Avenida 4), 350 m
  ☎ 66031 $13.50
- ★ Hotel Dino's, Avenida 3 (between Paseo 111 and 112), 300 m
  ☎ 62028 $13.50
- ★ Hotel Disi, Avenida 2 (between Paseo 107 and Paseo 108), 200 m
  ☎ 62245 $13.50
- ★ Hotel Edith, Paseo 109 (between Avenida 3 and Avenida 4), 350 m
  ☎ 62304 $13.50
- ★ Hotel El Cisne, Avenida 4 (between Paseo 102 and Paseo 104), 400 m
  ☎ 62289 $13.50
- ★ Hotel El Duri, Paseo 116 (between Avenida 2 and Avenida 3), 300 m
  ☎ 62551 $13.50
- ★ Hotel El Quijote, Avenida 2 (between Paseo 115 and Paseo 116), 300 m
  ☎ 62598 $13.50
- ★ Hotel Etna, Avenida 2 (between Paseo 107 and Paseo 108), 250 m
  ☎ 62442 $13.50
- ★ Hotel Hansa, corner of Alameda 205 and Calle 303, 300 m
  ☎ 68029 $13.50
- ★ Hotel Il Luppo, corner of Avenida 3 and Paseo 137, 300 m
  ☎ 66128 $13.50
- ★ Hotel Ispra, corner of Paseo 109 and beach front
  ☎ 62391 $13.50
- ★ Hotel Kaiken, corner of Avenida 2 and Paseo 121, 200 m
  ☎ 62791 $13.50
- ★ Hotel Kamati, Paseo 124 (between Avenida 2 and 3), 300m $13.50
- ★ Hotel La Helvetica, Avenida 1 (between Paseo 107 and 108), 150 m $13.50
- ★ Hotel Lilian, Avenida 3 (between Paseo 114 and Paseo 115), 300 m
  ☎ 62316 $13.50
- ★ Hotel Maracas, corner of Avenida 1 and Paseo 103, 150 m
  ☎ 62479 $13.50
- ★ Hotel Mariska, corner of Avenida 1 and Paseo 130, 100 m
  ☎ 66341 $13.50
- ★ Hotel Marisol, corner of Paseo 115, on beach front
  ☎ 62329 $13.50
- ★ Hotel Massa, Avenida 1 (between Paseo 107 and Paseo 108), 150 m
  ☎ 62226 $13.50
- ★ Hotel Mi Sueño, corner of Avenida 2 and Paseo 115, 200 m
  ☎ 62345 $13.50
- ★ Hotel Mon Amour, Avenida 1 (between Paseo 117 and Paseo 118), 100 m
  ☎ 62439 $13.50
- ★ Hotel Náutico, Paseo 119 (between Avenida 2 and Avenida 3), 250 m
  ☎ 62935 $13.50
- ★ Hotel Neptuno, Avenida 3 (between Paseo 127 and Paseo 128), 300 m
  ☎ 62376 $13.50
- ★ Hotel Oasis, Avenida 3 (between Paseo 119 and Paseo 120), 300 m
  ☎ 62204 $13.50
- ★ Hotel Panorama, Avenida 1 (between Paseo 119 and 120), 150 m
  ☎ 62263 $13.50
- ★ Hotel Piazza, Avenida 1 (between Paseo 116 and 117), 150 m
  ☎ 62661 $13.50
- ★ Hotel Portofino, corner of Avenida 3 and Paseo 116, 300 m
  ☎ 62202 $13.50
- ★ Hotel Posada del Sol, Avenida 4 (between Paseo 106 and Paseo 107, 450 m
  ☎ 62086 $13.50
- ★ Hotel Quetrihue, Paseo 141 (between Avenida 3 and Avenida 4), 300 m
  ☎ 63476 $13.50
- ★ Hotel Romina, corner of Avenida 1 and Paseo 140, 100 m
  ☎ 66074 $13.50

Villa Gesell

BUENOS AIRES PROVINCE

Accommodation in Villa Gesell—continued

★	Hotel Royal, Avenida 3 (between Paseo 110 and Paseo 110 bis), 350 m			
		✆ 62411	$13.50	♙
★	Hotel Sahara, Paseo 112 (between Avenida 1 and Avenida 3), 150 m			
		✆ 62208	$13.50	♙
★	Hotel Sekand, Avenida 1 (between Paseo 116 and Paseo 117), 150 m			
		✆ 62036	$13.50	♙
★	Hotel Silmar, Avenida 3 (between Paseo 137 and Paseo 138), 350 m			
		✆ 66065	$13.50	♙
★	Hotel Smyrna, Paseo 109 (on beach front)	✆ 62017	$13.50	♙
★	Hotel Sole Mio, Paseo 119 (between Avenida 3 and Avenida 4), 350 m			
		✆ 62832	$13.50	♙
★	Hotel Splendid, corner of Avenida 4 and Paseo 104, 400 m			
		✆ 62326	$13.50	♙
★	Hotel Tobrouck, Paseo 140 (between Avenida 1 and Avenida 2), 250 m			
		✆ 66079	$13.50	♙
★	Hotel Torremolinos, Paseo 111 (on beach front)	✆ 62389	$13.50	♙
★	Hotel Trio, Avenida 11 (between Paseo 105 and Paseo 106), 1000 m			
		✆ 62154	$13.50	♙
★	Hotel Victoria, Avenida 3 (between Paseo 114 and Paseo 115), 300 m			
		✆ 62775	$13.50	♙
★	Hotel Vireo, Avenida 3 (between Paseo 121 and Paseo 123), 300 m			
		✆ 62796	$13.50	♙
★★★	Hostería Posta Carretas, Avenida 1 (between Paseo 109 and Paseo 110), 100 m			
		✆ 62526	$18.50	♙
★★★	Hostería Querandi, Avenida 1 (between Paseo 126 and Paseo 127), 100 m			
		✆ 62707	$18.50	♙
★★★	Hostería Tequendama, corner of Paseo 109 and Avenida 1, on beach front	✆ 62829	$18.50	♙
★★★	Hostería Tirol, corner of Avenida 2 and Paseo 110, 250 m			
		✆ 62011	$18.50	♙
★★★	Hostería Zagreb, Cort. corner of 206 bis and Calle 307, 450 m			
		✆ 68040	$18.50	♙
★★	Hostería Alinel, Avenida 3 (between Paseo 116 and Paseo 117), 300 m			
		✆ 62023	$15.50	♙
★★	Hostería Alpina, corner of Calle 307 and Alameda 206, 300 m			
		✆ 68066	$15.50	♙
★★	Hostería El Velero, Avenida 3 (between Paseo 102 and Paseo 104), 300 m			
		✆ 62256	$15.50	♙
★★	Hostería Ete, Alameda (between Calle 309 and Calle 308), 300 m			
		✆ 68098	$15.50	♙
★★	Hostería Flor de Lis, Avenida 4 (between Paseo 104 and Paseo 105), 400 m			
		✆ 62529	$15.50	♙
★★	Hostería Gran Chalet, Paseo 105 (between Avenida 4 and Avenida 5), 400 m			
		✆ 62913	$15.50	♙
★★	Hostería Gran Danes, Paseo 126 (between Avenida 1 and Avenida 2), 150 m			
		✆ 62703	$15.50	♙
★★	Hostería Lindau, Avenida 3 (between Paseo 123 and Paseo 124), 300 m			
		✆ 62766	$15.50	♙
★★	Hostería Maxim, Alameda 201 (between Calle 306 and Calle 207), on beach front	✆ 68026	$15.50	2
★★	Hostería Santa Barbara, corner of Avenida 2 and Paseo 109, 100 m			
		✆ 63143	$15.50	♙
★	Hostería Aloha, Paseo 104 (between Avenida 1 and Avenida 2), 200 m			
		✆ 62510	$12.50	♙
★	Hostería Astrid, Paseo 141 bis (between Avenida 3 and Avenida 4), 400 m			
		✆ 66147	$12.50	♙
★	Hostería City Mar, Paseo 119 (between Avenida 3 and Avenida 4), 250 m			
		✆ 66179	$12.50	♙

Villa Gesell

Buenos Aires Province

Accommodation in Villa Gesell—continued

- ★ Hostería Colonial, corner of Avenida 5 and Paseo 106, 500 m
  ℓ 62351 $12.50
- ★ Hostería Conti, Paseo 109 (between Avenida 3 and Avenida 4), 350 m
  ℓ 62032 $12.50
- ★ Hostería Costa Azul, Paseo 141 (between Avenida 2 and Avenida 3), 300 m
  ℓ 66035 $12.50
- ★ Hostería Dakota, Paseo 119 (between Avenida 2 and Avenida 3), 250 m
  ℓ 62037 $12.50
- ★ Hostería El Faro, Avenida 3 (between Paseo 110 and Paseo 111), 300 m
  ℓ 62259 $12.50
- ★ Hostería Flipper, Paseo 138 (between Avenida 1 and Avenida 2), 200 m
  ℓ 66175 $12.50
- ★ Hostería Flor de Cactus, Alameda 205 (between Calle 308 and Calle 309), 200 m
  ℓ 68020 $12.50
- ★ Hostería Hamburgo, Avenida 3 (between Paseo 107 and Paseo 108), 300 m
  ℓ 62060 $12.50
- ★ Hostería Hawai, corner of Avenida 2 and Paseo 108, 300 m
  ℓ 62047 $12.50
- ★ Hostería Idaho, corner of Avenida 3 and Paseo 133, 300 m
  ℓ 66263 $12.50
- ★ Hostería Los Cedros, corner of Calle 303 and Alameda 212, 700 m
  ℓ 68211 $12.50
- ★ Hostería Los Troncos, Paseo 105 (between Avenida 4 and Avenida 5), 400 m
  ℓ 62220 $12.50
- ★ Hostería Mar Azul, Avenida 4 (between Paseo 106 and Paseo 107), 400 m
  ℓ 62457 $12.50
- ★ Hostería Molise, Paseo 142 (between Avenida 2 and Avenida 3), 250 m
  $12.50
- ★ Hostería Montecarlo, corner of Pasaje Costanero and Paseo 103 bis, 100 m
  ℓ 62587 $12.50
- ★ Hostería Parma, corner of Paseo 105 and Avenida 3, 350 m
  ℓ 62569 $12.50
- ★ Hostería Sajonia, Calle 20–51 (corner of Avenida Buenos Aires), 100m
  $12.50
- ★ Hostería San Marcos, corner of Avenida 1 and Paseo 104, 150 m
  ℓ 62232 $12.50
- ★ Hostería Vagabonde, corner of Avenida 2 and Paseo 134, 250 m
  ℓ 66115 $12.50
- ★ Hostería Zodiaco, Avenida 2 (between Paseos 107 and Paseo 108), 250 m
  ℓ 62015 $12.50
- **A** Hospedaje Aguas Verdes, Avenida 5 (between Paseo 104 and Paseo 105), 500 m
  ℓ 62040 $11.50
- **A** Hospedaje Albert, corner of Avenida 3 and Paseo 114, 350 m
  ℓ 62049 $11.50
- **A** Hospedaje Antonio, Avenida 4 (between Paseos 104 and Paseo 105), 450 m
  ℓ 62246 $11.50
- **A** Hospedaje Astoria, Avenida 5 (between Paseos 106 and Paseo 107), 500 m
  ℓ 62021 $11.50
- **A** Hospedaje Arglahu, Avenida 5 (between Paseos 104 and Paseo 105), 500 m
  ℓ 62377 $11.50
- **A** Hospedaje Barca, Avenida 3 (between Paseos 114 and Paseo 115), 350 m
  ℓ 62223 $11.50
- **A** Hospedaje Bella Vista, Paseo 114 (between Avenida 1 and Avenida 3), 150 m
  ℓ 62293 $11.50
- **A** Hospedaje Bell Motel, corner of Alameda 206 and Calle 303, 500 m
  ℓ 68033 $11.50

Villa Gesell

Accommodation in Villa Gesell—continued

- **A** Hospedaje Ceferino, Paseo 117 (between Avenida 2 and Avenida 3), 300 m — $11.50
- **A** Hospedaje Don Felix, Pasaje 3 bis (between Paseo 105 and Paseo 106), 400 m — $11.50
- **A** Hospedaje Elisan, corner of Avenida 6 and Paseo 105, 600 m — $11.50
- **A** Hospedaje Gran Mar, Avenida 1 (between Paseo 119 and Paseo 120), 150 m (62083 — $11.50
- **A** Hospedaje Islas Canarias, corner of Avenida 2 and Paseo 126, 250 m (62494 — $11.50
- **A** Hospedaje Jabali, Avenida 5 (between Paseos 104 and Paseo 105), 500 m (62318 — $11.50
- **A** Hospedaje La Almeja Loca, corner of Avenida 3 and Paseo 135 bis, 300 m (66116 — $11.50
- **A** Hospedaje La Estrella, corner of Avenida 5 and Paseo 110, 500 m — $11.50
- **A** Hospedaje La Loma, Avenida 5 (between Paseo 104 and Paseo 105), 600 m (62656 — $11.50
- **A** Hospedaje La Lomita, corner of Avenida 6 and Paseo 104, 700 m (62034 — $11.50
- **A** Hospedaje Las Dunas, Paseo 110 bis (between Avenida 3 and Avenida 4), 350 m — $11.50
- **A** Hospedaje Le Caravelle, corner of Avenida and Paseo 104, 350 m (62363 — $11.50
- **A** Hospedaje Los Abetos, Avenida 4 (between Paseo 105 and Paseo 10)6 400 m — $11.50
- **A** Hospedaje Los Medanos, Avenida 5 (between Paseo 105 and Paseo 106), 500 m (63205 — $11.50
- **A** Hospedaje Mar Azul, Avenida 4 (between Paseo 106 and Paseo 107), 450 m (62457 — $11.50
- **A** Hospedaje Mariel, Avenida 5 (between Paseo 104 and Paseo 105), 500 m — $11.50
- **A** Hospedaje Marino, corner of Avenida 1 and Paseo 112, 100 m (62436 — $11.50
- **A** Hospedaje Mohnen, Avenida 3 (between Paseo 116 and Paseo 117), 300 m (63095 — $11.50
- **A** Hospedaje Odisea, corner of Avenida 1 and Paseo 119, 100 m (62055 — $11.50
- **A** Hospedaje Olimpo, corner of Avenida 3 and Paseo 119, 300 m (62216 — $11.50
- **A** Hospedaje Onozu, Paseo 115 (between Avenida 5 and Avenida 6), 550 m (62523 — $11.50
- **A** Hospedaje Parque Hotel, corner of Avenida 3 and Paseo 102, 300 m (62298 — $11.50
- **A** Hospedaje Pino Azul, Avenida 8 (between Paseo 106 and Paseo 107), 800 m (63160 — $11.50
- **A** Hospedaje Playa Azul, corner of Avenida 3 and Paseo 126, 300 m (62010 — $11.50
- **A** Hospedaje Pourrally, corner of Avenida 3 and Paseo 134, 300 m (66160 — $11.50
- **A** Hospedaje Robert, Paseo 109 (between Avenida 3 and Avenida 4), 350 m (62304 — $11.50

Buenos Aires Province

Accommodation in Villa Gesell—continued

A	Hospedaje San Hector, Avenida 8 (between Paseo 106 and Paseo 107), 800 m	(62052	$11.50	♊
A	Hospedaje San Marino, Paseo 106 (between Avenida 5 and Avenida 6), 500 m	(62690	$11.50	♊
A	Hospedaje Sarymar, corner of Avenida 3 and Paseo 118, 300 m		$11.50	♊
A	Hospedaje Stelvio, corner of Avenida 5 and Paseo 106, 500 m	(62537	$11.50	♊
A	Hospedaje Stradum, Avenida 3 (between Paseo 114 and Paseo 115), 350 m	(62025	$11.50	♊
A	Hospedaje Tamune, Paseo 112 (on beach front) (62044		$11.50	♊
A	Hospedaje Villa Gesell, Avenida 3 (between Paseo 108 and Paseo 109), 300 m	(62393	$11.50	♊
A	Hospedaje Viya, Avenida 5 (between Paseo 105 and Paseo 106), 500 m	(62757	$11.50	♊
B	Hospedaje Bixie, Avenida 3 (between Paseo 106 and Paseo 107), 600 m		$8.50	♊
B	Hospedaje Ester, corner of Avenida 7 and Paseo 112, 700 m		$8.50	♊
B	Hospedaje Intihuasi, corner of Alameda 202 and Avenida Buenos Aires, 500 m	(68365	$8.50	♊
B	Hospedaje Mi Negro, Paseo 105 (between Avenida 4 and Avenida 5), 450 m	(62286	$8.50	♊
B	Hospedaje Vesubio, Avenida 4 (between Paseo 112 and Paseo 113), 500 m	(62748	$8.50	♊

- Restaurant El Casco, corner of Avenida Buenos Aires and Alameda 204
- Restaurant El 5, Avenida 5 (between Paseo 105 and Paseo 106)
- Restaurant El Con de Fermin, corner of Paseo 105 and Avenida 2
- Restaurant El Cortijo, corner of Paseo 140 and Avenida 2
- Restaurant El Establo, Avenida 3 (between Avenida Buenos Aires and Avenida 102)
- Restaurant El Estribo, corner of Avenida Buenos Aires and Alameda 203
- Restaurant El Quijote, corner of Avenida Buenos Aires, opposite tourist bureau
- Restaurant El Raviolon, corner of Paseo 104 and Avenida 4
- Restaurant El Reloj, corner of Avenida 3 and Paseo 114
- Restaurant Fortin 13, corner of Avenida 3 and Paseo 120
- Restaurant Gomez, Avenida 5 (between Paseo 107 and Paseo 106)
- Restaurant Gramajo, Paseo 106 (between Avenida 7 and Avenida 8)
- Restaurant Ilppo, corner of Avenida 3 and Paseo 137
- Restaurant La Estancia, Avenida 3 (between Paseo 105 and Paseo 106)
- Restaurant La Gondola, Avenida 3 (between Paseo 107 and Paseo 108)
- Restaurant La Jirafa Azul, corner of Avenida 3 and Paseo 102
- Restaurant La Taberna de Don Ramon, corner of Avenida 3 and Paseo 105
- Restaurant Los Airedales, corner of Avenida Buenos Aires and Avenida. Circunvalación
- Restaurant Los Hijos de López, corner of Avenida 3 and Paseo 119
- Restaurant Los Sobrinos, Avenida 4 (between Paseo 105 and Paseo 104)
- Restaurant Medina, corner of Avenida Buenos Aires and Alameda 203
- Restaurant Mickey, corner of Avenida 3 and Paseo 102
- Restaurant Mohnen, corner of Avenida 3 and Paseo 116
- Restaurant Papus, corner of Paseo 104 and Paseo Costanera
- Restaurant Pleno Sol, Avenida 3 (between Paseo 135 and Paseo 136)

Villa Gesell

BUENOS AIRES PROVINCE

- Restaurant Royal, Avenida 3–936
- Restaurant Saint George, Paseo 104 (between Avenida 2 and Avenida 3)
- Restaurant Sancho, Avenida 3 (between Paseo 104 and Paseo 105)
- Restaurant San Remo, corner of Avenida 1 and Paseo 107
- Restaurant Tala, Avenida 7 (between Paseo 105 and Paseo 106)
- Restaurant Tío Pancho, corner of Avenida Buenos Aires and Alameda 203
- Restaurant Viejo Munich, at the roundabout just outside Villa Gesell
- Restaurant Vilash, Avenida 3 (between Paseo 108 and Paseo 109)

Seafood

- Restaurant El Baston, Paseo 107 (between Avenida 3 and Avenida 2)
- Restaurant Hostal Del Mar, corner of Paseo 112 and Playa
- Restaurant Nichee, corner of Paseo Costanero and Paseo 111

Pizzerías

- Pizzería Bar Italia, corner of Avenida 3 and Paseo 105
- Pizzería Center, corner of Avenida 3 and Paseo 109
- Pizzería Cosco Inna, corner of Avenida 3 and Paseo 105
- Pizzería El Sanjuanino, corner of Avenida Buenos Aires and Alameda 203
- Pizzería Italiana, corner of Avenida 3 and Paseo 105
- Pizzería Los Marcianos, corner of Avenida 3 and Paseo 107
- Pizzería Mafalda, corner of Avenida 3 and Paseo 118
- Pizzería Michelangelo, corner of Avenida 3 and Paseo 105
- Pizzería Novechento, corner of Paseo 105 and Avenida 3
- Pizzería Pinocho, corner of Avenida 3 and Paseo 104
- Pizzería Ventura, Avenida Buenos (between and Avenida 10 and Avenida 11)
- Pizzería Ventura, corner of Avenida 3 and Paseo 121

Cafeterías

- Cafetería Atolon, corner of Avenida 3 and Paseo 105
- Cafetería Bacara, corner of Avenida 3 and Paseo 106
- Cafetería Barajas, corner of Avenida 3 and Paseo 104
- Cafetería Cachavacha, corner of Avenida 3 and Paseo 108
- Cafetería Dogos, corner of Paseo 104 and Avenida 2
- Cafetería El Angel de Oro, Avenida 3 (between Paseo 110 and Paseo 111)
- Cafetería El Estano, Paseo 105 (between Avenida 3 and Avenida 2)
- Cafetería Groobe, corner of Paseo 107 and Avenida 2
- Cafetería Il Tiempo, Avenida Buenos (between Avenida 3 and Avenida 4)
- Cafetería Jet Set, corner of Avenida 3 and Paseo 104
- Cafetería La Jirafa Roja, Avenida 3 (between Paseo 102 and Paseo 104)
- Cafetería Mini Golf, Avenida 3 (between Paseo 133 and Paseo 135)
- Cafetería Mono Cafetero, Paseo 105 (between Avenida 3 and Avenida 3 bis)
- Cafetería Nostalgias, Avenida 3 (between Paseo 105 and Paseo 106)
- Cafetería Quo Vadis, Paseo 105 (between Avenida 2 and Avenida 3)
- Cafetería Saint George, Paseo 104 (between Avenida 3 and Avenida 2)
- Cafetería Sagitario, corner of Avenida 3 and Paseo 140
- Cafetería Snoopy, corner of Avenida 3 and Paseo 105
- Cafetería Tía Vicenta, corner of Avenida 3 and Paseo 109
- Cafetería Tío Isidoro, corner of Avenida Buenos Aires and Avenida 4
- Cafetería Torino, corner of Avenida 3 and Paseo 104
- Cafetería Traca Traca, Avenida 3 (between Paseo 108 and Paseo 109)

Post and telegraph

- Post office: Encotel, Avenida 3 (between Paseo 105 and Paseo 106)
- Telephone: Cooperativa Telefonica, corner of Avenida 3 and Paseo 113

Financial

- Banco de la Provincia de Buenos Aires, Avenida (between Paseo 107 and Paseo 108). Cash advances on Visa card

Villa Gesell

BUENOS AIRES PROVINCE

🏠 Services and facilities
- Laundromat: Laverap, corner of Paseo 105 and Avenida 3

Ⓒ Clubs
- Chess: Circulo de Ajedrez, Avenida 3 (between Paseo 110 and Paseo 110 bis)

✈ Air services
- Aerolineas Argentinas, corner of Avenida Buenos Aires and Avenida 10 ℂ 68331. Several flights daily to Buenos Aires

🚌 Buses
The bus terminal is on the corner of Avenida 3 and Paseo 140.
- Buenos Aires: 26 services daily; 7 hours; Empresa Antón, Empresa Río de la Plata
- Mar del Plata: Fare $2.80; 8 services daily; 2 hours; Empresa Costamar
- Mar del Tuyú: Departs daily; 2½ hours; Empresa Costamar
- Pinamar: 8 services daily; ½ hour; Empresa Costamar

🚗 Motoring
- Service station: ACA, Avenida 3 (between Paseo 112 and Paseo 113)

⊕ Tours
- Costamar, Avenida 4 (between Paseo 104 and Paseo 105) ℂ 62340
- Tamar-tours, shop 11, Galería Taxco, ℂ 68489

⚽ Sport
- Golf: Villa Gesell Golf Club, Paseo del Golf ℂ 68249. Also tennis courts

Riding schools and horse hire
- Tante Puppi, corner of Boulevard and Avenida Buenos Aires
- Yoni, corner of Alameda 210 and Avenida Buenos Aires

Tennis
- Tennis Norte, corner of Alameda 205 and Calle 310 ℂ 68168
- Tennis Caravan, corner of Avenida Circunvalación and Paseo 101 ℂ 69259
- Tennis Carretas, Avenida 1 (between Paseo 109 and Paseo 110) ℂ 62526

🎭 Entertainment
- Disco Cariño, Avenida 2 (between Paseo 102 and Paseo 103)
- Disco Kopay, Avenida Buenos (between Avenida 8 and Avenida 10)
- Disco Palodu, corner of Paseo 103 bis and Avenida 1
- Disco Sabash, Paseo 103 (between Avenida 1 and Costanera)
- Disco Vraie, corner of Avenida 3 and Paseo 106
- Disco Whim, corner of Avenida 3 and Paseo 104

⚑ Excursions
- **Mar Chiquita** and **Pinamar**: Both are within easy reach of Villa Gesell by frequent buses

ZÁRATE

Postal code: 2800 • ℂ area code: (0328) • Population: 50,000
Distance from Buenos Aires: 89 km northwest on RN 9

Zárate is an important road and rail junction, and a highly industrialized city. It has refrigeration plants and paper factories, and the atomic energy center of Atucha is nearby. The Brazo Largo bridge over the **Río Paraná** is a major engineering feat and connects Buenos Aires province with Entre Ríos province. Buses and trains run frequently between Zárate and Buenos Aires.

ℹ Tourist information
- Palacio Municipal ℂ 2429

BUENOS AIRES PROVINCE

🛏 Accommodation in Zárate

★	Hotel Palace, 19 de Marzo 333	(4228	$13.50	♕
★	Hotel San Martín, Ameghino 773 ▣ ACA discount	(2713	$13.50	♕
★	Hotel Welcome, J Lima de Atucha 337 ▣ ACA discount	(2622, 4313	$13.50	♕
A	Hospedaje Doña María, General Paz 1575		$11.50	♕
A	Hospedaje Panambi, Ituzaingo 562	(2084	$11.50	♕
A	Hospedaje Real, corner of Mitre and Alem	(2590	$11.50	♕

🛒 Services and facilities

- Lavandería Laverap, Ituzaingó 677

🚌 Buses

- Buenos Aires: Fare $2.00; 6 services daily; 1 hour; Empresa Micro Mar
- Rosario: Fare $5.00; 6 services daily; 3 hours; Empresa Micro Mar

🚗 Motoring

The bridge toll over the Brazo Largo complex is $5.00.

🚆 Trains

Both F C General B Mitre and F C General Urquiza run fast trains from Zárate to Buenos Aire and Rosario–Santa Fé.

Zárate

CÓRDOBA PROVINCE

Plate 7 Map of Córdoba Province
- 143 Achiras
- 143 Agua de Oro
- 144 Almafuerte
- 144 Alpa Corral
- 144 Alta Gracia
- 146   Map
- 149 Arias
- 150 Arroyito
- 150 Ascochinga
- 150 Ballesteros
- 151 Bell Ville
- 151 Berrotarán
- 151 Bialet Massé
- 151 Canals
- 152 Candonga
- 152 Capilla del Monte
- 153 Cerro Colorado
- 154 Colonia Caroya
- 154 Córdoba
- 156   Map
- 166 Cosquín
- 169 Cruz Chica
- 169 Cruz del Eje
- 170 Déan Funes
- 171 Embalse

Córdoba Province

140

CÓRDOBA PROVINCE

- **172** General Cabrera
- **172** General Deheza
- **173** General Levalle
- **173** Huinca Renancó
- **173** Jesús María
- **174** La Calera
- **174** La Carlota
- **174** La Cruz
- **175** La Cumbre
- **176** Map
- **178** La Cumbrecita
- **178** La Falda
- **180** Map
- **185** La Granja
- **186** La Población
- **186** Laboulaye
- **186** Las Rabonas
- **186** Leones
- **186** Los Cocos
- **187** Los Hornillos
- **187** Marcos Juárez
- **187** Mina Clavero
- **189** Map
- **194** Miramar
- **194** Nono
- **195** Oliva
- **195** Oncativo
- **195** Pilar
- **197** Río Ceballos
- **197** Río Cuarto
- **198** Río Tercero
- **199** Salsipuedes
- **199** Sampacho
- **199** San Antonio de Arredondo
- **200** San Clemente
- **200** San Francisco
- **201** San José de la Dormida

Córdoba Province

CÓRDOBA PROVINCE

- 201 San Marcos Sierra
- 201 Santa Rosa de Calamuchita
- 202   Map
- 204 Taninga
- 204 Tanti
- 205 Unquillo
- 206 Vicuña Mackenna
- 206 Villa Allende
- 206 Villa Carlos Paz
- 208   Map
- 225 Villa Ciudad de América
- 225 Villa Cura Brochero
- 225 Villa de María de Río Seco
- 226 Villa de Soto
- 226 Villa del Dique
- 226 Villa Dolores
- 227   Map
- 229 Villa General Belgrano
- 230   Map
- 233 Villa General Mitre
- 233 Villa María
- 234 Villa Rumipal
- 235 Villa Tulumba
- 235 Yacanto de Calamuchita

Córdoba province is the geographical center of Argentina. It has an excellent road system and a range of good and popular tourist centers. Some of the biggest tourist resorts are centered around the many dams in the **Sierras de Córdoba**. Water sports and fishing in the rivers and artificial lakes are popular pastimes of the *Cordobanos*.

The eastern part of Córdoba is flat *pampa*. It is one of the richest agricultural areas of Argentina, partly because of the plentiful water supply, and is swiftly becoming the center of heavy industry in Argentina because of the ready availability of electricity from hydroelectric sta-

CÓRDOBA PROVINCE

tions such as San Roque, Cruz del Eje, Río Tercero, Los Alazanes and San Jeronimo. Many of the rivers flowing out of the *sierras* are dammed several times along their course to provide for irrigation and electricity generation. Exploitation of mineral deposits is limited to the extraction of minerals such as marmor and manganese.

The western mountainous part of Córdoba, the **Sierras de Córdoba**, contains the major tourist attractions. This is hiking country, particularly around **Cerro Champaqui**, at 2790 m the highest peak in the province, which is easily accessible from **Villa Dolores**. The *sierras* run for about 500 km north–south and are approximately 170 km wide. The three main ranges comprising the Sierras de Córdoba are the **Sierra Grande** in the center and the **Sierra Chica** with the *punilla* valley between them, and the **Sierra de Pocho** in the west. The higher peaks are snow-covered for part of the year. Some of the larger tourist towns are in the *punilla*, such as **Villa Carlos Paz** on **Lago San Roque**, **La Falda**, **Cosquín**, and **La Cumbre**. The climate in the *sierras* is sunny and dry throughout the year, and popular vacation pastimes include riding, walking, tennis, and golf, as well as swimming, fishing, and sailing in the numerous dams. Information can be obtained at the Dirección Provincial de Turismo in Córdoba.

Córdoba, the capital of the province, is 771 km northwest of the federal capital Buenos Aires.

ACA has excellent maps of the province and of the Sierras de Córdoba.

ACHIRAS

Postal code: 5833 • Altitude: 845 m
Distance from Río Cuarto: 70 km westwards on RP 1

Achiras is located in the southeastern part of the **Sierra de Comechingones**. Hiking in the nearby mountains is popular.

Accommodation
- Hospedaje Poffo, Cabrera 386. No single bedrooms
- Hospedaje Victoria, 24 de Setiembre 530
- Residencial Hostal de las Sierras, 24 de Setiembre 358

Buses
Buses run regularly to Río Cuarto.

AGUA DE ORO

Postal code: 5107 • Altitude: 605 m
Distance from to Córdoba: 46 km northwards

Agua de Oro is a small village located on the eastern slopes of the **Sierra Chica**.

Accommodation
★★ Hotel Estancia Agua de Oro, RP 53 (236 $18.00. Breakfast $2.50; open December–March

CÓRDOBA PROVINCE

Hospedaje San Leonardo ☎ 229 $10.00. Breakfast $1.50

ALMAFUERTE

Postal code: 5854 • area code: (0571) • Altitude: 432 m
Distance from Córdoba: 100 km southwards on RN 36

Almafuerte is located on the artificial lake **Piedras Moras**, 18 km from Río Tercero. The dam is 57 m high and 530 m long, and has a surface area of 830 ha. The water is used to irrigate an area of 60 000 ha. Forty-six million kilowatt/hours of electricity are generated each year.

Accommodation
- ★ Hotel Pettit, corner of Castelli and Salta ☎ 91343 $7.00. No single bedrooms
- ★ Hotel Siena, Pedro C Molina 473 ☎ 91336
- Hospedaje Lombard, Pedro C Molina
- Residencial Almafuerte, 25 de Mayo (corner of Pedro C Molina) $7.00
- Residencial San Carlos, Salvador Escabuzo 183

Buses
- Córdoba: departs 0635; 2 services daily; 2 hours; Empresa TOA

Sport
- Fishing and sailing

ALPA CORRAL

Postal code: 5801 • Altitude: 750 m
Distance from Río Cuarto: 70 km northwest on RN 36 then RP 11

Located in the foothills of the **Sierra de Comechingones**, Alpa Corral is a popular hiking area.

Accommodation
Hospedaje Don Alberto, Gobernador J Borda. No single bedrooms
Residencial El Puente. No single bedrooms

Buses
Buses run regularly to Río Cuarto.

ALTA GRACIA

Postal code: 5186 • Population: 27 000 • area code: (0547) • Altitude: 600 m
Distance from Córdoba: 38 km southwest on RP 5

Alta Gracia is situated in a wide valley east of the Sierra Chica where the valleys of the **Río Punillas** and the **Río Calamuchita** join. The town consists of two parts: the area west of Laguna Tajamar, containing the bus terminal, golf course, and a few hotels; and the center, where there are a Jesuit church, a casino, and hotels.

At the time of the Spanish invasion Alta Gracia was inhabited by the Comechingones who called the region "Paravachasca". The Inca empire had already begun expanding into this region when the European invasion cut it short. Owing to their small physique the Comechingones were no match for the invading Spaniards and soon succumbed.

Agua de Oro

CÓRDOBA PROVINCE

The town was founded in 1588 and was taken over by the Jesuits in 1643. The Jesuits left behind some remarkable buildings with walls over one metre thick.

Festivals
- Fiesta Nuestra Señora de la Merced (Festival of Our Lady of Mercy, the city's patron saint): 24 September
- Festival Manuel de Falla: November

Tourist information
- Tourist office inside clock tower by Laguna Trajamar (21455
- Tourist office at El Crucero, at the corner of RP 5 and San Martín

Camping
- Municipal, Barrio C Pellegrini, on the road to Rinconada

Camping in La Serranita
- El Caracol, RN 5
- El Diquecito, RN 5

Accommodation in Alta Gracia

★	Hotel Covadonga, Quintana 265	(21456	$6.00	
★	Hotel Liguria, Pellegrini 797 No single bedrooms	(21766		
★	Hotel Ritz, Avenida Belgrano 302	(21965		
★	Hotel Gran Savoy, Sarmiento 418 No single bedrooms	(21314	$11.00	
★	Hostería Alta Gracia, Avellaneda, 353 No single bedrooms	(21223	$11.00	
★	Hostería Colonial, Avellaneda 346	(21314		
★	Hostería Oberá, Vélez Sarsfield 55 Open December–March; no single bedrooms	(21475		
•	Hospedaje Asturias, Vélez Sarsfield 127 No single bedrooms	(21068, 23368	$6.00	
•	Hospedaje Buenos Aires, Giorello 269	(21832	$5.00	
•	Hospedaje Del Sol, RP 36 Km 800 No single bedrooms	(21643		
•	Hospedaje Fernandez, Franchini 138 No single bedrooms			
•	Hospedaje San Jorge, Belisario Roldan 68 No single bedrooms			
•	Residencial Flor de Lis, Avellaneda 306	(21111	$5.00	
•	Residencial Irma, Cochabamba 46 No single bedrooms	(21725	$5.00	
•	Residencial Reyna, Urquiza 139 No single bedrooms	(21724		

Accommodation outside Alta Gracia
- ★ Hotel Río Sierra, Villa los Aromos, 11 km south of town
  No single bedrooms
- • Hotel Rincón Serrano, La Paisanita, 10 km south of town
  Open December–March; no single bedrooms
- • Hostería Castro, La Serranita
- • Hospedaje La Serranita, La Serranita, 16 km south of town
  Open December–March; no single bedrooms
- • Residencial La Portena, La Serranita, 16 km south of town
  Open December–April; no single bedrooms

Alta Gracia

CÓRDOBA PROVINCE

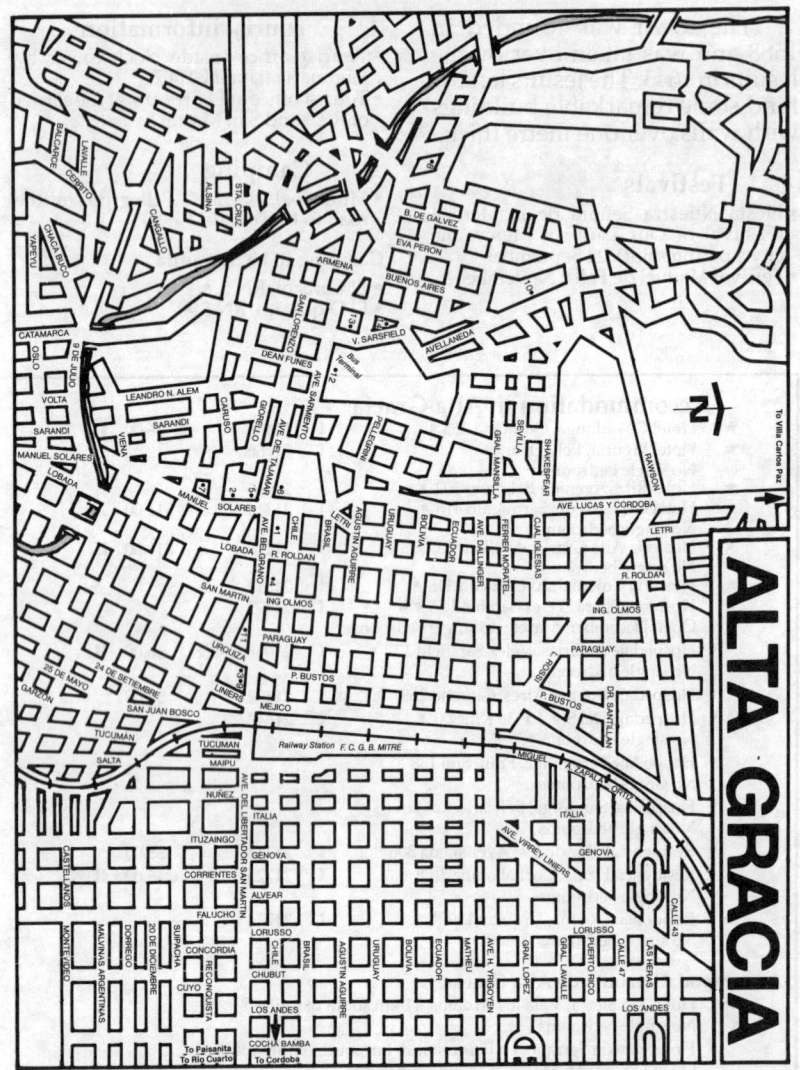

🍴 Eating out

- Restaurant AeroClub, Ruta C45
- Restaurant Albeñiz, Sarmiento 413. Seafood
- Restaurant Circulo Italiano, España 450
- Restaurant Don Carlos, corner of Sarmiento and Uriburu
- Restaurant El Amigo, corner of Sarmiento and Déan Funes

Alta Gracia

CÓRDOBA PROVINCE

Key to Map
1. Municipalidad
2. Iglesia Nuestra Señora de la Merced
3. Post office (Encotel)
4. Telephones (Entel)
5. Museo Histórico Nacional Casa del Virrey Liniers
6. Tajamar (Tourist information)
7. El Obraje
8. Museo Provincial Manuel de Falla
9. Casino
10. Casa del Che Guevara
11. Hotel Ritz
12. Hotel Gran Savoy
13. Hostería Oberá
14. Hostería Asturias

- Restaurant El Ancla, Paso Martir
- Restaurant El Gran Galetto, Libertador 1045
- Restaurant El Tajamar, Belgrano 163. Steakhouse
- Restaurant La Casona, corner of Avenida Sarmiento and Déan Funes. Steakhouse
- Restaurant La Cuevita, corner of Sarmiento and Vélez Sarsfield
- Restaurant Monte Grande, corner of Avenida Sarmiento and Déan Funes. Steakhouse
- Restaurant Nuevo Horizonte, corner of Avenida Sarmiento and Vélez Sarsfield
- Restaurant Pizza, corner of Avenida Sarmiento and Déan Funes
- Pizzería King, corner of Avenida Tajamar and Parravachasca. Hamburgers
- Cafetería Avenida Belgrano 231. Snacks
- Cafetería Carrasco, Belgrano 480
- Cafetería El Quijote, Belgrano 71. Tearoom
- Cafetería La Cholita, Libertador 783
- Cafetería La Chulita, Liniers 53
- Cafetería La Vienesa, Avenida del Tajamar (opposite Tajamar tower)
- Cafetería L'Orelle, Vélez Sarsfield 171
- Cafetería La Terminal, corner of Vélez Sarsfield and Sarmiento
- Cafetería Los Mineros, Urquiza 26
- Cafetería Lucky, Quintana 295
- Cafetería Manaos, Belgrano 77
- Cafetería Miguelito, España 107
- Cafetería Monte Grande, Sarmiento 449
- Cafetería Myosotis, corner of A Rodriguez and General Paz
- Cafetería New Saloon, Vélez Sarsfield 175
- Cafetería Nuevo Horizonte, Sarmiento 460
- Cafetería Oasis, Belgrano 79
- Cafetería Petit Colón, Belgrano 101. Pizzas
- Cafetería Roma, Belgrano 311
- Cafetería San Remo, Belgrano 131
- Cafetería Satan, Belgrano 83
- Cafetería S'Charus, Libertador 1100
- Cafetería Stuttgart, Belgrano 135
- Cafetería 20 de Junio, corner of L Córdoba and Diagonal Rossi
- Cafetería Wal-Mir, España 18

Eating out at El Crucero

There are sevaeral *cafeterías* and a restaurant at El Crucero.

Post and telegraph

- Post office: Encotel, Urquiza 2 (corner of Belgrano)
- Telephone: Entel, Avenida Belgrano 175

Services and facilities

- Delicatessen: Macaco, corner of Avenida Sarmiento and LN Alem
- Drycleaner: Su Prima Bologna, Vélez Sarsfield
- Supermarket: Becerra, corner of Belgrano and Bustos

Laundromats

- Laverap, corner of Belgrano and Maipú
- Laverap, España 422. Closed Sundays

Motoring

Service stations

- ACA, corner of Lucas V Córdoba and Lucio V Rossi
- Shell, Avenida Sarmiento block 200 (corner of Presidente Arturo Illia)
- YPF, El Crucero, corner of RP 5 and San Martín. Mechanic available

Alta Gracia

CÓRDOBA PROVINCE

🚌 Buses from Alta Gracia

The bus terminal is on the corner of Sarmiento and Vélez Sarsfield. Some buses do not enter the town, but stop at El Crucero; passengers then take a local bus the extra 3 km into town.

Destination	Fare	Depart	Services	Hours	Company
• Córdoba	$0.70	0640	15 services daily	1	ABLO, Satag, TOA
• Buenos Aires	$15.00	1840	3 services daily	12	ABLO, Chevallier, Urquiza
• La Paisanita		1130	Mon–Fri	1½	Satag
• La Serranita		0555	21 services daily	1	La Serranita, Satag
• Santa Rosa		0645	12 services daily	1½–2	S. de Calamuchita, TOA
• Villa Carlos Paz	$0.80	0800	4 services daily	1	COTAP
• Villa Ciudad de América		0645	12 services daily	½–1	Sierras de Caamuchital, TOA
• Villa General Belgrano	$1.50	0640	12 services daily	1–1½	Sierras de Calamuchita
• Villa Rumipal		0945	4 services daily	2½	TOA

🛍 Shopping
- Regionales El Gaucho, corner of Avenida Sarmiento and Déan Funes

🏌 Sport
- Golf: There is a nine-hole golf course in the center of town
- Aviation: Aero Club, RP C45 (road to Río Segundo past El Crucero)
- Walks: Alta Gracia is a good base for walks into the mountains

🍷 Entertainment
- Bingo, corner of Avenida Belgrano and Roldan
- New Casino, corner of Avenida Belgrano and Urquiza
- Disco Krajo's, corner of Pellegrini and Centenario
- Disco Krakatoa, Belgrano 145
- Disco Rose Marie, Belgrano 55
- Disco Sabotage, in the golf club in the center of town

📷 Sightseeing
- Iglesia Nuestra Señora de la Merced parish church is a mixture of Renaissance, baroque, and rococo styles. It took over a hundred years to build and was finally completed in 1762. Its roofs were impregnated with a substance which made them waterproof; the composition of that substance is unknown to this day
- El Obraje was a sort of school where Indians were taught weaving, agriculture, and the rudiments of Christianity under the Jesuits
- El Tajamar, La Huerta, and mill. The waters of the **Arroyo de los Paredones** were brought via underground conduits to the Tajamar weir and distributed to the fields near what is now called Lepri. This extensive project was completed by the Jesuits in 1659. The ruins of the flour mill can still be seen. Nowadays El Tajamar is part of a public park
- Los Paredones ("The Walls") were built by the Jesuits as part of the original channel project to conduct water to El Tajamar. One portion can still be seen 4 km from the city center

Alta Gracia

CÓRDOBA PROVINCE

- Museo Histórico Nacional Casa del Virrey Liniers (National Historical Museum Home of Viceroy Liniers) was the entrance to the convent, built between 1659 and 1735, and was converted into a museum in 1968. It is in colonial baroque style and has many rooms containing contemporary furniture. It was the home for a short while of viceroy Santiago de Liniers. Open Tue–Sun 0900–1200 and 1500–1800
- Museo Provincial Manuel de Falla (Manuel de Falla Provincial Museum), on Pellegrini (opposite the golf course), home of the famous composer. Open Tue–Fri 0900–1900
- Casa del Che Guevara (House of Che Guevara), Avellaneda. Home of the former revolutionary who died in Bolivia, fomenting a rebellion

Excursions

- **Embalse Los Molinos**: 35 km. Take RP 5 south, passing through **Villa Los Aromos**, **Villa Anizacate**, Villa La Serrania and **Villa Ciudad de América**. Five km west of Villa Ciudad de América at **Potrero de Garay** are archeological remains of the pre-Colombian population. On the lake itself you can enjoy aquatic sports. This spot is served by public transport
- **La Paisanita** and **La Serranita** are quiet little country villages with accommodation, 10–15 km south of Alta Gracia
- **Bosque Alegre** and observatory: Located in the **Sierra Chica** 24 km north of Alta Gracia. There are good views over Córdoba, Alta Gracia, and the Sierra Grande, extending as far east as the city of Córdoba. There is a satellite communications center at Bosque Alegre and a small archeological site nearby. Open Thurs 1600–1800 and Sun 1000–1200 and 1600–1800
- **San Clemente**: Located 50 km west of Alta Gracia at the gateway to the **Quebrada del Condorito** which opens into the **Cumbres de Achala** towards **Cerro Lindero**, at 2200 m the highest peak of this mountain range. This area has a wild scenic beauty. Proposals have been made to create a national park to preserve the flora and fauna of the area, including the few condors still living here. A mountain walk is possible starting on RN 20 8 km west of **El Cóndor**, following the headwaters of the **Río Condorito** and finishing at San Clemente. See San Clemente on page 200.

ARIAS

Postal code: 2624 • area code: (0462)
Distance from Córdoba (via Río Cuarto): 347 km south-west on RN 9 then RN 4 and RN 8

Arias is located in the south-eastern part of the province, 2 km off the main highway to Río Cuarto. This is flat *pampa*.

Accommodation
- Hospedaje Arias, Avenida Rivadavia 1122 (161 $11.00
- Hospedaje Mayo, San Martín 1022 $7.00
- Hospedaje Santa Teresa, Italia 1031 (122

Buses
Buses run regularly to Río Cuarto.

ARROYITO

Postal code: 2434 • (area code: (0576)
Distance from Córdoba: 114 km eastwards on RN 19

Arroyito is a small farming community in the eastern part of the province.

Accommodation
- ★★ Hostal del Arroyito, RN 19 Km 220 (130
- ★ Hotel Ona, corner of Boedo and Batalla $11.00. No single bedrooms

Buses
Buses run regularly to Córdoba.

ASCOCHINGA

Postal code: 5117 • Altitude: 734 m
Distance from Córdoba: 68 km north on RN 9 (via Jesús María)

The little township of Ascochinga is located in the eastern foothills of the **Sierras de Córdoba**. The road leading up to **La Cumbre** is very scenic. Ascochinga was founded in the middle of the seventeenth century, possibly as an offshoot of the Jesuit mission establishment in Jesús María, Santa Catalina convent, established in 1622.

Accommodation
There is a basic hotel.

Eating out
There are some restaurants.

Buses
Buses run the two-hour trip to Córdoba regularly.

Motoring
- Service staton: ACA, RN 156

Excursions
- Santa Catalina at **Jesús María**: 13 km north. The remains of the most important and largest Jesuit mission convent in the province of Córdoba. The church was begun in 1754 and the Jesuits were expelled in 1763. It was the home of the Jesuit historians Padre Lozano and Guevara. See Jesús María on page 173

BALLESTEROS

Distance from Córdoba: 168 km southeast on RN 9

Accommodation
- Residencial Titi, corner of Argentino and Belgrano $9.00. Breakfast $1.50

Arias

CÓRDOBA PROVINCE

BELL VILLE

Postal code: 2550 • (area code: (0534) •
Altitude: 132 m
Distance from Córdoba: 201 km southeast on RN 9

Bell Ville is an agricultural center of some importance. It is located in the *pampa*.

Accommodation
- ★★★ Hotel Bell Ville, José Pio Angulo 531 (24076 $19.00
- ★★ Hotel Central, José Pio Angulo 532 (24071 $12.00
- ★ Hotel Italia, corner of José Pio Angulo and Belgrano (24066 $16.00
- Hospedaje Santa Lucía, RN 9 Km 501 (24883. No single bedrooms

Buses
Buses run regularly to Córdoba and Buenos Aires.

BERROTARÁN

Postal code: 5817 • (area code: (0586) •
Altitude: 690 m
Distance from Río Cuarto: 79 km northwards on RN 36

Accommodation
- ★ Hotel Co-Ra-Se, corner of H Irigoyen and San Martín $11.00

BIALET MASSÉ

Postal code: 5158 • (area code: (0541) •
Altitude: 653 m
Distance from Córdoba: 44 km northwest on RN 38

Bialet Massé is located at the northern end of **Lago San Roque** in the **Río Punillas valley**. It is one of the quieter towns in the Punillas valley but is still within easy reach of all the tourist areas.

Accommodation
- ★ Hotel Elba, RN 38 Km 755 $10.00. Breakfast $2.00
- Hospedaje Bialet Massé, corner of R Indarte and Deheza $10.00. No single bedrooms
- Hospedaje Mi Herencia, Independencia 701. Open January–March; triples only

Buses
Buses run regularly to Villa Carlos Paz, Córdoba, and La Falda.

CANALS

Postal code: 2650 • (area code: (0463)
Distance from Córdoba (via Villa María): 272 km south-east on RN 9 then RN 4 and RN 8

Canals is located 4 km south of the main highway (RN 8) in flat *pampa*. It is a useful stopping off point.

Accommodation
- ★ Hotel Córdoba, 25 de Mayo 226 (165 $7.00
- Hospedaje San José, Sarmiento 332

Buses
Buses run regularly to Río Cuarto and Córdoba.

CÓRDOBA PROVINCE

CANDONGA

Postal code: 5111 • Altitude: 810 m
Distance from Córdoba: 55 km northwards on RP 55

Candonga is located on the eastern side of the **Sierra Chica**, about two hours' drive from Córdoba. The main attraction is the Jesuit chapel (now a national monument) which was built in 1730 to serve the Estancia Santa Gertrudis. Its style shows the influence of native artists. The winding and picturesque road continues up to La Falda.

Accommodation
- Residencial Candonga, Candonga

CAPILLA DEL MONTE

Postal code: 5184 • Population: 7200 • area code: (0548) • Altitude: 979 m
Distance from Córdoba: 106 km northwest on RN 38

This tourist resort is in the **Sierra Chica**. There are walks in the nearby mountains, one of which—**Cerro Uritorco** at 1950 m—dominates the little town.

There are medicinal waters, waterfalls and wide views. Despite its graffiti, **El Zapato rock** is particularly worth a visit.

Capilla del Monte's unusual microclimate is caused by a higher than usual negative ion

Accommodation in Capilla del Monte

★★ Hotel Roma, Corrientes 387	81083	$17.00	
Breakfast $2.00			
★ Hotel Plaza, Sarmiento 455	81028	$11.00	
Breakfast $1.00			
★ Hostería San Antonio, Ruta 38	81158	$11.00	
Breakfast $1.00			
★ Hostería Las Palmas, H Yrigoyen 187		$8.00	
Breakfast $1.00			
★ Hostería Lucy, San Luis 481	81268	$8.00	
Breakfast $1.00			
★ Hostería María Antonieta	81514	$8.00	
No single bedrooms			
• Hostería Suárez, San Luis 452		$8.00	
Open January–March; no single bedrooms			
• Hospedaje, Adrianita, Chubut 168			
Open December–March; no single bedrooms			
• Hospedaje Galicia, Salta	81366		
Open December–March; no single bedrooms			
• Hospedaje La Rosario, Dean Funes 487			
• Hospedaje Nuñez, Yrigoyen 355			
No single bedrooms			
• Residencial Fernandez, Pueyrredón 787	81331		
• Residencial Villa Teresita, Sarmiento 178			
No single bedrooms			
• Residencial Italiana, Rivadavia 539			
Open January–March; no single bedrooms			

Candonga

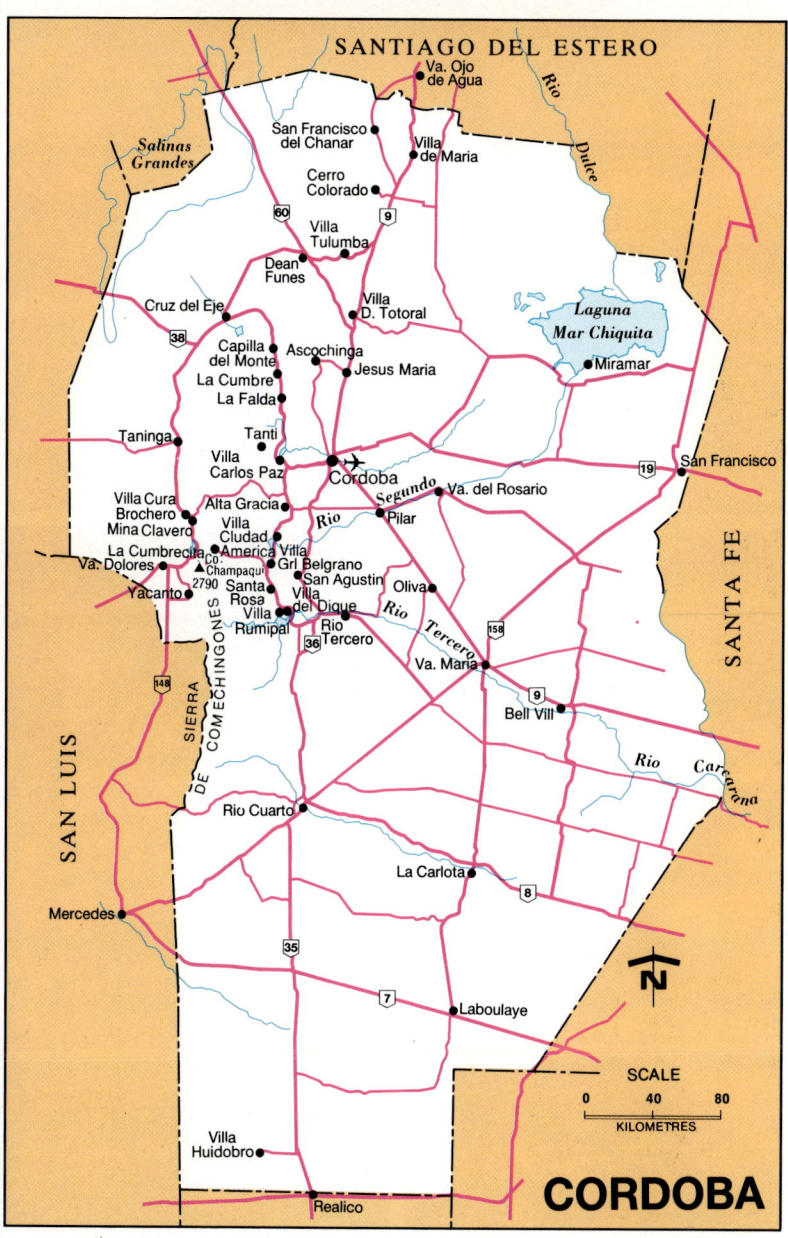

Plate 7
Map of Córdoba Province

Plate 8

Top: Valle de Calingasta, near Barreal, with the *cordillera* in the background
Bottom left: Río Paraná Delta
Bottom right: Carmen de Patagonés, across the Río Negro

CÓRDOBA PROVINCE

🚌 Buses from Capilla del Monte

Central bus terminal.
ABLO runs two buses daily to Rosario and Buenos Aires.

Destination	Fare	Depart	Services	Hours	Company
• Córdoba		0450	29 services daily	3	La Capillense, Primero de Mayo
• Cosquín		0450	29 services daily	1	La Capillense, Primero de Mayo
• Cruz del Eje	$1.20	1005	8 services daily	1	Primero de Mayo
• La Cumbre		0450	29 services daily	½	La Capillense, Primero de Mayo
• La Falda		0450	21 services daily	1	La Capillense, Primero de Mayo
• Villa Carlos Paz		0645	8 services daily	2	Primero de Mayo

content in the atmosphere, making the air very stimulating, a phenomenon also found in Merlo in San Luis province.

🅰 Camping

- Municipal Calabaluma, on the banks of the Río Calabaluma

🍴 Eating out

- Cafetería Terminal

📮 Post and telegraph

- Post office: Encotel, Corrientes 158
- Telephone: In the town hall

🚗 Motoring

RN 38 rises towards La Cumbre, reaching its highest point at La Cumbre (1142 m). The road narrows at Valle de la Punilla.
- Service station: ACA, B Mitre 1076

🛍 Shopping

Try the honey made from carob blossom, about $2.00 for 1 kg.

🌳 Excursions

- **Cerro Uritorco**: The summit can be reached by a winding path in 2½ hours. There are good views over much of the **Punilla** and the **Sierras de Córdoba**. Permission to walk must be obtained from a house beyond the river crossing. Fee $0.60
- **Los Alazanes**: It is a leisurely 3 hour walk over 11 km to this artificial lake where you can fish for *pejerrey*. There is a walking path to **Los Cocos** along the crest of the **Sierra Chica**
- **Tío Mayo**: Excellent trout fishing, one hour's drive from Capilla del Monte
- **San Marcos Sierra**: You can walk here on the 22 km direct dirt road. Parakeets abound here. There are many small farmhouses, and you will also see pretty views to the **Dique Cruz del Eje**

CERRO COLORADO

Postal code: 5205 • Altitude: 700 m
Distance from Córdoba: 160 km northwards on RN 9

CÓRDOBA PROVINCE

Cerro Colorado has the most accessible rock paintings in the area; here there are more than 30 000 rock paintings of the Comechingones Indians and earlier tribes. The small museum organized by the caretaker contains rock and mineral samples of the area, spearheads, fossilized wood, and semi-precious stones found in the mountains. The caretaker also acts as a tourist guide (fee $1.00).

In order to get to the hill containing the rock paintings after which the town is named you must ford a river—or if it is swollen you cross over a hanging bridge. Many tourist buses visit, especially on weekends.

Cerro Colorado is 10 km west of RN 9. The turnoff is at Santa Elena.

Accommodation

Cheap accommodation and camping are available in the Parque Arqueologico Cerro Colorado.

Eating out

Food is available in the local *comedors* and shops.

Buses

As far as I could ascertain there is only one bus service per week to and from Córdoba. The 10 km walk from **Santa Elena** (to which buses run frequently along RN 9) can be done in two hours, but at one stage you have to wade through a knee-deep fast-flowing river, depending on the season. The site may be best visited using a tour operator.

COLONIA CAROYA

Postal code: 5223 • area code: (0525) • Altitude: 530 m
Distance from Córdoba: 44 km northwards on RN 9

Located in the foothills of the **Sierra Chica**, Colonia Caroya was colonized by Friulanos from northern Italy from 1878 onwards.

Festivals
- Fiesta Provincial de la Vendimia (Provincial Grape Harvest Festival): Second week in March

Accommodation
- Hospedaje del Valle, San Martín 3092 $11.00

Buses
- Jesús María: departs 0040; 17 services daily; ½ hour; Empresa Cadol

CÓRDOBA

Postal code: 5000 • Population: 1 million • area code: (051) • Altitude: 440 m
Distance from Buenos Aires: 713 km northwest on RN 9

Córdoba is the capital of the province and the second largest city in Argentina. It was founded in 1573 by Jeronimo Luis de Cabrera, and its university which dates from 1613 was one of the first in the country.

Córdoba has retained a remarkable number of buildings from its Spanish past despite the fact that it is now a modern in-

CÓRDOBA PROVINCE

dustrial city—it is the hub of the Argentine car manufacturing industry—and an important commercial center. The center around Plaza San Martín may be described as a jewel of colonial art. The inner-city pedestrian malls are full of shops and restaurants, and the nightlife is quite dazzling. Culture is very important in Córdoba—there are plenty of theaters and museums.

Córdoba is situated on the **Río Primero**. To the west and south the **Sierras de Córdoba** rise to a height of over 2500 m, while to the east there is the seemingly endless flat *pampa*.

Festivals
- Foundation of the City: July 6
- San Gerónimo (St Jerome): September 30

Tourist information
- Dirección de Turismo Provincial, Tucuman 25 ℂ 33061
- Information center, Plaza San Martín
- Information center, Rosario de Santa Fé 39
- Tourist information on ground floor in bus terminal, open daily 0800–2000
- Club Andino. For information ring the Tarditis family ℂ 800693

Camping
- Municipal, Complejo Ferial Córdoba

Eating out
- Restaurant Cantina Buono, Obispo Trejo 169
- Restaurant Chino, San Gerónimo block 600 (corner of Avenida Presidente J D Perón). Chinese cuisine
- Restaurant Chino Oriente, San Gerónimo 351. Chinese cuisine
- Restaurant Circulo Italiano de Córdoba, Belgrano 137
- Restaurant Don Julio, 25 de Mayo block 200 (corner of Maipú). Steakhouse
- Restaurant Don Siriaco, Bulevar Illia 533. Steakhouse
- Restaurant El Buen Vientre, Vélez Sarsfield block 300 (corner of Bulevar San Juan). Steakhouse
- Restaurant El Meson, Rioja 390
- Restaurant Emir, Bulevar Illia 71
- Restaurant Galerías del Teatro, Vélez Sarsfield 370
- Restaurant Hermitage, Avenida General Paz block 100 (corner of 9 de Julio). Also theater
- Restaurant Il Gatto, Avenida General Paz block 100 (corner of 9 de Julio). Italian cuisine
- Restaurant La Casona del Tio, Bulevar Illia block 600 (corner of Allende). Steakhouse
- Restaurant Lago di Garda, Lima block 200 (corner of Maipu). Italian cuisine
- Restaurant La Mamma, Avenida Figueroa Alcorta 270. Italian cuisine; credit cards accepted
- Restaurant La Parrilla, Avenida Olmos 146. Steakhouse
- Restaurant La Perla, Bulevar San Juan 172
- Restaurant La Perla II, San Gerónimo block 100 (corner of Buenos Aires)
- Restaurant La Rueda, Olmos 371. Steakhouse
- Restaurant Las Hortalezas, Avenida General Paz 682. International cuisine
- Restaurant Los Australes, Avenida Olmos block 200 (corner of Alvear)
- Restaurant Los Troncos, Bulevar Illia block 300 (corner of Chacabuco). Steakhouse
- Restaurant Odeon Bar, Bulevar San Juan 126
- Restaurant Romagnolo, Avenida Presidente J D Perón block 100 (corner of San Jerónimo; opposite F C General B Mitre station)
- Restaurant Salon Rojo, Hotel Gran Dora, Entre Ríos 70
- Restaurant Vegetariano, corner of San Martín and 9 de Julio (upstairs)
- Restaurant Viejo Argamonte, Caseros 71
- Pizzería 100, Bulevar San Juan block 200 (corner of Obispo Trejo)
- Pizzería El Correo, Avenida General Paz block 200 (corner of Avenida Colón)

CÓRDOBA PROVINCE

CORDOBA

CÓRDOBA PROVINCE

- Pizzería Italiana, San Gerónimo block 600
- Pizzería La Candela, Entre Ríos block 600 (corner of Perón)
- Pizzería La Carreta, San Gerónimo block 400 (corner of Salguero)
- Pizzería Las Marías, Avenida General Paz 276
- Pizzería San Luis, Avenida General Paz block 300 (corner of La Rioja
- Pizzería Sorocabana, San Gerónimo block 0 (corner of Buenos Aires)
- Pizzería Vallier, General Paz block 400 (corner of La Rioja)
- Cafetería Bangoi, Sucrey block 400 (corner of La Rioja)
- Cafetería Blenders, Caseros block 300 (corner of Belgrano)
- Cafetería Café del Teatro, Vélez Sarsfield block 300 (corner of Bulevar San Juan)
- Cafetería Castelar, Vélez Sarsfield 78
- Cafetería Champagne, Sucre block 100 (corner of 9 de Julio)
- Cafetería Gallery, Avenida General Paz block 100 (corner of 9 de Julio)
- Cafetería Gente Bar, Jujuy block 200 (corner of Avenida Colon)
- Cafetería Juventud, Obispo Trejo block 200 (corner of Caseros)
- Cafetería Lancelot, Vélez Sarsfield block 0 (corner of Déan Funes)
- Cafetería La Tasca del Paseo, Obispo Trejo block 0 (corner of Déan Funes)
- Cafetería L'Expresso Cafe, San Gerónimo block 100 (corner of Buenos Aires)
- Cafetería Reggiao, General Paz block 300 (corner of Santa Rosa)
- Cafetería San Marino, Belgrano block 0 (corner of Déan Funes)

Continued on page 160

Key to map

1	Municipalidad
2	Catedral
3	Cabildo
4	Post office (Encotel)
5	Telephone (Entel)
6	Tourist information
7	Aerolineas Argentinas
8	Austral Lineas Aereas
9	Iglesia de San Francisco
10	Iglesia de la Compañía de Jesús
11	Capilla San Roque
12	Iglesia del Pilar
13	Basilica Santo Domingo
14	Iglesia de la Merced
15	Convento de Santa Teresa (Carmelite)
16	Convento de Santa Catalina
17	Casa del Obispo Mercadillo
18	Universidad Mayor de San Carlos
19	Museo Casa del Virrey Sobremonte
20	Coin Viajes y Cambio
21	Cambio Cash
22	Cambio Barujel
23	Museo de Ciencias Naturales B Mitre
24	Hotel Sussex
25	Hotel Gran Dora
26	Hotel Mediterraneo
27	Hotel Nogaro Córdoba
28	Hotel Gran Astoria
29	Hotel Viña de Italia
30	Hotel Waldorf
31	Hotel Argentino
32	Hotel Corona
33	Hotel Dallas
34	Hotel Felipe II
35	Hotel Heydi
36	Hotel Royal
37	Hotel Claridge
38	Hotel Damar
39	Hospedaje Florida
40	Hospedaje Wonder
41	Hotel Soledad
42	Hospedaje Entre Ríos
43	Hospedaje Susy
44	Hospedaje Sportsman
45	Hotel Albeñiz
46	Hotel Continental
47	Hotel Italiano
48	Hotel Castelar
49	Hotel Las Colonias
50	Hotel Junín
51	Hotel Gran Savoy
52	Hotel Valle
53	Hotel Yolanda
54	Hotel Cesar C Carman

Córdoba

CÓRDOBA PROVINCE

Accommodation in Córdoba

There are cheap hotels in the area next to the bus terminal (across the pedestrian bridge) and also in Alto Córdoba (Upper Córdoba) near F C General Belgrano station.

★★★★★	Hotel Sussex, Buenos Aires 59	29071	$35.00	
	No single bedrooms			
★★★★	Hotel Cesar C Carman, Avenida Sabattini 459	34516	$23.00	
	No single bedrooms; breakfast $3.00			
★★★★	Hotel Crillon, Rivadavia 85	46093	$32.00	
★★★★	Hotel Gran Dora, Entre Ríos 70	42030	$25.00	
★★★★	Hotel Mediterraneo, M T de Alvear 10	26025	$30.00	
	No single bedrooms			
★★★★	Hotel Nogaro Córdoba, San Jerónimo 137	24001	$32.00	
	Breakfast included			
★★★★	Hotel Windsor, Buenos Aires 214	24012	$22.00	
★★★	Hotel de la Cañada, M T de Alvear 580, along the Cañada			
	Breakfast included	31227	$27.00	
★★★	Hotel Gran Astoria, Avenida Colón 164	45091	$21.00	
★★★	Hotel Ritz, San Jerónimo 495	45031	$20.00	
★★★	Hotel Viña de Italia, San Jerónimo 611	45663	$17.00	
★★★	Hotel Waldorf, Avenida Olmos 513	28051	$20.00	
★★	Hotel Argentino, Entre Ríos 60	44609	$19.00	
★★	Hotel Corona, San Jerónimo 574 $13.00			
★★	Hotel Dallas, San Jerónimo 339	46091	$17.00	
	No single bedrooms			
★★	Hotel del Sol, Balcarce 144	33961	$12.00	
	Breakfast $1.50			
★★	Hotel Felipe II, San Jerónimo 279	44752	$17.00	
	No single bedrooms			
★★	Hotel Grand Bristol, Pasaje Corrientes 64	36222	$10.00	
★★	Hotel Heydi, Bulevar Illia 615		$15.00	
	Breakfast $1.50			
★★	Hotel Monte Carlo, Avenida Sabattini 1699	50158	$14.00	
	No single bedrooms			
★★	Hotel Plaza, Buenos Aires 85	45035	$18.00	
★★	Hotel Royal, Bulevar Perón 180 (opposite F C General Mitre rail station)			
	Breakfast $2.00	45000	$13.00	
★	Hotel Alex, Bulevar Illia 742	44350	$9.00	
★	Hotel Claridge, 25 de Mayo 218	45741	$10.00	
★	Hotel Damar, Bulevar Illia 518	33180	$10.00	
	No single bedrooms			
★	Hotel Dorrego, Transito Cáceres de Allende 485	21039	$10.00	
	No single bedrooms			
★	Hotel Gran Grisol, Avenida Sabattini 1012	20205	$10.00	
	No single bedrooms			
★	Hotel Los Vascos, H Yrigoyen 220		$11.00	
★	Hotel Paseo del Cesar, Rincón 173	25965	$8.00	
	No single bedrooms			
★	Hotel Riviera, Balcarce 72 (near the bus terminal)	23029	$13.00	
	No single bedrooms			
★	Hospedaje Cuyo, Obispo Trejo 647	38134	$6.00	
	Cheaper with shared bathroom			
★	Hospedaje Florida, Rosario de Santa Fé 459	26373	$6.00	
★	Hospedaje Garden, 25 de Mayo 35		$7.50	

Córdoba

CÓRDOBA PROVINCE

Accommodation in Córdoba—Continued

- ★ Hospedaje Gran Rex, Vélez Sarsfield 601 — $8.00
- ★ Hospedaje La Fragata, Vélez Sarsfield 621 — (30589
- ★ Hospedaje Mallorca, Balcarce 73 — (39234 — $6.50
  Near F C General B Mitre rail station and bus terminal
- Hotel Soledad, San Jerónimo 479
  For budget travelers
- Hospedaje Apolo, San Jerónimo 462
- Hospedaje Argentino, San Jerónimo 628
  For budget travelers
- Hospedaje Berlin, Entre Ríos (near bus terminal)
- Hospedaje Entre Ríos, Entre Ríos block 500 (corner of Balcarce, near bus terminal)
- Hospedaje Gran Terminal, Pasaje Corrientes 64, near bus terminal
- Hospedaje Mar-Del, Bvar Mitre 141 — (39733
- Hospedaje Meridiano, San Jerónimo 532 — (23284
- Hospedaje Palace, Buenos Aires 101
- Hospedaje Sportsman, San Jerónimo 590
  Near bus and railway stations; for budget travelers
- Hospedaje Suiza, Corrientes 559, near bus terminal
- Hosepdaje Susy, Entre Ríos 528
  For budget travelers
- Hospedaje Turin's, Vélez Sarsfield 671 — (33967 — $6.50
  No single bedrooms
- Hospedaje Vazquez, Santiago del Estero 188 — (38268 — $5.00
- Hospedaje Viena, Laprida 235 — $9.00
- Hospedaje Wonder, San Jerónimo 519 — (29322 — $13.50
  No single bedrooms
- Residencial Central, near bus station
- Residencial Mi Valle, Corrientes 586
- Pasajeros, Corrientes 564
- Plaza, Balcarce 336, near bus station
  For budget travelers

Accommodation in Alto Córdoba

Near F C General Belgrano station.

- ★★ Hotel Castelar, Avendida J L de Cabrera 265
  (719822 — $12.50
- Hotel Albeñiz, Avenida J L de Cabrera block 200 (corner of Rivadeo)
- Hotel Continental, Avenida J L de Cabrera block 200 (corner of Rivadeo)
- Hotel Italiano, Avenida J L de Cabrera
- Hotel Gran Savoy, Avenida J L de Cabrera 201
  No single bedrooms — (718050 — $17.00
- Hotel Junín, Avenida J L de Cabrera 163
  For budget travelers
- Hotel Las Colonias, Avenida J L de Cabrera
- Hotel Valle, Avenida J L de Cabrera block 100 (corner of Rivera Indarte)
- Hotel Yolanda, Avenida J L de Cabrera 285

Córdoba

CÓRDOBA PROVINCE

- Cafetería Schneider, Caseros block 0 (corner of Déan Funes)
- Cafetería Zhivago, Avenida General Paz block 100 (corner of 9 de Julio)
- Fast food: American Food, Tucumán 135. Hamburger $1.00
- Fast food: Dixie, 9 de Julio block 300 (corner of Tucumán)
- Fast food: Pi, Obispo Trejo block 100 (corner of 27 de Abril)
- Fast food: Pumpernic, Avenida General Paz block 100 (corner of 9 de Julio
- English-style pub: Cheers, corner of Jujuy and Avenida Colón

Eating out in Alto Córdoba

- Restaurant Córdoba, Avenida J L de Cabrera 235. Steakhouse
- Restaurant La Amistad, Avenida R S Peña 1523
- Comedor Albeñiz, Avenida J L de Cabrera block 200 (corner of Rivadeo)

Post and telegraph

- Central post office: Encotel, Avenida Colón 201. Parcel despatch from the ground floor
- Post office in bus terminal
- Telephone: Central Telefonica, Avenida General Paz 36. For international calls dial (000

Financial

- Avincor, Avenida Olmos 110 (27057
- Banco Alas, Ituzaingo 6. Cash advances on Visa card
- Bank of London and South America, Buenos Aires 23
- Cambio Barujel, San Martín 37 (downstairs). 5% discount on Thomas Cook travelers' checks
- Cash, Rivadavia 69 (39922
- Citibank, 25 de Mayo block 100 (corner of Rivadavia). Cash advances on Diners Club card; open 0730–1330
- Coin Viajes y Cambio, Rivadavia 100 (24723
- Exprinter, Rivadavia 39
- Maguitur, Rivadavia 30 (33388. Good rates
- Viacor, Buenos Aires 181 (35040

Services and facilities

- Drycleaner: San Gerónimo 600
- Health food: Hierbas Medicinales Aborigen, General Paz 387
- Medical services: Clinica Privada Nuevo Córdoba, Chacabuco block 700 (corner of Derqui)
- Supermarket: Americanos, Vélez Sarsfield 138

Laundromats

- Integral, Salguero 555
- La Burbuja, corner of Ituzaingo and San Lorenzo; Open Sun
- Laverap, corner of M T de Alvear and Belgrano
- Limpi-Mas, Vélez Sarsfield 56 (Edificio General Perez). Open Mon–Sat 0730–2130; $2.50

Photographic supplies

- Fotoscoop, Vélez Sarsfield 80. Good selection of photographic equipment
- La Casa de Fotografo, Déan Funes 159

Saunas

- Gymnasium Sendero, Tucumán 568 (corner of General Paz)
- Sauna Carribean, San Gerónimo block 100 (corner of Ituzaingo; downstairs)

Clubs

- British: British Council, San Juan 137. Has a good library
- French: Alliance Française, Ayacucho 46
- German: Goethe Institut, Avenida Illia 356; Mon–Fri 1700–2100
- Italian: Instituto Italiano Cultura, Vélez Sarsfield block 300 (corner of D Quiroz)

Visas, passports

- Visa extensions: Dirección de Migraciones, Caseros 680 (22740
- German consulate, Olmos 501 (33962
- Italian consulate, Ayacucho 131
- Peruvian consulate, Lugones 212. Open Mon–Fri 0900–1400
- Spanish consulate, Bulevar Chacabuco 875 (65013

Córdoba

CÓRDOBA PROVINCE

✈ Air services from Córdoba

Pajas Blancas airport, 15 km from the city, is modern and has a very good restaurant. The airport bus leaves from the bus terminal (local 6B) at the corner of Lugones and Avenida Perón half an hour before the plane leaves. Fares to the airport: bus $1.00; taxi $3.00

- Aerolineas Argentinas, Colón 520 ℂ 45003, airport ℂ 811418
- ALFA, Terminal de Omnibus, local 1 ℂ 38678, airport ℂ 816866)
- Austral, Buenos Aires 59 ℂ 34883, airport ℂ 810997)
- LADE, airport ℂ 814791

Destination	Fare	Depart	Services	Hours	Airline
• Bahía Blanca	$59.00	1435	Mon	2	Aerolineas
• Buenos Aires (Aeroparque Jorge Newbery)					
	$55.00	0810	6–14 services daily	1	Aerolineas, Austral
• Comodoro Rivadavia					
	$77.00	1655	Wed, Fri, Sun	4	Aerolineas
• La Rioja	$31.00	0810	Mon, Wed, Fri, Sun	1	Aerolineas
• Mar del Plata	$71.00	1655	daily	3	Austral
• Mendoza	$38.00	0825	2–3 services daily	1	Aerolineas, Austral
• Neuquén	$64.00	1655	Wed, Fri	3	Aerolineas
• Paraná	$71.00	1315	Mon, Wed, Fri	3	Austral
• Posadas	$64.00	1605	Mon	2	Aerolineas
• Puerto Iguazú	$75.00	1440	Mon, Thurs, Sat	3	
• Resistencia	$44.00	1250	Mon, Wed, Fri		ALFA
• Río Gallegos	$87.00	1655	Sat	5	Aerolineas
• Río Grande	$95.00	1655	Sat	6	Aerolineas
• Rosario	$35.00	1315	1–2 services daily	2	Aerolineas, Austral
• Salta	$52.00	1010	1–2 services daily	1	Aerolineas, Austral
• San Carlos de Bariloche					
	$90.00	0845	Mon, Wed, Fri–Sun	3	Aerolineas, Austral
• San Juan	$35.00	1920	daily	1	Aerolineas
• San Fernando de Catamarca					
	$30.00	0810	Mon, Wed, Fri	2	Aerolineas
• San Miguel de Tucumán					
	$41.00	0810	1–2 services daily	1	Aerolineas, Austral
• San Salvador de Jujuy					
	$58.00	0810	Mon–Wed, Fri, Sun	2	Aerolineas
• Santa Fé	$29.00	1415	Sun	1	Aerolineas
	$21.00	1250	Mon, Wed, Fri	1	ALFA
• Santa Rosa	$43.00	1445	Mon	1½	Aerolineas
• Termas de Río Hondo		1035	Tues, Thurs, Sat, Sun	2	Austral
• Villa Dolores	$10.00	1110	Mon, Fri	1	ALFA

🚌 Motoring

Service stations

- ACA, Humberto I block 200 (corner of General Paz)
- YPF, Rosario de Santa Fé block 600 (corner of Bulevar Guzman)

Car rentals

- A1 International, Hotel Dora, Entre Ríos 70 ℂ 42-036, 42-037, 42-038. Also at airport
- ALA, Obispo Trejo 586 ℂ 36020
- Avis, Corrientes 452 ℂ 27384. Also at airport

Córdoba

CÓRDOBA PROVINCE

🚌 Buses from Córdoba

The modern bus terminal is located Avenida Presidente J D Perón (between Avenida Illia and Avenida Lugones). It houses several cafeterias and restaurants, a tourist office, a post office, public telephones, shops, a bank (cash only at official rate), and clean restrooms with showers (soap and towel $1.00). It gets crowded at weekends when people travel to neighboring resorts.

Destination	Fare	Depart	Services	Hours	Company
• Alta Gracia	$0.70	0600	8 services daily	1	Sierras de Calamuchita
• Asunción	$25.00	1230	Wed, Sun	20	Cacorba
• Bahía Blanca		0830	3 services daily	15	TUP
• Buenos Aires	$21.00	1935	many services daily	10	ABLO, Cacorba, TA Chevallier
	$14.80		daily	13	Urquiza
• Capilla del Monte	$2.60	0430	29 services daily	3	La Capillense, Primero
• Chilecito					Cotil
• Clorinda	$24.00	1230	Wed, Sun	17	Cacorba
• Comodoro Rivadavia					
	$47.00	1200	daily	28	TUP
• Corrientes	$23.00	2000	Fri		El Serrano
• Cosquín	$1.50	0430	29 services daily	2	La Capillense, Primero de Mayo
• Cuesta Blanca		0415	9 services daily	2	COTAP
• El Condor		0700	7 services daily	3	EPA/El Petizo
• Formosa	$22.00	1800	Tues, Fri, Sun	15	Cacorba
• La Cumbre	$2.10	0430	29 services daily	2/2	La Capillense, Primero de Mayo
• La Falda	$2.00	0700	8 services daily	2	Primero de Mayo
• La Rioja		0645	3–4 services daily		Cotil, El Condor
• Mar del Plata	$21.00	1345	2 services daily		Expreso Córdoba
• Mendoza		1000	5 services daily	10	Colta, TAC
• Mina Clavero	$4.50	0700	7 services daily	4	EPA/El Petizo
• Montevideo (Uruguay)		1815	Fri–Wed		Cora-Encon, Onda
• Neuquén	$22.50		Fri–Wed	18	La Estrella, TUS
• Paraná		0745	5 services daily		El Litoral, El Serrano, Expreso Singer
• Paso de los Libres	$20.50	1230	daily		El Litoral, Expreso Singer
• Posadas		1230	daily	20	El Litoral, Expreso Singer
• Puerto Iguazú		1230	Mon–Fri	26	El Litoral, Expreso Singer
• Puerto Madryn		1200	daily	21	TUP
• Rawson	$32.50	1200	Wed, Fri, Sat		TUP
• Resistencia	$19.50	1930	1–2 services daily	13	Cacorba, La Estrella
• Rosario	$8.50	0700	10 services daily	7	ABLO, General Urquiza
• Saldan		0645	13 services daily	1	La Calera
• Salta	$25.00	0830	14 services daily	12	Expreso Panamericano, La Veloz del Norte
• San Antonio Oeste		1200	daily	9	TUP
• San Carlos de Bariloche					
	$32.00	1230	Fri–Wed	24	TUS
• San Fernando de Catamarca	$9.00	0645	7 services daily		Cacorba, Cotil, TA Chevallier
• San Juan	$14.40	1130	3 services daily		Socasa

Córdoba

CÓRDOBA PROVINCE

Buses from Córdoba—Continued					
• San Luis	1000		5 services daily		Colta, TAC
• San Martín de los Andes	$36.00	1230	Tues, Sat	25	TUS
• San Miguel de Tucumán	$12.50	0830	7 services daily		El Trebol, Tucumano, Panamericano, La Veloz del Norte
• San Salvador de Jujuy		1500	daily		Expreso Panamericano
• Santa Fé	$7.80	0745	4–5 services daily		El Litoral, El Serrano
• Santa Rosa (La Pampa province)	$12.00	0830	4 services daily	10	TUP
• Santa Rosa de Calamuchita	$2.40	0600	8 services daily	2	Sierras de Calamuchita
• Santiago del Estero	$9.50	0800	5 services daily	7	Cacorba
• Tanti		0345	9 services daily	1½	COTAP
• Termas de Río Hondo	$10.50	2300	2 services daily	7	Chevallier
	$11.50	0830	6 services daily	8	Panamericano
• Trelew		1200	daily	2	TUP
• Villa Allende		0820	2 services daily	1	La Capillense
• Villa Carlos Paz	$0.80	0700	half-hourly	1	COTAP, Primero de Mayo, EPA/El Petizo
• Villa Ciudad de América		0600	8 services daily	2	Sierras de Calamuchita
• Villa Dolores	$5.20	0700	25 services daily	5	EPA/El Petizo, Expreso Mina Clavero, Contal
• Villa General Belgrano	$2.40	0600	8 services daily	2	Sierra de Calamuchita
• Zapala	$28.50				TUS

- Liprandi Rent a Car, Chacbuco 185 ℓ 40426

Trains

Stations
- F C General B Mitre, Bulevar Perón 200
- F C General Belgrano, Avenida J L de Cabrera, Alto Córdoba district

Trains to Buenos Aires
Only "Rayo del Sol" has sleepers and Pullmans.
"El Norteño" connects with bus services to and from La Rioja and Catamarca.
Fares: Sleeper $23.70, Pullman $16.20, first class $11.00, tourist class $8.00
- "Rayo del Sol" (Train 296): Departs 2035 daily; 12 hours
- "Serranoche" (Train 298): Departs 2145; 12 hours
- Train 218: Departs 0930 Mon, Wed, Fri; 12½ hours
- "El Norteño": Departs 0745 Tues, Fri, Sat from Alto Córdoba station; 12 hours

Shopping

Córdoba is a good shopping city; it has a large area of pedestrian malls, but prices tend to be higher than in Buenos Aires.
- Antiguedades Monserrat, Caseros 88
- Antiguedades El Dolar de Oro, Rivera Indarte 253

Sport
- Squash Bar, Chacabuco 611. Bring your own gear; $4.00 per hour

Entertainment
- Disco La Barra, Lima 152

CÓRDOBA PROVINCE

- Nightclub Down, 9 de Julio block 200 (corner of General Paz)
- Nightclub Tramps Club, Bulevar Illia block 400 (corner of Salguera)
- Night Club Tropican, Sarmiento 255; Shows Fr-Sa-Su
- Peña La Marinera, Bulevar Illia 365
- Tanguería Musirama, Lima block 200
- Whiskería, Jujuy 296
- Whiskería Gioia, Tucuman 396

Sightseeing

The focal point of the city is Plaza San Martín, with the statue of the "Liberator", San Martín.

Public buildings

- The old Cabildo (City Council) building, on the western side of the Plaza, was the center of public life in colonial times and is now the provincial police headquarters. It was built by Juan Manuel López in 1785 during the reign of viceroy Marqués de Sobremonte
- The Universidad Mayor de San Marcos (St Mark's University), also called "Colegio Maximo", is located next to La Compañía in Trejo 242. It was administered by the Jesuits from 1600 until their expulsion in 1767
- La Casa del Obispo Mercadillo (Home of Bishop Mercadillo), Rosario de Santa Fé 39. This is the remainder of the building which was the home of Bishop Mercadillo when he relocated the bishopric from Tucumán to Córdoba in 1698. The most outstanding piece is the balcony which is made from hammered steel
- Jardín Zoológico (Zoo), in Parque Sarmiento, has a reptile house and a small waterfall
- Observatorio Astronómico de Córdoba (Cordoba Astronomical Observatory), south end of Calle General Ártigas

Churches

Churches are open in the mornings and after 1600 in the afternoon.

- La Catedral (Cathedral), on the Plaza, was begun in 1697 and consecrated in 1782. It is the most important example of colonial architecture in Córdoba. It is in the baroque style but shows strong Indian influences which makes it unique in the Americas. The paintings inside are by Octavio Pinto, Emilio Caraffa, and Genaro Perez, and on the portico there is a noteworthy wrought-iron trellis depicting angels blowing trumpets. The Cathedral is the resting place of Generals Paz and Déan Funes and the chapel of the Virgen de Nieva is the resting place of Fray Mamerto Esquiú, one of the apostles of America
- Iglesia y Convento de Santa Teresa (Church and Convent of Santa Teresa), Calle Independencia, between Caseros and 27 de Abril. It was founded in 1628 by Juan de Tejeda, the first native Argentinian poet, and now houses the Museo de Arte Religioso (Museum of

Córdoba

Religious Art). It has a beautiful doorway built in 1770
- Iglesia de la Compañía de Jesús (Jesuit Church), Calle Trejo 242 (corner of Caseros), dates from about 1650. Paraguayan cedar was used to construct the vault and the cupola
- Basilica de Santo Domingo, corner of Avenida Velez Sarsfield and Déan Funes
- Iglesia de la Merced (Church of Mercy), north of Plaza San Martín on the corner of Calle Rivadavia and 25 de Mayo. Building began in 1600 and was completed in 1826. The old colonial pulpit is well worth seeing
- Capilla San Roque (St Roque's Chapel), corner of Calle Obispo Salguero and San Jerónimo. This chapel has strong reinforced walls on the outside
- Iglesia San Francisco (St Francis' Church), corner of Plazoleta Buenos Aires and Entre Ríos. It was built between 1795 and 1813. In the vicinity are the graves of the descendants of the founders. San Francisco Solano and Fray Mamerto Esquiú spent some time here
- Iglesia del Pilar (Church of the Pillar), the corner of Avenida Olmos and Avenida Maipú. This was the seat of the Order of the Santa Hermandad which assisted those who were condemned to death. The most auspicous members were Déan Funes and governor Marqués de Sobremonte
- Convento de Santa Catalina (St Catherine's Convent), corner of Obispo Trejo and Déan Funes. Founded in 1613 by Bishop Trejo
- Iglesia del Sagrado Corazón (Church of the Sacred Heart), corner of Buenos Aires and Yrigoyen. The neogothic church was built in 1933 and is worth a visit

Museums

- Museo Casa del Virrey Sobremonte (Museum and Home of Viceroy Sobremonte), Calle Rosario de Santa Fé 218 (corner of Ituzaingó), east of the central Plaza. It may well be considered the most beautiful colonial house remaining in Córdoba. Built by Don José Rodriguez around 1750 it was the viceregal home of the Marques de Sobremonte until 1796, and now houses the Museo Provincial de Historia Marqués de Sobremonte (Marquess of Sobremonte Provincial History Museum). On exhibit are historical documents, medieval weapons, and furniture. Open Tue–Fri 0830–1300, 1500–1930, and Sat and Sun 0900–1200
- Museo de Ciencias Naturales "B Mitre" (B Mitre Natural Sciences Museum), Avenida Yrigoyen 115 is open Mon–Fri 0830–1230 and 1430–1830 and Sat, Sun 0900–1200
- Museo Mineralógico (Mineralogy Museum): There is a very interesting and well laid out museum of mineralogy at the Universidad de Ciencias Exac-

tas (University of Physical Sciences)
- Museo Provincial de Belles Artes "Emilio Caraffa" (Emilio Caraffa Provincial Fine Arts Museum), the theatre and the Olmos school are near the Plaza Vélez Sarsfield
- Museo Municipal de Bellas Artes "Genaro Peréz" (Genaro Peréz Municipal Fine Arts Museum), Avenida General Paz 33. Open Mon–Fri 0900–1300

Excursions
- **Dique San Roque**: This great dam protects the city from flooding, regulates the flow of the **Río Primero**, provides drinking water and electrical power, feeds two large irrigation systems, and forms a blue lake ringed by hills which has become a tourist resort
- **Cosquín**: A round trip from Córdoba to Cosquín and back again via **Cerro Pan de Azúcar** and the eastern side of **Lago San Roque** can be made by public transport in one day by taking the La Capillense bus from Córdoba terminal at 0820. The bus travels through **Argüello**, **Villa Allende**, and **Villa Alegre**, then enters the Cerro Pan de Azúcar pass road which winds through the mountains for 27 km before descending again into the **Río Punillas valley** near Cosquín. The highest point, 1250 m is reached near Cerro Pan de Azúcar (Cosquín is at about 1000 m). The return to Córdoba can be made on a La Calera bus directly via **Bialet Massé** and **Calera** along the eastern side of Lago San Roque following the **Río Primero**, which starts at the dam. Alternatively you could go via **Villa Carlos Paz**; see "Buses" above. See also Cosquín below

COSQUÍN

Postal code: 5166 • (area code: (0541) • Altitude: 720 m
Distance from Córdoba: 63 km northwest

Cosquín is located in the **Río Punillas valley** at the foot of the **Cerro Pan de Azúcar** (1260 m). There are easy walks in the beautiful surroundings. Cosquín is much frequented by Argentine tourists.

Festivals
- A folk festival is held during the last half of January

Tourist information
- San Martín, 560

Camping
- Caravana, López y Planes
- Río Cosquín, on the Pan de Azucar Road

Eating out
- Pizzería San Marino, San Martín 707
- Comedor Don Luis, San Martín block 1100 (corner of Ortiz). Pastas
- Comedor Familiar El Coco, San Martín block 1500
- Cafetería King's, San Martín 819
- Cafetería San Remo, corner of San Martín and Corrientes

CÓRDOBA PROVINCE

Accommodation in Cosquín

★★★	Hotel La Puerta del Sol, Buenos Aires 820	(51626	$24.00	♂♂
	Breakfast $2.00			
★★	Hotel Gran Sierras, San Martín 733		$20.00	♂♂
	Breakfast $2.00			
★	Hotel Alex Mar, San Martín 616 (corner of Catamarca)	(51322		
	Open January to March			
★	Hotel Carlitos, Juan B Justo	(51165	$11.00	♂♂
	Breakfast $1.50			
★	Hotel El Lago, Avenida General Paz	(51542	$15.00	♂♂
	Breakfast $1.50			
★	Hotel Folklore, F Sanchez 688	(52081		
★	Hotel Maiques, San Martín 1456	(52188	$16.00	♂♂
	Breakfast $2.00			
★	Hotel Menorca, A Sabattini 662	(51126		
	No single bedrooms			
★	Hotel Miramontes, G Mistral 829			
	No single bedrooms			
	Hotel Puerto El Cádiz, San Martín 351	(51299	$15.00	♂♂
	Breakfast $1.50			
★	Hostería Mary, Obispo Oro 545	(52095	$10.00	♂♂
	Breakfast $1.50			
★	Hostería Pardo, San Martín 1469	(52055	$11.00	♂♂
	Breakfast $1.50			
★	Hostería Roma, A Sabattini 554	(52023		
	No single bedrooms			
•	Hospedaje Cosquín, corner of Tucumán and Sabattini	(51222		
	No single bedrooms			
•	Hospedaje El Aguila, Obispo Bustos 956	(51749		
	Triple rooms only			
•	Hospedaje El Puente, Corrientes 360			
	No single bedrooms			
•	Hospedaje El Remanso, General Paz			
•	Hospedaje Esperanza, Buenos Aires 637	(51858		
	Open January–March; no single bedrooms			
•	Hospedaje Gisele, Santa Fé 1327			
	Triple rooms only			
•	Hospedaje Ideal, Buenos Aires 1159	(51644		
•	Hospedaje Italia, corner of Termango and Vertis		$11.00	♂♂
	Breakfast $1.50			
•	Hospedaje La Serrana, Ortiz 440, near bus station	(51306	$9.00	♂♂
	Breakfast $1.50			
•	Hospedaje Mary–Mar, Intendente Ternengo 1015			
	No single bedrooms			
•	Hospedaje Norita, corner of Mallín and Tucumán	(51474		
•	Hospedaje Rincón Serrano, Sabattini 739	(51311	$8.00	♂♂
	No single bedrooms			
•	Residencial Estelita, Catamarca 138	(51473		
	Triples only			

CÓRDOBA PROVINCE

Accommodation in Cosquín—Continued
- Residencial Palermo, San Martín 239 🛏 (51114
  No single bedrooms

Accommodation in Villa Bustos
Three km south of Cosquín
- Hospedaje Argentina, corner of San Martín and Rosario
  No single bedrooms

- Cafetería Via Veneto, block 800 (corner of Dr JC Geronico)

📬 Post and telegraph
- Post office: Encotel, Buenos Aires 746
- Telephone: Tucumán 1001

🛎 Services and facilities
- Laundromat: Laverap, Buenos Aires 385

🚗 Motoring
- Service station: Esso, corner of San Martín and Corrientes

🍸 Entertainment
- Disco Reviens, San Martín 845

🍁 Excursions
- **Cerro Pan de Azúcar**: From here you get a good view over the **Río Punillas valley**. Buses run from 0930–1630; otherwise you can take the chairlift or walk for two hours to the top
- **Capillo San José** (St Joseph's Chapel): 13 km east, on the road to Tanti. Built in 1670

🚌 Buses from Cosquín

Most buses to Córdoba go via Villa Carlos Paz taking the road on the western side of Lago San Roque (RN 20), but some turn east at Bialet Massé and follow the eastern side of Lago San Roque, passing by the dam and following the Río Primero.

Destination	Fare	Depart	Services	Hours	Company
Córdoba		0610	31 services daily	2½	ABLO, L Capillense, Primero de Mayo
Buenos Aires		0830	2 services daily	12	ABLO
Capilla del Monte		0545	29 services daily	1½	La Capillense, Primero de Mayo
Cruz del Eje		0835	8 services daily	2	Primero de Mayo
La Cumbre		0545	29 services daily	1	La Capillense, Primero de Mayo
La Falda	$0.60	0545	29 services daily	½	La Capillense, Primero de Mayo
Rosario		0830	2 services daily	7	ABLO
Villa Carlos Paz	$0.80	0800	8 services daily	1	Primero de Mayo
Villa María		0830	2 services daily	4	

Cosquín

CRUZ CHICA

Postal code: 5178 • Altitude: 1067 m

Cruz Chica is a charming little town surrounded by pine forests, 3 km north of La Cumbre in the **Sierra Chica**, and is a good starting point for hikes in the nearby *sierra*. There is an English boys' school here.

Accommodation
★★ Hotel Zapata, Ruta Provincial 🍽🛏 ☎ Los Cocos 58 $17.00 👥. Open December–April; breakfast $1.50
★ Hotel Cabor, Avenida Bartolomé Jaime 🍽🛏 ☎ 91052 $15.00 👥. Breakfast $1.50

Buses
Municipal run regular buses to La Cumbre.

CRUZ DEL EJE

Postal code: 5280 • ☎ area code (0549) • Altitude: 476 m
Distance from Córdoba: 115 km northwest on RN 38

Cruz del Eje is located in the north-western part of the province. It is the center of an olive-growing area, with more than a million olive trees in the vicinity. Cotton and grapes are also grown. During the summer vacation the artificial lake attracts many tourists for water sports and *pejerrey* fishing.

The drive to Cruz del Eje from Córdoba through the **Sierras de Córdoba** is very scenic.

Festivals
- Fiesta Nacional del Olivo (National Olive Festival): Second week in February

Accommodation
★ Hotel España, corner of Caseros and Alsina ☎ 2702
★ Hostería Cruz del Eje, corner of H Yrigoyen and Maipú ☎ 2431
★ Hostería Don Pepe, Alsina 146 🍽 ☎ 2406
• Hospedaje San Martín, San Martín 310 ☎ 2059. No single rooms

Accommodation outside Cruz del Eje
★★ Motel Vintage, corner of RN 38 and R Moyano 🍽🛏 ☎ 2517 $12.00 👥. No single rooms

Buses from Cruz del Eje
There is a central bus terminal.

Destination	Fare	Depart	Services	Hours	Company
• Córdoba		0430	8 services daily	4	Primero de Mayo
• Capilla del Monte		0430	8 services daily	1	Primero de Mayo
• Cosquín		0430	8 services daily	2½	Primero de Mayo
• Déan Funes	$1.10				
• La Cumbre	$1.20	0500	8 services daily	1½	Primero de Mayo
• La Falda		0430	8 services daily	2	Primero de Mayo
• Villa Carlos Paz		0500	8 services daily	3	Primero de Mayo

CÓRDOBA PROVINCE

🍽 Eating out
- Restaurant El Cordon, Sarmiento. Steakhouse
- Pizzería, corner of Sáenz Peña and Alvear

🏨 Services and facilities
- Laundromat: Laverap, Alvear 321

🚗 Motoring
- Service station: ACA, corner of Rivadavia and Sarmiento

🏊 Sport
There are fishing and aquatic sports at Cruz del Eje dam, 5 km outside town. The dam is 3 km long.

🌲 Excursions

Cruz del Eje is a good starting point for excursions into the northern **Sierras de Córdoba**, including **Capilla del Monte** and **La Cumbre**. There are frequent bus services.
- **La Cumbre**: RN 38 initially ascends gently towards the **Sierra Chica**, reaching 949 m at **Capilla del Monte**. **Cerro Uritorco** (1950 m), the highest mountain of the Sierra Chica, comes into view in the east. In the west is the **Sierra de Cuniputo**, slightly lower, with its highest peak **Cerro Pencales** at 1300 m. See also La Cumbre on page 175

DÉAN FUNES

Postal code: 5200 • ☎ area code (0521) • Altitude: 690 m
Distances
- From Córdoba: 124 km northwards on RN 9
- From Cruz del Eje: 70 km eastwards on RP 16

Déan Funes is located in the north-western part of the province on the main road to Catamarca (RN 60). Fifty km further north the huge Salinas Grandes begin.

🏨 Accommodation in Déan Funes

★★ Hotel San Jorge, España 88 (corner of Buenos Aires) 🛏 Breakfast $2.00	☎ 21174	$12.00	👥
• Hotel Valentini, Rivadavia		$3.00	👤
• Hospedaje Déan Funes, Alte Brown 365 🛏 Breakfast $1.00		$12.00	👥
• Hospedaje Mitre, Bulevar San Martín 347 🛏			
• Hospedaje Santa Fé, Santa Fé 291 (corner of Italia)	☎ 20223		
• Hospedaje San Martín, 25 de Mayo 230, on Plaza San Martín		$6.00	👥
• Hospedaje Samay Huasi, Independencia 428 No single rooms			
• Residencial Martinez, Santa Fé 425 🍽	☎ 21135		
• Residencial El Chino, Mitre 295 (corner of Santa Fé), opposite rail station 🍽		$3.00	👤
• Residencial San Martín, 25 de Mayo 1230 (corner of Plaza San Martín)		$3.00	👤

Cruz del Eje

CÓRDOBA·PROVINCE

🚌 Buses from Deán Funes

The bus terminal is on Cabrera.

Destination	Fare	Depart	Services	Hours	Company
• Córdoba	$2.20	0410	2–3 services daily	2	Cacorba
• Buenos Aires	$17.00	1915	daily	15	Cacorba
	$19.00	2340	daily	13	Cacorba Express bus
• Cruz del Eje	$1.10	0715	4 services daily		Cadol
• Rosario		1915	daily		Cacorba
• San Fernando de Catamarca	0545		4 services daily	5	Cacorba
• San Juan de la Dormida	$1.30		several services daily		Cadol
• Santiago del Estero		1055	Mon, Wed, Fri	6	Cacorba

🍴 Eating out

- Restaurant La Cartuja, Rivadavia
- Comedor Miguelito, Italia 66
- Comedor Moyano, corner of 25 de Mayo and España
- Comedor Fogón II, corner of H Yrigoyen and Santiago del Estero
- Cafetería El Puma, corner of 25 de Mayo and Sáenz Peña, on the Plaza San Martín
- Cafetería El Tabi, 25 de Mayo, on the Plaza San Martín. Snacks
- Cafetería Jumajo, 25 de Mayo, on the Plaza San Martín. Snacks
- Cafetería Terminal. Open 24 hours

✉ Post and telegraph

- Post office: Encotel, corner of Sáenz Peña and Rivadavia
- Telephone: Entel, corner of Cabrera and Rivadavia, on the Plaza San Martín

🛒 Services and facilities

- Delicatessen: Pablito, Italia 184 (corner of Rivadavia); Sandwiches
- Supermarket: Supercoop, corner of Morandini and Santa Fé

🚗 Motoring

RP 16 passes over the *punilla* on its way to the junction with RN 9 at **San José de la Dormida**. Once the highest point is reached it is fairly flat country until Villa Tulumba, where the road descends again.

Service stations

- ACA, corner of Rivadavia and Sarmiento
- Esso, corner of 9 de Julio and Italia (on the Plaza)
- YPF, corner of Rivadavia and Sáenz Peña

🚆 Trains

The station is on Mitre opposite Santa Fé. It is possible to travel by train to Alto Córdoba.

🌳 Excursions

- Cruz del Eje: RP 16 skirts the spurs of the **Sierras de Córdoba** on the southern side, staying in flat country throughout. To the north are the **Salinas Grandes**

EMBALSE

Postal code: 5856 • Population: 3500 • (area code (0571) • Altitude: 440 m
Distance from Córdoba: 120 km southwards on RN 36

Embalse is the tourist center of a string of lakes created by the damming of the **Río Tercero**.

CÓRDOBA PROVINCE

Many weekenders and yachting clubs have sprung up around the lake, which is a good place for fishing, swimming, and sailing. The dams are part of a hydroelectric scheme which supplies electricity to industry in Córdoba and irrigation water for the farms in the lowland.

🚌 Buses
Buses run regularly to Córdoba and Rio Cuarto.

🌳 Excursions
- Ruins of the Jesuit Estancia Santos Ejercicios, founded in 1726. Located on RP 23 7 km south of Santa Rosa de Calamuchita

GENERAL CABRERA

General Cabrera is located halfway between Río Cuarto and Villa Maria on RN 158.

🛏 Accommodation
Residencial Lucho, Avenida Belgrano 621 $9.00

GENERAL DEHEZA

General Deheza is located halfway between Villa María and Río Cuarto on RN 158.

🛏 Accommodation
★★★ Hotel Posada del Larriego, RN 158 ⑪ ✆ 196 $25.00. No single rooms

🛏 Accommodation in Embalse

★ Hotel La Perla, RP 5 km 711		✆ 99222	$13.00
★ Hostería Dolard, Barrio El Pueblito		✆ 99246	$9.00
• Hospedaje Ana Mar, Libertad 594 No single rooms			
• Hospedaje Aranda, Avenida Comercial No single rooms		✆ 99282	
• Hospedaje El Plato Volador, Barrio Comercial Triple rooms only		✆ 99270	
• Hospedaje Feuz, RP 5		✆ 99268	$14.00
• Hospedaje Garcia, Barrio Comercial Triple rooms only		✆ 99217	
• Hospedaje Gigena, Barrio Comercial Triple rooms only		✆ 99265	$9.00
• Hospedaje Irupe, Villa Irupe		✆ 99232	$8.00
• Hospedaje La Pampa, RP 5 No single rooms			
• Hospedaje San Cayetano, Barrio Comercial No single rooms		✆ 99331	

Embalse

GENERAL LEVALLE

General Devalle is located 43 km west of Laboulaye on RN 7.

Accommodation
Hospedaje Glasgow, Avenida Pellegrini 147 (176

HUINCA RENANCÓ

Postal code: 6270 • (area code: (0336)
Distance from Realicó (La Pampa province): 26 km northwards on RN 35

Huinca Renancó is an important east–west north–south road junction at the extreme southern point of the province.

Accommodation
- ★★ Hotel Los Vascos, H Yrigoyen 220 (583 $18.00
- Hospedaje Betty, Santa Fé 296 (627
- Hospedaje Petit Colón, A N Aguado 25 (442
- Hospedaje San Salvador, Ruta 35 Km 526 (518 $10.00

Buses
Buses run regularly to Río Cuarto and Realicó.

JESÚS MARÍA

Postal code: 5220 • Population: 18 000 • (area code: (0525) • Altitude: 530 m
Distance from Córdoba: 51 km northwards on RN 9

Jesús María is situated on the **Río Ascochinga** on the eastern side of the **Sierra Chica**.

It was founded in the middle of the seventeenth century as a Jesuit *estancia*; in the former convent building is a Jesuit museum, the Museo Jesuítico. **Colonia Caroya**, 5 km south, was part of the Jesuit land holding; its Jesuit Chapel has been preserved.

There is good fishing in the streams which come down from the **Sierra Chica**.

Sinsacate, 4 km north off the main road, was an important staging post on the road to Alto Perú during colonial times. The chapel and the old inn have been converted into a rural museum. Good wine is grown in the area.

Festivals
- Festival de Doma y Folklore: First half of January

Tourist information
- Dirección de Turismo, corner of San Martín and Olmos (2101

Accommodation
- ★★ Hotel Rizzi, Tucumán 662 (2580 $14.00
- ★ Hostería Costa Azul, San Martín 442. No single rooms
- Hospedaje del Plata, corner of Tucumán and Colón (23 $10.00. No single rooms

Accommodation outside Jesús María
- ★★★ Motel El Paso Viejo, RN 9 Km 753 (2174 $17.00
- ★★ Motel La Cabaña del Tío Juan, RN 9 Km 754 (2563 $17.00. Breakfast $1.50

CÓRDOBA PROVINCE

🍴 Eating out
There are three restaurants in Jesús María.

✉ Post and telegraph
- Post office: Encotel, Tucumán 510
- Telephone: Entel, San Ignacio de Loyola 455

🚌 Buses
- Córdoba: Departs 0010; 17 services daily; Empresa Cadol

🚗 Motoring
- Service station: ACA, corner of RN 9 and Corrientes

⚑ Excursions
- **La Cumbre**: Scenic drive or bus trip via **Ascochinga**. See La Cumbre on page 175
- **Convento Santa Catalina**: 38 km north. This Jesuit mission was the most important foundation of the Jesuits in Córdoba province

LA CALERA

Altitude: 500 m
Distance from Córdoba: 19 km northwest

La Calera is located on the northern outskirts of Córdoba on the road to Lago San Roque. Nearby are the ruins of a Jesuit chapel built in the eighteenth century.

🛏 Accommodation
- ★ Hotel Suquía, Saul Moyano 401 🍴📠 ☎96316 $17.00 ♂♂. Breakfast $1.50
- Hospedaje Parque, Avenida Stoechlin 60 📠 ☎96135 $10.00 ♂♂
- Hospedaje Suizo, N Avellaneda 685 ☎96105 $10.00 ♂♂

⚑ Excursions
- **Casa Bamba**: further up in the **Río Primero** valley

LA CARLOTA

Postal code: 2670 • ☎ area code: (0584) •
Altitude: 141 m
Distance from Córdoba: 255 km southwards on RP 9 then RP 4

La Carlota is located at the intersection of RN 8 with RP 4 and RP 50. It is a convenient stopover en route to Mendoza.

🛏 Accommodation
- Hospedaje Avenida, H Yrigoyen 155 📠 $12.00 ♂♂. Breakfast $1.50
- Hospedaje Ferrero, San Martín 255 ☎255 $8.00 ♂♂
- Hospedaje Ladrillo Duro, RP 8 Km 501 📠. No single rooms
- Hospedaje Sur, San Martín 348 $10.00 ♂♂

LA CRUZ

Postal code: 5859 • ☎ area code: (0546) •
Altitude: 584 m
Distance from Córdoba: 126 km southwards on RN 38

Formerly part of Calamuchita district, La Cruz is located on the **Río de la Cruz** just south of Embalse del Río Tercero.

🛏 Accommodation
- ★ Hostería Doña Laura, Avenida San Martín 🍴. No single rooms

La Cumbre

Postal code: 5178 • (area code: (0548) •
Altitude: 1141 m
Distance from Córdoba: 97 km northwest on RN 38

La Cumbre is a major tourist resort in the **Río Punillas valley**. The streams coming down from the mountains are well-stocked with trout. On the outskirts of town are lavender plantations.

La Cumbre has an airstrip.

Tourist information

- Dirección Municipal de Turismo, bus terminal (51154

Eating out

- Restaurant Cumbres Nevados, corner of B Jaime and Presidente Yrigoyen. Steakhouse
- Restaurant Casona del Toboso, Belgrano 349
- Restaurant El Cacique, Rivadavia 115
- Restaurant Juva, Belgrano 485 (corner of Déan Funes)
- Restaurant La Casa de José, 25 de Mayo 289
- Restaurant La Fonda de la Cruz Chica (on the road to Los Cocos)
- Restaurant La Peña, corner of General Paz and San Martín
- Restaurant La Perla, Caraffa 238
- Restaurant Petrocelli–Meson Español, Belgrano 433
- Restaurant Quincho Gloria, corner of San Martín and General Paz. Steakhouse
- Cafetería Black and White, corner of 25 de Mayo and Lopez y Planes
- Cafetería El Aguila, corner of Caraffa and Belgrano
- Cafetería Hoyo en Uno, Belgrano 264
- Cafetería La Gran Aldea, corner of Belgrano and 25 de Mayo
- Cafetería Macondo, 25 de Mayo 119
- Cafetería Queimada, Belgrano 228

Post and telegraph

- Post office: Encotel, 25 de Mayo 150 (corner of Belgrano)
- Telephone: Entel, Lopez y Planes 351 (corner of Colón)

Services and facilities

- Laundromat: Laverap, Belgrano 309 (corner of 25 de Mayo)

Supermarkets

- Ray, B Jaime
- Catalano & Cia, 25 de Mayo 190 (corner of López y Planes)

Buses

The bus terminal is on the corner of General Paz and San Martín, and is equipped with a restaurant and toilets.
- Córdoba: Fare $2.00; departs 0845; several services daily; Empresa Primero de Mayo

Sport

Swimming, 18-hole golf course, tennis. The trout-fishing season runs November–April.

Entertainment

- Casino Nacional, Tassano
- Disco Genesis, corner of Sarmiento and 9 de Julio
- Disco Koki, Caraffa 365 (corner of 25 de Mayo)
- Disco Toby's, corner of Dean Funes and López y Panes
- Night Club Nan-Kar, Presidente Yrigoyen

Excursions

- Cristo Redentor: 1 km from the town center. This walk goes past the Balneario Municipal up the riverbed and finishes at the natural mineral springs (**El Chorrito**)
- **Cruz Chica** and **Cruz Grande**: A 7 km walk over a well-paved road. The beautiful wide valley

CÓRDOBA PROVINCE

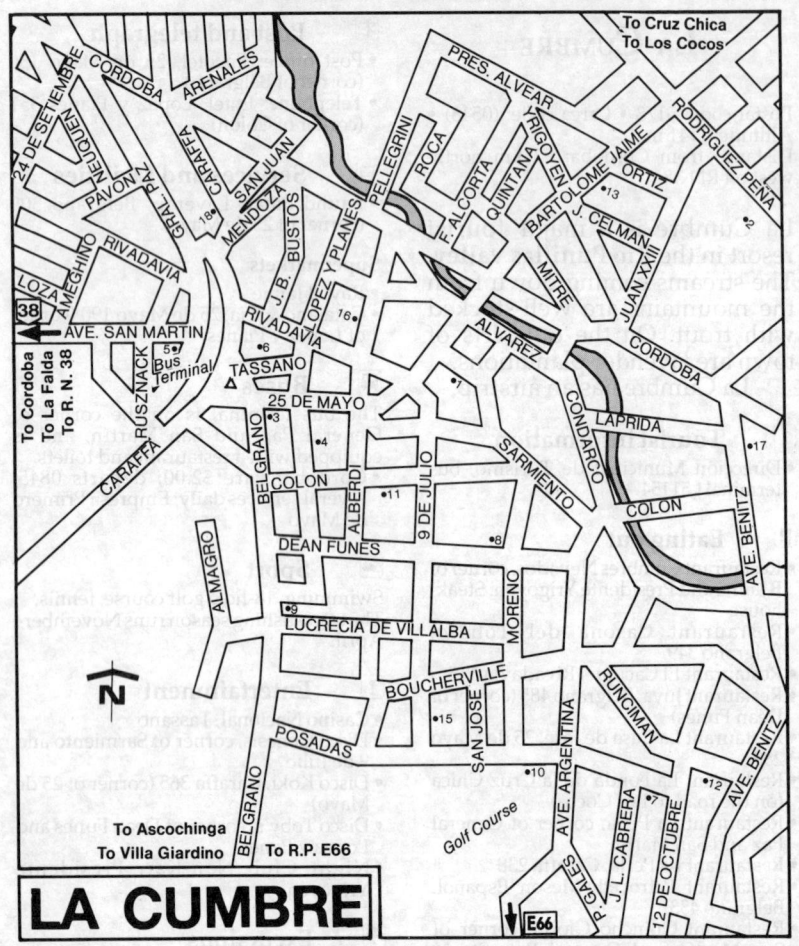

LA CUMBRE

full of summer residences with clusters of trees looks like parkland

- **Ascochinga**: The walk on the road to Ascochinga rises 1400 m within 4 km. The area is covered with pine and wild cherry trees. A little further on the water cascades from the weir at **Dique San Jerónimo**. You can fish in the pond. See also Ascochinga on page 150
- **Cuchi Corral**: A lookout 8 km west of La Cumbre, where hang-gliders sometimes practice

La Cumbre

CÓRDOBA PROVINCE

Key to map
1. Municipalidad
2. Iglesia
3. Post office (Encotel)
4. Telephone (Entel)
5. Tourist information
6. Casino Nacional
7. Hotel Gran Hotel La Cumbre
8. Hotel Lima
9. Hotel María Ines
10. Hotel Victoria
11. Hostería La Cartuja
12. Hostería Los Mimbres
13. Hostería El Cóndor
14. Hostería Granja Iris
15. Hostería La Cumbre
16. Hostería Norita
17. Residencial Los Montes
18. Hotel la Viña

Accommodation in La Cumbre

★★★	Hotel Gran Hotel La Cumbre, Posadas. Meals $7.00	(	51550	$50.00
★	Hotel La Viña, Caraffa 48. No single rooms	(	51338	
★	Hotel Lima, corner of Déan Funes and Moreno. Breakfast included	(	51727	$30.00
★	Hotel María Ines, Belgrano 599. Breakfast included	(	51270	$11.00
★	Hotel Victoria, Posadas. No single rooms	(	51412	
★★	Hostería La Cartuja, Colón 330. Breakfast included	(	51262	$30.00
★★	Hostería Los Mimbres, Brenciman	(	51039	$26.00
★	Hostería Carignani, corner of San Martín and General Paz			
★	Hostería Casablanca, Tucumán. No single rooms	(	51735	
★	Hostería El Cóndor, corner of Avenida Bartolomé Jaime and Celman. Breakfast $1.00	(	51596	$13.00
★	Hostería El Tandil, Presidente Alvear. Open January–April; No single rooms	(	51757	
★	Hostería Granja Iris, Río Negro. No single rooms			
★	Hostería La Cumbre, 9 de Julio 753. No single rooms	(	51736	
★	Hostería Norita, López y Planes 132. Open January–February; breakfast $1.00	(	51322	$7.00
★	Hostería Plaza, Entre Ríos 530. No single rooms	(	51252	
★	Hostería San Martín, Lopez y Planes 174. Breakfast included	(	51158	$19.00
•	Hospedaje Colonial, 25 de Mayo 426	(	51584	$3.00
•	Residencial Normandie, Bomberos Voluntarios. No single rooms	(	51120	
•	Residencial Peti, corner of General Paz and Rivadavia			$7.00
•	Residencial Los Montes, Juan Benitez. Breakfast included	(	51167	$16.00

La Cumbre

CÓRDOBA PROVINCE

LA CUMBRECITA

Postal code: 5194
Distance from Córdoba: 110 km southwest

La Cumbrecita is situated in the eastern part of the **Sierra de Comechingones** on the **Río del Medio** which flows into **Dique Los Molinos** dam. It has an alpine appearance and is much frequented by the German and Swiss communities in Argentina.

Accommodation
- ★★ Hotel La Cumbrecita $25.00
- ★★ Hotel Las Cascadas. Closed June
- ★ Hotel Tilcara $14.00. Open December–April; breakfast $2.00
- Hotel Las Verbenas $22.00. Breakfast $2.00
- Hotel Panorama $24.00. Breakfast $1.50

Buses
La Cumbrecita is best reached from Villa General Belgrano, 40 km away.

Sport
There are fishing and hiking in the hills.

Excursions
See "Excursions" under Villa Carlos Paz on page 224, and under Villa General Belgrano on page 233

LA FALDA

Postal code: 5172 • Population: 15 000 • area code: (0548) • Altitude: 933 m
Distance from Córdoba: 83 km northwest via Río Ceballos

La Falda is located on the slopes of the **Sierra Chica** and is the center of the *punilla* tourist area. The land on which it stands was originally part of a grant made by Jerónimo Luis de Cabrera to his loyal followers. La Falda was acquired by Dr Juan Bialet Massé in 1847 and gradually increased in size and importance until the first procession of the Inmaculada Concepción on December 8, 1868. This day is regarded as the foundation day of the city and celebrated each year with great aplomb. The real boost to the fledgling town came in 1897 with the construction of Hotel Eden. There are now over seventy hotels, making La Falda one of the largest tourist centres in the *punilla*.

The pure air is one of the attractions of La Falda. From November to February there is some rain.

La Falda is a good base for excursions into the surrounding area. Visit the nearby **Cerro El Cuadrado** (1500 m) and **Villa Giardino** on the **Río San Francisco**, with its mill constructed by the Jesuits.

Festivals
- Foundation Day: December 8
- Fiesta Nacional del Tango (National Tango Festival): February

Tourist information
- Secretaria de Turismo, Avenida España 50, in what was the rail station ℂ 22764
- Secretaria de Turismo, bus terminal ℂ 23186

CÓRDOBA PROVINCE

Camping

- Río Grande, on the beach at Morecabo. Follow Avenida Italia and turn to the right before crossing the bridge
- Siete Cascadas, on the beach at Siete Cascadas. Follow Avenida Italia, cross the bridge and take the small trail to the left passing by the dam

Eating out

- Restaurant Araxi, corner of Avenida Eden and Santa Fé
- Restaurant Caprí, Avenida Buenos Aires 305
- Restaurant El Bochin, España 117
- Restaurant El Chivito Dorado, Paraná 38. Goat's meat
- Restaurant El Cristal, San Lorenzo 39
- Restaurant El Cristal II, corner of Maipú and Avenida Kennedy
- Restaurant El Laurel, corner of Diagonal San Martín and Avenida España
- Restaurant La Falda, Avenida Buenos Aires 100
- Restaurant La Posta de Eden, Avenida Eden 560
- Restaurant Munich, Avenida España 147
- Restaurant Nor-Tomarza, Avenida Eden 1002
- Restaurant Petit Salon Azul, Uruguay 36
- Restaurant Rancho Criollo II, Avenida Eden 701
- Restaurant Rancho Grande, Avenida España 700
- Restaurant San Martín, Avenida Buenos Aires 114
- Restaurant Salzburgo, Camino Laguna de los Patos
- Pizzería Alpi, Avenida Eden 139
- Pizzería American, corner of Avenida Eden and La Plata
- Pizzería Bar Argentino, Avenida Eden 150
- Pizzería Bon, corner of Avenida Eden and Rivadavia
- Pizzería Copacabana, Avenida Buenos Aires
- Pizzería Gorosito, Parana 27
- Cafetería ACA, corner of Avenida España and Sarmiento
- Cafetería Atelier, Avenida Eden 337
- Cafetería Baviera, Avenida Eden 218
- Cafetería Bon-Con, Avenida Eden 348
- Cafetería Bon-Ter, bus terminal
- Cafetería Casablanca, Avenida Eden 574
- Cafetería Fra-Noi, Avenida Eden 570
- Cafetería Ki-Bon, Avenida Eden 444
- Cafetería Molino de Oro, Los Eucaliptos
- Cafetería Payp's, corner of Avenida Eden and San Geronimo
- Cafetería Schmidel, 25 de Mayo 417
- Cafetería Sir Lawrence, Avenida Eden 176
- Cafetería Strauss, corner of Avenida Eden and San Lorenzo

Post and telegraph

- Post office: Encotel, Diagonal San Martín
- Telephone: Entel, Diagonal San Martín 6

Services and facilities

- Laundromat: Laverap, Capital Federal 96 (corner of Avenida 25 de Mayo). Open Mon–Sat 0800–2000
- Bicycle hire: Bicicletería Loza, corner of Uruguay and 25 de Mayo

Motoring

- Service station: ACA, corner of Avenida España and Eden (22674
- Car hire: Mar-Per-Tur, corner of Sarmiento and Diagonal San Martín

Tours

La Falda, G L de Cabrera 206 (22740, operates a number of tours, all of which run daily and require a minimum of eight passengers.

- Ascochinga and Salsipuedes: Fare $10.00; departs 0830. Fare includes a barbecue
- Cosquín and Pan de Azucar: Fare $5.00; departs 1400
- Dique Cruz del Eje: Fare $5.00; departs 1400
- La Cumbre and Los Cocos: Fare $3.50; departs 1400
- Mina Clavero and Los Túneles: Fare $12.00; departs 0530
- Villa Carlos Paz and Tanti: Fare $4.00; departs 1400
- Villa General Belgrano and La Cumbrecita: Fare $11.00; departs 0600

La Falda

CÓRDOBA PROVINCE

LA FALDA

Key to Map
1. Municipalidad
2. Iglesia Santísimo Sacramento
3. Post office (Encotel)
4. Telephone (Entel)
5. Tourist information
6. Banco de la Nación
7. Bus terminal

La Falda

CÓRDOBA PROVINCE

Accommodation in La Falda

★★★★	Hotel Nor-Tomarza, Avenida Eden 1063	22004	$32.00	
	Breakfast $3.00			
★★★★	Hotel Tomaso di Savoia, Avenida Eden 732	23013	$34.00	
	Breakfast $5.00			
★★★	Hotel Araxi, Avenida Eden 1002	25172	$30.00	
	Breakfast $3.00			
★★	Hotel España, Pueyrredón 24	22001, 22344	$17.00	
	Breakfast $2.00			
★★	Hotel El Soberano, L de la Torre 411	22801	$16.00	
	Open December–March; breakfast $2.00			
★★	Hotel Fiumicino, Avenida Eden 735	23065	$15.00	
	Breakfast $2.00			
★★	Hotel Italia, Avenida Belgrano 420	22017	$17.00	
	Open December–March; breakfast $2.00			
★★	Hotel La Asturiana, Avenida Colón 835	22923	$16.00	
	Breakfast $2.00			
★★	Hotel Leon de Castilla, Avenida Buenos Aires 238	22878	$13.00	
	Open October–July; breakfast $2.00			
★★	Hotel Majestic, Capital Federal 149	22117	$11.00	
	Open December–February			
	Hotel Montecarlo, Avenida España 884	22650	$17.00	
	Breakfast $1.50			
★★	Hotel Ollantay, La Plata 236	22341	$21.00	
	Breakfast $2.00			
★★	Hotel Punilla, 9 de Julio 201 (corner of Bahía Blanca)	22121	$20.00	
	Open December–March			
★★	Hotel Sans Souci, Avenida 9 de Julio 1349	22228	$17.00	
	Breakfast $2.00			
★★	Hotel Scala, La Plata 59	23072	$27.00	
	Breakfast $2.00			
★★	Hotel Sorrento, Avenida Argentina 118	23577	$12.00	
	Includes breakfast			
★	Hotel Buenos Aires, Avenida Buenos Aires 139	22534	$15.00	
	Breakfast $1.50			
★	Hotel Colón, Avenida España 168	22209	$12.00	
	Breakfast $1.50			
★	Hotel El Piccolo, Avenida Uruguay 61	23343	$9.00	
	Includes breakfast			
★	Hotel Gure Echea, Bahia Blanca 258	22175	$14.00	
	Breakfast $2.00			
★	Hotel Galeon, Avenida Rosario 520	23033		
★	Hotel Ideal, Avenida General Güemes 297	22041, 22230		
	No single rooms			

Entertainment

- Disco Alkarim, Avenida Eden 513
- Disco Bon-Bai, Sarmiento 348
- Disco Gregor, Pasaje Cap de Villa
- Disco Peperina Bar, Avenida Eden 590

Sightseeing

- Hotel Eden: At the end of Avenida Eden. In its heyday, between 1904 and 1945, the

continued on page 184

La Falda

Accommodation in La Falda—Continued

★	Hotel La Asturiana, Avenida Argentina 119 ⌑	ℓ	22357	
	No single rooms			
★	Hotel La Falda, Alvear 107 ⌑⌑	ℓ	22990	$11.00 ⌑
	Breakfast $1.50			
★	Hotel La Favorita, Buenos Aires 207 ⌑	ℓ	22375	$10.00 ⌑
	Includes breakfast			
★	Hotel Las Violetas, Güemes 124 ⌑	ℓ	23322	$9.00 ⌑
★	Hotel Malvinas Argentinas, Güemes 117 ⌑	ℓ	22811	$14.00 ⌑
	Breakfast $1.50			
★	Hotel Matias, Sarmiento 256 ⌑	ℓ	23038	$8.00 ⌑
★	Hotel El Nogal, Estados Unidos 149 ⌑	ℓ	22477	
	No single rooms			
★	Hotel Mi Sueño, Avenida Argentina 157 ⌑	ℓ	22153	$11.00 ⌑
	Breakfast $1.50			
★	Hotel Marydor, Avenida Eden 868 ⌑⌑	ℓ	23510	$8.00 ⌑
★	Hotel Novelty, Las Heras 208 ⌑	ℓ	22922	$9.00 ⌑
	Open summer only; breakfast included			
★	Hotel Old Garden, Capital Federal 28 ⌑⌑	ℓ	22842	$13.00 ⌑
	Includes breakfast			
★	Hotel Mediterraneo (Patria), Avenida Patria 147 ⌑⌑	ℓ	22720	$10.00 ⌑
	Breakfast $1.50			
★	Hotel Peloso, Avenida España 242 ⌑⌑	ℓ	23201	$12.00 ⌑
	Breakfast $1.50			
★	Hotel San Remo, Avenida Argentina 108 ⌑	ℓ	22409	$8.00 ⌑
	Open December–April; breakfast $1.00			
★	Hotel Santa Ines, Avenida Rosario 102 ⌑	ℓ	22061	$13.00 ⌑
	Breakfast $1.50			
★	Hotel Sherop's, Avenida Eden 1100 ⌑⌑⌑	ℓ	22857	$13.00 ⌑
	Includes breakfast			
★	Hotel Villa del Rosario, Güemes 149 ⌑	ℓ	22958	$7.00 ⌑
	Open summer only			
•	Hotel Capri, Buenos Aires 315	ℓ	2714	
★★	Hostería El Mirador, Sargento Cabral 257 ⌑⌑⌑	ℓ	22710	$15.00 ⌑
	Breakfast $1.00			
★★	Hostería Viejo Castaño, Los Aromos ⌑⌑	ℓ	22875	$11.00 ⌑
	Open January–March; breakfast $2.00			
★★	Hostería Los Andes, corner of Pringles and Maipú ⌑⌑	ℓ	22044	$10.00 ⌑
	Open summer only			
★	Hostería Carlos Manuel, Victoria 299 ⌑	ℓ	22546	
	Open December–March; no single rooms			
★	Hostería El Paraiso, España 125 ⌑	ℓ		$11.00
	Included breakfast			
★	Hostería Fenix, 25 de Mayo 268 ⌑⌑	ℓ	22411	$12.00 ⌑
★	Hostería La Casona, Avenida Argentina 340 ⌑	ℓ	22498	$10.00 ⌑
	Includes breakfast			
★	Hostería Las Piedras, Güemes ⌑	ℓ	23155	$10.00 ⌑
	Includes breakfast			
★	Hostería Marina, Güemes 134 ⌑	ℓ	22640	$11.00 ⌑
	Open December–March; includes breakfast			
★	Hostería Mayo, 25 de Mayo 426 ⌑⌑	ℓ		$13.00
	Open January–April; breakfast $1.50			
★	Hostería Nuevo Achalay, Victoria 294 ⌑	ℓ	22318	$10.00 ⌑
	Breakfast $1.50			
★	Hostería Zurich, Río Negro 311 ⌑⌑	ℓ	22458	$9.00 ⌑
	Open January–February; includes breakfast			

La Falda

Accommodation in La Falda—Continued

- Hospedaje Ananke, Lamadrid 481 ✈   ℭ 22316 $8.00 ♂♀
  Open December–February
- Hospedaje Los Pinos, corner of Maipú and Kennedy ✈▲   ℭ 22353 $11.00 ♂♀
  Open January–March; breakfast $1.50
- Hospedaje Las Playas, Avenida Ferrarini 355 ✈ℭ   ℭ 22536 $7.00 ♂♀
  No single rooms
- Hospedaje 9 de Julio, 9 de Julio 155 ✈   ℭ 22173 $10.00 ♂♀
  Includes breakfast
- Residencial Llao Llao, Avenida Kennedy 356   ℭ 22225 $15.00 ♂♀
  Breakfast $2.00
- Residencial Rosa Roja, Avenida Argentina 239 ✈   ℭ 22549 $9.00 ♂♀
  Open January–April; breakfast $1.50
- Residencial Molino Azul, 25 de Mayo 402 (corner of Bahía Blanca) ⛟
  Breakfast $1.50   ℭ 22151, 22152 $10.00 ♂♀
- Residencial Piemonte, La Plata 239 ⛟   ℭ 23160
  No single rooms
- Residencial San Miguel, La Plata 160 ⛟   ℭ 22404 $8.00 ♂♀

Accommodation in Huerta Grande

The town of Huerta Grande has almost merged with La Falda. Although no prices can be given for individual hotels they are in line with those in La Falda.

- ★ Hotel Bellavista, Avenida San Martín 748 ⛟●▲
  No single rooms
- ★ Hotel El Molino, San Juan 100 ⛟▲   ℭ 23097
  No single rooms
- ★ Hotel El Portal, Avenida San Martín 1744 ⛟▲   ℭ 21051
  No single rooms
- ★ Hostería La Posada, R Cassaux 217 ⛟▲   ℭ 21793
  No single rooms
- ★ Hostería Panorama, G Battaglia ⛟▲
  No single rooms
- Hospedaje Los Troncos, Avenida San Martín 2256 ✈●
  Open December–February; no single rooms
- Residencial Dorado, Provincias Unidas 341 ✈
  No single rooms
- Residencial Huguito, Capitán Arrubarrena 1659 ✈
  No single rooms
- Residencial San Remo, Provincias Unidas 59 ⛟●

Accommodation in Valle Hermoso

Valle Hermoso is now virtually a southern suburb of La Falda. There are regular municipal buses linking La Falda, Huerta Grande, and Valle Hermoso.

- ★★ Hotel La Martucha, Gdor Carcano 161 ⛟▲   ℭ 21306
  No single rooms
- ★★ Hotel Tehuel, corner of General Paz and Argentina ⛟●▲   ℭ 21262
  No single rooms
- ★ Hotel Biondi's, General Paz 186 ⛟▲   ℭ 21252 $11.00 ♂♀
  Breakfast $1.50

CÓRDOBA PROVINCE

Accommodation in La Falda—Continued

Accommodation in Valle Hermoso—Continued

★	Hotel Lucerna, Rodriguez Peña 15	(21878	$13.00	♁
	Open January–March; breakfast $1.50			
★	Hostería La Rosita, Fleming 12	(23006	$8.00	♁
	Open January–April; breakfast $1.00			
•	Hospedaje Alex Mar, Alsina 140	(21757		
	Open January–March; no single rooms			
•	Hospedaje Carmencita	(22544		
	Triple rooms only			
•	Hospedaje Guindon, RN 38			
	Open December–March; triple rooms only			
•	Hospedaje Ivalu, Villa California			
	No single rooms			
•	Hospedaje Nuevo Venecia, RN 38 Km 779			
	No single rooms			
•	Hospedaje Santa Elizabeth, RN 38 Km 779			
•	Residencial Colonial, Pellegrini	(21176		
	Open November–March; no single rooms			
•	Residencial Galicia, Calderon de la Barca		$11.00	♁
	Breakfast $1.00			
•	Residencial Santa Rosa, Gdor Carcano 381			
	No single rooms			

Accommodation in Villa Giardino

Villa Giardino is located 5 km north of La Falda, of which it is virtually the northernmost suburb.

★★	Hotel Alto de San Pedro, Alto de San Pedro	
★	Hostería Avenida, corner of RN 38 and Augusto Fasi	
	No single rooms	
•	Hospedaje Anita, Dante Aleghieri	$8.00
	No single rooms	
•	Hospedaje Tina, Avenida Las Flores	
	Open January–March; no single rooms	

Hotel Eden was a self-sufficient unit with its own farm
- Model railway museum at the end of Avenida 25 de Mayo
- Old restored Capilla de San Antonio (St Anthony's Chapel) in Valle Hermoso

🍂 Excursions
- **Quebrada Chica**
- **Huerta Grande** (971 m): 3½ km on RN 38. A bathing resort with good fishing and medicinal waters
- **Cascadas de Olaen** (Olaen Falls) and Capilla de Santa Barbara (St Barbara's Chapel): Start at Avenida Italia and continue along the dirt road towards **Pampa de Olaen**. Twenty-two km past **Fundación San Roque** turn south, then at the signpost saying "Cascadas de Olaen" leave your car and walk 5 km to

La Falda

CÓRDOBA PROVINCE

Buses from La Falda

Destination	Fare	Depart	Services	Hours	Company
• Córdoba	$2.20	0530	28 services daily	2	Cotil, Primero de Mayo
• Buenos Aires	$26.70	0820	7 services daily		ABLO, T A Chevallier
• Capilla del Monte	$1.00	0905	12 services daily	1	Cotil, Primero de Mayo
• Chilecito	$9.50	2350	daily	7	Cotil
• Cosquín	$0.60	0545	8 services daily	½	Primero de Mayo
• Cruz del Eje	$1.80	0535	10 services daily	1½	Cotil
	$1.20	0905	8 services daily	1½	Primero de Mayo
• La Cumbre	$0.50	0905	12 services daily	½	Cotil, Primero de Mayo
• La Rioja	$8.00	1455	daily	6½	Cotil
• Rosario		0820	5 services daily	8	ABLO, TA Chevallier
• Villa Carlos Paz	$1.30	0635	8 services daily	2	Primero de Mayo

the waterfall. Alternatively, it is a one-day hike. Marble and limestone are mined here. At the time of the Spanish occupation this area was settled by Sanavirones Comechingones Indians. The waterfall is in a picturesque canyon and forms a small lake; it is a favorite outing for people from the *punilla* tourist resorts. The Capilla de Santa Barbara, built in 1747, has a venerated picture of St Barbara. Nearby are the ruins of a manorial building which belonged to a famous descendant of the founder of Córdoba, Dr Diego de Salguero y Cabrera

- **Dique La Falda**: A short walk following Avenida Italia on the outskirts of town. This weir dams up the **Río Grande de Punillas** and provides water for La Falda
- **Cerro El Cuadrado**: Follow Avenida Eden to the end and follow the signs to the left. From the "Balcony of the Clouds" just before the summit you have extensive views over the city and the **Río Punillas valley**

LA GRANJA

Postal code: 5166 • Altitude: 630 m
Distance from Córdoba: 56 km northwards on RN 9 via Caroya

La Granja is situated 6 km south of Ascochinga on the eastern side of the **Sierra Chica** on the **Río La Granja**.

(This La Granja is the one north of Córdoba, not to be confused with La Granja west of Alta Gracia.)

Accommodation

★ Hostería La Granja, RP 53 (297. Open January–March; no single rooms
★ Hostería Las Vertientes, RP 53 (216. No single rooms
• Residencial La Primavera

La Granja

CÓRDOBA PROVINCE

LA POBLACIÓN

Postal code: 5200
Distance from Villa Dolores: 26 km eastwards

La Población is situated in the western foothills of the **Sierra de Comechingones**.

Accommodation
- Residencial Champaqui. No single rooms

LABOULAYE

Postal code: 6120
Distance from Buenos Aires: 517 km westwards on RN 7

Laboulaye is located in the southern part of the province at the intersection of RN 7 (east–west) and RP 4 (north–south).

Accommodation
- ★★ Hotel Ranquel Maipú, RN 7 Km 489 (7466 $24.00
- Hospedaje Italia, Ameghino 10 (582
- Hospedaje Mar Azul, Moreno 1 (559 $5.00. Shared bathrooms
- Hospedaje Sanchez, Avellaneda 21
- Hospedaje Victoria, Alvear 10 (256 $14.00. Shared bathroom cheaper

Buses
Buses run regularly to Buenos Aires, Mendoza, and Córdoba.

LAS RABONAS

Postal code: 5885
Distance from Córdoba: 162 km south-west on RN 20

Las Rabonas is situated on the shore of the artificial lake **Lago Ingeniero A M Allende** on the western slope of the **Cumbres de Achala**. It is well situated for walks into the mountains and watersports on the lake.

Accommodation
- ★ Hostería Tajamar. Open December–April

LEONES

Postal code: 2594 • area code: (0472)
Distance from Córdoba: 277 km south-east on RN 9

Accommodation
- ★ Hotel Ideal, corner of Amadeo Bertini and Colón (8553

LOS COCOS

Postal code: 5181 • Altitude: 1220 m
Distance from Córdoba via Jesús María: 105 km north-west

Los Cocos is a small village in the northern part of the **Sierra Chica**. Although off the beaten track, it is within walking distance of La Cumbre and is a good base for easy walks in the Sierra.

Accommodation
- ★★ Hotel La Esperanza (16 $13.00. Breakfast $1.50

La Población

CÓRDOBA PROVINCE

★★ Hotel Los Pinos, Cecilia Grierson 🅘🅢🅐 (2 $13.00 ♨. Breakfast $1.50
★★ Hostería Ramos, Las Calas 🅘🅐 (49 $15.00 ♨. Breakfast $2.00
★ Hostería Zanier, Las Calas 🅢🅐. No single rooms
Hospedaje La Mamita, Las Margaritas 🅢🅐. No single rooms

🚌 Buses
- Buses run regularly to La Cumbre.

LOS HORNILLOS

Los Hornillos is set in the foothills of the **Sierra de Achala** near Villa Dolores, and is virtually the start of the picturesque Tras la Sierra road to Córdoba.

🛏 Accommodation
- Hospedaje Alta Montaña 🅘🅐 $16.00 ♨. Open October–February; breakfast $2.00
- Hospedaje Barrionuevo 🅢. Open July–October; no single rooms
- Residencial Dos Arroyos 🅘🅐. Open January only; no single rooms

MARCOS JUÁREZ

Postal code: 2580 • (area code: (0472) •
Altitude: 115 m
Distance from Córdoba: 255 km southeast on RN 9

Located in the *pampa*, Marcos Juarez is the center of an agricultural district. It is served by the F C General B Mitre railroad.

🚌 Buses
Buses run regularly to Córdoba and Rosario.

MINA CLAVERO

Postal code: 5889 • (area code: (0544) •
Altitude: 915 m
Distance from Córdoba: 140 km southwest on RN 20

Mina Clavero is located in the valley to the west of the **Sierra Grande** and the **Pampa de Pocho**. Seen from Córdoba city, it is "behind the mountains", whence the name of the region "Traslasierra". It is easily accessible from Córdoba and San Luis, and has good tourist facilities, al-

🛏 Accommodation in Marcos Juárez

★★	Hotel El Tropical, corner of RN 9 and Calle 4 🅘	(	25426	$15.00 ♨
★	Hotel Marcos Juárez, RN 9 Km 445 🅢	(	25558	
•	Hospedaje Bali-Cor, corner of RN 9 and Santiago del Estero	(	26131	
•	Hospedaje Dezotti, San Martín 764	(	26613	
•	Hospedaje Esmeralda, 9 de Julio 274 🅢	(	26565	
•	Hospedaje Samurai, RN 9 Km 436 🅢 No single rooms			

Mina Clavero

though some of the hotels are not open all year round. It is a good starting point for exploration and hiking in the mountains: **Cerro Champaquí**, at 2880 m the highest mountain of Córdoba province, is within easy reach of the town.

In 1573 the first Spanish expedition visited the area to assess the number and location of the indigenous population and to find gold. The expedition was made up of forty soldiers under the command of Capitán Hernán Mejías Miraval. Chroniclers report that the Contonavi Indian village headed by *Cacique* (or "Chief") Milac Navira was at the junction of the **Río Panaholma** and **Río Mina Clavero**. The present name is a corruption of the chief's name. From 1598 onwards some mines were worked in the area, and from 1890 there was a small flow of tourists to take advantage of the mineral waters which have similiar properties to those of Evian in France.

In pre-Hispanic times gold was mined near the aboriginal settlement on the **Río Panaholma**, suggesting that a branch of the Inca road finished there.

Some rain falls between December and March.

ℹ️ Tourist information
- Avenida Mitre 1191 ℡ 70001

▲ Camping
- Autocamping Dos Ríos, Avenida Merlo
- La Siesta, Avenida Santa Isabel

🍴 Eating out
- Restaurant Amadeus, San Martín block 1200 (corner of Belgrano)
- Restaurant Bardon Ramon, San Martín block 1000 (corner of Intendente Vila
- Restaurant Don Damian, San Martín 1144
- Restaurant Don Enrique, San Martín block 1200 (corner of Lugones)
- Restaurant El Altillo, San Martín 1076. Steakhouse

continued on page 192

Key to Map
1. Municipalidad
2. Iglesia
3. Post office (Encotel)
4. Telephone (Entel)
5. Bus terminal
6. Tourist information
7. Hotel los Aromos
8. Hotel la Morenita
9. Hospedaje Franchino
10. Residencial Asturias
11. Hostería Progreso
12. Hotel San Martín
13. Hotel Rossetti
14. Hostería Bellavista
15. Hotel Nuevo Fenix
16. Hotel Palace
17. Hostería Meliton Dominguez
18. Motel Ruta 66
19. Hotel Marengo
20. Hostería La Ideal
21. Hotel Vila
22. Hotel Mina Clavero
23. Hospedaje Italia
24. Hostería del Sol
25. Residencial El Porteño
26. Hospedaje Ferrari
27. Hostería Danubio
28. Hotel Oviedo
29. Residencial Pilla
30. Hostería Zazu
31. Hostería Tico Tico
32. Casino de la Traslasierra
33. Hospedaje Coronado
34. Residencial España

CÓRDOBA PROVINCE

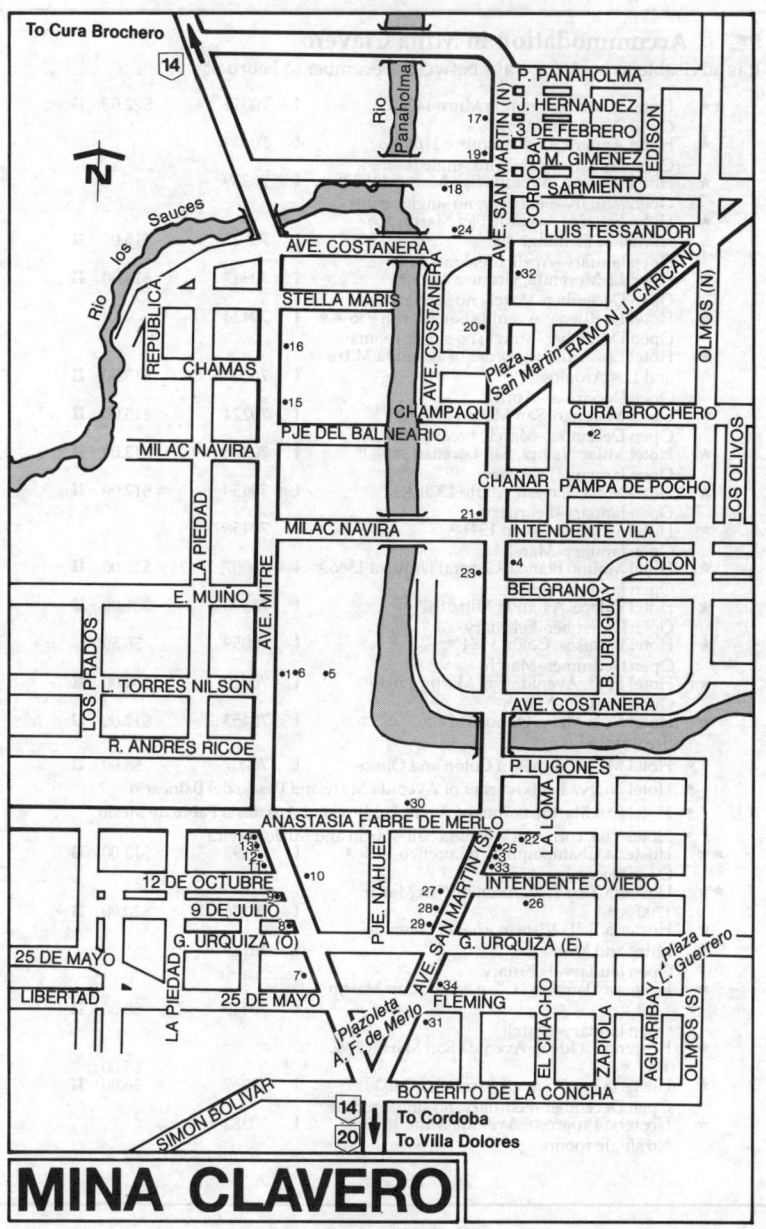

Mina Clavero

CÓRDOBA PROVINCE

🛏 Accommodation in Mina Clavero

It is advisable to book for stays between December to February.

★★	Hotel Rossetti, Avenida Mitre 1434	✆ 70012	$22.00	👥
	Open December–April			
★	Hotel Aguero, 12 de Octubre 1166	✆ 70439		
	Open January–March; no single rooms			
★	Hotel Aguirre, Avenida San Martín 1188	✆ 70239		
	Open January–February; no single rooms			
★	Hotel España, Avenida San Martín 1687 (corner of Fleming)	✆ 70123	$15.00	👥
	Open January–April; breakfast $1.00			
★	Hotel La Moreníta, Urquiza 1145	✆ 70347	$14.00	👥
	Open December–March; no single rooms			
★	Hotel La Rueda, Avenida San Martín 986	✆ 70424		
	Open December–March; no single rooms			
★	Hotel Los Aromos, corner of Avenida Mitre and Los Aromos	✆ 70200	$13.00	👥
	Open December–April			
★	Hotel Marengo, San Martín 598	✆ 70224	$15.00	👥
	Open December–March; breakfast $1.00			
★	Hotel Milac Navira, San Lorenzo 1407	✆ 70278	$13.00	👥
	Open January–February			
★	Hotel Mina Clavero, Merlo 1320	✆ 70450	$12.00	👥
	Open January–February			
★	Hotel Mirador, Colón 1941	✆ 70456		
	Open January–March			
★	Hotel Molino Blanco, General Urquiza 1366	✆ 70007, 70124	$15.00	👥
	Open January–April			
★	Hotel Palace, Avenida Mitre 847	✆ 70390	$21.00	👥
	Open December–February			
★	Hotel Paraisos, Colón 1584	✆ 70059	$6.50	
	Open December–March			
★	Hotel Petit, Avenida San Martín 1263	✆ 70019	$8.00	👥
	Open January–March			
★	Hotel Villa Mery, Olmos 1524	✆ 70453	$12.00	👥
	Breakfast $1.00			
•	Hotel Monti, corner of Colón and Olmos	✆ 70007	$8.00	👥
•	Hotel Nueva Fenix, corner of Avenida Mitre and Pasaje del Balneario			
•	Hotel San Martín, corner of Avenida Mitre and Anastasia Fabre de Merlo			
•	Hotel Vila, corner of Avenida San Martín and Milac Navira			
★★	Hostería Champaqui, San Lorenzo 1429	✆ 70393	$13.00	👥
	Open December–March			
★★	Hostería Tico Tico, Avenida San Martín 1700	✆ 70176	$20.00	👥
★	Hostería Bella Vista, corner of Avenida Mitre and Merlo	✆ 70165		
	Open January–February			
★	Hostería Danubio "C", Avenida San Martín 1482	✆ 70440	$8.00	👥
	Open January–March			
★	Hostería La Ideal, Avenida San Martín 706		$5.00	
★	Hostería Los Puentes, Sarmiento 1403	✆ 70357	$6.00	👥
	Open December–February; no single rooms			
★	Hostería Progreso, Avenida Mitre 1506	✆ 70382		
	No single rooms			

Mina Clavero

Accommodation in Mina Clavero—Continued

- ★ Hostería Sierras, Belgrano 1367 ☎   (70223 $4.00
  Open January–March; no single rooms
- ★ Hostería Zazu, Merlo 1241 🍽   (70449 $6.50
  Open December–March
- • Hostería del Sol, corner of Costanera and Avenida San Martín
- • Hostería Meliton Dominguez, Avenida San Martín
- ★★ Motel Du Soleil, corner of Avenida Mitre and
  La Piedad ☎●   (70066 $20.00 ♊
  Breakfast $2.00
- ★ Motel Ruta 66, Tessandori 1254 ☎   (70342 $18.00 ♊
- • Hospedaje Ana Maria, San Martín 1548 ☎   (91225, 70225
  Open December–March; no single rooms
- • Hospedaje Car Mar, Los Valles 1320, Barrio Santa Ana
  Triple rooms only   (70693 $5.50
- • Hospedaje Costa Azul, Urquiza 1142   (70347
  Open December–March; no single rooms
- • Hospedaje Coronado, corner of Avenida San
  Martín 1495 and San Lorenzo ☎
  Open January–March; no single rooms
- • Hospedaje Ferrari, San Lorenzo 1344 ☎   (91172, 70172 $5.00
  No single rooms
- • Hospedaje Franchino, Avenida Mitre 1544
  (corner of 9 de Julio) ☎   (70395
  Open December–March
- • Hospedaje Italia, San Martín 1176   (70232 $3.00
  Open January–March
- • Hospedaje La Primavera, Belgrano 1474 ☎   (70381 $5.00
  Open January–March and July–August
- • Hospedaje Las Moras, Urquiza 1361 ☎ $7.00 ♊
  No single rooms
- • Hospedaje Los Espinillos, Intendente Villa
  1465   (70356
  Open January–February; no single rooms
- • Hospedaje Nury, Merlo 1210 ☎   (70228 $6.00
  No single rooms
- • Hospedaje Oviedo, San Martín 1500 ☎ $5.00
  Open December–March; no single rooms
- • Hospedaje Pilla, San Martín 1540
  Open January–March; no single rooms
- • Residencial Aire y Sol, Rivadavia 551 🍽   (70226 $9.50 ♊
  No single rooms
- • Residencial Asturias, Avenida Mitre 1517 🍽   (70016 $9.50 ♊
  No single rooms
- • Residencial Buenos Aires, Los Alpes 581
  (corner of Edison) 🍽 $9.50 ♊
  Open January–February; no single rooms
- • Residencial El Parral, Avenida Intendente
  Vilas 1430   (70005
  No single rooms
- • Residencial El Porteño, San Martín 1441 🍽   (70235 $5.00
  Open January–March; no single rooms

CÓRDOBA PROVINCE

Accommodation in Mina Clavero—Continued

- Residencial España, corner of San Martín and Urquiza 🏨 — (70387
  Open December–March; no single rooms
- Residencial Llastaj-Sumaj, Sarmiento 1394 — (70074 — $5.00
  No single rooms
- Residencial Los Alpes, Sarmiento 1431 🏨 — (70191
  Open January–February; no single rooms
- Residencial Pilla, corner of Avenida San Martín and G Urquiza

Accommodation outside Mina Clavero

★ Hostería Santa María, RP 14 Pampa de Achala Km 126, 5 km north 🏨 — $5.00

- Restaurant El Mangrullo, San Martín block 1100 (corner of Intendente Vila). Steakhouse
- Restaurant El Platerito, San Martín block 1200 (corner of Lugones)
- ☞ Restaurant Escalera Real, San Martín block 1100 (corner of Intendente Vila, upstairs)
- Restaurant La Casa de Mi Abuela, San Martín block 1200 (corner of Belgrano)
- Restaurant La Mezquita, San Martín Norte block 700 (corner of Avenida Costanera)
- Restaurant Rincón Suizo, Champaquí 1200. International cuisine
- Pizzería El Capricho, San Martín block 1100 (corner of Intendente Vila)
- Pizzería El Obrero, San Martín block 1000 (corner of Intendente Vila)
- Pizzería Las Brasas, San Martín Norte (corner of Champaquí)
- Pizzería Las Palmeras, San Martín block 1200 (corner of Lugones)
- Pizzería Rumico, San Martín block 1200 (corner of Lugones)
- Cafetería Keops, San Martín block 1200 (corner of Belgrano)
- Cafetería Palenque, San Martín block 1100 (corner of Belgrano)
- Confitería Del Carmen, San Martín 1335

🚌 Buses from Mina Clavero

The bus terminal is behind the Municipalidad in Avenida Mitre 1191.

Destination	Fare	Depart	Services	Hours	Company
• Córdoba	$5.50	0720	10 services daily	4–5	Contal, EPA/El Petizo, 20 de Junio
• Buenos Aires	$24.50	1700	Mon–Thurs	16½	Chevallier, TAC
• Cruz del Eje					Contal
• El Condor		0805	7 services daily	1½	EPA/El Petizo
• Mendoza					TAC
• Merlo					TAC
• Río Cuarto					S Cordobesas, TAC, TA Chevallier
• Salsacate	$1.00	0720	2 services daily	1½	20 de Junio
• San Juan					20 de Junio
• Tantí	$4.50	0720	2 services daily	3½	20 de Junio
• Villa Carlos Paz	$4.00	0805	7 services daily	3	EPA/El Petizo
• Villa Dolores	$1.25	1050	8 services daily	1	EPA/El Petizo, Expreso Mina Clavero

CÓRDOBA PROVINCE

- Snack Bar Imperial, San Martín (corner of Champaqui)

Post and telegraph
- Post office: Encotel, Avenida San Martín 1464
- Telephone: Entel, Avenida San Martín 1149

Services and facilities
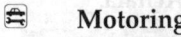
- Hospital, Fleming 1364 (70220
- Pharmacy: Farmacia López Romero, San Lorenzo 1501
- Supermercado: Stop, San Martín 729

Motoring

Service stations
- ACA, San Martín block 700
- Esso, corner of Mitre and Santa Ana

Sport
- Fishing: The rivers coming down from the Sierra are well-stocked with trout
- Golf: Hotel La Quebrada and Hotel Yacanto have nine-hole courses. They are both 15 km from Mina Clavero and 47 km from Merlo

Entertainment
- Bowling: Tico Tuco Ten Pin, San Martín block 1200 (corner of Belgrano)
- Casino de la Traslasierra, Avenida San Martín 785
- Discoteca Cabanna, corner of Champaqui and Avenida Costanera
- Discoteca Naturaleza, San Martín block 1100 (corner of Belgrano)

Excursions

See also "Excursions" under Villa Dolores on page 229

- **Villa Carlos Paz**: There is a good new road (not yet sealed) from Mina Clavero over the **Sierra Grande**. From **El Condor** onwards there are occasional spectacular glimpses of the city of **Córdoba**, **Lago San Roque**, and Villa Carlos Paz. There are magnificent vistas on this scenic drive. Although there is snow in winter the road is kept open. See also "Excursions" under Villa Carlos Paz on page 223
- **Museo Rocsen** (archeological and minerological museum) in **Nono**, 8 km south
- **El Cóndor**: The highest point in the **Pampa de Achala** with a view to **Lago San Roque**. There is a restaurant at El Cóndor but no accommodation. An 18 km hike north-west takes you to the Franciscan Collegio Padredose Marialiquens set against the **Sierra Grande** with views to **Cerro Los Gigantes** (2374 m)
- There are many beaches with camping grounds along **Río de los Sauces**
- **Lago Viña**

Archeological sites

There are several archeological sites in the area bearing witness to the pre-Columbian culture of the Comechingones, most of which are within walking distance of Mina Clavero.
- **Panaholma** site is on the track to **Las Maravillas**, 5 km north of Villa Cura Brochero
- **Campitos** site is 3 km south of Mina Clavero at the far end of the local airstrip on the property of the Charras family
- **Cañada Larga** site, 1 km east of the Campitos site: Here is a small cave with rock paintings where potsherds and stone mortars have been found

Mina Clavero

CÓRDOBA PROVINCE

MIRAMAR

Postal code: 5143
Distance from Córdoba: 200 km eastwards

Miramar is on the southern shore of **Laguna Mar Chiquita**. It is a very popular resort during the summer months. Laguna Mar Chiquita has no outlet, and is very swampy in the north where the **Río Dulce** enters.

The salt waters of Miramar are used in the treatment of rheumatic ailments and skin diseases.

Camping
- Autocamping Lilly

Motoring
Miramar is best reached by road from Córdoba.

NONO

Postal code: 5887
Distance from Córdoba: 147 km westwards on RN 20

Nono is located on the northern side of the artificial lake **Lago Ingeniero A M Allende** halfway between Villa Dolores and Mina Clavero. It is a good base for excursions to the western slopes of the **Cumbres de Achala**.

Accommodation
- ★★ Hostería La Lejania $14.00. Breakfast $2.00
- Hospedaje La Viña, Vicente Castro. Open January–February; no single rooms
- Residencial Del Alto, Alto del Monte. Open January; no single rooms
- Residencial La Quebrada, Casilla Correo 19
- Residencial Nono, Vicente Castro. Open January–March; no single rooms

Accommodation in Miramar

Hotel Savoy, Sarmiento — Full board	48	$10.00
Hotel Brazilia — Half board		$7.00
Hotel Marchetti, Córdoba — Breakfast $1.00	52	$3.50
Hospedaje Campomar		$3.50
Hospedaje Ethel	86	$3.00
Hospedaje Gatti		$3.00
Hospedaje Nover		$3.00
Hospedaje Hogar San Antonio		$3.00
Hospedaje La Porteña		$3.50
Hospedaje Mabel		$3.50
Hospedaje Merlino		$3.50
Hospedaje San Cayetano		$3.00

CÓRDOBA PROVINCE

Sightseeing
- Museo Rocsen, an archeological and mineralogical museum 5 km from the town center (towards the mountains), is open from 0900 till sunset daily

OLIVA

Postal code: 5980 • area code: (0532) • Altitude: 260 m
Distance from Córdoba: 93 km south-east on RN 9

Oliva is situated halfway between Córdoba and Villa María on RN 9 in the *pampa*.

Accommodation
★★ Hotel Ciudad de Oliva, Ruta 9 Km 612 (20668
Hospedaje El Panamericano, L N Alem 642

ONCATIVO

Postal code: 5986 • area code: (0572)
Distance from Córdoba: 78 km south-east on RN 9

Oncativo is located in the *pampa*. It is served by the F C General B Mitre railroad.

Accommodation
- ★ Hostería Permanelli, Belgrano 783 $11.00. Breakfast $1.50
- ★ Hotel La Posa, San Martín 1180 $14.00. Breakfast $2.00
- Hospedaje Franco, San Martín 1200 (66095 $9.00

PILAR

Postal code: 5972 • area code: (0572)
Distance from Córdoba: 44 km south-east on RN 9

Pilar is located in the *pampa* on the **Río Segundo**.

Accommodation
- Hospedaje El Puente, Juan B Alberdí $8.00
- Hospedaje La Taberna de Adan, Juan B Alberdí (91263 $9.00 No single rooms
- Hospedaje Pilar, RN 9 between Rioja and Catamarca. No single rooms
- Hospedaje Ruta 9, corner of Juan B Alberdí and T Garzon (91278

Accommodation in Río Segundo

Río Segundo is 5 km north of Pilar.
- Hospedaje Ri–So–Ra, RN 9 Km 737

RÍO CEBALLOS

Postal code: 5111 • area code: (051) • Altitude: 679 m
Distance from Córdoba: 33 km north

Río Ceballos is located on the eastern slopes of the **Sierra Chica** and is a favorite vacation resort with Argentines. There is a scenic drive to **La Falda** across the *sierra*.

Camping
- La Quebrada, on the artificial lake

Eating out
- Cafetería Faquie, Avenida San Martín 4526. Video bar

CÓRDOBA PROVINCE

Accommodation in Río Ceballos

- ★ Hotel California, Avenida San Martín 7888 — $15.00
  Open January–March; breakfast $1.50
- ★ Hotel Gure Echea, corner of Azcuenaga and Rivadavia — 951495 — $13.00
  Breakfast $1.50
- ★ Hotel Los Algarrobos, Avenida San Martín 5403 — 951026 — $13.00
  Breakfast $1.50
- ★ Hotel Namuncura, 3 de Febrero 38 — 951391 — $12.00
  Breakfast $1.00
- ★ Hotel Rama, Alte Brown 714 — 951028 — $10.00
  Breakfast $1.00
- ★ Hotel San Pedro, Avenida San Martín 3637 — 951305
  No single rooms
- ★ Hotel Stella Alpina, Avenida San Martín — 951179 — $10.00
  Open January–March; breakfast $1.50
- ★ Hostería Americano, Avenida San Martín 6302 — $10.00
  Breakfast $1.50
- ★ Hostería Anita, Avenida San Martín 4341 — 951008 — $13.00
  Breakfast $1.50
- ★ Hostería Los Mirlos, Avenida San Martín
  No single rooms
- • Hostería Elsa, Avenida San Martín 8178 — $7.00
  Triple rooms only; breakfast $1.5
- • Hostería La Gloria, Avenida San Martín 5495 — $6.00
- ★ Motel El Sidi, Alte Brown 273 — 951778 — $13.00
  Breakfast $2.00
- • Hospedaje Danubio Azul, Rivadavia 1020
  No single rooms
- • Hospedaje El Valle, C Pellegrini 171 — $9.00
  Breakfast $1.00
- • Hospedaje La Italiana, Rivadavia 1058 — 951155
- • Hospedaje La Selva Negra, Avenida 12 de Octubre
  No single rooms
- • Hospedaje Las Tias, Avenida San Martín 4564
  No single rooms
- • Hospedaje Michlochar, Avenida San Martín 4819
  No single rooms
- • Hospedaje Muñiz, corner of San Martín and Belgrano — 951492 — $7.00
  Breakfast $1.00
- • Hospedaje Santa Teresita, Avenida San Martín — 951235 — $7.00
  Cheaper with a shared bathroom
- • Residencial Are Kepay, Los Nogales Lote 11 Manzana 11 — $10.00
- • Residencial Catalunya, Ameghino 59 — $9.00
  Breakfast $1.00
- • Residencial Irupe, Los Sauces 74 — 951493
- • Residencial Lilian, J Ingenieros 11 — $11.00 Triple

Río Ceballos

CÓRDOBA PROVINCE

🚌 Buses
Buses run regularly to Córdoba.

RÍO CUARTO

Postal code: 5800 • Population: 70 000 • area code: (0586) • Altitude: 440 m
Distance from Córdoba: 220 km southwards on RN 36

Río Cuarto is situated on the river of the same name. It is a modern city with wide avenues and many parks and plazas. It is the center of an agricultural area, and has a university and a golf club. Río Cuarto is a good stopover point on the route between Buenos Aires and Mendoza.

🍴 Eating out
- Restaurant Cantina Italiana Sorrento. Pasta
- Restaurant Pizzería Costa Azul, Belgrano 67

✉ Post and telegraph
- Post office: Encotel, Plaza General Roca

Accommodation in Río Cuarto

★★★★	Hotel Opera, 25 de Mayo 55	24390	$25.00	
★★★	Hotel Cariel, Buenos Aires 364	24963	$17.00	
★★★	Hotel Crillon, General Paz 1043		$22.00	
★★★	Hotel Gran Hotel Río Cuarto, Sobremonte 725		$19.00	
★★★	Hotel Menossi, Avenida España 41	234321	$22.00	
★★★	Motel Sol, RN 8 Km 607		$22.00	
★★	Hotel City, Lamadrid 701	25322	$17.00	
★★	Hotel Versalles, Avenida España 55		$17.00	
•	Hospedaje Alihue, Vélez Sarsfield 58 Shared bathrooms cheaper		$9.00	
•	Hospedaje Central, General Paz 575			
•	Hospedaje El Bambi, Sobremonte 170 No single rooms; near bus terminal			
•	Hospedaje El Ciervo, Sobremonte 123 No single rooms; near bus terminal			
•	Hospedaje El Padrino, Pedernera 637 No single rooms			
•	Hospedaje Genova, Sargento Cabral 1076 Cheaper shared bathroom	24147	$11.00	
•	Hospedaje Mendoza, Constitución 483		$11.00	
•	Hospedaje Monge, Sobremonte 178 Near bus terminal			
•	Hospedaje Nogaro, Alsina 870 No single rooms	26357		
•	Hospedaje Urquiza, Urquiza 75		$11.00	
•	Hospedaje Victoria, Buenos Aires 183			
•	Residencial Cristal, Constitución 544 Cheaper shared bathroom		$11.00	
•	Residencial Royal, Avenida General Roca 898		$11.00	
•	Residencial Venecia, Bolivar 28		$11.00	

CÓRDOBA PROVINCE

💲 Financial
- Banco de la Nación, corner of Sobremonte and Rivadavia
- Maguitour, Buenos Aires 85 ✆ 30294

🚻 Services and facilities
- Laundromat: Laverap, Déan Funes 142

✈ Air services
- Buenos Aires (Aeroparque Jorge Newbery): Fare $49.00; departs 1655 daily; 1 hour; Aerolineas
- San Rafael: Fare $30.00; departs 1425 daily; 1 hour; Aerolineas

🚌 Buses
- Córdoba: Fare $6.00
- Buenos Aires: Fare $13.00
- Mendoza: Fare $8.60; Empresa TAC
- Villa Dolores: $5.50; Empresa Sierras de Córdoba

🚗 Motoring
- Service station: ACA, RN 8 Km 608

🚆 Trains
The F C General San Martín station is on Bulevar Ameghino opposite Bulevar General Roca. There are daily trains to Buenos Aires and Mendoza.

🅿 Excursions

The south-eastern part of the largely unknown **Sierra de Comechingones** is accessible from Río Cuarto. Places to visit are **Alpa Corral** (750 m), **Villa Chacay**, and **Achiras** (845m); accommodation is available at Alpa Corral and Villa Chacay. Alpa Corral can be reached direct via Paso del Río Seco on dirt roads (68 km north-west) or via Piedra Blanca.

RÍO TERCERO

Postal code: 5850 • ✆ area code: (0571) • Altitude: 387
Distance from Córdoba: 112 km southwards on RP 5

Río Tercero is located on the river of the same name, 18 km east of the artificial lake **Lago Piedras Moras**.

🛏 Accommodation in Río Tercero

★★★	Hotel Argentino, corner of Libertad and Fray Santa María de Oro 🅿	✆ 21468	$30.00	👥
★	Hotel Embajador, Santos Discepolo 50 🅿	✆ 22280	$16.00	👥
★	Hotel Río Tercero, Libertad 139 🅿	✆ 21531	$16.00	👥
★	Hotel Velez Sarsfield, Vélez Sarsfield 549 🅿●	✆ 21336	$15.00	👥
•	Hospedaje Aligomac, Cafferata 50	✆ 22110		
•	Hospedaje Avenida, Avenida San Martín 75 No single rooms			
•	Hospedaje La Paz, General Paz 1 🅿			
•	Hospedaje Las Violetas, corner of Calle 4 and Ceballos	✆ 21821		
•	Hospedaje Richard, Lavalle 186 🅿 No single rooms	✆ 22084	$13.00	👥
•	Hospedaje Sarmiento, Sarmiento 71 Breakfast $1.50		$16.00	👥

Río Cuarto

Buses

Buses run regularly to Córdoba and Río Cuarto.

Excursions

The **Río Tercero** hydroelectric scheme has created a string of artificial lakes which are frequented by tourists. Good *pejerrey* fishing and watersports. The dams are **Embalse Piedras Moras** (nearest to town), **Embalse del Río Tercero**, and **Embalse Cerro Pelado**.

SALSIPÜEDES

Postal code: 5113 • (area code: (051) • Altitude: 750 m
Distance from Córdoba: 40 km north

Salsipüedes is located on the eastern slopes of the **Sierra Chica**.

Accommodation

- ★ Hotel Piantino, corner of Güemes and Ruta 53 (16 $10.00
- Hospedaje Oro Verde, Güemes 137. Open January–February; no single rooms
- Residencial La Posada, Santa Rosa 228 (299 $11.00. Shared bathroom

Camping

- Bello Horizonte, Corro 112, 3 km outside town

SAMPACHO

Postal code: 5829 • (area code: (0582)
Distance from Río Cuarto: 46 km southwest on RN 8

Located in the south-western part of the province, Sampacho is served by the F C General San Martín railroad.

Accommodation

- Hospedaje Porasso, corner of Rivadavia and Sarmiento (70234. No single rooms
- Hospedaje San Fernando, corner of RN 8 and 9 de Julio. No single rooms

SAN ANTONIO DE ARREDONDO

Postal code: 5153
Distance from Córdoba: 44 km west on RN 20

San Antonio de Arredondo is located in the **Río Punillas valley** at the beginning of the Traslasierra road over the **Pampa de Achala**.

San Antonio is virtually a suburb of Villa Carlos Paz. It is the starting pont for a picturesque tour across the **Sierras de Córdoba** to Mina Clavero.

Accommodation

★ Hostería Los Pinos, RP 14. No single rooms

Accommodation in Villa Icho Cruz

Villa Icho Cruz is 3 km west of San Antonio de Arredondo.
★ Hotel Icho Cruz, Juan de Casaris $10.00. Breakfast $1.00

CÓRDOBA PROVINCE

SAN CLEMENTE

Postal code: 5187
Distance from Córdoba: 66 km west

San Clemente is located on the eastern slopes of the **Cumbres de Achala** in good hiking country.

Accommodation

★ Hotel La Granadilla, about 3 km outside the town
• Residencial El Vado. Open January–February only

Excursions

There are archeological sites in the area, including rock paintings.
• **Quebrada de los Condoritos**: A national park has been proposed to preserve this area's flora and fauna, particularly the condors

SAN FRANCISCO

Postal code: 2400 • (area code: (0564) •
Altitude: 141 m
Distance from Córdoba: 205 km eastwards on RN 19

San Francisco is situated in the north-eastern part of Córdoba province, almost on the border with Santa Fé.

(Do not confuse this San Francisco with San Francisco near the border with Santiago del Estero province.)

Services and facilities
• Laundromat: Laverap, Bulevar Buenos Aires 147

Buses
• Córdoba: Daily; Empresa TAC
• Mendoza: Fare $15.50; Empresa TAC
• San Miguel de Tucumán: Departs 0300 daily; 10 hours; Empresa La Estrella
• Santiago del Estero: Departs 0300 daily; 7½ hours; Empresa La Estrella
• Termas de Río Hondo: Departs 0300 daily; 9 hours; Empresa La Estrella

Accommodation in San Francisco

★★★	Hotel Libertador, 25 de Mayo 1783	(	24680	$25.00	ii
★★	Hotel Fundador, corner of Avellaneda and Paraguay	(	22515		
★★	Hotel Mediteraneo, 9 de Julio 2675	(	25566	$21.00	ii
★★	Hotel Menfis, 25 de Mayo 251	(	26677	$17.00	ii
•	Hospedaje Alex, Avenida Urquiza 1334				
•	Hospedaje Americano, Mitre 76			$13.00	ii
•	Hospedaje Dunhill, corner of Colón and Iturraspe				
•	Hospedaje Belgrano, Belgrano 2256	(	23976		
•	Hospedaje Majestic, 9 de Julio 2142	(	26133	$16.00	ii
•	Hospedaje Minazu, Entre Rios 1629 No single rooms				
•	Hospedaje Mitre, Mitre 83	(	24425	$15.00	ii
•	Hospedaje San Jorge, Castelli 2847				

CÓRDOBA PROVINCE

Motoring
- Service station: ACA, Alberti 57

SAN JOSÉ DE LA DORMIDA

San José de la Dormida is located on RN 9 in the northern part of Córdoba province. This is the starting point for walks to the **Cerro Colorado** archeological site.

Accommodation
Motel San José, RN 9. No single rooms

SAN MARCOS SIERRA

Postal code: 5282

San Marcos Sierra is situated at the northern end of the **Sierra Chica** on the **Río San Marcos**, one of the rivers which form the Cruz del Eje reservoir.

Accommodation
- Hospedaje Los Horneros, San Martin. No single rooms

Buses
Empresa La Falda and Empresa La Cumbre run regular buses to Córdoba and Cruz del Eje, through the Valle de la Punilla.

SANTA ROSA DE CALAMUCHITA

Postal code: 5196 • Population: 10 000 • area code: (0546) • Altitude: 615 m
Distance from Córdoba: 106 km southwards on RP 5

Santa Rosa de Calamuchita is located in the spurs of the **Sierra de Pocho** and **Sierra Chica** on the **Río Santa Rosa**, in the **Valle de Calamuchita**.

The town was named after Santa Rosa de Lima who was venerated here in 1700 in a little chapel on the banks of the river. Nowadays it is a tourist resort with good facilities. During the summer months the influx of tourists doubles the town's population.

The crystalline **Río Santa Rosa** has its source in the **Cerro Champaquí**. It is one of the main rivers feeding into the **Dique Río Tercero** dam.

Festivals
- Santa Rosa de Lima: August 30

Tourist information
- Centro Turistico de Santa Rosa, Libertad 189 (2277

Camping
- El Portezuelo, RP 5

Eating out
- Restaurant Berlin, just across the bridge. German cuisine
- Restaurant Venecia, Libertad 364. Italian cuisine
- Cafetería Mar Batt, Libertad 149

CÓRDOBA PROVINCE

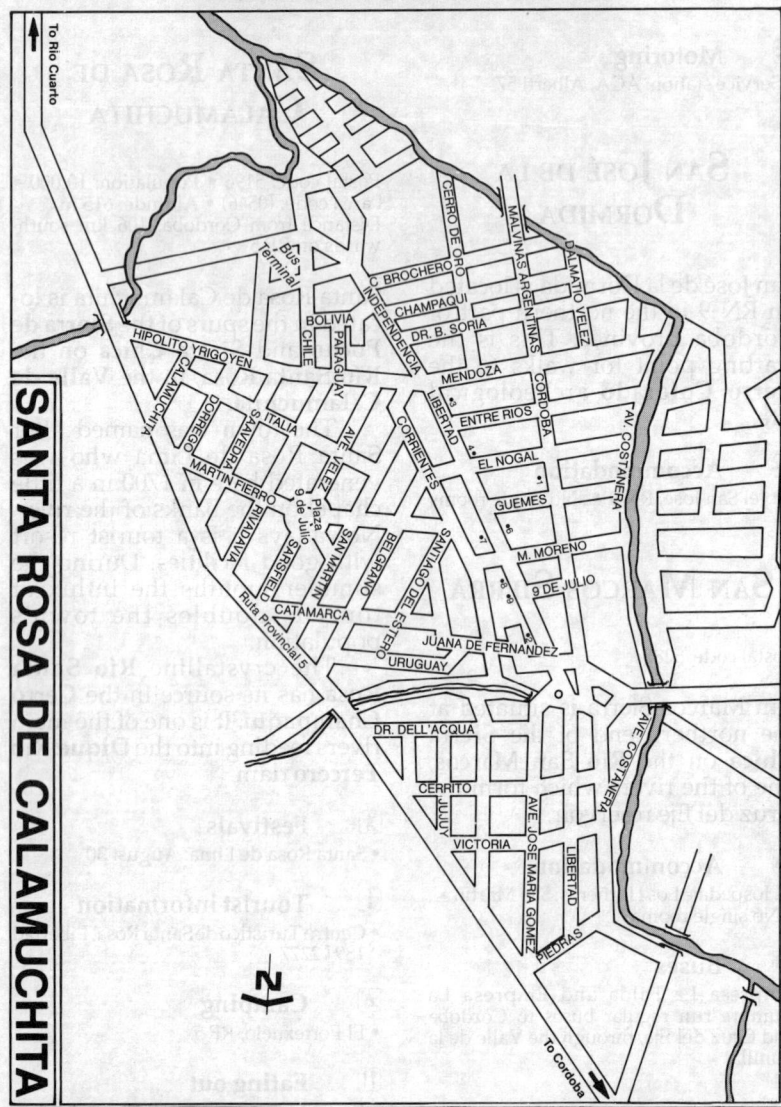

Key to Map
1. Municipalidad
2. Iglesia Santa Rosa de Lima
3. Post office (Encotel)
4. Telephones (Entel)
5. Tourist information
6. Hospedaje Torino
7. Hospedaje Rey Eduardo
8. Hospedaje Ana Mar
9. Hospedaje Aurora

Santa Rosa de Calamuchita

CÓRDOBA PROVINCE

Accommodation in Santa Rosa de Calamuchita

★★	Hotel Dunes, Parador de la Montaña			
	No single rooms			
★★	Hotel Santa Rosa, Entre Ríos 86	(2186	$16.00	
	Breakfast $1.50			
★★	Hotel Ypora Palace, RP 5	(2116	$16.00	
	Breakfast $2.00			
★	Hotel Gloria, Dalmacio Velez 50	(2214	$11.00	
	Breakfast $1.00			
★	Hotel Rex, corner of Libertad and Mendoza	(2226	$10.00	
	Open December–February			
★	Hotel Rex (Anex), Mendoza 27		$10.00	
	Open January–February			
★	Hotel Torino, Libertad 355	(2260	$10.00	
	Open November–April			
★	Hostería Avenida, Avenida Costanera	(2166		
	Open December–March; no single rooms			
★	Hostería Don Pedro, H Yrigoyen 535	(2264	$7.00	
	No single rooms			
•	Hospedaje Ana Mar, Libertad 594		$12.00	
•	Hospedaje Ariand, Malvinas Argentinas 83		$12.00	
	Triple rooms only			
•	Hospedaje Aurora, Libertad 600		$10.00	
	Triple rooms only			
•	Hospedaje Belverde, Corrientes 236			
	Open January and February			
	No single rooms			
•	Hospedaje Dany, Mendoza 128			
	Quadruple rooms only			
•	Hospedaje El Progreso, Independencia 301			
	No single rooms			
•	Hospedaje El Trebol, corner of Córdoba and M Moreno			
	No single rooms			
•	Hospedaje Parissi, Avenida Costanera, on the other side of the river		$3.00	
	Open December–March			
•	Hospedaje Rey Eduardo, Libertad 344	(2165	$15.00	
•	Hospedaje Santa Fé, Loma Hermosa			
	Quadruple rooms only			
•	Hospedaje Torino, Libertad (near Güemes)			
•	Residencial Angelita, Malvinas Argentinas 46	(2205	$7.00	Triple
•	Residencial Sierras, Avenida Costanera		$7.00	

Post and telegraph

- Post office: Encotel, corner of Libertad and Entre Ríos
- Telephone: Entel, corner of Libertad and El Nogal

Buses

- Córdoba: Departs 0500; 12 services daily; 2½ hours; Empresa Sierras de Calamuchita, Empresa TOA
- Alta Gracia: Departs 0500; 12 services daily; 1½–2 hours; Empresa Sierras de Calamuchita, Empresa TOA

Santa Rosa de Calamuchita

CÓRDOBA PROVINCE

- Villa Ciudad de América: Departs 0500; 12 services daily; 1 hour; Empresa Sierras de Calamuchita, Empresa TOA
- Villa General Belgrano: Fare $0.40; departs 1445; 13 services daily; ½ hour; Empresa Santa Rosa de Calamuchita, Empresa TOA

TANINGA

Altitude: 920 m
Distance from Córdoba: 136 km west on RP 20 then RP 28

Taninga is in the **Río Salsacate** valley, in the western part of the province. Nearby are the cones of the extinct volcanoes **Yerba Buena**, **Poca**, and **Boroa**.

Accommodation
- Hospedaje Cachimayo, RP 15. No single rooms

TANTI

Postal code: 5155 • Population: 4000 • area code: (0541)
Distances
- From Córdoba: 55 km westwards on RN 20
- From Villa Carlos Paz: 14 km northwards

Tanti is a picturesque little village located in undulating hills. It was already settled by indigenous tribes in pre-Colombian times, and in colonial times was a stop on the western road to Alto Perú.

ℹ️ Tourist information
- Inside bus terminal, San Martín

🅰 Camping
- Costas de Oro, corner of General Paz and Trejo

Accommodation in Tanti

★ Hotel Chez Nous (Escalada), San Martín 365 — No single rooms	98130	$8.00	
★ Hotel Tanti, General Paz 115 — Breakfast $2.00	98145	$13.00	
★ Hostería Caballito Blanco, Ruta 20 Km 756			
★ Hostería Capricornio, M Moreno 80			
★ Hostería Sierrasol, Santa Fé 62			
• Hostería Los Manantiales, Moreno 80	98147	$8.50	
• Hostería La Zulmita, Río Negro — No single rooms	98162	$7.00	
• Hospedaje Las Margaritas, Rosario	98187	$7.00	
• Hospedaje San Antonio, Güemes 112 — Open January–February; Triples only		$7.00	
• Hospedaje San Eduardo, Neuquén — No single rooms			
• Hospedaje Sans Souci, Tucumán — Open January–April	98178	$6.00	
• Residencial El Bosque, corner of Belgrano and RN 20	98160		
• Residencial Jesús de Nazareth, Santa Fé 62	98196		
• Hostal Solar de Piedra, RN 20 Km 753	98185		
• Residencial El Sol, Tucumán	98180	$10.00	

Santa Rosa de Calamucnita

CÓRDOBA PROVINCE

🚌 Buses from Tanti

The bus terminal is on the corner of Córdoba and San Martín.

Destination	Fare	Deaprt	Services	Hours	Comapny
• Córdoba	$1.50	0700	7 services daily	1½	COTAP
• Buenos Aires	$16.50	2142	daily	12	Chevallier
• Cosquin		0745	3 services daily		COTAP
• Rosario	$10.00	2142	daily		Chevallier
• Taninga	$3.50			3½	20 de Junio
• Villa Carlos Paz	$0.50	0700	7 services daily	½	COTAP
• Villa Dolores	$5.50			6	20 de Junio

- La Isla, by the stream at the end of General Paz
- Sans Souci, Tucumán

🍴 Eating out

- Restaurant Casa Vecchia, corner of Belgrano and General Paz
- Restaurant El Fogón
- Restaurant Hotel Tanti, General Paz 115
- Restaurant Hotel Escalada, San Martín 365
- Restaurant La Nonna
- Confitería Luky
- Confitería in terminal

📮 Post and telegraph

- Central post office, corner of Mendoza and San Martín
- Long-distance telephones, Belgrano 83

🏪 Services and facilities

- Pharmacy: Pierry, San Martín 265 ☏ 98068

🎯 Excursions

- **Mogote Los Gigantes**: 32 km on RN 20 west. At 2350 m, the highest peak in the Sierra Grande. Panoramic views, easy ascent. Take an Empresa 20 de Junio bus
- **La Cascada**: A 20 m waterfall situated 100 m above the Balneario El Diquecito, within the town
- **Río Los Chorrillos**: 6 km from town on RN 20. A 120 m waterfall
- **Laguna Brava**: Located in a horseshoe-shaped *cañon*, formed by the **Río Yuspe**. It is covered in thick vegetation, and there are caves formed by the river
- **San José de los Ríos**: A 16 km hike

UNQUILLO

Postal code: 5109 • ☏ area code: (051) • Altitude: 566 m
Distance from Córdoba: 25 km northwest

Unquillo is a small resort town on the eastern slopes of the **Sierra Chica**.

🏨 Accommodation

Hospedaje Bonelli, Cabaña Estafeta
Hospedaje La Susanita, San Martin 1900 $11.00. Open December–March
Hospedaje Sierras, Avenida San Martín 2186 $7.00. No single rooms

CÓRDOBA PROVINCE

🚌 Buses
Buses run regularly to Córdoba.

✱ Excursions
- **Cosquín**: A scenic drive over the **Sierra Chica** past **Cerro Pan de Azúcar**

VICUÑA MACKENNA

Vicuña Mackenna is situated on the RN 7 at the intersection with RN 35 in the southern part of the province. It is virtually no more than a railway station for the F C General San Martín railroad, with a few hotels, situated at an important crossroad. It is a convenient stopover between Buenos Aires and Mendoza.

🛏 Accommodation
Hospedaje Sercos, Intendente Gómez 744 ☏ 59
Motel Tala Penda, corner of RN 7 and RN 35 ☏ 142 $26.00

VILLA ALLENDE

Altitude: 505 m
Distance from Córdoba: 17 km

🛏 Accommodation
There are two basic hotels, one camping place, and two private accommodations.

🍽 Eating out
There are three restaurants, three tearooms, and three delicatessens.

🚗 Motoring
There are two mechanics, gas stations, and tire shops.

VILLA CARLOS PAZ

Postal code: 5152 • ☏ area code: (0541) •
Altitude: 640 m
Distance from Córdoba: 36 km westwards on RN 38

Villa Carlos Paz is a pleasant resort in the *punilla* valley, situated on the artificial **Lago San Roque** at the foot of a hill. It is the nearest vacation town to Córdoba.

The area on which Villa Carlos Paz stands was given to Juan de Nadal, who accompanied the founder of Córdoba, Juan L de Cabrera, in 1573. The area was then known by its aboriginal name of Valle de Quizquicate after the Comechingones people who inhabited the valley; it later became known as Estancia Santa Leocadia. In 1869 the land was acquired by two partners, Rudecindo Paz and Gabriel Cuello. Cuello sold out to the Paz family, whose vision made the farm prosperous. More families settled around the farm and a town planner was engaged in 1914. The old farm disappeared in the lake created by construction of the dam.

Villa Carlos Paz has excellent tourist facilities with scores of first-class hotels and restaurants. It is linked to the city of Córdoba by a six-lane 40 km long highway

Unquillo

CÓRDOBA PROVINCE

and may be considered as the "playground of the *Cordobeses*". The entertainment ranges from casinos and nightclubs to outdoor activities on the lake such as swimming, fishing, boating, windsurfing, and sailing. There are tennis courts, ice rinks, and even parachute jumps into the lake. For those wishing to spend a few quiet days there are many idyllic guesthouses scattered along the lakeshores within easy reach of the city. Many tour operators arrange day tours in the surrounding hinterland with its valleys and *sierras*.

The restaurants and eating places in Villa Carlos Paz have been rated by local authorities, in a similar manner to hotels.

Festivals
- Fiesta Provincial de los Lagos (Provincial Festival of the Lakes): January
- Fiesta Patronal Nuestra Señora del Carmen (Festival of the Patron Saint): July 16

Tourist information
You pass a tourist information kiosk in the central strip on San Martín when entering town from the Córdoba side.
- Secretaria Municipal de Turismo, San Martín 400, at the bus station ℂ 21624

Camping
- ACA, corner of Avenida San Martín and N Huapi. Huge complex
- Bahía del Gitano, corner of Artigas and Azopardo
- Carlos Paz, corner of Urquiza and Derqui
- Club Cazadores y Pescadores, corner of Gobernador Ferreyra and Avenida Atlantica
- Club de Pesca, corner of Esparta and Avenida Atlantica
- El Principito, Madrid near bridge
- La Ribera, corner of Ayacucho and Costanera
- Las Tolderias, Comechingones
- Los Angeles, corner of Avenida Carcano and Santa Teresa
- Los Pinos, corner of Curros Enriquez and Lincoln
- Mi Refugio, Becquer Block 300
- Sol y Río, corner of Gambartes and Costanera

Eating out
Restaurants in Carlos Villa Paz have been assigned ratings by the local tourist authority. The cheapest meals range from $2.50 to $3.00. A good average meal in a better-class restaurant ranges from $5.00 to $8.00, and in top-class restaurants from $10.00 to $15.00.

Restaurants
- ★★★★ Restaurant Casino, Lisandro de La Torre 58
- ★★★ Restaurant Alcala, General Paz 271
- ★★★ Restaurant Centro Italiano, corner of Libertad and Belgrano
- ★★★ Restaurant Club de Pesca, San Martín 200. Seafood
- ★★★ Restaurant Country Club, on the road to the dam
- ★★★ Restaurant El Dorado, San Martín 1500. Seafood
- ★★★ Restaurant El Galeon, Uruguay 721
- ★★★ Restaurant El Rancho de Porcel, Uruguay 700
- ★★★ Restaurant Hostal del Sol, Avenida San Martín 1991
- ★★★ Restaurant La Casa de Pedro, Uruguay 464
- ★★★ Restaurant Lago Azul, corner of Andrea del Sarto and San Martín. Fondue
- ★★★ Restaurant La Terminal, San Martín 400
- ★★★ Restaurant Mariel I, La Paz 135
- ★★★ Restaurant Tranquera, San Martín block 1400 (corner of Gutemberg). Seafood
- ★★ Restaurant Berrizbeitia, corner of San Martín and Esparta
- ★★ Restaurant Blanco y Negro, corner of Juan B Justo and Las Heras

Villa Carlos Paz

CÓRDOBA PROVINCE

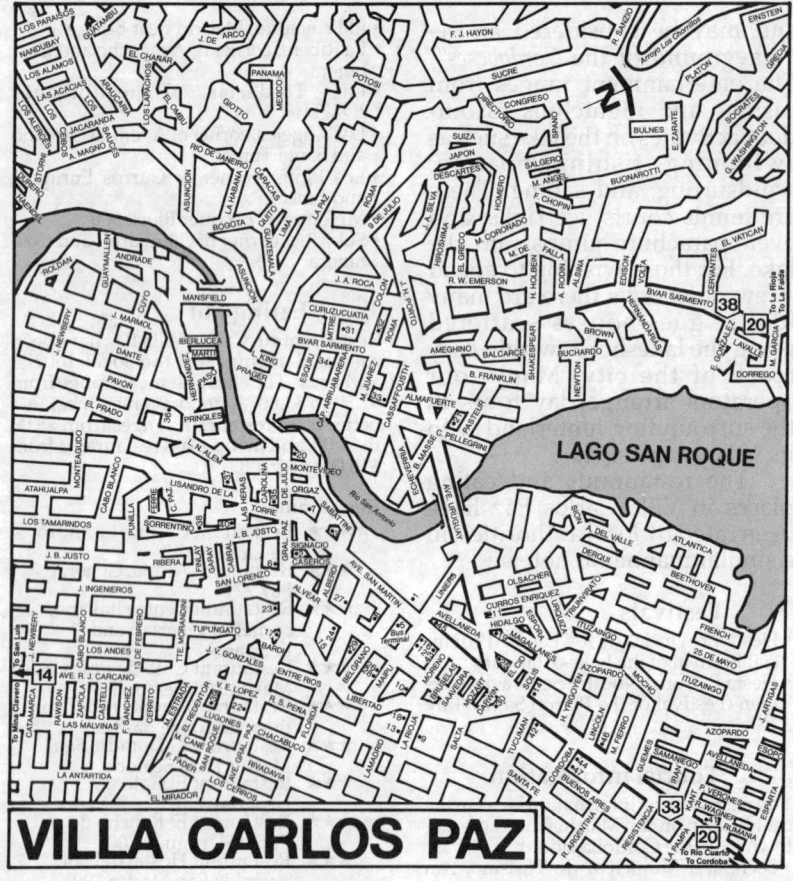

VILLA CARLOS PAZ

- ★★ Restaurant Brec, corner of San Martín and Yrigoyen. Big
- ★★ Restaurant El Mancla, H Yrigoyen 994
- ★★ Restaurant Il Gatto Freddy, corner of Uruguay and Liniers. Italian cuisine
- ★★ Restaurant Kan-Kun, corner of Atlantica and Lincoln
- ★★ Restaurant La Cabaña Cordobesa, 9 de Julio 21
- ★★ Restaurant La Casa de José, San Martín 1800
- ★★ Restaurant Mariel II, Libertad 357
- ★★ Restaurant Pastilandia, corner of San Martín and 9 de Julio (upstairs)
- ★★ Restaurant Stilo, Belgrano 144
- ★★ Restaurant Trattoria Don David, corner of Carcano and San Luis
- ★★ Restaurant Vieja Recova, General Paz 247
- ★ Restaurant La Bandeja, San Martín 1049
- ★ Restaurant Los Dos Amigos, Alberdí 158
- ★ Restaurant Mariel II, Libertad 357

Córdoba Province

Key to Map

1. Municipalidad
2. Iglesia
3. Post office (Encotel) and Telephone (Entel)
5. Tourist information
6. Banco de la Nación
7. Casino
8. Hotel Florida (center)
9. Hotel Linz (center)
10. Hotel Taormina (center)
11. Hotel Capvio (center)
12. Hotel Casino (center)
13. Hotel El Cid (center)
14. Hotel Mont Pelée (center)
15. Hostería El Bosque (center)
16. Hotel Brisas (center)
17. Hotel Coronado (center)
18. Hotel Dana (center)
19. Hotel Hawaii (center)
20. Hotel Italia (center)
21. Hotel Suiza (center)
22. Hotel Santander (center)
23. Hostería Augustus (center)
24. Hostería Le Blanc (center)
25. Hospedaje Dreams (center)
26. Hospedaje Grisabel (center)
27. Hospedaje Las Junturas (center)
28. Hospedaje Maipú (center)
29. Hospedaje Yolan (center)
30. Residencial Carlitos (center)
31. Hotel La Toscana (center north)
32. Hotel Luxor (center north)
33. Hotel Buenos Aires (center north)
34. Hotel Villa Alicia (center north)
35. Hotel Grand Prix (center west)
36. Hostería Los Espinillos (center west)
37. Hostería San Carlos (center west)
38. Hospedaje Mari Renée (center west)
39. Hospedaje Maury (center west)
40. Hospedaje Mogador (center west)
41. Hotel Grillet (center east)
42. Hotel Amanque (center east)
43. Hotel Florencia (center east)
44. Hotel Libertador (center east)
45. Hotel Los Sauces (center east)
46. Hotel Riviera (center east)
47. Hostería La Casona (center east)

★ Restaurant Montebianco, corner of Las Heras and L de la Torre
★ Restaurant Yo-Pa-Ma, General Paz 200
• Restaurant El Triangulo, Carcano 1700
• Restaurant Mario II, Libertador Block 900 (corner of Saavedra)
• Restaurant Onda Verde, Belgrano 183. Vegetarian

Parrillas

A *parrilla* is a charcoal grill.

★★★ Parrilla El Candil, San Martín 1290
★★★ Parrilla El Rancho Por'a, Uruguay 472
★★★ Parrilla La Casona, corner of San Martín and Gobernador Roca
★★★ Parrilla Tauro, General Paz 160
★★ Parrilla La Tranquera, San Martín 1506
★★ Parrilla La Posta, corner of San Martín and Tirzo de Molina
★ Parrilla El Cardon, San Martín 1262
★ Parrilla La Churrasquita, corner of 9 de Julio and Alem
★ Parrilla La Taberna de Julio, Uruguay 680
★ Parrilla Los Gauchos de Guemes, H Irigoyen 23
★ Parrilla Mingo, Uruguay 735 (opposite Hotel Uruguay)
• Parrilla El Mangrullo, Libertador block 900 (corner of Alvear)
• Parrilla El Meson de Leon, España
• Parrilla El Rancho de Jorge, San Martín block 1400 (corner of Esparta). Meal
• Parrilla Gringo's, Uruguay 686
☞• Parrilla La Casa de José, corner of San Martín and Gobernador Peña. Big
☞• Parrilla La Taba, Alberdi 53
• Parrilla Q'Pollos, corner of Carcano and Ayacucho
• Parrilla Quincho El Fantasio, Perito Moreno

continued on page 219

Villa Carlos Paz

CÓRDOBA PROVINCE

Accommodation in Villa Carlos Paz

Accommodation in the city center

South of the lake, between General La Paz and 9 de Julio at one end and Tucumán and H Yrigoyen at the other.

★★★	Hotel Eiffel, H Irigoyen 706	(23230		
	No single rooms			
★★★	Hotel Florida, Belgrano 45	(21905	$15.00	
	No single rooms; includes breakfast			
★★★	Hotel Linz, La Rioja 68	(22053	$23.00	
	No single rooms			
★★★	Hotel Mon Petit, Avenida Libertad 285	(21704		
	No single rooms			
★★★	Hotel Platino, Las Heras 60	(24077		
★★★	Hotel Sialdorf, corner of Avenida Uruguay and Liniers			
	No single rooms	(21158		
★★★	Hotel Taormina, Moreno 185	(21711	$23.00	
	No single rooms; includes breakfast			
★★	Hotel Avenida, General Paz 549	(24198		
	No single rooms			
★★	Hotel California, Avenida Libertador 359	(21706		
	No single rooms			
★★	Hotel Capvio, Curros Enriquez 15 (corner of Avenida Uruguay)	(23595	$13.00	
	No single rooms; includes breakfast			
★★	Hotel Casino, Maipú 90	(21670	$10.00	
	Includes breakfast			
★★	Hotel Catedral, Florida 377	(21506		
	German-speaking staff; no single rooms			
★★	Hotel Colonial, Florida 201	(21510		
	Open December–April; no single rooms			
★★	Hotel El Cid, H Yrigoyen 250	(21358	$13.00	
	No single rooms; includes breakfast			
★★	Hotel El Monte, Caseros 45	(22001		
	No single rooms			
★★	Hotel Enri Mar, H Yrigoyen 148	(21362		
	No single rooms			
★★	Hotel Marciala, Güemes 164	(23020		
	No single rooms			
★★	Hotel Mont Pelée, corner of Uruguay and Solis			
	No single rooms	(21011	$8.00	
★★	Hotel Plaza Huincul, Uruguay 832	(21109		
	No single rooms			
★★	Hotel Playa, 9 de Julio 162	(21467		
★★	Hotel Uruguay, Uruguay 730	(22335		
	No single rooms			
★★	Hotel Wanda, Alvear 479	(21760		
	Open November–April; no single rooms			
★	Hotel Argentina, Bruselas 26	(21557		
★	Hotel Arno, Moreno 39	(21691, 21619		
	No single rooms			
★	Hotel Belgrano, Belgrano 155	(21319		
	No single rooms			
★	Hotel Brisas, Maipú 50	(21587	$6.00	
	No single rooms			
★	Hotel Charicar, Hidalgo 20	(21211	$8.00	
	No single rooms; includes breakfast			

Villa Carlos Paz

CÓRDOBA PROVINCE

Accommodation in Villa Carlos Paz—continued

Accommodation in the city center—continued

★	Hotel Córdoba, Belgrano 175	(21963		
	No single rooms			
★	Hotel Coronado, General Paz 289	(22354	$10.00	♈
	No single rooms; includes breakfast			
★	Hotel Dana, H Yrigoyen 294	(23695	$9.00	♈
	Open December—March; no single rooms			
★	Hotel Durban, corner of Perito Moreno and Paris			
	Open December–February; no single rooms			
★	Hotel Escorial, Moreno 120	(22541		
	No single rooms			
★	Hotel Gisel, Salta 180	(24226		
★	Hotel Gran Victoria, La Rioja 87	(23267		
	No single rooms			
★	Hotel Hawaii, Uruguay 830	(22009	$10.00	♈
	No single rooms			
★	Hotel Hermitage, Alvear 570	(23897		
★	Hotel Hurlingham, corner of Alvear and General Paz			
	No single rooms	(22995		
★	Hotel Italia, 9 de Julio 155	(21811	$7.00	♈
★	Hotel Jorge Omar, Florida 416	(21512		
★	Hotel La Tebra, corner of Alem and Hernandez			
	Open December–April; no single rooms	(21536		
★	Hotel Los Angeles, Uruguay 1040	(22646	$6.00	♈
	No single rooms			
★	Hotel Santander, Avenida General Paz 401	(22359, 22309	$8.00	♈
	No single rooms			
★	Hotel San José, Alvear 193	(22372		
★	Hotel Vesubio, Entre Ríos 40	(21186		
	No single rooms			
★★★	Hostería El Ciervo de Oro, H Yrigoyen 995	(22498		
★★	Hostería Alpenrose, H Yrigoyen 615	(25595		
	Open December–April; triple rooms only			
★★	Hostería Arenales, Alberdi 43	(21112		
	No single rooms			
★★	Hostería Cerro Azul, Tucumán 298	(23946		
	Open July–April			
★★	Hostería Del Pedregal, Belgrano 128	(21035		
	No single rooms			
★★	Hostería Dora, H Yrigoyen 137	(21361		
	No single rooms			
★★	Hostería El Bosque, Libertad block 150 (corner of Florida)	(21906	$10.00	♈
★★	Hostería La Posada de Fredy, Perito Moreno	(24791		
	No single rooms			
★★	Hostería Las Vertientes, Santa Fé 1200	(21687		
	No single rooms			
★★	Hostería Panambi, Uruguay block 600 (corner of Liniers)	(22151		
	No single rooms			
★★	Hostería Rey, Belgrano 149	(23947		
	No single rooms			
★★	Hostería Roxana Haydee, San Martín 375	(22370		
	No single rooms			

Villa Carlos Paz

Accommodation in Villa Carlos Paz—continued

Accommodation in the city center—continued

- ★ Hostería Augustus, José Ingenieros 10
  (corner of Avenida General Paz) ✆ 22208 $7.00 ⚌
- ★ Hostería Classic, Tucumán 98 ✆ 21406
- ★ Hostería El Ciervo Manso, Florida 160 ✆ 22303
  No single rooms
- ★ Hostería Lalo, Florida 163 ✆ 21903
  No single rooms
- ★ Hostería Laura, Florida 190 ✆ 21683
- ★ Hostería Le Blanc, Alvear 199 ✆ 22268 $6.00 ⚌
- ★ Hostería Marili, Avenida Uruguay 870 ✆ 23424
  Open December–March
- ★ Hostería Portal del Sol, Fidel Lopez 150 ✆ 24750

- • Hospedaje Ana María, Florida 198
- • Hospedaje Casino, Maipú 90 ✆ 21670
  No single rooms
- • Hospedaje Charo, Alvear 655 ✆ 23999
  No single rooms
- • Hospedaje Don Carlos, Sabattini 55 ✆ 22597
  Triple rooms only
- • Hospedaje Dream's, Avenida Uruguay 848 ✆ 25804 $5.00 ⚌
  No single rooms
- • Hospedaje Elsita, Sargento Cabral 262 ✆ 24355
- • Hospedaje Elsy, Juan S Bach
  No single rooms
- • Hospedaje Grisabel, Maipú 145 ✆ 25976 $6.00 ⚌
  Triple rooms only
- • Hospedaje Las Junturas, Florida 181 ✆ 21625 $5.00 ⚌
  No single rooms
- • Hospedaje Las Lilas, La Rioja 79 ✆ 23497
  No single rooms
- • Hospedaje Maipú, Maipú 175 ✆ 21851 $3.00 ⚊
  Triple rooms only
- • Hospedaje Matacos, Matacos 88 ✆ 22424
  No single rooms
- • Hospedaje Nogarosa, L N Alem ✆ 23903
  No single rooms
- • Hospedaje Nora, Entre Ríos 79 ✆ 22398
- • Hospedaje Platero, General Paz block 300 (corner of Pasaje Bardi) ✆
  Open January–March; no single rooms
- • Hospedaje Porteña, corner of Florida and Alvear FH
  No single rooms ✆ 21907
- • Hospedaje Rodas, Avenida Libertad 31 ✆ 25655
  No single rooms
- • Hospedaje San Luis, Pasaje Carlos Paz 12 ✆ 21499
  No single rooms
- • Hospedaje Versailles, H Yrigoyen 699 ✆ 21106
  No single rooms
- • Hospedaje Yolan, Florida 136 ✆ 23794 $4.00
  Triple rooms only

Villa Carlos Paz

CÓRDOBA PROVINCE

Accommodation in Villa Carlos Paz—continued

Accommodation in the city center—continued

- Residencial Alvear, Alvear block 200 (corner of Belgrano)
- Residencial Asturias, San Lorenzo 99
  No single rooms
- Residencial Carlitos, Avenida Libertad 432 (23073 $7.00
  No single rooms
- Residencial Castelar, Avenida Libertad 56 (23445, 21705
  No single rooms
- Residencial Los Eucaliptus, Intendente Juan García 673

Accommodation in the center north

North of the lake, between 9 de Julio and Uruguay.

★★★	Hotel Gran Lourdes, Cassafousth 63	(23347	
	No single rooms		
★★	Hotel Amanda, La Paz 127	(21957	
	No single rooms		
★★	Hotel La Toscana, Mitre 63	(22746	$18.00
	No single rooms		
★★	Hotel Luxor, Colón 66	(23596	$12.00
	No single rooms		
★★	Hotel Montecarlo, Uruguay 120	(22251	
	No single rooms		
★★	Hotel Montecatini, Curuzú Cuatiá 100	(24160	
	No single rooms		
★★	Hotel Nahuel, Pasteur 44	(21059	
	No single rooms		
★★	Hotel Temú, Uruguay 150	(23899, 21044	
	No single rooms		
★★	Hotel Texas, Cassafousth 261	(23694	
	No single rooms		
★	Hotel Amancay, Avenida Uruguay 326	(21057	
★	Hotel Anita, Esquiú 52 Open January–March	(21938	
	No single rooms		
★	Hotel Bacara, 9 de Julio 486	(21977	
	No single rooms		
★	Hotel Buenos Aires, Cassafousth 181	(21389	$8.00
	No single rooms; includes breakfast		
★	Hotel City, Sarmiento 240	(21665	
★	Hotel Crovetto, Echeverria 126	(21679	
	No single rooms		
★	Hotel Dunes, Mitre 64	(21304	
★	Hotel El Mirador, Echeverría 69	(22350	
★	Hotel Enzo, Curuzú Cuatiá 43	(21695	
	No single rooms		
★	Hotel Giordano Polano, Sarmiento 438	(23749	
	Open January–February; no single rooms		
★	Hotel Imperial, Bialet Massé 386	(22749	
★	Hotel Italiano, Uruguay 253	(22202	
	No single rooms		
★	Hotel Leonard, Cassafousth 258	(22949	
	No single rooms		

CÓRDOBA PROVINCE

Accommodation in Villa Carlos Paz—continued

Accommodation in the center north—continued

★	Hotel Mar del Plata, Esquiú 47	(	22068	
★	Hotel Parque, Uruguay 338	(	22447	
	Open December–March; no single rooms			
★	Hotel Suiza, C Pellegrini 522	(	21174	
	No single rooms			
★	Hotel Villa Alicia, Arrubarrena 53	(	21451	$7.00
	No single rooms			
★★	Hostería Etna, Esquiú 56	(	21474	
	No single rooms			
★	Hostería Anayak, Avenida 9 de Julio 572	(	23997	
★	Hostería Estancia La Quinta, La Paz 39	(	21610	
★	Hostería Güemes, H Porto 23	(	25433	
	No single rooms			
★	Hostería Irupé, Roma 276	(	21412	
	No single rooms			
★	Hostería Paradise, 9 de Julio 1013			
	No single rooms			
★	Hostería Yuspe, La Paz 59	(	22678	
	No single rooms			
•	Hospedaje Antica, José H Porto 65	(	25964	
	No single rooms			
•	Hospedaje Astral, Mitre 65	(	22704	
	No single rooms			
•	Hospedaje Becerra, Pellegrini 154			
	No single rooms			
•	Hospedaje Colón, Colón 92			
	No single rooms			
•	Hospedaje Elena, C Pellegrini 58	(	21458	
	No single rooms			
•	Hospedaje Flamingo, Bialet Massé 216	(	23548	
	No single rooms			
•	Hospedaje Gilmar, Echeverría 30	(	21945	
	No single rooms			
•	Hospedaje Los Gigantes, José H Porto 79	(	24982	
	No single rooms			
•	Hospedaje Montreal, Sarmiento 70	(	21309	
	No single rooms			
•	Hospedaje Necochea, Esquiú 98	(	21402	
	No single rooms			
•	Hospedaje Paris, José H Porto 236	(	21160	
•	Hospedaje Punta del Este, Pellegrini 313	(	24461	
•	Hospedaje Ritz, Uruguay 38	(	22126	
	Triple rooms only			
•	Hospedaje San Roque, Cassafousth 102	(	21199	
	No single rooms			
•	Hospedaje Siel, Corner of 9 de Julio 910 and Roma			
	Open January–February; no single rooms			
•	Hospedaje Sumitas, Juan H Porto	(	21160	
•	Hospedaje Susy Bell, 9 de Julio 770	(	21934	
	Open December–April; no single rooms			

Villa Carlos Paz

Accommodation in Villa Carlos Paz—continued

Accommodation in the centre north—continued

- Hospedaje Venecia, Mitre 58
  No single rooms
- Residencial Estrella de Italia, Colón 77 🏨
  No single rooms
- Residencial Europa, Cassafousth 99 ▣ (21835
  No single rooms
- Residencial Iberia, Cassafousth 298 🏨▣ (21732
  No single rooms
- Residencial Lucca, Miguel Juarez 38 ▣ (21820
  No single rooms
- Residencial San Francisco II, H Porto 116 🏨
  Open December–March; no single rooms

Accommodation west of the city center

West of General Paz and 9 de Julio.

★★★	Hotel Grand Prix, Lisandro de la Torre 45 ▣●	(23745	$18.00 ♜
★★	Hotel Atalaya, Carcano 192 🏨●▣	(22209	
★★	Hotel Del Carmen, San Roque 274 ▣▣	(22698	
	No single rooms		
★★	Hotel Mendoza, Juan B Justo 314 🏨▣	(21046	
	Open December–March		
★★	Hotel Skorpios, Antartida 154 (corner of F Sanchez) 🏨		
	No single rooms	(24213	
★	Hotel Alcazaba, Estrada 193 🏨	(22054	
	No single rooms		
★	Hotel Bella Vista, Las Malvinas 351 🏨	(21420	
	No single rooms		
★	Hotel El Triangulo, Carcano 1300 ▣	(22570	$10.00 ♜
	No single rooms		
★	Hotel Maspalomas, José Ribera 30	(25216	
★	Hotel Monte Bianco, Lisandro de la Torre 103 🏨	(24727	
	No single rooms		
★	Hotel Savoy, Pasaje Sorrentino 73 ▣	(22595	
•	Hotel Yon Pedro, Avenida Estrada 300 (corner of Miguel Cane) 🏨▣	(22255	
★★	Hostería Covadonga, Lules 29 🏨●▣	(21577	$11.00 ♜
	No single rooms		
★★	Hostería Los Espinillos, Pavon 50 🏨●▣	(23495	$10.00 ♜
	No single rooms		
★	Hostería Aconcagua, Juan B Justo 200 🏨●	(21339	$7.00 ♜
	No single rooms		
★	Hostería Dany, Avenida Estrada 179 ▣	(24664	
	No single rooms		
★	Hostería Holiday, Avenida Carcano 58 ▣	(22196	
	No single rooms		
★	Hostería Intihuasi, Avenida Estrada 103	(22030	
★	Hostería Jocar, Juan de Garay 49 ▣●	(24015	
	Open December–February; no single rooms		
★	Hostería Lolita, Avenida Estrada 290 ▣	(225591	
	No single rooms		

Villa Carlos Paz

Accommodation in Villa Carlos Paz—continued

Accommodation west of the city center—continued

★	Hostería Los Manantiales, corner of Monteagudo and Pavon ▣	(	22600	
	Open December–March; no single rooms			
★	Hostería Michel, corner of Lugones and El Redentor ▣	(	22486	
	No single rooms			
★	Hostería Norvil, Los Eucaliptus 350 ▣	(	23976	
	Open December–April; no single rooms			
★	Hostería San Carlos, Lisandro de La Torre 139	(	21922	$6.00 ♛
★	Hostería Sonia, Avenida Carcano 499 ▣▲	(	24984	
★	Hostería Villa Andrea, Lugones 135 ▣	(	22122	
	No single rooms			
•	Hospedaje Alhambra, corner of Avenida Estrada and Las Malvinas	(	25461	
	No single rooms			
•	Hospedaje Ana, Lisandro de La Torre 195			
	Triple rooms only			
•	Hospedaje Bristol, Catamarca 35	(	24201	
•	Hospedaje Cerro Blanco, Cerro Blanco 348	(	21721	
	Triple rooms only			
•	Hospedaje Danubio, Zapiola 74 ▣	(	22011	
	No single rooms			
•	Hospedaje La Aldea, Juan B Justo 141 ▣	(	24063	$7.00 ♛
	Open December–April; no single rooms			
•	Hospedaje Las Heras, Las Heras 269 ▣●	(	24607	
	No single rooms			
•	Hospedaje Las Vegas, San Roque 237			
•	Hospedaje Liber, Las Malvinas 199	(	22204	
	Open January–February; triple rooms only			
•	Hospedaje Marbot, Estrada 290	(	22559	
•	Hospedaje Mari Renée, Juan B Justo 199 ▥	(	24590	$7.00 ♛
	No single rooms			
•	Hospedaje Maury, El Redentor 146 ▥	(	21691	$5.00 ♛
	No single rooms; includes breakfast			
•	Hospedaje Mogador, Juan B Justo 103 ▣	(	23948	$6.00 ♛
	No single rooms			
•	Hospedaje Nellian, Catamarca 94 ▥	(	24624	
	No single rooms			
•	Hospedaje Parque Carlos Paz, Santa Fé 50 ▣▲	(	25128	
•	Hospedaje Rosario, Florencio Sanchez 130 ●	(	22013	
	No single rooms			
•	Hospedaje San Cayetano, Los Andes 253	(	22639	
	Triple rooms only			
•	Hospedaje San Jorge, San Roque 66	(	22188	
	No single rooms			
•	Hospedaje Santa Cecilia, Ingenieros 299 ▣●▲	(	21258	
	Open December–March			
•	Hospedaje Sierras, Rawson 95 ▣	(	21740	
	Open January–March; no single rooms			

Villa Carlos Paz

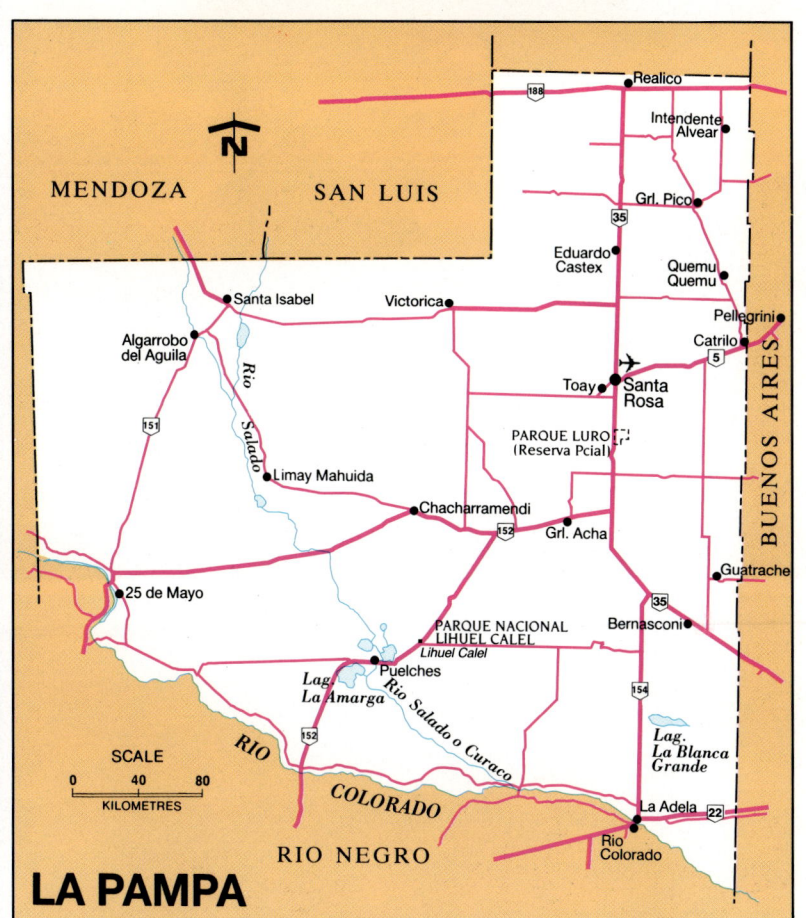

Plate 9
Map of La Pampa Province

Plate 10

Top: Cerro Fitz Roy, Patagonia
Bottom: Lago Argentino, with Glaciar Perito Moreno

CÓRDOBA PROVINCE

Accommodation in Villa Carlos Paz—continued

Accommodation west of the city center—continued

- Hospedaje Tierra del Fuego, San Roque 463 ☎ (24561
  No single rooms
- Hospedaje Torino, Carcano 56 ☎ (21852
  No single rooms
- Residencial Cosmos, San Roque 303 ⁞ (21125
  Triple rooms only

Accommodation east of the city center

Towards Córdoba.

★★★★	Hotel Portal del Lago, corner of Gobernador Alvarez and Cabrera ⑪●▲	(24931	$40.00	⁞⁞
★★★	Hotel Las Lajas, corner of Avenida San Martín and España ⑪●▲	(22134		
	No single rooms			
★★★	Hotel Macondo, corner of San Martín and G Mistral ⑪●▲	(22924		
	No single rooms			
★★★	Hotel Monaco, corner of Avenida San Martín and Zuviria ⑪●▲	(21242	$23.00	⁞⁞
	No single rooms; breakfast $1.50			
★★	Hotel Alfil, Avenida San Martín 1727 ☎▲	(22184		
	No single rooms			
★★	Hotel Amanque, Avenida San Martín 927 ⑪●▲	(21296	$8.00	⁞⁞
★★	Hotel El Tala, Roque Sáenz Peña 54 ☎▲	(23547		
★★	Hotel Florencia, San Martín 595 ☎●▲	(22599	$12.00	⁞⁞
	No single rooms; includes breakfast			
★★	Hotel Gladys, Roque Sáenz Peña 68 ☎	(22161		
	No single rooms			
★★	Hotel Gure Echea, Avenida San Martín 749 ☎●▲			
	Open December–April; no single rooms	(21469		
★★	Hotel Libertador, Avenida San Martín 1001 (corner of Córdoba) ☎●			
	No single rooms	(23330	$16.00	⁞⁞
★★	Hotel Los Sauces, Avenida San Martín 510 ⑪●▲			
	No single rooms	(21807	$12.00	⁞⁞
★★	Hotel Panamericano, Avenida San Martín 670 ☎●▲			
	No single rooms	(21662		
★★	Hotel Riviera, corner of Avenida San Martín and Lincoln ⑪▲			
	No single rooms; includes breakfast	(23494	$9.00	
★★	Hotel Victory, A del Sarto ☎●▲	(22279		
★	Hotel Graciela, Lincoln 114 ☎	(21094		
	No single rooms			
★	Hotel King, Avenida San Martín 2500 ☎▲	(21545		
	No single rooms			
★	Hotel Lucy, Martín Fierro 72 ☎	(25173		
	No single rooms			
★	Hotel Magú, corner of Buenos Aires and Tokio ☎▲			
	No single rooms	(22742		
★	Hotel Rolson, Avenida San Martín 1097 ☎	(21210		
	No single rooms			
★★★	Apart Hotel San Isidro, Tokio 150	(23256		
★★	Motel La Cuesta, Avenida San Martín block 1400 (corner of O Wilde) ☎			
		(23748		

Villa Carlos Paz

CÓRDOBA PROVINCE

Accommodation in Villa Carlos Paz—continued

Accommodation east of the city center—continued

★	Motel El Arbol, corner of Avenida San Martín and Gobernador Garzon			
	Open December–April	(	22339	
★★	Hostería El Grillo, Gobernador Ferreyra 212			
	Open December–April; no single rooms	(	21521	
★★	Hostería Minor, Avenida San Martín 1059	(	23291	
	No single rooms			
★★	Hostería La Casona, Córdoba 72	(	22870	$9.00
	No single rooms; includes breakfast			
★	Hostería Criced, Avenida San Martín 1396	(	22945	$7.00
	No single rooms			
★	Hostería Los Arrayanes, Buenos Aires 221	(	25577	$8.00
	No single rooms; includes breakfast			
★	Hostería Santa Rita, Buenos Aires 37	(	21698	
	No single rooms			
•	Hospedaje Alhoa, Martín Fierro 30	(	25755	
	No single rooms			
•	Hospedaje Cerro, Rosario 2190	(	22554	
•	Hospedaje Don Eduardo, corner of Beethoven and Güemes			
	No single rooms			
•	Hospedaje Lago di Como, corner of Güemes and 25 de Mayo			
	Open December–April; no single rooms	(	23174	
•	Hospedaje Lanus, Avenida San Martín 941	(	21251	
	No single rooms			
•	Hospedaje Mi Abuelita, Artigas 100	(	24552	
	Open January–April; no single rooms			
•	Hospedaje Saint Tropez, Avenida San Martín 2921			
•	Hospedaje San Marcos, Artigas 101	(	21967	
	No single rooms			
•	Hospedaje Silvia, corner of Lincoln and Avellaneda			
	No single rooms	(	24049	
•	Hospedaje Venado Tuerto, Artigas 320			
	Triple rooms only			
•	Residencial Cruz del Sur, Martín Fierro 91	(	21440	$8.00
	No single rooms; includes breakfast			

Accommodation outside Villa Carlos Paz

To the north.

★★★	Hotel Casa Blanca, Bulevar Sarmiento 1101	(	23924	
★★★	Hotel El Faro, Bulevar Sarmiento 1110	(	21151	$17.50
	Includes breakfast			
★★	Hotel Los Cerros, Bulevar Sarmiento 1002			
		(	21313	
★★	Motel Puente Negro, RN 20 Km 743	(	22162	
★★	Hostería Achalay, Sarmiento 999	(	21153	$13.00
	Open December–April; includes breakfast			
★	Hostería Norte, Emilio Zola			
	No single rooms			
★	Hostería Santiagueña, RN 20 Km 743	(	22996	
	No single rooms			

Villa Carlos Paz

CÓRDOBA PROVINCE

Comedors

A *comedor* is literally a dining room: see Glossary.

- ★★ Comedor Le Piaf Bistro, 9 de Julio 170
- ★★ Comedor Masticando Mas, corner of San Martín and Saavedra
- ★★ Comedor The Garden, Perito Moreno
- ★ Comedor Don Ciriaco, San Martín 1014
- ★ Comedor El Sol, Uruguay 127
- ★ Comedor La Casona del Negro, corner of Montevideo and Costanera
- ★ Comedor Mari Renée, Juan B Justo 199
- ★ Comedor Playas de Oro, España
- • Comedor Villa del Lago, RN 20 Km 743

Lomiterías

A *lomitería* is a small *parrilla*

- ★★★ Lomitería Que Tal, corner of Pasaje San Ignacio and General Paz
- ★★ Lomitería Acuarela, Libertad 31
- ★★ Lomitería El Ciervo, San Martín 35
- ★★ Lomitería Joy's, General Paz 50
- ★★ Lomitería La Tumba, Lisandro de La Torre. Snack bar
- ★★ Lomitería Legui's, General Paz 60
- ★★ Lomitería S'Friscos, General Paz 101
- ★★ Lomitería Recuerdos, General Paz 60
- ★★ Lomitería Chichi, corner of Florida and Alvear

Pizzerías

- ★★★ Pizzería Juancho, corner of 9 de Julio and San Martín
- ★★ Pizzería La Torre, Libertad 305
- ★★ Pizzería El Viejo Marconi, 9 de Julio 145
- ★ Pizzería Chiquini, San Martín 941
- ★ Pizzería La Tarrasca, Juan B Justo 106
- • Pizzería La Torre, corner of Libertador and La Rioja
- • Pizzería Mamma Mia, corner of Libertador and Salta
- • Pizzería New UFO, San Martín 42
- • Pizzería San Cayetano, Libertad 100
- • Pizzería Tu y Yo, Lisandro de la Torre 70

Confiterás

A *confitería* is literally a confectioner's shop, but is more like a tearoom.

- ★★★★ Confitería Casino Provincial, San Martín
- ☞ ★★★★ Confitería El Bosque, San Martín 1470
- ★★★ Confitería Badajoz, 9 de Julio 117 (in the *galería*)
- ★★★ Confitería Café del Sol, General Paz 262
- ★★★ Confitería Chez Ami, Alem block 0 (corner of Hernandez)
- ★★★ Confitería Kan-Kun, corner of Avenida Atlantica and Lincoln
- ★★★ Confitería Lagos y Sierras, 9 de Julio 97
- ★★★ Confitería La Taberna SA (Confitería del Bingo)
- ★★★ Confitería La Terminal, San Martín 400
- ★★★ Confitería Manhattan, corner of Las Heras and L de la Torre
- ★★★ Confitería Teatro Bar, General Paz 20
- ★★★ Confitería Tobok, General Paz 3
- ★★ Confitería Acapulco, San Martín 825
- ★★ Confitería Acuario Cafe, 9 de Julio 90
- ★★ Confitería Aerosilla, Florencia Sanchez
- ★★ Confitería Avenida, Uruguay 1030
- ★★ Confitería Augustus, General Paz 243
- ★★ Confitería Babieka, General Paz 2
- ★★ Confitería Café de Paris, 9 de Julio 35
- ★★ Confitería Café de la Villa, corner of Uruguay and Liniers
- ★★ Confitería Cervecería Alemana, 9 de Julio 50
- ★★ Cafetería Cervecería Alemana, 9 de Julio 21 (in the *galería*)
- ★★ Confitería Edelweiss, 9 de Julio 50 (in the *galería*)
- ★★ Confitería El Viejo Candil, Ruta 20 Km 743

Villa Carlos Paz

CÓRDOBA PROVINCE

★★ Confitería Iceberg, corner of Rosario and Tokio
★★ Confitería Isaura, corner of San Martín and Villalobos (attached to the service station)
★★ Confitería Kiwi, General Paz 270
★★ Confitería Mari Juan, Carcano 185
★★ Confitería Molino Carlos Paz, 9 de Julio 28
★★ Confitería Waikiki, Pasaje Carolina 12
★★ Confitería Rocas Vivas, Ruta 20 km 743
★★ Confitería Vaudeville, Libertad 14
★ Confitería Café Jardín, 9 de Julio 53
★ Confitería Cafetín, San Martín 135
★ Confitería El Barcito, Las Heras 265
★ Confitería El Triangulo, Carcano 1700
★ Confitería Isidoro, Carcano 349
★ Confitería La Bruja del Lago, H Yrigoyen 985
★ Confitería La Cabaña, Uruguay 476
★ Confitería Mi Viejo, General Paz 101 (in the *galería*)

- Confitería ACA, corner of San Martín and and Medrano (in the camping grounds)
- Confitería Bar Avenida, San Martín block 1000. Open 24 hours
- Confitería Cervecería Munich, General Paz 97
- Confitería Coronado, General Paz 289
- Confitería Charo, Libertad 30
- Confitería El Bar de Miguel, Uruguay 703
- Confitería Stop Bar, corner of Juan S Bach and Nahuel Huapí

Take-aways

- Take-away Rotisería Versailles, San Martín 709

Eating out in the center north

★★ Restaurant El Balcón del Cu-Cu, corner of Sarmiento and H Porto
★★ Restaurant El Ciervo Rojo, Uruguay 131
★★ Restaurant El Velero, 9 de Julio 318
★ Restaurant La Casa del Gitano, 9 de Julio 319
★★ Parrilla El Rincon Salteño, Sarmiento 472
★★ Parrilla La Querencia, Uruguay 55
★★ Parrilla Santa Fé, Uruguay 311
★ Parrilla El Patio de José, 9 de Julio 360
★ Parrilla La Cocina de la Chacra, Uruguay 129
★ Parrilla La Tuerca, Sarmiento 36
★ Parrilla Mingo y Octavio, corner of Uruguay and Pellegrini

- Parrilla Cabana, Sarmiento 553
  ★ Comedor Cu-Cu, Sarmiento 426
  ★ Comedor Danona, 9 de Julio 322
  ★★★ Pizzería La Corona, 9 de Julio 398
  ★ Pizzería Cu-Cu, Sarmiento 425
  ★ Pizzería El Sanjuanino, Sarmiento 423
- Pizzería Bristol, Sarmiento 296
- Pizzería El Viejo Brazilia, corner of Bulevar Sarmiento and Colón
  ★★★ Confitería Hermitage, 9 de Julio 469
  ★★★ Confitería Nautique, corner of Sarmiento and H Porto
  ★★ Confitería Le Blon, Sarmiento 258
  ★★ Confitería Vieja Recova, Sarmiento 402
  ★ Confitería Copacabana, Sarmiento 472

Eating out in Villa del Lago

On the road to La Falda

★★★ Parrilla Sierras, Sarmiento 560
★ Parrilla Copacabana II, Sarmiento 919
★ Parrilla El Rey del Cabrito, Sarmiento 553
★★★ Confitería Alakush, Sarmiento 1110
★★★ Confitería Portobello, Sarmiento 1111

Post and telegraph

- Post office: Encotel, San Martín 190
- Telephone: Entel, San Martín 150

Villa Carlos Paz

CÓRDOBA PROVINCE

Services and facilities

- Bakery: San Francisco, Bulevar Sarmiento 198 (in the center north of the city
- Fishing and camping gear: La Pirana, Avenida San Martín block 1300 (corner of Kant)
- Photographic supplies: Ital Foto, San Martín 92. Selection of photographic equipment
- Supermarket: Frucar, San Martín 67

Delicatessens

- Delicatessen Alemán, corner of Alvear and General Paz
- Delicatessen Al Queso, San Martín 37

Laundromats

- Lavandería Centro, Lisandro de la Torre 61; $2.50
- Laverap, Alberdí block 100 (corner of Libertad). Open daily 0800–2200
- Laverap, Pellegrini 267 (in the center north of town). Open Mon–Sat 0800–2100
- Laverap, H Yrigoyen 1812

Clubs

- German: Club Alemán, Independencia 201; Social
- Italian: Centro Italiano, corner of Avenida Libertad and Belgrano. Social club

Motoring

Service stations

- ACA, corner of Avenida San Martín and Medrano
- Esso, Avenida San Martín block 1100 (corner of Lincoln)

Buses from Villa Carlos Paz

The bus terminal is on the corner of Avenida San Martín and Belgrano. It houses a restaurant (upstairs), *confitería*, telephones, post office, clean restrooms and a luggage depot.

- ABLO (Rosario–Buenos Aires)
- Colta (San Luis–Mendoza)
- Costera Criolla (Buenos Aires–Mar del Plata)
- El Serrano (Santa Fé–Parana–Corrientes)
- General Urquiza (Rosario–Buenos Aires)
- Sierras de Córdoba (Rosario–Buenos Aires)

Destination	Fare	Depart	Services	Hours	Company
Córdoba		0825	15 services daily	1	EPA/El Petiza, Primero de Mayo
Alta Gracia	$1.00	0640	4 services daily	1	COTAP
Buenos Aires	$25.00	0955	4 services daily	11	TA Chevallier
Capilla del Monte		0750	8 services daily	2	Primero de Mayo
Cosquín	$0.80	0750	8 services daily	1	Primero de Mayo
Cruz del Eje		0750	8 services daily	3	Primero de Mayo
Cuesta Blanca		0345	daily every hour	½	COTAP
El Condor		0745	7 services daily	2½	EPA/El Petizo
La Falda	$1.30	0750	8 services daily	1½	Primero de Mayo
La Cumbre		0750	8 services daily	1½	Primero de Mayo
Mina Clavero	$4.00	0745	7 services daily	3	EPA/ El Petizo
Rosario		0955	4 services daily	7	TA Chevallier
Tanti	$0.50	0740	7 services daily	½	COTAP
Villa Dolores		0745	7 services daily	4	EPA/El Petizo

Villa Carlos Paz

CÓRDOBA PROVINCE

⊕ Tours

Tour operators

- Akivi Tours, corner of Avenida San Martín and Maipú ℂ 21645. Also in the bus terminal. Their buses usually park near the terminal on San Martín
- Ben-Tur, Avenida Libertad 55 ℂ 23445
- Cruce Tours, corner of Sabattini and San Martín
- Excursiones El Condorito, Maipú 90 ℂ 22547
- Quir Tours, Alberdí 51 ℂ 21353
- Turismo del Lago San Roque, corner of Sabattini and Orgaz

Bus tours

- Capilla del Monte and Los Cocos: Mon and Tues 1330–1930; fare $3.50
- City of Córdoba and environs: Sat 0800–1200; fare $2.00
- Embalse Río Tercero and Los Molinos: Sat 0700–1945; fare $5.50
- La Cumbrecita and Villa Ciudad América: Wed–Sat 0700–2000; fare $7.50
- Mina Clavero and Los Tuneles: Tues–Fri 0600–1930; fare $10.00
- Río Ceballos and Dique San Roque: Tues–Thurs 1330–1900; fare $3.00

Boat trips on the lake

- Turismo del Lago San Roque. Boats moor on Sabattini (the *Costanera*) between Orgaz and M Juarez. Catamaran tours (2½ hours) depart 1030 and 1530; fare $5.00
- Cruce Tours. Boats moor on the *Costanera* between 9 de Julio and Montevideo. Boats leave at 1020 and 1530 for a 2½ hour tour (fare $2.50); and at 1700 for a 1½ hour tour (fare $2.00)
- Quir Tours runs a *"nautibus"*, an amphibious tour vehicle running both on land and in the lake; two-hour excursion; fare $3.00

⊞ Shopping

Best buys are leather mats, bags, and pottery.

Sport

- Roller skating and optical illusions: La Casa de Caspar, El Redentor 350 (corner of M Cane)
- Tennis Ranch Carlos Paz, San Martín block 2200; 0800–2300. Tennis court illuminated ($3.00 per hour)

Boating

- Alas Argentinas, López y Planes. Sailing boat hire
- Asociación Clubes de Remo, J L de Cabrera. Rowboat hire
- Los 400 Yacht Club, Tagore
- Motonáutico Córdoba, J S Bach
- Náutico Córdoba, Vespucio

▼ Entertainment

- Aerosilla Carlos Paz tourist complex, F Sanchez 300. At the foot of the mountain there is a swimming pool with solarium. You can take a chairlift to the top ($3.00) where there is a cafeteria, a nightclub, and a miniature trainset, as well as great views over the city, Lago San Roque, and the mountains surrounding the city
- Complejo Turístico de Peko, on RN 20, 5 km north of town before the turnoff to Tanti, is a castle-shaped building which houses optical illusions, a small zoo, an aquarium, a garden maze and a *confitería*
- Complejo Turístico Ciudad Dorada, on the corner of San Martín and Gobernador Alvarez has a "Wild West" type complex and features country music in the saloons
- Complejo Turístico Montaña Magica (Magic Mountain Tourist Complex) at the end of Calle Córdoba (corner of Los Cerros). Tobogganing on artificial snow, swimming pool, solarium; views over the city and lake; *confitería*
- Bingo Sala Azul, Avenida 9 de Julio 53
- Casino, Lisandro de la Torre 37
- Casino Sala Dorada, Avenida 9 de Julio 26
- Casino Sala de los Espejos, Avenida San Martín 36
- Disco Bangkok, Echevarría 79 (center north)
- Disco Keop's, corner of RS Peña and Seneca
- Disco Khalama, Avenida Estrada 113

Villa Carlos Paz

CÓRDOBA PROVINCE

- Disco Matilde, El Mirador
- Disco Molino Rojo, Avenida 9 de Julio 623 (center north)
- Disco Salon Oscar's, corner of Montevideo and Avenida 9 de Julio (upstairs)
- Peña Bailable Los Creadores, corner of Montevideo and 9 de Julio
- Peña Canteral, corner of Florida and RS Peña
- English-style pub: Chez Ami, corner of LN Alem and J Hernandez
- English-style pub: Liberty Street, Avenida Libertad 30
- English-style pub: "N N " Avenida Libertad 45
- Tanguería El Mangrullo, corner of Avenida Libertad and Salta
- Teatro "Bar", Avenida General Paz 27
- Teatro Candilejas, Pasaje Carolinas
- Teatro Carlos Paz, Avenida 9 de Julio 282
- Teatro Comico, Avenida 9 de Julio 50
- Teatro de la Villa, a theater complex on the corner of Avenida Uruguay and Liniers. The two theaters within the complex are called the "Sala Verde" ("Green Room") and the "Sala Ocre" ("Ochre Room")
- Teatro del Lago, Belgrano 81
- Teatro del Sol, Avenida General Paz 242
- Teatro Estrellas, Avenida 9 de Julio 25
- Teatro La Sombrilla, Alberdí 50
- Teatro Marconi, Avenida 9 de Julio 160
- Teatro Moliere, Avenida San Martín 545
- Teatro Orfeo, Avenida General Paz 27
- Teatro Quijote, corner of Liniers and Avellaneda
- Teatro Yolanda, Avenida 9 de Julio 70
- Teatro Zorba, corner of Avenida Carcano and S Roque

Excursions

Tours on amphibious buses go as far as the two dams on the lake. From there there are 2½-hour launch trips around the lake; fare $2.40.

Between 0900 and 1900 a chairlift ($2.10) runs up the slopes to a tearoom and nightclub overlooking the valley.

- **Capilla del Monte**: This is the classic *Punilla* excursion travelling through **Lago Roca**, **Cosquín** (with **Cerro Pan de Azúcar** in the range to the east), **La Falda**, and **La Cumbre** to Capilla del Monte. Mondays and Tuesdays 1330; half-day tour (146 km return; fare $3.50
- **Mina Clavero** and **Los Túneles** via **Taninga**. This trip combines the so-called *"Túnel y Volcán"* (Tunnel and Volcano) excursions with the High Peaks road. From Villa Carlos Paz you travel north to the junction with RP 28 where the *Túnel y Volcán* road begins. The road passes through **Tanti**, then starts climbing towards **Mogote los Gigantes** (2376 m), the highest peak of the **Sierra Grande**. The Club Andino Córdoba has a mountain *refugio* for about 20 people near the peak. The road then descends to the **Río Yuspe** and **Pampa de San Luis**. After passing **Cuchilla Nevada** it passes through the **Valle del Río San Guillermo** and passes near **Dos Ríos**, the lowest part, which separates the **Sierra Grande** to the south and **Cumbres de Gaspar** to the north. On approaching **Taninga** the road becomes picturesque once again as the regular cones of the long-extinct volcanoes **Yerba Buena**, **Boroa**, and others become visible. After that the trip crosses the **Pampa de Pocho** on a straight road to **Las Palmas**. During the Spanish colonial period this was a larger settlement as the

Villa Carlos Paz

main road to the *altiplano* passed through here. Evidence of its importance is shown by an old colonial church, Capilla de las Palmas, which was built in 1639 and is one of the oldest buildings in the region. It was built of *adobe* in simplistic colonial style. From Las Palmas it is only a short distance to the *túneles*. Returning to Las Palmas you take the road south through the Pampa de Pocho; there are patches of Caranday palms along the road. Some 20 km east of Pocho is the **Laguna de Pocho**, whose waters are said to have medicinal properties. In 1882 the *gaucho* priest Brochero completed the first irrigation water reservoir in **Villa Cura Brochero**. The aqueducts can still be seen in the vicinity. From Mina Clavero RN 20 crosses the **Cumbres de Achala**; it is still unsealed but is a picturesque mountain-pass road with great panoramic views. The road curves gently uphill and reaches its highest point at **El Cóndor**. There is a cafeteria here, but no hotel. From this point the **Lago San Roque** and Villa Carlos Paz can be seen for the first time. Tour buses usually stop here for a meal break. From El Condor it is possible to reach the Franciscan *colegio* (school) along an 18 km trail. The *colegio* is situated on the western slopes of the **Sierra Grande** at the headwaters of the **Río Rugapampa**. Continuing the trip from El Condor to Villa Carlos Paz the road starts to curve, and between **Casilla Negra** and **Copina** passes through some particularly scenic country, with sweeping views over the **Río Icho Cruz** valley and the **Sierra Grande** to the north, with occasional glimpses of Lago San Roque. Road works are still in progress on this stretch. The bus arrives back in Villa Carlos Paz in late afternoon. You can do this trip with Akivi Tours (Tuesday and Fridays from 0600 to 1900; fare $10.00), or by yourself using buses run by Empresa 20 de Junio and El Petizo

- **La Cumbrecita**: This excursion brings you to the Swiss-style mountain retreat going south past **Embalse Los Molinos**, a huge artificial lake of about 2500 ha. The turn-off from the main road is just south of this lake near **Los Reartes**. From here it is 16 km to the first "Swiss" village of **Villa Berna**. The road winds along the valley with views of the **Sierra de Comechingones** and **Sierra de Achala**. La Cumbrecita (1480 m) is situated in mountains covered with pine forests. Akivi Tours runs trips on Saturdays departing at 0700; fare $8.00. See also La Cumbrecita on page 178

CÓRDOBA PROVINCE

VILLA CIUDAD DE AMÉRICA

Distance from Córdoba: 65 km southwards via Alta Gracia

Villa Ciudad de América is situated on the northern shore of **Embalse Los Molinos**. It has good tourist facilities and is a center for water sports such as waterskiing, fishing, and windsurfing.

Accommodation

★★ Hotel Lago Los Molinos, RP 5 Km 769

★ Hotel Fatima, RP 5 Km 770 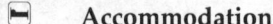. No single rooms

Buses

There are also buses to Río Cuarto via Villa General Belgrano and Villa Rumipal.
- Córdoba: Departs 0650; 4 services daily; 1½ hours; Empresa TOA
- Alta Gracia: Departs 0550; 12 services daily; ½ hour; Empresa Sierras de Calamuchita, Empresa TOA
- Villa General Belgrano: Departs 0645; 4 services daily; 1 hour; Empresa Sierras de Calamuchita

VILLA CURA BROCHERO

Postal code: 5891 • Altitude: 945 m
Distance from Córdoba: 142 km westwards on RN 20

Villa Cura Brochero is a vacation resort with good facilities. It is a good base for hiking and excursions into the **Cumbres de Achala**.

Buses

Buses run regularly to Córdoba and Villa Dolores.

VILLA DE MARÍA DE RÍO SECO

Postal code: 5248 • (area code: (0522) • Altitude: 315 m
Distance from Córdoba: 180 km north on RN 9

Accommodation in Villa Cura Brochero

- Hostería Cura Brochero, Tucumán 162 — $8.00
- Hospedaje Aluminé, Poeta Aguero 495 — $8.00
- Hospedaje Bibiloni, La Tablada 152
  No single rooms
- Hospedaje Casasnovas, General Paz 125
  No single rooms
- Hospedaje El Algarrobo, Juan Aguirre
  Triple rooms only
- Hospedaje Los Robles, Avenida Belgrano (91042
  No single rooms
- Hospedaje Los Cajones, Avenida Mina Clavero (91454
  Open December–March; no single rooms

CÓRDOBA PROVINCE

Villa de María is situated in the northernmost part of the province. It is the birthplace of Leopoldo Lugones, a poet of country life, whose house is now a museum. It is a convenient stopover en route to Santiago del Estero.

Accommodation
★ Hotel Samay Huasi, Avenida F Risuto $11.00. Breakfast $1.50

Buses
- Buses run regularly Córdoba and Santiago del Estero.

VILLA DE SOTO

Postal code: 5284 • Altitude: 530 m
Distance from Córdoba: 171 km northwest on RN 38

Villa de Soto is situated in the north-west near La Rioja province, close to the Salinas Grandes. It is one of the driest areas in Córdoba province.

Accommodation
★★ Hostería Martínez, J I Peralta (37
Hospedaje Costanera, J I Peralta 1078

Buses
Buses run daily to Córdoba and La Rioja.

VILLA DEL DIQUE

Postal code: 5862 • (area code: (0546)
Distance from Córdoba: 117 km southwest on RN 36

Villa del Dique is situated on the northern shore of the artificial lake **Embalse del Río Tercero**, the largest of a string of lakes on the Río Tercero. It is a good place for water sports.

Accommodation
★ Hotel Venecia, Bulevar Principal $15.00
Hostería Caribe $14.00
Hospedaje Santa Marta $12.00

VILLA DOLORES

Postal code: 5870 • Population: 10 000 •
(area code: (0544) • Altitude: 529 m
Distance from Córdoba: 187 km southwest on RP 14/20

Villa Dolores is situated in the **Río San Javier** valley on the **Río Los Sauces**, on the western side of the **Sierra de Comechingones**, also known as the *"Traslasierra"* (or "behind the mountains" from Córdoba). The town has views to **Cerro Champaquí** and is a good base for walks in the mountains. Wine, olives, tobacco, and walnuts are extensively grown in the area.

Tourist information
- Oficina de Informes y Turismo, in the bus terminal on Avenida España, also serves as ACA information office for the sale of maps. Señora Flora Ortiz Woodhouse (who does not speak English) is doing archeological surveys in the area.

Camping
- Piedras Pintadas, near Lago Los Sauces. 15 minutes by bus 1

CÓRDOBA PROVINCE

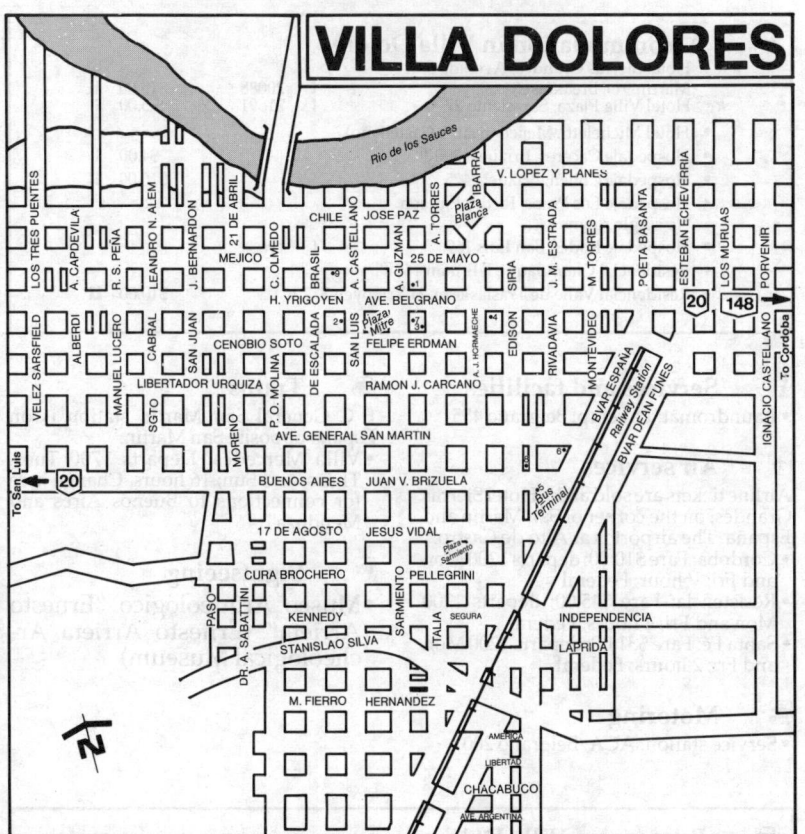

Key to Map
1. Municipalidad
2. Iglesia
3. Post office (Encotel)
4. Telephone (Entel)
5. Tourist information
6. Hotel Sierras Grandes
7. Hotel Villa Plaza
8. Hospedaje Cohen
9. Hotel Micheletti

Eating out
- Restaurant Don Santos, San Martín

Post and telegraph
- Post office: Encotel, Italia 299
- Telephone: Entel, Belgrano 340

Villa Dolores

CÓRDOBA PROVINCE

🛏 Accommodation in Villa Dolores

★★	Hotel Sierras Grandes, Avenida San Martín 9 🕾 Breakfast $1.50	✆ 20088	$15.00	👥
★	Hotel Villa Plaza, Sarmiento 27 ▣	✆ 21691	$ 5.00	👤

- Hotel Micheletti, Mejico (near A Castellano)
- Hospedaje Caceres, Brizuela 390 🕾 | | $4.00 | 👤
- Hospedaje Cohen, Brizuela 425 | | $10.00 | 👥
- Hospedaje Los Pinos, Piedra Pintada
  No single rooms
- Hospedaje Roder, San Luis 169 | ✆ 196 |
- Residencial Champaqui, F Erman 162 🕾
- Residencial Valle de Traslasierra, H Yrigoyen 317 🕾 | | $10.00 | 👥

🛒 Services and facilities
- Laundromat: Laverap, Belgrano 455

✈ Air services
Airline tickets are sold at the Hotel Sierras Grandes, on the corner of San Martín and España. The airport is at Alto de Castro.
- Córdoba: Fare $10.00; departs 1200 Mon and Fri; ½hour; Federal
- Resistencia: Fare $45.00; departs 1200 Mon and Fri; 4 hours; Federal
- Santa Fé: Fare $31.00; departs 1200 Mon and Fri; 2 hours; Federal

🚗 Motoring
- Service station: ACA, Belgrano 200

🚆 Trains
F C General San Martín station is on España opposite San Martín.
- Villa Mercedes: Departs 1700 Tues, Thurs, and Sun; 16 hours. Change here for connections to Buenos Aires and Mendoza

📷 Sightseeing
- Museo Arqueológico "Ernesto Arrieta" (Ernesto Arrieta Archeological Museum)

🚌 Buses from Villa Dolores

The bus terminal is on the corner of Brizuela and España, near the rail station.

Destination	Fare	Depart	Services	Hours	Company
• Córdoba	$5.50	0620	25 services daily	5	Contal, EPA/El Petizo, Expreso Mina Clavero
• La Toma	$2.50	1130	Mon, Wed, Fri, Sun		Sierras de Córdoba
• Mendoza	$10.00				TAC
• Merlo	$1.70	0645	daily		Sierras de Córdoba
• Mina Clavero	$1.40	0620	14 services daily	1	Contal, EPA/El Petizo, Sierras de Córdoba
• Río Cuarto					
via Santa Rosa	$4.70				Sierras de Córdoba
via Merlo	$5.50				Sierras de Córdoba
• San Juan	$6.20	0600	daily	6	Expreso 20 de Junio
• San Luis				5	
• Villa Carlos Paz		0620	13 services daily	4	Contal, EPA/El Petizo

CÓRDOBA PROVINCE

Excursions

- **Mina Clavero**: The road from Villa Dolores to Mina Clavero heads east towards the **Sierra de Comechingones** in an almost straight line. The airdrome and aero club are 3 km out of town. The road starts climbing at **Las Tapias**. There are vineyards on both sides of the road. From **Villa de las Rosas** (where Discoteca Los Cuartos is open during summer) the road turns north and runs parallel to the eastern side of the Sierra de Comechingones and enters hilly country. At **Los Pozos** there is a turn-off to the southern end of **Lago Ingeniero A M Allende**, at the **Dique de la Viña** dam. From Los Pozos the road heads eastwards for 5 km then veers north towards the highest part of the **Cumbres de Achala**. Just before **Los Hornillos** the road enters the valley and descends to Hostería Alta Montaña. Outside Los Hornillos we pass Hostería Dos Arroyos and Hostería Monte Perico, open only during summer. **Las Rabonas** is a small rural community with a sprinkling of villas, and the Hostería El Talamar. At **Huacle** there is Motel La Quebrada. From here onwards the countryside consists of shrub lands alternating with cultivated lands, where there are many apiaries. The Cumbre de Achala on the right hand side is now getting lower. At **Nono** there is a turn-off to Hotel del Alto, 3 km up on the right; 5 km from Nono is the Museo Rocse (Rocse Museum). After Nono the road follows the **Río de los Sauces**. The landscape here is not unlike that encountered in Australia. The road has a good surface, and the flat valley is followed on the western side by a low mountain range. Just before arriving at Mina Clavero is Santa Iñez camping grounds, near the river. See also Mina Clavero on page 187
- **Cerro Champaquí**: The best way to reach the top of this mountain is via **San Javier** and **Capilla Constancia**. The Municipalidad (Town Hall) in San Javier has names of guides. The walk goes through pine forests and walnut groves. From San Javier it is 8 km to the base of Cerro Champaquí. It is a four-hour walk to Constancia. It can be done in one day if you start early in San Javier
- **Lago Ingeniero A M Allende**: 23 km. Swimming, *pejerrey* fishing, and boat hire at the artificial lake

VILLA GENERAL BELGRANO

Postal code: 5194 • Population: 4500 • area code: (0546) • Altitude: 840 m
Distance from Córdoba: 85 km southwards on RN 36

Villa General Belgrano is situated in the pretty **Río Calamuchita valley** in western Córdoba

CÓRDOBA PROVINCE

BELGRANO

province, surrounded to the west by the **Sierra Grande** and to the east by the **Sierra Chica**. It is equidistant from two artificial lakes: **Embalse del Río Tercero** (19 km away) and **Embalse Los Molinos** (21 km away).

There are good tourist facilities, and the proximity of the *sierra* has made this town a favorite vacation resort, particularly among Argentina's German community. Further up the mountains are Swiss-style villages and hamlets such as **La Cumbrecita** and **Villa Berna**. There do not appear to be any regular buses between Villa General Belgrano and La Cumbrecita.

Villa General Belgrano has strong German roots. It was virtually founded by the crew of the *Graf Spee*, who were interned

Villa General Belgrano

CÓRDOBA PROVINCE

here during the Second World War and chose to remain afterwards.

Every year in October the beer festival is held, complete with Bavarian brass bands, German folkdances, and Weisswurst. At this time scores of Argentine Germans congregate here.

Villa General Belgrano is known locally as "Belgrano".

Festivals

- October 11 celebrates the arrival of the first German settlers and coincides with the Beer Festival
- Fiesta de La Masa Vienesa (Festival of the Viennese Cookies) coincides with Holy Week. A grand Viennese ball is held as the crowning event
- Tyrolian carnival: December and January

Tourist information

- Dirección Municipal de Turismo, Plaza San Martín (6215. Open daily 0730–1230 and 1600–2000

Camping

- Municipal camping grounds, on the banks of the River El Sauce near the bus terminal

Camping outside Villa General Belgrano

- Alta Vista, 14 km from town on the road to La Cumbrecita. Near the river
- San José, 5 km from centre on RP 5 (6496
- Tannenwald, 14 km from town on the road to Villa Berna (6299

Eating out

- Restaurant Bierkeller, RP 5, at the town entrance. German cuisine
- Restaurant Brisas Serranas. Steakhouse
- Restaurant Edelweiss, Hotel Edelweiss, corner of Avenida Los Incas and Ojo de Agua
- Restaurant El Monte
- Restaurant Halcon, Hostería Halcon
- Restaurant Il Mago. Italian cuisine

Accommodation in Villa General Belgrano

During the October beer festival it is advisable to book in advance. Señor Günter Meininghaus, the director of the Municipal de Turismo (City Tourist Department), speaks fluent English and German and will assist travellers (6317 or 6215.

★★★	Hotel Edelweiss, corner of Avenida Los Incas and Ojo de Agua	(6317	$25.00	
★	Hotel Rancho Grande, Avenida San Martín	(6358	$14.00	
★	Hotel Samay Huasi, Avenida Comechingones Includes breakfast	(6534	$10.00	
★	Hostería Chascomus, RP 14 north	(6625	$7.50	
★	No single rooms; includes breakfast Hostería El Mirador, Barrio Mirador	(6443	$30.00	
★	Open December–March; includes breakfast Hostería Halcon	(6289	$25.00	
★	Breakfast $1.50; meals $3.00 Hospedaje Alpino, corner of San Martín and La Toma	(6355	$11.00	
★	Hospedaje Champaqui	(6206	$4.50	
★	Hospedaje Dusseldorf, Julio A Roca	(6451	$25.00	

Villa General Belgrano

CÓRDOBA PROVINCE

- Restaurant Los Pinos
- Restaurant Munich, San Martín. German cuisine
- Restaurant Norma
- Restaurant Rancho Grande, Hotel Rancho Grande, Avenida San Martín
- Cafetería Alpengruesse, Avenida Champaquí
- Cafetería Ciervo Rojo
- Cafetería Don Miguel. Pizzeria
- Cafetería Ottilia

Post and telegraph
- Post office: Encotel, Plaza San Martín
- Telephones: Entel, Plaza San Martín

Services and facilities
- Supermarket: Autoservicio San Martín, San Martín

Motoring
- Service station: ACA, corner of RP 5 and Avenida Champaquí

Sport
- Flying: Aeroclub

- Swimming: There is a public swimming pool, and there are pools at most of the better hotels
- Tennis: Tennis courts at Hotel Edelweiss. Small fee for external users

Entertainment
- Disco Gerlind
- Disco Vikinger

Excursions
- **Dique Los Molinos**: This 61 km trip makes a complete circuit of the lake and takes a full day by car. Follow RP 5 north. Shortly before arriving at **Villa La Merced** you will see the lake on your left. It covers 2500 ha and was inaugurated in 1953. Water sports and *pejerrey* fishing are popular here. Continue to **Villa Ciudad de America** where you turn west, taking the road to **Potrero de Garay**, following the

Buses from Villa General Belgrano

The bus terminal is about five blocks from Plaza San Martín on Plaza Velez Sarsfield.

Destination	Fare	Depart	Services	Hours	Company
• Córdoba	$2.40	0500	16 services daily	2	Colta, Sierras de Calamuchita, TOA
• Alta Gracia	$1.50	0515	12 services daily	1½	Sierras de Calamuchita, TOA
• Buenos Aires	$15.00	1915	4 services daily	12	Colta, Sierras de Calamuchita
	$19.00	1900	daily	11	TA Chevallier
• La Cruz		1110	4 services daily	1½	TOA
• Mendoza	$12.50	2120	Mon, Wed, Fri	8	Colta
• Río Cuarto		0900	2 services daily		Colta
• Río Tercero		0625	3 services daily		Colta
• Rosario	$9.50	2000	daily	9	ABLO
• Santa Rosa de Calamuchita	$0.50	0800	8 services daily	½	Sierras de Calamuchita
• Villa Ciudad de América		0515	12 services daily	1	Sierras de Calamuchita, TOA
• Villa Rumipal		0500	5 services daily	1	TOA

Villa General Belgrano

northern lakeshore. At Potrero de Garay turn south. The road crosses **Río Espinillo** and **Río del Medio**, which flow from the **Sierra Grande** and are the main feeder streams of the lake. After **Los Reartes** it crosses **Río de los Reartes**, another major feeder of the lake. Continue until you return to Villa General Belgrano
• **La Cumbrecita**: 85 km, a full day by car. This trip takes you through an almost Alpine landscape: forests, clean streams, waterfalls. On leaving Villa General Belgrano take the direct road due north to **Los Reartes**. At Los Reartes turn west and follow the road past **Villa Berna** right up to La Cumbrecita, a transplanted Swiss Alpine village with a hotel. Return via Villa Berna but instead of continuing due east to Los Reartes take the turn-off to the south passing through **Intiyaco** and **Atos Pampa**. At Atos Pampa turn east until you reach the crossroads at **Capilla Vieja**, then turn south to bring you back to Villa General Belgrano. See also La Cumbrecita on page 178

VILLA GENERAL MITRE

Postal code: 5236 • Altitude: 569 m
Distance from Córdoba: 81 km

Accommodation

There is one basic hotel, one camping ground, and two private accommodations.

Eating out

There are two restaurants, two tearooms, and two shops.

Motoring

There are two petrol stations, two mechanics, and two tyre-repair places.

VILLA MARÍA

Postal code: 5900 • Population: 70 000 • (
area code: (0535) • Altitude: 200 m
Distance from Córdoba: 146 km southeast on RN 9

Villa Maria is a prosperous agricultural center situated in the fertile humid *pampa* on the **Río Tercero**. It is served by the F C General B Mitre railroad, and is an important town on the crossroads of the main Buenos Aires–Córdoba road and the most convenient highway route linking central Chile with Paraguay, Uruguay, and Brazil.

Festivals

• Festival de Peñas Folkloricos (Folksong Festival): first week in January

Eating out

• La Churrasquita

Post and telegraph

• Post office: Encotel, Catamarca 1190
• Telephone: Entel, J Ingenieros 151

Buses

Buses run regularly to Buenos Aires and Córdoba; TA Chevallier runs 9 services a day.

CÓRDOBA PROVINCE

📧 Accommodation in Villa María

★★★	Hotel Republica, 9 de Julio 58	(	21556	$25.00	♨
★★	Hotel City, Buenos Aires 1184	(	20948	$19.00	♨
★★	Hotel Palace, corner of Cabral and Mendoza	(	23331	$13.00	♨
★	Hotel Antares, Bulevar Alvear 191	(	24555	$15.00	♨
•	Hospedaje Alcazar, corner of Alvear and M Ocampo	(	22445		
•	Hospedaje Alvear, M T de Alvear 578				
•	Hospedaje Colonial, Corrientes 1150. No single rooms	(	21429		
•	Hospedaje Entre Ríos, H Yrigoyen 221				
•	Hospedaje Orazzi, Entre Ríos 1335				
•	Hospedaje Plaza, San Martín 141	(	23249		
•	Hospedaje San Martín, H Yrigoyen 127	(	20328		
•	Hospedaje San Remo, M T de Alvear 595. No single rooms	(	21750		

🌿 Excursions

On an island in the **Río Tercero** there is a flora and fauna reserve.

VILLA RUMIPAL

Postal code: 5864 • (area code: (0546) •
Altitude: 590 m
Distance from Córdoba: 126 km southwards on RN 36

Villa Rumipal is situated at the north end of the artificial lake **Embalse del Río Tercero**. It was founded by Gustav Riemann in 1930.

The climate is good all year round. The aboriginal inhabitants of this area were the Comechingones, but the only reminder of them is the name of the town: *rumi* means "stone" and *pal* means "star", possibly indicating a meteorite fall they witnessed in the area.

🏃 Festivals

- Festival Provincial del Lago (Provincial Lake Festival): January
- Magimundo: during the winter vacation
- Expo Rumipal: in September during Semana del Pueblo, an exhibition of crafts and archeology
- Motonáutica Interprovincial: A motorboat racing event

ℹ️ Tourist information

- Municipalidad de Calamuchita (98272.

📧 Accommodation

- ★ Hostería Cayzani, Bulevar Illia 394 $7.00 ♨. Full board $5.00
- Hospedaje Walter, Fuerza Aerea. No single rooms

⛺ Camping

There are several camping grounds along the lake shore.

🍴 Eating out

There are several restaurants, bars, and tearooms.

✉️ Post and telegraph

There is a post office and public telephones.

Villa María

CÓRDOBA PROVINCE

🚌 Buses from Villa Rumipal

Destination	Depart	Services	Hours	Company
• Córdoba	0525	5 services daily	3	Colta, TOA
• Alta Gracia	0525	4 services daily	2	TOA
• Buenos Aires				Sierras de Calamuchita, Colta
• Mendoza				Colta
• Rosario				ABLO, Monticas
• Santa Rosa	0420	5 services daily		TOA
• Villa Ciudad de América	0525	4 services daily	1½	TOA
• Villa General Belgrano	0420	5 services daily	1	TOA

✈ Air services
There is an airdrome for local flights only.

Sport
- Fishing: Good places to fish for the "king of fish", the *pejerrey*, are the banks near the river mouths of Río Santa Rosa and Río Quillinzo, and from boats
- Water sports: Boat hire, diving, swimming, waterskiing, sailing

Entertainment
Most of the discos and dancing spots are only open during the tourist season, December–February

VILLA TULUMBA

Postal code: 5203 • (area code: (0521) • Altitude: 650 m
Distance from Córdoba: 132 km northwards on RP 60 then RP 16

Villa Tulumba is located in the northern part of the province.

Accommodation
★ Hotel Las Vegas $4.50. The bus stops in front of the hotel

🚌 Buses
Empresa Cadol buses run regularly to Déan Funes, San José de la Dormida, and Córdoba.

YACANTO DE CALAMUCHITA

Postal code: 5877 • Altitude: 1100 m
Distance from Villa Dolores: 20 km northwest

Yacanto de Calamuchita is situated at at the foot of **Cerro Champaquí**, the highest mountain in the Sierra de Comechingones. The region is forested, has many waterfalls, and produces some wine.

The town's springs are said to contain curative waters.

Accommodation
★★ Hotel Yacanto (2 (San Javier) $43.00. Breakfast $2.00
★ Hostería Champaquí $8.00

Accommodation in San Javier
San Javier is 2 km north of Yacanto.
★ Hostería Gonzalez (6. Open December–February; no single rooms

CÓRDOBA PROVINCE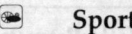

Buses
Buses run regularly to Córdoba, Merlo (Empresa San Luis), and Villa Dolores.

Sport
There is an 18-hole golf course.

Yacanto de Calamuchita

LA PAMPA PROVINCE

Plate 9 Map of La Pampa Province
- 238 General Acha
- 239 Map
- 241 General Pico
- 242 Map
- 241 Parque Nacional Lihuel Calel
- 243 Santa Rosa
- 244 Map

The name of this province, La Pampa, is derived from a Quechua word meaning "flat country". However, the landscape varies from flat steppe to undulating plains and low mountains. La Pampa is located in the centre of Argentina, and shares borders with Neuquén and Mendoza in the west, Córdoba and San Luis in the north, Buenos Aires in the east, and Río Negro to the south, with the Río Negro forming the border.

The main river is the **Río Negro** in the south. The highest mountain in the province is the **Cerro Negro**, 1188 m high, situated in the **Parque Nacional Lihuel Calel**. In the extreme west there are many salt flats.

The construction of large dams in the upper reaches and tributaries of the Río Salado in the provinces of Mendoza and San Luis has created deserts in the western part of the province.

The rain decreases from east to west, and in most parts of the province is insufficient for wheat crops. The highest rainfall is in the north-east, around 750 mm a year. Because of the shortage of

La Pampa Province

precipitation, most cities depend on bore water, which is usually of good quality. The temperature oscillates between 40°C in summer and –8°C in winter. Irregular rainfall and long periods of dry spells characterize this province, and because of these harsh living conditions the population density is low: there are few large cities, and even the capital Santa Rosa has only about 60 000 inhabitants.

Winters usually constitute the dry months, and can last until October. The wet season starts at the end of September and lasts until December. There is another short wet period towards the end of February.

Hot strong winds are common, and, according to the season, blow from the north and north-east. The *pampero* which comes up from the south brings cold weather. Sometimes the *sudestacada* blows from the southeast, bringing fogs and humidity.

The dry conditions have shaped the landscape: *algarrobo*, prickly *calden*, and *chañar* trees dominate.

La Pampa was formerly the home of semi-nomadic Tehuelche Indians who were formidable hunters. Around 1800, Araucanian peoples invaded the territory. Until the "pacification campaign" waged by the Argentines against the Araucanian people in 1879, Indian raiders made European settlement difficult. This changed after the Argentine army defeated the Indians and their famous leaders Pincen, Yanquetruz, Catriel Namuncura, and Calfucura. Between 1880 and 1890 most of the big *estancias* were established.

It was only in 1951 that La Pampa was elevated to the status of province, and **Santa Rosa**, some 600 km south-west of Buenos Aires, established as its capital.

The largest towns are **Santa Rosa** (population 65 000), **General Pico** (population 32 000), **Realico** (population 13 000), and **General Acha** (population 8000).

Although La Pampa is mostly a "transit" province for the tourist stream going south to Río Negro and Neuquén, it offers open, sparsely populated country for those seeking peace and quiet. You can travel for hours on excellent roads without seeing evidence of people on the landscape, especially in the western part.

The wide open spaces have a charm of their own. Some of the nature reserves are stocked with stags. The best known nature reserves are **Parque Provincial Luro** and **Parque Nacional Lihuel Calel**, both of which have prehistoric rock paintings.

GENERAL ACHA

Postal code: 8200 • (area code: (0952) •
Population: 8000
Distance from Santa Rosa: 103 km southwards on RN 35 then RN 152

La Pampa Province

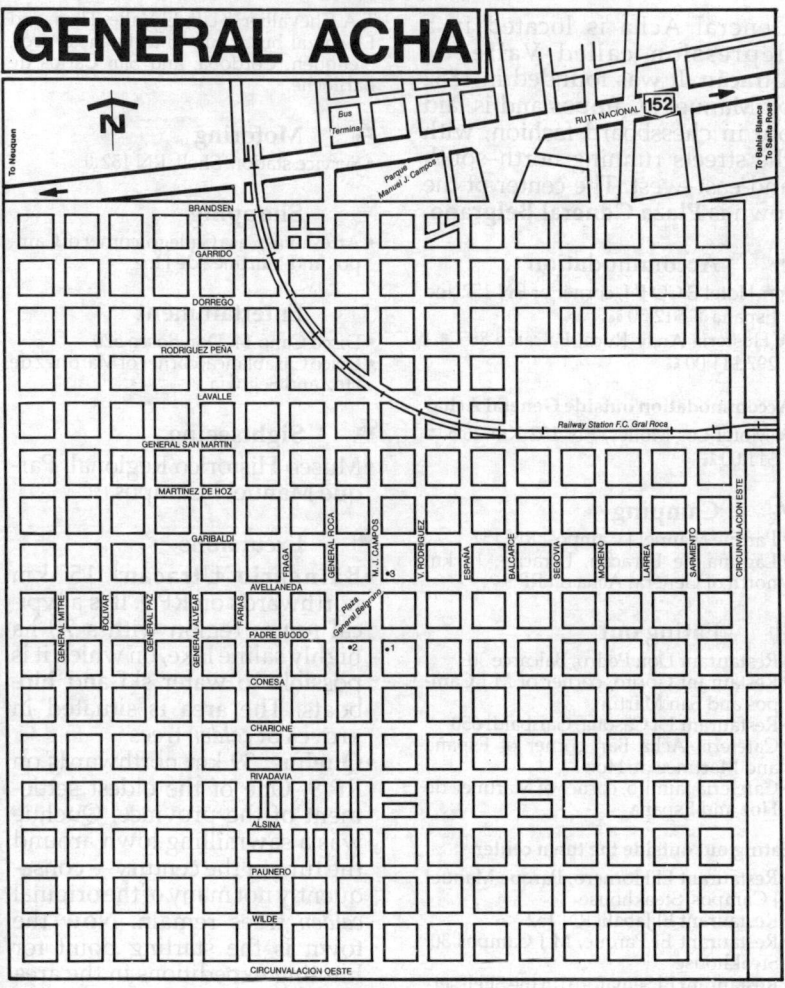

Key to Map	2	Iglesia
1 Municipalidad	3	Post office (Encotel)
	4	Bus terminal

General Acha

La Pampa Province

General Acha is located in a depression called **Valle de Utracán**. It was founded in 1882 by Manuel J Campos and is laid out in chessboard fashion, with the streets running north–south and east–west. The center of the town is **Plaza General Belgrano**.

🛏 Accommodation

- ★★ Hotel E CO P I, corner of RN 152 and España ⑪ $12.50 ♚
- ★ Hostería Anay Ruca, Balcarce 885 ▣ ☏ 297 $11.00 ♚

Accommodation outside General Acha

- ★ Motel Los Molles, RN 152 Km 26.5 ▣ $11.00 ♚

⛺ Camping

- Parque Manuel J Campos, RN 152
- Laguna de Utracán, Utracán, 14 km north of General Acha on RP 9

🍽 Eating out

- Restaurant Don Pedro, Balcarce 30
- Restaurant Gorito, corner of M J Campos and San Martín
- Restaurant La Casona, Garibaldi 650
- Cafetería Acha Bar, corner of España and Martinez de Hoz
- Cafetería Jaimito, corner of Martinez de Hoz and Espana

Eating out outside the town center

- Restaurant El Hornero, Parque Manuel J Campos. Steakhouse
- Restaurant El Jabali, RN 152
- Restaurant El Parque, M J Campos 30. Steakhouse
- Restaurant El Semaforo (in the Shell service station), RN 152

📬 Post and telegraph

- Post office: Encotel, Avellaneda 795

🚌 Buses

The bus terminal is on RN 152, opposite Parque Manuel J Campos.

T A Chevallier, TUP, El Valle, Tirsa, and El Zorzal buses run to to Buenos Aires, Neuquén, Córdoba, and San Carlos de Bariloche.

🚗 Motoring

- Service station: Shell, RN 152 ⑪

🛍 Shopping

- Artesanías Casa Gallego, corner of Campos and Martinez de Hoz

🎭 Entertainment

- Disco Cano 14, Don Bosco 520
- Disco Casablanca, corner of Martinez de Hoz and Segovia

📷 Sightseeing

- Museo Historico Regional, Parque Manuel J Campos

🌳 Excursions

- **Balneario Utracán**: 15 km northwards on RP 9. It is a typical *pampa* region with a 70 ha highly saline lake, on which it is possible to water ski and hire boats. The area is situated in groves of *calden* trees
- **Quehue**: 39 km northwards on RP 9. One of the oldest settlement of the province, Quehue was a sawmilling town around the turn of the century— consequently not many of the original *calden* trees remain. Now the town is the starting point for hunting expeditions in the area for wild boar and stags
- **Padre Angel Buodo**: Located at the intersection of RN 152 and RN 35, some 25 km east. Padre Buodo was a Salesian priest who worked as a missionary here. The museum is open daily 1000–1800

General Acha

LA PAMPA PROVINCE

GENERAL PICO

Postal code: 6360 • (area code: (0302) • Population: 33 000
Distance from Santa Rosa: 131 km northwest on RP 35 then RP 102

General Pico is located in the north-western part of the province. It is an important crossroads; RP 1 and RP 101 intersect here. The town was founded in 1905 by Eduardo de Chapeaurouge. The climate is moderate and dry, with temperatures of 45°C in summer and –13°C in winter. Most of the rain falls between October and April.

Accommodation
- ★★Hotel Pico, Calle 17 1013 (22446 $15.00
- ★★ Hostería Caui, corner of Calle 9 and Calle 104 (21435 $15.00
- ★★ Motel Brisa, corner of RP 1 and Calle 9 (22712 $12.50

Post and telegraph
- Post office: Encotel, corner of 9 de Julio and 20 de Setiembre

Services and facilities
- Laundromat: Laverap, General Belgrano (formerly Calle 20) 486

Air services
Lapa has regular flights in and out of General Pico.

Buses
- Santa Rosa: Fare $2.50; departs 2000 daily; 2 hours; T A Chevallier
- Buenos Aires: Fare $15.20; departs 0630 daily; 8 hours; Empresa T A Chevallier

Excursions
- **Intendente Alvear**: 54 km north on RP 1. A *gaucho* festival, Fiesta de la Doma y Folklore, is held here from the last Saturday in January until first Sunday in February
- **Bernardo Larroude**: 79 km north on RN 188. Municipal baths contain thermal water with curative properties

PARQUE NACIONAL LIHUEL CALEL

Postal code: 8201
Distance from Santa Rosa: 242 km southwest on RN 35 then RP 152

This national park of approximately 10 000 ha is located in the southern part of the province. It was created in 1977 to preserve the unusual flora encountered in this area. The backdrop to the park is the low **Sierra de Lihuel Calel**, forming a 15 km horseshoe. During the past century this was the last hideout of the Indian tribes who, under Chief Namuncura, invaded La Pampa from Chile. The caves and walls inside abound with rock paintings, indicating an unbroken occupation of the area from prehistoric times. The microclimate of the area allows species of widely different habitats to coexist in a very small area.

LA PAMPA PROVINCE

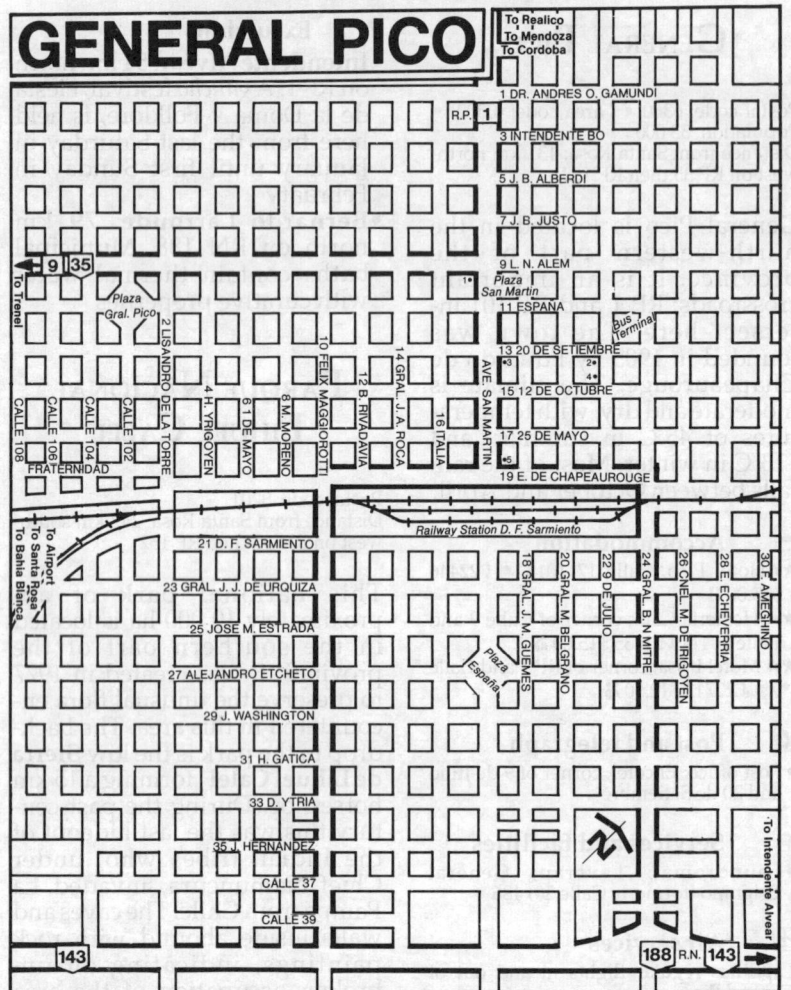

Key to Map
1. Municipalidad
2. Post office (Encotel)
3. Telephone (Entel)
4. Banco de la Nación
5. Hotel Pico

General Pico

LA PAMPA PROVINCE

Accommodation
At this stage it is unknown whether the ACA motel outside the national park entrance is open.

Post and telegraph
There is a post office at the ACA service station.

Buses
- Santa Rosa: Departs 0130; 2 services daily; 3 hours; Empresa T A Chevallier
- Neuquén: Departs 0140; 2 services daily; 5 hours; Empresa T A Chevallier

Motoring
- Service station: ACA

SANTA ROSA

Postal code: 6300 • Population: 65 000 • area code: (0954) • Altitude: 177 m
Distances
- From Bahía Blanca: 332 km north-west on RN 35
- From Buenos Aires: 619 km south-east on RN 5

Santa Rosa, the capital of La Pampa, is located in the central eastern part of the province, near **Laguna Don Tomas**. It was founded by Tomas Mason in 1892. The first settlement was **Estancia La Malvina**, some 3 km from the town center. In 1904 Santa Rosa became capital of the then Territorio Nacional La Pampa to replace the town of **General Acha**. Although it progressed slowly at first, Santa Rosa is now a modern city. The centre of town is Avenida San Martín between Avenida Luro (with the magnificent Casa de Gobierno) and the corner of Avenida Avellaneda and Mitre. Buses run frequently to Buenos Aires and Neuquén.

Tourist information
- Dirección Provincial de Turismo, corner of Avenida Luro and San Martín (25060

Camping
- Municipal Laguna Don Tomas, at the end of Avenida Uruguay

Accommodation in Santa Rosa

★★★★	Hotel Calfacura, San Martín 695	(23608	$31.00	
★	Hotel Calden, Avenida Spinetto 820	(25995	$14.50	
★	Hotel San Martín, Avenida Alsina 101 (opposite rail station)	(22549	$11.50	
★	Hostería French, French 346	(22033	$11.00	
★	Hostería Río Atuel, Avenida Luro 356	(22597	$11.00	
★	Hostería Santa Rosa, H Yrigoyen 696	(23868	$12.50	
•	Hospedaje Tredi, Spinetto 35			
•	Residencial Mitre, Mitre 76 (near bus terminal)		$5.00	

Accommodation outside Santa Rosa

★★★	Motel Calden, RN 35 Km 330	(24311	$21.00	
★★	Motel ACA, RN 5 Km 606	(24067	$13.50	
★	Hotel Los Lebreles, RN 5 Km 606	(27557	$13.00	

Santa Rosa

LA PAMPA PROVINCE

SANTA ROSA

LA PAMPA PROVINCE

🚌 Buses from Santa Rosa

The bus terminal is on corner of Corrientes and Avenida Luro, on the north side of the civic center. 🕐24hr 🚻. Clean restrooms.

Destination	Fare	Depart	Services	Hours	Company
• Bahía Blanca		0025	4 services daily		Andesmar, TUP
• Buenos Aires	$15.00	0315	3 services daily	10	T A Chevallier
• Córdoba	$12.00	0145	3 services daily		TUP
• Lihuel Calel	$5.00	0255	2 services daily	4	T A Chevallier
• Mar del Plata		2030	daily		El Rapido
• Mendoza		2234	daily		Andesmar
• Neuquén	$9.50	0255	4 services daily	7	T A Chevallier
	$9.50	0011	4–5 services daily	9	Alto Valle, El Valle, TIRSA, TUP
• Rawson		2145	Wed, Fri, Sat		TUP
• Rosario		0437	Mon, Wed		TIRSA
• San Carlos de Bariloche		0011	Mon, Sat		TIRSA
• San Juan		2133	Mon–Wed, Sat		TICSA
• San Luis		2133	Mon–Wed, Sat		TICSA

🍴 Eating out

- Restaurant Club Español, corner of H Lagos and Avellaneda
- Restaurant El Bato, corner of Avenida Luro and L de la Torre. Steakhouse; credit cards accepted
- Restaurant El Ciervo, corner of Corrientes and Santa Fé
- Restaurant Gran Paris, 9 de Julio 243. Local cuisine; cheap
- Restaurant La Taberna de José, Avenida Luro block 200 (corner of H Yrigoyen). Credit cards accepted
- Restaurant La Tablita, Urquiza 326. Steakhouse
- Restaurant Pocho, corner of O'Higgins and 25 de Mayo
- Restaurant Rancho La Ruta, Avenida Luro block 600 (corner of Pampeanos). Steakhouse
- ☞ Restaurant San Martín, Pellegrini 115. Credit cards accepted
- ☞ Restaurant Solos, Pellegrini 228. Expensive
- Comedor El Gallego, Alvear 42. Local cuisine
- Comedor La Cocina de Nora, Pellegrini 560. Local cuisine; cheap
- Comedor Universitario ULNPAM, Avenida Luro 143
- ☞ Pizzería Itati, Gil 265
- Pizzería Mar-Yor, España 87
- Pizzería Savarini, 25 de Mayo block 100 (corner of Mansilla)
- Pizzería Tano, corner of San Martín and Gil
- Cafetería ACA, corner of Gil and San Martín
- Cafetería Bar Quiroga, Avenida Luro block 200 (corner of H Lagos). Early breakfast

Key to Map

1. Municipalidad
2. Catedral
3. Post office (Encotel)
4. Telephone (Entel)
5. Tourist information
6. Banco de la Nación
7. Aerolineas Argentinas
8. Museo Provincial
9. Hotel Calfacura
10. Hotel San Martín
11. Hostería Río Atuel
12. Hostería Santa Rosa
13. Hospedaje Tredi
14. Residencial Mitre

Santa Rosa

LA PAMPA PROVINCE

- Cafetería Bariloche, Avenida Luro block 200 (corner of H Yrigoyen). Open 24 hours
- Cafetería de la "O", corner of H Yrigoyen and 25 de Mayo
- Cafetería El Centenario, corner of Avellaneda and Mansilla. Snacks
- Cafetería La Capital, corner of Avellaneda and H Yrigoyen
- ☞ Cafetería La Recova, Avellaneda block 200 (corner of H Lagos)
- ☞ Cafetería Nairobi Pub, 9 de Julio block 0 (corner of Avellaneda)
- Cafetería Pampa Bar, Gil block 300 (corner of San Martín)
- Takeaway: Listo El Pollo, San Martín block 500 (corner of Garibaldi)

Post and telegraph

- Post office: Encotel, corner of H Lagos and Rivadavia
- Telephone: Entel, corner of H Lagos and Rivadavia

Financial

- Banco de la Nación, corner of Avenida San Martín and B Mitre. Official exchange rate
- Banco Mercantil, C Pellegrini 98. Cash advances on Visa card

Services and facilities

- Laundromat: Laverap, Rivadavia 253. Open Mon–Sat 0800–2100, Sun 0900–1300
- Pharmacy: Farmacia Calamari, Avenida Luro block 0 (corner of Alvear)
- Photographic equipment: Foto Principe, San Martín block 100 (corner of 25 de Mayo)
- Supermarket: Luro, Avenida Luro block 0 (corner of Mansilla)

Clubs

- Spanish: Club Español, corner of H Lagos and Avellaneda

Air services

A taxi to the airport costs $3.50.

Airlines

- Aerolineas Argentinas, Rivadavia 266

Services

- Bahía Blanca: Fare $29.00; departs 1625 Mon; 2 hours; Aerolineas
- Buenos Aires (Aeroparque Jorge Newbery): Fare $52.00; departs 1915; 1–2 services daily; 1 hour; Aerolineas
- Córdoba: Fare $43.00; departs 1915 Fri; 1 hours; Aerolineas

Motoring

Service stations

- ACA, corner of San Martín and Gil. Maps available
- YPF, corner of B Mitre and Alem

Trains

The station is on Alsina, opposite Pellegrini. Trains arrive in Buenos Aires at Once station.

- Buenos Aires: Departs 1916 Sun–Wed, Fri; 13 hours

Tours

- Cintur Turismo, L de la Torre 400
- Turindio, Pellegrini block 0 (corner of Alsina)

Shopping

- Artesanías La Ruca, H Lagos block 0 (corner of Avellaneda)
- ☞ Souvenir shop, Pellegrini 86. Gaucho items

Entertainment

- Disco Jockey, 9 de Julio 130
- Tanguería El Rincón de los Amigos, Gil 31

Sightseeing

- Museo Provincial (Provincial Museum), Pellegrini 180. Local history and natural sciences
- Centro Recreativo Don Tomas (Don Tomas Recreation Center). Situated on the 350 ha Laguna Don Tomas, it is a reafforested area and camping spot

Santa Rosa

LA PAMPA PROVINCE

♣ **Excursions**

- **Parque Luro**: 33 km south of Santa Rosa on RN 35. Covering 7500 ha, it was acquired by the provincial government in 1965 and converted into a provincial reserve to preserve the flora and fauna prevalent in the area. There is a variety of wildlife such as pheasants, deer, and stags which proliferated after being imported from Europe. The *castilo* was built by Don Antonio Maura, a Spanish aristocrat. There is a visitors' center. Open Wed–Sun 0900–1800; small admission charge

Santa Fé Province

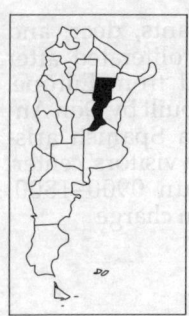

Plate 11 Map of Santa Fé Province
- 249 Melincué
- 249 Reconquista
- 250 Rosario
- 251 Map
- 259 San Lorenzo
- 259 Santa Fé de la Vera Cruz
- 260 Map
- 267 Venado Tuerto

Santa Fé province covers 133 000 square kilometers. It is completely flat and has no mountains of any significance. A large part of this province forms part of the Chaco–Pampa plains. It is dominated by the **Río Paraná** along which are many flood-prone areas.

Santa Fé province shares borders to the north with Chaco province, to the west with Santiago del Estero and Córdoba, to the south with Buenos Aires, and to the east with Entre Ríos and Corrientes. The main cities are **Santa Fé de la Vera Cruz** (often abbreviated to "Santa Fé", population 350 000), the provincial capital, and **Rosario** (population 1 000 000). Rosario and Santa Fé de la Vera Cruz are among the most heavily industrialized cities in Argentina.

The climate is temperate, with a dry season, to subtropical, with no dry season. The predominant trees in the north are the *quebracho* and the *algarrobo*.

Santa Fé is a major producer of prime beef and dairy products

Plate 11

Map of Santa Fé Province

Plate 12

Top: Valle de las Cuevas
Bottom: Los Penitentes ski resort

SANTA FÉ PROVINCE

as well as wheat. Together with Buenos Aires province it is the granary of Argentina.

The province has an extensive first-class road system. The **Río Paraná** is also navigable and ships ply between Buenos Aires and Santa Fé–Paraná.

For the tourist the city of **Santa Fé de la Vera Cruz**, founded in 1573 by Juan de Garay, is interesting. Sportsfishing in the rivers is possible at any time of the year. Cruising the Río Paraná is another possibility.

MELINCUÉ

Postal code: 2728
Distance from Rosario: 128 km southwest on RP 33 then RP 93

Melincué is situated on the northern shore of **Lago Melincué**. The lake is fed by thermal springs which are apparently beneficial for some forms of arthritis and rheumatism. There is a colonial church in the locality.

Accommodation
There are a few small hotels.

Buses
There are direct bus services to Rosario and Venado Tuerto.

RECONQUISTA

Postal code: 3560 • area code: (0776) •
Population: 35 000
Distance from Santa Fé de la Vera Cruz: 260 km northwards on RN 11

The city was founded in 1872 by Colonel Manuel Obligado. It is located some 15 km from its port on the Río Paraná.

Festivals
- Festival Folklórico del Noroeste Argentino (Folk Festival of the Argentine North-west): January

Accommodation
- ★★ Hotel Ichoalay, H Yrigoyen 802 20957
- Hotel Magui. On the main street
- Hotel Olessio $12.00. Opposite the bus terminal
- Residencial San Martín, B Mitre (corner of Bolivar) $8.00
- Motel Hostal del Rey, RN 11 $20.00. Just outside town

Services and facilities
- Laundromat: Laverap, Iturraste 434

Buses from Reconquista

Destination	Services	Hours	Company
• Santa Fé de la Vera Cruz	11 services daily	5½	Godoy
• Buenos Aires	15 services daily	12	La Internacional
• Clorinda	3 services daily	8	Brujula
• Formosa	3 services daily	6	Godoy
• Resistencia	5 services daily	3	La Internacional
• Rosario	11 services daily	8	Brujula

Santa Fé Province

✈ Air services
The military airbase is used as the airport and is 10 km from town.
- Buenos Aires (Aeroparque Jorge Newbery): $56.00; 1340 Tues, Thurs, Sat; 2 hours; Austral
- Santa Fé de la Vera Cruz: $36.00; 1340 Tues, Thurs, Sat; 1 hour; Austral

🚘 Motoring
- Service station: ACA, corner of Bulevar Galvez and Patricio Diez

⌂ Water transport
A ferry service runs from Puerto Reconquista to Goya in Corrientes province daily except Wed at 1500; fare $2.50. A bus runs from Reconquista to el Puerto: fare $0.50

Rosario

Postal code: 2000 • Population: 1 000 000 • (area code (041)
Distance from Santa Fé de la Vera Cruz: 147 km southwards on RN 11 (*autopista*)

Rosario, the third largest city in Argentina, is situated on the **Río Paraná** in the southern part of Santa Fé province. There is no official founding date for the city, which is quite unusual for Spanish colonial history. Its origin can be traced back to an *estancia*, and to its chapel to the Virgen del Rosario (Virgin of the Rosary) which stood here on the banks at the end of the seventeenth century. Settlers came from **Santa Fé la Vieja)** (or "Old Santa Fé") to escape the marauding Indians. The first landholder here was Capitán Luis Romero de Pineda, who took up his holding in 1689. In 1852 it became a city.

The Río Paraná is over 5 km wide here and ocean-going vessels can berth in Rosario. Agricultural products from the north-west are shipped from here, making it Argentina's second biggest trading port. It is both a university and an industrial city.

The town is laid out on a grandiose scale with wide avenues and boulevards, most of them tree-lined. Along the Río Paraná runs a splendid boulevard.

The Río Paraná is dotted with islands which can be reached by ferries and are weekend destinations for the *Rosarinos*.

Key to Map
1. Municipalidad
2. Catedral
3. Post office (Encotel)
4. Telephone (Entel)
5. Tourist information
6. Cambio Exprinter
7. Banco de la Nación
8. Museo Histórico Provincial
9. Museo Histórico Provincial
10. Museo de Arte Decorativo "Firma y Odilo Estevez"
11. Museo Municipal de Ciencias Naturales "Dr Angel Gallardo"
12. Museo Municipal de Bellas Artes "Juan B Castagnino"
13. Hotel Monumento
14. Hotel Nogaré
15. Hotel Buenos Aires

Santa Fé Province

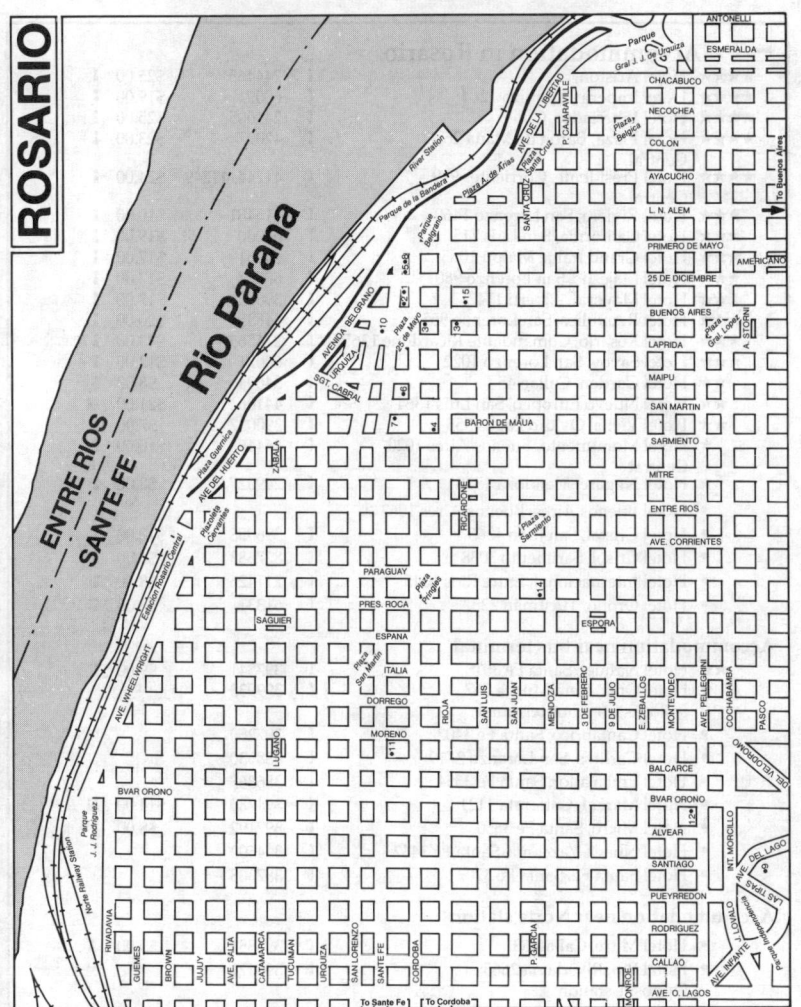

🚶 Festivals
- Fiesta de la Virgen de Rosario (Festival of the Virgin of the Rosary): October 7
- Día de la Bandera (Flag Day): July 20

ℹ️ Tourist information
- Dirección Municipal de Turismo, Santa Fé 581 (214972

Rosario

Santa Fé Province

🛏 Accommodation in Rosario

★★★★	Hotel Ariston,	(244465	$25.00	ℹ
★★★★	Hotel Imperio, Urquiza 1264	(60091	$19.00	ℹ
★★★★	Hotel Libertador, C	(241005	$25.00	ℹ
★★★★	Hotel Plaza, Baron de Maua 26 Central	(47097	$23.00	ℹ
★★★★	Hotel Presidente, Corrientes 919 ✉ Central	(41244, 41249	$24.00	ℹ
★★★	Hotel Riviera, San Lorenzo 1460	(213481	$10.00	ℹ
★★★	Hotel California, San Luis 715	(64000	$19.00	ℹ
★★★	Hotel Grand Italia, Maipú 1065	(60061	$17.00	ℹ
★★★	Hotel Majestic, San Lorenzo 980	(60027	$17.00	ℹ
★★★	Hotel Mayoral, Alberti 1142	(398924	$17.00	ℹ
★★★	Hotel Republica, San Lorenzo 955	(248351	$20.00	ℹ
★★★	Hotel Rosario, Comandante Ricardone 1365	(214565	$13.00	ℹ
★★★	Hotel Savoy, San Lorenzo 1022	(60071	$12.00	ℹ
★★	Hotel Garden, Callao 45	(34694	$8.00	ℹ
★★	Hotel Nuevo Europeo, San Luis 1364	(44106	$21.00	🍴
★★	Hotel Viena, Ovidio Lagos 555	(390037	$7.00	ℹ
★	Hotel Monumento, Buenos Aires 1020 Central	(46446	$10.00	ℹ
★	Hotel Nogare, Mendoza 1578	(249027	$8.00	ℹ
•	Hotel Buenos Aires, Buenos Aires 1063 🍴			
•	Hotel Cristal, San Juan 4065	(396058	$10.00	ℹ
•	Hotel Crisol, Sarmiento 3038	(827683	$6.00	ℹ
•	Hotel Internacional, Entre Ríos 1045	(211426	$8.00	ℹ
•	Hotel Oroño, Tucumán 2257	(61331	$8.00	ℹ

Accommodation near bus terminal

★★	Hotel Nahuel, Santa Fé 3618	(397341	$9.00	ℹ
★	Hotel Onix, Vera Mujica 757 5 blocks from bus terminal	(399933		
•	Hotel Cantabrico, Santa Fé 3402	(397250		
•	Hotel Carlitos, San Lorenzo 3719	(388530		
•	Hotel Embajador, Santa Fé 3554	(386367		
•	Hotel María I, Cafferata 1121	(394780	$14.00	🍴
•	Hotel Micro, Santa Fé 3650	(397192	$8.00	ℹ
•	Hotel Nueva Vazconia, Santa Fé 3432	(394502		
•	Hotel Santa Fé, Santa Fé 3202	(387388		

Accommodation near Norte station

•	Hotel Mitre, Callao 68	(393881	$5.00	ℹ
•	Hotel Río, Rivadavia 2665 Opposite station	(396421		

🍴 Eating out

Local cuisine
- Restaurant Agree, Santa Fé block 800
- Restaurant Colibri, San Luis block 1200

International cuisine
- Restaurant Brigadier Estanislao López, San Martín 1670
- Restaurant Chez Anton, Paraguay 746

SANTA FÉ PROVINCE

- Restaurant de Arturo, Pasco 1243
- Restaurant El Chaco, Mitre 1298
- Restaurant El Dandy, Avenida Pellegrini 1295
- Restaurant El Gallo de Oro, corner of Rivadavia and Rodriguez
- Restaurant El Sur, San Juan 2962
- Restaurant El Retiro, corner of Paraguay and San Juan
- Restaurant Gino, Maipú 1128
- Restaurant Las Leñas, Paraguay 632
- Restaurant La Taberna del Parque, Moreno 1793
- Restaurant La Torre del Reloj, Avenida Wheelwright
- Restaurant Lizabeth, Ríoja 1221
- Restaurant Los Años Locos, corner of Puccio and Costanera
- Restaurant Mercurio, Corrientes 750
- Restaurant Nuevo America, Córdoba 2402
- Restaurant Rich, San Juan 1131
- Restaurant San Miguel, Cafferata 1399
- Restaurant Sunderland, San Martín block 500
- Piano Bar Astorias, corner of Alvear and 9 de Julio

Chinese cuisine

- Restaurant Chino, San Luis 2170
- Restaurant El Gran Chino, Laprida 1145
- Restaurant Mei Hwa, Ríoja 940
- Restaurant Gran Chino, Rivadavia 3158

Italian cuisine

- Restaurant Caprí, San Luis 2591
- Restaurant Cesarin, Sarmiento 1999
- Restaurant Doña María, Santa Fé 1371
- Restaurant Familia Abruzzesa, Santiago 1334
- Restaurant Familia Piamontesa, Laprida 1350
- Restaurant La Trattoria, Tucumán 1479
- Restaurant La Cantina de Bruno, Ovidio Lagos 1599
- Restaurant Parrilla Porky, Bulevar Galvez block 2300 (corner of San Luis). Pasta; credit cards accepted

Spanish cuisine

- Restaurant Centro Gallego, Buenos Aires 1137
- Restaurant La Marina, corner of Ríoja and 1 de Mayo

Seafood

- Restaurant Al Papagallo, Avenida Pellegrini 1164. Seafood and pasta
- Restaurant Antonino, Avenida Pellegrini 796. Seafood and pasta
- Restaurant Centro Zaspirat Bat, Entre Ríos 261
- Restaurant Club Náutico Obras Publicas, behind the Canal Cinco (Channel 5) building
- Restaurant Copalo, Ayacucho 5402
- Restaurant Don Rodrigo, Santa Fé block 900
- Restaurant El Dorado, L M Drago 1309
- Restaurant Gran Paraná II, Pellegrini 2732
- Restaurant Il Piccolo Navio, San Luis 709
- Restaurant L'Auberge, corner of Freyre and Barrancas
- Restaurant Rivadavia, Rivadavia 3299 (*surubi*)

Steakhouses

- ☞ Restaurant Elizabeth, Ríoja block 1200 (corner of Mitre). At rear
- Restaurant Casa Uruguaya, Alvear 1162
- Restaurant Cortada, Comaandante Ricardone 1270
- Restaurant El Cid, San Juan 4200
- Restaurant El Churrasco, Avenida Pellegrini 598
- Restaurant El Naranjo, Corrientes 521
- Restaurant Emanuelle, corner of Guemes and Santiago
- Restaurant La Caleta, corner of Paseo Ribereno and A Luduena
- Restaurant La Chacra, corner of Bulevar Oroño and Rivadavia
- Restaurant La Estancia, Avenida Pellegrini 1510
- Restaurant La Herradura, Mendoza 2245
- Restaurant La Parrilla de Marcos, Peatonal Córdoba block 800
- Restaurant La Rural, Bulevar Oroño 2420
- Restaurant Las Espuelas, Bulevar Rondeau 1602
- Restaurant La Tablita, Bulevar Rondeau 1180
- Restaurant La Tapera, Avenida Pellegrini 2732
- Restaurant Los Tilos, Mendoza 351

Santa Fé Province

- Restaurant Mariscal Santa Cruz, Pasaje Santa Cruz 361
- Restaurant Parrilla de Marcos, Córdoba block 800 (corner of Laprida). Credit cards accepted
- Restaurant Parrilla Martín, corner of San Luis and 1 de Mayo
- Restaurant Paso de la Patria, Buenos Aires 1667

Pizzerias

- Restaurant Astral, Rioja 931
- Restaurant Giardino, Santa Fé 1100
- Restaurant Giovanino, Mitre 700
- Restaurant Pavarotti, Laprida 988
- Restaurant Pedrin, corner of Dorrego and San Juan
- Restaurant Torremolinos, corner of Zeballos and Entre Ríos
- Restaurant Via Appia, Pellegrini 955
- Pizzería Argentina, Rioja block 1400 (corner of Paraguay)
- Pizzería Austral, Rioja block 900 (corner of Maipú). Hamburgers

Other restaurants

- Restaurant Bridge, Sarmiento 859. Fixed menu
- Restaurant Don Otto, Wilde 1175. German cuisine
- Restaurant Fenix, Santa Fé 1113
- Restaurant Genesis, Mendoza block 900 (corner of Maipú)
- Restaurant La Ventana, Avenida del Huerto 1051
- Restaurant Le Monde, Peatonal Córdoba 1235. Self serve
- Restaurant Paso del Rey, Rioja block 900 (corner of San Martín)
- Restaurant Vatda, Entre Ríos 1253. Vegetarian cuisine
- Restaurant Victoria, Mendoza block 1500 (corner of Roca)

Cafeterias

- Cafetería Arca de Noe, corner of Laprida and Avenida Pellegrini
- Cafetería Abruzzo, Sarmiento 925
- Cafetería Bao Babs, Avenida Pellegrini block 1100
- Cafetería Cabotaje, corner of Buenos Aires and Avenida Belgrano
- Cafetería Café Correo, Córdoba block 800 (corner of Laprida)
- Cafetería Cafe Español, Sarmiento Block 500
- Cafetería Carrington, corner of Presidente Roca and Rioja
- Cafetería Casablanca, Córdoba 1435
- Cafetería Farmer, Córdoba 975
- Cafetería Junior's, Mitre 849
- Cafetería Que Sé Yo, Moreno 1739
- Cafetería La Cartuja, corner of Córdoba and España
- Cafetería La Farmacia, España 795
- Cafetería La Folie, corner of Entre Ríos and San Lorenzo
- Cafetería Lola, corner of Rioja and Corrientes
- Cafetería Nevada, Avenida Pellegrini block 1100
- ☞ Cafetería Natalie, Rioja 1022
- Cafetería Pago de los Arroyos, corner of Avenida Belgrano and Sargento Cabral
- Cafetería Privacia, Moreno 1605
- Cafetería Pasaporte, corner of Maipú and Urquiza
- Cafetería Pinocho, corner of Avenida Pellegrini and San Martín
- Cafetería Pipo II, corner of Entre Ríos and Rioja
- Cafetería San Telmo, Tucumán block 400
- Cafetería Señor Juan, corner of Laprida and 9 de Julio

Coffee lounges

- Azurro, corner of Buenos Aires and Rioja. Early breakfast
- Augustus, corner of Córdoba and Corrientes
- Café de Abalorios, Rioja 1450
- Café 1910, Corrientes 760
- Costanera Norte, corner Avenida Costanera and R Nuñez
- Epoca, Corrientes 779
- Eterna, Laprida 847
- Gin Tonic, Entre Ríos 779
- Luiggi, Santa Fé 1260
- Markoa, Avenida Pellegrini block 1100
- Paco Tío, Sarmiento 778
- Pico Fino, San Martín 783
- Remember, Rioja Block 1100
- Sugar, Tucumán 1334

Fast food

- Whimpy, Rioja block 1000 (corner of Sarmiento)

Rosario

SANTA FÉ PROVINCE

Milkbars
- La Lechería, Entre Rios block 300
- La Lechería Mitre, Mitre block 700

Piano bars
- Café del Sol, corner of Urquiza and Sarmiento
- Mariscal Santa Cruz, Pasaje Santa Cruz 361. Steakhouse

English-style pubs
- Pub A Tu Gusto, Italia 1452
- Buon Giorno, Santa Fé 1140
- Hans, Mitre 775
- La Birra, corner of Avenida Pellegrini and Sarmiento
- Star Bar, Rioja block 1300 (corner of Corrientes)

Post and telegraph
- Post office: Encotel, Córdoba 721
- Telephone: Entel, San Luis 936 (24 hours)

$ Financial
- Banco Credito, Corrientes 649. Cash advances on Visa card
- Bank of London and South America, La Rioja 1205
- Citibank, Santa Fé 1101
- First National Bank of Boston, corner of Córdoba and Mitre. Open 1000–1600
- Cambio Exprinter, Córdoba 960

Services and facilities
- Supermarket: Cosmos, Roca 967

Laundromats
- Mendoza 868. Open daily 0800–2000
- Laverap, San Martín 512

C Clubs
- English: Asociación Rosarina de Cultura Inglesa, Buenos Aires 1174
- German: Club Alemán Rosario, Paraguay 462, ℡218776
- Italian: Asociación Italiana, Mendoza 1355
- Spanish: Club Español, Rioja 1052

✈ Air services from Rosario

The airport is at Fisherton, 14 km west of the town center, via Autopista A008
- Taxi to airport $5.00
- Aerolineas Argentinas, Santa Fé 1410 ℡ 249292
- Austral Lineas Aereas, Paraguay 731 ℡ 64041
- Lineas Aerea Santafecinas, España 848 ℡ 213962

Destination	Fare	Depart	Services	Hours	Airline
Bahía Blanca	$65.00	1305	Mon, Fri	3	Austral
Buenos Aires (Aeroparque Jorge Newbery)	$32.00	0805	6–8 services daily	1	Aerolineas, Austral
Comodoro Rivadavia	$87.00	1305	Mon, Fri, Sat	5	Austral
Córdoba	$35.00	1235	Tues–Sun	1	Aerolineas
Mar Del Plata	$52.00	0830	Mon–Sat	2	Austral
Paraná	$17.00	1615	Mon–Sat	1	Austral
Puerto Iguazú	$67.00	1130	Wed, Thurs, Sat, Sun	2–4	Aerolineas, Austral
Resistencia	$52.00	1005	Sat	1	Austral
Salta	$72.00	1235	Tues, Wed, Fri	4	Aerolineas
San Carlos de Bariloche	$92.00	0810	Sun (2 services)	4	Aerolineas, Austral
San Miguel de Tucumán	$57.00	1235	Tues, Wed, Fri	3	
Trelew	$87.00	1305	Mon, Fri, Sat	4	Austral, Aerolineas

SANTA FÉ PROVINCE

✝ Churches
- St Bartholomew's Anglican Church, corner of Paraguay and Urquiza

🛂 Visas, passports
- German consulate, 5th floor, Córdoba 1437 ℂ 66546
- French consulate, San Luis 846, ℂ 67170
- Italian consulate, Bulevar Oroño 1591, ℂ 47021
- Swiss Consulate, Córdoba 1365, ℂ 61716

🚌 Buses from Rosario

The bus terminal is at Cafferata 702 (corner of Santa Fé, block 3400–3600).
Buenos Aires can be reached on RN 9, via San Nicolás and General Pacheco, or on RN 8 then 188, via Pergamino. This latter route is less frequented by trucks.

Destination	Fare	Depart	Services	Hours	Company
Santa Fé de la Vera Cruz	$3.60	0600	13–14 services daily		El Norte Bis, El Rapido, Kurtz, Micro
Asunción		1352	2 services daily		La Internacional
Bahía Blanca		1630	2 services daily		Central Argentino, Nandu del Sur
Buenos Aires	$7.00				TATA
Clorinda	$22.50				Godoy
Córdoba	$10.50	0015	10 services daily	7	Ablo, General Urquiza
Corrientes		1350	2 services daily	14	El Norte Bis, TA Chevallier
Formosa	$20.00	0007	3 services daily		Godoy
La Rioja		2023	Mon–Thurs		Ablo, General Urquiza, Cotil
Mar del Plata		1000	2 services daily		Empresa Argentina
Mendoza	$21.00	1900	2 services daily	14	Central Argentino, TAC
Montevideo		2345	Fri–Wed		Cora-Encon, Onda
Neuquén	$20.50	1200	Wed, Fri, Sun	18	T A Chevallier, Tirsa
Paraná		0820	6–7 services daily		El Norte Bis, El Rapido, Kurtz
Paso de los Libres		1300	1–2 services daily		El Norte Bis, Kurtz
Posadas		1300	2–3 services daily		El Norte Bis, Kurtz
Puerto Iguazú		1300	daily		El Norte Bis, Kurtz
Resistencia		1350	2 services daily		El Norte Bis
San Fernando de Catamarca		1625	daily	12½	TA Chevallier
San Carlos de Bariloche	$35.00	1200	Fri, Sun (2)	24	TA Chevallier, Tirsa
San Juan		1430	daily		Del Sur y Media
San Luis		1900	2 services daily	10	Central Argentino, TAC
San Miguel de Tucumán	$17.60	2042	daily	11	TA Chevallier
Santa Rosa		1200	Wed, Sun		Tirsa
Santiago del Estero		2942	2 services daily		La Unión, TA Chevallier
Termas de Río Hondo	$16.00	2042	daily	10	T A Chevallier

Rosario

Santa Fé Province

🚗 Motoring services

A new *autopista* runs to Santa Fé de la Vera Cruz.
- Service station: ACA, corner of Bulevar Oroño and 3 de Fébrero
- Car rental: Liprandi Rent-a-Car, San Martín 650 ℡ 210248

🚆 Trains

Stations
- Rosario Norte (F C General B Mitre), Avenida Wheelwright 1520
- Rosario Oeste (F C General M Belgrano), Paraná 1350 (corner of 9 de Julio)

Services
- Buenos Aires (express): Tourist class $4.50; 4 hours; 12 services daily

⚓ Water transport

- Excursion boats on the **Río Paraná** depart from Darsena de Cabotaje on Plaza A de Arias
- Ferry boats ply up the **Río Carbon Grande** to **Victoria** in Entre Ríos province

🏊 Sport

- Race course
- Alberdí boat club
- Arroyito boat club
- Saladillo golf club, beside the F C General B Mitre railroad
- Aero club, in the suburb of Fisherton
- Swimming at sandy Florida beach, about 8 km north of Rosario

🍸 Entertainment

Rosario has a very active night life, including some very good theaters.
- Show Cantina Don Victorio, corner of Circunvalación and Salvat
- Peña La Taba, 3 de Febrero 1653
- Peña La Salamanca, Mendoza 852
- Disco Atlantic, corner of San Martín and Lorenzo
- Disco Damasco, corner of Córdoba and Circunvalación
- Disco Mengano, corner of San Martín and Tucumán
- Disco Mongo Aurelio, Avenida de la Libertad 90
- Disco New York, Balcarce 430
- Disco Quinto Pirata, RN 9 (on the way to the airport)
- Disco Space, Mendoza block 3900
- Disco Lips, Italia block 1400
- Disco Uno Medio, Córdoba 1390
- Nightclub Whanna, Mendoza block 700 (corner of Laprida)

📷 Sightseeing

Monuments and parks

- **Monumento a la Bandera** (Monument to the Flag), situated in Parque Nacional a la Bandera on the river where Avenida Belgrano and 25 de Mayo intersect. Erected in honour of General Belgrano, who designed the Argentine flag and raised it on this spot for the first time. This building is the resting place of the famous general. Also in the hall housed in glass cabinets are the flags of all the nations of South America, symbolising the bonds between these countries. The tower flanking the building is 78 m high
- **Parque Independencia** is located in the center of the city, intersected by Bulevar Pellegrini and Bulevar Oroño. It was created in 1901 and considered one of the finest parks in the country. There are several artificial lakes with water-birds, a rose garden, and a large Spanish ceramic fountain. The park also contains sports clubs and museums
- **Parque Alem**, at the end of Bulevar Avellaneda on the

Rosario

corner of Cordiviola, on the banks of the Río Paraná. It has views over the river to the islands in the middle of the stream. In the grounds of the park is a fish breeding research station
- Parque Justo José de Urquiza, located on the Río Paraná, at the intersection of Bulevar Pellegrini and Chacabuco. Inside the park is the Observatorio Astronómico Municipal (Municipal Astronomical Obervatory)

Churches

- Nuestra Señora del Rosario cathedral, Buenos Aires 789 (on the corner of Plaza 25 de Mayo), was built in the baroque style. The image of the Virgin was brought from Cadiz in 1773

Museums

- Museo Histórico Provincial "Dr Julio Marc" (Dr Julio Marc Provincial History Museum), in Parque Independencia on the northern (Avenida Pellegrini) side. In the thirty-five exhibition rooms are pre-Columbian and colonial artefacts from Argentina and Spanish America, including weavings, archeological items, paintings, aand furniture. Open Thurs and Sat from 1500–1800, and Sun 1000–1200 and 1500–1800
- Museo de Arte Decorativo "Firma y Odilo Estevez" (Firma and Odilo Estevez Decorative Art Museum), Santa Fé 748, exhibits a collection of paintings, furniture, china, ceramics, silver, and carpets
- Museo Municipal de Ciencias Naturales "Dr Angel Gallardo" (Dr Angel Gallardo Municipal Natural Science Museum), Moreno 758, has fifteen rooms of zoological, botanical, mineralogical, palaeontological and anthropological exhibits
- Museo Municipal de la Ciudad de Rosario (Rosario City Municipal Museum), Bulevar Oroño 1540, gives an overview of the city's past and present
- Museo Municipal de Bellas Artes "Juan B Castagnino" (Juan B Castagnino Municipal Fine Arts Museum), Pellegrini 2202 (corner of Bulevar Oroño) exhibits in the 34 rooms more than 1600 paintings by outstanding Argentine and foreign artists
- Museo del Paraná y Islas, in the wharf building on the corner of Avenida Belgrano and Rioja, contains paintings by the famous artist Raul Dominguez, who captured vividly the life of the people living on the banks and the islands of the Río Paraná

◉ Excursions

- On weekends and holidays the boat *Ciudad de Rosario* runs a two-hour trip around the nearby islands on the **Río Paraná**. It leaves from the Estación Fluvial near the Monumento a la Bandera (Monument to the Flag) on Sat 1630, and on Sun 1400 and 1630; fare $1.50

SANTA FÉ PROVINCE

- A ferry service runs up the **Río Paraná** between Puerto General San Martín and **Victoria** in Entre Ríos province. There is a municipal camp site in Victoria
- **San Lorenzo**: Some 27 km upstream is an important historical site. Troops under San Martín fought the royalists here for the first time and won a decisive victory. The convent of San Carlos Boromeo is a national monument. Empresa 9 de Julio runs frequent services. See San Lorenzo below

SAN LORENZO

Postal code: 2200 • (area code: (0476)
Distance from Rosario: 27 km northwards on the *autopista*

San Lorenzo was founded in 1573. On February 3 1813 the troops of San Martín won their first victory over the royalist troops here, beginning the liberation campaign. The Convento de San Carlos Borromeo, now a national shrine, served as a field hospital; the cell where San Martín stayed can still be seen. Nowadays the town is an important industrial center, housing a petrochemical complex.

🚌 Buses
There are numerous buses to and from Rosario (Empresa 9 de Julio).

SANTA FÉ DE LA VERA CRUZ

Postal code: 3000 • (area code: (042) •
Population: 350 000
Distance from Paraná: 30 km westwards on RN 168 (via the Túnel Subfluvial Hernandarias)

Santa Fé de la Vera Cruz (generally abbreviated to "Santa Fé") is located on **Laguna Setúbal**, which is linked to the **Río Paraná** by the **Canal de Acceso**.
Santa Fé is the provincial capital and the center of a very fertile agricultural region. The original settlement was founded by Juan de Garay on November 15, 1573 in **Cayastá**, some 100 km north-east from its present site. Owing to constant attacks by Indian tribes and frequent flooding, it was relocated in 1650 to its present site. Six conventions were held in this city before the constitution was adopted in 1853. The city center is situated between Plaza San Martín and Plaza 25 de Mayo.
Santa Fé is linked with the city of **Paraná** in Entre Ríos province by the Túnel Subfluvial Hernandarias under the Río Paraná; see "Excursions" below.

🎭 Festivals
- Fiesta de la Doma: September, held in San Justo; see "Excursions" below
- San Gerónimo: September 30
- Beer festival: October, held in Esperanza; see "Excursions" below
- Foundation of the city: November 15

SANTA FÉ PROVINCE

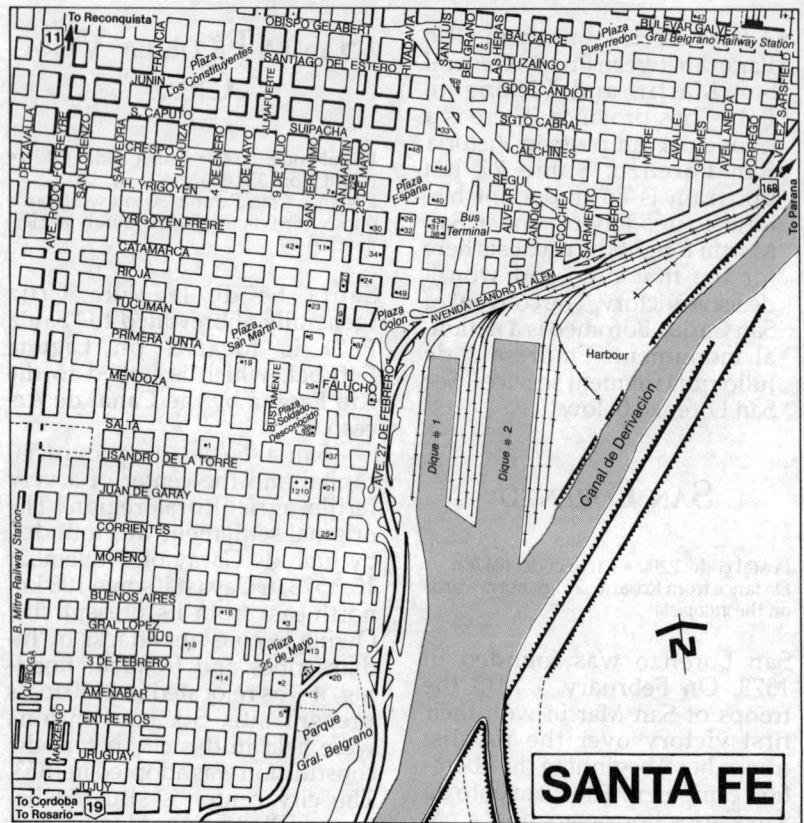

ℹ️ Tourist information

The tourist office is in the lobby of the bus terminal, on the corner of Belgrano and H Yrigoyen ● Open every day
- Dirección Provincial de Turismo, San Martín 1698 (corner of Amenabar) ☏ 37333

⛺ Camping

- Parque Manuel Belgrano: $1.00 per tent. Don't swim here—the water is contaminated
- Santo Tomé municipal camping ground, 10 km south of the city center on RN 11, on the beach 📖 $1.00 per tent

🍴 Eating out

Eating out in the city center

Try *surubí*, the local fish.
- Restaurant Aston, San Gerónimo 2619. Credit cards accepted
- Restaurant Carlucci, Avenida R Freyre 2350. Credit cards accepted
- Restaurant Chalet Suisse, Avenida General Lopez 3066. Credit cards accepted

Santa Fé de la Vera Cruz

Santa Fé Province

Key to Map

1. Municipalidad
2. Casa de Gobierno
3. Catedral
4. Post office and telephone
5. Tourist information
6. Banco de la Nación
7. Cambio Tourfe
8. Cambio Camsa
9. Cambio Cambatour
10. Aerolineas Argentinas
11. Austral Lineas Aereas
12. Aerolineas Federales Argentinas
13. Iglesia Nuestra Señora de los Milagros
14. Iglesia Santo Domingo
15. Convento de San Francisco
16. Casa Colonial de los Aldao
17. Museo Histórico Provincial
18. Museo Provincial de Bellas Artes "Rosa Galisteo de Rodriguez"
19. Museo Provincial de Ciencias Naturales "Florentino Ameghino"
20. Museo Etnográfico Colonial
21. Museo de Artes Visuales "Josefa Díaz y Clusellas"
22. Hotel Hostal Santa Fé de la Vera Cruz
23. Hotel Río Grande
24. Hotel El Conquistador
25. Hotel Corrientes
26. Hotel Zavaleta
27. Hotel España
28. Hotel Bertaina
29. Hotel Castelar
30. Hotel Emperatriz
31. Hotel Colón
32. Hotel Gran Carlitos
33. Hotel Brigadier
34. Hotel Niza
35. Hotel Hospedaje Nueva Tripolitania
36. Hotel Apolo
37. Hotel California
38. Hotel Cervantes
39. Hotel Il Tetto
40. Hotel Lucas
41. Motel Royal
42. Hotel San Gerónimo II
43. Hotel Gran Terminal
44. Hotel Umberto
45. Hospedaje Belgrano
46. Residencial Claridge
47. Residencial Güemes
48. Residencial Nuevo Suipacha

- Restaurant El Chanta, Yrigoyen Freire 2275. For budget travelers
- ☞ Restaurant el Quincho, Bulevar Pellegrini block 3200 (corner of Francia)
- Restaurant España, San Martín 2648. Credit cards accepted
- Restaurant Gran Parrilla Argentina, Bulevar Galvez 1849
- ☞ Restaurant Gran Parrilla Rivadavia, Rivadavia block 3200
- Restaurant La Brujula, San Martín 1945. Colonial-style house
- Restaurant La Ratatouille, 25 de Mayo 3452. Open Mon–Sat
- Restaurant Las Cuartetas, Bulevar Pellegrini 2577
- ☞ Restaurant Le Coq Au Vin, Santiago del Estero 3299. Credit cards accepted
- ☞ Restaurant Le Monde, Avenida R Freyre 2599. Credit cards accepted
- Restaurant Lucas, Belgrano. Opposite bus terminal
- Restaurant Mangrullo, Belgrano 2751
- Restaurant Parrilla Jaimito, La Rioja 2316
- Restaurant Parrilla Tia Ena, Junín 2613. Steakhouse
- Restaurant Super Grill, Belgrano block 2900. Opposite bus terminal
- Pizzería Caprií Bulevar Galvez 3421
- Pizzería El Imparcial, H Yrigoyen block 2900 (corner of 1 de Mayo)
- Pizzería La Cabaña, Bulevar Galvez block 1800 (corner of Candiotti)
- Pizzería Los Amigos, corner of Bustamente and Salta, opposite Plaza del Soldado Desconocido
- Pizzería Nicolás, J J Pazo block 3400 (corner of Avenida R Freyre)
- Pizzería Portofino, Avenida R Freyre 2000
- Pizzería Tío Pepin, Bulevar Galvez 2301
- Pizzería Tuyú, Bulevar Pellegrini 3101
- Comedor La Pisquita, Rivadavia 2775
- Comedor "Tu Menu", H Yrigoyen block 2800 (corner of 1 de Mayo)
- Chop Baviera, 25 de Mayo, 3287

Santa Fé de la Vera Cruz

SANTA FÉ PROVINCE

- Chopería D'Accord, J J Pazo 3358
- Chopería El Cabildo, 25 de Mayo block 3200 (corner of Junín). Credit cards accepted
- Chopería Los Faroles, Bulevar Galvez block 1200 (corner of Avellaneda)
- Chopería Santa Fé, Bulevar Galvez block 1200 (corner of Avellaneda)

Accommodation in Santa Fé

★★★★ Hotel Hostal de Santa Fé de Vera Cruz, San Martín 2954	21115	$22.00	
★★★★ Hotel El Conquistador, 25 de Mayo 2676	40195	$23.00	
★★★★ Hotel Río Grande, San Geronimo 2586	30147	$23.00	
Take bus 4, 5, 8, 10, 14, or 18			
★★★ Hotel Bertaina, H Yrigoyen 2255	32287	$20.00	
Near bus terminal			
★★★ Hotel Castelar, 25 de Mayo 2349	20141	$18.00	
★★★ Hotel Corrientes, Corrientes 2520	40126	$21.00	
★★★ Hotel España, 25 de Mayo 2647	21016	$21.00	
★★★ Hotel Zavaleta, H. Yrigoyen 2349	30104	$21.00	
★★ Hotel Colón, San Luis 2862	45167	$18.00	
Take bus 6 or 14			
★★ Hotel Emperatriz, Yrigoyen Freyre 2440	30061	$18.00	
Near bus terminal			
★★ Hotel Gran Carlitos, Yrigoyen Freyre 2336	31541	$15.00	
★ Hotel Brigadier, San Luis 3148	37387	$13.00	
Credit cards accepted; take bus 6			
★ Hotel de las Flores, Blas Parera 6790	60440	$9.00	
★ Hotel Niza, Rivadavia 2755	22047	$13.00	

- Hotel Apolo, Belgrano 2821
  Opposite bus terminal; for budget travelers
- Hotel California, 25 de Mayo 2190
- Hotel Cervantes, 25 de Mayo 2283
- Hotel Gran Terminal, Belgrano 2837 $7.00
  Opposite bus terminal; for budget travelers
- Hotel Hernandarias, Rivadavia 2684
- Hotel Hospedaje Nueva Tripolitania, Yrigoyen Freyre 2230
  For budget travelers
- Hotel Il Tetto, 25 de Mayo block 220 (corner of Salta)
- Hotel Lucas, H Yrigoyen 2226
  Near bus terminal; for budget travelers
- Hotel Royal, Yrigoyen Freyre 2   27359 $10.00
  Opposite bus terminal
- Hotel San Gerónimo II, San Gerónimo 2779
  For budget travelers
- Hotel Umberto, Crespo 2224
  Near bus terminal; for budget travelers
- Hospedaje Belgrano, Belgrano 3346
  For budget travelers
- Residencial Claridge, Belgrano 2174
  Near bus terminal; for budget travelers
- Residencial Güemes, Bulevar Galvez 1362
  Near rail station; for budget travelers
- Residencial Nuevo Suipacha, Suipacha 2381
  For budget travelers

Santa Fé de la Vera Cruz

SANTA FÉ PROVINCE

- Chopería Suiza, 25 de Mayo 3220
- Cafetería Bowling Club, San Martín block 1800 (corner of Moreno)
- Cafetería Chop Sur, Avenida General Lopez 1601
- ☞ Cafetería Exodo, Tucumán block 2400 (corner of 25 de Mayo)
- Cafetería Fausto, San Martín block 1800 (corner of Moreno)
- Cafetería La Mirage, San Martín 2421
- Cafetería Necochea, Bulevar Galvez 1945
- Cafetería Oriental, La Rioja 2600 (corner of San Geronimo)
- Cafetería Punto Talara, corner of San Martín and Corrientes
- Cafetería Santa Fé, Avenida R Freyre 1540. *Churros*
- Cafetería Status, Rivadavia 1501
- Cafetería Toneglia, San Martín Block 2600 (corner of La Rioja). Pizza

Eating out in Guadalupe

Guadelupe is a small beach resort to the north of the town center; see "Excursions" below. Around the intersection of Javier de la Rosa and Avenida Alm Brown (the *costanera*) are many good and fashionable restaurants. Take *colectivo* 16 from the city center.

- Restaurant El Quincho de Chiquito, Avenida Costanera 7100. Seafood
- Restaurant El Quincho de Don Pipo, Javier de la Rosa 223. Steakhouse
- Restaurant La Mia Mamma, Avenida Costanera. Italian cuisine

Post and telegraph

- Post office (Encotel), corner of Mendoza and Rivadavia
- Long distance telephone (Entel) corner of Mendoza and Rivadavia

Financial

- Banco Credito, corner of Bulevar San Lorenzo and Santa Fé. Cash advances on Visa cards
- Bank of London and South America, 25 de Mayo 2501. Mon–Fri 0715–1315
- Citibank, San Martín block 2600 (corner of La Rioja). Cash advances on Diners' Club cards
- Cambio Cambatour, corner of Tucumán and San Martín
- Cambio Tourfe, San Martín 2901 (39987
- Cambio Camsa, 25 de Mayo 2466 (27837

Services and facilities

- Dry-cleaner: Los Japoneses, Yrigoyen Freire 2730
- Pharmacy: Farmacia Irigoyen, San Martín 1698 (24 hours) (42036
- Photographic supplies: Colorama, San Martín block 2500 (corner of Tucumán)
- Sauna: New Force Gimnasio, Rivadavia 2957
- Sports shop: Camping Centro, Tucumán block 2800 (corner of 9 de Julio)
- Supermarket: Bienestar, Avenida R Freyre 2551. Open on Sunday mornings

Laundromats

- Laverap, San Martín 1786
- Laverap, Rivadavia 3150. Open Mon–Sat 0800–2000, Sat 0930–1230
- Laverap, San Jerónimo 1985
- Laverap, General Lopez 3477

Clubs

- Centro Cultural Provincial, Junin 2457
- French: Alliance Française, Bulevar Galvez 2101
- German: Club Alemán, Avenida General Paz 7073
- Spanish: Centro Español, Salta 2219
- Swiss: Helvecia Club, 25 de Mayo 3220
- ☞ Syrian–Lebanese: Club Sirio Libanes, San Martín 2748

Visas, passports

- German consulate, Salta 2763,

Motoring

The road south to Rosario (160 km) is a four-lane highway. The road north to Formosa (894 km) is sealed all the way.

- Car rental: Rent-a-Car, Juan de Garay 2657 (34294. Also at airport

Service stations

- ACA, Rivadavia block 3100 (corner of Suipacha)
- Esso, Bulevar Galvez block 1500 (corner of Mitre)

Santa Fé de la Vera Cruz

Santa Fé Province

✈ Air services from Santa Fé

The airport is at Sauce Viejo, 17 km south of the city center on RN 1.
- Aerolineas Argentinas, Lisandro de la Torre 2633 ℡ 22207
- Lineas Aereas Santafecinas (LAS), San Martín 2819 ℡ 22766. LAS provides many internal flights within the province, especially between Santa Fé and Rosario
- Federal (ALFA), Lisandro de la Torre 2673 ℡ 27174
- Austral Lineas Aereas, San Martín 2777 ℡ 35472

Destination	Fare	Depart	Services	Hours	Airline
Buenos Aires (Aeroparque Jorge Newbery)	$36.00	0815	2–3 services daily	1	Aerolineas, Austral
Córdoba	$29.00	1055	Sun	1	Aerolineas
	$21.00	0950	Mon, Wed, Fri	1	Federal
Goya	$36.00	1200	Mon, Wed, Sat	1	Austral
La Rioja	$46.00	1055	Sun	2	Aerolineas
Reconquista	$36.00	1200	Mon, Wed, Sat	½	Austral
Resistencia	$33.00	1410	Mon, Wed, Fri		Federal
Villa Dolores	$31.00	0950	Mon, Fri		Federal

🚆 Trains

F C General M Belgrano station is on Bulevar Galvez 1150 ℡ 40116. The F C General B Mitre line also serves Santa Fé. Although it is possible to travel north to Resistencia by train, it takes three times longer than by bus.
- Buenos Aires: Pullman $12.00, first class $7.20, tourist class $5.50; 5 services daily; 10 hours
- Rosario: $3.50; 5 services daily ; 4 hours

⚓ Water transport

Passenger boats no longer stop at Santa Fé, but only in Paraná.

🛍 Shopping

The main shopping street is San Martín, which is a pedestrian mall between Lisandro de la Torre and La Rioja.
- Artesanías Galería Saguir, San Martín 2022. Artefacts
- Artesanías La Casa de Marta, San Jeronimo 3455. Ceramics, leather
- Artesanías La Marca, San Martín. Leather
- Artesanías Nuñez, San Martín 2785

🏆 Sport

- Golf: There is an 18-hole golf course near the racecourse ℡ 60840 or 61581
- Racing: The jockey club holds Sunday race meeting with on-course betting

🎭 Entertainment

- Bowling: Santa Fé bowling club, Corrientes block 2600 (corner of San Martín)
- Discoteca Los Pinos, Parque del Sur, within the Parque General Belgrano. Open Fri–Sun 🕚
- Night Club Acuarelo, Yrigoyen Freyre 2630
- Night Club Bacan, 25 de Mayo 1998
- Night Club Carousel Super Star, Belgrano 2719
- Night Club La Posada, 25 de Mayo block 2000 (corner of L de la Torre)
- Shelter Pub, San Martín 1702. Credit cards accepted

📷 Sightseeing

The historical part of the city is around Plaza 25 de Mayo, between J J Paso and General López.

Churches

- Catedral (Cathedral), whose official name is Iglesia Matríz de Todos los Santos (First All

Santa Fé de la Vera Cruz

SANTA FÉ PROVINCE

🚌 Buses from Santa Fé

There is a modern bus terminal on the corner of Belgrano and Yrigoyen. This spacious modern building has a tourist office, cloakroom, clean restrooms, and a 24-hour cafeteria.

Destination	Fare	Depart	Services	Hours	Company
• Asunción	$22.00	0200	5 services daily		La Internacional
• Bahía Blanca		1340	2 services daily		Central Argentino, Nandu del Sur
• Buenos Aires	$11.00				
• Clorinda	$18.80				Godoy
• Córdoba	$7.80	0120	5–6 services daily	6	El Litoral, El Serrano, Encon
• Corrientes		0215	2 services daily		El Rapido, TA Chevallier
• Formosa	$16.00	0237	3 services daily		Godoy
• Mar del Plata	$22.60	2010	Tues, Fri		Zenit Turismo
• Mendoza	$20.50	2030	2 services daily		TAC, TA Villa Maria
• Montevideo	$21.70	0145	Sat–Thurs		Cora-Encon, Onda
• Paraná	$1.00			1	Etacer, T Fluviales
Buses from both companies run half-hourly					
• Paso de los Libres	$11.50	2200	daily		Federal
• Posadas	$20.50	1625	2–4 services daily		Ciudad de Posadas, El Litoral, El Norte Bis, Expreso Singer
• Puerto Iguazú	$30.50	1605	1–3 services daily (except Tues)		El Norte, Expreso Singer, Kurtz
• Resistencia	$12.20	0345	6 services daily		El Norte Bis, La Internacional
• Rosario	$3.60	0520	twice hourly		Micro, TATA-Rapido
Micro runs 5 services daily; TATA-Rapido runs twice-hourly to 2345					
• San Luis		2030	2 services daily		TAC, TA Villa María
• Santiago del Estero		2005	daily	10	La Estrella
• San Miguel de Tucumán	$17.00	2005	daily	12½	La Estrella
• Termas de Río Hondo		2005	daily	11	La Estrella

Saints' Church), Avenida Gral Lopez 2672 (corner of San Jeronimo). Construction began in 1661 and the outside was remodelled in 1747. It is the resting place of famous Argentines

• **Convento San Francisco** (St Francis Convent), corner of San Martín and Amenabar, was built in 1680. Some of the walls are nearly 2 m thick. This church represents one of the finest examples of Spanish colonial architecture. Particularly noteworthy are the carved wooden ceilings. A picture of *"El Nazareno"* ("The Nazarene") was given by Queen Maria Ana of Austria in 1650. Inside is the tomb of

Santa Fé de la Vera Cruz

SANTA FÉ PROVINCE

General Estanislao López and his wife
- Iglesia Nuestra Señora de los Milagros (Our Lady of the Miracles Church), also known as Iglesia de la Merced (Church of Mercy), corner of San Martín and Avenida General López. Built by the Jesuits in 1660, it is the oldest church in Santa Fé. Inside is a picture of the Holy Virgin which was painted in 1633 by a Jesuit friar in Santa Fé la Vieja
- Iglesia Santo Domingo (St Dominic's Church), corner of 3 de Fébrero and 9 de Julio.
- Iglesia Nuestra Señora de Guadalupe (Our Lady of Guadalupe Church), José de la Rosa, in the suburb of Guadalupe, has beautiful painted glass windows. It may be reached by bus 8 or 14 from the city center

Museums

- Casa de Gobierno (Government House), 3 de Febrero 2649. Built in 1906 on the old Cabildo site, it is the seat of the provincial government. In the old Cabildo the signing of the 1829 treaty with Brazil took place, as well as the federation treaty of 1831. Several other constitutional congresses were also held here
- Casa Colonial de los Aldao (Colonial Home of the Aldao Family), Buenos Aires 2865 (corner of 1 de Mayo). Built around 1711, it is a typical colonial house
- Museo del Convento de San Francisco (St Francis' Convent Museum), corner of San Martín and Amenabar
- Museo Histórico Provincial (Provincial Historical Museum), San Martín 1490. Built around 1660, it houses a great many historical objects and paintings from the Cuzco school, and a collection of contemporary weapons
- Museo Provincial de Bellas Artes "Rosa Galisteo de Rodriguez"(Rosa Galisteo de Rodriguez Provincial Fine Art Museum), 4 de Enero 1552 (corner of General López), has a collection of over 2000 paintings, maily by Argentine artists
- Museo de Ciencias Naturales "Florentino Ameghino", (Florentino Ameghino Natural Science Museum), Primera Junta 2895
- Museo Etnografico Colonial (Colonial Ethnography Museum), 25 de Mayo 1470. On exhibition are archeological items and items excavated at the ruins of Santa Fé la Vieja near Cayasta. The museum also houses a collection of official records of the years 1635–1852
- Museo de Artes Visuales "Josefa Diaz y Clusellas" (Josefa Diaz y Clusellas Visual Arts Museum), San Martín 2068. Permanent exhibition of paintings and drawings
- Granja La Esmeralda, Avenida Aristobulo del Valle 8700, a zoo and agricultural experimental station some 4 km north of the city center. A large area is

Santa Fé de la Vera Cruz

Santa Fé Province

devoted to local fauna and flora. Take bus 10 from the terminal or 16 along the *costanera*

Excursions

- **Cayastá**: Located some 80 km north of Santa Fé, Cayastá is where Santa Fé was originally founded by Juan de Garay in 1573, before relocation to its present site. The main item of interest is the excavated ruin of the San Francisco church and its cemetery. Amongst the graves identified were the tombs of Hernando Arias (known as "Hernandarias") and his wife Jerónima, daughter of Juan de Garay
- **Túnel Subfluvial Hernandarias**: The tunnel runs under the **Río Paraná**, linking Santa Fé with **Paraná**. This outstanding engineering feat encloses a four-lane highway and was completed in 1969. It is 32 m below the river and 2.4 km long. A toll is charged. Explosives and combustibles cannot be carried through the tunnel: they must be ferried across the river
- **San Justo**, 100km north on RN 11. Fiesta de la Doma is held in September
- **Esperanza**, 33 km north-west on RP 70. A *Fiesta de la Cerveza* (Beer Festival) is held in October
- **Guadelupe**: A small beach resort to the north of the town center. Bus 8 takes 20 minutes; fare $0.30. For the return trip take bus 16, which follows the *costanera* for some way. The Basilica de Guadelupe is a Catholic shrine and many pilgrims make their way here. Guadalupe has many good and fashionable restaurants; see "Eating out in Guadelupe" above. Take *colectivo* 16 from the city center

VENADO TUERTO

Postal code: 2600 • (area code: (0462) • Population: 60 000
Distance from Rosario: 164 km southwest on RN 33

Located in the south-western part of the province in the *pampa*, Venado Tuerto is a pleasant town with a fine country club at which race meetings and tournaments are held twice a year.

Accommodation

★★★ Hotel Riviera, Alvear 799 ⑪ (1700 ACA discount
B Residencial Alesandra, Azcuenaga 740 ⑤. ACA discount
B Residencial Salta, Saavedra 889 (2994. ACA discount

Accommodation outside town
★★★Hotel El Molino, RN 78 Km 368 ⑪ (1013. ACA discount

Buses

T A Chevallier runs frequent bus services to Buenos Aires, Rosario, and Córdoba.

PATAGONIA

Neuquén Province

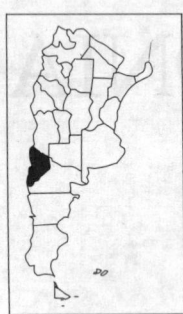

Plate 13 Map of Neuquén Province
- 272 Aguada Florencio
- 272 Aluminé
- 273   Map
- 275 Andacollo
- 276 Arroyito Challacó
- 277 Barrancas
- 277 Caviahué
- 278 Centenario
- 278 Cerro Bayó
- 279 Cerro Chapelco
- 281 Chos Malal
- 282   Map
- 283 Churriaca
- 283 Confluencia
- 283 Copahué
- 284   Map
- 286 Cutral-Có
- 287 El Huecu
- 287 Junín de los Andes
- 288   Map
- 291 La Rinconada
- 291 Las Lajas
- 292 Las Ovejas
- 292 Neuquén
- 293   Map

NEUQUÉN PROVINCE

299 Piedra del Águila
299 Primeros Pinos
300 Quillén
301 San Martín de los Andes
302   Map
309 Villa La Angostura
310   Map
311 Villa Traful
312 Zapala
313   Map

The province of Neuquén is landlocked. The northern border with Mendoza is formed by the **Río Barrancas** and the **Río Colorado**, and in the east and south **Lago Nahuel Huapí** and the **Río Limay** form borders with the province of Río Negro. To the west the chain of the Andes forms a natural border with Chile.

Before the arrival of the Spaniards Neuquén province was inhabited by warlike Indian peoples. They lived in the valleys, and the names of the mountains, mountain passes, lakes, and rivers are mostly in the Indian language. Neuquén was first colonized in 1551 by Jesuits and Franciscan monks, who had come across from Chile. They established a mission on Lago Nahuel Huapí, but constant attacks by local Indians eventually forced them to leave.

The province has an excellent road system and is also linked with Buenos Aires by rail.

The provincial capital is also called **Neuquén**, and is situated 1215 km south-west of Buenos Aires.

The major attractions of Neuquén province are the 20 or so lakes in the pre-Andean country, and the ski resorts, which are of world class. Two-thirds of Argentina's national parks are located in this region. The three main parks are: **Parque Nacional Lanín**, **Parque Nacional Nahuel Huapí**, and **Parque Nacional Laguna Blanca**.

Neuquén offers great opportunities for the outdoor enthusiast: mountain climbing and hiking in the national parks, skiing near San Martín de los Andes, on **Cerro Chapelco**, and, for the fisherman, an abundance of salmon and trout. Some of the best fishing spots are:

- **Río Paimún**, where it drains the **Lago Paimún**. Lago Paimún can be reached from Junín de los Andes
- **Lago Epulafquen** near the mouth of the **Río Escorial**. It is best reached from San Martín de los Andes

NEUQUÉN PROVINCE

- **Lago Huechulafquen** near the start of the **Río Chimehuin**, Bahía Tranack. Leave from Junín de los Andes
- **Lago Tromen** at the beginning of **Río Malleo**. It can be reached from San Junín de los Andes. This is also a good spot for camping
- **Río Chimehuin**, at the point where it leaves Lago Huechulafquen

Volcán Lanín has long been an attraction for mountain climbers. Its snow-topped, almost perfectly shaped cone can be seen from a long distance. This is an area of outstanding beauty. There are extensive forests and, at higher altitudes, glaciers. Recommended for experienced climbers only.

Neuquén province has three skiing regions:

- **Cerro Chapelco**, near San Martín de los Andes
- **Cerro Bayó**, near Villa La Angostura
- **Primeros Pinos** near Zapala

AGUADA FLORENCIO

Postal code: 8341
Distances
- From Junín de los Andes: 116 km northwards on RN 40
- From Zapala: 83 km southwards on RN 40

Aguada Florencio is located halfway between Junín de los Andes and Zapala on RN 40.

Accommodation
★ Hostería Aguada Florencia, RN 40 $8.00

Motoring
- Service station: ACA

ALUMINÉ

Postal code: 8345 • Population: 2000 • area code: (0942) • Altitude: 835 m
Distances
- From Junín de los Andes: 103 km northwards on RP 23
- From Zapala: 155 km westwards on RP 13 then southwards on RP 23

Located on **Río Aluminé** in the heart of *pehuenia* country— *pehuenia* is a type of araucaria tree which grows profusely in this area, and whose fruit used to be the staple diet of local Indians.

Tourist information
- Dirección Municipal de Turismo, corner of Avenida Cuatro de Caballeria and Gendarme Carruego

Accommodation
★★ Hostería Nid Car, corner of Joubert and Benigar (96031 $7.00
A Hospedaje Kengo, Islas Malvinas (96012

Accommodation outside Aluminé

★★ Hostería Aluminé, Lago Aluminé, on the lakeside near the junction of RP 13 and RP 23 (23731 $24.00. Includes breakfast
★★ Hostería Quillén, Rahué, 17 km south of Aluminé at the junction of RP 46 with RP 23 $25.00
A Hospedaje La Bella Durmiente, Lago Moquehue $16.00. Rooms with shared bathrooms are cheaper

Neuquén Province

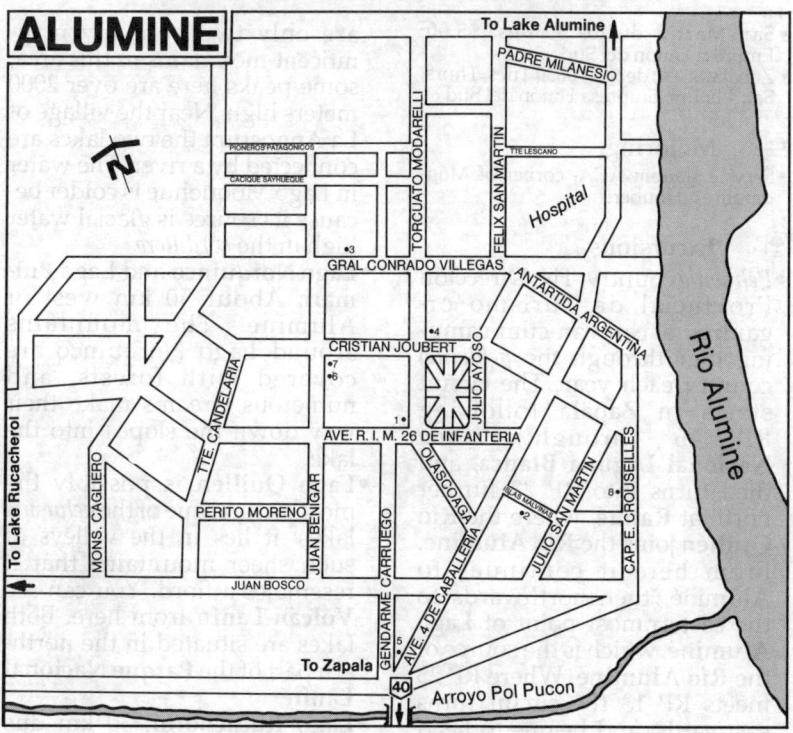

Key to Map
1. Municipalidad
2. Iglesia
3. Post office
4. Telephone
5. Tourist information
6. Bus stop
7. Hostería Nid Car
8. Hospedaje Kengo

🍴 Eating out
- Restaurant ACA, C Joubert
- Restaurant Antumalal, D Bosco
- Restaurant Kengo, Hospedaje Kengo, Islas Malvinas
- Restaurant Lago Aluminé, Hostería Aluminé, on the lakeside near the junction of RP 13 and RP 23
- Restaurant Nid Car, Hostería Nid Car, corner of Benigar and C Joubert

✉ Post and telegraph
- Post office: Encotel, Villegas
- Telephone: Entel, corner of Joubert and Modarell
- Public telephone, Joubert, opposite Plaza

🚌 Buses
The bus stop is at the corner of Benigar and Joubert, next to Hostería Nid Car

Aluminé

Neuquén Province

- San Martín de los Andes: $5.00; Empresa Unión del Sud
- Zapala: $6.00; departs 0830 Tues, Thurs, Sat; 4 hours; Empresa Unión del Sud

Motoring
- Service station: ACA, corner of Mondarelli and Joubert

Excursions

- *Pehuenia* country: The Dirección Provincial de Turismo organizes a caravan-cum-camping tour through the *pehuania* country each year. The circuit starts in **Zapala**, following RP 46 through **Parque Nacional Laguna Blanca**, and then turns into RP 23 further north at **Rahué**, where the **Río Quillén** joins the **Río Aluminé**. From here it continues to Aluminé, then northwards to the easternmost point of **Lago Aluminé**, which is the source of the **Río Aluminé**. Where RP 23 meets RP 13 the circuit turns eastwards, and begins to head back towards Zapala, passing through **Primeros Pinos** along the way. From here on the road is sealed. The total length of the trip is 300 km, and the duration eight days. An ACA vehicle also takes part to help out in case of breakdowns. Inquiries can be made in the tourist office in Neuquén; see "Tourist information" in Neuquén on page 292
- **Lago Aluminé** and **Lago Moquehue**: These lakes are about 50 and 70 km north of Aluminé respectively. Lago Aluminé stretches over 54 square km. **Piñihue** and **Batea Mahuida** are only two of many magnificent mountains in this area; some peaks here are over 2000 meters high. Near the village of **La Angostura** the two lakes are connected by a river. The water in Lago Moquehue is colder because its source is glacial water high in the *cordillera*
- **Lago Norquinco** and **Lago Pulmari**: About 50 km west of Aluminé. The mountains around Lago Norquinco are covered with forests, and numerous streams make their way down the slopes into the lake
- **Lago Quillén** is possibly the most picturesque of the *pehuenia* lakes: it lies in the valleys of such sheer mountains that it resembles a fiord. You can see **Volcán Lanín** from here. Both lakes are situated in the northern part of the **Parque Nacional Lanín**
- **Lago Rucachoroi**: 30 km due west of Aluminé. To reach it take RP 18, which actually finishes at the lake. This lake is also in the northernmost part of Parque Nacional Lanín. The road to it passes through the **Campo de Pulmari**, where a battle was fought against Indians. There is an Indian reserve, Aigo, on the shores of the lake. The Indians here are expert craftsmen, and make a variety of woven materials, including ponchos

Aluminé

NEUQUÉN PROVINCE

ANDACOLLO

Postal code: 8353 • Altitude: 1415 m •
(area code: (0948)
Distance from Chos Malal: 58 km northwest on RN 43

Andacollo is located in the upper **Río Neuquén valley**, where the **Río Varvarco** and **Río Lileo** join to form the Río Neuquén in the foothills of the **Cordillera del Viento**. In Quechua, Andacollo means "the best mineral", a reference to the gold still being found in the rivers and creeks of the surrounding country. The name was coined by Quechua-speaking miners who came here from northern Chile.

🛏 Accommodation

★ Hostería Andacollo, corner of Varvarco and Nahueve ✆ (94055 $10.00

🍽 Eating out

• Restaurant ACA, Varvarco

🚌 Buses

A bus to Neuquén costs $12.50.

⚑ Excursions

Andacollo can serve as a base for further exploration of the **Sierra del Viento**.

- **Volcán Domuyo** and **Laguna Varvarco Campos**: A trip for the adventurous. Hiking in this area should only be be undertaken by experienced bushwalkers. Provisions, which can be bought in Chos Mallal, and proper equipment, including a tent and sleeping bag, are essential. The best period to visit this area is from November to April
- **Huingancó**: A small village 5 km east of Andacollo. Although the surrounding landscape is bare and mountainous, the villagers in Huingancó have planted some 120 000 fir trees in their town and transformed it into a green oasis. For this reason it is called the "garden of the province". Many of the trees here have virtually been planted between rocks. The villagers are also skilled artesans, and produce woven materials and delicious sweets. There is also a goldmine nearby which is still operating, and produces 78 grams of gold per cubic meter
- **Las Ovejas**: 35 km further up the valley. This village derives its name from the huge flocks of sheep which used to graze around here. The Fiesta de San Sebastian attracts many visitors to Las Ovejas. From Las Ovejas a mountain trail leads to **Colo Michi-có**, an archeological site
- **Los Bolillos**: 15 km north. These extraordinary natural sculptures were created by wind and erosion
- **Epu-Lauquen**: A nature reserve 74 km north-west, near the Chilean border. It has been created to preserve araucanias and other trees which grow in the area, and covers about 7500 hectares. The tree-covered western slopes of the park contrast sharply with the eastern ranges, which are almost bare.

Neuquén Province

At the center of the park are the Epulafquen lakes: blue, crystal clear, and very cold. They contain an abundance of trout, and the fishing is excellent. The best spot is the connecting river between the two lakes. This is a trip for the adventurous and experienced angler only

- **Río Nahueve**: This river has its source in the Epu-laufquen lakes. There is good fishing for trout, *pejerrey*, and perch near the village of **Nahueve**
- **Lagunas Varvarco, Tapia, and Campos**: The Varvarco lakes are the source of the Río Varvarco. To reach them take the bus to Las Ovejas. From there it is about 120 km by unsealed road to the lakes. Take RP 54 rather than RP 1. The water of the lakes is clear and cold, and medium-sized trout and perch are plentiful. Be careful though: the banks are rocky and sometimes steep. Some of the peaks around the lakes are snow-covered. Four- wheel drive vehicles are necessary in this area, and bushwalking is only for the experienced
- **Volcán Domuyo**: 80 km north on RP 1. This is the highest point in the Patagonian Andes—just over 4700 meters. The mountain is bare of vegetation and the top is covered with snow all year round. There are also several glaciers in this region. The climate is harsh in winter and even in summer the climate can change abruptly. The attraction of the area is its volcanic activity: there are numerous hot springs, geysers, and fumaroles. Some of the geysers spout as high as 15 m. The temperature of the thermal springs averages 40°C, although one spring has a temperature of 95°C. **Los Tachos**, **Las Olletas**, and **El Humazo** are three of the better-known thermal springs in the area, but there are at least fifteen others. There are no tourist facilities here, but any lack of comfort is more than compensated for by the natural beauty of the gorges and waterfalls. This area is still unspoilt
- **Fortín Guañacos**: The ruins of this fort are 30 km south. It was one of many forts erected after the wars of 1882 to protect the Western frontier
- **Cordillera del Viento Este**: The best place to start hiking is **Tricao Malal**, which is 40 km north on RP 2. The **Sierra del Viento** starts from **Volcán Domuyo** and goes due south for 80 km, almost to Chos Malal. The top of the range is fairly flat throughout, and the highest point is about 3000 meters. Strong winds prevent the growth of vegetation, and in winter the Cordillera is completely covered with snow

Arroyito Challacó

Postal code: 8313
Distance from Neuquén: 50 km eastwards on RN 22

NEUQUÉN PROVINCE

Arroyito Challacó is located 3 km off Río Limay. Nearby is Arroyito dam.

Accommodation
★★★ Motel Posta Arroyito, RN 22 (Cabina Publica 19 $14.00

Eating out
- Restaurant Arroyito, RN 22. Cafeteria

Buses
The bus to San Martín de los Andes costs $10.00.

BARRANCAS

Postal code: 8353
Distance from Chos Malal: 140 km northwards on RN 40

This is the last township in Neuquén province before the border with Mendoza province.

Accomodation
★ Hospedaje Barrancas, RN 40 $13.00

Eating out
- Restaurant ACA
- Restaurant Ruta 40

Buses
- Neuquén: Fare $15.00; departs 0745 Sat; 11 hours; Empresa Unión del Sud

CAVIAHUÉ

Postal code: 8349
Distance from Neuquén: 375 km westwards on RN 22, then RP 23 and RP 70 (via Loncopue)

Caviahué is a developing ski resort, in the **Volcán Copahue** area, near the Chilean border. It is 16 km from **Copahué**, itself a thermal springs resort in summer. Caviahue is becoming better known as a ski resort, but has a summer season also. There are some 12 000 hectares of undulating country, interspersed with large flat areas, available for skiing. The terrain is very suitable for *langlauf*, or Nordic skiing. The skiing season starts in July and finishes in October. There are two ski-lifts.

Accommodation
Facilities here consist of a modern hotel (200 beds), one hostería, sixteen cabins, and two restaurants (both in the hotel). There is also a convention center. Skiing equipment can be hired.

Air services
The airstrip is only usable in summer.
- Neuquén: $23.00; departs 1300, Mon, Wed, Sat; 1 hour; Empresa TAN

Buses
The best plan is to book a package deal in Neuquén.

Motoring Services
- Service station: ACA

Sport
Club Andino Caviahué runs two skiing schools, one in alpine skiing, and one in *langlauf* skiing. The snow is dry powder, one meter deep at the base. There are cross-country skis of 10, 30, and 60 km, and an alpine run with a 300 m drop and a 20° slope.

Excursions
- Copahué: Summer only

Neuquén Province

Centenario

Postal code: 8309 • Population: 17 000

Centenario is located 15 km north of Neuquén on RN 234, and is virtually one of its suburbs. The motel here is excellent.

Accommodation
★★ Motel Sayhueque, RN 234 (91127 $16.00

Eating out
- Restaurant Centenario, Avenida Belgrano
- Restaurant Las Palmeras, P Pobladores 260. Pizzeria
- Restaurant Tío Lopez, P Pobladores 65. Pizzeria
- Cafetería Monaco, P Pobladores 157
- Cafetería Tobas, Intendente Ponds 245

Cerro Bayó

Altitude: 1780 m
Distances
- From Neuquén: 512 km south-west on RN 22 and RN 237, then north-west on RN 231
- From San Carlos de Bariloche: 90 km northwards on RN 237 then RN 231

Cerro Bayó is located 9 km northeast of Villa La Angostura, inside the **Parque Nacional Nahuel Huapí**. Six km off the main road is RN 231, which leads to Cerro Bayo via the shores of **Lago Nahuel Huapí**.

Cerro Bayó's easterly outlook makes skiing conditions perfect from June to September; the skiing season runs from July 1 to September 30. During that period the snow is dry and compact, but varies between powder and wet. The skiing slopes practically finish up on Lago Nahuel Huapí. They are suitable for intermediate to advanced skiers. There is a *refugio* at the base (1050 m), with a cafeteria, ski hire, repairs, cloak room, and a ski school run by the Ski Club Villa La Angostura.

A few figures on the slopes:
- The snow cover is 10 cm at the base and 80 cm at 1500 m
- The height difference between the top of the run and its base is 600 m
- The inclination of slopes is 35°
- The skiing area is 80 hectares
- The length of the ski courses is 1800

There are three ski-lifts:
- Poma: From base at 1050 m to 1492 m; length 1350 m; capacity 500 persons per hour
- Intermediate ski-lift from 1492 m to 1600 m with a capacity to transport 300 persons per hour
- Beginners' lift at the base; capacity 70 persons per hour

Accommodation
The nearest accommodation is in Villa La Angostura, with 200 beds. See "Accommodation" in Villa La Angostura on page 309

Eating out
A cafetería at the top (1500 m) offers light meals.

NEUQUÉN PROVINCE

CERRO CHAPELCO

Postal code: 8370
Distance from San Martín de los Andes: 20 km

Cerro Chapelco is Neuquén province's top winter resort, located some 20 km uphill from San Martín de los Andes. The eight lift installations transport up to 8600 skiers a day. The skiing season opens in the middle of June and continues up to the middle of October.

Cerro Chapelco is situated in the Chapelco chain which extends in a north–south direction for 40 km between Lago Lacar and Río Caleufu. Neuquén is 440 km south-west of here, via RN 234, and San Martín de los Andes is only 20 km away. Continue from San Martín on RN 234 for 12 km until you reach the junction with RP 19. A further 8 km along RP 19 brings you to the base of the Chapelco skiing region. This is the route you must take going uphill, but the return trip takes the old RP 19 which is only 16 km and is one-way. The road is kept free of snow by the roads department. During the skiing season local tour operators run regular bus services between San Martín and the snow-fields. There are also a few services in summer.

Skiing equipment can bought or hired either in San Martín or at Cerro Chapelco. The local skiing club is the Club Andino San Martín de los Andes (known as CASMA).

Visitors can stay in the Hotel Los Techos in Cerro Chapelco, but it has only sixteen beds and booking is recommended. Thirteen km away is the Hotel Sol de los Andes, which overlooks San Martín. It has 270 beds and is expensive, but also popular—booking is recommended here as well.

There is more choice when it comes to restaurants: there are four restaurants in Cerro Chapelco itself, and about 30 restaurants and cafeterias in San Martín.

An efficient system of lifts and cable cars has been installed at Cerro Chapelco, and skiers should not experience undue delays in getting to the ski runs. The system has the capacity to move 8600 persons per day, on eight installations: three chair lifts, four teleskis, and a cable car:

- Antuhue: A double chair lift which ascends from 1600 m to 1670 m. It is 400 m long, and can carry 1200 skiers per hour. A six-minute ride
- Culache: A triple chair lift which starts at 1250 m and reaches 1350 m. It is 450 m long, and can carry 1200 skiers per hour. The ride takes five minutes
- Rayen Lemu: A double chair lift which starts at 1350 m and climbs to 1720 m. It is 1700 m long, and can carry 832 persons per hour. The trip to the top takes 20 minutes
- Epuche: A T-bar lift which starts at 1600 m and goes up to 1720 m. It is 650 m long, and can

Neuquén Province

carry 1200 skiers per hour. The ride takes three minutes
- Palito: The upper baby lift. It starts at 1730 m and goes up to 1830 m. It is 330 m long, and can carry 719 skiers per hour. The ride takes four minutes
- Petro Hue: The lower baby lift for beginners. It starts at 1250 m and goes up to 1300 m. It is 400 m long, and can carry 800 skiers per hour. The ride takes three minutes
- Pire Lil: A *poma* lift which starts at 1720 m and ascends to 1980 m. It is 900 m long, and can carry 800 skiers per hour. A five-minute trip
- Cable car: This starts from the base at 1250 m and goes up to 1600 m. It takes five minutes to do the 1675 m trip. Each car takes six persons, and the system can transport 1800 skiers per hour

The longest ski run is 3800 m, and the total area available for skiing is 120 hectares.

The snow season lasts from June 20 to October 15. On average there is 40 cm of snow at the base and 1.5 m at 1000 m. The snow is dry powder of excellent quality. The inclination of the slopes varies between 10° and 45°. The snow-fields up to 1750 m are suitable for beginning and intermediate skiers, but only advanced skiers should venture beyond this altitude.

The ski instructors are mostly Austrians and, not surprisingly, teach what are basically Austrian techniques. However, where appropiate they have modified their methods to suit local conditions. Mono-skiing is one of the newer techniques being taught. You can hire the mono-skis, and any other skiing equipment, in Cerro Chapelco.

ℹ️ Tourist information
There is a tourist office in San Martín de los Andes.

🛏 Accommodation
Advance bookings, especially in season, are strongly recommended.
★★★ Hotel Los Techos ℡ (7664 $30.00 ⁂.
Half board. The hotel is located right at the ski-lift base.

🏷 Services and facilities
- Daily ski-lift ticket $21.00
- Weekly ski-lift ticket $125.00
- Hire of skiing gear (alpine) $13.00 a day
- Hire of skiing gear (Nordic) $8.00 a day
- Hire of ski boots $4.00 a day
- Alpine ski school $26.00 per person per lesson

✈ Air services
The airdrome is 10 km from San Martín, halfway on the road to Junín de los Andes. Air services are provided by TAN and Lade.

🚌 Buses
There are regular buses running direct from San Martín de los Andes to Neuquén, San Carlos de Bariloche, and Buenos Aires.
During the skiing season there is a minibus service between Villa La Angostura and the base of the mountain.

✤ Excursions
- **Lago Lacar** and **San Martín de los Andes** are close by. See San Martín de los Andes on page 301

Cerro Chapelco

NEUQUÉN PROVINCE

CHOS MALAL

Postal code: 8353 • Population: 6700 •
area code: (0942) • Altitude: 866 m
Distance from Zapala: 202 km
northwards on RN 40

Situated in the extreme northwest of the province on the **Río Curri Leuvu** (the upper reaches of the Río Neuquén), Chos Mallal was founded in 1887 as a military fort, and was the provincial capital until 1904. Today it still retains the charm of a frontier town.

The restored Fortín de la IV Division is now the Museo Historico Olascoaga.

Accommodation

★★ Hotel Chos Malal ACA, corner of General San Martín and Sarmiento (21165 and 21465 $13.00
★ Hostería El Torreón, Lavalle (21141 $10.00
A Hospedaje Lavalle, Lavalle (21193 $6.00

Eating out

- Restaurant ACA, San Martin 89
- Restaurant Andresito, corner of 25 de Mayo and Irigoyen
- Restaurant Bahía Cafe, corner of Sarmiento and Urquiza. Cafeteria
- Restaurant Caicallen, General Paz 345. Cafeteria
- Restaurant Mundialito 78, 25 de Mayo 715
- Cafetería El Torreón, 25 de Mayo 137. Snack-bar

Air services

- Neuquén: Fare $21.50; departs 1010 Mon–Wed, Fri, Sat; 1 hour; TAN
- Mendoza: Fare $42.00; departs 1010 Tues, Fri; 2 hours; TAN

Buses

- Neuquén: Fare $11.00; Empresa Unión del Sud
- Bariloche: Departs daily; 10 hours; Empresa TAC
- Malargüe: Departs daily; 9 hours; Empresa TAC
- Mendoza: Departs daily; 16 hours; Empresa TAC
- Zapala: Fare $7.00; departs 1045; 2 services daily; 5 hours; Empresa Unión del Sud

Motoring

RN 40 leading north is largely unsealed.

Sightseeing

- Museo Regional
- Antigua Casa de Gobierno (Old House of Assembly)

Sightseeing

- Museo Regional (Regional Museum)
- Antigua Casa de Gobierno (Old House of Assembly)

Excursions

- **Reserva Provincial Tromen**: 40 km north. **Lago Tromen** is at the center of the park. To get there from Chos Malal take RN 40 for 6 km, and then head north on RP 2. Follow RP 2 until Chapuá, then take the 20 km track which leads to the reserve. Part of **Volcán Tromen** (3980 m) lies within the boundaries of the park and its imposing outline dominates the whole area. This volcano features colorful rock formations, and, further down towards its base, rivers of solidified lava. Lago Tromen has no fish because sulphur is washed down

NEUQUÉN PROVINCE

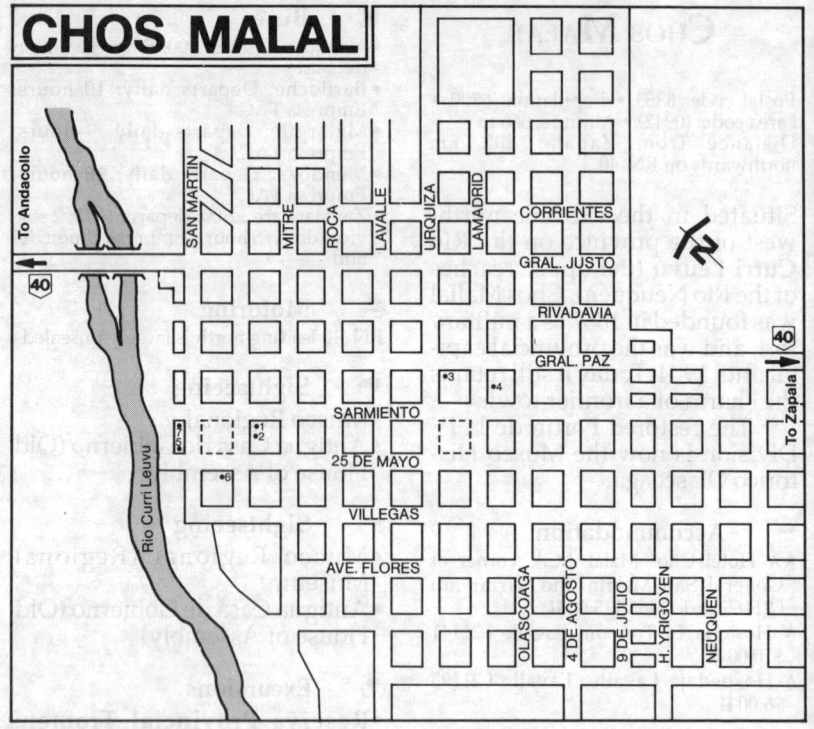

Key to Map
1. Municipalidad
2. Iglesia
3. Post office (Encotel)
4. Telephone (Entel)
5. Museo Regional
6. Antigua Casa de Gobierno
7. Hotel Chos Malal

from the surrounding volcanic rocks, making the water uninhabitable. The reserve was created to protect local birdlife, in particular the black-necked swan and the migrating flamingo

- **Andacollo** and the upper **Río Neuquén** valley: Located 58 km north-west, in the foothills of the **Sierra del Viento**. First take RP 43, then RP 1. The **Río Neuquén** is muddy for most of the year owing to the sediment it brings down from the Andes and Volcán Domuyo. This is a gold-mining area, and the local population still makes its living from prospecting, using water-driven crushing mills and

Chos Malal

282

NEUQUÉN PROVINCE

washing installations. The climate is harsh even in summer, and it is essential to bring warm, protective clothing to guard against sudden changes in the weather. This is good bushwalking country for those with experience and a sense of adventure. See Andacollo on page 275 for more details

- **El Cholar** and the valley of the **Río Trocoman**: 60 km west on RP 6. El Cholar nestles in a valley surrounded by high peaks. A fishing trip to **Vilú Mallín** on the Río Trocoman is recommended. The bumpy 15 km journey is worth it: this mountain stream is crystal-clear and teeming with trout and perch

CHURRIACA

Postal code: 8351
Distance from Chos Malal: 71 km southwards on RN 40

This small hamlet is in the far north of the province, quite close to the **Sierra de Churriacu**, which is over 2000 m high.

Accommodation
A Hospedaje Churriaca, RN 40 $12.00

Buses
- Neuquén: Fare $7.50
- Zapala: Fare $4.50

CONFLUENCIA

Distance from San Carlos de Bariloche: 66 km northwards on RN 237

Confluencia is located at the junction of the **Río Traful** with **Río Limay**.

Accommodation
Motel El Rancho, just before Confluencia

COPAHUÉ

Postal code: 8349
Distance from Zapala: 190 km northwards on RP 23 then RP 70

Copahué is located in the **Reserva Nacional Copahué**, about 380 km north-west of Neuquén, close to the Chilean border. The name itself is Araucanian for "sulphur place". The town lies in a horseshoe-shaped valley formed by glacial erosion, with the open end of the horseshoe facing east. The high altitude (1980 m) makes this a bleak place, and the only real attractions are the thermal springs and **Volcán Copahué** (2980 m). The resort is open from late November to April, but closed throughout winter.

To get to Copahué take RN 22 via Zapala, Las Lajas, and Loncopue.

The numerous thermal springs here are reputed to have excellent medicinal properties. This, and the high altitude, make

Neuquén Province

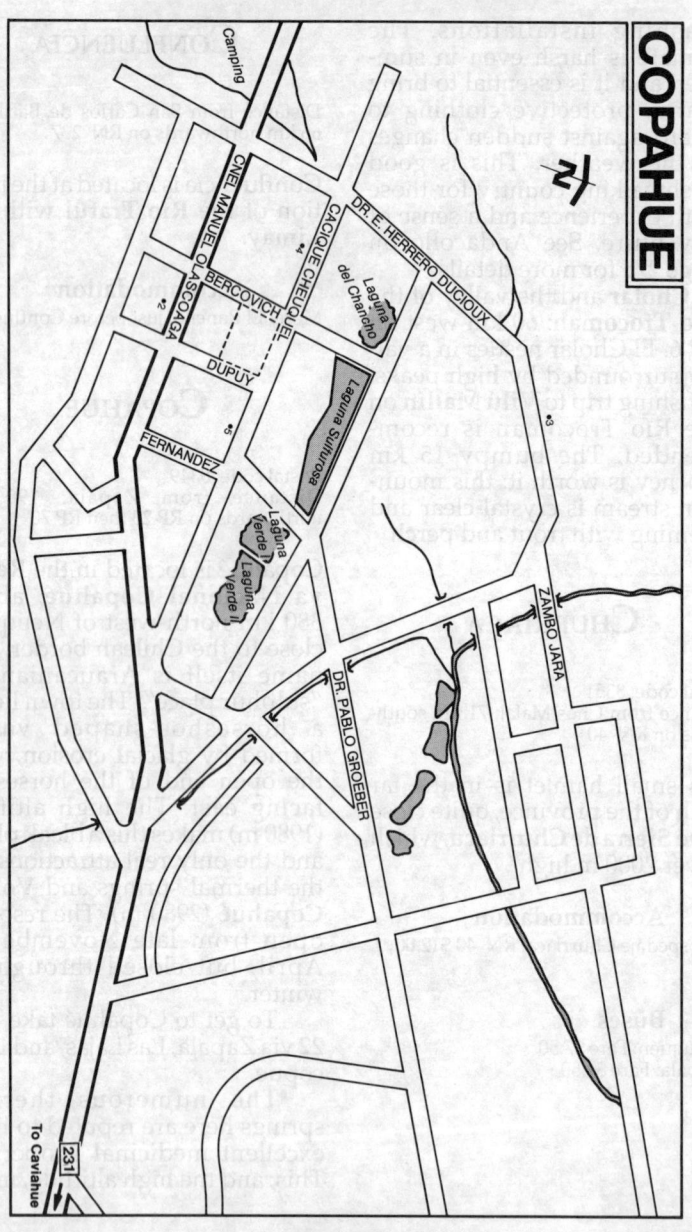

Copahué

NEUQUÉN PROVINCE

Key to Map
1. Tourist office
2. Hospital
3. Hotel Termas
4. Hotel Copahué
5. Hotel Santa Monica

it an ideal place if you suffer from arthritis, indigestion, high blood pressure, or skin or nervous disorders. The water in the springs can reach 90°C.

The thermal springs were known to the Indian population long before the arrival of Europeans. Havestadt was the first European to bring out word of their existence in 1752. Then in 1865 Dr Ortiz Velez received permission from *Cacique* Chenquel to inspect them. In 1887 the local Indians were subjugated by Colonel Olascoaga, and it became possible to study the springs without fear of harrassment. The first to do this scientifically were Dr Paul Groeber and Professor H Corti. The Reserva Nacional Copahué was established in 1940.

The largest and most spectacular thermal springs are right in Copahué itself, on Calle Chenquel. Others worth visiting are **Laguna Sulfurosa**, **Laguna Verde** and **Laguna Verde II**, and **Laguna del Chancho**, which is a good place for mud-baths.

At **Las Maquinas** near the banks of **Arroyo Blanco**, there is a small *laguna* with many geysers and blow-holes. These spout regularly and it is a good place to see volcanic activity. **Las Maquinitas**, also on the banks of the **Arroyo Blanco**, has some geysers as well.

Reserva Nacional Copahué covers 400 square km and is roughly square. Along its border with Chile are four passes over 2000 m high.

Bring warm clothes with you as the temperature can drop suddenly, and even snowstorms are not unknown in the middle of summer.

Eating out
- Restaurant Codihué
- Restaurant Copahué
- Restaurant El Dandy

Accommodation in Copahué

These hotels are only open from November to April.

★★★	Hotel Termas	(	95045
★★	Hotel Copahué	(	95085
★	Hotel Santa Monica	(	95022
A	Hospedaje Codihué	(	95031
A	Hospedaje El Dandy	(	95056
A	Hospedaje Hualcupen	(	95046
A	Hospedaje La Cabañita	(	95023

NEUQUÉN PROVINCE

- Restaurant La Cabañita
- Restaurant Santa Monica
- Restaurant Termas Hotel

Post and telegraph
- Post office: Encotel, Colonel Olascoaga

Buses
- Neuquén: Fare $9.50; departs 0900; 2 services daily, during summer only; 7 hours; Empresa El Petroleo, Empresa Unión del Sud
- Las Lajas: Departs 1430 daily, during summer only; 2 hours; Empresa El Petroleo
- Zapala: Fare $5.00; departs 1430 daily, during summer only; 4 hours; Empresa El Petroleo

Motoring
The road to Chile goes over the **Paso Copahué**, at an altitude of 1996 m. The Chileans call it Paso Pucón Mahuida.
The 69 km stretch of RP 70 along **Lago Caviahue** was being sealed at the time of writing.
- Service station: ACA. Camping ground attached

Shopping
So close is Copahué to the Chilean border that neighbouring Chileans hold a market here in Calle Dr Herrero Ducioux three times each week. They call it the *Feria de Chile*, and it is a good place to buy woven materials such as blankets and ponchos.

Sport
There is good fishing in the **Río Trolope**, about 11 km north, the **Río Hualcupen** and **Laguna Hualcupen**. Trout of 3 kg are common. There are no fish in this section of the **Río Agrio** because of the sulphur carried into it by thermal springs coming from **Volcán Copahué**. The best fishing spots on **Laguna Trolope**, **Laguna Achacosa**, and **Laguna Rincón** are all on private property.

Excursions
- **Reserva Nacional Copahué**: The national park is a good place for extended bushwalks
- **Caviahue** and **Laguna Hualcupen**: Good for trout-fishing enthusiasts
- **Río Agrio falls**: 20 km
- **Río Trolope valley** and **Laguna Trolope**
- **Los Pinos**, and the **Arroyo Blanco falls**
- **Lagunas de Chancho-Có** and **Trapa Trapa valley**: These are in Chile and can be reached via mountain trails. The 8 km trip takes 1 hour
- **Volcán Copahué** crater: This is a seven-hour walk each way. The trail follows **Arroyo Blanco** and passes the **Lagunas Las Mellizas**. The climb is about 1000 m, and along the way you have magnificent views of **Lago Caviahue**, Lagunas Las Mellizas and **Volcán Villarica** in Chile. The last 200 m from **Los Baños** are fairly steep. You should be reasonably fit to attempt this walk

CUTRAL-CÓ

Postal code: 8322 • area code: (0943) • Population: 32 000
Distance from Neuquén: 106 km westwards on RN 22

Cutral Co and its sister town **Plaza Huincul** are the center of oil and natural gas production in Neuquén province.

Copahué

Neuquén Province

🛏 Accommodation

Accommodation in Cutral-Có

- ★★★ Hotel Alfa, corner of Sáenz Peña and Alem ▨▨▨ (61119 $16.00 ♨
- ★ Hotel FB, Irigoyen 545 ▨ (61345 $11.00 ♨
- ★ Hostería Mapuche, corner of RN 22 and Santa Isabel ▨ (61360 $10.00 ♨
- A Hospedaje Arayen, Avenida del Trabajo 302 (61172 $9.00 ♨
- A Hospedaje Cutral Co, Sáenz Peña 670 (61087 $9.00 ♨

Accommodation in Plaza Huincul

- ★ Hostería Tunquelen, RN 22 (6423

🍴 Eating out

Eating out in Cutral-Có

- Restaurant Arayen, Avenida del Trabajo 302
- Restaurant Centro de Comercio, Roca 416. Steakhouse
- Restaurant Córdoba, corner of Permicik and Alem
- Restaurant Don Tito, Roca 980
- Restaurant La Parrilla de Coco, Sarmiento 86. Steakhouse
- Restaurant Pan Ambi, Moreno 364. Regional cuisine
- Cafetería Alexs, C H Rodriguez. Snack-bar
- Cafetería Bucky, P Moreno. Snack-bar
- Cafetería Poppy's, Olascoaga 834
- Cafetería Sayonara, corner of Roca and Sarmiento. Snack-bar
- Cafetería Suya Cafa, C H Rodriguez 77

Eating out in Plaza Huincul

- Restaurant Club YPF
- Restaurant La Rueda, RN 22. Steakhouse

🛎 Services and facilities

- Laundromat: Laverap, Avenida del Trabajo 709

🚌 Buses

There are several services each day to Neuquén and Zapala.

El Huecu

Postal code: 8349
Distance from Chos Malal: 93 km southwest on RP 26 then RP 23

El Huecu is located in the northern part of the province on RP 23. The Indians who lived here originally put up fierce resistance to the intrusion by the Europeans. Nearby is the battlefield of **Cerro de la Batería**, the site of one such clash.

🛏 Accommodation

- ★ Hostería El Hueco, RP 23 $10.00 ♨

🍴 Eating out

- Restaurant El Huecu, Hostería EL Huecu, RP 23

🚌 Buses

- Las Lajas: Departs 0700 Tues and Sat; 3 hours; Empresa Unión del Sud
- Loncopué: Departs 0700 Tues and Sat; 2 hours; Empresa Unión del Sud
- Zapala: $5.50; departs 0700 Tues, Sat; 5 hrs; Empresa El Petroleo, Empresa Unión del Sud

Junín de los Andes

Postal code: 8371 • Population: 7200 • (area code: (0944) • Altitude: 773 m
Distances
- From San Martín de los Andes: 41 km north-east on RN 234
- From Zapala: 199 km south-west on RN 40

Junín de los Andes is located on the **Río Chimehuin**, nestling between mountains and lakes. The township was originally a fort

Neuquén Province

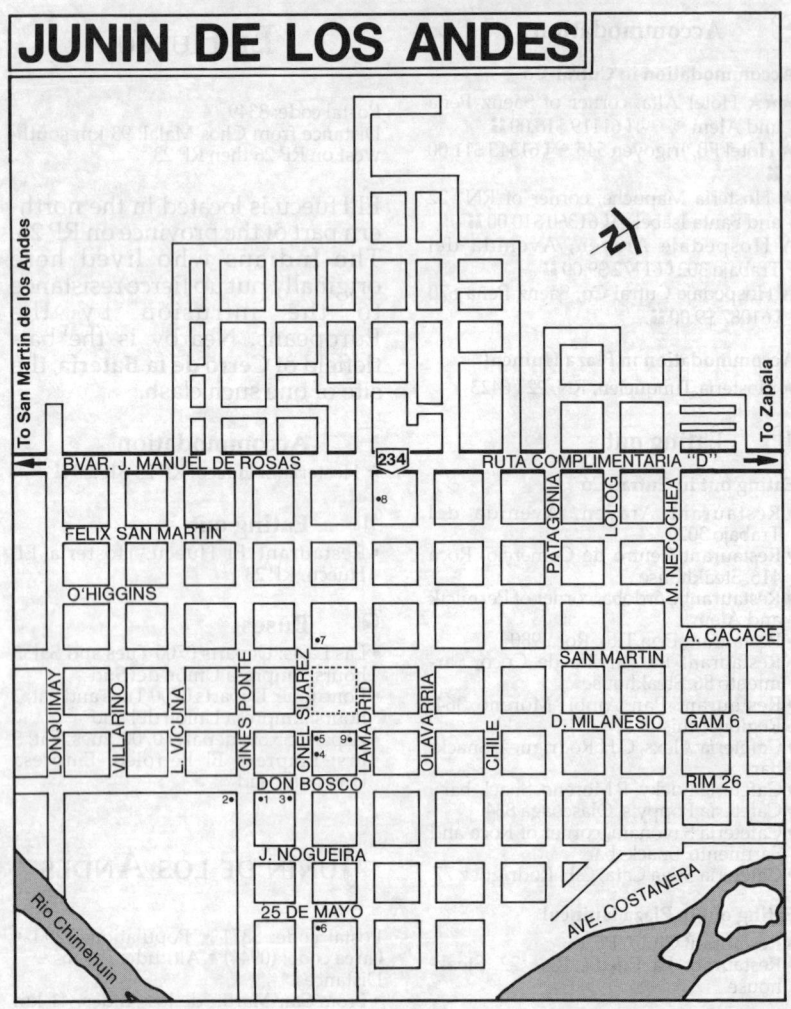

Key to Map
1. Municipalidad
2. Iglesia
3. Post office (Encotel)
4. Telephone (Entel)
5. Tourist information
6. Hotel Chimehuin
7. Hostería El Montanes
8. Hostería Rosters
9. Hospedaje El Cedro

Junín de los Andes

Neuquén Province

Accommodation in Junín de los Andes

★★	Hotel Alejandro I, RN 234	ℂ	91184	$17.00	ii
★★	Hotel San Jorge, Chacra 54	ℂ	91147	$17.00	ii
★	Hotel Chimehuin, corner of Suárez and 25 de Mayo	ℂ	91132	$16.00	ii
★★	Hostería El Montanes, San Martín 555	ℂ	91155	$11.00	ii
★	Hostería Rosters, Lamadrid 66	ℂ	91114		
A	Hospedaje El Cedro, Lamadrid 409	ℂ	91182	$9.00	ii
B	Hospedaje Marisa, J M de Rosas	ℂ	91175	$8.00	ii

Accommodation outside Junín de los Andes

★★★	Hostería Paimún, Lago Paimún	ℂ	91201	$32.00	i
	Full board available; open December–April				
★★★	Hostería San Huberto, Ruta "m", on the road to Tromen pass ●			$36.00	i
	Full board available; open December–April				
★	Hostería Refugio del Pescador, Puerto Canoa ●	ℂ	91132		

built in 1883. Nowadays it is the center of a cattle-raising district, and the pathway to the northern lakes region of the province. This area is famous for its trout fishing.

🛈 Tourist information

- Dirección Municipal de Turismo, corner of D Milanesio and Suárez, opposite the Plaza

🍴 Eating out

- Restaurant Centro Turismo, P Milanesio 589
- Restaurant El Refugio, Lamadrid 450. Pizzeria
- Restaurant El Rincón de Belisario, Colonel Suárez 559. Steakhouse
- Restaurant Fortín Huiliches, Commandante Peñinory
- Restaurant Hueney Ruca, P Milanesio 641
- Restaurant La Tablita, Republica de Chile
- Restaurant Los Tres Hermanos, P Milanesio 542
- Restaurant Tromen, Lamadrid
- Cafetería Cobu, Lamadrid 370
- Cafetería El Montañes, Lamadrid 555. Snack-bar
- Cafetería Ideal, Lamadrid

Eating out outside Junín de los Andes

- Restaurant El Mangrullo, Ruta "d". Steakhouse

✉ Post and telegraph

- Post office: Encotel, corner of Don Bosco and Suárez
- Telephone: Entel, corner of Suárez and Don Bosco

🚗 Motoring

- Service station: YPF, corner of Necochea and Manuel de Rosas (take the Zapala exit)

⊕ Tours

- Mutisia Viajes, corner of 25 de Mayo and Colonel Suárez ℂ 91132

Sport

- Fishing in the lakes
- Mountain hikes
- Hunting: There are many stags and red deer in this area. The hunting season starts on March 10. Pumas and wild boars can be found in the more remote mountain areas

🍸 Entertainment

- Disco Hotel Alejandro I

Junín de los Andes

Neuquén Province

🚌 Buses from Junín de los Andes

The bus terminal is on corner of Suárez and Milanesio, just around the corner from the tourist office.
From Junín de los Andes it is possible to travel to Chile with Empresa Transportes Igi-Laimi. See "Excursions" below.

Destination	Fare	Depart	Services	Hours	Company
• Neuquén	$9.50	1400	daily	6	T A Chevallier
• Buenos Aires	$40.20	1400	daily	22	T A Chevallier
• La Rinconada		1400	daily	1	T A Chevallier
• San Martín de los Andes	$1.50			½	
• Santa Rosa		1400	daily	13	T A Chevallier
• Villa La Angostura		0500	Mon, Wed, Fri	5	Unión del Sud
• Zapala	$8.00	1400	daily	3½	T A Chevallier

🍽 Excursions

- **Chile**: Empresa Transportes Igi-Laimi runs buses to Chile via Villarica, Temuco, Osorno, and Puerto Montt. En route you negotiate **Paso Tromen**, also known as Paso Mamuil Malal, and skirt **Lago Tromen** while still on RP 60. This route is less developed than that via Puyehué, and closes during heavy rain or snow. Parts of it are narrow and steep, and not recommended for the fainthearted. It is 64 km from Junín de los Andes to the pass, and the Argentine checkpoint is right at the pass. The Chilean checkpoint is at Puesco, some 16 km further on. There is an international bus, but officially it will only pick up passengers at Paso Tromen at departure time (0900); sometimes it will allow travelers to board at the customs checkpoint at Puesco, but this is at the discretion of the driver. From the border it is 45 km to Currahue. There are several buses a day from Currahue to Pucón (departing 0800 and 1400). On the Chilean side of the border is Parque Nacional Villarrica. You can camp here but bring your own food. Hitch hiking over the Paso Tromen is difficult

- **Lago Huechulafquen**, in the **Parque Nacional Lanín**: 20 km north-west on RP 63 (Ruta "h"). The lake has many small bays and inlets, while **Volcán Lanín** towers over the northern shore. In the far west of the lake is a narrow stretch of water, called "La Unión", which forms a passageway between **Lago Paimún** and Lago Huechulafquen. This area is of interest historically as it was the site of bloody running battles between Argentine troops and Indians. See also "Excursions" in San Martín de los Andes on page 307

- **Lago Tromen**: 54 km north-west on RP 60 (Ruta "m"). Not to be confused with the Lago Tromen north of Chos Malal. This lake is 19 km long and

Junín de los Andes

NEUQUÉN PROVINCE

7 km wide, and is so deeply cut into the basaltic rocks which form the surrounding mountains that it resembles a fiord. The water is greenish but clear, and the few beaches have volcanic sand and pebbles. The sheltered bays here make wonderful camping spots. Fishing is excellent in this lake, and attracts many local anglers. Be careful out on the lake: it can get very windy at short notice

- **Auca Pan** and **Atreuco**: Two of several native reservations in the area, both about 40 km north. An El Petroleo bus leaves San Martín de los Andes on Tuesdays 0900 for Aluminé, passing through Junín. Ask the driver to let you off at Río Malleo for Atreuco, another 9 km walk down the track. The Indians make handicrafts which are for sale
- **Epulafquen**: Thermal springs near here, close to the Chilean border
- **Fortín Huechu Lauquen** on Lago Huechulafquen, and **Fortín Mamuy Malal** on the road to Lago Tromen: Two of several forts in the area
- Pucón, on Lago Villarica in Chile, via the **Paso Tromen** (altitude 1200 m). Once in Chile you pass through the superb Parque Nacional Villarica, with views of Volcán Quetrupillan (2360 m) and, further on, Volcán Villarica (2840 m)

LA RINCONADA

Postal code: 8375 • (area code: (0944)
Distance from Junín de los Andes: 30 km eastwards on RN 234

La Rinconada is situated at the intersection of RN 40 and RN 234. The motel here overlooks the **Río Aluminé**.

🛏 Accommodation

A Motel La Rinconada ACA, RN 40 $8.00
⚌. Has a *confitería*

🚌 Buses

Empresa El Petroleo runs regular buses to Neuquén, San Carlos de Bariloche, and San Martín de los Andes.

LAS LAJAS

Postal code: 8347 • Population: 2500 •
(area code: (0942) • Altitude: 710 m
Distance from Zapala: 55 km north-west on RN 22

Las Lajas is located 55 km from the Paso Pino Hachado into Chile.

🛏 Accommodation

★ Hostería Las Lajas, Avenida Roca 22 $9.00 ⚌

🍴 Eating out

- Restaurant Las Lajas, Hostería Las Lajas, Avenida Roca 22

🚌 Buses

- Neuquén: Fare $4.00
- Zapala: Fare $1.20

Las Lajas

NEUQUÉN PROVINCE

LAS OVEJAS

Postal code: 8353
Distance from Andacollo: 26 km northwards on RP 1

Las Ovejas is located on the western slopes of the **Cordillera del Viento**. There is no accommodation here; the nearest is at Andacollo. There is good fishing and hiking in the **Volcán Domuyo** massif.

🚌 Buses
- Chos Malal: Departs 0715 Tues, Thurs, Sat; 4 hours; Empresa Unión del Sud
- Zapala: Departs 0715 Tues, Thurs, Sat; 9 hours; Empresa Unión del Sud

NEUQUÉN

Postal code: 8300 • ✆ area code: (0943) • Population: 130 000

The capital of Neuquén province, Neuquén is located at the junction of the **Río Limay** and the **Río Neuquén**. It is considered the fastest-growing city in Patagonia today, with good reason: heavy industries produce engineering and construction materials, and there are rich oil-fields to the west and irrigated fruit orchards in the valleys to the east. These orchards are sheltered by long rows of eye-catching windbreaks; the main crops are apples, pears, and grapes.

The main shopping street is Avenida Argentina, which has a center strip planted with trees: the benches under them are a pleasant place to rest or eat lunch.

Don't confuse San Martín and Felix San Martín—they are different streets entirely.

ℹ️ Tourist information
- Tourist office, Felix San Martín 182

Key to Map

#	Place	#	Place
1	Municipalidad	17	Hotel Ideal
2	Casa de Gobierno	18	Hotel Royal
3	Catedral María La Auxiliadora	19	Hotel Amucan
4	Post office (Encotel)	20	Hotel Charbel
5	Telephone (Entel)	21	Hotel Italia
6	Banco de la Nación	22	Hotel Nuevo Parque
7	Tourist information	23	Hotel Suizo
8	Aerolineas Argentinas	24	Hotel Cari Hue
9	Austral Lineas Aereas	25	Hostal Quime Quipe Ruca
10	LADE (airline)	26	Hospedaje Musters
11	Transportes Aereos Neuquinos (TAN)	27	Hospedaje Neuquén
12	Museo Histórico Provincial	28	Hospedaje Ingles
13	Hotel del Comahué	29	Hospedaje El Rey
14	Hotel Apolo	30	Hospedaje Monsa
15	Hotel Crystal	31	Hospedaje Pani
16	Hotel Iberia	32	Hospedaje Belgrano
		33	Hospedaje Premier
		34	Residencial El Vero

Las Ovejas

Neuquén Province.

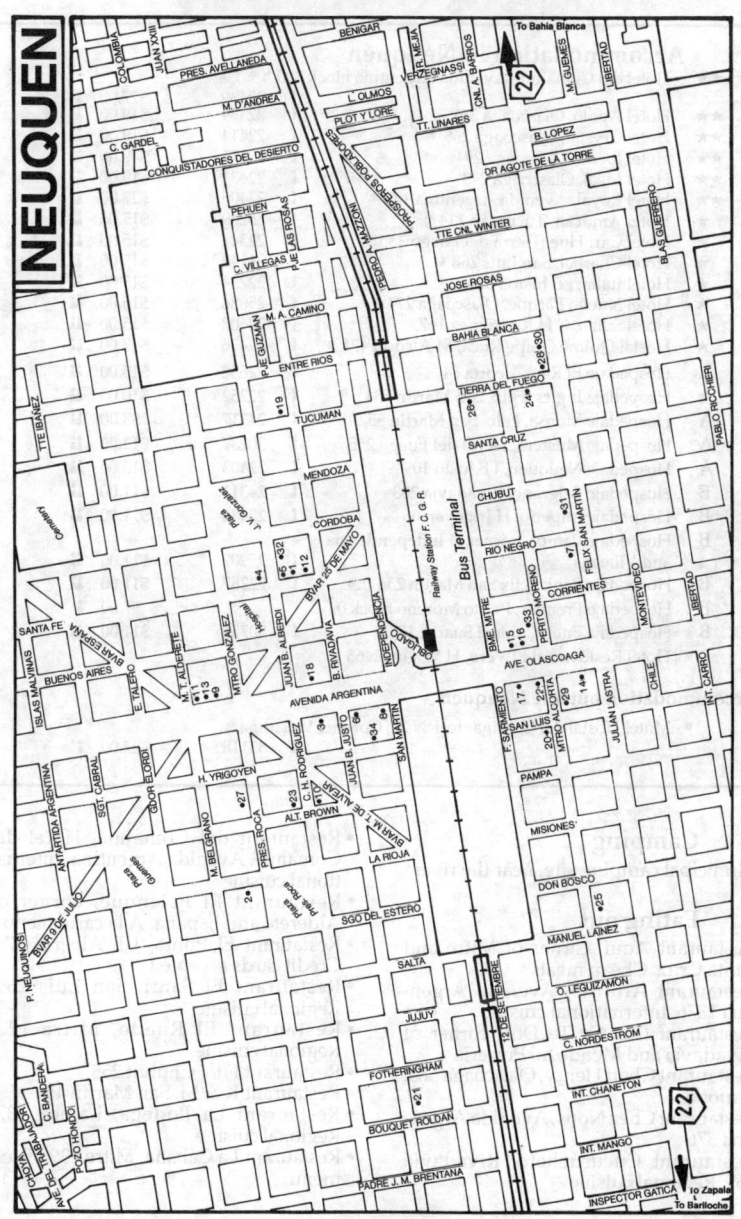

Neuquén

NEUQUÉN PROVINCE

Accommodation in Neuquén

★★★★	Hotel del Comahué, Avenida Argentina block 300	(22439	$27.00	
★★	Hotel Apolo, Olascoaga 361	(22334	$19.00	
★★	Hotel Crystal, Olascoaga 268	(22414	$19.00	
★★	Hotel Iberia, Olascoaga 294	(22372	$19.00	
★★	Hotel Ideal, Olascoaga 243	(22431	$19.00	
★★	Hotel Royal, Avenida Argentina 143	(22408	$22.00	
★	Hotel Amucan, Tucumán 114	(25209	$15.00	
★	Hotel Cari Hue, Tierra del Fuego 335	(2234	$15.00	
★	Hotel Charbel, San Luis 268	(24143	$15.00	
★	Hotel Italia, J B Justo 782	(22234	$15.00	
★	Hotel Nuevo Parque, Olascoaga 271	(25086	$15.00	
★	Hotel Suizo, C H Rodriguez 167	(22602	$15.00	
★	Hostal Quime Quipe Ruca, M Alcorta 474	(22436	$17.00	
A	Hospedaje El Rey, Alcorta 84	(22652	$13.00	
A	Hospedaje Ingles, Felix San Martín 534	(22252	$10.00	
A	Hospedaje Monsa, Felix San Martín 552	(24317	$8.00	
A	Hospedaje Musters, Tierra del Fuego 255	(30237	$12.00	
A	Hospedaje Neuquén, J B Justo 109	(22403	$13.00	
B	Hospedaje Belgrano, Rivadavia 283	(24311	$11.00	
B	Hospedaje Imperio, H Irigoyen 66	(22488	$11.00	
B	Hospedaje Pampa, corner of Independencia and Villegas	(25907	$11.00	
B	Hospedaje Pani, Felix San Martín 236	(22287	$11.00	
B	Hospedaje Premier, Perito Moreno block 0		$7.00	
B	Hospedaje Puel, Colonel Suarez 1518	(30757	$11.00	
•	Hotel Residencial El Vero, H Yrigoyen 65			

Accommodation outside Neuquén

- Motel Hostal del Caminante, RN 22, Coronel Valentina
(33118 $27.00

ⓐ Camping
- Municipal camping site, near the river

🍴 Eating out
- Restaurant Aqui, corner of Mitre and Santa Cruz. Cheap meals
- ☞ Restaurant Arturito, Avenida Argentina 1376. International cuisine
- Restaurant Cas Co Te Dos, corner of Rivadavia and Mendoza. Pizzeria
- Restaurant Cheff Henry, Olascoaga 583. Seafood
- Restaurant Chez Nous, Avenida Argentina 376
- Restaurant Cucurucheto, Rivadavia 265. Regional cuisine
- Restaurant del Comahué, Hotel del Comahué, Avenida Argentina. International cuisine
- Restaurant El Palenque, corner of Alderete and España. A la carte menu
- ☞ Restaurant El Punto, J B Alberdí 176. Credit cards accepted
- Restaurant El Santi, San Luis 265. Regional cuisine
- Restaurant El Ruedo, Mitre 123. Regional cuisine
- Restaurant Fito, Chubut 255
- Restaurant K & M, San Martín 45
- Restaurant La Bodega, Lainez 107. Regional cuisine
- Restaurant La Cabaña, Mitre 439. Fixed menu

Neuquén

NEUQUÉN PROVINCE

✈ Air services from Neuquén

The airport is 7 km from the center of Neuquén.
- Aerolineas Argentinas, Avenida Argentina block 0 (corner of Independencia)
- Austral, Avenida Argentina block 300 (corner of 25 de Mayo)
- LADE, Alte Brown block 100 (corner of C Rodriguez)
- Transportes Aereos Neuquén (TAN), Avenida Argentina 377 ℡ 24834

Destination	Fare	Depart	Services	Hours	Airline
Bahía Blanca	$41.00	1510	daily	1	Austral
	$35.00	1800	Wed	1	LADE
Buenos Aires (Aeroparque Jorge Newbery)					
	$72.00	0900	2–5 services daily	2	Aerolineas, Austral
	$58.00	1215	Tues, Wed, Fri	4–8	LADE
Caviahué	$23.00	1150	Mon, Wed, Sat	1	TAN
Chapelco	$26.00	1140	Tues, Wed, Sat, Sun	1	Aerolineas
	$19.00	1415	Mon, Wed	2	LADE
	$23.50	1130	daily	1	TAN
Chos Malal	$21.50	0900	daily except Sun	1	TAN
Comodoro Rivadavia					
	$46.00	1200	Tues, Wed, Thurs, Fri, Sat	2	Aerolineas
	$36.00	1155	Tues, Wed, Fri	4	LADE
Córdoba	$64.00	1125	Mon, Thurs	2½	Aerolineas
Esquel	$40.00	1130	Mon, Tues, Thurs, Fri Sat	2	Aerolineas, TAN
	$32.00	1155	Tues, Fri	2	LADE
Mar del Plata	$46.00	1215	Tues, Wed, Fri, Sat	2–7	LADE
Mendoza	$52.00	1125	Mon, Thurs	1	Aerolineas
	$49.00	0830	Tues, Wed, Fri, Sat	2½	TAN
Puerto Deseado	$38.00	1155	Tues, Fri	6	LADE
Puerto San Julián	$40.00	1155	Tues, Fri	6	LADE
Río de los Sauces	$14.00	0930	Tues, Sat	½	TAN
Río Gallegos	$41.00	1155	Tues, Fri	8	LADE
Río Grande	$49.00	1155	Tues, Fri	9	LADE
Salta	$99.00	1125	Mon, Thurs	5	Aerolineas
San Antonio Oeste					
	$20.00	1215	Tues	3½	LADE
San Carlos de Bariloche					
	$32.00	1200	Tues, Thurs, Sat, Sun	1	Aerolineas
	$26.00	1155	Mon, Tues, Wed, Fri	1	LADE
	$30.00	1130	Mon, Tues, Fri, Sat	2	TAN
San Miguel de Tucumán					
	$94.00	1125	Mon, Thurs	4	Aerolineas
San Rafael	$40.00	0900	Tues, Wed, Fri, Sat	2½	TAN
Santa Cruz	$42.00	1155	Tues, Fri	7	LADE
Trelew	$35.00	1155	Tues, Fri	3	LADE
Viedma	$27.00	1215	Tues, Sat	1–5	LADE
	$35.00	0800	Mon, Wed, Fri	1½	TAN
Zapala	$18.00	1415	Wed	1	LADE

Neuquén Province

🚌 Buses from Neuquén

Neuquén is the transport centre for Mendoza, Bahía Blanca, Buenos Aires, Zapala, Chile, and San Carlos de Bariloche. The bus terminal is on B Mitre, between Corrientes and Río Negro.

Destination	Fare	Depart	Services	Hours	Company
• Andacollo	$12.50				
• Bahía Blanca	$28.50	0600	6 services daily	10	El Valle; La Estrella, La Puntual
• Barrancas	$15.00				
• Buenos Aires	$24.00	1530	3 services daily	17–19	El Valle, La Estrella, TA Chevallier
• Chorriaca	$7.50				
• Chos Malal	$11.00				
• Comodoro Rivadavia	$24.00	0955	daily		Andesmar
• Copahué	$9.50	0645	2 services daily (summer only)	7	El Petroleo, Unión del Sud
• Córdoba	$22.50	1630	Mon, Thurs, Fri, Sat	18	La Estrella, TUS
• Cutral-Có	$2.00	0915	9 services daily	2	El Petroleo, Unión del Sud
• Junín de los Andes	$9.50	1315	2–3 services daily	7–8	El Petroleo, Unión del Sud
• Las Lajas	$4.00				
• Mendoza	$16.50	2043	1–2 services daily	14	Alto Valle, Andesmar
• Piedra de Aguila	$4.50	1100	1 services daily	4	El Petroleo, Unión del Sud
• Plaza Huincul	$2.00				
• Puerto Madryn	$13.00				Andesmar
• Rawson		0955	daily		Andesmar
• Rincón de los Sauces		0700	2 services daily	3	Alto Valle
• Rosario	$20.50	1930	Mon, Tues (2), Thurs, Sun	19	T A Chevallier, Tirsa
• San Carlos de Bariloche	$11.00	0630	4–6 services daily	9	El Valle, T A Mercedes, Tirsa, TUS
• San Martín de los Andes	$12.00	0620	Tues, Fri, Sat	6–7	La Estrella, TUS
	$11.00	1315	2–4 services daily	8–9	El Petroleo, El Valle, Unión del Sud
• San Rafael	$12.50	1850	1–2 services daily	11	Alto Valle, Andesmar
• Santa Rosa	$9.50	1644	2–4 services daily	9	Alto Valle, El Valle, Tirsa, TUS
• Temuco (Chile)	$20.00	0200	Mon, Tues, Thurs, Sat		Unión del Sud
Returns 0430 on Wed, Fri, Sun, Mon					
• Trelew	$14.00				Andesmar
• Villa El Chocón	$1.50	0800	2 services daily	1	Alto Valle
• Villa La Angostura		2200	Mon, Wed, Fri	12	Unión del Sud
• Viedma		1335	daily	10	Puntual
• Zapala	$4.50	0915	9 services daily	3	El Petroleo, El Valle, Unión del Sud

Neuquén

NEUQUÉN PROVINCE

- ☞ Restaurant La Casa de Mi Abuela, Santiago del Estero 41. International cuisine
- ☞ Restaurant La Estancia, corner of Lainez and Lastra. Steakhouse; credit cards accepted
- ☞ Restaurant La Nona, Diagonal 9 de Julio 65. *Trattoría*
- Restaurant La Posta de Don Juan, corner of Perticone and Río Negro. 24-hour service
- Restaurant La Principal, Mitre 167. Open 24 hours
- Restaurant La Raya, J B Alberdí 85. Steakhouse; credit cards accepted
- Restaurant La Rueda, Santa Cruz 245
- Restaurant Las Tres Marías, J B Alberdí 126. Steakhouse; credit cards accepted
- Restaurant Lo de Tito, Felix San Martín
- Restaurant Los Cipreses, corner of J J Lastra and Misiones. Steakhouse; credit cards accepted
- Restaurant Mavos, Avenida Argentina 130
- Restaurant Nonthue, Alcorta 116. Fixed menu
- Restaurant Origen, Avenida Argentina 344
- Restaurant Parrilla del Manolo, corner of J B Justo and H Yrigoyen
- Restaurant Pastilandia, Felix San Martín 246. Regional cuisine; credit cards accepted
- Restaurant Piazza Albertina, corner of Argentina and J B Alberdí. Pizzeria; credit cards accepted
- Restaurant Piccolo, corner of 25 de Mayo and Santa Fé. Regional cuisine
- ☞ Restaurant Rancho Grande, Felix San Martín 890. Steakhouse
- Restaurant Ruta al Chocón, Lastra 268
- Restaurant San Jorge, corner of Tierra del Fuego and Pa Santa Fé. Regional cuisine
- Restaurant Shanghai, Belgrano 66. Chinese cuisine; open Tues–Sun 1200–1500, 2000–0100
- ☞ Restaurant Via Lactea, corner of San Martín and Irigoyen
- Cafetería Atelier, Diagonal 25 de Mayo 45
- Cafetería Avenida, Avenida Olascoaga 269
- Cafetería Cafe Al Paso, San Martín 23
- Cafetería Coli Bar, Irigoyen 90
- ☞ Cafetería Cafe El Colonial, Roca 285. Good pizzas
- Cafetería Cafe Italiano, Galería Jardín (downstairs)
- Cafetería Cafe Victoria, corner of An Martín 23
- Cafetería Cafe de la Flor, Diagonal Alvear 59
- Cafetería Chez Nous, Avenida Argentina 376
- Cafetería del Comahué, Hotel del Comahué, Avenida Argentina 377
- ☞ Cafetería El Alamo, Elordi 100
- Cafetería El Arabe, JB Justo 66. Arabic meals; credit cards accepted
- Cafetería El Boliche de Manolo, Pigoyen 90
- Cafetería El Cafe, corner of Roca and Irigoyen
- Cafetería El Ciervo, Avenida Argentina 219
- Cafetería Fedra, 25 de Mayo 20. Cocktail lounge
- Cafetería Jimmy Bar, Avenida Olascoaga 261
- Cafetería Katango, J B Alberdí 32
- Cafetería La Terminal, Mitre 129
- ☞ Cafetería Matias, Rivadavia 96
- Cafetería Origen, Avenida Argentina 344
- Cafetería Paris Garden Pool, 1st floor, Galería Jardin. Pool tables
- Cafetería Que Tal Pascual, Gonzalez 20. Steakhouse
- Cafetería Quijote, San Martín 159
- Cafetería Rivadavia, Rivadavia 283. Snack-bar
- Cafetería Tijuana, Avenida Argentina 131
- Cafetería Village, Rivadavia 71
- Cafetería Vitral, Avenida Argentina 178

Eating out outside Neuquén

- Restaurant Aeropuerto Neuquén, at the airport
- Restaurant Domino, municipal swimming pool. Steakhouse
- ☞ Restaurant El Trebol, municipal swimming pool
- Restaurant Polo Club, RN 22 Km 1220. Regional food
- Restaurant Tennis Club, Olascoaga 1355. Regional cuisine

Neuquén

Neuquén Province

Post and telegraph
- Post office: Encotel, Rivadavia block 200 (corner of Santa Fé)
- Long distance telephones: Entel, J B Alberdí block 200 (corner of Córdoba)

Financial
- Banco Alas, Avenida Argentina 135. Cash advances on Visa card
- Casa de Cambio Pulman, Alcorta 140
- Casa de Cambio Olano, J B Justo 86
- ☞ Exterior Turismo, San Martín 29. Good rates

Services and facilities
- Dry cleaner: Paimún, Alte Brown 541
- Medical clinic: Clinica Pasteur, La Rioja 36
- Photographic supplies: Lutz Ferrando, Avenida Argentrina 26
- Sports shop: Ferracioli, corner of Río Negro amd P Moreno. Canoes, rubber rafts, tents, and skis
- Supermarket: La Anónima block 200 (corner of Brown)

Laundromats
- Laverap, Independencia 513
- Laverap, Alte Brown 350
- Marva, Roca 137. Open daily 0830–2100, Sun 1000–1400

Clubs
- Italian: Asociación Italiana, J B Alberdí block 0 (corner of Avenida Argentina

Churches
- Latter Day Saints, La Rioja block 100 (corner of J B Justo)

Visas, passports
- Italian vice-consulate, Independencia 350

Motoring
The road to Buenos Aires is sealed all the way.

Service stations
- ACA, corner of Bulevar 25 de Mayo and Buenos Aires
- Shell, corner of Perticone and Río Negro
- YPF, corner of Chubut and Mitre

Car rental
- A-1 Rent-a-Car International, Felix San Martín block 500 (corner of Bahía Blanca)
- Avis Rent-a-Car, Hotel del Comahue, Avenida Argentina 363 ℃ 30213. Also an office at the airport

Trains
The station is on the corner of Avenida B Mitre and Avenida Olascoaga.
- Buenos Aires (Constitución station): First class $20.00, tourist class $15.00; departs daily; 21 hours
- Zapala: "La Estrella del Valle"; first class $3.00, tourist class $21.50; departs daily; 5 hours

Tours
- Cardone Viajes, Yrigoyen 96 ℃ 23030. Weekend skiing packages to Primeros Pinos
- Domuyo SRL, Rivadavia 365 ℃ 24849
- Exterior, San Martín 29 ℃ 30359
- Mutisia Viajes, San Martín 359 ℃ 23641

Shopping
- Artesanías TYA, Avenida Argentina 235
- El Mangrullo, Avenida Argentina block 200. Handicrafts
- Artesanias Mapuche, M T de Alvear 65 (corner of Yrigoyen)

Sport
- Tennis courts: corner of Buenos Aires and Ibañez

Entertainment
- Cafetería Bailable, corner of Mitre and Tierra del Fuego. Tanguería
- Disco Blip, Salta
- Disco Mirrow, Diagonal 9 de Julio 58
- Disco Pirkas, RN 234
- Disco Roller, Rivadavia 421 (corner of Mendoza)
- Disco Sakoga, RN 22, Cipolletti district (2 km eastwards)
- Night Club Bagatelle, Mitre block 300 (corner of Chubut)

NEUQUÉN PROVINCE

📷 Sightseeing

- **Museo Histórico Provincial** (Provincial History Museum), Santa Fé 163. Open Mon–Fri 1000–1200 and 1500–1900

❋ Excursions

- **San Carlos de Bariloche**: The road south-west is now completely sealed. It is a pleasant drive through orchards to **Arroyito**, where there is a hotel. From there the road follows the northern rim of the **Embalse Ramos Mexia**, an artificial lake created by damming the **Río Limay**

PIEDRA DEL ÁGUILA

Postal code: 8315 • Population: 1700 • area code: (0942) • Altitude: 573 m
Distance from Neuquén: 228 km eastwards on RN 238

Piedra del Águila is located about 5 km from the **Río Limay**. It is a good spot for fishing.

🛏 Accommodation

★★★ Hotel Ranch, RN 237 ◉ $16.00 ⓘ. Half board

★ Hostería El Ciervo, Lanin ◉ ℂ 93267 $9.00 ⓘⓘ

A Hospedaje La Rueda, RN 237 ℂ 93046 $7.00 ⓘⓘ

B Hospedaje Piedra del Águila, RN 237 ℂ 93011 $7.00 ⓘⓘ

🍴 Eating out

- Restaurant Ayelen, Villegas. Steakhouse
- Restaurant Chamonix, Mitre. Cafeteria
- Restaurant El Águila Dorada, corner of P Pobladores and 9 de Julio
- Restaurant El Atalaya, Villegas
- Restaurant El Choique, Villegas. Cafeteria
- Restaurant El Cristal, corner of Roca and RN 237. Regional cuisine
- Restaurant Iturbide, corner of Villegas and Mitre
- Restaurant La Cipoleña, P Pobladores. Regional cuisine
- Restaurant La Terminal, at the bus terminal
- Restaurant Lo de Miguel, Belgrano. Regional cuisine
- Restaurant Los Amigos, Villegas
- Cafetería La Rueda, Ruta 237
- Cafetería Snack-bar, Mitre

🚌 Buses

Buses run regularly to Neuquén and San Carlos de Bariloche.

PRIMEROS PINOS

Altitude: 1000 m
Distances
- From Zapala: 45 km westwards on RP 13
- From Neuquén: 230 km westwards

The winter resort of Primeros Pinos, set in the foothills of the Andes among araucania forests, is a good place for beginner skiers. The resort itself comprises two parts: the base area Primeros Pinos at 1600 m, and **Cerro Quelli Mahuida** at 1810 m. There is a ski school, ski hire, restaurant, and cafeteria at base level, and a cafeteria, teleski, and ski lift above at Cerro Mahuida. The skiing season runs from July 1 to September 30. There are 6 ha of skiing area.

Neuquén Province

On an average day there is about 0.7 m of dry compact snow.

At the base, the slopes incline at an angle of about 20°. There is a height difference of only 30 m over a length of 200 m, which makes Primeros Pinos good for beginning and intermediate skiers.

Skiing equipment for Alpine skiing can be hired at Primeros Pinos. They have about 100 pairs of skis for hire. A sign at the base of the ski run indicates what services are available on a particular day.

Ski clubs with facilities here are: Club Andino Zapala, Caza y Pesca, and Club Andino Chachil.

Base area

Facilities in the base area, near the *hostería* include:
- Teleski Borer: 150 m long, can carry 600 skiers per hour, height difference 30 m
- School ski lift: 130 long, can carry 600 skiers per hour, height difference 20 m

Cerro Quelli Mahuida

Facilities in the upper area include:
- Teleski Borer: 300 m long, can carry 600 skiers, height difference 130 m
- School ski lift: 200 m long, can carry 600 skiers per hour, height difference 60 m

Accommodation

Booking is almost essential if you want accommodation right on the snow-fields. See also "Accommodation" in Zapala on page 314
- ★★ Hostería Primeros Pinos ((0942)21163 $35.00. 28 beds

Buses

- Empresa Unión del Sud operates buses from Neuquén and Zapala ((0942) 21363
- Empresa Alvarez Internacional, Avenida Trannack 1440, Zapala (21376. The address in Buenos Aires is 5th floor, 508 Avenida Santa Fé 1780 (410397. This company organizes skiing trips from Zapala twice a day in the skiing season. They leave Zapala at 1000 and 1300, and return from Primeros Pinos at 1045 and 1345. The trip takes about an hour, and a return ticket which includes lunch costs $20.00

QUILLÉN

Postal code: 8341
Distance from Zapala: 136 km westwards on RP 46

Quillén is located at the northern entrance to the **Parque Nacional Lanín**, about 3 km from Lago Quillén.

Accommodation

★★ Hostería Quillen, El Rahue $28.00. Includes breakfast

Excursions

- Parque Nacional Lanín. See "Excursions" in San Martín de los Andes on page 307

Primeros Pinos

NEUQUÉN PROVINCE

SAN MARTÍN DE LOS ANDES

Postal code: 8370 • Population: 13 000 • area code: (0944)
Distances
- From Junín de los Andes: 41 km south-west on RP 234
- From Zapala: 240 km south-west on RN 40 then RP 234

San Martín de los Andes is located at the eastern end of **Lago Lacar**. It is well geared for tourism with accommodation for over 3000 people in a variety of hotels. It is the best starting point to explore the **Parque Nacional Lanín**, with its idyllic lakes and wooded mountain valleys, all dominated by the snow-capped **Volcán Lanín**.

Walking through the park you can see red deer and stags which have been introduced from Europe.

The popular skiing resort of **Cerro Chapelco** is only 18 km from here, and can be reached on an excellent road which is kept open even after heavy snowfalls. Drivers should note that there is one way traffic on RN 234 as far as the turn-off east onto RP 19. For a shorter return route take RP 19 all the way north to San Martín. See Cerro Chapelco on page 279.

The surface of **Lago Lacar** covers 50 square km. It measures 24 km long and 3 km wide, and is 640 m above sea level. The deepest point is 77 m. The site of San Martín was once under the waters of Lago Lacar, at a time when the lake emptied into the Atlantic Ocean. The water level dropped, however, and the lake found an outlet into the Pacific Ocean.

ℹ Tourist information

- The tourist office is at Rosas 790, in the main square near the corner of San Martin. Open 0800–2400 in summer, 0800–2100 in winter. They frown upon anyone seeking private accommodation here
- National parks office, E Frey, opposite the Plaza. Good for information about hikes and cabins in the national parks

▲ Camping

- ACA Camping, RN 234 east. The kiosk is not open all year round. $1.40 per person
- Autocamping San Martín de los Andes. Camping $1.40 per person, cabins $5.00 per person
- Camping Municipal, corner of Juez del Valle and General Roca. The bridge across the river is barred to vehicular traffic
- Los Andes, Juez del Valle (7372

!! Eating out

Most restaurants start to serve dinner around 2100. There are some good restaurants here, and gourmets are well catered for.
- Restaurant Betty, San Martín 1203
- Restaurant Chapelco, Hotel Chapelco Ski, Belgrano 869
- Restaurant Cheval, Belgrano 876
- Restaurant Crismalu, Elordi 526
- Restaurant del Neuquén, Villegas 776. Regional cuisine
- Restaurant Don Eugenio, Mascardi 898 (corner of Villegas). Regional cuisine
- Restaurant Don Juan, corner of Elordi and General Roca. Regional cuisine
- Restaurant El Ciervo, Villegas 700. Regional cuisine
- Restaurant El Esquiador, Belgrano 883. Steakhouse
- Restaurant El Rancho, San Martín 1100

Neuquén Province

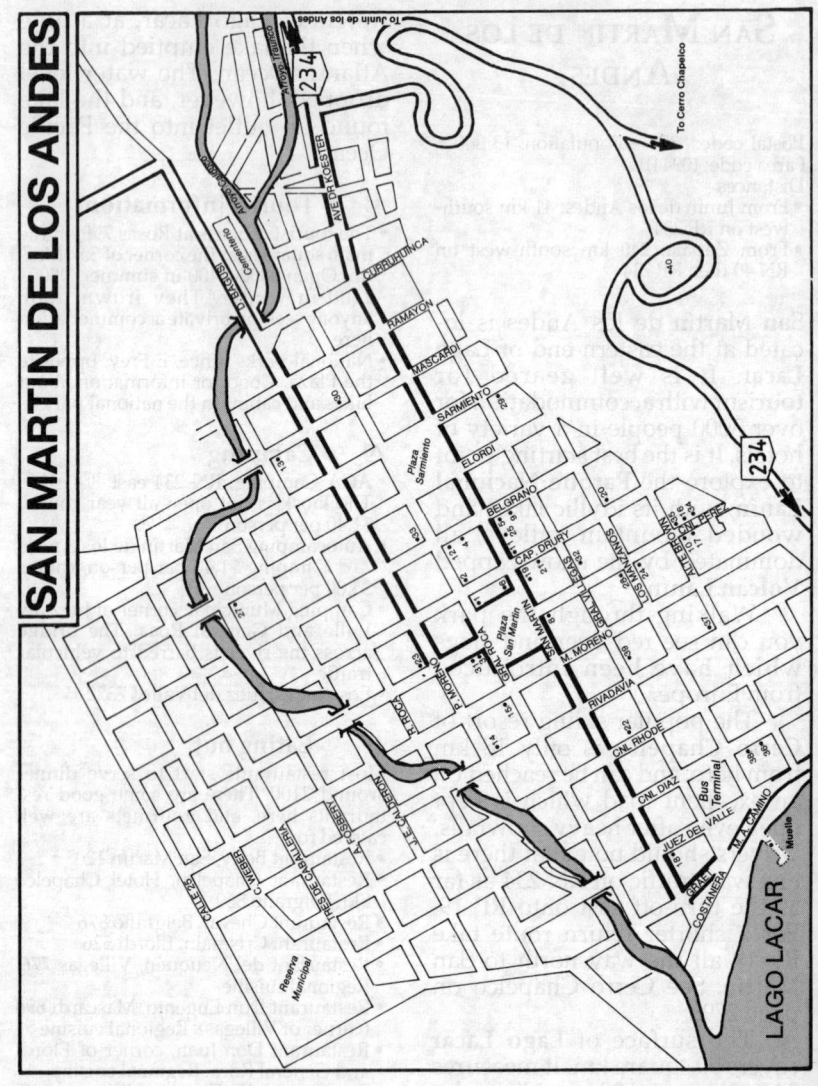

NEUQUÉN PROVINCE

Key to Map
1. Municipalidad
2. Iglesia
3. Post Office (Encotel)
4. Telephone (Entel)
5. Aerolineas Argentinas
6. Tourist information
7. Lake cruises
8. Banco de la Nación
9. Hotel Chapelco Ski
10. Hotel Berna
11. Hotel Nevegal
12. Hotel Tunqueley
13. Hotel Turismo
14. Hotel Curruhuinca
15. Hostería La Cheminee
16. Hostería La Raclette
17. Hostería Las Lengas
18. Hostería La Posta del Cazador
19. Hostería Tisu
20. Hostería La Masia
21. Hostería Anay
22. Hostería Hostal del Lago
23. Hostería Nevada
24. Hostería Hueney Ruca
25. Hostería Peumayen
26. Hospedaje Villa Biby
27. Hospedaje Cecchetto
28. Hospedaje Italia
29. Residencial Cumelen
30. Residencial Laura
31. Residencial Marily
32. Residencial Villa Lago
33. Cabañas Le Village
34. Cabañas Ojo del Agua
35. Cabañas El Rincón
36. Cabañas Vista del Lago
37. Cabañas Las Rucas
38. Cabañas del Chapelco
39. Cabañas Andina
40. Hotel Sol de los Andes

- Restaurant Fanfani, Rhode 786. Pasta; credit cards accepted
- Restaurant Jockey Club, Villegas 657. Trout and venison
- Restaurant La Masia, Hostería La Masia, Drury block 1000 (corner of Los Manzanos)
- Restaurant La Raclette, Perez 1170
- Restaurant La Tranquera, Villegas 985. Steakhouse
- Restaurant Mi Viejo Pepe, Villegas 725. Regional cuisine
- Restaurant Munich de los Andes, Elordi 761. International cuisine
- Restaurant Piscis, Villegas block 500 (corner of Moreno). Seafood; credit cards accepted
- Restaurant Sayhueque, corner of San Martín and Rivadavia. Steakhouse; credit cards accepted
- Pizzería Casa Blanca, corner of Mascardi and Villegas. Cheap
- Pizzería El Jabali, Juan del Valle 1000
- Pizzería La Strada, corner of San Martín 715 and Perez
- Rotisería Alemana, General Villegas 953. Takeaway
- Cafetería Chapelco, corner of Drury and Moreno. Tearoom
- Cafetería La Masia, corner of Obeid and Drury. Tearoom
- Cafetería La Revancha, Curruhuinca 725
- Cafetería Lyn y Su Familia, corner of Juez del Valle and Villegas
- Cafetería New Anyway, San Martín 737. Pizzeria
- Cafetería Olaf, C Perez 1130. Pool tables
- Cafetería Peumayen, San Martín 851
- Cafetería Tisu, Hostería Tisu, San Martín 771
- Pub: Ku-Bar, San Martín 737
- Pub: Olaf, Perez 1124. Pool
- Pub: Richards, Capitán Drury 813
- Pub: Tasca Pueblo, M Moreno 856

Eating out outside San Martín del los Andes

- Restaurant Arrayan, Ruta "d", 3 km from town center
- Restaurant El Pinito, RN 234
- Restaurant El Viejo Molino de Pulgarcito, Ruta "d", Km 4. Steakhouse
- Restaurant Hua Hum, RP 48. International cuisine
- Restaurant L'Auberge, RN 234 La Cascada
- Restaurant Hotel Sol de los Andes, RP 19. International cuisine

San Martín de los Andes

NEUQUÉN PROVINCE

🛏 Accommodation in San Martín de los Andes

As well as normal hotels, cabin-style accommodation known as "*cabañas*" is available in San Martín de los Andes. These cabins are built to accommodate from four to six persons, and have cooking facilities. They are quite a bargain if you have a family or are traveling with several people.

★★★★★	Hotel Sol de los Andes, RP 19 ☎Ⓣ🅿⬇		
	Overlooks the town. Rates are $120.00 👥 during July and August, and $60.00 👥 in June and September		
★★★	Hotel Caupolicán, San Martín 969	☏ 7658	$49.00 👥
★★★	Hotel Chapelco Ski, Belgrano 869 🍴☎		
★★★	Hotel del Viejo Esquiador, San Martín 1242 ☎		
★★★	Hotel Le Village, corner of Capitán Drury and General Roca 🅿		
		☏ 7698	$49.00 👥
★★	Hotel Berna, Teniente Coronel Perez 1127 ☎		
★★	Hotel Crismalu, Roca 975 ☎		
★★	Hotel Nevegal, San Martín 817 ☎		
★★	Hotel Tunqueley, corner of Roca and Belgrano 🍴		
		☏ 7381	$17.00 👥
★	Hotel Curruhuinca, Rivadavia 686	☏ 7224	$11.00 👥
★	Hotel Turismo, Mascardi 517	☏ 7592	$11.00 👥
★★★	Hostería Hostal del Esquiador, Colonel Rhode 975 ☎		
		☏ 7674	$20.00 👥
★★★	Hostería La Cheminee, corner of Roca and Moreno ☎🅿⬇	☏ 7617	$32.00 👥
★★★	Hostería La Masia, corner of Obeid 811 (formerly called Los Manzanos) and Capitán Drury	☏ 7688	$19.00 👥
★★★	Hostería La Posta del Cazador, San Martín 175 ☎	☏ 7501	$22.00 👥
★★★	Hostería La Raclette, Teniente Coronel Perez 1170 🍴☎		
★★★	Hostería Las Lengas, Teniente Coronel Perez 1175		
★★★	Hostería Tisu, San Martín 771 🍴☎		
★★	Hostería Anay, Capitán Drury 841 ☎		
★★	Hostería del Chapelco, corner of Alte Brown 297 and J del Valle ☎	☏ 7610	$13.00 👥
★★	Hostería Hostal del Lago, Colonel Rhode 854		
★★	Hostería Nevada, Moreno 590 Ⓣ		
★	Hostería Cumelen, Elordi 931 ☎🅿		
★	Hostería Hueney Ruca, corner of Obeid (formerly called Los Manzanos) and Teniente Coronel Perez	☏ 7499	$11.00 👥
★	Hostería La Posada, Rivadavia 1145		$17.00 👥
★	Hostería Peumayen, San Martín 851		
A	Hospedaje Cechetto, Fosbery 995	☏ 7384	$9.00 👥
A	Hospedaje Laura, Mascardi 632 ☎		
A	Hospedaje Los Pinos, Alte Brown 420 ☎		
A	Hospedaje Villa Biby, Colonel Díaz 1186 🅿		
A	Hospedaje Villa Lago, Villegas 717 ☎		
B	Hospedaje Casa Alta, C Obeid 659 ☎		
B	Hospedaje Italia, Teniente Coronel Perez 977	☏ 7590	$10.00 👥
B	Hospedaje Mi Ranchito, Rivadavia 341	☏ 7421	$9.00 👥
•	Residencial Cumelen, Elordi 931		
•	Residencial Laura, Mascardi 632 🍴		
•	Residencial Marily, Perez 567 🅿		$6.00 👤
	Central heating		
•	Residencial Villa Lago, General Villegas 717		

San Martín de los Andes

NEUQUÉN PROVINCE

Accommodation in San Martín de los Andes—continued

Cabañas

The prices indicated are for groups. The size of the group is given after the price.

★★★	Cabañas Humo Azul, R Roca 618	(7678	$32.00	5
★★★	Cabañas Le Village, corner of Drury and Roca	(7698	$39.00	5
★★★	Cabañas Ojo del Agua, corner of Teniente Coronel Perez and Almirante Brown	(7302	$25.00	5
★★	Cabañas del Abuelo, Los Cipreses 1541	(7539	$17.00	5
★★	Cabañas de la Isla, Rohde 380	(7411	$25.00	5
★★	Cabañas del Bosque, P Moreno 1420	(7607	$28.00	5
★★	Cabañas del Lacar, Rhode 1144	(7679	$25.00	5
★★	Cabañas El Rincón, Teniente Coronel Perez 1144 (booking office at 956 Rhode)	(7220	$30.00	5
★★	Cabañas Vista del Lago, Coronel Díaz 1125			5
★★	Cabañas Waldeck, P Moreno 1871	(7682	$25.00	5
★	Cabañas Andina, Villegas 567	(7242		
★	Cabañas del Chapelco, corner of Coronel Díaz and Brown	(7610	$22.00	5
★	Cabañas El Ciervo Rojo, Brown 445	(7220	$28.00	6
★	Cabañas El Silencio, corner of Rivadavia block 1100 and Brown			
★	Cabañas Las Rucas, Alte Brown 516	(7373		
★	Cabañas Los Cipreses, corner of Los Notros and Los Cipreses		$20.00	5
★	Cabaña Viejo Mio, Avenida Koessler 2205		$19.00	5

Accommodation outside San Martín de los Andes

★★★	Hostería del Bosque, on the road to Lago Lolog	((0943) 22943	$21.00	♣
★★	Hostería Parque Los Andes, RN 234	(7252	$19.00	♣
★	Hostería L'Auberge, RN 234, Vega Maipú district	(7723	$11.00	♣
★	Hostería El Pinito, RN 234	(7692	$11.00	♣
★★★	Apart Hotel Ruca Leufu, El Oasis Turn at Koessler block 2500		$39.00	5

Communication

- Post office: Encotel, corner of Roca and Perez
- Telephone: Entel, corner of Drury 761 and Roca

Services and facilities

- Bakery: Gustavo I, Elordi 485
- Delicatessen: corner of Drury and Moreno
- Dry-cleaner: Pilquitron, Belgrano 745
- Photographic supplies: Foto Thuman, corner of San
- Supermarket: Elordi, Elordi 367 (corner of P Moreno)

Laundromats

- Laverap, Drury 882
- Lavadero Lacar, Elordi 838

Pharmacies

- Farmacia Austral, Elordi 750
- Farmacia Lacar, corner of San Martín and Drury

Ski hire

- Andia Wedel, M Moreno 787
- Bums, corner of Moreno and Roca. Alpine skis $12.00 per day, Nordic skis $8.00 per day
- La Colina, San Martín 532. Also sells second-hand ski boots

NEUQUÉN PROVINCE

✈ Air services from San Martín de los Andes

Chapelco airport is some 20 km outside town on the road to Junín de los Andes. The airport can only handle small planes. Both TAN and LADE operate flights from here.
- Aerolineas Argentinas, corner of Avenida San Martín and Belgrano ℂ 7003
- LADE, Avenida San Martín 915 ℂ 7672
- TAN, Avenida San Martín 915 ℂ 7872

Destination	Fare	Depart	Services	Hours	Airline
• Neuquén	$23.50	1240	daily	1	TAN
• Buenos Aires (Aeroparque Jorge Newbery					
	$57.00	1050	Tues	9½	LADE
	$57.00	12		7	LADE
• Comodoro Rivadavia					
	$28.00	1635	Wed	3	LADE
• Esquel		1230	Mon, Fri	1½	TAN
• Mar del Plata	$49.00	1050	Tues	8	LADE
	$49.00	1200	Fri	5	LADE
• Neuquén	$19.00	1050	Tues, Fri	1–2	LADE
• San Antonio Oeste					
	$26.00	1050	Tues	5	LADE
• San Carlos de Bariloche					
	$15.00	1635	Mon, Wed	½	LADE
		1330	Mon, Tues, Fri, Sat	1	TAN
• Viedma	$32.00	1050	Tues	6	LADE
• Zapala	$15.00	1200	Fri	1	LADE

⛴ Water transport

Boats leave from General Villegas in the Parque Yapeyu. There are fewer services out of season. The ticket office is open 0930–1730, and managed by Señor Schneeberger, who speaks some German. See also "Excursions" below.

⊕ Tours

- Chapelco Turismo, Avenida San Martín 876 ℂ 7550
- Hua-Hum Turismo, General Roca 1397 ℂ 7616
- Navegación Lago Lacar ℂ 7682. Book at the pier or at the bus terminal
- Pucará Viajes y Turismo, San Martín 943 ℂ 7218
- Ruca Huelun, Belgrano 790 ℂ 7496
- Viajes Travel Agency, corner of Moreno and P Moreno. This agency also has automobiles for hire

🏬 Shopping

Artesanías

- Arruz, corner of Moreno and Brown
- Edelweiss, General Roca 645
- Melipal, San Martín 878
- Mercado Artesanal, JM de Rosas 770
- Stablo, Elordi 835
- Wald, Elordi 820

Ceramics

- Ceramicas del Bosque Encantado, Los Cipreses 2111
- Ceramicas San Martín, Capitán Drury 860

Chocolates

- Mamusia, corner of San Martín and M Moreno
- Fenoglio, San Martín 836

🎾 Sport

- Squash: Squash Cachito, P Moreno 846. $2.00 per half hour. Hamburgers are also available

San Martín de los Andes

Neuquén Province

🚌 Buses from San Martín de los Andes

The bus terminal is on the corner of General Villegas 251 and Capitán Drury. The rest rooms are clean.

Empresa Igi Llaimi and Empresa San Martín operate services to and from Chile. Destinations include Temuco, Pucon, and Villarrica. These buses start operating in mid-November and finish in May. The return times from Temuco are: Empresa San Martín Tues, Thurs, Sat at 0500; Empresa Igi-Llaimi Tues, Thurs at 0330

Transportes Ko Ko also operates a service from Junín de los Andes to Aluminé each Tuesday. The bus leaves at 0900 and costs $7.00. You pass an Indian reservation on the way.

Destination	Fare	Depart	Service	Hours	Company
• Neuquén	$11.50	1300	Mon, Wed, Fri, Sun	8	El Valle
	$12.00	0830	2–3 services daily	8	El Petroleo, Unión del Sud
	$12.00	0930	Mon (2), Wed, Thurs, Sat	7	T A Chevallier, TUS
	$12.00	1335	Sun	5	La Estrella
• Aluminé	$5.00	0800	Tues		El Petroleo
• Buenos Aires	$40.00	1200	Mon, Wed, Thurs, Fri	24	El Valle
	$42.00	1330	Mon, Wed, Sat	22	TA Chevallier
• Córdoba	$36.00	0930	Mon, Thurs	25	TUS
• Junín de los Andes	$1.50	0700	2 services daily	1	El Petroleo
• San Carlos de Bariloche	$6.50	0800	Mon–Wed, Fri, Sat	4–5	El Valle, Unión del Sud
• Temuco (Chile)	$15.00	0700	1–services Tues–Sat	8	Empresa San Martín, GAC, Igi Llaimi
• Valdivia (Chile)		0630	Sun		La Estrella/Sur
• Villa La Angostura	$4.00	0600	Mon–Wed, Fri	3	El Petroleo, Unión del Sud
• Zapala	$8.00	0830	2 services daily	4	El Petroleo

Skiing

There is skiing at Cerro Chapelco. Facilities include 32 chair lifts and ski-tows. The slopes and snow conditions here are excellent.
• Club Andino San Martín, Capitán Drury block 800 (corner of Villegas)

🍸 Entertainment

- Casino Provincial, Hotel Sol de Andes
- Cine Amancay, General Roca 1154
- Disco Crismalu, R Roca 1011
- Disco, Hotel Sol de los Andes
- Night Club Yamaina, corner of Elordi and Villegas

📷 Excursions

- **Parque Nacional Lanín**: This national park, on the edge of which San Martín stands, is in a spectacular setting. It is situated in high country, and extends to the summit of **Volcán Lanín** on the border with Chile. This volcano is snow-covered all year round and has numerous thermal springs. The park contains many lakes and rivers providing excellent trout fishing and canoeing. There is hiking and mountaineering on Volcán Lanín. The plentiful wildlife includes boars, deer, *pudu*, pumas, and wildcats
- **Zapala**: The four-hour trip is very scenic and highly recom-

San Martín de los Andes

NEUQUÉN PROVINCE

mended. Transportes Ko Ko and Empresa El Petroleo both provide services which leave at 0830. It is also a good trip to do by car, especially if you want to explore side routes. Soon after you pass through Junín de los Andes, the cone of **Volcán Lanín** looms on the left. This volcano is 3776 m high and usually snow-covered all year round. (If you are bound for Chile the turn-off to **Paso Tromen** is on the left, about five minutes' drive out of Junín de los Andes. It is called RP 60 but is little more than a dirt track.) The valley flattens out after a while, but you can see the snow-capped *cordillera* in the background. This mountain range forms a natural border between Argentina and Chile. The flatter land here is suited to grazing, and this is rich cattle country. At **La Rinconada** the road meets RN 40 and follows it north. At this point it is still 173 km to Zapala. You then begin to climb the **Cuesta La Rinconada**, a steep winding road which has been gouged out of the mountain-side. Once you have negotiated the small pass at the top there are sweeping views of the valley to the left—try to get a seat on the left-hand side of the bus if you can. The land up here is almost bare; you can see cows and horses grazing, but about all that grow are low shrubs and isolated clumps of grass. After this the road deteriorates, and ends up on a plain, or *meseta*. A little further on, an Isaura service station marks the junction with RP 24. It is a 20 km trip to **Las Coloradas** on this road, and you can continue through Las Coloradas to **Bajada Rahue**, and **Aluminé**, via part of **Parque Nacional Laguna Blanca**. At **Fortín Mayo** the main San Martín–Zapala road meets RP 46. The people in this region are still predominately Indian. After the junction with RP 46, RN 40 becomes a dirt road. This area is quite remote: at **Aguada Florencia** the only building is the ACA service station and cafeteria. The hills are bare, and even though the road is sealed after Aguada Florencia, it is full of pot-holes: be prepared for a bumpy ride. The turn-off to Parque Nacional Laguna Blanca is 10 km before Zapala, and from here on the road improves. There is usually a strong wind blowing over the *meseta* here, and the Andes, which were receding from view up to now, begin to loom larger again. See also Zapala on page 312

- **San Carlos de Bariloche**: Local buses take the longer, partially paved road via **Junín de los Andes** because it is open all year round. But the most scenic route is RN 234, via **Villa La Angostura**. The tour buses take 10 hours to do the 200 km journey, and en route pass **Lago Meliquina**, **Lago Falkner**, **Lago Traful**, and **Lago Espejo**, where RN 234 joins RN 231 coming from Chile. From here on the road skirts the shores of beauti-

San Martín de los Andes

Neuquén Province

ful **Lago Nahuel Huapí**. It is worth spending some time at Villa La Angostura to explore the surrounding countryside. Local buses operate services from here to Chile and Bariloche. See also Villa La Angostura below

- **Hua-Hum**, by boat: This trip is organized by Navegación Lago Lacar SA and costs $7.50. The boat leaves San Martín at 0930 and passes the northern shores of **Cerro Bandurias** and **Península Yuco**, and **Isla Santa Teresita**. The trip continues through La Angostura channel (also called "La Unión") into **Lago Monthue**, and stops ashore briefly to visit the **Cha-Chin** falls. There is a stop for lunch at **Hua Hum**; it is only 2 km to the Chilean border from here. The return trip after lunch includes a short visit to the mineral springs at **Quila-Quina**. You arrive back in San Martín at about 1730. Take plenty of film with you
- **Quila-Quina**: The boat leaves at 1500 and passes **Catritre** and **Cerro Abanico** beaches before docking at Puerto Quila-Quina. Here you can visit the mineral springs and nearby rock paintings. There is also a tearoom here, the Casa de Te El Establo. The boat arrrives back in San Martín at 1900. The fare is $4.00

Trips into Chile

San Martín is a good base for trips into neighboring Chile. Some suggestions are given below.

- **Hua-Hum**, **Paso Hua- Hum** on the border, Puerto Fuy, and Panguipulli
- **Paso Puyehue** on the border, and Osorno
- **Junín de los Andes**, **Paso Tromen** (or Paso de Mamuil Malal) on the border, Pucón, and Villarica

Villa La Angostura

Postal code: 8403 • Population: 2700 • area code: (0944) • Altitude: 845 m
Distance from San Carlos de Bariloche: 80 km north-west on RN 231

Accommodation in Villa La Angostura

It is possible to stay with families in private houses—check the tourist office for details.

★★★	Hotel Correntoso, RN 231		$46.00	
★	Hotel La Angostura, Villa La Angostura	(94161	$22.00	
	Apart Hotel Las Lomas del Correntoso, RN 231		$51.00	5
A	Hospedaje Don Pedro, El Cruce		$ 9.00	
B	Hospedaje La Cabañita, Belvedere			
A	Hospedaje La Granja, Villa La Angostura	(94193	$14.00	
A	Hospedaje Río Bonito, Topa Topa	(94110	$12.00	
•	Cabañas Rancho Bayo, El Cruce			

Neuquén Province

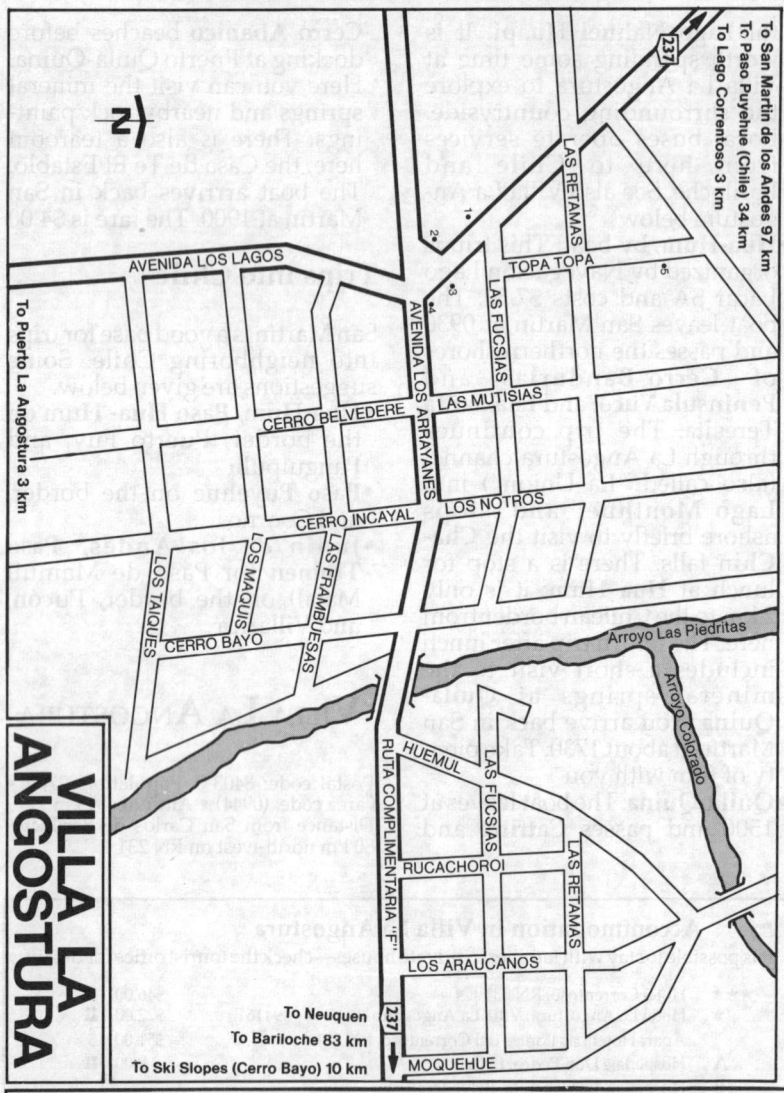

Key to Map
1. Municipalidad
2. Iglesia
3. Post office (Encotel)
4. Tourist information
5. Hospedaje Río Bonito

Villa la Angostura

Neuquén Province

Buses from Villa La Angostura

Destination	Fare	Depart	Services	Hours	Company
• Neuquén		1845	Tues, Thurs, Sun	12	Unión del Sud
• San Carlos de Bariloche	$5.00	0800	2–3 services daily except Sun	2–3	Algarrobal, Ayala, T A Mercedes
• Junín de los Andes		1845	Tues, Thurs, Sat	6	Unión del Sud
• Osorno (Chile)					
• Puerto Montt (Chile)		1100	Mon–Thurs, Sat	6	T A Mercedes
• San Martín de los Andes	$4.00	1845	Tues, Thurs, Sat	4	Unión del Sud

Villa La Angostura is a small and picturesque tourist resort village on the northern shore of **Lago Nahuel Huapí**, on the road to Chile. If you are heading towards San Martín de los Andes to visit the lakes area you pass through here.

Camping
- El Cruce
- Osa Mayor, 2 km along the road to San Martín de Bariloche. Open late December to mid-May
- Municipal Lago Correntoso

Eating out
- Restaurant Bianchi, corner of T Topa and Las Retamas
- Restaurant Correntoso, RN 231 (at the hotel). International cuisine
- Restaurant Don Pedro, C Belvedere
- Restaurant La Angostura, Hotel La Angostura, Villa La Angostura
- Restaurant Mi Ranchito, C Belvedere
- Restaurant Pichi Huinca, Avenida Los Arrayanes
- Cafetería Los Tres Mosqueteros, Villa La Angostura
- Cafetería Un Lugar del Jardín, Villa La Angostura

Motoring
- Service station: ACA, Lago Correntoso

Water transport
There are excursion boats on Lago Nahuel Huapí.

Tours
- Village, Avenida Arrayanes (94292

Sport
Skiing at Cerro Bayó is possible July–September; see Cerro Bayo on page 278

Villa Traful

Postal code: 8403
Distance from San Carlos de Bariloche: 100 northwards on RN 237 then RP 67

Located on the southern shore of picturesque **Lago Traful**, Villa Traful is very popular with holiday-makers in summer.

Accommodation
★ Hostería Rincón del Pescador, Villa Traful $27.00. Half board; for bookings write to Casilla correo 1168, San Carlos de Bariloche
★ Hostería Traful, Villa Traful $12.00
★ Cabañas Aiken Traful, Villa Traful
★ Cabañas Walnor, Villa Traful $28.00 for 8 persons

NEUQUÉN PROVINCE

🍴 Eating out
- Restaurant Rincón del Pescador, Hostería Rincón del Pescador, Villa Traful. Regional cuisine
- Restaurant Villa Traful, Hostería Traful, Villa Traful. Regional cuisine

🚌 Buses
There are regular daily services to San Carlos de Bariloche.

✤ Excursions
- **Parque Nacional Nahuel Huapí**: This park with its numerous lakes is recommended for bushwalking. You can camp anywhere in the park.

ZAPALA

Postal code: 8340 • Population: 25,000 • (area code: 0942 • Altitude: 1012 m
Distance from Neuquén: 185 km westwards on RN 22

Zapala was founded in 1913, and is located on a high plateau within easy reach of the western Andes in the center of the province. It is an important rail and road junction: here RN 40, which runs north–south, intersects with RN 22, which runs east–west. Much industry has been established here in recent years. Zapala has an excellent natural history museum and a ceramics school. For tourists it is the starting point for trips to the snow-fields and the **Parque Nacional Laguna Blanca**. It is also possible to visit the Indian reserves in the area. The main shopping street is San Martín.

ℹ️ Tourist information
- Delegación de Turismo, Avenida San Martín, between Avenida Chaneton and Mayor Torres, on the center strip (21938. Open Mon–Fri 0900–1300 and 1700–2000

⛺ Camping
- Municipal Camping, Avenida Avellaneda, next to rail line

🍴 Eating out
- Restaurant Catalunia, Roca 261
- Restaurant del Gimnasio, Avenida Avellaneda
- Restaurant Don Hector, Zeballos 774. Steakhouse
- Restaurant El Morocho, M Garayta block 100 (corner of Mayor Torres)
- Restaurant Fortabat, Avenida Avellaneda 662
- Restaurant Huincul, Roca 315. Steakhouse
- Restaurant La Singarella, corner of B Houssay and Paraguay
- Restaurant Las Brasas, Avenida Avellaneda. Steakhouse
- Restaurant Odetto's Grill, Ejercito Argentino 445
- Restaurant Pizzería El 55, Ejercito Argentino 648. Pizzeria
- Pizzería Bohemia, San Martín

Key to map
1. Municipalidad
2. Iglesia
3. Post office (Encotel)
4. Telephone (Entel)
5. Tourist information
6. LADE (airline)
7. Hotel Nuevo Pehuen
8. Hostería Coliqueo
9. Hospedaje Huincul
10. Hospedaje Odetto
11. Hospedaje Nevada
12. Residencial Don Hector

Zapala

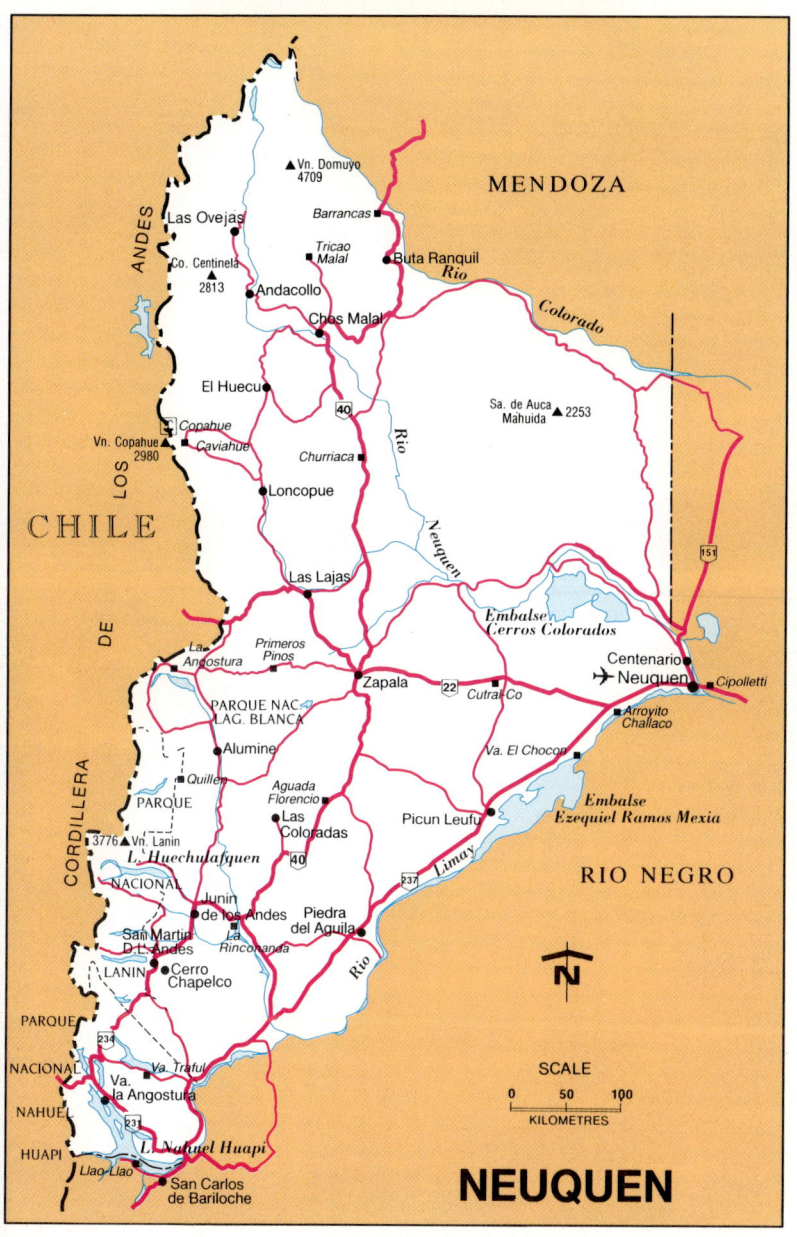

Plate 13
Map of Neuquén Province

Plate 14

Top: San Martín de los Andes
Bottom: Lago Nahuel Huapí, from Isla Victoria

Neuquén Province

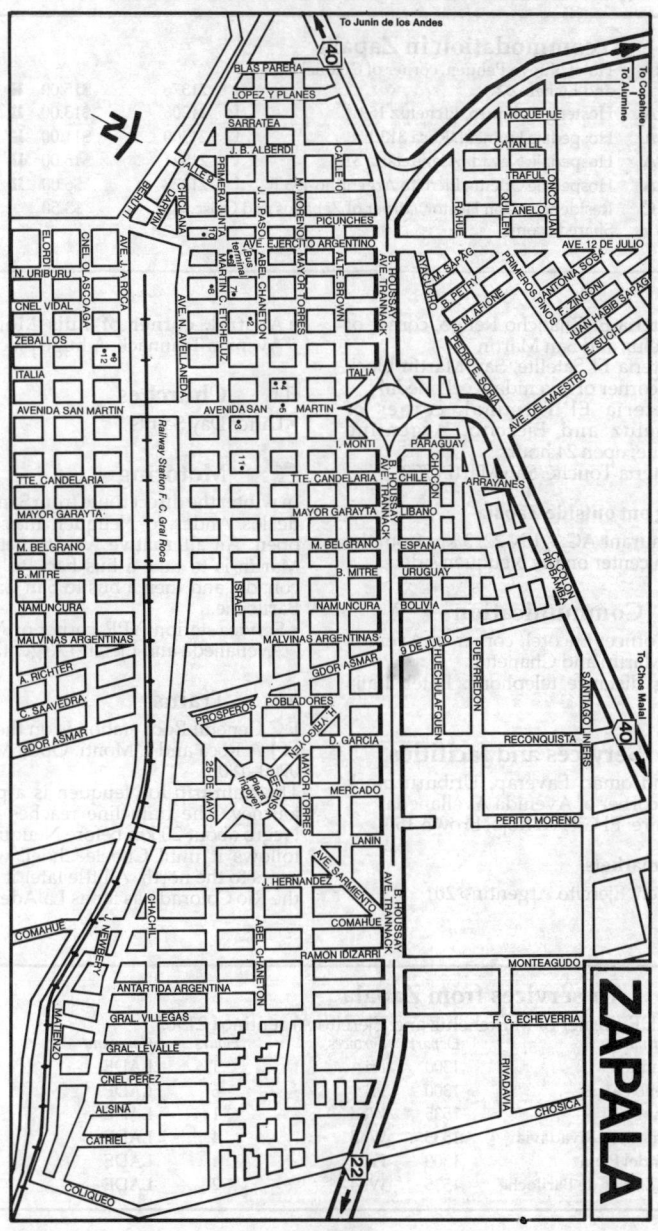

Zapala

NEUQUÉN PROVINCE

🛏 Accommodation in Zapala

★★	Hotel Nuevo Pehuen, corner of Colonel Vidal and Etcheluz	(	21376	$15.00	⚏
A	Hostería Coliqueo, Etcheluz 159	(	21308	$13.00	⚏
A	Hospedaje Huincul, Roca 313	(	21300	$11.00	⚏
A	Hospedaje Nevada, Candelaria 317	(	21321	$15.00	⚏
A	Hospedaje Odetto, Ejercito Argentino 455	(	21328	$6.00	⚏
C	Residencial Don Hector, corner of Zeballos and Olascoaga Shared rooms			$3.50	

- Cafetería El Chancho Rengo, corner of Etcheluz and San Martín
- Cafetería El Satelite, San Martín block 700 (corner of Avenida Avellaneda)
- Cafetería El Terminal, corner of Etcheluz and Ejercito. Argentine cuisine; open 24 hours
- Cafetería Touché, San Martín 773

Eating out outside Zapala

- Restaurant ACA, RN 22, 3 km from the town center on the Neuquén side

📞 Communication

- Post office: Encotel, corner of Avenida San Martín and Chaneton
- Long distance telephone: Entel, Italia 240

🛎 Services and facilities

- Laundromat: Laverap, Uriburu block 400 (corner of Avenida Avellaneda)
- Ski hire: El Ciervo Rojo, Brown 150

Supermarkets

- Ayelen, Ejercito Argentino 201

- Austral, corner of Luis Monti and Avenida Trannack. A huge place

✝ Churches

- Latter Day Saints

🚗 Motoring

In winter the direct route from San Martín de los Andes to Neuquén may not be open. An alternative way to get to San Martín is to take a bus back to La Rinconada, and then a bus to San Carlos de Bariloche.

- Service station: YPF, corner of Avenida Avellaneda and Ejercito Argentino

🚆 Trains

F C General Roca station is on the corner of J A Roca and L Monti. Open Mon–Sat 0900–1800.

The train trip to Neuquén is a pleasant journey. The train line reaches the Río Negro about 20 km before Neuquén, and follows it until Choele-Choel, where it veers to the north. A little later it follows the Río Colorado as far as La Adela.

✈ Air services from Zapala

- LADE, corner of M Etcheluz and Ejercito Argentino (21967

Destination	Depart	Services	Hours	Company
• Neuquén	1300	Fri	1½	LADE
• Buenos Aires	1300	Fri	6	LADE
• Chapelco	1535	Wed	1	LADE
• Comodoro Rivadavia	1535	Wed	4	LADE
• Mar del Plata	1300	Fri	4	LADE
• San Carlos de Bariloche	1535	Wed	2	LADE

Zapala

Neuquén Province

🚌 Buses from Zapala

The bus terminal is on the corner of Etcheluz and Ejercito Argentino. There is a 24-hour cafeteria here, a cloak room, and clean toilets. The staff in the information office is very helpful.

In summer buses to and from Temuco go via Paso Pino Hachado. In winter they go via Paso Puyehue.

Destination	Fare	Depart	Services	Hours	Company
• Neuquén	$6.00		19 services daily	3	El Petroleo, El Valle, Unión del Sud
• Aluminé	$6.00	1400	Mon, Wed, Fri	4	Unión del Sud
• Arroyito	$2.50				
• Bahía Blanca	$12.00	0600	3 services daily	12	El Valle
• Buenos Aires	$24.50	1720	1–2 services daily	19	El Valle, T A Chevallier
• Catriel	$5.00				
• Caviahué Summer only	$12.00				El Petroleo
• Chorriaca	$4.50				
• Chos Malal	$7.00	1400	2 services daily	5	Unión del Sud
• Copahué Summer only	$12.00	0950	daily	3	El Petroleo
• Córdoba	$28.50	1515	daily		TUS
• El Cholar		1400		7	Unión del Sud
• El Huecu	$10.00	1020	2–3 services daily	10	El Petroleo, Unión del Sud
• Junín de los Andes	$8.00	1315	2 services daily	8	El Petroleo
• Lago Moquehue Summer only	$7.50	0700	daily except Mon	4	Unión del Sud
Return trip	$7.50	2000	daily except Mon	4	Unión del Sud
• Laguna Blanca	$5.00	1400	Mon, Wed Fri		Unión del Sud
Return trip	$5.00	0800	Tues, Thurs, Sat		Unión del Sud
• Las Lajas	$1.20	0950	daily	1	El Petroleo
• Las Ovejas		1400	Mon, Wed, Sat	8	Unión del Sud
• Loncopue	$3.50	0950	daily	2	El Petroleo
• Malargüe		1800	Thurs		TAC
• Mendoza		1800	Thurs	18	TAC
• Moquehue	$6.00	0700	Mon, Wed, Sat	5	Unión del Sud
• Primeros Pinos Summer only	$3.00	0700	daily except Mon		Unión del Sud
• San Carlos de Bariloche	$12.00	0530	1–2 services daily	12	El Valle, TAC
• San Martín de los Andes	$8.00	0230	3 services daily	5	El Petroleo
• Santa Rosa (La Pampa province)	$14.50	1400	Mon, Thurs		TUS
• Tricao Malal	$8.50	1400	Tues	7	Unión del Sud
• Temuco (Chile)	$15.00	0400	Mon–Sat	7	Igi Llaimi, Ruta Sur, Unión del Sud
Returns Tues–Sun					
• Viedma		1445	daily		El Valle
• Villa Traful	$8.00			5	

315

Zapala

NEUQUÉN PROVINCE

- Neuquén: First class $3.00, tourist class $2.50; departs daily; 5 hours
- Bahía Blanca: First class $10.00, tourist class $7.50; departs daily
- Buenos Aires: "La Estrella del Valle"; first class $23.30, tourist class $17.50; 25 hours

Tours
- Alvarez International, Avenida A Trannack 1440 (21376

Shopping
- The ceramics school here produces high quality ceramics, and some very skillful weaving in the Indian style. Both are for sale
- Artesanías El Ciervo Rojo, Alte Brown 332

Sport
- Fishing: There is good fishing for perch in the **Río Agrio**. At this point the river has lost its salinity because of the number of freshwater streams flowing into it. The best spots are between Arroyo Codihue and Bajada del Agrio
- Shooting: Permits for hunting stag and wild boar can be obtained at Recursos Naturales, corner of Colonel Vidal and Avenida Avellaneda. A permit for the season costs $25.00

Entertainment
- Cabaret, Roca 797

Sightseeing
- Museo Profesor Dr Augusto Olsacher is a wonderful geology museum, with a priceless collection of minerals, fossils, shells, and rocks. Its collection attracts many experts from foreign countries. Among the prize exhibits is the complete crocodile-like jaw of a species of dinosaur called the peyrosaurus, which roamed the wetlands of Argentina 80-odd million years ago. There is also a fossilized fish from the Silurian era whose scales are impregnated with copper, and part of a meteorite found in Moravia

Excursions
- **Parque Nacional Laguna Blanca**: 30 km eastwards on RP 46, which passes through the southern part of the park. This park was established to protect the rare black-necked swans which live here. The area covers a vast 11 250 ha, most of which comprises volcanic flats. There is a biological research station and an observation post here, but the place is serene and undisturbed. The land further back from the lake is rather dry, and the flora consists mostly of low bushes and thorny plants. Rushes grow around the perimeter of the lake
- **Primeros Pinos**: 45 km westwards on RP 13. This is a recently developed skiing resort. The road is sealed all the way to Primeros Pinos. See Primeros Pinos on page 299
- San Martín de los Andes: See "Excursions" to Zapala in San Martín de los Andes on page 307

Zapala

Río Negro Province

Plate 15 Map of Río Negro Province
- 319 Balneario Las Grutas
- 320 Catriel
- 320 Cerro Catedral
- 321 Choele-Choel
- 322 Cipolletti
- 322 El Bolsón
- 325 Llao Llao
- 325 Parque Nacional Nahuel Huapí
- 326 Puerto Pañuelo
- 327 Río Colorado
- 327 San Antonio Oeste
- 329 San Carlos de Bariloche
- 331 Map
- 352 Viedma
- 353 Map

Río Negro shares borders with Chubut to the south, Neuquén to the west, La Pampa to the north, and Buenos Aires province to the north-east. In the south-east the **Golfo San Matias**, with its 400 km of beaches, opens onto the Atlantic Ocean.

The capital of Río Negro is **Viedma**, located some 970 km south of Buenos Aires.

Geographically the province can be divided into four distinct zones. These are, from east to

Río Negro Province

west: the coastal zone, the tableland, the pre-Cordillera, and the high Cordillera. Although most of the Atlantic coast consists of fine beaches, with the exception of those located near major settlements (Viedma, San Antonio Oeste, and **Punta Colorada**) they are not accessible. Near **San Antonio Oeste** the 45 km strip of white sandy beach is popular for skindiving. The Atlantic coast from **Balneario Bahía Rosas creek** southwards has good spots for scuba diving and spear fishing. The best time for fishing is from November to February. In the summer months beware of the schools of sharks that come south with the warm currents.

The interior of the province is part of the Patagonian Plateau, a vast dry stretch of land with small salt lakes and some canyons, where the rainfall is scanty and few rivers reach the sea. But the area has not always been desert. Millions of years ago it was forested with huge araucaria-like trees. However, a sudden and violent change to the earth's surface turned the climate of this area from subtropical to dry and caused volcanic eruptions which covered the forests. Nowadays the petrified wood found in the tablelands bears witness to the exuberant growth of the past. There are many archeological sites, mostly rock paintings in caves. Iron ore has been found near **Sierra Grande**, and a pelletizing plant converts the crushed ore into concentrates which are shipped through Punta Colorada. There are trout and salmonoids in the rivers and lakes and fishing is permitted from November onwards.

Further to the west in the pre-Andean is some of the most beautiful lake scenery in the world. Most of the lakes are navigable, and include **Lago Nahuel Huapí**, **Lago Mascardi**, **Lago Gutierrez**. Here are some of the best-known tourist centers of Argentina, such as **San Carlos de Bariloche** and **El Bolsón**. In winter these are skiing centers. This is good hiking country with many *refugios* available to the mountaineer. The main crest of the Andes forms the border with Chile.

For most of the year the climate is harsh in the interior of Río Negro. In the Patagonian tableland the temperature in winter can drop as low as –30 °C and in summer soar to 40 °C near the coast. The lowest temperature near the coast is –7 °C. Snowfalls are greatest in the Andean zone with up to 5000 mm annually, declining to 300 mm near the coast. The flora and fauna reflect this range of climatic conditions. The Patagonian forests in the high mountains gradually give way to savanna and then to a vegetation adapted to more desert-like conditions. Consequently the animal life also varies. The ostriches living in the mountain areas in the north-east are bigger than their counterparts in the tablelands. Pampas deer, condors, and pumas have

RÍO NEGRO PROVINCE

almost completely disappeared in the *meseta* and are now mostly found in the sierras to the north and west. *Guanacos*, *maras* ("Patagonian hares") and ostriches are plentiful and can frequently be seen from the highways. European hares and foxes have been introduced. Near **Punta Bermeja**, 60 km southeast of Viedma, is a Reserva Faunística (Animal Reserve) with a seal colony which totals about 3000 animals, the largest influx being in spring when the mating season starts. Sea lions, sea elephants, and the occasional whale can also be seen. Birdlife is well-represented by numbers of noisy *loros barranqueros* which nest in the rocky promontories. A further reserve, at **Caleta de los Loros** 125 km south-east of Viedma, also has a seal colony, albeit not as large as that at Punta Bermeja. Here the main attraction is the birdlife which feeds on the rich marine life found in this part of the Atlantic. The occasional sea lion visits in spring. The reserve is a research station which studies the habits of migratory birds in conjunction with other similiar research stations in North America.

The province is one of the major fruit producers of Argentina, and most of the orchards are on the banks of the 760 km **Río Negro**.

The pre-Hispanic inhabitants were called Tehuelches. They were hunters and fishers who roamed the pampas for approximately 10 000 years. By the time the Spaniards arrived these original inhabitants had been absorbed by Araucanians coming from the west. This admixture produced a very bellicose population which fiercely resisted the Spanish advance. With the introduction of the horse by the Spaniards the tribes became horse riders. The only continuous European settlement surviving from 1779 onwards was the urban nucleus of Viedma–Carmen del Patagonés. It was an isolated settlement as the only communication possible was by sea. By 1885 the Argentine army had completed its conquest of the desert and the resistance of the indigenous people was broken, and Patagonia was opened up for European immigrants on a large scale.

BALNEARIO LAS GRUTAS

Distance from San Antonio Oeste: 20 km southwards on RP 2

The seaside resort of Balneario Las Grutas (often referred to simply as Las Grutas), south of San Antonio Oeste on the **Golfo San Matias**, was developed in the 1960s. Its safe sandy beaches attract many visitors during the summer. The resort is open from December to March only, and is closed for the rest of the year.

Río Negro Province

🛏 Accommodation in Balneario Las Grutas

B	Hospedaje Antares, Pomona 864 (corner of Villa Regina) ℂ 97026	$6.00 ℹ
B	Hospedaje Choele Choel, Pichi Mahuida 849 (corner of Bariloche)	$6.00 ℹ
B	Hospedaje El Pobre Gaucho, Avenida Bariloche 842 (corner of Huergo) ℂ 97011	$6.00 ℹ
B	Hospedaje Las Grutas, Lamarque 871 (corner of Viedma)	$6.00 ℹ
B	Hospedaje Pekito, corner of Mainque and Huergo ℂ 97068	
B	Hospedaje Solana del Mar, corner of Avenida Costanera and Pomona	
B	Hospedaje Solmar, RP 2, on the access road to Las Grutas	$6.00 ℹ
★	Cabañas La Tour du Golfe, Avenida Bariloche 849 ℂ 97039	
★	Cabañas Unidad Turística ACA, Avenida Bariloche 85 (corner of Costanera)	

ℹ Tourist information
- Delegación Provincial de Turismo ℂ 97064

🅰 Camping
- La Entrada, access road to Las Grutas

🍴 Eating out
- Restaurant Bariloche, corner of Avenida Bariloche and Pomona. Steak house
- Restaurant Retorno II, corner of Avenida Costanera and Catriel
- Restaurant Sociedad Italiana, corner of Avenida Bariloche and Huergo
- Restaurant Vago's, corner of Pomona and El Bolsón
- Cafetería Arpeak, corner of Allen and Mainque
- Cafetería Jonoe's, corner of Pomona and Villa Regina

✉ Post and telegraph
- Post office: Encotel, Centro Municipal de Turismo
- Telephone: Entel, Centro Municipal de Turismo

🎭 Entertainment
- Disco Chimocha, corner of Avenida Bariloche and Allen
- Disco Status, corner of Allen and Mainque

CATRIEL

Postal code: 8307 • ℂ area code: (0943)
Distance from Neuquén: 130 km northwards on RN 151

Catriel is located on the **Río Colorado** in the northern part of the province.

🚌 Buses
- Mendoza: Departs 2330 daily; 11 hours; Empresa El Alto Valle
- Neuquén: Departs daily; 2½ hours: Empresa Andesmar, Empresa El Petroleo

CERRO CATEDRAL

Postal code: 8401
Distance from San Carlos de Bariloche: 24 km eastwards

Cerro Catedral is one of the most important skiing centers in Argentina. It is situated only 25 km west of San Carlos de Bariloche, with ample means of transport to and from the city. There are 32

Balneario Las Grutas

Río Negro Province

ski-lifts which can cope with 18 000 skiers per hour, 60 km of downhill ski runs, 15 km of cross-country skiing, and 400 skiing instructors. There are also snow-making machines, just in case the snow is late. The skiing season runs from mid-June to the end of September.

A weekly ski-lift ticket costs $65.00.

The Cerro Catedral area has accommodation for 1000 guests. Accommodation and most restaurants are at Villa Cerro Catedral, at the base of Cerro Catedral.

Skiing equipment may be hired from Nestor Ski or Carlos Oertle.

Tourist information
Parques Nacionales have an information center at the base of Cerro Catedral.

Accommodation
Hotels are open all year round, but prices increase during the skiing season.
- ★★★★ Hotel Catedral, Villa Cerro Catedral ✆ 22322 $21.00
- ★★★ Hotel Daulaghiri, Villa Cerro Catedral ✆ 25636 $17.00
- Hotel Pire Hue, Villa Catedral
- ★★★ Hostería del Cerro, Villa Cerro Catedral ✆ 22181 $17.00
- ★★★ Hostería de la Villa, Villa Cerro Catedral ✆ 26282 $17.00

Eating out
There are a few restaurants and cafeterias on the ski slopes at Refugio Lynch.
- Restaurant Catedral, Villa Cerro Catedral
- Restaurant del Cerro, Villa Cerro Catedral
- Restaurant Plaza Oertle, Villa Cerro Catedral. Steakhouse
- Restaurant Snowbar, Villa Cerro Catedral
- Cafetería Pire Hue, at the foot of Cerro Catedral
- Cafetería Punta Princesa, Cerro Catedral
- Cafetería Ski Ranch, at the foot of Cerro Catedral. Open all year; disco

Buses
Buses run regularly to the base of the ski-lifts from San Carlos de Bariloche.

Sport
There is an ice skating rink, where ice hockey is also played.

Excursions
Lifts operate all year round and walks can be made in the upper mountain regions. Hikes in the area are organized by the Club Andino Bariloche.

CHOELE-CHOEL

Postal code: 8360 • ✆ area code: (0946)
Distance from Neuquén: 182 km eastwards on RN 22

Choele-Choel is situated on the **Río Negro**. The town was officially founded in 1879 by Colonel Villegas, although it was mentioned during General Rosas' desert campaign in 1833.

The area is irrigated and produces large quantities of fruit. The Río Negro divides here to create the large island of **Isla Choele-Choel Grande**. The canal which carries water to San Antonio Oeste on the Atlantic coast starts here. There is good *pejerrey* fishing in the river.

🛏 Accommodation
- Hotel Rucantu, Republica del Uruguay 10. ACA members 10% discount
- Motel ACA, RN 22 Km 1006, on edge of town 🍴

⛺ Camping
- Municipal camp site beside Río Negro. No facilities

🚌 Buses
- Neuquén: Depart daily; 4½ hours; Empresa Andesmar

🚗 Motoring
- Service station: ACA, at the intersection of RN 22 and RN 250

CIPOLLETTI

Postal code: 8324 • (area code: (0943) •
Altitude: 265 m
Distance from Neuquén: 3 km eastwards on RN 22

Cipolletti is located on the **Río Negro** near its junction with the **Río Limay**. It was founded in 1903 and named after an engineer who spent most of his time looking for suitable places to construct dams to irrigate the fertile land. The town is the center of a huge irrigated fruit-growing area which produces apples and pears. The bridge which connects it with the neighboring city of Neuquén has become a real bottleneck during peak-hour traffic.

ℹ Accommodation
- Motel Cipolletti (ACA), corner of RN 22 and Avenida L Toschi (71827

$ Financial
- Banco de Credito, Yrigoyen 498. Cash advances on Visa card

🛠 Services and facilities
- Laundromat: Laverap, Roca 521

🚌 Buses
- Catriel: Departs daily; 2 hours; Empresa Alto Valle
- Mendoza: Departs daily; 13½ hours; Empresa Alto Valle
- Neuquén: Departs daily; ½ hour; Empresa Alto Valle

🚗 Motoring
- Service station: ACA, corner of Luis Toschi and RN 22

📷 Sightseeing
- Museo Ameghino, Yrigoyen 1047

EL BOLSÓN

Postal code: 8430 • area code: (0944) •
Population: 15 000
Distances
- From San Carlos de Bariloche: 125 km southwards on RN 258
- From Esquel: 156 km northwards on RN 40 then RN 258

El Bolsón is located in the southwestern part of Río Negro province, almost on the border with Chubut province and not far from the Chilean border, only 12 km from **Parque Nacional Lago Puelo** in Chubut province. Over the last decade or so it has developed into a substantial tourist resort in summer, and to a lesser degree, in winter as well.

The town is located in a wide valley surrounded by spectacular mountain scenery, in an area that invites the hiker. There are waterfalls everywhere and good fishing for trout and salmon in the clear mountain streams. This is orchard country where strawberries, cherries, and walnuts are grown, and it is also a center of hop production.

Excursions are possible to **San Carlos de Bariloche**, and **Lago Epuyen** is within half an hour's drive.

The summer season runs from January to the middle of March.

Festivals
- Fiesta del Lupulo (Hop Festival): first week of February

Tourist information
- Dirección Municipal de Turismo, corner of San Martín and Roca, on the Plaza Pagano (92204. Open daily 0900–2000. Sketch maps for walks available
- Club Andino Piltriquitron, corner of Avenida Sarmiento and Roca. Not always open

Camping
- El Sol, Balneario. $2.00 per person per tent

Camping outside El Bolsón
- Camping El Bolsón, RN 258, 2 km from town. $2.00 per person per tent
- Lago Puelo, 18 km south off main road. $2.00 per person per tent. Views across the lake to **Cerro Tres Pico**
- Mallin Ahogado, 12 km north off main highway
- Río Azul, 7 km west. $2.00 per person per tent

Accommodation in El Bolsón
Accommodation can be difficult to find during the high season.

★★	Hotel Arrayanes, San Martín	$20.00	ii
	Hotel Piltriquitron, corner of Avenida San Martín 2748 and Roca	$5.00	i
★★	Hostería Amancay, San Martín 3217 (corner of Hernandez) (92222	$13.00	ii
	Hostería La Posada de Hamelin, Intendente Granollers 2179	$10.00	ii
	Hostería Steiner, San Martín 70 (92224	$4.50	i
	Hostería Villa Turismo, RN 258 south	$3.50	i
	Residencial El Bolsón, Angel del Agua 364 (92594 Shared bathroom	$3.50	i
	Residencial Lostra, Sarmiento 3212 (corner of Hernandez)	$6.00	i
	Private accommodation: Szaniuk, RN 258 South	$4.00	i
	Private accommodation: Roberto Bobadilla, San Martín 1119	$4.00	i
	Private accommodation: Buchi family, Almirante O'Connor	$4.00	i
	Private Accommodation: Salinas, Roca Shared bathroom	$4.00	i
	Cabañas Paco Cruz, Villa Turismo	$20.00	5 persons
	Cabañas Bungalows Ricardo Guerra, Villa Turismo	$20.00	5 persons

Accommodation outside El Bolsón
- Motel La Posta, RN 258, 1 km north (92207 $5.00 i

Río Negro Province

Eating out
- Restaurant Achachay, corner of Avenida San Martín and Belgrano. Steakhouse
- Restaurant Don Diego, Hotel Amancay, Avenida San Martín 3221
- Restaurant La Cocinita, Avenida San Martín. Pizzeria
- Restaurant Lostra, Sarmiento 3212. Pizzeria
- Restaurant Puma, corner of Hube and Avenida San Martín
- Cafetería Candilejas, Hotel Piltriquitron, Avenida San Martín 2748 (corner of Roca)
- Cafetería El Chino, Avenida San Martín 2535. Sandwiches
- Cafetería H G, Galería Amancay, Avenida San Martín
- Cafetería Jauja, Avenida San Martín
- Cafetería Ricar-Dos, corner of Roca and P Moreno
- Cafetería Zulu, corner of Dorrego and Avenida San Martín
- Casa de Té Galés, Villa Turismo, 2 km south. Welsh tearoom

Services and facilities
- Laundromat: Laverap, Paso 425. Open Mon–Sat

Air services
Only small airplanes can land here.
- Esquel: Fare $15.00; departs 1100 Wed; 1 hour; LADE
- Comodoro Rivadavia: Fare $24.00; departs 1100 Wed; 4 hours; LADE
- San Carlos de Bariloche: Fare $11.00; departs 1325 Tues; 1 hour; LADE

Buses
- San Carlos de Bariloche: Fare $4.00; Empresa Don Otto

Motoring
- Service station: ACA, corner of Avenida San Martín and Bolívar

Shopping
El Bolsón is well known for its natural homemade berry jams. Goat yoghurt is also made here.

- Camping equipment: Casa Lirio

Fishing gear
- Casa Funes
- Casa Lirio. Also sells camping gear

Sport
- Skiing: **Cerro Piltriquitron**, 7 km from El Bolsón. The ski-lift was upgraded in 1987. There is a restaurant at the base. Skis and boots can be hired for $4.00 per day from Club Andino Piltriquitron
- Water-skiing: Lago Epuyen and Lago Puelo. Bring your own equipment

Entertainment
- Disco Barrabas, corner of P Moreno and Belgrano. Weekends
- Disco Life. Weekends

Excursions
- **Río Azul**: A 10 km easy hike
- **Lago Puelo**: 15 km south. Admission to the national park is $1.00. *Micros* depart at 0700, 1215, and 1800 and return at 0800, 1300, and 1900. The trip takes about 45 minutes: fare $0.75
- **Hoyo de Epuyén**: 18 km south on the RN 258. Hoyo de Epuyén can be reached by *micros* which run every Mon, Thurs, and Sat, leaving El Bolsón at 1330 and 1940, and returning from Hoyo de Epuyén at 1430 and 2040. The trip takes about one hour. Fare: $0.75. See also Hoyo de Epuyén on page 377
- **Lago Epuyén**
- Waterfalls in the area include: **Cascada Escondida**, 8 km north on the way to Mallín Ahogado; **Cascada de la Virgen Misionera**, 12 km north near Rinconada de Nahuel Pan; and

El Bolsón

RÍO NEGRO PROVINCE

Cascada Mallín, 12 km north near a camping spot
- **Complejo Invernal Perito Moreno** (Perito Moreno Winter Complex): 7 km north. It is possible to stay the night in the Club Andino Piltriquitron's *refugio*; however it is usually full of *andinistas*, so check beforehand

LLAO LLAO

Postal code: 8409 • area code: 0944
Distance from Bariloche: 24 km northwest on RN 237

Eating out
- Restaurant Amadeus, Avenida Bustillo Km 25
- Restaurant Atalaya, Avenida Bustillo Km 23.5
- Restaurant Il Gabbiano, Avenida Bustillo Km 24
- Cafetería Chez Bellevue, Avenida Bustillo Km 24.5

Buses
There is a regular 24 hour service to San Carlos de Bariloche.

Sport
- Golf: Eighteen hole golf links at Villa Arelauquen, Avenida Bustillo Km 16

PARQUE NACIONAL NAHUEL HUAPÍ

Parque Nacional Nahuel Huapí was created in 1943 and covers about 750 000 ha. It is part of the Patagonian *meseta*, but includes the eastern spurs of the Andes with the **Cerro Tronador** at 3554 m as the highest elevation. The area covered by this park has the largest concentration of lakes in Argentina and is therefore also known as the "lakes district". Wildlife is represented by *pudu* deer (a very rare dwarf variety), stags, and puma.

Tourist information
The park has stations in the following locations: Villa La Angostura, Brazo Blest, Villa Cerro Catedral, Cuyin-Manzano in the Valle Encantado, Lago Fonck, the western section of Lago Gutierrez, Lago Steffen, Isla Victoria, Mascardi, Puyehue, Villarino, Villegas, Huemul, Lago Espejo, and Pampa Linda (on the access road to Cerro Tronador).

Accommodation in Llao Llao

★★★★	Hotel Tunquelen, Avenida Bustillo Km 24	48233	$22.00	
★★★	Apart-Hotel Casablanca, Avenida Bustillo Km 23	48117	$17.00	
★★	Hostería Katy, Avenida Bustillo Km 24	48023	$10.00	
A	Residencial La Posada de La Flor, Avenida Bustillo Km 24.5	48070	$6.50	
★★★	Cabaña El Bouquet, Avenida Bustillo Km 24.4	48113	$17.00	
★★	Cabaña Cumelcan, Avenida Bustillo Km 24		$9.50	
•	Cabaña Nory, Avenida Bustillo Km 24	48284		

RÍO NEGRO PROVINCE

Accommodation
- Hotel Puerto Blest, Lago Nahuel Huapí (25443 (on the San Carlos de Bariloche exchange) The only access is by boat or by trail from Pampa Linda

Accommodation on Lago Gutierrez
- Hostería Los Peraltoches. Open November–March and June–August

Accommodation on Lago Mascardi
★★★ Hotel Tronador, Lago Mascardi $17.00

Accommodation on Lago Gutierrez
★★★ Hotel Los Coihues, Lago Gutierrez (22855 $17.00
★ Hostería Lago Gutierrez, RN 258 Km 15 $6.50

Accommodation on Lago Hess
B Residencial Cinco Lagos, Lago Hess $4.00

Camping
- Camping Lago Gutierrez
- Camping Lago Moreno
- Camping Lago Roca, Cascada Los Alerces
- Camping Las Carpitas, Lago Mascardi
- Camping Parque Doble "W", Lago Gutierrez

Excursions
- "Seven lakes" route: This is the most popular circuit. It covers the northern section of the park and also takes in part of **Parque Nacional Lanin**. The route goes via **Lagos Correntoso**, **Escondido**, **Hermoso**, **Machonico**, **Villarino**, **Falkner**, and **Meliquina**.
- Southern lakes area: The spectacular scenic route to **Lago Mascardi** follows a sealed road which branches off to the south near **Lago Los Moscos** to **Lago Roca** and the **Cascada Los Alerces**. This route can be varied by going west to **Villa Mascardi** on the RN 254 and then on to **Cerro Tronador** and **Glaciar Tronador**

PUERTO PAÑUELO

Postal code: 8409
Distance from San Carlos de Bariloche: 29 km westwards on RN 237

Situated on **Lago Nahuel Huapí** opposite **Isla Victoria**, Puerto Pañuelo is the starting point for all launch excursions on the lake.

Accommodation
Club Mediterranée seems to be about to open the long-closed Hotel Llao Llao.
★★★★ Hotel Tunquelen, Avenida Bustillo Km 24 (48233 $22.00
- Apart Hotel DUT, Avenida Bustillo Km 20.4 (48044

Buses
Buses run to and from San Carlos de Bariloche every 40 minutes.

Water transport
During the summer holidays launches and catamarans are usually very crowded.
The ticket office for catamarans is past the national park kiosk. The entry fee to the national park is $1.50.
The two most popular excursions are to **Puerto Blest** and **Isla Victoria** (with Arrayanes Forest).
Catamarans (which carry names of Río Paraná provinces) have no open deck. Open-deck boats are the MV *Modesta Victoria* and *Don Luis* operated by Turi Sur. All boats have cafeterias.

Parque Nacional Nahuel Huapí

RÍO NEGRO PROVINCE

RÍO COLORADO

Postal code: 8138 • (area code: (0931)
Distance from Viedma: 306 km northwest on RN 250, then northwards on RN 251 and eastwards on RN 22

The town of Río Colorado is in the north-eastern part of the province, on the **Río Colorado** opposite **La Adela** in La Pampa province.

🚌 Buses
- Bahía Blanca: Fare: $2.10; Empresa Don Otto

SAN ANTONIO OESTE

Postal code: 8520 • (area code: (0934) •
Population: 15 000
Distance from Viedma: 173 km westwards on RN 3

San Antonio Oeste is on the **Golfo San Matias**. The first known landing on the spot was made during the voyages of Juan de La Piedra in 1779, but it was not until 1905 that a small settlement began here.

The climate is mild all year round.

A fishing industry is based on shellfish, which is plentiful in these waters. Otherwise it is a summer holiday resort and fairly quiet outside the season. The extensive beaches of **Balneario Las Grutas** are nearby.

🍴 Eating out
- Restaurant Americano, San Martín 742
- Restaurant El Colonial, Motel Colonial, corner of RN 3 and RN 251
- Restaurant El Nautico, corner of San Martín and Costanera
- Restaurant El Patagonico, corner of Mitre and Sarmiento
- Restaurant España, Hospedaje España, corner of Sarmiento and H Yrigoyen
- Restaurant La Vieja Esquina, corner of San Martín and Avellaneda
- Restaurant Olaf, corner of Costanera and Sarmiento

Eating out outside San Antonio Oeste
- Restaurant El Cruce, corner of RN 3 and RN 251

✉ Post and telegraph
- Post office: Encotel, Brown 305
- Telephone: Entel, Pellegrini 295 (corner of Belgrano)

🚗 Motoring
RN 23 westwards to San Carlos de Bariloche is sealed throughout.

🚆 Trains
F C General Roca station is at R Mejia 9.
- Bahía Blanca: First class $6.00, tourist class $5.50; departs Mon–Fri; 10 hours
- Buenos Aires: First class $19.00, tourist class $14.00; departs Mon–Fri; 22 hours

⊕ Tours
- Triton Turismo, San Martín 1282 (21206

🏳 Excursions
- **San Carlos de Bariloche** via **Los Menucos** and **Ingeniero Jacobacci**: RN 23. The first 200 km of the journey is through bush country, which provides fodder for a few cattle, and there are views of the **Salina del Gualicho** salt flats. The drive over the Patagonian *meseta* is fairly monotonous until you reach Ingeniero Jacobacci. From here south-

RÍO NEGRO PROVINCE

🛏 Accommodation in San Antonio Oeste

★★	Motel Colonial, El Cruce (at the intersection of RN 3 and RN 251 🍴			
		(21360, 21047	$9.00	🚿
★	Hostería Huelen, corner of San Martín and Alem		$9.00	🚿
★	Hostería Kandava, corner of Sarmiento 240 and San Martín			
		(21340	$9.00	🚿
★	Hostería Rayen, 9 de Julio 378	(21474	$9.00	🚿
A	Hospedaje Santa Isabel, corner of Moreno 106 and H Yrigoyen			
		(21330	$4.00	🚿
B	Hospedaje El Vasquito, corner of H Yrigoyen and R Mexia			
		(21204	$6.00	🚿
B	Hospedaje España, corner of Sarmiento and H Yrigoyen 🍴			
		(21588	$6.00	🚿
B	Hospedaje Iberia, Sarmiento 241	(21376	$6.00	🚿
B	Hospedaje Premier, corner of H Yrigoyen 609 and Moreno			
		(21323	$6.00	🚿

wards the scenery become more interesting; here the road and the railroad run side by side for most of the way

- **Neuquén**: RP 2 meets the Zapala–Buenos Aires highway at **Choele-Choel**. This is a very monotonous trip until you reach the **Río Negro** at **Pomona**. From Choele-Choel it is 223 km to **Neuquén**, through an unbroken line of groves of small trees which shelter vineyards and orchards. The road follows the Río Negro valley, which through irrigation has been converted into a continuous apple and pear orchard. The 424 km from Neuquén to San Carlos de Bariloche skirts the entire length of the reservoir formed by the **Dique Ezequiel Ramos Mejía**. It then drops over an escarpment to cross the **Río Collón Curá**. The journey can be completed in 11 hours

✈ Air services from San Antonio Oeste

- LADE, corner of H Yrigoyen and Moreno (21500

Destination	Fare	Depart	Services	Hours	Airline
• Viedma	$16.00	1415	Thurs, Fri	1	LADE
• Bahía Blanca	$20.00	1415	Fri	2	LADE
• Buenos Aires (Aeroparque Jorge Newbery)					
	$41.00	1415	Tues, Fri	4	LADE
• Chapelco	$26.00	1255	Mon	5	LADE
• Comodoro Rivadavia					
	$32.00	1335	Thurs	4	LADE
• Mar del Plata	$37.00	1610	Tues	3	LADE
• Neuquén	$20.00	1255	Mon	3	LADE
• San Carlos de Bariloche					
	$27.00	1255	Mon	6	LADE
• Trelew	$19.00	1335	Thurs	1	LADE

San Antonio Oeste

RÍO NEGRO PROVINCE

Buses from San Antonio Oeste

Destination	Fare	Depart	Services	Hours	Company
• Viedma	$3.70	0915	2 services daily	3	T A Mercedes
• Bahía Blanca	$7.00		several services daily		Don Otto
• Buenos Aires	$22.00		several services daily		Don Otto
• Córdoba	$23.50	daily	9		T U P
• Puerto Madryn	$5.50		several services daily		
• San Carlos de Bariloche	$14.00	0730	2 services daily	13	T A Mercedes

- **Balneario Las Grutas**: It is claimed that the waters here are the clearest and most temperate along the Argentine coast. The sandy beach is also perfect for spending leisure hours basking in the sun. The battering of the sea has created huge caverns in the cliffs behind the sandy beach. See Balneario San Grutas on page 319
- **Bajo de Gualicho**: 44 km north of San Antonio Oeste. This depression is 73 m below sea-level. Some salt mining takes place here. As it is in the desert there can be extreme temperature differences between day and night. It is an area where pumas, wild boar, and ostriches can still be seen. There is hunting during the season. The area can be reached by tourist bus

SAN CARLOS DE BARILOCHE

Postal code: 8400 • Population: 80 000
• (area code: (0944) • Altitude: 790 m
Distances
- From Buenos Aires: 1675 km southwards on RN 5 then RN 152 and RN 237
- From Esquel: 310 km northwards on RN 258
- From Neuquén: 460 km southwards on RN 237

San Carlos de Bariloche, commonly known as Bariloche, is located on the southern shore of **Lago Nahuel Huapí**, at the foot of **Cerro Otto**. In the distance to the south are the **Sierra de la Ventana**, 1910 m high. Lago Nahuel Huapí was first mentioned by Capitan Don Francisco de Cesar who launched an expedition to find the town which was supposed to have been there. The Indians living in this area were the Vuriloches (whence the name "Bariloche") and Puelches, who were a very warlike people. From the mid-1600s until 1720 the Jesuits attempted to convert the Indian population to Christianity, but failed owing to the fierce resistance from the Indians. Most of the missionaries, such as Padre N Mascardi, were martyred. After 1720, the area was not visited by outsiders until 1860, when Perito Moreno launched an expedition from Argentina and Cox led a Chilean expedition into the area. This was followed by much unrest, and peace was not restored to the lakes area until the military expeditions (known as the "desert campaigns") under Roca and Villegas. From then onwards Europeans arrived and settled in the lakes area. The first house was built in 1895 by Karl Wiederhold; the city's official foundation date is May 3, 1902.

Bariloche is a picturesque town with steep streets leading up from the lake foreshore. It is the best center from which to explore the Parque Nacional Nahuel Huapí. In the tourist season it can become very crowded, and prices tend to rise. The best time to visit is either spring or fall, to avoid the big rush. Possibly the best months are from March to May, when there are no winds and the temperature is pleasant.

Bariloche can easily be reached from all parts of Argentina. The main road to the coast is sealed and open all year round. The tourist facilities are good with many first-class hotels and cafeterias, restaurants, and nightclubs. It is a summer and winter holiday resort, with a quiet season from March to June.

The main church dominates the town. It was built in 1946, but the interior is so far unfinished.

On top of Cerro Otto, 11 km from the city center, there is a viewing platform with sweeping views over the lake and the Andes.

ℹ️ Tourist information

- Secretaria Municipal de Turismo, Centro Civico ℓ 23022. Open Mon–Sat 0800–2000
- Club Andino Bariloche, 20 de Febrero 30. Open Mon–Fri 0900–1200 and 1500–2000. The club organizes club walks in

Key to Map

1	Municipalidad
2	Iglesia
3	Post office (Encotel)
4	Telephone (Entel)
5	Tourist information
6	Intendencia Parque Nacional Nahuel Huapí
7	Club Andino Bariloche
8	Banco de la Nación
9	Cambio Casa Piano
10	Hotel Aspen Ski
11	Hotel Apartur
12	Hotel Nahuel Huapí
13	Hotel Interlaken
14	Hotel Internacional
15	Hotel Los Andes
16	Hotel Sunset
17	Hotel Tres Reyes
18	Hotel King's
19	Hotel Las Piedras
20	Hotel Ayelen
21	Hotel Carlos V
22	Hotel Colonial
23	Hotel Cristal
24	Hotel Pilmayquen
25	Hotel Premier
26	Hotel Kentton
27	Hotel Andurina
28	Hotel Piuke
29	Hotel Cambria
30	Hotel Quetrihue
31	Hostería Casita Suiza
32	Hostería Miguelito
33	Hotel Sol Bariloche
34	Hotel Tivoli
35	Hostería Puyehue
36	Hostería Nontue
37	Aerolineas Argentinas and LADE
38	Austral

San Carlos de Bariloche

Río Negro Province

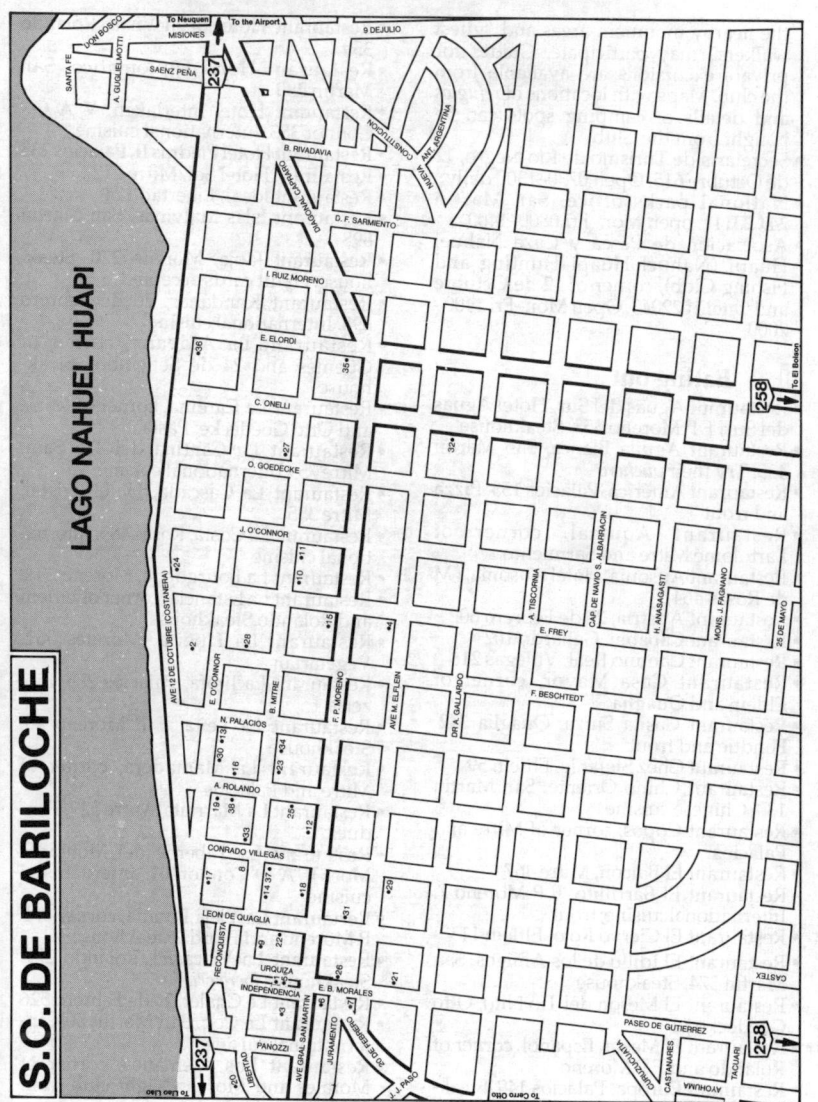

San Carlos de Bariloche

Río Negro Province

the nearby mountain areas and "guest walkers" may participate. Guides for private excursions are available from the club. Maps with locations of *refugios* and details of camping spots can be bought from the Club
- Secretaria de Turismo de Río Negro, 12 de Octubre 615. Open 0730–1300 daily
- National parks office, San Martín 24, ℓ 23111, open Mon–Fri 0800–1400
- Asociación de Pesca y Caza Nahuel Huapí (Nahuel Huapí Hunting and Fishing Club), corner of 12 de Octubre and Onelli ℓ 22043. Open Mon–Fri 1400–2000

🍽 Eating out

- Restaurant Aguas del Sur, Hotel Aguas del Sur, F P Moreno 353. Steakhouse
- Restaurant Aguila Blanca, San Martín 435. Try their *puchero*
- Restaurant América, Palacios 153. Pizza and trout
- Restaurant Aqumal, corner of Bartolomé Mitre and Sarmiento
- Restaurant Ausonia, Hotel Ausonia, J M de Rosas 464
- Restaurant Austria, 20 de Febrero 602
- Restaurant Cababhi, Gallardo 102
- Restaurant Camino Real, Villegas 216
- Restaurant Casa Mayor, corner of Elflein and Quaglia
- Restaurant Casita Suiza, Quaglia 342. Fondue and trout
- Restaurant Chez Stefanie, Elflein 59
- Restaurant Chino Oriente, San Martín 130. Chinese cuisine
- Restaurant Copos, corner of Mitre and Palacios
- Restaurant El Balcón, Mitre 467
- Restaurant El Barrillito, F P Moreno 7. Internationalcuisine; trout
- ☞• Restaurant El Ciervo Rojo, Elflein 115
- Restaurant El Idillo de los Amigos, San Martín 574. Steakhouse
- Restaurant El Mesón del Tío Nito, Otto Goedecke 82
- ☞• Restaurant El Mesón Español, corner of Rolando and F P Moreno
- Restaurant Europa, Palacios 149. Steakhouse
- Restaurant Fogón Criollo, Quaglia 425
- Restaurant Fondue Suiza, San Martín 74
- Restaurant Gran Roma, San Martín 102
- Restaurant Hotel Bella Vista, Rolando 359
- Restaurant Hotel Diplomatico, San Martín 280
- Restaurant Hotel Interlaken, V A O'Connor 383. International cuisine
- Restaurant Hotel Piedras II, Palacios 235
- Restaurant Hotel Sol, Mitre 212
- Restaurant Ideal, Libertad 121
- Restaurant Islas Malvinas, San Martín 898
- Restaurant Jauja, Moreno 220. Steakhouse; credit cards accepted
- Restaurant Kandahar, 20 de Febrero 698. International cuisine
- Restaurant La Aldeana, corner of Güemes and 24 de Setiembre. Steakhouse
- ☞• Restaurant La Cantina, corner of Mitre and Otto Goedecke. Pastas
- Restaurant La Cantina del Tío Sam, Mitre 759. International cuisine
- Restaurant La Cascada, Hotel Cristal, Mitre 355
- Restaurant La Costa, Rosas 485. International cuisine
- Restaurant La Bourgogne, Moreno 23
- Restaurant La Estancia, corner of Elflein and Rolando.Steakhouse
- Restaurant La Huerta, Morales 362. Vegetarian
- Restaurant La Jirafa, Palacios 288. Pizzeria
- Restaurant La Leña, F P Moreno 48. Steakhouse
- Restaurant La Mamadera, corner of Mitre and Palacios
- Restaurant La Marmita, Mitre 329. Fondues
- Restaurant La Taberna del Montanés Mor, V A O'Connor 401. International cuisine
- Restaurant La Vieja Posada, corner of F P Moreno and Elordi. Steakhouse
- Restaurant La Vizcacha, Rolando 279. Steakhouse; *locro criollo*
- Restaurant Le Chalet, 20 de Febrero 526
- Restaurant Le Coq, San Martín 503. International cuisine
- Restaurant Los Alemanes, corner of Morales and Moreno.Night club from 2230 onwards

continued on page 339

San Carlos de Bariloche

Río Negro Province

Accommodation in San Carlos de Bariloche

Hotel prices increase steeply in the skiing season.
The tourist office has an up-to-date price list of hotels, with a town map, and a listing of private homes which offer accommodation.
At the beginning of each season the Officina Municipal de Turismo publishes an up-to-date list of all accommodation available in Bariloche and Llao Llao, with a map and prices.
Bariloche is a high-class tourist resort, and hotels are not confined to the city but spread all the way to Llao-Llao, 24 km to the west along Lago Nahuel Huapí and its inlets.
Therefore for ease of reference accommodation has been grouped as follows:
- City center: From Calle Campichuelo in the west to 9 de Julio in the east as far as the southern part of Calle Anasagasti
- Bariloche west: Avenida de Los Pioneros, from Campichuelo to the Cerro Otto ski-lifts
- Lakeside: Avenida Bustillo, along the lake up to Km 5
- Barrio Melipal: 5 km west beTween Avenida Bustillo and Avenida Los Pioneros
- Central west: Avenida Bustillo, west of Barrio Melipal as far as Km 10
- Puerto Perito Moreno: Avenida Bustillo Km 10
- Outer west: Avenida Bustillo west of Puerto Perito Moreno to Km 23

For accommodation west of Km 23 see "Accommodation" in LlaoLlao on page 325 and in Puerto Pañuelo on page 326

Accommodation in the city center

From Calle Campichuelo in the west to 9 de Julio in the east as far as the southern part of Calle Anasagasti.

★★★★★	Hotel Bariloche Ski Hotel, San Martín 352	(22913	$52.00	
★★★★★	Hotel Edelweiss, San Martín 202	(26165	$39.00	
★★★★	Hotel Apartur, corner of Bartolomé Mitre and O'Connor	(26193	$22.00	
★★★★	Hotel Bella Vista, Rolando 351	(22435	$22.00	
★★★★	Hotel Interlaken, Alte O'Connor 383 (corner of Palacios)			
★★★★	Hotel Meridien, España 351	(26156	$22.00	
★★★★	Hotel Nahuel Huapí, F P Moreno 252	(23088	$22.00	
★★★★	Hotel Sunset, Rolando 132	(26146	$22.00	
★★★★	Hotel Tres Reyes, 12 de Octubre 135	(25177	$22.00	
★★★	Hotel Aconcagua, San Martín 289	(26124	$22.00	
★★★	Hotel Ausonia, Rosas 464	(24718	$17.00	
★★★	Hotel Ayelen, Libertad 157	(25401	$17.00	
★★★	Hotel Carlos V, Morales 426	(23611	$17.00	
★★★	Hotel Colonial, Quaglia 281	(25474	$17.00	
★★★	Hotel Cristal, Bartolomé Mitre 355	(26101	$17.00	
★★★	Hotel del Lago Ski, San Martín 645	(22442	$17.00	
★★★	Hotel El Candil, J M de Rosas 150	(26134	$17.00	
★★★	Hotel Epuyen, Morales 619	(24494	$17.00	
★★★	Hotel Kentton, corner of Morales and F P Moreno	(22148	$17.00	
★★★	Hotel Libertador, San Martín 441	(24583	$17.00	
★★★	Hotel Panamericano, San Martín	(26171	$17.00	
★★★	Hotel Piuke, Beschtedt 136		$17.00	
★★★	Hotel Presidente, San Martín 152	(23044	$17.00	
★★★	Hotel Quetrihue, O'Connor 315		$17.00	
★★★		(22061	$17.00	

San Carlos de Bariloche

Río Negro Province

Accommodation in San Carlos de Bariloche—continued

Accommodation in the city center—continued

★★★	Hotel Roma, San Martín 102	(22204	$17.00	
★★★	Hotel Slalom, Salta 190	(24574	$17.00	
★★★	Hotel Sol Bariloche, Bartolomé Mitre 202	(22507	$17.00	
★★★	Hotel Tivoli, Bartolomé Mitre 383	(26155	$17.00	
★★★	Hotel Torresol, España 462	(22484	$17.00	
★★	Hotel Andino, Palacios 129	(22732	$9.50	
★★	Hotel Aspen Ski, Bartolomé Mitre 651	(25537	$9.50	
★★	Hotel Austral, San Martín 425	(22178	$9.50	
★★	Hotel Concorde, Libertad 131	(24500	$9.50	
★★	Hotel Internacional, Bartolomé Mitre 171	(25938	$9.50	
★★	Hotel King's, F P Moreno 136	(22044	$8.50	
	Cheaper in the off-season			
★★	Hotel Los Andes, F P Moreno 594	(22222	$9.50	
	Shared bathroom		$6.50	
★★	Hotel Las Piedras I, Rolando 127	(26141	$9.50	
★★	Hotel Los Pinos, 20 de Febrero 640	(22823	$10.00	
★★	Hotel Monte Cervino, Ruiz Moreno 211	(23053	$9.50	
★★	Hotel Pilmayquen, 12 de Octubre 701	(26175	$9.50	
★★	Hotel Premier, Rolando 263	(23681	$10.00	
★★	Hotel 7 de Febrero, F P Moreno 534	(22244	$9.50	
★★	Hotel Val Gardena, Rolando 197	(25901	$9.50	
★★	Hotel Venezia, Morales 446	(22407	$9.50	
★	Hotel Aguas del Sur, F P Moreno 353	(22995	$6.50	
★	Hotel Alfil, Elflein 235	(24747	$6.50	
★	Hotel Antartida, Bartolomé Mitre 382	(23195	$6.50	
★	Hotel Arauco, Quaglia 647	(22180	$6.50	
★	Hotel Argentina Libre, Bartolomé Mitre 278		$6.50	
★	Hotel Arrayan, Elflein 1211	(23489	$6.50	
★	Hotel Belle Ville, Tiscornia 862	(23344	$6.50	
★	Hotel Carantania, San Martín 496	(25248	$6.50	
★	Hotel Copahué, V O'Connor 263	(25248	$6.50	
★	Hotel Cottbus, Villegas 444	(25440	$6.50	
★	Hotel El Jabalí, San Martín 130	(22256	$6.50	
	Chinese restaurant			
★	Hotel El Mirador, F P Moreno 658	(22221	$6.50	
★	Hotel Flamingo, Bartolomé Mitre 24	(22334	$6.50	
	Overlooks the lake			
★	Hotel Galería Arrayanes, Bartolomé Mitre 349	(22777	$6.50	
★	Hotel Gran Lago, V O'Connor 431	(22320	$6.50	
★	Hotel Grand Prix, Tiscornia 88	(22589	$6.50	
★	Hotel Gressoney, San Martín 447	(24626	$6.50	
★	Hotel Ideal Bariloche, Libertad 121	(22901	$6.50	
	Cheaper without private bath			
★	Hotel Las Piedras II, Palacios 235	(25594	$6.50	
★	Hotel Madinette, Morales 534	(22561	$6.50	
★	Hotel Marau Limac, 12 de Octubre 655	(25201	$6.50	
	Best views over the lake			
★	Hotel Milán, Beschtedt 120	(22624	$6.50	
	Closed in May			
★	Hotel Pacifico, F P Moreno 335	(23115	$6.50	
★	Hotel Pucón, Rolando 118 and (corner of Bartolomé Mitre)	(26163	$6.50	

San Carlos de Bariloche

RÍO NEGRO PROVINCE

Accommodation in San Carlos de Bariloche—continued

Accommodation in the city center—continued

★	Hotel Punta Nevada, Onelli 337 (corner of Elflein)		
		(24643	$6.50
★	Hotel Quillen, San Martín 415		$6.50
★	Hotel Remy, Bartolomé Mitre 1473	(22059	$6.50
★	Hotel San Fernando, 20 de Febrero 664 (corner of Pasaje Gutierrez)		
		(25150	$6.50
★	Hotel Sodas, 12 de Octubre 1915	(22050	$6.50
●	Hotel Plaza, corner of Bartolomé Mitre and Palacios		
★★★	Hostería Bonaria, Salta 422	(23136	$17.00
★★★	Hostería Godec, 24 de Setiembre 213	(23085	$17.00
★★★	Hostería La Pastorella, Belgrano 125	(24656	$17.00
★★★	Hostería Nontue, 12 de Octubre 969	(25276	$17.00
★★★	Hostería Tirol, Libertad 175	(26152	$17.00
★★	Hostería Aitue, Rolando 141	(22064	$9.50
★★	Hostería Andurina, Bartolomé Mitre 810	(22700	$9.50
★★	Hostería Arco Iris, Belgrano 127	(24656	$9.50
★★	Hostería Cambria, Elfein 183	(22511	$9.50
★★	Hostería Campaña, Belgrano 165	(22162	$9.50
★★	Hostería Casita Suiza, Quaglia 342	(26111	$10.00
★★	Hostería Diplomatic, San Martín 280	(22310	$9.50
★★	Hostería El Nire, O'Connor 94	(23041	$9.50
★★	Hostería Güemes, Güemes 715	(24735, 24785	$9.00
★★	Hostería Lagos del Sur, Quaglia 540	(22077	$9.50
★★	Hostería Las Amapolas, Rosas 598 (corner of España)		
		(22664	$9.50
★★	Hostería La Surena, San Martín 432	(22013	$10.00
★★	Hostería Los Alerces, España 327	(22369	$9.50
★★	Hostería Los Alpes, Diagonal Capraro 1034	(23416	$9.50
★★	Hostería Miguelito, Onelli 459	(26104	$9.50
★★	Hostería Marriott, España 456	(26112, 22561	$9.50
★★	Hostería Miralagos, Salta 514	(22788	$9.50
★★	Hostería Puyehue, Elordi 24	(22196	$9.50
★★	Hostería Quimelen, Gallardo 136	(22501	$9.50
★★	Hostería Quime Quipan, F P Moreno 1103	(22658	$9.50
★★	Hostería Selva Negra, San Martín 555	(24532	$9.00
★★	Hostería Split, corner of Gallardo and Frei		$9.50
★★	Hostería Sur, Beschtedt 101	(22677	$10.00
★★	Hostería Suyai, 12 de Octubre 855	(22726	$9.50
	View over the lake		
★	Hostería Abedules, Salta 375		$6.50
★	Hostería Americana, Juramento 182	(22710	$6.50
★	Hostería Bariloche, Quaglia 338	(26161	$6.50
★	Hostería Cabaghi, Quaglia 490	(22697	$6.50
★	Hostería Caprí, Tucumán 309	(25832	$6.50
★	Hostería Don Jacinto, Gallardo 946	(22890	$6.50
★	Hostería El Aguila, San Martín 435	(22423	$6.50
★	Hostería El Alcazar, Rolando 65	(25127	$6.50
★	Hostería El Manantial, 20 de Febrero 470	(22070	$6.50
★	Hostería El Radal, 24 de Setiembre 46	(22551	$6.50 [A]
★	Hostería El Viejo Aljibe, Frey 571	(23316	$6.50
★	Hostería Gracy Luz, Villegas 148	(23011	$6.50
★	Hostería Ivalu, Frey 535	(23237	$6.50

San Carlos de Bariloche

Río Negro Province

Accommodation in San Carlos de Bariloche—continued

Accommodation in the city center—continued

★	Hostería La Fontana, Saavedra 689 (corner of Plaza Belgrano) ▣	(22471	$6.50	♦
★	Hostería La Paleta del Pintor, 20 de Febrero 620 (corner of Pasaje Gutierrez)	(22220	$6.50	♦
★	Hostería Millaray, Libertad 195 ⑪▲ *Parrilla* restaurant	(22229	$6.50	♦
★	Hostería Munich, Tucumán 21	(22091	$6.50	♦
★	Hostería Nikola, Elflein 45	(22500	$6.50	♦
★	Hostería Panoramico, F P Moreno 645 Recommended	(23468	$6.50	♦
★	Hostería Portofino, Morales 439	(22795	$6.50	♦
★	Hostería Ruca Cheli, 24 de Setiembre 275	(24528	$6.50	♦
★	Hostería San Jorge, 20 de Febrero 549	(22032	$6.50	♦
★	Hostería San Remo, San Martín 457	(24628	$6.50	♦
★	Hostería Tejas Rojas, 20 de Febrero 526	(22956	$6.50	♦
B	Hospedaje Casa Fliz, Rosas 198	(22865	$4.00	♦
B	Hospedaje Mirador, F P Moreno 658 German spoken; views of the lake	(22221	$4.00	♦
B	Hospedaje Nahuel, Gallardo 454	(22552	$4.00	♦
B	Hospedaje/Residencial Matterhorn, Gutierrez 1122 German spoken	(22768	$4.00	♦
B	Hospedaje Victoria, Bartolomé Mitre 815 In back yard	(22220	$4.00	♦
A	Residencial Adquintue, V O'Connor 766	(22084	$5.00	♦
A	Residencial Alpino, Tiscornia 90	(24841	$5.00	♦
A	Residencial Andrea, Goedecke 443 ▣			♦
A	Residencial Arequepay, Palacios 276	(25774	$5.00	♦
A	Residencial Consular, San Martín 422	(25818	$5.00	♦
A	Residencial Continental, Diagonal Capraro 1398		$5.00	♦
A	Residencial Costa del Lago, 12 de Octubre 955	(25384	$5.00	♦
A	Residencial El Ciervo Rojo, Elflein 115 ▣	(23810	$5.00	♦
A	Residencial El Esquiador, Neumeyer 34	(22153	$5.00	♦
A	Residencial Elizabeth, J J Paso 117 German spoken	(24853	$5.00	♦
A	Residencial Huechu Ruca, F P Moreno 816 ▣	(22366	$5.00	♦
A	Residencial La Casa de Nogueira, Elflein 205	(23648	$5.00	♦
A	Residencial Lago Azul, Bartolomé Mitre 1361	(23407	$5.00	♦
A	Residencial Lila, Rolando 494		$5.00	♦
A	Residencial Olimpia, San Martín 950	(25194	$5.00	♦
A	Residencial Pehuen, Gallardo 360	(22633	$5.00	♦
A	Residencial Pequena Germania, Quaglia 425	(25288	$5.00	♦
A	Residencial Posta Alpina, Goedecke 62	(24437	$5.00	♦
A	Residencial Río Manso, Tiscornia 465	(23325	$5.00	♦
A	Residencial San Francisco, 20 de Febrero 493⑪		$5.00	♦
A	Residencial Tanahuen, Bartolomé Mitre 1647	(23398	$5.00	♦
A	Residencial Tito, V O'Connor 745	(24039	$5.00	♦
A	Residencial Zagreb, Quaglia 546 ▣	(22022	$5.00	♦
B	Residencial Adonay, San Martín 298	(25306	$4.00	♦

RÍO NEGRO PROVINCE

Accommodation in San Carlos de Bariloche—continued

Accommodation in the city center—continued

B	Residencial Belgrano, Güemes 648	23164	$4.00	
B	Residencial Cerro Villegas, Sáenz Peña 140	22773	$4.00	
B	Residencial Continental, Diagonal Capraro 1398	22087	$4.00	
B	Residencial Cuenca Lacustre, Anasagasti 845	23886	$4.00	
B	Residencial Cumelen, San Martín 580	24846	$4.00	
B	Residencial Dakana, Tacuari 95	22458	$4.00	
B	Residencial del Nahuel, San Martín 157		$4.00	
B	Residencial Elly, Pje. Gutierrez 65	22745	$4.00	
B	Residencial El Malagueno, Onelli 469	23445	$4.00	
B	Residencial La Luna, San Martín 519	22088	$4.00	
B	Residencial Los Olmos, Rivadavia 1187 (South)		$4.00	
B	Residencial Martín, 20 de Febrero 555	22055	$4.00	
B	Residencial Monte Grande, 25 de Mayo 1544 (South)		$4.00	
B	Residencial Nahuel, Gallardo 454	22552	$4.00	
B	Residencial Nogare, Elflein 58	22438	$4.00	
B	Residencial Peumayen, Bartolomé Mitre 106	22580	$4.00	
B	Residencial Roschec, Elflein 533	22645	$4.00	
B	Residencial Ruca 419, Elflein 419	22914	$4.00	
B	Residencial San Marco, Rolando 530 (through the yard)	23608	$4.00	
B	Residencial Topa Topa, 20 de Junio 530	24684	$4.00	
B	Residencial Torres, Tiscornia 747	23355	$4.00	
B	Residencial Wicriser, Arrayanes 270	24888	$4.00	
B	Residencial Wikter, Güemes 566	23248	$4.00	

- Residencial Antares, Güemes 763
- Residencial Aquumal, corner of Bartolomé Mitre and Sarmiento
- Residencial Bonaria, corner of Salta and Güemes
- Residencial Nevada, corner of Rolando and F P Moreno
- Private accommodation: Arriagada family, Gallardo 1025
  - 22296 $4.00
- Private accommodation: Lamaison family, John O'Connor 1481
  - 23229 $4.00
- Private accommodation: Nordestion family, Morales 430
  - 22421 $4.00
- Private accommodation: Señora Alicia Chavez de Perez, Anasagastí 840
  - 22360 $7.80

Accommodation in Bariloche west

Avenida de los Pioneros, from Campichuelo to the Cerro Otto ski-lifts.

★★★★	Hotel El Monasterio, Avenida de los Pioneros Km 4.6	24885	$22.00	
★	Hotel Edelil, Avenida de los Pioneros Km 4	23016	$6.50	
★★★	Hostería del Prado, Avenida de los Pioneros Km 4.5	22122	$17.00	
★★★	Hostería Las Vertientes, Avenida de los Pioneros Km 2.3	23341	$17.00	

San Carlos de Bariloche

RÍO NEGRO PROVINCE

Accommodation in San Carlos de Bariloche—continued

Accommodation in San Carlos de Bariloche west—continued

★	Hostería La Danesa, Avenida de los Pioneros Km 4			
		ℓ 24918	$6.50	ⓘ
★★★	Cabaña del Esquiador, Avenida de los Pioneros Km 8			
		ℓ 22408	$17.00	ⓘ
★★★	Cabaña Los Arcos, Avenida de los Pioneros Km 3.3		$17.00	ⓘ
★★★	Cabaña Torres Blancas, Avenida de los Pioneros Km 7.5		$17.00	ⓘ
★★★	Cabaña Tucapel, Avenida de los Pioneros Km 4.2			
		ℓ 23574	$17.00	ⓘ
★★	Cabaña del Faldeo, Avenida de los Pioneros Km 8			
		ℓ 23339	$9.50	ⓘ
★★	Cabaña Quila Leufu, Avenida de los Pioneros Km 4			
		ℓ 23283	$9.50	ⓘ
★	Cabaña Ojo De Agua, Avenida de los Pioneros Km 5		$6.50	ⓘ
•	Cabaña del Bosque, Avenida de los Pioneros Km 4.5			
		ℓ 23977		
•	Private accommodation: Señora Carlota Baumann, Avenida de los Pioneros 860			
		ℓ 24502	$4.00	ⓘ

Breakfast $1.00; kitchenette; free pickup from buses; English and German spoken

Lakeside

Avenida Bustillo, along the lake up to Km 5.

★★★	Hotel Huemul, Bustillo Km 1.5 ⛽	ℓ 22181	$17.00	ⓘ
★	Hotel Parque, Bustillo Km 1	ℓ 22316	$6.50	ⓘ
A	Residencial Cari Hue, Bustillo Km 5.2	ℓ 22420	$5.00	ⓘ
★	Cabaña El Yeti, Bustillo Km 5.6		$6.50	ⓘ
★	Cabaña Las Gaviotas, Bustillo Km 5.3		$6.50	ⓘ
•	Cabaña Los Retamos, Bustillo Km 5.2			

Accommodation in Barrio Melipal

Five km west, between Avenida Bustillo and Avenida de los Pioneros.

★★★	Hostería La Negra, Barrio Melipal		$17.00	ⓘ
★★	Hostería Lonquimay, Lonquimay 3672		$9.50	ⓘ
★	Hostería Alondra, Boock 199 (Melipal)	ℓ 22863	$6.50	ⓘ
★	Hostería Caballito Blanco, Copahué 4191	ℓ 22993	$6.50	ⓘ
★	Hostería Cristina, corner of Lanin and Boock	ℓ 25372	$6.50	ⓘ
★	Hostería Villa Encanto, Copahué 3459	ℓ 24913	$6.50	ⓘ
★	Hostería Villa Sokol, corner of Belgrano and Roca			
		ℓ 24076	$6.50	ⓘ
★	Cabaña El Manganga, Catedral 3343	ℓ 24943	$6.50	ⓘ
★	Cabaña Palito's, Tronador	ℓ 25084	$6.50	ⓘ
•	Cabaña Cecines, Melipal	ℓ 22888		
•	Cabaña Nelipeni, Barrio Melipal			

Accommodation in the central west

Avenida Bustillo, west of Barrio Melipal as far as Km 10.

★★★	Hotel del Viejo Molino, Bustillo Km 6.2	ℓ 22411	$17.00	ⓘ
★★★	Hostería del la Luna, Bustillo Km 7.5	ℓ 25720	$17.00	ⓘ
★★★	Hostería Hipocambo, Bustillo Km 7.2	ℓ 22181	$17.00	ⓘ
B	Residencial Los Celtas, Bustillo Km 6.5		$4.00	ⓘ

San Carlos de Bariloche

Accommodation in San Carlos de Bariloche—continued

Accommodation in the central west—continued

★★★	Cabaña San Isidro, Bustillo Km 5.8	✆ 23718	$17.00	🛏
★★	Cabaña del Catedral, Bustillo Km 8.6		$9.50	🛏
★★	Cabaña del Cruce, Bustillo Km 8.7		$9.50	🛏
★★	Cabaña La Cebra, Bustillo Km 7		$9.50	🛏
★★	Cabaña Peters, Bustillo Km 6	✆ 25720	$9.50	🛏
★	Cabaña Araucaria, Bustillo Km 8		$6.50	🛏
★	Cabaña Vuchalafquen Lien, Bustillo Km 7.2		$6.50	🛏
•	Cabaña Chiquilquen, Bustillo Km 7.5			
•	Cabaña Sumajohe, Bustillo Km 8.5	✆ 22220		

Accommodation in Puerto Perito Moreno

Avenida Bustillo Km 10.

★★★★	Hotel El Casco, Bustillo Km 11 🏨 German spoken	✆ 22532	$22.00	🛏
★	Hotel Altamira Del Lago, Bustillo Km 10.5	✆ 26130	$6.50	🛏
★★	Hostería Pajaro Azul, Bustillo Km 11 ✉	✆ 24131	$10.00	🛏
★★	Cabaña Nahuel Malal, Bustillo Km 12.4		$9.50	🛏
★	Cabaña Lisis, Bustillo Km 12.4		$6.50	🛏
•	Cabaña El Tigre, Bustillo Km 12.4			
•	Cabaña Nahuel-Có, Bustillo Km 12.4	✆ 25480		

Accommodation in the outer west

Avenida Bustillo west of Puerto Perito Moreno to Km 23.

★★★	Hostería Valle del Sol, Bustillo Km 18	✆ 48353	$17.00	🛏
B	Residencial Los Notros, Bustillo Km 20		$4.00	🛏
★★	Cabaña Playa Serena, Bustillo Km 13.1	✆ 22015	$9.50	🛏
★	Cabaña del Trebol, Bustillo Km 18	✆ 48072	$6.50	🛏
★	Cabaña Pichi Ruca, Bustillo Km 16.3		$6.50	🛏

- Restaurant Los Andes, Hotel Los Andes, F P Moreno 594
- Restaurant Los Tehuelches, Belgrano 46. Steakhouse
- Restaurant Malevil, Pasaje Pagano 275. International cuisine
- Restaurant Mangiare, Palacios 150. Pizzas
- Restaurant 1810, Elflein 167. Steakhouse
- Restaurant Nahuel Huapí, Hotel Nahuel Huapí, F P Moreno 252
- Restaurant Nikola, Elflein 49. Steakhouse
- Restaurant Pilmayquen, Hotel Pilmayquen, 12 de Octubre 701
- Restaurant Portal del Lago, San Martín 127. International cuisine
- Restaurant Pub del Lago, Costanera 180
- Restaurant San Francisco, corner of 20 de Febrero and JJ Paso
- ☞ Restaurant Sobremonte, corner of Bartolomé Mitre and Beschtedt
- Restaurant Tenedores, Elflein 301 (corner of Rolando). Steakhouse
- Restaurant Tres Reyes, Hotel Tres Reyes, 12 de Octubre 135
- Restaurant Venezia, Morales 446
- Restaurant Verde, Hotel Apartur, Bartolomé Mitre 685. International cuisine
- Restaurant Viejo Munich, Bartolomé Mitre 102 (corner of Quaglia)
- Restaurant Villegas, Villegas 363. Trout and venison

San Carlos de Bariloche

RÍO NEGRO PROVINCE

Restaurants on the Llao Llao road

Some of the Bariloche's best restaurants are on the road to Llao Llao.
- Restaurant Dirty Dick's Pub, Bustillo Km 5
- Restaurant Hotel El Casco, Bustillo Km 11. Steakhouse
- Restaurant La Tranquera, Bustillo Km 8.4. Steakhouse
- Restaurant Magari, Bustillo Km 5.2
- ☞ Pizzería El Mundo de la Pizza, Bartolomé Mitre 370
- Pizzería Gandhi, 20 de Febrero 406
- Pizzería La Andina, corner of Elflein and Quaglia
- Pizzería La Andinita, Bartolomé Mitre 56. Pizzas and *churros*
- Pizzería Oasis, F P Moreno 278
- Pizzería No Name, corner of Villegas and Tiscornia. Goulash with nockerl
- Pizzería Pin 9, corner of Rolando and V O'Connor
- Pizzería Pinocchio, Onelli 784
- Pizzería Piyin Ruca, Onelli 547
- Pizzería Pizza Al Comer, Morales 376
- Pizzería Raulito, Gallardo 920
- Pizzería Via Roma, Bartolomé Mitre 5
- ☞ Cafetería Bariloche, corner of Alte O'Connor and Onelli
- Cafetería Don Pancho, Bartolomé Mitre 148
- Cafetería El Cairo, F P Moreno 23
- Cafetería Friends, San Martín 104
- Cafetería Hola Nicolas, corner of Moreno 10 and Urquiza. Pastries and hot chocolate
- Cafetería Hottys, corner of Bartolomé Mitre and Beschtedt
- ☞ Cafetería Isidoro, Alte O'Connor 741
- Cafetería Kaffee Status, corner of Bartolomé Mitre and Rolando. Bariloche's meeting place; pool tables
- Cafetería La Mamadera, Bartolomé Mitre 358
- Cafetería Los Dandys, corner of Diagonal Capraro and Ruiz Moreno
- Cafetería Oso Pardo, corner of Quaglia and Bartolomé Mitre
- Cafetería Petit Cafe, Bartolomé Mitre 819
- Cafetería Piccolo, corner of F P Moreno and Quaglia
- Cafetería T-Bar, corner of Villegas and Bartolomé Mitre
- Fast food: Pumpernic, corner of Rolando and Bartolmé Mitre

Post and telegraph

- Post office: Encotel, Centro Civico
- Telephone: Entel, Elflein 554
- Public telephones: Quaglia 220

$ Financial

All banks charge commission on travelers' checks.
In an emergency some bus companies exchange cash.
- Banco Alas, F P Moreno 175. Cash advances on Visa card
- Banco Velox, Bartolomé Mitre 96
- Cambio Kivani's, Bartolomé Mitre 210
- Casa Piano, Bartolomé Mitre 131 ℓ 23733. Open 0900–1300 and 1600–2000
- Exchange Turismo, Villegas 292
- Kiosco Anri, Bartolomé Mitre 339. Travelers' checks and Chilean *pesos*
- Kiosco Arrayanes, Galería Arrayanes, Bartolomé Mitre 357
- Kiosco Suyoi, Elflein 87. Cash only

Services and facilities

Delicatessens

- Al Puro Huevo, 20 de Febrero 519
- Provaletto, corner of 20 de Febrero and J J Paso

Drycleaners

- Corner of Albarracin and O'Connor (Supermarket Dodo complex)
- Gatius, Villegas 146

Laundromats

- Mar-va, corner of San Martín and Berutti
- Lavamatic Mar-va, corner of Beschtedt and Bartolomé Mitre
- Laverap, corner of Onelli and Fagnano. Open Mon–Sat, 0900–2100
- Lave-Rapid, Quaglia 427

Medical centers

- Centro Médico Privado, Anasagasti 860 ℓ 23582
- Cruz Azul, Diagonal Capraro 1210

San Carlos de Bariloche

Río Negro Province

✈ Air services from San Carlos de Bariloche

The airport is 11 km from town; the taxi fare is $8.00.
There is an airport departure tax.

- Aerolineas Argentinas, Bartolomé Mitre 199 (22425. Provides a night flight to Buenos Aires; fare $60.00
- Austral Lineas Aereas, Rolando 157 (26126
- Empresa Catedral Turismo (25443. Has airport bus leaving one and half hours before each flight from Bartolomé Mitre 399; fare $1.25
- LADE, Bartlomé Mitre 199 (22355. Flights to Chile
- Transportes Aereos Coyaique, Mitre 150

Destination	Fare	Depart	Services	Hours	Airline
• Bahía Blanca	$63.00	1305	Tues, Thur, Fri		Austral
	$47.00	1645	Wed	2	LADE
• Buenos Aires (Aeroparque Jorge Newbery)					
	$95.00	0405	1–4 services daily	2–3	Aerolineas, Austral
	$76.00	1000	Tues, Wed, Fri, Sat	7	LADE
• Chapelco	$15.00	1000	Tues, Fri	1	LADE
• Comodoro Rivadavia					
	$38.00	1310	Tues, Thur, Sat, Sun	2	Aerolineas
	$35.00	1000	Tues, Wed, Fri	3	LADE
• Córdoba	$90.00	1105	Sat, Sun	3	Aerolineas
• El Bolsón	$12.00	1000	Wed	1	LADE
• Esquel	$19.00	0145	Tues–Thur, Sat	1	Aerolineas
	$16.00	1000	Tues, Wed, Fri	1	LADE
• La Plata	$67.00	1110	Wed, Fri, Sat	7	LADE
• Mar del Plata	$99.00	1320	Sun	3	Aerolineas
	$57.00	1000	Tues, Wed, Fri, Sat	6	LADE
• Mendoza	$68.00	1105	Sat, Sun	2	Aerolineas
• Neuquén	$32.00	1320	Tues, Thur, Sat, Sun	1	Aerolineas
	$26.00	1000	Tues, Wed, Fri, Sat	2	LADE
• Puerto Deseado	$36.00	1320	Tues, Fri	4	LADE
• Puerto San Julián	$37.00	1320	Tues, Fri	5	LADE
• Río Gallegos	$44.00	1320	Tues, Fri	6	LADE
	$55.00	2000	Sat	2	Aerolineas
• Río Grande	$47.00	1320	Tues, Fri	7	LADE
	$71.00	2000	Sat	3	Aerolineas
• Rosario	$93.00	1200	Sun	3	Aerolineas
	$93.00	1305	Sun	2	Austral
• Salta	$113.00	1105	Sat, Sun	6	Aerolineas
• San Antonio Oeste					
	$27.00	1000	Tues	6	LADE
• San Miguel de Tucumán					
	$100.00	1105	Sat, Sun	5	Aerolineas
• Santa Cruz	$38.00	1320	Tues, Fri	6	LADE
• Trelew	$35.00	1320	Tues, Fri	2	LADE
• Viedma	$48.00	1510	Mon, Wed, Fri	1	Aerolineas
	$38.00	1000	Tues	7	LADE
	$38.00	1655	Sat	2	LADE
• Zapala	$18.00	1110	Fri	2	LADE

San Carlos de Bariloche

RÍO NEGRO PROVINCE

🚌 Buses from San Carlos de Bariloche

There is no central bus terminal as yet.
- Bus Norte, Bartlomé Mitre 10 ℡ 22231
- Charter, Bartolomé Mitre 10 ℡ 22231
- Chevallier S A, Moreno 107 ℡ 23090
- Cooperativa El Valle, Palacios 243 ℡ 25443
- Don Otto S A, Bartlomé Mitre 1049
- Ko Ko, Moreno 107 ℡ 23090
- La Estrella, Palacios 246 ℡ 22140
- T A Mercedes, Bartolomé Mitre 161 ℡ 24269
- TAC International, Alte O'Connor 717
- TAC, Bartolomé Mitre 10 ℡ 22231
- Tas Choapa Internacional, San Martín 568 ℡ 22695
- TIRSA, Quaglia 161 ℡ 26076
- Turismo y Transportes Penimel, Moreno 138 ℡ 22318
- TUS, O'Connor 766 ℡ 24565

Destination	Fare	Depart	Services	Hours	Company
• Bahía Blanca	$18.50	1230	daily	16	El Valle
• Buenos Aires	$41.00	1345	daily	25	El Valle
	$41.00	1500	daily	21	La Estrella
	$44.20	1400	daily	22	Chevallier
• Chos Mallal			daily	9	TAC
• Comodoro Rivadavia	$30.00	0600	Tues–Sat	22	Don Otto
• Córdoba	$31.00	1000	Tues, Wed, Fri, Sun	25	TUS
• El Bolsón	$4.00	0700	4 services daily	4	T A Mercedes, Don Otto
• Epuyen	$6.50	0800	daily	6	T AMercedes
• Esquel	$11.50	0710	daily	9	Don Otto
	$10.50	0800	Mon, Wed, Fri, Sun	9	T A Mercedes
• Ingeniero Jacobacci	$4.00	1800	daily		T A Mercedes
• Llao Llao	$0.50		daily	½	municipal bus
• Malargüe	$25.70	1200	daily	19	TAC
• Mar del Plata	$32.00	1230	Mon–Fri	23	T A Mercedes
• Mendoza	$30.50	1200	daily	24	TAC
• Neuquén	$11.50	1000	6–8 services daily	6	TUS, Tirsa, T A Chevallier, La Estrella, La Puntual, T A Mercedes, El Valle
• Osorno	$17.50	0830	daily	6	Bus Norte
• Puerto Montt (Chile)	$14.00	0800	3–4 services daily	9	T A Mercedes, Penimel, Bus Norte, TAC, TAS-Choapa
• Rosarío	$35.00	1330	Tues–Sun	24	T A Chevallier, TIRSA
• San Martín de los Andes	$6.50	0800	Mon, Wed, Fri, Sun	5	El Valle, TUS
• San Rafael	$28.60	1200	daily	22	TAC
• Santiago de Chile (Chile)	$30.00			24	
• Villa La Angostura		0800	2–3 services daily		T A Mercedes, Ayala, Algarrobal
• Viedma	$19.00	0730	Mon–Thur	16	T A Mercedes
• Zapala	$8.70	1200	daily	6	TAC

San Carlos de Bariloche

RÍO NEGRO PROVINCE

Pharmacy
- Farmacia de Miguel, Mitre 130

Photographic supplies
- Centro de la Fotografia, Mitre 139
- Studio One, corner of Quaglia and B Mitre. Agfa film and photographic equipment

Ski hire
- Bambi, corner of Villegas and Moreno
- Salomon, corner of Mitre and J O'Connor. Also repairs

Sporting supplies
- Corner of Quaglia and Moreno. Camping, fishing and skiing equipment

Supermarkets
- Dodo, corner of Albarracin and O'Connor
- La Anónima, Quaglia 331

Clubs
- Italian: Sociedad Italiana, corner of Beschtedt and Bartolomé Mitre

Churches
- Latter Day Saints, corner of Frey and Elflein
- Lutheran: Frey 461
- Methodist: corner of J J Paso and Salta

Visas, passports
- Austrian vice-consulate, 24 de Setiembre 230. The consul is Ing. F Pirker
- Chilean consulate, Villegas 239 (23050
- French consulate, Villa Llao Llao (48094
- German consulate, F P Moreno 19 (22205. Open Mon–Fri 0900–1200
- Italian vice-consulate, shop 20, Mitre 120 (23764
- Spanish consulate, Rolando 252 (22179

Motoring

The road east to the coast via Neuquén is sealed all the way and is open all year round.

The road to Chile via Paso Puyehué is sealed as far as the turn-off at Nahuel Huapí. Roadworks are in progress after that. From here onwards the road is unsealed until Anticura in Chile.

The road south to Esquel is sealed as far as La Veraneda, past Lago Guillelmo.

Service stations
- ACA, 12 de Octubre 785. Maps and road information
- Esso, corner of Onelli and Mitre
- Isaura, corner of Alte O'Connor and Frey

Car rental

If you intend to travel to Chile in a hired car, you must obtain written permission.
- A-1 International Rent-A-Car, corner of Mitre and Quaglia
- Avis Rent-a-Car, Libertad 124 (25371. There is an extra charge of $35 for a permit to travel into Chile
- Chapi Car Rental, Libertad 120
- Hertz Rent-a-Car, San Martín 295 (24718. Open 24 hours
- Liprandi Rent-a-Car, Villega 137 (23714
- National Car Rental (also know as Lan-Car), Libertad 114 (24404
- Open Car, Villegas 137 (23714

Trains

F C General Roca station is on RN 237, 3 km east from the center of the city. The railroad information office is at San Martín 127 (26181
- Buenos Aires (Retiro station): "Expreso Lagos del Sur"; Pullman $44.00, sleeper $52.80, first class $29.00, tourist class $21.50; departs Mon, Tues, Fri; 31 hours

Water transport

All boats and catamarans leave from Puerto Pañuelo. See "Water transport" in Puerto Pañuelo on page 326
- Alimar, Moreno 69, Local 7 (24261. Bookings for M V Flecha del Plata

Tours

Tour operators

All tour operators charge the same prices, and tour buses pick up participants from their respective hotels.

San Carlos de Bariloche

RÍO NEGRO PROVINCE

Trips to Puerto Montt and Osorno in Chile can be organized through Varastur and Turismo Llao-Llao.
- Alun-Co Turismo, Mitre 22, first floor ℂ 22283. Also car hire
- Catedral Turismo, Bartolomé Mitre 399 ℂ 25443. Has its own fleet of *micros*, and organizes land and lake cruises
- Corre Caminos Turismo, Quaglia 197 ℂ 26076. Agent for Tas-Choapa bus to Chile
- Hider Turismo, Bartolomé Mitre 387 ℂ 25532. Caters for "adventure tourism"
- Patagonia Travel, Bartolomé Mitre 150 ℂ 24297
- Polvani Viajes y Turismo, Quaglia 268 ℂ 23286
- Safaris Acuáticos, 20 de Febrero 798 ℂ 25521. River rafting expeditions
- T A Mercedes, Mitre 161 ℂ 24269
- Turismo Algarrobal, San Martín 459
- Turisur, Quaglia 227 ℂ 26109. Catamarans on Lago Nahuel Huapí

Tours

- Cerro Catedral: $5.50
- Cerro López: $13.00
- Cerro Tronador and Cascada Los Alerces: $11.00
- Circuito Chico: $5.50
- Circuito Grande: $11.00
- El Bolsón and Lago Puelo: $12.00
- Lago Frías: $4.00
- Lago Hess and Cascada Los Alerces: $8.00
- Llao Llao: $3.00
- Puerto Blest: $12.00. Includes bus to Puerto Pañuelo
- San Martín de los Andes: $15.00

Shopping

Bariloche is best known for its sweaters and sweets.
- Artesanes, corner of Morales and Elflein

Sport

A wide range of sporting activities are possible in and around Bariloche.
- Fishing: A permit is required for trout fishing. The season begins in November
- Golf: Avenida Bustillo Km 16
- Grass skiing: Ruta 258 Km 18
- Hiking through the national parks: There are guides available but they are expensive. In the national parks there are huts with firewood. The Club Andino Bariloche also has huts; cost $3.00 per night. The club organizes weekend walks for the outdoor enthusiasts. Excursions are graded. Enquire at the club office. A list of huts is available at the club
- Hunting: Inquire at Club Caza y Pesca, corner of 12 de Octubre and Elordi. The hunting season runs from March 1 to the end of May. Hunting is not permitted in national parks. Animals which may be hunted include wild boar and European stag
- Ice skating: B Mitre 742. Summer and winter, daily from 1600 onwards
- Ice skating: Mitre 260 (corner of Otto Goedecke)
- Swimming: There is an indoor swimming pool on the corner of Villegas and Albarracín Open Mon–Sat 0830–2245
- Mountaineering: Club Andino Bariloche has mountain walks for members at weekends. Check with the club. See also "Tourist information" above. The club also provides guides for individual hikes and climbing excursions, but this is expensive. Don't forget to bring sun protection cream. In the national parks there are huts built above 1000 m. Firewood is provided and some of the huts are managed during the summer season. Maps and information regarding the location of huts can be obtained from Club Andino and from the Servicio Parque Nacional Nahuel Huapí
- Sailing and boating: Club Yatch Bariloche, Bustillo Km 13.6
- Scuba diving: Club Náutico, Avenida Bustillo Km 3.5. There are diving sites near Isla de las Gallinas and at Pichi Traful. Diving is restricted to 22 m
- Water-skiing: Practiced on Playa Bonita, Avenida Bustillo Km 8; Laguna El Trebol, Avenida Bustillo Km 18; and Lago Gutierrez, RN 253 Km 13
- Windsurfing: In Bahía Serena, Avenida Bustillo Km 12; Lago Gutierrez RN 253 Km 13; and Laguna El Trebol, Avenida Bustillo Km 18. For more information ring ℂ 26181, extension 429

San Carlos de Bariloche

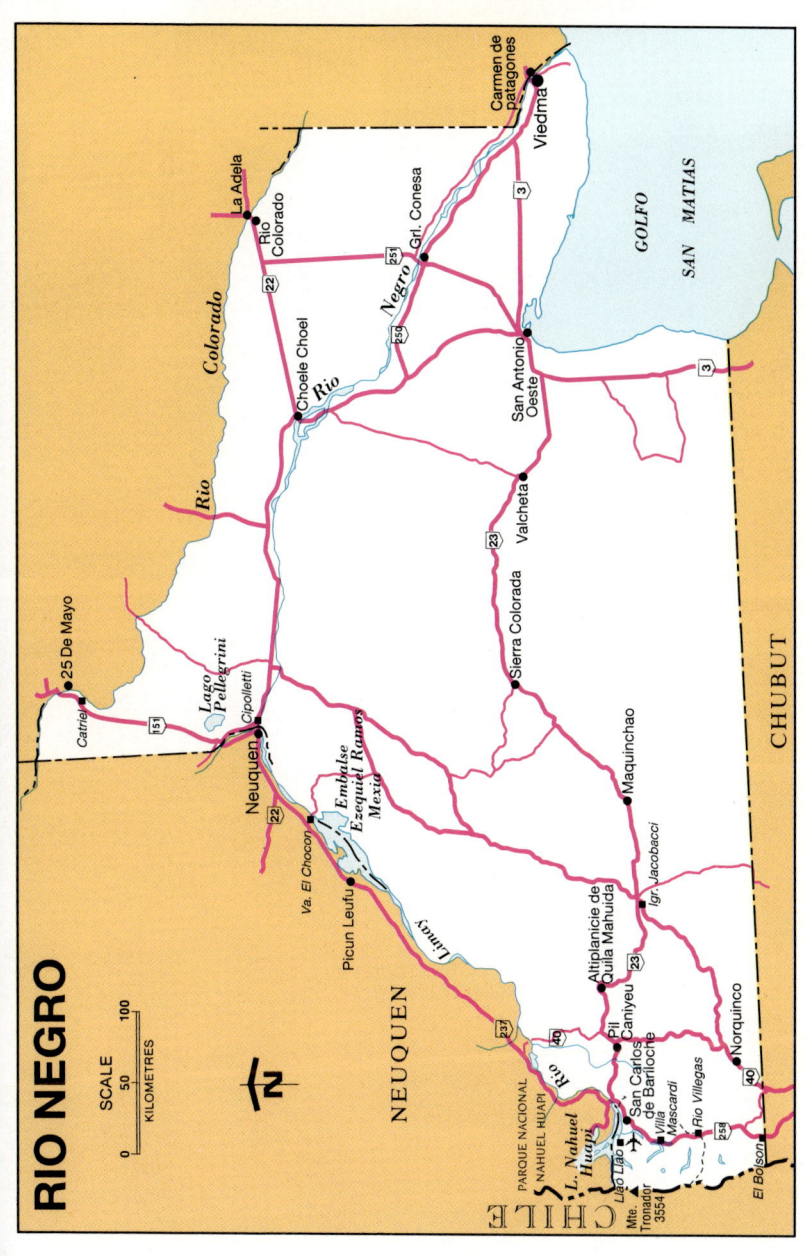

Plate 15

Map of Río Negro Province

Plate 16

Top: Buenos Aires Cathedral, with Tomb of General San Martín
Bottom: Bosque Petrificado José Ormachera, in Patagonia

RÍO NEGRO PROVINCE

Skiing

The skiing season runs from July to early October.

Ski equipment can be hired at Beschtedt 288 and Kivani Snow Gear, F P Moreno 146, in Bariloche

- Cerro Catedral: There are two commercial operations: Lado Bueno and Robles Catedral. They both run their own ski-lifts, hotels, restaurants, ski hire, etc. It is advantageous to book with a tour company because you may secure discounts for lift tickets. The favorite skiing slopes are on Cerro Catedral, 23 km east of Bariloche—see Cerro Catedral on page 320. The Mercedes bus company, Mitre 161, runs a bus service at one-hour intervals from 0800 to 1800; fare $3.00 return. The cable car, 2900 m long, operates from the base station Tues–Sun 0900–1200 and 1400–1700 all year round; fare $5.00 return. The Robles and Ladobueno chair-lifts operate only from June onwards. Walking trails from the top leading downhill are marked with red and yellow markers. The descent takes between three and four hours. Bus tours from Bariloche to the foot of Cerro Catedral allow for less than two hours to reach the mountain top; fare including lift ticket $6.00, weekly skilift tickets $65.00. Entrance to the Cerro Catedral ski slopes, below the snow line, cost $0.40.
- Cerro Otto: Only about 5 km from downtown Bariloche. Follow Avenida Pioneros, also known as Ruta de Faldeo. The cable car operates Mon–Sat 1400–1800; fare $5.00 return, local bus $1.50 return.
- For those interested in cross-country skiing, contact Club Andino Bariloche. The favorite areas are on Cerro López from Refugio Arroyo Challhuaco to Refugio Neumeyer on the Sierra de la Ventana

Entertainment

- Bowling del Lago, corner of Rolando and F P Moreno. Open from 1800 onwards
- Casino Centro, Edificio Bariloche, San Martín 127. Open daily 2130–0300
- Disco Bongo, Bartolomé Mitre 17
- Disco By Pass, Rolando 155 (corner of Bartolomé Mitre)
- Disco Cerebro, J M de Rosas 405
- Disco Feet Up, corner of Palacios and Bartolomé Mitre
- Disco Grisu, J M de Rosas 574
- Disco Gel, Pagano 270
- Disco Spazio, corner of Goedecke and V A O'Connor
- Night Club La Sirena, Elflein 149
- Piano Bar, Hotel Valgardena, corner of Rolando and Bartolomé Mitre
- Pub: Bar Glover, corner of Alte O'Connor and Palacios
- Pub: Kentton Hotel, Morales 230. Live entertainment from 2300
- Pub: Malevil, corner of Pagano and 0Libertad
- Peña Folklorica Casa del Deporte, corner of 12 de Octubre and Rolando. Open Fri from 2300; free admission
- Tanguería Centro Bariloche, Pagano 220. Tues, Thur, Sat 2300

Sightseeing

- Museo de la Patagonia, Centro Cívico. Open Tues–Fri 1000–1230 and 1400–1900, Sat 1000–1300. Has an interesting collection of Indian artefacts. Admission free
- Capilla Virgen de las Nieves: Take the bus to Llao-Llao from the city center and alight at Calle Los Pinos. The chapel is on the corner of Calle Los Pinos and Catedral

Excursions

- Osorno in Chile: The road eastward at first closely follows the north shore of **Lago Nahuel Huapí**, and Bariloche and **Cerro Tronador** are visible most of the way. If you are traveling by bus, there is usually a stop at the resort town of **Villa La Angostura** where the scenic lakes road to San Martín de los Andes

San Carlos de Bariloche

begins—see Villa La Angostura on page 309. The most picturesque part on the Argentine side is from **Correntoso** (where there is a camping site) onwards, when the climb starts through the **Río Blanco valley**. The Argentine passport control is a good hour's drive from the **Paso Puyehue**. As you enter Chile you are in the Parque Nacional Puyehue. Right at the Chilean passport control you are within striking distance of Volcán Puyehue and it is worth taking a picture from here. The best views on the Argentine side are on the left-hand side of the bus. On the Chilean side the best views are on the right hand side. The whole trip from Bariloche to Osorno is breathtaking: you are either passing along lakes with high mountains as a backdrop, or you are in the mountains with still higher mountains, or even volcanoes, on either side

- **Esquel**: Leave Bariloche by Avenida Onelli, which is the starting point of RN 258. Six km outside town is the turn-off east to the Refugio Neumeyer on Cerro Ñireco. Shortly afterwards you get your first view of **Lago Gutiérrez**. The road is well sealed and follows the eastern edge of the lake for about 9 km, passing on the way through the villages of **Ruca Lafquen**, **Villa Atalaya**, and **Quimey Mahuida**, all picturesque villages overlooking the lake. Some have hotels and restaurants and water sports facilities. There are views over the lake to **Cerro Catedral**, whose forests ascend to 2400 m. Four km after the bridge at the southern end of Lago Gutierrez is another picturesque lake, **Lago Mascardi**, which is larger and offers boat rides. There is a watershed between Lago Gutierrez and Lago Mascardi—water from Lago Gutierrez empties into Lago Nahuel Huapí whereas water from Lago Mascardi flows into the Río Manso. **Villa Mascardi** has a camping ground, Suyai, near the ACA service station. After crossing **Arroyo Guillermo** there is a hotel on the outskirts of Villa Mascardi. A little further on is the turn-off to the upper reaches of Lago Mascardi, onto an all-weather, narrow, gravel road. You can reach **Río Alerce** on good walking trails along this river, and **Río Frías**, past **Cerro Tronador**. Continuing on RN 258 after leaving Villa Mascardi, the road follows the eastern side of **Lago Guillelmo**. Here the road is curved and sometimes high above the valley. At the end of **Lago Guillelmo**, the road surface becomes gravel just before the full-scale descent into the **El Bolsón** valley. The trip from there onwards is quite interesting, as it descends and ascends several times to negotiate a difficult stretch. For a short distance the valley widens and the mountains appear lower. Near **Pampa El Toro** the road is particularly winding. The higher

RÍO NEGRO PROVINCE

mountain range is on the eastern side. Pampa El Toro itself is nothing more than a road workers' camp; here the road turns off to **Laguna Huata Hue** and **Lago Steffen**, both good for fishing. This area can get very cold even in summer. The river is about 300 m below the road level, and the road winds on its descent. At Km 65 waterfalls come into view. **Río Villegas** with a small road diner is near here. The scenery here is picturesque, with views over the valley below. Forty km before El Bolsón you reach the valley floor, where there is a cafeteria called Tacuifi. Shortly before reaching El Bolsón the usually snow- covered peaks of the **Cerro Ventisquero** come into view on the western side. At Km 95 there is a crossing over the **Río Foyel**. The valley narrows, but the mountains here are not terribly high. The road continues through a sort of canyon. On the left-hand side is the **Cascada de la Virgen**, and past this waterfall is a steakhouse, El Rancho de Fernando, just where two valleys intersect, forming a wide section. The river we are following is called **Río Los Repollos**. Thirteen km before reaching El Bolsón the road is sealed again. The valley is now very wide, made up of continuous river flats, and its slopes are forested on both sides. On the right-hand side is the turn-off to Mallin Ahogado. Just on the outskirts of El Bolsón near the river is El Bolsón camping ground. Motel La Posta on the left hand side looks good. The most picturesque part however is after **Cholila**, when the road enters the **Parque Nacional Los Alerces**. The T A Mercedes bus unfortunately arrives rather too late at this breathtaking part of the trip to take full advantage of the views. You should sit on the right-hand side of the bus when coming from Bariloche. In fact this trip is better made the other way, leaving Esquel in the morning so that you can enjoy the trip through the national park in broad daylight

- **San Martín de los Andes** via the northern route: Leave Bariloche on RN 237 which for the first 18 km follows **Lago Nahuel Huapí**. After you have crossed the bridge over the **Río Limay**, the mountains decrease in size and the land becomes drier. Three km past the Río Limay bridge is the turn-off onto Ruta "g" to Villa Angostura and on to Puerto Montt in Chile. The all-weather sealed road follows the Río Limay almost all the way to **Confluencia**. Before you cross the **Río Traful** at Confluencia there is the turn-off westwards onto Ruta "d" and later Ruta "l" to Lago Traful and on to Lago Correntoso and Chile. A bit further on overlooking the valley is the *hostería*. To take the more picturesque route, take the turn-off west *after* crossing the Río Traful. Tourist buses usually take this route, unless Córdoba pass

San Carlos de Bariloche

RÍO NEGRO PROVINCE

is impassable. Here wind and water erosion have created spectacular rock formations known as **Piedra del Viento**. Twelve km past Confluencia, the road turns north and follows the **Arroyo Córdoba** for some 8 km. The mountains on both sides of the road are in the 1800 m range. Vegetation here is reduced to small patches of grass. Shortly afterwards the ascent to the **Paso de Córdoba** begins, a picturesque 6 km stretch of winding mountain road. Signs along the road point out photogenic spots. The mountains again approach the 2100 m mark as we get closer to **Lago Meliquina** and the **Cerro Chapelco** skiing slopes. Twenty-six km past Lago Meliquina and over a very picturesque mountain road, we reach San Martín de los Andes. See also San Martín de los Andes on page 301

- **San Martín de los Andes** via RN 40 and RN 234. This is the less scenic route taken by bus services, but has the advantage that the road is sealed for most of the way and open all year round. At **Confluencia**, where there is an ACA service station on the left-hand side at the Traful junction where the **Río Traful** joins the **Río Limay**, cross the bridge over the Río Traful and turn east. For 42 km the road follows the northern rim of the **Río Limay**, which here almost forms a lake due to the water stored by dams such as Dique Alicura further down the valley. The first part is interesting as the valley is just wide enough for the river and the road, but it quickly becomes rather unattractive as most of the time the land is dry. Occasionally the rock formations have unusual shapes due to the strong forces of wind erosion. Across the river weir a feeble attempt has been made to plant conifers. After crossing **Río Collón Curá**, the road turns sharply northwards, becoming RN 40, which runs through undulating country almost bare of growth. **La Rinconada** is nothing more than a long narrow bridge over the **Río Aluminé**. Across the river on the western side is an ACA service station with a motel. We are now on RN 234. Once more the mountains rise higher—this is cattle country. The road ascends slightly and crosses the **Río Chimehuin** at **Junín de los Andes**. The valley which the road follows here is fairly wide and green. The mountains on either side steadily increase in height and are frequently snow-covered even in summer. Hotels on the city's outskirts mark the traveler's arrival in San Martín de los Andes

- **Safariland** and **Parque Luna Helada**: 21 km west. The turn-off to this 40 ha wildlife reserve is at Km 18.3 along the road to Llao-Llao. The park is bordered with 200-year old *coihue* and other trees. Condors, stags, and ostriches can be seen there. There is a cafeteria and a *pub* on

San Carlos de Bariloche

RÍO NEGRO PROVINCE

site. Take bus 0 from the city center

Lake excursions

T A Mercedes tourist buses leave Bariloche at 0900 from B Mitre 161 for Puerto Pañuelo to meet the catamarans; return fare $3.00.

Municipal buses leave Bariloche from the corner of Moreno and Sargento Rolando for Puerto Pañuelo; one-way fare $0.50. Buses are always crowded, so leave early, about 0830.

- **Lago Nahuel Huapí**: This lake has seven coves or *brazos*. At the entrance to **Brazo Puerto Blest** is **Isla Centinela** which contains the mausoleum of Don Francisco Perito Moreno, one of the trail-blazers of the national park. The island's original Indian name was "Nahuel Huapí", which means "tiger island", after the shape of the island. The lake covers 560 sq km, and its longest arm is 96 km long; its deepest point is 464 m; and it is 764 m above sea-level. A catamaran leaves Puerto Pañuelo at about 1030 daily and proceeds northwards, passing **Isla Victoria**
- **Isla Victoria** and **Bosque Arrayanes**: Departs Puerto Pañuelo 1000; fare $9.00
- **Puerto Blest**, including waterfalls: Departs Puerto Pañuelo 1000; fare $9.00
- **Puerto Blest**, waterfalls, and **Laguna Frías**: Departs Puerto Pañuelo 1000; fare $13.00
- **Isla Victoria**, **Bosque Arrayanes**, and **Villa La Angostura**: Departs Puerto Pañuelo Wed 0930; fare $10.00 for a full-day excursion
- **Cerro Tronador**: Departs Puerto Mascardi 1100; fare $8.50

Conducted tours

See also "Tours" above.
- **Cerro Catedral**: Half-day trip; departs 1330; fare $5.50
- **Cascada Los Alerces**: Half-day trip; departs 1330; fare $8.00
- **Cerro López**: Half-day; departs 1330; fare $7.50
- **Cerro Tronador** and **Cascada Los Alerces**: Departs 0800; fare $11.00
- **El Bolsón** and **Lago Puelo**: Departs 0800; fare $11.50
- **Cerro Tronador**: Full day trip; fare $12.00. Includes a walk to **Glaciar Negro** ("Black Glacier")
- Peulla in Chile via **Los Lagos**: Fare $33.00; Travel Agency Copa, Galería Via Firenze
- **Puerto Pañuelo** and **Puerto Blest** (by boat), **Puerto Alegre** by bus, **Puerto Frías** by launch, and **Cascada de los Cántaros**: Full day trip; fare $14.00
- **San Martín de los Andes**: Departs 0800; fare $15.00
- **Villa la Angostura** and Osorno in Chile: 8 hours one-way
- Seven-lakes trip, taking in **Río Limay**, **Valle Encantado**, **Lago Traful**, **Lago Correntoso**, **Villa La Angostura**, and **Paso Coihue**: 8 hours

Walking tours

- **Cerro Campanarío**: Chairlift Km 17.7 Bustillo. There are scenic views over lakes **Nahuel Huapí** and **Bariloche**. The chairlift runs daily from

San Carlos de Bariloche

Km 17.7 on Avenida Bustillo 0900–1200 and 1400–1800; fare $1.00
- **Llao Llao, Colonia Suiza, Cerro Catedral**, and return to Bariloche: Full day trip
- **Llao Llao, Colonia Suiza, Punto Panoramico**, and around **Lago Moreno**
- Rubber raft tour from Bariloche down the **Río Limay** to **Confluencia**, stopping for lunch at **Valle Encantado**: 9 hours; fare $16.00. Runs from mid-November to mid-April
- **Cerro Otto**: For a do-it-yourself trip, take a Transportes 3 de Mayo bus from the corner of Perito Moreno and Sargento Rolando. The cable car station is on Avenida de los Pioneros, 5 km from the city center. This is a steep two-hour walk uphill. Eight hundred meters up there is the station for the cable-car, which ascends to 1400 m. On top of the mountain there is a restaurant with a rotating viewing platform
- **Isla Victoria**: For a do-it-yourself one-day tour, take a Transporte 3 de Mayo bus from the corner of Moreno and Rolando, departing 0800 for **Puerto Pañuelo**. The boat leaves Puerto Pañuelo 1030. Total fares $7.00

Mountain walks

There are a number of *refugios*, from which beautiful mountain walks may be made. Below are just a few of them.

- Refugio Cerro López: Take a Colonia Suiza bus and alight at Puente Arroyo López. The trail starts on the left-hand side of the **Arroyo López** and follows the stream. You pass a waterfall and reach the *refugio* in about two hours' walk. From the *refugio* there is a walking trail to **Pico Turista** at 2050 m past a small tarn; the lake is an hour's walk, and Pico Turista a further hour and a half's walk. There is a road up to **Cerro López**, and from the carpark it is a short and easy walk to the mountain hut. The hut is at 1600 m and can accommodate 100 guests. There is also a small restaurant. The trails are marked red or orange
- Refugio Emilio Frey: Located in the **Cerro Catedral** massif on the shore of **Laguna Tonchek**. Take a bus from Bariloche to the base of Cerro Catedral, and from there the cable car to the summit. From the summit along the trail marked in blue and red it is a short, easy walk. The mountain hut is at 1700 m and has room for 40 people, and there is a restaurant. From here various peaks may be scaled. Walking from the base takes about three and a half hours, but taking the cable car cuts the time down to two hours
- Refugio Neumeyer, also referred to as Refugio Challhuaco: 3 km south on RN 258, a mountain road turns left to the *refugio*, for most of the way following the **Arroyo Challhuaco**. This trail can be used by small vehicles and is

San Carlos de Bariloche

RÍO NEGRO PROVINCE

about 14 km long, crossing four bridges. At the third bridge the Arroyo Challhuaco turns south. The mountain hut is at about 1300 m and is in a forested area. It can accommodate 60 tourists and has a small restaurant, and is open from early December to the end of April, depending on the weather. From the hut you can make several walks; all are easy, but the best views are from **Mirador**. To **Laguna Verde** it is an hour's walk

- Hostel Pampa Linda: During the summer season buses make the trip daily along the 86 km road from Bariloche. The hostel and camping grounds are located in the **Valle Vuriloche**. For 50 km the road is narrow and made of gravel. It is one-way to all the way to Hostel Pampa Linda at 1300 m, and is open to outward traffic from 1500. The hostel has accommodation for 150 persons, and dining room facilities for 60. **Pampa Linda** is the starting point for many wonderful hikes as well as for the trek up to Refugio Meiling, the **Paso de las Nubes** ("Cloud Pass"), **Las Nalcas waterfall**, **Glaciar Tronador**, and Hostel Los Ventisqueros

- Hostel Los Ventisqueros: Located at 1050 m at the foot of **Cerro Tronador** in the upper **Río Manso** valley. The starting point is 10 km further down at Pampa Linda. The hostel is open from early November until mid-April. This is the starting point for climbing **Cerro Argentino** and **Cerro Chileno**, and hikes to **Glaciar Negro**, source of the Río Manso, **Cascada Río Blanco**, and **Garganta del Diablo** ("Devil's Gorge") in the Tronador area. A more extensive two-day hike may be made to the Puerto Blest–Lago Frías tourist complex, but it should only be attempted by experienced hikers. From Puerto Blest you can return by ferry to Puerto Pañuelo

- Refugio Otto Meiling: The trail to this mountain shelter starts from **Pampa Linda**. If you intend to make a more extensive mountain hike (say to Paso de las Nubes) check with the national parks information service at the camping site, located at about 2000 m between the **Alerce** and **Castaño Overo glaciers**. At first the trail passes through a forested area where you follow the white arrows. Once you leave the forest behind there are red circles painted on the rocks. Do not take any short cuts! From Pampa Linda it is a 14 km easy climb taking about four and a half hours. The hut is open from early December to the end of April and caters for 60 people. There is also a small cafeteria and dining room. Refugio Otto Meiling is the starting point for climbs in the **Cerro Tronador** massif. At the base of the face of **Glaciar Castana Overo** there is a small waterfall which is the source of the **Arroyo Overo**. Likewise the **Glaciar Alerce** has

San Carlos de Bariloche

Río Negro Province

several waterfalls at its base which form the source of the **Arroyo Alerce**. This is marvellous hiking country but not without its danger

VIEDMA

Postal code: 8500 • **[**area code: (0920) •
Population: 20 000
Distance from Buenos Aires: 966 km south on RN 3

Viedma, the capital of Río Negro province, is situated on the **Río Negro**. Two bridges span the river, connecting Viedma with **Carmen de Patagonés** in Buenos Aires province.

The first Spanish vessel to sail up the Río Negro was the *Nuestra Señora del Carmen* commanded by Basilio Villarino in 1779. On April 22, 1779 Don Francisco de Viedma founded the colony of Mercedes on the spot where Viedma is today. Several months later the town was moved to the opposite shore of the Río Negro because of frequent flooding. This newly founded town was named Fuerte del Carmen de Patagonés. Nothing remains of the old Mercedes settlement as a violent flood in 1899 completely destroyed the site. The first settlers of Carmen de Patagones lived in the *cuevas maragatas* on arrival from Spain. A sign in Calle Rivadavia points to this site. A monument on a hill behind the city commemorates the repulse of a Brazilian naval attack by the citizens in 1827.

While Viedma (renamed in 1878 in honour of the Spanish nobleman) is a fairly modern city, the twin city of Carmen de Patagonés has retained its colonial charm. The climate is mild and particularly good in autumn.

The Viedma–Carmen de Patagonés area has been earmarked as the site of the future federal capital of Argentina, replacing Buenos Aires.

🎭 Festivals
- Kayacs del Río Regata: January. This annual kayak race between Neuquén and Viedma is broken into 11 legs over 15 days to cover the 1000 km

ℹ️ Tourist information
- Secretaria de Turismo, Garrone 245 **[**22146
- Information kiosk, RN3, just after crossing the Puente Nuevo bridge
- Information kiosk, Buenos Aires 356, in the park

Key to Map
1. Municipalidad
2. Casa de Gobierno
3. Cathedral
4. Post office (Encotel)
5. Telephone (Entel)
6. Tourist information
7. Banco de la Nación
8. Aerolineas Argentinas
9. LADE (airline)
10. Museo Antropologico
11. Museo del Río Negro

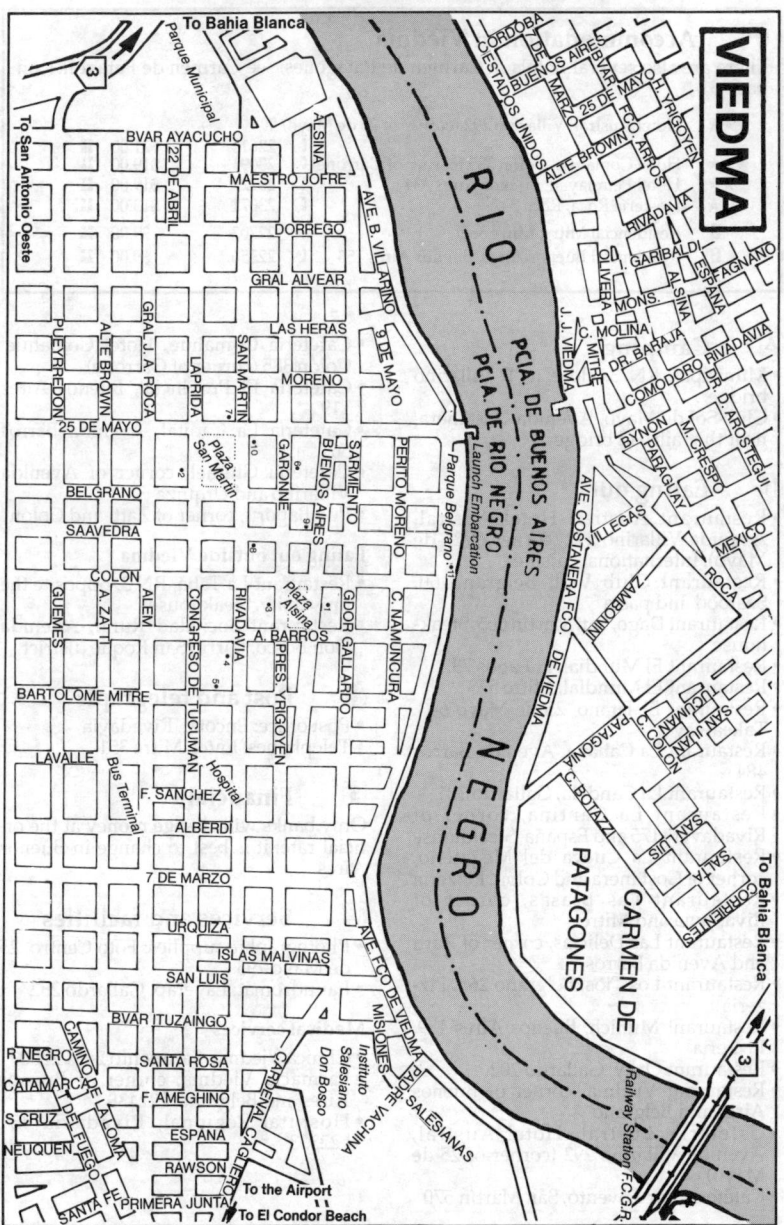

Viedma

RÍO NEGRO PROVINCE

🛏 Accommodation in Viedma

There are also several hotels in Carmen de Patagones; see Carmen de Patagonés on page 81

★★★	Hotel Austral, Villarino 292 (corner of 25 de Mayo) 🍴				
		(	22615	$21.00	👥
★★★	Hotel Comahue, Colón 385 (corner of Garrone)	(	23091	$19.00	👥
★★	Hotel Peumayen, Buenos Aires 334	(	25222	$19.00	👥
★	Hostería Roca, Roca 347	(	23071	$13.00	👥
B	Residencial Mitre, Mitre 562	(	22703	$9.00	👥
B	Residencial Buenos Aires, Buenos Aires 153	(	22356	$9.00	👥

⛺ Camping

- Municipal, RN 3, close to B Villarino bridge
- Club Sol de Mayo, Avenida Costanera, near the railroad bridge

🍴 Eating out

- Restaurant Austral, Hotel Austral, Avenida Villarino 292 (corner of 25 de Mayo). International cuisine
- Restaurant Club Vial, Belgrano 60. Seafood and pasta
- Restaurant Dago, San Martín 665. Steakhouse
- Restaurant El Mundial, H Lagos 732
- Restaurant El Mundial, Mitre 573
- Restaurant El Titano, 25 de Mayo 643. Takeaway
- Restaurant La Cabaña, Avenida Barros 484
- Restaurant La Candela, Gallardo 181
- Restaurant La Cantina, corner of Rivadavia 1175 and España. Steakhouse
- Restaurant La Cueva del Megaterio, corner of Costanera and Colón. Pizzeria
- Restaurant Las Brasas, corner of Rivadavia and Mitre
- Restaurant Las Delicias, corner of Zatti and Avenida Barros
- Restaurant Los Tios, Belgrano 265. Pizzeria
- Restaurant Munich, Buenos Aires 159. Pizzeria
- Restaurant Oaky, Gallardo 202
- Restaurant Viedma, corner of Buenos Aires and Belgrano
- Cafetería Austral, Hotel Austral, Avenida Villarino 292 (corner of 25 de Mayo)
- Cafetería Bar Lovento, San Martín 570
- Cafetería Comahue, Hotel Comahue, Colón 385 (corner of Garrone)
- Cafetería El Provincial, Buenos Aires 119
- Cafetería La Capital, Avenida Barros 561
- Cafetería Ghimel, corner of Avenida Villarino and Urquiza
- Pub Baporu, corner of Zatti and Colón

Eating out outside Viedma

- Restaurant La Taba, RN 3, opposite the university. Steakhouse
- Restaurant Sociedad Rural, Avenida Don Bosco, Barrio San Roque district

✉ Post and telegraph

- Post office: Encotel, Rivadavia
- Telephones: Entel, Mitre 351

$ Financial

Only banks will change money at the official rate; it is best to change in Buenos Aires.

🛎 Services and facilities

- Photographic supplies: Foto Centro, 25 de Mayo 793
- Laundromat: Laverap, Gallardo 282

Medical services

- Clinica Viedma, Sarmiento 243 (22509
- Farmacia Viedma, corner of Buenos Aires and Belgrano, (22438
- Hospital Regional, Rivadavia 351 (22333

Viedma

RÍO NEGRO PROVINCE

✈ Air services from Viedma

Gobernador Castello airport is 2 km from the town center and can only be reached by taxi.

- Aerolineas Argentinas, corner of San Martín and Saavedra ✆ 22018
- LADE, corner of Garrone and Saavedra ✆ 22020
- TAN, Namuncura 78 ✆ 22131

Destination	Fare	Depart	Services	Hours	Airline
• Bahía Blanca	$20.00	1510	Fri	1	LADE
• Buenos Aires (Aeroparque Jorge Newbery)					
	$60.00	1445	1 service daily	2	Aerolineas
	$50.00	1510	Tues, Fri, Sat	3	LADE
• Chapelco	$32.00	1200	Mon	6	LADE
• Comodoro Rivadavia					
	$39.00	1100	Thurs, Fri	6	Aerolineas
	$41.00	1120	Sun	1	LADE
• Esquel	$38.00	1100	Fri	4	LADE
• Mar del Plata	$38.00	1705	Tues, Sat	1	LADE
• Neuquén	$27.00	1100	Mon, Fri	1–4	LADE
• Puerto Deseado	$44.00	1100	Fri	6	LADE
• Puerto San Julián	$45.00	1100	Fri	7	LADE
• Río Gallegos	$49.00	1100	Fri	9	LADE
• Río Grande	$50.00	1100	Fri	10	LADE
• San Antonio Oeste					
	$16.00	1200	Mon, Thurs	1	LADE
• San Carlos de Bariloche					
	$39.00	1100	Mon, Fri	2–7	LADE
	$48.00	1330	Mon, Wed, Fri	2	Aerolineas
• Santa Cruz	$46.00	1100	Fri	8	LADE
• Trelew	$39.00	1100	Thurs, Fri	2–5	LADE

Supermarkets

- La Anonima, Rivadavia 450 (corner of Alberdi)
- Supercoop, corner of Avenida Barros and O'Higgins

🚗 Motoring

Service stations

- ACA, RN 3
- YPF, corner of Avenida Barros and Tucumán
- Servisaura Viedma, Avenida Rivadavia 298
- Vidrieria Morete, Gallardo 882. Windscreens

🚆 Trains

F C General Roca station is 20 blocks from the city center on the southern side across the Río Negro (Barrio San Roque). Road access to the station is from Avenida Cardinal Cagliero.

⚓ Water transport

There are regular ferry services on the Río Negro connecting Carmen de Patagonés with Viedma, leaving from Parque Belgrano at the end of 25 de Mayo.

⊕ Tours

- Triton, Namuncura 78 ✆ 22131

🛍 Shopping

- Regionales, Mishquíhue, 25 de Mayo 393
- Regionales Casa del Turista, San Martín 117

Viedma

RÍO NEGRO PROVINCE

🚌 Buses from Viedma

The bus terminal is at Zatti 350. It has a restaurant, clean rest rooms, and a cloak room ($0.50).

Ceferino urban transport, at Schieroni 883, runs transport to the beaches. In winter buses to El Cóndor depart only once a day, and to Loberia on weekends only.

Destination	Fare	Depart	Services	Hours	Company
• Bahía Blanca	$14.00	0600	4 services daily		La Puntual
• Buenos Aires	$21.50	El Cóndor			
• Comodoro Rivadavia	$19.00	0250	Tues, Thurs, Sat, Sun		Don Otto
• Neuquén	$13.00	1330	daily	10	La Puntual
• Carmen de Patagonés	$0.40				Trans Benitez
• Puerto Madryn	$13.50				El Cóndor
• Playa El Cóndor	$0.70			½	Empresa Ceferino
Last return bus 1730					
• Rawson		0127	Mon, Tues, Thurs, Sat		La Puntual
• San Carlos de Bariloche	$19.00	2000	Tues, Fri		T A Mercedes

🎭 Entertainment

- Centro Municipal de Cultura (Municipal Cultural Center), Avenida Villarino
- Disco Maroco, corner of Avenida Caseros and Mexico

📷 Sightseeing

- Museo Gobernador Eugenio Tello, San Martín 263
- Museo Cardenal Cagliero, Rivadavia 34
- Museo del Río (River Museum), corner of Avenida Costanera and Colón. Open Mon–Fri. This museum gives an overview of the geological development of the valley and also the changes made along the **Río Negro** since the founding of the first Jesuit missions in the eighteenth century

♣ Excursions

- River cruises on the catamaran *Curru Leuvu*, from the pier under the railway bridge
- **Balneario El Cóndor**: 30 km. This small seaside resort on the Atlantic coast is near the mouth of the **Río Negro**. There is camping, restaurants, and small *residencial*. At low tide there is good fishing near the lighthouse. The lighthouse, "Los Pozones", is one of the oldest in Patagonia and was built in 1883. It is a slim tower of 13 m and can be visited. Take an Empresa Ceferino bus from the Plaza
- **Balneario Lobería**: 30km further south from Balneario El Cóndor. Camping and restaurants. Take a Ceferino bus from the Plaza. Both *balnearios* function only in summer

Viedma

Chubut Province

Plate 18 Map of Chubut Province
- 359 Alto Río Senguerr
- 359 Balneario Rada Tilly
- 360 Camarones
- 361   Map
- 362 Cholila
- 362 Comodoro Rivadavia
- 364   Map
- 368 Esquel
- 370   Map
- 375 Gaimán
- 376   Map
- 377 Hoyo de Epuyén
- 378 La Hoya
- 379 Los Altares
- 379 Parque Nacional Los Alerces
- 381 Puerto Madryn
- 385   Map
- 387 Puerto Pirámides
- 388 Punta Tombo
- 389 Rawson
- 390   Map
- 391 Río Mayo
- 392 Sarmiento
- 393   Map

Chubut Province

- **394** Trelew
- **395** Map
- **399** Trevelín
- **400** Map

Chubut with 225 000 square km is the largest Patagonian province. The geographical features differ from one region to another: in the east the Atlantic coastline, in the centre the Patagonian *meseta* or plateau, and in the west the Andes. The fringe of the Andean *cordillera* consists of wooded mountains, lakes, and year-round rivers, and has a stimulating climate and many natural attractions for the tourist. **Esquel**, near **Lago Futalaufquen**, is the gateway to the **Parque Nacional Los Alerces**, which, with the **Parque Nacional Lago Puelo** is the major attraction of the Andean region. Esquel is also a ski resort. The Patagonian *meseta* alternates with river basins, valleys, and glens. Here the soil is sandy and vegetation is sparse. Despite the dryness of the Patagonian tableland, the **Río Chubut** basin has been transformed into a valuable agricultural region by the **Dique Florentino Ameghino**, 129 km from Trelew, which supplies water for both irrigation and hydro-electricty. Another important hydro-electric scheme is the Futaleufú power station near Esquel.

This province was, in the main, opened up by Welsh colonists who arrived from 1865 onwards. The towns with populations of largely Welsh descent are **Puerto Madryn**, **Dolavon**, **Gaimán**, and **Trelew**. The major cities are Puerto Madryn, Trelew, and **Rawson**, all on the coast and founded by Welsh colonists, and **Comodoro Rivadavia** in the far south. Rawson, the provincial capital, 1455 km south from Buenos Aires, is a quiet unassuming town of little interest to the tourist. Trelew is a commercial center. Puerto Madryn is the gateway to the **Península Valdés**, and Comodoro Rivadavia is the center of petrol production. The road system covers approximately 7000 km, 2100 km of which is sealed.

On the Atlantic Ocean are long stretches of beaches where there are breeding grounds for sea lions, seals, and penguins. The Península Valdés is especially abundant in marine life, and from August to March is visited by whales. The interior is sparsely populated by sheepfarmers. Of the rivers only the **Río Chubut** reaches the sea; most others end up in inland lakes such as **Lago Musters**, **Lago Colhué Huapi**, or **Gran Laguna Salada**. There is good fishing in Lago Musters and Lago Colhué Huapi.

Chubut Province

Of economic importance are the oil and gas deposits in the south. A well-established fishing industry, with crab and shrimp the main catch, supplies canning factories located in Rawson and Comodoro Rivadavia. The mineral wealth is considerable. Uranium is mined near **Cerro Santa Ana** with a concentrating plant at **El Chalet**, and there are also deposits of copper, manganese, gold, silver, and iron ore.
- Major places of interest to tourists are:
- Worth a visit: **Península Valdés** and **Parque Nacional Los Alerces**
- Worth a detour: **Parque Nacional Lago Puelo**, **Esquel**, and **Puerto Madryn**
- Of interest: **Puerto Pirámides**, **Camarones**, and **Comodoro Rivadavia**.

Alto Río Senguerr

Postal code: 9033 • Population: 1500
Distances
- From Comodoro Rivadavia: 356 km westwards on RN 26 then RN 20, RN 22, and RN 40
- From Río Mayo: 97 km north-west on RN 40

Alto Río Senguerr is located on the **Río Senguerr** in the *pre-cordillera*. The wildlife in the area includes deer, puma, and mountain cat.

Accommodation
There is a small hotel with a restaurant.

Air services
- Comodoro Rivadavia: Fare $17.00; departs 1045 Mon, Fri; 2 hours; Empresa LADE
- Río Mayo: Fare $13.50; departs 1220 Mon, Fri; ½ hour; Empresa LADE

Buses
Empresa Giobbi runs buses to Esquel, Río Mayo, and Comodoro Rivadavia.

Excursions
- **Lago Fontana** and **Lago La Plata**: 51 km westwards on RP 21. For this fishing and camping trip you need your own transport, preferably a four-wheel drive. The main attraction is the trout fishing and the large numbers of deer. The river floods in springtime and the road is usually impassable in several places. The best time to visit is from December to March. Take warm clothes as the temperature drops considerably at night.

Balneario Rada Tilly

Postal code: 9001 • (area code: (0967)
Distance from Comodoro Rivadavia: 14 km southwards on RN 3

Balneario Rada Tilly (commonly known as "Rada Tilly") is located about 12 km south of **Comodoro Rivadavia** on a 4 km long bay. It is enclosed at the northern end by **Cerro Punta Piedras** and at the southern end by the rocky promontory of **Cerro Punta del Marqués**, where there is a seal colony. The sandy beach is 300 m wide. Rada Tilly was named in 1789 by the Malaspina expedition, a Spanish foray into Patagonia, in honor of the Marqués Everardo de Casa Tilly who fought the Portuguese in 1776 over the possession of the La Plata area. Rada Tilly is the home of Comodoro Rivadavia's affluent.

Accommodation
- Hotel Rada Tilly, corner of Piedrabuena and Fragata Argentina

Camping
- Next to Hotel Rada Tilly; use the hotel facilities. Pebbly ground

Eating out
- Cafetería Los Troncos, Avenida Costanera

Entertainment
- Disco Alexia, Avenida Costanera
- Disco Jonathan, Primera Avenida
- Disco Naranja, Avenida Costanera
- Disco Ronano, Avenida Primera

Sightseeing
- Museo Regional, Tercera Avenida

Excursions
- **Punta Marqués**: Located on the far southern side of the bay where there is a *lobería* or seal colony. A road runs to the top of the promontory and you can descend on foot some distance towards the seals

CAMARONES

Postal code: 9111
Distances
- From Trelew: 300 km southwards on RN 3 then RP 30
- From Comodoro Rivadavia: 277 km north-east on RN 3 then RP 30

The area around Camarones produces a particularly fine variety of merino wool. The highest elevation is **Cerro Dos Bahías** at 182 m. The major attraction is the natural reserve 27 km to the south-east, reached by a dirt road and open only during the tourist season. There is also is a sea lion nursery nearby, open in summer; bring binoculars.

Accommodation
- Hotel Kau-i-Keuken ⑪ $3.50 ⚑
- Pension Mar Azul ⑪ $2.50 ⚑ $3.50. Full board

Camping
- Municipal camping ground, near the beach. $1.00 per tent per person

Eating out
- Restaurant Kau-i-Keuken, Hotel Kau-i-Keuken

Buses
Camarones is best reached from Trelew, but transport is infrequent.
- Trelew: Fare $6.00; departs Mon and Fri; Empresa Don Otto

Motoring
RP 30 from the turn-off near Garayalde is unsealed until the approach to Camarones.

Balneario Rada Tilly

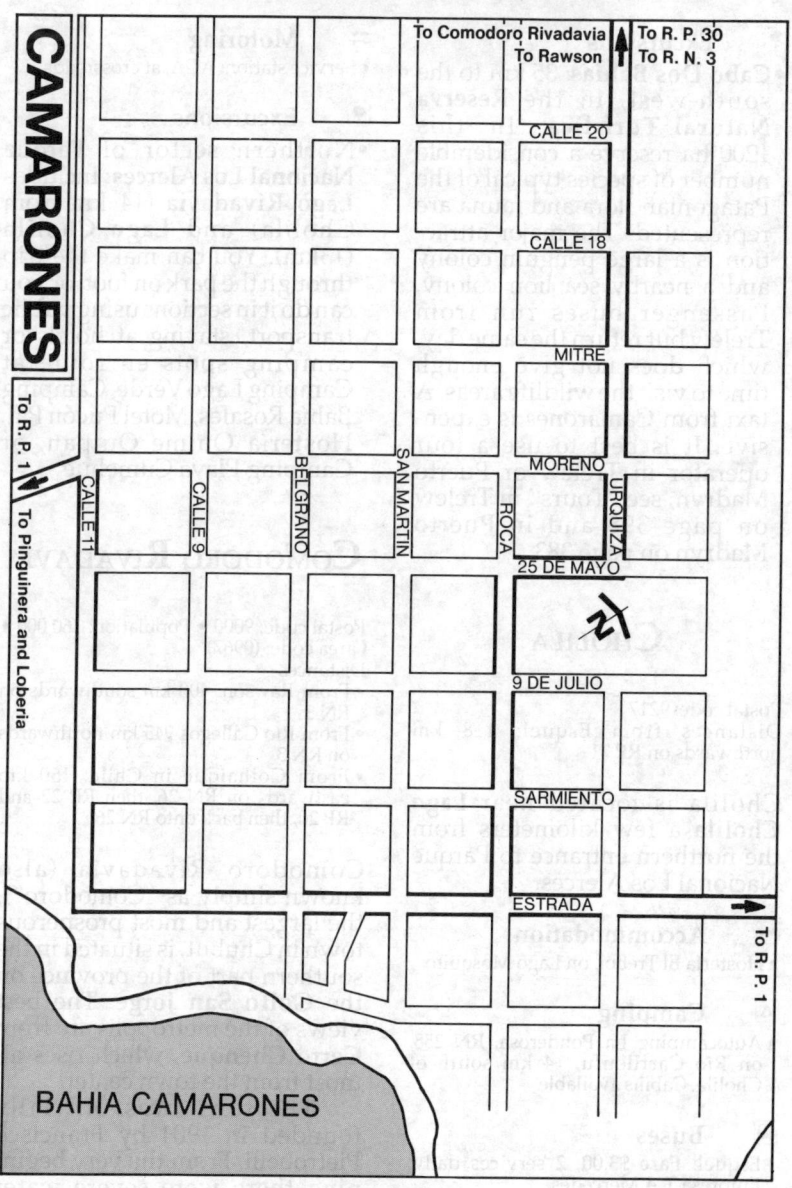

Carmarones

CHUBUT PROVINCE

🌳 Excursions

- **Cabo Dos Bahías**: 35 km to the south-west, in the **Reserva Natural Turística**: In this 1200 ha reserve a considerable number of species typical of the Patagonian flora and fauna are represented. The major attraction is a large penguin colony and a nearby sea lion colony. Passenger buses run from Trelew but return the same day, which does not give enough time to visit the wildlife areas. A taxi from Camarones is expensive. It is best to use a tour operator in Trelew or Puerto Madryn; see "Tours" in Trelew on page 398 and in Puerto Madryn on page 383

CHOLILA

Postal code: 9217
Distances from Esquel: 118 km northwards on RP 71

Cholila is located near **Lago Cholila** a few kilometers from the northern entrance to Parque Nacional Los Alerces.

🛏 Accommodation

- Hostería El Trebol, on Lago Mosquito

⛺ Camping

- Autocamping La Ponderosa, RN 258, on Río Carrileufu, 14 km south of Cholila. Cabins available

🚌 Buses

- Esquel: Fare $3.00; 2 services daily; Empresa T A Mercedes

🚗 Motoring

- Service station: ACA, at crossroads

🌳 Excursions

- Northern sector of **Parque Nacional Los Alerces**: Includes **Lago Rivadavia** (14 km from Cholila) and **Lago Cholila** (13km). You can make the trip through the park on foot; or you can do it in sections using public transport, staying at hotels or camping spots en route at Camping Lago Verde, Camping Bahía Rosales, Motel Pucón Pai, Hostería Quime Quipan, or Camping Playa Cumehue

COMODORO RIVADAVIA

Postal code: 9000 • Population: 160 000 • ℓ area code: (0967)
Distances
- From Rawson: 400 km southwards on RN 3
- From Río Gallegos 945 km northwards on RN 3
- From Coihaique in Chile: 450 km eastwards on RN 26, then RP 22 and RP 20, then back onto RN 26

Comodoro Rivadavia (also known simply as "Comodoro"), the largest and most prosperous town in Chubut, is situated in the southern part of the province on the **Golfo San Jorge**. The best views of the metropolis are from **Cerro Chenque**, which rises almost from the town center.

The town was officially founded in 1901 by Francisco Pietrobelli. From the very beginning there were severe water

Camarones

CHUBUT PROVINCE

shortages. In 1907 while drilling for water, oil was discovered and oil-fields now extend far beyond Comodoro Rivadavia. There are two industrial parks in the town, with most enterprises geared towards the oil industry. A pipeline carries gas north to Buenos Aires. The fishing port is in **Caleta Córdoba**, 13 km north of Comodoro, and a fishing industry based on shrimp and calamari is increasing. The mean temperatures are 20 °C in January and 4 °C in July. Humidity is 65% in July. **Balneario Rada Tilly**, 12 km south on a bay, is a beach resort.

Festivals
- Foundation day of Comodoro Rivadavia: February 23
- Foundation day of Chubut: July 28
- Petroleum day: December 13

Tourist information
- Tourist office, located in the bus terminal, corner of Pellegrini and Ameghino (23263
- Dirección Provincial de Turismo, corner of Avenida Rivadavia and Pellegrini

Accommodation in Comodoro Rivadavia

★★★	Hotel Austral, Rivadavia 190	(21021	$21.00
★★★	Hotel Comodoro, corner of 9 de Julio 770 and Rivadavia	(22061	$21.00
★★	Hotel Atlantico, corner of Alem 32 and Necochea	(23145	$16.00
★★	Hotel Azul, Sarmiento 724	(24874	
★★	Hotel del Sur, Maipú 1083	(24119	$16.00
•	Hotel Lisboa, corner of San Martín and Francia For budget travelers		
B	Hospedaje Belgrano, Belgrano 546	(24313	$5.00
B	Hospedaje Cocos, Sarmiento 759		$5.00
B	Hospedaje Colón, San Martín 341		$7.00
B	Hospedaje Derby, San Martín 1046 Shared bathroom		$8.00
B	Hospedaje Italiano, Rivadavia 481		$5.00
B	Hospedaje Sevilla, Ameghino 750		$5.00
C	Hospedaje Diana, corner of Belgrano and Rawson		$3.00 per bed
•	Hospedaje Español, 9 de Julio 940		
•	Hospedaje Hamburgo, B Mitre (near bus terminal)		
★	Residencial Chubut, Belgrano 738	(24767	$8.50
★	Residencial Comodoro, España 919	(22582	$9.00
B	Residencial Cari-hue, Belgrano 563	(22946	$5.00
B	Residencial Comercio, Rivadavia 341	(22341	$4.00

Accommodation outside Comodoro Rivadavia

★★★★	Hotel Su Estrella, RN 3 south (near the airport and flying club)	(22482	
★	Motel El Patagon, RN 3 south	(25394	$9.00

CHUBUT PROVINCE

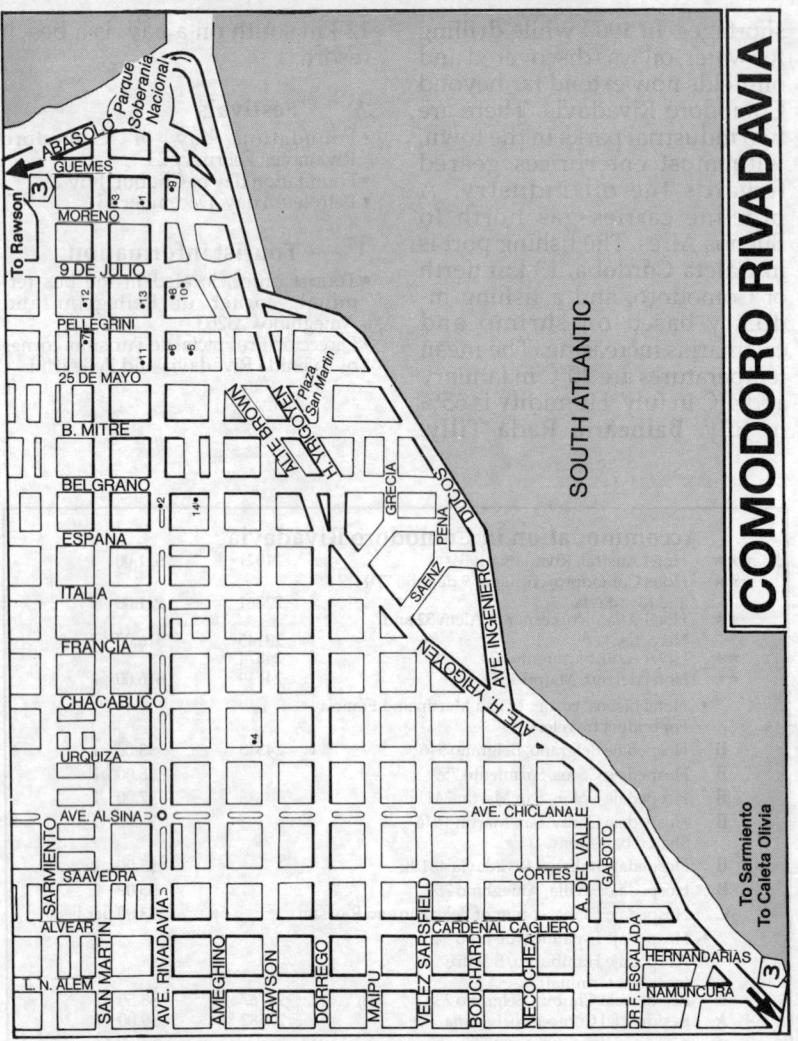

🍴 Eating out

The normal dinner time is from 2200 onwards.
- Restaurant Bon Bife, España 832. Grill
- Restaurant El Jabali, Belgrano 960
- Restaurant El Nautico, Paseo Costanera. Seafood
- Restaurant El Submarino, corner of Belgrano and Sarmiento. Grill
- Restaurant Hamburgo, corner of B Mitre and Brown

CHUBUT PROVINCE

Key to Map
1. Municipalidad
2. Catedral
3. Post office (Encotel)
4. Telephone (Entel)
5. Bus terminal
6. Tourist information
7. Aerolineas Argentinas
8. LADE (airline)
9. Hotel Austral
10. Hotel Comodoro
11. Hospedaje Italiano
12. Hospedaje Colón
13. Residencial Comercio
14. Residencial Chubut

- Restaurant La Estancia, Urquiza 863. Grill
- Restaurant La Fontana di Trevi, San Martín 601
- Restaurant La Minuta, Alem 35. Grill
- Restaurant La Nueva Parrilla, corner of B Mitre and Rawson
- Restaurant La Rastra, Rivadavia 340. Credit cards accepted
- Restaurant La Tradición, corner of Mitre 675 and Ameghino. Grill
- Restaurant Mesón Español, San Martín 674
- Pizzería El Nazareno, corner of San Martín and España
- Pizzería Giulietta, Belgrano 851
- Pizzería Romanella, 25 de Mayo 840
- Cafetería A Mi Estilo, corner of Avenida San Martín and B Mitre
- Cafetería Austral, Rivadavia 190
- Cafetería Bowling, Avenida San Martín 371
- Cafetería Crazy's, corner of B Mitre and San Martín
- Cafetería Dhanus, corner of Avenida Rivadavia and Moreno
- Cafetería Lowibar, Hotel Comodoro, 9 de Julio 770
- Cafetería Pleno Centro, 9 de Julio 860
- Cafetería Reencuentro, Avenida San Martín 371
- Cafetería Scorpios, corner of Belgrano and San Martín
- Cafetería Silvania, corner of Avenida Rivadavia and 25 de Mayo

Eating out outside Comodoro Rivadavia

- Restaurant El Ancla de Oro, Caleta Cordóba, RN 3, 18km north
- Restaurant La Recova Asados, corner of Ruta 3 south and Ramos Mejia. Grill

Post and telegraph
- Post office: Encotel, corner of Avenida San Martín and Moreno. Open 0800–2000
- Post office in bus terminal
- Telephone: Entel, corner of Urquiza and Rawson. Long distance calls 0700–2200

Financial
- Banco de la Nación, corner of San Martín and Abasalo. Cash only
- Bank of London and South America, Rivadavia 264. Cash and travelers' checks; commission is charged on checks. No exchange transactions after 1000
- Casa de Cambio Casa Ostoich, corner of 25 de Mayo and San Martín

Services and facilities
- Hospital: Sanatorio de la Asociacion Española, B Mitre 860 ☏ 22027
- Laundromat: Laverap, corner of 9 de Julio and Rivadavia
- Pharmacy: Farmacia La Ley, corner of Rivadavia and España ☏ 23639 24 hours
- Photographic supplies: Expo Color SRL, L N Alem 729
- Supermarket: La Anónima, corner of San Martín and Guemes

Visas, passports
- Belgian vice-consulate, Rivadavia 283
- Chilean consulate, corner of Avenida Rivadavia and B Mitre
- Italian vice-consulate, Belgrano 1053 ☏ 22753
- South African vice-consulate, Rawson 757
- Spanish consulate, Mesón Español, corner of San Martín and Belgrano

Comodoro Rivadavia

CHUBUT PROVINCE

✈ Air services from Comodoro Rivadavia

Aeropuerto General Mosconi is located off RN 3 south, halfway to Rada Tilly. The bus to airport from outside bus terminal is bus 6, marked "Palazzo", and takes 45 minutes; fare $0.30. An airport bus also leaves from the Aerolineas office. Taxi fare to the airport is $6.00. There is an airport tax of $1.00.

- Aerolineas Argentinas, Avenida San Martín 421 ℡ 24781; airport ℡ 22126
- Austral Lineas Aereas, Avenida San Martín 291 ℡ 22605
- LADE, Avenida Rivadavia 360 ℡ 24934

Destination	Fare	Depart	Services	Hours	Airline
• Alto Río Senguerr	$17.00	1015	Mon, Fri	1	LADE
• Bahía Blanca	$52.00	0950	1–2 services daily	2	Aerolineas, Austral
	$49.00	0930	Wed, Fri	6	LADE
• Buenos Aires (Aeroparque Jorge Newbery)					
	$77.00	0830	4–6 services daily	3	Aerolineas, Austral
	$78.00	0930	Wed, Fri, Sat	9	LADE
• Chapelco	$28.00	0900	Fri	2	LADE
• Córdoba	$77.00	0945	Mon, Thurs, Sat	4	Aerolineas
• El Bolsón	$24.00	0900	Tues	4	LADE
• Esquel	$27.00	0900	Tues, Wed, Sat	2	LADE
	$28.00	1515	Tues, Thurs, Sat	1	Aerolineas
• Gobernador Gregores					
	$17.00	0945	Mon, Thurs	2	LADE
• Lago Argentino	$20.00	0945	Mon	3	LADE
• Mar del Plata	$71.00	1730	Tues, Thurs, Sat, Sun	3	Aerolineas, Austral
	$58.00	0900	Wed, Fri, Sat	8	LADE
• Mendoza	$80.00	0945	Mon, Thurs, Sat	3	Aerolineas
• Neuquén	$46.00	0945	Mon, Tues, Thurs, Sat	2	Aerolineas
	$36.00	0900	Wed, Fri, Sat	5	LADE
• Perito Moreno	$15.00	0945	Mon, Thurs	1	LADE
• Puerto Deseado	$17.00	1030	Mon, Tues, Fri	1	LADE
• Puerto San Julián	$25.00	1030	Mon, Tues, Fr	2	LADE
• Río Gallegos	$39.00	0930	1–2 services daily	2	Aerolineas, Austral
	$35.00	0930	Mon, Tues, Thur, Fri	3	LADE
• Río Grande	$49.00	0930	Mon–Wed, Fri–Sun	3	Aerolineas, Fri, Sat, Sun
	$42.00	0945	Mon, Tues, Fri	6	LADE
• Río Mayo	$13.00	1015	Mon, Fri	1	LADE
• Salta	$102.00	0945	Mon, Thurs, Sat	7	Aerolineas
• San Antonio Oeste					
	$33.00	0930	Fri	3	LADE
• San Carlos de Bariloche					
	$38.00	0900	Tues–Sat	2	Aerolineas, LADE
• San Miguel de Tucumán					
	$95.00	0945	Mon, Thurs, Sat	6	Aerolineas
• Santa Cruz	$28.00	1030	Mon, Tues, Fri	3	LADE
• Trelew	$25.00	0315	1–2 services daily	1	Aerolineas, Austral
	$22.00	0930	Wed, Fri, Sat	2	LADE
• Ushuaia	$36.00	0945	Mon	7	LADE
	$55.00	1120	Tues, Wed, Fri–Sun	3	Aerolineas
• Viedma	$39.00	1305	Sun	1	Aerolineas
	$41.00	0930	Fri, Sat	5	LADE
• Zapala	$28.00	0900	Fri	3½	LADE

Comodoro Rivadavia

CHUBUT PROVINCE

🚗 Motoring

The inland road to Sarmiento and Río Mayo, RN 26, RP 20, and RP 22, is sealed as far as Sarmiento, and partially sealed to Río Mayo.

The coastal road north, RN 3, is surfaced all the way to Buenos Aires.

The coastal road south, RN 3, follows the seashore until Caleta Olivia. After Caleta the road veers inland and runs through mostly dry, flat, and very monotonous Patagonian landscape. The well-surfaced road appears as a straight line disappearing on the horizon.

- Service station: ACA, corner of Alvear and Dorrego
- Car rental: Autorent, Avenida Rivadavia 120. Credit cards accepted

⊕ Tours

- Ceferino, San Martín 372. Also money exchange
- Giobbi, Terminal
- Puelche, Rivadavia 439 ℡ 23012
- Solytur, Rivadavia 827 ℡ 21489

🛍 Shopping

Comodoro Rivadavia would be the last cheap shopping town on your way south, as prices tend to rise steeply the further south you go.

🍸 Entertainment

- Casino de Comodoro Rivadavia, San Martín 847
- Whiskería La Botica, corner of Belgrano and Ameghino

🚌 Buses from Comodoro Rivadavia

The bus terminal is on the corner of Pellegrini and Alte Brown. There is a tourist office inside.

- Cooperativa La Unión: Taxis to Caleta Olivia
- Cooperativa Sportman: Buses to Pico Truncado, Puerto Deseado, and Las Heras
- Empresa Ortiz: Buses to Tinogasta, in Catamarca province
- Empresa Robledo: Fiambalá, in Catamarca province

Destination	Fare	Depart	Services	Hours	Company
• Rawson	$13.00	1300	daily	6	Transporte Patagónico
• Balneario Rada Tilly	$0.40		daily every half hour		Municipal
• Buenos Aires	$42.00	1300	1–2 services daily	32	Puntual/Cóndor, Don Otto
• Caleta Olivia			daily every 15 mins.	1	Empresa La Unión
• Camarone		2400	Wed		Don Otto
• Coihaique (Chile)	$15.00	0100	Mon, Wed, Fri		Empresa Giobbi
Return		0830	Tues, Thurs, Sat		
• Esquel	$17.00	2230	Tues–Thurs, Sat, Sun	9	Don Otto, Empresa Giobbi
• Mendoza		0300	4 services per week		Andesmar
• Neuquén		0300	4 services per week		Andesmar
• Pico Truncado			3 services daily		Don Otto
• Puerto Deseado		0600	Mon, Wed, Fri		La Unión
• Puerto Madryn	$12.00				Transporte Patagónico
• Río Gallegos	$28.00	0515	Sun, Mon, Wed, Fri	14	Transporte Patagónico
• Río Mayo	$7.50		Wed, Sat		Empresa Giobbi
• San Carlos de Bariloche (via Esquel)		2000	Thurs, Sun	22	Don Otto
• San Fernando del Valle de Catamarca	$46.00	1930	Mon, Thurs		Empresa Ortiz
• Sarmiento	$3.80	0700	3 services daily	2	Empresa Trevisan
• Trelew	$9.50		4 services daily	6	Don Otto

Comodoro Rivadavia

Chubut Province

Sport
- Flying: Aero Club Rivadavia, corner of RN 3 south and Belgrano 778 (24671. The club has six airplanes which can be hired for joy flights over Patagonia
- Golf: Santa Lucía golf club, Santa Lucía, N Avellaneda, 3 km from town. Also has tennis courts
- Scuba diving: At Punta Marquez in Balneario Rada Tilly, a beach resort just out of Comodoro Rivadavia. Initial tuition takes about 3 hours
- Water-skiing: Club Náutico Espora, Avenida Costanera

Sightseeing
- Museo Regional Patagonico (Patagonian Regional Museum), formerly the Hotel de Turismo building. Open daily 0900–1200 and 1500–1900
- Museo Paleontológico (Paleontology Museum), Astra RN 3 Km 20
- **Cerro Chenque**: stroll up for panoramic views over the town, and return via Parque Saavedra, which is like a green oasis

Excursions
- **Balneario Rada Tilly**: A summer beach resort 12 km south. There are frequent buses, leaving from the terminal. See Balneario Rada Tilly on page 359
- **Camarones**: 277 km north. At the **Cabo Dos Bahias** nature reserve you can see penguins and sea lions. See Camarones on page 360. Puelche Turismo runs a one-day day tour for $55.00 each, minimum five persons
- **Bosque Petrificado José Ormachea** (José Ormachea Petrified Forest): 145 km west. Take the Trevisan bus to Sarmiento; fare $7.50. Ring Señor José Valera on (0967) 93317 to arrange transport from Sarmiento to Ormachea; fare $19.50 both ways. Alternatively Puelche Turismo organizes minibus tours for $45.00, minimum five persons. See "Excursions" in Sarmiento on page 394
- **Bosque Petrificado Victor Szapelis** (Victor Szapelis Petrified Forest): 172 km west, near **Río Senguerr**. Best reached via Sarmiento. Szapelis is 60 km south of Sarmiento on a gravel road.

Esquel

Postal code: 9200 • Population: 18 000 • (area code: (0945) • Altitude: 540 m
Distance from San Carlos de Bariloche: 291 km southwards on RN 258 then RN 40

Esquel was founded in 1904 by descendants of Welsh colonists from the coast. It is a modern town, is served by many road and air services, and has good facilities. In the nearby **Cordón de Esquel**, which has mountains over 2000 m, a major skiing resort has been opened at **La Hoya**, 15 km north-east of the Esquel. Esquel is also the gateway to the **Parque Nacional Los Alerces** with its many lakes, mountain trails, and ancient *alerces* trees, many of which are 500 years or more old. The area is rewarding for bushwalkers and all outdoor enthusiasts.

It is noteworthy that all rivers from the Esquel area drain to the Pacific Ocean. The Cordón de Esquel, and not the main range of the Andes, is the watershed between the Pacific and the Atlantic. This unusual Andean formation gave rise to a border dispute with Chile, which was settled by an English umpire in favour of Argentina, as the area had in the main been settled by Welsh colonists who had moved up from the coast—the *Rifleros Galeses* or Welsh Rifles formed a major contingent within the Fontana expedition sent by the Argentine government to lay claim to the disputed area.

Tourist information

- Club Andino Esquel, Belgrano, has skiing information
- Jefatura Turismo, corner of Alvear and Fontana, in the bus terminal ℡ 2369. Closed Saturday afternoon and all day Sunday in the off-season

Camping

There are many camping grounds located on the lakes and rivers in the Parque Nacional Los Alerces; see page 379. Camping permits and fishing permits must be obtained from the park ranger.

- Autocamping Municipal Esquel, RN 259, the eastern access road to the park

Eating out

- Restaurant Ahla Wasahla, corner of San Martín 1100 and Sarmiento
- Restaurant Club de Pescadores, Ameghino 108. Grill
- Restaurant El Fogón, Irigoyen 1530. Grill
- Restaurant El Mesón, Rivadavia 1034. Grill; credit cards accepted
- Restaurant Jockey Club, Alvear 949. International cuisine
- Restaurant La Estancia, 25 de Mayo 539. Grill; credit cards accepted
- Restaurant La Tour d'Argent, Hostería La Tour d'Argent, San Martín 1063. International cuisine
- Restaurant 9 de Julio, corner of 9 de Julio and Sarmiento
- Restaurant Tehuelche, Hotel Tehuelche, 9 de Julio 961 (corner of Belgrano)
- Restaurant Vascongada, Hotel Vascongoda, corner of B Mitre and 9 de Julio
- Pizzería Don Pipo, Rivadavia 924
- Pizzería La Zeta, corner of San Martín and Darwin
- Pizzería Los Troceros, corner of 9 de Julio and B Mitre
- Cafetería Atelier, Sarmiento 630. Video
- Cafetería Croesso, Avenida Alvear 1021
- Cafetería El Jabalí Rojo, Sarmiento 530
- Cafetería El Padrino, corner of 25 de Mayo and San Martín
- Cafetería Esquel, San Martín with Fontana
- Cafetería Exedra, corner of 25 de Mayo and Alvear
- Cafetería Grisu, corner of B Mitre and 9 de Julio
- Cafetería Jazz, 25 de Mayo 672
- Cafetería Maika, 25 de Mayo 507
- Cafetería Pantalla Gigante, corner of Sarmiento and Rivadavia
- Cafetería Quijotes, Rivadavia 730. Video
- Cafetería Ski, San Martín 1063
- Cafetería Sol del Sur, 9 de Julio 1086. Video
- Cafetería Tehuelche, corner of 9 de Julio and Belgrano
- English-style pub: El Jabalí Rojo, Sarmiento with Rivadavia
- Tearoom: Casa Suiza, Antartida Argentina 569. German spoken

Post and telegraph

- Post office: Encotel, corner of Avenida Alvear and Fontana
- Telephone: Entel, San Martín 850

Financial

- Turismo Via Sur, corner of 9 de Julio and 25 de Mayo. Money exchange
- Banco de la Nación, corner of Güemes and San Martín. Cash and travelers' checks (charges commission on checks); open Mon–Fri 1000–1300

Services and facilities

- Laundromat: Laverap, B Mitre 543

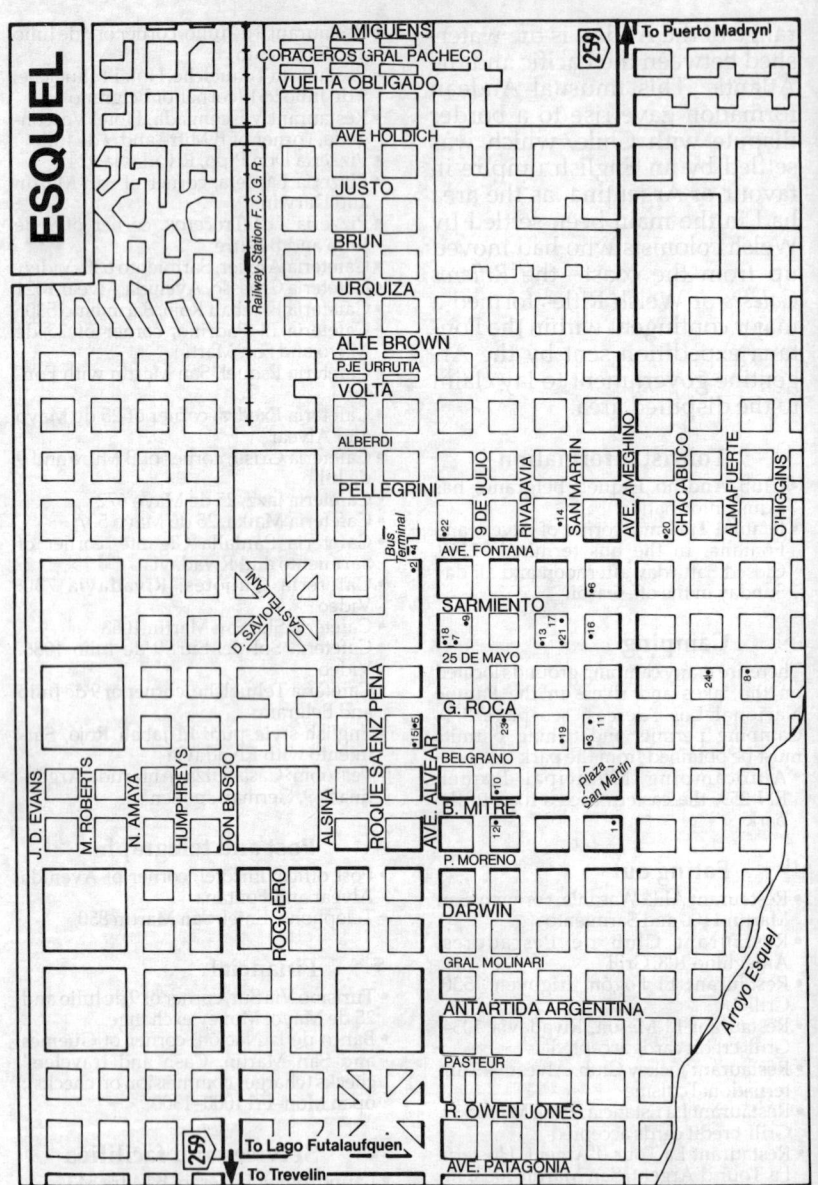

Esquel

Chubut Province

- Pharmacy: Farmacia El Cóndor, Roca 671
- Photographic supplies: Foto Stuttgart, corner of 9 de Julio and 25 de Mayo

Supermarkets

- La Plaza, corner of San Martín and B Mitre
- La Torinesa, corner of B Mitre and San Martín

Motoring

Service stations

- ACA, corner of Ameghino and 25 de Mayo
- YPF, corner of Rivadavia and Fontana

Trains

Esquel is the southernmost point in the Argentine rail system. F C General Roca station is on the corner of Roggero and Urquiza. Traveling to and from Buenos Aires involves changing trains in Ingeniero Jacobacci.

- Buenos Aires: First class: $33.50, tourist class $25.00; departs 2200 Thurs and Sun. Change in Ingeniero Jacobacci
- Nahuel Pan: Fare: $6.00; departs 1500 Mon or on demand

Water transport

Launch services on the lakes

Normally launches leave from **Puerto Limanao** on the western side of **Lago Futalaufquén** and go right up to **Lago Verde** through the channel linking the lakes. Regular launch services run only during the summer months (December–February) and after that only as required. The owners may be contacted at Motel Pucón Pai (on the eastern side of Lago Futalaufquén) if there are at least ten persons. In very dry seasons when the water level is low the launches leave from Motel Pucón Pai. See "Excursions" below, and Parque Nacional Los Alerces on page 379. The cruise departs at 1000 and returns to Puerto Limanao approximately 1900; fare $14.00.

Tours

- Esquel Tours, Fontana 754 ℂ 2704. Organizes lake tours
- Sol del Sur, Hotel Sol de Sur, 9 de Julio 1089 ℂ 2189
- Tehuelche Safaris, corner of 9 de Julio and Roca ℂ 3217
- Turismo Via Sur, 9 de Julio 1027 ℂ 2757

Shopping

Locally manufactured jams and jellies and liqueurs are well known for their quality.

- Olgbrun Artesanias, San Martín 1137. Good souvenir shop

Sport

- Fishing: The fishing season runs from November to April. Permits can be obtained from the tourist office or from kiosks in the national park

---

Key to Map

1. Municipalidad
2. Post office (Encotel)
3. Telephone (Entel)
4. Tourist information
5. Banco de la Nación
6. Aerolineas Argentinas
7. LADE (airline)
8. Hospital
9. Hotel Sol del Sur
10. Hotel Tehuelche
11. Hotel Ski
12. Hotel Vascongada
13. Residencial Hotel Argentino
14. Hostería Los Troncos
15. Hostería Angelina
16. Hostería La Tour d'Argent
17. Residencial Esquel
18. Residencial Huemul
19. Residencial Huenu
20. Residencial Los Tulipanes
21. Residencial Maika
22. Residencial Mayo
23. Residencial Zacarias
24. Hospedaje Beirut

Esquel

Chubut Province

🛏 Accommodation

The tourist office has addresses of private accommodation.

★★★	Hotel Sol del Sur, 9 de Julio 1089	✆ 2189	$19.00	👤
★★★	Hotel Tehuelche, corner of 9 de Julio 961 and Belgrano	✆ 2420	$22.00	👤
★★	Hotel Ski, San Martín 1063	✆ 2795, 2254	$10.00	👤
★	Hotel Vascongada, corner of 9 de Julio and Mitre	✆ 2361	$9.00	👤
	Credit cards accepted; cheaper with shared bathroom			
★★★	Hostería Los Troncos, corner of San Martín and Fontana	✆ 2423	$12.00	👤
★★	Hostería Angelina, corner of Avenida Alvear 758 and Belgrano	✆ 2753, 2763	$9.00	👤
★★	Hostería La Tour d'Argent, San Martín 1063	✆ 2530	$15.00	👤
•	Hospedaje Beirut, 25 de Mayo 246	✆ 2886		
★★	Residencial Esquel, San Martín 1042	✆ 2534	$10.00	👤
★	Residencial Arrayanes, Antartida Argentina 767	✆ 2082	$7.00	👤
★	Residencial Huemul, corner of Alvear 1009 and 25 de Mayo	✆ 2533, 2149	$9.00	👤
★	Residencial Huentru Niyeu, Chacabuco 606 (corner of Perito Moreno)	✆ 2576	$7.00	👤
★	Residencial Hueñu, San Martín 822	✆ 2589	$9.00	👤
★	Residencial Los Tulipanes, Avenida Fontana 365	✆ 2748	$8.00	👤
★	Residencial Maika, corner of San Martín and 25 de Mayo	✆ 2457	$10.00	👤
A	Residencial Hotel Argentino, 25 de Mayo 862	✆ 2237	$8.00	👤
B	Residencial Zacarias, Roca 636	✆ 2270	$4.50	👤
C	Residencial Al Sol, Chacabuco 762		$5.00	👤
•	Residencial Adriatico, Rivadavia 477	✆ 2751		
•	Residencial Mayo, corner of Fontana and Alvear			
•	Vacation apartments: DUT Esquel, corner of Rivadavia and Alberdí	✆ 2496		
	Credit cards accepted			
•	Vacation apartments: Artesanías Olgbrun, Sarmiento 1137			

Accommodation outside Esquel

★★	Motel La Hoya, corner of Ameghino 2296 and Libertad (1 km on airport road)	✆ 2473	$12.00	👥
★★	Cabañas Rayen Hue, corner of Avellaneda and Avenida Miguen	✆ 2677, 2185	$29.00	4
•	Vacation apartments: Turisol, Patagonia 1503 Holiday apartments	✆ 2601		

- Hunting: The hunting season for red fox and wild boar runs from April to August
- Skiing: At La Hoya, 13 km from Esquel
- Ski hire: Tehuelche Safaris, corner of 9 de Julio and Roca

🎭 Entertainment

- Bowling: Zorba, corner of Ameghino and 25 de Mayo
- Disco Ver Club, 25 de Mayo 510
- Disco Step, 9 de Julio 730
- Disco Ragtime, corner of Rivadavia and Sarmiento (upstairs)

Esquel

CHUBUT PROVINCE

✈ Air services from Esquel

The airport is 20km east of town reached on a paved road.
A taxi to the to airport costs $10.00; a bus costs $4.00.
- Aerolineas Argentinas, corner of Sarmiento and San Martín ✆ 2539
- LADE, 25 de Mayo 777 ✆ 2227
- TAN, 25 de Mayo 777

Destination	Fare	Depart	Services	Hours	Airline
• Bahía Blanca	$47.00	1535	Wed	3½	LADE
• Buenos Aires (Aeroparque Jorge Newbery)					
	$95.00	0300	daily	3	Aerolineas
	$76.00	1535	Wed, Sat	6	Empresa LADE
• Comodoro Rivadavia					
	$28.00	1405	Tues, Thurs, Sat	1	Aerolineas
	$27.00	1230	Tues, Wed, Fri	2	LADE
• El Bolsón	$12.00	1150	Tues	1	LADE
• Mar del Plata	$57.00	1535	Wed, Sat	5	LADE
• Neuquén	$33.00	1535	Mon–Sat	2	LADE
	$40.00	1440	Mon, Tues, Thur–Sat	2	Aerolineas, TAN
• Puerto Deseado	$33.00	1420	Tues, Fri	3	LADE
• Puerto San Julián	$35.00	1420	Tues, Fri	4	LADE
• Río Gallegos	$42.00	1420	Tues, Fri	5	LADE
• Río Grande	$46.00	1420	Tues, Fri	6	LADE
• San Carlos de Bariloche					
	$18.00	0300	Mon–Sat	1	Aerolineas, TAN
	$14.00	1150	Tues, Wed, Sat	2	LADE
• Santa Cruz	$37.00	1420	Tues, Fri	5	LADE
• Trelew	$36.00	1340	Mon, Wed, Fri, Sun	1	Aerolineas
	$27.00	1420	Tues, Fri	1½	LADE
• Viedma	$24.00	1535	Sat	3	LADE

📷 Sightseeing

- Museo, corner of Belgrano and Ameghino. Open Mon–Fri 0900–1200 and 1800–2100, Sat 1900–2100. Entrance free

🌳 Excursions

- **Trevelín**: 21 km westwards on RN 258. A charming still very Welsh community with many tearooms. There are regular buses to and from Esquel. See Trevelín on page 399
- **Nant y Fall** falls: 11 km from Trevelín. Take a Don Otto bus to **La Balsa**
- **Futalaufquén hydro-electric scheme**: Situated on the **Río Futalaufquén**, the dam is 600 m long and 120 m high, creating a lake of 9200 ha which supplies electricity to the aluminum smelter in Puerto Madryn by means of two 330 kw power lines
- **La Hoya**: Situated in the **Cordón de Esquel** with mountains reaching over 2000 m. A modern skiing resort has been developed. Regular bus services ply between Esquel and the base of the slopes; in sum-

Esquel

Chubut Province

🚌 Buses from Esquel

The bus terminal and main taxi rank is on the corner of Fontana and Alvear ✆ 2233. There are no direct buses to Buenos Aires—it is best to go via San Carlos de Bariloche. During winter Empresa Mercedes runs only three services a week to Bariloche.

Destination	Fare	Depart	Services	Hours	Company
• Bahía Blanca	$29.00				
• Balsa (on the Chilean border)					
	$1.50	1400	Mon, Wed, Fri	2	Empresa Don Otto
• Carrenleufú	$3.50	0900	Tues, Thurs Sat	4	Don Otto
• Cholila	$4.50	0800	Mon–Sat	3	Mercedes
• Comodoro Rivadavia					
	$17.00	1430	Tues, Thur, Sat, Sun	9	Don Otto
	$17.00	0600	Tues, Fri, Sun	15	Angel Giobbi
• Lago Futalaufquen	$1.20	0630	Mon (2), Thurs–Sat		Transporte Esquel
• Parque Nacional Los Alerces					
	$2.80	daily			
• Río Mayo	$12.80	0600	Tues, Fri, Sun	10	Angel Giobbi
• San Carlos de Bariloche via El Maitén					
	$10.50	0800	Mon, Tues, Thur, Sat	9	Mercedes
via Lago Futalaufquen					
	$10.50	0800	Mon–Sat	9	Mercedes
• Trelew	$13.50	1900	Mon, Thurs	11	Don Otto
	$15.00	2130	Thurs–Sun	10	Chubut
via Languiñeo	$15.00	0700	Wed	11	Chubut
• Trevelín	$0.60	daily			

mer they are less frequent. See La Hoya on page 378

- **Parque Nacional Los Alerces** lake tour: Launch cruises depart from **Puerto Limanao** on the western side of **Lago Futalaufquén**, and cruise up the fjord-like lake to the far northern end where the **Río Arrayanes** forms the connection between **Lago Verde** and Lago Futalaufquén. The launch continues into Lago Verde. There you disembark and make your way on foot to **Lago Menéndez** where you board another vessel. The cruise on Lago Menendez includes superb views of the **Glaciar Torrecillas**—take your camera. The forests around this lake are much denser than those on the *meseta*, resembling the forests on the Chilean side of the Andes. The trees are mainly conifers and giant fern trees. The most exciting trees however are the *alerces* or *alerzal* trees, 40 m tall and 3 m in diameter, some of which are estimated to be a thousand years old and still growing.

Trips are organized by tour operators in Esquel; see the "Tours" and "Water transport" sections above. If you prefer to spend more time in the park there are several hotels, motels, and camping grounds; see Parque Nacional Los Alerces on page 379

- **Nahuel Pan**: If you are traveling by tourist train the trip takes three hours. In the summer season a regular train departs every Tuesday at 0900 from

Esquel

CHUBUT PROVINCE

Esquel. A special train ride can be organized for a minimum of 20 persons. Fare $3.50

- **Parque Nacional Lago Puelo**: This is a 382 km return trip. Take RN 258 north passing **Lago Futalaufquén** and **Lago Rivadavia**. At the village of Lago Rivadavia you can stay at Cabañas Carrinleufú 300 m down from the road on the river. In the village, check at the sign post whether there are any vacancies. Five km further on is **Cholila** with Hostería El Trebol on **Lago Pellegrini**. From here you continue north, passing **Lago Lezama**. The road goes alternately over *mesetas* above 600 m, and through valleys which are only 250 m above sea-level. For this reason plants can be cultivated which normally grow only in warmer climates. The country around **Epuyén** is heavily forested; timber is the backbone of the local economy. You can take a day trip organized by tour operators in Esquel; see "Tours" above. Alternatively you can take local buses and make frequent stops, staying overnight in camping spots such as those on the shores of Lago Futalaufquén and Lago Verde

- Futalaufquén in Chile: Take a Don Otto bus to **La Balsa**. Two km before la Balsa there is a steep road leading uphill on the left to a caravan park overlooking the valley and the snow-capped border mountains. A raft takes you across the **Río Futalaufquén** which is approximatly 200 m wide and fast-flowing; the raft operates 0800–2000, during summer only. Once across the river the border post is only short distance from the ferry. Usually Chilean *colectivos* are waiting to pick up passengers to Futalaufquén; fare $16.00. On the Chilean side the river forms waterfalls and cascades. From Futalaufquén you can continue on to Puerto Ramirez and visit Lago Yelcho. The return to Argentina may be made via Palena. The border is on the **Paso Carrenleufú**. Return via **Corcovado** on a Don Otto bus to Esquel. This trip may take two to three days

- **Lago Fontana** and **Lago La Plata**: 385 km south. Take a Giobbi bus to Alto Río Senguerr. The attractions of the lakes include trout fishing and large numbers of deer. See "Excursions" in Alto Río Senguerr on page 359

GAIMÁN

Postal code: 9105 • (area code: (0965) •
Population: 4200
Distances from Trelew: 16 km westwards on RN 25

Gaimán was founded in 1885 on the north bank of the **Río Chubut** and was the first Welsh municipality in the lower Chubut valley. Of all the Welsh towns in Chubut, Gaimán has best retained its Welsh character.

Chubut Province

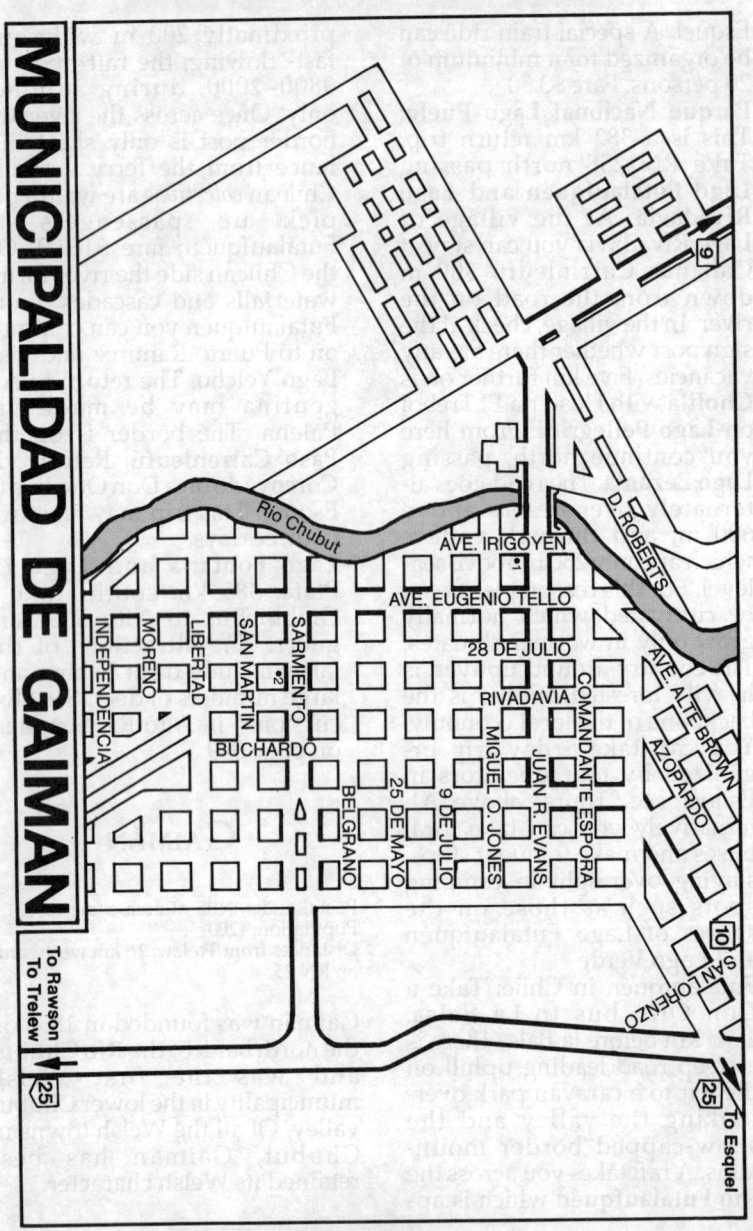

Gaimán

CHUBUT PROVINCE

Key to Map
1. Municipalidad
2. Museo

🚶 Festivals

Eisteddfod (Welsh Festival of Arts): Early August

⛺ Camping
- Municipal, corner of H Yrigoyen and Libertad on the banks of the Río Chubut

✉ Post and telegraph
- Post office: Encotel, Libertad
- Telephone: Entel, Tello 456

🍴 Eating out

Tearooms
- Eima, Eugenio Tello 571
- Gaimán, corner of H Yrigoyen and Sarmiento
- Plas y Coed, Michael D Jones
- Ty Draw Ir Avon, Juan C Evans
- Ty Gwyn, 9 de Julio 147
- Ty Nain, H Yrigoyen 283

🚌 Buses

Colectivos from Trelew take 45 minutes and depart every 15 minutes.
- Trelew: Fare $0.50; 10 services daily; Empresa 28 de Julio

📷 Sightseeing
- Welsh historical museum, corner of Sarmiento and 28 de Julio. Open Mon–Fri 0700–1300 and 1600–2100
- Museum of the colony. Open during winter Tues, Thurs, Sat 1500–1800
- Bethel Chapel
- First house built in Gaimán, in 1874

🎯 Excursions
- **La Angostura**: 10 km from the center of Gaimán. Here the **Río Chubut** runs through a narrow valley leaving just enough space for a road and irrigation channel

HOYO DE EPUYÉN

Postal code: 8431 • Population: 1200 • (area code: (0944) • Altitude: 200 m
Distance from Esquel: 210 km northwards; take RN 259 eastwards, then RN 40 northwards, RP 70 south-west, and finally RN 258 northwards again

Hoyo de Epuyén is situated in the **Río Epuyén valley** in the *precordillera*, halfway between San Carlos de Bariloche and Esquel. The name *"Hoyo"* ("Pit") which the first settlers gave to the spot is fitting as it resembles a hole in the middle of the mountains. The climate favors berry fruits which are extensively cultivated and made into delicious jams by the locals. The many hanging bridges over the Río Epuyén are an interesting feature.

🛏 Accommodation
★ Hotel La Carreta 🍴
★ Bungalows La Catarata 🍴

CHUBUT PROVINCE

▲ Camping
- Near La Catarata, 3 km from Hoyo de Epuyén
- Puerto Patriada on Lago Epuyen, 14 km from Hoyo de Epuyén

✉ Post and telegraph
- Post office: Encotel, Islas Malvinas
- Telephone: Entel, corner of Islas Malvinas and Las Almendras

🚌 Buses
- Comodoro Rivadavia: Fare $6.30
- San Carlos de Bariloche: Fare $4.50; 2 services daily; Empresa T A Mercedes

🚗 Motoring
- Gas station RN 258 south

♣ Excursions
- **La Catarata**: This waterfall, which plunges 81 m, is just 3 km out of town. A steep path leads up through pine forests to where the falls start, giving impressive views over the cultivated valley below. The cascade forms a little pool which is a good spot for swimming. Nearby are the bungalows and camping ground. Around the waterfall is a 13 ha nature reserve
- **Laguna del Plesiosauro**: 15 km south on RN 258. It is hidden from the road by trees and shrubs, so ask the locals. A good swimming spot
- **Puerto Patriada**: 14 km, on **Lago Epuyén**. There is a sandy beach on this part of the lake. A good spot for camping, and for water sports and fishing
- **Parque Nacional Lago Puelo**. See "Excursions" in Esquel on page 375

LA HOYA

Distance from Esquel: 13 km northwards

Skiing in La Hoya is possible until the end of October. The best months are August and September.

The skiing slopes range from between 1300 and 1700 m, and can be reached using ski-lifts and T-bars. In summer the area is a favorite walking region, with water tumbling down from the lofty heights, forming cascades and little brooks. There are panoramic views over Esquel.

Lift tickets cost $35.00 for a weekly ticket, or $7.50 for a day ticket. Ski and ski boot hire costs $7.00 per day. A half-hour group ski class costs $4.50 per person.

Some figures on the ski lifts:
- Chairlift: Length 1000 m, carries 600 skiers per hour
- T-Bar: Length 550 m, carries 600 skiers per hour
- T-Bar: Length 450 m, carries 600 skiers per hour
- Poma: Length 300 m, carries 400 skiers per hour
- Poma: Length 150 m, carries 400 skiers per hour

ℹ Tourist information
- The Club Andino Esquel has a tourist office at the base.

🛏 Accommodation
- ★ Hotel La Hoya, at the base ⁂ open July–October $23.00 ✦ half board

🍴 Eating out
- Restaurant at the base

- Confitería La Piedra at the end of the chairlift

🚌 Buses

In winter there are regular ski buses from Esquel to the base of chairlifts.

LOS ALTARES

Postal code: 9207 • Population: 600
Distances
- From Trelew: 291 km westwards on RN 25
- From Esquel: 324 km eastwards on RN 40 then RN 25

Huge blocks of rocks in the vicinity which look like cyclopean altars have given rise to the name of Los Altares, which means "The Altars".

When passing through, do not miss the rock paintings in the vicinity.

🛏 Accommodation
- Motel Los Altares (ACA), RN 25 Km 321

🚌 Buses

Road transport is provided by Empresa Chubut which runs daily buses between Esquel and Trelew.

🚗 Motoring
- Service station: ACA

📷 Excursions
- There are important rock paintings showing the artistic talents of the pre-Columbian population within easy walking distance from the village on the main road. The main painting, 1 m high by 50 cm wide, is painted with mineral pigments and is believed to date from the tenth century AD

PARQUE NACIONAL LOS ALERCES

Distance from Esquel: 60 km westwards on RN 259 then RP 71

Parque Nacional Los Alerces is located west of Esquel. The entrance to the park is at **Arroyo Los Coihues**; the entrance fee is $1.00.

The natural attractions of the eastern side of Los Alerces are similar to those of Parque Nacional Nahuel Huapí and Parque Nacional Lanín in Neuquén province (see "Excursions" in San Martín de los Andes on page 307), but it is much less developed for tourism than these parks.

The trip via **Trevelín**. following the **Río Futaleufú**, takes you through an interesting part of the park. Because of the Futaleufú hydro-electric dam you can go only a short distance into the park this way, and **Lago Situación** is closed off to the public. Entry to Futaleufú dam is only allowed at 1500, under police supervision; photography is not permitted, except on top of the dam itself.

The trees in the park are interesting: there are hundred-year-old larches, *coihues*, and

CHUBUT PROVINCE

arrayanes some of which are 500 years old.

The fishing season on **Lago Futalaufquen** begins on November 15.

Festivals

A fishing festival is held at Motel Pucón Pai to open the fishing season.

Accommodation

- Hotel Futalaufquen, on the west side of Lake Futalaufquen, 65 km from Esquel just north of Puerto Limanao $28.00 half board
- Hostería Cume-Hue, RP 71 on the east side of Lago Futalaufquen, 85 km from Esquel $23.00 full board. Closed in winter
- Hostería Los Tepues, RP 71 on the eastern side of Lago Futalaufquen, 70 km from Esquel $13.50 half board
- Hostería Quime Quipán, RP 71 on the east side of Lago Futalaufquen, 65 Km from Esquel $20.00 half board. Closed in winter
- Motel Pucón Pai, RP 71 on the east side of Lago Futalaufquen, 69 km from Esquel $12.50 half board. Open all year round; ACA 10% discount
- Cabañas Tejas Negras, RP 71 on the eastern side of Lago Futalaufquen, 71 km from Esquel $42.00 for 5

Camping

- Autocamping Bahía Rosales, RN 258 on the eastern side of Lago Futalaufquen, 72 km from Esquel (between Arroyos Centinela and Pedregoso). Room for 40 tents
- Autocamping Los Maitenes, on the southern side of Lago Futalaufquen on the **Río Desaguadero** on the road to Puerto Limanao, 63 km from Esquel. The national park headquarters is 200 m upriver, where fishing permits are available. Closed in winter
- Autocamping Pucón Pai, Motel Pucón Pai, RN 258 on the eastern side of Lago Futalaufquen, 69 km from Esquel. Room for 20 tents
- Cerro Riscoso, RN 258 on the east side of Lago Futalaufquen, just before Laguna Verde. 18 ha of camping grounds; no facilities
- Lago Rivadavia, RN 258 on eastern side of **Lago Rivadavia**, near the *guardaparque* kiosk, 25km south of Cholila. No facilities. The camping area is 10 ha
- Laguna Verde, RN 258 on the eastern side of Lago Futalaufquen, 83 km from Esquel (30 km from Cholila). No facilities. A *guardaparque* (park ranger) kiosk is nearby. This beautiful spot overlooks the **Río Rivadavia** as it emerges from Lago Rivadavia and flows into **Lago Verde** (which really is emerald green). The area set aside is 10 ha and there is room for 40 tents
- Playa Francés, RN 258 on the east side of Lago Futalaufquen, on the north arm. No facilities
- Punta Matos, RN 258 on the east side of Lago Futalaufquen, at the beginning of the north arm. No facilities
- Río Rivadavia, RN 258 on the east side of Lago Futalaufquen, at the southern end of the eastern side of Lago Rivadavia, 30 km south of Cholila. No facilities. The camping area is 20 ha

Buses

RP 71 passes through the park connecting all the lakes. Empresa Transportes Mercedes runs buses on this route to and from San Carlos de Bariloche stopping at all hotels and most camping sites.

- Esquel–Los Alerces: Fare $4.00; departs 0630 daily in summer. Last bus returns 1800
- Esquel–Puerto Limanao: Served by two daily *micros* during the tourist season
- San Carlos de Bariloche–Lago Futalaufquen: Fare $8.50; departs 0830 daily in summer. During the off-season a bus goes to the southern tip of the lake only; fare $5.15. A taxi costs $72.00

Water transport

There are launch trips on the lakes; see "Excursions" below.

Sport

Local guides hire outboard motor boats for fishing.

Parque Nacional Los Alerces

Chubut Province

⚘ Excursions

See also "Excursions" in Esquel on page 373.

All tours to the park can be arranged in Esquel; see "Tours" in Esquel on page 371.
- **Cinco Saltos** and **El Dedal**: Good walks from Hotel Futalaufquen
- **Lago Menéndez**: A launch trip departs from **Puerto Limanao** at 1000, goes along the **Río Arrayanes** to **Lago Verde** and on to Lago Menéndez. Continue by another launch to the northwestern end of Lago Menéndez passing **Cerro Torrecillas** and the **Glaciar Torrecillas**. From there it is a short walk to **Lago Cisne** which has views to the main chain of the Andes. This trip can be booked through Tehuelche Safaris in Esquel. The fare is $15.00; book early

Puerto Madryn

Postal code: 9120 • ✆ area code: (0965) • Population: 32 000
Distances
- From Esquel: 668 km eastwards on RN 40, then RP 62, RN 25, and RN 3
- From Río Gallegos: 1075 km northwards on RN 3
- From Viedma: 437 km southwards on RN 3

Puerto Madryn, on the **Golfo Nuevo**, was the starting point for Welsh colonization when, in 1865, Sir Jones Parry arrived with 150 Welsh families. It was named after a castle in Wales. The town is the gateway to the nature reserve on the **Península Valdés**.

Originally the small port served the solely agricultural community of the **Río Chubut** valley. Tourism, however, has changed the modern town beyond recognition. In order to broaden the economic base an aluminum smelter is located on the outskirts. Electricity comes from the Futaleufú hydroelectric power station near the Chilean Border via two 330 kv power lines. The town has good nightlife and facilities for water sports such as sailing and diving. Within easy reach is one of the most important wildlife reserves in the world where sea elephants, killer whales, right whales, and seals gather in the mating season and give birth to their young. Whales can even be sighted from the seaside promenade in Puerto Madryn in September and October.

兴 Festivals
- Foundation Day of the Welsh Colony: July 28

ℹ Tourist information
- Jefatura de Turismo, Sarmiento 386 ✆ 71514. Open 0800–1300
- Information kiosk, J A Roca, on the beachfront

▲ Camping
- ACA site, Punta Cuevas, 6 km south of town. Caravan $4.00 for 4 persons; tent hire $3.50 per day
- Balneario Acuario
- Camping Municipal Sur, Alte Brown, at Punta Loma, near the *lobería* $2.50

Chubut Province

🛏 Accommodation in Puerto Madryn

Hosterías usually have private bathrooms; *hospedajes* with an "A" rating always have private bathrooms; those with a "B" rating always have shared bathrooms. Book in advance for summer accommodation in the better hotels.

★★★★	Hotel Península Valdés, J A Roca 165 Includes breakfast	(71292	$30.00
★★★	Hotel Costanera, Brown 759	(72234, 7103	$21.00
★★★	Hotel Playa, J A Roca 181 🍴 Credit cards accepted	(71446	$21.00
★★★	Hotel Tolosa, R S Peña 253	(71850	$18.50
★★★	Hotel Yanco, J A Roca 626	(71581	$16.00
★★	Hotel Carreras, Zar 852	(71531	$16.00
★★	Hotel Hostal del Rey, Brown 681 (on the beach)	(71156	$16.00
★★	Hotel Gran Madryn, Lugones 40	(71728	$16.00
★★	Hotel Gran Palace, 28 de Julio 390 🍴	(71009	$14.00
★★	Hotel Mora, Justo 654 🍴	(71424	$16.00
★	Hotel Atalaya, García 149		$12.50
★	Hotel Azul, Gobernador Maiz 545		$12.50
★	Hostería Anclamar, 25 de Mayo 880	(71809	$9.50
★	Hostería La Posta, J A Roca 33	(71839	$9.50
★	Hostería Tandil, Justo 770 🍴	(71017	$9.50
A	Hospedaje Petit, Alvear 845	(71460	$6.00
A	Hospedaje San Francisco, Sarmiento 1290	(71712	$6.00
A	Hospedaje Suyay, 9 de Julio 57	(71539	$5.50
B	Hospedaje Aguila, corner of Zar and Peña		$5.00
B	Hospedaje Argentino, 25 de Mayo 253		$5.00
B	Hospedaje El Antiguo, 28 de Julio 147		$5.00
B	Hospedaje El Dorado, San Martín 545	(71046	$5.00
B	Hospedaje España, corner of San Martín and Belgrano		$5.00
B	Hospedaje Jo's, Bolívar 75	(71433	$5.00
B	Hospedaje Paris, corner of 25 de Mayo 101 and Peña	(72241	$5.00
B	Hospedaje Paula's, Albarracín 249	(72384	$9.50
B	Hospedaje Vaskonia, 25 de Mayo 43	(71427	$5.00
•	Apart Hotel Palma, corner of J A Roca and H Yrigoyen	(72044	
★★	Motel ACA, Ribera Marítima Norte 🍴	(71452	$14.00
★★	Motel Hipocampo, Vesta 33	(73605	$11.00
★★	Motel El Cid, 25 de Mayo 852	(71416	$16.00

🍴 Eating out

- Restaurant Aguila, corner of Zar 75 and Peña. Seafood
- Restaurant Cantina El Náutico, J A Roca 790 (corner of Lugones). Seafood
- Restaurant Club Náutico Atlántico Sur, Costanera Norte
- Restaurant Comedor ACA, Costanera Norte
- Restaurant Costanera, Hotel Costanera, Brown 759. Seafood
- Restaurant "2½", J A Roca 680. Pizzeria
- Restaurant Hermandad del Escrofano, corner of J A Roca and Gales. Seafood
- Restaurant Hueney, Peña 38. Grill
- Restaurant La Caleta, San Martín 156. Seafood
- Restaurant Mar Azul, Gales 494. Seafood

Chubut Province

- Restaurant Marejada, Rawson. Seafood
- Restaurant Mora, Hotel Mora, Justo 654. Paellas
- Restaurant Palace (Hotel), corner of 28 de Julio and San Martín
- Restaurant Paris, corner of Peña and 25 de Mayo. Seafood, pastas
- Restaurant Poseidon, corner of García and Salta. Seafood
- Restaurant Ricardito, J A Roca 150. Pizzería
- Restaurant Tandil, Hotel Tandil, Justo 770
- Restaurant Vaskonia, Hospedaje Vaskonia, 25 de Mayo 43
- Restaurant 25 de Mayo, 25 de Mayo 639. Seafood
- Restaurant Zenon, Zar 752. Grills, pastas
- Pizzería Cabildo, H Yrigoyen 38
- Pizzería El Viejo Almacen del 900, 9 de Julio 240
- Pizzería Loco's, corner of San Martín and 28 de Julio
- Pizzería Quine, corner of Peña and 25 de Mayo
- Pizzería Roselli, corner of J A Roca and Peña
- Cafetería Cielo Azul, corner of B Mitre and R S Peña. Chess players
- Cafetería Italia, corner of 28 de Julio and 25 de Mayo
- Cafetería La Calesita, corner of J A Roca and 9 de Julio. Milk bar
- Cafetería Península Valdés, J A Roca 161
- Cafetería Playa, corner of 28 de Julio and J A Roca
- Cafetería Pleno Centro, corner of 28 de Julio and 25 de Mayo
- Cafetería San Marco, corner of 28 de Julio and B Mitre
- Cafetería Torremar, corner of J A Roca and 9 de Julio. Opens early; good coffee
- Tearoom La Goleta, J A Roca 69. Welsh afternoon teas 1700–1900
- Tearoom La Casa de Dora, Zar 717. Open from 1600 onwards

Post and telegraph

- Post office: Encotel, corner of Gobernador Maiz 293 and Belgrano
- Telephone: Entel, Avenida 28 de Julio 338

Financial

There are no *cambios* in Puerto Madryn. Travel agencies, banks, and hotels give poor rates even for cash dollars. The nearest town with *cambios* is Trelew; otherwise stock up in Buenos Aires before coming south.

- Banco Alas, R S Peña 76. Cash advances on Visa card

Services and facilities

- Bicycle rental: corner of J A Roca and H Yrigoyen
- Dry cleaner: Los Tres Hermanos, Avenida Zar 176

Laundromats

- Prestolav, corner of Bulevar Guillermo Brown and Avenida Galés
- Burbúja, Gobierno Maiz 440. Also dry-cleaning and ironing

Photographic supplies

- Petrel Foto Cine, Galería Castilla, corner of 28 de Julio and 25 de Mayo
- Photographic supplies: Foto Stuttgart, B Mitre 160

Supermarkets

- Madryn, corner of 28 de Julio and 25 de Mayo
- La Anónima, corner of H Yrigoyen and 25 de Mayo

Air services

The airport is near Trelew.

Motoring

- Car rental: Patagónico Rent a Car, corner of Avenida Galés and Piedrabuena (71797
- Service station: ACA, corner of Avenida Zar and H Yrigoyen

Tours

- Coyun-Có Turismo (Mar y Valle), J A Roca 37 (72872
- Golfo Nuevo Travel Agency, corner of 28 de Julio and J A Roca
- Pu-Ma, 28 de Julio 40 (71482. Also hires mini-buses with driver for day trips

Puerto Madryn

Chubut Province

Key to Map
1. Municipalidad
2. Iglesia
3. Post office (Encotel)
4. Telephone (Entel)
5. Tourist information
6. Banco de la Nación
7. Casino
8. Hotel Península Valdés
9. Hotel Costanera
10. Hotel Playa
11. Hotel Tolosa
12. Hotel Yanco
13. Hotel Hostal del Rey
14. Hotel Gran Madryn
15. Hotel Gran Palace
16. Hostería La Posta
17. Hospedaje Suyay
18. Hospedaje Aguila
19. Hospedaje El Antiguo
20. Hospedaje España
21. Hospedaje Vaskonia
22. Apart Hotel Palma
23. Motel ACA

- Receptivo Puerto Madryn, J A Roca 141 ℡ 72418
- Tour-Mar, 25 de Mayo 157 ℡ 71581

Shopping
- Regionales Tehuelche, 28 de Julio 113. Ceramics, carpets, and leather goods
- Madryn Mar SRL, J A Roca 620. Nautical sports equipment
- La Botica de Agata, Galería Castilla, 28 de Julio. Souvenirs

Sport
- Sailing: Conditions in the **Golfo Nuevo** favor sailing. The centres for sailing are **Puerto Madryn** and **Puerto Pirámides**, on the **Península Valdés**. There are several clubs, such as Club Náutico Atlántico Sud and Club Náutico Achernar, both in Puerto Madryn
- Scuba diving: The clear waters of the Golfo Nuevo attract skin divers from all over the world. The Centro Nacional Patagónico welcomes inquiries from experienced scuba divers. Hire of diving equipment is $15.00 per day. For those who have never dived before underwater training sessions are organized by the following operators:

Safari Submarine, Mitre 80. Equipment hire

Cressi Sub, H Yrigoyen 200 ℡ 71649. Equipment hire

Complejo Náutico Ferramar, corner of

Buses from Puerto Madryn
The bus terminal is on the corner of H Yrigoyen and San Martín.

Destination	Fare	Depart	Services	Hours	Company
• Bahía Blanca	$14.00	0700	daily	12	Empresa Don Otto
• Buenos Aires	$27.00		daily	24	El Cóndor, Costera Criolla
• Comodoro Rivadavia	$11.00				Don Otto
• Córdoba			daily	21	TUP
• Mar del Plata	$15.00				La Puntual
• Mendoza					Andesmar
• Neuquén	$13.00				Andesmar
• Puerto Pirámides	$4.00	0855	Tues, Thur, Sat, Sun		28 de Julio
Last return bus 1825					
• Río Gallegos	$33.50		1–2 services daily	24	Costera Criolla, Don Otto
• Trelew	$1.50		11 services daily	1	28 de Julio
• Viedma	$4.60				El Cóndor

Puerto Madryn

Chubut Province

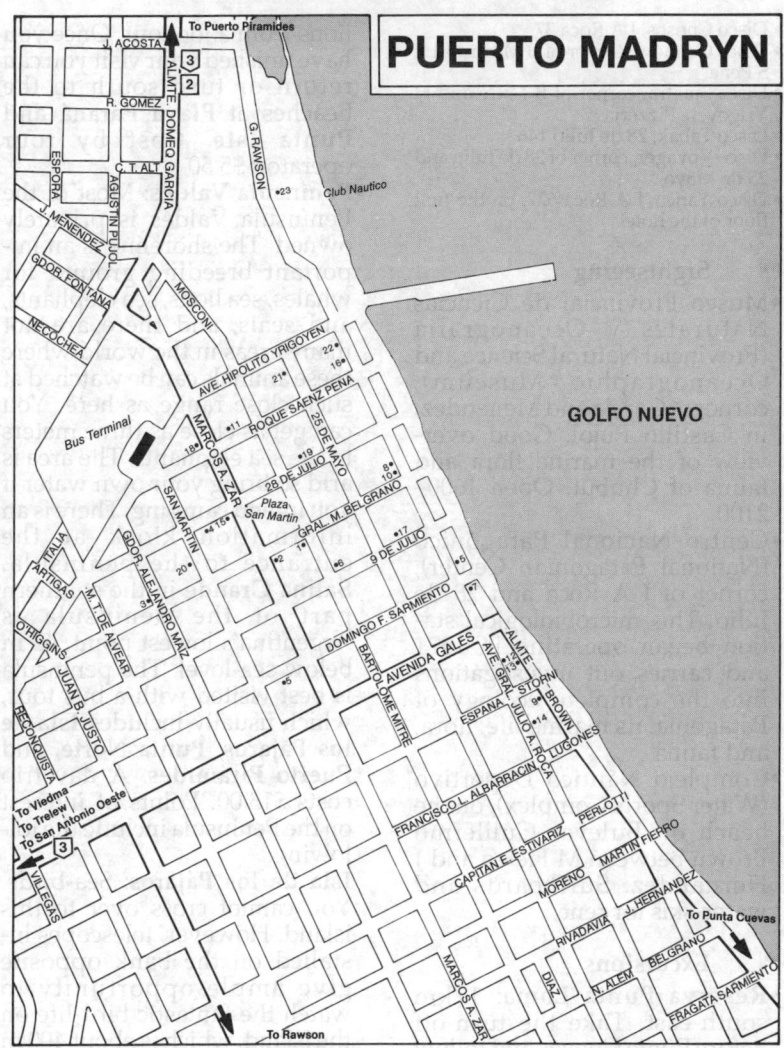

Bulevar Brown and Martín Fierro (Primera Rotunda)
Peke Sosa, Albarracin 290 (71291. "Adventure" trips with scuba diving excursions

🍷 Entertainment

- Cabaret Negro El 29, corner of Avenida Zar and R S Pena. Also hold *peñas*
- Casino, corner of J A Roca 516 and Sarmiento, on the beach front

Puerto Madryn

- Disco Cnosos, J A Roca 37
- Disco Gennow, corner of B Mitre and R S Peña
- Disco Sinatra, corner of B Mitre and H Yrigoyen. Pizzeria
- Disco Tabak, 28 de Julio 146
- Disco Voyager, corner of 28 de Julio and 25 de Mayo
- Disco Yanco, J A Roca 627, on the first floor of the hotel

Sightseeing

- Museo Provincial de Ciencias Naturales y Oceanografia (Provincial Natural Science and Oceanographic Museum), corner of Garcia and Menendez, in Castillo Pujol. Good overview of the marine flora and fauna of Chubut. Open 1600–2100
- Centro Nacional Patagónico (National Patagonian Center), corner of J A Roca and 28 de Julio. This microbiological station began operating in 1971 and carries out investigations into the complete ecology of Patagonia, its marine life, flora, and fauna
- Complejo Náutico Deportivo (Water Sports Complex), on the beach on Bulevar Guillermo Brown between M Fierro and J Hernandez. Surfboards and water-skis for rent

Excursions

- **Reserva Punta Loma**: 17km south-east. Take the turn-off before Punta Cuevas and follow the dirt road. Open 0800–1200 and 1500–2000; small admission fee. There is a colony of seals some 700 m from the visitors' center. You can observe sea lions from a lookout. Once you have finished your visit you can return or turn south to the beaches at **Playa Paraná** and **Punta Este**. Cost by tour operator: $5.50
- **Península Valdés**: Most of the Península Valdés is privately owned. The shoreline is an important breeding ground for whales, sea lions, sea elephants, and seals, and there are not many areas in the world where these animals can be watched at such close range as here. You can get as close as three meters to the sea elephants. The area is arid so bring your own water if you intend camping. There is an information kiosk at the entrance to the peninsula. **Salina Grande** in the southern part of the peninsula is Argentina's lowest point, 42 m below sea-level. The peninsula is best visited with a bus tour, which usually includes **Isla de los Pájaros**, **Punta Norte**, and **Puerto Pirámides**. A day trip costs $13.00. Points of interest on the Peninsula include the following:

Isla de los Pájaros: Sea-birds. You cannot cross over to this island. However, telescopes installed on the bank opposite give ample opportunity to watch the fantastic bird-life on the island, which is about 400 m offshore. *Guanacos* mix with visitors around the telescopes

Punta Pirámides: Sea lions. This is a small settlement on the Golfo Nuevo. The observation point is perched on a cliff and is

Puerto Madryn

Chubut Province

a 10 minute walk from the ACA hotel
Golfo Nuevo: Right whales
Golfo San José: Killer whales
Punta Norte: 176 km north—killer whales and sea elephants. The best time to visit is between November and March at low tide when the tour operators run daily buses to the peninsula. Breeding time begins in the middle August
- **Punta Tombo**: 200 km south on RP 1. Tour operators combine this trip with a short visit to **Rawson**, the provincial capital. See Punta Tombo on page 388
- **Dique Florentino Ameghino**: 170 km south-west. This dam is on the **Río Chubut**. A day excursion by tour operator costs $13.00

Puerto Pirámides

Postal code: 9121 • Population: 100
Distance from Puerto Madryn: 100 km northwards on RN 3 the RP 2

Puerto Pirámides is located on the **Golfo Nuevo** across the bay from Puerto Madryn and is the main township on the **Península Valdés**. Settlement here began in 1898 when the inland *salinas* were exploited for salt. The salt leases expired in 1918 and the township declined. It has a good beach and clear water, and attracts many scuba divers.

Accommodation
- Hostería Puerto Pirámides (ACA), Avenida Julio A Roca
- Hospedaje Libanés, Avenida Julio A Roca $3.50
- Hospedaje Torino, Avenida Julio A Roca $10 $3.50
- Posada del Mar

Camping
Camping is possible along the seashore. However the water supply on the peninsula is unreliable so take your own.

Eating out
- Restaurant Puerto Pirámides. Run by the ACA
- Cantina El Salmon, on the beach. Seafood.

Buses
- Trelew: Departs 0745, Tues, Thurs, Sat, Sun; Empresa Mar y Valle, Empresa 28 de Julio

Motoring
The road to Puerto Madryn is sealed. Roads on the Península Valdés are generally good.

Shopping
- Casa Torino, Avenida J A Roca. Souvenirs and *artesanías*

Sport
- Fishing and scuba diving: **Punta Pardelas** approximately 12 km south of Puerto Pirámides on the RP 2 is ideal for fishing and scuba diving. You can also reach it by walking along the coast
- Scuba diving: Hydro Sport rents diving gear and small boats, and organizes land and sea wildlife tours. It has a small restaurant attached

Excursions

To cover all areas of interest on the peninsula you need your own transport and plenty of water. Otherwise, it is best to do a day tour covering most of the peninsula with a tour operator in Puerto Madryn. A full day trip costs $17.00. See "Tours" in Puerto Madryn on page 383.

- **La Lobería**: 4 km. Here the vantage point on the rocks overlooks a rocky promontory where there is a colony of sea lions. It is very spectacular view.
- **Punta Delgada**: 71 km northeast on RP 2. On the way you pass **Salina Grande**, 42 m below sea-level and the largest depression in Argentina. An old light house there adds to the general atmosphere of abandonment. The views are superb
- **Punta Norte**: Located at the extreme north of the peninsula, some 77 km through desolate country. Here is one of the biggest sea elephant colonies on the South American continent. A concerted effort is being made by Argentina to safeguard this almost extinct species, even going to the extent of having the colony fenced in
- **Caleta Valdés**: Here a 30 km long sandbar starts, and forms a narrow water channel which widens into a lagoon at Caleta Valdés. This part of the peninsula is also extensively populated by sea elephants, and in the mating season, September–March, by dolphins and whales.

PUNTA TOMBO

Distance from Trelew: 120 km southwards on RP 1

The promontory at Punta Tombo, a 210 ha wildlife reserve, is possibly the biggest penguin reserve outside Antarctica, with more than one million birds. Besides penguins there are several types of cormorants, *ñandus*, *guanacos*, sea lions, and *maras* (a Patagonian hare).

The penguin season runs from September to March. The first to arrive are the male penguins who start building nests. More than 40 per cent of the penguins return to the previous year's nest site. Two eggs are laid at the beginning of October, and hatch at the end of October, but generally only one young penguin survives. In December the young penguins have their first swim. In late March, as the penguins prepare to leave, the breeding grounds are off-limits, so check with the tourist office.

The reserve can get a bit crowded in the tourist season, with both birds and humans. There are no tourist facilities at Punta Tombo. It is best to visit it with a tour operator from either Puerto Madryn or Trelew (see "Tours" in Puerto Madryn on page 383 and in Trelew on page 398); the fare is $12.00.

CHUBUT PROVINCE

RAWSON

Postal code: 9103 • (area code: (0965) • Population: 15 000
Distance from Trelew: 20 km eastwards on RN 25

Rawson, the capital of Chubut province and the first Welsh settlement, was founded in 1865. It was named after Dr William Rawson who organized the immigration. It is a quiet administrative center without much nightlife. **Puerto Rawson** is about 5 km down river. There is a good beach at **Playa Unión**.

Festivals
- Foundation of Chubut: July 28
- Petroleum day: December 13

Tourist information
- Dirección de Turismo, corner of 9 de Julio 64 and Moreno (81113 and 81383

Accommodation
- Hotel Provincial, Mitre 551 (81300 $14.00
- Residencial Esquel, Moreno 901

Eating out
- Restaurant Provincial, Hotel Provincial, Mitre 551
- Pizzería Tu Lugar, corner of Rivadavia and H Yrigoyen
- Cafetería Welcome, Plaza G Rawson, corner of M Moreno and B Vacchina

Post and telegraph
- Post office: Encotel, Moreno 650 (corner of Vacchina)
- Telephone: Entel, Federici 50

Services and facilities
- Laundromat: Laverap, Rawson 577

Air services
- Aerolineas Argentinas, corner of M Moreno and G Maiz

Motoring
- Service station: ACA, Libertad 321

Sightseeing
- Capel Berwyn (Welsh Historic Chapel). Named after the donor of that portion of land in 1881

Buses from Rawson

Buses to and from Trelew stop at Plaza G Rawson, on the corner Moreno and A Maiz.

Destination	Fare	Depart	Services	Hours	Company
Bahía Blanca	$13.50	1818	Mon, Thurs, Fri		Don Otto, La Puntual
Buenos Aires					
Comodoro Rivadavia	$32.00	0932	daily	6	Transportes Patagonico, Andesmar, La Puntual
Córdoba	$32.50	1200	Tues, Fri, Sun		TUP
Mendoza		0645	daily		Andesmar
Neuquén		0645	daily		Andesmar
Río Gallegos		1930	Tues, Thurs, Sun		Don Otto
Change in Comodoro Rivadavia					
Santa Rosa		1200	Tues, Fri, Sun		TUP
Viedma		1818	Mon, Thurs, Fri		La Puntual

Chubut Province

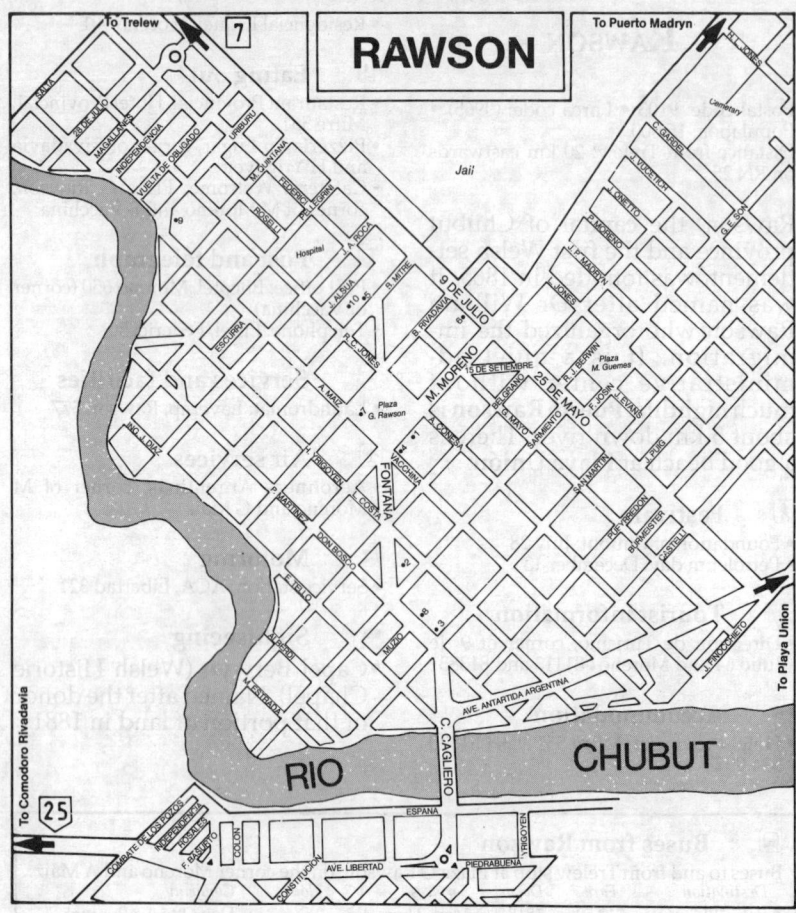

Key to Map
1. Municipalidad
2. Casa de Gobierno
3. Iglesia
4. Post office (Encotel)
5. Telephone (Entel)
6. Tourist information
7. Buses to Trelew
8. Museo Regional
9. Welsh historic church
10. Hotel Provincial

Rawson

Chubut Province

- Museo Regional, in the original parish church. Memorabilia of the desert wars, minerals, and an archeological collection

Excursions

- **Playa Unión**: A beach 6 km south-east

Río Mayo

Postal code: 9030 • Population: 2000
Distances
- From Coihaique in Chile: 177 km eastwards on RN 26
- From Esquel: 427 km southwards on RN 40
- From Perito Moreno: 123 km northwards on RN 40

The town is in the valley of the **Río Mayo**, situated in a depression which shelters it from the harsh Patagonian winds. It is an important road junction on RN 40, which runs north–south, and RN 26 to Chile, and is the best place to break the long dusty journey between Perito Moreno and Esquel.

Accommodation

Río Mayo is an oil exploration center and crews are lodged in the town, sometimes making tourist accomodation difficult.
B Hotel Covadonga ℂ 214
B Residencial San Martín ℂ 265
B Residencial Pingüino, San Martín 640

Air services

Empresa LADE's offices are at Avenida San Martín 520 ℂ 260
- Alto Río Senguerr: Fare $13.00; departs 1135 Mon and Fri; 1 hour; Empresa LADE
- Comodoro Rivadavia: Fare $12.00; departs 1305 Mon and Fri; 1 hour; Empresa LADE

Buses

There are no bus services southwards on RN 40 to Perito Moreno.
- Coihaique (Chile): 3 services weekly; Empresa A Giobbi
- Comodoro Rivadavia: Fare $7.50; departs 1530 Tues, Fri, Sun; 6 hours; Empresa A Giobbi
- Esquel (via Alto Río Senguerr): Fare $12.80; departs 0640 Mon, Thurs, Fri; 10 hours; Empresa A Giobbi

Motoring

- RN 26 to the Chilean border is a dirt road
- RP 20 and RP 22 to the coast is intermittently sealed to Sarmiento and completely sealed from Sarmiento to Comodoro Rivadavia
- RN 40 south to Perito Moreno is a dirt road
- RN 40 north to Esquel is unsealed as far as the junction with RP 20 and from there onwards intermittently sealed until Esquel

Excursions

- **Sarmiento** and **Comodoro Rivadavia**: The bus travels down RP 22, makes a detour to **Estancia Facundo** in the **Río Senguerr** valley, and then joins RP 20. After leaving the Río Senguerr valley the scenery becomes interesting again as the road passes through a wide valley between the **Sierra de San Bernardino**, which has areas with aboriginal rock paintings. The land is bare until you reach the vicinity of **Lago Musters**. Oil pumps along the road signal your arrival in Comodoro Rivadavia

CHUBUT PROVINCE

- The area between Esquel and Río Mayo west of the RN 40 is full of lakes and mountain scenery and is almost untouched by tourism. The only roads are feeders to *estancias* in the area. In general most of the lakes in the region are inaccessible unless you have your own transport. When hiking through these areas take warm clothes, a tent, and a sleeping bag as it gets very cold at night. Interesting areas include **Lago General Vintter**, which extends into Chile as Lago Palena, and **Lago Fontana**, which is reached via Alto Río Senguerr
- Chile: The country towards the Chilean border is *pre-cordillera*
- **Lago Blanco**: 110 km. Some 30 km south of Río Mayo, RP 55 turns west. Because of its inaccessibility and lack of facilities, Lago Blanco is a place for the outdoor enthusiast only. Activities include hiking, and fishing for salmon and rainbow trout in the *pre-cordillera* streams. Take camping gear and warm clothes. There is no public transport to Balmaceda in Chile
- **Alto Río Mayo**, near the Chilean border: There is a small hotel here which serves meals. Flamingos, swans, and other bird life can be seen en route to the Chilean border in the little *lagunas*. A rewarding side trip can be made from **La Aldea**, provided you can arrange transport, to the little lake of **Las Margueritas** near **Triana**. Wildlife in the forests includes deer, wild boar, and the occasional puma

SARMIENTO

Postal code: 9020 • Population: 6000 • area code: (0967)
Distance from Comodoro Rivadavia: 150 km westwards on RN 26 then RP 20

Sarmiento, also known as Colonia Sarmiento, is located near **Lago Musters** and **Lago Colhué Huapí**.

Accommodation
★★ Hostería Los Lagos, corner of J A Roca and Alberdí ☎ 93046 $11.00
B Hotel Lago Musters, corner of Moreno and Coronel $6.00
B Hotel Colón, Moreno 645 $6.00

Camping
- Municipal: 1 km outside town on Lago Musters

Eating out
- Restaurant El Gaucho, Access Route 20
- Restaurant Los Lagos, Hostería Los Lagos, corner of J A Roca and Alberdí

Buses
The office of Empresa Trevisan is on the corner of San Martín and Alberdí.
- Comodoro Rivadavia: $3.70; 3 services daily; 3 hours; Empresa Trevisan
- Esquel via Río Mayo: Fare $15.00; Empresa A Giobbi
- Río Mayo via Facundo: $3.70; 3 hours; Empresa A Giobbi

Motoring
The first 210 km to Esquel is sealed; from then on the surface is dirt, much of which is passable even in bad weather.

Plate 17

Top: Coastline on Península Valdés
Bottom left: Wildlife on Península Valdés
Bottom right: Seal colony on Península Valdés

Plate 18
Map of Chubut Province

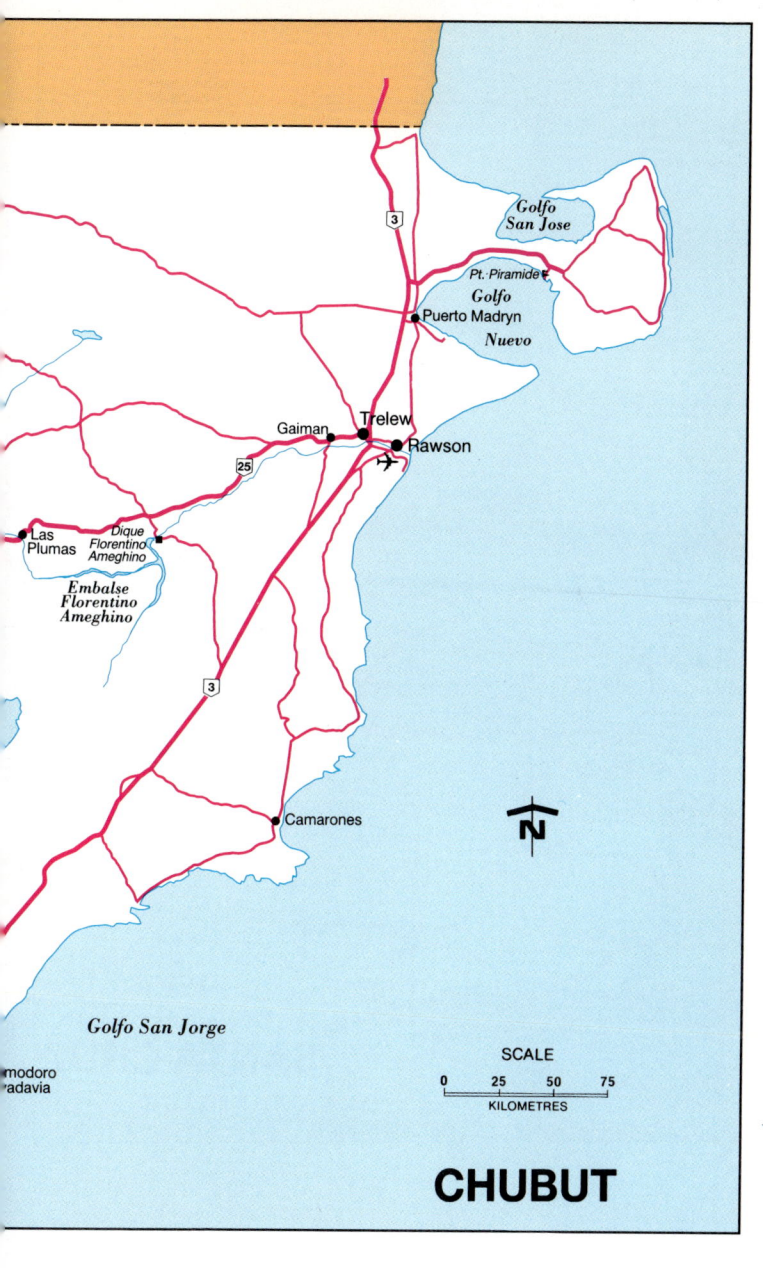

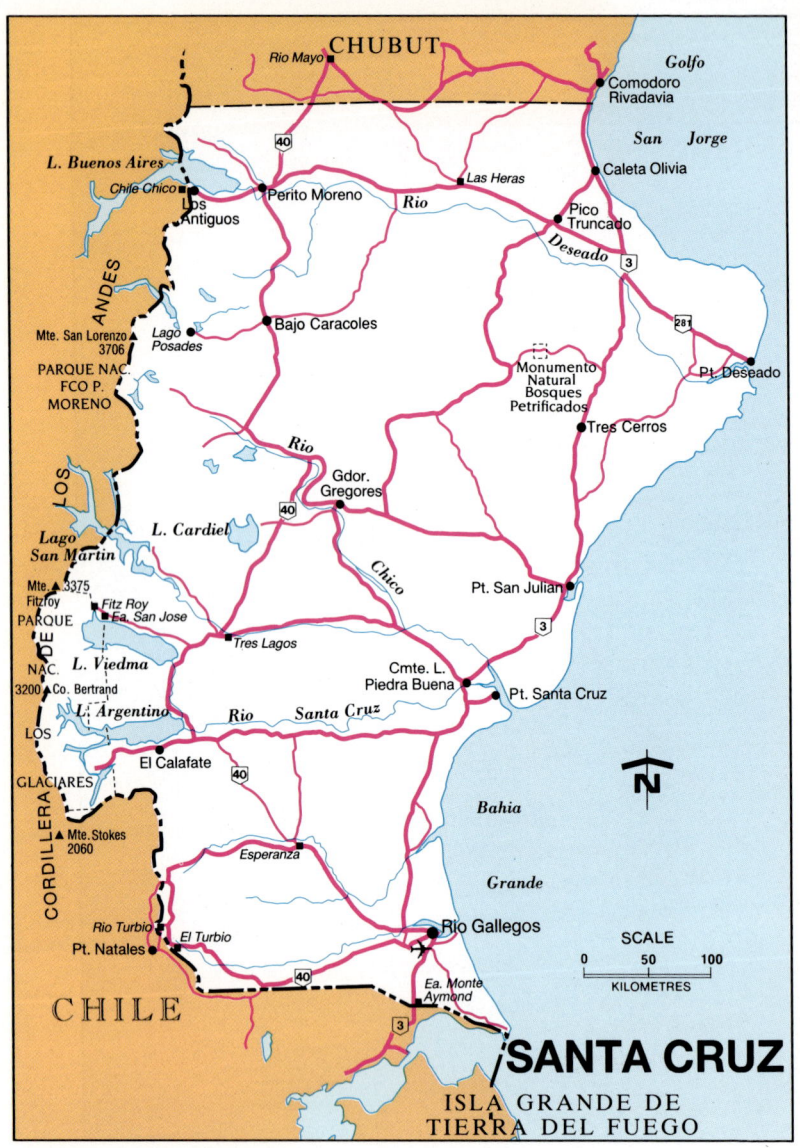

Plate 20
Map of Santa Cruz Province

Chubut Province

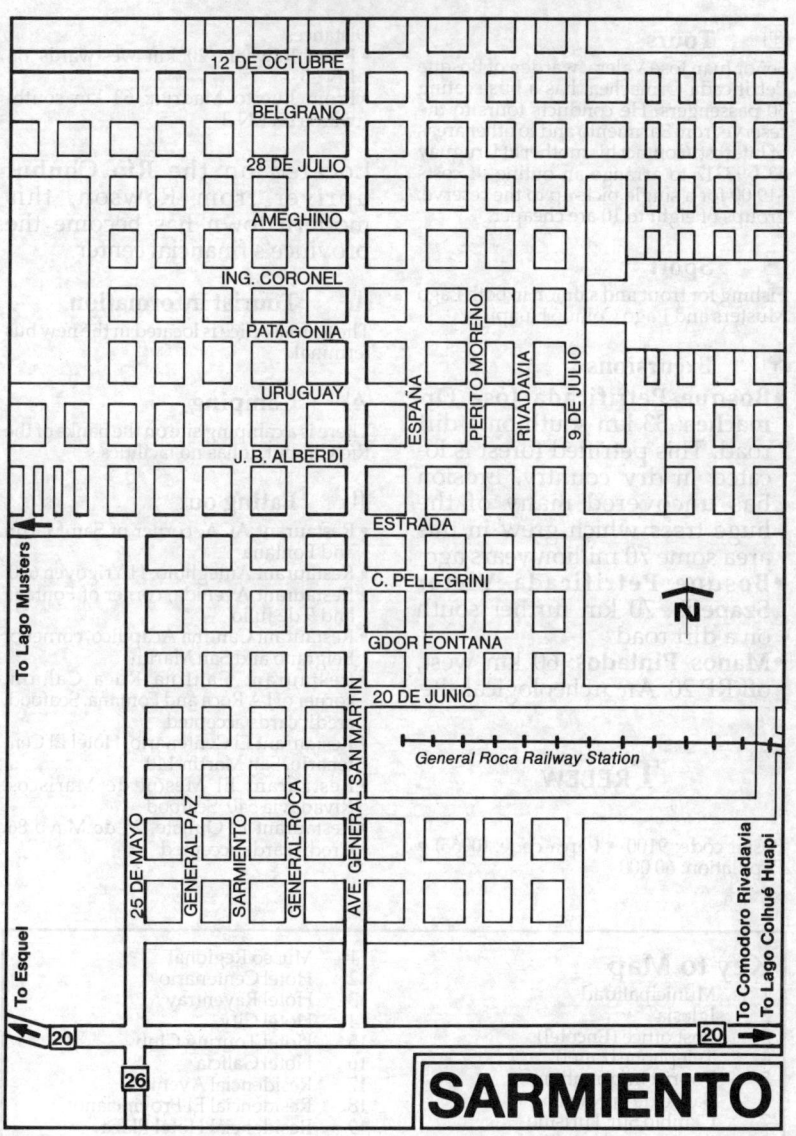

Chubut Province

⊕ Tours

Señor Juan José Valera, warden of Bosque Petrificada Ormachea, has a bus seating 30 passengers. He conducts tours to the reserve from Sarmiento and to other areas of interest. Contact his mother at Uruguay 33 ℂ 93317 to arrange an outing. It costs $19.00 for a single pick-up to the reserve; groups of eight to 10 are cheaper.

🍴 Sport

Fishing for trout and salmon in both Lago Musters and Lago Colhué Huapi.

🌳 Excursions

- **Bosque Petrificada José Ormachea**: 33 km south on a dirt road. This petrified forest is located in dry country. Erosion has uncovered many of the huge trees which grew in this area some 70 million years ago
- **Bosque Petrificada Victor Szapelis**. 70 km further south on a dirt road
- **Manos Pintados**: 60 km west, off RP 20. An archeological site

TRELEW

Postal code: 9100 • ℂ area code: (0965) • Population: 60 000

Distances
- From Rawson: 20 km westwards on RN 25
- From Puerto Madryn: 63 km southwards on RN 3

Located on the **Río Chubut** upriver from Rawson, this modern town has become the province's financial center.

ℹ Tourist information

The tourist office is located in the new bus terminal.

⛺ Camping

There is a camping site on the banks of the Río Chubut. It has no facilities.

🍽 Eating out

- Restaurant ACA, corner of San Martín and Fontana
- Restaurant Ameghino, H Yrigoyen 610
- Restaurant Avenida, corner of Fontana and 9 de Julio
- Restaurant Cantina Acapulco, corner of Belgrano and San Martín
- Restaurant Cantina Ruca Cahuin, corner of J A Roca and Fontana. Seafood; credit cards accepted
- Restaurant El Centenario, Hotel El Centenario, San Martín 140
- Restaurant El Mesón de Mariscos, Rivadavia 540. Seafood
- Restaurant El Quijote, 25 de Mayo 86. Credit cards accepted

Key to Map

1. Municipalidad
2. Iglesia
3. Post office (Encotel)
4. Telephone (Entel)
5. Tourist information
6. Banco de la Nación
7. Cambio Sur Turismo
8. Aerolineas Argentinas
9. Austral Lineas Aereas
10. LADE (airline)
11. Museo Regional
12. Hotel Centenario
13. Hotel Rayentray
14. Hotel City
15. Hotel Touring Club
16. Hotel Galicia
17. Residencial Avenida
18. Residencial El Provinciano
19. Residencial Hotel Plaza
20. Residencial Mitre
21. Residencial Urquiza

Sarmiento

Chubut Province

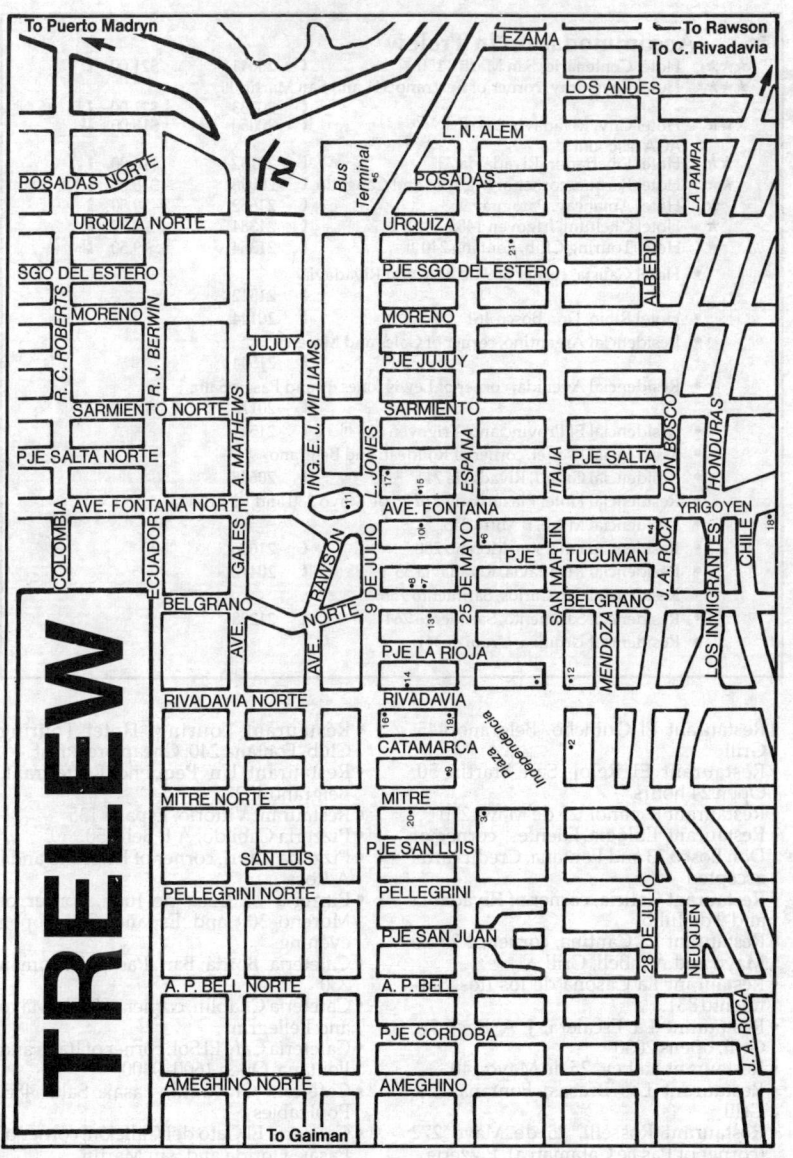

Trelew

Chubut Province

🛏 Accommodation in Trelew

★★★	Hotel Centenario, San Martín 150	✆	20041	$21.00	👤
★★★	Hotel Rayentray, corner of Belgrano 341 and San Martín	✆	20233	$21.00	👤
★★	Hotel City, Rivadavia 254, ACA discount	✆	20050	$18.00	👥
★★	Hotel Libertador, Rivadavia 73	✆	20132	$16.00	👤
★★	Hotel Parque, corner of Irigoyen and Cangallo	✆	20098	$16.00	👤
★	Hotel Amancay, Paraguay 953	✆	21662	$9.50	👤
★	Hotel Cheltum, Irigoyen 1485	✆	21384	$9.50	👤
★	Hotel Touring Club, Fontana 240	✆	21354	$9.50	👤

- Hotel Galicia, corner of 9 de Julio and Rivadavia ✆ 21512
- Hotel Riolo, Don Bosco 461 ✆ 20144
- Residencial Argentino, corner of Gales and Moreno ✆ 21544
- Residencial Avenida, corner of Lewis Jones 49 and Pasaje Salta ✆ 20172 $5.50 👤
- Residencial El Provinciano, Yrigoyen 625 ✆ 21544
- Residencial Esquel, corner of Rondeau and Belgrano
- Residencial Grand, Rivadavia 711 ✆ 20648
- Residencial Hotel Plaza, corner of 25 de Mayo 230 and Rivadavia
- Residencial Mitre, B Mitre 245
- Residencial Paterson, Moreno 280 ✆ 21636
- Residencial Rivadavia, Rivadavia 55 ✆ 20472
- Residencial San Carlos, Sarmiento 758
- Residencial Sarmiento, Sarmiento 264 ✆ 21228
- Residencial Urquiza, Urquiza 341

- Restaurant El Quincho, Belgrano 445. Grill
- Restaurant El Reloj, San Martín 50. Open 24 hours
- Restaurant Español, 25 de Mayo 270
- Restaurant Eulogia Fuentes, corner of Don Bosco 23 and Fontana. Credit cards accepted
- Restaurant Galicia, corner of Rivadavia and 9 de Julio
- Restaurant La Cantina, corner of 25 de Mayo and A P Bell. Grill
- Restaurant La Casona de los Itos, Sarmiento 331
- Restaurant La Escalera, J A Roca 70. Grill; opens 2030
- Restaurant La Ley, 25 de Mayo 140
- Restaurant Las Brasas, Fontana 220. Grill
- Restaurant Rosselli, 25 de Mayo 272 (corner of Pasaje Catamarca). Pizzeria
- Restaurant Ruca Cahuin. J A Roca 74. Seafood
- Restaurant Touring, Hotel Touring Club, Fontana 240. Cheap breakfast
- Restaurant Un Pequeño Restaurant, Belgrano 453
- Restaurant Vittorio, Espaná 135
- Pizzería Cabildo, A P Bell 350
- Pizzería Caprí, corner of Belgrano and J A Roca
- Pizzería La Casa de Juan, corner of Moreno 300 and España. Only open evenings
- Cafetería Borda Bar, Pasaje Tucumán 230
- Cafetería Chaplin, corner of 25 de Mayo and Pellegrini
- Cafetería Cafe El Sol, corner of Italia and Fontana. Open 1600–0400
- Cafetería Giovanni, Pasaje Salta 486. Pool tables
- Cafetería El Gato del Callejón, corner of Pasaje Florida and San Martín
- Cafetería La Reina, corner of Fontana and 25 de Mayo

Trelew

Chubut Province

- Cafetería Napoli, corner of Rivadavia and 9 de Julio
- Cafetería Seres, Belgrano 376
- Cafetería Rayentray, Hotel Rayentray, Belgrano 341 (corner of San Martín)
- Cafetería Tennis Club, Belgrano 450. Pool
- Milk bar: La Montevideana, corner of Rivadavia and 25 de Mayo
- Milk bar: Wimpy, corner of 25 de Mayo and Rivadavia
- English-style pub: Zodiac, corner of Belgrano and 25 de Mayo
- Tearoom: Quo Vadis, corner of España and Sarmiento

Eating out outside Sarmiento

- Restaurant Don Pedro, intersection of RN 3 with RN 25. Grill
- Restaurant Martin Fierro, intersection of RN 3 with RN 25 north. Grill

$ Post and telegraph

- Post office: Encotel, corner of 25 de Mayo and Mitre
- Telephone: Entel, corner of J A Roca and Pasaje Tucumán

$ Financial

- Banco Alas, Belgrano 489. Cash advances on Visa card
- Banco de Londres, corner of 9 de Julio and Belgrano
- Sur Turismo, Belgrano 330, ℂ 20550. Travelers' checks

✈ Air services from Trelew

- The airport is 5 km from the center. Buses to and from Puerto Madryn stop at the airport whenever a plane arrives or departs.
- Aerolineas Argentinas, Belgrano 286 ℂ 21297
- Austral Lineas Aereas, 25 de Mayo 259 ℂ 20386
- LADE, Fontana 227 ℂ 20440 and 20144

Destination	Fare	Depart	Services	Hours	Airline
• Bahía Blanca	$41.00	1010	daily	1	Aerolineas, Austral, LADE
• Buenos Aires (Aeroparque Jorge Newbery)					
	$69.00	0430	2-3 services daily	2	Aerolineas, Austral
	$45.00	1235	Wed, Fri, Sat	6	LADE
• Comodoro Rivadavia					
	$25.00	0130	1–3 services daily	1	Aerolineas, Austral
	$22.00	1525	Tues, Thurs, Fri	1	LADE
• Esquel	$36.00	1215	Mon, Wed, Fri, Sun	1	Aerolineas
	$27.00	1430	Wed, Sat	1	LADE
• Mar del Plata	$58.00	1430	Wed, Sat	6	LADE
	$61.00	1840	Tues, Thur, Sat, Sun	2	Aerolineas, Austral
• Neuquén	$35.00	1430	Wed, Sat	3	LADE
• Puerto Deseado	$27.00	1530	Tues, Fri	2	LADE
• Puerto San Julián	$31.00	1530	Tues, Fri	3	LADE
• Río Gallegos	$52.00	0040	daily	3	Aerolineas, Austral
	$38.00	1530	Tues, Fri	4	LADE
• Río Grande	$59.00	0825	Sun	3	Austral
	$44.00	1530	Tues, Fri	5	LADE
• San Antonio Oeste	$19.00	1235	Fri	1	LADE
• San Carlos de Bariloche					
	$35.00	1430	Wed, Sat	2	LADE
• Santa Cruz	$34.00	1530	Tues, Fri	3	LADE
• Ushuaia	$60.00	1010	daily	3	Aerolineas
• Viedma	$40.00	1235	Fri, Sat	2–4	LADE

CHUBUT PROVINCE

🚌 Buses from Trelew

The bus terminal is on the corner of L Jones and Urquiza.

Destination	Fare	Depart	Services	Hours	Company
• Rawson	$ 0.40	0600	every 15 minutes		Chubut
• Bahía Blanca	$13.50	0600	daily	11	Don Otto
• Buenos Aires	$29.00	1900	daily	25	La Puntual, El Condor
• Camarones	$6.00	0800	Mon, Fri		Don Otto
• Comodoro Rivadavia	$9.50	1030	1–2 services daily	6	Don Otto, Transportes Patagonicos
• Córdoba			daily	22	T U P
• Dique Ameghino Returns 1830		0800	Sun		Chubut
• Esquel	$13.50	1100	Tues, Thurs, Fri, Sat, Sun	11	Don Otto
via Languineo	$13.50	0700	Mon	12	Chubut
via Tecka	$13.50	2130	Tues, Wed, Thurs, Fri, Sun		Chubut
• Gaimán	$ 0.50		10 buses daily	20 min	28 de Julio
• Neuquén	$14.00				Andesmar
• Puerto Madryn	$ 1.50		17 buses daily	1	28 de Julio
• Río Gallegos via Puerto Deseado	$22.00	2005	Tues, Thurs, Sun		Don Otto

🧺 Services and facilities

- Dry-cleaner: Tokio, corner of B Mitre and J A Roca
- Laundromat: Laverap, corner of B Mitre and J A Roca
- Pharmacy: Farmacia Chubut, corner of España and Fontana
- Photographic supplies: Fotorama, corner of España and Fontana
- Supermarket: Supercoop, corner of 9 de Julio 386 and Pellegrini

🚗 Motoring

- Service station: ACA, corner of San Martín and Fontana. Road maps available

Car rental

- Alquilauto Fiorasi, corner of España and Urquiza ℂ 21344
- National Car, Belgrano 471
- Rent A Car Patagonico, Aeropuerto Ate Zar ℂ 32289

🌐 Tours

- Nievemar Tours, Italia 20 ℂ 20114. Organizes excursions to Península Valdés and Punta Tombo
- Cambio Sur Turismo, Belgrano 320

🛍 Shopping

- Jaguel, corner of Estados Unidos and Belgrano. Souvenirs and *artesanias*
- Roger's Souvenir shop, Moreno 463. Serves Welsh afternoon teas

🎭 Entertainment

- Bowling Bolo, 9 de Julio 562. Six lanes
- Disco Casablanca, corner of H Yrigoyen and Cangallo
- Disco La Recova, intersection of RN 3 with RN 25
- Disco Kapaúma, Alem 486
- Disco Kangaroo, Ruta 7
- Disco Cafe La Flor, 25 de Mayo 140
- Whiskería, B Mitre 235

Trelew

CHUBUT PROVINCE

📷 Sightseeing
- Museo Regional, 9 de Julio with Fontana
- In the cemetery are the graves and tombstones of many of the Welsh settlers who arrived in 1865

🌳 Excursions
- **Camarones**: 270 km south on the RN 3 then RP 30. The turn-off is 16 km before Garayalde, where there is an ACA service station. Make bookings for seats at Uruguay 590; the bus returns from Camarones on Tuesday and Saturday. If you want to continue to Comodoro Rivadavia wait for the bus at the junction of RN 3 and RP 30. The wildlife reserve at **Cabo Dos Bahías** is 30 km south. See Camarones on page 360

Excursion tours
Nievemar Tours (see "Tours" above) runs the following excursion tours:
- Puerto Madryn and Península Valdés: Fare $20.00, 12 hours
- Punta Tombo, 120 km south: Fare $14.00; 6 hours
- Rawson and Playa Unión and Gaimán: Fare $9.00; 4 hours
- Dique Florentino Ameghino: $Fare 17.00; 10 hours

TREVELÍN

Postal code: 9203 • Population: 5500 • (area code: (0945) • Altitude: 390 m
Distance from Esquel: 23 km southwards on RN 259

The first Welsh settlers arrived in Trevelín from the coast in 1888. Some of the pioneers came with Colonel Fontana as members of the *Rifleros del Chubut* (Chubut Rifles).

ℹ️ Tourist information
- Oficina de Informes, Plaza 28 de Julio

🛏️ Accommodation
B Residencial Trevelín, San Martín 295 (8102 $5.00 ⁞
- Residencial Estefania, Perito Moreno (8148 $6.00 ⁞

⛺ Camping
- Autocamping La Granja Trevelín: 4 km north on RN 259, on the Esquel side. Horse riding
- Autocamping Aiken Leufú: 12 km on the road to Futaleufú power station ⛺. Tent hire, boat hire, horse riding; $2 per person
- Autocamping Rio Grande: On the road to the Chilean border just before the Río Futaleufú ferry crossing. $4.00 per person

🍴 Eating out
- Restaurant El Quincho, corner of Fortin Refugio and Brown. Grill
- La Cabana, 7 km outside town on the road to Lago Futalaufquen
- Tearoom El Adobe, at the entrance to town
- Tearoom: La Muticia, San Martín 170
- Tearoom: La Pantera, Rotonda Trevelín
- Tearoom: Té Nain Maggie, Perito Moreno 159

✉️ Post and telegraph
- Post office: Encotel, corner of San Martín and Brown
- Telephone: Entel, San Martín. Automatic exchange

🚌 Buses
The bus terminal is on Libertad opposite J A Roca. There are frequent services to and from Esquel.

Chubut Province

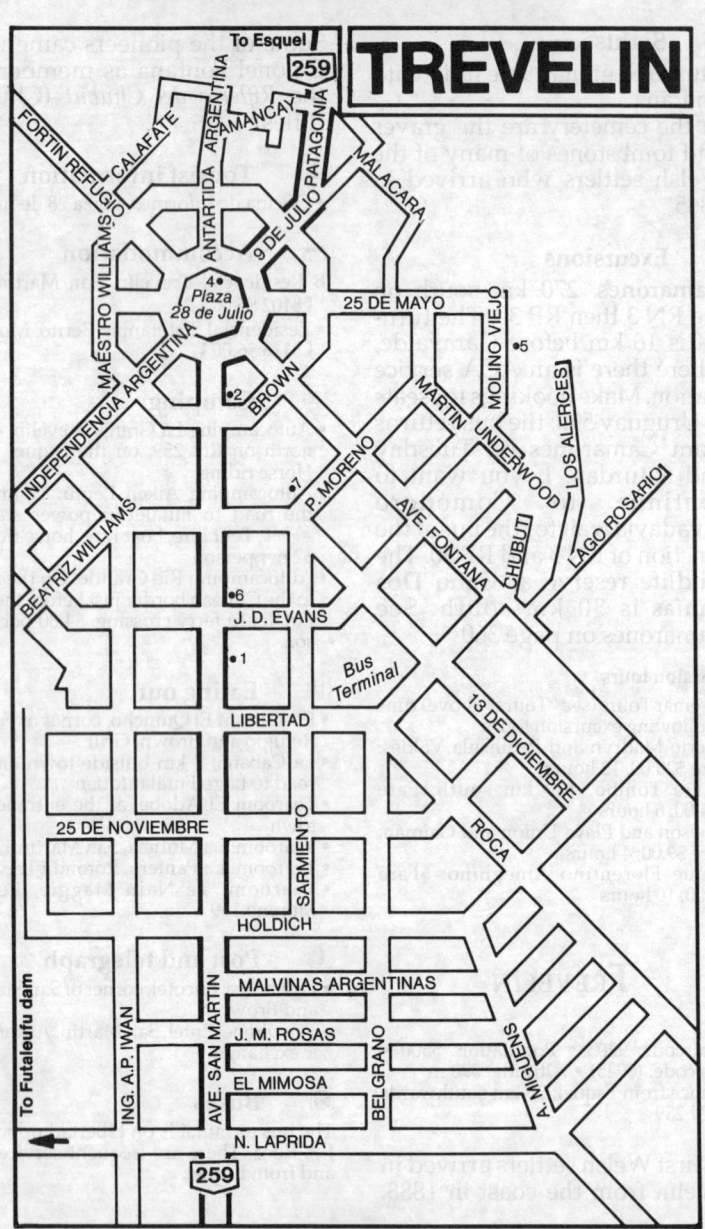

Trevelín

Chubut Province

Key to Map
1. Municipalidad
2. Post office (Encotel)
3. Telephone (Entel)
4. Tourist information
5. Museo Historico Regional
6. Residencial Trevelín
7. Residencial Estefania

Motoring
- Service station: YPF, corner of San Martín and John Evans

Sightseeing
- Molino Viejo (Old Mill). The name "Trevelín" means "mill village".
- Escuela no 18 (School no 18), outside the town, was used in 1902 for a plebiscite to decide the nationality of the area

Excursions
- **Parque Nacional Los Alerces**. See Parque Nacional Los Alerces on page 379
- **Mapuche Indian reserve** on **Laguna Rosario**: 35 km south RP 17. Artistic tapestries and woollen clothes are made here by the local Indians. **Nant y Fall** is on the river which flows out of Laguna Rosario: there are seven waterfalls in all, which are reached by a walking trail. Fishing in the lake is possible
- **La Balsa**, and Futaleufú in Chile

Trevelín

Santa Cruz Province

Plate 20 Map of Santa Cruz Province
- **403** Bajo Caracoles
- **404** Caleta Olivia
- **405** Comandante Luis Piedra Buena
- **406** Map
- **407** El Calafate
- **408** Map
- **413** Esperanza
- **414** Fitz Roy
- **414** Gobernador Gregores
- **415** Las Heras
- **416** Los Antiguos
- **416** Parque Nacional Los Glaciares
- **417** Perito Moreno
- **419** Pico Truncado
- **420** Puerto Deseado
- **421** Puerto San Julián
- **422** Map
- **425** Puerto Santa Cruz

Santa Cruz Province

Santa Cruz Province

427 Río Gallegos
426 Map
432 Río Turbio
433 Tres Cerros

Santa Cruz is the second largest province of Argentina. It extends from the Atlantic coast to the southern Andes chain and the Chilean border, and in the far south it is bounded by the Estrecho de Magallanes, known in English as the Straits of Magellan. In the north it shares a border with Chubut province. The capital is Río Gallegos, 2750 km south of Buenos Aires.

The province is sparsely populated. Agriculture is restricted to sheep farming in the Patagonian plateau. However, it is rich in mineral deposits. Oil is found in the extreme north near **Caleta Olivia** and in the extreme south near the Chilean border. Coal is mined at **Río Turbio**. The climate is dry and harsh. At times the *pampero* blows and stirs up dust clouds. Vegetation consists mostly of thorn bushes.

On the coast there are attractive beaches along the **Golfo San Jorge**. There are sea lion breeding grounds near **Cabo Blanco** and **Punta Quilla**, and penguin colonies at various points along the coast.

One of the major tourist attractions of Argentina is the **Glaciar Perito Moreno** on **Lago Argentino** near El Calafate in the **Parque Nacional Los Glaciares**. Also very scenic, and of interest to mountain hikers, is **Cerro Fitz Roy** on Lago Viedma, also in the Parque Nacional Los Glaciares. The tourist season is restricted to the summer months owing to the harsh climatic conditions in winter, and these resorts are very crowded at that time. **Parque Nacional Perito Moreno** is further north and can be reached via Gobernador Gregores, but you require your own vehicle.

There are aboriginal rock paintings on **Río Pinturas** and petrified wood in the **Parque Nacional Bosque Petrificado** near Laguna Grande.

Of interest to tourists are:
- Make an effort: **Parque Nacional Los Glaciares**
- Very interesting: **El Calafate**, **Río Pinturas**, and **Parque Nacional Perito Moreno**
- Of interest: **Puerto Deseado**, **Puerto San Julián**, **Río Gallegos**, and **Río Turbio**

Bajo Caracoles

Postal code: 9315
Distance from Perito Moreno: 128 km southwards on RN 40

Bajo Caracoles is located in the *pre-cordillera*. The Andes are clearly visible from here. **Cerro**

SANTA CRUZ PROVINCE

San Lorenzo at 3706 m is the highest mountain in the province.

Accommodation
B Hotel Bajo Caracoles $4.00

Eating out
- Hotel Bajo Caracoles

Buses
- San Julián: Fare $16.50; departs 0700 Wed; Empresa Cerro San Lorenzo
- Gobernador Gregores: Fare $9.00; departs 0700 Wed; Empresa Cerro San Lorenzo

Motoring
RN 40 north to Perito Moreno is a gravel road. There are a few interesting sections halfway along, when a low pass has to be negotiated. The chain of the Andes is visible to the west all the way. It takes about three hours from Bajo Caracoles to Perito Moreno. Very few trucks or cars pass through between March and November.

Excursions
- **Río Pinturas valley**: If you can obtain transport to Estancia Elisa, it is possible to visit the cave paintings here. The turn-off is 4 km north of Bajo Caracoles, and the cave can be reached from the Estancia on foot. Because of the difficulty of obtaining transport, most excursions are organized from Perito Moreno. Another possibility is a lengthy hike from Bajo Caracoles. Señor Antonio Barria is the caretaker and acts as guide. In summer he operates a small eating place at the site.
- **Lago Posadas**: 72 km west. There is a small country hotel here. Buses from Puerto San Julián run once a week only. The area around Bajo Caracoles is rarely visited by tourists.

CALETA OLIVIA

Postal code: 9011 • Population: 14 000 • area code: (0967)
Distances
- From Río Gallegos: 667 km northwards on RN 3
- From Comodoro Rivadavia: 70 km southwards on RN 3
- From Pico Truncado: 54 km north-east on RP 501

Caleta Olivia is the urban center for important oil fields stretching as far west as Las Heras, 134 km away. The gas from the field near **Pico Truncado** is piped to Buenos Aires.

Accommodation
★ Grand Hotel, corner of Mosconi and Chubut (61393 $4.00
A Hotel Caprí, José Hernandez 1145 (61132 $6.50
A Hotel San Julián, corner of RN 40 and Don Bosco $5.50
★★ Residencial Robert, San Martín 2151 (61452 $8.00

Eating out
- Restaurant Grill Royal, Independencia 1070

Buses
- Comodoro Rivadavia: Fare $1.80; Empresa Comi
- Los Antiguos (on the Chilean border): Fare $11.00; departs 0700 Mon and Thurs; Empresa Comi
- Perito Moreno: Fare $8.20; departs 0700 Mon and Thurs; Empresa Comi

SANTA CRUZ PROVINCE

🚗 Motoring

The road south is typical Patagonian tableland. Occasionally there are white patches over *lagunas* indicating that the soil is salty. Seventy km south of Fitz Roy is the turn-off eastwards to the petrified wood area of **Laguna Grande**. At Tres Cerros there is an ACA service station with a cafeteria. Usually buses make a meal break here. In the distance a few hills can be seen.

COMANDANTE LUIS PIEDRA BUENA

Postal code: 9303 • Population: 4000 • ☏ area code: (0962) • Altitude: Sea-level
Distances
- From Puerto Santa Cruz: 40 km westwards on RN 288 then northwards on RN 3
- From Tres Lagos: 218 km eastwards on RN 288

Comandante Luis Piedra Buena (commonly referred to simply as "Piedra Buena") is located off the main highway on the **Río Santa Cruz estuary**.

🛏 Accommodation

B Hotel Internacional, Gobernador Ibañez 99 ☏ 7197 $6.50 ⓘ
B Hotel Paso, Gobernador Ibañez ⏽ $6.50 ⓘ
★ Hostería Hayen, Belgrano Oeste at the entrance to town ⏽
* Motel ACA, RN 3 Km 2404, opposite turn-off into town ⏽ ☏ 7245 $10.00 ⓘ. Discount for ACA members

⛺ Camping

There are camp sites north of town.

⏽ Eating out

- Restaurant Select
- Pizzería Zorba II, corner of San Martín South and 21 de Noviembre
- Motel ACA, RN 3 Km 2404

🚌 Buses

- Río Gallegos: 5 hours; Transporte Ruta 3
- Puerto San Julián: 3 hours; Transporte Ruta 3

🍸 Entertainment

- Disco Genesis, corner of San Martín east and 25 de Noviembre

● Excursions

- **Puerto Santa Cruz**: Just south of town there is a crossing over the **Río Santa Cruz**. There are two bridges: the little island between them in the middle of the river was the site of the landing in 1859 of Comandante Luis Piedra Buena in the *Nancy* to claim Patagonia for Argentina. Seven km from the bridge is the turn-off to Puerto Santa Cruz, the original capital of the province. Long-distance buses do not usually enter Santa Cruz. See also Puerto Santa Cruz on page 425
- **El Calafate**: 272 km on RP 1603. The turn-off eastwards is 18 km further south of the turn-off to Puerto Santa Cruz. The road is unsealed and runs through typical Patagonian country over flat windswept plateaus. Occasionally the **Río Santa Cruz** can be seen to the right. Shortly after Estancia La Fortaleza the road descends into the valley, where there is a bridge over the **Río Bote**. RN 3 continues from the Río Bote southwards to the **Río Gallegos**

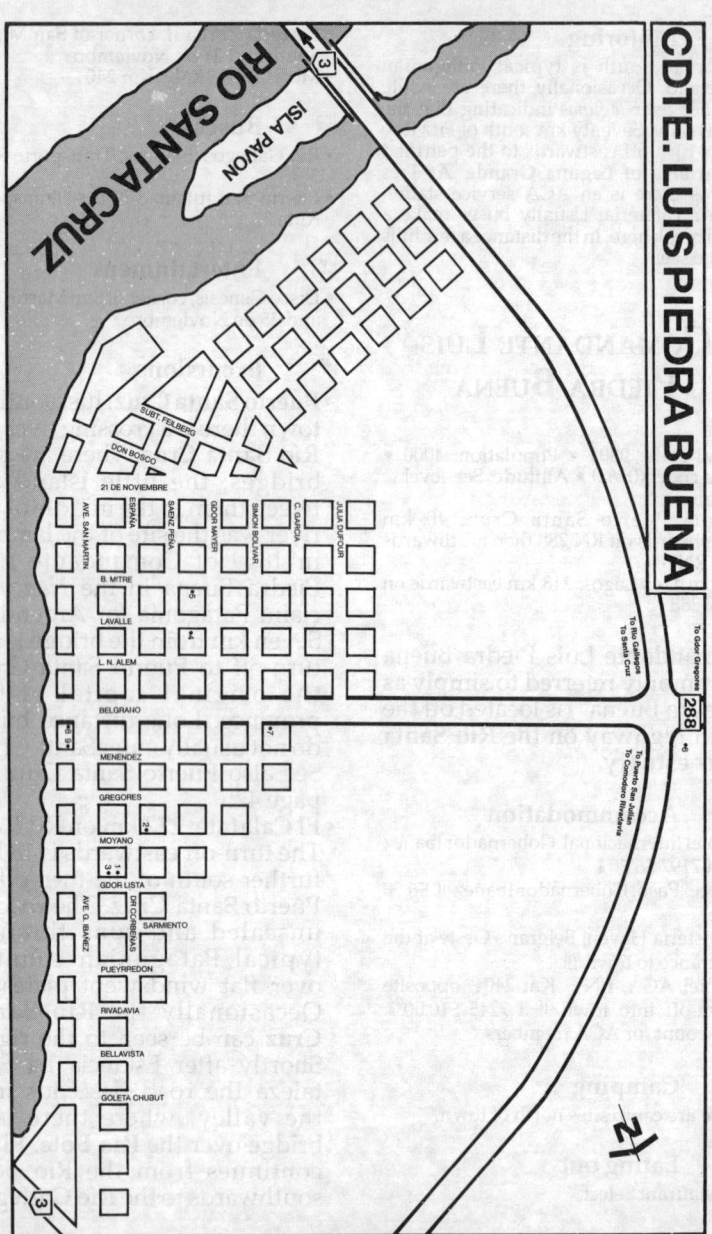

Santa Cruz Province

Key to Map
1. Municipalidad
2. Iglesia
3. Post office (Encotel)
4. Telephone (Entel)
5. Hospital
6. Hostería ACA
7. Hostería Hayen
8. Hotel
9. Hotel

through the mainly flat Patagonian landscape and crosses it over a dilapidated one-lane bridge. This river valley is unusually green for Patagonia. Just after the crossing is the turn-off to El Calafate, the beginning of RN 40 in Patagonia, which ends just before La Quiaca near the Bolivian border. On the left after the bridge is a police checkpoint. See also El Calafate below.

El Calafate

Postal code: 9405 • Population: 2000
Distances
- From Río Gallegos: 315 km north-west on RN 40
- From Perito Moreno: 630 km southwards on RN 40
- From Puerto Santa Cruz: 291 km eastwards on RP 1603

El Calafate (often just called "Calafate") is located in the *pre-cordillera* on the southern shore of **Lago Argentino**. It was officially founded in 1927. The lake softens the harsh Patagonian conditions, and El Calafate enjoys a temperate microclimate. The wet season is usually between the end of March and May, but the best months to visit are from November to April. During the December–January holiday period the town and the surrounding district are packed with tourists, when the town's facilities are especially strained, and it is advisable to book in advance for both accommodation and air travel. At present the only sealed road and paved sidewalks are on Avenida San Martín. El Calafate is the starting point for all excursions into the **Parque Nacional Los Glaciares**, the southern entrance being only 50 km away; the northern entrance is at Lago Viedma.

At the western end of the lake, 80 km away, is the **Ventisquero Moreno**, one of the few glaciers in the world which is increasing in size—its face is 60 m high and 5 km wide. Pieces break off and float away as icebergs, or *"tempanos"*. Respect the warning signs and do not go to the edge of the lake, as these large ice chunks cause waves and people occasionally get washed off the nearby rocks.

continued on page 410

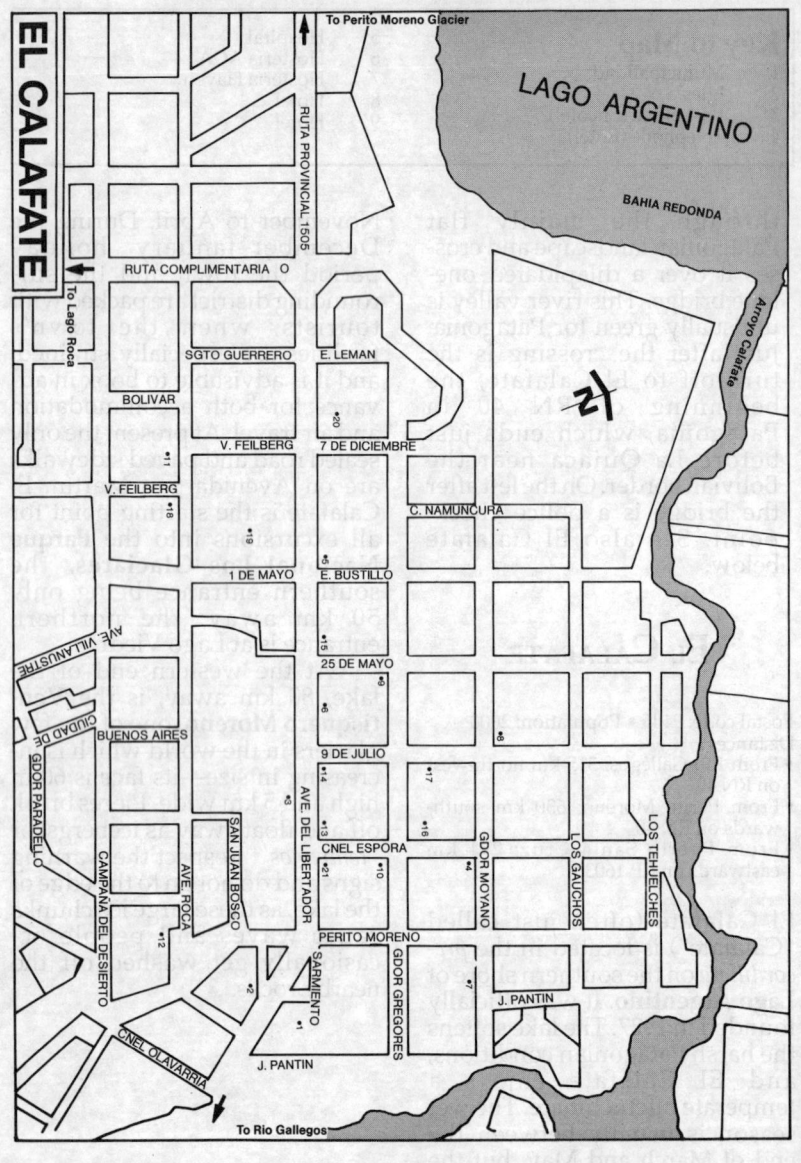

SANTA CRUZ PROVINCE

Accommodation in El Calafate

Most non-ACA hotels are open only from October to April.

★★★	Hotel Los Alamos, corner of Gobernador Moyano and Bustillos ⒯	✆ 74	$23.00	♁
★★	Hotel ACA El Calafate, corner of 1 de Mayo and Feilberg ⒯	✆ 04	$17.50	♂
	Motel		$30.00	♁
★★	Hotel El Quijote, Gobernador Gregores 1191 (corner of 25 de Mayo) ⒯	✆ 17	$18.00	♁
★★	Hotel Michelangelo, corner of Gobernador Moyano and Espora, ⒯	✆ 45	$16.00	♁
	Poor rates for travelers' checks			
★	Hotel Carlitos, Espora 991	✆ 88	$15.00	♁
★	Hotel Glanesa, Libertador 1108 ⒯✆	09	$15.50	♁
★	Hotel Tehuel Aike, Avenida Libertador 992 ⒯	✆ 91	$11.50	♁
★	Hotel Upsala, Espora 139	✆ 75	$14.00	♁
A	Hotel Amado, corner of San Martín and 9 de Julio	✆ 23	$9.00	♁
★★★	Hostería Kaiken, corner of Feilberg and Roca ⒯ ✆	73	$17.50	♁
	Credit cards accepted			
★★	Hostería Kau-Yatun, 25 de Mayo (across Arroyo Calafate in a former *estancia*)	✆ 59	$19.50	♁
★★	Hostería La Loma, corner of Roca and 15 de Febrero ⒯●	✆ 16	$21.00	2
	Bookings can be made in Buenos Aires; breakfast included			
★	Hostería Kapenke, Gregores 1194	✆ 93	$14.00	♁
	Breakfast $2.00			
B	Hospedaje Jorgito, Moyano 943		$5.50	♂
	Shared rooms			
B	Residencial Avenida, San Martín 83	✆ 83	$6.50	♂
	Shared rooms with and without bath			
★	Cabañas Nevis, RN 1505 (extension of Avenida del Libertador)		$36.00	5
B	Private accommodation: Del Norte family, Los Gauchos 813		$11.00	
C	Private accommodation: Los Lagos family, 25 de Mayo 220		$5.00	♂
	Shared rooms			
C	Private accommodation: Borquez family, 25 de Mayo 345		$4.50	♂
	Shared rooms			

Key to Map

1. Municipalidad
2. Iglesia
3. Post office (Encotel)
4. Telephone (Entel)
5. Tourist information (national parks)
6. Transportes Patagonicos
7. Hospedaje Jorgito
8. Hotel Michelangelo
9. Hotel El Quijote
10. Hotel Carlitos
11. Hospital
12. Hostería La Loma
13. Hotel Tehuel Aike
14. Hotel Amado
15. Hotel Glanesa
16. Hotel Upsala
17. Hostería Kapenke
18. Hostería Kaiken
19. Hotel ACA El Calafate
20. Hotel Los Alamos
21. Residencial Avenida

El Calafate

SANTA CRUZ PROVINCE

✈ Air services from El Calafate

A new airport is being built 25 km to the west. The airport is listed in itineraries as Lago Argentino (not as El Calafate) and is being upgraded. In winter when the weather is bad there are often no flights for weeks.

- LADE, corner of San Martín and 25 de Mayo

Destination	Fare	Depart	Days	Services	Airline
Río Gallegas	$15.00	1320	1–2 services daily		LADE
Comodoro Rivadavia	$20.00	1235	Tues	3	LADE
Gobernador Gregores	$14.00	1235	Tues	1	LADE
Perito Moreno	$15.00	1235	Tues	2	LADE
Río Grande	$18.50	1320	Mon, Tues, Wed, Thurs	1	LADE
Ushuaia	$22.00	1320	1–2 services daily	3	LADE

ℹ Tourist information

- Intendencia Parque Nacional Los Glaciares, corner of Bustillo and Libertador 05. It is advisable when travelling to the national park to obtain camping and fishing permits here. You can also find out whether *refugios* are open and how to get there. There are maps available but information is not always up to date. Camping is permitted only in designated areas
- The national park office also serves as the tourist office. A list of hotel prices and private accommodation is available here
- Hotel Glanesa has information about camping on Lago Roca

⛺ Camping

- Municipal camp site $1.00

Camping in the Parque Nacional

When camping and hiking in the national park take plenty of food and drink with you. The use of *refugios* is free, but obtain permission to use them from the *Intendancia* in Calafate.

- The nearest camping site is 8 km from Glaciar Perito Moreno
- Camping site on Lago Roca, 55 km west
- Autocamping and *hostería* near Lago Viedma, 74 km north on RN 40
- Río Túnel, Subintendancia de Parques Nacionales, located at the foot of Cerro Fitz Roy, on the north side of Lago Viedma, 216 km north on RP 524

🍽 Eating out

- Restaurant ACA, corner of 1 de Mayo and Roca. Grill
- Restaurant El Mirador del Lago, Libertador
- Restaurant Hotel El Quijote, corner of Gobernador Moyano and Bustillos
- Restaurant Hotel Michelangelo, Espora 213 (corner of Moyano)
- Restaurant Hotel Tehuel Aike, Avenida Libertador 992
- Restaurant Kaiken, Hostería Kaiken, corner of Feilberg and Roca
- Restaurant La Tablita, corner of Commandante Rosales and Libertador, near municipal camping ground. Grill
- Restaurant Glanesa, Residencial Glanesa, Libertador 1108
- Pizzería Onelli, Avenida del Libertador 1100
- Cafetería Kasbah, Avenida del Libertador 1002
- Tearoom: La Casita de la Loma
- Tearoom: Mac Tub, Ave del Libertador 960

✉ Post and telegraph

- Post office: San Martín
- Telephone: Gobernador Commandante Espora 194 (corner of Moyano)

El Calafate

Santa Cruz Province

💲 Financial

Money changing in El Calafate is expensive. There is a steep surcharge by both the ACA Motel and the Banco de la Provincia de Santa Cruz.
Lake Travel changes and accepts travelers' checks.

🗒 Services and facilities

- Bakery: 25 de Mayo 1260
- Supermarket: Gobernador Gregores 1101

✈ Border crossing

The Cancha Carrera border post is open from December to April.

🚌 Buses

Bus companies

- Empresa Ruta 3
- Transportadora Patagonica, San Martín

Services

- Río Gallegos: Fare $9.50; departs 0615 Sun–Tues, Thurs, Fri; Empresa Transportadora Patagonica
- Fitz Roy: Fare $22.00; departs 0700 or on demand (car); Lake Travel
- Glaciar Perito Moreno: Fare $10.00; departs daily
- Glaciar Upsala: Fare $25.00; departs 0700 daily; Empresa Nova Terra. Transport is by bus to Punta Bandera and by boat from there

🚗 Motoring

- ACA, at Hotel ACA El Calafate, gives information about road conditions to Lago Viedma and Gobernador Gregores, and advises on alternative trips using your own vehicle.

⊕ Tours

- Alvaro Viajes, corner of Avenida del Libertador and Thomas Espora. Runs an excursion to Glaciar Moreno; fare $10.00, including entrance to Parque Nacional. English spoken

- Interlagos, Libertador 1175. Excursions and car rental; daily trips to Glaciar Moreno
- Lake Travel Services, Avenida del Libertador 997 ℭ 92. Excursions to Glaciar Moreno ($10.00) and Cerro Fitz Roy ($20.00). English, French, and German spoken
- Nova Terra, 25 de Mayo 73

🛍 Shopping

- Los Glaciares *artesanía* shop, corner of Gregores and Moyano

🎭 Entertainment

Film shows about the Glaciar Perito Moreno are held nightly at 1915 in the Restaurante La Posada de los Alamos, corner of Gobernador Moyano and Bustillo.

- Tío Cacho Discotheque, corner of Gobernador Gregores and 9 de Julio

🏞 Excursions

All of the excursions listed below are in the **Parque Nacional Los Glaciares**. See also Parque Nacional Los Glaciares on page 416.

- **Cerro Fitz Roy**: 230 km, at the northern end of the park. The road to **Lago Viedma** has recently been upgraded. At **Paso Río La Leona** there is a small *posada*, or *gaucho* bar, which also offers shared accommodation for $4.00 per person. There is a bridge over the **Río La Leona**, which drains Lago Viedma. From Estancia San Agustín the road roughly follows the northern edge of the lake for 35 km. Shortly after crossing the Río Fitz Roy you arrive at the base camp. Here is the northern entrance to the park, with a ranger station. The Hostería

El Calafate

SANTA CRUZ PROVINCE

Lago Viedma is open from the end of September until April 20. If you are going on a hiking trip through the Fitz Roy you have to make your own arrangements in El Calafate for own transport and when to be picked up. You will pay double the full fare. You can also arrange pickup through the national park rangers, who can radio to El Calafate. You can lodge at Hostería Viedma and make day trips to various areas. The trail to Glaciar Viedma begins behind the *hostería*. Another trail leads up the **Río Fitz Roy** to the glacier lake and along the eastern side of a small mountain tarn—this is my favourite hike in this area. Beware of sudden forceful gales coming down from the mountain. Further up there is a *refugio*, but check first with the *guardaparque* (or park rangers) what state it is in. You can easily reach **Glaciar Torre** in one day, and camp at 2500 m in full view of the glacier in superb Andean scenery

- **Glaciar Perito Moreno** by minibus from El Calafate. This is a full day's outing organized by several tour operators. After following the lake shore for 25 km the trip goes up a dirt road through hilly country into the Andes. Take protection against the strong wind which blows all year round, such as a hat and protective skin cream. You arrive for lunch at 1200 at the ACA tourist complex which overlooks part of the glacier. The tourist complex consist of 16 huts, and costs $25.00 for ACA members. Buses return to El Calafate at 1630. For a close view take the trail behind the complex leading along the lake and finishing at the large parking lot. The glacier dips into the lake over a 5 km face and divides **Lago Argentino** at its narrowest part. The melt-water is prevented from escaping and over a two to three year period rises to more than 30 m. By then the water pressure is so strong that the ice barrier crumbles, and this "breaking" attracts tourists and scientists from all over the globe. The sight of this huge mass of ice is an overwhelming spectacle. Occasionally you can see ice chunks separating to float down the lake as icebergs. No trip to Argentina is complete without seeing this glacier

- **Glaciar Upsala**, at the extreme western end of **Lago Argentino**, by bus and boat via Punta Bandera. This excursion is organized by several tour operators, but does not take place every day; the boat fare is $22.50. It is a full day's outing—the boat trip alone takes four hours. Bring your own lunch and sun lotion. The ship usually carries about a hundred passengers, and goes through the **Boca del Diablo** ("Devil's Mouth") into the northern arm of Lago Argentino and into the **Canal Upsala**. In the off-season smaller boats are used. The first landing is usually at **Bahía Onelli** in order to make a short

El Calafate

SANTA CRUZ PROVINCE

walk up to **Lago Onelli**, from where you can view **Glaciars Onelli** and **Agassiz**. How close you sail to the glacier depends on the captain. The glacier extends into Chile and is part of the 500 km Patagonian ice shield. If you plan to make the trip towards the end of the tourist season, say in April, you may have to arrange your own transport from El Calafate to Punta Bandera. There are no regular buses to Punta Bandera, 51 km away
- **La Gerónima** and **Laguna Frías**: 80 km south. In order to reach this part of the national park you need your own transport as far as Laguna Roca, as no regular excursion buses go there. During the summer holidays you may get a lift to the camping spot near Laguna Roca. From there it is a 30 km walk to the Río Frias. Trout and salmon fishing, climbing, and camping are possible
- **Laguna de los Cisnes**, across Arroyo Calafate. This is a bird sanctuary with crimson flamingoes
- **Punta Gualichu** caves: Approximately 9 km east. The cave is about 2 m deep and 7 m high. The Argentine explorer Perito Moreno sought shelter here after he was shipwrecked in Lago Argentino. The aboriginal cave paintings are mostly abstracts with a few painted hands. Vandals have done some damage
- **Parque Nacional Los Glaciares** and Parque Nacional Torres del Paine in Chile: A hike combining these neighbouring parks is at present possible only with lengthy and exhaustive paperwork at both embassies in your home country, and then only for a large group such as bushwalking or mountaineering clubs. Should you be able to obtain such a special visa you have to present yourself at the police in Puerto Natales in Chile and again at the police station in El Calafate. The road to Paso Baguales is not completed to the border on the Argentine side

ESPERANZA

Postal code: 9401
Distances
- From Río Gallegos: 147 km north-west on RN 40
- From El Calafate: 170 km south-east on RN 40
- From El Turbio: 188 km north-east on RP 1707

Esperanza is situated on the **Río Coig** halfway between Río Gallegos and El Calafate.

Accommodation
- ACA motel. Confitería

Motoring
The 77 km stretch between La Esperanza and Cerrito is now sealed.
- Service station: ACA

Santa Cruz Province

Fitz Roy

Postal code: 9019
Distance from Comodoro Rivadavia: 140 km southwards on RN 3

Fitz Roy is a tiny town named after the captain of Darwin's *Beagle*, and is not much to look at. It is a convenient stopover on the way to Puerto Deseado or Río Gallegos.

🛏 Accommodation
There are two tiny *hosterías*.

🚗 Motoring
The road north to Comodoro Rivadavia is sealed.

📍 Excursions
- **Reserva Natural Laguna Grande**: 140 km south-west. Follow RN 3 south for 85 km and turn westwards rather than taking the direct route 10 km south of the Río Deseado bridge. Here there is a petrified forest, made up entirely of the *Araucaritis mirabilis* species; it is estimated to be at least 40 million years old. Some of the petrified tree trunks are 3 m thick and 20 m long. To get here you need your own transport or a taxi

Gobernador Gregores

Postal code: 9311 • (area code: (0962)
Distances

- From Bajo Caracoles 222 km southwards on RN 40 then RP 521
- From Puerto San Julián: 220 km westwards on RP 521
- From Puerto Santa Cruz: 228 km north-west on RN 288 then RP 1301
- From Tres Lagos: 176 km north-east on RN 40 then RP 2310

Located in the **Río Chico valley**, Gobernador Gregores is a typical Patagonian township. It lies in a sheltered position in the river valley, with dusty unsealed streets and sidewalks. The town is almost deserted in winter, when many of the townsfolk shut up their houses and travel north to escape the climate.

All roads in the area are unsealed and transport is sometimes Unreliable in winter.

There is a modern agricultural college, and a salmon cannery.

🛏 Accommodation
- ★ Hotel Universal. Cheapest in town
- ★★ Hostal Adelino, RP 521, just at the entrance to the town (91039 $17.00 ȉ
- B San Francisco, San Martín 463 $8.50 ȉ. Open all year round

🍴 Eating out
- Restaurant Cañadón León
- Bar El Ultimo Gaucho. Señor Julio Lopez is a local character and considers himself the last of the *gauchos*, hence the name of his establishment. His wife speaks German

🚌 Buses
Transportes Cerro San Lorenzo buses stop outside Bar El Ultimo Gaucho.
- Bajo Caracoles: Fare $9.00; departs 1330 Thurs; Empresa Cerro San Lorenzo
- Puerto San Julián: Fare $7.50; departs 0700 Thurs, Sat; 4 hours; Empresa Cerro San Lorenzo

Fitz Roy

SANTA CRUZ PROVINCE

✈ Air services from Gobernador Gregores

Destination	Fare	Depart	Services	Hours	Airline
• Río Gallegos	$16.00	1215	Mon, Thurs	2	LADE
• Comodoro Rivadavia	$17.00	1340	Tues, Thurs	2	LADE
• Lago Argentino	$14.00	1215	Mon	1	LADE
• Perito Moreno	$14.00	1340	Tues, Thurs	1	LADE
• Río Grande	$17.00	1215	Mon	4	LADE
• Ushuaia	$22.00	1215	Mon	5	LADE

🚐 Motoring

Just outside Gobernador Gregores the road links up with RN 40, which here is nothing more than a dirt track.
On the way north there is a hotel at Riera and another at Las Horquetas. A narrow bridge crosses the Río Olnie; here there is a small inn.
• Service station: YPF

🎣 Sport

• Fishing: A salmon fishing competition is held on Lago Cardiel in April. Because the water is slightly salty there are no trout

⚑ Excursions

• **Lago Cardiel**: Some 65 km east on RP 2310, and the home of delicious salmon. The lake has no visible outlet. In April the local fishing club sponsors a competition which attracts large numbers of anglers
• **Parque Nacional Francisco Perito Moreno**, **Lago Belgrano**, and **Lago Escondido**: The area is home to numerous herds of *guanacos* and *ñandus*. You can only reach the park with your own vehicle. The nearest bus stop is at Hotel Las Horquetas, where there is a small hotel and restaurant, 90 km from the entrance to the park.

• **Bajo Caracoles** and **Lago Posadas**: The trip from Gobernador Gregores to Bajo Caracoles is more varied than the rather dull trip from the coast to Gobernador Gregores. En route the bus stops at **Tamal Aike** (where there is a police station), **Hotel Las Horquetas**, and **Río Olnie**, where there is an inn. The bus terminaTes at Lago Posadas, where there is a hotel, and returns next morning via Bajo Caracoles to Puerto San Julián on the coast.

LAS HERAS

Postal code: 9017 • ✆ area code: (0967)
Distances
• From Comodoro Rivadavia: 165 km south-west on RP 502
• From Perito Moreno: 188 km eastwards on RP 520

Las Heras is a convenient stopover on the way to Perito Moreno and on to Chile.

🛏 Accommodation

★ Hotel Suyai, O'Higgins 171 ✆ 94117 $14.00

A Hotel Lo del Tordoc, Gobernador Gregores (94097 $6.50

🚌 Buses
- Caleta Olivia: Empresa Co-Mi
- Los Antiguos: Empresa Co-Mi

LOS ANTIGUOS

Postal code: 0941
Distances
- From Chile Chico (Chile): 8 km eastwards on RP 520
- From Perito Moreno: 60 km westwards on RP 520

Located on the Río Los Antiguos, on the south side of the Lago Buenos Aires, Los Antiguos is surrounded by high mountains in a picturesque setting. The climate is mellowed by the influence of the lake.

🛏 Accommodation
A Hotel Argentino, Avenida 11 de Julio ⓝ $7.50 ℹ

⚠ Border crossing
The Argentine border post is about 1 km from the town. From here onwards the road is a track leading through the wide river bed. If using your own vehicle, be sure to follow somebody who knows the route through the river. The Chilean immigration post is on the other side of the river.

🚌 Buses
- Caleta Olivia: Fare $11.00; departs Tues, Fri; Empresa Co-Mi
- Chile Chico (Chile): Fare $1.50. It is possible to hitch-hike, as private cars pass through daily; Chileans charge $1.50 for a ride

PARQUE NACIONAL LOS GLACIARES

The Parque Nacional Los Glaciares is located in the extreme west of Santa Cruz province along the *cordillera* and borders Chile. The length of the park is 350 km and the width varies between 40 and 60 km. It covers an area of 600 000 ha. It is the major tourist attraction of the province and perhaps of Argentina itself. Owing to its natural beauty and unique flora and fauna it has been declared a world heritage area. El Calafate, some 80 k east from the southern entrance to the national park, is the major tourist centre. The main attractions in the southern section are **Glaciar Perito Moreno**, **Glaciar Upsala**, and **Lago Argentino**, with its many arms extending far into the high sierra. In the northern section **Lago Viedma** and the peaks of **Cerro Fitz Roy** at 2275 m are a major attraction for hikers and climbers. Rare and endangered animals can be found here, such as the *huemul* (the South American deer) and the *pudu* (dwarf deer), which grows only 40 cm high. The condor and various species of eagles can also be seen. The rivers abound with trout and salmon, which makes this area a paradise for anglers.

Santa Cruz Province

◘ Accommodation

★ Hostería Lago Viedma, on the Río Fitz Roy 7 km from Lago Viedma $12.00. Open from December to the end of April
• Unidad Turistica ACA Ventisquero Perito Moreno, RP 1506, on Peninsula Magallanes overlooking the Lake Argentino and part of the Glaciar Perito Moreno ⊞▣ $35.00 for five

◉ Excursions

Hostería Lago Viedma is the starting point for excursions into the Cerro Fitz Roy area, including **Cerro Fitz Roy**, **Glaciar del Torre**, **Lago Torre**, and **Glaciar Viedma**. There is a restaurant here, but bring your own provisions. It is 216 km north of El Calafate and 122 km east of Tres Lagos. Take Ruta "o" for 33 km to the junction with RN 40, and then turn north into RN 40 at the intersection which crosses the **Río Santa Cruz** and cross a second bridge over the **Río Leona** some 15 km further along. Follow the Río Leona due north for 53 km until you reach **Paso Río La Leona**. Just before the bridge the Hostería Paso Río Leona is on the right; it has shared accommodation and cafeteria-cum-country inn atmosphere—local *gaucho* characters indulge in their drinking bouts here. After crossing the bridge continue on RN 40 to the intersection with RP 524. Follow RP 524 for 88 km due west along the northern rim of **Lago Viedma** until you reach the Hostería Lago Viedma.

See also "Excursions" in El Calafate on page 411.

PERITO MORENO

Postal code: 9040 • Population: 2000 • Altitude: 400 m
Distances
• From Caleta Olivia: 305 km west on RP 501 then RP 520
• From Los Antiguos (on the Chilean border): 60 km eastwards on RP 520
• From Río Mayo: 123 km southwards on RN 40
• From Tres Lagos: 455 km northwards on RN 40

Perito Moreno is located near Lago Buenos Aires, which crosses the border into Chile and is called Lago General Carrera by the Chileans. To the south are Lago Belgrano and Lago Burmeister. Although the town is located in Santa Cruz province it is dominated by Comodoro Rivadavia in Chubut province.

ⓘ Tourist information

• Tourist information, Avenida San Martín 1059. Open Mon–Fri 0800–2000 and every day in holiday season.

◘ Accommodation

Some hotels are only open between December and April.
★ Hotel Austral, Avenida San Martín 1381 ℂ 42 $12.50 ⚹
★ Hotel Belgrano, Avenida San Martín 1001 ⊞ ℂ 19 $12.00 ⚹
★ Hotel Santa Cruz, Belgrano 1565. Cheap
B Hospedaje Argentino, Buenos Aires 1276 $4.00 ⚹. Basic
B Hospedaje Fenix, Avenida San Martín 1302 (corner of Mitre) $4.00 ⚹. Basic

⛺ Camping

• Parque Laguna, near the center of town, also serves as an offshoot of the tourist office. If nobody is there contact Señor Luis Garcia who lives on Avenida San

Santa Cruz Province

Martín 665 opposite the police station on the road to Bajo Caracoles. Cabins cost $4.50 per person, and tent rental costs $1.00 per person
- Recreo Municipal, 2 km from town near the road workers' camp. Free camping by the river

Eating out
- Restaurant El Americano, Avenida San Martín 1327. Also arranges transport to Caleta Olivia and to Los Antiguos on the Chilean border
- Restaurant El Cisne, corner of Sarmiento and B Mitre
- Restaurant La Tranquera, Sarmiento 1598 (corner of Rivadavia)
- Cafetería, 9 de Julio 1443

Post and telegraph
- Post office
- Telephone: corner of 9 de Julio and Rivadavia

Financial
Banks do not accept travelers' checks.
US dollars can be exchanged at the Hotel Austral at good rates, and at the Hotel Belgrano.

Services and facilities
- Bakery: Don Adolfo, corner of Avenida San Martín and Buenos Aires
- Laundry: Buenos Aires 1332
- Supermarket: Central, corner of Avenida San Martín and Rivadavia

Buses
There is no central bus terminal.
There are no regular bus services north to Río Mayo (RN 40) or south to Bajo Caracoles (RN 40) and to the Río de las Pinturas.
Hitchhiking is difficult outside the tourist season, December to March.

Bus companies
- Empresa Comi, in Hotel Argentina, Buenos Aires 1276
- Empresa Los Antiguos, in Bar Americano, Avenida San Martín 1339

Services
- Caleta Olivia: Fare $8.20; departs 1000 Tues, Fri; Empresa Co-mi
- Los Antiguos: Fare $2.80; departs 1330 daily; Empresa Co-mi, Empresa Los Antiguos
- Río de las Cuevas Pintadas: $55.00 bus hire, costs shared amongst passengers; departs 0700 or as required; private company

Motoring
RN 40 northwards and southwards is unsealed and is rough going.
RP 520 to Los Antiguos on the Chilean border is being extensively upgraded.
- Service station: ACA, corner of 9 de Julio and Rivadavia

Tours
The tourist office or Hotel Belgrano will arrange transport and tours.

Air services from Perito Moreno
- LADE, San Martín 1207

Destination	Fare	Depart	Services	Hours	Airline
Río Gallegos	$17.00	1105	Mon, Thurs	3	LADE
Comodoro Rivadavia	$14.00	1450	Tues, Thurs	1	LADE
Gobernador Gregores	$14.00	1105	Mon, Thurs	1	LADE
Lago Argentino	$15.00	1105	Mon	2	LADE
Río Grande	$21.00	1105	Mon	5	LADE
Ushuaia	$25.00	1105	Mon	6	LADE

Perito Moreno

SANTA CRUZ PROVINCE

Excursions

- **Lago Buenos Aires**: 25 km westwards. The lake extends into Chile as Lago General Carrera. This huge sheet of water moderates the climate of the area: the closer to the lake the greener the countryside becomes. The lake is surrounded by high mountains but opens onto undulating country in the eastern or Argentine section. These mountains also form the border between the two countries. The road is sealed, and the views are magnificent. All cultivated fields are strips of 100 by 300 m bordered by willow trees. At **Estancia Las Chilcas** there is an archeological site; see below.
- **Los Antiguos**: 67 km westwards on RP 520, on **Lago Buenos Aires**. Orchards and *pejerrey* fishing. There is a daily bus
- **Estancia Las Chilcas**: 30 km westwards on RP 520. There is an archeological site nearby with prehistoric cave paintings
- **Cerro El Volcán**: On leaving Perito Moreno southwards take the first dirt road on your left after the police station. From here it is a 15 km walk to the crater, which is on private property
- **Las Cuevas de las Manos** ("Caves of the Hands"): 124 km south, on the **Río Pinturas**. Turn off into the canyon 3 km north of Bajo Caracoles, and travel north-east on a dirt road. The paintings of human hands and animals inside the caves are said to be 10 000 years old. The drive through the canyon is very picturesque. For public transport check with the tourist office. Private buses usually leave at 0700, as required, and return the same evening; the cost is $55.00 per bus, shared amongst the passengers
- **Coihaique in Chile, via Chile Chico**: Take the bus to Los Antiguos, and cross the border at Chile Chico by wading through the river or by four-wheel drive. From there a twice-weekly ferry goes across Lago General Carrera (Lago Argentino in Argentina) to Puerto Ingeniero Ibañez, where you can board the waiting bus for Coihaique
- **Coihaique in Chile, via Río Mayo**: 300 km. See Río Mayo on page 391
- **Coihaique in Chile, via Río Gueuguel**: 170 km, over the **Paso Huemules**

PICO TRUNCADO

Postal code: 9015 • area code: (0967)
Distances
- From Río Gallegos: 687 km northwards on RN 3 then RP 520
- From Comodoro Rivadavia: 123 km southwards on RN 3 then RP 501
- From Perito Moreno: 251 km eastwards on RP 520
- From Puerto Deseado: 184 km northwest on RN 281 then RP 520

Pico Truncado is the center of a vast oil and gas field. It is a convenient stopover for travelers

SANTA CRUZ PROVINCE

going westwards, but there is little of interest for tourists.

🛏 Accommodation
A Hotel J O, Rivadavia 45 ✆ 92245 $4.00
B Hotel La Paz, Avenida San Martín 596 ✆ 92029 $7.00

PUERTO DESEADO

Postal code: 9050 • Population: 4000 • ✆ area code: (0967) • Altitude: Sea-level
Distance from Comodoro Rivadavia: 270 km south-east on RN 3 then RN 281

Puerto Deseado is at the mouth of the **Río Deseado**, which drains Lago Buenos Aires. The town was founded in 1884, and the harbor can accommodate ocean-going vessels. There are panoramic views from here over the Bahía Uruguay and the Atlantic Ocean.

🎭 Festivals
- Fiesta de San Juan Bosco (Feast of St John Bosco): January 31
- Fiesta de la Raza: October 9

🛏 Accommodation
A Hotel Colón, Almirante Brown 450 ✆ 7304 $13.00
** Hostería Los Acantilados, Espora 1611 (corner of Pueyrredon) ✆ 7167 $16.00

🚌 Buses
Autotransportes La Unión and Don Otto buses run regularly between Puerto Deseado and Comodoro Rivadavia.

🚗 Motoring
RN 281 is sealed for most of the 130 km to the junction with RN 3, 8 km south of Fitz Roy.

🎣 Sport
Fishing along the coast and in the Bahía Uruguay, which is the mouth of the Río Deseado.

✈ Air services from Puerto Deseado

Destination	Fare	Depart	Services	Hours	Airline
• Río Gallegos	$28.00	1140	Mon, Tues, Fri	2	LADE
• Bahía Blanca	$49.00	1220	Wed	6½	LADE
• Buenos Aires (Aeroparque Jorge Newbery)					
	$79.00	1220	Wed, Sat	9½	LADE
• Comodoro Rivadavia					
	$17.00	1220	Mon, Wed, Fri, Sat	1	LADE
• Esquel	$32.00	1220	Wed, Sat	3	LADE
• Mar del Plata	$58.00	1220	Wed, Sat	8	LADE
• Neuquén	$38.00	1220	Wed, Sat	5½	LADE
• Puerto San Julián	$17.00	1140	Mon, Tues, Fri	1	LADE
• Puerto Santa Cruz					
	$22.00	1140	Mon, Tues, Fri	1	LADE
• Río Grande	$35.00	1735	Tues, Fri	3	LADE
• San Carlos de Bariloche					
	$36.00	1220	Wed, Sat	4	LADE
• Trelew	$28.00	1220	Wed, Sat	2	LADE
• Viedma	$44.00	1220	Sat	6½	LADE

Pico Truncado

SANTA CRUZ PROVINCE

Excursions

- **Cañadón de las Bandurrias**: 3 km west of RN 281 on the outskirts of town. Forty meter high "grotto of Lourdes"
- **Isla de los Pájaros** and **Bahía Uruguay**: Launch trips to Isla de los Pájaros, where there is a penguin colony, and to Bahía Uruguay, where the unique grey cormorant can be seen on the islands

PUERTO SAN JULIÁN

Postal code: 9310 • Population: 4600 • area code: (0962)
Distances
- From Río Gallegos: 316 km northwards on RN 3
- From Comodoro Rivadavia: 426 km southwards on RN 3
- From Gobernador Gregores: 207 km eastwards on RP 521

The first Christian mass in Argentina was held here when Magellan landed and executed a member of his crew. The spot, situated on a little island at the entrance to the bay, is nowadays known as "Banco Justicia" ("Justice Bank"). Sir Francis DRake also executed one of his crew here.

The first attempt to found a town here was made by Antonio de Viedma in 1780: he called it Colonia de Florida Blanca. It was abandoned in 1784—its ruins are 10 km west near the airport. Puerto San Julián was founded in 1901 and is situated on the **Bahía San Julián**. It is halfway between Comodoro Rivadavia and Río Gallegos, and has good facilities for breaking the monotonous journey through Patagonia. There is wildlife in the area such as *guanacos*, red and grey foxes, and *ñandus*. The hinterland is used for sheep raising. Canning fish and kaolin production are other sources of income.

Puerto San Julián is commonly known simply as "San Julián".

Tourist information

- Tourist information, corner of San Martín and Rivadavia (2485. Open Mon–Fri 0800–1500. Ask for Señora Lucía E Del Valle de Lombardich
- In summer the tourist office is open in the center strip of San Martín near Rivadavia

Camping

- Autocamping Municipal, Costanera between Rivadavia and Roca (2160 $1.00 per person, $2.00 per car. Very clean, with telephone and all facilities

Eating out

- Restaurant Aconcagua, corner of Sarmiento and Vieytes. Cheap
- Restaurant Avenida, San Martín 1375
- Restaurant El Águila, San Martín 527 (corner of Rivadavia)
- Restaurant Elazo, corner of Cevallos and Mitre
- Restaurant La Rural, corner of Ameghino and Urquiza
- Restaurant La Taza de Oro, corner of Urquiza and Piedrabuena
- Restaurant Sportsman, Mitre 311 (corner of 25 de Mayo)
- Confitería Nos Amis, Ameghino 1091

Eating out outside Puerto San Julián

- Astra, on RN 3 north, about 1 km from crossroad

Puerto San Julián

Santa Cruz Province

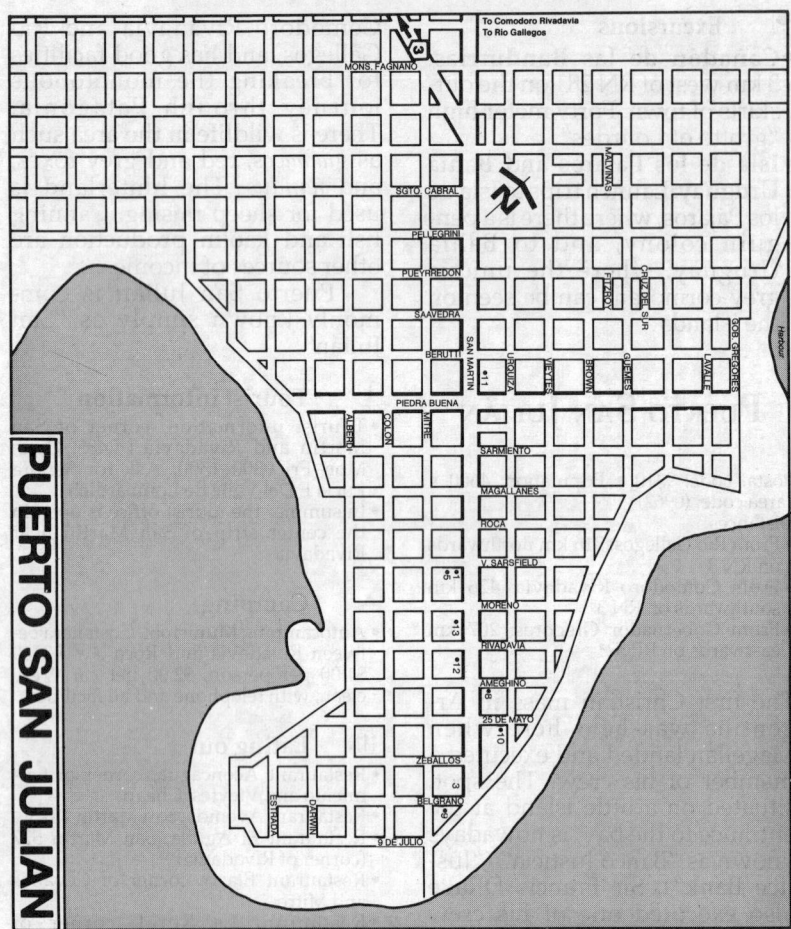

Key to Map
1. Municipalidad
2. Iglesia
3. Post office (Encotel)
4. Telephone (Entel)
5. Tourist information
6. Transportadora Patagónica
7. Transportes Cerro San Lorenzo
8. Transportes Ruta 3
9. Museum
10. Hotel Municipal de Turismo
11. Residencial Sada
12. Hotel Gran Colón
13. Hotel El Aguila

Puerto San Julián

SANTA CRUZ PROVINCE

🛏 Accommodation in Puerto San Julián

★★	Hotel Municipal de Turismo, 25 de Mayo 917 (corner of Costanera)	2300	$13.00	
A	Hotel Gran Colón, San Martín 301	2428	$9.50	
A	Residencial Sada, San Martín 1112 (corner of Piedra Buena)	2013	$11.50	
B	Residencial Águila, corner of San Martín and Rivadavia.		$4.50	
B	Residencial Argentino, corner of Urquiza and Saavedra. Family hotel; shared bathrooms		$4.50	
C	Residencial Asturias, Mitre 362. Family hotel; shared bathrooms		$4.50	

✉ Post and telegraph
- Post office, corner of Belgrano and San Martín
- Telephone: Moreno block 600 (corner of Mitre)

$ Financial
Ask at the tourist office—see "Tourist information" above.

🗒 Services and facilities
- Bakery: La Pancha, Mitre 478
- Hospital: Costanera between Roca and Magallanes
- Supermarket: Paul & Mary

🚌 Buses

Bus companies
- Transporte Ruta 3, Ameghino 953 (corner of San Martín)
- Transportadora Patagonica, corner of Sarsfield and San Martín (2082
- Transportadora Upsala
- Transportes Cerro San Lorenzo, Mitre 150 (2403

✈ Air services from Puerto San Julián

A taxi to the airport costs $3.00.
- LADE, San Martín 2137 (corner of Berutti) (2137

Destination	Fare	Depart	Services	Hours	Airline
• Río Gallegos	$22.00	1240	Mon, Tues, Fri	1	LADE
• Bahía Blanca	$50.00	1130	We	7	LADE
• Buenos Aires (Aeroparque Jorge Newbery)					
	$80.00	1130	Wed, Sat	8	LADE
• Comodoro Rivadavia					
	$25.00	1130	Mon, Wed, Fri, Sat	2	LADE
• Esquel	$35.00	1130	Wed, Sat	4½	LADE
• Mar del Plata	$61.00	1130	Wed, Sat	8½	LADE
• Neuquén	$39.00	1130	Wed, Sat	6	LADE
• Puerto Deseado	$17.00	1130	Mon, Wed, Fri, Sat	1	LADE
• Río Grande	$28.00	1825	Tue, Fri	2	LADE
• San Carlos de Bariloche					
	$37.00	1130	Wed, Sat	5	LADE
• Trelew	$31.00	1130	Wed, Sat	2½	LADE
• Viedma	$45.00	1130	Sat	7	LADE

Puerto San Julián

Santa Cruz Province

Services
- Río Gallegos: Fare $10.00; departs 0500; 2 services daily; Transporte Ruta 3, Transportadora Upsala
- Bajo Caracoles: Fare $16.50; departs 0700 Tues; Transportes Cerro San Lorenzo
- Comandante Luis Piedra Buena: Fare $3.50; departs 0500 daily; Transporte Ruta 3
- Gobernador Gregores: Fare $7.50; departs 0700 Tues–Sat; Transporte Cerro San Lorenzo
- Puerto Santa Cruz: Fare $4.00; departs 0500 daily; Transporte Ruta 3

Motoring
RN 3 southwards is sealed in places. It crosses the **Río Chico** (which originates in the Parque Nacional Francisco Perito Moreno) 90 km south of Puerto San Julián. The Río Chico valley is about 4 km wide.
RP 521 westwards to Gobernador Gregores is unsealed from the turn-off just outside town.
- Service station: YPF, corner of Piedrabuena and San Martín

Shopping
- Artesanias de San Julián, corner of Moreno and Mitre

Sport
Fishing in the **Bahía San Julián** requires a fishing permit. Fishing is good all year round but least good in winter. The fish encountered mostly are *robalo* (*Eleginus maclovinus*), up to 50 cm long and weighing up to 8 kg with delicious flesh; and *pejerrey* in the summer only. Punta Caldera is a popular fishing spot.

Entertainment
- Disco Galaxia, corner of Mitre and 25 de Mayo
- Bowling: Boliche de Pin, at the *hostería* on Avenida Costanera

Sightseeing
- Museo Regional (Regional Museum), including the Museo Arte Marino (Museum of Marine Art), corner of 9 de Julio and Mitre. Open daily 0800–1200; entry free

Excursions
- **Gobernador Gregores**: About an hour along the road there is the overpriced Hotel Bella Vista which lets rooms for $10.00. It is mostly flat, windswept, Patagonian *meseta* country. Along the road small flocks of *ñandus* or rheas can be seen, as well as the *mara* or Patagonian hare. Shortly before Gobernador Gregores the road enters the wide valley of the **Río Chico**. The inhabitants of Patagonia grow hedges and lines of trees to protect them against the continual harsh winds. As you wind down into the valley you get a good view of Gobernador Gregores. See also Gobernador Gregores on page 414
- **Florida Blanca**: 10 km. The ruins of a colony founded in 1780 by Antonio Viedma. Arrange your trip with a guide from the tourist office in the center strip of San Martín near the taxi stand
- **Cabo Curioso**: 18 km north. A beach with an attractive natural cave. There is camping here, but facilities are poor
- **Islas de los Pingüinos**: For excursions by launch to this island (whose name means "Penguin Island") contact the tourist of-

PUERTO SANTA CRUZ

Postal code: 9300 • Population: 3000 • (area code: (0962) • Altitude: Sea-level
Distances
- From Río Gallegos: 228 km northwards on RN 3
- From Comodoro Rivadavia: 524 km southwards on RN 3

Located off the main highway at the mouth of the **Río Santa Cruz**, which has its source in Lago Argentino, Puerto Santa Cruz was founded in 1878 and was the provincial capital until 1904.

It has one of the best harbors in the south, well protected from the fierce Patagonian winds. **Punta Quilla**, 22 km further downstream, is now a growing deep-water port. The main shopping street is Avenida Roca.

Puerto Santa Cruz is commonly known simply as "Santa Cruz".

Accommodation
B Hotel Anel Aike, corner of San Martín and 25 de Mayo (8206 4.50
★★ Hostería ACA, 25 de Mayo 659 (8146 $11.00. 20% discount to ACA members

Buses
Transporte Ruta 3, Alvarez Ballestra block 400
- Río Gallegos: 3 hours
- Puerto San Julián: 2 hours

Excursions
- **Isla Monte León**: 70 km southwards on RN 288 then RN 3. Turn east 18 km past the junction of RN 288 with RN 3 onto a dirt track. There are walruses and penguins, good beaches, fishing, and camping facilities

Air services from Puerto Santa Cruz

Destination	Fare	Depart	Services	Hours	Airline
• Río Gallegos	$17.00	1330	Mon, Tues, Fri	½	LADE
• Bahía Blanca	$50.00	1055	Wed	8	LADE
• Buenos Aires (Aeroparque Jorge Newbery)					
	$80.00	1055	Wed, Sat	11	LADE
• Comodoro Rivadavia					
	$28.00	1055	Mon, Wed, Sat	2	LADE
• Esquel	$37.00	1055	Wed, Sat	5	LADE
• Mar del Plata	$61.00	1055	Wed, Sat	9	LADE
• Neuquén	$42.00	1055	Wed, Sat	7	LADE
• Puerto Deseado	$22.00	1055	Mon, Wed, Sat	1	LADE
• Río Grande	$25.00	1900	Tues	1	LADE
• San Carlos de Bariloche					
	$38.00	1055	Wed, Sat	5	LADE
• Trelew	$34.00	1055	Wed, Sat	3	LADE
• Viedma	$46.00	1055	Sat	8	LADE

Santa Cruz Province

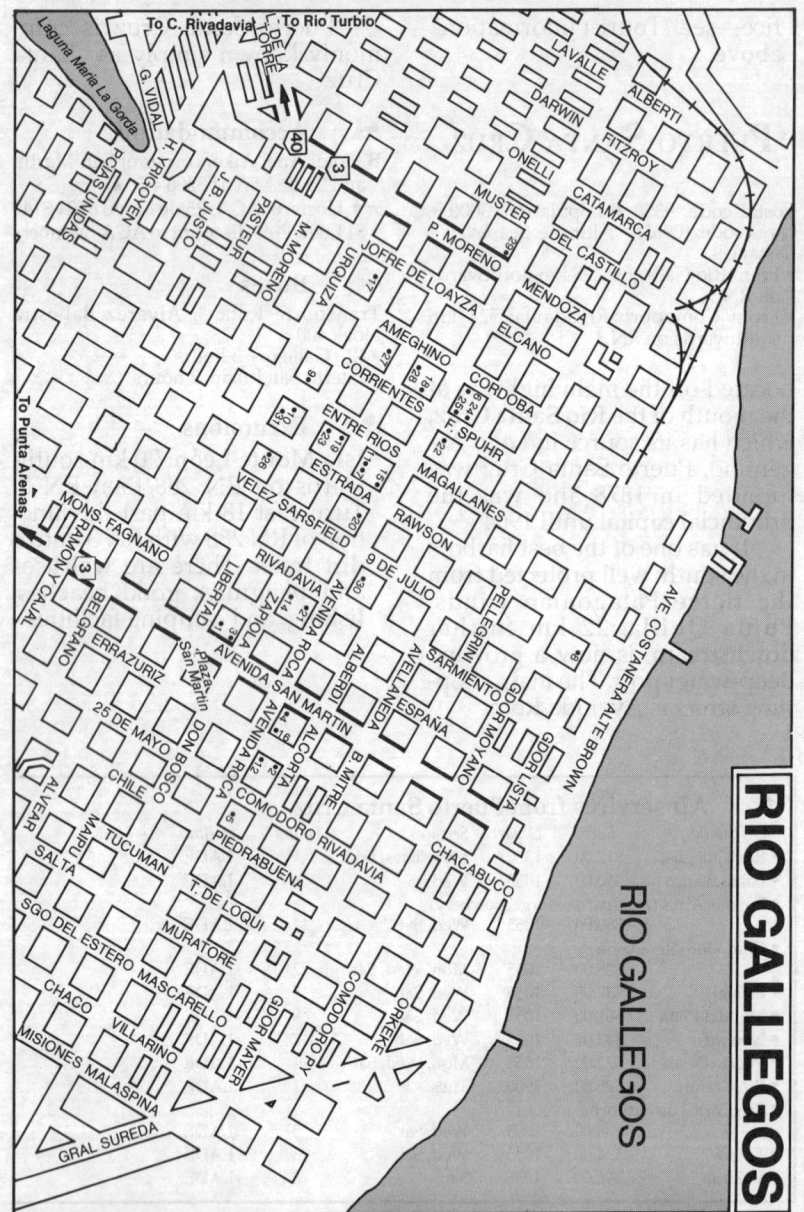

Río Gallegos

Santa Cruz Province

Río Gallegos

Postal code: 9400 • Population: 50 000 •
area code: (0966)
Distances
- From Comodoro Rivadavia: 1034 km southwards on RN 3
- From El Calafate: 319 km south-east on RN 40
- From Puerto Natales (Chile): 187 km eastwards on RN 40
- From Punta Arenas (Chile): 263 km northwards on RN 255 the RN 3

Río Gallegos is the capital of Santa Cruz province and is located on the estuary of **Río Gallegos**. It was founded in 1885. The town is an important center for transport to El Calafate and Ushuaia, and to Punta Arenas and Puerto Natales in Chile. During spring waves on the river may run as high as 16 m. Río Gallegos used to be the port for coal shipments from the Río Turbio mine, but a new deep-water facility has been built at **Punta Loyola**. The town's economic foundation rests on wool, sheepskin, and coal exports.

Festivals
- Foundation day: December 9

Tourist information
- Subsecretaria de Turismo Provincial, Roca 1151 (corner of Córdoba). Open Mon–Fri 0800–1400. Señor Eduardo Gabriel Aguirre speaks English and is very helpful
- Municipal tourist office, Piedra Buena, on the riverside. Open daily 0900–1200 and 1500–1900.

Camping
- It is possible to camp near the intersection of San Martín and Italia, a fair distance from the town. There are no facilities; cost $1.00 per tent

Eating out
- Restaurant British Club, corner of Roca and San Martín
- Restaurant Díaz, Roca 1157
- Restaurant El Palenque, Corrientes 73. Credit cards accepted
- Restaurant Hotel Carrera. Early breakfast
- Restaurant La Casa de Miguel, Roca 1284

Key to Map
1 Municipalidad
2 Casa de Gobierno
3 Iglesia
4 Post office (Encotel)
5 Telephone (Entel)
6 Tourist information
7 Transporte El Pingüino
8 Transportadora Patagonica
9 Transporte San Ceferino
10 Transporte Ruta 3
11 Cambio El Pingüino
12 Banco de la Nación
13 Aerolineas Argentinas
14 Austral Lineas Aereas
15 Hotel Comercio
16 Hotel Santa Cruz
17 Hotel Oviedo
18 Hotel Alonso
19 Hotel Río Turbio
20 Hotel Covadonga
21 Hotel Paris
22 Hotel Punta Arenas
23 Residencial Entre Ríos
24 Residencial Internacional
25 Residencial Ampuero
26 Residencial Laguna Azul
27 Residencial Esmeralda
28 Pension El Gaucho
29 Museo Regional
30 Pension Maddelana
31 Hotel Yugoslavia

Santa Cruz Province

🛏 Accommodation in Río Gallegos

There is a shortage of accommodation, especially in the lower price range, because of free spending by oil crews. Hotel prices rise in January and February.

★★★	Hotel Comercio, Roca 1302	☎ 2172	$19.50	ℹ
	Credit cards accepted; 10% discount to ACA members			
★★★	Hotel Santa Cruz, corner of Avenida Roca and Comodoro Rivadavia ☎ $	☎ 8601	$19.50	ℹ
	Credit cards accepted; 10% discount to ACA members			
★★	Hotel Oviedo, Libertad 746 ☏	☎ 8118	$14.00	ℹ
★★	Hotel Yugoslavia, Urquiza 431	☎ 2997	$17.50	ℹ
★	Hotel Alonso, Corrientes 33	☎ 2414	$17.50	ℹ
★	Hotel Río Turbio, Zapiola 486, opposite Expreso Pingüino ☎ ●			
	Shared bathroom $9.00	☎ 2155	$14.50	ℹ
A	Hotel Cabo Vírgenes, Rivadavia 256	☎ 2141	$16.00	ℹ
A	Hotel Covadonga, Roca 1244	☎ 8190	$15.00	ℹ
	Shared bathroom $9.50			
A	Hotel Paris, Roca 1040	☎ 8111	$14.50	ℹ $8.50
	Shared bathroom			
A	Hotel Punta Arenas, Sphur 55	☎ 2743	$14.00	ℹ
	Cheaper with shared bathrooms			
B	Residencial Ampuero, Sphur 18 (corner of Roca), in the same building as the pizzeria	☎ 2189		
B	Residencial Colonial, corner of Rivadavia and Urquiza ☎	☎ 2329	$11.00	ℹ
B	Residencial Fer Mar, 25 de Mayo 196	☎ 8098	$12.50	ℹ
	Cheaper with shared bathrooms			
B	Residencial Florida, Roca 1200 (corner of Sarsfield)	☎ 8210	$8.00	ℹ
B	Residencial Laguna Azul, Estrada 298 (corner of Urquiza)		$8.00	ℹ
	Shared bathroom			
B	Residencial Puerto Santa Cruz, Zapiola 238 (corner of Rivadavia)			
	Shared bathroom	☎ 8099	$6.50	ℹ
	Shared bathroom			
B	Residencial Sacha's, Rivadavia 122 ☏		$5.50	ℹ
	Shared rooms			
B	Residencial Viejo Lafuente, Sarsfield 64	☎ 8304	$11.00	ℹ
	Cheaper with shared rooms			
•	Residencial Entre Ríos, Entre Ríos 170			
•	Residencial Esmeralda, Zapiola 636			
	For budget travellers			
•	Residencial Internacional, Sphur 78 (corner of Roca)			
C	Pension Belgrano, Belgrano 119 ☏			
	Cheap and clean			
C	Pension Carrera, corner of España and Roca			
C	Pension El Gaucho, Zapiola 627	☎ 2166	$8.00	ℹ
	Shared rooms			
C	Pension Maddelena, Roca 1127			
	Central			
C	Pension Miramar, Roca 1630	☎ 8197	$8.00	ℹ
	Shared rooms			

Río Gallegos

Santa Cruz Province

- Restaurant La Fusta, corner of Rawson and Alberdí
- Restaurant Monte Carlo, Zapiola 558. Seafood
- ☞ Restaurant Oviedo, corner of Libertad and Loayza
- Restaurant Sacha's, Rivadavia 122
- Restaurant Safari, corner of Corrientes and Libertad. "Menú económico"
- ☞ Pizzería El Porteño, corner of Moreno and Zapiola
- Pizzería Hotel Ampuero, corner of Sphur and Roca
- Pizzería Viejo, corner of Corrientes and Roca
- Cafetería Copacho, corner of Entre Ríos and Zapiola
- Cafetería Tit, corner of Roca and Sarmiento. Pancakes

Post and telegraph

- Post office: Roca 893 (corner of San Martín)
- Telephone: Roca 600

$ Financial

There are poor exchange rates in El Calafate and cash only is taken, so change money and checks here.
- Sur Cambio, corner of San Martín and Roca. Cash only
- ☞ Cambio El Pingüino, corner of Zapiola and Estrada (next to Transportes La Pingüina) accepts some European currencies as well as US dollars

Services and facilities

- Camping equipment: Casa del Camping, corner of Entre Ríos and Zapiola

Laundromats

- Aike Lavar, coRner of Corrientes and Libertad
- Corner of Estrada and Zapiola

Photographic supplies

- Foto Cine
- Tommy Color, corner of Roca and Sarmiento

Buses from Río Gallegos

There is no central bus terminal.
- Expreso Pingüino, Zapiola 455. Open Mon–Fri 0800–1250 and 1500–1930, Sat 0800–1230 and 1530–1900
- Transportadora Patagónica and Don Otto, Gobernador Lista 330 ℓ 2330
- San Ceferino, Entre Ríos 371, runs buses departing at 2150 on Tues, Thurs, and Sat which connect in Comodoro Rivadavia with buses to Rawson, Trelew, Puerto Madryn (a 24 hour trip), and Bahía Blanca
- Transportes Ruta 3, Entre Ríos 354. Daily buses depart at 1500 for to Puerto San Julián, Puerto Santa Cruz, and Comandante Luis Piedrabuena

Destination	Fare	Depart	Services	Hours	Company
• Calafate	$9.50	1500	Sat–Mon, Wed, Thu	6	319 km Transportes Patagonicos, San Ceferino
• Comodoro Rivadavia	$27.60	2130	Mon, Tues, Thurs, Sat	14	Transportes Patagonicos, Don Otto
• Puerto Natales	$10.00	0830	Sat		
• Punta Arenas	$11.00	0900, 1400 Mon–Sat		5	Expreso Pingüino
• Río Turbio	$9.00	1230	Mon–Sat		Expreso Pingüino, San Ceferino, Transportes Patagonicos

Río Gallegos

SANTA CRUZ PROVINCE

✈ Air services from Río Gallegos

There is an airport tax of $1.00.
A taxi to the airport costs $4.00.
- Aerolineas Argentinas: Cheap night flights to Buenos Aires (Sat) and to Río Grande (Tues)
- Austral Airlines, corner of Roca and Rivadavia
- LADE, Fagnano 53 ℡ 8912

Destination	Fare	Depart	Services	Hours	Airline
• Bahía Blanca	$35.00	1005	Wed	9	LADE
	$66.00	1320	2–3 services daily	3	Aerolineas, Austral
• Buenos Aires (Aeroparque Jorge Newbery)					
	$83.00	0145	4–7 services daily	4	Aerolineas, Austral
	$81.00	1005	Wed, Sat	12	LADE
• Comodoro Rivadavia					
	$34.00	1445	Mon–Sat	4	LADE
	$39.00	1320	Fri–Wed	1	Aerolineas, Austral
• Córdoba	$87.00	0845	Sun	5	Aerolineas
• Esquel	$42.00	1005	Wed, Sat	5	LADE
• Gobernador Gregores					
	$16.00	1130	Tues, Thurs	2	LADE
• Lago Argentino	$15.00	1130	1–2 services daily	1	LADE
• Mar del Plata	$62.00	1005	Wed, Sat	10	LADE
	$77.00	1600	Sun	4	Aerolineas
• Mendoza	$83.00	0845	Sun	4	Aerolineas
• Neuquén	$46.00	1005	Wed, Sat	7	LADE
• Perito Moreno	$17.00	1130	Tue, Thu	3	LADE
• Puerto Deseado	$28.00	1005	Mon, Wed, Fri, Sat	2	LADE
• Puerto San Julián	$22.00	1005	Mon, Wed, Fri, Sat	1	LADE
• Puerto Santa Cruz	$17.00	1005	Mon, Wed, Sat	1	LADE
• Río Grande	$18.00	0145	3–5 services daily	1	Aerolineas, Austral
	$17.00	1435	Mon–Fri	1	LADE
• Río Turbio	$17.00	1115	Mon, Tue, Wed, Thu, Fri	1 hr	LADE
• Salta	$118.00	0845	Sun	8	Aerolineas
• San Carlos de Bariloche					
	$44.00	1005	Wed, Sat	6	LADE
	$55.00	0845	Sun	2	Aerolineas
• San Miguel de Tucumán					
	$110.00	0845	Sun	7	Aerolineas
• Trelew	$38.00	1005	Wed, Sat	4	LADE
	$52.00	1520	Fri–Wed	2	Aerolineas, Austral
• Ushuaia	$21.00	1055	14 services daily	2	Aerolineas, LADE
• Viedma	$49.00	1005	Sat	9	LADE

Supermarkets
- La Anónima, corner of Roca and España
- Sados, corner of Estrada and Zapiola

🛂 Visas, passports
- Chilean consulate, Moreno 144, Mon–Friday 0900–1300 and 1500–1700

Río Gallegos

Santa Cruz Province

🚗 Motoring

RN 3 to Puntas Arenas in Chile is unsealed but good.
RN 40 to El Calafate is sealed to Cerrito, 209 km away.

- Car parts and repairs: Repuestos Sarmiento, Sarmiento. Owner friendly and helpful

Service stations

- ACA, corner of Orkeke and Chacabuco
- YPF, corner of Entre Ríos and Libertad

Car rental

- A1 Rent-a-Car International, corner of Entre Ríos and Moreno
- Gotti-Riestra, Entre Ríos 375 ℂ 2453

⛴ Water transport

Occasionally ships depart for Buenos Aires.

🛍 Shopping

- Sheep skins and leather: Señor Szasack, Zapiola 122 sells tanned sheep skins and warm leather coats
- Handicrafts: Market at Roca 658, open 1300–2000
- Souvenirs: El Orfebre, Avenida Roca 1348 (corner of Estrada). Good range

🎭 Entertainment

- Nightclub Zeus, corner of J de Loayza and Libertad (upstairs). Shows
- Video Bar Studio 54
- Whiskería Yemu, corner of San Martín and Zapiola

📷 Sightseeing

- Museo Regional Provincial (Provincial Regional Museum), corner of Perito Moreno and Avenida Roca. The emphasis is on geology and archeology, but it also has fine collections of flora and fauna

♣ Excursions

- **Río Turbio**: The 300 km road goes through very flat but gReen country and crosses the narrow gauge line used to bring coal to the harbour several times. The closer to the Andes (which are very low in this part of South America) the greener it gets. It is a dusty trip as the road is not sealed. There are Patagonian geese all along the road. See Río Turbio below
- **El Calafate**: At **Esperanza**, two hours away, is an ACA Motel and service station; see Esperanza on page 413. After Esperanza the country becomes hilly, culminating in a narrow and winding road over the **Cuesta El Aguay**, which has been declared a fauna reserve for its abundant wildlife. Shortly afterwards you cross the **Río Bote** over a ramshackle bridge, at the small Hotel Río Bote, known locally as a *gaucho* inn. See also El Calafate on page 407
- **Cabo Vírgenes**: 114 km southwards on RP 526. A penguin colony. On the way you pass an oil treatment plant. Escalatur runs trips in summer only, when the birds are nesting
- **Reserva Provincial Laguna Azul**: 60 km south, 4 km off RN 3. This area is of volcanic origin. **Lago Azul** itself occupies the site of an extinct volcano, an abrupt depression from the tableland. There is a surprising absence of vegetation. A visit is only possible with your own vehicle or

Río Gallegos

through a travel agency. If you are hitchhiking ask to be set down about 9 km from the border post
- **Punta Loyola**: 30 km east. Near here is the wreck of the sailing ship *Kently* which foundered here in 1910. This is also a good fishing spot

RÍO TURBIO

Postal code: 9407 • Population: 6000
Distances
- From Río Gallegos: 239 km westwards on RN 40
- From Puerto Natales (Chile): 37 km northwards

Río Turbio is located near the Chilean border. Argentina's largest coal fields are near here. Some of the coal is shipped by train to Río Gallegos and some is used for power generation in Río Turbio itself.

With the development of the **Mina Uno** ski slopes Río Turbio has also become a small winter sports center.

Fishing is possible in nearby brooks and some *lagunas*.

Tourist information
- Señor Raul Antonio Pereyra in Residencial El Azteca

Accommodation
- ★★ Hotel Capipe, Paraje Julia Dufour, on the outskirts of town on the Río Gallegos road. $18.00
- B Hotel Gato Negro, R S Peña on Plaza del Castillo (91226 $13.00 Shared bathroom $8.00. Expensive

- Residencial El Azteca, J Newbery 98 (91285 $7.00

Eating out
- Restaurant El Ringo, Teniente Castillo
- Restaurant El Vasco, corner of Del Castillo and R S Peña
- Restaurant Papulis, corner of J Newbery and Gregores
- Restaurant Quri, corner of Del Castillo and J Newbery
- Cafetería Gato Negro, Plaza del Castillo

Post and telegraph
- Post office, R S Peña

Services and facilities

Laundromats
- Lavarefe, corner of Del Castillo and Yrigoyen. $2.00
- Lavandería, corner of Del Castillo and Gobernador Moyano

Border crossing
Border formalities are 3 km uphill, past the ski-lifts, and are very quick on both sides. At the Argentine border control the Puerto Natales bus is waiting to take you to Chilean passport control about 4 km further on. From there it is a scenic 14 km down hill drive to Puerto Natales, with views over the Pacific Ocean.

Air services

Airlines
- LADE, Avenida del Minero 375 (91224

Services
- Río Gallegos: Fare $17.00; departs 1230 Mon–Fri; 1 hour; LADE

Buses
Individual bus companies have their own terminals and stops from which buses depart.
The bus arriving from Río Gallegos connects with the bus to Puerto Natales in Chile.

Santa Cruz Province

Border buses leave from corner of Avenida de los Mineros and J Newbery. On Sundays the first bus leaves about 1000; during the week at 0900. It takes about half an hour to reach the border post, after a scenic drive up the mountain.

Bus companies

- Expreso Pingüino, corner of Newbery and Del Minero
- Empresa Ceferino and Austral, Del Castillo
- Transportes Patagonicos, Del Minero opposite Pellegrini
- Empresa Alvarez and Empresa Cootra depart from the corner of Del Minero and Ramon Castillo for Puerto Natales in Chile

Services

- Río Gallegos: Fare $9.00; departs 0630 Tues, Thurs, Sat; Transportes Patagonicos
- El Calafate: $20.00 bus hire; departs as required; Empresa Travel
- Puerto Natales (Chile): $1.50; several services daily; Empresa Cootra

Motoring

The road north to El Calafate via Esperanza is in bad condition and may be cut in bad weather.
The road west to Puerto Natales is also a dirt road but is kept open all year round.

- Service station: YPF, corner of Del Castillo and Ramon Castillo

Trains

- Río Gallegos: It is possible to get a lift with the coal freight trains leaving early in the morning. No charge; 11 hours

Sport

Río Turbio is promoting its **Mina Uno** ski resort located 4 km uphill from the township and only 1 km from the Chilean border. It is operated by the Club Andino Río Turbio. The skiing season runs from June 1 to September 15. The area is good for both alpine and cross country skiing, with 90% powder snow. It is possible to ski from 0900 until 2200, as the snowfields are illuminated.

- The ACA operates an *albergue*-cum-restaurant at the snow-fields. At the resort there is also a disco, Las Lengas. At present the following ski-lifts are in operation:
- Teleski del Arco: 70 m long; carries 300 people an hour; for beginners
- Teleski de la Base (Poma): 300 m long; carries 450 people an hour
- Teleski del Bosque (Poma): 300 m long; carries 450 people an hour

Alpine ski runs:
- "Mulla": 400 m long
- "Mirador": 900 m long
- "Piren": 1400 m long
- "Valle Hermoso" 2500 m

Cross country circuits:
- "Circuit Monte Ñire": 10 500 m long
- "Circuit Monte Lenga": 6200 m long

Excursions

- Puerto Natales in Chile
- Parque Nacional Payne in Chile, via the **Cancha Carrera** border post

Tres Cerros

Postal code: 9050
Distance from Comodoro Rivadavia: 270 km southwards on RN 3

Tres Cerros is nothing more than a convenient stop-over on the way south from Comodoro Rivadavia to Río Gallegos, to break the monotony of the Patagonian plain.

Accommodation

- ACA Hotel, RN 3 Km 2082 $12.00. Discount for ACA members

Motoring

A new road is under construction 42 km north which will lead to the petrified wood area in the Reserva Nacional Laguna Grande, 90 km away.

Tierra del Fuego

Plate 21 Map of Tierra del Fuego
- 435 Kaiken
- 436 Lago Escondido
- 436 Lapataia
- 436 Río Grande
- 438 Map
- 441 San Sebastián
- 442 Ushuaia
- 443 Map

Tierra del Fuego is part of the Territorio Nacional de Tierra del Fuego, Antártida, e Islas del Atlántico, and as such is governed directly by the federal government. The territory includes the islands in the South Atlantic as well as that part of Antarctica claimed by Argentina ("Antártida Argentina"). The island of Tierra del Fuego proper ("Isla Grande de Tierra del Fuego") is split between Chile and Argentina. Chile has the western part and Argentina has the eastern part, bounded by the **Estrecho de Magallanes** (Straits of Magellan) in the north, the South Atlantic in the east, and the **Canal Beagle** in the south. The largest town and administRative center is **Ushuaia**, the southernmost city in the world.

The northern part of the island is flat whereas the southern part is fairly mountainous. The highest mountain is **Cerro Olivia** which is 1470 m high.

The climate is harsh in winter with temperatures dropping as low as –20°C. Skiing is possible from early April to late October.

Tierra del Fuego

TIERRA DEL FUEGO

Tierra del Fuego has very little agriculture except for sheep farming. However the economy has been boosted with the discovery of petroleum oil in the northern and eastern part of the island, and with the movement of high-tech industries, such as computers, from the mainland to places such as **Río Grande**. Logging is carried out in the forests in the south.

Among the tourist attractions is the **Parque Nacional Tierra del Fuego** which is only a short distance away from Ushuaia towards the Chilean part of the island. The aboriginal tribes, the Onas, Alacufes, and Yamanas, are all extinct. Cruises to the Argentinian Antarctic bases are organized by the National Tourist Organisation. The best time to visit is between December and March.

Tierra del Fuego is linked with the mainland by flights from Ushuaia and Río Grande. Air services may be cut in harsh winteR conditions. There is no direct airlink between Ushuaia and Puntas Arenas in Chile. Road transport between Rio Grande and Ushuaia runs daily, and between Rio Grande and Porvenir in Chile three times a week. Most roads are dirt roads. A massive road upgrading program is underway stretching from San Sebastian on the Chilean border to Río Grande. Boat services between Ushuaia and Isla Navarino in Chile across the Canal Beagle are unreliable.

The main areas of interest to the tourist are:
- Worth a visit: **Ushuaia**
- Worth a detour: **Parque Nacional Lapataia**
- Very interesting: **Kaiken** and **Lago Fagnano**, and **Lago Escondido**
- Of interest: **Río Grande** and **San Sebastián**

KAIKEN

Distances
- From Ushuaia: 101 km westwards on RN 3
- From Río Grande: 121 km southwards on RN 3

Kaiken is located on a promontory on the eastern part of **Lago Fagnano**. Buses usually take a meal break at this very picturesque spot.

Accommodation
★★ Hostería Kaiken ⑪ (Ushuaia 19 $15.00 $29.00 per cabin. ACA hostería; views over lake; credit cards accepted; 10% discount for ACA members; open all year

Buses
Los Carlos buses coming from Río Grande take a half hour meal break here.
- Ushuaia: Fare $4.00; departs 1400; 2 services daily; 2 hours
- Río Grande: Fare $4.50; departs 1400; 2 services daily; 2 hours

Motoring
- Service station: ACA

TIERRA DEL FUEGO

⌖ Excursions
- Fifteen km south past Kaiken there are hot springs; turn off to the left

LAGO ESCONDIDO

Distance from Ushuaia: 60 km northwards on RN 3

Lago Escondido is one of the most picturesque lakes in Tierra del Fuego. Access to the lake is off the main highway.

⌂ Accommodation
★★ Hostería Petrel, on southern end of Lago Escondido ⑪ $18.00. Views over lake

🚌 Buses
Contact the tourist office in Ushuaia; see page 442

LAPATAIA

Distance from Ushuaia: 19 km westwards on RN 3

Lapataia is situated inside the **Parque Nacional Tierra del Fuego**, which is a region of lakes, dense forests, and high mountains. Its serene tranquillity is reflected in the lakes and rivers, which are crystal clear. The setting of **Lago Roca** is very picturesque with the mountains coming right down to the edge. Half of the lake is in the Chilean sector. Along the north- western side of the lake is a trail which leads to the Chilean border, signified by some planks of wood. There is no problem continuing the trail on the other side of the border into the Chilean national park. There are plenty of salmon and trout in the waters of the park. The introduction of beavers into the park from Canada has had an unbalancing effect on nature and the park authorities are trying to remove the beavers.

⌂ Accommodation
- Hostería Alakush, on RN 3 ⑪. Open from December 1 to March 31

🚌 Buses
El Cóndor conducts bus services from Ushuaia; a ¾ hour trip.

RÍO GRANDE

Postal code: 9420 • Population: 15 000 • Altitude: sea level • (area code: (0964)
Distances
- From Ushuaia: 222 km north-east on RN 3
- From Porvenir (Chile): 239 km eastwards on RN 3

Río Grande is the economic capital of Argentine Tierra del Fuego, situated in a plain on the often windswept eastern coast. It was settled in 1894 and is a modern, clean port town with wide avenues. Winds from the Antarctic occasionally make life miserable. Not far from the town are oilfields, with some drilling carried out offshore. The district consists mostly of sheep farms;

kaiken

TIERRA DEL FUEGO

one of the biggest slaughterhouses can be visited between February and June. The town is expanding to the south, with electronic industries being set up in an industrial park.

Festivals
- Trout festival: 3rd Sunday in February
- Snow festiva: 3rd Sunday in July
- Fiesta de la Lenga (Woodsman Festival): 1st Sunday in December, at Aserradero Laguna Verde

Tourist information
- Municipalidad, Elcano overlooking the ocean

Eating out
- Restaurant Club de Pesca, corner Elcano and San Martín. On the seaside
- Restaurant Comedor Porteño, corner 9 de Julio and Rosales
- Restaurant Das Segel, San Martín 754
- Restaurant El Castor, corner Lasserre and Fagnano
- Restaurant Fiori, Elcano 537
- Restaurant Hotel Frederico Ibarra, Rosales 357 (corner of Fagnano)
- Restaurant Hotel Los Yaganes, Belgrano 319
- Restaurant La Rambla, corner Elcano and Belgrano
- Restaurant La Vieja Casona, corner of Elcano and J Newbery
- Restaurant Las Malvinas, Rosales 443
- Restaurant Los Leños, Islas Malvinas 375. Grill
- Restaurant Miramar, Hospedaje Miramar, Mackinlay 595 (corner of Belgrano)
- Restaurant Paris, Rosales 448 (corner of Espora). Grill; closed Wed
- Cafetería Ciclos, San Martin 649
- Cafetería Le Rendezvous, P Moreno block 100 (corner of Don Bosco)
- Cafetería Roca, Roca 629
- Pizzería El Trebol, Belgrano 557 (corner of Lasserre)
- Pizzería La Pamilia, Lasserre 769 (corner of Estrada)
- Pizzería Via Veneto, Lasserre 566 (corner of Belgrano)

Post and telegraph
- Post office: Encotel, corner of Ameghino and Piedrabuena

Services and facilities
- Laundry: San Martín 985 (corner of 25 de Mayo)
- Sauna: San Martin block 600 (corner of Belgrano)

Supermarkets
- La Anónima, San Martin block 500 (corner of Belgrano)
- Supe, corner of Estrada and San Martín

Buses
There is no central bus terminal.

Bus companies
- Empresa Senkovic, San Martín 959. Book in advance
- Transporte Los Carlos, Estrada 568

Services
- Ushuaia: Fare $8.20; departs 1200; 2 services daily; 5 hours; Transporte Los Carlos
- Kaiken: Fare $4.50; Transporte Los Carlos
- Laguna Verde: Fare $6.00; Transporte Los Carlos
- Lago Escondido: Fare $6.50; Transporte Los Carlos
- Porvenir (Chile): Fare $10.00; departs 0600 Wed–Sat; 5 hours; Empresa Senkovic

Motoring
The road from Río Grande to Porvenir in Chile is being upgraded on the Argentine side, but it is still a rough trip through Chilean Tierra del Fuego. There is a passport control point at San Sebastián.
The road to Ushuaia is sealed as far as Punta María on the coast.
- Service station: ACA, San Martín block 400 (corner of Rivadavia)

Río Grande

TIERRA DEL FUEGO

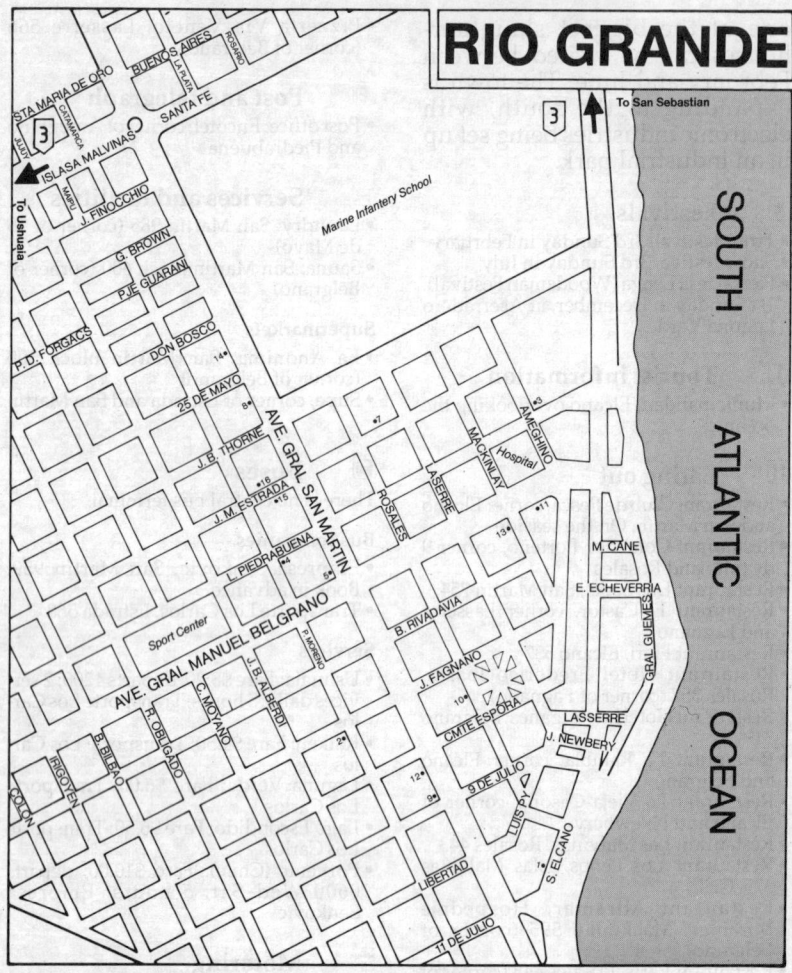

Key to Map
1. Municipalidad
2. Iglesia
3. Post office (Encotel)
4. Telephone (Entel)
5. Aerolineas Argentinas
6. LADE (airline)
7. Transporte Los Carlos
8. Transporte Senkovic
9. Banco de la Nación
10. Hotel Federico Ibarra
11. Hotel Los Yaganes
12. Hospedaje Villa
13. Hospedaje Miramar
14. Hospedaje La Cabaña
15. Hospedaje Irmary
16. Residencial Rawson

Río Grande

TIERRA DEL FUEGO

Accommodation in Río Grande

Accommodation is very difficult to find between January and March. Also, most of the cheap accommodation is taken up by itinerant oil workers.

★★★	Hotel Federico Ibarra, Rosales 357 (corner of Fagnano) 🛏 Breakfast extra	(21071	$35.00	ii
★★★	Hotel Los Yaganes ACA, Belgrano 319 🛏	(2372	$35.00	ii
B	Hostería Arboleas, Rivadavia 649	(22323	$9.00	i
B	Hospedaje Antares, Rosales 835, (Echeverria 50)	(21517	$9.00	i
B	Hospedaje Miramar, Mackinlay 595 (corner of Belgrano) 🛏 Shared bathrooms	(22452	$12.00	ii
B	Hospedaje Villa, San Martin 277 Shared rooms	(22312	$8.50	i
C	Hospedaje Argentino, San Martín 64 Shared rooms	(22365	$3.50	i
C	Hospedaje La Cabaña, 9 de Julio 1025 Shared rooms		$5.50	i
•	Hospedaje Irmary, Estrada 743 Near Senkovic bus office			
•	Motel Sur, corner Belgrano and Elcano		$12.00	i
•	Residencial Las Lenguitas, Piedrabuena block 400 (corner of Mackinlay) Shared bathroom		$13.50	ii
•	Residencial Rawson, Estrada 750			

- Car rental: Rent-a-Car International, corner Belgrano block 200 and Ameghino

Tours
- Turismo Bulvare, corner of Lasserre and Rivadavia
- Turismo Yaganes, San Martín 641

Sport
- Ice skating: There is an ice rink
- Fishing: Salmon fishing in the Río Grande. Catches of up to 8 kg are common

Entertainment
- Nightclub Cabaret Show, Piedrabuena 888

Excursions
- **Ushuaia**: Travel along the sealed coastal road to **Punta María**. From **Rio Fuego** there is an unsealed road until shortly before Ushuaia. As you travel further south the trees clustered in farmland become forests. From **Río Ewan** the road turns inland again and the scenery changes to parkland: rolling hills and open spaces, used for grazing, interspersed with lakes and forests. Patagonian geese abound. Soon the **Sierra Lucio Lopez** comes into view. Many of the mountains carry snow all year round although they are under 1500 m. There is logging

in the area, especially around **Tolhuin**. Most of the houses are built from timber which gives them an alpine look. After Tolhuin the road starts to climb. At Hostería Kaiken, an ACA *hostería* at **Kaiken**, is **Lago Fagnano**. Buses stop for refresh-

---

✈ Air services from Río Grande

The airport is on Ruta "c", turning off Ave Islas Malvinas 5 km west. A taxi to the airport costs $2.00.

There is no municipal bus service, only Los Carlos buses to and from Ushuaia.
- Aerolineas Argentinas ℂ 22749
- LADE, MacKinlay 560, behind Hotel Yaganes ℂ 21151. Open Mon–Fri 09.00–12.00 and 15.00–19.00.
- Rent-A-Plane, at airport. $36.00 per hour

Destination	Fare	Depart	Services	Hours	Airline
• Bahía Blanca	$64.00	0900	Wed	10	LADE
	$85.00	1245	Mon–Sat	3	Aerolineas, Austral
• Buenos Aires (Aeroparque Jorge Newbery)					
	$100.00	0205	3–4 services daily	4	Aerolineas
	$100.00	1245	daily	5	Austral
	$90.00	0900	Wed, Sat	13	LADE
• Comodoro Rivadavia					
	$38.50	0900	Tues, Wed, Sat	4	LADE
	$54.00	1245	Mon, Wed, Fri	4	Austral
	$54.00	1830	Mon–Wed, Fri, Sat	3	Aerolineas
• Córdoba	$105.00	0740	Sun	6	Aerolineas
• Esquel	$51.50	0900	Wed, Sat	6½	LADE
• Gobernador Gregores					
	$18.50	1000	Tue	3½	LADE
• Lago Argentino	$18.50	1000	Tue, Wed, Thu	2½	LADE
• Mar del Plata	$74.50	0900	Wed, Sat	11	LADE
• Mendoza	$98.50	0740	Sun	5	Aerolineas
• Neuquén	$54.50	0900	Wed, Sat	8½	LADE
• Perito Moreno	$23.50	1000	Tue	4½	LADE
• Puerto Deseado	$39.50	0900	Wed, Sat	3	LADE
• Puerto San Julián	$24.50	0900	Wed, Sat	2½	LADE
• Río Gallegos	$20.50	0205	3–5 services daily	1	Aerolineas, Austral
	$16.00	1000	Tue–Thur	1	LADE
• Salta	$142.00	0740	Sun	9	Aerolineas
• San Carlos de Bariloche					
	$79.00	0740	Sun	7	Aerolineas
	$51.50	0900	Wed, Sat	7	LADE
• San Miguel de Tucumán					
	$131.00	0740	Sun	8	Aerolineas
• Santa Cruz	$22.50	0900	Wed, Sat	1½	LADE
• Trelew	$48.50	0900	Wed, Sat	5	LADE
	$65.00	1215	Sun	3½	Austral
• Ushuaia	$11.00	1210	daily	½	Aerolineas
	$13.50	1600	Mon–Thurs	½	LADE
• Viedma	$54.50	0900	Sat	10	LADE

Río Grande

Plate 21

Map of Tierra del Fuego

Plate 22

Top: Lago Roca, Tierra del Fuego
Bottom left: Grazing *guanacos*, Santa Cruz province
Bottom right: Lago Roca, Tierra del Fuego

TIERRA DEL FUEGO

ments here allowing time to take a few scenic photographs of the lake, which, with the mountains in the west, must rank as a first-rate tourist attraction. After Kaiken the road starts its climb towards **Paso Garibaldi**. The road is very winding and passes the turn-off to **Lago Escondido** with an *hostería* at the southern end. The road follows a deep gorge on the western side. Most of the mountain peaks are covered with ice or snow. Near Paso Garibaldi is another small lake. At 3015 km you look down into the **Valle Tierra Mayor** valley, which has a ski run and the Hostería Valle Tierra Mayor. After crossing the **Río Olívia**, the road descends sharply to the **Canal Beagle**, passing waterfalls, fern gullies, and views of **Cerro Olivia**. Six km before Ushuaia the road reaches the Canal Beagle, providing the first glimpse of Ushuaia. The stretch between Lago Fagnano and Ushuaia would be one of the most scenic trips in Tierra del Fuego

- Salesian mission: 11 km north on RN 3. The mission was founded by Monsignor Fagnano. There is an interesting regional museum which is housed in the original chapel. Exhibits consists mostly of Ona artefacts, and there are a lot of them! There are also fossils and Salesian mission memorabilia

SAN SEBASTIÁN

Postal code: 9420
Distances
- From Río Grande: 79 km north-west on RN 3
- From Porvenir (Chile): 160 km eastwards on Ruta i

San Sebastián is a small town with an oil refinery and a border control point.

Accommodation
★ Hostería San Sebastian ACA $15.00. 10% discount for ACA members

Eating out
- Cafetería La Frontera. On the Chilean side

Border crossing
San Sebastián is an Argentine and Chilean border control point. The border is open 24 hours all year round.

Buses
There is a Transportes Senkovic office.
- Río Grande: Fare $3.50; Transportes Senkovic
- Porvenir (Chile): Fare $6.50; Transportes Senkovic

Motoring
On the Argentine side the road to Río Grande improves slightly and road works are in progress. From Km 2780 onwards the road is sealed intermittently. Along the road there are many "oil dogs" pumping the crude oil and a maze of pipelines. The countryside is dotted with oil rigs and there are some rigs out to sea. The land is very flat and the road is a straight line. On the southern horizon you can see mountains which are usually snow-capped.

TIERRA DEL FUEGO

USHUAIA

Postal code: 9410 • (area code: (0964) • Population: 50 000

Ushuaia is situated on the slopes of the **Cerro Martial** around **Bahía Encerrada** overlooking the **Canal Beaglel**. It is the largest town of the Argentine part of Tierra del Fuego and is the southernmost city in the world.

In winter the temperature drops as low as −12°C, and in summer rises to 25°C. Snowfalls in summer are not unusual. It is possible to ski on the slopes of **Cerro Martial** as early as April.

The area is densely forested and the timber industry is very strong. Fishing, sheep raising, and tourism are the pillars of the economy.

Although Ushuaia is expensive and desperately short of accommodation in the lower price bracket, this town with its Nordic appearance is well worth a visit. The vistas from the town of the snow-clad mountains are splendid.

Ushuaia is the gateway to the **Parque Nacional Tierra del Fuego** and for excursions around the **Canal Beagle** and to neighboring Isla Navarino in Chile.

i Tourist information

- Dirección de Turismo Territorial, San Martín 512. Open daily 0800–2000. Has a large chart of hotels with prices
- Tourist office at airport has hotel information
- Club Andino, Solis 50, has information on hiking, skiing, and climbing
- National park administration office, corner of Patagonia and San Martín

🍴 Eating out

Centolla (king crab) and *cholga* (giant mussels) are the specialty food of the town.

- Restaurant Bar Ideal, San Martín 391 (corner of Roca). Seafood and pizzas; cheap
- Restaurant Centro Deportivo, corner of Maipú and 12 de Octubre. International cuisine; *centolla*
- Restaurant Club Nautico, Maipú (opposite Belgrano). International cuisine
- Restaurant Don Pancho, corner of San Martín and Yaganes
- Restaurant Hotel Antartida, San Martín 1600. International cuisine; cheap

Key to Map

1. Municipalidad
2. Casa de Gobierno
3. Iglesia
4. Post office (Encotel)
5. Telephone (Entel)
6. Tourist information
7. National parks administration
8. Banco de la Nación
9. Aerolineas Argentinas
10. LADE (airline)
11. Transporte Los Carlos
12. Transporte El Cóndor
13. Museo Territorial
14. Hotel Las Lengas
15. Hotel Canal Beagle
16. Hotel Albatros
17. Hotel Cabo de Horno
18. Hotel Antartida
19. Hotel Maiten
20. Hostería Mustapic
21. Hospedaje Cesar
22. Hospedaje Caprí
23. Hospedaje Fernandez
24. Hospedaje Hispano
25. Sanchez private accommodation

Tierra del Fuego

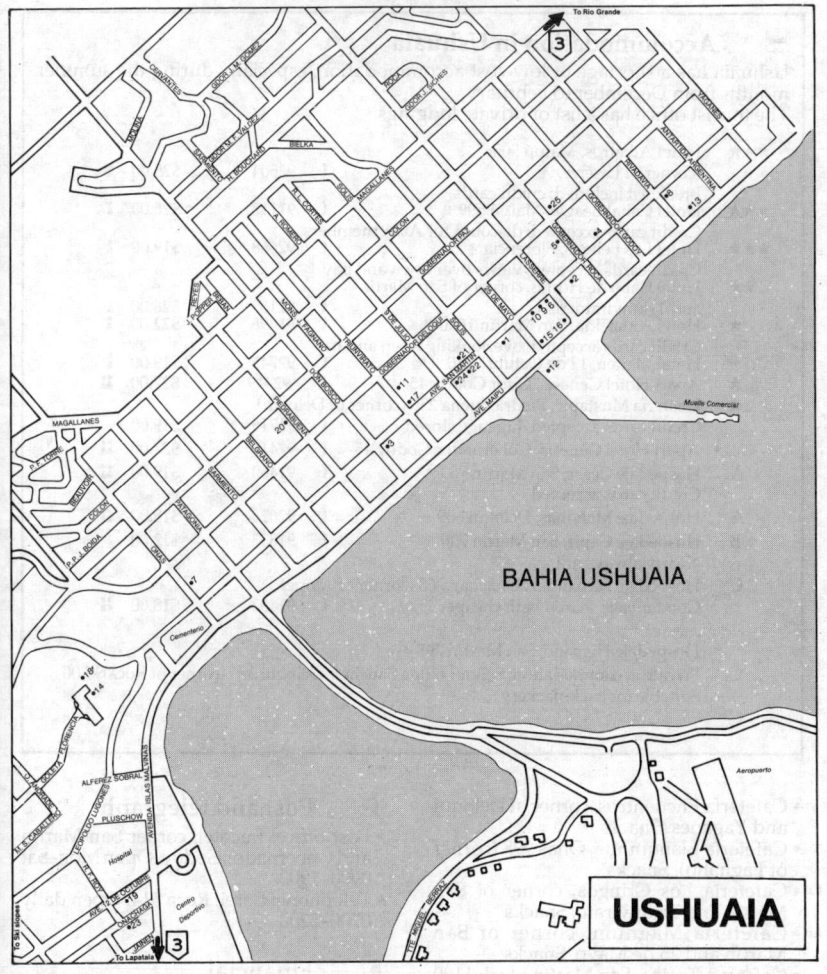

- Restaurant HoTel Canal Beagle, Maipú 599. International cuisine
- Restaurant Los Canelos, Maipú 823 (corner of 9 de Julio). Seafood (*centolla*)
- Restaurant Moustacchio, corner of San Martín and Godoy. Seafood; menu in English
- Restaurant Tante Elvira, San Martín 238. Seafood (*centolla*)
- Restaurant Tío Carlos, corner Colón and 9 de Julio. Grill
- Restaurant Tío Rico, corner of Belgrano and Gdor Deloqui
- Cafetería at airport. Snacks
- Cafetería Acuario, San Martín 124. Snacks
- Cafetería El Trebol, corner of San Martín and 9 de Julio. Snacks

Ushuaia

TIERRA DEL FUEGO

🛏 Accommodation in Ushuaia

Ushuaia has a shortage of low-cost accommodation, especially during the summer months from December to February.
The tourist office has a list of private lodgings.

★★★	Hotel Albatros, Maipú 505 (corner of Laserre)	ℓ 92504	$25.00	👤
	Breakfast included; credit cards			
★★★	Hotel Canal Beagle, Maipú 599	ℓ 91117	$26.00	👤
	Credit cards accepted; discount for ACA members			
★★★	Hotel Las Lengas, Florencia	ℓ 92668	$19.00	👤
	Credit cards accepted; views over town and bay			
★★	Hotel Cabo de Horno, corner of San Martín and Triunvirato	ℓ 92187	$26.00	👤
★	Hotel Antartida, San Martín 1600	ℓ 91896	$22.00	👤
	Credit cards accepted; overlooking town and bay			
★	Hotel Maiten, 12 de Octubre 140	ℓ 92745	$19.00	👤
★	Apart Hotel Genesis, Gdor Godoy 45	ℓ 92419	$27.00	👥
★	Hostería Mustapic, Piedra Buena 230 (corner of Deloqui)			
	Credit cards accepted; luggage stored	ℓ 91718	$19.00	
•	Apart Hotel Genesis, Gobernador Godoy 45	ℓ 92419	$27.00	👥
A	Hospedaje Cesar, San Martín 753	ℓ 91460	$19.00	👥
	Credit cards accepted			
A	Hospedaje Malvinas, Deloqui 609	ℓ 92626	$18.00	👥
B	Hospedaje Caprí, San Martín 720	ℓ 91833	$12.00	
	Nearly always full			
C	Hospedaje Fernandez, Onachaga 68 (corner of Alope)			
	Good meals; shared bath cheaper	ℓ 91453	$18.00	👥

- Hospedaje Hispano, San Martín 798
- **C** Private accommodation: Señora Hilda Sanchez, Deloqui 395 (corner of Roca) $5.00
  Suitable for back-packers
- **C**

- Cafetería Encuentros, corner of Deloqui and Yaganes. Snacks
- Cafetería Llanquihue, Onas 998 (corner of Fagnano). Snacks
- Cafetería Los Gringos, corner of San Martín and Triunvirato. Snacks
- Cafetería Magnum, corner of San Martín and 25 de Mayo. Snacks
- Cafetería Troika, San Martín block 1100 (corner of Belgrano). Snacks
- Cafetería Yoppen, Corner of Gdor Deloqui and Rivadavia. Snacks
- Take away: Fried Chicken, San Martín 261 (corner of Gdor Godoy)
- Take away: Putantan, San Martín 1133 (corner of Belgrano)

📬 Post and telegraph

- Post office: Encotel, corner San Martín and Gobernador Godoy. Open Mon–Sat 0900–1900
- Telephone: Entel, Roca 514. Open daily 0700–2200

💲 Financial

Cash and travelers' checks are exchanged at the official rate only. Banks are open 0800–1300.

- Banco de la Nación, corner of San Martín and Rivadavia
- Banco de la Provincia de Santa Cruz, Laserre 140. Cash at no commission

Ushuaia

TIERRA DEL FUEGO

✈ Air services from Ushuaia

- Aerolineas Argentinas, San Martín 524 (91218. Open Mon–Fri 0900–1200 and 1500–1800
- LADE, Galería Albatros, San Martín 546 (91123

The airport is across the Bahía de Ushuaia, some 2 km from the center of Ushuaia. Bus no 2 goes from the center to the airport. A taxi to the airport costs $1.50.

On taking off you get spectacular views over the city, Isla Navarino in Chile, and the **Canal Beagle** with its boats appearing as numerous little specks in the water. For the first ten minutes the plane flies over snow-clad mountain ranges.

Flights in winter are sometimes cancelled due to bad weather.

Flying in and out of Ushuaia is a problem at the best of times. During the main tourist season, between December and March, the planes are constantly booked out well in advance. The alternative is to take a bus to Río Grande and board a flight from there. When using LADE flights it is more interesting to go straight to Lago Argentino (the airport for El Calafate) rather than alighting in Río Gallegos.

There are no direct air services between Ushuaia and Punta Arenas in Chile. The only possibility is crossing the Canal Beagle to Puerto Williams on Isla Navarino. However this is fraught with complications as there is at present no regular ferry service between the two ports. Also air services between Punta Arenas and Puerto Williams are irregular and frequently booked out.

None of the airlines accepts credit cards.

Destination	Fare	Depart	Services	Hours	Airline
• Bahía Blanca	$83.00	1330	2 services daily	5	Aerolineas
• Buenos Aires (Aeroparque Jorge Newbery)					
	$96.00	1330	2 services daily	6	Aerolineas
• Comodoro Rivadavia					
	$36.00	0900	Tues	7	LADE
	$55.00	1440	Tues, Wed, Fri–Sun	3	Aerolineas
• Gobernador Gregores					
	$22.00	0900	Tues	5	LADE
• Lago Argentino	$20.00	0900	1–2 services daily	3	LADE
• Mar del Plata	$87.00	1440	Sun	6	Aerolineas
• Perito Moreno	$25.00	0900	Tue	5	LADE
• Río Gallegos	$21.00	1330	2 services daily	2	Aerolineas
	$18.00	0900	1–2 services daily	2	LADE
• Río Grande	$12.00	0900	Tues–Thu	½	LADE
	$10.00	1330	daily	½	Aerolineas
• Trelew	$60.00	1400	daily	3	Aerolineas

🗎 Services and facilities

- Delicatessen: San Martín 1479. Specialty cheese shop
- Hospital: corner of Maipú and 12 de Octubre
- Laundromat: Laverap, Triunviarato 155
- Ski hire: Rincón Popper y Jimmy Button
- Tent hire: Parque Nacional Lapataia

Supermarkets

- Autoservicio Dimar, corner of San Martín and Rivadavia
- Sados, San Martín
- Supercoop, corner of San Martín and Solís

▣ Visas, passports

On arrival from Puerto Williams on Isla Navarino, report to Investigaciones at Kuanip 787.

- Chilean consulate, Malvinas Argentinas 244 (corner of Kuanip)

Ushuaia

TIERRA DEL FUEGO

🚌 Buses

Bus companies
- Transporte El Cóndor. Buses leave from the corner of Maipú and 25 de Mayo, opposite customs
- Transporte Los Carlos, Triunvirato 57
- Transporte Rumbo Sur, San Martín 350 (office)

Services
- Río Grande: Fare $8.00; departs 1200; 2 services daily; Transporte Los Carlos
- Lapataia (in Parque Nacional Tierra del Fuego): Fare $4.00 return; departs 1000; 4 services daily; Transporte El Cóndor
- Aerosilla: Fare $2.00 return; departs 1000; several services daily till 2000; Transporte Rumbo Sur

🚗 Motoring

The road between Ushuaia and Río Grande via Paso Garibaldi is not sealed. The pass is kept free of snow during winter.
- Car rental: Austral, Gobernador Paz 1022

Service stations
- ACA, corner of Avenida Maipú and 25 de Mayo. Road maps available
- ACA, corner of Malvinas and Jainen
- YPF, corner of Maipu and 12 de Octubre

⊕ Tours
- Antartur, San Martín 1200 ℓ 92668. Boat tours to Antarctica
- Onas Turismo, 25 de Mayo 50 ℓ 92002
- Rumbo Sur, San Martín 342 ℓ 91139
- Tiempo Libre, San Martín 154 ℓ 91273. Adventure trips

🏬 Shopping

Duty free shopping is no longer available in Tierra del Fuego.

Sport

There is a sports complex at the corner of Malvinas Argentinas and Onachaga, on Bahía Encerrada, with an indoor heated swimming pool.
- Diving: Information from Club de Actividades Subacuaticas
- Fishing: Contact Asociación de Caza y Pesca, corner of Maipú and 9 de Julio
- Ice skating: Rink at Ushuaia gymnasium
- Sailing: Club Náutico, corner of Maipú and Belgrano

Skiing
- Cross country skiing: Valle Tierra Mayora, 20 km east of Ushuaia. Equipment rental, snowmobiling and cafeteria
- Downhill skiing: The skiing season on Cerro Martial runs from June to August. Club Andino runs a chair lift, cafeteria, and equipment rental

🎭 Entertainment
- Discoteca Katutinka, corner of Maipú and Gobernador Godoy
- Cine General San Martín, corner of San Martín and 25 de Mayo
- Bingo games: Corner of Deloqui and Yaganes
- Bowling: Corner of Lassere and San Martín

📷 Sightseeing

- Museo Territorial (Territorial Museum), also called Museo del Fin del Mundo (Museum of the End of the World), Maipú 181 (corner of Rivadavia). Open daily 1500–2030. The collection of memorabilia from the early days of European settlement is extremely interesting. The artefacts made by the now extinct local tribes are well worth seeing. Admission $0.50

🌱 Excursions

- **Parque Nacional TierRa del Fuego**: The route follows Islas Malvinas and then RN 3 westwards. The entrance to the national park is about half an hour's drive from Ushuaia. Behind the entrance on the right-

Ushuaia

TIERRA DEL FUEGO

hand side is a picnic area with fireplaces and tables. Further on at **Lapataia**, 18 km from Ushuaia, beside the forested shore of **Lago Roca**, is the Cafetería Casita del Bosque. Next to it is the Arua Ovando Camping, with facilities for cars and tents ▫▫▫▫ open from December to March; backpackers are welcome. Weather can be cold so be prepared. Rangers in the park are friendly and will put people up for a couple of days and advise them on the sights. A trail leads along the northern shore of the lake: after about one hour's walk you come to a wooden fence which marks the border between Argentina and Chile—it is possible to continue on the Chilean side. The national park is a region of lakes, forests, and snow-covered high mountains. Its serene tranquillity is reflected in the mirroring lakes. Water in the rivers and lakes is crystal clear and of good drinking quality. The rivers and lakes abound with trout and salmon. Beavers may be seen in the park near the Chilean border. El Cóndor runs conducted tours to the park. Hitchhiking is easy in the summer months with passing motorists or national park staff offering lifts

- **Cascadas de Río Pipo**: On the road to the Parque Nacional, 4 km from Ushuaia. There is a free camp site; it has no facilities but is beside a restaurant. Take an El Cóndor bus or hitchhike
- **Monte Susana**: 10 km west. Camping
- **Ensenada**: 14 km west. Camping
- **Río Olivia**: 12 km east. Waterfalls, fern gullies, camping
- Fish hatchery: 7 km east. Open Tues and Thus 1000–1200 and 1400–1800. Take an eastbound bus no. 1; travel to the end of the route then walk 2 km further
- **GlaciaR Martial**: 7 km behind town. This is a three-hour scenic walk along a mountain trail starting from Hotel Antartida. Nearby is a small dam. There is also a chairlift to the glacier, which operates Tues–Sun. Club Andino Ushuaia operates a *confitería* near the ski slopes which is open daily 1600–2400. Take a Rumbo Sur bus
- **Islas Bridges**
- **Isla Redonda**: A government-run *guanaco* breeding program
- Indian cemetery: 5 km west of town. Site archeologists will inform you about Indian history
- **Bahía Lendegaia** and **Bahía Lapataia**
- Punta Arenas in Chile via Puerto Williams on Isla Navarino in Chile: This trip is possible at present with the easing of tensions between the two countries. Cross by means of ferry from Ushuaia to Puerto Navarino, and take a bus to Puerto Williams in Chile. Usually you have to spend a night in Puerto Williams and board a flight to Punta Arenas the next day. These flights are irregular—check the flight timetable with a tourist agency

Ushuaia

TIERRA DEL FUEGO

or the Chilean consul in Ushuaia
- **Antártida Argentina** (Argentine Antarctica): An 11-day trip to the scientific bases during January and February. $2400.00
- **Lago Fagnano** and **Lago Escondido**: $14.00
- **Canal Beagle**: A 30-minute aerial tour; fare $25.00
- **Puerto Almanza** and **Harberton**: $34.00 for the five-hour trip
- **Isla Gable**: A seven-hour trip by bus and boat; fare $26.00
- Puerto Williams in Chile: Fare $26.00
- **Lago Escondido**: A three to four hour trip; fare$8.00
- **Glaciar Martial**: Fare $8.00
- **Isla de los Lobos**: A three- hour boat trip; fare $16.00
- Les Eclaireurs lighthouse: A three-hour boat trip; fare $16.00

Ushuaia

Cuyo
Provinces

Mendoza Province

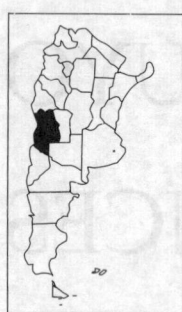

Plate 23 Map of Mendoza Province
- 453 Cacheuta
- 453 General Alvear
- 454 Las Cuevas
- 454 Las Leñas
- 456 Los Molles
- 456 Los Penitentes
- 457 Luján de Cuyo
- 458 Maipú
- 458 Malargüe
- 459   Map
- 463 Mendoza
- 464   Map
- 476 Potrerillos
- 477 Puente del Inca
- 477 Rivadavia
- 478   Map
- 480 San Carlos
- 480 San Martín
- 481 San Rafael
- 482   Map
- 486 Termas Villavicencio
- 487 Tunuyan
- 488   Map
- 490 Tupungato
- 490 Uspallata

MENDOZA PROVINCE

Mendoza is located in the central western region of Argentina. The Andean *cordillera* forms the border with Chile. In the south-west Mendoza adjoins Neuquen Province, in the east La Pampa and San Luis, and in the north San Juan.

The main areas of tourist interest in the province are:
- Worth a visit: **Mendoza city**; and **Las Leñas** and the **Valle Hermoso**
- Worth a detour: **Las Cuevas valley** between Uspallata and Las Cuevas, incorporating the **Los Penitentes ski resort**; **Cacheuta–Vallecitos–Potrerillos**; and the **Cañon San Rafael** and **Cañon del Atuel**
- Interesting: **Tunuyan**; **Tupungato**; **Malargüe;** and **El Sosneado** and the upper **Río Atuel valley**

Several Indian tribes inhabited the area before the arrival of the Incas and the Spaniards. The Huarpes lived in the north, Picunches in the east, Araucanos in the west, and Puenches and Pehuenches in the south-west. It is believed that the Incas subjected the aboriginal population around 1480, without completely gaining control of them. Remains of an Inca road are still visible in some places, as are relics of *tambos* (staging posts for Inca runners) such as the one near **Uspallata**. The first Spaniard to pass through Mendoza was Diego de Almagro, who traveled along the Inca road as far as the Río Maule in Chile, the southernmost border of the Inca empire.

Mendoza was founded as part of Chile and until 1776 belonged to the Gobernación de Chile. With the creation of the Virreinato del Río de la Plata, Mendoza, along with the other Cuyo provinces San Juan and San Luis, became part of the Intendencia de Córdoba. It was in Mendoza that General San Martín prepared his crossing of the Andes to invade the Spanish-held part of South America.

Nowadays Mendoza is the largest wine-producing province in Argentina. Grapes are grown on 330 000 ha, in over 60 000 vineyards, and produce 30 million hectoliters of wine in a good year. Vines were first planted by the Jesuits in 1556. Without water channeled from the high sierras very little agricultural activity could be sustained. A visit to a winery in Mendoza is a must.

Mendoza is one of the most scenic areas of Argentina and tourism is well developed. Mountaineering—**Cerro Aconcagua**, the highest mountain of the Americas, is within easy reach of the city of Mendoza—enjoys an ever-increasing popularity. Trout fishing is also a very popular sport. Mendoza has major winter sports centers such as **Las Leñas** in the **Valle Hermoso**, **Los Penitentes**, or **Vallecitos**.

Mendoza claims 350 days of sunshine per year!

The eastern part of Mendoza consists largely of plains. To the

Mendoza Province

south within easy reach of Malargüe is **Laguna de Llancanelo**, rich in birdlife. Further to the south are the mountains of the **Borde Alto** (highest peak **Cerro Payún**), 3 680 m, a volcanic region rich in fauna, hardly touched by tourism.

Near the Chilean border two nature reserves have been created: the 71 000 ha **Parque Provincial Aconcagua**, with **Cerro Aconcagua** as its highest mountain, and to the south the 120 000 ha **Parque Provincial Volcán Tupungato**. The two parks are separated by the **Río de las Cuevas**. Both reserves have more than a dozen peaks over 6000 m high, and many glaciers such as **Glaciar Horcones Superior, Glaciar Cuerno, Glaciar Gussfeldt,** and **Glaciar Horcones Inferior,** which are the source of crystal-clear mountain streams. In the southern part of **Parque Provincial Volcán Tupungato** are many hot thermal springs; most of them are in the **Toscas** and **Taguas valleys** but are inaccessible to the ordinary tourist. Some areas have been earmarked for development, for example, the **Río de las Cuevas valley**, **Los Penitentes**, **Puente del Inca**, and **Las Cuevas**. In another development, the **Río Tupungato valley** is to be developed for hydroelectricity generation.

The many artificial lakes are another source of enjoyment for the tourist. The biggest is **Dique El Nihuil**, in a beautiful setting in the **Cañon del Atuel** near San Rafael with the chain of the Andes beckoning in the west, providing water sports and accommodation. **Dique El Carrizal** on the **Río Tunuyan** also attracts a large following of water sport enthusiasts.

The western part of Mendoza is taken up by the *cordillera*, containing the highest peaks in the Americas (**Cerro Aconcagua** 6959 m). This is one of the best areas for mountain climbing, hiking, and fishing.

If you wish to scale **Cerro Aconcagua**, you must obtain a permit from the Dirección de Deportes, Recreación y Turismo Social, Estadio Malvinas Argentinas, Mendoza. This permit is issued in duplicate; the group leader must keep the original and hand the duplicate to the Chief of Police in Uspallata. The best time for mountaineering is from January to the beginning of March.

Mendoza is well endowed with thermal springs. Many have excellent facilities, such as **Cacheuta** (not far from Mendoza city), **Los Molles**, and **Termas Villavicencio**. Hikes through the mountains will reveal many more, one of the most picturesque being at **Puente del Inca** on the road to Chile.

For those interested in archeology, you can see the remains of the old Inca road with ruins of an Inca *tambo* in the **Río de las Cuevas valley** past Uspallata.

For the fishing enthusiast there are countless rivers, moun-

Mendoza Province

tain streams, lakes, and *lagunas*. The fishing season runs from November 1 to April 30 for salmonoids, and until July 31 for *pejerrey*, *bagres*, perch, and carp. The best places are the **Río de las Cuevas** and **Río Mendoza** and their tributaries **Río Uspallata**, **Arroyo San Alberto**, and **Río Picheuta** for trout; **Dique El Carrizal** for *pejerrey*, trout, and *bagres*; **Valle de Uco** and its tributaries **Arroyo Las Pircas** and **Arroyo El Grande de la Quebrada** for arco iris and brook trout; **Dique El Nihuil**, and **Lago Valle Grande** near San Rafael for brook trout, arco iris, and Patagonian and Gran Parana *pejerrey*; and in the **Malargüe** area in **Río Atuel**, **Río Barrancas**, **Río Cobre**, **Río Poti Mallal Chico**, **Río Poti Mallal Grande**, **Río Salado**, **Río Tordillo**, and **Río Valenzuela** for trout fly fishing.

CACHEUTA

Postal code: 5549 • Altitude: 1200 m
Distance from Mendoza: 32 km westwards on RN 7

Cacheuta is situated in the lower narrows of the **Río Mendoza valley**. The hot springs at Cacheuta have valuable therapeutic properties.

A modern spa incorporates the original buildings in its lift tower. A hotel is also planned.

🍴 Eating out
• Restaurant Mi Montaña

🚌 Buses
Turismo Mendoza, Las Heras 559 (230316, runs a daily bus service leaving Mendoza at 0900 daily.
• Mendoza: 3 services daily; 1 hour; Expreso Uspallata
• La Cuevas: 2 services daily; 4 hours; Expreso Uspallata
• Uspallata: 3 services daily; 1 hour; Expreso Uspallata

GENERAL ALVEAR

Postal code: 5620 • (area code (0625)

Located in the **Río Atuel** valley, General Alvear is an important crossroads (RN 143 north–south and RN 188 east–west).

🛏 Accommodation in General Alvear

★★	Hotel Buenos Aires, Ingeniero Lange 54 Central	(	2972	$9.00
★★	Hotel Grosso, Ingeniero Lange 31 Central	(	2393	$9.00
•	Hotel Avenida, General Alvear Este 254 Central	(	2535	
•	Hotel Salamanca, Alvear Este 302 Includes breakfast	(	2700	$7.00
•	Hospedaje Argentina, Avenida Alvear Este 765			
•	Hospedaje Boetto, Paso de los Andes 125			
•	Hospedaje La Alhambra, Sarmiento 55			
•	Hospedaje San José, Sarmiento 132			

MENDOZA PROVINCE

🍴 Eating out
- Restaurant Amici, Diagonal Carlos Pellegrini 184
- Restaurant Club Español, Avenida Alvear Este 41
- Restaurant Doña Olga, Independencia 67
- Restaurant Islas Canarias, Avenida Alvear Este 162
- Restaurant Julian, Avenida Alvear Oeste 427
- Restaurant La Llagada, Avenida Alvear Este 499
- Restaurant Las Brasa, corner of 26 de Julio and Paso de los Andes. Grill
- Pizzería Roma, Diagonal C Pellegrini 80

🚌 Buses
Buses run regularly to Mendoza and to Santa Rosa in La Pampa province.

🚗 Motoring
- Service station: ACA, corner of Avenida Libertador and Granaderos

📷 Sightseeing
- Museo de Historía Natural (Natural History Museum), San Rafael 48

LAS CUEVAS

Postal code: 5557 • Altitude: 3151 m
Distance from Mendoza: 198 km westwards on RN 7

Las Cuevas is the last Argentinian settlement before crossing into Chile (see "Visas, passports" below). Shortly after leaving the township, the road enters a tunnel (toll $10) and reemerges in Chile.

The area is ideal for hiking, such as to Cristo Redentor, 9 km away, at an altitude of 4000 m. The mountains surrounding Las Cuevas are about 6000 m high. It is a ski resort, and in winter snow chains must be used or you may not be permitted to continue. Both the Chilean and Argentinian automobile associations sell snow chains.

🛏 Accommodation
Hotel Las Cuevas may not be open, so check. If not, try Puente del Inca; see page 477.

📇 Visas, passports
If you are continuing to Chile, have your passport processed at Punta de Vaca by the Argentinian border guards, 32 km back *before* Las Cuevas.

🚌 Buses
Expreso Uspallata runs two buses daily to Mendoza.
See also "Tours" in Mendoza on page 473.

♦ Excursions
- Cristo Redentor: This monument to Christ the Redeemer was cast in 1904 from cannons of the Andean Army by the sculptor Alonso. To see the magnificent views from here you must climb 900 m over a 9 km track

LAS LEÑAS

Postal code: 5612 • (area code: (0627) • Altitude: 2250 m
Distances
- From Mendoza: 437 km southwards on RN 40 and RN 143 then RP 222
- From Malargüe: 70 km northwards on RN 40 then RP 222

General Alvear

MENDOZA PROVINCE

This ski resort which has all the usual facilities is situated in the **Valle Hermoso** at the junction of **Arroyo Blanco** and **Arroyo Las Leñas**.

There is year-round access from Buenos Aires by road, rail or plane to San Rafael and thence by bus. Las Leñas is also worth visiting in summer. It is the most modern ski resort in South America, with a skiing area of 3300 ha and 57 km of ski runs from 350 m to over 7 km long.

The main skiing season runs from June to October, but there may be snow as early as May and as late as November.

There are six ski-lifts and four T-bars between 240 m (Teleski Eros) to 1670 m (Telesilla Vulcano). A higher chairlift, Telesilla Juno, goes up to 3360 m. The lifts are capable of transporting a total of 6800 skiers per hour.

Skiing conditions for beginners, intermediate skiers, and advanced skiers are all excellent.

Accommodation

Accommodation must be booked on a weekly basis, from Saturday to Saturday. The price includes transport to and from Buenos Aires, half-board accommodation, and ski-lifts. All units are built of stone. All hotels may be reached on ℓ71100.

★★★★ Hotel Escorpio $1050.00 ♨ Off season price: $680.00 ♨
★★★★ Hotel Geminis $ 680.00 ♨. Off season price: $410.00 ♨
★★★★ Hotel Piscis International $1650.00 ♨. Off season price: $1150.00 ♨
• Department Atenas
• Department Corintos

Eating out
Hotel rates include meals.
• Restaurant Acuario, Hotel Acuario. International cuisine)
• Restaurant Bankett. International cuisine
• Restaurant Escorpio, Hotel Escorpio. International cuisine
• Restaurant Geminis, Hotel Geminis. International cuisine
• Restaurant La Salamandra
• Cafetería Bacus, at the end of Telesilla Neptuno (2660 m) ℓ ♨
• Cafetería at the end of T-Bar Minerva (2320 m)

Post and telegraph
Post office and public telephones in Centro Comercial La Piramide allow direct dialling within Argentina and internationally.

Financial
There is an exchange bureau in Centro Comercial La Piramide.

Services and facilities
There is a shop hiring skis and other equipment at the base of the ski slopes; and a complete medical center in the ski village.

Buses
A TAC bus connection between San Rafael and Mendoza links with a shuttle bus service at the intersection of the road from Valle Hermoso and RN 40. Bus services to Malargüe, although closer, are less reliable.

Motoring
• The best route to Buenos Aires is to return to Mendoza on RN 40 and then take the sealed RN 7 to San Luis. The short cut to San Luis via San Rafael has a few bad stretches on RN 146 between Monte Comán and Puente Las Horquetas
• YPF service station just before the ski village, southwards on RP 222

Las Leñas

Mendoza Province

Sport
Lift tickets are included in the price for those staying a week or more. Daily lift tickets cost $11.50 for one-day skiers from Malargüe, San Rafael, or Mendoza.

Entertainment
Las Leñas operates five closed-circuit television channels, one in English and one with programs for children.
- Casino in Hotel Piscis
- Disco Cleopatra
- Angelo's Piano Bar, Centro Comercial

Excursions

The resort is ideally located in the Andes for summer hikes, walking, or horse riding.
- **Laguna del Valle** and **Río del Cobre**
- **Los Molles**, a thermal spring, and **Laguna Niña Encantada**. There is a camping ground
- **Laguna del Valle Hermoso**. Windsurfing is popular

Los Molles

Postal code: 5613 • area code: (0625) • Altitude: 1980 m
Distance from to Malargüe: 60 km northwards on RN 40 then RP 222

Los Molles is a winter resort with good ski runs. Since the opening of Las Leñas it has lost much of its sparkle. The thermal springs of **Termas Lahuen-Có** are on the right bank of the Rio Salado a short distance away. Los Molles is surrounded by high mountains and is a good summer hiking area.

Accommodation
C Hotel Lahuen-Có ⑪ (2491 $14.00. Mostly shared bedrooms

Buses
There are several buses a day from the junction of RP 222 and RN 40 up the Las Leñas valley.

Excursions
- **Las Leñas**: 23 km, a highly developed winter sport resort; see page 454
- **Termas Lahuen-Có**: 1.5 km
- **Pozo de las Animas**: 9 km, a geological depression
- **Laguna de la Niña Encantada**: 9 km, remains of a geyser, thermal water

Los Penitentes

Postal code: 5539 • Altitude: 2580 m
Distance from Mendoza: 154 km westwards on RN 7

Los Penitentes is a ski resort, located in the upper **Río de las Cuevas valley** on the main road to Chile, accessible all year round. Construction of a new tourist project "Ayelen" is planned with a hotel complex and extension of the present ski-lifts.

Accommodation
- Apart Hotel Horcones (timesharing), RN 7 Km 164
- Apart Hotel Juncal (timesharing), RN 7 Km 154
- Apart Hotel Lomas Blancas, RN 7 Km 154 (240442 $68.00 Half board; weekly rate

Las Leñas

Mendoza Province

- Hotel Los Penitentes, RN 7 Km 151 E
  (227095 $36.00 ⁑ Half board $43.00

Accommodation outside Los Pentitentes

A number of clubs have branches here: Club Cruz de Caña, Club Sociedad Eslovena (Slovenian Association), and the Asociación Mendocina de Actividades de Montaña. See "Clubs" in Mendoza on page 472.

Services and facilities

Ski equipment hire $10.00 a day, lift ticket $15.00 a day.

Buses

There is no bus terminal. Hotels have copies of bus timetables.
- Mendoza: 2½ hours; Expreso Uspallata
- Uspallata: $1.70; Expreso Uspallata

Sport

At the moment the following lifts operate: a beginners' lift near the base, a chairlift Las Pircas, and a T-bar Slalom going up to 3020 m.

LUJÁN DE CUYO

Postal code: 5507 • (area code: (061)
Distance from Mendoza: 15 km southwards on RN 40

Luján de Cuyo is located in the **Río Mendoza valley** and forms part of greater Mendoza. It is a retreat for upper-class *Mendocinos* and boasts many splendid villas. Some of the biggest *bodegas* or wineries in the province are also located here.

Accommodation

- ★★ Motel Hotel San Francisco, Pueyrredon 2865 (960110 $13.50 ⁑. Includes breakfast
- ★ Motel Nuevo Chacras, Pueyrredón 2401 (960877/960747 $10.00 ⁑. Includes breakfast
- ★ Hotel Patricios, Patricios 421 (980060 $6.50 ⁑. Shared bathroom cheaper
- Hotel España, Alvear 165 (980411. ACA discount 10%

Eating out

- Restaurant Copacabana, RN 40 Km 37, Luján de Cuyo
- Restaurant Costa Brava, corner of Bustamente and Colombres, Luján de Cuyo
- Restaurant Don Omar, Ruta Panamericana Km 18, Luján de Cuyo
- Restaurant Edelweiss, San Martín 3696, near Museo Fader. International cuisine
- Restaurant El Alero de los Cuatro, San Martín 4180, Mayor Drummond
- Restaurant El Pollín, San Martín 28
- Restaurant Ganimedes, RN 7, La Puntilla
- Restaurant La Primavera, Colombres 235
- Restaurant Los Feudales, Ruta Panamericana, La Puntilla
- Restaurant Los Jardines de Carlos V, Ruta Panamericana. Grill
- Restaurant Mariani, Ruta Panamericana Km 26
- Restaurant N'Ontue, Ugarte 314, La Puntilla
- Restaurant San Felipe, Loria 5801, Chacras de Coria
- Restaurant San Telmo, Ruta Panamericana, La Puntilla. Grill
- Restaurant Tio Carlos, Balcarce 76
- Restaurant Tobac, Ruta Panamericana, La Puntilla

Buses

Buses to Mendoza depart every 15 minutes.

Sport

Trout fishing in **Dique Cippolletti**, 7 km away. ACA *hostería* and camping.

Mendoza Province

🎭 Entertainment
- Disco Afrika, Ruta Panamericana, Luján de Cuyo
- Disco Al Diablo, Bernardo Ortiz, Vistalba
- Disco Aloha, Bernardo Ortiz, Vistalba
- Disco Barok, Bernardo Ortiz, Vistalba
- Disco Natan, Ruta International Km 23, Blanco Encalada
- Disco Sketch, Sáenz 501, Vistalba
- Disco Viva María, Bernardo Ortiz 2671, Vistalba
- Show El Amasijo, Ugarte 802 (corner of Aliaga), La Puntilla

📷 Sightseeing
- Museo Municipal (Municipal Museum), San Martín 250. Colonial-style *hacienda*
- Antique church, a historical monument
- Museo Bellas Artes "Emiliano Guiñazu" (Emiliano Guiñazu Fine Arts Museum), RN 40 3251. Dedicated to an Argentine artist, the museum is surrounded by sculptures in the garden. Entry is free

🍷 Excursions
- **Dique El Carrizal**: On the **Río Tunuyan**, 37 km south. Fishing and water sports. The lake provides a combined hydroelectric and irrigation scheme

MAIPÚ

Postal code: 5515 • ☏ area code: (061)

🍴 Eating out
- Restaurant El Amigo, Padre Vazquez 174c
- Restaurant La Esmeralda, Patricias Argentinas 310

✝ Churches
- Latter Day Saints, Barcala 148

🚌 Buses
There are regular bus services to Mendoza.

🛍 Shopping
- Bodega Giol, Ozamis

📷 Sightseeing
- Museo Arqueológico Municipal (Municipal Archeology Museum), corner of Sarmiento and Patricias Mendocinas

MALARGÜE

Postal code: 5613 • Population: 18 000 • ☏ area code: (0627) • Altitude: 1410 m
Distance from Mendoza: 421 km southwards on RN 40

Key to Map
1. Municipalidad
2. Catholic church
3. Post office
4. Telephone
5. Tourist information
6. T A C bus station
7. Transportes Expreso Malargüe
8. Hotel Turismo
9. Hotel Bambi
10. Residencial Scheryl
11. Residencial Theis
12. Residencial Sakura
13. Residencial España
14. Hotel Rioma
15. Hotel Valle Hermoso

Luján de Cuyo

Mendoza Province

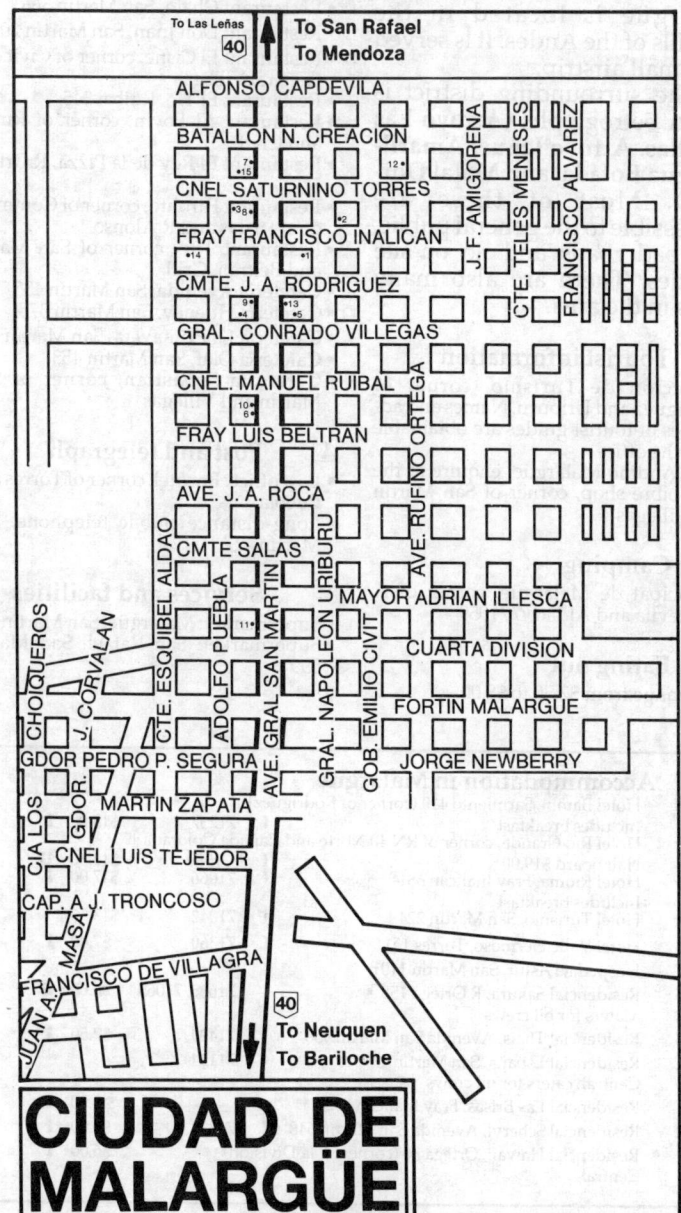

Malargüe

MENDOZA PROVINCE

Malargüe is located in the foothills of the Andes. It is served by a small airstrip.

The surrounding district is rich in petroglyphs (**Arroyo Las Mesillas**, **Arroyo Jaguel Amarillo**, **Agua Botada**, and **Malal Dormido**). Most of these are inaccessible to the general public, with bad roads and no on-site facilities. There are also many mines in the area.

🛈 Tourist information

- Dirección de Turismo, corner of Rodriguez and Uriburu. Names and addresses of tourist guides are obtainable from the office
- Club Andino Malargüe: enquire at the Aire Libre shop, corner of San Martín and Villegas

▲ Camping

- Municipal de Malargüe, corner of A Capdevila and Aldao ✆ 71059

🍽 Eating out

Meals range from $2.50 to $8.00.

- Restaurant Chalo, San Martín 566
- Restaurant Don Juan, San Martín 209
- Restaurant El Cisne, corner of Civit and General Villegas
- Restaurant El Tío, Ruibal 345
- Restaurant El Poyin, corner of Ruibal and Civit
- Restaurant El Rey de la Pizza, R Ortega 517
- Restaurant Farolito, corner of Commandante Salas and R Alonso
- Restaurant Tito, corner of San Martín and Beltran. Grill
- Cafetería Avenida, San Martín 435
- Cafetería Hueney, San Martín 378
- Cafetería La Primavera, San Martín 445
- Cafetería Olaf, San Martín 453
- Cafetería Sebastian, corner of San Martín and Villegas

✉ Post and telegraph

- Post office: Encotel, corner of Torres and Puebla
- Long-distance public telephone, San Martín 427

🏢 Services and facilities

- Supermarket: Malargüe, San Martín 863
- Supermarket: San Rafael, San Martín 599

🛏 Accommodation in Malargüe

	Name	Phone	Price	
★★	Hotel Bambi, Sarmiento 410 (corner of Rodriguez) Includes breakfast	✆ 71237	$13.00	👤
★★	Hotel Río Grande, corner of RN 40 Norte and Cañada Colorada 🍽 Half board $19.00	✆ 71589	$13.50	👥
★★	Hotel Rioma, Fray Inalican 68 Includes breakfast	✆ 71066	$17.00	👤
★★	Hotel Turismo, San Martín 224	✆ 71042	$13.50	
B	Hotel Valle Hermoso, Torres 151	✆ 71360	$7.00	👤
C	Hospedaje Astur, San Martín 1101			
B	Residencial Sakura, R Ortega 158 Caters for oil crews	✆ 71665, 71065	$6.00	👥
B	Residencial Theis, Avenida San Martín 938	✆ 71429	$7.50	👤
C	Residencial España, San Martín 409 Central; caters for oil crews	✆ 71124		
C	Residencial Las Brisas, Fray Inalican 582		$4.00	👤
C	Residencial Scheryl, Avenida San Martín 648	✆ 71337	$6.00	👤
•	Residencial Hawaii, Ortega 30 (corner of 4a Division) Central		$6.00	👤

Malargüe

MENDOZA PROVINCE

🚌 Buses from Malargüe

The TAC office is at San Martín 680.
TAC runs daily services to La Rioja, Chos Malal, and San Carlos de Bariloche (19 hours).
Buses no longer run to Talca in Chile as the road has been destroyed on the Chilean side. In the skiing season there is a direct daily bus to Las Leñas leaving Malargüe at 0830 and returning at 1730. Buses leaving 1200 and 1600 connect with buses for Las Leñas in Río Salado.

Destination	Fare	Depart	Services	Hours	Company
• Mendoza	$6.50	0500	3 services daily	6½	TAC
• Bardas Blancas	$1.50	1630			TAC
• Chos Mallal			daily	10	TAC
• Las Leñas (via Río Salado)	$1.50	0850	4 services daily	2	
Return bus		0850			
• San Carlos de Bariloche			daily	19	TAC
• San Rafael	$3.20	0600	5 services daily	3	TAC
• Tunuyan	$5.00		daily		TAC
• Zapala			daily	13	TAC

• Bakery: Real, corner of San Martín and Las Vegas

✈ Air services

The airport is on RN 40, just on the south side of town. Transportes Aerios Neuquinos (TAN) is planning a service flying between Neuquén, Chos Mallal, Malargüe, and Mendoza.

🚗 Motoring

• Service station: YPF

🎣 Sport

Fishing for trout and salmonoids is possible in many mountain lakes and rivers. Fishing licenses may be obtained from the Dirección de Bosques y Parques Nacionales, RN 40. The season runs from November 1 to April 30 for trout, and for *pejerrey* until July 31. Perch fishing in **Río Salado**, and **Laguna Blanca** for *pejerrey*.

📺 Entertainment

• Whiskería Tabaris, Fortin Malargüe 260

📷 Sightseeing

• Museo de Ciencias Naturales (Natural Sciences Museum), RN 40 north, in the building of the Dirección de Bosques y Parques Provinciales. This, together with the old mill, was part of the *hacienda* "La Orteguiña", which belonged to the colorful General Rufino Ortega, who took part in the Desert Campaign. The museum includes archeological exhibits (a mummy, spearheads), minerals, and paleontological pieces (15-million-year-old ammonites)

🌿 Excursions

The area is largely by-passed by ordinary tourists and has thus preserved much of its original character. Mountain hikes to **Laguna de Llancanelo** 65 km east of Malargüe, with its abundant

Malargüe

MENDOZA PROVINCE

bird life, or to the volcanic regions with sulfur thermal springs are just a few of the possibilities.

- **Las Leñas**, including **Pozo de Las Animas**, **Laguna de la Niña Encantada**: Guided tour $5.00, minimum of ten persons
- **Termas de Azufre**, **Termas de Cajón Grande**, **Caverna de las Brujas** (see below), and **Llano Blanco** petrified forest: Guided tour $5.00, minimum of ten persons
- **Fortín Malal-Hue**: 12 km south, off RN 40. This was apparently a fortified ranch house erected about 1870 and not a military fort as originally thought, although a military detachment camped here in 1833 during the first desert campaign. After his pardon last century, Indian *Cacique* Fraypan raised cattle here
- **Termas de Azufre**: Located in the westernmost part of the **Valle Las Leñas** almost on the Chilean border. The track leading up is only suitable for four-wheel drive vehicles, and not passable in winter. However a good road is planned to link the spot to Valle de Las Leñas, Valle Noble, and Valle Hermoso
- Fishing in the upper reaches of the **Río Grande**: This is one of the largest rivers in the southern part of the province and flows all year round. It is one of the head-waters of the **Río Colorado**
- **Caverna de las Brujas** (Witches' Cave): Located on **Cerro Mogol**, approximately 8 km north of Bardas Blancas. The cave entrance is at 1900 m. The cave was inhabited from earliest times. So far only five kilometers have been mapped and explored. Huge stalagmites and stalactites have been formed through the action of water seeping through fissures in the rock. Some underground halls have been named, such as Sala de la Virgen and Sala de las Flores
- **Laguna de la Niña Encantada** (Lake of the Bewitched Child): Located on the left bank of the **Río Salado**, this lake is about 80 m in diameter and is filled with clear bluish water. It may be the crater of an extinct volcano, and is surrounded by black basaltic rocks which give it a forbidding aspect. The lake is alive with trout and fishing is permitted in season. It is located within hiking distance of Los Molles
- **Laguna de Llancanelo**: Situated 65 km south-east. The basin covers about 300 square kilometers. The size of the Laguna (or more properly *Salina*) varies with the amount of water entering from the rivers which feed it. It has no visible outlet. It has been declared a fauna reserve for abundant bird life, which includes flamingos and black-necked swans. Access is via RP 186 by guided tour only
- **Payún Matrú** and **Payún Liso**: These volcanic ranges are located about 120 km south-east. Access is difficult. The highest elevation is **Cerro Payún** at

Malargüe

MENDOZA PROVINCE

3680 m. The mountains consist of brownish basalt rock, with vast areas consisting simply of lava giving them a moon-like appearance. Because of their isolation they remain ecologically unique. Amongst the fauna are guanacos, pumas, and abundant bird life (including eagles)
- **Los Castillos de Pincheira**: 30 km west, near the junction of the **Río Pincheira** with **Río Malargüe** on the road to La Valenciana mine. Glaciation has carved out tower-shaped outcrops resembling fortresses. It is said this was the hide-out of Chief Pincheira and his band of Indians last century. Spearheads can be found here
- **Río Barrancas**: A picturesque alternative route for four-wheel drive vehicles goes via the **Portezuelo de Choique**. Turn off near Manzano onto the Camino de Calmuco, an 85 km unsealed road, and rejoin RN 40 near Laguna Blanca
- **Llano Blanco**: A petrified forest. Turn off to this site 6 km south of Bardas Blancas for petrified araucarias (monkey-puzzle trees), said to be 120 million years old

MENDOZA

Postal code: 5500 • Population: 600 000 • area code: (061) • Altitude: 756 m
Distances
- From Buenos Aires: 1060 km westwards on RN7
- From Santiago de Chile: 250 km eastwards on RN7

Mendoza is situated in the **Río Mendoza valley** in the *pre-cordillera*. It was founded in 1561 by Don Pedro del Castillo as he crossed the Andes from Chile. During the Liberation Campaign, José de San Martín crossed the Andes from here, defeating the Spanish Royalist troops in Chile and Peru. In 1861 the town was completely destroyed by an earthquake, and severely damaged by a lesser one in 1985.

Mendoza is a modern, beautiful, well-laid-out, thriving Western-style metropolis, lying in a perfect setting against the Andes. Because the city sits on an earthquake fault, there are few high rise buildings. Very little rain falls in this region, but irrigation has transformed Mendoza into a green oasis. Agriculture comprises vineyards and orchards.

Mendoza is linked to Buenos Aires by a sealed road, and to Santiago de Chile by an all-weather road.

Greater Mendoza embraces parts of the following departments:
- **Maipú** (incorporating the suburbs of Maipú and Luzuriaga), notable for its wineries
- **Luján** (incorporating Luján de Cuyo, La Puntilla, Chacras de Coria, and Mayor Drummond), notable for its motels
- **Las Heras** (incorporating El Challao and Las Heras), notable

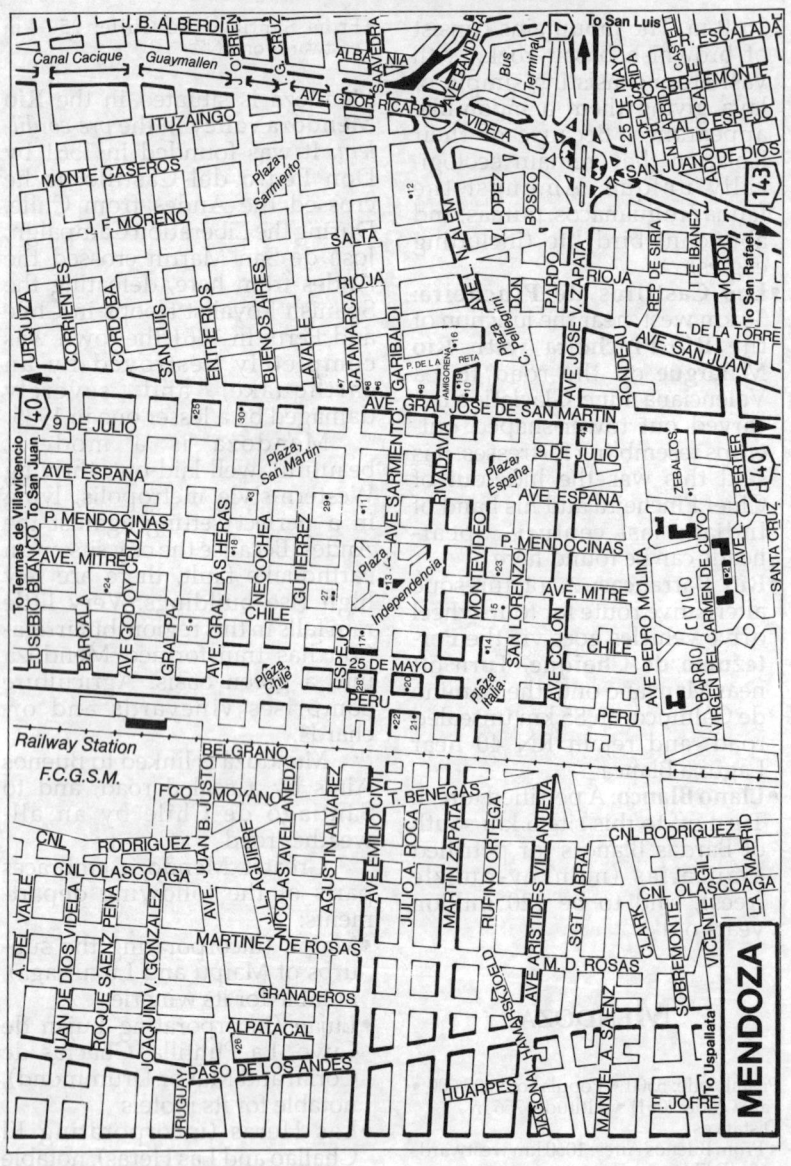

Mendoza

Mendoza Province

for its camping grounds and night clubs
- Guaymallen (incorporating Dorrego, San José, Villa Nueva, Rodeo de la Cruz, El Sauce, and Bermejo), notable for its hotels and restaurants
- Godoy Cruz, notable for its restaurants

✱ Festivals

- Crossing of the Andes festival: January 18
- Fiesta de la Vendimia (Grape Harvest Festival): March. The highlight of the event is the crowning of the Queen of the Grape Harvest, held in the Amphitheatre of the Parque San Martín
- Santiago (St James): July 25
- Virgen de Carmen del Cuyo: September 8. Catholic festival in honor of the Virgin

ℹ Tourist information

- Tourist Office at San Martín 1143, ℂ 242800. Has a list of private accommodation, translators, baby-sitters and so on in the bus terminal
- Cruz de Caña Club (Federación de Andinismo y de Esqui), Las Heras 694, Local 19, ℂ 257775. Has a ski lodge at Los Penitentes. Information on and walks in the Andes

▲ Camping

The nearest camp sites are at El Challao, about 8 km north from the city; take bus 15.
- El Challao, Avenida Champagnat, El Challao (in the northern part of Mendoza) ℂ 292019
- Huerto del Carmen, Avenida Champagnat, El Challao (in the northern part of Mendoza) ℂ 311283
- Non-Quen, RN 7, Acceso Este Km 23, Fray Luis Beltran, Maipú (in the eastern part of Mendoza) ℂ 221768
- Parque Suizo, Avenida Champagnat,, El Challao ▲⊕ (in the northern part of Mendoza; take bus 15) ℂ 255755 $4.00 per person/tent
- La Perla del Cuyo, Bandera de los Andes 5380, Rodeo de la Cruz (a locality in the suburb of Guaymallen)
- Saucelandia, Tirasso, El Sauce, Guaymallen ℂ 263699

🍴 Eating out

Some of the best restaurants are located in Luján de Cuyo; see "Eating out" in Luján de Cuyo on page 457.
I recommend these local wines: "Cruz de Sur" and "Tinto Seco" from Bodega Arizú; and Valroy's "Cuesta de Parsal", burgundy (*borgono*), cabernet sauvignon, and "Viejo Toro".
- Restaurant Aconcagua, San Lorenzo 545
- Restaurant Adrian, Las Heras 457. Grill
- Restaurant Ajadrez, San Martín 814

continued on page 468

Key to Map

1	Municipalidad
2	Casa de Gobierno
3	Cathedral
4	Post office
5	Telephone
6	Tourist information
7	Cambio Maguitur
8	Cambio Santiago
9	Aerolineas Argentinas
10	Austral airlines
11	ALFA airlines
12	Hospital
13	Museo de Historía Natural
14	Museo del Pasado Cuyano
15	Hotel Aconcagua
16	Hotel Huentala
17	Hotel Plaza
18	Hotel Balbi
19	Hotel Cervantes
20	Hotel Crillon
21	Hotel Gran Ritz
22	Hotel Internacional
23	Hotel Nutibara
24	Hotel Acapulco
25	Hotel Alcor
26	Hotel América
27	Hotel Argentino
28	Hotel San Martín and Hotel Argentino
29	Hotel Gran Mendoza
30	Hotel Palace

MENDOZA PROVINCE

🛏 Accommodation in Mendoza

See also "Accommodation" in Luján de Cuyo on page 457.

★★★★	Hotel Aconcagua, San Lorenzo 545	✆ 242321, 242450	$47.00	👥
	Includes breakfast			
★★★★	Hotel Huentala, Primitivo de la Reta 1007 24hr	✆ 240766	$47.00	👥
★★★★	Hotel Plaza, Chile 1124	✆ 233000	$47.00	👥
	Includes breakfast			
★★★	Hotel Balbi, Las Heras 328	✆ 233500	$18.00	👤
	Includes breakfast			
★★★	Hotel Cervantes, Amigorena 65 24hr	✆ 244700	$18.00	👤
★★★	Hotel Crillon, Perú 1065	✆ 45525, 244070	$18.00	👤
★★★	Hotel Gran Ritz, Perú 1008 (corner of Rivadavia) 24hr			
	Central	✆ 248506	$18.00	👤
★★★	Hotel Internacional, Sarmiento 720	✆ 245600	$18.00	👤
★★★	Hotel Nutibara, Mitre 867 24hr	✆ 244658	$18.00	👤
	Central			
★★★	Hotel Acapulco, Patricias Mendocinas 1785			
	Includes breakfast	✆ 250771	$13.50	👤
★★	Hotel Alcor, Paz 86	✆ 234800	$13.50	👤
	Central; includes breakfast			
★★	Hotel América, Justo 812	✆ 256514	$13.50	👤
	Includes breakfast			
★★	Hotel Argentino, Espejo 455	✆ 254000	$13.50	👤
	Includes breakfast			
★★	Hotel Gran Ariosto, Infanta Mercedes San Martín 48 24hr			
	Central; includes breakfast	✆ 293051	$17.00	👤
★★	Hotel Carollo, 25 de Mayo 1184	✆ 234537	$13.50	👤
★★	Hotel Gran Mendoza, España 1210 (corner of Espejo) 24hr			
	Central; includes breakfast	✆ 252000	$18.00	👤
★★	Hotel Milena, Babilonia 17	✆ 240284		
★★	Hotel Palace, Las Heras 70	✆ 234200	$13.50	👤
	Central			
★★	Hotel Rex, J B Justo 367			
★★	Hotel Primero de Mayo, Garibaldi 80	✆ 248820	$12.00	👤
	Central			
★★	Hotel San Martín, Espejo 435	✆ 251349	$13.50	👤
	Central; includes breakfast			
★★	Hotel Vecchia Roma, España 1619	✆ 232529	$13.50	👤
★★	Hotel 27 de Agosto, Amigorena 36	✆ 246031, 246035	$13.50	👤
	Central; includes breakfast			
★★	Hotel Vendimia, Godoy Cruz 10	✆ 256075	$13.50	👤
	Central			
★★	Apart Hotel El Pino Azul, San Martín 2872	✆ 304593	$11.50	👤
★	Hotel Casino, Gutierrez 688	✆ 256666	$9.00	👤
	Central; includes breakfast			
★	Hotel Castelar, Gutierrez 598	✆ 234245	$9.00	👤
	Central			
★	Hotel Castillo, Gutierrez 572	✆ 257370	$9.00	👤
★	Hotel City, General Paz 95	✆ 251343	$8.00	👤
	Central; includes breakfast			
★	Hotel España, Peru 1525	✆ 231481		
	Central			
★	Hotel Horizonte, Gutierrez 565	✆ 253998	$9.00	👤
	Central			
★	Hotel Margal, J B Justo 75	✆ 252013	$9.00	👤
★	Hotel Mesidor, Alberdi 690	✆ 314013	$13.50	👤

Mendoza Province

Accommodation in Mendoza—continued

★	Hotel Petit, Peru 1459 Near railway station	(	232099	$9.00	
★	Hotel Provincial, Belgrano 1259 ▣24hr⊕	(	258284	$13.50	
★	Hotel Republica, Necochea 541 Central; breakfast included	(	253501	$9.00	
★	Hotel Rex, J B. Justo 367	(	253560		
★	Hotel Rincón Vasco, Las Heras 590 Central; breakfast included	(	233033	$9.00	
★	Hotel Rosario, Chile 1579 (corner of Las Heras) Central; breakfast included	(	254765	$9.00	
★	Hotel Royal, Las Heras 145 ● Central	(	243526	$9.00	
★	Hotel San Remo, Godoy Cruz 477 ⊕ Central; breakfast included	(	234068	$7.50	
★	Hotel William, Patricias Mendocinas 1643	(	231341		
★	Apart Hotel Cordillera, J B Justo 144 ⅲ▣●$				
A	Hospedaje Aragon, Godoy Cruz 212 Breakfast included	(	232474	$7.00	
A	Hospedaje Balcarce, San Martín 1446 ● Cheaper if you share the bathroom	(	252579	$7.00	
A	Hospedaje Center, Alem 547 (near bus terminal) Breakfast included	(	241184	$7.00	
A	Hospedaje Denur, Patricias Mendocinas 866	(	248492	$9.00	
A	Hospedaje El Libertador, Avenida España 347 Breakfast included	(	290921	$7.00	
A	Hospedaje Embajador, J B Justo 365	(	259129, 259229	$7.00	
A	Hospedaje Escorial, San Luis 263 Central; includes breakfast	(	254777	$7.00	
A	Hospedaje Ferroviario, J B Justo 154	(	230490, 215490	$6.00	
A	Hospedaje Gutelcas, J B Justo 67	(	252811	$7.00	
A	Hospedaje Ideal, J B Justo 270 ⅲ Central	(	256842	$7.00	
A	Hospedaje Imperial, Las Heras 88 ⊕ Central	(	234671	$9.00	
A	Hospedaje La Marchigiana, Patricias Mendocinas 1528	(	251518	$7.00	
A	Hospedaje Lendi, R E de San Martín 2265	(	255831	$7.00	
A	Hospedaje Mallorca, Roca 719	(	233079	$7.00	
A	Hospedaje Marconi, J B Justo 28	(	233636, 214104	$7.00	
A	Hospedaje Mayo, 25 de Mayo 1265	(	254424	$7.00	
A	Hospedaje Presidente, Perú 1469	(	234808	$9.00	
A	Hospedaje Quijote, San Juan 1407 ⅲ Central; includes breakfast	(	256286, 234696	$7.00	
A	Hospedaje San Cayetano, Chile 1739	(	255402	$7.00	
A	Hospedaje Venus, Perú 1155	(	254147	$7.00	
A	Hospedaje Villa Ines, Sobremonte 648	(	245968	$9.00	
A	Hospedaje Viña del Mar, Rioja 1776	(	234696	$7.00	
A	Hospedaje Zamora, Perú 1156 Central	(	257537	$6.00	
B	Hospedaje Avellaneda, N Avellaneda 810	(	230208	$6.00	
B	Hospedaje Belgrano, Belgrano 965 Includes breakfast	(	247978	$8.00	

MENDOZA PROVINCE

Accommodation in Mendoza—continued

B	Hospedaje Delta, Maza 39		$6.00	
B	Hospedaje La Posta del Cuyo, Godoy Cruz 463	(233730	$6.00	
B	Hospedaje Las Viñas, Martinez de Rosas 1668	(232501	$5.00	
B	Hospedaje Vigo, Necochea 749	(250208	$8.50	
B	Hospedaje Villa Mary, Santiago del Estero 464	(307595	$6.00	
C	Hospedaje Alberdi, Alberdi 51	(234110	$4.00	
C	Hospedaje Andino, Gonzalez 162	(252484	$4.00	
C	Hospedaje Benegas, T Benegas 1864	(255402, 234588	$4.50	
C	Hospedaje Canciller, San Luis 451	(250013	$5.00	
C	Hospedaje Central, 9 de Julio 658	(291361	$4.00	
C	Hospedaje Dardex, Perú 1735	(252670	$4.00	
C	Hospedaje España, Viecente Lopez 420	(244955	$4.00	
C	Hospedaje Forli, Plaza 515	(234651	$4.00	
C	Hospedaje Galicia, San Juan 881 Central	(249619	$4.00	
C	Hospedaje Libano, General Paz 227		$4.00	
C	Hospedaje Lucense, Chile 756 Central	(245937	$4.00	
C	Hospedaje Nevada, Perú 1525 Near railway station	(217598		
C	Hospedaje Premier, J B Justo 804 Central	(250743	$4.00	
C	Hospedaje Ruiz, Salta 1351		$4.00	
C	Hospedaje Savoy, Belgrano 1337		$4.00	

Accommodation in Guaymallen

★	Hotel Panamericano, A Calle 895, Dorrego	(312168	$13.00	
A	Hospedaje Balear, Mitre 992, San José (CP 5519)			
		(230710	$7.00	
A	Hostería Pucara, Saavedra 523, San José (CP 5519)			
		(310253	$6.00	

- Restaurant Alba, Perú 3332
- Restaurant Alba II, Aguirre 489
- Restaurant Brinco's, Buenos Aires 80
- Restaurant Cap Polonio, E Civit 267
- Restaurant Cocram, Remedio Escalada de San Martín 2055
- Restaurant Colony, Lavalle 144
- Restaurant Copihue, Las Heras 651. Grill
- Restaurant Don Esteban, Patricias Mendocinas 1472
- Restaurant Dorgan, San Juan 1331
- Restaurant El Cipres, corner of P Mendocinas and Gutierrez
- Restaurant El Cortijo, Sarmiento 716. Spanish cuisine
- Restaurant El Dragon de Oro, 25 de Mayo 1553
- Restaurant El Escorial, Primitivo de la Reta 1007
- Restaurant El Fogón, San Juan 1556. Grill
- Restaurant El Mangrullo, Parque General San Martín
- Restaurant El Molico, Catamarca 208
- Restaurant El Motivo, Gutierrez 277
- Restaurant El Nuevo Rincón Gaucho, P Molina 591 (corner of 25 de Mayo). Grill
- Restaurant El Platense, Buenos Aires 273
- Restaurant El Restaurant de Enrique, San Martín 827
- Restaurant El Tío Paleto, Belgrano 805
- Restaurant Estrasburgo, Belgrano 886
- Restaurant Facundo, Paso de los Andes 1048. Grill

Mendoza

Mendoza Province

- Restaurant Kimei Kipan, Las Heras 450
- Restaurant La Cordillera, Patricias Mendocinas 1642
- Restaurant La Vieja Recova, San Martín 924. Seafood and pasta
- Restaurant Las Mil y Una, Córdoba 305
- Restaurant Le Notaire, Patricias Mendocinas 756
- Restaurant Los Aromos, Parque General San Martín. Grill
- Restaurant Los Dos Amigos, Santa Fé 402
- Restaurant Papollo, San Martín 776. Grill
- Restaurant Patricia, Libertador. Grill
- Restaurant Los Pipones, Zapata 60
- Restaurant Los Tres Molinos, Avenida España 968
- Restaurant Michele, Avenida España 744
- Restaurant Mi Querencia, Las Heras 523
- Restaurant Pic-Nic, Las Heras 475
- Restaurant Pippo, Garibaldi 80. Grill
- Restaurant Quijote, Hospedaje Quijote, San Juan 1407
- Restaurant Sancho, Amigorena 65
- Restaurant Tarascon Al Pollo, Emilio Civit 396
- Restaurant Timarai, Boulogne sur Mer 241
- Restaurant Trevi, Hotel Palace, Las Heras 70. International cuisine
- Restaurant Trattoria Aveni, 25 de Mayo 1158
- Restaurant Tristan Barraza, Sarmiento 657. Grill
- Restaurant Vecchia Roma, Hotel Vecchia Roma, España 1619. Italian cuisine
- Restaurant Vieja Recova, San Martín 924
- Restaurant Vikingo, San Luis 357
- Restaurant Vladimiro, 25 de Mayo 1221
- Restaurant Zamba, Mitre 1468
- Pizzería Capri, Lavalle 109
- ☞ Pizzería de Un Rincón de la Boca, Las Heras 485
- Pizzería Firenze, Amigorena 52
- Pizzería La Buona Pizza, Sarmiento 785
- Pizzería La Mendocina, General Paz 229
- Pizzería La Pizza Nuestra, Sarmiento 777
- Pizzería La Strega, Colón 646
- Pizzería La Veneciana, San Martín 719
- Pizzería Los Andes, Paso de los Andes 70
- Pizzería Los Inmortales, Sarmiento 695
- Pizzería Lucky, General Paz 124
- Pizzería Monge, Alem 219
- Pizzería Pan Claus, Sarmiento 695
- Pizzería Pantagruel, San Martín 1046
- Pizzería Piu, San Martín 1273
- Pizzería Qué Sé Yo, San Juan 1271
- Pizzería Quince Estrellas, Pueyrredon 604
- Pizzería Rincón de la Boca, Las Heras 485 (corner of Chile)
- Pizzería Riviera, P Molina 423
- Pizzería Rodicar, San Martín 1744
- Pizzería Sebastian, L N Alem 431
- Pizzería Tío Carry, Mitre 552
- Pizzería Trentino, Godoy Cruz 43
- Pizzería Trento, Lavalle 102 (corner of San Juan)
- Cafetería Automobile Club, San Martín 953 (corner of Amigorena)
- Snack-bar: Don Claudio, Benegas 740. Sandwich shop
- Snack-bar: Mankie, corner of Las Heras and Mitre
- Snack-bar: Juan Sebastian, A Villanueva 757
- Snack-bar: Tiempo, J A Roca 635
- Tearoom Solanas, Sarmiento 68. Self-serve; hamburgers, cocktails

Eating out in Godoy Cruz

- Restaurant El Alamo, Ruta Panamericana 3275
- Restaurant El Ceibo, Lavalle 10
- Restaurant El Lomo Campeon, corner of Ruta Panamericana and Río Negro. Grill
- Restaurant El Lomo Loco, San Martín Sur 3001. Grill
- Restaurant La Nueva Parrala, Colon 83
- Restaurant Marujone, corner of Republica de Siria and E Civit
- Restaurant Pollo Top, San Martín 303. Grill, chicken
- Restaurant Rincón Gaucho, Ruta Panamericana 2901. Grill
- Restaurant San Jorge, Chacabuco 19
- Restaurant Viña del Mar, San Martín 996
- Pizzería Cascote, San Martín 1095
- Pizzería Da Vinci, Montes de Oca
- Pizzería Pizzaiola, San Martín 610
- Pizzería Scala, San Martín Sur 898
- Beergarden Schoenbrunn, San Martín 996

Eating out in Guaymallen

Excellent restaurants are also run by national clubs; see "Clubs" below

Mendoza

Mendoza Province

✈ Air services from Mendoza

Plumerillo Airport is 10 km from the city center. Bus 6 from the corner of San Juan and Alem takes you close to the airport.
- Aerolineas Argentinas, San Martín 850 ℡ 246214 (airport ℡ 306927)
- Aerolineas Federal Argentina (ALFA), Espejo 222 ℡ 255078
- Austral, San Martín 921 ℡ 249078
- Ladeco, Espejo 214 ℡ 250670 (to Santiago de Chile)
- Transportes Aereos Neuquinos TAN), San Martín 1143 ℡ 242800

Destination	Fare	Depart	Services	Hours	Airline
Buenos Aires (Aeroparque Jorge Newbery)					
	$72.00	0900	2–4 services daily	2	Aerolineas
	$79.00	1820	Wed, Fri, Sun	3	Aerolineas
Chos Mallal	$42.00	1250	Tues, Fri	2	TAN
Comodoro Rivadavia					
	$79.00	1820	Wed, Fri, Sun	3	Aerolineas
Córdoba	$38.00	0955	1–5 services daily	1	Aerolineas, Austral
Mar del Plata	$74.00	1545	daily	4	Austral
Neuquén	$49.00	1105	Tues, Wed, Fri, Sat	2–3	TAN
	$52.00	1820	Wed, Fri	½	Aerolineas
Resistencia	$58.00	1140	Tues, Thurs, Sun	5	ALFA
Río Gallegos	$83.00	1815	Sat	4½	Aerolineas
Salta	$77.00	1255	Mon, Thurs, Sat, Sun	3½	Aerolineas
San Carlos de Bariloche					
	$68.00	1815	Sat, Sun	½	Aerolineas
San Juan	$10.00	1530	Sun	½	ALFA
San Miguel de Tucumán					
	$44.00	1140	Tues, Thurs, Sun	2	ALFA
	$69.00	1255	Mon, Thurs, Sat, Sun	3	Aerolineas
San Rafael	$10.00	1310	Sun	½	ALFA

- Restaurant Blanco, Correa Saa 1694 (corner of Soler), San José
- Restaurant Cantina de Padovani, Godoy Cruz 2751 (corner of Sarmiento), San José
- Restaurant Don Mario, corner of 25 de Mayo 1324 and P de los Patos, Dorrego
- Restaurant Don Venancio, Rosales 300, Dorrego
- Restaurant El Cóndor, Uspallata 480, Dorrego
- Restaurant Manolo, Godoy Cruz 1815, San José
- Restaurant Nahuel, corner of Acceso Este and C Alegre, San José
- Restaurant Nuevo Horizonte, Feria de Guaymallen Local 2
- Restaurant Welcome, Bus Terminal, San José
- Pizzería 007, Costanera Norte 2309, San José
- Pizzería Bambi, Godoy Cruz 705, San José
- Pizzería Campos, Godoy Cruz 708, San José
- Pizzería Che Bartolo, Alberdi 135, San José
- Pizzería City, P Molina 113, Pedro Molina
- Pizzería de un Rincón de la Boca, Avenida Libertad 920, Villa Nueva
- Pizzería Etna, Godoy Cruz 2480, San José
- Pizzería Internacional, Bandera de los Andes 291, San José

Eating out in Las Heras
- Restaurant El Castillo, Avenida Champagnat, El Challao
- Restaurant Turi, Roca 653
- Pizzería Bambi, J A Roca 610

Mendoza Province

🚌 Buses from Mendoza

The bus terminal is on the corner of Costanera and Alberdí, Guaymallen ℂ 258982

Destination	Fare	Depart	Services	Hours	Company
• Bahía Blanca		1200	daily		Andesmar
• Buenos Aires	$32.70				TAC
• Comodoro Rivadavia	$70.00	2000	daily	36	Andesmar
• Córdoba	$10.50	1000	5 services daily	9	ABLO, TAC, Colta
• Corrientes		0700	Tues, Thurs, Sat		COTAL
• La Rioja	$17.00	0700	3–4 services daily		COTAL, La Estrella, T A Libertador
• La Serena (Chile) via San Juan and the Agua Negra Pass—Summer only					
• Neuquén	$16.50	2000	daily	14	Alto Valle, Andesmar
• Paraná		1900	2 services daily		TAC, T A Villamaría
• Posadas		0700	Tues, Thurs, Sat		COTAL
• Puente del Inca	$3.50				Expreso Uspallata
• Puerto Iguazú		0700	Tues, Thurs, Sat		COTAL
• Rawson		2000	daily		Andesmar
• Resistencia		0700	Tues, Thurs, Sat		COTAL
• Rosario	$21.00	1700	2 services daily	13	TAC, C Argentino
• San Carlos de Bariloche	$32.50	0900	Tues	27	TAC
• San Fernando del Valle de Catamarca	$12.50	0700	2–3 services daily	12	COTAL, La Estrella
• San Juan	$3.00	0600	9 services daily	2	TAC, COTAL, La Estrella, T A Libertador
• San Luis	$7.00	1200	7 services daily		TAC, T A Villamaría, Centro Argentino
• San Miguel de Tucumán	$18.00	1300	daily	16	La Estrella
• San Rafael		2000	Tues, Thurs, Sun	4	TAC, Andesmar
• Santa Fé	$20.50	1900	2 services daily		TAC, T A Villamaria
• Santa Rosa		1200	daily		Andesmar
• Santiago (Chile)	$10.00	0800	12–13 services daily	10	Nevada, TAC, T A Choapa, Nueva O'Higgins, Fenix-Pullman, Chi-Ar, CATA
• Santiago del Estero		0700	1–2 services daily		TAC, T A Libertador
• Termas de Río Hondo	$20.00	1930	daily	19	
• Tupungato	$1.50	0645	7 services daily		
• Uspallata	$3.00				Expreso Uspallata

Buses to Chile

All buses pass through the new tunnel which is open for traffic 0800 to 1300 and 1300 to 1800.

A return ticket (available in Santiago or Mendoza) is slightly cheaper than two singles.

Passengers are normally collected from their hotels.

Mendoza

MENDOZA PROVINCE

Post and telegraph
- Central post office: Encotel, San Martín 678 (corner of Colón)
- Telephone and cables: Entel, Chile 1574

Financial
- Banco Alas, General Espejo 131. Cash advances on Visa card
- Bank of London and South America, San Martín 1498 (corner of Las Heras) ℂ 233900
- Banco de la Nación Argentina, Necochea 127 (corner of 9 de Julio) ℂ 258733
- ☞ Bank of America, corner of San Martín and Alem ℂ 249974. Good rates
- Banco de Mendoza, corner of Gutierrez and 9 de Julio ℂ 251200
- Cambio Cash, San Martín 1173 ℂ 240813
- Cambio Cash, corner of Lavalle and San Martín, ℂ 255919
- Cambio Exprinter, corner of San Martín and Espejo ℂ 231026
- ☞ Cambio Maguitur, San Martín 1203 (corner of Catamarca) ℂ 251575
- Cambio Mundial, Catamarca 12
- Cambio Santiago, Galería Tonsa, San Martín 1177 ℂ 248277
- Master Card, corner of Gutierrez and 9 de Julio ℂ 251200

Services and facilities
- Bicycle and motorcycle hire: Bicicletas y Motocicletas, Las Heras 683
- Laundromat: Laverap, Colon 543
- Supermarket: Supermarcado Lider, Avenida San Martín 821

Ski hire
- Las Heras 431
- Las Heras 516
- 25 de Mayo 1510
- Mitre 2002 ℂ 23791

Clubs
- German: Club Alemán, Olmedo 1921, Dorrego (a locality in Guaymallen) ℂ 264410
- German: Goethe Institut, Moron 265 ℂ 249407. Shows German movies
- Spanish: Club Español, Avenida España 948 ℂ 245313
- Syrian: Club Sirio, Córdoba 339 ℂ 257333
- Chess: Club de Ajedrez Mendoza, San Martín 814

Churches
- Latter Day Saints, E Civit 232 (corner of Olascoaga) ℂ 223314

Visas, passports
- Visa extensions: Migración, Avenida España 1425
- Belgian consulate, Barcala 249 ℂ 230840
- Bolivian consulate, Lavalle 382, Godoy Cruz ℂ 220430
- Chilean consulate, E Civit 296 ℂ 255024
- Danish consulate, Sanchez 435, Godoy Cruz ℂ 223588
- French consulate, Chile 1754 ℂ 234614
- Italian consulate, Necochea 363 (corner of Perú) ℂ 250886
- Peruvian consulate, Perú 8185, Carrodilla (a locality in Luján de Cuyo) ℂ 226524
- Spanish consulate, Alvarez 455 ℂ 253947
- Swedish consulate, Necochea 363 ℂ 242963
- Swiss consulate, San Martín 103 ℂ 247576
- West German consulate, Montevideo 127 ℂ 242539

Border crossing
The Argentinian border control point is at **Punta de Vacas**, 30 km from Las Cuevas. Chilean passport control is just on the other side of the tunnel. There is an exchange bureau in the Chilean border control building which gives good rates for cash and travelers' checks.

Trains
Passenger trains no longer run to Chile. A new service called *Tren a la Nieve* will follow the old route to Chile as far as the border, linking some of the major holiday centers in the Río Mendoza–Las Cuevas valley.
- Buenos Aires: Sleeper $36.00, Pullman $27.20, first class $17.80, tourist class $13.50. "El Libertador" departs 2015 Mon and Fri; 14 hours. "El Aconcagua" departs 1600 daily; 17 hours. "El Cóndor" departs 1845 Sun; 15 hours
- San Juan: "El Aconcagua"; first class $1.50; departs 1400; 2 services daily; 3–4 hours

Mendoza

Plate 23

Map of Mendoza Province

Plate 24
Puente del Inca, towards the Chilean border

MENDOZA PROVINCE

🚗 Motoring

- Service station: ACA, corner of Amigorena and San Martín, opposite Hotel Cervantes. Will supply maps

Car rental

- Avis Rent-a-Car, Espejo 228 ℓ 257802
- Liprandi Rent-a-Car (also known as Cuyo Car Rental), Garibaldi 186 ℓ 248317
- Rent a Car Lis Car, San Lorenzo 110 ℓ 291416
- Rent a Car Mendoza Cars, Paso de los Andes 1073 ℓ 251925

⊕ Tours

- Incatour, shop number 28, Avenida Mitre 1448 (corner of Avenida Las Heras)
- Transportadora Turistica Luján, Galería Via del Sol, Las Heras 426 ℓ 232828
- TTA Tours, 9 de Julio 968 ℓ 241984
- Turismo Condor, 25 de Mayo 1537 ℓ 234019
- Turismo La Cumbre, Necochea 543 ℓ 234652
- Turismo Mendoza, Las Heras 559 ℓ 257743
- Turismo Vitar, Las Heras 494 ℓ 232876

🛍 Shopping

The wine-making season runs from March to April. Wineries, or *bodegas*, are open to visitors, but opening times may change depending on the season. Prices at the *bodegas* are not necessarily cheaper than in other retail outlets.

- Bodega Arizú, San Martín 1515, Godoy Cruz. Bus 7 from the city center
- Bodega Escorihuela, Belgrano 1086, Godoy Cruz. Bus 15 from the city center
- Bodega Giol is one of the world's biggest wineries. Take bus 16, 17, or 18 (every hour). Visits are possible on weekdays
- Bodega Toso, Alberdi 808, San José. Walking distance from city center

🏆 Sport

- Golf Club Andino, south section of Parque General San Martín ℓ 240410
- Golf Club de Campo, corner of E Gonzales and Tuyuti, San Francisco del Monte, Godoy Cruz ℓ 228623
- Mendoza Tennis Club, corner of Parque General San Martín and Avenida Boulogne sur Mer

🎭 Entertainment

Good discos and night clubs are also located in Luján de Cuyo; see "Entertainment" in Luján de Cuyo on page 458.

- Casino, 25 de Mayo 1123, daily from 2200–0300
- Concert Cafe Liceo, A Villanueva 444. Has pool tables
- Disco Bim-Bam-Bum, General Paz 690
- Disco Blow Up, Mitre 1520
- Disco Califa, Garibaldi 7 (corner of San Martín)
- Disco Caribe, Lavalle 174
- Disco Carolina, General Paz 688
- Disco Crazy Horse, 9 de Julio 1724
- Disco Flash, General Paz 25
- Disco Jeeny's, Necochea 40
- Disco Kalatraba, Peru 1779
- Disco Kangaroo, Rivadavia 430
- Disco Saudades, corner of San Martín and J Barraquero
- Disco Tango Bar, San Juan 1484
- Disco Taxi Girls, J F Moreno 2405
- Disco The Cat, Chile 1265
- Disco Topless, General Paz 680
- Disco Vishnu, Villa San Agustín
- Night Club El Grillo, Chile 1243
- Strip La Noche, corner of Salta and Ayacucho
- Strip Studio 55, Catamarca 23
- Strip Tiffany's, Avenida España 1022
- Tanguería Tangomania, Belgrano 1443
- Teatro Mendoza, San Juan 1427
- Teatro Municipal, Plaza Independencia
- Teatro Opera, Lavalle 54

Entertainment in Las Heras

- Disco Acuario, Avenida Champagnat, El Challao
- Disco Galaxi, Avenida Champagnat 48, El Challao
- Disco Jucarama, Avenida las Delicias
- Disco La Chimere, corner of Quintana and San Esteban, Algarrobal
- Disco Sir Lancelot, La Virgen, El Challao
- Disco Tempo, El Challao

Entertainment in Godoy Cruz

- Show La Casona, San Martín Sur 905
- Strip Copacabana, corner of Cervantes and Alberdí

Mendoza Province

Entertainment in Guaymallen
- Disco Bisanzio, Avenida de Acceso 1081, Dorrego
- Disco Piscis, M Hoyos 5915, El Sauce
- Show La Bodega del 900, corner of Avenida de Acceso and Urquiza, Villa Nueva

Sightseeing

Parque General San Martín is located about ten blocks uphill from the city center. It is a huge public space, well laid out, with a one-kilometer watercourse where the local regatta club holds races. Other club facilites located in the park include a race course, golf club, and tennis club; close by is the Meteorological Observatory. Take bus 3 from the city center.

Further west is the stadium, and at the foot of **Cerro de la Gloria** is the Zoological Garden. On top of Cerro de la Gloria is an impressive monument depicting the crossing of the Andes by General San Martín. On the rectangular block there are life-size scenes of this historic event. At night it is floodlit and can be seen from afar. Well worth a visit. A cafeteria is situated on the hilltop.

- Museo Arqueológico (Archeology Museum), Centro Universitario, Avenida del Libertador (256551
- Museo de Arte Moderno (Modern Art Museum), San Martín 1143
- Museo de Bellas Artes Fader (Fader Fine Arts Museum), RN 40 South, Mayor Drummond/Luján
- Museo del Pasado Cuyano (Cuyo History Museum), Montevideo 544 with Chile, has a collection on San Martín and the history of Mendoza
- Museo del Vino (Wine Museum), Centro Civico, Peltier
- Museo de Historia Natural (Natural History Museum), in the center of Plaza Independencia has interesting colonial exhibits, but specializes in Argentinian plants and animals. Open Tues–Fri 0900–1300 and 1500–2000, Sat–Sun 1600–2000
- Museo Histórico General San Martín (General San Martín History Museum), R E de San Martín 1846
- Museo Mineralógico Tellechea (Tellechea Minerals Museum), Parque General San Martín
- Acuario Municipal (Municipal Aquarium), corner of Buenos Aires and Ituzaingo. Open Mon–Fri 1000–1200 and 1530–2100. Admission $0.50
- Roof-top observation platform, 9 de Julio 500. No charge
- Convento de San Francisco: Ruins of a Franciscan convent and church, near Plaza Pedro de Castillo. Destroyed by earthquake in 1861

Excursions

- **Cacheuta**: A spa 42 km west on RN 7. New facilities have recently been constructed at the hot springs in a very attractive setting. Empresa Uspallata runs three one-hour services a day.

Mendoza

Mendoza Province

Short walks in the gorge. See Cacheuta on page 453

- Popular resorts near the city include El Borbollon (north-east) and El Challao (north-west) with many popular night clubs. Local buses
- **Los Penitentes**: A small ski resort 170 km from Mendoza, with hotels, restaurants, ski-lifts, and a 6.5 km ski run. Day tours are organized by tour operators during the skiing season. For a do-it-yourself trip, see "Buses" above. See also Los Penitentes on page 456
- **Puente del Inca** and Cristo Redentor: Tour operators run trips daily for $13.00. The trip follows the **Río Mendoza** and **Río de las Cuevas** and passes through **Cacheuta**, **Potrerillos**, **Uspallata** (stopping for breakfast, and visiting **Puente Histórico Picheuta** off the main highway), **Polvaredas**, **Punta de Vacas** (visiting the natural stone arch of **Puente del Inca**, and the adjacent thermal springs with the old baths hewn out of the rock), **Mirador del Cerro Aconcagua** (providing a full view of Aconcagua), **Las Cuevas** (on the Chilean border), and finally climbs the winding road to the statue of Christ which marks the border between the two countries. The bus leaves Mendoza daily at 0700 and returns at 2000. See also Puente del Inca on page 477. For a do-it-yourself trip, see "Buses" above.
- **Cañon del Atuel**: Tour operators organize day trips for $19.00, leaving Mendoza at 0530 and returning at 2000. The trip includes a visit to **San Rafael**, **Río Diamante valley**, up the Atuel gorge, the dams at **Dique Valle Grande** (with a visit to the power-stations), and Dique El Nihuil. Lunch at the Motel Cañon del Atuel. Return to Mendoza on RN 40 via Cuesta de los Terneros. For a do-it-yourself trip, see "Buses" in San Rafael on page 484
- **Las Leñas**: In the skiing season tour operators organize weekend day trips for $20.00. Buses usually leave at 2400 and arrive in Las Leñas at dawn. Ski hire in town or in Las Leñas (more expensive). Buses leave Las Leñas about 1700. See also Las Leñas on page 454. For a do-it-yourself trip, see "Buses" in San Rafael on page 484 and in Malargüe on page 461
- **Termas Villavicencio**: Tour operators organize half-day trips for $6.00, leaving Mendoza at 0800, visiting the Finca Histórico Del Pino (Del Pino Historic Estate, named after the first bishop of Mendoza) and the winding roads of Villavicencio. Several stops are made en route to enjoy impressive vistas. Stops for lunch at Gran Hotel Villavicencio and a visit to the thermal springs. Continues up to El Balcón (a short stop) and up to the **Cruz de Paramillos**. Returns through the **Quebrada del Toro** and **Garganta del Diablo** (Devil's Gorge)
- City tour: Includes the ruins of the Convento de San Francisco

Mendoza

and Parque General San Martín, **Cerro de la Gloria**, El Challao, and museums. Buses leave at 0800 and return at 1200. During the tourist season there is also an afternoon tour

- **Potrerillos**: During winter, tour operators organize trips to this ski resort via the Vallecito ski runs at **Piedra Grande** and **Cordón del Plata**, and Refugios San Antonio (2800 m), San Bernardo (3000 m), and La Canaleta (3200 m). Buses leave Mendoza at 0900 and return at 2000. During summer there are two half-day tours. For a do-it-yourself trip, see "Buses" above. See also Potrerillos below
- **Manzano Histórico**: Organized half-day tour of 219 km (fare $8.00). The trip passes through Chacras de Coria (visiting a *bodega* and the Museo Casa de Fader, and passing through the oil drilling field **Los Cerillos**, **Valle del Jaurua** (walnut plantations), **Tupungato**, **Valle de Uco**, **La Arboleda** (stopping for lunch), **Arroyos Grandes**, **Las Pircas**, and Manzano Histórico, and returns via **Vista Flores** and **Tunuyan**. Summer only. See also Tunuyan on page 489
- Winery tour: Tour operators organize visits to a great number of *bodegas*; the programs vary from one tour operator to another. One afternoon tour includes a visit to Bodega Peñaflor, **Dique Cippolletti**, and Carrodilla Church, dedicated to the patron saint of vineyards, leaving 1430; fare $4.00

POTRERILLOS

Postal code: 5549 • Altitude: 1351 m
Distances
- From Mendoza 52 km westwards on RN 7
- From Cacheuta 13 km westwards

Potrerillos is a holiday resort much frequented by *Mendocinos*. The **Vallecitos** ski slopes are 26 km away, and are best reached by tour buses from Mendoza.

Accommodation
★★★★ Hotel Gran Potrerillos 24hr (233000 $27.50. Half board $41.00
- Hotel Los Pinos, Avenida Los Condores 34

Camping
- Don Domingo, Km 48, RN 7 on the western side of town
- El Montañes, RP 82, Las Chacritas
- ACA Potrerillos, Km 50, RN 7 on the western side of town

Eating out
- Restaurant Armando, RP 86
- Restaurant Delfy, RN 7
- Restaurant Potrerillos, RP 75

Excursions
- **Termas de Cacheuta**: 13 km downhill. This is an easy two hours' walk through a very scenic gorge. Return trip by Expreso Uspallata (3 services daily; 15 minutes). New facilities at the hot springs

MENDOZA PROVINCE

PUENTE DEL INCA

Postal code: 5555 • Altitude: 2718 m
Distance from Mendoza: 160 km westwards on RN 7.

Situated in one of the most scenic areas in Mendoza Province, Puente del Inca is a center for mountaineering in the Andes and for winter sports.

Accommodation
- Hostería Puente del Inca, RN 7 ☏ 233500 $19.00. Half board $23.00

Eating out
- Restaurant Club Cruz de Caña, RN 7 Km 151
- Restaurant Puente del Inca, RN 7

Buses
- Mendoza: $3.50; Expreso Uspallata
- Las Cuevas: $1.00; Expreso Uspallata
- Uspallata: $2.00; Expreso Uspallata

Motoring
- Service station. Also has accommodation

Sport
It is possible to start your hikes to **Cerro Aconcagua** from here.

Sightseeing

Just 100 m from the main road is the natural stone archway **Puente del Inca** after which this settlement is named. One of the natural wonders of South America, it was formed by sulphur-bearing hot springs. Inside the rock underneath the bridge are galleries hewn into the rock where the hot sulphur springs emerge. The natural arch spans the **Río de las Cuevas** at a height of 19 m, and is 27 m wide. There are many more natural springs within a radius of 200 m.

Excursions

Puente del Inca is the best starting point for excursions to the higher Andean valleys and hikes in the nearby **Parque Provincial Aconcagua**.
- **Los Penitentes**: 6 km downhill on foot or on horseback
- **Laguna de los Horcones**: Underground lake; 5 km
- **Statue of Cristo Redentor**: 16 km uphill, set above La Cumbre

RIVADAVIA

Postal code: 557 • Population: 18 000 • ☏ area code: (0623) • Altitude: 660 m
Distance from Mendoza: 55 km southeast on RN 7

Rivadavia is located in the irrigation belt about 100 km east of the *cordillera*. It was founded in 1884 on the "Indian salt road", over which salt was transported northwards from the southern *salinas*. The climate is desert-continental, with temperatures reaching in 39°C in summer and plunging as low as 5°C in winter. The annual rainfall is about 200 mm. The **Río Tunuyan** meanders slowly through the department after its torrential beginnings in the high sierras. Its waters are stored in the **Dique El Carrizal**

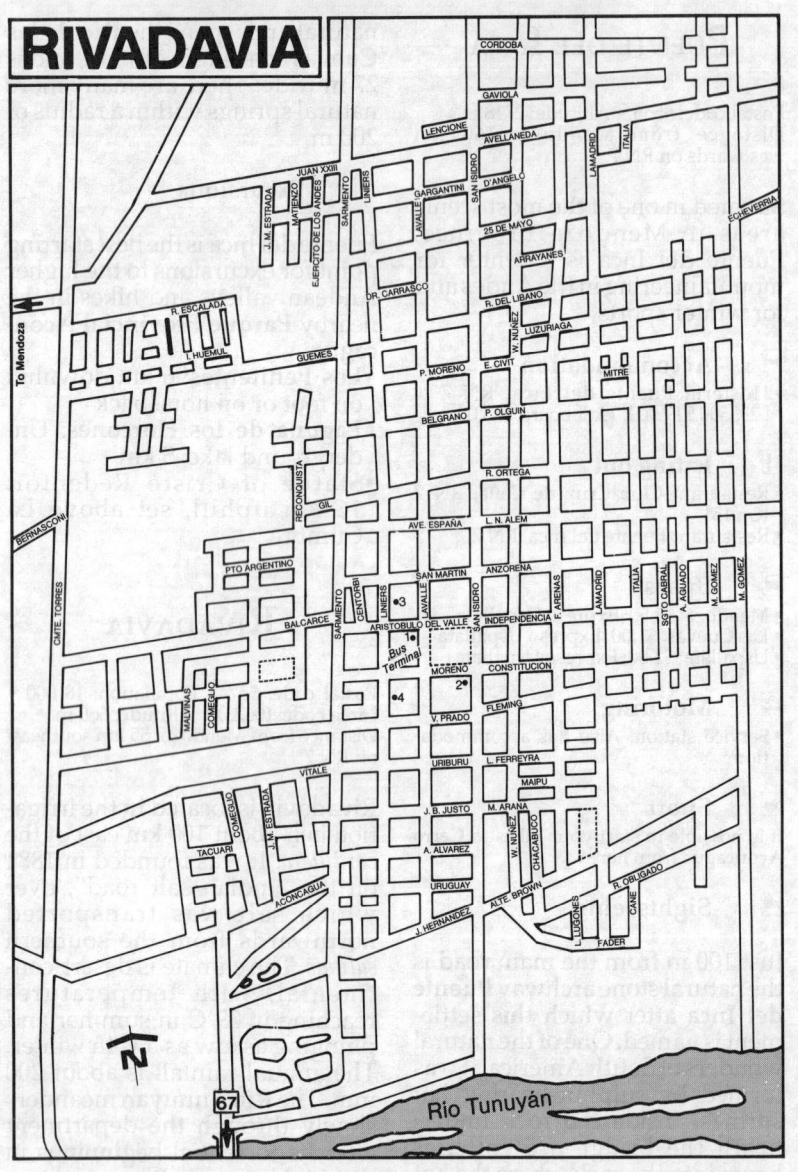

MENDOZA PROVINCE

dam where they are used extensively for irrigation, supplemented by bore water. Rivadavia is the center of a wine-producing region.

Festivals
- Fiesta de la Vendimia (Grape Harvest Festival): March
- Festival de Folklore Cuyano, a fiesta celebrating the settlement of the Cuyo provinces: first week in December

Accommodation
- Hospedaje Palace, San Isidro Labrador 1049

Eating out
- Restaurant Boulevard, corner of Sargento Cabral and Constitución
- Restaurant Centro San Agustín Alvarez, Lavalle 540
- Restaurant Club San Mariano Moreno, San Isidro 541
- Restaurant Don Pablo, corner of W Nuñez and Maza. Grill
- Restaurant El Tío Calambre, San Isidro 963
- Restaurant Hostería del Lago Municipal, RP 67 (corner of Brandsen)
- Restaurant San Francisco, San Isidro 327
- Pizzería Italia, San Isidro 875
- Pizzería Santa Rita, bus terminal
- Cafetería Encuentros, San Isidro 701 (corner of Anzorena)
- Cafetería La Posada, A Del Valle 170
- Cafetería Miroba, San Martín
- Cafetería Monacos, Galería Centorbi, Lavalle 742
- Cafetería Nuevo Tropical, San Isidro 632
- Cafetería Stilo SRL, San Isidro 1360

Post and telegraph
- Post office: Encotel, corner of Liniers and San Martín

- Long distance telephones: Entel, corner of Liniers and Constitución

Buses
Buses run regularly to Mendoza.

Entertainment
- Disco Salon Ducal, Lavalle 740
- Disco Salon Star Five, San Isidro 635
- Disco Zeus, corner of Commandante Torres and I Estrella

Sightseeing

There is a new tourist recreation complex on the banks of the **Río Tunuyan** which includes an artificial lake, camping grounds in a shaded area, and barbecue areas. In the same complex is the Anfiteatro (Amphitheatre) where *fiestas* are staged, a sports center, tennis courts, a cultural center, and other facilities.

Excursions

Dique El Carrizal, an artifical lake, is a favorite weekend resort which has many clubs and restaurants around its shore. Water sports include sailing, wind-surfing, and diving. Follow RP 67 for 40 km west alongside the Río Tunuyan, passing a smaller reservoir **Benegas** (where there are camping grounds), through typical Mendoza countryside—olive groves, vineyards, and irrigation channels lined with willow trees. The lake is 15 km long and 3 km

---

Key to Map
1. Municipalidad
2. Iglesia
3. Post office (Encotel)
4. Telephone (Entel)

MENDOZA PROVINCE

wide, and covers an area of 8000 ha. On the eastern side the forestry and provincial park commission has created a forested recreational area with barbecue facilities, camping grounds, and boat ramps. A tourist resort is planned, with hotels, motels, restaurants, tennis courts, etc. For the fishing enthusiast there are *pejerrey* and trout.

SAN CARLOS

Postal code: 5569 • Altitude: 943 m
Distance from Mendoza: 106 km southwards on RN 40

San Carlos began in 1770 as the **Fuerte San Carlos** (San Carlos Fort). It was here that General San Martín parleyed with the local Indians. In the vicinity are thermal springs. San Carlos is an old-style town possessing many early Spanish adobe houses.

Festivals
• Fiesta de la Tradición

Eating out
• Restaurant Arias, San Martín 102, Eugenio Bustos (2 km south of the town on RN 40)
• Restaurant Avenida, San Martín 20, La Consulta (7 km from town on the road to Valle de Uco dam)
• Cafetería Bongolo, corner of B Quiroga, Echevarria, and Eugenio Bustos
• Cafetería El Triangolo, corner of RN40 and Eugenio Bustos

Buses
TAC runs regular bus services to Mendoza and San Rafael.

Excursions
• Ruins of the **Fuerte San Carlos** (San Carlos Fort): 13 km
• **Baños de Capiz**: 12 km north; follow the unpaved road on the right bank of the river
• **Manzano Histórico** (Historic Apple Tree): Scenic drive with a 5 km side trip to **Valle de Uco dam**. See also "Excursions" in Tunuyan on page 489

SAN MARTÍN

Postal code: 5570 • (area code: (0623)
Distance from Mendoza: 43 km eastwards on RN 7

San Martín was founded in 1816. The original town plan was drawn up by General San Martín. RN 7 runs right through the centre of the town. It is the capital of the San Martín department and the center of a fruit and wine producing region.

Accommodation
★★ Hotel San Pedro, RN 7 Km 1036 (22429 and 22425 $12.50
★ Hotel Libertador, Boulogne sur Mer 256 (22633 $7.00
B Hospedaje Santa Rosa, Alem 357 (21470 $5.00. Central
• Hotel Italia, 25 de Mayo 154 (21066

Eating out
• Restaurant Albirrojo, Lavalle
• Restaurant del Este, L N Alem 447
• Restaurant Italia, 25 de Mayo 168. Grill
• Restaurant La Cigarra, 25 de Mayo 461
• Restaurant Malvinas Argentinas, Terminal de Omnibus
• Restaurant Kukinazo, Lima 314. Grill
• Pizzería Mauro, 25 de Mayo 130
• Pizzería Mayo, 25 de Mayo 531

Rivadavia

Mendoza Province

🚌 Buses
Buses run regularly to Mendoza and San Luis.

📷 Sightseeing
- **Museo Histórico Las Bovedas**: At one stage this was the home of General San Martín, and for a time the headquarters of the Liberation Army prior to the crossing to Chile
- **Chacra de los Barriales**: Local archeological finds

San Rafael

Postal code: 5600 • Population: 60 000 • (area code: (0627) • Altitude: 688 m
Distance from Mendoza: 232 km southwards on RN 40 and then RN 143

San Rafael is situated on the **Río Diamante** in an otherwise arid region. Only irrigation makes large-scale fruit-growing possible in the valley. The modern town is well laid out with good facilities, and provides a good base for excursions to **Dique El Nihuil** and **Lago Valle Grande**, which form part of the **Río Atuel** hydroelectric scheme.

Fuerte San Rafael (San Rafael Fort) was founded in 1805 in what is now the suburb of **Villa 25 de Mayo**. The town was the capital of the department until 1903.

Petroleum has been found in the vicinity, and oil prospecting crews still operate in the flat lands to the east.

🎉 Festivals
- Fiesta de la Vendimia (Grape Harvest Festival)

ℹ️ Tourist information
- Dirección de Turismo, Suarez 145 (terminal complex) (24217. Closed Saturday and Sunday afternoons

⛺ Camping
- Isla Río Diamante ACA, Ingeniero Ballofet (Parque Mariano Moreno), 6 km from town

🍽️ Eating out
- Restaurant ACA San Rafael, Balloffet
- Restaurant Churrasqueria Antaño, H Irigoyen 830
- Restaurant Club Español, Salas 173
- Restaurant El Arca de Noe, Espinola 1331
- Restaurant El Cortijo, H Yrigoyen 999. Grill
- Restaurant El Estribo, Castelli 64. Grill
- Restaurant Gimenez, Godoy Cruz 120
- Restaurant La Cabaña, Los Andes
- Restaurant La Casa de los Andinos, Olascoaga 61. Grill
- Restaurant La Taberna de Nicolás, Pellegrini 17
- Restaurant La Vieja Posada, Pellegrini 15
- Restaurant Las Vegas, San Martín 226. Grill
- Restaurant Lazaro Hermanos, Coronel Suarez 149
- Restaurant Mi Rincín, Godoy Cruz 123
- Restaurant San Marcos, Day 46
- Restaurant San Martín, San Martín 481. Grill
- Restaurant Tennis Club, Sobremonte 737
- Pizzería Cuartetas, Chile 27
- Pizzería El Rey de la Pizza, San Martín 132
- Pizzería Internacional, Sarmiento 825
- Pizzería Leo, Chile 53
- Pizzería Munich, Rivadavia 292

💲 Financial
- Mundial Cambio, Galería Gijón, H Yrigoyen 24

Mendoza Province

Key to Map
1. Municipalidad
2. Cathedral
3. Post office
4. Telephone
5. Tourist information
6. Aerolineas Argentinas
7. Mundial Cambio
8. Hotel España II
9. Hotel Kalton
10. Hotel Dali
11. Hotel Los Alamos
12. Hotel Regine
13. Hotel Viñas
14. Hotel Luis I
15. Hotel Rex
16. Hospedaje Cerro Nevado
17. Hospedaje El Turista
18. Hospedaje España
19. Hospedaje Santa Ana
20. Hospedaje Tonin
21. Hospedaje Turis Hotel
22. Bus terminal

San Rafael

MENDOZA PROVINCE

Accommodation in San Rafael

★★	Hotel España II, San Martín 292 Central	(24055	$12.50	♂
★★	Hotel Kalton, H Yrigoyen 120 Central; ACA discount 10%	(22568	$12.00	♂
★	Hotel Dali, Belgrano 44	(22929	$9.00	♂
★	Hotel Los Alamos, Salas 47 ▣24hr⊕ ACA discount 10%	(22732	$13.00	♂♂
★	Hotel Regine, Independencia 627	(21470	$11.00	♂♂
★	Hotel Viñas, Mitre 441 ACA discount 10%	(24355	$8.50	♂
A	Hotel Luis I, España 23	(25387	$4.00	♂
A	Hotel Rex, H Yrigoyen 56	(22177	$5.50	♂
A	Hospedaje Cerro Nevado, H Yrigoyen 376	(28209	$7.00	♂
A	Hospedaje El Turista, Chile 641	(27061	$5.00	♂
A	Hospedaje España, San Martin 270 Corner of España Central	(21192	$5.50	♂
A	Hospedaje Santa Ana, B de Irigoyen 337	(22596	$4.50	♂
A	Hospedaje Tonin, San Martín 327	(22499, 25802	$9.00	♂
A	Hospedaje Turis Hotel, Condarco 340	(28090	$6.00	♂
B	Residencial Copacabana, Las Heras 129	(23740	$4.50	♂
B	Hospedaje Ideal, San Martín 192 Central	(22301	$5.00	♂
B	Hospedaje La Esperanza, Avellaneda 263 Includes breakfast	(22382	$6.00	♂
C	Hospedaje El Viajero, Rivadavia 120		$4.50	♂
C	Hotel Martinez, Coronel Suarez 124	(21083	$5.00	♂
C	Hospedaje Petit Nihuil, B de Irigoyen 420	(24950	$4.50	♂
•	Hospedaje Antolinez, Las Heras 446			
•	Hospedaje Montaña, El Libertador 686			

Services and facilities
- Laundromat: Lavandería Laverap, Moreno 79

Motoring
The road over the El Pehuenche Pass to Talca (Chile) is closed.
- Service station: ACA, corner of H Yrigoyen and 9 de Julio

Tours
Tours can be organized for six participants or more.
- Empresa Buttini, Corrientes 494 (21413
- Hotel Los Alamos, Commandante Salas 51

Entertainment
- Disco Magic Night, A Calle
- Disco Prestige, Olascoaga 26
- Disco Sugar, Commandante Salas 1700, Cuadro Nacional
- Disco weekend, A Calle, El Cerrito

Sightseeing
- Museo Municipal de História Natural (Municipal Natural History Museum), corner of Avenida San Martín and Francia, in Parque Mariano Moreno: Situated in a botanical garden, the museum has an extensive collection of minerals, fossils, archeology, anthropology, and paleontology
- Parque Hipólito Yrigoyen, corner of RN 143 and Marqués

San Rafael

Mendoza Province

✈ Air services from San Rafael

The half-hour taxi trip to the airport costs $4.00.
- Aerolineas Argentinas, Day 95 ☏ 22267
- Transportes Aereos Neuquén, Commandante Salas 287 ☏ 22121

Destination	Fare	Depart	Services	Hours	Airline
• Mendoza	$10.00	1430	Sun	1	Federal
• Buenos Aires (Aeroparque Jorge Newbery)					
	$71.00	1545	Mon–Thurs	3	Aerolineas
• Resistencia	$62.00	1430	Sun	6	Federal
• Río Cuarto	$30.00	1545	daily	1	Aerolineas
• San Juan	$20.00	1430	Sun	1	Federal
• San Miguel de Tucumán					
	$53.00	1430	Sun	4	Federal

de Sobremonte, 15 blocks from the town center. Contains a sports centre and an amphitheatre with a seating capacity of 10 000 spectators where plays are staged. The annual grape festival takes place here

● Excursions

- **Cuesta de los Terneros**: 33 km. This is a steep and winding section of RN 144 going west. Not far from the beginning of the ascent a trail leads northwards to **Arroyos de la Pintada**, which has good camping spots in scenic surroundings. This area

🚌 Buses from San Rafael

The bus terminal is on the corner of Avellenada and Súarez. Andesmar runs a daily bus service to Bahia Blanca and Santa Rosa departing at 1645.

Destination	Fare	Depart	Services	Hours	Company
• Mendoza	$ 4.20	0300	14 trips daily		TAC
• Bardas Blancas	$ 4.50				TAC
• Barrancas	$ 8.50				TAC
• Buenos Aires	$22.60				Rojas
• Comodoro Rivadavia					
	$40.00	2325	daily		Andesmar
• Córdoba	$15.00				Rojas
• El Nihuil	$ 1.50	0545	several trips daily		TAC
Return trips run 1430 to 1830					
• General Pico		1525	Tues, Thurs, Sun		Andesmar
• Los Molles	$ 3.50	1000	several trips daily		TAC
Return trips run 1530 to 1730					
• Malargüe	$ 3.25				3½ TAC
• Neuquén	$13.50	2100	2 services daily	11	Andesmar, T Alto Valle
• Trelew		2325	daily		Andesmar
• Valle Grande	$ 0.75	0720	3 trips daily	1	T Iselin
Return trips run 0920 to 2000					

San Rafael

has many archeological sites including rock paintings. Further up are panoramic views over the city

- **Dique El Nihuil** (El Nihuil Dam) (75km) and **Lago Valle Grande**: Fourteen kilometers further on from the Cuesta del Ternero is the turn-off south to El Nihuil dam and lake. The dam forms an artifical lake of nearly 10 000 ha, and supplies a string of power stations in the gorge of the **Cañon del Atuel**. The power generated is used by an iron and steel plant nearby. The lake is a favourite weekend retreat, and many clubs line its shore. There is good fishing (*pejerrey* and trout), as well as sailing and water-skiing, and a hotel with a restaurant, Hotel El Nihuil. From Lago El Nihuil there is an interesting 21 km walk down through the gorge of **Cañon del Atuel**. On the way down you pass power-stations Nihuil I, II, and III, Lagos Aisol, and Tierras Blancas. In the valley, on the left-hand side between power-station II and III, is Motel Cañon del Atuel (with bungalows or cabins, a restaurant, and a swimming pool). At Valle Grande lake is the Club Náutico Valle Grande with a restaurant and boat hire. A good spot for fishing, windsurfing, and diving. From Lago Valle Grande onwards the road is sealed, and regular buses return to the city. Tour operators run organized day tours ($12.50) which include **Feria Artesanal**, **Dique Valle Grande**, a visit to the power stations, and Dique El Nihuil, leaving San Rafael at 1030 and returning at 1900
- **Villa 25 de Mayo** and the **Río Diamante valley**: Founded in 1805 as **Fuerte San Rafael** (San Rafael Fort), Villa 25 de Mayo was the first settlement in the district. Nowadays it is a quiet suburb which has retained some of the charm of the past century, with its adobe houses and tree-lined streets. Nearby is one of the main dams on the Río Diamante which distributes the water for irrigation. Near **Cerro Bola** are thermal springs, and the biggest uranium mine in Argentina. There are regular bus services to and from the city. Further up the valley in a narrow gorge is the **Los Reyunos** hydro-electric scheme. The dam forms a lake of 800 ha, with fishing and water sports, but no other facilities. The biggest dam in the Río Diamante valley is **Dique Agua del Toro** with a 128 m concrete wall producing a lake of over 1000 ha. Follow the partially sealed road westwards from Villa 25 de Mayo to the intersection with RN 40 and turn south for 7 km. Fishing and water sports are available, but no other facilities. Tour operators organize day trips ($12.50) including a visit to Villa 25 de Mayo, **Dique El Tigre**, Los Reyunos private club, and a three-hour boat trip on the lake. The tour bus leaves San Rafael at 1030 and returns at 1900; lunch is included

San Rafael

Mendoza Province

- **Las Leñas** and **Valle Hermoso**: During the summer months tour operators organize day trips for $25.00. The tour includes a visit to **El Sosneado**, **Laguna de la Niña Encantada**, **Pozo de las Animas**, **Los Molles**, Las Leñas, and Valle Hermoso. The return trip from Valle Hermoso includes a short visit to the Las Leñas complex (hotels, bars, and cafeterias). Lunch at La Niña Encantada. The bus leaves San Rafael at 0830 and returns at 2130. During winter, day skiing trips are available. For budget-minded travelers regular tour buses are available. See also Las Leñas, page 454
- **El Sosneado** and the upper **Río Atuel valley**: Take the sealed roads of the RN 144 and then RN 40 to El Sosneado; go through semi-desert country towards El Sosneado. In the far distance the snow-capped peaks of the Andes are clearly visible. From El Sosneado RP 220 continues up the Río Atuel valley to the thermal springs at **Termas El Sosneado**. There are no facilities apart from the pool and springs, but accommodation and food are available at the Estancia El Sosneado near the head of the valley. This is an unspoilt area of outstanding scenic beauty with views of **Cerro Sosneado** (5189 m) and the main range of the Andean chain. Transport services are irregular, but you may get a lift with a truck or car going to the mines
- **Caverna de las Brujas** (Witches' Cave): Tour operators organize day trips for $25.00, which include a visit to **Malargüe**. During a three-hour guided tour in the caves you descend to 170 m to see stalactites and stalagmites. The bus leaves San Rafael at 1000 and returns at 2000

Termas Villavicencio

Postal code: 545 • Altitude: 1850 m
Distances
- From Mendoza: 45 km northwards
- From Uspallata: 56 km eastwards

Located in a picturesque valley in the *pre-cordillera* with a delightful climate, Termas de Villavicencio is famous for its curative thermal water with a temperature ranging from 37 °C to 48 °C.

Accommodation
- Hotel Termas. Open only during the short summer season

Buses
A bus makes a round trip to Mendoza on Wednesdays and Sundays, leaving at 0800 and returning at 1330 ($3.50).

Excursions
- **Canota-Monument**: 16 km. Where San Martín divided his army before crossing the Andes into Chile
- **Las Higueras**: 20 km. Thermal springs
- **Bosque Petrificado Carlos Darwin** (Charles Darwin Petrified Forest): 23 km

San Rafael

MENDOZA PROVINCE

TUNUYAN

Postal code: 5560 • Population: 40 000 •
area code: (0622) • Altitude: 873 m
Distance
- From Mendoza: 82 km southwards on RN 40
- From San Rafael: 160 km northwards on RN 40

Tunuyan is located on the **Río Tunuyan** at the foot of the Andes, which rise up in a series of chains (**Cordón del Portillo** and **Cordón del Marmolejo**) to nearly 7000 m at the Chilean border. Tunuyan was founded in 1880 when the Territorio del Uco was split into Tunuyan and Tupungato. The name is derived from an Araucanian word meaning "trembling earth"—**Cerro Bravard** (5913 m) and **Cerro San Juan** (6111 m) are extinct volcanoes. At the time of the Spanish invasion there was a large aboriginal settlement on the shores of the Río Tunuyan. Nowadays the river is dammed in several places and its waters used to irrigate some 100 000 ha. Temperatures in the mountains can fall to –17°C. The usual minimum city temperature in winter is 13°C and in summer it can climb to 40°C. Since 1920 apple trees have been planted, to create an important fruit juice industry in the region. Softwood plantations supply wood for the fruit boxes. Besides apple plantations large areas are planted with apricots, plums, cherries, and pears.

One of the best ski runs is located in the **Río Manantiales valley**, some 67 km west of Tunuyan. It is claimed that you can ski here for nine months of the year; there are no facilities as yet but a major ski center is planned. The skiable area is 340 ha (or 1100 ha if the **Río Guanaquitas valley** is included), with 45 km of ski runs from 2 km to 5 km in length and 2800 m to 3100 m in altitude. For the time being check out the Club Andino in Tunuyan, which has an artificial snow piste.

A new hydro-electric scheme "Los Blancos" will soon dam the **Río Los Blancos** and **Río Los Tordillos** in the upper Tunuyan valley.

Festivals
- Fiesta de la Vendimia (Grape Harvest Festival) and song festival, held concurrently

Tourist information
- Oficina de Turismo, Centro Cívico, corner of Republica de Siria and H Yrigoyen
- Club Andino Tunuyan. Owns Refugio Lemos in the mountains

Accommodation
- ★ Hotel Mestre, San Martín 1386 (22555 $6.50. Central
- ★ Hotel Sancer, San Martín 651 (corner of Marinelli) (22229 $6.50
- A Hospedaje San Luis, J A Roca 943 (23042 $6.50. Shared bathroom
- A Hospedaje Tunuyan, Roca 949 $5.00

Camping
- Manzano Histórico: ACA camping ground. See "Excursions" below

MENDOZA PROVINCE

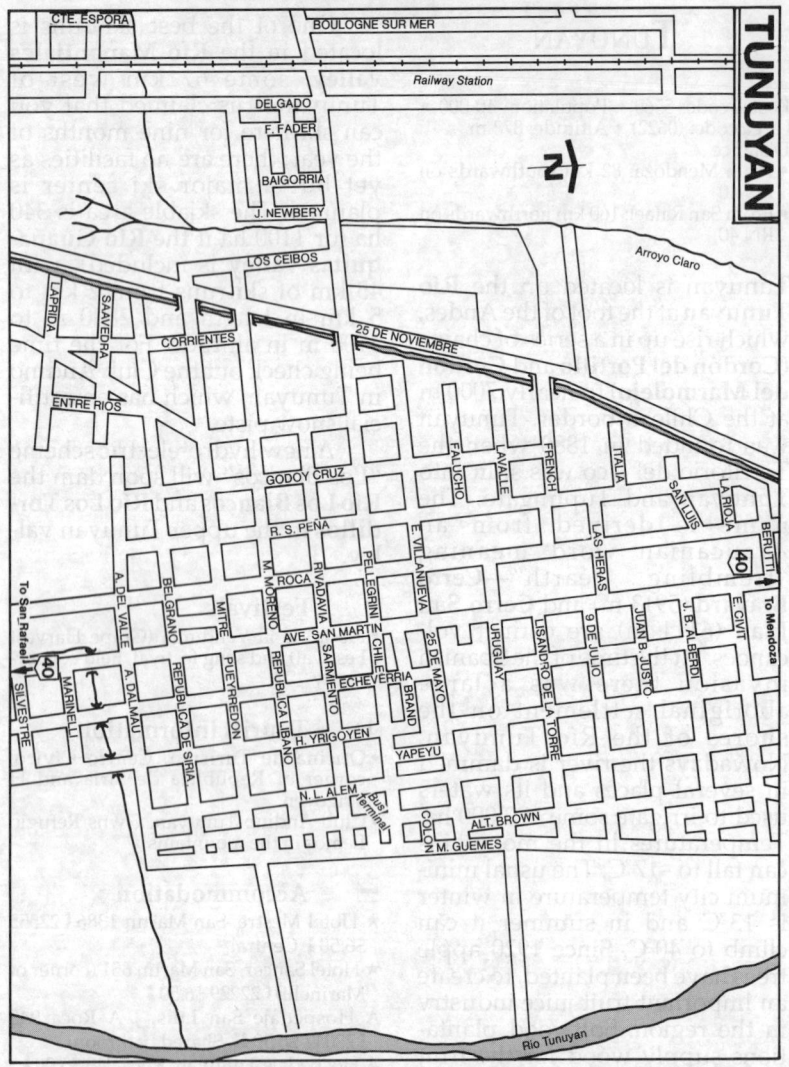

🍴 **Eating out**
- Restaurant Alfredito, San Martín 600
- Restaurant Colón, San Martín 1164
- Restaurant Juancho, San Martín 1827
- Restaurant Los Choiques, Chile
- Restaurant Los Compadres, RN 40 Km 35. Grill
- Restaurant Los Manantiales, corner of Pellegrini and Godoy Cruz

Tunuyan

MENDOZA PROVINCE

- Restaurant Sociedad Española, San Martín 973
- Restaurant Sosa, San Martín 1776
- Restaurant Tío Carlos, San Martín Sur 104
- Pizzería Ilo, corner of San Martín and L de la Torre
- Cafetería Bar Sky, San Martín 1190
- Cafetería Carioca, corner of San Martín and Rawson
- Cafetería Don Pepe, San Martín 1055
- Cafetería El Esquí, San Martín 1186
- Cafetería El Pirulo, corner of San Martín and Rivadavia (sector Sur)
- Cafetería La Cabaña, San Martín 1156
- Cafetería La Terminal, corner of Chile and Alem
- Cafetería Mozart, San Martín 1396
- Cafetería San Martín, San Martín 1060

Post and telegraph

- Post office: Encotel, corner of San Martín and Rivadavia

Buses

The bus terminal is at Alem block 1100 (corner of Sarmiento)
- Mendoza: Empresa ECLA
- Malargüe: Fare $5.00; Empresa TAC
- Neuquen: Empresa Alto Valle
- Rivadavia: Empresa Andesmar
- Tupungato: Transportes General B Mitre

Motoring

Service stations

- Shell, corner of San Martín and L de La Torre
- YPF, corner of San Martín and E Villanueva
- YPF, San Martín 1137

Sport

- Horse trekking: Cabalgata Andina, San Martín 1080 Trekking in the *pre-cordillera*

Entertainment

- Night Club Kobaru, corner of RN 40 and Callejon Lemos
- Night Club Kua Kua, corner of RN 92, Reina, and Colonia Las Rosas
- Night Club Malake, RN 92, Vista Flores, 15 km west of Tunuyán
- Night Club Tijuana, Juan de Dios Videla, Vista Flores

Excursions

- **Manzano Histórico** (Historic Apple Tree): Located 40 km westwards on RP 92, this is an historic site where General de San Martín camped on his way over the Andes to Chile. A monument called Retorno a la Patria is erected here. The site also serves to celebrate various festivals such as the grape harvest and song festival. RP 92 from Tunuyan follows the **Río Carocas**. The closest camping spots along the river are in Colonia Las Rosas, after passing La Botella de Armani. Some 15 km from the town center is the suburb **Vista Flores**. Nineteen kilometers from town is another camping spot. **Los Higuerales**, 25 km from Tunuyan, is aptly named because of the fig trees (*higueras*) in the area. Further on on the left is the monument to "La India Muerta", commemorating an Araucanian legend. The weekend resort of **Arroyo Grande** is 35 km from town. Nearby is the San Antonio chapel. At the Manzano Histórico is an ACA camping spot with toilets and hot water. You may visit the nearby trout hatchery. Transportes ECLA and TAC run bus services in this area. If you have your own transport you can return via **Los Arboles** to either Tunuyan or Tupungato

MENDOZA PROVINCE

- Andes: From Manzano Histórico, take the trail through the **Quebrada del Arroyo Grande** into the high Andes. This is hiking and climbing area par excellence. There are several *refugios* (mountain huts or chalets) here run by the Club Andino, such as Refugio Capitan Lemos and Refugio Doctor Scaravelli. Pass the junction of **Río Llaretas**, **Río Manantiales**, and **Río Cuanaquitas** and you are in the **Quebrada de las Llaretas**, over 4000 m above sea level. At **Portillo Argentino** is an incomplete water tunnel known as the **Río Palomares**, which was to have linked the valley of the Arroyo Grande with the upper Río Tunuyan valley

TUPUNGATO

Postal code: 5561 • area code: (0622)
Distance from Mendoza: 78km southwest on RP 86

Located in the **Río Uco valley**, and surrounded by snowcapped peaks to the west with views of **Cerro Tupungato** (6800 m), Tupungato is a good base for exploring the countryside and for hikes.

Accommodation

★★ Hotel Turismo Tupungato, Belgrano 1066 88421 $10.50
A Residencial Italia, Belgrano 542 88176 $5.00
B Residencial Nieto, Brown 1200 (near the bus terminal) $4.00

Eating out

- Restaurant Hotel Turismo Tupungato, Belgrano 1066
- Restaurant Ilo, Belgrano 703
- Restaurant La Ideal, Belgrano 498
- Restaurant Valle del Tupungato, Belgrano 542

Buses

From the bus terminal Transporte General B Mitre runs seven services daily to Mendoza: the first first bus leaves at 0530, and the last at 1930 ($1.50)

Motoring

- ACA service station, Belgrano 808 (corner of General Mosconi)

Entertainment

- Disco Cuore, M Argentina with C Urquiza
- Disco Moncloa, Roca
- Disco Playboy I, Liniers
- Disco Playboy II, Belgrano

Excursions

- **Manzano Histórico**, 40 km on an unsealed road: See "Excursions" in Tunuyan on page 489

USPALLATA

Postal code: 5545 • Altitude: 1900 m
Distance from Mendoza: 105 km northwest on RN 7

Uspallata is the last sizeable town before the Chilean border. During the war of independence Fray Luis Beltran forged weapons here for San Martin's army before crossing the Andes.

Tourist information

- Oficina de Turismo Uspallata, Centro Comercial

Tunuyan

MENDOZA PROVINCE

- Señor Ricardo Elias Jatib, owner of Restaurant Don Elias, is also a mine of information on the district

Accommodation

- Hotel Gran Uspallata, RN 7 west of the town center (3 $14.00. Includes breakfast
- Hostería Los Condores, corner of La Heras and RN 7 (2 $7.00. Includes breakfast
- Hostería La Montaña, RN 7 (981832 $7.00

Camping

- Uspallata, RN 7
- Camping Uspallata ACA, RN 7 Km 1184 (244901

Eating out

- Restaurant Casa de Don Elias, Cerro Barrauca, where the bus stops
- Restaurant El Motivo, RN 7
- Restaurant Hosteria Los Condores, corner of Las Heras and RN 7
- Restaurant Uspallata, RN 7
- Pizzería El Fogon, corner of Las Heras and Tupungato

Buses

Expreso Uspallata stops at Restaurant Don Elias.
- Mendoza: $3.00; 3 services daily; 2½ hours; Expreso Uspallata
- Los Penitentes: $1.70; Expreso Uspallata
- Las Cuevas: 2 services daily; 2½ hours; Expreso Uspallata
- Puente del Inca: $2.00; Expreso Uspallata
- San Juan (via Barreal); $10.50; Sat; Empresa TAC

Motoring

It is possible to travel to Mendoza via the Termas Villavicencio road.

Excursions

- **Puente Histórico Picheuta**: A bridge constructed by General San Martín to move his troops over the Andes
- **Ruins of Las Bovedas**: A ruined city built by the Huarpe Indians under the Jesuits, and also an Inca *tambería*
- **Barreal** and **San Juan** in San Juan province: See "Buses" above

Uspallata

San Juan Province

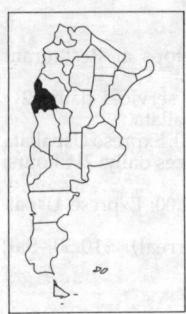

Plate 25 Map of San Juan Province
- 494 Barreal
- 495 Calingasta
- 496 Difunta Correa
- 496 Huaco
- 497 Pismanta
- 497 Rodeo
- 498 San Agustín del Valle Fértil
- 499 San José de Jáchal
- 500 San Juan
- 501 Map

San Juan has an area of 96 000 square km. It shares borders with La Rioja province in the north and east, San Luis province in the east, Mendoza in the south, and the spine of the Andes forms the border with Chile.

The centers of traditional *artesanías* (weaving, potting, and so on) are in the Andean region—such as **San José de Jáchal**, **Iglesia**, and **San Agustín del Valle Fértil** in the east.

The provincial capital is **San Juan**, located some 1130 km north-west from Buenos Aires.

San Juan is a dry province and has to optimize use of its water resources. The rainfall decreases the further east one goes. Most of the rivers are dammed, the biggest water storage system being on the **Río San Juan** not far from the capital itself. Here the water sports facilities of **Gran Presa de Embalse Quebrada de Ullum** attract

San Juan Province

San Juan Province

thousands of tourists. There are other reservoirs with similar facilities, such as **Dique Los Cauquenes**.

Most of the industry is centered in greater San Juan, which includes **Albardón** in the north, **Villa Santa Rosa** in the east, **Villa Media Agua** in the south, and **Rivadavia** in the west.

The areas of interest to the tourist include the capital city, the **Río de los Patos valley**, **Valle Fértil** department with the **Ischigualasto** provincial reserve, the thermal springs at **Pismanta**, **Iglesia**, and **San José de Jáchal**. There are several archeological sites in the province, such as the pre-Columbian village near Angualasto 20 km north of Rodeo.

San Juan is rich in minerals. Copper is found on the **Río de Pachón** near the Chilean border.

The only road to Chile is RP 150 from Las Flores to La Serena in Chile, via the **Paso del Agua Negra** (4770 m). This road is usually impassable very early in the winter season. During the tourist season there are buses from San Juan to La Serena.

San Juan is a mountainous province. Only about a tenth of the total area is arable, and this only because of irrigation. The water descending down from the high *sierras* is collected in numerous dams to be used for irrigation and electricity production. The irrigated area is used mainly for viticulture; San Juan produces some of the best wine grapes and is one of the biggest wine-producing provinces in Argentina.

San Juan is a region for mountaineering. Its scenic beauty is outstanding, and many mountain valleys still await the arrival of the first tourist.

The province has innumerable thermal springs, such as **Termas de Agua Hedionda** ("Stinking Water"), **Termas de Agua Negra**, **Pismanta**, **Termas de Talacasto**, and **Baños La Laja**, to name just a few of the more accessible ones. Only Termas de Pismanta has adequate facilities.

Fishing in San Juan

The rivers and many artificial lakes provide an opportunity to indulge in water sports and fishing. The two major fishing rivers are the upper reaches of the **Río San Juan** (**Río de los Patos** and **Río Castaño**), providing good catches of salmon and *arco iris* trout. From San Juan take RP 12, 180 km sealed road, to Calingasta. From there take either the northern road to the township of Castaño or the southern road to the township of Barreal. In the Río Castaño the fishing season runs from November 15 to April 15.

In the many lakes, such as the **Gran Presa de Embalse Quebrada de Ullum** and **Dique Los Cauquenes**, lower **Río San Juan**, and rivers in the **Valle Fértil**, the main varieties fished are *pejerrey*, *bagre*, perch, and carp. Fishing in the lakes is permitted all year round.

SAN JUAN PROVINCE

carp. Fishing in the lakes is permitted all year round.

Only 15 km from the city of San Juan is the **Gran Presa de Embalse Quebrada de Ullum**. It is the biggest tourist attraction in the province and much frequented by the townspeople. The major aquatic sports are windsurfing, boating, and fishing. All the main fish varieties listed above are encountered in the lake: *pejerrey*, trout, *bagre*, and carp.

Further fishing grounds are located near **San Agustín del Valle Fértil**, some 247 km northeast from the provincial capital. The facilities are sufficiently good to make the stay pleasant. Here fishing is mostly for giant *bagre*, *pejerrey*, and Mojarra *plateada*. Fishing is forbidden from September to November and during March and April. Fishing licences are obtainable from the Oficinas de Fiscalización, Parque de Mayo, San Juan; alternatively, park inspectors issue day permits. Note that these permits or licences are issued for "sectors" of rivers only, that is, for defined lengths, usually between two branches or tributaries.

BARREAL

Postal code: 5405 • (code: (0648) • Altitude: 1650 m
Distance from San Juan: 180 km westwards on RP 12 then 412

Barreal is situated 43 km south of Calingasta in the Pampa Negra on the **Río de los Patos**, also known as the Valle de Calingasta. A concerted effort is being made by the municipality to upgrade its tourist facilities. A case in point are the fine cabins recently finished in the municipal camping grounds.

The history of Barreal goes back to pre-Hispanic days, when the Inca trail from Cuzco in Peru passed through this valley to Chile over the Uspallata pass. Vestiges of this trail are still visible. Barreal is a good base for excursions up the Valle de Calingasta. Views the of snowcapped **Cerro Aconcagua** (6960 m) and **Cerro Mercedario** (6770 m) are visible from the village.

Unlike most villages and towns, Barreal is a long stretched-out village with no real center. Most shops and the town hall are located in the northern end of town, and the church is 2 km further south.

ⓘ   Tourist information

In the absence of a local tourist office, the best source of tourist information is Don Jorge of the Hotel Jorge almost opposite Hotel Barreal.

⌂   Accommodation
- Hotel Barreal ⑪ $7.00 ☎. Meals $3.00; breakfast included
- Hostería Posada San Eduardo $8.00 ☎. Converted hacienda open only in summer. Huge rooms heated by open fireplaces. Meals $4.50, breakfast U$1.00
- Residencial Hotel Jorge 41048 $3.00 ☎. Shared bathroom; breakfast $S0.80. Also runs a small shop

San Juan Province

▲ Camping
There is a municipal camping ground, near the church. Cabins for six $13.00

🍽 Eating out
- Restaurant Hotel Barreal

🚌 Buses
There is no bus terminal. There is a TAC ticket office in the reception area of the Hotel Barreal. Book early on Friday.
- San Juan: Fare $3.50; departs 1330; 1–2 services daily; 4 hours; Empresa TAC
- Uspallata: Departs 1130 Fri; 2 hours; Empresa TAC

📷 Sightseeing
- Private museum of Señora Iñez Herrera. Walk up from the Plaza. All the pre-Columbian artefacts on display have been unearthed in the area while plowing the fields

🌳 Excursions
- **Pampa del Leoncito**: 20 km south of the village. The Pampa del Leoncito was formerly a lake. Now it is dry and forms an almost perfect, unrippled plain. The flatness of the surface has given rise to a local sport known as *carrovelismo*: a vehicle is fitted with a sail and driven by the strong winds. RP 412 to Uspallata passes through these flats. Eight km further on is a turn-off into the **Arroyo de las Cabeceras**, at the end of which there is the Observatorio Astronomico El Leoncito. Unusually clear skies all year round have prompted the erection of this observatory

- **Río de los Patos valley** (also known as Valle de Calingasta) towards Aconcagua: There is a well-defined 55 km walking track as far as the junction of the Río de los Patos with **Arroyo Aldeco** and beyond. This is the domain of anglers and mountain hikers. Here the valleys are narrow and glaciers come into view. The upper reaches of the Río de Los Patos and **Río Blanco** belong to the sports and fishing club of San Juan, which runs the Refugio Las Hornillas, a fishing lodge with basic facilities. The area has been described as an angler's paradise. The fishing season is open here all year round. If you intend to hike extensively through this area, buy your supplies in San Juan. A tent and sleeping bag are required as the nights are very chilly even in summer

CALINGASTA

Postal code: 5403 • ✆ area code: (0648) Altitude: 1375 m
Distance from San Juan: 109 km westwards on RP 12

Located in the wide and fertile Valle de Calingasta where the **Río Castaño Viejo**, the **Río de los Patos**, and the **Río Calingasta** meet to form the **Río San Juan**. It is the center of a fruitgrowing area, particularly grapes and apples; cider is produced in large quantities. There are also many

SAN JUAN PROVINCE

copper deposits. Calingasta is an angler's paradise, as the crystal-clear and icy waters abound with fish, particularly trout and salmon.

🍴 Festivals
- Apple cider festival: April

ℹ️ Accommodation
★★ Hotel Minar, RP 20, 4 km outside town on the Barreal side. New

🍽 Eating out
- Restaurant La Capilla

🚗 Motoring
Because of the narrowness of the road, traffic between San Juan and Calingasta on RP 20 is restricted to traffic traveling uphill to Calingasta between 0600 and 1200, and from 1200 till 1800 to vehicles descending from Calingasta.
- Service station: ACA, RP 20 on the San Juan side

🌴 Excursions
- **Cerro Hilario**: Near Tamberías, 14km south of Calingasta, you cross the Río de los Patos on a foot bridge and arrive at the village of Hilario. On the mountain are pre-Columbian remains. It appears this was a *tambo* or runners' staging post on the Inca trail penetrating into what is today Chile
- **Castaño Viejo**: Located on the upper reaches of the **Río Castaño**, Castaño Viejo ("Old Castaño", to distnguish it from Castaño Nuevo, or "New Castaño", through which you will pass on your way), and is at the end of a dirt road. This area is much frequented by Argentine anglers. It is beautiful, and unspoilt by mass tourism

DIFUNTA CORREA

Postal code: 5443
Distance from San Juan: 60 km eastwards on RP 141

At this famous religious site, a shrine in the desert commemorates a baby who survived miraculously for three days by living off its dead mother's milk. Thousands of pilgrims flock here, especially at Easter and May 1. In the vicinity are also several hot mineral springs.

There are no tourist facilities in Difunta Correa.

🚌 Buses
Buses run regularly to and from San Juan.

HUACO

Postal code: 5463 • Altitude: 1000 m
Distance from San José de Jáchal: 32 km eastwards on RP 40

Huaco is located in the **Río Huaco valley** 6 km south of the main road. The main attraction is the **Termas de Agua Hedionda** (you can't miss the smell—the name means "Stinking Water"!)). It is a typical *gaucho* place where time appears to have stood still. The area has been made famous by the writings of the Argentinian poet Buenaventura Luna, who is buried here.

Calingasta

SAN JUAN PROVINCE

Accommodation

At this stage it is unknown whether the local Hostería Provincial de Turismo is open for business.

Buses

Buses run frequently to and from San Juan.

Excursions

- **Dique Los Cauquenes**: A dam halfway between Huaco and San José de Jáchal. Good for fishing and boating

PISMANTA

Postal code: 5467 • Altitude: 2000 m
Distance from San Juan: 182 km northwards on RP 436 then RP 150

Pismanta, also known as Termas de Pismanta, is located in the foothills of the *pre-cordillera* in a dry area. It consists only of a few isolated homesteads and *estancias* plus the thermal complex. The thermal water emerges at 42°C and is slightly radioactive, and has a pleasant taste. Not far away are the thermal springs of **Termas de Centenario** which are on private property and have no facilities.

The complex consists of a two-star hotel with a thermal spa, cabins, a swimming pool with 40°C water, a casino, and an excellent dining room. The pergola set in the front garden is used for evening functions. The complex consists of two sections; although the newer section is slightly dearer ($20 for half board, with reduced prices Sun to Thurs), try to get acommodation there. Tip the attendant at the spa who checks your pulse.

Accommodation

★★ Hotel Termas de Pismanta $18.50. It is possible to book in San Juan and Buenos Aires. Lower rates apply from Sun to Thurs

Buses

Empresa Iglesia runs services to and from San Juan, leaving San Juan Mon, Wed, Fri, and Sun at 0720 and arriving in Pismanta at 1330; fare $3.50.
- San Juan: Fare $3.50; departs 1500 Mon, Wed, Fri, Sun; 4 hours; Empresa Iglesia
- San José de Jáchal: Fare $1.80

Motoring

- Service station: ACA, in Las Flores, 4 km from Pismanta

Excursions

- **Angualasto**: 32 km north in the Río Jáchal valley; see "Excursions" section San Juan on page 508. Empresa Iglesias runs daily buses

RODEO

Postal code: 5465 • Altitude: 1600 m
Distance from San Juan: 197 km northwards on RP 40 then 436

Rodeo is situated on an elevated plain surrounded by mountains in the far distance. Rodeo would be a stopping point for those who are interested in visiting the archeological site at Angualasto.

Accommodation
C Residencial Las Vegas 🍴 $2.00 ℹ. Basic facilities only

🅰 Camping
- Municipal Rodeo

🍴 Eating out
- Comedor Las Vegas, in the main street. Rather in the style of a "*gaucho* bar"

🚌 Buses
Empresa Iglesia runs daily services to and from San Juan via Termas de Pismanta. Services also run up to Angualasto.
Empresa TAC runs services to San Juan via San José Jáchal, and to Termas de Pismanta.

Excursions
- **Pismanta** : See Pismanta on page 497
- **Angualasto**: Aboriginal ruins. See "Excursions" San Juan on page 508

SAN AGUSTÍN DEL VALLE FÉRTIL

Postal code: 5449
Distance: From San Juan: 247 km northeast on RP 141 then RP 510

San Agustín del Valle Fértil is located in a valley formed by the **Río del Valle**. It was founded in 1788 by Pedro Pablo de Quiroga. Tourism and weaving provide the population's main income. The setting is very picturesque; the **Sierra del Valle Fértil** to the west reaches its highest point with **Cerro Colorado** at 2350 m.

The flora is subtropical and partially covers the mountainsides.

Accommodation
- Hostería Valle Fértil , RP 293 Km 1155 🍴 ₡125. Run by the ACA
- Residencial Andacollo
- Residencial Los Olivos

🅰 Camping
- Camping ACA, below the Hostería Valle Fértil
- Municipal camping ground

🚌 Buses
Buses going either to San Juan or to La Rioja are usually full.
Empresa T A Libertador runs daily buses to Santiago del Estero (11 hours) and Termas de Río Hondo (12 hours).
- San Juan: Fare $4.00; 2 services daily; 5 hours; Expreso Valle Fértil
- La Rioja: Depart daily; 3 hours; Empresa TA Libertador
- Mendoza: Depart daily; 6½ hours; Empresa TA Libertador

🚗 Motoring
- Service station: ACA . Hires four-wheel drive vehicles for a day trip to Ischigualasto: $20.00 including driver

Shopping
Homespun articles made from wool and alpaca-wool ponchos are good buys. The skills are usually part of a family tradition going back centuries.

Sport
There is *pejerrey* fishing in the nearby artificial lake.

Excursions
- **Ischigualasto**, also called Valle de la Luna (Valley of the Moon): 60 km north of San Agustín, 18 km beyond Los Baldecitos. This is a graveyard of long-extinct dinosaurs from the

SAN JUAN·PROVINCE

Mesozoic era. Petrified prehistoric araucanias and fern trees can also be seen. Best visited with a Tour operator. Some of the fossils are on display at the Museo Bernardino Rivadavia in Buenos Aires. Erosion has created some grotesque rock formations. The entrance fee is $1.00, and includes a guide. A car trip round the reserve takes two or three hours. Guided tours run by Yafar Turismo leave from San Juan and La Rioja. Or hire a jeep with a driver from ACA for $20.00. There is an ACA campsite

- **Parque Nacional Talampaya**: See "Excursions" in Chilecito on page 568

SAN JOSÉ DE JÁCHAL

Postal code: 5460 • (area code: (0647) • Altitude: 1162m
Distances
- From Chilecito in La Rioja province: 246 km southwards on RP 40, via Cuesta de Miranda, a mountain pass
- From San Juan: 162 km northwards on RP 40

San José de Jachál was founded by Capitán Juan de Echegaray in 1751.

Tourist information
- Tourist office, in the Municipalidad (Town Hall), San Juan (on the Plaza)

Accommodation
- Hotel Plaza, San Juan 546 (directly up from the bus terminal) $6.00. Cheaper without a bath
- Hotel San Martín, Echegaray $4.00

Eating out
- Comedor La Cabaña, D F Sarmiento 538 (on the Plaza)
- Comedor Mary, D F Sarmiento (on the Plaza). Has three bowling lanes

Post and telegraph
- Post office: Encotel, corner of San Martín and Rawson

Buses
The bus terminal is on the corner of Obispo Zapata and San Juan.
- San Juan: Fare $3.30; departs 0545; 4 services daily; 3 hours; Empresa TAC
- Chilecito (via Cuesta de Miranda): Fare $8.50; departs 0030 daily; 7 hours; Empresa TAC
- Iglesia: Departs 1010 Mon, Wed, Fri, Sun; 2 hours; Empresa TAC
- Mendoza: Fare $6.30; departs daily; Empresa TAC
- Pismanta: Fare $1.70; departs daily; Empresa TAC

Motoring
RP 40 north to Villa Unión is sealed for part of its 144 km. The landscape is varied, mostly dry and desertlike interrupted by green oases with olives, grapes, and fruit trees.

Excursions
- **Pismanta**: There is a hotel here. See "Excursions" in San Juan on page 508
- **Termas de Agua Negra**: 7km. There are no tourist facilities
- **Termas de Agua Hedionda** ("Stinking Water"): 29 km. See Huaco on page 496
- **Huaco**: 33 km. See Huaco on page 496
- **Dique Los Cauquenes**: 33 km. Fishing in the dam. See "Excursions" in Huaco on page 497
- **La Huerta de Huachi**: 32 km. Mountain walks.

SAN JUAN PROVINCE

SAN JUAN

Postal code: 5400 • Population: 400 000 • area code: (064) • Altitude: 650 m
Distances
- From Córdoba: 510 km westwards on RP 20
- From La Rioja via Olta: 520 km southwest on RP 38 then 79 and 141
- From Mendoza: 166 km northwards on RP 40

The capital of San Juan province is located in the *pre-cordillera* on the **Río San Juan** in the southern part of the province. It was founded in 1562 by Don Juan Jufre de Loayza y Montese, emissary of the Chilean viceroy, on his way from Chile to found Spanish towns on the eastern side of the Andes. The center was destroyed by a devastating earthquake in 1944 but has since been completely rebuilt.

San Juan is the birthplace of Domingo F Sarmiento, the eminent historian, educationist, and president from 1868 to 1874. The house in which he was born is now a museum. The town is also strategically situated near the artificial lake **Gran Presa de Embalse Quebrada de Ullum** (also known as Dique José Ignacio de la Roza). Here water sports such as sailing, windsurfing, and fishing can be enjoyed.

The town itself is a good base for exploring the mountainous regions to the west and north, some of which exceed 5000 m in height, as well as the number one attraction of the province, **Ischigualasto** (also called Valle de la Luna). Several thermal spas are also located in the province, the best known being **Pismanta**.

Note that Avenida General San Martín divides the town into north and south. Street names are the same and the building numbers start afresh at the Avenida, distinguished only by the affix "N" for "Norte" (or North) and "S" for "Sur" (or South). Similar-

Key to Map
1. Municipalidad
3. Catedral
4. Post office (Encotel)
6. Tourist information
7. Cambio Bolsa de Comercio
8. Aerolineas Argentinas
9. Austral Lineas Aereas
10. Bus terminal
11. Museo Sarmiento
12. Convento Santo Domingo
13. Hotel Nogaro
14. Hotel Alhambra
15. Hotel Plaza
16. Hotel Provincia
17. Hotel Selby
18. Hotel America
19. Hotel Brescia
20. Hotel Bristol
21. Hotel Petit Jardín
22. Hotel Embajador
23. Hotel Hispano Argentino
24. Hotel La Toja
25. Hotel Marsella
26. Hotel San Francisco
27. Hotel Austria
28. Hotel Apolo
29. Hotel El Mendocino
30. Hotel 9 de Julio
31. Hotel Roy
32. Hotel Sussex
33. Residencial Alemania
34. Hotel Moreno
35. Hotel Central

San Juan Province

ly Avenida Mendoza divides the city into east and west, and building numbers start afresh at this Avenida distinguished only by the affix "O" for "Oeste" (or West) and "E" for "Este" (or East). In the *Travel Companion* the affixes are given following the street number.

🎭 Festivals
- Fiesta Nacional del Sol (National Sun Festival): August

ℹ Tourist information

The Dirección Provincial de Turismo, Sarmiento 24 (S), opposite Sarmiento museum, arranges tours, and distributes excellent leaflets on the main tourist centers of Calingasta, Pismanta, Ischigualasto, and San José del Valle Fértil.

San Juan

San Juan Province

Ⓐ Camping
- Municipal Rivadavia, 19km west of town center
- Zonda, 18km west of town center
- El Pinar, 11 km west of town center

🍴 Eating out
- Restaurant Avenida, corner of San Martín (O) and España. Steakhouse
- Restaurant Brescia, Hotel Brescia, Ave España 336 (S)
- Restaurant Casa España, Rivadavia 32 (E). Spanish cuisine
- Restaurant Central, corner of Avenida I de la Roza (E) and Tucumán. Steakhouse
- Restaurant Centro Valenciano, corner of General Acha and R del Libano. Spanish cuisine
- Restaurant Club Sirio Libanés, Entre Rios 33 (S). Arab cuisine
- Restaurant Comedor Amicci, corner of Rawson (S) and I de la Roza
- Restaurant Comedor Central, Avenida I de la Roza 179 (E)
- Restaurant Don Serapio, Avenida I de la Roza 174 (E). Credit cards accepted
- Restaurant El Internacional, Terminal de Omnibus
- Restaurant El Mendocino, Avenida España 344 (S)
- Restaurant El Rincón Cuyano, Sarmiento 394 (N)
- Restaurant Grill Sportman, Avenida Rawson 643 (S). Steakhouse
- Restaurant Jáchal, corner of Avenida I de la Roza (O) and Sarmiento. Steakhouse
- Restaurant La Estancia, corner of General Paz and A del Valle. Steakhouse
- Restaurant La Fusta, Avenida la Rioja
- Restaurant La Soprilla, corner of España (S) and Mitre. Steakhouse; credit cards accepted
- Restaurant Listo El Pollo, corner of Avenida San Martín and Santiago del Estero
- Restaurant Los Faroles, corner of Mendoza and Belgrano
- Restaurant Los Gorditos, Laprida 285 (E). Pizzeria
- Restaurant Los Paraisos, San Martín 1101 (E). Grill
- Restaurant Mi Vieja Bodega, Avenida España 186 (S)
- Restaurant Nogaro, I de la Roza 132 (E)
- Restaurant Oviedo, San Martín 1101 (E)
- Restaurant Pa-Ma, corner of Avenida Rioja and M Moreno
- Restaurant Seul, San Martín 177 (O). Korean cuisine)
- Restaurant Un Rincón de Napoli, Rivadavia 175 (O) Pizzeria
- Restaurant Victoria, Mendoza 422 (S)
- Restaurant Yafar, corner of España (S) and Rivadavia. Steakhouse
- ☞ Cafetería Amadeus Bar, corner of General Acha (S) and Rivadavia
- Cafetería Bon Jour, corner of Jujuy (S) and Rivadavia
- Cafetería Café de la Plaza, corner of General Acha (S) and I de la Roza
- Cafetería Café do Brazil, Mendoza 184 (S)
- ☞ Cafetería Capriccio, 9 de Julio 673 (E)
- Cafetería El Águila, Mitre 20 (O)
- Cafetería Felipe, corner of General Acha (S) and Laprida
- ☞ Cafetería Forum, Rivadavia 478 (E)
- Cafetería Hamburgo, corner of Mendoza (S) and Laprida. Pool table
- Cafetería Hawaii, corner of General Acha and I de la Roza
- Cafetería Jack Pool, corner of Rivadavia and Tucumán
- ☞ Cafetería Karam, Santa Fé 84 (E)
- Cafetería La Casita del Suizo, Rivadavia 173 (E)
- Cafetería Los Douglas, corner of Tucumán (S) and Mitre. Open 24 hours during summer
- Cafetería Mathias, corner of Rivadavia and Entre Ríos
- Cafetería Monaco, corner of Tucumán and Libertador
- Cafetería Morgan, corner of San Martín and General Acha
- Cafetería Mitre 500, corner of Mitre and Aberastain
- Cafetería Morocco, corner of Rivadavia and Sarmiento
- Cafetería Pekos, corner of Rivadavia and Jujuy
- Cafetería Piccolo, corner of General Acha (S) and Mitre
- Cafetería Simbabwe, Mendoza 157 (N)
- Cafetería Star II, Rivadavia 358 (E)
- Chopería Alaska, Santa Fé 2 (E)

San Juan Province

🛏 Accommodation in San Juan

Hotel bookings: Hotel Termas de Pismanta, Sarmiento 24 (S) ℓ 224466.

★★★	Hotel Nogaro, Ignazio de la Roza 132 (E)	ℓ 227501	$23.00	🛉
★★	Hotel Alhambra, General Acha 180 (S)	ℓ 228280	$10.00	🛉
★★	Hotel Lido, 9 de Julio 429	ℓ 211825	$11.00	🛉
★★	Hotel Plaza, Sarmiento 344 (S)	ℓ 225179	$10.00	🛉
★★	Hotel Provincia, Mitre 31 (E)	ℓ 225122	$10.00	🛉
	10% discount for ACA members			
★★	Hotel Selby, Rioja 183 (S)	ℓ 224777	$10.00	🛉
★	Hotel América, 9 de Julio 1052 (E)	ℓ 222514	$9.00	
	Near the bus terminal			
★	Hotel Brescia, España 336 (S) 🍴	ℓ 225708	$8.00	🛉
	Near the railway station. Known to the locals as "El Pepe"			
★	Hotel Bristol, Entre Ríos 368 (S)	ℓ 222629	$10.00	🛉
•	Hotel Petit Jardín, 25 de Mayo 345 (E)	ℓ 211825		
	10% discount for ACA members			
A	Residencial Embajador, Rawson 25 (S)	ℓ 225520, 221243	$6.00	🛉
A	Residencial Hispano Argentino, Estados Unidos 381 (S)		$5.00	🛉
	Near the bus terminal			
A	Residencial La Toja, Rivadavia 494 (E)	ℓ 222584	$7.00	🛉
A	Residencial Marsella, Sarmiento 8 (N)	ℓ 227195, 227196	$5.00	🛉
	Cheaper with shared bathroom			
A	Residencial San Francisco, España 284 (S)	ℓ 223760	$5.00	🛉
	Near the railway station			
B	Residencial Apolo, España 10 (S) 🍴		$4.00	🛉
	Has a pizzeria			
B	Residencial Austria, Sarmiento 234 (N)	ℓ 210274	$4.00	🛉
B	Residencial El Mendocino, España 344 (S) 🍴	ℓ 225930	$9.00	🛉🛉
	Near the railway station; cheaper with shared bathroom			
B	Residencial Favimon, Córdoba 2253 (E)	ℓ 250050		
B	Residencial Lara, Rivadavia 213 (O)	ℓ 227973	$4.00	🛉
B	Residencial Nueve de Julio, 9 de Julio 147 (O)	ℓ 222717	$7.00	🛉
B	Residencial Roy, Entre Ríos 182 (S)	ℓ 224391	$4.00	🛉
B	Residencial Sussex, España 402 (S) 🍴			
	Near the railway station; has a pizzeria			
•	Pension Central, Mitre 131 (E)	ℓ 223174	$5.00	🛉
	Shared bathroom			
•	Pension La Alemana, Cordoba 193 (E)	ℓ 228606	$3.00	🛉
•	Pension Las Vegas, Puerredón 603 (S)	ℓ 220261		
•	Pension Moreno, General Acha 633 (S)	ℓ 222988	$6.00	🛉
	Often still known by its earlier name, "Mon Petit Hotel". Cheaper with a shared bathroom			
•	Pension Tajamar, Jujuy 45 (N)	ℓ 213871	$6.00	🛉🛉

- Chopería Matias, corner of Rivadavia (O) and Entre Ríos
- Fast food: Carlitos, corner of General Acha 84 (S) and Laprida
- ☞ Snackbar: El Clavel, corner of Santa Fé (O) and Mendoza
- Snackbar: Equus, corner of Mitre (O) and Sarmiento

Eating out in the suburbs

- Restaurant Ausonia, I de la Roza 2174 (O)

San Juan

San Juan Province

- Restaurant Don Tristan, San Martín 5057 (O). Grill
- Restaurant El Fortin, Ruta 20 Km 5. Grill
- Restaurant Hostería de Zonda, Parque Rivadavia
- Restaurant Kincho Dorado, corner of Avenida de Circunvalación (S) and I de la Roza
- Restaurant La Fusta, corner of Avenida La Rioja and A Tapia. Grill
- Restaurant Las Cubas, corner of San Martín and Moreno. Grill
- Restaurant Lawn Tennis Club, Felix Aguilar 76 (N)
- Restaurant Las Palmeras, corner of Juan Jufre and Tucumán. Grill
- Restaurant Rancho II, San Martín 1665 (O). Grill
- Restaurant Rancho Grande, corner of Acceso Sur and RP 40. Grill
- Restaurant Wiesbaden, corner of Avenida Circunvalavión and Libertador

Post and telegraph

- Central post office: Encotel, I de la Roza 259 (E)
- Telephones: Compañía Argentina de Telefonos, General Acha 29 (S)

Financial

- Banco Popular Argentino, corner of General Acha and B Mitre. Cash advances on Visa card
- Cambio Cash, Tucumán 210 (S) ℂ 223450
- Cambio Santiago, General Acha 52 (S) ℂ 212132
- Casa de Cambio Bolsa de Comercio, corner of General Acha (S) and I de la Roza. Open 0830–1330

Services and facilities

- Bakery: Mauri, corner of Santa Fé (E) and Tucumán
- Cardiac emergency hospital: Caseros 160 (S) ℂ 226088
- Delicatessen: Casa del Jamón, Rivadavia 472 (E)
- Dry cleaner: Lavaseco de San Juan, Laprida 685 (E)
- Hospital: Hospital Rawson, corner of Rawson and General Paz
- Laundromat: Laverap, Rivadavia 499
- Pharmacy: Farmacía Central, San Martín block 100 (E) (corner of General Acha)
- Supermarket: Tilbas, Mendoza 279 (S)

Clubs

- German: Goethe Institut, Santa Fé 114 (E)
- Italian: Sociedad Italiana Dante Aleghieri, España 70 (S)

Motoring

RP 40 between San Juan and Mendoza runs for the most part in a straight line and is in excellent condition.
The road to La Rioja, RP 141 and 150, via San Agustín del Valle Fértil has been improved.

Service stations

- ACA, corner of General Acha 667 (S) and 9 de Julio
- ACA, corner of 9 de Julio 113 (E) and Rawson

Trains

F C General San Martín station is on Avenida España block 200 (S)

- Buenos Aires: Sleeper $39.80, Pullman $31.00, first class $20.50, tourist class $15.20; 19 hours
- Mendoza: Pullman $4.00, tourist class $2.00; 3 hours

Tours

- Yafar Turismo, Aberastain 102 (S) ℂ 226176

Shopping

- Mercado Artesanal, 25 de Mayo 1215 (O)
- Mercado de las Pulgas ("Flea Market"), corner of Plaza Laprida and San Martín

Sport

- Bowling alley: Bowling San Juan, Laprida 34 (O)

Entertainment

- Cabaret Tiffany's, corner of Laprida and Aberastain

Plate 25
Map of San Juan Province

Plate 26

Top: Valle de Calingasta, near Barreal
Bottom left: Colonial spa building, Puente del Inca
Bottom right: Main plaza, San Juan

San Juan Province

- Cabaret Le Baron, corner of Laprida and Navarro
- Casino de San Juan, Libertador San Martín 862 (O)
- Disco Alberto, corner of Laprida and Entre Rios
- Night Club Poka Toc, corner of Avenida San Martín and Marquezado
- Night Club Rogelio, corner of Avenida San Martín and Marquezado
- Night Club Samoa, Sarmiento 46 (S)
- Night Club Saudades, at the southern exit to RP 40
- Night Club Siroco, corner of Avenida I de La Roza and Rivadavia
- Night Club Sortilege, corner of Cano and A Tapia
- Tango Club, corner of Mendoza and San Luis

Sightseeing

- Casa Natal de Domingo F Sarmiento (Birthplace of Domingo F Sarmiento), Sarmiento 21 (S): Innumerable memorabilia of this great man are well exhibited in about ten rooms, including archives and furniture of the period
- Museo Arqueológico La Laja (La Laja Archeological Museum): Located in the suburb of Albardón, 10 km from the city center across the Río San Juan, on the corner of La Laja and Sarmiento. The mummies on exhibit come from Cerro Los Morillos and Cerro Del Toro. There are frequent municipal buses
- Museo de Ciencias Naturales (Natural Sciences Museum, corner of San Martín and Catamarca: Open daily 0830–1230 and 1530–1930. Admission $0.15
- Centro Cultural de San Juan (San Juan Cultural Center), General Acha 737 (E): Exhibition of paintings and sculptures by Argentinian artists
- Museo Geográfico Einstein (Einstein Geographical Museum), Túnel de Zonda, Municipalidad de Rivadavia
- Convento de Santo Domingo (Dominican Convent), corner of Avenida del Libertador and Entre Rios
- Parque de Mayo, San Martín (past the railroad line): This park is an oasis in the middle of town with an artificial lake

Air services from San Juan

Airport Chacritas, is 14 km south-west off RN 20 ℂ 250486.
- Aerolineas Argentinas, Mendoza 468 (S) ℂ 220205
- ALFA, Sarmiento 24 (S) ℂ 221212
- Austral Airlines, Entre Rios 219 (S) ℂ 227227

Destination	Fare	Depart	Services	Hours	Airline
• Buenos Aires (Aeroparque Jorge Newbery)					
	$71.00	0925	2 services daily	2	Aerolineas, Austral
• Córdoba	$35.00	2035	daily	1	Aerolineas
• Mendoza	$10.00	1220	Sun	½	Federal
• Resistencia	$53.00	1620	Sun	4	Federal
• San Miguel de Tucumán					
	$40.00	1620	Sun	2	Federal
• San Rafael	$20.00	1220	Sun	1½	Federal

San Juan Province

🚌 Buses from San Juan

The bus terminal is on the corner of Estados Unidos 492 (S) and General Paz. Cotal runs buses to Resistencia, Posadas, and Puerto Iguazú, departing at 0930 on Tues and Sat.

Destination	Fare	Depart	Services	Hours	Company
• Angualasto					Empresa Iglesia
• Bahía Blanca		1430	daily		TICSA
• Barreal	$3.50	0700	daily		TAC
• Buenos Aires	$22.60	2200	daily	16	Rojas, Auto Transportes San Juan
• Calingasta	$2.50	0700	daily	5	TAC
• Chepes	$4.50				La Estrella
• Chilecito	$11.00	0900	daily except Mon	9	TAC
• Córdoba	$14.40	1130	3 services daily		Socasa
• Corrientes		0930	Tues, Sat		COTAL
• Iglesia	$4.50	0720	Mon, Wed, Fri	4	Empresa Iglesia
• Ischigualasto	$4.60	0730	2 services daily	6	Expreso Valle Fértil
• La Rioja	$10.80	0930	3–4 services daily	7	COTAL, La Estrella, T A Libertador
• La Serena (Chile)	$22.00	0800	Fri	24	Covalle
• Mar del Plata	$26.80	0730	Wed, Sat		Auto Transportes San Juan
• Mendoza	$3.50	0600	11 services daily	2	COTAL, Del Sur y Media Agua, TAC, T A Libertador
• Rosario	$19.00	1530	daily		Del Sur y Media Agua
• San Agustín del Valle Fértil	$4.00	0730	2 services daily	5	Expreso Valle Fértil
• San Fernando del Valle de Catamarca	$12.20	0930	2–3 services daily	2	COTAL, La Estrella
• San José de Jáchal	$3.50	0700	4–5 services daily	2	TAC
• San Luis		1300	3–4 services daily		Auto Transportes San Juan, Del Sur y Media Agua, Rojas, TICSA
• San Miguel de Tucumán	$16.50	1540	2 services daily		La Estrella
• Santa Rosa		1430	daily		TICSA
• Santiago del Estero	$40.00	0930	1–3 services daily	14½	COTAL, TA Libertador
• Termas de Río Hondo		2210	daily	16	T A Libertador
• Uspallata	$7.80	0700	Fri		TAC
• Villa Dolores	$6.20			6	Expreso 20 de Junio
• Villa Unión	$8.50	0900	Tues, Wed, Fri–Sun		TAC

(where you can hire a boat), and a soccer stadium for 10 000 spectators

🍀 Excursions

- **Difunta Correa**: A Catholic shrine at Vallecito, 61 km eastwards on RP 141. See Difunta Correa on page 496

SAN JUAN PROVINCE

- **Paso del Agua Negra**: The road over the pass to La Serena in Chile has been closed by the Chileans, but as you approach the border the mountain scenery is superb.
- **Calingasta** and **Barreal**: Leave San Juan on the Avenida Ignacio de la Roza, which becomes RP 20. Just before Zonda is the seismological institute. The road passes the **Gran Presa de Embalse Quebrada**, and from here onwards the road winds its way up through the narrow and picturesque **Río San Juan valley**. After crossing the **Río Saisa** the valley widens. The slopes of the mountains are bare except for a type of round cactus. Where the **Río Uruguay** joins the Río Saisa there is a brief glimpse of snow-covered mountains on the left-hand side. For long stretches the road consists of only one lane; for this reason the road is open to traffic ascending westwards 0600–1200, and from 1200–1800 it is open to traffic descending eastwards, but from 1800 onwards it is open to traffic in both directions. From Río Uruguay onwards the road becomes patchy and bumpy with a bad spot at Km 95 where it has been destroyed by landslides. The highest point is the **Portezuelo El Tambor** at 1050 m. From here the road descends to the valley floor. After the small township of **Pachaco** (where there is an *hostería*), the valley narrows considerably. The river flats are covered with waist-high shrubs. There are bauxite mines in the district. Gradually the snow-capped **Cordillera de la Totora** comes into view. Outside Calingasta is an ACA service station. Calingasta is located on the **Río de los Patos**; see Calingasta on page 495. About 4 km outside town on the Barreal side is the Hotel Minar. From **Tamberías** onwards you can catch occasional glimpses of **Cerro Aconcagua** on the right-hand side. You can visit on foot the archeological site of **Cerro Hilario**, where there are remains of an Incan *tamberia* or runners' staging post. From here onwards is magnificent mountain scenery set in orchards and vineyards which continue to Barreal; see Barreal on page 494. The mountain streams are ice-cold and abound with trout and salmon.
- **Valle Fértil** and **Ischigualasto**: A guided tour costing $21.00 leaves at 0400 and returns at 2000. It includes a visit to the shrine **Difunta Correa** (see Difunta Correal on page 496 and Ischigualasto national reserve (also called Valle de la Luna); see "Excursions" in San Agustín on page 498. The trip returns to San Juan the same day
- **Huaco** and **Pismanta**: A guided tour costs $16.00. The highlight of this trip is the spa complex of Termas de Pismanta, 181 km north of San Juan; see Huaco on page 496 and Pismanta on page 497

San Juan

San Juan Province

- **Quebrada de Zonda**: Located only 17 km west of the city center, this 4 km long canyon is also known as Parque Rivadavia. In the middle of the valley's groves and meadows is a camping ground on the *estero* brook. The **Parque de los Poetas** forms part of the area. Nearby is a 3.2 km car-racing circuit. The mountain slopes are bare of growth
- **Angualasto** via **Pismanta**: Transporte Iglesias runs a daily service from the bus terminal. Angualasto is located on the former Inca road in the **Río Jáchal valley**, and the remains of a pre-Colombian settlement and of a *tambo* or runners' staging post can still be seen in the vicinity. There is also a monument to the Indian people. There is no accommodation here and archeology enthusiasts are advised either to camp out or to return to Pismanta, which has a hotel with a thermal spa. There is good fishing in the river. The bus leaves San Juan at 0745 and initially travels through flat countryside. At Talacasto is the turn-off north-west to RP 436. Twelve kilometers after the turn-off are the thermal springs of **Termas de Talacasto**, on the right-hand side of the road at the foot of **Cerro El Sapo**; there are no tourist facilities. The spring is situated at a height of 1150 m, and the water temperature is 25 °C. The road gradually climbs up to the **Portezuelo del Colorado**, passing a flat area called **Pampa de Gualilan**. At the pass there are huts for the road maintenance crew, which can be used as shelter. From the pass there are splendid views of the snow-covered **Cordillera de Collanguil** in the distance. After the pass the road descends again and there is a long stretch of *salina* along the road. Then the valley widens, and the mountains on the western side become higher. It is very dry country. At **Las Flores** is an ACA service station with a cafeteria. Here is the turnoff to the Paso del Agua Negra and Chile, RP 150. Not far away on the left-hand side are the **Termas de Centenario**, hot springs with no facilities. The large Pismanta spa complex comes into sight; see Pismanta on page 497. Accommodation is available in the little town of **Rodeo**, 12 km further up the valley; see Rodeo on page 497. From the turn-off up the **Río Jáchal** the road deteriorates considerably
- **Ischigualasto** (also called Valle de la Luna): Located 75 km north of San Agustín del Valle Fértil; see "Excursions" in San Agustín on page 498

SAN LUIS PROVINCE

Plate 27 Map of San Luis Province
- 510 Balde
- 511 Carolina
- 511 Concarán
- 511 Cruz de Piedra
- 512 El Volcán
- 512 Hipólito Yrigoyen
- 512 La Toma
- 513 Mercedes
- 514   Map
- 515 Merlo
- 516   Map
- 519 Potrero de los Funes
- 520 Quines
- 520 Renca
- 520 San Francisco del Monte de Oro
- 521 San Gerónimo
- 521 San Luis
- 522   Map
- 525 Santa Rosa del Conlara
- 526 Tilisarao
- 526 Trapiche
- 526 Villa Elena

San Luis Province

San Luis Province

When entering San Luis province from the east, and even more so from the south, the first impression is that of a desert. However, on closer look we discover that the province is dotted with some 200 lakes in the far south and has some very high mountains in the north interspersed with lovely valleys and palm groves. The climate is enjoyable all year round.

San Luis is not a very rich province: some cattle farms, orchards, and market farming are the agricultural activities. Few mineral deposits are worked. San Luis is, however, a major producer of onyx which is used for production of ornamental objects.

Landlocked San Luis shares borders with La Pampa in the south, Mendoza in the west, San Juan in the north-west, La Rioja in the north, and Córdoba in the east. Through the center stretches the **Sierra de San Luis** with **Cerro Tomolasta** the highest mountain at 2018 m. In the east it shares with Córdoba province the **Sierra de Comechingones**. Most of the rivers finish in salt lakes. Many dams have been constructed to preserve the precious water and these water storage dams attract many tourists for water sports and fishing, mostly for *pejerrey*.

One of the most pleasant resorts is located on **Lago Cruz de Piedra** with the four star Hotel Potrero de los Funes on its shores. San Luis also has many thermal springs, the best known being in **Balde** and **San Gerónimo**, both of which have small hotels.

The major tourist areas are the capital, San Luis city, the surrounding region, and the northeastern part near Córdoba province at the foot of the **Sierra de Comechingones**. There the city of **Merlo**, which boasts a unique microclimate, is particularly popular.

San Luis province was founded and settled from the Chilean part of the Spanish empire.

In colonial days it was renowned for its gold production. A substantial archeological site is situated near **Inti Huasi** where the Michilingue culture once flourished, and rock paintings can be found in caves nearby.

San Luis can easily be reached by road or plane from Buenos Aires, Córdoba, or Mendoza.

Balde

Postal code: 5724
Distance from San Luis: 34 km westwards on RN 7 then RP 15

Although Balde is located in arid country, it has thermal water which emerges at 43°C and has medicinal properties.

Accommodation
A Hostería Termas de Balde ⒣ $5.00 ⚑.
  Thermal water

SAN LUIS PROVINCE

🚍 Buses
Buses run regularly to San Luis.

CAROLINA

Postal code: 5757 • Altitude: 1610 m
Distance from San Luis: 84 km northwards on RP 20 then RP 9

Carolina is located in the mountainous part of San Luis in the central north. It is perched against **Cerro Tomolasta**, at 2018 m the highest mountain in the province. It was founded in 1792 by the Marqués de Sobremonte, and during colonial times was an important gold mining center. Some of the underground mines can be visited and even today the locals pan the rivers for gold.

🛏 Accommodation outside Carolina
A Hostería Las Verbenas, Valle de Pancanta ⑪ $7.00 ⓘ. 13 km south of Carolina on RP 9

🚍 Buses
Buses run regularly to San Luis, and also along the scenic drive to San Francisco del Monte de Oro.

♣ Excursions
- **Gruta de Inti Huasi**: About 28 km east. The center of an important prehistoric culture; traces of human habitation there go back 8000 years. It is in a very picturesque mountainous area

CONCARÁN

Postal code: 5770 • Altitude: 672 m
Distance from San Luis: 163 km northeast on RP 20, then eastwards on RP 10 and north-east on RN 148

Concarán is located in the north-eastern part of the province on the **Río Conlara**.

🛏 Accommodation
★ Hostería de Concarán 🅿🅰 ℂ 238 $6.50 ⓘ

🚍 Buses
Buses run regularly San Luis and Santa Rosa del Conlara.

CRUZ DE PIEDRA

Postal code: 5701 • Altitude: 915 m
Distance from San Luis: 16 km north-east on RP 20

Cruz de Piedra is located on the artificial lake of the same name.

🛏 Accommodation
★ Hotel Cabaña de San Francisco ⑪

🚍 Buses
Buses run regularly to San Luis.

♣ Excursions
- **Potrero de los Funes**, passing through the **Quebrada de los Cóndores**, a narrow and picturesque gorge. See Potrero de los Funes on page 519

SAN LUIS PROVINCE

EL VOLCÁN

Postal code: 5409 • Altitude: 915 m
Distance from San Luis: 17 km north-east on RP 20

El Volcan is located on the artificial lake **Cruz de Piedra**, in an area renowned for century-old walnut groves.

Accommodation
★ Hotel Villa Andrea ⚑ (23860 $8.50
A Residencial El Puente ⚑ $5.50

Camping
- El Volcán
- Río Volcán

Eating out
- Restaurant Villa Andrea, Hotel Villa Andrea

Buses
Buses run regularly to San Luis.

Sport
There are swimming, fishing, and boating in the artificial lake.

Excursions
- Estancia Grande and El Durazno are farms which date from the colonial period and are found in the mountainous country around **Cerro Quijada**, whose height is 1640 m.

HIPÓLITO YRIGOYEN

Postal code: 5703 • Altitude: 803 m
Distance from San Luis: 74 km northwards on RP 3, via Villa de la Quebrada

Hipólito Yrigoyen is located on the western slopes of the **Sierras de San Luis**. It is also known by its earlier name of Nogolí.

Accommodation
A Hostería 17 de Octubre ⚑ $3.00

Buses
Buses run regularly to San Luis.

Excursions
- **Laguna Brava** and hikes into the valleys around **Cerro Barroso**, 1905 m high

LA TOMA

Postal code: 5750 • (area code: (0655) • Altitude: 892 km
Distance from San Luis: 84 km north-east on RP 20

La Toma is the center of the green onyx polishing industry. This semiprecious stone is found in the nearby hills.

Accommodation
- Hotel Gran Italia
★ Hostería La Toma ⚑ $6.50
A Residencial El Indio (92 $5.50
- Residencial Days, Graciarena 158

Services and facilities
- Laundromat: Laverap, corner of Belgrano and RN 20

Buses
- Villa Dolores: Fare $2.50; Empresa Sierras Córdoba

San Luis Province

🛍 Shopping

La Toma is the cheapest place to buy green onyx, which is mined locally.

🌵 Excursions

- **Cerros del Rosario**, 1450 m: 16 km north-west
- **San José del Morro**: 28 km eastwards on RP 10 then southwards on RN 148. Located in the **Sierra del Morro**. The highest mountain is **Cerro Alumbre**, which is 1639 m high and of volcanic origin. Rose quartz is found here

MERCEDES

Postal code: 5730 • ✆ area code: (0657) • Altitude: 515 m
Distances
- From San Luis: 94 km south-east on RN 7
- From Buenos Aires: 693 km westwards on RN 7

Mercedes, also known as Villa Mercedes, is located in the east of the province, near Córdoba province. About 65 km beyond Mercedes towards San Luis the rolling hills typical of San Luis begin and further towards San Luis are stretches of woodland.

A railroad line runs northwards to Villa Dolores in Córdoba province.

🛎 Services and facilities

- Laundromat: Laverap, Pringles 126

✈ Air services

Villa Reynolds airport is 10 km from the town center.
- Buenos Aires: Departs 1025 Mon, Wed, Fri; Austral

🚌 Buses

- Buenos Aires: Fare $20.00
- Mendoza: Fare $6.50; Empresa TAC

🚗 Motoring

- Service station: ACA, RN 7 Km 689

🚆 Trains

F C General San Martín station is on Aviador Origone at the intersection of Avenida Mitre. There is also a line to Río Cuarto in Córdoba province.
- Buenos Aires: "El Aconcagua"; first class $12.20; departs 2224 daily; 10 hours
- Mendoza: "El Aconcagua"; first class $4.20; departs 0728 daily; 7 hours

🛏 Accommodation in Mercedes

★★	Hotel Centro, Junín 46	✆1212	$14.00	
★★	Hotel Piero, Junín 85	✆2256	$14.00	
★★	Hotel San Martín, Lavalle 435	✆2358	$14.00	
★	Hotel Bonino, Avenida Mitre 1701	✆1720	$11.00	
★	Hotel del Sol, corner of Ruta 7 and Las Heras	✆1320	$13.50	
★	Motel El Fortín Parque Hotel, corner of RN 7 and Calle 148	✆1805	$14.00	
★	Hotel Lavalle, Lavalle 417	✆1442	$13.50	
★	Hotel Lincoln, España 207	✆2812	$13.50	
★	Hotel Libertador, Pedernera 990	✆2930	$11.00	
A	Hotel Printz, Avenida Mitre 1169	✆2935	$11.00	
A	Hotel Avenida, Avenida Mitre 1668	✆1248	$11.00	

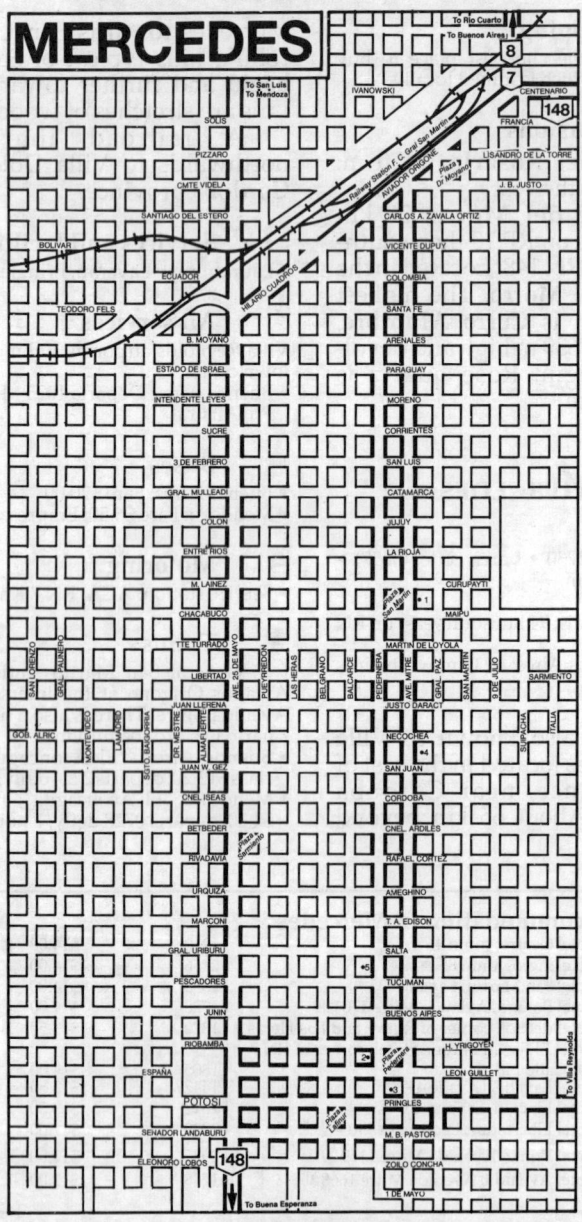

Mercedes

San Luis Province

Key to Map
1. Municipalidad
2. Iglesia San Roque
3. Post office (Encotel)
4. Telephone (Entel)
5. Banco de la Nación

- Villa Dolores: "Automotor"; departs 0745 Tues, Thurs, Sat; 5 hours

Merlo

Postal code: 5881 • Population: 5000 • area code: (0220) • Altitude: 900 m
Distances
- From San Luis: 196 km north-east on RP 20, then RP 10, RN 148, and RP 5
- From Córdoba: 245 km south-east on RN 14, then RN 148 and RP 5

Merlo is located in the north-eastern part of the province on the western slopes of the **Sierra de Comechingones**. It was founded by Captain Juan de Videla in 1797 by order of the governor of Córdoba, Marqués de Sobremonte. Merlo enjoys a microclimate which makes it a tourist mecca all year round. Its average annual temperature is 20°C, and it is moderately dry throughout the year. Its microclimate is caused by an excess of negatively charged ions over positively charged ions, and is confined to an area of 30 km by 3 km. Near **Rincón de Papagayos**, 35 km south, are *caranday* palm groves which are to be declared a national park.

Other areas of interest are **Villa Elena** to the south and **La Estanzuela**, formerly a Jesuit *estancia*, which was the home of Spanish general Marco del Pont, ex-President of Chile, until his death in 1821.

ℹ Tourist information
- Dirección de Turismo de Merlo, Coronel Mercau 605 (155. Open Mon–Sun 0800–1300 and 1500–2000
- Casa Merlo in Buenos Aires has information, and can make hotel bookings

▲ Camping
- Balneario Municipal, Avenida del Deporte 702
- Don Juan, El Rincón
- El Molino, El Rincón

🍴 Eating out
- Restaurant Casino, Avenida 2 Venados 1100. Grill
- Restaurant Clima, Hotel Clima Tres, Avenida del Sol 416
- Restaurant El Balneario, Avenida del Deporte 702
- Restaurant El Dragón Rojo, P Becerra 547
- Restaurant Elefante Blanco, P Becerra 573
- Restaurant El Hornero, Avenida de Los Cesares 1456
- Restaurant El Sol, Avenida del Sol 137. Grill
- Restaurant Flamingo, Hotel Flamingo, Avenida Dos Venados 941
- Restaurant La Casona, Janson 101
- Restaurant Los Pinos Avenida de Los Cesares 1842
- Restaurant Parque, Hotel Parque, Avenida del Sol 821
- Restaurant Piedra Blanca, Avenida Norte. Grill
- Restaurant Plaza, España 58
- Cafetería Blue Moon, Coronel Mercau 677

San Luis Province

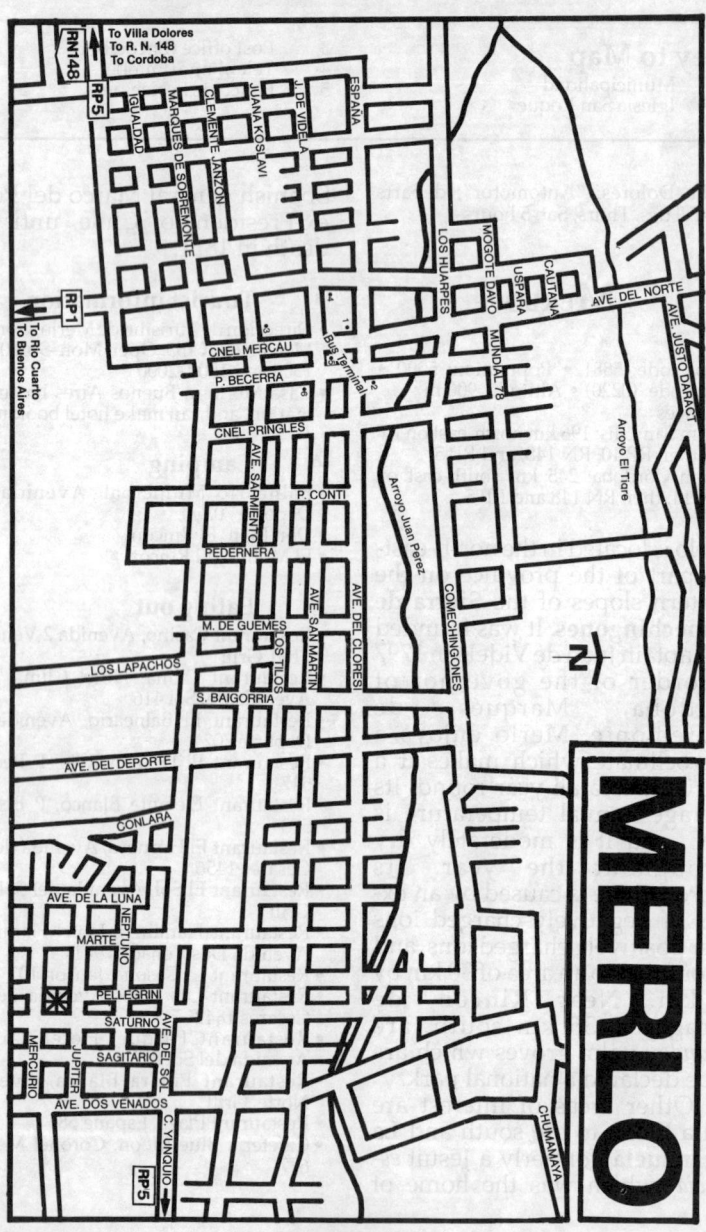

Merlo

San Luis Province

Accommodation in Merlo

★★	Hotel Clima Tres, Avenida del Sol 416	(197	$17.50	
★★	Hotel Flamingo, Avenida Dos Venados 941	(173	$17.50	
★★	Hotel Parque, Avenida del Sol 821	(110	$17.50	
★	Hotel Casablanca, Avenida del Sol 50	(384	$12.50	
★	Hotel Contilo, corner of Conti and Los Tilos	(293	$11.00	
★	Hotel San José, Avenida Dos Venados 698			
★★	Hostería El Hornero, Avenida Los Cesares 1456	(220	$15.00	
★	Hostería Bosque Alegre, Los Almendros 1008	(121	$ 4.50	
★	Motel 78, Avenida del Deporte 549	(195	$13.00	
A	Residencial Conlara, Avenida del Deporte 437	(183	$13.00	
A	Residencial La Argentina, Los Almendros 110		$8.50	
A	Residencial Malu, Avenida del Sol 51	(341	$4.00	
A	Residencial Plaza, J de Videla 49	(159		
B	Residencial Amancay, Avenida del Sol 500		$7.00	
B	Residencial Castelar, Avenida Comechingones 21 Shared Bathroom	(206	$9.50	
B	Residencial Mirasierras, Pedernera	(343	$7.50	
•	Residencial Piscu Yaco, Avenida Del Sol 231	187	$11.50	
•	Hospedaje Egle, P Lugones Shared bathroom; full board	(168	$10.50	
•	Hospedaje El Castaño, Avenida del Sol 584		$3.50	
•	Hospedaje La Llegada, Avenida Los Almendros 500	(205		
•	Hospedaje Oviedo, Coronel Mercau 795		$4.00	
•	Hospedaje Sierras Verdes, Avenida del Sol 458		$10.50	
•	Hospedaje Villegas, Avenida Los Cesares 1496			

Accommodation outside the city center

★★	Hotel El Cóndor, El Rincón	(103	$7.50	
★★	Hotel Piedra Blanca, Avenida de los Incas 3000, Piedra Blanca Full board	(226	$13.00	
★	Hotel El Rincón, El Rincón del Este			
A	Residencial Choay, Avenida Los Incas, Piedra Blanca	(317	$6.00	
B	Residencial Mercedes, El Rincón			
A	Residencial San Luis, El Rincón		$10.00	
•	Hospedaje El Molino, El Rincón			

Key to Map

1. Municipalidad
2. Iglesia
3. Post office (Encotel)
4. Telephone (Entel)
5. Bus terminal
6. Banco Provincial

Merlo

San Luis Province

- Cafetería Crin, Capitán Juan de Videla 41
- Cafetería La Terminal, Pringles 533
- Cafetería Yungulo, Coronel Mercau 655
- Cafetería Montecarlo, Sarmiento 100
- Cafetería La Posada del Sol 2, Avenida del Sol 2. Pizzeria
- Country Club Chumamaya tourist complex, Avenida Dos Venados 900

Eating out outside the city center

- Restaurant El Manantial, Avenida de los Incas, Piedra Blanca. Grill
- Restaurant El Molino, Hospedaje El Molino, Rincón del Este
- Restaurant El Rincón, Hotel El Rincón, Rincón del Este
- Restaurant El Cóndor, Hotel El Cóndor, Rincón del Este

Post and telegraph

- Post office: Encotel, Coronel Mercau 579
- Telephones: Coop Telefónica Merlo, J de Videla 112

Services and facilities

- Delicatessen: Osmar, Poeta Agüero 503
- Laundromat: Laverap, Coronel Mercau 925
- Pharmacy: Farmacia Guadalupe, P Becerra 724
- Photographic supplies: Foto REI Postales, España 118
- Supermarket: Ceballos, Coronel Mercau 866

Clubs

- Casa de la Cultura, Poeta Agüero 380

Buses

Bus companies

- Chevallier
- ETAD
- TAC

Services

- San Luis: Fare $2.50; departs 0610 daily; Empresa Jocoli
- Villa Dolores: Fare $1.70; Empresa Sierras de Córdoba

Motoring

Service stations

- ACA, Poeta Agüero 391
- YPF, Avenida del Sol 307

Tours

- Turismo Merlo, Avenida Norte 1499

Shopping

The area is rich in semiprecious stones, which are cut and polished in the district.

- Carpets: M Ceballos, Coronel Mercau 971
- Onyx: Palmero, España 74
- Semiprecious stones: Casa de las Piedras, Avenida del Sol 51
- Wood carvings: Ver-Mer, Avenida del Sol 115

Sport

- Swimming: Municipal swimming pool, Avenida del Deporte 702
- Tennis: Club Casino Tenis, Poeta Agüero 1099, (106

Entertainment

- Bowling Blue Moon, Coronel Mercau 677
- Casino Dos Venados, Avenida Dos Venados 1300
- Cinema Fenix, P Becerra 729
- Disco Crash, Barrio Pellegrini
- Disco Piedras, Avenida Dos Venados
- Disco Privado, Los Lapachos
- Disco Vaipasse, El Rincón
- Disco Halloween, Avenida Norte
- Pool Godoy, J Videla 118
- Pool Robledo, P Becerra 768

Sightseeing

- Capilla de la Virgen del Rosario (Chapel of the Virgin of the Rosary): This chapel is older than the town itself and was completed in 1740. The walls of the chapel are nearly 1 m thick, and inside are pictures painted during the same era

Merlo

SAN LUIS PROVINCE

♣ Excursions

Some easy to medium mountain climbs can be made from Merlo.

For information on excursions from Merlo speak to Señor Miguel Angel Flores or Señorita Martha Quiñonez at the Dirección de Turismo, Delegación Merlo, Coronel Mercau 605.

- **El Rincón**: About 6 km east in the **Sierra de Comechingones** at 1500 m. Follow the **Río Molino** to arrive at the **Salto del Tabaquillo** (15 m). Near the small dam there is a camping ground, and it is possible to swim in the lake. Mountaineers can continue on a path to **Río El Manzano** and **Las Cañas** via **Cuesta El Mogote Bayo**. Both rivers are stocked with trout and there is a lot of birdlife
- **Pasos Malos**: 7 km north-east. You can walk to the **Cascada Olvidada** in 2 hours. It is surrounded by high mountains and there are scenic views from 1680 m. Mountaineers can continue to **Cerro de la Oveja** at 2350 m through the **Cuesta de Pasos Malos**
- **Cuesta de Cerro de Oro**: 5 km south. It leads to **Cerro Aspero**. There is a tungsten mine nearby
- **El Talar**: A natural beach 12 km south, near **Los Molles**
- **Villa Elena**: 20 km south is the turn-off to the east into the **Valle Cortadera** where there is a gorge with a clear mountain stream and forest
- **El Papagayo**: 43 km south. This exotic palm grove is located in the middle of the mountains. The locals produce artefacts from palm fibre

POTRERO DE LOS FUNES

Postal code: 5701 • Altitude: 985 m
Distance from San Luis: 18 km north-east on RP 20 then RP 18

Portrero de los Funes is located on the artificial lake of the same name, only a short distance from the provincial capital. Nearby is the **Quebrada de los Cóndores**. It is a holiday resort with excellent hotels.

⊟ Accommodation

★★★★ Hotel Potrero de los Funes ⏼⏼⏼ ☏ 23898 $20.00 ⁞
★ Hotel Fernando ⏼⏼ $10.00 ⁞
★ Motel Yunka Taky ⏼ $6.00 ⁞

⛺ Camping

- El Potrero ⏼⏼⏼

🍴 Eating out

- Hotel Fernando
- Hotel Potrero de los Funes
- Motel Yunka Taky

🚌 Buses

Buses run regularly to San Luis.

🏊 Sport

The artificial lake is excellent for *pejerrey* fishing, swimming, and sailing.

♣ Excursions

- **Quebrada de los Cóndores**: The road going through this

San Luis Province

narrow gorge was blasted out of the granite rocks. There is magnificent mountain scenery with vistas to the artificial lake and the surrounding mountains
- **Quebrada del León Colgado** ("Canyon of the Hanged Lion"): Can be reached on horseback. It has sweeping views to the west

QUINES

Postal code: 5711 • (area code: (0651) •
Altitude: 481 m
Distance from San Luis: 154 km northeast on RN 146

Quines is the center of date palm plantations in the extreme north. Five km south are the thermal springs of **Baños del Zapallar**.

Accommodation
★ Hostería de Quines

Buses
Buses run regularly to San Luis, and once a week to La Rioja.

RENCA

Postal code: 5775 • Altitude: 775 m
Distance from San Luis: 120 km northeast on RP 20 then RP 23

Renca is located on the **Río Conlara** on the eastern side of the **Sierra de San Luis**. It was founded in the early eighteenth century. In the old chapel is a picture of El Señor de Renca, which has been venerated by pilgrims from all over the country since the seventeenth century. Eleven km southwest is the **Lago San Felipe**.

Festivals
- Fiesta del Señor de Renca (Festival of the Lord of Renca): May 3

Camping
- Balneario de Renca
- Camping San Felipe: 13 km south on the eastern side of the lake

Sport
Swimming, fishing, and water sports in the lake.

SAN FRANCISCO DEL MONTE DE ORO

Postal code: 5705 • Altitude: 776 m
Distance from San Luis: 115 km northwards on RN 146

San Francisco del Monte de Oro is located in the wide valley of the **Río San Francisco** at the foot of the **Sierra de Michilingue**. The river divides the town: the southern half is the older part with narrow streets and colonial houses. Nearby is the narrow gorge **Quebrada de López** and **Balneario El Palmar**. Also worth a visit is **Punta del Agua**, with walnut plantations and gorges with crystal clear water. The house where Juan Domingo Sarmiento taught class at the age of 15 is a national shrine.

Potrero de los Funes

San Luis Province

🚌 Accommodation
★ Hostería San Francisco ⑪

🅰 Camping
- Camping Laguna Esteco, south of town

🚌 Buses
Buses run regularly to San Luis.

San Gerónimo

Postal code: 5719
Distance from San Luis: 26 km north-west on RP 147

San Gerónimo is located in a very dry zone. Its only tourist attraction is the strong thermal springs which help arthritis and rheumatic disorders.

🚌 Accommodation
A Hostería La Perseveranza ⑪ $3.00 ℹ. Thermal water
★ Hostería Termas de San Gerónimo ⑪ $5.00 ℹ. Thermal water

🚌 Buses
Buses run regularly to San Luis.

San Luis

Postal code: 5700 • Population: 87 000 • ☎ area code: (0652) • Altitude: 765 m
Distances
- From Mendoza: 264 km eastwards on RN 7
- From Mercedes: 98 km north-west on RN 7

San Luis, the capital of San Luis province, is located at the southern end of the **Sierra de San Luis**. It was founded in 1594 by José Jufre by order of the governor of Chile, Martín de Loyola. Despite its modern appearance it has retained a colonial aspect, particularly because of the low houses.

ℹ Tourist information
- Dirección de Turismo, corner of Avenida Quintana and Junín ☎ 23957

⑪ Eating out
- Restaurant El Circulo, Rivadavia 563
- Restaurant El Galeon, Gran Hotel San Luis, Quintana 470
- Restaurant El Polo, Avenida Quintana 352
- Restaurant Guay Curu, General Paz 882
- Restaurant La Cigueña, San Martín 729. Grill
- Restaurant La Nona, San Martin 743
- Restaurant La Porteña, corner of Junín and General Paz. Pizzas
- Restaurant Los Venados, corner of Colón and Bolívar
- Restaurant Michell, corner of Avenida Lafinur and Avenida España
- Restaurant San Antonio, corner of Avenida España and Ejercicio de los Andes
- Restaurant Suany, Bolívar 921
- Restaurant Terminal, at the bus terminal
- Restaurant Venezia, corner of Pringles and Chacabuco
- Restaurant Vitic, Pringles 1070
- Cafetería Aranjuez, corner of Pringles and Rivadavia
- Cafetería El Foro, corner of Rivadavia and 9 de Julio
- Cafetería Mastropiero, Pringles 820
- Cafetería Oba Oba, Junín 942
- Cafetería Ocean, San Martín 698
- Cafetería Palace Hotel, Rivadavia 657
- Cafetería Singara, Junín 952
- Pub Pippa's, corner of Avenida España and Chile

Eating out outside San Luis
- Restaurant El Chacho, RN 7 east. Grill
- Restaurant La Strega, RP 20 El Chorillo

San Luis Province

- Restaurant Las Palmeras, RN 7 east
- Restaurant Mi Rancho, corner of Falucho and RP 20. Grill
- Restaurant "801", RN 7 km 801. Grill
- Restaurant Piro's, RP 20 Puente Blanco. Grill
- Restaurant Viejo Mateo, RN 7 Km 795. Grill
- Drive in: El Chorrillo, RP 20, El Chorrillo
- Drive in: Braten, RP 20, El Chorrillo

Post and telegraph

- Post office: Encotel, corner of San Martín and Pedernera, on Plaza Pringles

Financial

- Casa de Cambio Ausonia Viajes, corner of Rivadavia and Ayacucho
- Casa de Cambio Gentour, corner of San Martín and Pedernera

San Luis

SAN LUIS PROVINCE

Key to Map
1. Municipalidad
2. Palacio de Gobierno
3. Catedral
4. Post office (Encotel)
5. Telephone (Entel)
6. Tourist information
7. Banco de la Nación
8. Aerolineas Argentinas
9. Hotel Dos Venados
10. Hotel Aiello
11. Hotel Gran San Luis
12. Hotel Regidor
13. Hotel Gran España
14. Hotel Castelmonte
15. Hotel Gran Palace
16. Hotel Huarpes
17. Hotel Mitre
18. Residencial Iguazú
19. Residencial Buenos Aires
20. Residencial Conlara
21. Residencial Los Andes
22. Residencial Royal
23. Residencial Casablanca
24. Residencial Royal
25. Residencial 17
26. Residencial San Antonio
27. Convento Santo Domingo
28. Residencia Rivadavia

Accommodation in San Luis

There are cheap hotels in the vicinity of the bus terminal.

★★★	Hotel Aiello, Avenida Quintana 431	25609	$17.00	
★★★	Hotel Dos Venados, corner of Avenida Sucre and República del Libano	22312	$17.00	
★★★	Hotel Gran San Luis, Avenida Quintana 470	25049	$17.00	
★★★	Hotel Regidor, San Martín 804	24756	$17.00	
★★	Hotel Gran España, Avenida Quintana 300	25051	$14.00	
★	Hotel Castelmonte, Chacabuco 769	24963	$13.00	
★	Hotel Cesar I, Falucho 163	24334	$8.00	
★	Hotel Comesa, Colún 657	22996	$11.00	
★	Hotel Gran Palace, Rivadavia 657	22059	$11.00	
★	Hotel Huarpes, Belgrano 1560	25597	$13.00	
★	Hotel Mitre, Mitre 1043	24599	$11.00	
★	Hotel Residencial Iguazú, Avenida Ejercito de los Andes 1582	22129	$9.00	
•	Hotel El Encuentro, corner of Ejercito de los Andes and España			
A	Residencial Buenos Aires, Buenos Aires 834	24062	$8.00	
A	Residencial Conlara, Mitre 1058	24453		
A	Residencial Grisel, Bolívar 321	23584	$7.00	
A	Residencial Los Andes, Ejercicio de los Andes 1180, near the bus terminal	22033	$6.00	
A	Residencial Rivadavia, Estado de Israel 1070, opposite the bus terminal	22437	$8.00	
B	Residencial Casablanca, Belgrano 1406	23206	$7.00	
B	Residencial 17, Estado del Israel 1475, opposite the bus terminal	23387	$7.00	
B	Residencial Royal, Colón 878	22022	$7.00	
B	Residencial San Antonio, corner of Ejercicio de los Andes and España		$7.50	

San Luis Province

🚌 Buses from San Luis

Municipal buses have a flat fare of $0.15.
The bus terminal is on the corner of España and Estado de Israel.

Destination	Fare	Depart	Services	Hours	Company
• Bahía Blanca		1922	Wed, Fri		TICSA
• Buenos Aires	$18.50				Colta
• Córdoba		0845	4 services daily		Colta, TAC
• La Rioja		0900	Fri		COTIL
• La Toma	$1.50	1400	daily		Dasso
• Mar del Plata		1150	Wed, Sat		Auto San Juan
• Mendoza	$7.00	0242	6 services daily		Expreso Jocoli, T A Villa María
• Merlo	$3.80	0610	3 services daily		Expreso Jocoli
• Paraná		0003	2 services daily		TAC, T A Villa María
• Rosario		2045	daily		TAC
• Salinas del Bebedero		0500	4 services daily		
• San Fernando del Valle de Catamarca	$16.00				
• San Juan		0145	1–3 services daily		Auto San Luis, Del Sur y Media Agua, Rojas, TICSA
• San Rafael	$5.60	1530	Fri		TAC
• Santa Fé		0003	4 services daily		Auto San Juan, Centro Argentino, TAC, T A Villa María
• Santa Rosa		1922	Wed, Fri		TICSA
• Villa Dolores	$5.00		several services daily		TAC

🗒 Services and facilities

- Dry cleaner: Rivadavia 978

Laundromats

- Laverap, Colón 624
- Laverap, Rivadavia 1036
- Laverap, Sucre 789

✈ Air services

The airport is 3 km from town and costs about $2.50 by taxi.

- Buenos Aires (Aeroparque Jorge Newbery): Fare $63.00; departs 1035 daily; 1 hour; Aerolineas

🚗 Motoring

- Service station: ACA, corner of Avenida Quintana and Constitución

🚆 Trains

- Buenos Aires: "El Aconcagua"; tourist class $10.20; departs 2006 daily; 12 hours
- Mendoza: "El Aconcagua"; tourist class $3.50; departs 0942 daily; 2 hours

⊕ Tours

- Dasso Viajes, Tomás Jofre 590 ☏ 25386; and at the bus terminal
- Pachacamac Viajes, corner of Colón and Pedernera. Minimum of eight passengers

🛍 Shopping

- Mercado de Artesanías Puntanas, RP 20 km 9, Chorillo. Pottery, blankets, wood carvings, leather goods. Open Mon–Sat 1000–1200 and 1900–2200, Sun 1000–1200

🎭 Entertainment

- Disco Boykot, RP 20, El Chorrillo

San Luis

San Luis Province

- Disco Flay, corner of Rivadavia and Belgrano
- Disco Jiakopos, Chacabuco 671 (corner of Pringles)
- Disco Selquet, RP 20, El Chorrillo
- Disco Zeus, RP 20, Cruz de Piedra

Sightseeing

On the hill overlooking the town is a *Via Crucis*. The Stations of the Cross are sculpted in white marble.

Excursions

Señorita Martini Yamile, at the Dirección de Turismo, is very helpful.

- **El Volcán**: Following RP 9 is a picturesque trip passing through **Cruz de Piedra**. Fishing is possible in the rivers and dams, and at **Cañada Honda** you can pan for gold. There are daily buses
- **La Toma**: 29 km north-east. The center of the onyx mining. There are day excursions with Empresa Dasso; fare $1.50
- **Carolina**: Full day round trip excursion to Carolina via **La Florida** dam, **Paso del Rey**, and **Gruta de Inti Huasi**. Here you can visit the old goldmine. Return through **Valle Pancanta** and **Los Tapiales**, where there is a monolith to Colonel Pringles. Tour fare: $9.00
- **Merlo**: Full day round trip excursion via **La Toma**, and **Villa Elena**. At Merlo there is a visit to the Capilla del Rosario; see also Merlo on page 515. Return via **Piedra Blanca** and **Rincón del Este**. Tour fare: $18.00
- **Salinas del Bebedero**: Half day excursion to the salt mines. Tour fare: $5.00
- **Hipólito Yrigoyen**: Half day round trip excursion via **Villa de la Quebrada**, where there is a visit to Señor de la Quebrada, and the *Via Crucis*, with a visit to Balneario. Return the same way. Tour fare: $4.00. See Hipólitio Yrigoyen on page 512

Santa Rosa del Conlara

Postal code: 5777 • area code: (0544) • Altitude: 605 m
Distance from San Luis: 194 km north-east on RP 10, then RP 20 and RN 148

Santa Rosa del Conlara is located in the north-western part of the province, on the border with Córdoba province.

Accommodation
★ Hostería Santa Rosa 012 $6.50

Buses
Buses run regularly to San Luis.

Trains
Santa Rosa del Conlara is on the rail line connecting Villa Dolores in Córdoba province with Mercedes. There are trains to Mercedes on Tues, Thurs, and Sat departing at 1700 and arriving at Mercedes at 2135 to link up with "El Aconcagua" departing at 2224 for Buenos Aires. Only first class fares available.

San Luis Province

Tilisarao

Postal code: 5773 • Altitude: 751 m
Distance from San Luis: 140 km north-east on RP 20 the RP 23

Tilisarao is located in the **Río Conlara valley** in the north-western part of the province.

Accommodation
★ Hotel Udine ⑪ ℂ 213 $4.50

Buses
Buses regularly to San Luis and to Villa Dolores in Córdoba province

Trapiche

Postal code: 5701 • Altitude: 1050 m
Distance from San Luis: 40 km north-east on RP 20 then RP 9

Trapiche is located in the **Sierra de San Luis** near the western end of **Embalse La Florida** in the **Río Quinto valley**. There are fishing and water sports on the lake. Trapiche lies in the heart of the Sierra de San Luis, with clear mountain streams and green valleys full of walnut trees. It is a good starting point for excursions to the surrounding area such as to **Río Grande**.

Accommodation
★ Hostería Los Sauces ⑪ $12.50
A Hostería El Trapiche $11.50
A Residencial El Ciervo $7.00
A Residencial La Cabaña de Johnny $11.50

Camping
- Camping Municipal
- Camping Schmid

Eating out
- Restaurant Hostería Los Sauces
- Restaurant Residencial La Cabaña

Buses
Buses run regularly to San Luis.

Excursions
- **Embalse La Florida**: Water sports
- Round trip to **Río Grande, Carolina, Inti Huasi,** and **Paso del Rey**, returning via **La Florida**

Villa Elena

Postal code: 5883
Distance from San Luis: 204 km north-east on RP 20, RP 10, and RN 148, then eastwards on RP 6 and northwards on RP 1

Villa Elena is located on the western slopes of the **Sierra de Comechingones**.

Accommodation
Hotel Villa Elena ⑪ $4.50
Hostería Magdalena ⑪ $5.00

Buses
Buses run regularly to Concarán and Merlo.

Tilisarao

North-Western Provinces

Catamarca Province

Plate 29 Map of Catamarca Province
- 531 Ancasti
- 531 Andalgalá
- 534 Antofagasta de la Sierra
- 536 Balcosna
- 536 Belén
- 540 Chumbicha
- 540 Concepción
- 541 El Alto
- 541 El Rodeo
- 542 Fiambalá
- 544 Hualfín
- 544 La Merced
- 545 Las Juntas
- 545 Londres
- 546 Pomán
- 546 Recreo
- 547 San Antonio
- 547 San Fernando del Valle de Catamarca
- 548   Map
- 554 San Isidro
- 554 Santa María
- 556 Tinogasta

CATAMARCA PROVINCE

Catamarca province is situated in the north-west of Argentina. The word "Catamarca" is derived from a Quechua word meaning "Fortress on the Slopes", and could well refer to any of the many pre-Columbian fortress-towns located in the **Sierra de Aconquija**.

The province is shaped like a tilted triangle. The border with Chile forms the western side; along the north-eastern side are Salta, Tucumán, and Santiago del Estero; while La Rioja lies along the south-western border.

The capital of Catamarca is **San Fernando del Valle de Catamarca**. Within Catamarca its name is generally abbreviated to "San Fernando", but outside Catamarca its name is often abbreviated to "Catamarca", particularly on public transport. It is well worth a visit.

The other main places of interest to tourists in this province are Andalgalá and Belén. Both are worth the detour involved in reaching them. Santa María and Tinogasta are also very interesting.

Catamarca is a province of contrasts: to the west along the border with Chile are some of the highest peaks in the Andean *cordillera*; to the east are fertile and productive valleys. The northern region is almost completely barren and covered with salt lakes such as **Salar de Antofalla**, **Salina de la Laguna Verde**, and, closer to the capital San Fernando, **Salar de Pipanaco**.

Catamarca has a dry climate and because of its low annual rainfall depends heavily on irrigation for its agriculture. Sheep and goats are the predominant farm animals.

The province's mineral wealth is considerable, but the deposits of copper, manganese, gold, and silver are not mined because of the lack of road connections and electricity. The Diaguitas were already using copper and gold to manufacture ornaments and utensils in pre-Incan times; around 1470 they came under Inca domination, and today they are almost extinct.

In the smaller villages hand weaving is still practised.

The road network and bus services are adequate, particularly in the eastern part of the province. Towards the Chilean border most roads are unsealed, and rivers are generally crossed by ford. During the spring thaw, roads in these distant regions are sometimes cut. Bus services into neighbouring provinces are good. Only San Fernando has connecting flights to and from other provinces.

Besides the capital, there are no large urban centres in Catamarca. Most towns are connected by roads, but there still are quite a number of outlying villages which can only be reached on horseback.

Catamarca province is still largely unexplored, and in the more remote areas you may well be the first European visitor.

Catamarca Province

When eating out, be aware that in Catamarca soup is served *after* the main course.

The main areas of tourist interest in the province are:
- Worth a visit: **San Fernando del Valle de Catamarca**
- Worth a detour: **Andalgalá** and **Belén**
- Very interesting: **Santa María** and **Tinogasta**

Pre-Hispanic culture

Catamarca is considered the cradle of most pre-Hispanic cultures in Argentina. Traces of two cultures which flourished in the paleolithic era—the Ampajango and Ayampín cultures—have been discovered in this region. These people were nomadic hunter-gatherers. The period known as the Early Pottery Era began in 500 BC and lasted until 550 AD, during which time llamas were domesticated the first urban centers established. The best examples of these settlements are at **Cóndor Huasi** and **Falda Ciénaga** in the department of Belén and **Alamito** in the department of Andalgalá. By the time the Ciénaga culture arose about 200 AD its people were already expert metalworkers. From around 600 AD until 900 AD the Aguada culture flourished. The Santa María culture began around 950 AD in the **Río Yokavil valley**, and soon spread over the whole Calchaqui area, encompassing large areas of Tucumán province and the southern part of Salta province. These were very warlike people who in effect led the 1643 uprising against the Spanish. They were defeated and the vanquished population was forcibly resettled in small groups in Cordoba and Buenos Aires provinces. In pre-European times the Incas had used a similar strategy against unruly or recently-conquered tribes, and the Spanish adopted it from them. In recent years some of the pre-Incan cities which were abandoned in this way have been restored, such as **Quilmes** in Tucumán province. Other archaeological sites from the Santa María culture are **Loma Rica**, **La Paya**, and **Punta de Balasto**. As well as being fine potters these people were also expert metallurgists and metalworkers, as were the people of the Belén culture which flourished at about the same time.

The **Nevados del Aconquija** ranges contain several pre-Columbian towns, some of which have barely been explored. The best known is **Las Chacritas** near Buena Vista; there are others in the **Río Calchaqui valley**.

Thermal springs

There are hundreds of thermal springs in Catamarca, most of them with therapeutic properties, but very few with tourist facilities. A list of the most important follows; none has any facilities.

Catamarca Province

Ambarto department
- **Agua de la Puerta**

Andalgalá department
- **Nacimiento del Río Alumbrera** (or "Source of the Alumbrera River")
- **Vis-Vis**

Belén department
- **Cura Fierro**
- **Dionisio**
- **La Colpa**
- **Llampa**
- **Villa Vil**
- **Ojo Dulce de Choya**
- **Salada de Choya**

Capayán department
- **Agua de Coneta**
- **Agua Blanca**

Capital department
- **El Carrizal**
- **El Jumeal**

Fray Mamertu Esquiú department
- **Aguaditas de San José**

Paclín department
- **El Rosario**

Santa Rosa department
- **Termas Lavalle**

Tinogasta department
- **Baño de Higueritas**
- **Nacimientos de Hualfín**
- The impressive **Termas de Fiambalá**

ANCASTI

Postal code: 4701
Distance from San Fernando del Valle de Catamarca: 85 km southwards on RP 13 then RP 2

Located on the eastern side of the **Sierra de Ancasti** in attractive surroundings, Ancasti was founded by Don Pedro Pablo Acosta in 1735. The town has many orchards, and *pejerrey* fishing is popular in the nearby **Dique Ibizca**.

Festivals
- Festival of the Patron Saint: December 24

Accommodation
- Hostería de Turismo de Ancasti $5.00 **i**. Shared bathroom

Excursions
- **Lago Ibizca**: 20 km south. Swimming and fishing in the dam
- Jesuit ruins of **Ancastillo**: 48 km east
- **Anquincila**: 10 km north. Archeological site

ANDALGALÁ

Postal code: 4740 • Altitude: 962 m
Distances
- From San Fernando del Valle de Catamarca via Chumbicha: 250 km north-west on RN 25 then RN 38
- From San Fernando del Valle de Catamarca via Singuil: 195 km north-west on RP 1 then RP 65
- From Belén: 85 km eastwards on RP 46

Andalgalá

CATAMARCA PROVINCE

- From Santa María via Capillitas: 140 km southwards on RP 47. Very scenic but a bad road

Located at the foot of the **Nevado del Candado** (5450 m), Andangalá's origins go back to 1658 when General Don Francisco de Nieva y Castilla established a fort here as a base from which to fight rebellious Indians in the region. It is the second largest city in Catamarca.

The climate is pleasant throughout the year. The maximum temperature in summer is 42C, and the average minimum temperature in winter is 4C.

A variety of wildlife still lives in the nearby mountains: marmots in the higher reaches, mountain cats, *vizcachas*, condors, mountain turkey, deer, and the occasional puma.

The area produces olive oil and walnuts, and aniseed in Chaquiago 3 km north of Andangalá. There are rich mineral seams in the Aconquija chain, and in the nearby Minas Capillitas manganese, silver, and copper are mined. The semiprecious stone rhodochrosite (known as "Rosa del Inca") is also found. Some logging and forestry are carried out.

Festivals

Catamarca province has a very strong folk tradition.
- Fiesta del Fuerte de Andalgalá (Festival of Andalgalá Fort): Early January

Accommodation

There is a shortage of good accommodation in Andalgalá.

- Hotel de Turismo Andalgalá, Avenida Sarmiento 35 $7.00 **i**. At the start of RP 25 south
- Hotel Galileo, Nuñez del Prado 757 (corner of Lopez) $5.00 **i**. Includes breakfast

Camping

- Autocamping Municipal La Aguada (near La Usina), is 3 km north of town on the banks of the Río Andalgalá, which flows all year round. To get to the grounds, go past the water treatment plant, and continue into the foothills of the **Nevado del Candado**

Eating out

- Restaurant Club Andalgalá, in the Plaza
- Restaurant Don Cacho, corner of Nuñez del Prado and San Martin
- Restaurant El Tío, corner of Belgrano (to the north of the Plaza) and Nuñez del Prado. Steakhouse
- Restaurant El Americano, Nuñez del Prado 348
- Restaurant Hotel de Turismo, Avenida Sarmiento
- Restaurant La Terminal
- Comedor Figueroa, Nuñez del Prado 778
- Cafetería El Aconquija, corner of Perez de Zurita and Belgrano
- Cafetería El Nevado, Nuñez del Prado 662 (on the Plaza)

Post and telegraph

- Post office: Encotel, corner of Rivadavia and Mercado
- Telephone: Entel, corner of Rivadavia and Perez de Zurita

Shopping

- Cut rhodochrosites (semiprecious stones)
- Carvings made from *cardon* wood
- Woven textiles and carpets

Sightseeing

- Museo Provincial de Arqueologia (Provincial Archaeology Museum), San Martín Sur

Andalgalá

CATAMARCA PROVINCE

🚌 Buses from Andalgalá

The bus terminal is in Barcena Oeste.
- Empresa Bosio runs a service from Andalgalá to San Fernando del Valle de Catamarca via Pomán and Chumbicha
- Empresa La Calera runs a service from Belén to San Fernando del Valle de Catamarca via Andalgalá
- Empresa Gutierrez runs a service from Tinogasta to San Miguel de Tucumán via Belén, Andalgalá, and Alpachiri
- Empresa Lazo runs a service from Andalgalá to San Fernando del Valle de Catamarca via Singuil

Destination	Fare	Depart	Services	Hours	Company
• San Fernando del Valle de Catamarca		1–3 services daily		6	Bosio, Lazo
via Saujil	$5.50	1000			Lazo
via La Puerta	$5.50		Tues, Thurs, Sat		Lazo
• Belén	$2.50	8000	Tues, Thurs–Sun	2½	Bosio, La Calera, Gutierrez
• Cerro Negro	$4.80	1325	Sat		Gutierrez
• Córdoba		1745	Wed, Fri, Sun		La Galera
• Londres	$3.00	1325	Tues, Sat	3½	Gutierrez
• San Miguel de Tucumán	$6.00	0800	Mon, Wed, Fri	7½	Gutierrez
• Santa María	$7.50	1120	Fri, Sun	7	Bosio
• Tinogasta	$6.00	1325	Sat	5½	Gutierrez

110 (on the south side of the town center, on the corner of Perez de Zurita). This museum contains many items from the pre-Columbian cultures which flourished in the area
- Museo Arqueologico Malli (Malli Archaeological Museum), southern extension of San Martín, in Malli district. This is a private museum

● Excursions

This area is very mountainous, and ideal for hiking. There are many thermal springs in the surrounding valleys.
- **Belén**: The road from Andalgalá to Belén becomes a dirt road soon after leaving town. For most of the way it skirts the edge of the mountain range to the north, and the **Salar de Pipanaco**. All river crossings are by ford and roads may be cut off when the rivers flood during spring. The mountains are covered in shrubs. A signpost indicates the turn-off into the **Valle Amanao**, in the upper part of which are hot springs. Springs such as these are common throughout these ranges, most of them being in the vicinity of the **Farellón Negro** copper mine. As the road follows the edge of the mountain range the slopes become bare, with only a few cacti surviving on the hills. Small armadillos can be seen hiding as the bus approaches. Near the **Río Pozo** the road climbs a small pass known as **Cuesta de Belén**, at an elevation of 1140 m,

Andalgalá

where eagles live. Descending again into flat country the road fords many small rivers which emerge from the mountains only to disappear into the Salar de Pipanaco. In the distance the **Sierra de Belén** and the **Sierra de Fiambalá** come into view. Just before **La Puntilla** the sealed road starts again, more farm houses appear, and as a result of extensive irrigation the countryside turns green again. Almost abruptly the road reaches the bridge crossing over the **Río Belén**. Here the valley is very wide, and the town of Belén is located on the western bank of the river. A huge statue of the Virgin is erected on a hill overlooking the town

- **Salta**, via **Antofagasta de la Sierra** and **San Antonio de los Cobres**: The adventurous with their own transport can do the complete trip over the *altiplano*, turning eastwards off the **Puerta de Corral Quemado** 13 km before Hualfín. Hualfín is your last chance to fill up with gas for this gruelling 600 km stretch. Before undertaking this trip check with bus drivers at Andalgalá about road conditions to Antofagasta de la Sierra, and again with the locals at Antofagasta before continuing further north. The road is more than 3000 m high and the nights are cold. There are archeological sites en route at **Laguna Blanca** and **Falda Ciénaga**. See also Salta on page 626, and Antofagasta de la Sierra below

- **Capillitas**: 54 km north. A large mining camp, run by the military, Capillitas is one of the few places where the semiprecious stone rhodochrosite is found. It is possible to visit the mine, but authorization must be obtained from the Dirección General de Fabricaciones Militares. Not far from Capillitas are the hot springs of **Choya Ojo Dulce**, which emerge from the ground at a temperature of 19C. There are no tourist facilities here

- **Valle Amanao**: There are many hot springs about 14 km past Amanao, as well as further up the valley

- **Ojo Dulce de Choya**: Thermal springs on the road to Capillitas mine, at an elevation of 1300 m

- **Aguas Amarillas** ("Yellow Water"): These are mineral springs in the **Cañon Aguas Amarillas** (3000 m)

- **El Pucará**: 58 km eastwards

- The following mountain passes (*"cuestas"*) are within easy reach of Andalgalá: **La Chilca** (1933 m), **El Clavillo** (1846 m), and **Minas Capillitas** (3100 m)

- Other worthwhile excursions are into the **Cañon Chilca**, and to **El Potrero de Santa Lucia**

Antofagasta de la Sierra

Postal code: 4705 • Population: 900 • Altitude: 3 600 m
Distance from San Fernando del Valle de Catamarca: 540 km north-west

Catamarca Province

Antofagasta de la Sierra is located on the **Río Punillo** in the *altiplano*. It is the main township of the north-west, and in one of the most underdeveloped regions of Catamarca, if not Argentina.

Agriculture here is restricted to growing potatoes and some maize, and raising herds of alpaca and sheep.

This region was added to Catamarca by ministerial decree in 1943, when the previous Territorio de los Andes was dissolved and divided between the provinces of Catamarca and Salta. There are deposits of onyx, sulfur, and mica in the area, yet only a few mines are operating. The Mina Inca-Huasi is one such mine, extracting gold. There are also extensive salt lakes, most of which are only partially filled. **Salar del Hombre Muerto** and **Salar de Antofalla** are two examples. Most of the local rivers disappear into these salt lakes.

The inhabitants are descendants of the Diaguitas and speak a colloquial Spanish of their own. Although devout Catholics they see no contradiction in making offerings to their ancestral gods such as Pachamama, the earth goddess. Their dialect and customs distinguish them from the rest of the *Catamarqueños*, and make them more akin to their cousins in the *altiplano* in neighboring Salta, Jujuy, and even Bolivia.

The archeological heritage of this part of Argentina is considerable, and traces of life from the earliest stone-age period right through to the last days of the Inca empire have been found. The remoteness of the region has certainly helped to preserve most of these sites, most of which are inaccessible to the average tourist. Some of the outstanding sites are:
- **Gruta Salamanca**, with petroglyphs
- **Pucará de la Alumbrera**
- **Ruinas de Cayparcito**

Facilities here are very basic: Antofagasta de la Sierra has no hotel at all. Only private accommodation or *hospedajes* are available.

Accommodation
- Hospedaje La Florida. Shared bathroom
- Hospedaje Pipito. Shared bathroom
- Hospedaje Guzman. Shared bathroom
- Private accommodation: Díaz family. Shared bathroom
- Private accommodation: Mamani family. Shared bathroom
- Private accommodation: Vasquez family $7.00

Eating out
Most *hospedajes* also serve simple food for their lodgers.
- Bar Pipito

Buses
There is no bus route between Antofagasta de la Sierra and San Antonio de los Cobres in Salta province.
- Belén: $11.70; departs 0600 Sun; 12 hours; Empresa Bosio

Motoring services
- Service station: YPF

Antofagasta de la Sierra

CATAMARCA PROVINCE

Sport
- Fishing: There is good trout fishing in the Río Punilla and Río Calacaste. Trout up to 4 kg are not unusual

Excursions
- **Reserva Natural Laguna Blanca**: 100 km south. It covers an area of 900 000 ha, most of it above 3200 m. The area is classified as high-altitude desert. Most rain falls in summer, and winters are usually dry and extremely cold, with isolated snowfalls and strong winds
- The landscape around Antofagasta de la Sierra is dotted with salt lakes and there are many peaks over 6000 m. You can see pink flamingos on the salt lakes at certain times of the year. In the surrounding countryside *guanaco*, *vicuñas*, chinchillas, and foxes can also be spotted. The gold in the surrounding hills had already been mined before the Spanish arrived. This region is sparsely populated

BALCOSNA

Postal code: 4719
Distance from San Fernando de Catamarca: 95 km northwards on RP 1, via La Puerta

Balcosna is located in the department of Paclín. It is a popular resting point between San Fernando del Valle de Catamarca and San Miguel de Tucumán. You will sometimes see the name spelt "Balcozna".

Accommodation
- Hostería de Balcozna, in Las Lajas, on the outskirts of town $15.00

Buses
Daily buses run to Catamarca.

BELÉN

Postal code: 4750 • Population: 18 000 • Altitude: 1200 m
Distances
- From Andalgalá: 85 km westwards on RP 3
- From Santa María: 177 km south-west on RN 40

Belén is situated just inside the **Cañon Belén**, where the river emerges from the mountains and dissipates in the **Salar de Pipanaco**. It was founded in 1681 by the priest Bartolomé de Olmos y Aguilera. Overlooking the town is a statue of Nuestra Señora de Belén (Our Lady of Belén). From here there are views over the city, the gorge, and the beginning of the salt flats, where the river first splits up into smaller rivulets before disappearing. The surrounding district produces wine, pepper, and aniseed. The abundance of water from both rivers and irrigation makes this a lush area. Roads in the Cañon Belén may be cut off temporarily during the wet season in January and February.

Festivals
- Fiesta Nuestra Señora de Belén (Festival of Our Lady of Belén): December 20 to January 6

Antofagasta de la Sierra

Plate 27
Map of San Luis Province

Plate 28

Top: Chapel at Puente del Inca
Bottom: Natural arch and hot springs, Puente del Inca

CATAMARCA PROVINCE

🚌 Buses from Belén

The bus terminal is on the corner of Sarmiento and Rivadavia.

Destination	Fare	Depart	Services	Hours	Company
• San Fernando del Valle de Catamarca					
via Andalgalá	$8.50	1200	Tues, Fri, Sun	9	Bosio
via Aimogasta	$6.50	1200	daily	6	Bosio
• Andalgalá	$2.80	0600	Wed, Thurs, Sat, Sun	2	Bosio, Gutierrez
• Antofagasta de la Sierra	$11.70	0600	Fri	12	Bosio
• Concepción	$7.20	0600	Wed	8	Gutierriez
• Córdoba	$13.50	1600	Wed, Fri, Sun	13	La Calera
via Chumbicha and Déan Funes			5 services a week		La Calera
• Hualfín		1335	Tues, Fri, Sat	2	Bosio
• Londres	$0.50	several services daily		½	El Cóndor
• Salta		0600	Thurs	11	El Indio
• Santa María	$5.20	1300	Mon, Tues, Wed, Fri, Sun		Cayetano
• San Miguel de Tucumán	$8.50	0600	Wed, Sun	½	Gutierrez
• Tinogasta	$3.40	1550	Sat	3	Gutierriez

🛏 Accommodation

- Hotel de Turismo Belén, corner of Belgrano and Cubas $5.50 🛉
- Hotel Samaj, Urquiza 349 $8.00 🛉
- Residencial Doña Pilar, Lavalle 462 $4.00 🛉
- Residencial Gómez, Calchaquí 213
- Residencial Dalesi, corner of Belgrano and Sarmiento

🍴 Eating out

- Restaurant El Forastero, Sarmiento 321. Grill
- Restaurant El Unico, General Roca 315 (corner of Sarmiento). Grill
- Restaurant Hotel Provincial de Turismo
- Restaurant Sorrento, Belgrano 240. Pizzeria
- Cafetería La Terminal. Open daily until 0100

📮 Post and telegraph

- Post office: Encotel, San Martín 543
- Telephone: Entel, corner of Lavalle and General Paz

✈ Air services

There is no public airport. The airport 8 km south of town, halfway to Londres, used to provide regular air services to San Fernando del Valle de Catamarca, but these were suspended in 1986. Now only private planes use the runway.

🚗 Motoring services

RN 40 south to Tinogasta, via Londres and Cerro Negro, is in bad condition all the way.
- Service station: YPF

🛍 Shopping

Belén is the home of traditional Catamarcan weaving. This art has been handed down for generations from mother to daughter. Materials used include the wool from sheep, *alpaca*, and *vicuña*.
- Feria Artesanal, on the main square. Sells fine quality ponchos and rugs

🎭 Entertainment

- Disco Hotel Provincial de Turismo. Only open during the tourist season

📷 Sightseeing

- Museo Provincial Cóndor Huasi. On exhibition here are many fine relics of the ancient

Belén

Belén culture which once thrived at nearby Londres. This is also a good place to obtain information on archeological sites in the area
- Nuestra Señora de Belén (Our Lady of Belén): A statue on the top of **Cerro Tiro**, 450 m above the city. There are splendid views over the city and valley from here: you can see the river breaking up into little streams just south of the city and disappearing into the sand
- Bodega Don Juan, San Martin 498. A commercial wine cellar

Excursions

- **Santa María** via **Hualfín**: RP 40. The road is unsealed until just before Santa María. A few kilometers outside Belén the narrow and beautiful **Cañon Belén** begins. The road follows the western side of the river and gradually winds uphill. At Km 800 is the **Gruta de la Virgen** (Virgin's Grotto). From here on the scenery becomes very picturesque as the mountains close in and leave just enough room for the river and the road. The valley widens again just before **San José**. Here a rapid river coming down from the **Cerro El Mojón** massif joins the **Río Belén**. This river can be forded, a distance of about 880 m, though it may not be fordable during the spring thaw between September and November. Across the river is the turn-off to **Cóndor Huasi**, whose predominately Indian population is descended from the Diaguitas. For the hardy bushwalker a hike to the thermal springs located further up an eastern tributary nearby may be rewarding, but it is definitely only accessible to back-packers. At Km 816 the bridge crossing the river has been washed away. This region, with its huge windmills, is known as **La Ciénaga**. From here onwards the mountains recede and the road meanders through undulating country, occasionally fording small streams. In the north the **Sierra Chango Real** comes into view. Just before San Fernando there is a small pass to negotiate before descending to the village. The peak to the west which has been visible for most of the trip is **Cerro Morado**. At 4920 m it is snow-covered all year round. The landscape changes at this lower altitude to savannah country, densely covered with grass, but with few trees. After the ford over the **Río El Bolsón** the country becomes bare again and is severely eroded. The **Río Belén** here is only a small stream, although the riverbed is still very wide; during the spring thaw in the mountains the roads are often flooded and cut off. After **El Eje** the road winds down to the level of the riverbed. A short distance outside El Eje is the turn-off to **Antofagasta de la Sierra**. The trip to Antofagasta de la Sierra is a long and arduous one up into the Argentine *altiplano*, a bleak and arid

CATAMARCA PROVINCE

region, sparsely populated by descendants of the Diaguita Indians. The turn-off is well signposted, and Empresa Bosio runs a 12-hour service which leaves from Belén on Friday, returning on Sunday. There is no bus service beyond Antofagasta de la Sierra. About 6 km past this junction is Hualfín, a good hiking area with many hot springs. There is an ACA service station with a cafeteria here. Beyond Hualfín the **Campo Arenal** ("Sandy Field") starts. Looking east across this huge flat valley basin, it is possible to get splendid views of the towering **Sierra de Aconquija** mountain range, whose peaks reach over 5450 m. 13 km past Hualfín is a road junction: to the west is a 3 km access road to the thermal springs of **Los Nacimientos**, and to the east is the turn-off to **Los Farellones** mines. It is possible to get a lift up to the mines, from where you can hike through the **Valle Amanao** to Andalgalá—this is for intrepid bushwalkers only. On the walk look for unusual rocks: they may be rhodochrosites or "Rosa del Inca", a semiprecious stone. Further on is a valley junction where the fast flowing **Río Chango Real** is forded. This river starts at Cerro Laguna Blanca, and flows through the very pretty **Río Chango valley**. Almost imperceptibly the valley rises to form a watershed between the **Río Santa María** and the **Río Belén**. Campo de Arenal further north is known as **Campos de los Pozos** (or "Field of Wells") because of the many bores which tap the underground water there. From Km 883 the road descends gently and the valley becomes the intersection of several valleys. At **Guanacoyacu** the turn-off to the left leads to **Aguas Amarillas**. The plains become grassy again here. After entering the Río Santa María valley, the road veers to the east: here the **Sierra de Quilmes** starts. The road follows the eastern side of the river as far as Santa María, fording numerous streams along the way. As the Río Santa María valley begins to narrow the area becomes more lush. Just before **Punta de Balasto** is a junction with the Capillitas road leading to Andalgalá—a rough but very scenic drive. From Punta de Balasto the valley is densely populated and there is a continuous string of villages until the town of Santa María. See also Santa María on page 554

- **La Ciénaga**: 12 km west of RN 40 going north. An archeological site. Through the gorge at 1150 m are thermal springs with a temperature of 30C. There is a bus service
- Other thermal springs in this area include: **Fuente de Cura Fierro** (1400 m), which has strongly alkaline water, and produces a good table water; and **La Colpa** (1190 m,), which has moderately warm bicarbonate-alkaline water

Belén

CATAMARCA PROVINCE

- **Diversionary dam**: A few kilometers north of the city, in the gorge. The water redirected by this dam is used to irrigate the plains to the south and east of Belén
- **Londres**: An archaeological site 15 km south of town. The first bus leaves at 0630. Empresa El Cóndor runs five services each weekday. See also Londres on page 545
- **Gruta de la Virgen** (Virgin's Grotto): A 20-minute walk north of town
- **Salta** via **Antofagasta de la Sierra** and **San Antonio de los Cobres**: A trip over the *altiplano* for the adventurous. For a description see "Excursions" in Andalgalá on page 534

CHUMBICHA

Postal code: 4728 • Altitude: 450 m
Distance from San Fernando del Valle de Catamarca: 66 km south- west on RN 38

Chumbicha is located near the intersection of RN 60 and RN 38 in the south-western part of the province. The **Sierra de Ambato** is within easy reach of here.

There are many thermal springs in the Sierra de Ambato, but none of them have tourist facilities.

⚐ Festivals
- Fiesta Provincial de la Mandarina (Mandarine Festival): June

⚐ Camping
- La Toma

⚐ Eating out
- Restaurant Nueva Conetta
- Restaurant San Martín
- Cafetería Americano
- Cafetería Valencia

Buses
Buses run regularly to San Fernando del Valle de Catamarca.

⚐ Sport
- Fishing: There is trout fishing in the **Río Los Angeles** and **Río Concepción**

CONCEPCIÓN

Postal code: 4726
Distance from San Fernando del Valle de Catamarca: 47 km south- west on RN 38

Concepción is in the eastern foothills of the **Sierra de Ambato**, in the department of Capayán. The turn-off is at Huillapima, 35 km south-west of San Fernando del Valle de Catamarca. The region produces walnuts and olives, and there are a number of hot springs in the area.

⚐ Accommodation
- Hostería de Turismo Concepción $12.00 **i.** Full board

⚐ Buses
Buses run regularly to San Fernando del Valle de Catamarca.

⚐ Excursions
- A good area for walking. There are some easy walks up the valleys, and the narrow gorges and

Belén

CATAMARCA PROVINCE

small forests are also worth exploring

EL ALTO

Postal code: 4235 • Population: 4000 • Altitude: 950 m
Distance from San Fernando del Valle de Catamarca: 82 km eastwards on RP 42

El Alto is located in the east of Catamarca province, in the department of El Alto, near the border with the neighbouring province of Santiago del Estero. Europeans had established farms here as early as 1692. The parish was founded in 1748. The area is fairly dry and agriculture depends on irrigation.

Accommodation
- Hostería de Turismo El Alto $4.00 **i**. Shared bathroom

Eating out
- Restaurant Cuello
- Restaurant Gómez
- Restaurant Hostería de Turismo

Post and telegraph
There is a post office and public telephones in the Municipalidad.

Buses
Empresa La Paz runs daily bus services between San Fernando del Valle de Catamarca, Frías, and El Alto.

Excursions
- **Dique Collagasta**: 12 km on RP 39. You can camp here but there are no facilities. It is a good place for fishing and water sports

EL RODEO

Postal code: 4715 • Altitude: 1275 m
Distance from San Fernando del Valle de Catamarca: 34 km northwards on RP 4

Located in the foothills of the **Sierra de Ambato**, the village of El Rodeo was founded in 1614. It is a popular weekend resort for the wealthy of San Fernando because of its cool climate and pleasant scenery. The center of town is dominated by holiday villas. The streets are named after flowers, which are the major crop of the region. This area is in the foothills of the Sierra de Ambato, with elevations of between 1200 and 1600 m. It is good hiking country. Wildlife in the area includes deer, *vizcachas*, wild boar, mountain turkeys, falcons, and

Accommodation in El Rodeo
- Hotel de Turismo El Rodeo — $20.00 **ii**
- Hostería Doña Chicha, Los Gladiolos — $6.00 **i**
- Hostería Santa Rosa, Las Maravillas
- Hostería Stella Maris, Las Hortensias
- Hostería Vidal, corner of Las Hortensias and Las Margaritas — $10.50 **ii**
- Hostería Villafañez, RP 4

El Rodeo

CATAMARCA PROVINCE

eagles. If you are very lucky you might see a puma.

🅰 Camping
- Municipal "El Rodeo", on the left bank of Río Ambato. Fire-places available

🍴 Eating out
- Restaurant Hotel Provincial
- Restaurant Hostería Vidal
- Restaurant Hostería Villafañez

🚌 Buses
Empresa Acevedo runs services between San Fernando del Valle de Catamarca, El Rodeo, and Las Juntas daily on Mon, Tues, Wed, and Fri; and twice daily on Thurs, Sat, and Sun.

🏅 Sport
- Fishing: Trout and salmon fishing in rivers
- Hiking: Cumbre del Huaico
- Horse riding: Cumbre del Huaico
- Mountaineering: Cerro El Manchao (4550 m)

🚩 Excursions
- The statue of Christ on **Cerro El Manchao**

FIAMBALÁ

Postal code: 5345 • Altitude: 1600 m
Distances
- From Paso de San Francisco (on the Chilean border): 203 km south-east on RN 60
- From Tinogasta: 49 km northwards on RN 60

Fiambalá is situated in the wide desert-like valley of the **Río Abaucan**, whose huge shifting sand dunes contrast strangely with the high, encircling mountains. The town was founded in 1702 by Don Diego Frites de Carrizo. The old mission church is dedicated to San Pedro (Saint Peter), whose image was brought here from Bolivia. The church was built in 1770—you can still see the date inscribed above the door. From here to the Chilean border the land is sparsely populated and the terrain alternates between high mountains and *salinas*.

Fiambalá was originally established as a *reducción*, a reservation for those few Indians who had survived the European invasion. These missions were usually run by Jesuit or Franciscan monks. These days the inhabitants grow wine in the valley. There are also many thermal springs in the area.

🛏 Accommodation
Fiambalá is a very friendly town. Finding accommodation in private houses is no problem.
- Hostería Fiambalá
- Residencial San Francisco $2.50
- Private accommodation: Cabur family
- Private accommodation: Cargio family

🍴 Eating out
- Comedor Silvia

🚌 Buses
- San Fernando del Valle de Catamarca: Fare $6.50; departs 0530; 2 services daily; 5½; Empresa Gutierrez
- Córdoba: Departs 1515 Tues, Wed, Fri; 12 hours; Empresa El Cóndor, Empresa Robledo
- Cerro Negro: Departs 0530 daily; Empresa Gutierrez
- La Rioja: Fare $5.50; departs 1515 Tues, Wed, Fri; Empresa El Cóndor

El Rodeo

CATAMARCA PROVINCE

- Tinogasta: Fare $1.00; 1 hour; Empresa Gutierrez

Motoring services

The road to Copiapó in Chile, via Paso San Francisco (4726 m), is unsealed, and carries very little traffic.
- Service station: YPF

Shopping

Fiambalá is famous for its exquisite hand-woven fabric.

Sightseeing

- Old mission church dedicated to San Pedro built in 1770

Excursions

- Fiambalá hot springs: A 16 km hike over a road partly covered by shifting, crescent-shaped sand dunes, which begin almost as soon as you leave town. The bridge over the **Río Abaucán** was swept away by a recent flood, and only four-wheel drive vehicles and those on foot can cross the sandy ford through the usually dry river bed. Once across the river the road ascends gently, obstructed now and then by huge drifting sand dunes, until you reach **Quebrada de los Árboles**. The name means "Canyon of Trees", but there are no trees here at all! Signposts on the track point to mines inside the gorge. From here on the road descends gently into the valley. Fiambalá remains in view for the entire walk. Near an abandoned village with an old church you see the first sign of a thermal spring. Follow the stream uphill for a short distance until you find a rock pool with a comfortable temperature. Located at 1570 m, the spring emerges at 54°C. This hot spring is at present generally only used by the locals and is so far unspoilt. However a study is presently under way to determine the feasibility of building a hotel here. Although the walk is not difficult, it is a long one, so take precautions against the fierce sun. The heat is intensified by the reflection on the bare hills and sand in the valley
- **Troya**: A pre-Hispanic site in the **Río Troya** valley. There is a signpost on the main road halfway to Tinogasta
- **Saujil**: 15 km north on RP 34. Hot springs, located at 2000 m. The temperature is 21°C. A track continues a further 32 km up the valley to **Palo Blanco**. By this time you are in the *puna*, a high altitude arid tableland; only private accommodation is available
- Copiapó, in Chile: RN 60 goes through the **Río Chaschuil** valley over the **Paso San Francisco**, past **Cerro de Incahuasi**, 6620 m high, with views of **Volcán Negro**, 5420 m high. The road is unsealed but passable on the Argentine side. The Chilean side, however, is far worse

Fiambalá

CATAMARCA PROVINCE

HUALFÍN

Postal code: 4751
Distance
- From Belén: 61 km northwards on RN 40
- From Santa María: 117 km south-west on RN 40

Hualfín is a small village with a very old church dedicated to the Virgen del Rosario (Virgin of the Rosary). There are many thermal springs in this area, some of which are within walking distance of the village. There are no tourist facilities, but private accommodation is available. Hualfín is also the site of important finds from the pre-Columbian era. One of the biggest mining ventures in the province is in **Farellón Negro**, 38 km westwards. Manganese, silver, and gold are mined.

Eating out
There is a small snack bar, near the old church and bus stop

Buses
- Antofagasta de la Sierra: Departs Fri; Empresa Bosio
- Belén: Departs Tues, Thurs, Sun; 2 hours
- Santa María: Departs Mon, Wed, Fri; 3 hours

Motoring services
The roads south to Belén and north to Santa María are dirt roads, and all rivers are crossed by fords. The road to Antofagasta de la Sierra (turn off west, 9 km south of Hualfín) is occasionally cut off during spring.
- Service station: ACA, on RN 40 on the road north, 3 km from the town center

Sightseeing
- Iglesia de la Virgen del Rosario (Church of the Virgin of the Rosary). Coming from the south, this quaint church is on the left, built on a small hill. Unfortunately a large and ugly building has recently been constructed right next to the church; it is virtually impossible to exclude this building when photographing the church

Excursions
- **Termas Los Nacimientos**: 17 km north-west. No tourist facilities
- **Farellón Negro**, **Valle Amanao**, and **Andalgalá**: A three-day hike, for the fit and experienced only. Buy your supplies in Andalgalá or Belén. Catch a lift to the Farellón Negro mine with one of the trucks and cars which come to Hualfín from there frequently. Near the mine are several hot springs. There are no tourist facilities, but you may be able to sleep in the mining village

LA MERCED

Postal code: 4718 • Altitude: 881 m
Distance from San Fernando del Valle de Catamarca: 59 km northwards on RN 38

La Merced is a summer holiday resort located in the foothills of the **Sierra de Graciana** in the department of Paclín. It is the center of a tobacco-growing area.

CATAMARCA PROVINCE

🛏 Accommodation
- Hostería de Turismo La Merced $7.00 👥. Shared bathroom

🍴 Eating out
- Restaurant Barrientos, Figueroa
- Restaurant Carlitos, RN 38
- Restaurant El Embrujo, RN 38
- Restaurant La Huella, RN 38. Regional cuisine

🚌 Buses
- San Fernando del Valle de Catamarca, via Balcosna: Departs daily; Empresa Menecier. Via Santiago del Estero: Departs daily; Empresa Bosio. Via San Miguel de Tucumán: Departs daily; Empresa Bosio

📍 Excursions
- **La Viña**: 24 km north on RN 38, the main highway between Catamarca and Tucumán. This is a very picturesque trip; it goes over the mountainous terrain of the **Cuesta del Totoral**, and the road is very winding

LAS JUNTAS

Postal code: 4715
Distances from San Fernando del Valle de Catamarca: 54 km northwards on RP 4

Las Juntas is an idyllic place in the foothills of the **Sierra de Manchao**, in the department of Ambato. For mountaineers **Cerro Manchao** (4550 m) and **La Silleta** are nearby.

🎭 Festivals
- Festival of the patron saint Santa Teresita del Niño Jesús: October

🛏 Accommodation
- Hostería de Turismo El Bolsón $10.00 👥
- Hostería Los Sauces $11.00 👥

⛺ Camping
There is an unofficial camping site without any facilities at Punta del Camino, opposite the race course on the Río Las Juntas.

🍴 Eating out
- Restaurant Hostería Los Sauces
- Restaurant Vega
- Cafetería El Junteñito

🚌 Buses
- San Fernando del Valle de Catamarca, via El Rodeo and Las Piedras Blancas: Departs 1730 daily; Empresa Acevedo

🚗 Motoring services
RP 4 is sealed all the way southwards to San Fernando del Valle de Catamarca. The section which runs north to the junction with RP 1 at Los Varela is a dirt road.

🎣 Sport
- Mountaineering: There are several guides in the village
- Fishing: Trout and salmon abound in the **Río Las Juntas** and **Río Las Salvias**

LONDRES

Postal code: 4753
Distance from Belén: 15 km southwards on RP 3

Located on the **Río Quimivil**, Londres is the second oldest town in Argentina. It was founded in 1558 by Juan Perez de Zurita, to celebrate the marriage of Phillip II to Mary Tudor in 1554. This was to be the site of the new provincial capital, but because of the uprising of the Calchaquies tribes the city had to be abandoned. Artefacts of the early Belén culture have been discovered in the many archaeological sites in the area.

⛺ Camping
- Balneario Municipal, on Río Quimivil. Kiosk only open in summer

🍴 Eating out
- Cafetería La Tranquera, near Plaza Colombres

🚌 Buses
- Belén: 6 services daily; Mon–Sat. Fewer services on Sun

◆ Excursions
- **El Shincal**: Ruins of a pre-Columbian village, a 20-minute walk. Check with the police or municipal offices for directions

POMÁN

Postal code: 5315
Distance from San Fernando del Valle de Catamarca: 159 km southwards on RN 38, then westwards on RN 60, and finally northwards on RN 25

Located on the western side of the **Sierra de Ambato**, Pomán was founded in 1633 by Jerónimo Luis de Cabrera—yet another attempt by the Spaniards to found a permanent provincial capital. In 1898 it was completely destroyed by an earthquake. A few colonial buildings such as the church have survived. Agricultural products are olives, wine, and walnuts.

🎉 Festivals
- Fiesta de San Sebastian, the town's patron saint: January

🛏 Accommodation
- Hostería de Turismo de Pomán $8.50. Shared bathroom

🍴 Eating out
- Restaurant Hostería de Turismo

🚌 Buses
- San Fernando del Valle de Catamarca, via Andalgalá and Chumbicha: 2 services daily; Empresa Bosio
- Córdoba, via Andalgalá and Déan Funes: 3 services per week; Empresa La Calera

◆ Excursions
- Hikes in the nearby **Sierra de Ambato**

RECREO

Postal code: 5260
Distance from San Fernando del Valle de Catamarca: 180 km southwards on RP 13 then eastwards on RP 111

Recreo is located right on the border with Santiago del Estero province, close to the **Salinas Grandes**. This area is part of the department of La Paz; it is so dry here that it is virtually desert.

🎉 Festivals
- Festival del Cabrito (Kid Festival): February

CATAMARCA PROVINCE

🛏 Accommodation
- Residencial Recreo $9.00 ♦♦

🚗 Motoring services
- Service station: YPF

SAN ANTONIO

Postal code: 4701
Distance from San Fernando del Valle de Catamarca: 19 km north-east, just off RN 38

San Antonio is situated on the eastern side of the **Sierra de Graciana** in the department of La Paz, near the border with Tucumán province. It is a pretty spot, and has many archaeological ruins that have not yet been excavated.

🛏 Accommodation
- Hostería La Paz $6.00 ♦

🚌 Buses
Buses run regularly to San Fernando del Valle de Catamarca.

SAN FERNANDO DEL VALLE DE CATAMARCA

Postal code: 4700 • Population: 30 000 • area code: (0833) • Altitude: 520 m
Distances
- From La Rioja: 153 km north-east on RN 38
- From San Miguel de Tucumán: 240 km southwards on RN 38

San Fernando del Valle de Catamarca is located in a large fertile valley formed by the **Sierra de Ambato** in the west and the **Sierra de Ancasti** in the east.

There were two attempts to establish a provincial capital elsewhere before San Fernando del Valle de Catamarca was chosen. In 1559 Juan Perez de Zurita founded **Londres** in the **Valle Quimivil**. This was not a success, however, and a second attempt to re-establish Londres as the capital in 1591 by Ramirez Velazco failed also. San Fernando del Valle de Catamarca was founded in 1683 by Don Fernando Maté de la Luna.

Within Catamarca the name of this city is generally abbreviated to "San Fernando", but outside Catamarca its name is often abbreviated to "Catamarca", particularly on public transport.

San Fernando is the provincial capital. Its wide avenues give the city a charm that is reminiscent of colonial days. It is laid out in the conventional square pattern, with the hub of town being Plaza 25 de Mayo. There are numerous old churches and museums, and the city has a rich cultural life. Tourist facilities are good, with many first-class hotels and open-air coffee shops. For those interested in nightlife there is a casino, and several nightclubs and discos. Parque Adan Quiroga is a large park in the center of town.

The climate is one of San Fernando's attractions for visitors: it is mild all year round. There is some rain in October,

CATAMARCA PROVINCE

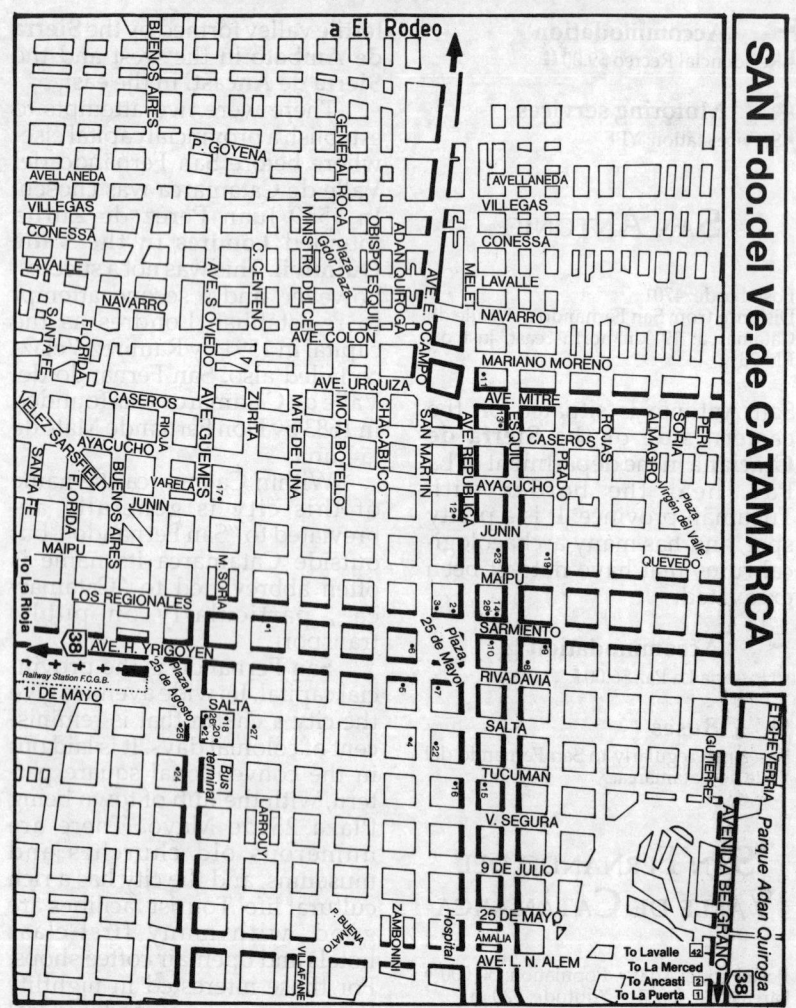

and during July and August there is a strong, dry mountain wind, called the *zonda*.

🎭 Festivals

- Fiesta Nuestra Señora del Valle (Festival of Our Lady of the Valley): 15 days after Easter
- Festival del Poncho: July. The main events are held near the office of the Dirección de Turismo. There are exhibitions of handicrafts, and four nights of

San Fernando del Valle de Catamarca

Catamarca Province

Key to map
1. Municipalidad
2. Casa de Gobierno
3. Catedral
4. Post office (Encotel)
5. Telephone (Entel)
6. Tourist information
7. Banco de la Nación
8. Convento de San Francisco
9. Museo Arqueologico Adam Quiroga
10. Hotel Ancasti
11. Hotel Grand Hotel
12. Hotel Inti Huasi
13. Hotel Pucara
14. Hotel Sumaj Huasi
15. Hotel Colonial
16. Hotel Comodoro
17. Hotel Güemes
18. Hotel Sol
19. Hotel Tempo
20. Residencial Venecia
21. Residencial Avenida
22. Residencial Delgrado
23. Residencial Esquiú
24. Residencial Familiar
25. Residencial Menem
26. Residencial Sirio
27. Hospedaje Jocar
28. Aerolineas Argentinas

Accommodation in San Fernando del Valle de Catamarca

★★★	Hotel Ancasti, Sarmiento 520	25001	$16.00	
	ACA members 10% discount			
★★★	Hotel Grand Hotel, Camilo Melet 41	26715	$12.00	
★★★	Hotel Inti Huasi, Republica 297	24664, 25293	$12.00	
	ACA members 10% discount			
★★★	Hotel Pucara, Caseros 501	23898	$12.00	
★★	Hotel Sumaj Huasi, Sarmiento 547	25199	$10.00	
	ACA members 10% discount			
★	Hotel Colonial, Republica 802	23502	$10.00	
★	Hotel Comodoro, Republica 851	23490	$8.50	
	Shared bathroom cheaper			
★	Hotel Güemes, Junín 189 (formerly Carlos I)	23203	$14.00	
★	Hotel Sol, Salta 1142	24134	$10.00	
★	Hotel Tempo, Prado 367	25023	$10.00	
A	Residencial Venecia, Tucumán 1115	24748	$6.00	
	Near bus terminal			
B	Residencial Avenida, Güemes 754	22139	$5.00	
	Near bus terminal; shared bathroom cheaper			
B	Residencial Delgado, San Martín 788	26109	$4.00	
	Shared bathroom			
B	Residencial Esquiú, Esquiú 365	22284	$5.00	
B	Residencial Familiar, Güemes 841	22142	$4.00	
	Near bus terminal			
B	Residencial Menem, Güemes 793 (corner of Tucumán)			
	Near bus terminal	24755	$5.00	
B	Residencial Sirio, Salta 1184	24144	$6.00	
	Two blocks from bus terminal; shared bathroom cheaper			
B	Residencial Yunka Suma, Segura 1255	23034	$4.00	
C	Hospedaje Jocar, Zurita 740			

Accommodation outside San Fernando del Valle de Catamarca
★★★★	Hotel Sussex, RN 38 south of town, in La Viña	22368	$16.00	

San Fernando del Valle de Catamarca

CATAMARCA PROVINCE

Andean music with open-air *peñas*, featuring groups of local folk musicians and dancers
- Semana del Turismo (Tourism Week): September
- Fiesta Nuestra Señora del Valle (Festival of Our Lady of the Valley): November 23 to December 8. The festival culminates in a large procession around Plaza 25 de Mayo

Tourist information

- Tourist office, San Martín 555. Leaflets detailing various trips around San Fernando are available here
- Dirección de Turismo, corner of General Roca and Urquiza (22999
- Agrupación de Montaña Calchaqui (also known as the "Coordinación de Montaña") can provide guides for mountain treks in the **Sierra de Ambato** and **Sierra de Aconquija**

Camping

- Parque Adan Quiroga, Avenida Belgrano 1100. Central location
- Autocamping Municipal, Quebrada de El Tala. This pretty spot is situated in a forested area 5 km from town, on the right as you go out along RP 4
- El Calvario, Quebrada de El Tala. Take RP 4. El Calvario is on the left

Eating out

- Restaurant Al Diente Libre, Sarmiento 740. Steak house; set price, eat as much as you like
- Restaurant Don Pedro, Caseros 386
- Restaurant El Encuentro, Hotel Angasti, Sarmiento 520
- Restaurant La Abuela, Sarmiento block 500 (corner of Esquiú). Steakhouse
- Restaurant La Farola, Rivadavia block 1100 (corner of Güemes). Credit cards accepted
- Restaurant La Tinaja, Sarmiento block 500 (corner of Esquiú). Steak house
- Restaurant Mementos, Junín 1189
- Restaurant Quincho Chirot, República 750. Steakhouse
- Restaurant Sociedad Italiana, corner of Camilo Melet and M Moreno
- Comedor Amicci, V Segura 618
- Comedor Cachito, Avenida H Yrigoyen 1743
- Comedor Chichi, Esquiú 905
- Comedor Club Español, Avenida Urquiza 725
- Comedor Club Italiano, M Moreno 152
- Comedor Don Luigi, Sarmiento 564
- Comedor El Barrilito, corner of Avenida Ocampo and Colón
- Comedor El Peregrino, San Martín 494
- Comedor Güemes, Avenida Güemes 813
- Comedor Segli, Avenida Güemes 875
- Comedor Tucumano, Sarmiento 836. Local cuisine
- Pizzería La Antartida, Ayacucho 21
- Pizzería La Cabaña, Tucumán 1115
- Pizzería Las Cuartetas, Tucumán 625
- Pizzería Las Malvinas, Rivadavia 341
- Pizzería Los Maestros, Rivadavia 973
- Pizzería Marielli, Esquiú 467
- Pizzería Marcos, Rivadavia 974
- Pizzería Monte Carlo, Rivadavia block 500 (corner of Esquiú)
- Cafetería Amadeus, San Martín 425
- Cafetería Bahia, República 500
- Cafetería Bambino, 25 de Mayo 1025. Billiards
- Cafetería Cristal, Rivadavia 618
- Cafetería Diogenes, San Martín 674. Billiards
- Cafetería Ego, República 419. Video games
- Cafetería El Bambi, Tucumán 612
- Cafetería El Mordisco, República 510
- Cafetería Esquiú, Esquiú 461
- Cafetería Flojos, Maté de Luna 659. Pool tables
- Cafetería Hotel Ancasti, Sarmiento 520
- Cafetería La Cascada, Rivadavia 558
- Cafetería La Farola, Rivadavia 1199
- Cafetería La Gringa, V Segura 1144
- Cafetería La Terminal, Avenida Güemes 850
- Cafetería Legislatura, corner of República and Ayacucho
- Cafetería Matias, Avenida Güemes 821
- Cafetería Mi Copetín, Rivadavia 1123
- Cafetería Nubes, Rivadavia 587. Snack bar
- Cafetería Oasis, Esquiú 1274
- Cafetería Quorum, corner of República and Ayacucho
- Cafetería Richmond, República 534
- Cafetería Roxalex, Gral Roca 33
- Cafetería Tabare, Rivadavia 853

San Fernando del Valle de Catamarca

CATAMARCA PROVINCE

🚌 Buses from San Fernando del Valle de Catamarca

Buses operate to Córdoba, from where there is a rail service to Buenos Aires. The bus terminal is on the corner of Avenida Güemes and Tucumán. It has a post office and a cloakroom.

Destination	Fare	Depart	Services	Hours	Company
Andalgalá					
via Balcosna	$5.50	0500	Mon, Thurs, Sat		Lazo
via La Puerta	$5.50	0500	Mon, Thurs, Sat		Lazo
via Saujil	$5.50	0530	2 services daily	6	Bosio
Belén					
via Aimogasta	$6.50	1330	daily	7	Bosio
via Andalgalá	$8.50	0530	Tues, Fri, Sun	9	Bosio
Buenos Aires	$28.00	1900	3 services daily	18	Cacorba, TA Chevallier
Chumbicha		1000	Tues, Thurs–Sat	8	San Luis
Córdoba	$9.00	1000	5 services daily	6	Cacorba, Cotil
Corrientes		1945	Tues, Thurs, Sat		
El Bolsón, via La Puerta		0600	Sun		Lazo
El Rodeo			1–2 services daily		
Fiambalá	$6.50	1130	2 services daily	7	Gutierrez
Frías	$5.00	0800	1–2 services daily	5	Salles
La Rioja	$2.50	0045	7 services daily	2	La Estrella, Cotil, Bosio
Las Juntas	$1.50	1245	1–2 services daily	½	Acevedo
Los Varela, via Balcosna		1330	Wed		Lazo
Mendoza	$13.50	0055	1–2 services daily		Cotil, La Estrella
Posadas		1945	Tues, Thurs, Sat		Cotil
Puerto Iguazú		1945	Tues, Thurs, Sat		Cotil
Resistencia		1945	Tues, Thurs, Sat		Cotil
Rosario		1900	daily		TA Chevallier
San Juan	$10.50	0055	2–3 services daily		La Estrella, Cotil
San Luis	$18.00				
San Miguel de Tucumán	$5.00	0025	9 services daily	5	La Estrella, Bosio
Santa María					
via Acheral	$8.50	1130	Mon, Wed, Fri		Bosio
via Belén	$13.50	0530	Fri, Sun		Bosio
Santiago del Estero	$6.00	0530	3 services daily	5½	Coop Catamarca, Bosio
Singuil, via La Puerta		1800	Mon, Tues, Fri		Lazo
Tinogasta	$5.50	1130	2 services daily	5½	Lazo

- Bar Nuevo Cabildo, República 580

Eating out outside San Fernando del Valle de Catamarca
- Restaurant El Mangrullo, Presidente Castillo 576. Grill

📬 Post and telegraph
- Post office: Encotel, San Martín 753
- Telephones: Entel, Rivadavia 758

💲 Financial
There are no bureaux de change in San Fernando.

🗄 Services and facilities
- Delicatessen: Centro, corner of República and Rivadavia
- Dry-cleaner: Japonesa, San Martín 733

San Fernando del Valle de Catamarca

CATAMARCA PROVINCE

- Laundromat: Laverap, Mota Botello 345. There are only four machines here—be prepared for a long wait
- Sauna: Junín 10, between Perú and Almagro
- Supermarket: TIA, Rivadavia block 1100 (corner of Güemes)

✈ Air services

The airport is 27 km south of San Fernando. Aerolineas Argentinas runs a minibus service from town; a taxi costs $11.00.

Airlines

- Aerolineas Argentinas, Sarmiento 589 (corner of República)

Services

- Buenos Aires (Aeroparque Jorge Newbery): Fare $69.00; departs 1020; 1–2 services daily; 2 hours; Aerolineas
- Córdoba: Fare $31.00; departs 1020 Mon, Wed, Fri; 1 hour; Aerolineas
- Neuquén: Fare $82.00; departs 1245 Tues, Wed, Sat, Sun; 2 hours; Aerolineas

🚗 Motoring

- Car rental: Adbeca, Sarmiento 766 ℂ 28959

⊕ Tour operators

- Turismo Adbeca, Sarmiento 760
- Turismo Turi-Cat, República 832 ℂ 25499. Three buses
- Yokavil Turismo, Galería Catamarca, Rivadavia 648 ℂ 28717. Two buses

🛍 Shopping

Catamarca province is famous for its hand-woven ponchos and for its preserves, especially one made from the fruit of a cactus.

- Casa del Tongio
- Cuesta del Portezuelo, Sarmiento block 500 (corner of República). Local handcrafts
- Regionales Maika, Sarmiento block 500 (corner of República)
- Regionales Servita, Sarmiento 511. Good selection of ponchos and Catamarcan handcrafts

⚽ Sport

- Hiking: The **El Rodeo–La Puerta** region is very popular for hikes, which take one to two days. There are many archaeological sites in this area
- Mountaineering: For experienced mountaineers **Cerro Manchao** is a three- to four-day climb

🍸 Entertainment

- Casino, Club Villa Cubas, Ocampo 500
- Disco Ancasti Hotel
- Disco Sussex Hotel
- Peña Folklorico Asociación Flor de Tusca ("Tusca Flower Folk"), corner of Quiroga and General Navarro. Open from May to October 12. After 2200 each night regional cuisine is served in the dining room

📷 Sightseeing

- Museo Arqueológico "Adan Quiroga" (Adan Quiroga Archeological Museum), in the Esquiú cultural institute, Sarmiento 446. This museum was named after a famous Argentine archeologist. The archeological section has displays of artefacts from each culture which flourished in the province, starting from the preceramic period in 6000 BC. The colonial period is also well represented. There is also a good mineralogy section. Open daily 0800–1300 and 1530–2130, Sat and Sun 0830–1230. Admission $0.50
- Museo Folklórico Juan Alfonso Carrizo, Paseo General Navarro
- Iglesia y Convento de San Francisco (Franciscan Church and Convent), corner of Rivadavia and Esquiú

San Fernando del Valle de Catamarca

CATAMARCA PROVINCE

◆ Excursions

- **Andalgalá**: The road initially goes through the flat part of the ever-widening **Valle Catamarca**, following the contours of the **Sierra de Ambato** as far as **Chumbicha**. Here the mountain ranges fade and the road turns northward following RN 60 for 50 km. After the intersection with RP 25 the road starts climbing. On reaching **Pomán** the bus turns into the mountainous region to serve the scattered villages such as **Rosario de Colona** situated on the western slope of the Sierra de Ambato, and rejoins the main road again near Saujil. These mountain villages are very picturesque with the 4400 m range directly behind them. On the western side are sweeping views over the **Salar de Pipanaco** into which several rivers flow and disappear. From **Saujil** onwards the road skirts the edge of the mountain eventually descending onto the plain. There are fords over most rivers, rather than bridges. As the **Sierra de Manchao** is left behind the **Sierra de Aconquija** comes into view ahead. The town of Andalgalá is perched against the 5450 m high **Nevado del Candado**. See also Andalgalá on page 531

- Copiapó in Chile, via **Chumbicha**, **Tinogasta**, and **Paso San Francisco** (4726 m): This route follows RN 38 and RN 60. The road is sealed as far as the intersection with RN 60; from there it is sealed patchily to Tinogasta, and after **Fiambalá** it is a gravel road for 750 km. For more details see "Excursions" in Fiambalá on page 534

- **Dique Las Pirquitas** (Las Pirquitas Dam): 33km north on RP 1, about one hour by municipal bus (fare $0.50) from the terminal. The valley is narrow, and the mountains covered with fairly dense subtropical vegetation. At the bus stop is the Hostería Provincial de Turismo. There is also camping near the river. The first bus leaves San Fernando at 0630 and the last bus leaves Dique las Pirquitas at 2200

- **Cuesta del Portezuelo** pass: This is a 20 km stretch of steep winding road. Follow RN 38 for 18 km east until you cross the **Río del Portezuelo**. The turn-off to this mountain pass road is on the right shortly after crossing the Río del Portezuelo. The splendid views over the valley, and the winding road with its hairpin bends make this an exhilarating trip. The highest point is 1680 m, aptly named **Alto del Portezuelo** (Portezuelo Height). Tour operators run half-day excursions leaving at 0900 which cost $7.00

- **El Rodeo** and **Gruta de la Virgen del Valle** (Grotto of the Virgin of the Valley): Tour buses do this half-day tour each day, leaving at 1500. It costs $7.00. You can also take a local Empresa Acevedo bus from the bus terminal. See also El Rodeo on page 541

San Fernando del Valle de Catamarca

CATAMARCA PROVINCE

SAN ISIDRO

Postal code: 4707 • Altitude: 590 m
Distance from San Fernando del Valle de Catamarca: 6 km eastwards on RN 38

Because it is so close to San Fernando—only separated by the **Río del Valle**—San Isidro is virtually a suburb of San Fernando. It was founded in 1668. The climate is subtropical.

Accommodation
- Hostería Valle Viejo, Sant Rosa (6 km from San Fernando) $13.50

Camping
- Parque Autoctono, Santa Rosa

Eating out
- Cafetería El Chopp
- Cafetería Hawaii

Post and telegraph
- Post office: Encotel, Villa Dolores
- Telephone: Entel, Tres Puentes

Motoring services
- Service station: YPF, RN 38, Tres Puentes

Entertainment
- Disco Cabala, Tres Puentes
- Disco Cantry, San Isidro

SANTA MARÍA

Postal code: 4139 • Population: 18 000
Distances
- From San Miguel de Tucumán: 179 km westwards on RP 338 then RP 337
- From San Fernando del Valle de Catamarca, via Aimogasta: 350 km south-west on RN 38, north-west on RN 60, then north-east on RN 40. Change buses at Cerro Negro

Santa María is located in the **Río Santa María valley** formed by the **Sierra de Quilmes** on the western side and the **Sierra de Aconquija** on the east. The area is rich in archeological sites, with rock paintings and Indian fortifications. Santa María was part of the Calchaquies Indian federation which put up a massive resistance against the Spanish occupation. Ambrosio Nuñez Cancinos founded the town as a Spanish settlement in 1710.

Festivals
- Nuestra Señora de la Candelaria (Our Lady of the Lamp)

Accommodation
There is a shortage of accommodation in Santa María.
- ★★Hotel de Turismo Santa María, corner of San Martín and 1 de Mayo (240 $13.00
- Hotel Plaza, San Martín 350 (on the Plaza) (309 $6.50
- Residencial Alemán, T M de la Quintana 146 (226 $5.00
- Private accommodation: Domingo Isidro Maturano, Belgrano 146 $3.00

Camping
You can camp at the far end of Belgrano, past Alsina. Water and barbecue facilities are available

Eating out
- Restaurant El Rancho de Fredo, Moreno 332
- Restaurant Esquiú, Esquiú 358
- Restaurant Hotel Turismo Santa María
- Restaurant Yokovil, corner of Mitre and Sarmiento

CATAMARCA PROVINCE

🚌 Buses from Santa María

There is no central bus terminal.
- Empresa Aconquija, Belgrano 220
- Empresa Bosio, DF Sarmiento 415
- Empresa El Indio, Belgrano 271

Destination	Fare	Depart	Services	Hours	Company
• San Fernando del Valle de Catamarca					
via Acheral	$8.50		Tues, Thurs, Sun	9	Bosio
via Belén	$13.50		Mon, Sat		Bosio
• Amaicha del Valle			3 services daily	1	Aconquija
• Andahuala			several services daily		local bus
• Andalgalá	$7.50	0530	Mon, Thurs, Sat		Bosio
• Belén	$5.20	0530	Mon, Thurs, Sat	5	Bosio
• Cafayate	$2.20	1200	Tues, Thurs, Sat	2	Aconquija
	$2.50	0700	daily		El Indio
• Colalao del Valle			2 services daily	1	Aconquija
• Quilmes			2 services daily	½	
• Ríos			several services daily		local bus
• Salta		0700	daily	11	El Indio
• San José	$0.50	hourly			local bus
• San Miguel de Tucumán	$5.20	0600	Mon–Sun	6	Aconquija
• Tafí del Valle	$2.50		3 services daily	3	Aconquija

- Cafetería El Águila, San Martín 231 (on the Plaza)

✉️ Post and telegraph
- Post office: Encotel, T M de la Quintana 375
- Long-distance telephones: Belgrano 103

🚗 Motoring
- Service station: YPF, corner of Esquiú and Sarmiento

⊕ Tours
- The Hotel Turismo Santa María operates tours to **San José** and the pre-Hispanic city of **Loma Rica**. The trip takes three hours
- Tours can also be made to **Fuerte Quemado**, another pre-Hispanic city. This is also a three-hour trip

🛍️ Shopping
- Regionales Lizi, corner of Esquiú and T M de la Quintana

📷 Sightseeing
- Museo Arqueológico Eric Bohman (Eric Bohman Archeological Museum), Sarmiento 271, in the Municipalidad

● Excursions
- **Tafí del Valle**: The road from Santa María is sealed as far as **Amaicha del Valle**. Near Amaicha del Valle the local bus takes a convoluted route in order to take in some distant villages before returning to Amaicha. The dirt road from Amaicha starts climbing and is winding and narrow. It can get very cold here; rivers freeze over in winter. There are huge cacti on the steep mountain slopes. This is beautiful country, particularly around

Santa María

CATAMARCA PROVINCE

Abra de Infiernillo. Further down is **Carapunco**, which was an Inca outpost. Soon after the road crosses **Paso El Infiernillo** you get your first glimpses of Tafí del Valle with its artificial lake. Many mountain streams join the **Río Tafí** here. Some houses along this road are still thatched with straw. Reafforestation with pine trees is in progress. Shortly before Tafí the road becomes sealed again
- **Cerro Pintado**: 8 km to these colored sandstone mountains
- **Loma Rica**: 18 km south off RN 40. Important ruins
- **Ampajango**: 20 km south, off RN 40. Interesting petroglyphs can be seen here.
- **Quilmes**, in Tucumán province: 32 km north on RN 40. From the turn-off it is a well-signposted 5 km walk to the ruins of this once formidable pre-Hispanic fortification. It has been restored, and there is a small museum. There are also camping facilities and a guide at the site. See Quilmes on page 590
- **La Hoyada**: In the **Río Saladillo** valley. There are irregular buses from Santa María

TINOGASTA

Postal code: 5340 • Population: 8000 • Altitude: 1500 m
Distances
- From San Fernando del Valle de Catamarca: 277 km north-west on RN 38 then RN 60
- From Chilecito: 156 km northwards on RN 40
- From Copiapó (Chile): 522 km southeast on RN 60

Tinogasta is located in the **Río Abaucan valley** near the junction with the **Río Las Lajas** in the western part of the province. It was officially founded in 1713 by the Governor Don Esteban de Nieva y Castilla.

Wine and olives are the main crops grown in the area, but mining is the mainstay of the economy. The green valley contrasts starkly with the bare mountains rising sharply on the western side.

The town's population is predominately Indian, and most work in the copper mines.

In the vicinity of Tinogasta are several interesting archeological sites, hot springs, and some beautiful mountain scenery. The best time to visit the area is from November to May.

✶ Festivals
- Fiesta Provincial de la Vendimia (Provincial Grape Harvest Festival): February

⊟ Accommodation
- ★★ Hotel de Turismo Tinogasta, corner of Moreno and Gordillo $12.00 ⁑
- Hotel Familiar, General Uriburu 231
- Residencial El Viajante, RN 60 south of town center $2.50 ⁑. Situated at the entrance to the town, opposite the service station; no hot water
- Residencial Persegoni, Tristan Villafañez 415
- Residencial Rivadavia, corner of 25 de Mayo and Rivadavia $3.50 ⁑. Breakfast only

CATAMARCA PROVINCE

- Residencial San José, Antonio del Pino 419. For budget travelers

Accommodation outside town

- ☞ A Hostería Novel, Cordoba, RN 60 north of the town center, near the airport $5.50

Camping

- Los Filtros, Santa Rosa, RN 60, 4 km north
- Olivo Centenario, San Roque, RN 60, 8 km north. No facilities, but near thermal springs

Eating out

- Restaurant Hotel de Turismo, corner of Moreno and Gordillo
- Restaurant La Ivone, Antonio del Pino 490
- Restaurant Persegoni, Villafañez 375
- Restaurant Rancho Huayra-Puca, corner of Moreno and Copiapó. Steakhouse
- Restaurant San Francisco, 25 de Mayo block 400 (corner of 6 de Setiembre)
- Restaurant Virgen del Valle, corner of Catamarca and Tristan Villafañez
- Comedor Copayapu, corner of 6 de Setiembre and 25 de Mayo
- Pizzería Virgen del Valle, corner of Villafañez and Catamarca
- Cafetería Bar Carlitos, corner of Uriburu and Copiapó
- Cafetería Fama Las Vegas, 25 de Mayo 346
- Cafetería La Bomba, 25 de Mayo 349. Pizzeria, hamburgers
- Cafetería Los Amigos, 25 de Mayo 335
- Cafetería Saris, Antonio del Pino

Post and telegraph

- Post office: Encotel, Moreno 605 (corner of Constitución)
- Telephone: Entel, Antonio del Pino 739

Buses from Tinogasta

There is no bus terminal. Empresa El Cóndor and Empresa Santa Rita operate from Residencial Rivadavia, on the corner of 25 de Mayo and Rivadavia. Empresa Robledo has its terminal on the corner of Uriburu and Rivadavia. Empresa Ortiz and Transportes Gutierrez have their offices next to each other on the main Plaza on the corner of Moreno and 25 de Mayo.

Destination	Fare	Depart	Services	Hours	Company
San Fernando del Valle de Catamarca	$5.50	0645	2 services daily	5½	Gutierrez
Aimogasta				3	El Cóndor
Andalgalá	$6.00	0830	Sun	5	Gutierrez
Belén	$3.40	0830	Sun	3	Gutierrez
Caleta Olivia Robledo					
Chilecito via San Blas	$5.20	1100	Sun		Santa Rita
via Santa Cruz	$6.50	1530	Mon, Fri		Santa Rita
Comodoro Rivadavia			once a week		Ortiz
Concepción (in Tucumán)	$10.50	0830	Sun	11	Gutierrez
Córdoba	$12.00	0915	2 services daily	13	El Cóndor
Fiambalá	$1.00				Gutierrez
La Rioja	$4.50	0915	2 services daily	5	El Cóndor
San Miguel de Tucumán	$11.80	0830	Sun	12	Gutierrez
Termas de Santa Teresita	$3.00				El Cóndor

Catamarca Province

Motoring services

The 61 km road over the Cuesta de Zapata to Londres is not sealed. Buses do not take this shorter route, but instead take the detour via Cerro Negro.

Service stations

- ACA, corner of Moreno and Rivadavia. Enquire here for information about trips to Copiapó in Chile, and also for photocopies of road maps of the route to Chile. Very helpful
- YPF, corner of RN 60 and Tristan Villafañez. South of town

Sport

- Fishing: There is trout fishing in the **Río Chaschuil**, past Fiambalá, at an altitude of 4000 m. To reach it take RN 60 north for 120 km

Entertainment

- Disco Amigos, 25 de Mayo 238

Sightseeing

- Museo Tulio Ribaudi, Constitución. A private collection of archeological artefacts

Excursions

- **Fiambalá**: RN 60 follows the **Río Abaucan valley** north. As you make your way up the valley it narrows and the mountains grow larger on the western side. The scenery is spectacular around here; occasionally a few snow-covered peaks are visible. It can get very cold at night but the days are warm even during winter. There are many hot springs in the area just outside Tinogasta, but none of them have facilities. Two of them just a few km north of town are **San Roque** and **San José**. Both are well signposted on the main highway. The airstrip outside town is no longer used for commercial flights. The valley widens as you proceed north and passes through olive groves and vineyards. **Las Aguaditas de San José** are thermal springs, just past San José. Further on the road passes through a narrow gap between the **Sierra de Fiambalá** on the east and the range on the west, and emerges onto a plain which gets wider and wider, and begins to look like a desert because of the sand dunes which shift across its surface. The road fords the **Río Troya** which is flowing from the west. A signpost on the road points to the archaeological site of **Troya** (also known as Batungasta) further up in the Río Troya valley. The road becomes very patchy and all the rivers are forded. Just before entering Fiambalá the vineyards begin again. See also Fiambalá on page 542
- **Las Aguaditas de San José**: 15 km north, off RN 60. Thermal springs. There is a pool and changing rooms
- **Troya** (or Batungasta): 20 km north, off RN 60. Archaeological ruins, halfway between Tinogasta and Fiambalá in the **Río Troya valley**

Tinogasta

LA RIOJA PROVINCE

Plate 31 Map of La Rioja Province
- 560 Aimogasta
- 562 Anillaco
- 562 Chamical
- 563 Chepes
- 563 Chilecito
- 564   Map
- 569 Famatina
- 570 La Rioja
- 572   Map
- 577 Nonogasta
- 577 Olta
- 578 Patquía
- 578 Salicas
- 579 Termas Santa Teresita
- 580 Ulapes
- 580 Villa Castelli
- 581 Villa Sanagasta
- 581 Villa Unión
- 582 Vinchina

La Rioja province is located in the north-western part of Argentina. It borders with Catamarca to the north and east, Córdoba to the east, San Luis to the south, San Juan to the south-west, and Chile to the west. It measures 92 000 square km and

La Rioja Province

has approximately 200 000 inhabitants, about half of which live in and around the capital, La Rioja city.

La Rioja is classified as a "Pampa-Andean" province. It is green towards the west where the pre-Andean hills begin, but is dry in the east, which consists of salt-bush steppe interrupted by many salt lakes such as **Salina La Antigua** and **Salinas Grandes**, which is shared with Córdoba province. Vegetation in the dry east consists mostly of cactus and acacia-like trees. Typical of the flora is the *palo boracho* tree, which has a wide-bellied trunk similiar to the Australian bottle-tree.

In summer the temperature can rise to 40°C. In winter the average temperature is 12°C in the low-lying parts of the province. In the higher regions it can get very cold in winter, with snow covering the peaks **Sierra de Velasco**, **Sierra de Famatina**, and of course the peaks of the Sierra de los Andes which reach over 6000 m. A hot wind sweeping down from the *chaco* can bring sudden rises in temperature.

In the mountain valleys the soil is fertile and yields an abundance of crops such as grapes, citrus fruit, figs, and olives. The pastures are too dry to run cattle, so the only animals kept are goats and sheep. In the northern part of the province small herds of llamas and alpacas are kept, whose wool supports a unique original weaving industry.

The province is rich in minerals. Gold and silver deposits in particular were already exploited by the Incas. However the Incas' dominance over the region was only superficial. The many *pucarás* bear witness that the original inhabitants did not submit easily.

The province has good roads and most towns provide good accommodation. It is at present still "undiscovered" by tourists, even the Argentines. Besides the varied landscape another attraction is the colorful fiestas.

The rewarding tourist spots are the capital **La Rioja**, **Chilecito**, **Parque Provincial Talampaya**, and the thermal spa **Termas Santa Teresita**. For the mountaineer and the adventurous the area north of **Villa Unión** is of interest. The **Río Bonete valley** is particularly rewarding: here are La Rioja's highest peaks: **Cerro Bonete Chico** (6850 m) and **Monte Pissis** (6780 m). The starting point for trips into this area is from Vinchina or Alto Jagüé; buses run to Villa Unión.

AIMOGASTA

Postal code: 5310 • Population: 6000 • Altitude: 830 m
Distance from La Rioja: 130 km northwards on RP 1

Aimogasta is located in the *precordillera* on an irrigated plain intensively used for the cultiva-

La Rioja Province

tion of olive trees. In the nearby village of **Arauco** is the oldest olive tree in Argentina, planted in the sixteenth century.

Festivals
- Fiesta Nacional del Olivo (National Festival of the Olive): May 24

Accommodation
- ★ Hostería Aimogasta, San Martín 512 $13.00. Central
- Hostería Brigitte, on the Plaza $9.00

Eating out
- Restaurant El Turco
- Restaurant Santa Rita. Steakhouse

Post and telegraph
There is a post office and public telephones in the center of town.

Buses
There is no central bus terminal. Both transport companies have their offices next to each other on the main plaza
- La Rioja: Via Villa Mazán: Fare $2.50; departs 1200 daily; 2 hours; Empresa El Cóndor. Via Aminga: departs 0800 daily; Empresa El Cóndor
- San Fernando del Valle de Catamarca: Empresa Gutierrez
- Termas Santa Teresita: Fare $2.00; departs 1930 daily; Empresa El Cóndor
- Tinogasta: Departs 0730 daily; 3 hours; Empresa El Cóndor

Motoring
- Service station: YPF, southern entrance to Aimogasta. Excellent 24-hour cafeteria

Shopping
This is the place for lovers of delicious, huge olives, both green and black.

Excursions
- **San Fernando del Valle de Catamarca**: RN 60 eastwards passes through flat country cultivated mostly with olive trees, before entering the narrow gorge of **Villa Mazán**, which, although only about 5 km long, is very scenic. Past the gorge you arrive at Villa Mazán, with a turn-off to **Termas Santa Rita**, a thermal resort with a hotel. The road follows the **Río Salado** southwards between the **Sierra de Mazán** and the **Sierra de Ambato**, both medium-size mountain ranges. The river gradually but visibly loses strength, occasionally forming little pools in the river flats before finally disappearing completely in the **Desagüe del Río Salado**, both mountain ranges are left behind and it is all flat country with nothing growing but a few cacti. Near **Bazán** RP 9 joins RN 38, the main road linking La Rioja with San Fernando del Valle de Catamarca. At this stage La Rioja is only 24 km away to the west. Running north-east, RN 38 follows roughly the southern length of the **Sierra de Ambato**. **Chumbicha**, just across the border with Catamarca, and off the main road, is the "mandarine capital". As we follow the Sierra de Ambato northwards the mountains grow in height until they reach 4400 m. The range is of volcanic origin, attested to by the many thermal springs encountered there. The best

Aimogasta

LA RIOJA PROVINCE

known is **Termas Concepción** (with an *hostería*) 36 km before San Fernando. The **Sierra de Ancasti** approaches on the eastern side, forming the beautiful **Valle Catamarca**; here the valley is covered with shrubs and small trees. Just before entering San Fernando there is the Hotel Casino on the right-hand side. See also San Fernando del Valle de Catamarca on page 547

- **Termas Santa Teresita**: Take the bus to Mazán and alight at the ACA service station at the crossroad. The attendant is very helpful. Wait here to arrange a lift. El Cóndor runs a daily bus. From here it is 11 km

ANILLACO

Postal code: 5301 • Population: 700 • Altitude: 1380 m
Distance from La Rioja: 92 km northwards on RP 1

Anillaco is located 3 km off RP 75 between La Rioja and Aimogasta.

Accommodation
★★ Hostería Anillaco, Avenida Coronel Barros Reyes $15.00 ♨. ACA discount 20%

Post and telegraph
There is a post and telegraph office.

Excursions
- **Señor de la Peña**: 24 km east. A huge isolated rock in which the faithful believe they see the image of Christ

- **Chuquis**: 12 km southwards on RP 1. The Museo del Solar de Castro Barros, once home of the independence hero, exhibits memorabilia of the eighteenth century

CHAMICAL

Postal code: 5380 • Population: 6500 • Area code: (0826) • Altitude: 467 m
Distance to La Rioja: 132 km southwards on RN 38

Chamical, also known as Gobernador Gordillo, is situated at the intersection of RN 38 and RN 79. Nearby is the testing ground for missiles developed by the airforce. Vineyards and orchards surround the town.

Festivals
- Fiesta de la Virgen del Rosario (Festival of the Virgin of the Rosary): last Sunday in February

Accommodation
★★ Hotel Victoria, San Juan 274 (212 $15.00 ♨. ACA discount
★ Hostería Chamical, Rivadavia 100 $13.00 ♨. ACA discount

Eating out
- Restaurant Comedor El Potro, Sarmiento 251
- Restaurant El Quincho de Carlos, D de Arroyo 346
- Restaurant Victoria, Hotel Victoria, San Juan 274

Communication
There are post, telephone, and telegraph offices.

Aimogasta

La Rioja Province

🚌 Buses
- La Rioja: Fare $3.00; departs 0740; 2 hours; Empresa ABLO
- Chilecito: Fare $4.20; departs 0740 daily; 3 hours; Empresa ABLO

🚗 Motoring
- Service station: ACA

⚐ Excursions
- **Polco**: 7 km, a small picturesque village in the foothills of the **Sierra de los Llanos**. The Fiesta de Polco runs from the last Sunday in September till the first Sunday in October

CHEPES

Postal code: 5470 • Population: 5000 • Altitude: 652 m
Distance from La Rioja: 255 km southwards on RP 38, then RP 27, 28, and 29

Chepes, in the southern part of the province, is an important crossroad, situated halfway between Córdoba and San Juan, south of the foothills of the **Sierra de Argañaraz**. It was founded towards the end of the eighteenth century. *Quebracho* timber is felled and milled here. On the outskirts of Chepes is a modern ACA tourist complex.

🛏 Accommodation
★★ Motel Chepes, corner of J V González and Las Heras ⑪ $15.00 ⁑. ACA discount 20%

🍴 Eating out
- Restaurant Motel Chepes
- Restaurant Don Luis, corner of Avenida San Martín and RP 20
- Restaurant Yelpes Huasi, San Martín 1050

✉ Post and telegraph
There are post, telephone, and telegraph offices.

🚗 Motoring
- Service station: ACA, RN 20. Mechanic on duty

⚐ Excursions
- **Chepes Viejo**: 9 km north on a dirt road, Chepes Viejo (or "Old Chepes") has a small museum, Museo de los Caudillos (Museum of the Leaders), which exhibits memorabilia linked to the history of the province

CHILECITO

Postal code: 5360 • Population: 23 000 • Area code: (0825) • Altitude: 1100 m
Distances
- From La Rioja: 192 km eastwards on RN 38 then RN 74
- From Tinogasta: 149 km southwards on RN 11 then RN 40
- From Villa Unión: 109 km eastwards on RN 40

Chilecito is located in a wide valley between the **Sierra de Velasco** and **Sierra de Famatina**. The **Nevado Famatina** (6200 m) rises sharply behind the town, its crest snow-covered for part of the year. The climate is pleasant all year round.

Chilecito was founded on February 19, 1715 by Don

LA RIOJA PROVINCE

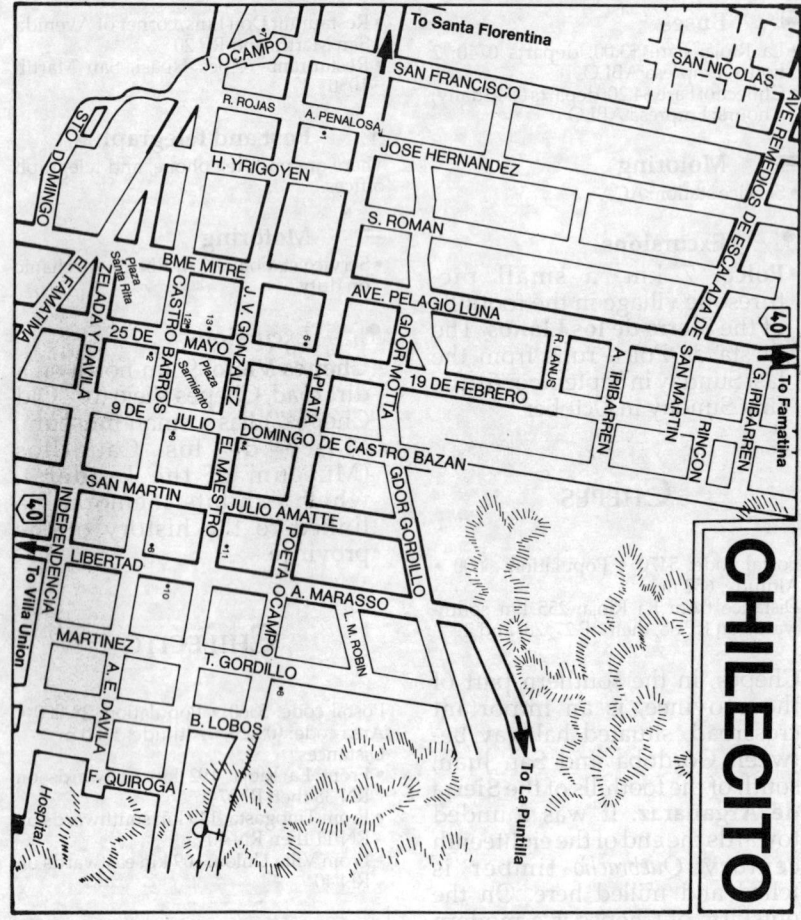

Key to map
1. Municipalidad
2. Iglesia
3. Post office (Encotel)
4. Telephone (Entel)
5. Bus terminal
6. Tourist information
7. Molino de San Francisco (Museum)
8. Hotel Chilecito (ACA)
9. Hotel Bel-Sa-Vac
10. Residencial Americano
11. Residencial Bellia
12. Residencial Riviera
13. Residencial Wamatinag

Chilecito

La Rioja Province

Domingo de Castro y Bazan, under the name of Santa Rita. The new name, meaning "Little Chile", reflects the Chilean miners living here after World War I. The period between 1895 and 1905 saw the city's greatest prosperity, when the cable car was installed to bring the rich ore down from the Mejicana mine.

Festivals
- Chilecito week, celebrating the city's foundation: starts February 19

Tourist information
- Delegación de Turismo, corner of Libertad and Independencia (2688. Maps available. Very helpful

Camping
- Santa Florentina, 6 km along Calle de la Plata; take an Empresa Santa Rita bus
- Los Talas, 8 km along Calle de la Plata; take an Empresa Santa Rita bus
- Guanchín, 15 km from Chilecito, near the Jesuit *estancia* established in 1652; take an Empresa Santa Rita bus

Eating out
- Restaurant Caprí, corner of J V González and Mitre
- Restaurant Rancho Grande, corner of 25 de Mayo 89 and Castro Barros. Steakhouse
- Restaurant El Quincho, corner of J V González and De Castro Bazan. Steakhouse
- Restaurant Ferrito, Avenida Pelagio B Luna 661
- Restaurant Toscanini, corner of Santa Rosa and San Martín. Pizzeria
- Restaurant El Gallo, corner of Avenida A Illia and Prensa Argentina
- Cafetería Bel-sa-vac, corner of Davila and 9 de Julio
- Snack-bar: Chaplin, 25 de Mayo and J V González

Post and telegraph
- Post office: Encotel, corner of J V González and Mitre
- Telephone: Entel, Castro y Bazan 27

Services and facilities
- Hospital Eleazar Herrera Motta, Independencia 600 (2511
- Laundromat Lave-Tec, B Mitre 55. $2.00
- Supermarket: Autoservicio Sancor, El Maestro 110

Air services
The airport is at Anguinán, some 6 km from town. At present there are no commercial services.

Accommodation in Chilecito

★★	Hotel Chilecito, corner of Poeta Ocampo and T Gordillo	(2201	$15.00	♂♂
	ACA discount 20%			
★	Hotel Bel-Sa-Vac, corner of 9 de Julio and Davila			
	Central	(8277	$13.00	♂♂
•	Residencial Americano, Libertad 68	(8104	$5.00	♂♂
•	Residencial Bellia, El Maestro block 200 (corner of Marasso)		$5.00	♂♂
•	Residencial Riviera, Castro Barros 133		$10.00	♂♂
•	Residencial Wamatinag, 25 de Mayo 37	(2510	$5.00	♂
	In arcade near bus terminal			

LA RIOJA PROVINCE

🚌 Buses from Chilecito

The bus terminal is on the corner of La Plata and 19 de Febrero, one block from the city center. The facilities are poor.

Destination	Fare	Depart	Services	Hours	Company
• La Rioja	$3.80	1130	daily	4	COTIL
• Buenos Aires	$27.50	1900	daily	18	ABLO
• Córdoba	$8.80	1900	2 services daily	8	ABLO, COTIL
• Famatina	$0.80	0700	4 services daily	1	Santa Rita
• Jáchal	$8.50	0900	Tue–Thur, Sat, Sun	7	TAC
• Rosario		1900	daily	14	ABLO
• San Juan	$11.00	0900	Wed, Sun	9	TAC
• Tinogasta					
via Campanas	$5.20	0600	Mon, Fri	5	Santa Rita
via Salicas	$6.50	1300	Sat	6	Santa Rita
• Villa Unión	$3.50	0900	Tues–Thurs, Sat, Sun	3	TAC

🚗 Motoring

Service stations

- ACA, corner of El Maestro and 9 de Julio
- Esso, corner of Libertad and Santa Rosa

⊕ Tours

- El Montones, shop 10, Galería Quintana, Adolfo E Davila 19

🛍 Shopping

- Regionales Peralta Davila, El Maestro 90

🎭 Entertainment

- Disco Status, corner of 25 de Mayo and Castro Barros

📷 Sightseeing

- Molino de San Francisco (St Francis' Mill), also called Museo de Chilecito (Chilecito Museum), Ocampo 63. A colonial building dating back to 1700, which belonged to the founder of the city. For nearly two hundred years it was used as a flour mill. Nowadays it has been converted to a museum exhibiting antique weapons, documents, and weavings. It is also used as an auditorium where dances and plays are staged. Open daily 0900–1300 and 1800–2000
- Plaza Santa Rita, corner of B Mitre and Zelada y Davila. This historic Plaza was the site of the first church to be built in Chilecito

⬥ Excursions

- **Villa Unión**: RN 40 runs over the **Cuesta de Miranda**, a mountain pass road. The trip is very picturesque, passing through narrow valleys. See also Villa Unión on page 581
- **La Rioja**: RN 74 initially makes a long detour southwards to circumvent the **Sierra de Velasco**, only to return northwards up the eastern side of the range for an equal distance as RN 38 to La Rioja. At first the valley is very wide, but it narrows considerably near the **Sierra de los Colorados**. Just 13 km south of

LA RIOJA PROVINCE

Chilecito is **Nonogasta**, famous for its *artesanías* or handicrafts, such as those made by the group calling itself Artesanías Marca Huasi. Where the river ends in salty marshes, the valley is also known as **Bajo de Santa Elena**. Further south, just before arriving at **Patquía**, is a low rock outcrop of unusual shapes and sizes known as **Los Mogotes Colorados**, which has been declared a natural monument. Inside this rock labyrinth is a cave called the Cueva del Chacho, which during the Wars of Independence served as a hideout for General Peñalosa. Also in the Mogotes are hot springs forming a rock pool, whose temperatature is 34°C. The **Sierra de los Colorados** interposing between **Sierra de Velasco** and **Sierra de Sanogasta** terminates abruptly, and the road emerges onto a wide plain. Following RN 74 south from Patquía for 10 km, you pass the turn-off to the date-palm center of **Guayapa**. From Patquía RN 38 runs directly northwards at first, along the **Desagüe de los Colorados**, with no sideroads. This plain collects the water from the nearby mountains during spring, but is fairly dry the rest of the year. Shrubs and small trees cover the plain densely and give shelter to a variety of colorful birdlife—nearly every tree along the road has at least one bird's nest. From **Talamuyuna** onwards the Sierra de Velasco rises visibly as the road runs alongside. See also La Rioja on page 570

- **La Mejicana mine**, a copper and silver mine, not currently worked. The base station is at **Santa Florentina**, 6 km west on RP 14. A cable car was installed in 1904 by a German firm, and it has since been extended by 34 km with nine stations. Near Santa Florentina a taxi ride away, are the ruins of the colonial ore foundries

- **Samay Huasi**: 3 km from the city center; Empresa Santa Rita buses go past. Samay Huasi was the country retreat of Joaquín V González, founder of La Plata university, and is now a museum. The building is surrounded by parks and orchards, and a path leads up to the hill behind the mansion. The museum has natural history sections; there is an interesting exhibit of beetles and butterflies, including a particularly good essay on the *vinchuga* beetle, the carrier of Chagas' disease. There are also well-endowed mineralogy and archeology sections. Open 0800–1200 and 1500–1800. You can walk back to the city across a low hill, emerging near the hospital, or take an Expreso Santa Rita bus

- **Los Sarmientos**: A small town to the north. The main attraction is the Santa Clara chapel, completed in 1764. The massive doors are carved from *algorrobo* wood. Take an Empresa Santa Rita bus

La Rioja Province

- **Tilimuqui**: 10 km east. This very old township has the remains of a colonial ore foundry and a chapel to the Virgen del Rosario de los Federales. Take an Empresa Santa Rita bus
- **Malligasta**: 11 km east. The chapel built in the seventeenth century contains a collection of colonial Indian carvings. Take an Expreso Santa Rita bus
- **Anguinán**: 6 km south-east. Founded in the early 1600s, it was the first urban center in the area. The church was built in the middle of the seventeenth century. Take an Empresa Santa Rita bus
- **La Cuadra**: Located between San Miguel and Anguinán. The birthplace of Francisco Ortiz de Ocampo, first general of the Argentinian army. Take an Empresa Santa Rita bus
- **San Nicolás**: 6 km north on RN 40. The Jesuit mission church contains a priceless altar and altar-piece, carved by the Indians of the Jesuit mission and covered with gold leaf. Take an Empresa Santa Rita bus
- **Guanchín**: 19 km west on RP 15. A pleasant village with a good climate. Nearby is an *estancia* founded by the Jesuits in 1652. Walnuts, quinces, and apples are cultivated. The road from Chilecito climbs a slope with panoramic views. The clear streams offer good fishing. Medicinal plants abound. Empresa Santa Rita, Cotil, and TAC buses all run past here
- **Sañogasta**: 16 km south of Guanchín along RP 15 via **Los Manzanos**. It is located at the beginning of the scenic drive over the Cuesta de Miranda. The climate is cool. It has vast walnut orchards, and the walnut festival in March attracts many visitors. There is a local festival in honour of the patron saint Sebastian
- **Nonogasta**: 11 km past Sañogasta along RN 40. It is a typical mountain village with large vineyards. The Jesuit chapel dates back to the eighteenth century. Dr Joaquín V Gonzáles was born there in 1863, and the house is still preserved. Bodega Nacari, which makes excellent wine, is worth a visit. Take an Empresa Santa Rita bus; fare $0.75. See also Nonogasta on page 577
- **Famatina**: 33 km north on RN 40 then RP 11, in the Famatina valley; see Famatina below. Take an Empresa Santa Rita bus
- **Laguna Brava**: North-west, at an altitude of 4200 m. There is a large flamingo colony
- **Tambo del Inca**: Behind the cemetery. An archeological site, with excavation of pre-Colombian houses, and possibly the remains of an Inca *tambo*
- **Valle de la Luna** (Valley of the Moon): Tour operators run round trips of this area, taking in **Nonogasta**, **Cuesta de Miranda**, **Villa Unión**, and **Los Baldecitos**
- **Parque Provincial Talampaya**: The road over the **Cuesta de**

Chilecito

Plate 29
Map of Catamarca Province

Plate 30

Top: Belén
Bottom left: Colonial church, Hualfín
Bottom right: Fiambalá

La Rioja Province

Miranda follows a narrow stream to **Pagancillo**, and for much of the way is hewn from the rock. The only way you can visit the park is to be driven by a guide in a vehicle provided; the cost is $40, plus $1 entrance fee. Before entering the park you must register at the police station, 28 km from Pagancillo on RP 26, and leave some form of official identification. The whole of the area now comprising the park was once under water, and two strata are now visible, known as the Tarjado and the Talampayo. There are interesting geological formations, as well as petroglyphs of animals which are 6000 years old. In one part of the park you enter a canyon whose walls overhang like balconies. Many medicinal plants grow in the area and are collected by local people. Three buses a week travel along RP 26 from Chilecito to San Juan; drivers will stop at the park entrance—you can get a lift back to Pagancillo or Villa Unión. The nearest hotel is at Villa Unión in the Hostería Provincial. Guided tours of the park run by Yafar Turismo leave from San Juan and La Rioja. See also "Excursions" in Villa Unión on page 582

Famatina

Postal code: 5365 • Population: 1500 • Altitude: 1580 m
Distance
- From Chilecito: 31 km northwards RN 40 then RP 11
- From Tinogasta: 118 km southwards on RN 40 then RP 11

Famatina is located in the valley formed by the **Sierra de Famatina** to the west and the **Sierra de Velasco** to the east. It is one of the most beautiful and accessible regions of the province. The mountain peaks surrounding the city are high enough to be snow-covered for most of the year. Because of the high altitude the weather is cool all year round.

The valley is intensively cultivated using irrigation, mostly producing walnuts and apples. The town has to a large extent preserved the colonial houses and the narrow streets which go with them. Easter celebrations are vey colorful. The large image of Christ venerated in the church of San Pedro is thought to have originated in Peru, from the Cuzco school, in the seventeenth century. The townsfolk are also very artistic; weavers produce ponchos and blankets.

Festivals
- Colorful Holy Week festivities
- Pilgrimages are also held in honour of the infant Jesús de Hualco in December, and the Virgen de Andacollo

Accommodation
★ Hostería Famatima, RN 40 Km 624 $13.00 ACA discount 20%

Eating out
- Restaurant Hostería Famatima, RN 40 Km 624

Post and telegraph
There are post, telephone, and telegraph offices.

LA RIOJA PROVINCE

🚌 Buses
- Chilecito: Departs 0430; 4 services daily; 1 hour; Expreso Santa Rita
- Tinogasta: Departs 0700 Mon, Fri; 4 hours; Expreso Santa Rita. Via San Blas: Departs 1340 Sat; 5 hours; Expreso Santa Rita

🚗 Motoring
- Service station: ACA, RN 40 Km 624

🛍 Shopping
Homemade blankets and ponchos.

📷 Sightseeing
In the local school there is a collection of rock samples found in the mountains around Famatina.

🌳 Excursions
- **La Greda** hydroelectric scheme with a 70 m waterfall
- Hermitage at **Plaza Vieja**
- Near **Carrizal** two streams merge: one is crystal clear and the other of strong ochre-yellow colour, possibly of volcanic origin
- Several hills around town can be climbed easily. One of them has a cross on top with scenic views over the town and the surrounding district

LA RIOJA

Postal code: 5300 • Altitude: 500 m • Area code: (0822) • Population: 60 000
Distance
- From Córdoba: 460 km north-west on RN 60 then south-west on RN 38
- From San Juan: 515 km north-east on RN 150 then north on RN 38
- From San Fernando del Valle de Catamarca: 154 km south-west on RN 38

La Rioja is located on the eastern side of the **Sierra de Velasco**, a mountain chain rich in hot mineral springs. The town was founded in 1591 by Spaniards under the command of Juan Ramirez de Velasco pushing down from Peru.

The city is the capital of La Rioja province. Some colonial buildings have survived the disastrous earthquake of 1894. Otherwise, it is a fairly modern city with wide avenues and modern buildings. The commercial district centers around Plaza 25 de Mayo and spreads into Avenida B Mitre and Pelagio B Luna.

There are many interesting historical relics from the past, such as the Convento de Santo Domingo (Convent of St Dominic).

There are many *bodegas* as the province is a large dry wine producer.

Most streets are lined with the *palo borracho* tree, a typical *chaco* tree, similar to the Australian bottle tree.

Streets change their names as they cross Avenida B Mitre.

The former Hotel Provincial de Turismo is now the town hall.

Famatina

La Rioja Province

🛏 Accommodation in La Rioja

During Holy Week celebrations, Semana de Rioja in May, and in July, book hotels in advance.

★★★★	Hotel de Turismo La Rioja, corner of Avenida Presidente Juan D Perón and Quiroga	(25283	$27.00	
★★★★	Hotel King's, Avenida J F Quiroga 1070	(25272	$27.00	
★★★★	Hotel Plaza, corner of 9 de Julio and Avenida B Mitre Central	(25215	$27.00	
★★★★	Hotel Sussex, O de Ocampo 1551	(25413	$27.00	
★★	Hotel Libertador, Buenos Aires 253 Central	(27474	$15.00	
★	Hotel Savoy, Roque A Luna 14 (corner of Avenida B Mitre)	(26894	$13.00	
★	Hotel Talampaya, Avenida Presidenete Juan D Perón 951	(24010	$13.00	
C	Residencial Sumaj Kanki, corner of Barros and Lagos Shared bathroom		$7.00	
•	Residencial El Gringo, Lagos 427			
•	Hospedaje Margarita, Sarmiento 419			
•	Private accommodation: Señor Carreño, Becar Vareza 461	(27563	$5.00	

Private accommodation:
- Señora Blanca de Barros, Choque A Luna 40 (27045 $5.00

Accommodation outside La Rioja

★★	Motel Yacampis, Avenida R de Velazco, Km 8 ACA discount 20%	(25216	$15.00	

🎭 Festivals

The city celebrates many religious festivals which always attract a large number of people.
- Fiesta de la Chaya: A carnival
- Semana de Rioja (Rioja Week): May 20. Commemorates the foundation of the city. Celebrated with great pomp and fireworks, and an exhibition of *artesanías*
- Fiesta de San Nicolás, and El Niño Alcalde: From December 31 to January 3. These constitute a major religious festival. On December 31 at noon there is the encounter of El Niño Alcalde with San Nicolás, the patron saint of the city. The crowning event is when the two processions meet.
- Festividad de Nuestra Señora de los Naturales: October

ℹ️ Tourist information

Dirección de Turismo, corner of Avenida Perón 401 and Urquiza (28834. Open Mo–Fri 0700–2100. Maps and pamphlets on the tourist attractions of Chilecito and La Rioja are available.

🍴 Eating out

- Restaurant Doña Hortensia, Dalmacio Velez
- Restaurant El Candil, Rivadavia 459. Credit cards accepted
- Restaurant El Milagro, corner of Avenida Presidente Juan D Perón and Remedios de Escalada
- Restaurant El Quijote, Santa Fé 801
- Restaurant El Viajante, corner of Avenida J F Quiroga and San Martín
- Restaurant El Viejo Boulevard, Ortiz de Ocampo 1306. Steakhouse

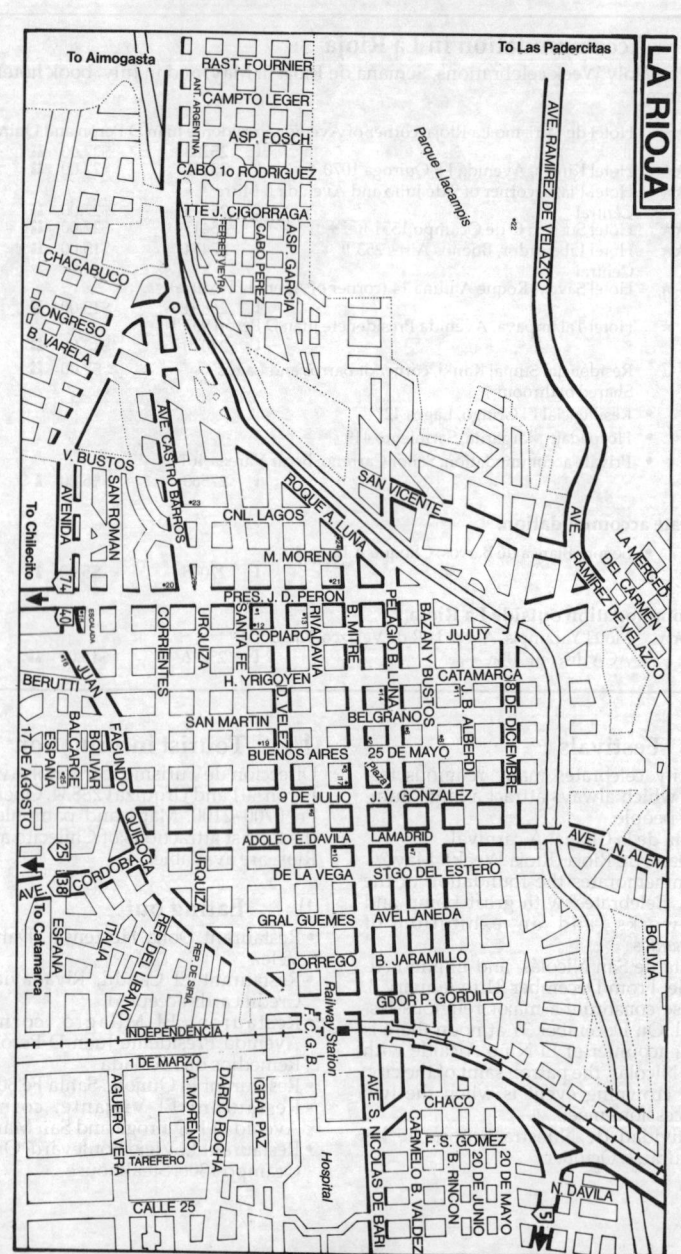

La Rioja Province

- Restaurant Encuentro, Urquiza 977. Local cuisine
- Restaurant Facundo, F Quiroga 1131 (corner of Avenida Presidente Juan D Perón). Steakhouse
- Restaurant Hotel de Turismo, corner of Avenida Presidente Juan D Perón and Avenida J F Quiroga
- Restaurant Hotel Sussex, Avenida Ortiz de Ocampo 1000
- ☞ Restaurant La Cantina de Juan, Yrigoyen 190 (corner of D Velez). Spanish cuisine
- Restaurant La Churrería, J V González 261
- Restaurant La Gran Ruleta, Rivadavia 461
- Restaurant La Herradura, corner of San Martín and Urquiza
- Restaurant La Posada de Arturo, Rivadavia 919
- Restaurant Lomoteca, Copiapó 350. Pizzeria
- Restaurant Mi Ranchito, Avenida F O de Ocampo block 700. Steakhouse
- Restaurant Sociedad Española, 9 de Julio 200
- Restaurant Vidal, Avenida Presidente Juan D Perón 500. Pizzeria
- Pizzería Bar Ideal, Avenida Presidente Juan D Perón 400
- Pizzería Centro, P B Luna 441
- Pizzería Club Social Facundo, corner of Avenida Presidente Juan D Perón and Dalmacio Velez
- Pizzería El Palacio de la Pizza, Avenida Presidente Juan D Perón 356
- Pizzería El Parque, Avellaneda 70
- Pizzería El Timón, Avenida Presidente Juan D Perón 454
- Pizzería Giovanni, Santa Fé 645
- Pizzería La Italiana, corner of Avenida Presidente Juan D Perón and Corrientes
- Pizzería Rivadavia, corner of Rivadavia and Buenos Aires
- Pizzería Veneto, corner of Rivadavia and Buenos Aires
- Cafetería Dickens, corner of Rivadavia and San Martin
- Cafetería El Ciervo, J V Gonzáles
- Cafetería Rio, corner of Avenida B Mitre and San Martín
- Cafetería Sorocabana, corner of 25 de Mayo and Avenida B Mitre
- Cafetería Talampaya, corner of Avenida Presidente Juan D Perón and Corrientes
- Snack-bar: VIP, P B Luna 523

Eating out outside the city center
- Restaurant Diente Libre, Ruta 75 Km 4
- Restaurant El Farolito, Avenida Benavidez
- Restaurant Facundo II, Avenida Ramirez de Velasco Km 2
- Restaurant Pecko's, Avenida L N Alem
- Restaurant La Estancia (opposite the stadium)
- Restaurant La Tablita, RN 75 Km 6

Post and telegraph
- Post office: Encotel, Avenida Presidente Juan D Perón 764
- Telephones: Entel, corner of P B Luna and J V González

Financial Services
There is no bureau de change in La Rioja.

Key to Map
#	
1	Municipalidad
2	Casa de Gobierno
3	Catedral
6	Banco de la Nación
7	Iglesia y Convento de Santo Domingo
8	Convento de San Francisco
9	Iglesia La Merced
10	Museo Histórico de la Provincia
11	Museo Arqueológico Inca Huasi
12	Museo de Bellas Artes
13	Casa de Joaquín V González
14	Mercado Artesanal
15	Hotel de Turismo La Rioja
16	Hotel King's
17	Hotel La Plaza
19	Hotel Libertador
20	Hotel Talampaya
21	Hospedaje Margarita
22	Motel Yacampis
23	Residencial Sumaj Kanki
24	Hotel Savoy
25	Bus terminal
26	Tourist information

La Rioja Province

🖃 Services and facilities
- Delicatessen: Fiambres Ital-Argentino, corner of P B Luna and Lamadrid
- Drycleaner: Superjet, V Sarsfield 750
- Supermarket: Americano, corner of Avenida B Mitre and Pasaje Diaguita

Laundromats
- Laverap, Avenida B Mitre 24
- Laverap, Rivadavia 1035

C Clubs
- Italian: Sociedad Italiana, Copiapó block 600 (corner of V Sarsfield)

✝ Churches
- Latter Day Saints Church, corner of San Martín and Quiroga

🖃 Visas, passports
- Italian vice-consulate, corner of Avenida Presidente Juan D Perón and Santa Fé

✈ Air services
The airport is 8 km north of town. The taxi fare is $3.50.

Airlines
- Aerolineas Argentinas ℡ 26307

Services
- Buenos Aires (Aeroparque Jorge Newbery): Fare $69.00; departs 0925 Tues, Thurs, Sat, Sun; Aerolineas
- Córdoba: Fare $30.00; departs 1310 Sun; 1 hour; Aerolineas

🚌 Buses from La Rioja

The bus terminal is on the corner of España and Artigas, eight blocks south of the city center.

Cotal runs buses to Corrientes, Posadas, Puerto Iguazú, and Resistencia, departing at 1651 on Tues, Thurs, and Sat.

Destination	Fare	Depart	Service	Hours	Company
• Aimogasta	$2.50				El Cóndor
• Buenos Aires				17	
• Chilecito	$4.50	1130	daily	4	Cotil
• Córdoba	$11.00	0800	4–5 services daily	7	Cotil, El Cóndor
• Famatima					
• Mendoza	$12.50	0311	3–4 services daily	9½	Cotal, La Estrella, T A Libertador
• Rosario	$21.50	2000	1–2 services daily	13	General Urquiza, ABLO/Cotil
• Salta		0515	daily		Bosio
• San Agustín del Valle Fértil	$5.00				
• San Fernando del Valle de Catamarca	$3.00	0027	8–9 services daily	3	La Estrella, Cotal, Cotil, Bosio
• San Juan	$11.00	0311	3–4 services daily	7	Cotal, La Estrella, T A Libertador
• San Luis		1000	Thur		Cotil
• San Miguel de Tucumán	$8.50	0027	3 services daily	7½	Bosio, La Estrella
• Santiago del Estero		0500	daily	3	T A Libertador
• Termas Santa Teresita (via Carrizal)	$2.00	0630	daily		El Cóndor
• Tinogasta	$5.50		3 services per week	4	

La Rioja

LA RIOJA PROVINCE

- San Fernando de Catamarca: Fare $16.00; departs 0915 daily; 1 hour
- Santa Fé: Fare $46.00; departs 1310 Sun; 2 hours; Aerolineas

Motoring

RN 38 to San Fernando del Valle de Catamarca is sealed and for most of the way runs through flat country.
- Service station: ACA, corner of Velez Sarsfield and Copiapó. Maps available
- Car rental: Liprandi Rent-a-Car (also known as Car Rental Autotour), Buenos Aires 244 ℂ 24065 and 25218. Also in the Hotel Plaza

Trains

The F C General M Belgrano station is on Gobernador P Gordillo, opposite Rivadavia. Passenger trains no longer run to Buenos Aires. Buy a combined bus-train ticket and change at Córdoba.

Tours

- Yafar Turismo, Lamadrid 170 ℂ 23053. Run tours to Parque Provincial Talampaya and Valle de la Luna
- Marco Polo, in the Hotel de Turismo, corner of Avenida Presidente Juan D Perón and Avenida J F Quiroga ℂ 25283
- Tur Rioja, Galería Sussex, 25 de Mayo 76 ℂ 26997

Shopping

Dates and date liqueurs are locally produced and only obtainable in La Rioja. Since they're very hard to find even in Buenos Aires, buy them here if you're interested.
- Regionales Facundo, Avenida J F Quiroga 726. Dates and date liqueur
- Regionales El Changuito, Avenida B Mitre 315
- Regionales Su Vineria, 9 de Julio 41. Wines
- Mercado Artesanal, Pelagio B Luna 790. In an old senorial house. On exhibit are samples of local craftmanship: ceramics, silver jewelry, wood carvings, and leather goods. Open Tues–Fri 0900–1200 and 1500–2000, Sat–Sun 0900–1200

Entertainment

- Bowling: Confitería Kalalo, P B Luna block 500 (corner of 25 de Mayo)
- Casino de Rioja, in Hotel Sussex, O de Ocampo 1551. It is also night club

Sightseeing

- Catedral, corner of Avenida B Mitre and Buenos Aires, completed in 1899. The remains of Pedro Ignacio de Castro Barros, one of the heroes of the independence wars, rest here
- Museo Folklorico (Folk Museum), Pelagio B Luna 811, in an authentic colonial house built in 1850. It gives a good idea what life was like in La Rioja during the last century
- Iglesia y Convento de Santo Domingo (Dominican Church and Convent), Pelagio B Luna, block 300 (corner of Lamadrid). Built in 1623 by Diaguita Indians under the guidance of the Dominicans. The main entrance is carved out of *algarrobo* wood—a priceless piece of art
- Iglesia de San Francisco (Franciscan Church), 25 de Mayo 218: Inside is the orange tree (now dead) which was planted by San Francisco Solano when he arrived in 1592 in La Rioja. The monk's cell in which he stayed can be visited
- Museo Arqueológica Inca Huasi, J B Alberdí 650 has a collection of over 10 000 items of archeological and paleantological items, including funerary urns and wide-bellied jars possibly belonging to the Florescent Era about 100 AD. Open

La Rioja

LA RIOJA PROVINCE

Mon–Fri 0900–1300 and 1600–1900, Sun 0900–1300.
- Museo de Bellas Artes (Fine Arts Museum), Copiapó 245. Paintings and sculptures housed in a restored colonial building. Open Mon–Fri 0700–1400 and 1430–2130, Sat and Sun 0900–1200
- Casa de Joaquín V González, Rivadavia 952, was the home of J V González, one of the great philosophers and literati of Argentina, born in Nonogasta in 1863
- Museo Histórico de la Provincia (Provincial History Museum), Adolfo E Davila 79. Open Sat and Sun only

◆ Excursions

- **Parque Provincial Talampaya**: This is a full day's trip (460 km) visiting en route **Patquía** and **El Chiflón**. The turn-off onto RP 26 is 14 km past El Chiflón (or 3 km before Los Baldecitos). Follow the road northwards for about 58 km; the turn-off east is well signposted. Follow the road for another 14 km to the **Puerta de Talampaya**, one of nature's wonders, with narrow canyons and isolated rock columns produced by the erosive forces of wind and water. This trip is best made through a tour operator; the cost is $25.00 each for a minimum of nine persons. Regular buses run between La Rioja and San Juan via Patquía, but there are no regular buses between Los Baldecitos and Villa Unión on Ruta 26. The visit to the reserve can also be made from Villa Unión, or from Chilecito via Villa Unión. Yafar Turismo runs guided tours. See also "Excursions" in Chilecito on page 568
- **Villa Sanagasta**: 80 km. A half-day excursion visiting **Las Padrecitas**, **Dique Los Sauces**, and Sanagasta. Through a tour operator the trip costs $8.00 for a minimum of nine persons. This trip can also be made using public buses as there are regular services up the **Río Grande Valle** to **Aminga**. See also Villa Sanagasta on page 581
- **Chilecito**: 490 km. This is a full day excursion. Tour operators include a visit to the rock formation **Los Mogotes Colorados** (with **Cueva del Chacho**), a visit to a winery in **Nonogasta**, a short drive up the **Cuesta de Miranda** over a narrow and winding road, and Samay Huasi museum outside Chilecito. Guided tours cost $19.00 for a minimum of nine persons. See also Chilecito on page 563
- **Ischigualasto** (also called Valle de la Luna) in San Juan province: 500 km. This is a full day trip. The route is the same as for the trip to Talampaya as far as the turn-off before Los Baldecitos. Tour operators sometimes combine the Talampaya trip with the Ischigualasto trip, but this can be rather tiring. The entrance to the park is 17 km north of the turn-off from los Baldecitos. Tours to this park are also organized from San Juan; $13.00 each for a minimum of nine persons). Budget

La Rioja

La Rioja Province

travelers can try to hitch a lift from the Baldecitos turn-off. Yafar Turismo runs guided tours. See "Excursions" in San Agustín del Valle Fértil on page 498

- **Anillaco**: 250 km. An eight-hour trip which includes **Dique Los Sauces**, **Villa Sanagasta**, **Cuesta de Huaco** (a winding road between Huaco and Las Penas), **Chuquis**, **Anillaco**, and a side trip to **Señor de la Peña**, a Catholic shrine with a rock bearing a resemblance of a face. Guided tours cost $13.00 for a minimum of nine persons. This trip can be made using regular buses (marked "La Costa"). You can stay overnight in the ACA complex in Anillaco. See Anillaco on page 562
- **Las Padrecitas** Jesuit church: 7 km west on RP 26. This is one of the oldest Jesuit adobe churches in the province. Here San Francisco Solano baptized the Indians
- **Dique Los Sauces**: 15 km west on RP 1. Swimming, fishing, waterskiing, and sailing. This is a favorite weekend retreat for the *Riojanos* or citizens of La Rioja. Municipal buses run here regularly
- **Cerro de la Cruz**: 1680 m high. Good views over La Rioja. The 13 km road to the top turns off to the left just before Dique Los Sauces. It is a very bad stretch and before attempting with your own vehicle check with the Policia Caminera (Road Police). Occasionally you can see hang gliders practice here
- **Parque Yacampis**: On Avenida R de Velasco, opposite the Autodrome, 3 km from the city. There is a lookout here from which you can see over the city. In the park is the monument to the Indian. ACA has a tourist complex here

Nonogasta

Postal code: 5372 • Population: 2400 • Altitude: 934 m
Distance from Chilecito: 16 km southwards on RN 40

Nonogasta is a typical mountain village 3 km off the main highway. It has a Jesuit chapel founded in the seventeenth century. Visit Nacari wine producers, makers of excellent wines. Nonogasta is the birthplace of Dr Joaquín V González. The **Cuesta de Miranda** road to Villa Unión begins here.

Post and telegraph
There are post, telephone, and telegraph offices.

Buses
Empresa Santa Rita buses run regularly to Chilecito.

Motoring
There is a petrol station.

Olta

Postal code: 5383 • Population: 2000 • Altitude: 530 m
Distance from La Rioja: 172 km south-east on RN 38 then southwards on RN 79

LA RIOJA PROVINCE

Olta is a small town in the south of the province. It is surrounded by the low mountains of the **Sierra de los Quinteros**, and the area is the center of fruitgrowing. During the independence wars several battles were fought here. General Angel Vicente Peñalosa (known as "El Chacho") was killed here on **Loma Blanco** 3 km from town.

Accommodation
- Hostería de Turismo, Castro Barros 298 $5.00
- Residencial Olta, Castro Barros 201 $5.00

Post and telegraph
There are post, telephone, and telegraph offices.

Motoring
There is a petrol station.

Excursions

Olta dam is 5 km from town; there is good fishing.

PATQUÍA

Postal code: 5386 • Population: 1000 • Altitude: 431 m
Distance from La Rioja: 69 km southwards on RN 38

Patquía is located south of the **Desagüe de los Colorados**, an evaporation plain, usually dry, for the rivers coming down from the nearby sierras in spring. Forestry is a flourishing industry. During the independence wars this was the base of General Angel Peñalosa (know as "El Chacho"). In **Guayapa**, 13 km south-west, is one of the biggest date palm plantations in South America; the road to the plantation turns off RN 150 10 km outside town.

Festivals
- Fiesta de Santa Rosa de Lima, patron saint of Patquía: August

Eating out
There is a cafeteria in the bus terminal.

Post and telegraph
There are post, telephone, and telegraph offices.

Buses
The bus terminal is situtated on the highway at the northern entrance to the town.
- La Rioja: Departs 0400 daily; Empresa T A Libertador

Motoring
There is a petrol station.

SALICAS

Postal code: 5327 • Population: 600 • Altitude: 1000 m
Distance from Tinogasta: 71 km southeast on RN 60 then RN 40

Salicas is located in the foothills west of the **Sierra de Velasco**. It has a mild climate all year round. Clear mountain streams descend from the Sierra. The surrounding district is orchard country. It is a good hiking area.

Olta

LA RIOJA PROVINCE

🛏 Accommodation
★ Hostería Salicas, RP 11 Km 117 🍴 $13.00 ⚙. ACA discount

🍴 Eating out
- Restaurant Hostería Salicas, RP 11 Km 117

🚌 Buses
Buses run regularly to Tinogasta and La Rioja.
- Chilecito: Departs Sun; Empresa Santa Rita
- Tinogasta: Departs Sat; Empresa Santa Rita

🚗 Motoring
It is 71 km to Tinogasta, with a 7 km unsealed stretch from Salicas.
There is a petrol station.

⚑ Excursions
- **San Blas**: 5 km south, the departmental capital
- **Schaqui**: 15 km south. This is the last outpost in the province where the pre-Christian Pachamama cult is still celebrated. In the center of the village is a *pucará*, or indigenous fortification. The inhabitants are descendants of the Diaguitas

TERMAS SANTA TERESITA

Postal code: 5313 • Altitude: 700 m
Distance to La Rioja: 110 km north-east on RP 38 then northwards on RP 9 and 10

The thermal spa of Termas Santa Teresita is situated in the utmost north-eastern corner of the province, 11 km off RN 60 between Tinogasta and San Fernando de Catamarca, near Villa Mazán. The climate is mild all year round and the modern ACA hotel is very comfortable. It is only a small village with a few scattered homesteads.

🛏 Accommodation
★★ Hostería Termas Santa Teresita, RP 10 Km 44 via Villa Mazán 🍴 $15.00 ⚙. Full board; ACA discount 20%

🍴 Eating out
- Hostería Termas Santa Teresita, RP 10 Km 44

🚌 Buses
- La Rioja: Fare $2.00; Empresa El Cóndor
- Tinogasta: $3.00; departs 0830 daily; Empresa El Cóndor

⚑ Excursions
- **Tinogasta**: RN 60. The bus makes a pickup trip to the *hostería* and returns to **Villa Mazán** reaching the main highway at the ACA service station. As far as Villa Mazán the hills are covered with shrubs; near here groves of olive trees start. Just west of the township the road enters the narrow gorge of the **Cuesta de Mazán**, carved out of the mountain by the **Río Salado**; however, most of the river's water is now canalled to provide water to irrigate the olive groves near Villa Mazán. South of Villa Mazán the Río Salado disappears in the **Desagüe del Río Salado**, a marshy plain some 40 km east of La Rioja. After passing this pic-

La Rioja Province

turesque gorge the road traverses a wide plain which gradually becomes studded with olive plantations as you approach **Aimogasta**; beyond Aimogasta is the **Sierra de Velasco**. After leaving Aimogasta the road is still sealed but becomes patchy in places, especially near rivers, all of which must be forded, such as **Río de los Sauces**. The road closely follows the contours of the Sierra de Velasco. At **Cerro Negro** there is an important crossroad, the intersection with RN 40 which goes right through to Patagonia and finishes in Jujuy province near the Bolivian border. It is possible to catch buses here north to Belén and Santa María; check timetables carefully as there is no accommodation here. After Cerro Negro the mountains close in again. This is now the **Río Colorado** valley, in its upper reaches called **Río Abaucan**. At this point the mountains on either side are not very high but increase in height rapidly the further north you get. Vineyards start to appear again, and the road becomes very uneven after **La Puntilla** until you reach Tinogasta

- **Villa Mazán** and the Mazán gorge: 15 km. Here the **Río Salado** has carved its course through the Sierra. The Quebrada is approximately 10 km long and quite narrow in some parts
- **Aimogasta**: 42 km. See Aimogasta on page 560

Ulapes

Postal code: 5473 • Population: 900 • Altitude: 450 m
Distance from La Rioja: 291 km southwards on RN 38 then RN 79

Ulapes is located in the extreme south of the province in fairly dry country. Further south on the border with San Luis province there are *salinas*.

🚭 Accommodation
- Residencial Oasis $4.00 ⋮⋮. Full board

🚘 Motoring
The road south to San Luis province is slightly better than the road north.

Villa Castelli

Postal code: 5355 • Population: 1000 • Altitude: 1250 m
Distance from La Rioja: 304 km westwards on RP 76 and RN 40 then northwards on RP 26

Villa Castelli is located in the **Río Vinchina valley**, at the river's junction with the **Río Potrero Grande**.

🚭 Accommodation
- Residencial Villa Castelli $4.00 ⋮⋮

📮 Post and telegraph
There are post, telephone, and telegraph offices.

🚌 Buses
- Chilecito: Departs daily; Empresa Cotillas

Terrmas Santa Teresita

La Rioja Province

- Villa Unión: Departs daily; Empresa Cotillas

🚗 Motoring
Petrol available.

VILLA SANAGASTA

Villa Sanagasta, RJA
Postal code: 5301 • Population: 1300 • Altitude: 1000 m
Distance from La Rioja: 31 km northwards on RP 1

Villa Sanagasta is a summer holiday resort and weekend retreat of the *Riojanos*, or citizens of La Rioja, situated in the **Río Huaco** valley. It has retained many of its colonial buildings, such as the Capilla de la Virgen de las Mercedes (Chapel of the Virgin of Mercy), and the narrow streets give it a peculiar charm. There are many vantage points for photography.

🎭 Festivals
- Pilgrimage of the Virgencita India de Sanagasta (Little Indian Virgin of Sanagasta) to La Rioja: Starts here on the last Friday in September

🛏 Accommodation
★ Hostería Hachay Sacat $14.00 ♨

🍽 Eating out
- Restaurant Villa Sanagasta

✉ Post and telegraph
There are post, telephone, and telegraph offices.

🚌 Buses
Buses run regularly from La Rioja.

VILLA UNIÓN

Postal code: 5350 • Population: 2400 • Area code: (0825) • Altitude: 1240 m
Distances
- From Chilecito: 106 km westwards on RN 40, over the Cuesta de Miranda
- From San José de Jáchal: 140 km northwards on RN 40

A small village in a wide valley basin on the **Río Bermejo**, Villa Unión is the center of a wine-growing and horticultural area. From a vantage point above the village there are panoramic views over Villa Unión and the valley.

🎭 Festivals
- Fiesta del Vinador: Wine festival with the election of a queen, held in March

ℹ Tourist information
Señor Werner Lorentz, of the Hostería Villa Unión, has information about Parque Provincial Talampaya and Ischigualasta (Valle de La Luna) in San Juan province.

🛏 Accommodation
- Hostería Villa Unión, N Davila 61 ℡ 7271 $13.00 ♨

✉ Post and telegraph
There are post, telephone, and telegraph offices.

🚌 Buses
- Chilecito: Fare $3.50; departs 1600 Tues, Sat; Empresa TAC

🚗 Motoring
- Service station: ACA, RN 40 Km 480

La Rioja Province

🟊 Excursions

- **Laguna Brava**: Hiking area. See "Excursions" in Vinchina below
- **Parque Provincial Talampaya**: 73 km south on RP 26, located 14 km off the main road. Wind and water erosion has formed some very strange rock formations: El Fraile (The Monk) and El Castillo (The Castle) are just two. At the **Puerta de Talampaya** is a checkpoint of the provincial tourist office where guides through the park can be hired. Inside the **Quebrada de Talampaya** there are many rock paintings executed by long-extinct tribes who lived here in pre- Hispanic times. Tour operators run round trips taking in **Nonogasta**, **Cuesta de Miranda**, and **Villa Unión**. Buses to La Rioja stop at this national park; see also "Excursions" in Chilecito on page 568
- **Cuesta de Miranda**: This narrow winding road with nearly 800 curves climbs over a pass to **Chilecito**, winding through the mountains over a 10 km stretch. At its highest point, 2020 m, is a plaque to the engineer in charge of building this splendid mountain road

VINCHINA

Postal code: 5357 • Population: 1100 • Altitude: 1480 m

Distance from La Rioja: 335 km westwards RP 76 and RN 40, then northwards on RP 26

Vinchina is a small town situated at the junction of the **Río Jague**, which from the junction becomes **Río Vinchina**. This is the gateway to the unexplored western mountainous part of the province towards the Chilean border. Lack of tourist facilities makes this area accessible only to the outdoor enthusiast who is prepared to hike in the area.

🛏 Accommodation
- Parador Vinchina: $5.00

✉ Post and telegraph
There are post, telephone, and telegraph offices.

🚌 Buses
There are irregular bus services to Villa Unión.

🟊 Excursions

- **Laguna Brava**: A five-day hike. Go to Alto Jagüe, from where it is 34 km on a track, passable to four-wheel drives only, to **Punta de Agua**. Hike alongside the **Río del Peñon** to Laguna Brava, where there are *flamingos rosadas*. Do not attempt this trip during the wet season
- **Cañadón de la Escarcha**: Hikes. A tent and warm gear are necessary

Villa Unión

Tucumán Province

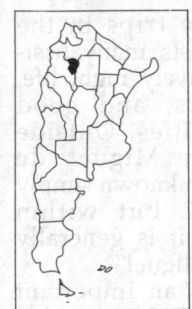

Plate 33 Map of Tucumán Province
- 585 Amaicha del Valle
- 586 Chicligasta
- 586 Colalao del Valle
- 587 Concepción de la Ramada
- 587 Dique El Cadillal
- 588 Dique Escaba
- 588 Ibatín
- 589 Juan B Alberdí
- 589 Los Pizarros
- 589 Lules
- 590 Parque Aconquija
- 590 Parque Provincial El Cochuna
- 590 Quilmes
- 592 Raco
- 592 San Miguel de Tucumán
- 594 Map
- 604 San Pedro de Colalao
- 605 Simoca
- 605 Taco Ralo
- 606 Tafí del Valle
- 608 Trancas
- 609 Villa Nougués

Tucumán Province

Tucumán is the smallest province in Argentina. In area it is only 22 500 square kilometers, and has a population of only 1.3 million. In spite of its compactness it offers the tourist a wide variety of scenery: there are plains in the east and high mountains in the west. Among the higher mountains are the **Cumbres de Calchaquies**, **Nevados del Aconquija** with the highest peak in the province, **Cerro El Bolsón** at 5550 m. The eastern slopes of the ranges are covered in beautiful forests which contain walnut trees, Tucumán cedars, and *lapachos rosados*.

Tucumán shares borders to the south and west with Catamarca, to the north with Salta, and to the east with Santiago del Estero.

The central region, which is traversed by the **Río Salí**, is the most important and most fertile part of the province. Here is the agricultural heart of Tucumán, where crops such as sugarcane, citrus fruit, soya beans, and cotton are grown.

Tucumán has several large hydro-electric schemes, such as the **Lago Escaba** and **Lago El Cadillal** dams, which produce both energy and water for irrigation. This is the base of a progressively growing industrialization. The artificial lakes produced by the dams have become centers of tourism, offering a variety of water sports.

The capital, **San Miguel de Tucumán**, is the ideal starting point for many trips in the province. It boasts many first-class hotels, a lively night life, beautiful parks, and good transport facilities. Outside Tucumán, San Miguel de Tucumán is often known simply as "Tucumán", but within Tucumán itself it is generally known as "San Miguel".

Tucumán is an important seat of learning. The Universidad de Tucumán in San Miguel has ten schools.

The road network contains about 4100 km, of which 900 km are sealed and about 1000 km are compacted. Outside San Miguel, the most important urban centres are **Tafí Viejo**, **Monteros**, **Juan B Alberdí**, **Concepción de la Ramada**, and **Tafí del Valle**.

Tucumán has many archeological and historical sites which for the most part are easily accessible and provide reasonable accommodation.

In the extreme south of the province are many thermal springs such as those at **Taco Ralo** and **La Madrid**. These springs are part of the same system of thermal water which surfaces in the neighbouring province of Santiago del Estero.

Places of interest to the tourist include:
- Worth a visit: **San Miguel de Tucumán**
- Worth a detour: **Tafí del Valle**, **Ruinas de Quilmes**
- Very interesting: **Amaicha del Valle**, **Parque Provincial El Cochuna**

TUCUMÁN PROVINCE

- Of interest: **Lago Escaba**, **Lago El Cadillal**

Scenic drives include: RP 338 and 380 between **Yerba Buena** and **Anta Muerta**, between Anta Muerta and **Villa Nougués**, and between Villa Nougués and **San Pablo**; RP 307 between **Casa de Piedra** and **Amaicha del Valle**; RP 308 (which is continued in Catamarca province as RP 9) from **Boca de la Quebrada** onwards past Lago Escaba; RP 330 (which also extends into Catamarca province) from **El Potrerillo** through **Parque Provincial El Cochuna** to **Cuesta del Clavillo**.

AMAICHA DEL VALLE

Postal code: 4137 • Area code: 0892
Distance
- From San Miguel de Tucumán: 144.5 km westwards on RN 38 then RP 307
- From Cafayate in Salta province: 67 km southwards on RP 340 then 307
- From Santa María in Catamarca province: 24 km northwards on RP 337

Amaicha del Valle is located in the extreme south of the **Río Calchaqui valley** on the **Río Amaicha**, in the western part of Tucumán. It is the only wine-producing area in the province, and also produces woollen textiles.

Amaicha del Valle is the only Indian community left in the province which has preserved its pre-Columbian traditions. These traditions may be seen demonstrated at a regional fair.

Festivals
- Fiesta de la Pachamama: February. This festival goes back to pre-Columbian times
- Fiesta Patronal de San Ramon: August. Festival of the town's patron saint

Accommodation
- Hostería Turística Amaicha del Valle ACA, corner of C Cavo and E Padilla (21019
- Pension Albarracín

Camping
- Municipal camp site, Juan Bautista Alberdí

Buses
- San Miguel de Tucumán: Fare $6.50; 4 services daily; 5 hours; Empresa El Aconcagua
- Cafayate: Fare $2.50; 2 services daily; 3 hours; Empresa El Aconcagua
- Quilmes: Fare $1.00; 2 services daily; 1 hours; Empresa El Aconcagua
- Santa María: Fare $1.50; 2 services daily; 1 hour; Empresa El Indio
- Tafí del Valle: Fare $4.00; 4 services daily; 2 hours; Empresa El Aconcagua

Motoring services

A very winding and picturesque road goes over the 3040 m **Paso Infiernillo**, 21 km from Tafí de Valle and 28 km from Amaicha del Valle. The road is sealed intermittently over this stretch, and also over the stretch between Amaicha del Valle and the junction of RN 40, which leads northwards to Cafayate. RN 337 southwards to Santa María is fully sealed.

TUCUMÁN PROVINCE

CHICLIGASTA

Postal code: 4174
Distance from San Miguel de Tucumán: 90 km southwards on RN 157 then RP 327 at San Antonio

Chicligasta is a small village on the **Río Gastona** just before it empties into the **Embalse Río Hondo**. It has an old church which has been declared a national monument, but because it is off the beaten track it is rarely visited. The date inscribed above the door reads 1797, but it is thought that the church's original foundation was 200 years earlier. The walls are painted with religious murals and there is an old image of the Virgen del Candelaria (Virgin of the Candle) which is venerated. San Francisco Solano, South America's first saint, preached here.

It is only possible to visit on guided tours unless you are prepared to walk 15 km from Atahona (on the main road, passed by buses). To get there by car turn east from RN 157 at km 1207 near San Antonio. There are no tourist facilities.

COLALAO DEL VALLE

Postal code: 4141 • Population: 400
Distance
- From Cafayate: 33 km southwards on RN 40
- From Tafí del Valle: 87 km northwards on RP 307 then RN 40

Colalao del Valle is located in the northern **Río Calchaqui valley**, near the border with Salta province. (It is not to be confused with San Pedro de Colalao also in Tucumán but situated on the eastern slopes of the Cumbres de Calchaquies.) It is a small rural Indian community not far from the archeological site of Quilmes.

Festivals
- Fiesta del Antigal: January. This festival goes back to pre-Columbian times
- Fiesta del Poncho: July
- Fiesta Patronal Nuestra Señora del Rosario (Festival of the Patron Saint Our Lady of the Rosary): August

Tourist information
Señor Lucio Ruben Vera of the Hostería has information on the valley, and he says there are more abandoned ruined pre-Columbian villages hidden in the Cumbres de Calchaquies.

Accommodation
- Hostería Comunal Colalao del Valle, northern end of town $7.00

Bus services
Empresa El Aconquija runs daily services between San Miguel de Tucumán and Cafayate, and also to Santa María. Buses go past the turn-off to Quilmes ruins; fare $0.80.

Motoring services
- Service station: YPF

Excursions
- **Quilmes** ruins: See Quilmes on page 590

Chicligasta

CONCEPCIÓN DE LA RAMADA

Postal code: 4146 • Area code: (0865) •
Population: 30 000
Distance from San Miguel de Tucumán:
65 km southwards on RN 38

Concepción de la Ramada is situated on the **Río Gastona**. Its name is commonly abbreviated to "Concepción". It is the center of a sugarcane farming area, having many sugar mills, and is also a timber milling center. Visit the Benedictine monastery 5 km outside town, where you can buy Benedictine liqueur and other regional products.

Accommodation
- Hotel Colonial, Colón 61

Buses
- San Miguel de Tucumán: 2 hours
- Andalgalá: Fare $4.70; departs 0810 Tues, Thurs, Sat; 5 hours
- Belén: Fare $7.20; departs 0810 Tues, Sat; 8 hours; Empresa Gutierrez
- Londres: Fare $7.50; departs 0810 Tues, Sat; 8 hours; Empresa Gutierrez
- Tinogasta: Fare $10.50; departs 0810 Sat; 11 hours; Empresa Gutierrez

Excursions
- **Dique El Molino**: A dam on the **Río Gastona** 10 km upstream, near **Itico**
- **Parque Provincial El Cochuna**: 60 km on RP 329 then RP 330. The area is most interesting from **El Potrerillo** onwards. Buses run by Gutierrez to Tinogasta pass through the Parque Provincial and over the **Cuesta del Clavillo**. The park is densely forested with many subtropical species. Trout fishing in the streams is permitted in season

DIQUE EL CADILLAL

Postal code: 4122
Distance from San Miguel de Tucumán:
26 km northwards on RN 9 then RP 347

The damming of the **Río Salí** has created a huge artificial lake known as Dique El Cadillal, a very popular resort among the *Tucumeños*. Many sports clubs have retreats here. The Complejo Turístico Río Loro on the south side of the lake has beaches, wooded areas, tables, and kiosks.

Camping
- ACA camping ground with recreation area

Bus services
Buses run frequently to and from San Miguel de Tucumán; return fare $1.00.

Sport
Water sports, such as sailing, boating, water-skiing, and swimming, and fishing are all popular.

Sightseeing
- Museo Arqueológico Ernesto Padilla (Ernesto Padillo Archeological Museum), near the amphitheatre
- Amphitheatre where plays are staged during the summer months

TUCUMÁN PROVINCE

Excursions

See "Excursions" in San Miguel de Tucumán on page 602

DIQUE ESCABA

Postal code: 4158 • Altitude: 630 m
Distance from Juan B Alberdí: 24 km westwards on RP 308

Dique Escaba is an artificial lake covering approximately 535 ha. The Escaba hydro-electric and irrigation scheme is one of the largest in the country. The waters come from the **Cumbres de Narvaez**, whose highest point is **Cerro Moros** at 1920 m, and **Cumbres de Santa Ana**. The lake provides good fishing, especially for *pejerrey*; trout which have been released into the lake have always migrated further up the streams where the water is colder.

The word *Escaba* is a Quechua word meaning "where the rivers come together, and is a fitting description of the location. It has become one of the favourite tourist centers in the province, providing for all kinds of water sports as well as sport fishing. Boats may be hired from the Club de Regatas de Tucumán.

Accommodation

The local *hosteria* at the moment has only a few rooms and several cabins between the road and the main building. It is definitely not geared for a large influx of tourists, and does not cater well to foreign tourists.

Eating out

Bring your own food, as the cafeteria is usually closed.

Visas, passports

There is a police checkpoint at Escaba, below the *hosteria*, where documents are checked and recorded, so bring your passport or identification.
There are several daily buses from Juan B Alberdí; return fare $1.50

Excursions

This is interesting hiking and camping country.
- The road up to the lake first passes through flat sugarcane country and tobacco farms. After **Boca de la Quebrada** it begins to climb, and past the Batiruana power station it becomes very winding and narrow. Every 100 m or so there is a widening in the road to permit oncoming traffic to pass. The drive through the lush subtropical canyon is exhilarating. At one stage the road passes over the crest of the dam to serve **Escaba de Arriba** at the northern end, and returns from there to terminate at **Escaba de Abajo** at the southern end. See also "Excursions" in San Miguel de Tucumán on page 603

IBATÍN

Distance from San Miguel de Tucumán: 52 km southwards on RN 38

Ibatín is the site where the original Tucumán was founded

Dique El Cadillal

in 1565. The outlines of the original buildings can still be traced. It is also known as Tucumán Viejo.

Bus services

El Trebol runs regular bus services from Tucumán to Ingenio Santa Rosa; return fare $2.50. See "Excursions" in San Miguel de Tucumán on page 603.

JUAN B ALBERDÍ

Postal code: 4158 • Population: 10 000 • Area code: (0865)
Distance from San Miguel de Tucumán: 95 km southwards on RN 38

Juan B Alberdí is a small town surrounded by sugarcane farms. It is a stopover for changing buses up to Dique Escaba.

Accommodation
• Residencial Hoffmann

Eating out
• Cafetería Bar Yuliano, on the main Plaza
• Cafetería Bar Náutico, on the main Plaza. Also Bosio buses
• Cafetería Bar Camarun, corner of Rivadavia and Córdoba, on the main Plaza

Bus services
• San Miguel de Tucumán: Fare $2.20
• Dique Escaba: Fare $0.80

Excursions
• **Dique Escaba**. See Dique Escaba on page 588, and "Excursions" in San Miguel de Tucumán on page 603

LOS PIZARROS

Postal code: 4162
Distance from San Miguel de Tucumán: 120 km southwards on RN 38

Los Pizarros is located in the southern part of Tucumán about 5 km west of La Cocha. Its only claim to fame is the Jesuit mission church of San Ignacio built in 1746. The church, located in a cemetery, has been completely restored. It is a national monument and worth a visit.

There is good *pejerrey* fishing in the nearby **Río San Ignacio**.

Buses
• San Miguel de Tucumán: Fare $2.80
• Juan B Alberdí: Fare $0.70

LULES

Postal code: 4128 • Altitude: 415m • Area code: (081) • Population: 12 000
Distance from San Miguel de Tucumán: 20 km south-west on RP 380

Just out of Lules on the north side are the Jesuit mission ruins of San José de Lules. The mission was founded in 1613 and was a flourishing center until the expulsion of the Jesuits in 1658. After years of neglect the monastery was acquired in 1781 by the Dominican friars, who built a new church. Only the church has remained of all the former buildings.

To reach the **Quebrada de Lules**, take the turn-off to the hydro-electric plant, 8 km past San Pablo. Here the **Río Lules** runs for some distance through a narrow passage. Nearby are the factories of Papel de Tucumán; the water from there onwards is heavily polluted.

Buses

There are regular municipal bus services from San Miguel de Tucumán.

PARQUE ACONQUIJA

Distance from San Miguel de Tucumán: 24 km east on RP 338

The Parque Aconquija is a place of outstanding scenic beauty, quite close to San Miguel de Tucumán. In the park is a restaurant. Past **Yerba Buena** a steep winding road leads up to **Anta Muerta**, at 1220 m, with a small *hostería* at the crest. Nearby is a statue of Cristo Redentor (Christ the Redeemer). It is a very scenic drive, especially near **San Javier**. It is possible to use public transport but it is worth going by tour bus.

Accommodation

★★ Hotel St James, RP 338. Good views over the Parque Aconquija

PARQUE PROVINCIAL EL COCHUNA

Distance from Concepció de la Ramada: 48 km westwards on RP 329

The Parque Provincial El Cochuna is situated in the **Río Cochuna valley**. RP 329 branches off RN 38 at Concepción and passes through the park on its way to the neighbouring Catamarca province. The most picturesque part is the splendid views up the valley after crossing the **Río Vallecito** bridge. Shortly after **La Banderita** the road reaches its highest point at **Cuesta del Clavillo**, from where it descends into the **Río Grande del Campo** valley in Catamarca. Empresa Gutierrez runs four buses a week through the park to Belén and Andalgalá in Catamarca province. This is a place for the hiker and camper, with mountain scenery of the **Nevados del Aconquija** reaching 5550 m in the **Cerro del Bolsón**. The vegetation is substropical. There are no tourist facilities.

Buses

If you intend to hike in the park, Señor Pedro Pablo Gutierrez, owner of the transport company at Avenida Avellaneda 327 in San Miguel de Tucumán will be pleased to give up-to-date advice on bus services available to and from the national road services camp, and on to Belén in Catamarca province.

QUILMES

Postal code: 4111
Distance
- From Amaicha del Valle: 22 km northeast on RN 40 then RP 307
- From Cafayate: 53 km southwards on RN 40

Lules

TUCUMÁN PROVINCE

- From Santa María: 32 km northwards on RN 40

Quilmes is one of the major archeological sites in Tucumán and indeed in the whole of Argentina. It is located 5 km east of RN 40; the turn-off is well signposted.

Quilmes was the place where the Calchaquies peoples staged their final resistance against the invading Spaniards. This fortress town was built on the slopes of the horseshoe-shaped **Cerro Alto del Rey**—a steep hill—with vanguard points along the rim of the horseshoe and small fortifications on the slopes. Clever use was made of rock formation to build the defense installations, some of them subterranean. Rather than risking a frontal attack which would have been disastrous for their troops the Spanish outflanked the defenders by climbing the hills and attacking them from above.

When the fortress fell the survivors were dispersed over Argentina, in the same way that the Incas had done with unruly conquered peoples. The biggest contingent of survivors was settled near Buenos Aires where to this day a suburb is called Quilmes. It is also the brand name of a well-known brewery.

The remains of the fortress are known as the *Ruinas de Quilmes* (Ruins of Quilmes). The federal government has made a commendable effort to restore the ruins and has constructed paths up the rather steep hill on which the fortress stands.

The visit to Quilmes is definitely one of the highlights of a tour through Argentina.

ℹ Tourist information

The administration building has an information desk, guides, and a kiosk for refreshments. Outside the main tourist season it is not always open.

🚌 Buses from Quilmes

Empresa Aconquija runs services to and from San Miguel de Tucumán, either direct or via Santa María; there are three services daily during summer, and two during winter. For the budget tourist the best starting point is Cafayate, where a bus leaves at 0600 arriving at the turn-off at around 0700. From the road junction it is 45 minutes' brisk walk over a gravel road. This gives keen photographers an opportunity to take pictures of the ruins when the sun is rising. An extensive visit right up to the highest point of the ruined town and inspection of the bastions and trails leading to them would take three or four hours, giving the tourist a chance to return to the main road and catch a bus either to Santa María or San Miguel de Tucumán and Tafí del Valle.

Destination	Fare	Services	Hours	Company
• San Miguel de Tucumán		2 services daily	6½	El Aconcagua
• Amaicha del Valle	$0.80	2 services daily	1	El Aconcagua
• Cafayate	$1.50	2 services daily	1	El Aconcagua
• Colalao del Valle	$0.80	2 services daily	½	El Aconcagua
• Santa María	$0.80	2 services daily	1	El Indio
• Tafí del Valle	$3.00	2 services daily	3	El Aconcagua

TUCUMÁN PROVINCE

Tours
Conducted tours are available from San Miguel de Tucumán and to a lesser degree from Salta.

RACO

Postal code: 4105
Distance from San Miguel de Tucumán: 52 km north-west on RP 338 then RP 340

Located on the upper **Río Tapia**, Raco's foundation goes back to the seventeenth century. Its mild climate attracts many visitors all year round. Trout fishing is possible in the **Río Raco** and **Río Siambon**. The monks in the nearby Benedictine monastery keep bees for the production of royal jelly. Local crafts include leather chairs and woven quilts.

SAN MIGUEL DE TUCUMÁN

Postal code: 4000 • Population: 450 000 • Area code: (081) • Altitude: 447 m
Distance
- From Buenos Aires: 1312 km north-west on RN 9
- From Salta: 288 km southwards on RN 9
- From Santiago del Estero: 160 km north-west on RN 9

San Miguel de Tucumán is situated on a wide plain overshadowed in the west by the magnificent **Sierra de Aconquija**. It is the provincial capital.

San Miguel was initially founded in 1565 in Campos de Ibatín by Don Diego de Villaroel, but was transferred to its present location in 1685. There are fine modern buildings and large plazas and parks such as Parque Avellaneda and Parque 9 de Julio with an artificial lake. The house of Bishop Colombres, founder of Argentina's sugar industry, is here; Colombres introduced the first milling machine early last century. It has an important university and a lively night life.

Plaza Independencia is the city's center. In its vicinity there are still some colonial houses to be seen. On the west side of the Plaza is the government palace, and on the south are major banks, the cathedral, and San Francisco church. Most of the houses are single-storied; above them rise the silhouettes of the city's churches, some with multicoloured tiled domes.

Running south from Plaza Independencia is Calle Congreso. Here is the Casa de Independencia (Independence Building), where at the Congreso de Tucumán Argentina declared its independence from Spain. The Casa is described under "Sightseeing" below.

Plaza Belgrano, south-west of Plaza Independencia at the intersection of Bolívar and Bernabé Araoz, is named in honour of the General who defeated the royalist troops outside San Miguel in 1812. His statue stands in the center of the plaza.

Calle San Martín is a pedestrian mall between 25 de Mayo and Maipú. Intersecting

Quilmes

TUCUMÁN PROVINCE

San Martín is Calle Buenos Aires, also a pedestrian mall running between San Martín and 24 de Setiembre, and between San Martín and Mendoza.

San Miguel is well served by road, rail, and air, and has excellent tourist facilities and good transport connections to tourist sites throughout the province. The ACA provides an excellent map of the province.

Outside Tucumán province, San Miguel de Tucumán is often known simply as "Tucumán", but within Tucumán itself it is generally known as "San Miguel".

Because of the hot summers, a siesta time is widely observed. It runs from 1200 to 1600 during the summer months, during which time most shops, services, and banks are closed.

Festivals

- Batalla de Tucumán (Battle of Tucumán): September 24

Tourist information

- Secretaria del Estado de Turismo, 24 de Setiembre 484, on the Plaza Independencia ℂ 218591. Open daily (including Sundays) 0700–2300. Very helpful

Camping

- Camping Municipal, Parque 9 de Julio

Eating out

- Cervecería del Norte. Makes excellent fermented "hop juice"
- Restaurant Ali Baba, Junín block 300 (corner of San Juan)
- Restaurant Barrio Norte, Monteagudo block 600 (corner of Corrientes)
- Restaurant Benito II, corner of 9 de Julio and General Paz. Steakhouse
- Restaurant Casa Libanesa, Chacabuco 51
- Restaurant Chin-San, Sarmiento 749. Chinese cuisine
- Restaurant Cien Puntos, Hotel Grand Hotel de Tucumán, Soldatti. International cuisine
- Restaurant Club Sirio, Maipú 575
- Restaurant Del Centro, San Martín block 200 (corner of Laprida). Credit cards accepted
- Restaurant del Lago, Parque 9 de Julio, beside Lago San Miguel
- Restaurant Don Quijote, Laprida block 300 (corner of Córdoba)
- Restaurant Don Zenon, Laprida 623. Steakhouse
- Restaurant El Alto de la Lechuza, 24 de Setiembre 1199. Steakhouse
- Restaurant El Duque, San Lorenzo 440
- Restaurant El Fondo, Laprida 846. Steakhouse
- Restaurant El Gallego, 9 de Julio block 0 (corner of Alvarez)
- Restaurant El Jardín, Mendoza 477. Steakhouse
- Restaurant El Mangrullo, corner of Congreso de Tucumán and General Paz
- Restaurant El Quincho de Carlos, corner of Laprida and Córdoba
- Restaurant El Rancho Grande, corner of Maipú and España
- Restaurant El Viejo Almacen, San Martin block 1100 corner of M Avellaneda. Steakhouse
- Restaurant Erula, Sarmiento 709. Credit cards accepted
- Restaurant Escrúpulos, corner of Mendoza 996 and Salta. Steakhouse
- Restaurant Escudero, San Juan 1101. Steakhouse
- Restaurant La Cantina, San Martín 750
- Restaurant La Esquina, Laprida 205. Also pasta
- Restaurant La Franco Argentina, 9 de Julio block 500 (corner of General de Lamadrid)
- Restaurant La Gran Via, corner of 25 de Mayo 398 and San Juan
- Restaurant La Leñita, 25 de Mayo block 300 (corner of San Juan)
- Restaurant La Recova, 24 de Setiembre block 0. A plaque says that Juan B Alberdí's birth place stood here

San Miguel de Tucumán

TUCUMÁN PROVINCE

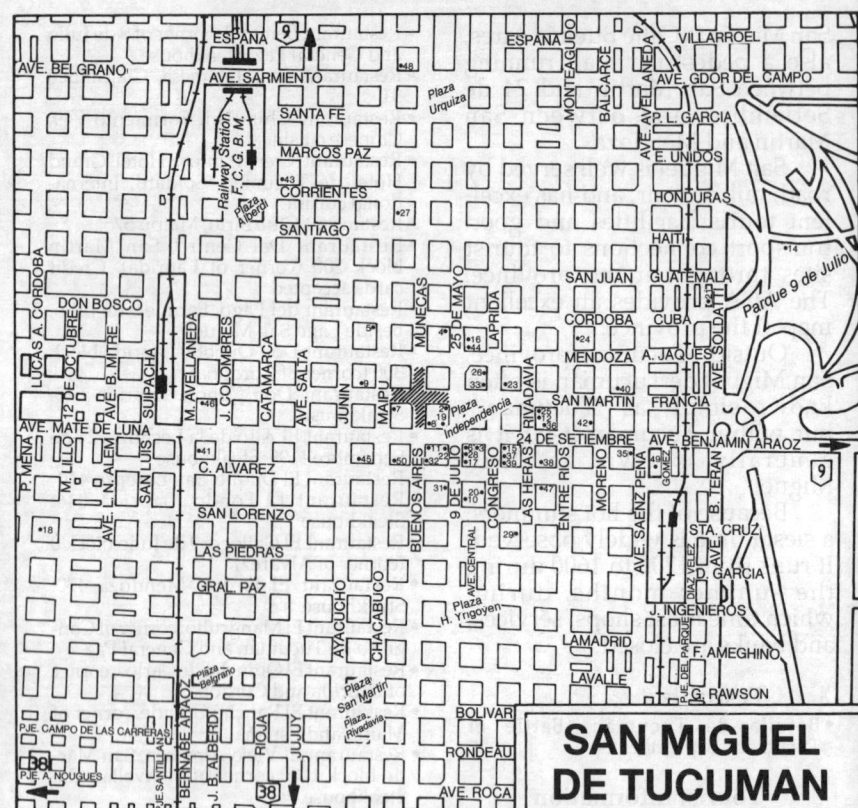

SAN MIGUEL DE TUCUMAN

- Restaurant La Terraza, Córdoba block 700 (corner of Junín). Steakhouse
- Restaurant La Vieja Casa, Córdoba 680. Local dishes
- Restaurant Lisandro, 25 de Mayo 453. Steakhouse
- Restaurant Los Angeles, Mendoza block 100 (corner of Monteagudo)
- Restaurant Los Dos Gordos, 24 de Setiembre 450
- Restaurant Mi Abuela, Maipú 942
- Restaurant Mi Estancia, 25 de Mayo 566. Steakhouse
- Restaurant Mi Jardín, Mendoza block 400 (corner of Laprida). Steakhouse
- Restaurant Mi Refugio, Maipú 492
- Restaurant Nuevo Italia, Congreso de Tucumán 32
- Restaurant Risco, corner of Araoz and Avellaneda (opposite bus station)
- Restaurant Parrilla del Centro, San Martín 391. Steakhouse
- Restaurant Pascualito, Laprida 187
- Restaurant Sorrento, Alvarez (near 9 de Julio). *Peña* every night; patronized by locals
- Restaurant Su Rincón Miana, Monteagudo 169
- Pizzería Amigos, corner of 24 de Setiembre and Rivadavia. English pub style

San Miguel de Tucumán

TUCUMÁN PROVINCE

Key to Map

2	Casa de Gobierno
3	Catedral
4	Post office (Encotel)
5	Telephone (Entel)
6	Tourist information
7	Banco de la Nación
8	Cambio Noroeste
9	Cambio Maguitour
10	Aerolineas Argentinas
11	Austral Lineas Aereas
12	Iglesia de la Merced
13	Iglesia San Francisco
14	Casa del Obispo Colombres
15	Museo Histórico de Provincia Presidente Nicolás Avellaneda
16	Museo de Antropologia, Prehistoria, y Arqueologia
17	Museo Provincial de Bellas Artes
18	Museo del Instituto Miguel Lillo
19	Museo Folklórico Provincial Manuel Belgrano
20	Casa de la Independencia
21	Hotel Grand Hotel de Tucumán
22	Hotel Metropol
23	Hotel del Sol
24	Hotel Presidente
25	Hotel República
26	Hotel Bristol
27	Hotel Claridge
28	Hotel Gran Corona
29	Hotel Embajador
30	Hotel Mayoral
31	Hotel Premier
32	Hotel Versalles
33	Hotel Plaza
34	Hotel Residencial Francia
35	Residencial Alcazar
36	Residencial Palace
37	Residencial Congreso
38	Residencial Impala
39	Residencial Asturias
40	Residencial Colonial
41	Residencial Crillon
42	Residencial Independencia
43	Residencial Italia
44	Residencial La Rida
45	Residencial Petit
46	Residencial Royal
47	Residencial Veco
48	Casino de Tucumán
49	Bus terminal
50	Hotel Garden

- Pizzería Cinta, corner of 24 de Setiembre and Congreso de Tucumán
- Pizzería Don Mostacho, 24 de Setiembre 508
- Pizzería Mr Pool (formerly called La Mamina), San Martín 941. Pasta
- Pizzería Momentos, 9 de Julio 513
- Pizzería Napoli, Catamarca block 800 (corner of Sarmiento)
- Pizzería Scorpa, San Martín 356
- Pizzería Via Flaviana, Muñecas block 100 (corner of Mendoza)
- Cafetería Ambato, San Martín 153
- Cafetería Augustus, 24 de Setiembre block 600 (corner of Buenos Aires)
- Cafetería Cafe de la Plaza, corner of Laprida and San Martín (on the Plaza)
- Cafetería Candy, Córdoba 513. *Churros*
- Cafetería Colonial, Maipú 453
- Cafetería Crillon, Mendoza 452
- Cafetería El Buen Gusto, 9 de Julio 29. Snacks
- Cafetería El Colonial, Congreso de Tucumán block 100 (corner of San Lorenzo)
- Cafetería El Juglar, Congreso de Tucumán 36
- Cafetería Emiliano, Congreso de Tucumán block 0 (corner of C Alvarez)
- Cafetería Gaston, Congreso de Tucumán block 0 (corner of C Alvarez)
- Cafetería Glass, 9 de Julio 96
- Cafetería La Carpa, Sarmiento block 700 (corner of Junín). Hamburgers
- Cafetería La Oca Express, Laprida block 500 (corner of Santiago)
- Cafetería La Pamera, Muñecas 692
- Cafetería Los Escudos, 25 de Mayo 286
- Cafetería Manuela, Junín 667
- Cafetería Petrus, 9 de Julio block 200 (corner of San Lorenzo)
- Cafetería Quetrihue, Mendoza 232
- Cafetería Regatas, 9 de Julio 477
- Cafetería Sebastian, Congreso de Tucumán block 200 (corner of Piedras)
- Cafetería Swazi, Congreso de Tucumán 210
- Cafetería Vera Cruz, Soldatti 686
- Cafetería Whimpy, Mendoza 352. Pasta

San Miguel de Tucumán

TUCUMÁN PROVINCE

🛏 Accommodation in San Miguel de Tucumán

Cheap accommodation can be found just around from the bus terminal at Residencial Cristal and Residencial Estrella, suitable for budget travelers only.

★★★★★	Hotel Grand Hotel de Tucumán, Proceres 380	ℓ 245000	$35.50	
★★★	Hotel del Sol, Laprida 32	ℓ 245555	$18.00	
★★★	Hotel Metropol, 24 Setiembre 524	ℓ 221180	$21.50	
★★★	Hotel Presidente, Monteagudo 249	ℓ 212414	$18.00	
★★★	Hotel República, Rivadavia 71	ℓ 219480	$18.00	
	Credit cards accepted			
★★	Hotel Bristol, Laprida 154	ℓ 219320	$14.00	
★★	Hotel Claridge, Maipú 545	ℓ 229360	$14.00	
★★	Hotel Embajador, Las Heras 250	ℓ 215264	$14.00	
★★	Hotel Gran Corona, 24 de Setiembre 498		$10.00	
★★	Hotel Mayoral, 24 de Setiembre 354	ℓ 218025	$14.00	
	Credit cards accepted			
★★	Hotel Premier, Alvarez 510	ℓ 21983	$14.00	
★★	Hotel Versailles, Alvarez 481	ℓ 229760	$14.00	
★	Hotel America, Santiago del Estero	ℓ 214209	$10.50	
★	Hotel California, Corrientes 985	ℓ 229259	$8.50	
★	Hotel Garden, C Alvarez 627	ℓ 221246	$10.50	
★	Hotel Miami, Junín 580	ℓ 222265	$10.50	
★	Hotel Plaza, San Martín 435	ℓ 215502	$10.50	
★	Hotel Residencial Francia, Alvarez 465		$10.50	
A	Residencial Congreso, Congreso 74	ℓ 221477	$8.50	
A	Residencial Impala, C Alvarez 277	ℓ 225371	$6.50	
	Breakfast $1.20			
A	Residencial Kings, Chacabuco 18	ℓ 219210	$8.50	
A	Residencial Universo, Santiago del Estero 1060	ℓ 216136	$8.50	
B	Residencial Astoria, Congreso 88	ℓ 217876	$6.50	
B	Residencial Colonial, San Martín 35	ℓ 211523	$6.50	
B	Residencial Crillon, B Araoz 36	ℓ 213507	$5.00	
B	Residencial Elton, Maipú 342	ℓ 229740	$6.50	
B	Residencial Florida, corner of 24 de Setiembre and 9 de Julio			
		ℓ 221785	$6.50	
B	Residencial Independencia, Balcarce 50	ℓ 217038	$5.00	
B	Residencial Italia, Catamarca 601 (corner of Corrientes)			
	Near F C General Bartolomé Mitre station	ℓ 229913	$5.00	
B	Residencial La Rida, Mendoza 437			
B	Residencial Petit, Alvarez 765	ℓ 213902	$6.50	
B	Residencial Royal, San Martín 1186	ℓ 218802	$5.00	
B	Residencial Viena, Santiago del Estero 1054	ℓ 224004	$5.00	
C	Residencial Boston, RS Peña 77			
	A bit rough, but acceptable for budget travelers			
C	Residencial Ritz, Congreso de Tucumán 75		$5.00	
	Suitable for budget travelers			
C	Residencial Veco, C Alvarez 244		$4.00	
	For budget travelers			

- Residencial Alcazar, R S Peña 3, opposite the bus terminal
- Residencial Palace, 24 de Setiembre 233

San Miguel de Tucumán

TUCUMÁN PROVINCE

Accommodation in San Miguel de Tucumán—continued

Accommodation outside San Miguel de Tucumán

See also "Accommodation" in Parque Aconquija on page 590

- ★ Motel Posta de los Arrieros, RN 9 in the northern part of town, Km 1301 (219608 $10.50
- ★ Motel Tucumán, corner of Salta and Mexico (226099

Post and telegraph

- Post office: Encotel, corner of 25 de Mayo and Córdoba
- Telephone: Entel, corner of Muñecas 226 and Córdoba 720

Financial

Tucumán province issues its own currency ("*bonos*") valid only within Tucumán itself. Banks open from 0700 to 1300, close during the siesta, and open again from 1600.

- Banco Alas, San Martín 578. Cash advances on Visa card
- ☞ Noroeste Cambios SA, 24 de Setiembre 549. Good rates
- ☞ Maguitur, San Martín 765 (211284. Checks and cash; good rates
- Turismo Pandorama, Mendoza 348. Not particularly good rates for travelers' checks
- Cambio Dinar, San Martín 678 (215741

Services and facilities

- Dry cleaner: Nipon, 24 de Setiembre 832
- Emergency medical services: 9 de Julio 712
- Sauna: Ivan Gym, Mendoza 880
- Sports equipment: Martin Pescador, Junín block 500 (corner of Santiago del Estero)

Laundromats

- Laverap, Santiago del Estero 414. Open Mo–Sat 080–2200
- Laverap, 9 de Julio 510. $2.00

Photographic supplies

- Camera repairs and photograph service, Alberdí 54
- Fotografía Norte, 24 de Setiembre block 500 (corner of 25 de Mayo). Stocks Agfa and Kodak film

Clubs

- French: Alliance Française, Mendoza 255
- German: Goethe Institut, Santiago 1220

Visas, passports

- Visa extensions: Imigraciones, Buenos Aires 2715. Take bus 6
- German vice-consulate, B Rivadavia 105, 3rd floor
- Italian vice-consul, 24 de Setiembre (in the Edificio Italia on the corner of Catamarca)

Motoring

Service stations

- ACA, C Alvarez block 900 (corner of Jujuy). An excellent map of the province is available from here

Car rental

- Movil Renta, San Lorenzo 370 (218635
- A1 International Rent-a-Car, Hotel Gran Casino, corner of Soldatti and Guatemala
- Avis Rent-a-Car, Hotel El Sol, Laprida 32 (245555. Also at the airport
- Liprandi Rent-a-Car, San Lorenzo 642 (corner of Congreso de Tucumán) (213760
- Noroeste Rent-a-Car, Hotel Versailles, C Alvarez

Trains

Two railroad lines run to San Miguel de Tucumán.

San Miguel de Tucumán

TUCUMÁN PROVINCE

✈ Air services from San Miguel de Tucumán

Aeropuerto Benjamin Matienzo is 9 km from the center of the city.
There are discounts for night flights.
- Aerolineas Argentinas, 9 de Julio block 100 (corner of San Lorenzo) (228747
- Austral Airlines, 24 de Setiembre 537
- Aerolineas Federal Argentina, Hotel Gran Corona, 24 de Setiembre 498

Destination	Fare	Services	Hours	Airline
Buenos Aires (Aeroparque Jorge Newbery)	$77.00	4–9 services daily	2	Aerolineas, Austral
Comodoro Rivadavia	$95.00	Wed, Fri, Sun	7	Aerolineas
Córdoba	$41.00	2–3 services daily	1	Aerolineas, Austral
Mendoza	$44.00	Tues, Thurs, Sun	2	Federal
	$69.00	Wed, Fri, Sun	3	Aerolineas
Neuquén	$94.00	Mon, Wed, Fri	5	Aerolineas, Austral
Resistencia	$40.00	Tues, Thurs, Sun	2	Federal
Río Gallegos	$110.00	Sat	7	Aerolineas
Río Grande	$118.00	Sat	8	Aerolineas
Rosario	$57.00	Mon, Tues, Thurs	3	Aerolineas
Salta	$23.00	1–2 services daily	1	Aerolineas
San Carlos de Bariloche	$100.00	Sat, Sun	5	Aerolineas
San Juan	$40.00	Sat	1	Federal
San Rafael	$53.00	Sun	3	Federal
San Salvador de Jujuy	$25.00	Mon–Fri, Sun	1	Aerolineas

F C General M Belgrano

The station is on the corner of Avenida Peña and Charcas, opposite the bus terminal. From here "El Norteño" departs Mon, Thurs, and Fri for Retiro station in Buenos Aires, via Córdoba.

F C General B Mitre

The station is on M Avellaneda. The following trains depart from here for Retiro station in Buenos Aires:
- "Independencia" departs Thurs and Sun, via La Banda and Córdoba. The trip takes 18 hours
- "Ciudad de Tucumán" departs daily, via Córdoba
- Train 216 departs Mon, Wed, and Fri, via La Banda

Fares to Buenos Aires

- "Independencia": Sleeper $41.50; Pullman $32.00
- Other trains: Pullman $25.50; first class $18.20; tourist class $12.60

⊕ Tours

- Delfin Turismo, 24 de Setiembre 370
- Turismo Mi Pais, C Alvarez 449 (211045
- Turismo Tucumán, 24 de Setiembre 440 (228773

🛍 Shopping

Although most shops are closed during the siesta, San Miguel is a place to shop. Most of the trading activities center around Plaza Independencia and in the pedestrian malls in Calle San Martín and Muñecas.
- Feria Artesanías Tucumános, 24 de Setiembre block 300 (corner of Congreso de Tucumán)
- Regionales El Coyuyo, Congreso de Tucumán 130
- Regionales Falchi, Congreso de Tucumán 86

TUCUMÁN PROVINCE

🚌 Bus services

The bus terminal is on R S Peña. Urban buses begin at 0530 and run until 0100.

Destination	Fare	Depart	Services	Hours	Company
• Andalgalá	$6.00	0630	Tues, Thurs, Fri Sat	7	Gutierrez
• Belén	$8.50	0630	Tues, Sat	9½	Gutierrez
• Buenos Aires	$26.00	2100	daily	16	T A Chevallier
• San Miguel de Catamarca	$5.00	1300	2 services daily	5	Bosio
• Cerro Negro	$10.50	0630	Sat		Gutierrez
• Concepción de la Ramada	$1.60	0630	Tues, Thurs, Fri, Sat	1½	Gutierrez
• Córdoba	$12.00	0014	9 services daily	8	El Trebol, Expreso Panamericano, La Veloz del Norte, T A Chevallier
• Corrientes	$14.00	1900	2 services daily	14½	El Rayo
• La Rioja	$7.30	1225	3 services daily	9	Bosio, La Estrella
• Londres	$8.90	0630	Tues, Sat	10	Gutierrez
• Los Pizarros	$2.80				San Cristobal
• Lules	Departs every 20 minutes from Platform 6				
• Mar del Plata	$37.40	1130	2 services daily	26	La Estrella
• Mendoza	$21.00	1300	2 services daily	16	La Estrella
• Paraná	$14.00	1900	daily	13	
• Presidencia Roque Sáenz Peña	$10.50	1900	daily	11	El Rayo
• Resistencia	$14.00	1900	2 services daily	14	El Rayo
• Rosario	$17.00	2100	daily	14½	T A Chevallier
• Salta	$7.50	0630	7 services daily	5	Expreso Panamericano
• San Francisco	$12.50	2000	daily	10	La Estrella
• San Juan	$16.50	1300	2 services daily		La Estrella
• San Pedro de Colalao	$1.80	0600	Mon, Fri		San Pedro de Colalao
• San Salvador de Jujuy	$8.30	0017	6 services daily	6	Expreso Panamericano, La Veloz del Norte
• Santa Fé	$17.00	1930	2 services daily	12	La Estrella
• Santa María	$5.20				El Indio
• Santiago del Estero	$2.80	0430	34 services daily	2	El Ranchilleño, El Rayo, El Santiagueño, La Estrella, La Unión
Express service	$3.80		7 services daily	1	Expreso Panamericano, La Estrella
• Tafí del Valle	$2.50	0500	daily	3	El Aconquija
• Termas de Río Hondo	$1.50	0430	29 services daily	1	El Ranchilleño, El Rayo, La Estrella, La Unión
• Tinogasta	$11.80	0630	Sat	12½	Gutierrez
• Trancas	$2.00	0600	4 services daily	3	

San Miguel de Tucumán

- Regionales Valencia, Congreso de Tucumán 116
- Regionales El Legiaro, Congreso de Tucumán block 0 (corner of C Alvarez)
- Regionales 9 de Julio, 9 de Julio 83

Sport

- Golf: Golf Club Alpa Sumaj, La Rinconada 12 km west of the city. Follow RP 338 as far as Yerba Buena and then turn south. Has a swimming pool
- Ice skating: Winner Club, Junín 629

Entertainment

- Casino de Tucumán, corner of Avenida Sarmiento and Maipú. Open all year round
- Night Club Harlem, Balcarce block 100 (corner of Mendoza)
- Night Club Iceberg, Laprida block 200 (corner of Mendoza)
- Peña El Alto de la Lechuza, 24 de Setiembre 1199. Regional music every night
- Peña El Motivo, Combate de las Piedras 393
- Tango Bar, Prospero Garcia 88. Open Fri, Sat, Sun, and public holidays from 2100
- La Peña, C Alvarez 464 (upstairs). Open daily with restaurant and bar; regional music

Sightseeing

Public buildings

- Casa de Gobierno (House of Assembly), 25 de Mayo (on the Plaza Independencia), the seat of provincial legislation
- Casa de la Independencia (Independence Building), Congreso 151. The Congreso de Tucumán met here on July 9, 1816 with delegates from all the Argentine provinces to declare Argentina's independence from Spain and to draft a constitution. On the wall is a painting of the delegates who participated in this grand *reunión*. Most of the original building was destroyed, but the room where the declaration of independence was signed has survived and has been incorporated into the newer building which is now a museum. Many other historical events took place here and are re-enacted each evening in the garden at 2030 in a son-et-lumière show. Buy your tickets for this function at the tourist office at 24 de Setiembre. Open Tues–Sun 0830–1200 and 1730–2000

Churches

- Catedral, on Plaza de la Independencia. The original wooden cross of the first foundation at Ibatín is preserved here
- Iglesia de la Merced (Church of Mercy), corner of Rivadavia and 24 de Setiembre. La Virgen de la Merced (Virgin of Mercy) was declared General of the Argentine forces by General Belgrano
- Iglesia San Francisco on Plaza de la Independencia. This historical building served as the accommodation for the participants of the Congreso de Tucumán

Museums

Museums are open daily 0900–1200 and 1600–2000. Admission is free.

San Miguel de Tucumán

Plate 31
Map of La Rioja Province

Plate 32

Top: Tucumán
Bottom: Menhir park, Tafí del Valle

TUCUMÁN PROVINCE

- Casa del Obispo Colombres (Bishop Colombres' House), Parque 9 de Julio, an eighteenth-century construction which belonged to the bishop José E Colombres, the founder of Tucumán's sugar industry. There is on exhibit the first sugar mill, built around 1821
- Calle Campo de las Carreras, near Plaza Belgrano, where the battle of Tucumán was fought in 1812
- Museo Folklórico Provincial Manuel Belgrano (Manuel Belgrano Provincial Folklore Museum), 24 de Setiembre 565, used to be the home of the family of Bishop Colombres. Open Wed–Sun 0800–1230 and 1730–2030. Must visit
- Museo del Instituto Miguel Lillo, Miguel Lillo 205, has a herbarium containing 700 000 items, and paleontological, geological, and other scientific collections. The library possesses a copy of the rare and valuable original edition of Von Humboldt's *Travels in Spanish America*
- Museo de Antropologia, Prehistoria, y Arqueologia (Anthropolgy, Prehistory, and Archeology Museum), 25 de Mayo 265, founded by Frenchman Alfred Metraux. On exhibit are archeological artefacts from the region (especially of the Tafí, Candelaria, and Santa María cultures), and also funeral urns and ceramics from Peru, Bolivia, and the Americas in general. Good exhibits on the Chaco peoples, the Chiriguanos, and the Tobas
- Museo Provincial de Bellas Artes (Provincial Fine Arts Museum), 9 de Julio 44
- Museo Histórico de Provincia Presidente Nicolás Avellaneda, Congreso 56, has exhibits on the history of Tucumán province from the earliest times to the twentieth century
- Casa de los Padilla, 25 de Mayo 36, a nineteenth-century mansion, now Museo de la Ciudad y Arte Decorativo (City and Decorative Arts Museum)

Parks

- Parque 9 de Julio, bounded to the south by Avenida Benjamin Araos, to the north by Avenida Gobernador del Campo, to the east by Avenida General Suarez, and to the west by Avenida Soldatti. Approximately 100 ha, the park was designed by a French architect. The outline of this beautiful garden follows geometrical designs. The summer residence of Bishop Colombres is near the Avenida Soldatti entrance, and is now a museum, paying tribute to the pioneer of sugarcane farming in Tucumán and probably Argentina. On exhibit are the first sugarcane crushing machines used until a modern steam-driven crushing plant was installed. There are also portraits of the Governors of Tucumán, painted by Lola Mora. The park is a favorite sports ground for

San Miguel de Tucumán

TUCUMÁN PROVINCE

Tucumeños, as the residents of San Miguel are known, with a sports complex and a lawn tennis club. You can go boating on the peaceful little Lago San Miguel. Kiosks and small restaurants cater for the hungry and thirsty. There are two camp sites near the river

Excursions

- **Dique El Cadillal** (El Cadillal Dam): Travelling 26 km north through mostly citrus orchards you arrive at the gorge of the **Río Salí** which was dammed to supply electricity and water for the city and to irrigate some 60 000 ha of otherwise unusable land. This is a favourite weekend retreat of the *Tucumeños* with yachting, water-skiing, fishing, and swimming facilities. There are many camp sites (such as that run by the ACA) and restaurants but no hotel. The lake has frequent bus services to and from Tucumán bus terminal ($0.60). There is an amphitheatre near the lake in which plays are performed during summer. In the fish hatchery area tapirs roam freely. Nearby is an archeological museum. Tour operators run three-hour tours, including one along the **Río Tapia valley** up to **Raco**, a summer holiday village in the mountains, and another to the Benedictine monastery Cristo Rey; fare $7.70. See also Dique El Cadillal on page 587

- **Villa Nougués**: 36 km west, an hour's bus ride up the mountainside, at 1250 m. It has a picturesque little church. The road runs through flat country until **Mundo Nuevo**, from where it starts climbing the mountain twisting steeply and giving ever more sweeping views over the plain of Tucumán and the city itself. Tour operators run trips to Cristo Redentor—a statue of Christ the Redeemer near **Anta Muerta**—and **Valle San Javier**; fare $7.70. Bus services are not very frequent. See also Villa Nougués on page 609

- Some tour operators combine the trips to **Dique El Cadillal** and **Villa Nougués** trip as a day tour costing $14.00

- **Tafí del Valle**: This is one of the most interesting trips from San Miguel. The road first passes through the sugarcane belt and then turns west into RP 307 near Acheral. Gradually the road enters the mountains, here covered with dense subtropical growth. At **La Angostura** the valley and **Lago El Mollar** are reached. Just past the village on the left is the turn-off to the archeological site **Parque Menhir**. There are frequent daily buses ($2.50). Tour operators organize 10-hour day trips for $10.00. See Tafí del Valle on page 606

- **Amaicha del Valle** and **Quilmes**: Some tour buses include Amaicha del Valle, an Indian community that holds colourful fiestas, and the Quilmes ruins. See Amaicha del Valle on page 585 and Quilmes on page 590.

San Miguel de Tucumán

TUCUMÁN PROVINCE

There are frequent buses to Quilmes from San Miguel de Tucumán; fare $3.50. A combined tourist excursion costs $15.00, including lunch

- **Ibatín**: This trip can be made by local bus. Just before Famailla RP 308 joins RN38. Most of the trip is through sugarcane fields. At **Ingenio Santa Rosa** where the bus stops is a sign pointing to Ibatín. This is a 5 km or 1 hour's brisk walk. The entrance to the archeological site has a mural inscribed "Ibatín"
- **Los Pizarros**: Off RN 38 from La Cocha. You can visit the Jesuit mission church of San Ignacio dating from 1746, a national monument surrounded by an old cemetery. There are direct bus services daily to Los Pizarros from the terminal; fare $2.60, three hours
- **Dique Escaba**: An interesting excursion can be made to the hydro-electric scheme at Dique Escaba in the **Silleta de los Higueras** mountains. Take the bus from the bus terminal to Juan B Alberdí (fare $2.00), where you change buses to ascend the mountain (fare $0.80). The bus follows RP 308 and fords the **Río Marada** near **Corralito**. Most houses in this area have straw-thatched roofs. This is very fertile country, mostly used for sugarcane growing. Near **Boca de la Quebrada** we enter the Escaba gorge and the next 13 km run steeply uphill on a narrow winding road. The scenery is most impressive with the mountain slopes densely covered with shrubs. Most of the water from the river is channeled into irrigation canals. Not far from the electricity plant (near Batiruana) there is an excellent picnic area with barbecue facilities. From here onwards the road is carved out of the mountain and rocks overhang the road forming quasi-tunnels; it becomes so narrow that only one vehicle can pass. For the best views sit on the right-hand side of the bus; here the road "hangs" 400 m above the valley floor. Little mountain streams cascade everywhere, and orchids cover the valley and mountainside. At one spot the river has carved a deep U-turn into the mountain—the panorama here is breathtaking. Shortly afterwards you reach the highest point, with views over the lake, backed by the Aconquija chain. The bus continues to Escaba via the dam and returns to the hamlet of **Escaba de Abajo**. On the road to Escaba de Abajo is a police checkpoint where foreigners have to identify themselves. Opposite the police checkpoint is a small *hostería* ($5.00 per bed) with cabins (not open all year round) and a camp site. Bring your own food as the restaurant has closed. This is an excellent area for hiking and camping, and there is good *pejerrey* fishing in the lake. The word *Escaba* is Quechua meaning "rivers which unify themselves", a very apt description. See also Dique Escaba on page 588

San Miguel de Tucumán

TUCUMÁN PROVINCE

- **San Pedro de Colalao** at the junction of the **Río Tipas** and the **Río Tacanas**. The area is fairly densely covered with subtropical vegetation which gives shelter to an immense variety of birdlife: parakeets, loros, and a colorful finch. Locals claim that in the mountains there are still condors, *vicuñas*, and definitely *alpacas*. The highest point is **Cerro Alto de la Mina** at 4762 m. Up to 3000 m the mountains are covered with shrubs, and above that they are bare. In winter the range is covered with snow. The air is crystal clear and unpolluted. Outside town on the road to Las Tacanas is a little cave on the left-hand side which is venerated as a Catholic shrine. This is mostly cattle-raising country but there are a number of walnut orchards. A trip can also be made to **Hualinchay** where the mountain trail starts across the range into the **Río Calchaqui valley** near Tolombón in Salta province. See also san Pedro de Colalao below

SAN PEDRO DE COLALAO

Postal code: 4124 • Population: 1500 • Altitude: 1190m
Distance from San Miguel de Tucumán: 90 km northwards on RN 9 then RP 311

San Pedro de Colalao is an agricultural community located in a mountainous region on the Río Tipas near its junction with the **Río Tacanas**, with the **Cumbres de Santa Barbara** forming a backdrop. It is a good base for excursions into the **Cumbres de Calchaquies**. Although the climate is rather cool, the air is fresh and clean. Sometimes during summer heavy rains cause the rivers to rise suddenly.

In the surrounding district are natural swimming pools set in groves suitable for camping. Willow trees along the banks of the clear rivers and brooks and commercially grown walnut trees are the hallmark of the region.

San Pedro is famous for its handicrafts.

The area is full of archeological sites of pre-Columbian Calchaquies tribes.

Festivals
- Fiesta de la Nuez (Walnut Festival): first half of April
- Fiesta de San Pedro: 29th June. Festivities on the occasion of the town's patron saint last for a week and are very colorful

Accommodation
★ Hostería Provincial El Lapacho (13 S5.00. Full board 10.50. Situated just before crossing the Río Tacanas on the left hand-side of the highway at the entrance to the village

Camping
- Auto Camping Municipal, on Río Tacanas. Cabins

Eating out
- Restaurant Hostería El Lapacho

San Miguel de Tucumán

TUCUMÁN PROVINCE

🚌 Buses
- San Miguel de Tucumán: Fare $1.80; departs daily; 3 hours; Empresa San Pedro de Colalao
- Hualinchay: Fare $0.50; departs 0900 Mon, Fri

🛍 Shopping
Hand-made leather goods, walnuts.

🏔 Sport
- Mountaineering: Some of the mountains can be easily scaled, such as Cumbres de Santa Barbara
- Hiking: Two-day hike to Hualinchay and Tolombón in Salta province. There is a trail leading over the Cumbres de Calchaquies. Return bus (Empresa San Pedro Calalao) from Hualinchay to San Pedro de Colalao leaves 1000 on Mon and Fri

✤ Excursions
- Monastery at **Hualinchay**: 16 km
- **Quebrada de los Laureles** and **Quebrada Chulca**: Picturesque gorges
- Jesuit church at **Trancas**: Access by bus
- **La Ovejeria**: 8 km. Archeological site with petroglyphs
- **Quebrada de Anta**

SIMOCA

Postal codes: 4172 ‹ Population: 4500
Distance to San Miguel de Tucumán: 44 km southwards on RN 157

The village of Simoca is located in the sugarcane belt south of Tucumán. It was founded towards the end of the seventeenth century. Nowadays it is well known for its colorful Saturday morning markets, where the villagers from the district sell their produce from makeshift stands.

TACO RALO

Postal code: 4242 • Population: 800
Distance to San Miguel de Tucumán: 120 km southwards on RN 157

Taco Ralo is located in the southern part of the province in flat *chaco* country. The climate is mainly dry; the rainfall rarely exceeds 500 mm a year, and falls mainly between November and March. Taco Ralo is best known for its thermal springs which are slightly radioactive, and have a temperature of 42°C. They belong to the same type of springs as those at neighbouring Termas de Río Hondo. They are claimed to have curative properties for rheumatism sufferers, and can help relieve kidney stones. Among the many thermal springs located on the **Río Marada** flats, the best known is **Pozo de Baez**, some 12 km from Taco Ralo railroad station. This water has a temperature of 48°C, is slightly radioactive, and contains rare elements such as vanadium, lithium, and rubidium.

🛏 Accommodation
There are some *hospedajes* and *residenciales* in town but they are not of a high standard. I recommend that you make a day excursion from San Miguel de Tucumán instead.

TUCUMÁN PROVINCE

Buses
Buses run frequently to and from San Miguel de Tucumán.

TAFÍ DEL VALLE

Postal code: 4137 • Altitude: 2000 m • Area code: (0867) • Population: 4500
Distance from San Miguel de Tucumán: 107 km south-west on RN 38 then north-west on RP 307

Tafí del Valle is one of the main tourist centers in the province. It is located in the beautiful **Río Tafí** valley, with the **Sierra de Aconquija** in the west and **Cumbres de Calchaquies** in the north forming a chain of high *sierras*. In the southern part of the valley is the artificial lake **Lago La Angostura**, and the valley center is dominated by **La Pelada** hill, rising sharply from the banks of the lake to a height of 2680 m.

The best time to visit is during spring and autumn. Summers are very wet, and winters are dry and cold with occasional frost and snow. The average temperature in July is 6°C, and there is some fog in July and August. Nights are usually cold. The Tafí area is perfect hiking country.

Archeologists confirm that this valley was inhabited by Diaguita peoples long before the Spaniards arrived—at least since 400 BC. The strategic position between the mountain peoples and the *chaco* peoples, and the consequent exchange of goods and ideas gave rise to the advanced Diaguita-Calchaquie civilization. They planted corn and domesticated llamas, and lived in small communities throughout the valleys. Proof that the area became affiliated with Inca Empire is **Carapunco**, a *tambo* located 18 km uphill towards El Infiernillo pass. In 1617 the Calchaqui peoples were conquered by Alonso de Mercado and Villacorte. Around 1700 the Jesuits arrived, who in a short period of time (until their expulsion in 1767) reorganized the communities and substantially raised the Indians' standard of living. The Jesuits' successors could not keep up the rate of westernization and during the eighteenth century the valley fell from European knowledge. Only since the establishment of a road link with San Miguel de Tucumán in 1943 has the area been opened to Western development. The many archeological sites bear witness to the advanced state of civilization of the pre-Hispanic population. The menhirs, or carved stone monoliths, of **El Mollar**, a hill some 8 km south of Tafí overlooking the lake, are well known.

The lake itself offers good fishing for trout and *pejerrey*, and water sports. El Mollar has now also become a tourist resort in its own right, and many rich *Tucumeños* have their weekend retreats up here.

Festivals
• Fiesta de La Ciénaga (Marsh Festival): January

Taco Ralo

TUCUMÁN PROVINCE

- Fiesta del Queso (Cheese Festival): February
- Fiesta de la Verdura: April. Held in El Mollar
- Fiesta Patronal Nuestra Señora del Carmen: July
- Fiesta del Canto de los Valles: July
- Fiesta de la Tradición: November
- Fiesta Patronal Nuestra Señora de Covadonga: November. Held in El Mollar

ⓘ Tourist information
- Municipalidad (Town Hall)

🛏 Accommodation

During the main tourist season from December to March is a shortage of accommodation.
- Hotel Colonial, corner of Avenida Belgrano and Faroles (21083 $5.00 ⓘ. Near the bus station
- Hostería ACA, corner of Avenida San Martín and Gobernador Campero 🍴 (21027 $8.50 ⓘ. ACA members 20% discount
- Hostería ATEP, corner of Los Menhires and Gobernador Campero
- Hospedaje La Cumbre, Diego de Rojas (21016 $4.00 ⓘ

Accommodation outside Tafí del Valle
- Cabañas El Pinar de los Ciervos, RP 307 Km 68, uphill $9.00 ⓘⓘ. On the north side of the town center, overlooking the valley

Accomodation in El Mollar and La Angostura
- Hostería La Angostura, La Angostura, RP 307. On the south side of the town center, 1 km from the menhirs. Not open all year round
- Hostería FEIA, El Mollar 🍴 $13.00 ⓘⓘ

⛺ Camping
- Auto Camping Municipal Los Sauzales, Los Palenques (21023. Also has cabins

🍴 Eating Out
- Restaurant El Portal
- Restaurant Hostería ACA
- Restaurant El Rancho de Felix, corner of Diego de Rojas and Belgrano
- Restaurant El Pabellón, Centro Cívico
- Restaurant El Colonial, corner of Belgrano and Los Faroles
- Restaurant las Ruedas, Avenida Critto
- Restaurant Peñas Azules, corner of Avenida Critto and Patria
- Restaurant Rancho del Cruce, corner of RP 307 and Avenida Patria
- Cafetería El Rodeo, Peatonal Los Faroles
- Cafetería El Eden, Peatonal Los Faroles
- Cafetería Aconquija, Avenida Campero (at the bus terminal)
- Cafetería Ochoa, Calle Los Palenques
- Cafetería El Oriental, Calle Los Palenques
- Cafetería Los Palenques, Calle Los Palenques

Eating out in El Mollar
- Restaurant FEIA
- Cafetería Montoya

🚌 Buses from Tafí del Valle

The bus terminal is on Avenida Campero. A local bus runs to El Mollar.

Destination	Fare	Depart	Services	Hours	Company
• San Miguel de Tucumán	$2.50		4 services daily	3	El Aconquija
• Amaicha del Valle			3 services daily	1	El Aconquija
• Cafayate	$4.60		2 services daily	5	El Aconquija
• Colalao del Valle	$3.80		2 services daily	4	El Aconquija
• Quilmes	$3.30		2 services daily	3½	El Aconquija
• Santa María	$2.50		3 services daily	3	El Aconquija

Tafí del Valle

TUCUMÁN PROVINCE

- Cafetería D'Agata

🚗 Motoring

The trip down to San Miguel de Tucumán is over a sealed road and has some spectacular vistas, especially on reaching the subtropical rain forest.
- YPF service station

🛍 Shopping

Tafí del Valle is famous for its cheeses.

🍸 Entertainment

- Disco Kham Nokha, Avenida Patria
- Pub El Ciervo, Avenida Diego de Rojas

🍽 Excursions

- **El Mollar**: A pre-Colombian menhir park some 10 km south on the slopes of Nuñorco; the menhirs are reminiscent of those in San Agustín in southern Colombia. Some of the 129 menhirs were brought from other locations. The whole site is well laid out with paths leading to the top of the hill, from where there is a splendid view over the lake and menhirs on the slope and the **Sierra de Aconquija** in the background. Some menhirs are 2.5 m high; the most interesting one on top of the hill has some incisions which look like some kind of writing. Down on the road, across the river from the *hostería*, is the Ambrosetti museum. There are facilities for fishing and sailing, an a fish hatchery. A suggested walk is from Tafí along the eastern side of the lake to the menhir park; return by bus to Tafí, but check the bus timetable for the last bus. There are regular municipal buses to El Mollar from Tafí, and it can also be reached on foot
- **Museo La Banda**: 10 minutes from Tafí. This Jesuit chapel was acquired by the national trust and after renovations in 1978 now serves as a museum. It is one of the most important Jesuit buildings in north-east Argentina, and shows the distinctive layout of buildings preferred by the Jesuits. There is also an archeological museum and a handicraft market
- **Carapunco**: 13 km uphill on RP 307. An important archeological site. Take the bus going to either Cafayate or Santa María and ask the driver to set you down at Carapunco. It is a pleasant walk all the way back down to Tafí with superb views over the **Río Tafí** valley
- **La Quebradita**: In the Zalba curve 2 km above Tafí, La Quebradita is an excavated indigenous dwelling. Take the local bus

TRANCAS

Postal code: 4124 • Population: 1500 • Altitude: 782m
Distance to San Miguel de Tucumán: 70 km northwards on RN 9

Located in the northern part of the province near the border with Salta, Trancas is a commercial center. About 2 km from the modern township is Villa Vieja,

Tafí del Valle

TUCUMÁN PROVINCE

the original foundation of Trancas.

When Don Mercado y Villacorta arrived here during his conquest of the Calchaqui peoples, the first baptism of Indians were carried out here. Around this place a small village grew and became a parish. The vanguard of the royalist troops were captured here in 1812. In 1816 in front of the church the republic of Tucumán was proclaimed by General Bernabé Araoz. He was executed in 1824 and his remains rest to the right of the main altar.

Buses
- San Miguel de Tucumán: Fare $2.00; departs 1200; 4 services daily; 2½ hours; Empresa San Pedro de Colalao

Excursions
- **Villa Vieja**: Hermitage of San Francisco Solano. Nearby are the remains of a Jesuit mission church, built in 1761 and destroyed by an earthquake in 1827. It is a national monument

VILLA NOUGUÉS

Postal code: 4105 • Altitude: 1250 m
Distance from San Miguel de Tucumán: 28 km westwards on RP 338

Villa Nougués is located in the **Cumbres de San Javier**. Because of its altitude it has a very enjoyable climate all year round and many *Tucumeños* have built their summer cottages here. The pretty gothic-style church is a curiosity and very photogenic.

Most tour operators include Villa Nougués on their itinerary because of the scenic drive leading there; see "Excursions" in San Miguel de Tucumán on page 602.

Villa Nougués

Salta Province

Plate 34 Map of Salta Province
- 613 Aguaray
- 613 Aguas Blancas
- 614 Angastaco
- 614 Cachi
- 616 Cafayate
- 617   Map
- 620 Coronel Moldes
- 620 Embarcación
- 621 General Güemes
- 621 Iruya
- 622 Metán
- 622 Molinos
- 623 Orán
- 623 Parque Nacional Baritú
- 624 Parque Nacional El Rey
- 624 Pocitos
- 625 Rosario de la Frontera
- 626 Salta
- 627   Map
- 640 San Antonio de los Cobres
- 642 San Carlos
- 642 San Lorenzo
- 642 Santa Victoria
- 643 Tartagal

Salta Province

Salta is one of the most interesting provinces of Argentina, and was first settled by Spaniards descending from Peru. The landscape is very varied: from the *altiplano* with its Indian population to subtropical valleys and huge dams—Salta has it all. The best time to visit is during spring and fall.

Crescent-shaped Salta shares borders with Chile on the western horn and Bolivia and Paraguay on the northern; Jujuy province nestles in the northwestern inner curve; and on the outer curve from north-east to south-west are Formosa, Chaco, Santiago del Estero, Tucumán, and Catamarca.

The climate of the north-eastern region ranges from tropical to subtropical, and **Salta city** and the **Río Lerma valley** are moderate to subtropical. The western region consists of the *altiplano*, with a fairly cold climate, and mostly inhabited by the descendants of the Diaguita Indians.

The provincial capital, also called **Salta**, is located 1617 km north-west from Buenos Aires. The road network covers approximately 9000 km, of which about half is sealed.

The highest mountains of the province are around **San Antonio de los Cobres** and **Cachi**, where many peaks exceed 6 000 m, such as **Llullaillaco** at 6723 m, **Nevado del Cachi** at 6720 m, **Nevado del Chani** at 6200 m, and **Nevado Queva** at 6130 m.

Salta province is still largely agricultural. Its main crops are *poroto*, maize, sugarcane, and wine. Its mineral products include oil and natural gas, and to a lesser degree silver, lead, onyx, and gemstones. Beef cattle are farmed, and there are approximately 15 000 head of llamas and alpacas. Forest products are also of great importance, and include *quebracho blanco*, cedar, and timber for railroad sleepers.

In and around **San Antonio** is the original chinchilla fur production area. Textiles made from alpaca and vicuña wool are manufactured here; they are very expensive.

The Jesuits left their legacy in the form of mission churches which are scattered all over the province. There are also some fortresses and *pucarás* built by the local Diaguita people to defend themselves against the invading Incas.

Salta province issues its own currency (*"bonos"*), which is not accepted outside the province.

National Parks

Salta has three national parks: **Parque Nacional El Rey**, **Parque Nacional Los Cardones** and **Parque Nacional Baritú**. The most accessible is Parque Nacional El Rey with an area of 44 000 ha, located some 106 km east of Salta city. The flora includes *palo borracho*, *palo barroso*, and giant cedars. The wildlife includes spiny anteaters, monkeys, pumas, jaguars, eagles, mountain turkeys, and snakes, notably cascabel and coral snakes. In the rivers are *bagres* and *dorados*. Near the park entrance is an *hostería*.

Parque Nacional Los Cardones is 71 000 ha in area. It includes the **Cuesta del Obispo**, the **Valle Encantado**, **Cachipampa**, and the straight of **Tin-Tin** on the road to Cachi. It is 13 km from Payogasta and 25 km from Cachi. This is a mountainous park whose peaks reach from 2700 m to the 5000 m **Cerro Macante**. At this altitude there are no dense woods or tall trees, but only scrub and grassland. The fauna includes the almost extinct northern *huemul* (a type of stag), pumas, foxes, *vizcachas*, mountain cats, and condors.

Parque Nacional Baritú is the least accessible of the parks, and measures 72 000 ha in area. It is located 70 km north of Orán. It consists mostly of tree savanna. The fauna includes pumas, monkeys, tapirs, and squirrels.

From Salta to the Chilean Border

The road from Salta passes through the **Quebrada de los Toros**, following the railroad as far as **Puerta Tastil**. The Quebrada de los Toros is a very scenic trip. At **Abra Muñano** (4160 m) the road and railroad meet again and continue together to San Antonio de los Cobres.

The railroad runs from Salta to San Antonio de los Cobres and on via the **Salar Pocitos** through the **Arizaro** to **Socompa** on the Chilean border. **Abra Muñano** at 4165 m is the highest rail station in Argentina. The line zigzags up the hill to Abra Munano, and on the other side of the ridge you arrive at **El Alisal** and **Chorrillos**. From here onwards is the Argentine *altiplano*; most of it is 3300 m above sea-level, and is quite barren. It is sparsely populated by the descendants of the Diaguita Indians, who are closely related to the Indians of Bolivia. The train ride is more spectacular than the bus ride but bypasses **Santa Rosa de Tastil**, where there is an interesting archeological site. The train does not go as far as Chile; if you want to continue check with the rail office in Salta whether there are connecting trains on the Chilean side.

Although Empresa Quebradeno runs a bus service between Salta and San Antonio, it is not very reliable. There is no water in the mountains, so if you plan to hike take your own. From San Antonio de los Cobres to Cauchari the road and rail run more or less parallel. The road reaches its highest point at the Chilean border, at **Paso de la Laguna Sico** at an altitude of 4079 m, from where it descends to San Pedro de Atacama in Chile. The trip across the salt lakes with their flamingos and the impressive deserts is very beautiful, but can be cold and uncomfortable. The road is in

SALTA PROVINCE

reasonable condition on the Argentine side, but on the Chilean side it is often very steep. There are no service stations between San Antonio de los Cobres and Calama in Chile. Because of snow this route is passable for only part of the year. A bus service runs from Salta to San Pedro de Atacama in Chile every Saturday, and returns on Wednesday. Over the stretch between **Campo Quijano** in the Quebrada and San Antonio de los Cobres the road fords several streams which during spring carry enough water to cut the road; the train is then the only means of getting through.

AGUARAY

Postal code: 4566
Distance from Tartagal: 32 km northwards on RN 34

Aguaray is a small village on the road to the Bolivian border. Just outside town across the railroad there are some hot springs. There are no tourist facilities.

Accommodation

B Residencial Los Angeles, corner of Britos and Yrigoyen [8

Border crossing

Just outside Aguaray is a checkpoint where all buses coming from the border are stopped and luggage is searched for contraband.

Buses

Empresa Balut and Empresa Atahualpa run several buses daily to the border and to Salta and Jujuy.

Excursions

See excursions from Pocitos on page 624

AGUAS BLANCAS

Postal code: 4531
Distance from Salta: 324 km north-east on RN 34 then RN 50

Aguas Blancas is a border town with Bolivia. There is no accommodation.

Eating out

• Restaurant El Rinconcito de Los Amigos

Financial

If you have any remaining Bolivian money, spend it here; it is not accepted further in at Orán.

Visas, passports

The passport office is open 0700–1200 and 1500–1900. There is a one-hour time difference between Bolivia and Argentina

Buses

• Salta: Departs 1100 daily
• Orán: Departs 1615; 3 services daily

Buses in Bolivia

To Bermejo: Fare $2.00; 2 services daily; 6 hours

SALTA PROVINCE

ANGASTACO

Postal code: 4427 • Altitude: 1990 m
Distance from Salta: 258 km south-west on RN 68 then RN 40, via Cafayate

Angastaco is located in the upper **Río Calchaqui valley**, 2 km off the main road. It has recently been relocated to its present site and looks really good. The new church is built in the old Jesuit style and is very picturesque. **Angastaco La Vieja** (Old Angastaco) is about half a kilometer down towards the canyon. The original Jesuit mission church still stands, and has been declared a national monument.

There is no electricity at night time. Also, be prepared for cold nights.

The local wine is known as "Vino Patera"; the grapes are crushed by treading in vats.

Tourist information

Señor Gabriel S Soloaga, manager of the YPF service station, has information on the area and will also conduct group excursions.

Accommodation

A Hostería Municipal, on the main Plaza $5.50

C Residencial Bastran, off the main Plaza $2.00. Serves meals $1.20; shared bathroom

Buses

- Molinos: Fare $1.50; departs 0600 Fri; 2 hours; La Rueda
- Cachi: Fare $3.50; departs 0545 Fri; 4 hours; La Rueda
- Cafayate: Fare $2.00; departs daily; 3 hours; El Indio

Motoring

The unsealed road to Cachi passes through many semi-desert sandy stretches which become boggy during rain; at such time the road may become impassable. The valley is very wide, and the mountains on the western side are close and very rugged.
Hitchhiking to Cachi is difficult as there is very little traffic. The best time is early in the morning: ask the manager of the YPF service station if he is aware of anybody going to Cachi.
- Service station: YPF, just before the main Plaza

Excursions

- The *quebradas* and mountains to the west of Angastaco are worth exploring. It appears that there are pre-Colombian settlements in the valleys
- **Molinos**: Has a beautiful restored Jesuit mission church

CACHI

Postal code: 4417 • Population: 4000 • Altitude: 2280 m
Distance from Salta: 157 km westwards on RP 33, a very picturesque drive

Cachi is located near the origins of the **Río Calchaqui** in a beautiful, wide valley with the snow-capped peak of **Nevado del Cachi** beckoning behind the town. The town's origins apparently go back to pre-Columbian times ("Cachi" means "salt" in Quechua). The climate is healthy and invigorating all year round, with cold spells between June and August. The townspeople are renowned for their weaving skills. Cachi is also

Angastaco

Salta Province

the center of a pepper-growing area ("*pimenton*"). Time seems to stand still in Cachi. It is a good base for hikes in the nearby sierra and canyons. Street names are not displayed.

Tourist information

There is a tourist information office in the *Municipalidad*. Ask for Señor Ramos Raul Santiago.

Accommodation

Cachi suffers from a shortage of accommodation, especially during the holiday seasons.

★★ Hostería Cachi ACA, Avenida ACA ⑪. Superb location on a hill overlooking the town, with vistas of Nevado del Cachi

B Residencial Nevado de Cachi, around the corner from Marcos Rueda bus station ⑪ $3.50 ⓘ. Good restaurant

- Albergue Juvenil, at the sports ground $1.50 ⓘ. Mostly occupied by visiting sports groups; shared bedrooms

Camping

- Camping Municipal at the sports ground. $2.00 per tent and person

Eating out

- Restaurant Hosteria Cachi
- Restaurant Nevado del Cachi, in the Residencial Nevado de Cachi, next to the Marcos Rueda bus station

Buses

- Salta: Fare: $5.20; departs 0900 daily; 5 hours; Marcos Rueda
- Molinos: Fare: $2.00; departs 0700 daily except Tues; 8 hours; Marcos Rueda
- Angastaco: Fare $3.50; departs 1300 Thurs; 10 hours; Marcos Rueda
- La Poma: Fare $2.50; departs 1430 Wed and Sat; 3 hours; Marcos Rueda

Motoring

- Service station: ACA, RN 40 Km 1237

Sightseeing

- Archeological museum: On the main Plaza; worth a visit
- Church: The floors and roof are built from cactus wood

Excursions

- **Salta**: The trip between Salta and Cachi is an absolute must when you are visiting Salta province. The road over the **Cuesta del Obispo** first crosses the **Río Calchaqui** and follows it on the eastern bank for quite some time. At **Payogasta** RP 33 joins RN 40 which runs directly northwards to San Antonio. Gradually the road ascends, affording splendid views of the **Nevado del Cachi**—for the best views sit on the left-hand side of the vehicle. As you reach the *altiplano* at an altitude of over 3000 m, you cross a wide plain covered with *ichu* grass, a type of spinifex grass indicating the habitat of alpacas and llamas; here the road is known as the **Straight of Tin-Tin**. Just before the long winding descent there is a rest-house where the bus drivers usually have a break before descending abruptly into the **Cuesta de Escoipe**. As the road winds down steeply into the valley, little streams emerge from beneath the rocks to become waterfalls on both walls of the canyon. Many canyons join the main valley, until halfway down the slope it is several kilometers wide but the road is still a long way above the valley floor. Halfway down is the

Cachi

SALTA PROVINCE

Hostería Ichicoana where bus drivers stop for lunch. The most spectacular part of the drive is from the rest-house at the top of the **Quebrada de Escoipe** to Ichicoana, but it is still interesting all the way to the township of **Chicoana** in the **Río Lerma valley**. Needless to say the water coming down from the mountains is cold and crystal-clear. It is good hiking country. Just before the junction of two rivers there is an interesting church perched on a cliff. Immediately after this view you cross the river over a dilapidated bridge and the road narrows once more as it reaches the valley floor. The road is sealed as far as Chicoana. Entering **Chicoana** you cross the river again, and on leaving the town the bus crosses this bridge once again. In Chicoana there is the Hostería Chicoana on the corner of the main Plaza and Calle España. See also Salta on page 626

- **Nevado del Cachi**: Cachi is the starting point for scaling the Nevado del Cachi, and for walks in the mountainous area to the west

- **La Poma**: Local buses run further up the **Río Calchaqui valley**. The mountain scenery is impressive, with the **Sierra de Pastos Grandes** forming the western side of the valley. The mountain peaks reach between 5500 and 6000 m—**Cerro Ciénaga Grande** is 6030 m high

CAFAYATE

Postal code: 4427 • Population: 9000 • area code: (0868) • Altitude: 1660 m
Distances
- From Salta: 198 km south-west on RN 68
- From San Miguel de Tucumán: 255 km north-west on RN 38 then RN 307 and RN 40

Cafayate is located in the **Río Calchaquies valley**. It enjoys a good climate all year round with low rainfall. It is a favorite destination with Argentine tourists, and has good tourist facilities. It is well known for the quality of the wines produced in the valley.

[i] Tourist information

- Officina de Turismo, in the Mercado Artesanal building on the Plaza, on the corner of General Güemes. It appears to

Key to Map
1. Municipalidad
2. Iglesia
3. Post office (Encotel)
4. Telephone (Entel)
5. Tourist information
6. Museo Arqueológico Señor Rodolfo Bravo
7. Hotel Confort
8. Hotel Asturias
9. Hotel Gran Real
10. Hotel Asembal
11. Hotel Emperador
12. Residencial Briones
13. Residencial Colonial
14. Residencial Güemes
15. Residencial Arroyo
16. Hostería Cafayate ACA
17. Transporte El Indio
18. Transporte Aconquija

Cachi

Salta Province

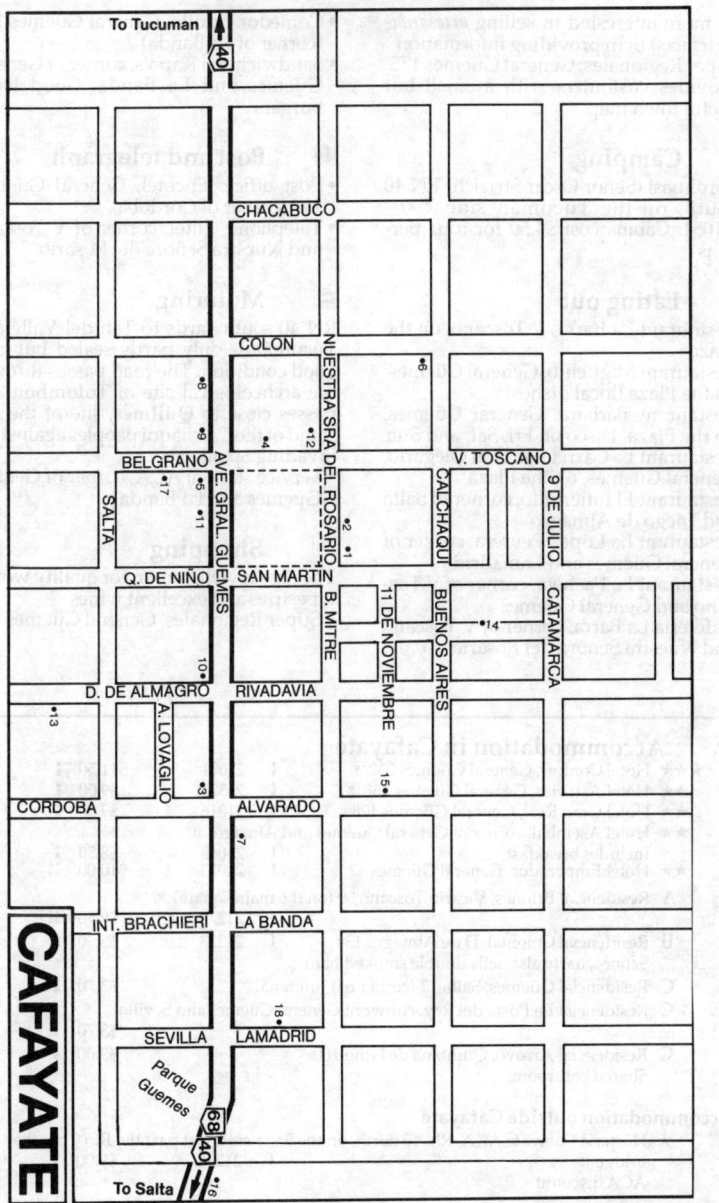

Cafayate

617

SALTA PROVINCE

be more interested in selling *artesanías* (artefacts) than providing information
- Super Regionales, General Güemes 175. Provides customers with a small but useful town map

🅰 Camping
- Lorohuasi (Señor Oscar Strizich) RN 40 south, on the Tucumán side ☎21051. Cabins cost \$4.50 for four persons

🍴 Eating out
- Restaurant La Barra, V Toscano, on the Plaza
- Restaurant Miguelito, General Güemes, on the Plaza (local dishes)
- Restaurant Barbara, General Güemes, on the Plaza. Disco on Fri, Sat, and Sun
- Restaurant La Carreta de Don Olegario, General Güemes, on the Plaza
- Restaurant El Infiernillo, corner of Salta and Diego de Almagro
- Restaurant La López Peyrera, corner of General Güemes and Lamadrid
- Restaurant La Pacheta, corner of V Toscano and General Güemes
- Cafetería La Barra, corner of V Toscano and Nuestra Señora del Rosario
- Comedor Criollo, General Güemes 254 (corner of La Banda)
- Sandwichería Kapo's, corner of General Güemes and La Banda. Good hamburgers

✉ Post and telegraph
- Post office: Encotel, General Güemes 197 (corner of Córdoba)
- Telephone: Entel, corner of V Toscano and Nuestra Señora del Rosario

🚗 Motoring
RN 40 southwards to Tafí del Valle and Tucumán is only partly sealed but is in good condition. The road passes through the archeological site of **Tolombon** and passes close to **Quilmes**, site of the last stand of the Calchaqui peoples against the invading Spaniards.
- Service station: ACA, corner of General Güemes and La Banda

🛍 Shopping
The area is well known for quality woven tapestries and excellent wines.
- Super Regionales, General Güemes 175

🛏 Accommodation in Cafayate

★★★	Hotel Confort, General Güemes 232	☎ 21091	\$11.50	👤
★★	Hotel Asturias, General Güemes 158	☎ 21328	\$9.00	👤
★★	Hotel Gran Real, General Güemes 128	☎ 21016	\$9.00	👤
★★	Hotel Asembal, corner of General Güemes and Almagro 🍴 Includes breakfast	☎ 21065	\$8.50	👤
★★	Hotel Emperador, General Güemes 42	☎ 21023	\$10.00	👥
A	Residencial Briones, Vicario Toscano 80 (on the main square)	☎ 21270	\$9.50	👥
B	Residencial Colonial, D de Almagro 134 Señor Duarte also sells double smoked ham	☎ 21233	\$5.50	👤
C	Residencial Güemes, Salta 13 (corner of Quintana)		\$3.70	👤
C	Residencial La Posta del Rey, corner of General Güemes and Sevilla		\$3.70	👤
C	Residencial Arroyo, Quintana de Nino 160 Shared bathroom		\$3.00	👤

Accommodation outside Cafayate

★	Hostería Cafayate ACA, RN 40 north, on the Salta side, just past the Río Chuscha bridge 🍴 ACA discount	☎ 21296	\$9.00	👤

Cafayate

SALTA PROVINCE

- *Platería* or silversmithy of Jorge Barraco, Colon 157, for silverware and gemstones
- Bodega Domingo Hnos, General Güemes, on the Tucumán side
- Bodega Arnaldo Etchart, Finca La Florida, RN 40 5 km south of town. Excellent wines. Conducted tours. The manager speaks German

Entertainment
- Disco Gipsy, corner of Calchaqui and Buenos Aires; operates on weekends only

Sightseeing
- Museo Arqueológico Señor Rodolfo Bravo (Señor Rodolfo Bravo Archeological Museum), corner of Colón and Calchaqui: Most artefacts on exhibit have been found in and around Cafayate, once apparently densely populated by Calchaqui peoples
- Museo del Vino (Wine Museum), corner of General Güemes with Chacabuco. A bit disappointing. Small admission charge

Excursions
- **Tolombon**: 18 km southwards on RN 40. In the vicinity is an archeological site
- **Quilmes**: A 5 km turn-off leads 54 km south of Cafayate to this interesting and well restored pre-Inca city of a Calchaqui people. The ruins have been restored with great care by Argentine archeologists. The site is 5 km east of the main road (45 minutes' easy walk) and is built in a horseshoe-shaped basin. This was the site of the last stand of the united Calchaquies peoples against the invading

Buses from Cafayate

Cafayate has no central bus terminal.
There are no direct bus services to Cachi. To get to Cachi take a bus to Angastaco with El Indio and from there catch a La Rueda bus to Cachi. Check timetables for connecting buses beforehand.
During summer Empresa Aconquija increases its services to San Miguel de Tucumán via Tafí del Valle.
- Empresa El Indio, corner of Belgrano and General Güemes
- Empresa Aconquija, corner of Lamadrid and General Güemes

Destination	Fare	Depart	Services	Hours	Company
Salta	$4.50		2 services daily	4	El Indio
Amaicha	$2.50		2 services daily	2½	Aconquija
Angastaco	$2.00	1100	daily	3	El Indio
Colalao	$2.00	0600	Wed, Fri, Sun	1	Aconquija
Quilmes	$1.50	0600	Wed, Fri, Sun	1½	Aconquija
San Miguel de Tucumán	$6.90	0600	Wed, Fri, Sun	8	Aconquija
Santa María	$2.50	0600	Tues, Thurs, Sat	2	Aconquija, El Indio
Tafí del Valle	$4.50	0600	2 services daily	5	Aconquija
San Carlos	$0.50			1	El Indio

SALTA PROVINCE

Spaniards. See Quilmes on page 590. Take the Aconquija bus on Wednesdays leaving at 0600; there is a return bus on the same day about noon, but check beforehand as it only runs during summer. It is possible to hitch a ride back with a truck. If you cannot make it back to Cafayate you can stay in Colalao del Valle at the *hostería*, which has a restaurant

- **Angastaco** and **Cachi**: A 250-km trip on RN 40 passing through the wide **Río Calchaqui valley**. The valley is fairly dry, but wherever there is water there are vineyards. At first the mountains are lower and further away on the eastern side. Here the valley floor is already 2000 m above sea-level. At **Animaná** there is a municipal camping ground. The road descends to the level of the river which carries very little water outside the rainy season and during the thaw, as most of it is channelled into reservoirs for irrigation—you pass several irrigation schemes on the way. From Animaná, the **Nevado del Cachi** starts to come into view. Dry stream beds open from gorges in the west. In many places the road has been cut through a mixture of lava and pebbles, betraying the land's volcanic origin. After **La Merced** the road crosses the **Río Caichaquies** over a long narrow bridge and enters the extremely scenic **Quebrada de Salta** (watch for falling rocks). The narrowest section of this *quebrada* is called "Corte de Ventisquero" ("Snowdrift Cut")

CORONEL MOLDES

Postal code: 4421
Distance from Salta: 62 km southwards on RN 68

The main attraction of Coronel Moldes is the artificial lake **Cabra Corral**, about 22 km east. Covering approximately 11 000 ha, this lake irrigates 32 000 ha of farmland and generates electricity. It is stocked with *pejerrey*, and attracts many visitors for sailing and water-skiing. See also "Excursions" in Salta on page 638

Accommodation
★★★ Hostería Cabra Corral, Avenida Sarmiento (219311

Buses
Buses run regularly to and from Salta.

EMBARCACIÓN

Postal code: 4550
Distance from Salta: 270 km eastwards on RN 34

Although it is a small town, Embarcación is an important rail and road junction.

Accommodation
The cheaper hotels are near the rail station.
- ★ Hotel Posta Norte, Avenida España
- **B** Residencial Universal, corner of H Yrigoyen and 9 de Julio $4.50
- Residencial Moderna, corner of H Yrigoyen and 9 de Julio
- Residencial Sarmiento

Cafayate

Salta Province

🍴 Eating out
- Cafetería El Escorial, corner of Belgrano and España, on the main Plaza

📬 Post and telegraph
- Post office: Encotel, 24 de Setiembre, on the main Plaza
- Telephone: Entel, Belgrano on the main Plaza

🚌 Buses
The bus terminal is on the corner of Belgrano and Independencia.
- Orán; Fare $1.00; 1 hour
- Pocitos (on the Bolivian border): Fare $2.40
- Rosario de la Frontera: Departs daily; 6 hours; Veloz del Norte
- San Miguel de Tucumán: Departs daily; 7½ hour; Veloz del Norte
- Tartagal: Departs daily; 1 hour; Veloz del Norte

🚆 Trains
Atahualpa in conjunction with the railroad runs a motor coach service to Formosa on Mon and Fri at 1325, taking 21½ hours. It is usually suspended during the wet season and replaced by a bus service, which may also get bogged down.
- Salta: Departs 0100 Thurs; 10 hours

General Güemes

Postal code: 4430 • (area code 087) • Altitude: 733 m
Distance from Salta: 52 km eastwards on RN 34 then 9

🛏 Accommodation
- Hotel Roman, San Martín 596 (911471

🚌 Buses
- Salta
- Orán: Fare $4.00
- Rosario de la Frontera: Fare $2.50

Iruya

Postal code: 4633 • Altitude: 2730 m
Distance from Humahuaca (Jujuy province): 69 km northwards on RP 9 then 13

Iruya is a picturesque mountain village. Although it is located in Salta province its only access is from Jujuy province

🎉 Festivals
- Fiesta Nuestra Señora del Rosario (Festival of Our Lady of the Rosary): October

ℹ Accommodation
There are no hotels in Iruya, but there is private accommodation.

🚌 Buses
There are twice-weekly buses from Jujuy via Hipólito Yrigoyen.

⚘ Excursions
- **Ticonte**: A 9 km hike to this archeological site

Metán

Postal code: 4440 • (area code: (0876) • Altitude: 860 m
Distance from Salta: 134 km southwards on RN 34

Metán was founded in 1859. Nearby is the site of the battle de las Piedras.

🎉 Festivals
- Fiesta Patronal de San José (Festival of the Patron Saint Joseph): March 19

SALTA PROVINCE

Accommodation
- Hotel Metán, RN 34
- A Residencial Solis, 20 de febrero 41 ℂ 20050
- B Residencial Metán, RN 34 ℂ 20063

Buses
There are regular bus services to Salta and San Miguel de Tucumán

Excursions
- **Posta de Yatasto**: 6 km south of Metán. The historic meeting between the liberation Generals San Martín, Güemes, and Belgrano took place here in January 1814.
- **Metán Viejo** (Old Metán): Metán was originally founded here, some 4 km south-west of town

MOLINOS

Postal code: 4419 • Altitude: 2020 m
Distances
- From Salta: 210 km westwards on RN 33 then 40
- From Angastaco: 46 km northwards on RN 40

Molinos is a very picturesque little village located in the **Río Lurancato valley** not far from the junction with the Río Calchaquies. In the background **Cerro Inca Huasi** rises to 5260 m. The little church was built in 1720 by the Jesuit mission, Candelaria; a national monument, it has recently been carefully restored. The remains of Coronel Severo Siqueira de Isasmendi y Echalar, the last governor appointed by the Spanish crown, rest here. The area abounds in archeological sites and opportunities for interesting short hikes into the nearby valleys. Unfortunately, accommodation is in short supply.

Accommodation
There is a small *residencial* ⊞ $3.00 ⚹. Shared bedrooms

Buses
- Cachi: Fare $2.10; departs 0645 daily except Wed; 2½ hours; Empresa Marcos Rueda

Excursions

Take a pleasant walk down from the church, crossing the stream and then climbing a gentle hill from which there are good views of Molinos and the surrounding countryside.
- **El Churcal**: This archeological site is nearby, where there are the remnants of a fifteenth-century pre-Hispanic settlement

ORÁN

Postal code: 4530 • ℂ area code: (0878) • Altitude: 326 m
Distance from Salta: 276 km north-east on RN 34 then 50

Orán's full name is San Ramón de la Nueva Orán. It was the last city founded by the Spanish in South America. Coming down from Bolivia it is the first town you come to with first-class hotels. Orán is a good starting point for trips to almost untouched areas,

Metán

such as the **Parque Nacional Baritú** with its fast-flowing rivers and abundant fish life. The subtropical climate and good rainfalls create an exuberant greenhouse, a paradise for the nature-lover and outdoor enthusiast.

Festivals
- Fiesta de San Ramón Nonato: August 31; festival of the patron saint

Accommodation
- ★★★ Hotel Gran Orán, Pellegrini 671 (21214 $15.50
- A Residencial Colonial, corner of Pizarro and Colón (21103
- A Residencial Crillon, 25 de Mayo 225 (21101
- B Residencial Centro, Pellegrini 332 (21500
- B Residencial Internacional, López y Planes 485 (21783
- Residencial Avenida, López y Planes 124 (21563

Eating out
- Pizzería Petrakos, Coronel Egues 355

PARQUE NACIONAL BARITÚ

The Parque Nacional Baritú is almost untouched by the onslaught of civilization—it has no tourist facilities at all. It is the last refuge in this part of Argentina for a variety of wildlife—pumas, tapirs, jaguars, squirrels, and monkeys. Most of the rainfall occurs during summer, but plenty of rain falls throughout the year, producing in parts of the park a dense jungle traversed by rivers such as the **Lipeo**, **Baritú**, and **Pescado** before they join the **Río Bermejo**.

See also "National Parks" on page 611.

Buses from Orán

Destination	Fare	Depart	Services	Hours	Company
• Salta	$4.75	0130	9 services daily		Atahualpa
• Agua Blanca	$1.60			2	Atahualpa
• Embarcación	$1.00			1	Atahualpa
• Formosa		1130	Tues, Thurs		Atahualpa
• General Güemes	$4.00				Atahualpa
• Jujuy		1200	daily		Balut
• San Miguel de Tucumán	$9.00	2210	daily		Veloz del Norte
• Tartagal	$3.50	0630	4 services daily		Atahualpa

SALTA PROVINCE

PARQUE NACIONAL EL REY

Postal code: 4434
Distances
- From Rosario de la Frontera: 160 km northwards on RN 34/9, then eastwards on RP 5 and northwards on RP 20
- From Salta: 196 km southwards RN 34/9, then eastwards on RP 5 and northwards on RP 20

The Parque Nacional El Rey is a 44 160 ha forest and wildlife reserve set among hills ranging from 900 to 1500 m, with clear streams providing good fishing. It has a colorful birdlife.

See also "National Parks" on page 611.

Accommodation
- Hostería El Rey, 10km from park entrance (220837

POCITOS

Postal code: 4568 • Altitude: 530 m • (area code: (0875
Distance from Salta: 426 km northwards on RN 34

Pocitos (also known as Salvador Mazza) is a border town across from Yacuiba in Bolivia. The wet season runs from the end of June to the end of August. It is of tourist interest only for the border crossing.

Accommodation
I do not recommend any of *residenciales*. I suggest you take the bus at least as far as Aguaray, where there are hot springs and a reasonable *residencial*, or Tartagal, where there are plenty of good hotels. Better still, travel directly to Salta or Jujuy.

$ Financial
- Dinar SRL, Salta 440 (71034

Visas, passports
- Bolivian consulate, Güemes 446

Border crossing
The border for travelers from Bolivia to Argentina is open between 0800 and 1800. The border for those traveling from Argentina to Bolivia opens half an hour later. This is a land crossing.

Buses
The bus terminal is one block from the border crossing.
There are daily buses from Yacuiba in Bolivia to Camiri, from where you can catch more frequent buses to Tarija.
- Salta: Fare $7.20; Empresa Atahualpa
- Embarcación: Fare $2.40; 3 hours; Empresa Balut
- San Salvador de Jujuy: Fare $6.25; departs 0900 daily; Empresa Balut

Trains
As trains no longer cross the border, take the *colectivo* (a ½-hour trip for $1.50) from the border to Yacuiba rail station for connection to Santa Cruz.

Excursions
- **Aguaray**: The road south from Pocitos is initially a dirt road and follows the **Río Carabar**. The shallow valley is called the **Valle de Tartagal**, but the low hills on the eastern side disappear shortly while the right hand side remains hilly. The vegetation is tropical. Aguaray is a small place about an hour's drive south, and just before

SALTA PROVINCE

turning into the village there is a checkpoint where literally all parcels are opened by the police. At Aguaray there are some hot springs which can be reached crossing the railroad. The water is only luke-warm and there are no tourist facilties. From Aguaray onwards the eastern side of the road is flat *chaco* country. See also Aguaray on page 613

ROSARIO DE LA FRONTERA

Postal code: 4190 • Altitude: 769 m • area code: (0876)
Distance from Salta: 173 km southwards on RN 34/9

Rosario de la Frontera is a popular resort from June to September. Eight kilometers away there are sulphur springs, famous for their curative properties.

There is a casino in the Hotel Termas. The thermal resort is about 4 km east of Rosario.

An exinct volcano forms a backdrop to Rosario.

Accommodation

B Residencial Real, Güemes 185 (81067 $ 5.00

Accommodation outside Rosario

★★ Hotel Termas, RN 34 (81004 $25.00. Full board. Situated on a hill overlooking the countryside, 6 km from the bus station. It is best reached by taxi ($6.00)

★★ Hostería Termal ACA, RN 34 (81143. One km before Hotel Termas

Eating out
• Cafetería Viejo Molino

Motoring

Service stations
• ACA, RN 34 Km 1293
• YPF, RN 34, on the north side of town

Sport
• Golf: between the Hostería Termal ACA and the Hotel Termas is a nine-hole golf course; it is divided by the road
• Across the road from the Hostería Termal ACA is an artifical lake, owned by Caza Y Pesca Club; ask in your hotel for permission to fish there. Picnic grounds

Buses from Rosario de la Frontera

Destination	Fare	Depart	Services	Hours	Company
• Salta	$4.00	0502	several services daily	2	Veloz del Norte
• Córdoba			7 services daily	11	Expreso Panamericano, Veloz del Norte
• Embarcación			daily	5½	Veloz del Norte
• Güemes	$2.50		several services daily		
• San Miguel de Tucumán		0502	several services daily	2½	Veloz del Norte
• San Salvador de Jujuy			daily	3	Veloz del Norte
• Santiago del Estero		0502	daily	4	Veloz del Norte
• Tartagal			daily	7	Veloz del Norte

SALTA PROVINCE

SALTA

Postal code: 4400 • Population: 345 000 • area code: (087) • Altitude: 1200 m
Distance from Buenos Aires: 1600 km north-west on RN 9

Located on the **Río Arias** in the **Lerma valley**, Salta is surrounded by mountains; some of the residential areas are built on the lower slopes of **Cerro San Bernardo** (1460 m). From the viewing platform on top of Cerro San Bernardo, which you can reach by sealed road or on foot along Via Crucis, there are splendid vistas over the city and valley to the distant *cordillera*. Salta was founded in 1582 by Don Hernando de Lerma on his descent from Peru. It is a city of fine plazas, convents, churches, and colonial buildings, especially around Plaza 9 de Julio, the hub of the town. Several streets in the center have been converted to pedestrian malls and are paved with interesting ceramic tiles which invite you to stroll around.

The climate is excellent all year round—cool summers and temperate winters with plenty of sunshine.

The diocese of Salta is the oldest in Argentina.

Because of earthquakes, city buildings are limited to two or three stories.

Festivals
- Battle of Tucumán and Salta: Sept 24
- *Gaucho* parade: June 16. Folk music by youngsters. All the *gauchos* wear the traditional red ponchos with black stripes. The gathering is around the statue of Güemes in Paseo Güemes. A very colorful event
- Carnaval (Mardi Gras): Salta celebrates a very lively *carnaval* with a procession of floats and thousands of participants. Themes are historical and caricatures of

Key to Map
1. Municipalidad
2. Casa de Gobierno
3. Catedral
4. Post office (Encotel)
5. Telephone (Entel)
6. Tourist information
7. Banco de la Nación
8. Cambio Maguitour
9. Aerolineas Argentinas
10. Convento y Iglesia de San Francisco
11. Cabildo y Museo Histórico del Norte
12. Museo de Ciencias Naturales
13. Museo Provincial de Bellas Artes
14. Casa José Evariste Uriburu (museum)
15. Casino
16. Hotel Provincial
17. Hotel Salta
18. Hotel California
19. Hotel Crystal
20. Hotel Victoria Plaza
21. Hotel Plaza
22. Hotel Regidor
23. Hotel Cabildo
24. Residencial Astur
25. Residencial El Provincial
26. Residencial Elena
27. Residencial Napoli
28. Residencial Candilejas
29. Residencial Florida
30. Residencial Centro
31. Residencial España
32. Residencial Güemes
33. Residencial Italia
34. Residencial 20 de Febrero
35. Residencial Royal
36. Museo Antropológico Juan Martín Leguizamón

Salta

Salta Province

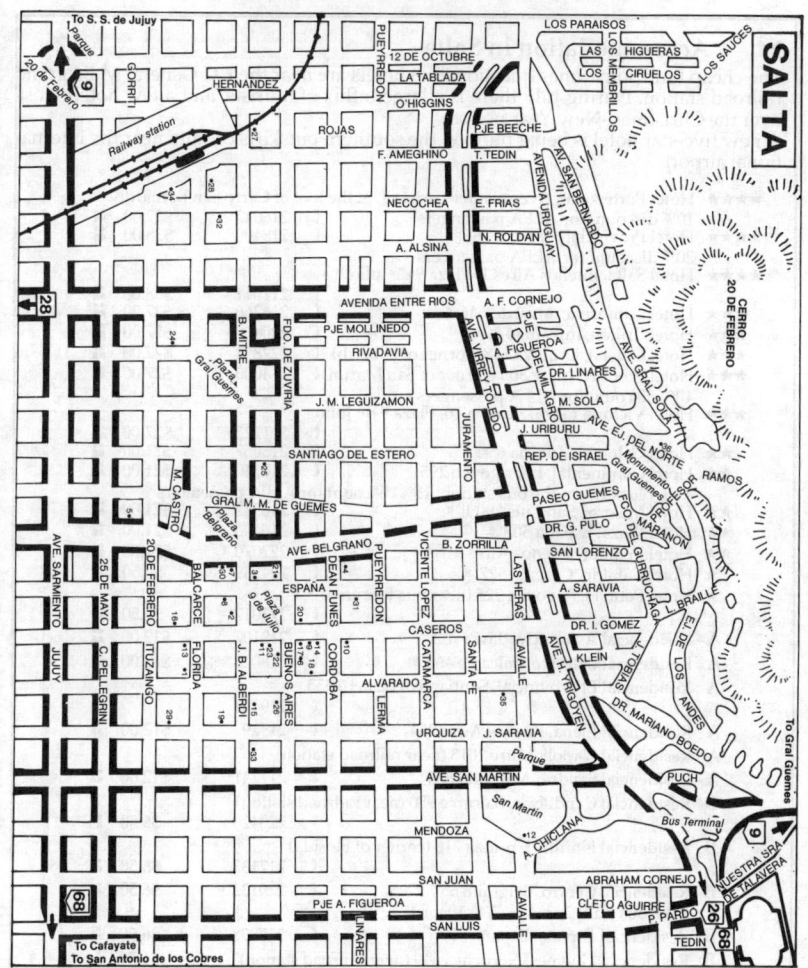

public figures. Also much "waterbombing" of unsuspecting passers-by!

ℹ Tourist information

The Dirección Provincial de Turismo, Buenos Aires 93 ✆ 215927 has maps and addresses of private accommodation.

▲ Camping

- Camping y Balneario Municipal Carlos Xamena, Avenida Republica del Libano, on the Río Arenales, about 3 km from the city center) ✆ 231341. Take bus no. 13. There is no signposting

SALTA PROVINCE

Accommodation in Salta

The cheap (and sometimes questionable) hotels are near the F C General M Belgrano railroad station. During July there is a large influx of tourists, and a few hotels close over the Christmas–New Year period.

A new five-star hotel is being built on the southern outskirts of Salta near the international airport.

★★★★	Hotel Portezuelo, Avenida del Turista 1, at the foot of Cerro San Bernardo			
	10% discount for ALFA passengers	(216047	$37.00	
★★★★	Hotel Provincial, Caseros 786	(218400	$38.00	
	20% discount for ALFA passengers			
★★★★	Hotel Salta, Buenos Aires 1, Plaza 9 de Julio			
		(211011	$38.00	
★★★	Hotel California, Alvardo 646	(216266	$27.00	
★★★	Hotel Crillon, Ituzaingó 30	(220400	$27.00	
★★★	Hotel Crystal, Urquiza 618 (corner of Alberdí)	(222854	$27.00	
★★★	Hotel Premier, Jujuy 305 (corner of San Martín)	(214000	$27.00	
	40% discount for ALFA passengers			
★★★	Hotel Victoria Plaza, Zuviria 16, Plaza 9 de Julio			
		(211222	$27.00	
★★	Hotel Colonial, Zuviria 6	(213057	$21.00	
★★	Hotel Continental, H Yrigoyen 295	(210340	$21.00	
	Two blocks from the bus station; 15% discount for ALFA passengers			
★★	Hotel Misoroj, San Luis 190	(218542	$21.00	
★★	Hotel Plaza, España 508	(216400	$21.00	
★★	Hotel Regidor, Buenos Aires 9	(222070	$21.00	
★	Hotel Cabildo, Caseros 527	(224589	$9.50	
★	Hotel Petit, H Yrigoyen 225 (near bus terminal)			
		(213012	$9.50	
A	Residencial Astur, Rivadavia 752	(212107	$12.00	
A	Residencial Balcarce, Balcarce 460	(218023	$12.00	
A	Residencial El Provincial, Santiago del Estero 555			
		(219438		
A	Residencial Elena, Buenos Aires 254	(21529	$12.00	
A	Residencial Napoli, Mitre 1013 (near railroad station)			
A	Residencial Sandra, Alvarado 630	(211241	$12.00	
B	Residencial Candilejas, Balcarce 980 (near railroad station)			
		(220426	$6.50	
B	Residencial Florida, Urquiza 718 (corner of Florida)			
		(212133	$6.50	
B	Residencial Centro, Belgrano 657	(220132	$6.50	
	Take bus no 1, 2, 3, 4, 6, 7, 8, 10, or 12			
B	Residencial España, España 319	(217898	$6.50	
B	Residencial Güemes, Necochea 649 (near railroad station)		$6.50	
B	Residencial Italia, Alberdí 210	(214050	$6.50	
B	Residencial Provincial, Santiago del Estero 555	(219438	$6.50	
B	Residencial Sanyor, Avenida San Martín 994	(214440	$6.50	
B	Residencial 20 de Febrero, 20 de Febrero 940 (near railroad station)		$6.50	
C	Residencial Royal, Alvarado 109 (corner of Lavalle, near bus terminal)			
C	Residencial Camiri, Tobias 66 (near bus terminal)			
	Shared rooms and bath			
C	Residencial Viena, Florida 18			

Salta

SALTA PROVINCE

Accommodation in Salta—continued

Accommodation outside Salta
- ★★★ Motel Huaico, corner of Bolivia and Patrón Costas, Campo Castanares
  Near the university, north of the city center ☏ 210211

🍴 Eating out

During the cooler season many restaurants serve at least once a week a kind of stew called *locro*—very tasty. Try the local wines.

Near the bus terminal is a string of *parrillas* or steak houses. There are cheap restaurants in Balcarce block 900, near the railroad station.

- ☞ Restaurant Aida de Castro, Leguizamon 711
- Restaurant Alvarez, corner of Buenos Aires and San Martín. Also pizzeria
- ☞ Restaurant Barcelona, Alvarado 624
- Restaurant Churrasqueria Don Emilio, Virrey Toledo 145
- Restaurant Don José, Urquiza 484. Steakhouse
- Restaurant El Antigal, Balcarce 935, near the railroad station (*peñas* at weekends)
- Restaurant El Emir, Caseros 870. Pizzas and Arabic meals
- Restaurant El Lago, Parque San Martín
- ☞ Restaurant El Mesón de Pepe, Rivadavia 774. Seafood; one of the best in town
- Restaurant El Monumento, Gurruchaga 20, next to the Güemes monument ◐
- Restaurant El Paraíso, Zuviria 64
- Restaurant El Pibe, San Martín block 500 (corner of Alberdí). Cheap meals
- Restaurant El Rey De Bife, corner of H Yrigoyen and San Martín. Steakhouse
- ☞ Restaurant El Rincón de López, corner of Virrey Toledo and O'Higgins. Steakhouse
- Restaurant El Tarco, Alvarado 614
- Restaurant Fausto, Avenida San Martín 481. Steakhouse
- ☞ Restaurant Fogón Criollo, corner of O'Higgins and Virrey Toledo. Steakhouse
- Restaurant Gimnasia y Tiro (Rifle club), corner of V López and Entre Ríos
- Restaurant Grill Salta, 1st floor Hotel Salta, Buenos Aires 1. International cuisine
- ☞ Restaurant Italiano, Buenos Aires 95, upstairs
- Restaurant J A, corner of H Yrigoyen and San Martín. Steakhouse
- Restaurant Jockey Club de Salta, General Güemes 452. International cuisine
- Restaurant La Casona, Caseros 511. Steakhouse
- Restaurant La Castiza, Alberdí 134. International and regional cuisine
- ☞ Restaurant La Madrileña, España 421. ACA discount
- Restaurant La Posta, España 476. Steakhouse; pastas
- Restaurant Lion D'or, Hotel Victoria Plaza, Zuviría 16
- Restaurant Mi Rancho, Mitre 301 (corner of General Güemes). Local cuisine
- Restaurant Parrilla a la Plaza, B Mitre block 300. Cheap
- Restaurant Parrilla Em Sudem, Balcarce 290. Steakhouse
- Restaurant Parrilla Luján, Santiago del Estero 526. Steakhouse
- Restaurant Peche Mitre, Victorino de la Plaza (opposite the bus terminal)
- Restaurant Pepito, Jujuy 1116
- Restaurant Rubero "88", Buenos Aires 88. Also cafeteria and pizzeria
- Restaurant Teby, Virrey Toledo block 800 (corner of Necochea). Credit cards accepted
- ☞ Pizzería Don Pedro, Alvarado 1101 (corner of Jujuy). Credit cards accepted
- Pizzería El Rincón Salteño, corner of Alvarado and Moldes
- Pizzería La Cantarella, corner of Corrientes and Jujuy
- Pizzería La Colonial, Balcarce 32
- Pizzería La Bella Tutta, Jujuy 465
- Pizzería La Fontana, Alberdí block 100 (corner of Urquiza)
- Pizzería La Monumental, Avenida Entre Ríos block 100 (corner of V López)

Salta Province

- Pizzería Marquez, Santiago del Estero block 100 (corner of Juramento)
- Pizzería La Selecta, Belgrano 511
- Pizzería Roque I, corner of San Martín and Alberdí
- Pizzería Roque II, Balcarce 55
- Pizzería Sucre, Urquiza 645
- Cafetería Cabildo, Caseros 529
- Cafetería Cafe Al Paso, B Mitre 55
- Cafetería Cafe del Paseo, Hotel Colonial Zuviria 6, Caseros 499 (corner of Urquiza). Open 24 hours
- Cafetería Cafe de la Fé, B Mitre 105
- Cafetería Cafeto, Caseros block 700 (corner of Florida)
- Cafetería Casablanca, Alvarado block 600 (corner of Alberdí)
- Cafetería Dixie, Urquiza 686
- Cafetería El Candil, Urquiza 894
- Cafetería El Paraiso, Buenos Aires 64
- Cafetería Frisco, Alvarado 640
- Cafetería Iberia, Urquiza block 500 (corner of Alberdí)
- Cafetería La Casa de las Empanadas, B Mitre block 200 (corner of Belgrano)
- Cafetería Mariver, corner of Alberdí and San Martín
- Cafetería Mickey, Alvarado block 200 (corner of Santa Fé)
- Cafetería Mil y Mil, España block 700 (corner of Balcarce). Video bar
- Cafetería Palpi, Leguizamon block 500 (corner of Mitre)
- Cafetería Regidor, Buenos Aires 2
- Cafetería Río, Mitre 41. Milk shakes and nice cakes
- Cafetería San Martín, Buenos Aires 298
- Cafetería Tobias, Caseros 515 (inside the arcade)
- Cafetería Topsy, Belgrano block 800 (corner of Sarmiento)
- Cafetería 25 de Mayo, B Mitre block 200 (corner of General Güemes). Snooker
- Cafetería Via del Cerro, General Güemes 118
- Cafetería Victoria Plaza, Buenos Aires 24
- Cafetería Zumo, Hotel Victoria plaza, Zuviria 16

Eating out outside Salta

- Restaurant El Ciervo, Avenida Reyes Catolicos 1465
- Restaurant El Circo, Hotel El Huaico, RN 9
- Restaurant El Rey del Pollo al Limon, Avenida Paraguay 1253
- Restaurant El Ruedo, Avenida Paraguay 1279. Steakhouse
- Restaurant La Loma, Entre Rios 2049. Steakhouse
- Restaurant Milemi, Avenida Chile 1448, near Camping Municipal
- Restaurant La Casa de las Empanadas, 12 de Octubre 720

Post and telegraph

- Post office: Encotel, Déan Funes 140 (corner of España)
- Telephones: Compañiá Argentina de Telefonos, Belgrano 824

Financial

- Maguitur, España 678, ℂ 216780. Cash only
- Banco de la Nación, corner of Mitre and Belgrano ℂ 213553. Exchanges money only between 0730 and 1000; accepts cash and travelers' checks
- Banco Provincial de Salta, Plaza 9 de Julio, España 526. Changes travelers' checks at the official rate
- Dinar S R L, España 609 ℂ 215561. Cash and travelers' checks; good rates
- Banco Credito, Alvarado 746. Cash adsvances on Visa card
- Banco Francés, España 642. Cash advances on Visa card
- Diner's Club office, Déan Funes block 300 (corner of General Güemes)

Services and facilities

- Bakery: La Europa, General Güemes block 100 (corner of España)
- Shoemaker: Dorcha, Vicente López 1046. Shoes and boots to measure

Dry cleaners

- Japon, Balcarce 413
- Japonesa, Urquiza 624
- Limpieza Güemes, 20 de Febrero block 100 (corner of Belgrano)

Laundromats

- Laverap, Alvarado 70. Open daily 0830–2000, $2.00
- Laverap, Juramento 315. Open daily 0800–1300 and 1500–2000

Salta

SALTA PROVINCE

Medical services
- Clinica Córdoba, Rivadavia 630
- Clinicas Medicas (specialist center), Rivadavia 220
- MAS (medical emergencies), corner of Puerreydon and Rivadavia (216243
- Policlinico San Bernardo, Tobias 69 (224000

Photographic supplies
- Foto y Film Enry Mar, Caseros 401
- Lindow, B Mitre 271

Saunas
- Sauna Club, Ituzaingó 106
- Sauna Finlandes, Balcarce block 0 (corner of España)

Supermarkets
- Cavanna, Caseros 542
- TIA, corner of Alberdí and Alvarado

C Clubs
- Casa de la Cultura (Cultural Center), Caseros 460. Runs cultural programs, including slide shows
- British: Asociación Cultural Argentino Británico, Caseros 139
- French: Alliance Française, Santa Fé 20
- Italian: Sociedad Italiana, Santiago del Estero block 400 (corner of Déan Funes).
- Spanish: Asociación Español, Balcarce block 600 (corner of Entre Ríos)

† Churches
- Latter Day Saints, corner of Boedo and San Martín

Visas, passports
- Bolivian consulate, Santiago del Estero 179. Open Mon–Fri 0900–1300 @ 211927
- Chilean consulate, Ejercito del Norte 312 (210827
- French consulate, Santa Fé 20 (213336
- Italian consulate, Zuviria 380 (212560

✈ Air services from Salta

El Aybal international airport is on RN 51, the road to Campo Quijano.
- Lloyd Aereo Boliviano, Caseros 376 May 12, (217753
- Aerolineas Argentinas, Caseros 475 (214757
- Aerolineas Federales Argentina (ALFA), Buenos Aires 88
- Austral, Buenos Aires 46 (224590
- SEAL, Lerma 162 (222333. Runs services to Iquique in Chile and Asunción in Paraguay

Destination	Fare	Depart	Services	Hours	Airline
Buenos Aires (Aeroparque Jorge Newbery)	$83.00	0320	2–6 services daily	2–3	Aerolineas, Austral
Comodoro Rivadavia	$102.00	1345	Wed, Fri, Sun	7½	Aerolineas
Córdoba	$52.00	1145	1–3 services daily	1–2	Aerolineas, Austral
Mendoza	$77.00	1345	Wed, Fri–Sun	4	Aerolineas
Neuquén	$99.00	1345	Wed, Fri	6	Aerolineas
Paraná	$94.00	1145	Mon, Wed, Fri	5	Austral
Resistencia	$41.00	1110	Wed, Sat	2	Federal
Río Gallegos	$118.00	1345	Sat	8½	Aerolineas
Río Grande	$128.00	1345	Sat	9½	Aerolineas
Rosario	$71.00	1145	Mon–Fri	4	Aerolineas,
San Carlos de Bariloche	$13.00	1345	Sat, Sun	6	Aerolineas, Austral
San Miguel de Tucumán	$23.00	0320	1–2 services daily	1	Aerolineas

Salta Province

🚌 Buses from Salta

The bus terminal is on the corner of Avenida H Yrigoyen and Puch.
From Salta there are daily buses to the Bolivian border, weekly buses to Antofagasta in Chile and weekly buses to Asunción in Paraguay.
Empresa Atahualpa runs a Saturday service to Asunción via Clorina, leaving Salta at 0830.

Municipal bus services

- Bus terminal–City center: Bus 1A, 1B, 1C, 11A, 11B
- Bus terminal–City center–Mercado Artesanal: Bus 3, 7
- Bus terminal–City center–Railroad station: Bus 4, 5, 6
- Bus terminal–City center–Railroad station–Castanares–University: Bus 10, 14
- Bus terminal–City center–Railroad station–Tres Cerritos: Bus 12
- City center–Railroad station: Bus 13
- City center–Railroad station–Mercado Artesanal–Tres Cerritos: Bus 2

Country and inter-city bus services

Destination	Fare	Depart	Services	Hours	Company
• Santa Rosa de Tastil				3	El Quebradeño
• Agua Blanca	$5.50	2200	daily	6	Atahualpa
• Antofagasta		1600	Wed		Atahualpa
Tickets from Balturis					
• Belén		0700	Wed	11	El Indio
• Buenos Aires		1200	1–2 services daily		La Veloz del Norte
The "Independencia" leaves at 1200 on Tues, Thurs, and Sat; and "La Estrella" at 1340 daily					
• Cachi	$5.20	0700	2 services daily except Wed and Fri	5	M Rueda
• Cafayate	$4.50	1130	daily	4	El Indio
• Calama (Chile)					Balturis
Only runs during summer					
• Córdoba		0715	4 services daily		Expreso Panamericano, La Veloz del Norte
• Embarcación		0600	4 services daily		Atahualpa
• Formosa	$24.00	0830	Mon, Wed, Fri	21	Atahualpa
• Humahuaca		0730	Fri, Sun		Atahualpa
• La Quiaca	$11.50	0630	3 services daily	8	Atahualpa
• La Rioja	$14.00	0730	daily		Bosio
• Orán	$6.50	0600	9 services daily	6	Atahualpa
Buses connect with Tarija buses to Bolivia					
• Pocitos (on the border)	$7.20	0600	4 services daily		Atahualpa
• Presidencia Roque Sáenz Peña	$16.00	2015	daily		La Veloz del Norte
• Resistencia	$15.50	1700	daily	15	La Veloz del Norte
• Rosario de la Frontera	$4.00	0700	5 services daily	3	La Veloz del Norte
• San Antonio de los Cobres	$4.50	0815	Tues, Thurs, Sat, Sun		El Quebradeño
Departs 0815 Thurs, 1500 Tues and Sat, 1900 Sun					
• San Fernando del Valle de Catamarca		0730	daily		Bosio

Salta

SALTA PROVINCE

Buses from Salta—continued

Destination	Fare	Depart	Services	Hours	Company
• San Lorenzo	$0.50				
• San Miguel de Tucumán	$7.50	0715	12 services daily	5	Expreso Panamericano, La Veloz del Norte
• San Salvador de Jujuy	$2.00	0600	16 services daily	3	Atahualpa
• Santa María		0700	daily		El Indio
• Santiago del Estero		0715	3 services daily		Expreso Panamericano, La Veloz del Norte
• Tartagal	$9.25	0600	7 services daily		Atahualpa
• Termas de Río Hondo	$9.00	0715	3 services daily	6	Panamericano

- Paraguayan consulate, Los Almendros 161 ℂ 212562
- Spanish consulate, Las Heras 1229 ℂ 221420
- West German consulate, 3rd floor, España 671, ℂ 220916

Motoring

The road trip to Jujuy can be made either via General Güemes (on RN 9) or direct via the *cornisa*, 92 km heading due north.

Service stations

- ACA, corner of Mitre and Rivadavia. Maps available
- Esso, corner of San Martín and Pellegrini

Car rental

- Avis Rent-a-Car, Alvarado 537 ℂ 216394. Also at airport
- Liprandi Rent-a-Car, Caseros 489 ℂ 224409
- Rent a Car–López Fleming, General Güemes 92 ℂ 211381. Also at airport
- Rent Auto Salta, Alvarado 30
- Salta Rent Car, Caseros 225 ℂ 212069
- A1 International, Caseros 221 and 489 ℂ 214871. Also at airport. Cars may be returned to San Salvador de Jujuy or San Miguel de Tucumán

Tours

Tour operators

- Balturis, Lerma 170 ℂ 210431. During summer runs buses to Antofagasta, Calama, and Arica in Chile
- Green Tours, Córdoba 46
- Saltour Turismo, Caseros 525 ℂ 215741. Multilingual staff
- Travel house, España 680 ℂ 214402 (Señor Giampiero Marchesi)

Tours

The following tours are descibed in detail under "Excursions" below.

- Parque Nacional El Rey: Two-day excusion, covering 400 km; fare $25.00 (excluding accommodation and food); departs 0700
- San Antonio de los Cobres: One-day excursion; fare $17.50; departs 0700
- Cabra Corral: Five-hour excursion, covering 220 km
- Cafayate: 12-hour excursion, covering 390 km; fare $15.00; departs 0700
- Cuesta del Obispo: Seven-hour excursion, covering 230 km; fare $11.00; normally departs 1300
- Cachi: 12-hour excursion, covering 320 km; fare $16.50; departs 0700
- Río Calchaqui valley: Two-day excursion, covering 520 km; fare $33.00 (excluding accommodation and food)
- Quebrada de Humahuaca: One-day excursion; fare $18.00
- Termas de Reyes and Lagunas de Yala: One-day excursion; fare $15.00

Salta

Salta Province

🚆 Trains from Salta

The F C General M Belgrano station is at Ameghino 690.

There are no direct services to Buenos Aires or San Salvador de Jujuy; instead there is a local service to General Güemes.

The "Tren a las Nubes", a tourist train, runs to **Polvarillo** viaduct and returns to Salta. Here you can enjoy a breathtaking panoramic spectacle in the comfort of a heated carriage. The train leaves Salta at 0700 and returns about 2140; the fare is $10.00. In July it runs daily; for the remainder of the year check with Belgrano station. The line to **Huaytiquina** was built under the American engineer Richard Maury who envisioned a connection between north-western Argentina and the Pacific. The work was started in the late 1920s and completed in the 1940s. It is interesting to note that one migrant worker from Yugoslavia by the name of Josip Broz worked on that project returning to Yugoslavia at the outbreak of war—he became known as Marshall Tito and headed the first post-war government in Yugoslavia. See also San Antonio de los Cobres under "Tours" below.

"El Norteño" departs 0700 Mon, Wed, and Fri for Buenos Aires via San Miguel de Tucumán and Alto Córdoba.

Destination	Fare	Depart	Services	Hours
• Alto Córdoba		0755	Mon, Wed, Fri	24
First class	$13.00			
• Buenos Aires (Retiro station)				
		0755	Mon, Thurs, Fri	36
First class	$23.00			
Tourist class	$17.50			
• La Quiaca				
Change at General Güemes				
• Mendoza					40
Change at Villa María				
• Pocitos (Salvador Mazza station)				
		1900	Wed	17
First class	$6.50			
Catch the Bolivian train to Santa Cruz at Pocitos by walking across the border to Yacuiba				
• Salar de Pocitos		1615	Wed	12
First class	$5.20			
• San Antonio de Los Cobres				
	$3.50	1615	Wed	8
• San Miguel de Tucumán				
		0755	Mon, Thurs, Fri	9
First class	$5.50			
• Socompa (on the Chilean border)				
		1615	Wed	21
First class	$9.00			

🛍 Shopping

- Antiguedades Enrique VIII, Puerreydon 4
- Artesanías La Casona, España 406. Souvenirs and onyx
- Artesanías Yunque, Caseros 505. Onyx
- Onyx factory, Avenida Chile 1663, near the municipal camping ground
- Mercado Municipal, corner of San Martín and Florida. Meat, fish, and vegetables. Closed 1200–1700 and Sun
- Mercado de Artesanía, Casa El Alto Molino, San Martín 2550. The house in which the market is located was built towards the end of the eighteenth century. The building has been completely restored and gives a good picture how

Salta

Salta Province

the rich of that period lived. All items displayed are of excellent quality. Although it is a long way out of town (almost at the intersection of San Martín with Circunvalación past the rail crossing) it is worth a visit. Open daily 0800–1930. Take bus 2, 3, or 7 from the city center
- El Potro, Urquiza 653. Local products and articles made from llama products
- Platería Cabildo, Caseros 507. Silver wares

Sport
- Salta polo and golf club, Caseros 525

Entertainment

Most discos and nightclubs are in the suburb of Tres Cerritos.
- Café Concert Birimbon, General Güemes 521
- Casino Provincial, Alberdí 235, in the pedestrian mall
- Disco Afrika, Tres Cerritos
- Disco Ego II, Tres Cerritos
- Disco Birimbau, General Güemes 517
- Disco Caligula, Jujuy 251. Open from 2200 onwards
- Disco Karthom, Tres Cerritos
- Disco Mao Mao, RN 51 Km 3, on the south side of the city center
- Disco Nacho I, Tres Cerritos
- Disco Tarot, Tres Cerritos
- Disco Ufa, Hotel Huaico, RN 9, on the north side of the city center
- Night Club La Cueva del Topo, Santa Fe 140
- Peña Boliche Balderrama, San Martín 1126
- Peña Daniel Toro, in Restaurant La Cason, Caseros 511, Cabildo
- Peña Española, B Mitre 389
- Peña José Manuel, Caseros 406
- Peña Gauchos de Güemes, Uruguay 750. Open nightly from 2100
- English-style pub: Lions, corner of Córdoba and Alvarado. Bar

Sightseeing

The historical part of the town is best explored on foot. There are a few old houses in Puerreydon which were spared in the 1884 earthquake; number 112 was built in 1739.
- Casa de Gobierno (House of Assembly), on the eastern side of Plaza 9 de Julio. The guard of honor is dressed in red ponchos with black stripes the historical uniforms of the Gauchos de Güemes. The changing of the guard takes place at 1200

Public buildings
- Complejo Museológico del Norte (Museum Complex of the North), Caseros 549–575, Cabildo was built in 1676, and includes the Museo Colonial Histórico (Colonial History Museum). It provides a good overview of Salta's past. Open daily, but check opening hours. Small admission charge
- Monument to General Güemes, situated at the end of Paseo Güemes at the foot of Cerro San Bernardo. This is a massive statue by the artist Victor Carino in honor of the Gaucho general who between 1814 and 1821 repelled and defeated the royalist troops coming down from Bolivia seven times

Museums
- Museo Provincial de Bellas Artes (Provincial Fine Arts Museum), Casa Arias Rengel, La Florida 20
- Casa José Evariste Uriburu, Caseros 417, was the home of a well-known nineteenth-century *Salteña* family, and con-

Salta

tains memorabilia of the family and the period
- Museo de Ciencias Naturales (Natural Science Museum), Mendoza 2, has an interesting ornithological section. Open daily
- Museo Antropológico Juan Martín Leguizamon (Juan Martín Leguizamon Anthropology Museum), Ejercito del Norte 750 (corner of Polo Sur), behind the Güemes monument. Many of the archeological pieces come from Santa Rosa de Tastil: Ceramics, wooden implements, weavings, and a disk made of silver and gold. Open Mon–Fri 0800–1230 and 1500–1800; Sat and Sun 0900–1200

Churches

- Cathedral and bishop's palace, on the north side of the Plaza 9 de Julio, were completed in 1878. The interior of the cathedral is decorated in red and gold. The late baroque altar and the images of the Cristo del Milagro (Christ of the Miracle) brought from Spain in 1592 and of the Virgin Mary are worth a visit. A disastrous earthquake which struck the city on September 13 1692 was miraculously stopped when the townsfolk paraded the two images through the streets
- San Bernardo convent, corner of Caseros and Santa Fé. The wooden portal dates from 1762
- Convento y Iglesia de San Francisco (Franciscan Convent and Church), corner of Caseros and Córdoba, was founded by Fray Bartolomé de la Cruz. The first part of the convent and church was completed in 1625. By 1674 a bigger church was constructed, which later fell victim to a fire. The present church was completed in 1880. The bells were made from the cannon used in the Battle of Salta. The steeple is 53 m high and one of the loftiest in South America. Inside the church are some famous paintings such as *Nuestra Señora de las Nieves* and a picture of San Francisco de Asissi, founder of the brotherhood. In the library there are numerous old volumes of inestimable value

Excursions

The "Tren a las Nubes" runs daily between March and July; see "Trains" above.
- **San Salavador de Jujuy** via the *autopista*: This is a three-hour trip if you go by Atahulapa bus. The 132 km road is sealed all the way. Leave the eastern suburbs of Salta on RN 9, skirting Cerro San Bernardo. Most buses make a short detour to serve the town of General Güemes. Turn off onto RN 34. The first township in Jujuy is **Pampa Blanca** where there is a police checkpoint. Most of the way you pass cultivated fields, growing such crops as tobacco, and orchards. Further on you pass through **Lapachos**, and **El Cadillal** with the airport serving San Sal-

SALTA PROVINCE

vador. This is primarily tobacco-growing country. The last townships before entering San Salvador are **Ciudad Perico** and **Palpalá**. See also San Salvador de Jujuy on page 654

- **San Salvador de Jujuy** via the *cornisa*. Although nearly 40 km shorter (total 94 km) than the route described above, it too takes three hours by Atahualpa buses since there are more stops. The road passes through scenic landscape whose hills and mountains are densely covered with shrubs and trees. You leave Salta on Avenida Bolivia going straight north. Twenty-five km north you pass through **El Carmen**, which is a wheat- and vegetable-growing area. Nearby is the **Dique La Ciénaga**, renowned for good *pejerrey* fishing. A little further north is **Abra Santa Laura**, on the border with Jujuy. Going past **Dique Campo Alegre** you see sailing boats on the lake. There is good fishing here too. Five km past the lake is **La Caldera**, which you can't miss since the huge 25 m high statue of Christ is visible from afar. At **La Baquera** are many camping spots with kiosks where you can buy *asados* (meals). The hills here are densely overgrown and difficult to penetrate. This is a very winding and picturesque road but is subject to being made impassable from rockfalls and during the wet season. See also San Salvador de Jujuy on page 654

- **Cerro San Bernardo**: 1466 m high. It is possible to reach the summit of this mountain by car. From the viewing platform there are panoramic views over the city and the distant *cordillera*. It is also possible to walk to the top along a mountain trail which commences at the General Güemes monument. This is a via crucis with stations leading to the top of the mountain. A cable car runs from Parque San Martín to the summit, where there is a restaurant

- **Fuerte Cobos**: On the right bank of the **Río Mojotoro** in the **Valle de Siancas**, halfway between Salta and General Güemes. This fort was erected as a first-line defense against the attacks of the Chaco Indians. At first it was only an outpost to give warning to Salta of an impending attack, but in 1690 it became a fully-fledged defense bastion under the governor of Salta, Don Diego Díaz Gómez. Despite this the Tobas and Mocovies crossed the lines of forts established along the Río Bermejo and continued to harass the settlers. They used the so-called Macomitas Trail which by-passed the fortifications and attacked Tucumán and Salta. The defensive character of Fuerte Cobos was enlarged in 1733 under governor Gerónimo Matorras. Despite a peace treaty between the Spanish and the Chaco peoples there was another large-scale invasion in 1775 and the fort was overrun. As the Indians

SALTA PROVINCE

were defeated in successive campaigns the fort lost its importance. During the Wars of Liberation General Manuel Belgrano stayed in Cobos on two occasions: in 1812 when he withdrew from the battle zone to Tucumán, and again in 1813 when he marched to the battle of Salta. At present the historic place consists solely of a two-story building

- **Coronel Moldes**: 26 km south of Salta. The **Cabra Corral dam** is a huge artificial lake and has become a weekend retreat for the *Saltenos*, who enjoy waterskiing and fishing there. Restaurant El Mirador has international cuisine and serves *pejerrey* from the lake. See also Coronel Moldes on page 620
- **San Lorenzo**: A picturesque village some 11 km north-west of Salta, at the beginning of the Quebrada. It can be reached by the frequent buses from Salta run by the Luis B Chavez company. The road is sealed throughout. Just before arriving at the Quebrada is the prestigious Restaurant El Castillo, which serves traditional and international cuisine and has occasional impromptu *peñas*. The staff speaks English. Camping is possible further up at the picnic grounds but there are no facilities
- **Polvarillo viaduct**: A highly-rcommended day trip by train
- **Cafayate**: The trip to Cafayate through the **Lerma valley** along a sealed raod and later through the **Quebrada de Cafayate** goes through a very scenic and wild part of the province. Most rivers are forded except the **Río Chunapa**. You pass through semi-arid landscapes and canyons with strange rock formations (**Los Castillos**, **El Fraile**, **El Obelisco**, and **El Anfiteatro**, a gorge)—most of these rock formations are signposted. Wildlife encountered are rheas and armadillos. The mountains are occasionally covered with shrub as the road winds its way gradually up through the canyon. The ruins of **Toquipili**, a pre-Columbian settlement, are across the river on the northern side. Just before arriving at Cafayate the Quebrada opens into the wide **Río Calchaqui valley**. See also Cafayate on page 616

Tours

For durations, distances, fares, departure times, and addresses of tour operators see "Tours" above.

- **Parque Nacional El Rey** via **Lumbreras**: An excursion into the lush eastern part of the province. There is opportunity to fish in the clear mountain streams and observe tropical birds such as toucans
- **San Antonio de Los Cobres**: Follows RN 51. Shortly after **Campo Quijano** the bus follows the **Río Blanco** through the **Quebrada de los Toros**. Almost immediately the moun-

SALTA PROVINCE

tains close in and the climb starts, and the sealed road gives way to a dirt road. The riverbed is very wide here but there is little water. Near the Km 28 mark the valley narrows, leaving just enough space for the one-lane road. The railroad is on the left-hand side and the first rail bridge appears. This is tremendous mountain scenery: steep walls, bare except for the round tree-like cacti which grow right up to the mountain peaks. Near the Km 36 mark the road and the railroad intersect at an unprotected level crossing. The *quebrada* becomes even narrower and almost all river crossings are by ford. At Km 41, just before **El Candado**, is another rail bridge; and after the village is still another rail bridge and a ford. At Km 49 is **Chorrillos**, a small Indian community consisting of half a dozen dwellings and a church. The **Río Incamayo** joins the river from the right. This is the valley through which the Inca road passed in pre-Hispanic times. The scenery is spectacular. The swift-running river is forded again and the valley widens at the junction of the two rivers. On the valley base are a few *chacras* or maize fields. After **El Antigal** there are some strangely-eroded rock formations which make excellent photographs. As we approach the *altiplano* the wind increases—again a very scenic spot, with views down into the valley where the railroad runs.

The mountains on the left-hand side dissolve into isolated hills. You are now entering the Quebrada del Toro, the last steep section before finally reaching the *altiplano*. Just before this the bus stops for a break at the El Huaico restaurant. Nearby an old white church contrasts beautifully with the mountains in the background; another photograph opportunity! In the Quebrada del Toro, just before **Santa Rosa de Tastil** (a partly-excavated archeological site) are some picturesque old deserted houses. There is no accommodation at Santa Rosa de Tastil. At **Abra Muñano**, a village of about 20 homesteads and a church, you reach the highest point of the trip: 4200 m. One of the most scenic railroads follows the road. The tour goes as far as San Antonio de Los Cobres in the typical *altiplano* country, with vistas of snow-capped peaks and *salinas* in the distance. Fare $17.50. See also San Antonio de los Cobres below; and "Tren a las Nubes" under "Trains" above

- **Cabra Corral**, the second largest artificial lake in Argentina: The trip follows RN 68 to **El Carril** and on to the village of Cabra Corral. The lake surface is in sharp contrast with the bare mountains encircling the site
- **Cafayate**: 390 km. The highlight of the trip is the passage through the **Quebrada del Río de las Conchas** (or "River of

Salta

Salta Province

Shells") and **Quebrada de Cafayate**. On arrival in Cafayate the tour visits a wine tasting at one of the *bodegas*. See also Cafayate on page 616

- **Cuesta del Obispo** ("Bishop's Slope"). The tour goes via **El Carril**, and after **Pulares** the road enters the **Quebrada de los Laureles** and the **Quebrada de Escoipe**. It is a seemingly endless uphill drive along a winding road, fording little crystalline mountain streams on the way up, but it provides panoramic views. The bus goes as far as **Piedra del Molino**, from where the outline of the **Nevado del Cachi** (6380 m) can be seen
- **Cachi**: The bus follows RP 33 through the **Quebrada de los Laureles** and **Escoipe** but after Piedra del Molino continues through the **Straight of Tin-Tin**, a flat stretch of about 30 km, passing through **Payogasta** and arriving in Cachi after crossing the **Río Calchaqui**. At Cachi, a visit to the museum and lunch at the ACA *hostería*, from where there are vistas of the surrounding countryside. See also Cachi on page 614
- **Río Calchaqui valley**: The trip goes via the **Cuesta del Obispo** to **Cachi**. From Cachi it follows RN 40 along the Río Calchaqui passing through **Molinos** (where there is an exquisitely restored Jesuit mission church dating from the seventeenth century) and **Angastaco**, **San Carlos**, and **Cafayate**. The return trip passes through the **Quebrada de las Conchas** and the **Quebrada de Cafayate** which has weird rock erosions and multicoloured rock formations
- **Quebrada de Humahuaca**: This excursion visits **San Salvador de Jujuy** and the pre-Inca city of **Tilcara**
- **Termas de Reyes** and **Lagunas de Yala**: Visits **San Salvador de Jujuy** and continues on to Jujuy province's best-known thermal resort. The Lagunas de Yala are a string of small lakes to the north of Reyes

San Antonio de los Cobres

Postal code: 4411 • Population: 3000 • Altitude: 3760 m
Distances
From Salta: 165 km north-west on RN 51
From Antofagasta (Chile): 606 km eastwards on RN 51

San Antonio de Los Cobres is situated in the desert-like *altiplano*. It was capital of the Gobernación de los Andes until 1958, when the Gobernación was split up between Jujuy, Salta, and Catamarca provinces. It is not a particularly beautiful town, but its situation in the *altiplano* is superb: vistas of salt lakes, snow-covered peaks, and many hot springs nearby. It is the home of the remaining Diaguitas Indians, who are distant cousins to the *altiplano* Indians in Bolivia. The

SALTA PROVINCE

economic activity of the area centres around the many zinc, copper, and silver mines, some of them operated on a shoe-string basis by single families. It is cold all year round and at night the temperature drops below 0°C, so bring your warm gear, especially if you intend to camp outside.

Accommodation

C Hospedaje Belgrano, Belgrano ⑴ $2.50
C Hospedaje Los Andes, Belgrano, on the Chilean exit road ⑴ $2.00. Shared bathroom

Buses

Empresa Quebradeno has its ticket office in the Hospedaje Belgrano.
A weekly bus service runs during the summer months between San Antonio and San Pedro de Atacama in Chile.
- Salta: Fare $4.50; departs 1000 Tues, Wed, Fri, Sun; 6 hours; El Quebradeno
- Mina Tincalayu: Fare $6.00; departs 0040 Thurs and Sun; 5 hours; El Quebradeno

Trains

There are trains coming from Paso Huaitiquina and Socompa on the Chilean border, but they do not follow a fixed timetable. You could be waiting half the night under chilling conditions for the arrival of the train back to Salta. The "Tren a las Nubes" (a tourist train) runs through San Antonio on its way to the Polvarillo viaduct. When using the passenger train on the down-hill journey sit on the right-hand side for the best views.
- Salta: Fare $3.70; departs 1840 daily; 10 hours; it usually has only one carriage, unheated. Another departs 0450 Fri; 11 hours; it comes from Socompa and is invariably late

Excursions

- Chile via the **Paso de la Laguna Sico**: This is a completely new road, replacing the one over the Paso Haytaquina and a considerable improvement. Fill up on petrol in San Antonio as there is none until **San Pedro de Atacama**. Cars have to be in good condition to complete the journey successfully; make sure you have a spare tyre, antifreeze, and plenty of water. The *altiplano* trip is rather monotonous, and passes many *salinas*, but it is scenically very beautiful on the Chilean side. Flamingo colonies live on the *salinas*. For those who appreciate desert scenery
- **Mina La Concordia**: La Concordia mine, 20 km west of San Antonio, is one of the biggest copper, zinc, and silver mines in the area. From the mine it is a 20-minute walk to **Polvarillo viaduct**, which was built for the railroad to Chile
- **Termas de Pompeya**: Located about 8 km west of San Antonio on RN 51. The turn-off to the hot springs is well signposted ("Baños Pompeya 1 km, Mina La Concordia 10 km"). The track to the right past the bridge can be used by cars. The stream is slightly sulfurous, pointing to its volcanic origin. Follow the track until you can see the houses on your right, then cross the river towards the houses. The hot springs are directly behind the houses, and emerge at about 35°C. The water is brought to the houses in rusted pipes. There are no tourist facilities. Some 100 m further behind is a pond which owes its

San Antonio de los Cobres

existence to thermal springs, and is the source of the stream. This is a 2½-hour hike through splendid *altiplano* country; on the way you can see wild llamas
- **Termas de Incachuli**, with the **Nevado de Queva** right behind it: This is a 30 km trip westwards on RN 51. Fourteen km past San Antonio is the turn-off to the Termas along RP 129. There are no buses, so hitch a lift with mining trucks
- **Susques**: The drive north is a hazardous trip. Susques is better reached via Jujuy; buses go by this route. See also Susques on page 665

SAN CARLOS

Postal code: 4427 • Altitude: 1660 m
Distances
- From Salta: 212 km south-west on RN 33 then RN 40
- From Cafayate: 24 km southwards on RN 40

Accommodation
- Hostería San Carlos (ACA), Belgrano on the main Plaza ⑪ $7.50 ⓘ

Camping
- Municipal campsite
- Camping by the roadside is possible anywhere

SAN LORENZO

Altitude: 1400 m
Distance from Salta: 11 km north-west on RP 28

San Lorenzo is a summer holiday resort and weekend retreat of *Salteños* on the **Río San Lorenzo**.

Accommodation
★★★ Hostería San Lorenzo, corner of A Gauffin and F Arias ℓ 921337

Eating out
- Restaurant El Castillo, near the Quebrada

Buses
Buses run regularly from Salta, turning round at the *quebrada* and returning; fare $0.30.

SANTA VICTORIA

Postal code: 4651
Distance from La Quiaca: 118 km eastwards on RP 7 then RP 5

Santa Victoria is located in the extreme north of the province on the **Río Santa Victoria** near the Bolivian border. It can only be reached from La Quiaca in Jujuy via Yaví on a gravel road. It was founded in 1803. There are no hotels but the road is of particular scenic beauty, especially after passing the **Sierra de Santa Victoria** which forms the provincial border with Jujuy and whose peaks reach over 5000 m.

Festivals
- Fiesta Patronal Santiago Apostol (Festival of the Patron Saint James the Apostle): July 25
- Fiesta Patronal Virgen de Santa Victoria: November 17

Tartagal

Postal code: 4560 • Population: 36 000 • (area code: (0875) • Altitude: 500 m
- Distance from Salta: 365 km north-west on RN 34

Tartagal owes its expansion to the petrol discoveries made in the district. Founded only in 1925, it is geared to the promotion of adventure tourism, and to visiting Franciscan Indian mission centers such as **Carapari**, the **Río Bermejo** and the *selva* areas of the *chaco*. Tartagal has good tourist facilities.

Accommodation

★★★ Hotel Gran Argentino, San Martín 54 (21325
★★ Hotel Espinillo, San Martín 122 (21007
A Residencial City, Alberdí 79 (21558
B Residencial Premier, Rivadavia 571 (21036

Eating out

- Cafetería Jonathan, San Martin 156. Whiskeria
- Restaurant Circulo Argentino, Rivadavia 241
- Restaurant El Lapacho, Alberdí 565. Pastas
- Restaurant El Rincon de Pichon, Cornejo 474. Steakhouse

Buses from Tartagal

The Atahualpa bus terminal is on Avenida 20 de Febrero. The restrooms are not well kept. The restaurant is open 24 hours. Note that Atahualpa buses which are supposed to run to Pocitos are combined here and only one bus goes to the border which is usually full. You also will lose your seat if you are on the bus which is cancelled here.
- Salta: Departs daily; Atahualpa
- Embarcación: Departs daily; ½ hour; Empresa Atahualpa
- Rosario de la Frontera: Departs daily; 7 hours; Empresa La Veloz del Norte
- San Miguel de Tucumán: Departs daily; 9 hours; Empresa La Veloz del Norte

Motoring

The road to Salta initially passes through flat country. Just before Embarcación it gets hilly on the north side
- Service station: ACA, corner of RN 34 and República

Jujuy Province

Plate 34 Map of Jujuy Province
  646 Abra Pampa
  647 Casabindo
  648 Cieneguillas
  648 Humahuaca
  650 La Quiaca
  651   Map
  653 Maimará
  653 Parque Nacional Calilegua
  654 San Salvador de Jujuy
  655   Map
  665 Susques
  666 Tilcara
  667   Map
  668 Tumbaya
  668 Uquía
  669 Yaví

Jujuy is the northernmost province of Argentina. It shares borders with Bolivia in the north and west, Chile in the west, and Salta province in the south and east. Most of the people have a similiar ethnic origin to the people of Bolivia.

The area covers 53 000 square km with a population of 480 000. Most of the province forms part of the *altiplano*. The eastern section consists of subtropical lowlands while the area around the capital has a temperate climate.

Jujuy Province

JUJUY PROVINCE

The economic backbone of the province is mining. The biggest single mining enterprise is Minera Aguilar, which operates mines in **Molino**, **Tres Cruces**, and **Veta Mina**, employing about 10 000 staff.

The capital of Jujuy is **San Salvador de Jujuy**. Within Jujuy its name is generally abbreviated to "San Salvador", but outside Jujuy its name is often abbreviated to "Jujuy", particularly on public transport.

This is a very traditional province where pagan elements and Christian elements walk side by side. Many of the population in the *altiplano* still cling to traditions going back to pre-Columbian times, and thus have a very vivid and colorful folklore which is best observed during fiestas such as Carnaval and the Fiesta de Mamapacha, both held in towns throughout the province.

From its earliest pre-Hispanic days Jujuy seems to have been on the invasion route of conquering armies. It has been established that the province formed part of the Inca Empire or "Collasuyo" since approximately 1480 AD. The domination by the Incas brought the Quechua language to this part of the empire, and it is still used today in the *altiplano* villages. With the arrival of the Spaniards pushing down from Peru in the middle of the sixteenth century a new era was ushered in: Christianity was introduced and embraced willingly by the populace, but with an admixture of paganism which has been accepted by the Church.

One of the customs brought by the Spaniards is still practised in this part of Argentina: the bullfight. But whereas in Spain and Mexico it is a bloody affair, here it is a question of skill: to remove a string of silver coins attached to the bull's horns without being gored.

In line with a long historic past there are many archeological sites bearing witness to an uninterrupted past. The foremost archeological site is **Tilcara**, where a pre-Columbian city fortress is being painstakingly pieced together by archeologists. However, other sites abound in and about **Humahuaca** where a type of *chullpa* (a pre-Hispanic burial site) is found which connects the area with the Tiahuanacu period, about 900–1100 AD. Most of these places are out of the reach of the average tourist, but for those interested in archeology the tourist office in San Salvador de Jujuy and the archeological museums in Tilcara and Humahuaca will provide information.

The province's road network is considerable. One of the latest feats is the construction of a road to **Paso de Jama** on the Chilean border. It will eventually be extended on the Chilean side to link up with the road going to San Pedro de Atacama, thus providing a link to the Pacific Ocean. On the Argentine side the road passes through **Lipan**, **Salinas Grandes**, and **Susques**.

JUJUY PROVINCE

The highest mountain in Jujuy is **Cerro Zapaleri**, which forms the border between Bolivia, Argentina, and Chile.

The areas of interest for the tourist are:
- Worth a detour: The capital **San Salvador de Jujuy**; the **Quebrada de Humahuaca**; and **Tilcara**
- Very interesting: **Parque Nacional Calilegua** near Libertador General San Martín; **Termas de Reyes**; and the **Lagunas de Yala**

For the intrepid outdoor enthusiast places such as **Laguna Pozuelos** with its flamingo population, and **Yaví** and **Iruya** in neighbouring Salta province with their Jesuit mission churches in splendid scenic mountainous country are recommended. Also the trip to **Susques** via the **Laguna Guayatayoc** is recommended, although the accommodation is less than comfortable in those areas and nights are definitely chilly.

Typical meals in Jujuy
- *Picante de pollo* (spicy chicken): $2.00
- *Locro* (a stew containing meat and vegetables): $1.00
- *Cabrito* (goat): $2.50
- *Lechón* (sucking pig): $3.00
- *Cayote solo* (a dessert based on squash): $0.70
- *Cayote con nueces* (a dessert with nuts): $1.00
- *Quesillo con miel de caña* (cheese with sugarcane sap): $0.70
- *Cuaresmillos* (Lenten cookies): $1.00

ABRA PAMPA

Postal code: 4640 • Altitude: 3484 m
Distance
- From San Salvador de Jujuy: 217 km northwards on RN 9
- From La Quiaca 75 km southwards on RN 9

Abra Pampa is an important mining town located in the *altiplano*. It is the gateway to places in the most north-western part of the province (and of Argentina) such as **Laguna Pozuelos** with its flamingo colonies. Accommodation is not very satisfactory: it is suitable only for the intrepid budget traveler. It gets very cold at night and warm clothing is a must. Snowfalls in summer are not uncommon.

Festivals
- Festival del Huancar: February
- Carnaval
- Fiesta de Mamapacha

Accommodation
C Residencial Sol de Mayo, Senador Perez 144 (corner of Sarmiento) $5.00. Shared bathroom
C Residencial El Norte, Sarmiento $4.50. Shared bathroom; the owner runs the Restaurant Terminal

Eating out
- Restaurant Terminal

JUJUY PROVINCE

🚌 Buses

The services to Casabindo are sometimes interrupted for weeks during the wet season, from January till April.
- San Salvador de Jujuy: Fare $6.50; 6 services daily; 5 hours; Expreso Panamericano
- Humahuaca: Fare $2.80; 6 services daily; 2 hours; Expreso Panamericano
- La Quiaca: Fare $1.80; 6 services daily; ½ hour; Expreso Panamericano
- Tilcara: $3.10; 6 services daily; 3 hours; Expreso Panamericano

Buses to the north-west

Empresa Vilte runs buses from their offices on the corner of Sarmiento and Macedonia Graz, and also from the bus terminal, into the north-western part of the province into areas hitherto untouched by tourism. Roads are bad and can be impassable during heavy rains. Suggested only for the hardy and intrepid.
- Casabindo: $1.50; departs 1030 Tues, Thurs, Sat. The bus continues to Tusaquilla, arriving at 1330, and returns to Abra Pampa
- Coranzuli: Fare $2.80; departs 1000 Mon, Wed, Fri. The bus returns the same day, leaving at 1430
- Laguna Pozuelos (eastern side): Fare $2.00; departs 0630 Mon, Wed, Sat. The bus continues to La Quiaca, arriving at 1000
- Laguna Pozuelos (western side, via Lagunillas): $2.00; departs 1030 Tues, Thurs, Fri. The bus continues to Guayatayoc, arriving at 1300, and then returns to Abra Pampa

🍷 Excursions

- **Cochinoca**: 25 km west
- **Casabindo**: 62 km. An *altiplano* village more reminiscent of Bolivia than Argentina
- **Laguna Pozuelos**: 60 km west on a dirt road, Laguna Pozuelos has been declared a natural monument and flamingo reserve. The parks office is situated on the **Río Cinsel**. Empresa Vilte runs buses there

CASABINDO

Postal code: 4641
Distance from Abra Pampa: 49 km southeast on RP 11

Casabindo is a small *altiplano* village with no hotels. It was founded around 1590. In pre-Hispanic times the Inca road to Chile passed through here. The church was built in 1772 and inside are pictures of the Cuzco school. The *fiestas* however are the big attraction here.

🎭 Festivals

- Nuestra Señora del Rosario (Our Lady of the Rosary): August 15. This *fiesta* is steeped in pre-Columbian customs: *suri* dancers in the morning and in the afternoon the *vincha* bullfight. This is one of the few places in Argentina where some form of bullfight has survived. The bullfight is held in the Plaza in front of the church and the *torero* (bullfighter) has to remove a string of money attached to the horns of the bull without getting hurt

🚌 Buses

The services to Casabindo are sometimes interrupted for a month when it rains.
- San Salvador de Jujuy: Depart 1700 Mon, Wed, Fri; 5½ hours; Expreso El Quiaqueño
- Abra Pampa: Departs 0710 Mon, Wed, Fri; 1 hour; Empresa El Quiaqueño

🍷 Excursions

- **Sorcuyo**: On **Laguna Guayatayoc**, some 23 km south, are

Casabindo

JUJUY PROVINCE

the remains of a pre-Hispanic city

CIENEGUILLAS

Postal code: 4653
Distance from La Quiaca: 36 km westwards on RP 5

Festivals
- Fiesta del Cambalache: February

Buses
Buses run regularly from La Quiaca.

HUMAHUACA

Postal code: 4630 • Altitude: 2940 m
Distance from San Salvador de Jujuy: 126 km northwards on RN 9

Humahuaca is located in the **Quebrada Humahuaca** on the **Río Grande**. Because of the high altitude the nights are cold even in summer. The town is very Indian, and many pre-Hispanic traditions are still preserved behind a mantle of Christianity.

The center of town is Plaza Sargento Gómez. The church was begun in the seventeenth century, but was remodelled and completed only in 1880. At 1200 the figure of San Francisco Solano appears at the clock tower and blesses the town. Stairs lead up to the large *Monumento a la Independencia* (Independence Monument) on a hill in the middle of town.

Festivals
- Serenata de los Cerros (Serenade of the Mountains): January 13–15. A folk festival, with local musical groups and dancing
- Fiesta de la Virgen de la Candelaria: February
- Fiesta de la Chicha y la Copla: February
- Holy week celebrations: April
- Solstice celebrations: June. Fires called *luminarias* are lit on the mountains
- Manca Fiesta (Festival of the Pots): October 17–24, when Indians from Jujuy and Bolivians from the *altiplano* sell handmade pots
- Fiesta de Mamapacha
- Carnaval

Accommodation
★★ Hotel Provincial de Turismo, corner of Buenos Aires and Entre Ríos $16.00

★ Hotel Humahuaca, Buenos Aires 184 $12.50

B Residencial Colonial, corner of Entre Ríos and Corrientes (near bus terminal) $8.50

B Residencial Humahuaca, Córdoba 40 (near bus terminal) $8.50

B Residencial Río Grande, Corrientes 480 (behind bus station) $9.00

Camping
- Municipal camp site, situated beside the river, over the bridge near the railway station. The modest fee includes the use of the facilities

Eating out
- Restaurant El Cardón, corner of Santa Fé and Salta, up the stairs near the Monumento a la Independencia
- Restaurant El Fortín, corner of Buenos Aires and Salta. Local cuisine
- Restaurant El Norte, Belgrano 342
- Restaurant El Rancho, corner of General Belgrano and Cordoba. *Peña* at weekends
- Restaurant Humahuaca Colonial, Tucumán 22

Casabindo

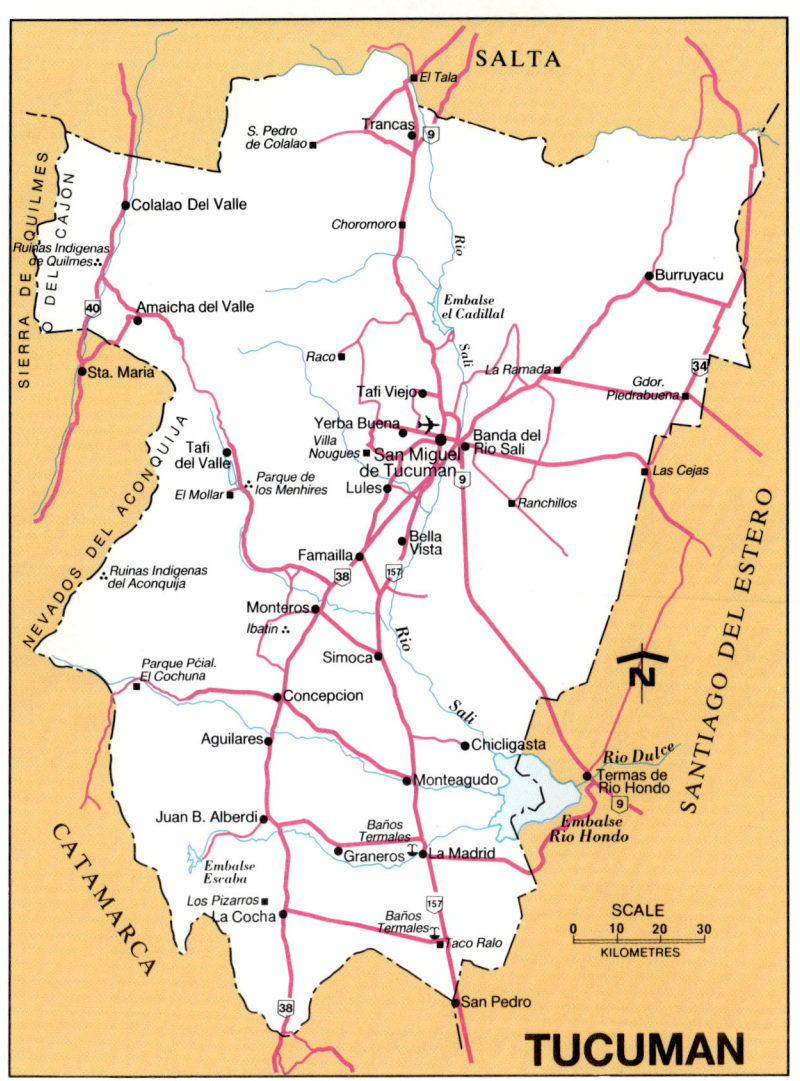

Plate 33
Map of Tucumán Province

Plate 34
Map of Salta and Jujuy Provinces

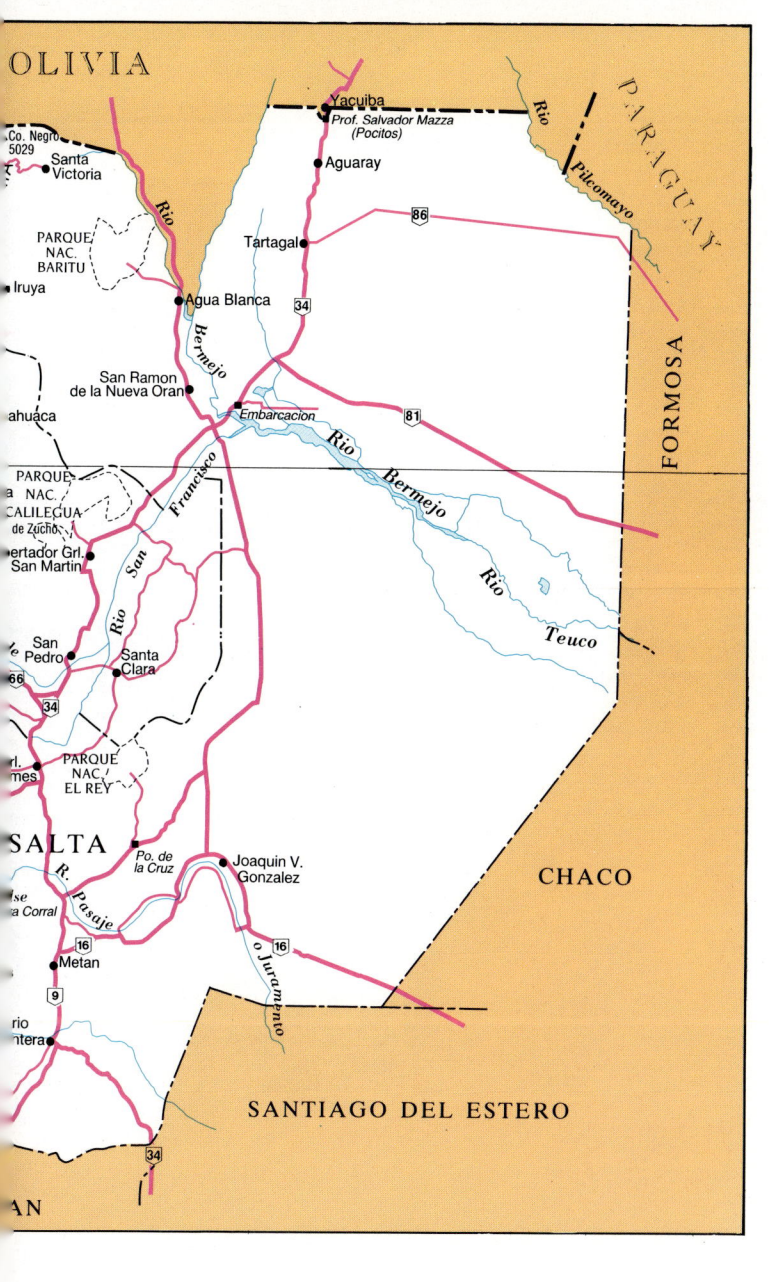

Plate 36

Top: Colonial church, Los Pisarros
Bottom: Pre-Inca ruins at Quilmes

JUJUY PROVINCE

- Restaurant La Cacharpaya, Jujuy 295 (corner of Santiago del Estero). Local Cuisine and music
- Restaurant Rosita, Belgrano 294. Local cuisine
- Restaurant Terminal

Post and telegraph
- Post office: Encotel, Plaza Santiago Gómez, Buenos Aires
- Telephone: Entel, Hotel de Turismo, Buenos Aires

Clubs

The Instituto de Cultura Indígena (Institute of Native Culture), Buenos Aires 740, under the guidance of its director Señor Sixto Vázquez Zuleta, makes a vigorous effort to preserve and promote the traditions and language of the native population in the *altiplano*. It serves as a cultural center for the local population, and offers public courses in the Quechua language. The library, open to the public, specializes in anthropology, folklore, history, and archeology. Guided tours are available.

Buses

The bus terminal is on the corner of General Belgrano and Entre Ríos
- San Salvador de Jujuy: Fare $3.50; 6 services daily; 3 hours
- Abra Pampa: Fare $2.80; 6 services daily; 2 hrs
- La Quiaca: Fare $5.30; 6 services daily; 4½ hours
- Tilcara: Fare $1.20; 6 services daily; 1 hour

Motoring
- Service station: ACA, corner of Belgrano and Entre Ríos

Trains
- San Salvador de Jujuy: First class only $2.75; departs 1455 Tues, Fri, Sun
- La Quiaca: First class only $3.00; departs 1423 Mon, Thurs, Sat

Shopping

At the market near the railway station *collas* sell Indian herbal teas.

Sightseeing
- Museo Folklórico Regional (Regional Folklore Museum), Plaza Sargento Gómez, corner of Buenos Aires and E Padilla
- Estudio Museo Ramoneda, a combined studio and museum; entrance $0.50
- Museo del Carnaval Norteño (Northern Carnival Museum). Interesting
- Church: The pictures in the church are said to be authentic works of the Cuzco School, executed by the painter Marcos Sapaca in 1764

Excursions
- **Hornaditas**: 18 km on the road to La Quiaca, on the **Arroyo Chorrillos**
- **Incacueva**: There are several caves along the **Arroyo Inca Cueva**, about 4 km from its junction with the **Río Grande**, with rock paintings and sites of pre-Hispanic implements
- **Rinconada**
- **La Cueva**: 17 km. Turn off from the main road 6 km from town
- **Iruya** in Salta province: 74 km north, at an elevation of 2730 m. A bus leaves three times a week from H Yrigoyen on the corner of RP 13. There is a festival in October. See also page 621
- **Coctaca**: Pre-Columbian ruins 8 km east of town. You can make this trip on foot as there is little traffic. Cross the river and

Humahuaca

JUJUY PROVINCE

take the first road on your left, which at first follows the river and then turns east. On arrival in the village ask at the school for further directions. The ruins are located 100 m above the **Río Coctaca** in a very strategic position. The remains of the **Pucará de Yacoraite** are on top of the hill, and the villagers lived at the base of the *pucará* or fortification. It was destroyed possibly during the advancement of the Incas. Some artefacts found point to Incan origin

LA QUIACA

Postal code: 4650 • ☏ area code: (0885) • Altitude: 3442 m
Distance
- From San Salvador de Jujuy: 292 km northwards on RN 9
- From Humahuaca: 167 km northwards on RN 9
- From Villazón in Bolivia: 3km southwards on RN 9

La Quiaca is located directly on the Bolivian border, and almost merges with its Bolivian neighbor Villazón. There is a very active border trade for goods which are in short supply in Bolivia.

It is the highest town in Argentina with a very dry climate—most rain falls in November but you need warm clothing all year round.

🎭 Festivals
- Manca Fiesta (Festival of the Pots): October 17–24. Indians from Jujuy and the Bolivians from *altiplano* sell all sorts of pots

ℹ️ Tourist information
There is a tourist information office right at the Argentine customs office.
The ACA service station a kilometer from the border post has good road maps of Argentina for sale. Discounts for ACA members.

🛏 Accommodation
Note that accommodation in Villazón in Bolivia is not of the same standard as in La Quiaca. It is suggested that you check out travel arrangements into Bolivia while you stay a day in La Quiaca. This may also help those who have to get accustomed to traveling at high altitudes.

★★ Hotel de Turismo La Quiaca, corner of Arabe Siria and San Martín ☏ 243 $9.60 ⛌

A Residencial Cristal, Avenida Sarmiento 539 ☏ 255 $5.50 ⛌

C Residencial Victoria, Sarmiento (opposite rail station) $3.00 per bed. Shared bedrooms

C Residencial Belén, Santiago del Estero 320, in a convent $3.00 ⛌. Shared bathroom

- Residencial Argentina, corner of Belgrano and República Arabe Siria

Key to Map
1 Municipalidad
2 Iglesia
3 Post office (Encotel)
4 Telephone (Entel)
5 Tourist information
6 ACA service station (road maps)
7 Banco de la Nación
8 Hotel de Turismo La Quiaca
9 Residencial Cristal
10 Residencial Argentina
11 Transport El Quiaqueño

Humahuaca

Jujuy Province

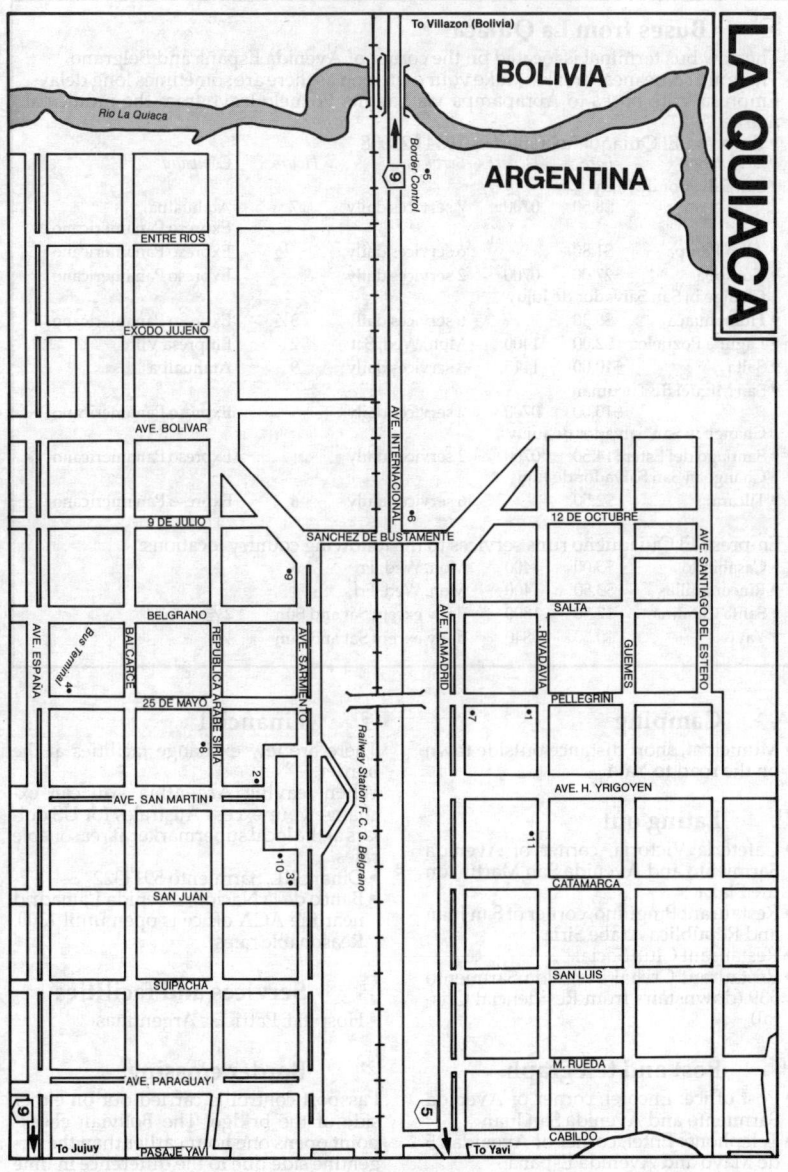

La Quiaca

JUJUY PROVINCE

🚌 Buses from La Quiaca

The new bus terminal is located on the corner of Avenida España and Belgrano. There are some meal breaks—take your own food as there are sometimes long delays. Empresa Vilte buses to Abrapampa via Laguna Pozuelo leave from the municipal market.

- Empresa El Quiaqueño, Güemes 1034 ✆ 23008

Destination	Fare	Depart	Services	Hours	Company
• San Salvador de Jujuy	$8.50	0700	7 services daily	7	Atahualpa, Expreso Panamericano
• Abra Pampa	$1.80		6 services daily	½	Expreso Panamericano
• Córdoba *Change in San Salvador de Jujuy*	$27.00	0700	2 services daily		Expreso Panamericano
• Humahuaca	$5.30		6 services daily	3½	Expreso Panamericano
• Laguna Pozuelos	$2.00	1400	Mon, Wed, Sat	2	Empresa Vilte
• Salta	$10.00	1115	3 services daily	9	Atahualpa
• San Miguel de Tucumán *Change in San Salvador de Jujuy*	$10.00	0700	2 services daily		Expreso Panamericano
• Santiago del Ester	$14.50	0700	2 services daily		Expreso Panamericano
Change in San Salvador de Jujuy					
• Tilcara	$2.50		6 services daily	6	Expreso Panamericano

Empresa El Quiaqueño runs services to the following country locations:

• Casabindo	$3.00	1400	Mon, Wed, Fri	3
• Rinconadillas	$3.50	1400	Mon, Wed, Fri	4
• Santa Catalina	$2.50	1800	daily except Sat and Sun	2½
• Yaví	$0.50	0840	daily except Sat and Sun	½

⛺ Camping

- Municipal, short distance outside town on the road to Yaví

🍴 Eating out

- Cafetería Victoria, corner of Avenida Sarmiento and Avenida San Martín, on the Plaza
- Restaurant Pingüino, corner of San Juan and República Arabe Siria
- Restaurant Club Social
- Restaurant Cristal, Avenida Sarmiento 539 (downstairs from Residencial Cristal)

✉ Post and telegraph

- Post office: Encotel, corner of Avenida Sarmiento and Avenida San Juan
- Telephone: Entel, corner of Avenida 25 de Mayo and Avenida España

$ Financial

There are few exchange facilities at the border.

When leaving Argentina you can exchange your excess Australes for US dollars at the local supermarket at reasonable rates.

- Dinar SRL, Sarmiento 591 ✆ 322
- Banco de la Nación, Avenida Lamadrid near the ACA office is open until 1300. Reasonable rates

🛏 Services and facilities

- Hospital: Patricias Argentinas

⚔ Border crossing

Passport control is carried out on either side of the bridge. The Bolivian checkpoint opens one hour earlier than the Argentine side due to the difference in time zones. The Bolivian and Argentine lunch

La Quiaca

JUJUY PROVINCE

times coincide. The Argentine checkpoint is open 0800–1800. After that you may enter Bolivia without a passport check, to check out and arrange travel into Bolivia, but may not take your luggage with you. It is a long walk uphill from the Bolivian customs to the center of Villazón, so it is advisable to hire a porter (at very reasonable rates) to help you with your luggage. On the way up you pass scores of money exchange offices; most of them accept only cash but a few also take travelers' checks.

Motoring
- Service station: ACA, at the intersection leading to the border. Has maps and information on road conditions

Trains
The F C General M Belgrano station is on Sarmiento, about 3 km from the border. Passengers wanting to continue by train in Bolivia must alight here take a taxi to the Bolivian station in Villazón.
Going south the railroad goes over a pass near **Tres Cruces**, at an elevation of 3692 m. Be prepared with warm clothing, as it can get bitterly cold and delays occur in the wet season. Change trains again in Jujuy to continue to Buenos Aires.

Shopping
La Quiaca is a huge supply base for all goods which are in short supply in Bolivia. Thousands of Bolivians are engaged in carrying anything from long-life milk cartons to laundry powder on their backs to the border; most of these goods are destined for the market in La Paz. Here is your last chance to stock up on items which are hard to come by in Bolivia.

Excursions
- **Yaví** : 19 km east. The church has been declared a national monument. Take an El Quiaqueño bus from Güemes 1034. There is a morning and an afternoon service. See also Yaví on page 669
- **Santa Catalina**: 65 km west on RP 5. Take an El Quiaqueño bus from Güemes 1034

MAIMARÁ

Postal code:4622
Distance from San Salvador de Jujuy: 124 km northwards on RN 9

Maimará is a Quechua word meaning "Field of Stars", most likely pointing to a meteorite fall in historical times.

Festivals
- Festival del Choclo y del Folklore (Maize and Folk Festival): March
- Festival de la Tijtincha: August

Buses
Buses run regularly to San Salvador de Jujuy.

PARQUE NACIONAL CALILEGUA

Distance from San Salvador de Jujuy: 135 km south-east on RP 56 then north on RN 34

The Parque Nacional Calilegua is located on the eastern slopes of the **Serrania Calilegua**. The entrance is 23 km north of Libertador General San Martín. This national park was created in 1974 to protect the unusual flora and fauna of the region. It covers an area of 76 000 ha, but has no tourist facilities. The flora is subtropical in the lower part where the elevation is only 450 m. Alpine-type meadows grow up to 1800 m, and the highest peaks reach about 2500 m.

There are frequent buses from San Salvador de Jujuy to Libertador General San Martín, but there are few cars going into the national park area. Hikers could take a cab to the park headquarters, but the best bet would be to make the trip with a tour operator.

See also "Excursions" in San Salvador de Jujuy on page 663

SAN SALVADOR DE JUJUY

Postal code: 4600 • Population: 200,000 • (area code: (0882) • Altitude: 1260 m
Distances
• From La Quiaca: 292 km southwards on RN 9
• From Salta: 132 km northwards on RN 9

San Salvador de Jujuy was founded in April 1593 by Don Francisco de Argañaraz y Murguia. The first attempts by the Spaniards to found a city were foiled by the Indians in 1565 and again in 1575. It is located at the junction of the **Río Xibi Xibi** and the **Río Grande**, which descends from the Quebrada de Humahuaca. Plaza Belgrano is the oldest part of town. Around the Plaza—as in days gone by—are the public buildings. Despite many earthquakes and wars there are a few historic buildings left. The city suffered heavily during the Wars of Independence; in 1812 as the Royalist troops advanced the citizens abandoned the town in a move known as the "Exodo Jujeño" (or "Jujuy Exodus").

The mountain ranges around San Salvador de Jujuy are covered by scrub and forest, and

Key to Map

1	Municipalidad
2	Casa de Gobierno
3	Catedral
4	Post office (Encotel)
5	Telephone (Entel)
6	Tourist information
7	Museo Histórico Provincial
8	Cabildo (police)
9	Museo Darwin de Paleontologia y Minera
10	Capilla Santa Barbara
11	Residencial Los Andes
12	Residencial Río de Janeiro
13	Residencial Vaquera
14	Hotel Purmamarca
15	Hotel Fenicia
16	Hotel Avenida
17	Residencial 19 de Abril
18	Hotel Gran Panorama
19	Residencial Luxor (formerly Residencial Santa Fé)
20	Hotel Savoy
21	Residencial Aramayo
22	Hotel Jujuy Internacional
23	Hotel Augustus
24	Hotel Sumaj
25	Hotel Asor's
27	Residencial San Carlos
28	Residencial Lavalle
29	Residencial Chung King
30	Residencial Norte
31	Aerolineas Federales Argentinas

JUJUY PROVINCE

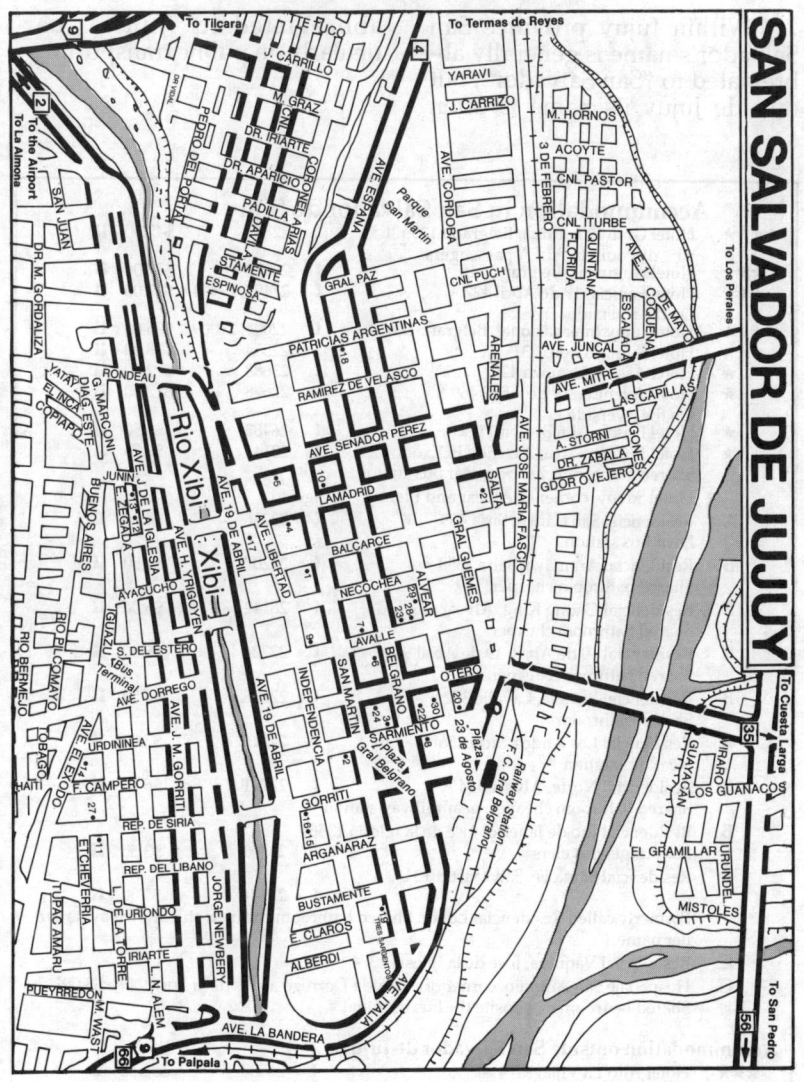

provide a very picturesque scenic setting for the provincial capital.

There are height restrictions on buildings as the city is in an earthquake zone. Most of the streets are lined with orange trees.

San Salvador de Jujuy

Jujuy Province

Within Jujuy province San Salvador's name is generally abbreviated to "San Salvador", but outside Jujuy its name is often abbreviated to "Jujuy", particularly on public transport.

Accommodation in San Salvador de Jujuy

★★★★	Hotel Gran Panorama, Belgrano 1295	(22832	$42.00	
	10% discount to ALFA passengers			
★★★	Hotel Augustus, Belgrano 715	(22930	$32.00	
★★★	Hotel Fenicia, 19 de Abril 427	(27492, 27494	$21.00	
	On the riverside			
★★★	Hotel Jujuy Internacional, Belgrano 501	(22004, 22009	$25.00	
★★	Hotel Sumaj, Otero 231	(22554	$18.00	
★	Hotel Asor's, Urquiza 428	(23688	$12.50	
★	Hotel Avenida, 19 de Abril 469	(22678	$12.50	
	On the riverside			
★	Hotel Brisas, Alte Brown 1127	(26483	$8.50	
★	Hotel Purmamarca, Avenida El Exodo 825	(23141	$8.75	
	Shared bathroom cheaper; near bus station			
•	Hotel Savoy, corner of Alvear and Plaza 23 de Agosto			
A	Residencial San Carlos, Siria 459	(22286	$8.50	
	Near bus station			
B	Residencial Aramayo, Salta 1058	(23207	$4.50	
	Shared bathroom cheaper			
B	Residencial Chung King, Alvear 627	(28142	$6.00	
	Shared bathroom cheaper			
B	Residencial 19 de Abril, 19 de Abril 943	(23224	$6.50	
	Shared bathroom cheaper			
B	Residencial Lavalle, Lavalle 372	(22698	$4.50	
	Shared bathroom			
B	Residencial Los Andes, Siria 456	(24315	$7.00	
	Near bus station			
B	Residencial Norte, Alvear 444	(22721	$6.50	
	Shared bathroom cheaper; near railway station			
B	Residencial Río de Janeiro, José de la Iglesia 1356			
	For budget travelers	(23700	$3.50	
B	Residencial Santa Fé, San Martín 134			
		(23714	$5.00	
	Formerly called Residencial Luxor. Shared bathroom cheaper; still known by its earlier name			
C	Residencial Vaquera, José de la Iglesia 1374			
C	Hospedaje San Antonio, corner of Avenida Dorrego and L de la Torre		$3.00	
	Shared bedrooms; opposite the bus terminal			

Accommodation outside San Salvador de Jujuy

★★★	Hotel Alto La Viña, RP 4	(26588	$32.50	
	On a hill			
★★	Hotel Huaico, RN 9 Km 3 north, on the road to Humahuaca			
		(22274	$11.50	
A	Residencial El Balcón, El Fortiniz, RP 57, in the Perales district			
		(29853	$6.50	

San Salvador de Jujuy

Calle Belgrano, formerly called Real, is the main shopping street.

🚶 Festivals

- Foundation of Jujuy: April 19
- Festival de Locro: July. *Locro* is a thick vegetable soup
- Fiesta de la Pachamama: August 1
- Exodo Jujeño ("Jujuy Exodus"): August 23 and 24

ⓘ Tourist information

- Consejo Provincial de Turismo, Belgrano 690 (corner of Lavalle). Very helpful

⛺ Camping

- Complejo Los Alisos, San Antonio, RP 2, 14 km south-west of the city. Has 30 cabins

🍴 Eating out

- ☞ Restaurant Balcarce, Balcarce 336
- Restaurant Brujas, Belgrano 855
- Restaurant Chino, Independencia 678. Chinese cuisine
- ☞ Restaurant Chungking, Alvear 627
- Restaurant Don Giuseppe, Avenida Senador Perez. Italian cuisine
- ☞ Restaurant El Exodo, Avenida El Exodo 199
- Restaurant La Royal, Belgrano 772
- Restaurant La Ventana, Belgrano 751 (downstairs)
- ☞ Restaurant Micuy Huasi, Balcarce 155
- Restaurant Parrilla El Mesón, Salta 799. Steakhouse
- Restaurant Parrilla La Casona, Alvear 1346. Credit cards accepted
- ☞ Restaurant Parrilla Livia, San Martín block 1000. Credit cards accepted
- Restaurant Parrilla Manuelita, Avenida El Exodo 652
- Restaurant Parrillada Estación de Cerveza, corner of Pueyrredón and L N Alem
- Restaurant Sirio Libanés, General Lamadrid 568
- Restaurant Sociedad Española, Belgrano block 1100 (corner of Perez)
- Restaurant Tablita, L N Alem 974
- Restaurant Victoria, Avenida El Exodo 640
- Pizzería El Condado, L N Alem block 800 (corner of Urdininea)
- Pizzería Independencia, Independencia 488
- Pizzería La Fuente, San Martín block 100 (corner of Bustamente)
- Cafetería Alvear, Alvear 630
- Cafetería Americano, Avenida Dorrego block 300 (corner of L N Alem). Open 24 hours
- ☞ Cafetería Cafe Dos Chinos, Alvear block 700 (corner of Lavalle). Big
- ☞ Cafetería Carenas, Balcarce block 200 (corner of Belgrano)
- Cafetería Gorriti, Republica de Siria 732
- ☞ Cafetería España, Belgrano block 1100 (corner of Velasco). Small
- Cafetería Jujuy, Belgrano block 900 (corner of Lamadrid)
- Cafetería La Cabaña, Belgrano 620
- Cafetería La Royal, Belgrano 732
- Cafetería Reno, San Martín block 700 (corner of Lavalle)
- Snack-bar: Las Mil Noches, Urdininea 332
- Takeaway: Granja San Jorge, L N Alem block 900 (corner of Urdininea). Chicken
- Bar-restaurant: Sociedad Obrera, Balcarce 357
- Los dos Gorditos, Alvear near railway

✉ Post and telegraph

- Post office: Encotel, General Lamadrid block 100 (corner of Independencia)
- Telephone: Entel, Avenida Senador Perez 141

$ Financial

- Banco Comercial del Norte, Alvear block 800 (corner of Necochea). Cash advances on Mastercard
- Banco Credito, Senador Perez 243. Cash advances on Visa card
- Banco de Galicia, Alvear block 700 (corner of Necochea). Cash advances on American Express card
- Cambio Dinar SRL, Belgrano 711 ℡ 25353
- Cambios Noroeste, Belgrano block 500 (corner of Otero). Cash and travelers' checks
- Horus Turismo, Belgrano 722 ℡ 27247

San Salvador de Jujuy

JUJUY PROVINCE

Services and facilities

- Bakery: Independencia, Independencia 416
- Batteries: Optica Savio, Belgrano block 1000 (corner of Senador Perez). Sells Duracell batteries
- Dry-cleaner: Tokio, Belgrano 1118
- Pharmacy: Farmacia Central, (corner of Belgrano and Necochea)
- Laundromat: Marva, Independencia 1031. Open Mo-Sa 0900- 2100 ($2.00)
- Supermarket: Iñiguez, Avenida Gorriti 836

Motoring

The trip to Salta can be made via Güemes on the *autopista* (RN 9 and RN 66), or over the *cornisa*.
RN 9 to La Quiaca is sealed only as far as Humahuaca.

Service stations

- ACA, Avenida Senador Perez block 400 (corner of Alvear)
- Esso, corner of Avenida Dorrego and L N Alem

Car rental

- A-1 Rent-a-Car, Belgrano 580 ℡ 29697. Cars may be returned to Salta or San Miguel de Tucumán
- Avis Rent-a-Car, Gran Hotel Panorama, Belgrano 1295 ℡ 22832. Also at the airport
- Lavalle Rent-a-Car, Lavalle 288 ℡ 28405

Clubs

- French: Alliance Française, General Lamadrid 242
- Italian: Sociedad Italiana, Avenida José María Fascio block 1000
- Spanish: Club Español, Belgrano block 100 (corner of Senador Perez)

Visas, passports

- Visa extensions: Migración, Belgrano 499
- Bolivian consulate, Güemes 828 ℡ 22010
- Italian consulate, Fascio 660 ℡ 23199
- Spanish consulate, Ramirez de Velasco 362 ℡ 28193
- West German consulate, Salta 947

Air services

El Cadillal airport is 40 km east of town or 45 minutes by bus. TEA Turismo, San Martín 734, runs buses to the airport for $2.00; taxis cost $15.00

Airlines

- Aerolineas Argentinas, Otero 310 ℡ 23897
- Aerolineas Federal Argentina, Avenida Senador Perez 325 ℡ 29875

Services

- Buenos Aires (Aeroparque Jorge Newbery): Fare $85.00; departs 0320; 2–3 services daily; 3 hours; Aerolineas Argentinas
- Córdoba: Fare $58.00; departs 1050 Mon–Wed, Fri, Sun; 2 hours; Aerolineas Argentinas
- La Paz (Bolivia): Departs 0810 Sat; 1 hour; Aerolineas Argentinas
- Salta: Fare $5.00; departs 1030 Wed, Sat; Federal. Fare $6.00; departs 1925 Sun; ½ hour; Aerolineas Argentinas
- San Miguel de Tucumán: Fare $25.00; departs 0320 Sun–Fri; 1 hour; Aerolineas Argentinas

Trains

The F General M Belgrano station is on Plaza 23 de Agosto.
The trains to Buenos Aires are always full, so book early. Trains no longer run directly to Salta and Bolivia.

- Buenos Aires (Retiro station) via Tucumán: "El Norteño"; First class $20.00, tourist class $14.00; departs 0825 Mon, Thurs, Fri; 36 hours. Very crowded and plagued by endless delays
- La Quiaca: First class $4.00, tourist class $2.60; departs 0900 Mon, Thurs, Sat; 8 hours
- San Miguel de Tucumán: First class $6.00, tourist class $4.00; departs 0745 Wed, Sun; 8 hours

Tours

- Horus, Belgrano 722 ℡ 27247
- Turismo Lavalle, Belgrano 636

San Salvador de Jujuy

Jujuy Province

🚌 Buses from San Salvador de Jujuy

The bus terminal is on the corner of Avenida Dorrego and Iguazú, and has a 24-hour restaurant, clean toilets, and left luggage facilities which cost $0.20.

Empresa Balut runs daily services to Embarcación via San Pedro and Libertador San Martín.

Empresa Purmamarca runs services to Susques in the *altiplano* via Purmamarca on Wed and Sat at 1330, returning Thurs and Sun at 1200, crossing the Abra Potrerillos and the Salinas Grandes of Jujuy.

Destination	Fare	Depart	Services	Hours	Company
• Abra Pampa	$5.00	0600	5 services daily	5½	Expreso Panamericano
• Córdoba	$16.50	1400	3 services daily	14	Expreso Panamericano
• Formosa	$21.00	1030	Tues, Thurs	20	Atahualpa
• Humahuaca	$3.00	0600	7 services daily	3	Expreso Panamericano
• La Quiaca (on the Bolivian border)					
	$7.00	0100	3 services daily	6	Atahualpa
	$7.00	0600	5 services daily	6½	Expreso Panamericano
• Liberatador General San Martín					
	$2.80	0500	18 services daily	2½	Balut
• Oran	$3.50				Balut
• Pocitos (on the Bolivian border)					
	$5.50				Balut
• Purmamarca	$1.60				
• Salta	$2.50	0700	5 services daily	2	Atahualpa
• San Miguel de Tucumán					
	$8.30	0630	6 services daily	5	Expreso Panamericano, Veloz del Norte
• Santiago del Estero					
	$14.50	0800	4 services daily	7½	Expreso Panamericano
• Termas de Reyes	$0.60				Bus 14
• Termas de Río Hondo					
	$9.60	1400	3 services daily	6	Expreso Panamericano
• Tilcara	$2.00	0600	7 services daily	2	Expreso Panamericano

🏛 Shopping

The main shopping streets are Alvear and Belgrano.
- Regionales Incallacta, Avenida 19 de Abril 427 (next to Hotel Fenicia)

🍸 Entertainment

- Restaurant Chung King, Alvear 627. *Peñas* and tangos
- Peña Folklorica El Coya Bolivar, L N Alem 634

📷 Sightseeing

Start your sight-seeing walk on Plaza Belgrano.

Museums and galleries

- Museo Histórico Provincial, Lavalle 266. This house belonged originally to Doraliza Blas de Zenarruza, wife of one of the governors of Jujuy. It is a colonial home and was declared a national monument in 1962. General Lavalle was murdered in the doorway here in 1848. The original doorway is in Buenos Aires. The museum is organized into seven rooms, each dealing with an important epoch in the history of Jujuy.

San Salvador de Jujuy

JUJUY PROVINCE

The rooms are *Sala General Lavalle*, *Sala Independencia* ("Independence Room"), *Sala Doraliza Blas de Zenarruza* (which has on exhibit the piano from the original chapel in Humahuaca dating back to 1745), *Sala de Arte Religioso y Colonial* ("Room of Religious and Colonial Art"), *Sala de los Gobernadores* ("Room of the Governors"), *Sala del Vestido Siglo XIX* ("Room of Nineteenth Century Costume"), and *Sala del Exodo Jujeño* ("Room of the Jujuy Exodus"). It is one of the best-preserved colonial houses, with two patios and *galerías* surrounding it. Worth a visit
- Museo Darwin de Paleontologia y Mineralogia (Darwin Paleontology and Mineralogy Museum), corner of Independencia and Lavalle
- Galería del Arte (Art Gallery), Balcarce 264
- Palacio de Gobierno (Governor's Palace), on the south side of Plaza Belgrano. On the first floor is the *Salon de la Bandera*, where the first flag of Argentina is kept
- The Cabildo (Council Chambers) is located on the north side of the Plaza. Built in the late eighteenth century, it now houses the police headquarters

Churches

- The Iglesia Catedral (Cathedral Church) is located on the western side of Plaza General Belgrano. The cathedral was built in 1750 and has been declared a national monument. It contains such fine images as *Nuestra Señora de Río Blanco* (Our Lady of Río Blanco) and *El Cristo Yacente*. The pulpit is made of wood and is gold plated; some of the confessionals were built by Indian craftsmen. The church constitutes an exceptional colonial art treasure
- Iglesia San Francisco (Franciscan Church)

Excursions

- **Termas de Reyes**: 19 km northwest, 45 minutes by bus; elevation 1750 m. The main attraction is the hot springs set in magnificent scenery in the **Río Reyes** valley. The Hotel Termas de Reyes has good facilities and the spring water (at a temperatue of 52 °C) is well known for its curative properties. The vistas from the dining room over the river and the mountains are particularly impressive. There are walks to the **Lagunas de Yala** at an elevation of 2036 m.

Linea 14 (Empresa General Lavalle) runs seven services daily from Central Municipal bus terminal, on 19 de Abril between Necochea and Lavalle, and also from the corner of Dorrego and L N Alem; the trip takes an hour. The last bus returns to San Salvador de Jujuy at 2240. The road is sealed right up to the hotel, but may be cut during heavy rain. Ten minutes past the Hotel Termas are two municipal thermal spas; it is from here that you catch a bus to San Salvador de Jujuy. The hotel has a fixed-menu restaurant and a cafeteria. There is a swimming pool on the ground floor, and there are also individual spas. There are 50 rooms, with central heating and thermal water in all rooms. Double

San Salvador de Jujuy

JUJUY PROVINCE

rooms including breakfast cost $21.00. A dip in the thermal pool costs $0.70, and a private thermal spa $1.00. It is open all year round. The main holiday season runs from June until the middle of August, during which time doctors and nurses are employed. During this period bookings are advisable

- **Lagunas de Yala**: 27 km from San Salvador de Jujuy and 12 km from the village of Yala. There are no direct bus services to these lakes. Take the *autopista* north as far as the village of **Yala** (elevation 1445 m) where the sealed road ends at the bridge crossing the **Río Yala**. Yala is a holiday resort with many weekend retreat villas, many of them with swimming pools in the back. From here onwards the road ascends, following the Río Yala with its crystal clear waters for most of the way. This river carries water all year round in large quantities, forming many waterfalls and cascades with inviting spots for camping. The valley widens and there are many fern trees along the slopes. Everything is green around here: a subtropical paradise. It is a truly enchanting landscape through which the road winds itself upward until we arrive at the *laguna* situated at an altitude of 2200 m. At the crossroads you can go to **Laguna Desaguadero**, the first of the Yala *lagunas*, where there is a trout hatchery. Fishing in Laguna Desaguadero is prohibited. The next *laguna* is **Comodoro**, completely surrounded by trees such as huge willows, laurels, and fern trees. The last *laguna* in the system is called **Laguna de Rodeo**. Fishing is permitted in Laguna Comedoro and Laguna de Rodeo on Sat and Sun between 0700 and 2000. There are however no trout, only *pejerrey*. The rivers which contain trout are the **Río Tesorero**, **Río Guerrero**, and the upper reaches of the **Río Reyes** . On the banks of Laguna de Rodeo is a new *hostería*—see below. Past the *hostería* are a few camping grounds on the *laguna*, with tables and barbecue facilities, but no toilet facilities. Tour operators combine Termas de Reyes and Lagunas de Yala in a five-hour hour excursion; fare $6.50

- **Hostería de Yala**, Abonado 41 (27432. Although small (only six double bedrooms), it is in an enchanting position. It has a fixed-menu restaurant, and all rooms have a private bathroom. It has marvellous views from the terrace

- **Iruya** in Salta province: via Hipólito Yrigoyen. Iruya is in a mountainous region, and its Jesuit church is the main attraction. See also Iruya on page 621.

Expreso Panamericano runs buses departing daily at 1045 and 1700, and arriving in Hipolito Yrigoyen at 1435 and 2035 respectively. From Hipólito Yrigoyen, Empresa Estanislao Mendoza runs services to Iruya departing 0800 Tues and Sat and 1500 Wed; the trip takes 2½ hours. Buses make the return trip from Iruya to Hipólito Yrigoyen departing 1200 on Tues, Thurs, and Sat. Accommodation in Iruya and Hipólito Yrigoyen is a problem, but private accommodation can be found—ask the bus drivers

San Salvador de Jujuy

JUJUY PROVINCE

- **Susques**: 219 km north-west. At the moment no tour operators organize trips so it is largely a do-it-yourself excursion by public transport, but it is a first-class excursion. Leaving San Salvador de Jujuy on RN 9 north, you cross the **Río Reyes** bridge 6 km further on, at a good camping spot. Seven km further on you arrive at the **Río Yala**, and follow it until you reach **Posta de Lozano**. At this stage it is not known whether the *hostería* is open or not. Past the village is the **Río Lozano**. After crossing the **Río Kalayo**, you arrive in **León**, which has a small local museum in a historic building. From here you pass through apple orchards until **Volcán**, the first village in the **Quebrada de Humahuaca**. Here the road starts to climb. Thirteen km past **Tumbaya**, with its mission church built in 1796, you leave RN 9 and enter RP 16. Four km uphill—the road becomes quite winding and steep—you arrive at **Purmamarca**, with its beautiful mission church. Time seems to have stood still in this picturesque village with its narrow streets and adobe houses with straw-thatched roofs. The people are quite Indian-looking. The mountain behind the village shines in seven different colours—hence its name, **Cerro de los Siete Colores** ("Mountain of the Seven Colors"). The mountains here are still densely covered in vegetation, being covered halfway up with shrubs, which then thin out and are replaced towards the peaks with cacti. After Purmamarca there is a 2 km rock-fall zone which can be closed during bad weather. Constant road works are in progress. From Purmamarca onwards there are no villages for nearly six hours, only isolated homesteads tucked away in the valley. As the road zigzags higher the trees and shrubs are left behind, giving way to desert-type plants. The bare parts of the mountains show all shades from green to gray to reddish. Past **La Ciénaga** there is a narrow bridge crossing over the **Río Huachichocana**. Small flocks of goats, sheep, llamas, and *vicuñas* appear. Hawks circle in the thin air. At the **Cuesta de Lipan** the road reaches its highest altitude, 4170 m, making hairpin turns to gain height. It is a fabulous sight to look down on the road which you have just negotiated. **Abra Blanca** is the highest point. From here **Cerro Chañi**, 6200 m high, and many salt lakes can be seen in the distance. Not far away is the junction of RN 40 coming up from Patagonia and joining with RN 9 south of Abra Pampa. Now the road traverses an immense high-altitude plain (*puna* or *altiplano*) with the **Salina Grande**, 525 square km, one of the largest in the north. From the junction the road becomes a straight line for almost 40 km until you arrive at the **Quebrada del Mal Paso**

JUJUY PROVINCE

("Canyon of the Bad Pass"), where the road becomes very narrow. Here because the sunlight cannot penetrate into the *cañon* the water flowing down the slopes is usually frozen. As you emerge from the *cañon* road works are under way to forge a link via the **Paso de Jama** with Chile. Your arrival in Susques is announced by huge white-painted parabolic antennas which contrast with the surrounding area. Susques is a cold place, and is windy all year round. The adobe houses are small and straw-thatched. The main street is planted with trees, and contains the main public buildings such as post office, station, school, town hall, and the small historic chapel. The chapel is in perfect condition. Inside is an altar made entirely from cactus wood, behind which is a smaller chapel with an image of the Virgen de Belén (Virgin of Bethlehem). The walls are painted white and bear murals of saints. The church tower stands apart from the church. This little Indian settlement has a constant electricity supply and telephone connection with the outside world; apart from this Susques may be regarded as a "time capsule". The long trip—eight hours—is mostly over bad roads but is exhilarating. The bus is usually packed full as villagers carry huge parcels to and from the low lands, including animals such as dogs, cats, and chickens. This trip is suggested for the hardy and intrepid—a real Andean experience. See also Susques on page 665. There are no hotels, but accommodation in private homes is available—there are only six rooms available in the whole village. It is possible to contact Señora Luisa Vazquez, Calle San Luis 33, via police radio to arrange accommodation beforehand. She runs a small hospedaje, offering bed and all meals. Most accommodation is taken up by the road gang working on the Paso de Jama road. In an emergency the school director may help out too.

- **Tiraxi**: 40 km north at the junction of the **Río Tesorero** and **Río Tiraxi**. This is considered a natural monument because of the natural beauty of the many narrow valleys. The trip goes via **Lozano**, where RP 29 begins, over an unsealed road. There are no direct buses so you have to improvise if you want to go there; ask at the bus terminal. Río Tiraxi flows west into the **Río Candelaria**. This is hiking country
- **Parque Nacional Calilegua**. This national park is situated 135 km east of San Salvador de Jujuy and 23 km north of Libertador General San Martín. The road is sealed all the way. You leave San Salvador de Jujuy via RN 56, arriving at **San Pedro de Jujuy**. The area is planted with sugarcane and alfalfa. At San Pedro take RN 34 through the villages **El Quemado** and **Chalicán** to the **Río San Francisco**. At **Ledesma** is the largest sugarmill in Argentina, processing 18 000 tonnes of sugar daily, and an offset paper production plant which makes

San Salvador de Jujuy

JUJUY PROVINCE

as a by-product 25 000 000 liters of alcohol a year. Shortly after, you arrive in **Libertador General San Martín**. The whole area is a citrus orchard, producing some of the best oranges in the country. This is also tropical fruit country, growing fruit such as *cherimoyas*, bananas, mangoes, and avocados. The bus terminates at the village of **Calilegua**. From here onwards you proceed northwards on RP 83 through dense tropical vegetation. You need at least three days to get to know this national park; if you intend to hike get in touch beforehand with the park supervisor, who can arrange for horses, as the trails are in very bad condition and can't be used by vehicles. (For the supervisor's contact address, see below.) There is a lot of rain during the summer months, so the best time to visit is between March and October, although even then you could get caught in a rainstorm. The vegetation is tropical with walnuts, laurels, and *lapachos rosados* predominating, and many orchids. In some areas the forest is so dense that the sun cannot penetrate. The rivers are clear and have many *dorados*, *surubí*, and *pejerrey*, but fishing and hunting are not allowed. Camping is allowed. At present no guided tours are conducted. See also Parque Nacional Calilegua on page 653. Park supervisor: Señor Luis Canteros, Intendencia del Parque Nacional Calilegua, Edificio Ex Soltería Calilegua in San Lorenzo ((0886) 22046. Balut Hermanos run direct buses daily from the bus terminal to the national park, every two hours. Traveling time is three hours, and a return ticket costs $6.00

- **Quebrada de Humahuaca**: Tour operators organize day trips leaving Jujuy at 0800 via RN 9 north. The first of the Quebrada towns is **Volcán**, at 2980 m. Nearby is the small **Laguna de Volcán**, where there is good *pejerrey* fishing. Seven km further on is **Tumbaya** where you visit the Jesuit chapel dating back to 1700. La Posta de Hornillos, founded in 1772, was a stage coach post where horses were exchanged for the long and tiresome journey to Alto Perú, in what is today Bolivia; it is now a national museum. Further on is **Tilcara**, also known as the "archeological capital of Jujuy". Here you visit the famous *pucará* or pre-Hispanic fortress. Thirteen km further north you pass near **Huacalera**, on the Tropic of Capricorn, marked with a monolith. The mission church of **Ucalera**, dating back to 1720, is also visited. **Humahuaca** is the highlight of the Quebrada tour with its narrow streets lined with adobe houses, most of which date back to the colonial period. Also notable is the huge Monumento a la Guerra de la Independencia Hispanoamérica (Monument to the Spanish- American War of Independence) overlooking the Plaza. At 12 noon San Francisco Solano appears at the clocktower and gives his blessings.

San Salvador de Jujuy

Jujuy Province

See also Humuhuaca on page 648. The bus returns about 1800. The fare is $12.00. The budget traveler can make this trip by public transport
- **Salta** via the *cornisa*. Tour operators organize a 10-hour day tour to Salta leaving Jujuy via RN 9 south; fare $12.00. Budget travelers see "Buses" above. See also Salta on page 626

Susques

Postal code: 4641 • Population: 800 • Altitude: 3600 m
Distance from San Salvador de Jujuy: 217 km northwards on RN 9, then wesrwards on RN 52 and RP 16. 149 km are over rough *altiplano* roads

Susques is situated in the heart of the *altiplano*, and is not easy for the average tourist to reach. The history of this part of Argentina is checkered to say the least. The inhabitants are the descendants of Aymara and thus have a common language with Indians in Bolivia. As a matter of fact until 1899 Susques was part of Bolivia. Until 1943 it formed part of the Territorio de los Andes which was divided amongst the provinces of Jujuy, Salta, and Catamarca, thus fragmenting a cultural unit. Although at a subsistence level, the town has electricity and running water and is connected to the outside world by a microwave transmitter. In pre-Hispanic times it was on the Inca road from Bolivia which went as far as the Río Maule in Chile. The people tend their flocks of llamas and *alpacas* just as their ancestors did, and are not very talkative. Occasionally the men work in the mines which abound in the area.

For additional information see "Excursions" in San Salvador de Jujuy on page 662

Festivals
- Virgen de Belén (Virgin of Bethlehem): January 23. This is the major event of the year and starts with a colorful procession during which the *Virgencita* (or "Little Virgin") is carried through the streets. A very lively *fiesta* ensues after the procession

Accommodation
There is no official *hostería*, but townsfolk will put you up for the night. Also the police are very helpful.

Buses
Susques is served by buses from San Salvador de Jujuy via Purmamarca. They pass through on Wed and Sat and return to San Salvador de Jujuy on Thurs and Sun.

Sightseeing
- Chapel: Built by the inhabitants about 1590 under the instruction of a visiting priest from Bolivia. It has been declared a national monument. According to legend the image of the Virgen de Belén was found on the very spot where the chapel now stands. The tower stands apart from the church. The two bells were brought from Sucre in Bolivia (then called Chuquisaca)

JUJUY PROVINCE

✱ Excursions

The environment of Susques features many *lagunas* and *salares*, which are populated for part of the year by thousands of flamingos.

- **San Antonio de los Cobres**: Southwards on RN 40. A four wheel drive vehicle is advisable

TILCARA

Postal code: 4624 • Altitude: 2461 m
Distance from San Salvador de Jujuy: 84 km northwards on RN 9

Tilcara is located in the **Quebrada de Humahuaca** on the eastern bank of the **Río Grande** at its junction with the **Río Huasamayo**. There is only one bridge for vehicular traffic into town. The town was the center of heavy fighting during the wars of independence. The monolith at the town entrance, near the YPF service station, indicates the dates of all the major battles fought in and around Tilcara. The pre-Columbian population were called "Fiscaras", and were deft farmers and fierce warriors.

The climate is mild all year round with little rainfall. The average temperature is 15°C in winter and 22°C in summer, and nights are cool. The area has many interesting walks within easy walking distance, interesting museums and archeological sites, and colorful fiestas. It has good tourist facilities although these can get somewhat strained during the main holiday season.

Tilcara is the major archeological site in Jujuy province.

🏃 Festivals
- Enero Tilcareño (Tilcara January): January

🛏 Accommodation
- ★★ Hotel de Turismo Tilcara, Belgrano 590 ℡2 $16.50
- **B** Residencial Eden, Rivadavia, one block from the Plaza $3.00
- **A** Residencial El Antigal, corner of Rivadavia and Jujuy ℡ ℡ 20 $6.00

⛺ Camping
- Camping El Jardín, RN 9, 2 km north of the town entrance $0.80 per person

🍴 Eating out
- Cafetería El Antigal, corner of Belgrano and Rivadavia, on Plaza Alvarez Prado
- Pucará, on main square

✉ Post and telegraph
- Post office: Encotel, Rivadavia, on Plaza Alvarez Prado
- Long distance telephone: Entel, Belgrano, next to the Hotel de Turismo)

🚌 Buses
- Abra Pampa: 6 services daily; 3½ hours; Expreso Panamericano
- Humahuaca: Fare $1.20; 7 services daily; 1 hour; Expreso Panamericano
- La Quiaca: 6 services daily; 4½ hours; Expreso Panamericano
- Purmamarca: Fare $1.00
- San Salvador de Jujuy: Fare $2.00; 7 services daily; 2 hours; Expreso Panamericano

🚗 Motoring
- Service station: YPF, on RN 9 just before the bridge crossing into town

JUJUY PROVINCE

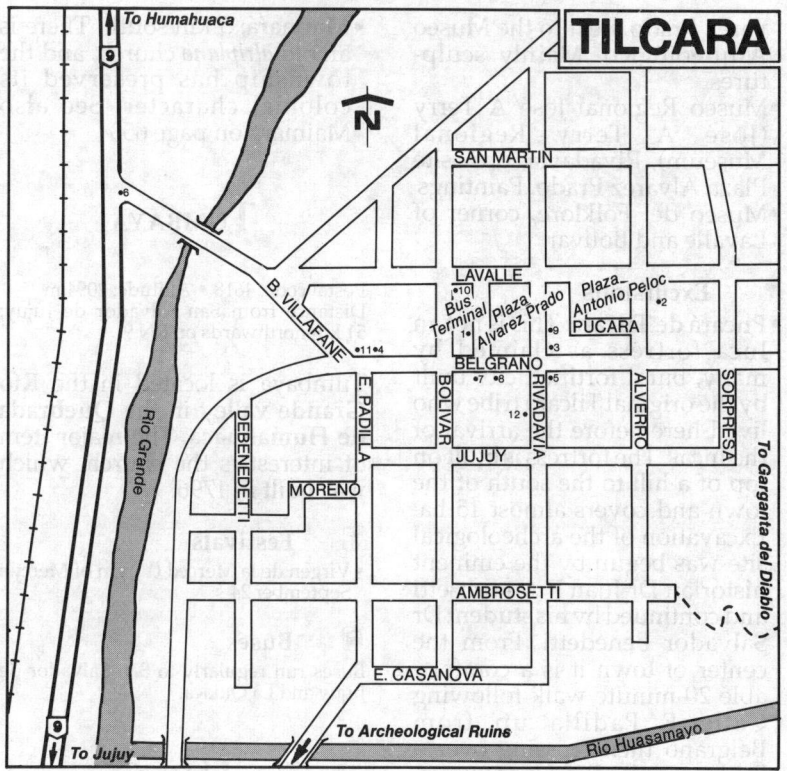

Key to Map
1. Municipalidad
2. Iglesia
3. Post office (Encotel)
4. Telephone (Entel)
5. Tourist information
6. Monolito (dates of battles)
7. Museo Arqueológico
8. Museo Soto Aveldaño
9. Museo Regional José A Terry
10. Museo del Folklore
11. Hotel de Turismo Tilcara
12. Residencial El Antigal

Sightseeing

- Museo Arqueológico (Archeological Museum), Belgrano, opposite Plaza Alvarez Prado. This museum, run by the Universidad Bueños, abounds with implements and items found in the *pucará*. Closed in June
- Museo Soto Aveldaño, Belgrano, opposite Plaza Al-

Tilcara

varez Prado, next to the Museo Arqueológico. Mainly sculptures
- Museo Regional José A Terry (José A Terry Regional Museum), Rivadavia, opposite Plaza Alvarez Prado. Paintings
- Museo del Folklore, corner of Lavalle and Bolívar

Excursions

- **Pucará de Tilcara**: This is not an Inca fortress as claimed by many, but a fortified city built by the original Tilcara tribe who lived here before the arrival of the Incas. The fortress is built on top of a hill to the south of the town and covers almost 15 ha. Excavation of the archeological site was begun by the eminent historian Dr Juan P Ambrosetti and continued by his student Dr Salvador Benedetti. From the center of town it is a comfortable 20-minute walk following Calle E Padilla up from Belgrano then crossing over a bridge on the Río Huasamayo. Shortly after the bridge you can take a trail up a small mountain from the top of which you have splendid views over the valley and the adjoining countryside. Before the entrance to the archeological complex there is a botanical garden which is also worth a visit. In the back of the garden is a "musical" rock
- **Garganta del Diablo** ("Devil's Gorge"): 7 km west in the upper reaches of the **Río Huasamayo**, which here forms a very narrow gorge with many waterfalls
- **Maimará**: 5 km south. There is an old *altiplano* church, and the township has preserved its colonial character. See also Maimará on page 653

Tumbaya

Postal code: 4618 • Altitude: 2094 m
Distance from San Salvador de Jujuy: 51 km northwards on RN 9

Tumbaya is located in the **Río Grande** valley in the **Quebrada de Humahuaca**. The major item of interest is the church, which was built in 1796.

Festivals
- Virgen de la Merced (Virgin of Mercy): September 24

Buses
Buses run regularly to San Salvador de Jujuy and La Quiaca.

Uquía

Postal code: 4626 • Altitude: 2900 m
Distance from San Salvador de Jujuy: 120 km northwards on RN 9

Uquía is a small *altiplano* village of pre-Hispanic origin located in the **Quebrada de Humahuaca** just 8 km south of Humahuaca. The church was one of the first built in the province, 1691.

Tilcara

JUJUY PROVINCE

❄ Festivals
- Fiesta de la Cruz (Festival of the Cross): May 3. In honor of St Madero and San Francisco de Paula

🚌 Buses
Buses run regularly to San Salvador de Jujuy and La Quiaca.

🌱 Excursions
- **Peñas Blancas**: This archeological site of a pre-Hispanic township is located on a hill (a white hill—hence the name) on the left bank of the **Río Grande**. Curiously formed buildings near the terraced fields may be the remains of crop storage barns

YAVÍ

Postal code: 4651
Distance from La Quiaca: 16 km eastwards

Yaví is so close to La Quiaca, on a good road, that you should not miss it simply for the sake of hurrying on to Bolivia. Its main attraction is a fine mission church, dedicated to San Francisco, with magnificent gold decorations. The church is normally closed, but the caretaker will open it and show you around for a small tip.

Opposite the church is the colonial house of a Spanish nobleman, the Marqués Campero y Trejo.

There are acheological sites near Yaví Chico, and halfway between Yaví and the turn-off to Suri Pujlo, 14 km away, is a cave on the north side of the road.

🛏 Accommodation.
There is a three-room *hostería*.

🌱 Excursions
- **Santa Victoria**: An Indian village in a rainforest valley. A 107 km track leads to the church; only for the intrepid

Chaco Provinces

FORMOSA PROVINCE

Plate 37 Map of Formosa Province
  673 Clorinda
  676 Comandante Fontana
  676 Formosa
  677   Map
  682 Ingeniero Guillermo N Juárez

Formosa is Argentina's northernmost province. It shares a border with Paraguay along the **Río Pilcomayo** and **Río Paraguay**. Chaco province lies to the south, and Salta to the west.

Formosa has a tropical climate. The area suffers from extended dry periods, up to six months of each year, at the end of which the rain comes down like a tropical deluge. To make good agricultural use of the land is therefore difficult. The ground water is saline, and in summer the rivers dry up and water has to be carted to the townships from the nearest source. In summer the temperatures can rise to 50 °C.

The province still consists partially of impenetrable forest where pumas, jaguars, alligators, and deer roam. The flora is very colorful, and includes many varieties of orchids. Due to "progress", however, some of the former *quebracho* forests have given way to large cotton plantations. Although the inhabitants refer to the interior as *"monte"* (mountain), the whole province is mostly flat.

Parque Nacional Río Pilcomayo, near **Clorinda**, is 60 000 ha in area and is certainly worth a visit. There are very few tourist facilities there, other than camping areas.

Formosa Province

FORMOSA PROVINCE

The remnants of the original Chaco tribes live in this province. They are still hunters and gatherers and are relatively untouched by European civilization.

Formosa is also the name of the capital, some 1200 km north of Buenos Aires.

The best time to visit Formosa is during the winter months of June, July, and up to mid-August.

CLORINDA

Postal code: 3610 • (area code: (0718)
Distances:
- From Formosa: 115 km northwards on RN 11
- From Asunción (Paraguay): 46 km eastwards

Clorinda was founded by Manfred Hertelendy in 1900 on the site where **Fuerte Fotheringham** had previously existed, on the **Río Alto Paraná**.

It is a cosmopolitan mixture of European, Indian, and Paraguayan influences. Everything of importance in Clorinda is on Avenida San Martín, the hub of the town. Most of the male population seems to be engaged in money-changing operations!

From the town center it is only 3 km north to the Puente Internacional Ignacio de Loyola which spans the **Río Pilcomayo**. The junction of Río Pilcomayo and **Río Paraguay** is 13 km south, near **Puerto Pilcomayo**. **Río Alto Paraná** is shallow and has many islands which are continuously shifting after the floods.

Clorinda is a border town, with road and ferry services to and from Paraguay. It is the main center of a banana- and rice-growing area.

🍴 Festivals
- Banana festival: Early October
- Fiesta Patronal de Nuestra Señora de los Angeles (Festival of the Patron Saint Our Lady of the Angels): August 2

ℹ️ Tourist information

There is no municipal tourist information bureau in Clorinda. The best bet is Señor Juan Simancas Sevilla, proprietor of Simancas Sevilla tourist agency, San Martín 492, who speaks some English and is very helpful and knowledgable about off-beat excursions and bus services to remote areas.

🛏 Accommodation
- ★ Hotel Embajador, San Martín 166, opposite the bus terminal (21148 $10.00
- C Residencial Helen, San Martín 320 $4.50
- Residencial Mario, Sarmiento 620 (21112 $6.00
- Residencial Rosarío, San Martín 775 (21932 $4.00

🍽 Eating out
- ☞ Restaurant El Jardín, San Martín 548
- Restaurant Faloppas, San Martín block 700 (corner of Italia)
- Restaurant Las Mercedes, San Martín 772
- Restaurant Maxim, corner of San Martín and 25 de Mayo
- Cafetería El Reloj, 25 de Mayo 1127

✉ Post and telegraph

Long-distance telephone: Entel, Plaza San Martín corner of J F Cancios and Alberdí

FORMOSA PROVINCE

💲 Financial

The streets are full of money changers streets but only cash US dollars are exchanged. Banks do not accept travelers' checks but good rates for these can be obtained in Asunción in Paraguay: *Australes*, *Guaraníes* (Paraguayan currency), and *Cruzados* (Brazilian currency). Currencies can also be exchanged on the bridge at the Paragayan border checkpoint.

Services and facilities

- Supermarket: Iñiguez, corner of San Martín and Corrientes

Visas and passports

- Paraguayan consulate, J F Cancios 1393. A $3.00 fee is payable for a ninety-day Paraguayan visa

Border crossing

The Argentine border control is directly on the Puente Internacional Ignacio de Loyola, only about 100 m from the municipal bus stop. The municipal buses go past the border control. The border is open twenty-four hours a day. You can walk across the bridge to the Paraguayan customs. A bus leaves from Clorinda every hour or so for Asunción. There are some money changers there whose rates are reasonable.

Motoring

- Service station: YPF, corner of J F Cancios and San Martín

Ferry services

There is a ferry service from Puerto Pilcomayo in Argentina to Ita Enramada in Paraguay, across the Río Paraguay. As an alternative to the road trip to Asunción, take the bus to Puerto Pilcomayo (a one-hour trip costing $0.60), and there board the ferry to Ita Enramada (a one-hour trip). From Ita Enramada take a bus to the center of Asunción (a 1½-hour trip). One of the best hotels in Asunción is not far from the landing pier.

Excursions

- **Formosa**: The trip south on RN 11 mostly passes through flat

🚌 Buses from Clorinda

The bus terminal is at the southern end of town, off San Martín.

Empresa Tigre-Salomon, corner of L Fernandez and Concio, runs buses to Belgrano, 142 km west on RN 86 which is sealed as far as Espinillo.

The local bus goes from the town center, past the Puente Internacional, to a new suburb of Clorinda every half an hour; fare $0.40.

The municipal bus to the Puerto Pilcomayo and to the ferry across Río Paraguay to Ita Enramada, leaves from corner of Buenos Aires and San Martín every forty minutes; fare $0.50. From Clorinda you can take the municipal bus to the border and alight 200 m before the passport control point; fare $0.20. On the Paraguyan side you can catch another *micro* to Asunción.

Destination	Fare	Depart	Services	Hours	Company
• Formosa	$2.50	0415	8 services daily	2	Godoy, La International
• Asunción	$2.00	0935	daily		Godoy
• Buenos Aires	$29.00	1024	3 services daily		Godoy
• Córdoba	$24.00	1425	Tue, Wed, Thur, Fri	17	Cacorba
• Resistencia	$6.50	0800	5 services daily	5	Godoy
• Rosarío	$22.50	1024	3 services daily		Godoy
• Salta		1040	Mon		Atahualpa
A rough ride through the *chaco* region					
• Santa Fá	$18.80	1024	3 services daily		Godoy

Clorinda

FORMOSA PROVINCE

country, with the landscape continually changing from swamps to *lagunas* to little farms and back to swamps. Along the road there are palm trees which are similar to those growing in Corrientes province. Although very little of the original *chaco* forest is left, there is a lot of birdlife, including some curious long-necked white birds strutting around among the cebu-like cattle grazing in the fields. The farmers in the district get their water from wells sunk into the ground which are checked at least once a year by the government. The road is mostly elevated to prevent it from being flooded during the rainy season; it is sealed and in perfect condition. It is permitted to camp along the road. Just before entering the city of Formosa there is a road check. After crossing the **Río Formosa**, you enter the city itself. Formosa is built in low-lying country which has been built up to avoid flooding. See also Formosa on page 676

- Asunción in Paraguay: An interesting round trip can be made to by first taking the road transport via the Puente Internacional (International Bridge) and then returning by ferry via **Ita Enramada** and **Puerto Pilcomayo**. The road to Asunción is sealed all the way. Take either an Empresa Godoy or an Empresa La Internacional bus from the terminal in town, or catch a local bus from the center of town to the bridge. Walk across the bridge and then take another bus to Asunción. The trip takes approximately two hours and is 50 km long. Shortly before Asunción, you cross **Río Paraguay** over a long bridge
- **Parque Nacional Río Pilcomayo**: Situated on the **Río Pilcomayo** which forms the border between Argentina and Paraguay, approximately 50 km west of Clorinda. The 60 000 ha plain is intersected with waterways which are forever changing after each rainy season. The park's wildlife is the most representative of the Formosan wetlands, including colorful toucans and small monkeys. Unfortunately the park does not include the whole of the **Laguna Blanca** with its many varieties of water birds. There are a lot of *caranday* palms, with white fronds and trunks. Due to the lack of funds, there are no personnel to look after this large tract of land, but there is a park information center. Also, there are picnic areas, toilets, places to swim and fish, and a boat ramp where boats can be hired. Empresa Tigre, corner of L Fernandez and Concio, runs five service a day to Laguna Blanca, and then as far as **General Belgrano** and **Comandante Fontana**. The first bus leaves Clorinda at 0615

Clorinda

FORMOSA PROVINCE

COMANDANTE FONTANA

Postal code: 3620   Distance from Formosa: 196 km north-west on RN 81

Comandante Fontana was founded in 1912. It is located on RN 81 which is the main route connecting Formosa province with Salta and Jujuy provinces.

This would be the best spot for a break in the rather monotonous journey to or from Salta, as there are such tourist facilities as *residenciales*, gas stations, and road and rail transport.

🚌 Buses

Buses run regularly to Formosa and Ingeniero Guillermo N Juárez.

FORMOSA

Postal code: 3600 • ✆ area code: (0717) • Population: 45 000

Distance from Buenos Aires: 1204 km northwards on RN 11

Formosa, the provincial capital, is located on the **Río Paraguay**, in a flood-prone alluvial plain some 240 km north of Corrientes.

Formosa was founded in 1879 by Comandante Luis Fontana, whose ashes lie in the cathedral. The name "Formosa" was derived from early Spanish descriptions of the river which takes a sweeping bend (*"vuelta hermosa"*) where Formosa is now located.

The climate is tropical and the vegetation is lush. There are two rainy seasons, one from February to May and a short one from August to September. Summers are very hot and humid. Mosquito nets are used all year round.

The river rises during the months of June, July, and August.

Key to Map

1	Municipalidad
2	Catedral
3	Casa de Gobierno
4	Post office (Encotel)
5	Telephone (Entel)
6	Banco de la Provincia
7	Tourist information
8	Ferries to Paraguay
9	Aerolineas Argentinas
10	Aerolineas Federales Argentinas
11	Empresa Brújula and Empresa Godoy terminal
12	Transportes Giroldi
13	Empresa Atahualpa
14	Empresa Cacorba
15	Transporte El Tigre
16	Transporte San José
17	Hotel Internacional de Turismo
18	Hotel Royal
19	Hotel Colón
20	Hotel Castellano
21	Hotel San Martín
22	Hotel Skorpio
23	Residencial City
24	Residencial Colonial
25	Residencial España
26	Residencial Iberia
27	Residencial Ideal
28	Residencial Las Vegas
29	Residencial Real
30	Residencial Rivas
31	Hospedaje La Familia

Comandante Fontana

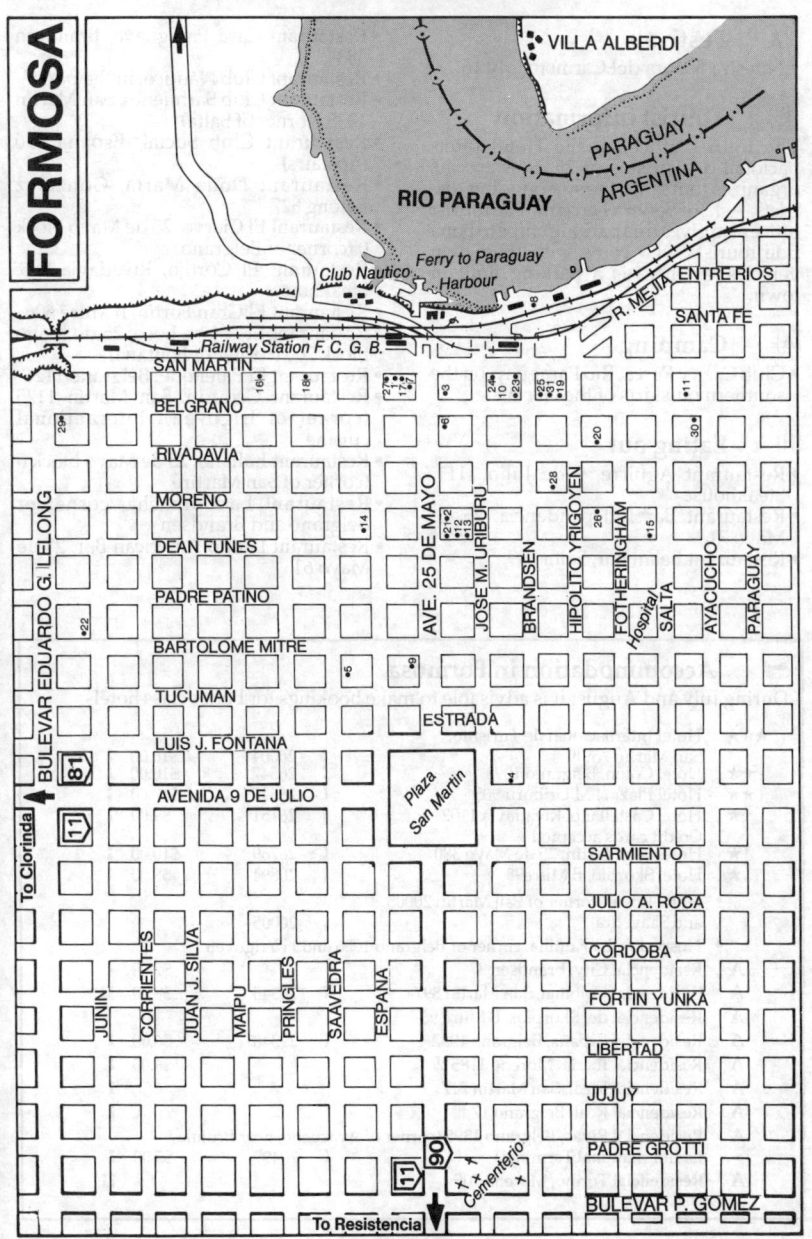

FORMOSA PROVINCE

FORMOSA PROVINCE

🎯 Festivals
- Nuestra Señora del Carmen: July 16

ℹ️ Tourist information
The tourist office, in the Hotel Internacional de Turismo at 25 de Mayo 40, organizes tours into the surrounding districts. Ask for Señora Ferreira. The tourist office also gives free parking chips to bona fide tourists who come with their own vehicles, as there is a parking limit in town.

⛺ Camping
- Club Caza y Pesca, Río Paraguay, on the southern outskirts of the city

🍴 Eating out
- Restaurant Aguirre, 9 de Julio 1111. Steakhouse
- Restaurant Bar Independencia, 25 de Mayo 71
- Restaurant Belán Bar, Salta 399
- Restaurant Casa Paraguaya, Brandsen 383
- Restaurant Club Náutico, in the port
- Restaurant Club Sarmiento, San Martín 1338 (corner of Salta)
- Restaurant Club Social, España 210 (upstairs)
- Restaurant Doña María, Gonzalez Lelong 827
- Restaurant El Ciervo, 25 de Mayo block 0 (corner of Belgrano)
- Restaurant El Cortijo, Rivadavia 886. Steakhouse
- Restaurant El Gran Fortín, B Mitre 606
- Restaurant El Pajaro Loco, 25 de Mayo block 700 (corner of Fontana)
- Restaurant El Palenque, Belgrano 1126
- Restaurant Gerardo, San Martín 1125 (corner of Irigoyen). International cuisine
- Restaurant Italiano, 25 de Mayo block 0 (corner of San Martín)
- Restaurant La Corbacha, corner of Belgrano and Brandsen
- Restaurant Latino American Bar, 25 de Mayo 61

🛏️ Accommodation in Formosa
During July and August it is advisable to make bookings for better class hotels.

★★★	Hotel Internaciónal de Turismo, San Martín 759	✆ 26004	$16.00	
★★	Hotel Colón, Belgrano 1098	✆ 26547	$10.00	
★★	Hotel Plaza, J M Uriburu 905	✆ 26547	$10.00	
★	Hotel Castellano, Rivadavia 1102 Credit cards accepted	✆ 26151	$9.00	
★	Hotel San Martín, 25 de Mayo 380	✆ 26769	$10.00	
★	Hotel Skorpio, B Mitre 98	✆ 20894	$8.00	
•	Hotel Royal, corner of San Martín 20005 and Saavedra	✆ 20005		
•	Hospedaje La Familia, corner of Belgrano 1056 and H Yrigoyen			
A	Residencial City, Brandsen 37		$7.00	
A	Residencial Colonial, San Martín 897	✆ 26345	$8.00	
A	Residencial del Skorpios, B Mitre 98			
A	Residencial España, Belgrano 1032	✆ 29348	$6.00	
A	Residencial Iberia, Moreno 1185		$6.00	
A	Residencial Ideal, San Martín 717			
A	Residencial Real, Belgrano 17			
A	Residencial Rivas, Belgrano 1395 (corner of Ayacucho, near Brujula/La International Terminal)	✆ 20499	$5.00	
A	Residencial Torino, Moreno 705			

Formosa

Formosa Province

- Restaurant Los Tres Mosqueteros, 9 de Julio 1044. Steakhouse
- Restaurant Moreno, Moreno 1150
- Restaurant Ser San, 25 de Mayo 280 (corner of Moreno)
- Restaurant Super Kiosko, Salta block 100 (corner of San Martín). Steakhouse
- ☞ Restaurant Tropicana Grill, España 252
- Restaurant Via Veneto, Rivadavia 774. Pizzeria
- Pizzería Aranjuez, 25 de Mayo block 200 (corner of Rivadavia)
- Pizzería La Farola, J M Uriburu 152
- Pizzería Las Palmas, España 301
- Cafetería Caacupe, Belgrano 1325
- Cafetería Cascote, 25 de Mayo 293
- Cafetería Casimiro, 25 de Mayo 133
- ☞ Cafetería Chichin, Rivadavia 884. Hamburgers
- Cafetería Dogs, España block 100 (corner of Rivadavia). Hamburgers
- Cafetería El Condado, Belgrano 687. Twenty-four hour service
- ☞ Cafetería El Fortin, B Mitre 602
- Cafetería Hotel de Turismo, 25 de Mayo 10
- Cafetería La Candela, Belgrano 1298
- Cafetería La Tropicana, España 246
- Cafetería La Viga, 25 de Mayo 273
- Cafetería Las Palmas, M Moreno 693
- Cafetería Le Prive, Brandsen 178
- Cafetería Los Mil Sanwiches, corner of Rivadavia and 25 de Mayo
- English-style pub: Baviera, Comandante Fontana 866
- English-style pub: Campito, Brandsen 874

Post and telegraph

Post office: Encotel, 9 de Julio 930
- Long-distance telephone: Entel, Saavedra 656

Financial

There are no *cambios* in Formosa.
- Banco de la Provincia de Formosa, corner of 25 de Mayo and Belgrano. Travelers' checks are changed

Services and facilities

- Laundromat: Laverap, Eva Páron 907. Mon–Fri 0800–2000; $2.00
- Sauna: Belgrano 671 (upstairs)
- Supermarket: Supermarcado El Diamante, Belgrano block 900 (corner of Brandson)

Fishing equipment hire

- Soto Pesca, San Martín
- Dupuy, corner of Déan Funes and Saavedra

Clubs

- Italian: Asociación Italiana, 25 de Mayo block 300 (corner of Moreno)
- Spanish: Asociación Español, Moreno 643

Border crossing

The passport control is open from 0700 – 1830 to coincide with the ferry service. The passport control is located on a moored boat from which you board the ferry to Isla Alberdí in Paraguay.

✈ Air services from Formosa

El Tucu airport is 4 km south of the center of the town; taxi fare $5.00.
- Aerolineas Argentinas, corner of B Mitre 779 and 25 de Mayo ℡ 29392

Destination	Fare	Depart	Services	Hours	Airline
Buenos Aires (Aeroparque Jorge Newbery)					
	$66.00	0950	Mon, Tues, Wed, Fri, Sat	2	Aerolineas
	$41.00				Aerolineas
Night flight; check departure time with the airline					
Corrientes	$13.00	0950	Tues	1	Aerolineas
Jujuy	$41.00	0850	Sat	2	Federal
Resistencia	$11.00	1800	Sat	1	Federal

FORMOSA PROVINCE

🚌 Buses from Formosa

Formosa has no central bus terminal; the various bus companies are scattered throughout the city.
- Empresa Atahualpa, Padre Patiño 969. To Salta—a rough trip)
- Empresa Brújula and Empresa Godoy, Belgrano 1346 (cornerof Salta)
- Empresa Cacorba, España 307
- Transporte El Tigre, corner of Déan Funes and Salta
- Transporte San José, San Martín 450. To Herradura
- Transportes Giroldi, Déan Funes 864. To Ingeniero Juárez and El Colorado

Destination	Fare	Depart	Services	Hours	Company
• Asunción (Paraguay)	$6.00	0550	4 services daily		Godoy
• Buenos Aires	$27.00	1248	3 services daily		Godoy
• Clorinda	$2.50	0750	5 services daily	2	Godoy
• Córdoba	$22.00	1608	Tue, Wed, Thur, Fri	15	Cacorba
• Embarcación	$18.00	1305	Thurs, Fri, Sat	17	Atahualpa
• General Belgrano	$10.00	0500	daily		El Tigre
• Puente Internacional		0430	5 services daily		Godoy
• Resistencia	$3.50	0630	5 services daily	3	Godoy
Buses to Resistencia are always crowded					
• Rosarío	$20.00	1248	3 services daily		Godoy
• Salta	$24.00	1305	Thurs, Fri, Sat	21	Atahualpa
• Santa Fá	$16.00	1248	3 services daily		Godoy

🚗 Motoring

- The 150 km road north to Clorinda and Asunción, via the new toll-bridge which crosses the Río Paraguay, is sealed all the way
- The 200 km road south to Resistencia is sealed for most of the way and is as straight as an arrow. See "Excursions" below
- Avenida 25 de Mayo becomes RN 11

Service stations
- Shell, corner of B Mitre and 25 de Mayo
- YPF, corner of Padre Patiño and 25 de Mayo

🚆 Trains from Formosa

F General M Belgrano station is on the corner of Avenida San Martín and Avenida 25 de Mayo, near the port. The Río Paraguay runs behind the station building.
There is a railroad line across the *chaco* to Embarcación with a so-called *"cochemotor"* or railmotor service, departing Wed, Thurs–Sun at 1200. It is advisable to buy the ticket two hours before departure. The trip to Embarcación goes through real *chaco* country. The trip takes you first through rather swampy countryside with plentiful birdlife, but from Comandante Fontana, it becomes a dusty trip.
- Embarcación: First class $10.50, tourist class $8.00; 19 hours
- Ingeniero Guillermo N Juárez: First class $7.00, tourist class $5.20

⌑ Water transport

A ferry to Isla Alberdí in Paraguay leaves at 0700 daily; the trip lasts half an hour and costs $0.75

⊕ Tours

- Turinort, 25 de Mayo 221 ℡ 27011
- Turismo de Castro, Belgrano 661 ℡ 27483

🛍 Shopping

- La Casa de Artesanía Aborígines, corner of 25 de Mayo and San Martín at the harbor entrance. This is an Indian cooperative which sells Indian artefacts such as bows and arrows and baskets.

Plate 37
Map of Formosa Province

Plate 38
Map of Chaco Province

Plate 40
Menhir with inscriptions, Tafí del Valle

Formosa Province

They also give information on visiting Toba Indians around Ingeniero Guillermo N Juárez
- Exposición de Cultura Artesanía Criolla, San Martín block 800 (corner of Uriburu)

Entertainment

- Bowling: Cafetería Class, corner of Belgrano and Saavedra
- Casino, España 210 (upstairs)
- Cine Argentino, Comandante Fontana 898
- Cine Italia, 25 de Mayo 349
- Disco Amadeus, Belgrano 550
- Disco Karamba, H Yrigoyen 240
- Disco "Z", 25 de Mayo 349
- Night Club Caramba, corner of H Yrigoyen and Belgrano
- Whiskería Très Bien, 25 de Mayo block 200 (corner of Rivadavia)

Sightseeing

- Museo Histórico Provincial (Provincial Historical Museum), 25 de Mayo 84. The museum was formerly the residence of Don Ignacio Fotheringham. It has been converted to house the museum but its colonial character has been left untouched.

Excursions

- **Resistencia**: The road south passes through flat swampy country where there is plentiful birdlife and cebu-like cattle can be seen grazing. There is a police checkpoint at **Tatane**, at the junction of RP 1, which goes to **San Francisco de Laishi**, an Indian community. At the turn-off to RP 5 to the Río Paraguay, there is a small camping spot, unfortunately without facilities. At **Puerto Vélaz** on the **Río Bermejo**, just before the bridge which crosses into Chaco province, there is a small roadside inn. The river is 100 m wide at this point but it floods in the rainy season. The river water is usually not fit for human consumption, so the locals use water from bores which must reach a depth of 30 m before they reach good water. Further south the road passes through palm groves and through **Margarita Belén**, and then enters the outer suburbs of Resistencia. See also Resistencia on page 688
- **Isla Alberdí in Paraguay**: If you have a multiple-entry visa, you can make a trip from the port to this duty-free island; you cannot continue on into Paraguay. The first launch to Isla Alberdí leaves at 0700 and last one at 1800. The last launch returns from Isla Alberdí at 1830
- **Herradura**: 40 km south. Take RN 11 for 31 km until the turn-off at **Tatane**. From here it is another 12 km to the beach on the **Río Paraguay**. The ACA has a camping spot there and Club de Vialidad has facilities. Herradura is an exotically tropical spot. Empresa San José, at San Martín 450, runs a bus service here
- **San Francisco de Laishi**: 64 km south-east on RP 1. To visit this Franciscan Indian mission take RN 11 south for 31 km to **Tatane**. From here follow RP 1 east for another 33 km on a dirt road. The old sugar mill which was constructed by the Franciscans is still operational and the

Formosa

FORMOSA PROVINCE

original church and some of the older buildings are still preserved. Take a bus leaving Formosa at 0600 or 1317 for General J de San Martín in Chaco province

- **Colonia General Fotheringham**: Some 140 km south-east on the **Río Paraguay**, across from the Paraguayan town of Pilar. Take RN 11 for 72 km until **Puerto Vélaz** on the **Río Bermejo**. Just before the bridge which crosses the Río Bermejo there is the turn-off onto RP 9, a dirt road following the river most of the way to its junction with **Río Paraguay**. The surroundings are luxuriantly tropical. The provincial government is planning to build a tourist complex here

INGENIERO GUILLERMO N JUÁREZ

Postal Code: 3636

Ingeniero Guillermo N Juárez (commonly known as Juárez) is located in the district of Matacos in the far west of Formosa province, some 60 km from the border with Salta province. Since the discovery of oil north of the town, near the border with Salta in the district of Ramon Lista, the pace in Juárez has accelerated. A pipeline has been laid from the oilfields to Juárez, which has as a result become an oil town. Juárez leans more more towards Salta province than to Formosa.

Festivals
- Fiesta Aniversario de la Fundación (Foundation Day Festival): July 21
- Fiesta Patronal de Nuestra Señora de la Merced (Festival of the Patron Saint Our Lady of Mercy): September 24

Accommodation
- Motel Ingeniero Juárez (ACA), RN 81

Buses
Empresa Atahualpa runs two services weekly between Salta and Formosa, stopping at Juárez.

Trains
Trains run to Embarcación and to Formosa.

Excursions
- **Reserva Natural Formosa**: Approximately 50 km south. It is very difficult to reach

Formosa

Chaco Province

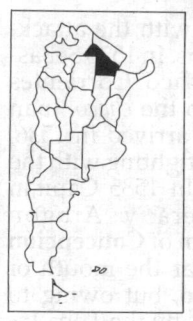

Plate 38 Map of Chaco Province
   685 Barranqueras 🚌 🏨
   685 Presidencia Roque Sáenz Peña
   686 Map
   688 Resistencia
   691 Map

Chaco province is still a pioneer province. Large tracts of the *chaco* are still covered with dense forest, and logging of *quebracho* wood is an important industry. In area it is 100 000 square km and there are approximately 700 000 inhabitants.

Agriculture forms the basis of economic activity. The *chaco* is the main cotton-producing region in Argentina, although in some areas, because of soil exhaustion, sunflower is replacing cotton. The second place is taken by forestry, especially felling of *quebracho*, not only for wood but also for tannin production. Until quite recently the *chaco* was impenetrable, but in recent years many roads have been built, most of them just tracks to exploit the natural riches. These roads have also opened up the province for tourism, although facilities in remote ares have not yet reached a standard for sophisticated tourists. For the time being the *chaco* remains the realm of the adventurer and nature-lover.

Any rain that falls generally does so in winter, with most of it in the eastern part, decreasing towards the west. Water is scarce in the center and in the western regions of the province. In summer the temperature can exceed 45°C for days on end. Extended periods of drought are the bane of the *chaco* and in some parts water has to be carted to the

Chaco Province

townships by truck or train. The underground water is mostly saline. When the rains do come, always in winter and chiefly in the eastern part of the *chaco*, they cover hundreds of kilometers of low-lying land. Thus the *chaco* is a country of extremes: one day there is no water, next day there is a flood.

Chaco province shares borders in the south-east with Corrientes, the south with Santa Fé, the south-west with Santiago del Estero, the north-west with Salta, the north-east with Formosa along the Ríos Teuco and Bermejo, and for a short distance in the east, along the Río Paraguay, with Paraguay.

In 1870 the first North Italian immigrants arrived, followed later by German immigrants. After the World War II many Ukrainians chose the *chaco* as their new home. The center of economic life is greater **Resistencia** which encompasses the provincial capital Residencia as well as the port of **Barranqueras** and the industrial suburb of **Puerto Vilelas**, some 1000 km north of Buenos Aires.

The history of the *chaco* is fascinating. The first European to set foot in the *chaco* was Alejo Garcia, who was shipwrecked on the Brazilian coast in 1526. He joined a band of Chaco Indians roaming the country, and it is claimed that he was with this tribe when it attacked an eastern outpost of the Inca Empire—reports reached Huayna Capac, who resided at that time in Quito, that a bearded white man was with the attacking Chaco Indians. In 1528 Sebastian Cabot reached Corrientes and crossed into the *chaco*. Juan de Ayolas, who arrived in 1536, was involved in fighting with the Chaco Indians. In 1585 Capitán Alonso de Vera y Aragon founded the town of **Concepción del Bermejo** near the mouth of the **Río Bermejo**, but owing to incessant attacks by the Toba Indians this fort had to be abandoned in 1632. In 1750 a settlement on the site of Resistencia under the name of **Reducción de San Fernando del Río Negro** was founded, but again this attempt at colonization had to be abandoned in 1773. In 1780 an expedition from Salta under the command of Colonel Francisco Gavino de Arias founded **Reducción de la Cangayé** and nearby **Reducción de San Bernardo de Vértiz**, neither of which lasted beyond 1804. A new wave of colonization began in 1863. With the exploitation of the rich *chaco* forests, the military established forts along the **Río Negro** and beyond. Around 1880 full-scale European settlement began.

In the north-western part of the *chaco* some of the original wildlife remains. Pumas, *ñandus*, and tapir can still be seen occasionally. For the tourist a visit to the **Parque Nacional Chaco** near Presidencia de la Plaza is suggested, as well as to various ruined Spanish settlements such as **Reducción de la Cangayé** near Fortin Lavalle (off RN 95).

CHACO PROVINCE

BARRANQUERAS

Postal code: 3503 • (area code: (0722)
Distances
• From Santa Fé: 600 km northwards on RN 11

Barranqueras is located on a bluff on the western bank of the **Río Paraná** near its junction with the **Río Negro**. Only 8 km from Resistencia, it is the port and now virtually a suburb of Resistencia. Regular buses run between the two towns. From the bridge over the Río Negro it is a short walk to the ruins of **San Buenaventura del Monte Alto**.

PRESIDENCIA ROQUE SÁENZ PEÑA

Postal code: 3700 • ₵ area code (0714)
Distances
• From Resistencia 169 km westwards on RN 16

Presidencia Roque Sáenz Peña was founded in 1912. It is situated in the dry *chaco* and the underground water is mainly saline. Hot springs have been found here and a substantial tourist resort has developed. It is the center of cotton-growing area.

This town is known locally simply as "Peña", and elsewhere as "Sáenz Peña" or "Roque Sáenz Peña". It is often written as "P R S Peña".

Some Toba Indian families still live in and around Presidencia Roque Sáenz Peña and produce a wide range of arts and crafts, such as weaving, basket-making, and pottery.

Originally the streets were given numbers, but these have gradually been replaced by names, so that streets now bear both numbers and names. However, in many cases the street sign for either the number or the name is missing, so the form in the *Travel Companion* follows whatever the remaining street sign has on it. Often both signs are missing; go back to the nearest intersection with a street sign.

ⓘ   Tourist information
• Turismo Municipal, Casa de la Cultura, corner of San Martín and 9 de Julio (22135.

▲   Camping
• El Descanso municipal camping ground, 1 km from city center

⑪   Eating out
• Restaurant El Fogón, Moreno 202. Steakhouse
• Restaurant Hotel Gualok, Gran Hotel Nogaro Gulok, San Martín 1200. International cuisine
• Restaurant Roma, corner of Calle 13 and Calle 14
• Cafetería Polito, corner of San Martín and Chacabuco, on the Plaza
• Cafetería Sarava, corner of San Martín block 400 and 9 de Julio

✉   Post and telegraph
• Post office: Encotel, corner of Mitre and M Moreno
• Telephone: Entel, corner of Rivadavia and 25 de Mayo

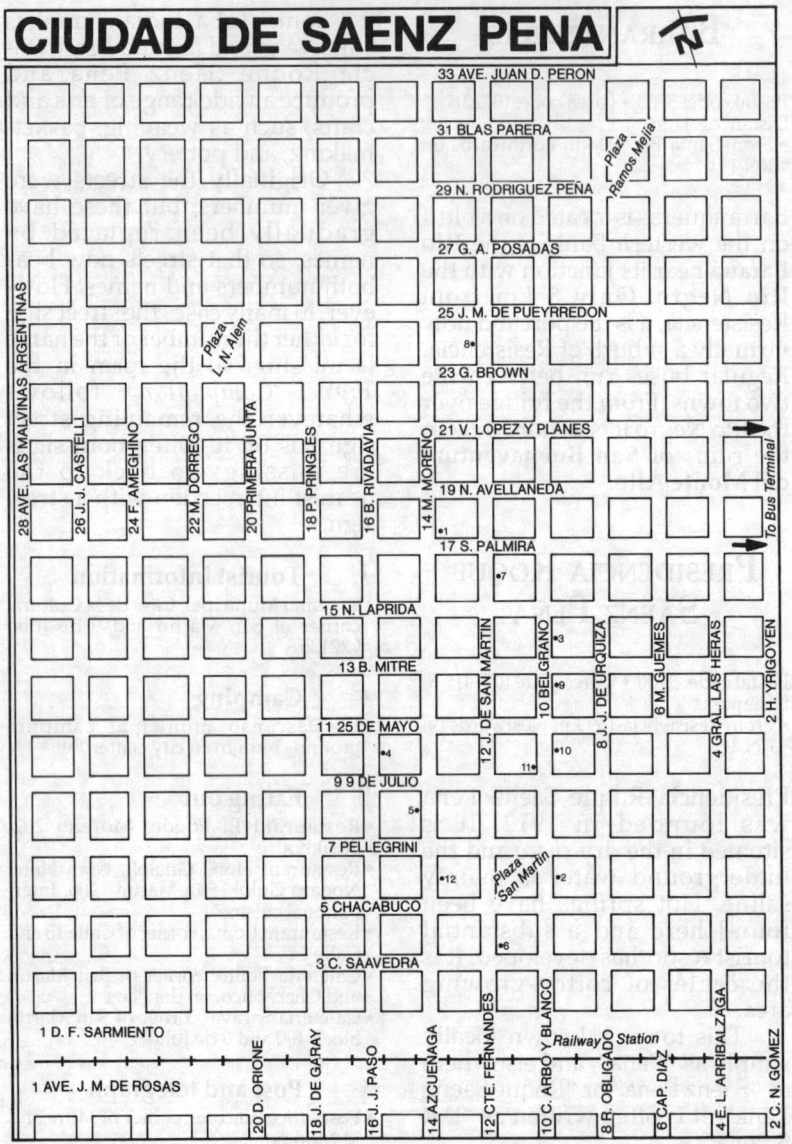

Chaco Province

🛏 Accommodation in Presidencia Roque Sáenz Peña

★★★★★ Gran Hotel Nogaro Gualok, San Martín 1200 🆔📶📺♨
Breakfast $1.50 — ℂ 20521 — $19.50
- Hotel Augustus, Belgrano 483 — ℂ 22068 — $7.50
  Shared bathroom $4.50
- Residencia Asturias, Belgrano (also called Calle 9) 411
- Hotel Orel, San Martin 130 — $7.00
- Residencial Augustus, corner of Belgrano and 9 de Julio — $4.50
  Annex to Hotel Augustus; shared bathroom
- Residencial El Colono, San Martín 755 📺 — $3.00
  Shared bathroom
- Residencial Premier, Belgrano 589
- Residencial Santa Fé, M Moreno 343 — $3.00
  Shared bathroom; for budget travelers

🍽 Services and facilities
- Supermarket: Derka, San Martin 849

🚂 Trains

The F C General M Belgrano station is on the corner of Avenida D F Sarmiento (formerly Calle 1) and J J de Urquiza, opposite Belgrano.
- Resistencia: Tourist class $3.00
- Santa Fé: First class $11.80, tourist class $9.00
- Buenos Aires (Retiro station): "El Chaqueño"; first class $21.80, tourist class $14.50

🚗 Motoring

The road through the *chaco* to Salta via Monte Quemado can be cut during the wet season.
- Service station: ACA, corner of Rivadavia and 25 de Mayo

📷 Sightseeing
- Museo Arqueológico Juan A Martinet

♣ Excursions
- **Campo del Cielo** (Field of Heaven): Approximately 350 km south-east, in the vicinity of **Gancedo**, this site derives its name from a meteorite shower which landed here. Some of the biggest meteorites are now on display in museums in New York and Buenos Aires. Fragments can still be found. Empresa Nueva Estrella runs a daily service from Presidencia Roque Sáenz Peña to Gancedo, departing at 1500 and taking four hours, fare $3.50. There is a return bus at 0600. Check with Hotel Nogaro to see if there is also a tourist bus

Key to Map
1. Municipalidad
2. Catedral
3. Post office (Encotel)
4. Telephone (Entel)
5. Tourist information
6. Hotel Orel
7. Residencial El Colono
8. Hotel Complejo Termal
9. Residencial Premier
10. Residencial Augustus
11. Hotel Asturias
12. Residencial Santa Fé

CHACO PROVINCE

🚌 Buses from Presidencia Roque Sáenz Peña

The bus terminal is at Calle 304, some 10 blocks from the city center.

Destination	Fare	Depart	Services	Hours	Company
• Resistencia					Central Sáenz Peña
• Buenos Aires	$20.00	2000	daily	19	La Internacional, TATA, Nueva Estrella
• Castelli					Central Sáenz Peña
• Córdoba					La Estrella
• Gancedo					Nueva Estrella
• Salta	$16.00	2000	daily	13	Veloz del Norte
• Santiago del Estero	$6.00	2215	daily	9	El Rayo
• San Miguel de Tucumán	$10.50	2215	daily	11	El Rayo
• Termas de Río Hondo	$7.70	2215	daily	10	El Rayo
• Villa Río Bermejito					Central Sáenz Peña

- Ruinas de **Concepción del Bermejo**: Alfonso de Vera y Aragón founded this town in 1585, but it was abandoned because of attacks by Chaco Indians. It was rediscovered in 1943 by Alfredo Martinet. The actual site of the ruins is near **Estancia El Estierro**. This trip is recommended for those interested in history and archeology. Empresa Central Sáenz Peña runs a daily service to Km 71, departing at 0915 and taking two hours; fare $3.50. Take water with you and check with the bus driver for directions. The return bus leaves at 0700 next day

- **Villa Río Bermejito**: Located on the banks of the **Río Bermejito**, which is a tributary of the **Río Bermejo**, this is one of the most remote and relatively unspoilt parts of the Argentine *chaco*. There are few visitors to its clear waters and sandy beaches. The area still abounds in wildlife, including colorful birds, *yacares* (caymans), gray foxes, and wildcats. There are many Indian settlements here. An adventure trip for nature-lovers; remember to take a tent and mosquito repellent. Empresa Central Sáenz Peña runs a daily service departing at 0915 and taking four and half hours; fare $3.50. The Villa Río Bermejito camping ground is directly on the river

RESISTENCIA

Postal code: 3500 • Population: 204 000 • (area code: (0722) • Altitude: 52 m

Modern and busy Resistencia, capital of Chaco province, is located on the **Río Barranqueras**, 7 km up from its junction with the **Río Paraná**.

In 1750 the Jesuit **Reducción de San Fernando del Río Negro** was founded, only to be abandoned in 1773. The real colonization of the province began in 1870, and the town of Resistencia began to grow from 1878 on-

Chaco Province

wards when the first Friulan immigrants arrived from northern Italy.

The 2 km Puente General M Belgrano (General M Belgrano Bridge) crosses the Río Paraná to link Resistencia with Corrientes. A feature of the town is the many statues of nudes in the streets. Most industry is located in nearby Barranqueras.

ⓘ Tourist information
- Tourist office, corner of Remedio de Escalada 85 and M T de Alvear ℡ 23547. Open 0800–2000

▲ Camping
- Parque 2 de Febrero municipal camping ground, corner of Avenida Lavalle and Avenida Avalos, 2 km from the city center; tent hire

🍴 Eating out
- Restaurant Casa Vieja, corner of Rawson and Ameghino
- Restaurant Charly, Güemes 215
- Restaurant Charolay, Avenida 25 de Mayo block 300 (corner of Necochea)
- Restaurant Circulo Residentes Santafecinos, Vedia 152. Local cuisine
- Restaurant Clemente, Santiago del Estero block 0, at the bus terminal. Steakhouse
- Restaurant Club Progreso, H Yrigoyen 412
- Restaurant Club Social, Avenida Alberdí 295
- ☞ Restaurant Comedor El Buen Gusto, Avenida Moreno 50
- Restaurant Continental Grill, Santa María de Oro block 400 (corner of Moreno)
- Restaurant Don Tito, Santiago del Estero block 0, at the bus terminal. Steakhouse
- ☞ Restaurant El Farol, Güemes block 200 (corner of Don Bosco). Credit cards accepted
- ☞ Restaurant El Yate, Avenida 25 de Mayo block 300 (corner of Donovan)
- Restaurant Irupe, San Martín 145. Steakhouse
- Restaurant La Biela, Güemes block 600 (corner of Córdoba)
- Restaurant La Estancia, 25 de Mayo 1745
- Restaurant La Fragata, Hotel Lemirson, Rawson 173
- Restaurant La Rueda, corner of Güemes and Brown
- Restaurant La Vieja Esquina, Rawson 402
- Restaurant Marymer, Vedia 260
- Restaurant Metro, Avenida Sarmiento 408. Pizzeria
- Restaurant Nuevo Crystal Palace, corner of Santa Maria de Oro and Sgo del Estero, near bus terminal
- Restaurant Pajaro Loco, Güemes 232
- Restaurant Parrilla Family, Güemes block 100 (corner of and Brown)
- Restaurant Por La Vuelta, corner of Obligado Block 0 and Alberdí
- ☞ Restaurant Residentes Santafecinos, Vedia 152
- Restaurant Sociedad Italiana, H Yrigoyen 204. Italian cuisine
- Restaurant Veredes, Güemes Block 100 (corner of Brown)
- Restaurant Viva El Rey, opposite the Triangle
- Restaurant W & N, Club de Gourmet, Avenida Sarmiento 141. Seafood
- Restaurant Yapu Guazú, J A Roca 1448. Seafood
- Pizzería Alvear, Santiago del Estero 145
- Pizzería La Tuerca, Avenida 25 de Mayo block 100 (corner of Vedia)
- ☞ Pizzería Napoli, Avenida 25 de Mayo block 200
- Pizzería Nevada, Juan D Perón block 100 (corner of Vedia)
- Pizzería Zan-En, Rawson block 0 (corner of Avenida 9 de Julio)
- ☞ Cafetería Americana, Rawson block 100 (corner of J B Justo)
- Cafetería Angelo, Güemes 175
- Cafetería Bacarat, J A Roca 165
- Cafetería Barbas, Rawson 125
- Cafetería Blues, Juan D Perón 163
- Cafetería Cafe Bar Sis, Pellegrini block 0 (corner of 9 de Julio)
- Cafetería Casa de Postre, corner of Santa María de Oro and Salta
- Cafetería Center Pool, corner of Avenida 9 de Julio and French. Pool
- Cafetería Doria, Santa María de Oro 175

Resistencia

Chaco Province

- Cafetería El Colome, Juan D Perón 187
- Cafetería El Molino, Antartida Argentina 147. Closed Sunday
- Cafetería El Super Chavo, Avenida 25 de Mayo block 100 (corner of Santa María de Oro
- Cafetería Factura's, corner of J A Roca and Avenida Alberdi
- Cafetería Gallery, corner of Sarmiento and Ayacucho
- Cafetería Kilo Cafe, Santa María de Oro 182
- Cafetería La Vieja Estrella, Pellegrini block 100 (corner of Brown)
- Cafetería Las Vegas, Juan D Perón 216. Pool
- Cafetería San José, main Plaza. Pizzeria
- ☞ Cafetería Reviens, corner of Güemes and H Yrigoyen
- Cafetería Veredes, Güemes 172
- Cafetería Zan-en, Rawson 15
- Heladería Wendy, corner of Juan D Perón block 200 and Vedia. Ice-cream

Post and telegraph

- Post office: Encotel, corner of H Yrigoyen and Güemes
- Long distance telephone: Entel, J M Paz block 200 (corner of J B Justo)

Financial

There are no *cambios* in Resistencia.
- Banco Alas, Tucumán 152. Cash advances on Visa card
- Banco del Chaco, Antartida Argentina 253, cashes travelers' checks at 3% commission

Services and facilities

- Bakery: La Central, Rawson block 300 (corner of Obligado)
- Delicatessen: Autoservicio, Güemes 223. Credit cards accepted
- Drycleaner: Nipon, Avenida 9 de Julio block 100 (corner of Rawson)
- Laundromat: Laverap, Juan D Perón 598. Open Mon–Sat 0800–2200; cost $2.00
- Pharmacy: Farmacia Sanchez, Rawson block 0 (corner of Avenida 9 de Julio)
- Photographic supplies: Fotocolor Valsechia, corner of J M Paz and Antartida Argentina. Sells Fuji and Kodak film
- Sports equipment: El Pescador, Juan D Perón 489
- Supermarket: Funcional, Salta block 300 (corner of Necochea)
- Vegetarian food supply: Vida Sana, Antartida Argentina block 600 (corner of Arbo y Blanco). Sells pollen

Clubs

- Club Social, Avenida Alberdi 295. Visitors welcome for meals
- Club Yapu Guazu, Roca 1448
- French: Alliance Française, R S Peña 451
- Italian: Sociedad Italiana Dante Aleghieri, H Yrigoyen 204. Italian-style meals; visitors welcome

Key to Map

1. Municipalidad
2. Casa de Gobierno
3. Catedral
4. Post office (Encotel)
5. Telephone (Entel)
6. Tourist information
7. Bus terminal
8. Banco de la Nación
9. Museo Histórico Ichoalay
11. Aerolineas Argentinas
12. Austral Lineas Aereas
13. Lineas Aereas Paraguayas
14. Hotel Covadonga
15. Hotel Lemirson
16. Hotel Sahara
17. Hotel Alfil
18. Hotel Colón
19. Hotel Esmirna
20. Residencial Alvear
21. Residencial Bariloche
22. Residencial El Diamante
23. Residencial Hernandarias
24. Residencial Marconi
25. Residencial San José
26. Residencial Santiago del Estero
27. Hospedaje Anita
28. Hospedaje Paraná

Chaco Province

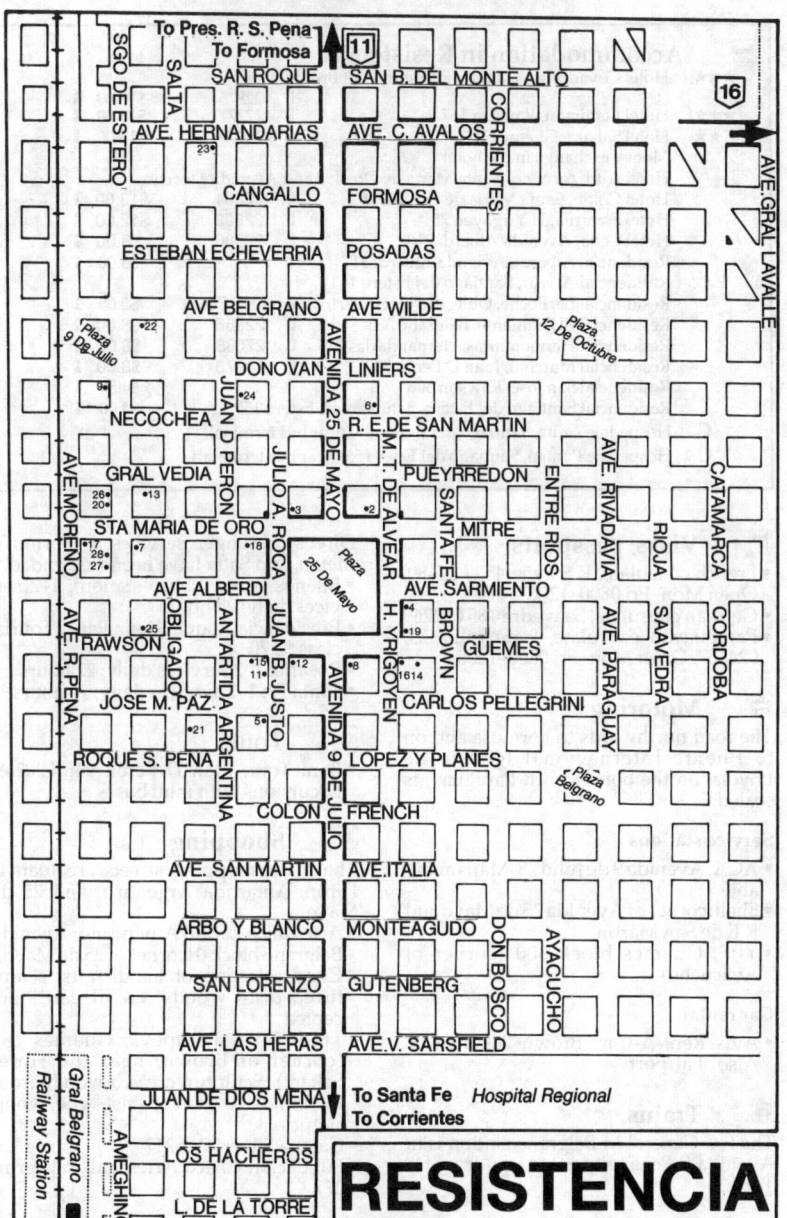

RESISTENCIA

Chaco Province

📭 Accommodation in Resistencia

★★★	Hotel Covadonga, Güemes 200 (corner of Brown)	(22875	$15.00	
★★★	Hotel Lemirson, Rawson 167	(22277	$15.00	
★★	Hotel Sahara, Güemes 160	(22970	$15.00	
	Money exchange in the hotel			
	Hotel Alfil, corner of Santa María de Oro 499 and Avenida Moreno			
	Hotel Colón, Santa María de Oro 149	(22861	$13.00	
	Hotel Esmirna, H Yrigoyen 75	(22898	$12.00	
	Hotel Celta, Avenida Alberdí 210	(22986	$ 8.00	
	Residencial Alberdí, Avenida Alberdí 317		$5.00	
	Residencial Alvear, Santiago del Estero 143			
	Residencial Bariloche, Obligado block 200 (corner of R S Peña)		$5.00	
	Residencial El Diamante, Belgrano 383	(22866	$8.00	
	Residencial Hernandarias, Hernandarias 215	(27088	$8.00	
	Residencial Marconi, Juan D Perón 332	(21978	$8.00	
	Residencial San José, Rawson 306		$4.50	
	Residencial Santiago del Estero, Santiago del Estero 155		$4.00	
C	Hospedaje Anita, Santiago del Estero 45 (near bus terminal)			
C	Hospedaje Paraná, Santiago del Estero 55 (near bus terminal)			

📭 Visas, passports

- French consulate, R S Peña 453 (24480. Open Mon–Fri 0800–1200
- German consulate, Saavedra 185 (22269
- Paraguayan consulate, 9 de Julio 326 (24667. Open Mon–Fri 0800–1200

🚗 Motoring

The road northwards to Formosa and on to Puente Internacional Ignacio de Loyola, on the border with Paraguay, is sealed.

Service stations

- ACA, Avenida 9 de Julio 78. Maps available
- Shell, corner of Avenida 25 de Mayo and R E de San Martín
- YPF, Güemes block 300 (corner of Ayacucho)

Car rental

- Avis Rent-A-Car, Brown 209 (29935. Also at airport

🚆 Trains

The F C General M Belgrano station is in Avenida R Peña, opposite Lisandro de la Torre.

Direct passenger services to Formosa, Metan, and Salta have been suspended.

- Buenos Aires (Retiro station): 1–2 services daily; 28 hours
- Presidencia Roque Sáenz Peña: Tourist class $2.70
- Rosario: 1–2 services daily; 22 hours
- Santa Fé: 1–2 services daily; 16 hours

⊕ Tours

- Boni Tour, Juan D Perón 946 (20238. Excursions with mini buses

🛍 Shopping

The main shopping streets are Juan D Perón, Antartida Argentina, and 25 de Mayo.

- Artesanías Latino Americano, Avenida Belgrano block 0 (corner of 25 de Mayo). Good selection of handicrafts, sculptured *chaco* woods; credit cards accepted
- Tradicional Pompeya, Güemes 154 (corner of Brown, near the Hotel Sahara). Sculptured *chaco* woods from Domingo Arenas; cubist-type wood statues
- Galería Silver, Paz 217
- Fundación Chaco Artesanal, Pellegrini 272

Chaco Province

✈ Air services from Resistenca

The international airport is 8 km south of the city near Villa Barberan. The airport bus to Resistenca costs $1.50; the airport bus to Corrientes costs $3.00.

- Aerolineas Argentinas, J B Justo 136 ☏ 22854
- ALFA (Aerolineas Federales Argentinas, formerly Aero-Chaco), Güemes 70 ☏ 25274
- Austral, Rawson 99 ☏ 25921
- Lineas Aereas Paraguayas (LAP), Vedia 331 ☏ 27627

Destination	Fare	Depart	Services	Hours	Airline
Buenos Aires (Aeroparque Jorge Newbery)					
	$58.00	0930	2–3 services daily	2	Aerolineas, Austral
Comodoro Rivadavia					
	$107.00	1140	Sat	7	Austral
Córdoba	$44.00	0800	Mon, Wed, Fri	3	ALFA
Formosa	$11.00	0800	Sat	½	ALFA
Mar del Plata	$77.00	1140	Sat	4	Austral
Mendoza	$58.00	0700	Tues, Thur, Sun	5	ALFA
Posadas	$22.00	0700	Tues	1	ALFA
	$26.00	0855	Sun	1	Austral
Puerto Iguazu	$30.00	0700	Tues, Thur	2	ALFA
Rosario	$52.00	1140	Tues, Thur–Sat	1	Austral
Salta	$41.00	0800	Wed, Sat	3	ALFA
San Juan	$53.00	0800	Sun	4	ALFA
San Miguel de Tucumán					
	$41.00	0700	Tues, Thurs, Sun	2	ALFA
San Rafael	$62.00	0800	Sun	6	ALFA
San Salvador de Jujuy					
	$41.00	0800	Wed, Sat	3	ALFA
Santa Fé	$33.00	0800	Mon, Wed, Fri	2	ALFA
Trelew	$104.00	1140	Sat	6	Austral
Villa Dolores	$45.00	0800	Mon, Fri	4	ALFA

- Cooperativa Toba, Barrio Toba RN 11 north. Handicrafts are sold by Toba Indians
- La Lechuza Quemada, Tucumán 1600

🏊 Sport

- Golf: Chaco golf course (18 holes), corner of Avenida 9 de Julio and Cartero Ramirez. Take bus 1 from the corner of J A Roca and Santa María de Oro, opposite the cathedral; it's the same bus that goes to Barranqueras. Ask the driver to let you off near the YPF service station

🍸 Entertainment

- Disco Revolución Zero, corner of Obligado and Rawson
- Disco Cripton, Güemes 240
- Disco El Yate, corner of Avenida 25 de Mayo and Donovan
- Peña Nativa Martin Fierro, corner of Ave 9 de Julio and Gutemberg
- Whiskería La Casa de Mario, Obligado block 100 (corner of J M Paz). Nightclub; open 2300–0500
- Whiskería Reviens, H Yrigoyen block 0 (corner of Güemes)

📷 Sightseeing

There are many modern statues, mostly female nudes, promoted by the Fogón de los Arrieros, along the streets.

- Museo Histórico Ichoalay, Donovan 425, in the Escuela

Chaco Province

🚌 Buses from Resistenca

The bus terminal is on Santiago del Estero, between Vedia and Santa María de Oro. Ataco Norte Buses to Corrientes leave from the corner of Santa María de Oro and Santiago del Estero every half hour 0600–2400.

Destination	Fare	Depart	Days	Hours	Company
• Asunción (Paraguay)		0300	3 services daily	5	Godoy, La Internacional
• Buenos Aires		1248	3 services daily	16	Godoy, La Internacional
• Clorinda	$6.50	0300	3 services daily	5	Godoy, La Internacional
• Córdoba	$19.30	1230	Tues–Sun	13	La Estrella, Cacorba
• Formosa	$4.00	0500	7 services daily	3	Godoy, La Internacional
• La Rioja		1311	Wed, Sat		COTAL
• Mendoza		1311	Wed, Sat		COTAL
• Posadas		1028	Wed, Fri, Sun		COTAL
• Presidencia Roque Sáenz Peña	$2.70	1940	daily	2½	El Rayo
• Puerto Iguazú		1028	Wed, Fri, Sun		COTAL
• Rosario		2015	daily		El Norte Bis
• Salta			daily		La Veloz del Norte
• San Fernando del Valle de Catamarca		1311	Wed, Sat		COTAL
• San Juan		1311	Mon, Wed, Sat		COTAL
• San Miguel de Tucumán	$15.00	1940	daily	14	El Rayo
• Santa Fé	$12.20	2015	daily		El Norte Bis
• Santiago del Estero	$10.50	1311	1–2 services daily		COTAL, El Rayo
• Termas de Río Hondo	$11.70	1940	daily	12½	El Rayo

Mixta Sarmiento. Of particular interest are the references to the Friulan immigration

- Museo de Ciencias Naturales del Chaco (Chaco Natural Science Museum), corner of B Mitre and Corrientes. The seven halls give a good overview of the flora and fauna of the *chaco*. There is a piece of meteorite from the Campo del Cielo on display here

🌳 Excursions

- **Corrientes**: Across the **Río Paraná**. The Puente General M Belgrano (General M Belgrano Bridge), nearly 3 km long, crosses the river, joing Corrientes with Resistencia. There is a splendid view from the Avenida Costanera General San Martín in Corrientes. See also Corrientes on page 726
- **Makallé**: 67 km westwards on RN 16. During last century a string of fortifications were built across the *chaco* to secure the land to the south from incursions by Chaco Indians. The remains of such a fort can still be seen in the vicinity of Makallé
- **Parque Nacional Chaco**: The main access to the park is from **Capitán Solari** on RP 9, some

Resistencia

Chaco Province

16 km north of **Colonia Elisa**. The park covers approximately 15 000 ha and is almost completely in its natural state. The wildlife includes monkeys, mountain cats, foxes, and birds in all colors and sizes. Most of the *chaco* forests are concentrated in the center, east, and south of the park. The western part consists of a typical savanna with *caranday* palms predominating. The south-east around the **Laguna Panza de Cabra** consists chiefly of typical wetlands vegetation, where the flora includes *quebracho*, *ceiba*, palm trees, and orchids. There is a vehicle trail of about 3 km, and four-wheel drive vehicles can do another 15 km on a dirt track; keep to the trails and tracks. There is an information office in the park, and there are picnic areas, extensive walking trails, camping, and toilet facilities. Park attendants provide guided tours for a small fee. Inside the park is a camping ground. Transport La Nueva Estrella runs a daily bus from Resistencia to Colonia Elisa departing at 0630, 1230, and 1730, taking approximately three hours; fare $2.00

- **Isla del Cerrito**: This island is located at the junction of the **Río Paraná** with the **Río Paraguay**, approximately 52 km northeast. The island is a provincial reserve, covering 12 000 ha. Its climate is subtropical and benign all year round. At the big road intersection just before the General M Belgrano bridge to Corrientes go straight on to **Puerto Antequeras**. From here onwards the road deteriorates but is still passable, following the **Riachuelo Antequera** and **Carpincho** for 20 km until it crosses the Cerrito bridge. From the bridge it is a further 17 km to the holiday resort, where the road is sealed once more. After the War of the Triple Alliance, the island was occupied by Brazilian forces for 10 years, before it was finally surrendered to Argentina. It is very picturesque with its typical *chaco* flora. Various guest houses, with a total of approximately 400 beds, cater for the influx of tourists, especially during September, the month of the *dorado* fishing season, organized by the Federación Chaqueña de Pesca. Guest houses usually charge per bed. Across the Río Paraguay is Paraguay, which can be visited from Isla del Cerrito. Ferries cross the Río Paraná daily to **Paso de la Patria** in Corrientes province. It is possible to return via Paso de la Patria to Corrientes or continue to Posadas. There are no bus services between Resistencia and Isla del Cerrito

Resistencia

Santiago del Estero Province

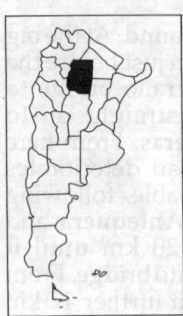

Plate 41 Map of Santiago del Estero Province
- 699 Añatuya
- 699 Frías
- 700 Guasayán
- 700 La Banda
- 701 Quimilí
- 701 Santiago del Estero
- 702   Map
- 708 Sumampa
- 708 Termas de Río Hondo
- 711   Map
- 718 Villa Ojo de Agua

Santiago del Estero is the oldest province in Argentina. It is part of the southern *chaco*, and has very few mountain ranges of any significance. Near the western border with Catamarca is the **Sierra de Guasayán**, and the **Sierra de Sumampa** is in the extreme south near Villa Ojo de Agua.

Land-locked Santiago del Estero shares borders with Salta in the north-west, Chaco in the north-east, Santa Fé in the south-

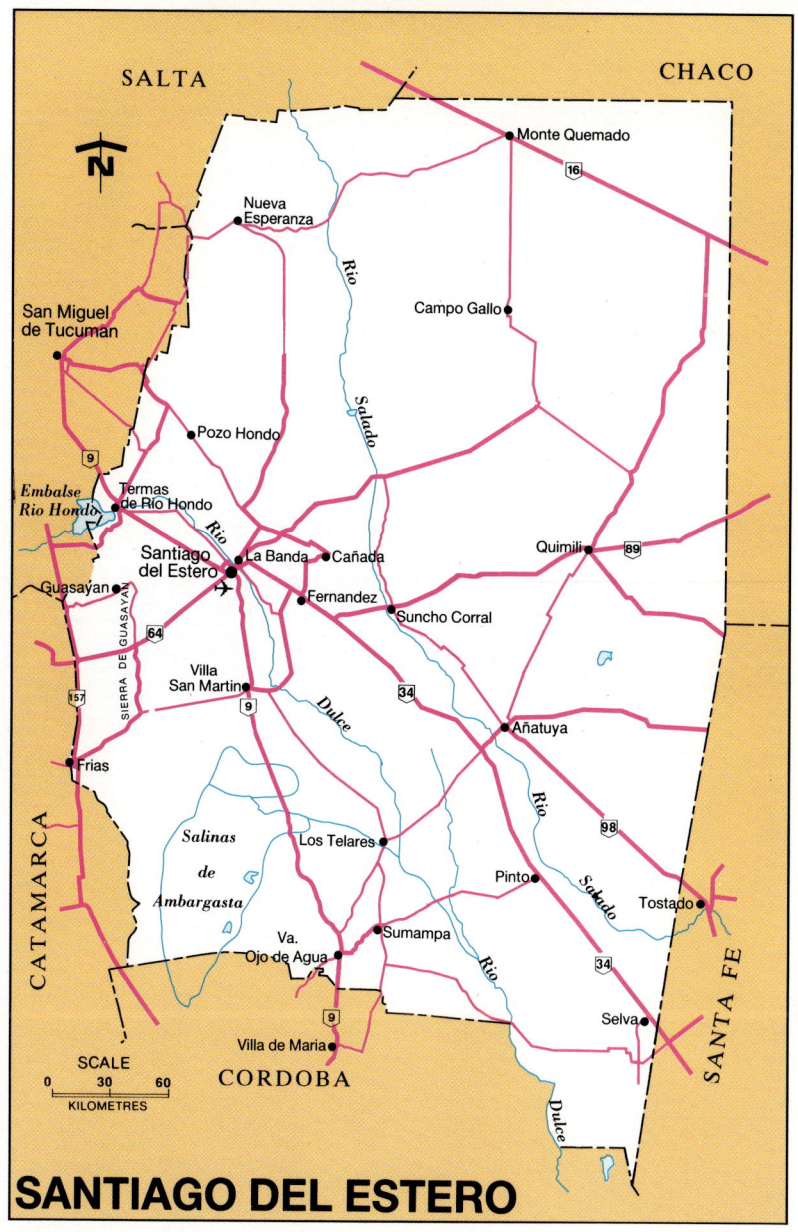

Plate 41

Map of Santiago del Estero Province

Plate 42
Rock paintings near Sumampa

SANTIAGO DEL ESTERO

east, Córdoba in the south, and Catamarca and Tucumán in the west.

The provincial capital is **Santiago del Estero** (often just called "Santiago"), with about 150 000 inhabitants. It is 1194 km distant from the federal capital Buenos Aires.

The main rivers are the **Río Dulce**, originating at the Río Hondo weir, and the **Río Salado**, coming from Salta province. Both rivers flow through extensive marshes. The Río Dulce flows through several *bañados* or lagoons, and eventually finishes up in Mar Chiquita in Córdoba province. Most of the rivers are forced into irrigation channels to enhance agricultural production. The province has also some very large *salinas*, such as the **Salinas de Ambargasta**.

Santiago del Estero province has Argentina's biggest single thermal spa in **Termas de Río Hondo** and this, next to the provincial capital, is the province's main tourist attraction.

The road network is extensive and the major through roads, RN 9 and RN 64 through the **Sierra de Guasayán** to San Miguel de Tucumán and RN 34 to Santa Fé, are in reasonable condition. The roads, which pass mostly through level country, run in a straight line over long distances. The landscape is unchanging *chaco* country. The most remarkable tree in this area is the *quebracho* ("axe-breaker"), so called because of its hard timber.

The climatic conditions of Santiago del Estero are much the same over the whole province. The hottest months are December to February, and during this time the average temperature climbs to 36 °C; the summer months also experience some rainy periods. During these months the sun burns down on a saltbush steppe, where temperatures up to 50 °C are not uncommon. The winters are mild, averaging 6 °C; the winter months are also the driest ones.

The subtropical climate of the north-eastern part of the province gives rise to dense forest cover, which is exploited commercially. The most sought-after timber is the *quebracho*.

In the north-west huge underground natural water reservoirs are being tapped. Some of the wells yield 100 000 liters an hour.

Some gypsum mining is carried out in the **Sierra de Guasayán**, and salt is mined from the *salinas* or salt pans. The economy of the province chiefly depends on two activities: agriculture and tourism.

Santiago del Estero is Argentina's hottest province. There are many salt lakes, the largest being **Salinas de Ambargasta**, near the border with and extending into Córdoba province. Because of the lack of water, many of the inhabitants are forced to seek employment in other better-endowed provinces, such as cotton harvesting in

SANTIAGO DEL ESTERO

Chaco province and sugarcane harvesting in Tucumán.

The most important engineering feat in the province was the erection of the 27 metre high dam at **Embalse Río Hondo**, which enabled the irrigation of extensive areas.

History

Santiago del Estero was the transit road for Chaco peoples and ideas moving to and from the high sierras. The first inhabitants left their mark some 12 000 years ago. They were food-gatherers who lived in the hilly areas of **Sumampa** and **Ambargasta**. Some 8000 years ago traces of a hunting people appear, mostly in the **Sierra de Guasayán**. This was apparently a very rich zone for gathering food and for hunting, although the lifestyle was still very basic.

About 4000 to 5000 years ago the indigenous people supplemented their meat dishes with ground grains, as evidenced by the discovery of many flat grinding stones. Around 1000 BC the agricultural period started, but the population did not create permanent settlements. Some animals were domesticated during this period.

About 500 AD the so-called early pottery period started, indicating that the population now had fixed dwelling places and were already *agricultores* or "cultivators". Agriculture was the main food source, supplemented by hunting and fishing. The earliest known culture is known as the Mercedes culture, thought to have originated in Catamarca. Most archeological sites of this culture are in the **Río Dulce valley** and the Sierra de Guasayán.

From about 900 AD onwards we find the intermediate pottery period, represented by the Sunchituyoj culture. In this period the pottery became more elaborate.

Around 1100 AD the late pottery period commenced. This was still the predominant culture when the Spaniards arrived. Most artistic was the Averías culture, which is thought to show the influence of the Andean Diaguitas.

The first Spanish arrival in the province was in 1543 under Capitán General Diego de Rojas, who was killed by a poisoned arrow in western Santiago del Estero, near the Tucumán border. In 1550 he was followed by Capitán General Juan Nuñez del Prado, who founded several small villages. In 1553 Capitán General Francisco de Aguirre founded the city of **Santiago del Estero**. At this time the aborigines still preserved their own culture, but accepted new ideas from the Europeans. Their culture centered around **Matara** on the central **Río Salado**.

The main bearers of Spanish influence were the Jesuits, who founded the first Indian *reducción* in Santiago del Estero. The Jesuit influence remained strong until their expulsion in 1767.

Santiago del Estero

During the colonial period the Río Salado was the last frontier against the warring Chaco peoples. To protect the Spanish colony a series of forts were erected along the so-called Salado fortification line.

Tourist attractions

Santiago del Estero has many thermal springs such as those at **Termas de Río Hondo**, and **La Punta**. The most fashionable is certainly Termas de Río Hondo, which boasts international-standard hotels to which Argentines and many tourists from other countries flock. The city of Termas de Río Hondo has an inexhaustible flow of hot thermal springs, which has made it the foremost winter tourist centre in the north-west.

The whole province is rich in folklore, expressed in colorful carnival celebrations and fiestas which are deeply rooted in pre-Columbian myths.

The best time to visit this province is in winter.

The chief tourist attractions are:
- Very interesting: City of **Santiago del Estero** with its historical and cultural interests; and **Termas de Río Hondo**, a thermal spa with water sports
- Interesting: **San Pedro** (in Guasayán department, near the Tucumán border), thermal springs; **Villa Ojo de Agua**, where there are aboriginal rock paintings; and **Sumampa** ("Sumampa Viejo"), which has aboriginal rock paintings, a religious festival, and an unspoilt back country

AÑATUYA

Postal code: 3760
Distance from Santiago del Estero: 200 km south-east on RN 34

Añatuya is located at the junction of RP 21 and RP 6. The area around the town—known as **Bañados de Añatuya**—is marshy. This is the source of the **Río Salado**.

🎭 Festivals
- Festival de la Chacarera: Date proclaimed each year

🛏 Accommodation
- Hospedaje Los Gringos (2198 $9.00 ⋕
- A Residencial Casablanca, 25 de Mayo $13.00 ⋕
- A Residencial Santa Rita, Avenida España 74 (21419 $13.00 ⋕
- C Residencial Añatuya, Avenida España 54 (2113 $10.00 ⋕

FRÍAS

Postal code: 4230 • (area code: (0854) • Altitude: 330 m
Distance from Santiago del Estero: 143 km southwards on RN 24 then RP 64

Frías is located at the intersection of RN 157 and RP 24 in the extreme west of the province, right on the border with Catamarca province.

Frías

Santiago del Estero

Accommodation in Frías

★	Hotel Biarritz, Avenida San Martín 70	(	21429	$15.00	♂♀
★	Hotel Petit, corner of Mitre and Alvear	(	21229	$15.00	♂♀
★	Hotel San Jorge, Rivadavia 300	(	21349	$15.00	♂♀
•	Hospedaje Rivadavia, Rivadavia 258	(	21377	$10.00	♂♀
•	Hospedaje Alvarez, Cordoba 269			$10.00	♂♀
B	Residencial Centro, Corrientes 485			$10.00	♂♀
B	Residencial El Viajante, Jujuy 119	(	21253	$11.00	♂♀
C	Residencial America, Dorrego 172			$10.00	♂♀

Festivals
- Fiesta Nacional del Bombo: November

Buses
- Santiago del Estero: Daily; 2 hours; Empresa T A Libertador
- Catamarca: Fare $5.00; 1-2 services daily; 4½ hours; Empresa Salles
- La Rioja: Daily; 5½ hours; Empresa T A Libertador
- Termas de Río Hondo: Daily; 3 hours; Empresa T A Libertador

GUASAYÁN

Postal code: 4238
Distance from Santiago del Estero: 101 km westwards on RN 64 then RP 3

Guasayán is located at the northern end of the **Sierra de Guasayán**.

Accommodation
- Hospedaje Achalay, Libertad $9.00 ♂♀

LA BANDA

Postal code: 4300 • (area code: (085)
Distance from Santiago del Estero: 7 km north-east on the *autopista*

La Banda is separated from the city of Santiago del Estero by the **Río Dulce**. Its only importance is as a railhead for trains to and from Buenos Aires, Tucumán, and Salta.

Festivals
- Festival Folklórico (Folk Festival): September

Accommodation
- ★★ Hotel Presidente, España 510 ⁅ (271051 $21.00 ♂♀
- ★ Hotel Trento, corner of Mitre and Besares ⁅ (271642 $17.00 ♂♀
- Hospedaje Comercio, Belgrano 55 (271725 $9.00 ♂♀. Some cheaper rooms with shared bathrooms
- A Residencial San Martín, Belgrano, opposite the rail station (271188 $13.00 ♂♀. Shared bathroom $11.00
- C Residencial Avellaneda, Avellaneda 73 (272178 $10.00 ♂♀. Shared bathroom $9.00

Eating out
- Hotel Presidente, España 510
- Cafetería Alhambra, corner of Besares and Belgrano

Buses
Municipal buses leave for Santiago del Estero every 20 minutes.

Santiago del Estero

🚆 Trains

The railroad station is at Besares block 300, at the intersection with Sáenz Peña.
- San Miguel de Tucumán: Tourist $4.50

Trains to Buenos Aires
- "Independencia": Pullman $31.20; departs 1945 Sun, Tues, Thurs; 14 hours.
- "Estrella del Norte": First class $16.50, tourist class $12.20; departs 2052 daily.
- "Ciudad de Tucumán": Sleeper $41.50, Pullman $24.80; departs 2245 daily;

QUIMILÍ

Postal code: 3740 • Altitude: 134 m
Distance from Santiago del Estero: 203 km eastwards on RN 34 then RN 89

Quimilí is located in *chaco* country at the intersection of RN 89, RP 6, and RP 116 in the western part of the province.

🛏 Accommodation

★ Hotel Parodi, 25 de Mayo 184 ✆ 66 $15.00 ⛉
- Hospedaje Almendra, 25 de Mayo ✆ 29 $9.00 ⛉
- Hospedaje Cadenas, 25 de Mayo 108 ✆ 28 $10.00 ⛉
- Hospedaje La Arboleda, Bulevar Roca Sur $10.00 ⛉
- Hospedaje Rivadavia, Avenida Rivadavia 465 ✆ 54 $10.00 ⛉

SANTIAGO DEL ESTERO

Postal code: 4200 • ✆ area code: (085) • Population: 165 000
Distance from Termas de Río Hondo: 65 km south-east on RN 9

Santiago del Estero was founded in 1553 by Capitán Don Francisco de Aguirre, coming south from Peru with settlers.

Santiago del Estero is in the southern *chaco*, on the banks of the **Río Dulce** which separates it from its twin city of La Banda. Both cities are linked by two modern bridges.

Most of the sparse rainfall occurs in January. The driest and coldest months are June, July, and August, which average 6 °C. December, January, and February are the hottest months, reaching 36 °C.

Some streets are marked "Norte" or "N" (North), "Este" or "E" (East), "Sur" or "S" (South), or "Oeste" or "O" (West), in relation to the Plaza.

The hub of the town is Plaza Libertad, flanked by the *Municipalidad* and the cathedral.

🎭 Festivals

- Carnaval de las Trincheras: A very colorful carnival celebration reminiscent of the carnival in Humahuaca in Jujuy.
- Día de la Autonomía (Independence Day), celebrated throughout the province: April 27
- Fiesta Santiago Apostol (Festival of Saint James the Apostle), The foundation day of the city, marking the start of Semana Santiago del Estero (Santiago del Estero Week): July 24. Lots of folk music

ℹ Tourist information

The tourist office, at Libertad 417 (corner of Tucumán, on the Plaza Libertad) is open 0800–2000 daily. In order to stimulate tourism in the city, the tourist office runs three free sight-seeing walking tours every day at 1000. Enquire at the Departamento de Turismo, Independencia 58, 2nd floor ✆ 211390.

SANTIAGO DEL ESTERO

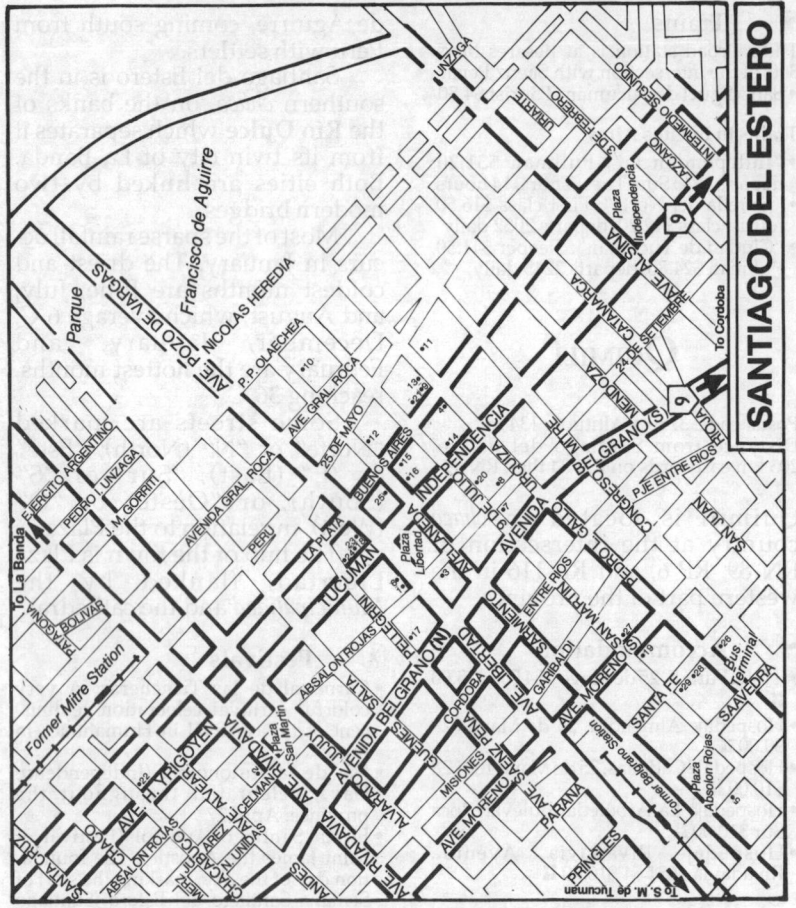

- Tour 1: Plaza Libertad, Museo Histórico (Historical Museum), and Iglesia y Convento de Santo Domingo (Dominican Church and Convent)
- Tour 2: Iglesia y Convento de San Francisco Solano (Church and Convent of Saint Francis Solano), Museo de Arte Sacro (Museum of Sacred Art), the cell of Saint Francisco de Solano, Parque Aguirre (Aguirre Park), and Museo Arqueológico Provincial (Provincial Archeological Museum)
- Tour 3: Cabildo (City Hall), cathedral, Iglesia de la Merced (Church of Mercy), Museo Andrés Chazarreta, Museo de Bellas Artes (Fine Arts Museum)

Most of these are described under "Sightseeing" below.

⛺ Camping

- Las Casuarinas, Avenida Costanera on the Río Dulce (8 blocks from the city center near Parque Aguirre)

SANTIAGO DEL ESTERO

Key to Map
1. Municipalidad
2. Casa de Gobierno
3. Catedral
4. Post office (Encotel)
5. Telephone (Entel)
6. Tourist information
7. Banco de la Nación
8. Cambio Noroeste
9. Aerolineas Argentinas
10. Iglesia y Convento de San Francisco Solano
11. Iglesia y Convento de Santo Domingo
12. Museo Arqueológico Provincial
13. Museo Histórico de la Provincia
14. Museo Provincial de Bellas Artes
15. Casa de los Taboada
16. Hotel Grand Hotel
17. Hotel Premier
18. Hotel Palace
19. Hotel Bristol
20. Hotel Centro
21. Hotel Embajador
22. Hotel Coventry
23. Hotel Florida
24. Residencial Savoy
25. Residencial City
26. Residencial Rodas
27. Residencial Iovino
28. Residencial Iovino II
29. Residencial Santa Fé

Accommodation in Santiago del Estero

★★★★	Hotel Grand Hotel, corner of Avellaneda and Independencia	214400	$40.00	
★★★	Hotel Bristol, Avenida Moreno 67	218387	$34.00	
★★★	Hotel Centro, 9 de Julio 131	214098	$34.00	
★★★	Hotel Libertador, Catamarca 47	218730	$34.00	
★★★	Hotel Palace, Avenida Tucumán 19	212700	$34.00	
★★★	Hotel Premier, Pellegrini 39 *Residencial* attached	218987	$34.00	
★★	Hotel Coventry, corner of H Irigoyen and Chacabuco	213477	$21.00	
★★	Hotel Embajador, Buenos Aires 60	214949	$21.00	
★	Hotel Florida, Libertad 355	211877	$17.00	
•	Hospedaje Palermo, Libertad 1057	213444	$9.00	
A	Residencial City, Avellaneda 278	218415	$15.00	
A	Residencial Rodas, Pedro Leon Gallo 432	219745	$15.00	
A	Residencial Savoy, Avenida Tucumán 39 Shared bathroom $13.00	211234	$15.00	
B	Residencial Iovino, Avenida Moreno (S) 602 Shared bathroom $10.00	213311	$11.00	
C	Residencial Iovino II, Santa Fé 273 Shared bathroom $9.00		$10.00	
C	Residencial Petit Colonial, La Plata 165 Shared bathroom $9.00	211261	$10.00	
C	Residencial Premier, Pellegrini 39 Annex to Hotel Premier	21488	$13.00	
•	Residencial Santa Fé, Santa Fé 255			

Santiago del Estero

Santiago del Estero

Prime location. Run by the town council.

🍴 Eating out

- Restaurant Florida, Hotel Florida, Libertad 355
- Restaurant Gran Hotel, Independencia block 100 (corner of Avellaneda)
- Restaurant Halley, corner of Pedro Gallo and Entre Rios. Credit cards
- Restaurant Jockey Club, Independencia block 0 (corner of Libertad)
- ☞ Restaurant Los Pinos, 9 de Julio block 300 (corner of 25 de Mayo)
- Restaurant Marqués, corner of Avellaneda and Belgrano (S)
- ☞ Restaurant Tartufo, corner of Oleachea and Mitre
- Pizzería Casullo, San Martín block 0 (corner of Avenida Roca)
- Pizzería El Toldito, corner of Belgrano (S) and San Martín
- Pizzería La Boca, Pellegrini 268
- Pizzería La Merced, corner of Belgrano (S) and 9 de Julio
- Pizzería La Tarantella, corner of Moreno (S) and Sarmiento
- Pizzería Napoli, Galería Leonardo, A Rojas block 100 (corner of Libertad)
- Pizzería Pica, corner of Rivadavia Oeste and Perú
- Pizzería Sissy, Avenida H Yrigoyen 499
- Cafetería Avestruz, Avellaneda block 100 (corner of Independencia)
- Cafetería Chachara, Sarmiento block 0 (corner of Begrano South)
- Cafetería Ciros Dos, corner of Alsina and Independencia
- Cafetería Espartago, Avellaneda 248
- Cafetería Felipe, corner of Belgrano (S) and Libertad
- Cafetería H P, corner of Belgrano (S) and Urquiza. Open 24 hours
- Cafetería La Cafetera, Libertad block 400 (corner of Avenida Tucumán)
- Cafetería La Esquina, Avenida Tucumán block 300 (corner of Salta)
- Cafetería Premier, Hotel Premier, Pellegrini 39
- Cafetería Sam Café, Avellaneda 17
- Cafetería Scorpio, corner of Avenida Alsina and Belgrano
- Cafetería Shopping, Córdoba block 0 (corner of Libertad)
- ☞ Cafetería Siglo XX, Avellaneda block 100 (corner of Independencia)
- ☞ Cafetería Sossegos, corner of Belgrano (S) and Libertad
- Chopería Noesigual, A Rojas 327. Pizzas
- Chopería Popeye, Avellaneda block 200 (corner of Buenos Aires)

✉ Post and telegraph

- Post office: Encotel, Buenos Aires 350

Telephones

- Entel, corner of Mendoza and Independencia
- Entel, Avenida Colón block 500 (corner of San Martín, near Plaza Absalon Rojas)

$ Financial

- Banco Financiero Argentina, 24 de Setiembre 256. Exchange
- Cambio Noroeste, 24 de Setiembre 220

🛄 Services and facilities

- Dry-cleaner: Don Quijote de la Mancha, Córdoba 30

Laundromats

- Laverap, 9 de Julio 173. Open every day
- Laverap, Independencia 267. Open every day

Supermarkets

- Centro, Pellegrini block 200 (corner of Avellaneda)
- T I A, A Rojas block 100 (corner of Salta)

C Clubs

- Spanish: Sociedad Española, Independencia block 200 (corner of 9 de Julio) 🍴

✈ Air services

The Aerolineas Argentinas office is on the corner of Buenos Aires and Avellaneda (213300.

- Buenos Aires (Aeroparque Jorge Newbery): Fare $71.00; departs 1240 daily; 2 hours; Aerolineas Argentinas

Santiago del Estero

🚌 Motoring

Service stations
- ACA, corner of Avenida Belgrano (S) and Sáenz Peña
- Esso, corner of Rivadavia (O) and Belgrano

🚆 Trains

Both the F C General M Belgrano and the F C General B Mitre stations in Santiago have been closed for passenger services. All trains to and from Buenos Aires arrive and depart from La Banda, located just across the Río Sali. There are regular municipal bus services for the 20 minute trip between the two cities.

🚍 Buses from Santiago del Estero

The bus terminal is located on the corner of Pedro El Gallo and Saavedra; it has a post office and a cloakroom. Local buses to La Banda for trains to Buenos Aires leave from platform 49.

Destination	Fare	Depart	Services	Hours	Company
• Añatuya		0430	4 services daily	4	Sol
• Buenos Aires	$22.00			17	T A Chevallier
	$22.30	1710	1 service daily	18	La Unión
• Córdoba	$9.50	0010	6 services daily	7	Cacorba, T A Chevallier
• Corrientes	$10.80	1230	3 services daily	12	El Rayo
• Frías	$2.80	1400	daily	2	T A Libertador
• La Banda	$0.15	every 20 minutes		½	municipal bus
• La Rioja		1400	Sun–Tue, Thu, Fri	7½	T A Libertador
• Mailín		1045	Mon, Sat	3	Sol
• Mar del Plata		1400	daily		La Estrella
• Mendoza		1400	Mon, Wed, Thu, Fri, Sun	17½	TA Libertador
• Paraná		2157	daily		La Estrella
• Posadas		0038	Wed, Fri, Sun		Cotal
• Presidencia Roque Sáenz Peña	$7.60	2130	daily	9	El Rayo
• Puerto Iguazú		0038	Wed, Fri–Sun 1–2 services daily		Cotal
• Resistencia	$10.50	1230	3 services daily	11½	El Rayo
• Rosario		1710	3 services daily		La Unión, T A Chevallier
• Salta		0445	3 services daily		Panamericano
• San Fernando del Valle de Catamarca	$5.50	0530	3 services daily	5½	Bosio, Coop Catamarca
• San Juan		1400	Mon, Wed–Fri, Sun	15	TA Libertador
• San Miguel de Tucumán	$2.80	0530	24 services daily	2	El Rayo, El Santiagueño, La Estrella, La Unión
	$3.00	0630	5 services daily	2	El Ranchilleno
• San Salvador de Jujuy		0445	3 services daily		Panamerican
• Santa Fé		2157	daily		La Estrella
• Sumampa	$4.00	1130	Mon, Wed, Fri	4	Cacorba
• Termas de Río Hondo	$1.30	0430	29 services daily	2	El Ranchilleño, El Rayo, La Estrella, La Unión, T A Libertador

Santiago del Estero

SANTIAGO DEL ESTERO

⊕ **Tours**
- Estero Tour, 24 de Setiembre 220

🛍 **Shopping**
- Centro de Artesanías Santiagueñas (Santiago Craft Center), Avenida Roca block 800 (corner of Urquiza)

🍸 **Entertainment**
- Disco Safari, 9 de Julio block 0 (corner of 24 de Setiembre)

📷 **Sightseeing**

Museums

- Museo Arqueológica Provincial (Provincial Archeological Museum), Avellaneda 355, has many objects, mostly pottery, from the *Santiagueña* pre-Columbian cultures such as the Mercedes culture, which flouriched between 400 and 700 AD. This culture lived on rivers and *lagunas* and buried their dead in urns or directly in the soil. Their remains include flint and bone implements used for agriculture and fishing. The Medio period is represented by the Sunchituyoj culture, which flourished between 800 and 1100 AD, and whose members engaged in agriculture and fishing, and domesticated animals. The Tardio period is represented by the Averias culture, which flourished between 1100 and 1500 AD, and whose members buried their dead in urns. Rock paintings near Ojo de Agua, Las Mangas, Pozo Grande, El Cajón, Barrealito, and La Pitada are reproduced in displays. Open Mon–Fri 0700–1300 and 1700–1930, Sat 0930–1200
- Museo Histórico de la Provincia (Museum of Provincial History), Urquiza 354, located in the former mansion of the Díaz Gallo family. A window into the past, it displays meticulously arranged furniture in its rooms. This museum is a jewel of Spanish colonial art. Open Mon–Fri 0800–1200 and 1530–1830, Sat 0800–1200
- Museo Provincial de Bellas Artes (Provincial Fine Arts Museum), Independencia 222. Soldi, Policastro, and Spilimbergo are just a few of the artists on display
- Museo Andres Chazarreta (Andres Chazarreta Museum), Mitre 127 (corner of 24 de Setiembre). The house of the former researcher into Argentine folklore
- Casa de los Tobeada, a colonial mansion belonging to the Tobeada family

Churches

- Iglesia La Merced (Church of Mercy), corner of 24 de Setiembre and Urquiza. The insignia for the transmission of authority in the province are kept in this church
- Iglesia y Convento de San Francisco Solano (Church and Convent of Saint Francis Solano), Avenida Roca (S) 716 (corner of Avellaneda). The oldest part of this convent dates back to 1566. The church was founded in 1590 by San Francisco Solano,

Santiago del Estero

Santiago del Estero

patron saint of Tucumán. Over the centuries the original church and convent underwent substanial alterations and additions. Inside the Convent is the Museo de Arte Religioso (Museum of Religious Art), which possesses religious objects pertaining to Saint Francisco Solano who used to preach here. The tour culminates with a visit to the cell which was occupied by the saint
- Catedral, 24 de Setiembre 55 (corner of Libertad). Erected in 1876 on the spot where the first church in Argentina was built in 1581. It was also the first bishopric in Argentina. The new Corinthian-style temple was built by the Italian Agustin Canepa in 1876. All in all there were five churches built on this spot
- Iglesia y Convento de Santo Domingo (Dominican Church and Convent), corner of 25 de Mayo and Urquiza. A copy of the Holy Shroud of Turin is kept here, donated by King Phillip II as a royal gesture to his American colonies
- Capilla de la Montanera, corner of Catamarca and 24 de Setiembre. Chapel of the patron saint of the brotherhood of the Montaneros, founded by the veterans of the battle at Pozo de Vargas

Parks

- Parque Francisco de Aguirre, on the river banks with huge old trees. The municipal swimming pool is here
- Across from the Convento de San Francisco de Solano there is a small zoo in the park and a monument built in honour of Saint Francisco Solano

Excursions

- **Córdoba**: The trip south to Cordoba on RN 9 goes through *chaco* country with shrubs and small trees on either side of the road, interrupted occasionally by a *hacienda* building. The country is quite flat. After **Monte Redondo** the road traverses the **Salinas de Ambargasta** and **Río Saladillo** for the next 59 km. The road is elevated to prevent flooding when the rivers rise. A low mountain range, the **Sierra de Ambargasta**, can be seen to the west. Shortly afterwards the **Sierra de Sumampa**, also very low, comes into view. At the intersection with RN 98 is **Villa Ojo de Agua**, a small *chaco* town with a hotel-restaurant and an ACA service station. Here is the turn-off to **Sumampa**, where there is a much venerated shrine which attracts many pilgrims; see "Excursions" in Sumampa on page 710. After crossing into Córdoba province the country becomes hillier and greener, with clusters of palm trees, as the road winds through the little mountains. There are few homesteads in sight. Before arrival in Villa de María mountains can be seen on the eastern

Santiago del Estero

and southern horizon. Most of the trip goes through semi-arid country with long, straight stretches of road along the **Sierras de Córdoba** in the west. Only just before Córdoba does the country become greener again. The road is sealed all the way from Santiago del Estero to the city of Córdoba
- Termas de Río Hondo: See Termas de Río Hondo below
- Sumampa: see Sumumpa below

SUMAMPA

Postal code: 4201 • Altitude: 244 m
Distance from Santiago del Estero: 240 km southwards on RN 9 then RP 13

Originally a Jesuit mission, Sumampa is located to the east of the **Sierra de Sumampa**, a low mountain range. One of the original landholders was of Portuguese origin. He asked for an image of the Holy Virgin to be sent from Brazil in 1630, and built the original chapel to house it. The existing church construction dates from 1720 and was built by landholder Saa.

Festivals
- Fiesta de la Virgen de la Consolación de Sumampa: September 11-26. Thousands of pilgrims flock to this sanctuary and hotels are completely booked out. See "Excursions" below

Accommodation
C Residencial Nuevo Sumampa, Avenida San Martín $10.00

- Hospedaje La Negrita, Avenida San Martín $9.00
- Hospedaje El Amanecer $9.00
- Hospedaje Imperio, Avenida San Martín $9.00
- Hospedaje Spedale $4.50. Breakfast included. Señor Spedale also escorts tourists to the rock paintings at Piedras Pintados

Buses
- Santiago del Estero: fare $4.00; 2 services daily; Empresa La Unión
- Córdoba: Departs 0730 daily; Empresa Cacorba

Excursions
- Santuario de la Virgen de Nuestra Señora de la Consolación (Sanctuary of the Virgin of Our Lady of Consolation): This much-venerated shrine, 3 km east of Sumampa at Sumampa Viejo, attracts thousands of pilgrims every September. Thermal springs form a large rockpool just in front of the church
- **Piedras Pintadas** (Painted Rocks): 3 km past the church, in scrub country. The area was settled in pre-Columbian times by Indian tribes who left many rock paintings all over the Sierra de Sumampa. A bit disappointing, however, and only of interest to archeology buffs

TERMAS DE RÍO HONDO

Postal code: 4220 • Population: 20 000 • area code: (0858) • Altitude: 265 m
Distances
- From Santiago del Estero: 65 km northwest on RN 9

SANTIAGO DEL ESTERO

- From San Miguel de Tucumán: 90 km south-east on RN 9

Termas de Río Hondo is located on the **Río Dulce**, which was dammed 4 km below the city in 1966 to create **Embalse Río Hondo**. The surface of the lake covers 33 000 ha. The dam is 30 m high and over 4 km long.

The location was known to the Indians as "miraculous hot waters". These hot springs intrigued the pre-Columbian Indians as well as the new Spanish arrivals. It is known that the area was settled by an aboriginal population 2000 years ago. Around 500 AD the Mercedes culture, best identified by its painted pottery, developed on both sides of the Río Dulce. Several Spanish families settled in the Termas de Río Hondo area but not much has come down to us from the colonial period. Its rise to fame began in 1914 when the first modest pensions were opened. Another milestone was the opening of the casino in 1928, when a railroad was completed.

During the winter months, which is the tourist high season, the town boasts a cultural program, staged in the Centro Cultural San Martín (San Martín Cultural Center).

Termas de Río Hondo sits on fourteen different layers of thermal waters ranging from 30 to 65 °C. The curative water is recommended for high blood pressure and rheumatism. All public swimming pools contain thermal water.

The town has excellent tourist facilities, with more than 150 hotels, including three four-star hotels. Road transport is concentrated in a modern bus terminal, where there are departures and arrivals on a twenty-four hour basis.

The nearby lake lends itself to practice sailing, fishing, and windsurfing.

The district's climate is subtropical.

Festivals
- International sailing competition organized by Club Náutico: August
- Motorboat racing competition: May

Tourist information
- Dirección Municipal de Turismo, Caseros 132 (21571
- Delegación Provincial de Turismo, J B Alberdí 245 (21571

Camping
- ACA Buenos Aires, on the northern side of the river near the dam, 3 km from the city. Thermal water
- El Mirador, corner of RN 9 and Urquiza (21392. Thermal spring
- La Olla, corner of H Yrigoyen and RN 9. Thermal water. Tent $1.00
- Municipal, corner of H Yrigoyen and RN 9. Thermal water. Cabin $2.00; tent $1.00

Eating out
Termas Río Hondo is famous for *alfajores*, or sweets.

Open all year round
- Restaurant Almada, corner of Fleming and Pasaje Besares. Local cuisine
- Restaurant Club Náutico, at the dam. Seafood
- Restaurant El Cóndor, corner of San Martín and Fleming

Termas de Río Hondo

Santiago del Estero

Key to Map

1	Municipalidad	45	Hotel San Carlos
2	Iglesia	46	Hotel San Remo
3	Post office (Encotel)	47	Hotel Suiza
4	Telephone (Entel)	48	Hotel Venezia
5	Tourist information	49	Residencial Austral
6	Banco de la Nación	50	Residencial Bitar
9	Casino	51	Residencial Charito
10	Hotel Los Pinos	52	Residencial Hurlingham
11	Hotel Grand Hotel	53	Residencial Inti Yacu
12	Hotel Grand Palace	56	Residencial Lancaster
13	Hotel Ambassador	57	Residencial Madrid
14	Hotel América	58	Residencial Malibu
16	Hotel Eduardo V	59	Residencial Michel
17	Hotel El Hostal del Sol	60	Residencial Mi Casita
18	Hotel Nuevo Río Hondo	61	Residencial Monaco
19	Hotel Termal Río Hondo	62	Residencial Namuncura
20	Hotel Borelli	64	Residencial Peña
21	Hotel Castelar	65	Residencial Provincial
22	Hotel Cervantes	66	Residencial Rosita
23	Hotel Dora	67	Residencial San Francisco
24	Hotel Jonathan	68	Residencial Santa Clara
25	Hotel Los Felipe	69	Residencial Sarmiento
26	Hotel Gran Hotel Los Incas	70	Residencial Savoy
27	Hotel Mar del Plata	71	Residencial Sevilla
28	Hotel Nuevo Emperatriz	72	Residencial Alicia
29	Hotel Premier	73	Residencial Bariloche
30	Hotel San Lorenzo	74	Residencial Daives
31	Hotel Semiramis	75	Residencial Pucara
32	Hotel Shalotel	76	Residencial Sierras
33	Hotel Termas Naranjo	77	Residencial Telma
34	Hotel Bilbao	78	Residencial Alemar
35	Hotel City	79	Residencial Christy
36	Hotel Enricar	80	Residencial La Perla
37	Hotel Florida	81	Residencial Messina
38	Hotel Gran Habana	82	Residencial Norma
39	Hotel Los Olivos	83	Residencial Petit Colonial
40	Hotel Majestic	84	Residencial San Juan
41	Hotel Miami	85	Pension Graciela
42	Hotel Miramar	86	Pension La Esperanza
43	Hotel Patric	87	Pension La Morocha
44	Hotel Roma	88	Hospedaje Elsita
		89	Hospedaje Luis I
		90	Hospedaje Rumania

- ☞ • Restaurant El Rancho de Doña María, corner of J B Alberdí and H Yrigoyen. Steaks
- Restaurant El Timón, F Solano 167. International cuisine
- Restaurant Hotel América. International cuisine
- Restaurant La Cabaña de los Changos, corner of Libertad and J B Alberdí. Local cuisine; steaks
- Restaurant La Estancia, J B Alberdí. Local cuisine; steaks
- Restaurant La Huerta, Sarmiento block 100 (corner of J B Justo). Vegetarian
- Restaurant La Recova, Sarmiento 44

Termas de Río Hondo

SANTIAGO DEL ESTERO

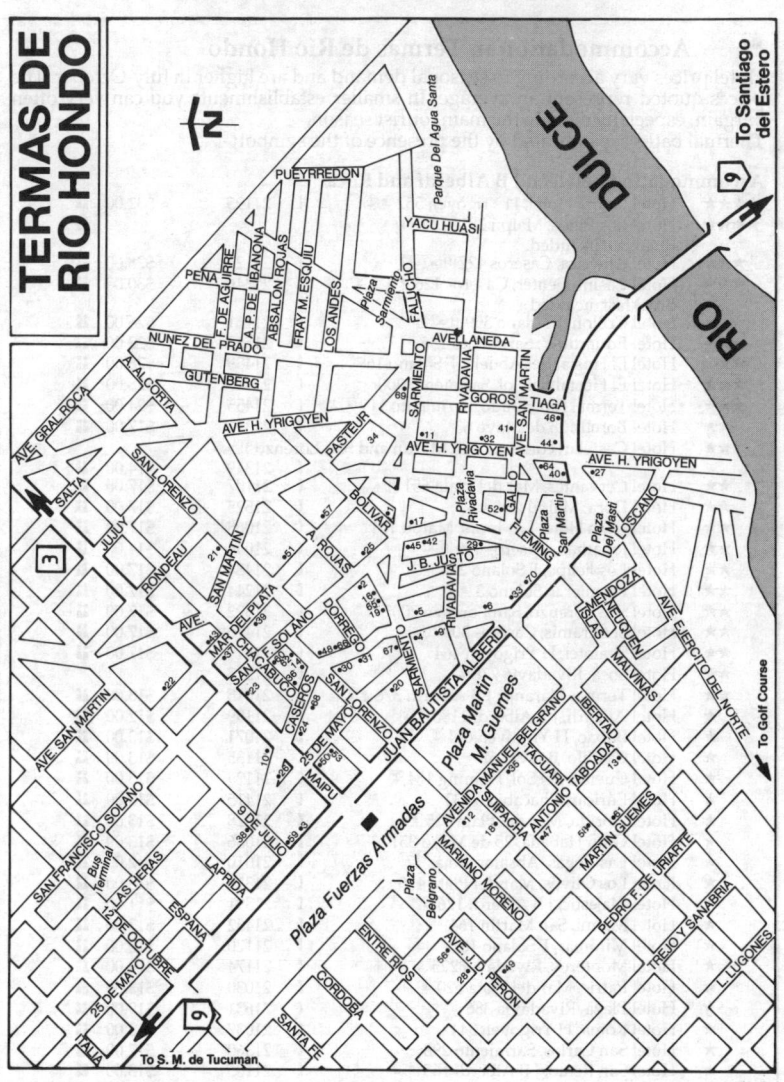

- Restaurant Las Brasas, J B Alberdí 576. Steaks
- Restaurant Los Gallegos, corner of Maipú and J B Alberdí. International cuisine
- Restaurant Monaco, Güemes 390

Coninued on page 715

Termas de Río Hondo

Santiago del Estero

🛏 Accommodation in Termas de Río Hondo

Hotel prices vary according to seasonal demand and are higher in July-October. The prices quoted represent an average. In smaller establishments you can very often bargain, especially outside the main tourist season.
Thermal baths are indicated by the presence of the symbol ♨.

Accommodation between J B Alberdí and Roca

★★★★	Hotel Grand Hotel, H Yrigoyen 552	(	21195	$32.00	♂♀
★★★★	Hotel Los Pinos, Maipú 201				♂♀
	Breakfast included				
★★★	Hotel América, Caseros 422	(	21123	$28.00	♂♀
★★★	Hotel Casino Center, Caseros 126	(	21346	$30.00	♂♀
	Breakfast included				
★★★	Hotel Crillon, F Solano 399	(	21161	$26.00	♂♀
★★★	Hotel Eduardo V, Sarmiento 135	(	21555	$22.00	♂♀
★★★	Hotel El Hostal del Abuelo, F Solano 168	(	21489	$28.00	♂♀
★★★	Hotel El Hostal del Sol, Sarmiento 300	(	21020	$28.00	♂♀
★★★	Hotel Termal Río Hondo, Sarmiento 119	(	21455	$24.00	♂♀
★★	Hotel Borelli, 25 de Mayo 63	(	21310	$17.00	♂♀
★★	Hotel Castelar, corner of San Martín and San Lorenzo				
		(	21349	$14.00	♂♀
★★	Hotel Cervantes, Mar del Plata 651	(	21107	$17.00	♂♀
★★	Hotel Dora, Maipú 264	(	21525	$17.00	♂♀
★★	Hotel Gran Hotel Los Incas, Maipú 101	(	21068	$17.00	♂♀
★★	Hotel Jonathan, Caseros 459	(	21044	$14.00	♂♀
★★	Hotel Los Felipe, F Solano 230	(	21484	$17.00	♂♀
★★	Hotel Premier, F Solano 3	(	21244	$17.00	♂♀
★★	Hotel San Lorenzo, San Lorenzo 200	(	21322	$17.00	♂♀
★★	Hotel Semiramis, Caseros 303	(	21416	$17.00	♂♀
★★	Hotel Shalotel, H Yrigoyen 464	(	21619	$17.00	♂♀
★★	Hotel Sosa, Rivadavia 778	(	21213		
★★	Hotel Termas Naranjo, J B Alberdí 378	(	21015	$13.00	♂♀
★	Hotel Alberdí, J B Alberdí 1180	(	21199	$12.00	♂♀
★	Hotel Bilbao, H Yrigoyen 641	(	21071	$13.00	♂♀
★	Hotel Castillo, Bolívar 67	(	21135	$13.00	♂♀
★	Hotel Cuenca del Sol, Fleming 184	(	21129	$13.00	♂♀
★	Hotel Enricar, Chacabuco 232	(	21415	$13.00	♂♀
★	Hotel Florida, Mar del Plata 515	(	21228	$13.00	♂♀
★	Hotel Gran Habana, 25 de Mayo 351	(	21086	$13.00	♂♀
★	Hotel Las Vegas, Absalon Rojas 17	(	21010	$12.00	♂♀
★	Hotel Los Olivos, Mar del Plata 455	(	21313	$13.00	♂♀
★	Hotel Majestic, J B Alberdí 126	(	21391	$11.00	♂♀
★	Hotel Miami, San Martín 164	(	21452	$13.00	♂♀
★	Hotel Miramar, F Solano 181	(	21120	$16.00	♂♀
★	Hotel Monterey, Rivadavia 225	(	21174	$19.00	♂♀
★	Hotel Patric, Mar del Plata 520	(	21030	$13.00	♂♀
★	Hotel Plaza, Rivadavia 386	(	21631	$19.00	♂♀
★	Hotel Roma, H Yrigoyen 344	(	21037	$13.00	♂♀
★	Hotel San Carlos, Sarmiento 298	(	21360	$12.00	♂♀
★	Hotel San Remo, J B Alberdí 165	(	21105	$13.00	♂♀
★	Hotel Victoria, Mar del Plata 251	(	21421	$13.00	♂♀
★	Hotel Venezia, Caseros 396	(	21480	$14.00	♂♀
•	Hospedaje Constanzo, Mar del Plata 512	(	21272		
•	Hospedaje El Alto, J B Alberdí 1200			$7.00	♂♀
•	Hospedaje Esquiú, Fray M Esquiú 125			$7.00	♂♀

Termas de Río Hondo

Santiago del Estero

Accommodation in Termas de Río Hondo—continued

Accommodation between J B Alberdí and Roca–continued

	• Hospedaje Gorostiaga, Gorostiaga 54		$7.00	
	• Hospedaje Luis I, Alberdí block 800 (corner of Laprida)		$7.00	
	• Hospedaje Rumania, corner of 12 de Octubre and Las Heras (near bus terminal)		$7.00	
	• Hospedaje Santa Rita, Caseros 451	21240	$7.00	
A	Residencial Bitar, 25 de Mayo 181	21344	$11.00	
A	Residencial Bristol, Rivadavia 300	21039	$11.00	
A	Residencial California, Pasaje Dorrego 47	21343	$11.00	
A	Residencial Chabe Ross, J B Justo 89	21381	$11.00	
A	Residencial Charito, Mar del Plata 376	21034	$11.00	
A	Residencial Florencia, corner of J B Alberdí and Italia	21095	$9.00	
A	Residencial Hurlingham, P L Gallo 116	21006	$11.00	
A	Residencial Insua, N Avellaneda 174	21402	$11.00	
A	Residencial Inti Yacu, 25 de Mayo 171			
A	Residencial Iruña, Pasaje Dorrego 49	21232	$10.00	
A	Residencial Italia, Rivadavia 747	21004	$11.00	
A	Residencial Jímenez, P L Gallo 28	21490	$11.00	
A	Residencial La Loma, J B Alberdí 296	21212	$16.00	
A	Residencial Lencina, Pasaje Dorrego 23	21251	$11.00	
A	Residencial Madrid, Mar del Plata 258	21080	$11.00	
A	Residencial Mi Casita, Chacabuco 255	21157	$11.00	
A	Residencial Michel, J B Alberdí 780	21396	$12.00	
A	Residencial Namuncura, San Lorenzo 255	21006	$11.00	
A	Residencial Norte, Sarmiento 423	21776	$11.00	
A	Residencial Peña, corner of San Martín and Fleming	21182	$11.00	
A	Residencial Provincial, Sarmiento 127		$10.00	
A	Residencial Rosita, Caseros 346 (corner of Dorrego)		$14.00	
A	Residencial San Francisco, Sarmiento 75	21160	$11.00	
A	Residencial Santa Clara, Caseros 457	21178	$11.00	
A	Residencial Sarmiento, Sarmiento 555	21214	$11.00	
A	Residencial Savoy, J B Alberdí 340	21404	$11.00	
A	Residencial Sipos, Rivadavia 812	21409	$11.00	
B	Residencial Bariloche, Chacabuco 45	21462	$9.00	
B	Residencial Daives, Sarmiento 521	21076	$9.00	
B	Residencial Fleming, Fleming 53	21181	$9.00	
B	Residencial Pucara, J B Alberdí 956	21734	$9.00	
B	Residencial Rivadavia, Rivadavia 320	21003	$9.00	
B	Residencial Telma, San Lorenzo 267		$9.00	
B	Residencial Tío Albert, Absalon Rojas 32	21708	$9.00	
C	Residencial Agua Santa, Yacu Huasi 55		$7.00	
C	Residencial Alemar, España 152, near bus terminal	21349	$7.00	
C	Residencial Amalia, Tacuari 141		$7.00	
C	Residencial California, Sarmiento 167		$7.00	

Termas de Río Hondo

SANTIAGO DEL ESTERO

Accommodation in Termas de Río Hondo—continued

Accommodation between J B Alberdí and Roca–continued

C	Residencial Christy, P L Gallo 122	21072	$7.00	
C	Residencial Claudy, Pasteur 36		$7.00	
C	Residencial El Coya, Absalon Rojas 20	21492	$7.00	
C	Residencial Gloria, Absalon Rojas 435		$7.00	
C	Residencial La Perla, San Martín 328	21329	$7.00	
C	Residencial Marta, Fray M Esquiú 135		$7.00	
C	Residencial Messina, San Lorenzo 147		$7.00	
C	Residencial Perez, Fleming 35	21074	$7.00	
C	Residencial Petit Colonial, Chacabuco 328		$7.00	
C	Residencial Roberto, Nuñez del Prado 233		$7.00	
C	Residencial San Juan, 25 de Mayo 167		$7.00	
B	Pension Graciela, San Lorenzo 69	21363	$8.00	
B	Pension La Esperanza, 9 de Julio 102	21242	$8.00	
B	Pension La Reyna, Fray M Esquiú 127		$8.00	
B	Pension Parsado, P L Gallo 33	21305	$8.00	
B	Pension Villa Lourdes, Chacabuco 403		$8.00	
A	Apart Hotel Aranjuez, J B Alberdí 280	21108	$16.00	
A	Apart Hotel Dora, Chacabuco 267	21525	$13.00	
A	Apart Hotel La Recova, Sarmiento 44	21208	$16.00	
A	Apart Hotel Paz, Bolivar 117	21641	$14.00	
A	Apart Hotel Phinos, Caseros 186	21353	$15.00	
A	Apart Hotel Siglo VI, F Solano 256	21719	$16.00	
B	Apart Hotel Carlitos, Sarmiento 21	21775	$11.00	
B	Apart Hotel Continental, Sarmiento 531 (corner of H Yrigoyen)		$11.00	
B	Apart Hotel Coria, A Rojas 153			
B	Apart Hotel Elba, Rivadavia 742	21733	$11.00	
B	Apart Hotel Juárez, F Solano 371	21378	$11.00	
B	Apart Hotel Victor Hugo, Absalon Rojas 57		$11.00	
C	Apart Hotel Salvatierra, Absalon Rojas 152		$8.00	
C	Apart Hotel Tío Cotelesso, Nuñez del Prado 248		$8.00	

Accommodation between J B Alberdí and Pedro F Uriarte

★★★★	Hotel Grand Palace, Belgrano 367	21089	$32.00	
★★★	Hotel Ambassador, Libertad 184	21196	$28.00	
★★★	Hotel Nuevo Río Hondo, Suipacha 77	21113	$26.00	
★★	Hotel Mar del Plata, H Yrigoyen 289	21124	$15.00	
★★	Hotel Nuevo Emperatriz, Juan D Perón 132			
		21746	$19.00	
★	Hotel City, Belgrano 245	21018	$13.00	
★	Hotel Haway, Islas Malvinas 448	21115	$11.00	
★	Hotel Suiza, A Tabaoda 399	21128	$13.00	
•	Hospedaje Chochita, Ejercito del Norte 425		$7.00	
•	Hospedaje Danielito, Ejercito del Norte 600			
•	Hospedaje Elsita, Ejercito del Norte 445		$7.00	
•	Hospedaje Los Patos, Juan D Perón 673			
•	Hospedaje Richard, Ejercito del Norte 321		$7.00	
•				

Termas de Río Hondo

SANTIAGO DEL ESTERO

Accommodation in Termas de Río Hondo—continued

Accommodation between J B Alberdí and Pedro F Uriarte—continued

A	Residencial Austral, M Güemes 687	(21495	$11.00	♝
A	Residencial Lancaster, Juan D Perón 100	(21319	$11.00	♝
A	Residencial Malibu, Tacuari 148	(21481	$11.00	♝
A	Residencial Monaco, M Güemes 360	(21523	$13.00	♝
A	Residencial Sevilla, Libertad 80	(21246	$11.00	♝
B	Residencial Alicia, Ejercito del Norte	(21009	$9.00	♝
B	Residencial Gallo Blanco, A Taboada 649	(21101	$9.00	♝
B	Residencial Sierras, Suipacha 287	(21130	$9.00	♝
C	Residencial Amalia, Tacuari 141		$7.00	♝
C	Residencial Las Brisas, M Güemes 669		$7.00	♝
C	Residencial Norma, Ejercito del Norte 421		$7.00	♝
B	Pension La Morocha, Ejercito del Norte 245		$8.00	♝
A	Apart Hotel Anush, Libertad 37	(21607	$12.00	♝
A	Apart Hotel Atenas, Juan D Perón 267	(21834	$12.00	♝
A	Apart Hotel Gulfi, Belgrano 287	(21158	$14.00	♝
A	Apart Hotel Ka Ri Ve, Belgrano 161	(21042	$11.00	♝
A	Apart Hotel Oasis, Belgrano 153		$12.00	♝
A	Apart Hotel Río Dulce, corner of Belgrano 195 and Tacuari	(21208	$16.00	♝
B	Apart Hotel El Parque, corner of Belgrano and Libertad	(21673	$11.00	♝
B	Apart Hotel Maranatha, H Yrigoyen 249	(21553	$10.00	♝
B	Apart Hotel Mary, M Güemes 752	(21388	$11.00	♝
B	Apart Hotel Moreno, Juan D Perón 237		$11.00	♝
B	Apart Hotel Rojas, Tacuari 183		$11.00	♝
B	Apart Hotel San Antonio, Belgrano 12	(21781	$11.00	♝
B	Apart Hotel San Javier del Valle, M Güemes 376	(21045	$11.00	♝
B	Apart Hotel Sheraton, Pedro F Uriarte 695		$11.00	♝
C	Apart Hotel Belgrano, Belgrano 485		$8.00	♝
C	Apart Hotel Elisa, Islas Malvinas 452	(21193	$8.00	♝
C	Apart Hotel Gianelli, Juan D Perón 250		$8.00	♝
C	Apart Hotel Güemes, M Güemes 394		$8.00	♝
C	Apart Hotel Santa Tecla, Tacuari 160			

- Restaurant Namuncura, J B Alberdí, Villa Balnearia district. Local cuisine
- Restaurant Nido del Condor, San Martín 485. Local cuisine
- Restaurant Patricios, Gorrostiaga 168. Steaks
- Restaurant Pizzalandia, corner of F Solano and Rivadavia
- Restaurant Pub del 40, Caseros block 0 (corner of Rivadavia)
- Restaurant Punto y Banca, España 152. Local cuisine
- Restaurant Rancho de Doña María, J B Alberdí 130. Local cuisine
- Restaurant Sabut, Caseros 66. Pastas
- Restaurant San Remo, San Martín 439
- Restaurant Sandra, J B Alberdí 1100 (corner of 12 de Octubre). Local cuisine; goat meat
- Restaurant Sarita, Pasaje Carlos Gardel. Local cuisine; steaks

Termas de Río Hondo

Santiago del Estero

- Pizzería El Ultimo Café, corner of Laprida and J B Alberdí
- Pizzería La Ponderosa, corner of España and 25 de Mayo
- Pizzería Los Inmortales, Caseros 26
- Pizzería Río, corner of J B Alberdí and Libertad
- Pizzería San Cayetano, Tacuari 149
- ☞ Pizzería Sandra, J B Alberdí block 1000 (corner of 12 de Octubre)
- Cafetería Aranjuez, corner of J B Alberdí and Pasaje Correa
- Cafetería Avenida, corner of San Martín and Rivadavia
- Cafetería El Cortijo, Hotel Los Pinos, Maipú 201. Snack bar
- Cafetería Jockey Club, Caseros block 100 (corner of Rivadavia)
- Cafetería La Placita, corner of Rivadavia and F Solano
- Cafetería La Posta del Viajante, corner of J B Alberdí and Maipú
- Cafetería Lajta Sumay, corner of Libertad and J B Alberdí, in the park
- Cafetería Santa Rita, corner of F Solano and Rivadavia

Open only during the tourist season

- Restaurant Don Quijote, corner of Sarmiento and Caseros. International cuisine; pastas
- Restaurant El Chivito, F Solano 154. Local cuisine; goat meat
- Restaurant El Gran Sergio, H Yrigoyen. Local cuisine
- Restaurant El Indio, J B Alberdí. Local cuisine
- Restaurant El Rey de la Parrilla, Gorostiaga 188. Local cuisine; steaks
- Restaurant La Cacerola, Caseros 124. Pizzería
- Restaurant La Casa de Don Avila, Belgrano 143. Local cuisine
- Restaurant La Huerta, corner of Sarmiento and J B Justo. Vegetarian
- Restaurant Naturalia, Rivadavia 380. Vegetarian
- Restaurant San Cayetano, Sarmiento 69. Steakhouse

Post and telegraph

- Post office: Encotel, corner of J B Alberdí and 9 de Julio
- Telephone: Entel, corner of Caseros and Sarmiento

Services and facilities

- Bicycle hire: corner of M Moreno and A Taboada ($0.75 per hour)
- Dentist: Dr Daives, Sarmiento 507 ☏ 21270
- Dry-cleaner: Yokohama, corner of Sarmiento and J B Justo
- Pharmacy: Del Pino, Rivadavia 736 ☏ 21717
- Supermarket: Oasis, corner of Sarmiento and Gorrostiaga

C | Clubs

- Centro Cultural San Martín (San Martín Cultural Centre), corner of Suipacha and Belgrano

Air services

All air services are via Santiago del Estero or San Miguel de Tucumán. See "Air services" on pages 704 and 598.
- Aerolineas Argentinas, Hotel Casino Center, Caseros 126
- Austral, Sarmiento 115 ☏ 21588

Motoring

RN 9 from Termas de Río Hondo to Santiago del Estero is sealed all the way.
- Service station: YPF, corner of Alberdí and Chacabuco

Tours

Tour operators

- Excursiones Arias, Sarmiento 138 ☏ 21493
- Turismo Vega, Rivadavia 515

Tours

- Santiago del Estero: Half-day tour; fare $3.50; departs 1400 daily
- San Fernando del Valle de Catamarca: Full-day tour; fare $13.00 (including lunch); departs 0700 daily
- San Miguel de Tucumán: Full-day tour; fare $8.00 (including lunch); departs 0800 daily
- Tafí del Valle: Full-day tour, fare $10.00 (including lunch); departs 0800 daily

Termas de Río Hondo

SANTIAGO DEL ESTERO

🚌 Buses from Termas de Río Hondo

The bus terminal is at the corner of Las Heras and 12 de Octubre, eight blocks from the city center.

Destination	Fare	Depart	Services	Hours	Company
• Santiago del Estero	$1.30	0605	26 services daily	1½	El Ranchilleño, El Rayo, La Unión
	$1.40	1230	3 services daily	1½	La Estrella, T A Libertador
• Buenos Aires	$22.50	1410	2 services daily	17	Chevallier
	$19.00	1600	1 service daily	19½	La Unión
	$22.00	1800	Wed, Sat	18½	La Unión
• Córdoba	$10.50	1410	2 services daily	7	Chevallier
	$10.50	0130	6 services daily	8	Panamericano
• Corrientes	$12.00	2020	1 service daily	13	El Rayo
• Frías	$4.00	1230	daily	3½	T A Libertador
• La Rioja	$10.00	1230	daily	9	TA Libertador
• Mar del Plata		2120	daily	12	La Estrella
• Mendoza	$20.00	1230	daily	19	T A Libertador
• Paraná		2055	daily	11½	La Estrella
• Presidencia Roque Sáenz Peña					
	$9.00	2020	daily	11	El Rayo
• Resistencia	$11.70	2020	daily	12½	El Rayo
• Rosario de la Frontera					
	$5.60				Panamericano
• Salta	$9.00	0015	3 services daily	6	Panamericano
• San Juan	$19.00	1230	daily	16½	TA Libertador
• San Miguel de Tucumán					
	$1.50	0545	27 services daily	1	El Ranchilleño, Panamerica, La Estrella, La Unión
• San Salvador de Jujuy					
	$9.60	0315	3 services daily	6½	Panamericano
• Santa Fé		2055	daily	11	La Estrella

🛍 Shopping

The main shopping centers are in Rivadavia and Caseros.
- La Catamarqueña, F Solano 11. Regional *artesanías* or handicrafts

🎣 Sport

- Fishing: In the lake for *bagre* and *dorado*, some over 12 kg
- Golf: Nine-hole golf course
- Tennis: Courts available
- Water-skiing and skindiving: In the lake. Instruction provided for novices by Club Náutico de Termas

🎭 Entertainment

- Bowling Termas, Sarmiento 114
- Casino, Rivadavia 57 (corner of Caseros). Open daily 2100–0300. Roulette and card games
- Disco Alexander, corner of Fleming and P L Gallo. Open daily
- Disco Casino, corner of Rivadavia and Caseros (downstairs)
- Disco Golden Glow, corner of Rivadavia and Caseros. For young people
- Disco Llajta Sumaj, Parque Miguel de Güemes. Open daily; for adults
- Disco Maracaibo, corner of Caseros and Rivadavia. For young people
- Peña Lo Nuestro, San Martín 252. Folk dancing and singing; local cuisine, specializing in *locro*
- Peña La Querencia, Gorostiaga 168. Open daily

Termas de Río Hondo

SANTIAGO DEL ESTERO

- Recreo San Telmo, corner of P Loscano and H Yrigoyen. Dancing
- Centro Cultural San Martín, corner of Sarmiento and Belgrano. Caters for exhibitions, concerts, and live theater

Excursions

- **Santiago del Estero**: Just past the Río Dulce crossing, the spillway of the Río Hondo dam comes into full view. There are no hotels on the other side of the river, but around the artificial lake there are many camping spots. To the south the shrub-covered *chaco* savanna predominates, extending as far as 4km before Santiago del Estero. Isolated homesteads can be seen. The road becomes a straight line running through flat country right down to Santiago del Estero. There are no mountains in sight to break the monotony. In the shrub *loros*, a type of parakeet with very colourful plumage, can be seen. See also Santiago del Estero on page 701
- **Embalse Río Hondo**: The nearby dam on the Río Dulce forms a 33 000 ha lake which is used for sailing and fishing
- **Río Dulce**: This river runs 320 km south-east of Santiago del Estero into the shallow Mar Chiquita on the southern edge of the *chaco*. Despite its name ("sweet") it has a slightly salty taste which the locals are partial to
- **Mar Chiquita**: This 80 by 25 km lake is naturally salty (*"mar"* means "sea") and the water is warm. No river drains it, but during the flood season two rivers flow into it from the Sierras de Córdoba
- **Vieja Villa Río Hondo** (Old Río Hondo Town): 22 km south of Termas de Río Hondo. Before it was submerged in the lake the original village was the second oldest Spanish settlement in the province. The village was shifted to its new location in 1966. In the past this was an important thoroughfare to Alto Perú in present Bolivia. It was also a Jesuit mission church, and one of the places which San Francisco Solano visited

VILLA OJO DE AGUA

Postal code: 5250
Distance from Santiago del Estero: 209 km southwards on RN 9

Villa Ojo de Agua is situated in the southern part of the province halfway between the cities of Córdoba and Santiago del Estero. The **Sierra de Sumampa**, a range of low hills in the vicinity, is of archeological importance.

Accommodation

B Residencial Albergue C Argentino, RN 9 $11.00
B Residencial El Tala, RN 9 Km 956 $13.00
C Residencial Los Camioneros, RN 9 $10.00
C Residencial Mony, Sarmiento $10.00

Termas de Río Hondo

Santiago del Estero

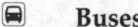 **Buses**

- Santiago del Estero: Fare $3.50; departs 0130; 7 services daily; 4 hours; Empresa Cacorba

- Córdoba: Departs 0120; 7 services daily; 4 hours; Empresa Cacorba

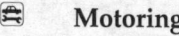 **Motoring**

- Service station: ACA, RN 9

MESOPOTAMIA

Corrientes Province

Plate 43 Map of Corrientes Province
- **725** Alvear
- **725** Bella Vista
- **726** Corrientes
- **729** Map
- **734** Curuzú Cuatiá
- **734** Empedrado
- **735** Esquina
- **735** Goya
- **737** Itá Ibaté
- **737** Itatí
- **738** Ituzaingó
- **739** Map
- **740** Mercedes
- **741** Monte Caseros
- **741** Paso de la Patria
- **742** Map
- **744** Paso de los Libres
- **745** Map
- **747** Santa Ana de los Guácaras
- **748** Santo Tomé
- **749** Yapeyú

Corrientes Province

Corrientes province is located in the north-eastern corner of Argentina. It forms part of the area generally known as Mesopotamia, between Río Paraná and Río Uruguay. The capital of the province, also called Corrientes, is located in the north-western corner on the Río Paraná.

Corrientes is almost entirely surrounded by rivers. In the east the Río Uruguay forms a border with Uruguay and with Brazil. In the west the Río Paraná forms a border with Santa Fé province and with Chaco province to the north-west; it then turns eastwards near the city of Corrientes in the extreme north-west of the province and forms a border with Paraguay to the north. To the north-east, between the Río Paraná and the Río Uruguay, is the brief border with Misiones province; and to the south, between the same two rivers, the border with Entre Ríos province.

Corrientes has an area of 88 000 square km and a population of nearly 700 000. Most of the population live in towns. The landscape is flat, and a large part of the interior is a waterlogged area called **Esteros del Iberá**, which was probably once the waterway of the Paraná. Some areas consist of *lagunas*, home of the *yacarés* or Argentine caymans. This *estero* and its outlet, the Río Corrientes, divide the province into two sections. The few mountains in the north are a continuation of the **Sierra Iman** in neighboring Misiones province.

Corrientes was involved in the War of Triple Alliance in 1868–1870 between Argentina, Uruguay, and Brazil on one side and Paraguay on the other.

The wet season is during March and April, the driest months being July and August. Annual rainfall can reach 2000 mm, but this drains off quickly and is not uniformly distributed throughout the year. The prevailing wind is northerly and north-easterly. If the wind swings around to a southerly direction it usually brings a sharp drop in temperature. The climate is humid for most of the year, and the province is well-forested, with palm trees following the many waterways. The southern part is cool and can be cold in winter, and is mostly used for pastoral grazing. The weather in the northern part is mild.

Corrientes is a major producer of rice, tea, tobacco, soya beans, citrus fruit, and cotton.

A large portion of the central part consists of swampland. The biggest swamps surround the lake–swamp complex of **Esteros del Iberá**, which normally covers some 12 000 square km but expands during the wet season. Those with an adventuresome spirit can visit the local wildlife. Many South American species such as *coatis*, white and black eagles, deer, and multicolored parrots can still be seen here in their natural habitat. The streams

CORRIENTES PROVINCE

and lakes abound in tropical fish such as *pejerrey*, *dorado*, and *surubí*, all good eating fish. The area is an angler's paradise, and it is being promoted by the provincial tourist office as a *Ruta de las Aventuras* or "Adventure Trail".

The eastern part of the province along the **Río Uruguay** is known as the *litoral* or coast, and with its many white sandy beaches and the wide river it looks like a coastal area, the only difference being that the water is not salty. This is the most historically interesting part of the province, still showing the early incursions of the Jesuits in places such as Yapeyú, Santo Tomé, and La Cruz. Some of the biggest post-independence battles were fought in this area. It was also the birthplace of the great son of Argentina, Don José de San Martín. The provincial tourist corporation promotes this area as the *Circuito Ruta de los Jesuitas* or "Jesuit Circuit"

The western and northern part of the province along the **Río Paraná** is promoted as the *Circuito Turístico de los Ríos* or "Tourist River Circuit". Here fishing enthusiasts from all over the world congregate to try for *surubí*, *pacú*, and *dorado* of immense size, as well as other game fish. Best known is the fishing competition held in **Paso de la Patria**. The sandy banks of the Río Paraná can reach 60 m high. The most interesting part of the Río Paraná is south of Corrientes near Manuel Derqui.

The original inhabitants of Corrientes were the Abipone, Guaycurue, and Guaraní. The Guaraní still make up a large proportion of the population, speaking their own language, but they are gradually being absorbed into the mainstream of Argentine life. During Juan de Ayola's epic journey upriver, a sub-branch of the Guaycurue people, who were excellent river navigators, attacked his convoy, and in punishment he destroyed 250 of their boats. In the area of the Ibera lived the Caracaras people who established small villages. Among the many peoples that formerly lived in Corrientes province, the Guaraní were most amenable to European influences. At the university in Corrientes the Guaraní language is still taught.

The General Belgrano bridge over the Río Paraná links the city of Corrientes with Resistencia in Chaco province.

A huge dam construction project is being undertaken with Paraguay on the Río Paraná. While construction is going on the management conducts free sightseeing trips from Ituzaingó. Once the dam is completed the **Saltos del Apipé** (Apipé Rapids) will disappear and the lake created will go past Posadas in Misiones province. At the same time sluices will enable large vessels to go up to Foz do Iguaçu in Brazil.

During January and February one of the most colorful

Corrientes Province

CORRIENTES PROVINCE

and peaceful carnivals in Argentina is celebrated here.

Along the **Río Uruguay** there are ruins of Jesuit missions dating back to the sixteenth century. The most important mission settlements were Yapeyú, Santo Tomé, and La Cruz, all near the Río Uruguay. They decayed after the expulsion of the Jesuits in 1768. This part of the province along the Río Uruguay is the most historically interesting part of Corrientes—it is promoted by the provincial tourist office as the *"Circuito Ruta de los Jesuitas"*.

Places of interest to the tourist include:
- Worth a visit: **Corrientes**
- Worth a detour: **Yapeyú**
- Of interest: **Itatí**, **Santo Tomé**, **Ituzaingó**, and **San Carlos**

Mercedes is a key town for visiting the **Esteros del Iberá**.

In some of the waterways a carnivorous fish called *palometa* is found. This is a relative of the piranha and has become a real pest. The cause of its proliferation is the indiscriminate slaughter of the *yacaré* which kept the *palometa* population at manageable proportions.

The *yaguareté* or jaguar has become rare, but in the swampy areas there is an abundance of *carpinchos*, anteaters, and tapirs.

From 1855 onwards a vigorous immigration policy was pursued to attract European settlers. First among the new arrivals were some French settlers who founded a small colony near the capital. Next came the German Swiss who founded **Palmira**.

ALVEAR

Postal code: 3344 • (area code: (0772)
Distance from Posadas: 231 km southwards on RN 105 then RN 14

Alvear is located on the Río Uruguay opposite the Brazilian town of Itaqui. There are daily launch and ferry services between the two cities.

Accommodation
Hospedaje Mamito, on the main street

Buses
Buses run frequently to Posadas and Paso de los Libres.

Excursions
- **La Cruz**: 16 km south on RN 14. Jesuit mission ruins

BELLA VISTA

Postal code: 3432 • (area code: (0777)
Distance from Corrientes: 141 km south on RN 12

Founded in 1825, Bella Vista is located directly on the **Río Paraná**. It is aptly named "Beautiful View" for its panoramic views over the mighty river flowing between sandy cliffs for about 30 km. *Dorado* fishing attracts many visitors. South of Bella Vista is **Punta Cuevas**, where during the War of the Triple Al-

CORRIENTES PROVINCE

liance an allied squadron attacked a Paraguayan battery in 1865 at a location now marked with a large commemorative wooden cross.

Bellas Vista is the center of an orange growing area. Fishing trips can be made from here.

Festivals
- Fiesta Provincial de la Naranja (Provincial Orange Festival): October and November

Accommodation
★★ El Triangulo, corner of Buenos Aires and RP 27 (125 $10.00

Buses
Buses run regularly to Goya, Paraná, and Corrientes

Motoring
- Service station: El Triangulo, RP 27

Sport
- Launch hire: El Dorado, corner of Buenos Aires and 25 de Mayo

CORRIENTES

Postal code: 3400 • (area code: (0783) •
Population: 150 000
Distance from Buenos Aires: 1041 km northwards on RN 12

Corrientes, the capital of Corrientes province, is located on the **Río Paraná**, here about 2 km wide, some 50 km south of the junction with the Río Paraguay. It is situated opposite the city of Resistencia in Chaco province, and is connected to it by a bridge. The city has retained much of its colonial charm and many fine mansions are still preserved. The tourist office is located in one of these renovated colonial mansions.

In 1527 the master mariner Sebastian Caboto reached the present site of Corrientes, and described the seven hills after which it is named. In 1588 the capital was founded here by Juan Vera y Aragón as San Juan de Vera de las Siete Corrientes.

Temperatures in summer can rise to 40°C and go occasionally as low as 0°C but winters are generally pleasant.

Prices in Corrientes are slightly higher than in Resistencia, and there is less accommodation in the lower brackets.

Festivals
The *carnaval* is one of the most colorful in Argentina and attracts many visitors.

Tourist information
- Tourist office, Rioja 475 (corner of Quintana) (27200. Open 0700–2100
- Automovil Club Argentino, corner of 25 de Mayo and Mendoza

Camping
- Camping Club Teléfono Corrientes, Avenida Maipú, near combined bus and railway terminal

Eating out
- Restaurant Asociación Italiana, C Pellegrini 1037
- Restaurant Canton Dorado, H Yrigoyen 1329
- Restaurant El Galeno, Mendoza 1428
- Restaurant Gigante, San Lorenzo 765 (corner of 9 de Julio). Steakhouse

CORRIENTES PROVINCE

🛏 Accommodation in Corrientes

During the carnival season make hotel reservations well in advance; otherwise stay in Resistencia, which is cheaper.

★★★★	Hotel Gran Guaraní, Mendoza 970	(	23090	$18.50
★★★★	Hotel Hostal del Pinar, P Martinez 1090 (corner of San Juan, overlooking river)	(	61089	$18.50
★★★	Hotel Gran Corrientes, Junín 1549	(	65025	$13.00
★★★	Hotel Gran Buenos Aires, C Pellegrini 1058	(	22065	$13.00
★★★	Hotel Orly, San Juan 867	(	27248	$13.00
★★★	Hotel San Martín, Santa Fé 955	(	60983	$13.00
★★★	Hotel de Turismo Provincial, Entre Ríos 650	(	23841	$13.00
★	Hotel Colón, Rioja 437	(	24527	$8.00
★	Hotel Sosa, España 1050 (corner of H Yrigoyen 1676)	(	62151	$8.00
•	Hotel Robert, La Rioja 415			
B	Residencial Avenida, Avenida 3 de Abril			$6.50
•	Residencial S O S, H Yrigoyen 1771	(	60330	$7.50

Accommodation outside Corrientes

There are regular public buses to the city center.

- Hotel Auel SA, Avenida Maipú 2183, near bus terminal
- Hotel Caribe, Avenida Maipú 2596, opposite bus terminal 🍴
  Breakfast included; credit cards accepted (63227 $11.00
- Hotel Pavon, Avenida Maipú Km 3, opposite bus terminal
  (62537 $8.00
- Hotel Waikiki, Gobernador A Ruiz 2260 (corner of Pujol, where Gobernador A Ruiz becomes RN 12 east) (23171 $8.00
- Motel Cadena de Oro, Las Heras 1896 (RN 12, on road to bus terminal)
- Motel G Carlos, 25 de Mayo 2526

- Restaurant Gran Hotel Turismo, Entre Ríos 650
- Restaurant Gran Restaurant, Avenida España 1050 (corner of H Yrigoyen)
- Restaurant La Criollita, San Juan 878
- Restaurant Las Espuelas, Mendoza 847. Steakhouse
- Restaurant Las Vegas, San Juan 939
- Restaurant Maximiliano, H Yrigoyen 1331. Late dinners
- ☞ Restaurant Michelangelo, corner of C Pellegrini and Catamarca
- Restaurant San José, corner of Avenida España and H Yrigoyen
- Restaurant Tía María, Catamarca block 800 (corner of Junín)
- Restaurant Vigón, Buenos Aires block 800 (corner of 9 de Julio)
- Restaurant Yapeyú, Vera 1352

- Pizzería Corrientes, Hotel Corrientes, Junín 1549 (corner of Santa Fé)
- Pizzería La Estrada, 9 de Julio 1261
- Pizzería Los Pinos, Catamarca 1202 (corner of Bolivar)
- Pizzería Rotterdam, Maipú 37
- Pizzería San José, H Yrigoyen block 1700 (corner of España)
- Cafetería Angel Bar, San Juan 671
- Cafetería Café Kraus, H Yrigoyen block 1300 (corner of Córdoba)
- Cafetería Cafe Paris, shop 13, Galería Paris
- Cafetería Cristal, 9 de Julio 1027
- Cafetería Exocet, Junín 1428
- Cafetería Hipocampo, Junín 1342. Tables on sidewalk
- Cafetería IUS, Salta block 400 (corner of P Martinez). Student meeting place
- Cafetería Kaunas, Junín 1122

Corrientes Province

- Cafetería La Facultad, Galería Corrientes
- Cafetería La Fusta, San Juan 935
- Cafetería Mecca, Junín 1266
- ☞ Cafetería Petit Valencia, Tucumán block 1100 (corner of Bolivar)
- Cafetería Pucará, San Lorenzo 765 (corner of 9 de Julio)
- Cafetería Viejo Cafe, Rioja 719
- Chopería Leos, Santa Fé 1226
- Chopería Viejo Cafée, La Rioja 712
- Ice-cream parlor: Italia, 9 de Julio 1301
- Ice-cream parlor: Trieste, corner of Avenida Italia and Quintana

Eating out outside the city center

- Restaurant Casa Mir, Avenida Maipú block 2500 (corner of Valparaiso, opposite the bus and rail terminal)
- Restaurant Che Cambá, Independencia 4134
- Pizzería San Jorge, H Yrigoyen 2365
- Cafetería La Terminal, Maipú 2590

Post and telegraph

- Post office: corner of San Martín and San Juan
- Long distance telephone: Entel, corner of Junín and Córdoba
- Telephone: Catamarca block 1300 (corner of Moreno)

$ Financial

- Banco Credito, Junín 1326. Cash advances on Visa card

Services and facilities

- Dry-cleaner: Los Mil Colores, San Juan 560
- Hospital: Hospital General San Martín, corner of Avenida G Ferre and Córdoba
- Pharmacy: Farmacia del Norte, corner of Catamarca and 9 de Julio. Open 24 hours
- Photographic supplies: Fotocine Mandri, Pellegrini 699
- Sauna: Instituto Masters, Rioja 924. Sauna, turkish bath and water massage. Men: Mon, Wed, Fri 1300–1500 and 2100–2300; women: Tues–Thurs, Sat 1600–2100. Entry $2.20

Fishing and camping gear

- Centro Náutico Corrientes, La Rioja block 700 (corner of 9 de Julio). Also hires kayaks
- Unger, Mendoza 830

Laundromats

- Laverap, Camba Cua, 25 de Mayo 620. Open Mon–Sat 0800–2200
- Laverap, San Martín 1614 (corner of Santa Fé). Open Mon–Sat– 0800–2200
- Marva, Córdoba block 900 (corner of H Yrigoyen). Open daily 0700–2100. $2.00

Key to Map

1. Municipalidad
2. Catedral
3. Casa de Gobierno
4. Post office (Encotel)
5. Telephone (Entel)
6. Tourist information
7. Buses to Resistencia
8. Municipal bus terminal
9. Aerolineas Argentinas
10. Austral Lineas Aereas
11. Banco de la Provincia
12. Old Cabildo
13. Iglesia de la Merced
14. Iglesia de la Cruz de los Milagros
15. Iglesia y Convento de San Francisco
16. Museo Franciscano
17. Museo de Ciencias Naturales
18. Museo de Bellas Artes
19. Museo Colonial e Historico
20. Casa del Gobernador
21. Hotel de Turismo Provincial
22. Hotel Gran Corrientes
23. Hotel Guaraní
24. Hotel San Martín
25. Hotel Gran Buenos Aires
26. Hotel Orly
27. Hotel Hostal del Pinar
28. Hotel Colón
29. Casino de Corrientes

Plate 43

Map of Corrientes Province

Plate 44
Garganta del Diablo, Cataratas del Iguazú

Corrientes Province

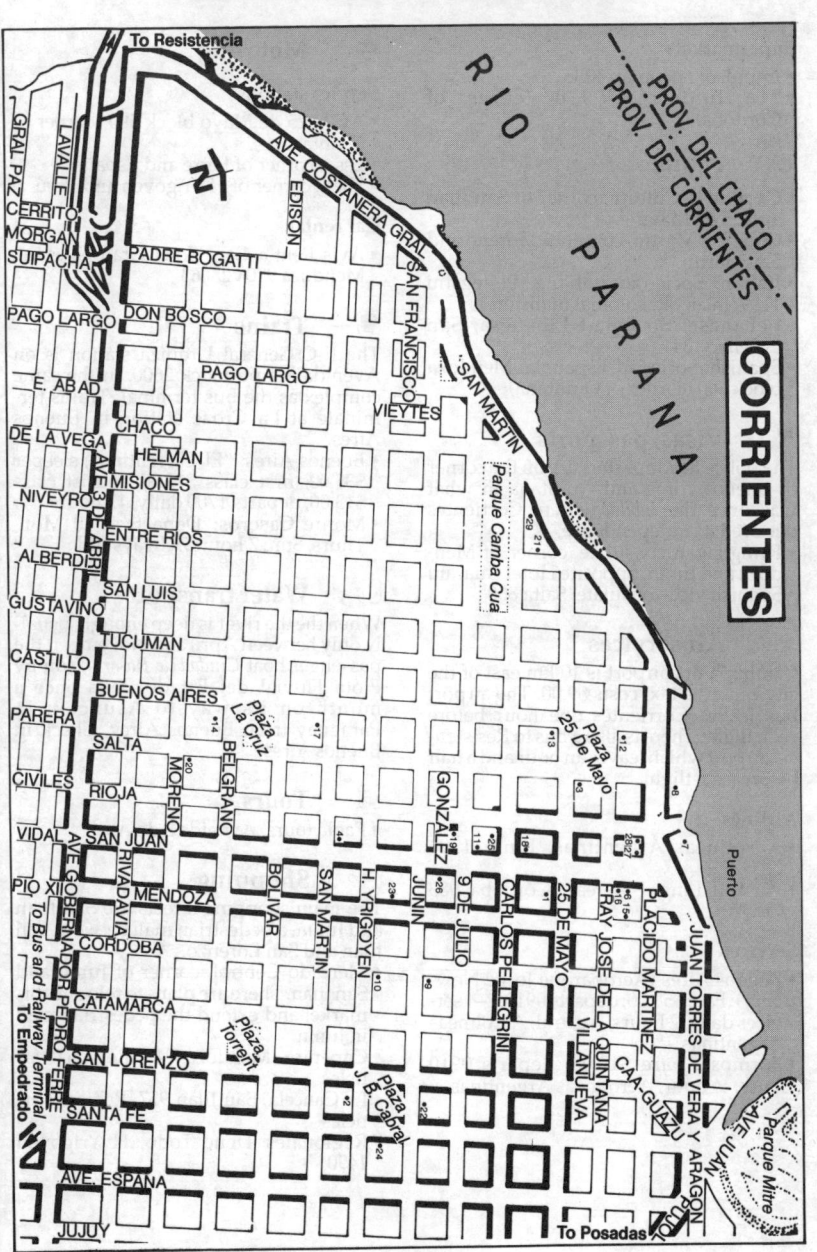

Corrientes

CORRIENTES PROVINCE

Supermarkets
- Impulso, Tucumán 1236
- TIA, Junín block 1300 (corner of Córdoba)

C Clubs
- Casa de la Cultura, corner of San Juan and 25 de Mayo
- Club San Martín, corner of Moreno and San Martín
- Italian: Sociedad Italiana, Pellegrini 1139. In an old colonial mansion
- Lebanese: Sociedad Libanesa, San Lorenzo 1341
- Spanish: Sociedad Española, Mendoza block 500 (corner of Quintana)

Visas, passports
The police headquarters are on the corner of Buenos Aires and Quintana in what was once the *cabildo* where Corrientes declared its independence.
- Paraguayan consulate, corner of Mendoza and Junín, opposite Hotel Guaraní
- Spanish vice-consulate, Salta 860

✈ Air services
Camba Punta airport is 10 km east of the city center; a taxi costs $9.00. The airport bus leaves Corrientes one hour before each flight. There is also a bus to Resistencia airport which leaves an hour and a half before each flight.

Airlines
- Aerolineas Argentinas, Junín 1301 ☎ 23850
- Austral Lineas Aereas, Córdoba 983 ☎ 22570

Services
- Buenos Aires (Aeroparque Jorge Newbery): Fare $58.00; departs 0910; 2–4 services daily; 2 hours; Austral, Aerolineas Argentinas
- Formosa: Fare $13.00; departs 0910 Tues; ½ hour; Aerolineas Argentinas

Motoring

Service stations
- ACA, 25 de Mayo block 500 (corner of Quintana)
- Esso, corner of Ferré and España
- Shell, corner of H Yrigoyen and Perú

Car rental
- Avis Rent-a-Car, Hotel Gran Guaraní, Mendoza 970 ☎ 23663

Trains
The F C General Urquiza station is on Avenida Maipú block 2600, in the same complex as the bus terminal. Trains terminate at La Croze station in Buenos Aires.
- Buenos Aires: "El Correntino"; sleeper $35.00, first class $17.50, tourist class $13.00; departs 1700 daily; 17 hours
- Monte Caseros: Departs 2040 Mon, Thurs, Sun; 7 hours. Always full

Water transport
When the the river is deep enough, usually only between April and November, the passenger boat *Ciudad de Rosario*, run by Flota Fluvial del Estado, calls once a month on its way to Asunción in Paraguay from Buenos Aires. Check in Buenos Aires

Tours
- Paola tours, Avenida 3 de Abril

Shopping
The main shopping streets are San Juan and Junín, a pedestrian mall between San Juan and San Lorenzo.
- Mercado Central, corner of Junín and San Juan. There are plans to relocate this market and extend the pedestrian mall in Junín
- Capepire, Mendoza 949. Regional articles
- La Cancela, San Juan 957. Regional articles
- Regionales Tiene Todo, H Yrigoyen 1490

Corrientes

CORRIENTES PROVINCE

🚌 Buses from Corrientes

The urban transport terminal, for local buses and *colectivos* to Resistencia, is at the corner of Costanera and Salta.

The long-distance bus and railway terminal is on Avenida Maipú block 2600, 4 km south of the city center. Municipal buses 6 and 11 travel between the two terminals every 20 minutes.

Destination	Fare	Depart	Services	Hours	Company
• Buenos Aires	$21.50	1730	2 services daily	12	T A Chevallier
• Córdoba	$19.00	1900	Tue, Wed, Fri, Sun		Tala
• Curuzú Cuatiá	$5.40	0530	3 services daily		Tala
• Esquina	$5.20	1400	2 services daily		Tala
• Goya	$3.50	0500	6 services daily	5	Tala
• Itatí	$1.20	0530	8 services daily		Itatí
• Ituzaingó	$4.00	0910	daily	4	Ciudad de Posadas
• La Rioja		1230	Mon, Wed, Sat		Cotal
• Mendoza		1230	Mon, Wed, Sat		Cotal
• Mercedes	$3.80	0530	2 services daily		Tala
• Paraná		1730	5 services daily		Tala-Rapido, T A Chevallier
• Paso de la Patria	$0.70	0730	3 services daily		Paso de la Patria
• Paso de los Libres	$5.80	0430	2 services daily		Paso de los Libres
• Posadas		0640	2 services daily	7	C de Posadas
• Presidencia Roque Sáenz Peña	$3.00	1900	daily	3	El Rayo
• Puerto Iguazú		2340	daily		Ciudad de Posadas
• Resistencia	$0.40		every 15 mins	¾	local bus 22
• Rosario	$18.00	1730	5 services daily		Tala-Rapido, T A Chevallier
• San Fernando del Valle de Catamarca		1230	Mon, Wed, Sat		Cotal
• San Juan		1230	Mon, Wed, Sat		Cotal
• San Miguel de Tucumán	$13.50	1900	daily	14½	El Rayo
• Santa Fé	$14.50	1730	5 services daily	9	T A Chevallier, Tala-Rapido
• Santiago del Estero	$10.80	1230	1–2 services daily		Cotal, El Rayo
• Santo Tomé	$6.50	0910	daily	6	Ciudad de Posadas
• Termas de Río Hondo	$12.00	1900	daily	13	El Rayo

🏆 Sport

- Golf: 18-hole golf course, Santa Ana district, 20 km east of town
- Racing: Jockey Club Corrientes, corner of Mendoza and H Yrigoyen
- Tennis: Tennis Club Corrientes, corner of Avenida Artigas and San Martín

Sailing

- Centro Náutico Correntino Campodonico, Poncho Verde 1920
- Club de Regatas Corrientes, in Parque Mitre

🍸 Entertainment

Most night clubs are open only from Thursday to Sunday.

Corrientes

- Chess club, corner of Bolívar and J A Roca
- Casino de Corrientes, corner of Pellegrini and Costanera. Open Tues–Sun 2200–0300
- Disco Ka Ko Si, Mendoza 1239
- Disco Killer, Pellegrini 808 (corner of Buenos Aires)
- Disco Metal, Junín 777
- Disco Savage, Junín 1511
- Night Club Claxon, Pellegrini 615
- Teatro Oficial Juan de Vera, San Juan. Opened in 1861
- Cine Teatro Corrientes, Cordoba

Sightseeing
- Costanera: A walk along the Costanera gives a good view of the photogenic Río Paraná and the Belgrano bridge across the river. On the Costanera there is a memorial built by the Italian community to Sebastian Caboto, the Italian navigator in the service of Spain, who sailed up the Río Paraná and passed this point in 1527

Churches
- Iglesia de la Cruz de los Milagros (Church of the Cross of Miracles), built in 1808, houses a miraculous cross placed there by the city's founder
- Iglesia de la Merced (Church of Our Lady of Mercy). Construction began in 1628 and the present building is the result of successive alterations and additions
- Catedral, H Yrigoyen opposite Plaza Cabral, is in renaissance style. The tombs of famous Argentines like General Joaquin Madariaga (see Paso de los Libres on page 744) and Coronel Beron de Astrada are in the church. It is a national monument
- Iglesia y Convento de San Francisco (Franciscan Church and Convent), corner of Mendoza and Quintana. Founded in 1600, construction was started in 1607. From 1797 to 1854 the building housed the school of arts, until it was rebuilt in 1871. Fray José de la Quintana taught here. The entrance to the Museo Franciscano is here
- Iglesia Jesús de Nazareno (Church of Jesus of Nazareth), corner of Pellegrini and San Lorenz
- Iglesia María Auxiliadora, corner of San Juan and 9 de Julio; also the Colegio Don Bosco
- Capilla Santa Rita (Chapel of Saint Rita), corner of Córdoba and Bolívar

Museums
- Museo de Ciencias Naturales "Amado Bompland" (Amado Bompland Natural Sciences Museum), corner of Buenos Aires and San Martín. This was the first museum in the city, founded in 1852
- Museo Franciscano. Access is through the Convento de San Francisco in Mendoza. Religious exhibits
- Museo Colonial e Histórico (Museum of Colonization and History), corner of 9 de Julio and La Rioja. Inaugurated in 1894

CORRIENTES PROVINCE

- Museo de Bellas Artes (Fine Arts Museum), San Juan 634 (corner of Pellegrini)

Public buildings and parks

- Casa de Gobierno (House of Assembly), corner of Salta and 25 de Mayo. Constructed in 1881
- Casa del Gobernador (Governor's House), Salta block 1300 (corner of Moreno). This was the first government house and seat of provincial government in 1814. After that it was the school of arts and hospital during the War of the Triple Alliance and again in 1871 during the yellow fever epidemic. The building serves now as a *comedor* or dining room for students
- Puente de la Batería (Battery Bridge), on the approaches to Parque Mitre. Constructed in 1851, this was the scene of heavy fighting during the war with Paraguay in 1865
- Monument to John Caboto, the first man to navigate the Río Paraná in 1529
- Palacio Municipal, corner of 25 de Mayo and San Juan. Built in 1728, this was originally the seat of the Dominican order and probably the base of the Inquisition. The original chapel was dedicated to Pius V. Some of the original interior constructions remain. Since 1828 it has housed the public offices. The façade dates from 1882
- Old colonial manor, corner of Quintana and Salta (Casa de la Artesania)
- Plaza 25 de Mayo. In the center is a statue of San Martín
- There is a small zoo on the Costanera, on the approaches to the bridge to Resistencia, which displays local wildlife
- Plaza de la Cruz has a statue to the doctors who perished during the yellow fever epidemic in 1871
- Plaza Sargente Cabral, corner of Junín and H Yrigoyen has a statue to the sergeant who saved General San Martín's life during the battle of San Lorenzo
- From Parque Mitre there are good views over the Río Paraná

Excursions

- **Goya**: Southwards on RN 3. The trip passes mostly through flat low-lying country with swampy areas. There are many citrus orchards but much of the area is still shrub-covered. The road is sealed all the way to Paraná and there are long straight stretches. Some of the land has been turned into pine plantations. The bus calls at Empedrado, Bellavista and Santa Lucía
- **Santa Ana de los Guácaras**: 20 km on RN 12. The seventeenth-century chapel built in honour of Santa Ana by Guacara Indians is a national shrine. On the way, there are many little *lagunas* amid lush vegetation. See Santa Ana de los Guácaras on page 747
- **Paso de la Patria**: 38 km on RN 12. Fishing. It is served by Empresa Paso de la Patria

buses. See Paso de la Patria on page 741
- **Itatí**: 73 km on RN 12. Catholic shrine. See Itatí on page 737
- **Ituzaingó**: 250 km on RN 12. You can visit the huge dam construction across the Río Paraná. See Ituzaingó on page 738

CURUZÚ CUATIÁ

Postal code: 3460 • (area code: (0774)
Distance from Corrientes: 314 km southwards in RN 12m then south-east on RN 123 and southwards on RN 118

Curuzú Cuatiá is located in the south-eastern part of the province at the intersection of RN 119 and RP 126. Some 23 km west is the battlefield of **Pago Largo**.

Accommodation
- ★★★ Hotel de Turismo, Duarte Ardoy 666 (2037 $14.00. ACA discount
- ★★ Hotel Continental, Caa Guazú 841, (2038 $10.00
- ★ Hotel Avenida, B de Astrada 1699 (2737 $8.00
- Hostal Curuzú Cuatiá, B de Astrada 957

Camping
- Municipal camping ground

Eating out
- Restaurant Anahí, B de Astrada 591
- Restaurant Continental, B de Astrada 841
- Restaurant Chabra, B de Astrada 1614
- Restaurant Don Ricardo, Caa Guazú 550
- Restaurant La Rural, B de Astrada 765

Buses
- Buenos Aires: Departs 2045 daily; 9 hours; Expreso Singer
- Concordia: Departs 2045 daily; 3 hours
- Gualeguaychú: Departs 2045 daily; 5 hours

Motoring
- Service station: ACA, corner of Beron Astrada and R Perrazzo

Entertainment
- Disco Crazy, B de Astrada 888

EMPEDRADO

Postal code: 3418 • Population: 24 000
Distance from Corrientes: 52 km south on RN 12 (sealed)

The **Fuerte Santiago Sánchez** was built in the seventeenth century against the marauding Chaco Indians. Later a small settlement developed on the banks of the **Rió Empedrado**, which was wiped out by the Chaco Indians in the eighteenth century. A new settlement grew about 1806 around a chapel with an image of the *Señor Hallado* carved of local wood by Guaraní Indians. Empedrado was officially refounded in 1825 by General Pedro Ferré.

The town is situated on the eastern bank of **Río Paraná**. It has retained its colonial character, enhanced by window gratings on many of the colonial mansions. Nearby are beaches which, despite the number of tourists, remain uncrowded. Most visitors come here to try *dorado* fishing.

Corrientes

CORRIENTES PROVINCE

The river runs here through abrupt sand hills. Most streets are unsealed.

Emperado is the centre of a citrus and rice growing region.

Accommodation

Hotel de Turismo, outside town ⊞▣ ℂ 47 and 48 $13.00

★ Hotel Rosario, B Mitre 1246 ▣ ℂ 30 $8.00

Camping

- There is a camp site 1½ km outside town on RN 12 south

Buses

The bus terminal is in the town center with regular services to Corrientes and Paraná.

Motoring

- Service station: Esso, corner of Piragini and RN 12

Trains

Empedrado is situated on the F C General Urquiza line connecting Buenos Aires and Corrientes.

Sport

Launch hire
- Casa Molina, General Paz 450
- El Doradito, Balneario Municipal

ESQUINA

Postal code: 3196 • ℂ area code: (0777)
Distance from Corrientes: 330 km southwards on RN 12

Esquina is located on the Río Paraná. To the north is mostly swamp.

Esquina is a fishing resort, well-known for its *dorado* and *surubí*.

Accommodation

★★★ Hotel de Turismo, corner of Mitre and San Martín ℂ 60220 $13.00

★★ Cabana del Pescador, RN 12, Casilla 27, outside town ℂ 60290 $10.00

Eating out

- Restaurant, B Lamela 675

Buses

The terminal has a 24-hour cafeteria.
- Corrientes: Fare $5.20; 2 services daily; Empresa El Tala

Motoring

Service stations
- YPF, corner of Caseros and Santa Rita
- Shell, RN 12

Sport

Launch hire for fishing
- Juanjo, San Martín 229
- Vira Bebe, Constitución 671

GOYA

Postal code: 3450 • ℂ area code: (0777) •
Population: 50 000
Distance from Corrientes: 191 km south on RN 12

Founded in 1807, Goya is located on the eastern bank of the **Río Paraná** near the junction with the **Río Santa Lucía**, and has developed into the second largest city in Corrientes province. It is the centre of a rice and tobacco growing area. In the region are

CORRIENTES PROVINCE

palm groves such as at **El Cocal** and **El Cocalito**.

Fishing excursions to the islands are one of the attractions of the town. With good tourist facilities and historic attractions it draws many tourists throughout the year.

Note that street numbering does not start from the central Plaza.

Festivals

- *Surubí* fishing competition: May
- Fiesta Nacional del Tabaco (National Tobacco Festival): February 18

Tourist information

The tourist office is on the *Barcasse*, anchored at the end of Calle M A Llosa, which serves as the dock for ferry services to and from Reconquista in Santa Fé province.

Eating out

- Restaurant El Colonial, M A Llosa 415
- Restaurant El Quijote, José Gómez 723
- Restaurant Hotel de Turismo, M I Lloza 471
- Restaurant La Nuit, M A Llosa 447
- Restaurant La Rueda, J J Rolón 1112
- Restaurant La Terminal, José Gómez 979
- Restaurant Parrilla Española, José Gómez 827. Steakhouse
- Pizzería Don Ata, José Gómez 958 (opposite bus terminal)
- Cafetería El Aljibe, José Gómez block 800 (corner of M A Llosa)
- Cafetería La Pucu, M A Llosa block 500 (main Plaza)
- Cafetería Leonardo's, corner of Martinez and Colón
- Cafetería Monterrey, Colón block 900 (corner of España)

Post and telegraph

- Post office: Encotel, Belgrano block 900 (on the main Plaza)
- Long distance telephone: Entel, Tucumán block 900 (corner of España). Open 080–2400

Services and facilities

- Laundromat: Laverap, Colón 1041 (corner of España)
- Supermarket: Autoservicio Itati, M A Llosa 364

Air services

The airport is 8 km north of the city.

Airlines

- Austral airlines, Martinez 370

Services

- Buenos Aires: Fare $56.00; departs 1300 Mon, Wed, Sat; 3 hours; Austral
- Reconquista: Fare $11.00; departs 1300 Mon, Wed, Sat; 1 hour; Empresa Austral
- Santa Fé: Fare $36.00; departs 1300 Mon, Wed, Sat; Austral

Accommodation in Goya

★★★	Hotel de Turismo, Mitre 880 — ACA discount	2560, 2561	$12.50	
★★★	Hotel Gran Cervantes, José Gómez 723	22445	$12.50	
★★	Hotel Gran Goya, Colón 929	22887	$10.00	
★	Hotel Alcazar, José Gómez 848	366	$6.50	
★	Hotel Colón, Colón 1077	22682	$8.00	

- Hotel Plaza, España block 500 (corner of Colón, opposite park)
- Hotel Sportman, España 831 — Shared bathroom — 2141 — $6.50
- Hospedaje Gracielita, Sarmiento 550
- Residencial Sugar, Tucumán 759

CORRIENTES PROVINCE

🚌 Buses

The bus terminal is on José Gómez block 900 (corner of España)
- Corrientes: Fare $3.50; departs 0430; 6 services daily; 5 hours; Empresa El Tala
- Paraná: Fare $7.00; departs 2030 daily; 6 hours; Empresa T A Chevallier

🚗 Motoring

The road north from Goya to Empedrado and Corrientes is sealed.
- Service station: Shell, corner of Colón and 25 de Mayo

⚓ Water transport

A launch to Reconquista leaves from the pier in 12 de Octubre at the end of M A Llosa. Services Mo–Fri at 0700; fare $2.50, 2½ hours. The bus to Reconquista picks up passengers at landing pier; fare $0.50, ½ hour. The return launch leaves from Reconquista pier at 1500.
Some river boats on their way south to Buenos Aires or north to Asunción in Paraguay call here for passengers when the river level is high enough.

🎣 Sport

Launch hire
- La Cueva del Pescador, España 220
- Pira Yagua, Belgrano 776

🏞 Excursions

- **Santa Lucía**: 21 km north on RP 12. Founded in 1616 by Hernando Arias de Saavedra (kown as "Hernandarias"). The church dates from 1770 and is a national monument
- **Colonia Carolina**: Capilla del Diablo (Chapel of the Devil) with exotic carvings made from *urunduy* wood. There is an aboriginal cemetery here on the banks of the **Río Miní**

ITÁ IBATÉ

Postal code: 3480 • ✆ area code: (0783)
Distance from Corrientes: 157 km eastwards on RN 12

Itá Ibaté is located on the **Río Paraná** halfway between Itatí and Ituzaingó. It is only a small village but the fishing, mainly for *dorado* and *surubí*, is good.

🛏 Accommodation

- Hospedaje Criollita, corner of San Martín and Uruguay
- Hospedaje El Hogar, San Miguel
- Hospedaje El Rancho de Aponte, on RN 12

🚌 Buses

- Corrientes: Fare $3.00; departs 0645; 5 services daily; 2 hours; Empresa Ciudad de Posadas
- Posadas: Fare $4.00; departs 0155; 7 services daily; 2½ hours; Empresa Ciudad de Posadas

🚗 Motoring

- Service station: ACA, RN 12 at the town entrance

ITATÍ

Postal code: 3414 • Population: 6000
Distance from Corrientes: 65 km west on RN 12

Itatí is a small port on the **Río Paraná**.

In 1615 Fray Luis Bolaños established a mission here. A statue of the *Virgen de Itatí* was brought here in 1859, and has been venerated ever since. In her honor a *fiesta* is held each year.

Itatí

CORRIENTES PROVINCE

🍴 Festivals
- Fiesta de la Virgen de Itatí: July 16. The procession begins in San Luis de Palmar, 53 km south-west of Itatí.

🚌 Buses
Corrientes: Fare $1.20; 8 services daily; Empresa Itatí

🚗 Motoring
- Service station: YPF, at the intersection of RN 12 and the road to the village

🎣 Sport
- Fishing gear: Casa Maciel, Avenida San Luis del Palmar

ITUZAINGÓ

Postal code: 3302 • (area code: (0752)
Distance from Corrientes: 231 km east on RN 12

Until the **Complejo Hidroeléctrico Yacyretá Apipé** (Yacyretá–Apipé Hydroelectric Project) began, Ituzaingó was a sleepy forgotten village on the banks of the **Río Paraná**, about 2 km off the main road with 3000 inhabitants. Now there is a modern satellite town housing 15 000 workers and their families. The dam is being built by a French–Italian consortium and will benefit Paraguay and Argentina in many ways: generating electricity, providing irrigation, and opening up the upper Paraná for shipping. The lake will reach to the twin cities of Posadas and Encarnación 60 km upstream, and will inundate the low-lying areas of both cities.

There are two distinct wet seasons: In October, and in April and May. The annual rainfall is a high 2800 mm.

The majority of streets are unsealed.

ℹ️ Tourist information
- The Complejo Hidroeléctrico Yacyretá Apipé public relations office, Tranquera de Loreto, conducts free guided tours of the project—see "Excursions" below

🏨 Accommodation
- ★★ Hotel Yaciretá, corner of Iberá and Entre Ríos (90129 $11.70
- ★ Hotel Geminis, corner of Buenos Aires and Antartida Argentina (90324 $9.00
- Hotel Máximo, near bus terminal (90408
- Residencial Hotel Sosa, corner of Buenos Aires and Sudamerica (90233 $6.00

🍴 Eating out
- Restaurant Apipé, in the works complex on the banks of the Río Paraná, 8 blocks from the public relations office

🛂 Visas, passports
- Paraguayan consulate, Buenos Aires 225 (90114. Open Mon-Sat 0900-1200

Key to Map
1. Municipalidad
2. Public relations officer for the Complejo Hidroeléctrico Yaciretá Apipé
3. Bus terminal
4. Hotel Yaciretá
5. Hotel Geminis
6. Hotel Sosa
7. Hotel Máximo

CORRIENTES PROVINCE

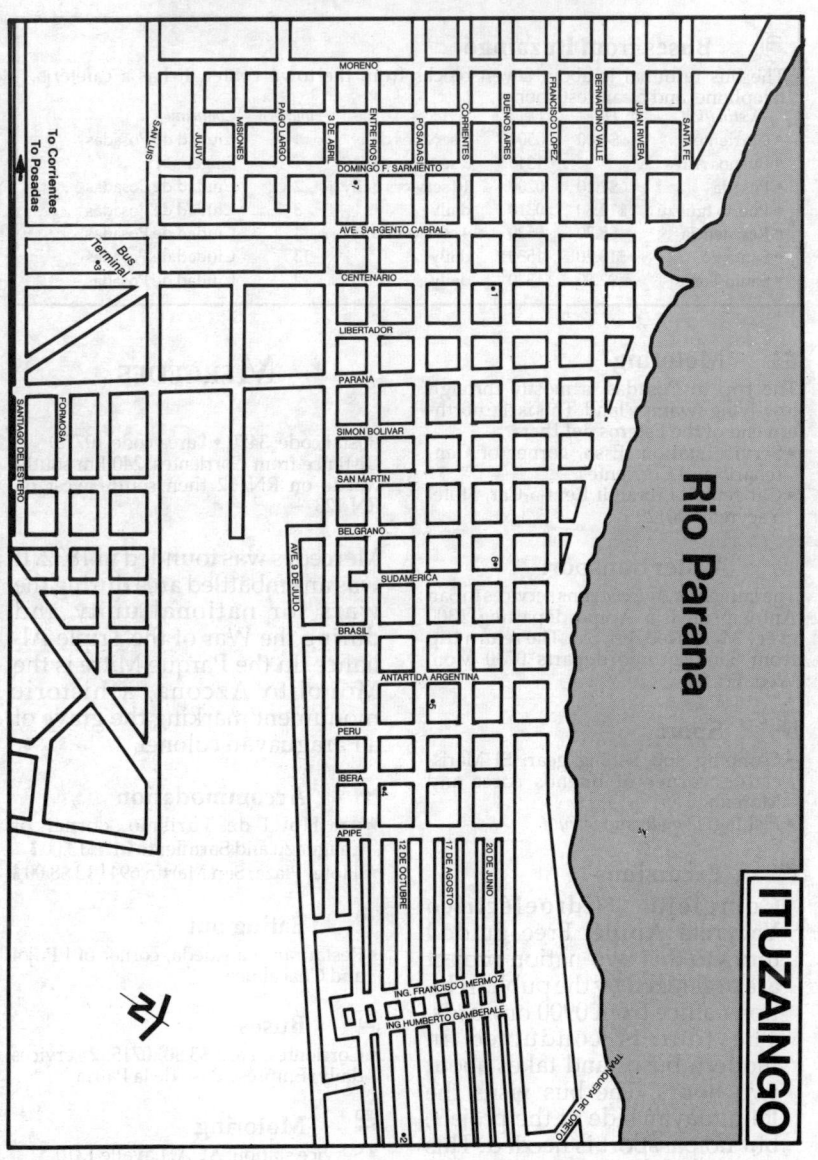

Ituzaingó

CORRIENTES PROVINCE

🚌 Buses from Ituzaingó

The bus terminal is about seven blocks from the town center. It has a cafeteria, telephone, and clean rest-rooms

Destination	Fare	Depart	Services	Hours	Company
• Corrientes	$4.00	0500	8 services daily	4	Ciudad de Posadas
• Buenos Aires		1340	3 services daily		Singer
• Posada	$2.20	0200	10 services daily	2	Ciudad de Posadas
• Puerto Iguazú	$12.80	0310	daily	8	Ciudad de Posadas
• Resistencia	$8.30	0520	4 services daily	4	Ciudad de Posadas
• Santa Fé	$18.20	1530	daily	13	Ciudad de Posadas
• Santo Tomé	$2.60	1320	daily	2	Ciudad de Posadas

🚙 Motoring

The trip to Posadas is mostly through low-lying swampy land. This is the northern end of the **Esteros del Iberá**.
- Service station: Esso, corner of Centenario and Corrientes
- Car rental: Liprandi Rent-a-Car, Hotel Yacyretá ℂ 90129

⚓ Water transport

The launch *La Apipeña* runs services to San Antonio on Isla Apipé departing 1300 every Mon, Wed, Fri, Sat. The return trip from San Antonio departs 0730 Mon, Wed, Fri, Sat

🎣 Sport

- Camping and fishing gear: El Mariscador, corner of Buenos Aires and Moreno
- Fishing: *Dorado* and *surubí*

🚩 Excursions

- **Complejo Hidroeléctrico Yacyretá Apipé**: Free guided tours to this two-nation project are organized by the public relations office from 0900 onwards. The tour is conducted in modern buses and takes about two hours. The bus visits the Paraguayan side of the project, but no passport is needed. This massive project will take about eight years to complete

MERCEDES

Postal code: 3470 • ℂ area code: (0773)
Distance from Corrientes: 240 km southwards on RN 12 then south-west on RN 123

Mercedes was founded in 1832. It was an embattled area during the wars for national unity and during the War of the Triple Alliance. In the Parque Mitre is the Monolito Azcona, a historic monument marking the grave of a Paraguayan colonel.

🛏 Accommodation

- ★★★ Hotel de Turismo, corner of Caaguazu and Sarmiento ℂ 17 $13.00 ≞
- ★ Hotel Plaza, San Martín 694 ℂ 13 $8.00 ≞

🍴 Eating out

- Restaurant La Rueda, corner of J Pujol and Chacabuco

🚌 Buses

- Corrientes: Fare $3.80; 0715; 2 services daily; Empresa Paso de la Patria

🚙 Motoring

- Service station: ACA, Lavalle 1310

Ituzaingó

CORRIENTES PROVINCE

📷 Sightseeing
- Museo Municipal de Ciencias Naturales (Municipal Natural Sciences Musuem)

🚶 Excursions
- **Colonia Carlos Pellegrini** on **Laguna Iberá**: 105 km north on RP 40. This is the starting point for boat trips in the Esteros del Iberá. The **Esteros del Iberá** have been declared a provincial natural reserve and Pellegrini has been earmarked as a tourist center. At the moment there is only a camping ground there. The road is bad and mostly runs through swampy area. A three-star hotel is planned

MONTE CASEROS

Postal code: 3220 • ☎ area code: (0775)
Distance from Corrientes: 406 km southwards on RN 12, south-east on RN 119 and RN 14, and eastwards on RP 129

Monte Caseros is situated on the **Río Uruguay** on the border with Brazil and Uruguay, opposite the border towns of Barra do Quarai in Brazil and Bella Unión in Uruguay. From here northwards the Alto Río Uruguay forms the border between Argentina and Brazil.

🛏 Accommodation
- ★★ Hotel Paterlini, corner of Colón and Salta ☎ 219 $11.00
- ★ Hotel Conte, Salta 463 $8.50

🚌 Buses
Buses run regularly to Corrientes and Posadas in Misiones province.

🚆 Trains
- Corrientes: "El Correntino" departs 0100 Mon, Thu, Sat
- Buenos Aires: "El Correntino" and "El Gran Capitan" depart daily
- Posadas: "El Gran Capitán" departs daily

PASO DE LA PATRIA

Postal code: 3409 • ☎ area code: 0783
Distance from Corrientes: 45 km north on RN 12

Located opposite the junction of the **Ríos Paraguay** and **Paraná**, about 10 km off RN 12, Paso de la Patria was founded in 1872. The area was an active war zone during the War of the Triple Alliance. Now it is a paradise for *dorado* anglers who congregate here once a year for the annual competition. The river at this point is more than 1½ km wide. On the Paso de la Patria side there are some rocky banks, but most of it consists of sandy stretches. The town opposite in Paraguay is also called Paso de la Patria.

🎉 Festivals
- *Dorado* fishing competition which attracts many anglers: First week in August. Most accommodation is booked out

ℹ Tourist information
- Dirección de Turismo, corner of 25 de Mayo and Bolívar

🛏 Accommodation
- Hotel Dorado, corner of San Martín and Córdoba $7.50 ⚠

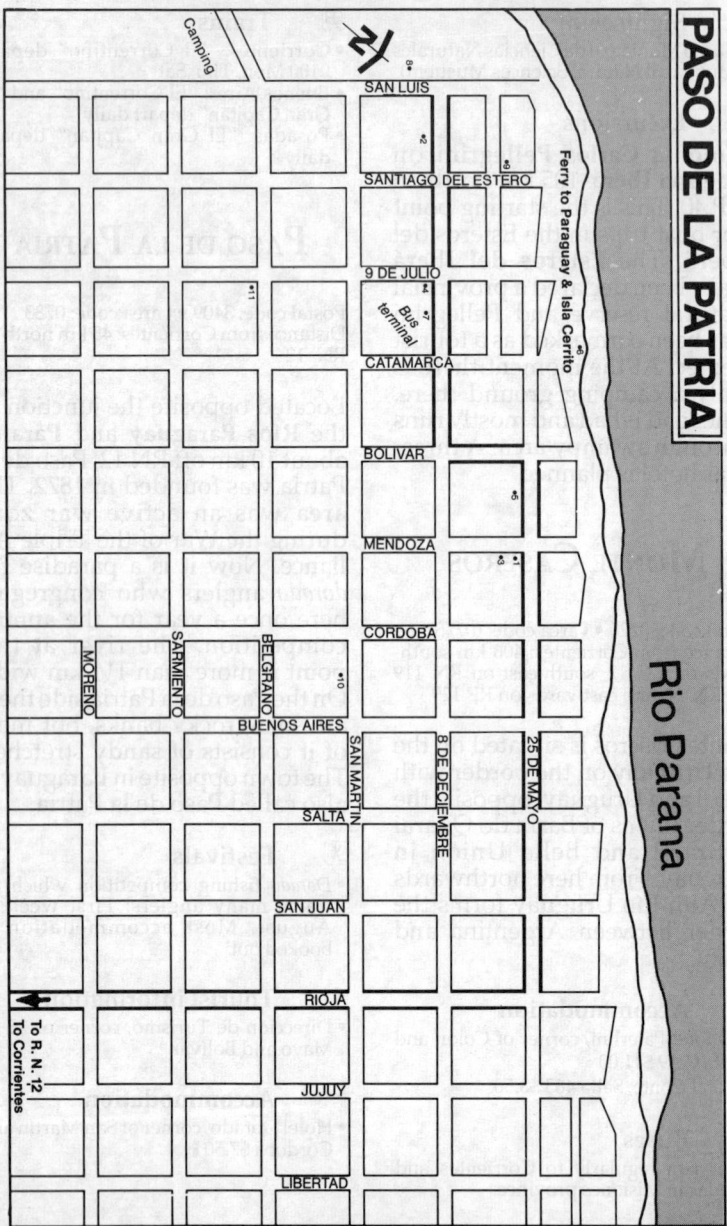

Paso de la Patria

CORRIENTES PROVINCE

- ★★ Hostería F A T S A ⑪ (94006 $21.00 ♣♣. Breakfast $1.20
- Residencial Casa Mersch, corner of Belgrano and 9 de Julio $3.00 ♣. Private bathroom
- Residencial Casa Sicardi, corner of Santiago del Estero and 25 de Mayo $2.50 ♣. Shared bathroom

Accommodation outside Paso de la Patria

- ★★★ Cabaña Don Julián, 2 km outside town, on the river ⑪ (94021 $15.00 ♣♣. Boat hire
- Cabañas Bigotes Ranch, 1 km before Don Julián $9.50 for four. Outside town

▲ Camping

- Municipal camping ground, on the road to Cabaña Don Julián

⑪ Eating out

- Restaurant Hotel F A T S A
- Snackbar Mauri, corner of 8 de Diciembre and San Luis. Hamburgers

✉ Post and telegraph

- Post office: Encotel, corner of Mendoza and 25 de Mayo
- Telephon: Entel, corner of 8 de Diciembre and 9 de Julio

🚌 Buses

The bus terminal is on the corner of 8 de Diciembre and Catamarca.
- Corrientes: Fare $0.75; 1 hour; Empresa Paso de las Patria

🚗 Motoring

- Service station: Casa Gímenez, corner of 25 de Mayo and Buenos Aires

⚓ Water transport

Launch services to Paso de la Patria in Paraguay run three times a week, on Mon, Wed, and Fri, leaving Paso de la Patria at 1400. Return trip the following day. You would have to stay overnight in Paraguay.

🎣 Sport

Fishing

Dorado fishing is not permitted between October and the end of February. During the fishing season only two *dorados* are allowed per person per day
- Todo Trolling, corner of San Luis and 25 de Mayo (94105. Launch hire, fishing gear. Ask for Martín N Kansourian
- Cabañas Don Julián. Launch hire $52.00 per day
- Launch hire for 2 hours (3 persons) $20.00

🎭 Entertainment

- Disco Veleros, corner of 8 de Diciembre and San Luis. Weekends only

♦ Excursions

- **Isla del Cerrito**: This island can be reached by daily ferry services departing 0700, 1500, and 1730. This service is free. Information from port officials. The island is part of Chaco province to which it is connected by a bridge; see "Excursions" in

Key to Map

1	Municipalidad
2	Iglesia Immaculada Concepción de María
3	Post office (Encotel)
4	Telephone (Entel)
5	Tourist information
6	Ferry to Paraguay and Isla Cerrito
7	Bus terminal
8	Hotel F A T S A
9	Residencial Casa Sicardi
10	Hotel Dorado
11	Residencial Casa Mersch

Resistencia on page 695. The island has an interesting history. At the end of the War of the Triple Alliance (Argentina, Uruguay, and Brazil versus Paraguay), the Brazilians occupied the island. Only after 10 years of negotiations did the Brazilians withdraw

PASO DE LOS LIBRES

Postal code: 3230 • ✆ area code: (0772) •
Population: 25 000
Distance from Monte Caseros: 126 km northwest on RP 25, then northeast on RN 14 and RN 117

In 1843 General Madariaga crossed the Río Uruguay here with his 108 liberators to annnex Corrientes province to Argentina.

The town is located on a little hill overlooking the **Río Uruguay** which is about 1 km wide here. It is linked by a modern road and rail bridge with the Brazilian town of Uruguaiana. At the bridge there is a huge ACA service station and cafeteria. On the Plaza Independencia is a monument with the names and ranks of the 108 liberators.

🎭 Festivals
- Famous *carnaval* season
- Fiesta de San José, patron saint of the town: March 19

ℹ️ Tourist information
- Municipal Tourist Office, corner of Madariaga and Mitre, on the Plaza

⛺ Camping
- Autocamping Laguna Mansa, near Puente Internacional overlooking the Río Uruguay

🍴 Eating out
- Restaurant El Encuentro, Madariaga 1081
- Restaurant El Motivo, Colón block 900 (corner of Rivadavia)
- ☞ Restaurant La Victoria, Colón 583. Steakhouse
- Pizzería Casa Rola, corner of Mitre and Madariaga

🛏 Accommodation in Paso de los Libres

★★★★	Hotel Alejandro I, Coronel Lopez 502 (corner of Pago Largo)	✆ 21000	$14.00	
	Air-conditioned; ACA discount			
★★★	Hotel Madariaga, Pago Largo 954	✆ 21501	$16.00	
★★	Hotel Buen Confort, Lopez 1091	✆ 21184	$8.00	
A	Residencial Colón, Colón 1055		$6.00	
A	Residencial Las Vegas, Colón 546		$5.50	
A	Residencial Uruguay, Uruguay 1252, 5 blocks from railway station	✆ 21672	$6.00	
B	Residencial 26 de Febrero, Uruguay 1297 (corner of Reguel)	✆ 22050	$3.00	

Accommodation outside the city center

★★★	Hotel de la Amistad, Puente Internacional	✆ 21100	$10.00	
•	Residencial Caprí, corner of Santiago del Estero and Pellegrini, opposite bus terminal		$5.50	

CORRIENTES PROVINCE

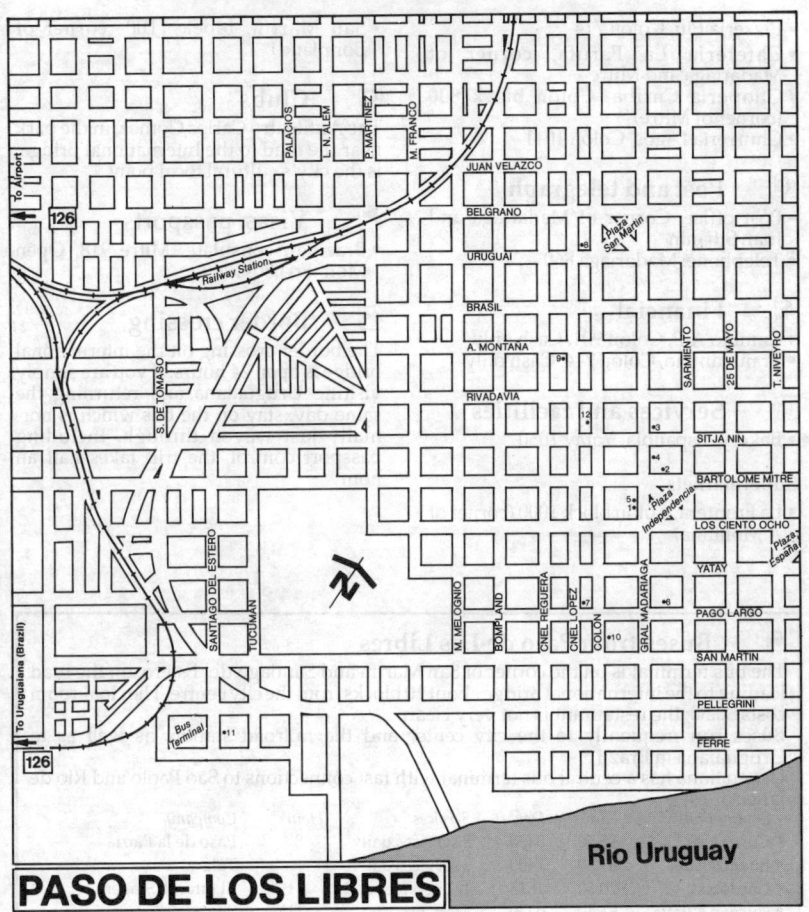

PASO DE LOS LIBRES

Key to Map
1. Municipalidad
2. Iglesia San José
3. Post office (Encotel)
4. Telephone (Entel)
5. Tourist office
6. Hotel Madariaga
7. Hotel Alejandro I
8. Residencial Uruguay
9. Hotel Buen Confort
10. Hotel Las Vegas
11. Residencial Caprí
12. Residencial Colón

Paso de los Libres

Corrientes Province

- Pizzería Piu, Colón 714
- Cafetería La Farula, corner of Madariaga and Mitre
- Chopería Cariba, Colón block 800 (corner of Mitre)
- Churrería Lagos, Colón 1011

Post and telegraph

- Post office: Corner of Madariaga and Juan Sitjanin
- Telephone: Madariaga 860

Financial

- Cambio A P, Colón 901. Cash only
- Transcambio, Colón 744. Cash only

Services and facilities

- Bakery: Española, Yatay 1050

Supermarkets

- La Frontera, Colón block 1000 (corner of A Montana)
- San Martín, block 1100 (corner of Bonpland)

Clubs

The Anfiteatro Carlos Gómez, in the park near the road to the International Bridge, is the city's cultural focal point.

Visas, passports

- Brazilian consulate, Mitre 918. Open Mon–Fri 080–1200

Border crossing

The border crossing on the international bridge is open 24 hours. If you are simply visiting Uruguaiana and returning the same day, stay on the bus which is normally just waved through. Including passport control, the trip takes half an hour.

Buses from Paso de Los Libres

The bus terminal is on the corner of San Martín and Santiago del Estero, on the road leading to the international bridge about 10 blocks from the city centre. The cloakroom costs $0.50; the restaurant is not very clean.

Buses run frequently to the city center and the railroad station, as well as to Uruguaiana in Brazil.

Uruguaiana has a central bus terminal with fast connections to São Paolo and Rio de Janeiro.

Destination	Fare	Depart	Services	Hours	Company
Corrientes	$5.50	0430	3 services daily	8	Paso de la Patria
Buenos Aires	$9.50	1400	3 services daily		Tala
Córdoba	$20.50	1815	1–2 services daily		El Litoral, Singer
Curuzú Cuatiá	$1.40	0730	Mon, Fri	1½	Silvia
Mercedes	$1.90		daily		Paso de la Patria
Paraná		2115	1–2 services daily		Federal, Kurtz
Posadas	$7.20	0300	5–6 services daily		Crucero del Norte, Singer, Kurtz
Puerto Iguazú		0300	1–2 services daily		Singer, Kurtz
Rosario		2300	1–2 services daily		El Norte Bis, Kurtz
Santa Fé	$11.70	1810	2 services daily		El Litoral, Singer, Federal, Kurtz
Santo Tomé	$3.70	0300	3 services daily	4	Crucero del Norte
Uruguaiana (Brazil)	$0.50		daily except Sun	½	Perini S A
Yapeyú	$1.50	0300	3 services daily	2	Crucero del Norte

Paso de los Libres

CORRIENTES PROVINCE

✈ Air services

- Buenos Aires (Aeroparque Jorge Newbery): Fare $44.00; departs 1140 daily; 2 hours; Empresa Aerolineas
- Concordia: Fare $19.00; Departs 1140 Mon, Tues, Thurs, Sat; ½ hour; Aerolineas Argentinas

🚗 Motoring

The road to Corrientes via Mercedes is sealed most of the way.
RN 17 trip to Yapeyú crosses the international bridge and passes through many planted eucalyptus forests. It is sealed throughout.

Service stations

- ACA, on the approaches to the international bridge. Information and maps
- Esso, Colón block 400 (corner of Pago Lago)

🚆 Trains

The railroad station is in Tucumán block 1300 (corner of Belgrano). The railroad connecting Buenos Aires with Posadas runs through Paso de Los Libres. Municipal buses run directly between the railroad station and the bus terminal. The trains running through here are "El Gran Capitán" and "Cataratas". They are always full, and it is not possible to book a seat.

- Asunción (Paraguay): Departs 1930 Fri; 28 hours
- Buenos Aires (Lacroze station): Pullman $17.00, first class $11.50, tourist class $8.00; departs 0513; 2 services daily; 11 hours
- Concordia $3.30
- Posadas: Pullman $8.50, first class $5.80, tourist class $4.00; departs 0209 daily; 6 hours

🛍 Shopping

The main shopping street is Colón.

⚽ Sport

- Racecourse

🎭 Entertainment

- Casino Provincial
- Night Club Kanela, Mitre 1072
- Peña La Vieja Pulteria, corner of Mitre and Coronel Reguera. Traditional

📷 Sightseeing

- Museo Municipal (Municipal Museum)
- Monolito a los 108. Memorial to the "liberators" during the campaign against the dictator Rosas in 1843
- Monolito de la Batalla de Yatay (Battle of Yatay Memorial). In memory of the battle of Yatay during the War of the Triple Alliance in 1865
- Tourist complex, including Victoria zoo

🌳 Excursions

- Uruguiana in Brazil. Take a Muñoz or Perini bus
- Yapeyú. A bus trip to the Jesuit mission and birthplace of General San Martín

SANTA ANA DE LOS GUÁCARAS

Postal code: 3401
Distance from Corrientes: 20 km eastwards

Santa Ana de los Guácaras is a seventeenth-century settlement with well-preserved colonial architecture. It was founded in 1660 by Franciscan monks after the destruction of Concepción de la Buena Esperanza, when they

CORRIENTES PROVINCE

resettled the Guácara Indians in Santa Ana.

Buses

Buses run frequently to and from Corrientes.

SANTO TOMÉ

Postal code: 3340 • (area code: (0756)
Distance from Posadas: 147 km south on RN 14 on a sealed road

Santo Tomé was officially founded in 1863, but its origins go back to the seventeenth century as a Jesuit mission after the founding of Yapeyú. After the expulsion of the Jesuits the settlement decayed and was sacked by the Portuguese in 1817.

Festivals
- Festival Correntino de Folklore (Corrientes Folk Festival): December
- Foundation day: August 27

Accommodation

During the holiday season book in advance for the better hotels.
- ★★★ Hotel Santo Tomé (ACA), corner of Beltran and Belgrano, 6 blocks from town center near the water tower (20161 $10.00
- A Residencial Che-Roga, Uruguay 936 (corner of San Martín, opposite the bus terminal) $4.50
- A Residencial Pucará, San Martín 557 (3 blocks from the bus terminal) $6.00
- B Residencial Paris, Mitre 890 (corner of Beltrán) $5.50. Back-packers

Eating out
- Restaurant Aidel, corner of Uruguay and San Martín
- Restaurant Bar Española, San Martín 535
- Restaurant Terminal

Buses from Santo Tomé

The bus terminal is at the corner of Uruguay and San Martín.
El Litoral runs services to Córdoba, Paraná, and Santa Fé.
El Norte Bis runs services to Rosario, Puerto Iguazú, and Santa Fé
Expreso Singer runs services to Buenos Aires, Córdoba, Posadas, Porto Alegre in Brazil, and Puerto Iguazú.
- Corrientes: Fare $6.50; departs 2200 daily; 6 hours; Empresa Ciudad de Posadas
- Apóstoles: Fare $2.00; departs 0040; 3 services daily; 1½ hours; Empresa Tigre Iguazú, Expreso Singer
- Ituzaingó: Fare $2.70; departs 2200 daily; 2 hours; Empresa Ciudad de Posadas
- Posadas: Fare $2.20; departs 0450; 3 services daily; 2½ hours; Empresa Tigre Iguazú, Expreso Singer
- Yapeyú: Fare $2.20; departs 1820 daily; 3 hours; Empresa Tigre Iguazú

Motoring

The road between Santo Tomé and Apóstoles runs through flat swampy country.
- Service station: YPF, Mitre block 400

Water transport
- Ferries across the Río Uruguay to the Brazilian town of San Borja leave from Puerto Hormiguero 10 km south, which can be reached by municipal bus 2. The ferry operates Mon–Fri 0730–1630 and Sat–Sun 0700–1500

Sport
- Fishing

Sightseeing
- Museo Histórico Regional (Museum of Regional History), Navajas 844

Santa Ana de las Guácaras

CORRIENTES PROVINCE

- Museo Miguel J Centeno, Blanco 869. Exhibits of local history
- The main church has a baptismal font which dates back to the Jesuit mission of 1688

Excursions
- A few kilometers south of town are the remains of a Jesuit mission

YAPEYÚ

Postal code: 3232 • (area code: (0772)
Distance
- From Paso de los Libres: 76 km northwards on RN 14 on a paved road
- From Santo Tomé: 144 km south on RN 14 on a sealed road

Yapeyú was founded in 1626 as the capital of the Jesuit Guaraní missions. It soon became a flourishing community. By the time the Jesuits were expelled from South America there were 60 000 head of cattle here and the population was over 8000. The present village is only a faint echo of its former glory—it was not only a prosperous rural community but also a renowned seat of learning, and the second city after Buenos Aires in the Gobernacion del Río de la Plata. After the expulsion of the Jesuits, Spanish civil and military governors took control, but it became clear that they could not match the talents of the Jesuits. In 1775 the father of Don José de San Martín became military governor in Yapeyú. He moved into the little fortress which was then the residence of the governors, and it was here that Don José, the future liberator of half of South America, was born. In those days the region was under constant threat by marauding Portuguese and it was against these invasions rather than the local indigenous people that the Spanish had to guard.

Yapeyú was almost destroyed by fire in 1817 when a Portuguese army invaded the township under the command of the Marquis of Alderete.

In 1860 Yapeyú was refounded as José de San Martín in honor of the Liberator, but was renamed Yapeyú for historical reasons in 1889.

Accommodation
From July to the middle of August accommodation is scarce.

★★★ Alejandro I, corner of Paso de los Andes and José de San Martín, overlooking Río Uruguay (93056 $15.00. Air-conditioned bungalows

★ Hostería del Yapeyú (formerly ACA), corner of Matorras and Cabral (93066 $5.00

Eating out
- Comedor del Bicentenario, overlooking the river

Buses
- Paso de los Libres: Fare $1.60
- Santo Tomé: Fare $2.60; departs 1700 daily; 3 hours; Empresa Crucero del Norte

Motoring
The road to Santo Tomé runs through much swampy country, especially between La Cruz and Alvear.

CORRIENTES PROVINCE

📷 Sightseeing

The whole settlement is alive with historical mementos: Jesuit inscriptions on rocks, temple columns on street corners, and references to José San Martín, like the 300-year-old fig tree which was a contemporary of the young San Martín.

- La Casa de San Martín (House of San Martín). Painstaking excavation by archeologists has located the house in which San Martín was born. The house is now inside a larger building and the whole place is kept in immaculate condition
- Museo Sanmartiniano (San Martín Museum). The gardens surrounding the museum is a replica of the garden in Boulogne-Sur-Mer in France where San Martín spent his last years in a self-imposed exile. Next to the remains of his birthplace there is a reconstructed black Jesuit structure which serves as a museum. Here you can view documents belonging or referring to San Martín during his lifetime
- Village church, a nineteenth-century neo-gothic building
- A partially completed arch erected after the disastrous Islas Malvinas (Falkland Islands) war, to commemorate the fallen. Most units serving in the war were from Corrientes. The arch will be completed when the islands are restored to Argentina
- Museo de Cultura Jesuítica (Jesuit Museum). Many objects and implements used during the Jesuit time and found in this area are gathered here. There are also columns with inscriptions in Spanish and Guaraní

Yapeyú

Entre Ríos Province

Plate 45 Map of Entre Ríos Province
- **753** Bovril
- **753** Chajarí
- **754** Colón
- **755** Map
- **757** Concepción del Uruguay
- **759** Map
- **762** Concordia
- **763** Map
- **766** Crespo
- **766** Diamante
- **767** Federación
- **768** Federal
- **768** Gualeguay
- **769** Gualeguaychú
- **770** Map
- **773** La Paz
- **774** Map
- **775** Nogoyá
- **775** Paraná
- **776** Map

Entre Ríos Province

782 Parque Nacional El Palmar
783 Rosario del Tala
783 Viale
783 Victoria
785 Villa Libertador General San Martín
785 Villaguay

Entre Ríos means "between rivers", an apt description of this province's location between the **Río Uruguay** and the **Río Paraná**. To the east, the Río Uruguay forms the border with Uruguay; the Río Paraná forms the border with Santa Fé province to the west, and to the south with Buenos Aires province. To the north is Corrientes province, the border formed by a series of smaller rivers. Other important rivers are the **Río Gualeguaychú** and the **Río Gualeguay**. The terrain in Entre Ríos province is uniformly flat, except for the so-called "**Cuchillos**" ("Knives") in the center. Not surprisingly, a considerable part of this low-lying country is swampy and marshy, especially along the Río Paraná as it approaches its junction with the Río Uruguay to form the Río de la Plata in the south-east corner of the province.

The climate is temperate, with an average annual rainfall of 1000 mm. Even though summer is the wettest season, the rainfall is spread fairly evenly throughout the year.

The provincial capital is **Paraná**, some 480 km north-west of Buenos Aires. Built on the high banks of the Río Paraná, it is an important river trading center. The hinterland is very fertile and produces rice, corn, sorghum, wheat, citrus fruit, peanuts, and many other crops.

The province covers an area of 79 000 square km. The population is almost one million, and comprises a variety of ethnic groups. A great many Wolga Germans settled in the province after the war.

The original inhabitants of Entre Ríos were the Guaranís. Many descendants of this people still live in the province, and in some areas a Guaraní dialect has survived.

The province is linked by the Complejo Ferrovial Zárate–Brazo Largo (Zárate–Brazo Largo Bridge Complex) with Buenos Aires province, which consists of a bridge over the **Río Paraná de las Palmas**, and another over the **Río Paraná Guazú**. The entire complex is built some 10 m above the swamp, all the way from Paraná de las Palmas to the Río Paraná Guazú bridge. This sys-

ENTRE RÍOS PROVINCE

tem enables trains and buses to make the journey from Paraná to Buenos Aires in less than eight hours.

Entre Ríos is an angler's paradise, and numerous fishing competitions are held here. The most sought after fish is the *dorado*, a type of giant goldfish.

A number of Argentina's most impressive engineering structures are in this province:
- The Complejo Ferrovial Zarate–Brazo Largo, mentioned above, which crosses the two arms of the **Río Paraná** and links Entre Ríos with Buenos Aires province
- The 2400 m long Túnel Subfluvial Hernandarias (Hernandarias River Tunnel) under the Río Paraná, linking Paraná with Santa Fé city
- The bridge over the **Embalse Salto Grande** on the **Río Uruguay**, built in conjunction with Uruguay
- The Puente Internacional Libertador General José de San Martín (Liberator General José de San Martín International Bridge) over the Río Uruguay. This bridge is 5400 m long, and links the town of **Gualeguaychú** with Fray Bentos in Uruguay
- Near **Salto Grande** there is a huge hydroelectric power station built in co-operation with Uruguay

The main attractions of Entre Ríos for the tourist are its excellent fishing, casinos, and golf courses, and the **Parque Nacional El Palmar** near Concordia, which has camping facilities right on the Río Uruguay. The towns of **Paraná**, **Concordia**, **Federación**, **Gualeguaychú**, and **Colón** are also worth visiting.

BOVRIL

Postal code: 3142 • (area code: (0438)
Distance from Paraná: 129 km north-east on RN 12 then RN 127

⌹ Accommodation
A Residencial Sayonara, Avenida San Martín 262 (173 $11.50 ⁞⁞

CHAJARÍ

Postal code: 3228 • (area code: (0456)
Distances
- From Concordia: 77 km northwards on RN 14
- From Paraná: 350 km eastwards on RN 18 then northwards on RN 14

Chajarí is a relatively new town, and began to flourish when citrus plantations were established in the area. It is located in the north-eastern sector of the province, about 18 km west of **Embalse Salto Grande**.

The average temperatures range from 27°C in summer to 14°C in winter.

Despite the neat, ordered citrus plantations, patches of virgin bush can still be found. Many streams wind their way through the area, and the surrounding plains have been partially reafforested with pine trees.

ENTRE RÍOS PROVINCE

Festivals
- Fiesta Provincial del Folklore "Ciudad de Chajarí" ("Chajarí City" Provincial Folk Festival): January
- Fiesta Provincial de la Citricultura (Provincial Citrus- Growing Festival): November

Accommodation
★ Hotel Caribe, Entre Ríos 3155 $14.00
B Residencial Central, Belgrano 990 $9.50
B Residencial,Regina, Sarmiento 2863 (1031 $9.50

Accommodation outside Chajarí
★ Motel Suiza, RN 14, Km 426 $14.00

Camping
- Balneario Municipal "Ciudad de Chajarí", 17 ha on the banks of Embalse Salto Grande. Cabins are available

Sightseeing
- Museo Regional "Camila Quiroga", corner of Respetto and Fochezatto. An old mansion with an exhibition of artefacts from Chajarí's past

COLÓN

Postal code: 3280 • (area code: (0447) • Population: 15 000
Distances
- From Paraná: 261 km eastwards on RN 18 then south-east on RN 130
- From Concepción del Uruguay: 37 km northwards on RN 14

The tourist resort of Colón was founded in 1863. It is situated on the **Río Uruguay**, and the long, white beaches along the river here attract many visitors. There are imposing cliffs along some parts of the river in this area; they can be seen from a considerable distance and are very picturesque. A toll bridge (toll $2.00) now links Colón with Paysandú in Uruguay. Temperatures average 30 °C in summer and 9 °C in winter.

Much of the population here is of Swiss-French origin.

San Martín is the main shopping street, and streets intersecting San Martín change their names after crossing it. Only the main streets are sealed. The **Río Uruguay** is about 1 km wide here, and the flow of water is regulated by the flood gates at the **Embalse Salto Grande**.

Festivals
- Fiesta Nacional de la Artesanía (National Craft Festival): February

Tourist information
- Centro Municipal de Turismo, corner of Avenida Costanera and E Gouchon (21233

Camping
- Autocamping Municipal, at the end of Lugones and Ferrari. Cabins are available

Eating out
- Restaurant Bamboche, Urquiza 116
- Restaurant El Dragón, 3 de Febrero 169
- Restaurant El Faro, San Martín east. Steakhouse
- Restaurant El Mangrullo, Balneario Municipal "S Inkier"
- Restaurant El Quincho, corner of Andrade and Mitre
- Restaurant JR, corner of Urquiza and Alem. Steakhouse
- Restaurant La Cumbre, Club A Campito, on the beachfront. Steakhouse

Entre Ríos Province

COLON

Key to Map
1. Municipalidad
2. Iglesia Santos Justo y Pastor
3. Post office (Encotel)
4. Telephone
5. Centro de Turismo
6. Banco de la Nación
7. Cambio Turismo Colón
8. Hotel Quirinale I and Casino
9. Hotel Nueva Plaza
10. Hotel Palmar
11. Hotel Vieja Calera del Rincón de Espiro
12. Residencial Aridan
13. Residencial Holimasú
14. Residencial Paysandú
15. Residencial Ver-Wei

Entre Ríos Province

Accommodation in Colón

★★★★★	Hotel Quirinale I, Avenida H Quiros	(21133	$48.00	
	Includes breakfast; on the beach			
★★	Hotel Nuevo Plaza, corner of 12 de Abril and Belgrano			
		(21043	$18.50	
★★	Hotel Palmar, Ferrari 295	(21948	$18.50	
★	Hotel Vieja Calera del Rincón de Espiro, Bolívar 344 (corner of Maipú)			
		(21139	$14.00	
A	Residencial Aridan, Alvear 50 (corner of San Martín)			
		(21830	$11.50	
A	Residencial Holimasú, Belgrano 28	(21305	$11.50	
B	Residencial Paysandú, corner of Paysandu and Maipú			
		(21140	$9.50	
B	Residencial Ver-Wei, 25 de Mayo 10	(21972	$9.50	

Accommodation outside Colón

★	Motel Colón, RN 14 12 Km south	$13.00	
	ACA discount; access to international bridge		
B	Residencial Las Colonias, San José, 5 km north, Centenario de la Colonia		
		$9.50	

- Restaurant La Rueda, San Martín 150. Steakhouse
- Restaurant Los Aventureros, corner of E Berga and 12 de Abril
- Restaurant Los Caudillos, San Martín 365. Steakhouse
- Restaurant Piedras Coloradas, on the beachfront. Steakhouse
- Pizzeria La Cabaña, 9 de Julio
- Pizzeria Omar, 12 de Abril 350
- Cafetería El Ciervo de Oro, corner of San Martín and Sourigues. Hamburgers
- Cafetería El Palmar, Bulevar Ferrari 295
- Cafetería Libertad, 12 de Abril 293
- Cafetería Nuevo Hotel Plaza, corner of 12 de Abril and Belgrano
- Cafetería Zalacain, corner of Urquiza and Lugones

Financial

- Casa de Cambio Sosa, corner of Alem and 12 de Abril

Visas, passports

- Uruguayan consulate, San Martín 103 (21350. Open Mon–Fri 0700–1500

Border crossing

There are border checkpoints on both sides of the international bridge, but procedures are fairly relaxed. Visitors passing into Uruguauy must pay a toll to use the road.

Motoring

Service stations

- ACA, junction of RN 14 and the turn-off to Colón, on the access road to the town
- Shell, corner of San Martín and Salta

Tours

- Náutica Río Uruguay, Maipú 364 (21696. This company organizes sailing trips on the Río Uruguay for $8.00 an hour or $20.00 for a half day. Señor Alvarez is the manager
- Turismo La Flecha, Moreno 408 (21295
- Turismo Paccot, 12 de Abril 280 (21900

Shopping

- La Casona, corner of 12 de Abril and J J Paso. The Fiesta de la Artesanía is held here in February

ENTRE RÍOS PROVINCE

🚌 Buses from Colón

The bus terminal is on the corner of Sourriges and Paysandú.

Destination	Fare	Depart	Services	Hours	Company
• Paraná	$5.00	0345		5	San José
• Buenos Aires	$7.50	0015	5 services daily		El Rápido, TATA
• Concepción del Uruguay	$1.00	0645	11 services daily		Expreso Girardot
• Concordia	$2.50	0505	3 services daily		Itapé
• Córdoba	$12.50	2000	Mon, Thurs, Fri, Sun		El Litoral
• Gualeguaychú	$1.00				Ciudad de Gualeguaychú
• Parque Nacional El Palmar	$1.30	0645			
• Paysandú (Uruguay)	$1.80	0845	3 services daily		Linea Internacional

Sport
- Bowling: El Cid, 3 de Febrero 72

Entertainment
- Casino Hotel Quirinale, Brown
- Disco Kaiman, Laprida east
- Disco Topo's, Urquiza 240

Excursions
- **Molino Forclaz**: 4 km. Built by Juan Bautistas Forclaz, a Swiss-French immigrant. This building was built in 1890 and was the first flour mill in the area
- **Palacio San José** and **Concepción del Uruguay**: An organised tour costs $6.00. See Concepción del Uruguay below
- **Parque Nacional El Palmar**: Approximately 50 km northwards, halfway to Concordia. See Parque Nacional El Palmar on page 782. To get to the park from Colón take a bus to Ubajay (fare $1.50), and let the driver know you want to get off at the entrance to the national park. The ticket office is about 200 m from the main road, and hikers are admitted free. A well-maintained dirt road crosses the park, and several minor tracks lead off it to the north and south. On the banks of the Río Uruguay is the rangers' office where you can get leaflets and information on flora and fauna in the park. Tour companies operate half-day excursions from Colón for $6.00
- **Paysandú and Termas de Guaviyú**, both in Uruguay: Tour companies operate a 10-hour excursion to neighbouring Uruguay, crossing the **Río Uruguay** at the Puente Internacional General Artigas (General Artigas International Bridge). There is a toll of $10.00 to cross the bridge. Expreso Itapé runs bus services from Colón to Paysandú for $1.80

CONCEPCIÓN DEL URUGUAY

Postal code: 3260 • ☎ area code: (0442) • Population: 50 000
Distances
- From Paraná: 288 km eastwards on RN 14
- From Buenos Aires: 320 km north-west on RN 12 and RP 39

Entre Ríos Province

The large river port of Concepción del Uruguay is located on an arm of the **Río Uruguay**, called the Riacho Itapé. It was founded in 1783 by Don Tomás de Rocamora and was the provincial capital until 1883.

The city center is the Plaza General Francisco Ramirez, named after the man known as *"El Supremo Entrerriano"*, an untranslateable phrase meaning "the greatest resident of Entre Ríos" or "the great man from Entre Ríos". A pyramid has been erected in the plaza in his honor.

There are 5 km of sandy beaches within walking distance of the city center. The average temperature in summer is 30°C, and in winter 18°C.

Festivals
- Carnaval: February
- Fiesta Federal: February 3
- Fiesta Provincial de la Playa (Provincial Beach Festival): January. Held in Banco Pelay, just outside Concepción

Tourist information
- Oficina Municipal de Turismo, 9 de Julio 844 ℅ 7152

Camping
- Camping Banco Pelay

Eating out
- Restaurant Canguro, corner of Rocamora and Reibel
- Restaurant Carlos V, corner of San Martín and Presidente Perón
- Restaurant El Buen Pollo, Leguizamón 33. Chicken
- Restaurant El Carrito, Rocamora 657. Set price, eat as much as you like
- Restaurant El Peregrino, Rocamora 826
- Restaurant El Picuru, Bulevar Martinez 52
- Restaurant Filippini, Rocamora 654 (corner of Eva Perón). Steakhouse
- Restaurant Isondu, Eva Perón 90 (corner of Rocamora)
- Restaurant La Costera, Bulevar H Yrigoyen 150
- Restaurant La Delfina, corner of Eva Perón and Rocamora
- Restaurant La Herradura, corner of Rocamora and I Torres
- Restaurant La Taberna, corner of Evita Perón and 8 de Junio
- Restaurant Los Verdes Años, Mitre 778. Vegetarian
- Restaurant Sarao, Rocamora 627
- Restaurant Super Lomo, corner of 8 de Junio and Leguizamón
- Restaurant Terminal, Bulevar Martinez, between block 50 and block 100
- Pizzería La Casona del Tano, J D Perón 585
- Pizzería La Peatonal, corner of Peatonal and Urquiza. Pizza
- Pizzería La Rusita, Galarza 1581
- Pizzería Napoli, Reibel 113
- Pizzería San Remo, 9 de Julio 841
- Pizzería Santa Lucía, Rocamora 583
- Cafetería La Delfina, corner of San Martín and 3 de Febrero
- Cafetería La Taberna, Eva Perón 135

Key to Map
1. Municipalidad
2. Catedral
3. Post office (Encotel)
4. Telephone
5. Tourist information
6. Cabildo
7. Museo Delio Panizza
8. Hotel Carlos I
9. Grand Hotel
10. Hotel General Francisco Ramirez
11. Apart Hotel Maximus
12. Apart Hotel Grumette
13. Residencial My House
14. Hospedaje Italiano
15. Hospedaje Soledad
16. Residencial T C

Concepción del Uruguay

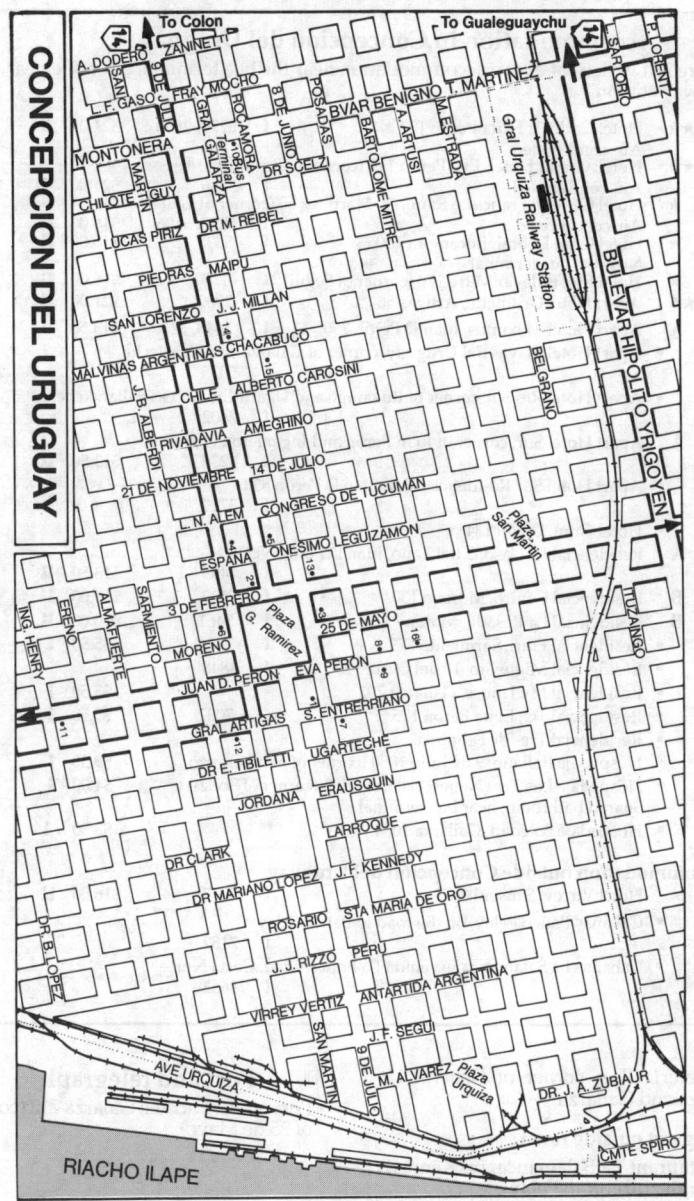

Entre Ríos Province

Accommodation in Concepción del Uruguay

There is a variety of cheap accommodation near the bus terminal, but none near the railway station.

★★	Hotel Carlos I, Evita Perón 133	(6776, 2850	$21.00	♁
★★	Hotel: Grand Hotel, Eva Perón 110 (corner of Rocamora)			
	Air-conditioned	(5586	$21.00	♁
★	Hotel General Francisco Ramirez, Martinez 60 (corner of Gallarza)			
	Air-conditioned	(5985, 5106	$16.00	♁
★	Hotel Gran Litoral, Rocamora 1406	(5035	$16.00	♁
	Near the bus terminal			
★	Hotel Río, Bulevar Mitre 170 (corner of Segui)	(6755	$16.00	♁
★★	Apart Hotel Grumette, Artigas 56	(2962	$21.00	♁
A	Apart Hotel Máximus, Juan D Perón 290	(3448, 3260	$13.50	♁
•	Apart Hotel Playas del Uruguay, corner of Galarza and Ugarteche			
		(5035		
•	Apart Hotel Río Sol, corner of Ituzaingó and Ugarteche, access to Banco Pelay			
		(7602		
A	Apart Hotel Sur, corner of Juan Perón and Ingeniero Pereyra			
		(4230	$13.50	♁
•	Apart Hotel Sur Residencial Tca, Juan D Perón 830			
		(3729		
•	Hotel Gran, Colón 134			
A	Residencial La Casona del Tano, Juan D Perón 585			
		(4405	$13.50	♁
B	Residencial Centro, Moreno 130	(7429	$10.00	♁
B	Residencial La Posada, Moreno 116	(5461	$10.00	♁
•	Residencial Fiuri, Sarmiento 779	(7016	$5.50	♁
•	Residencial Miguelito, 10 del Oeste 190	(4848		
•	Residencial My House, Gallarza 792		$3.50	♁
•	Residencial TC, Evita Perón 175	(7032	$5.50	♁
•	Residencial Tres de Febrero			
•	Hospedaje Italiano, 9 de Julio 1080 (corner of San Lorenzo)		$3.50	♁
•	Hospedaje Los Tres Nenes, Galarza 1233 (corner of Scelzi)		$4.00	♁
	Shared bathroom; near bus terminal			
•	Hospedaje Soledad, Gallarza 1034		$3.50	♁

Accommodation outside Concepción del Uruguay

★	Hotel Virrey, Sansoni 2075	(5017	$16.00	♁
•	Cabañas Banco Pelay, on the road to Banco Pelay			
		(7152		
•	Cabañas La Salamanca, Avenida La Fraternidad, Costa Norte			
		(4662		

- Cafetería Rys, corner of General Urquiza and Gallarza

Eating out outside town

- Restaurant La Salamanca, on Kennedy near the turnoff to Pelay

Post and telegraph

- Post office: Encotel, Galarza 712 (corner of 25 de Mayo)

Concepción del Uruguay

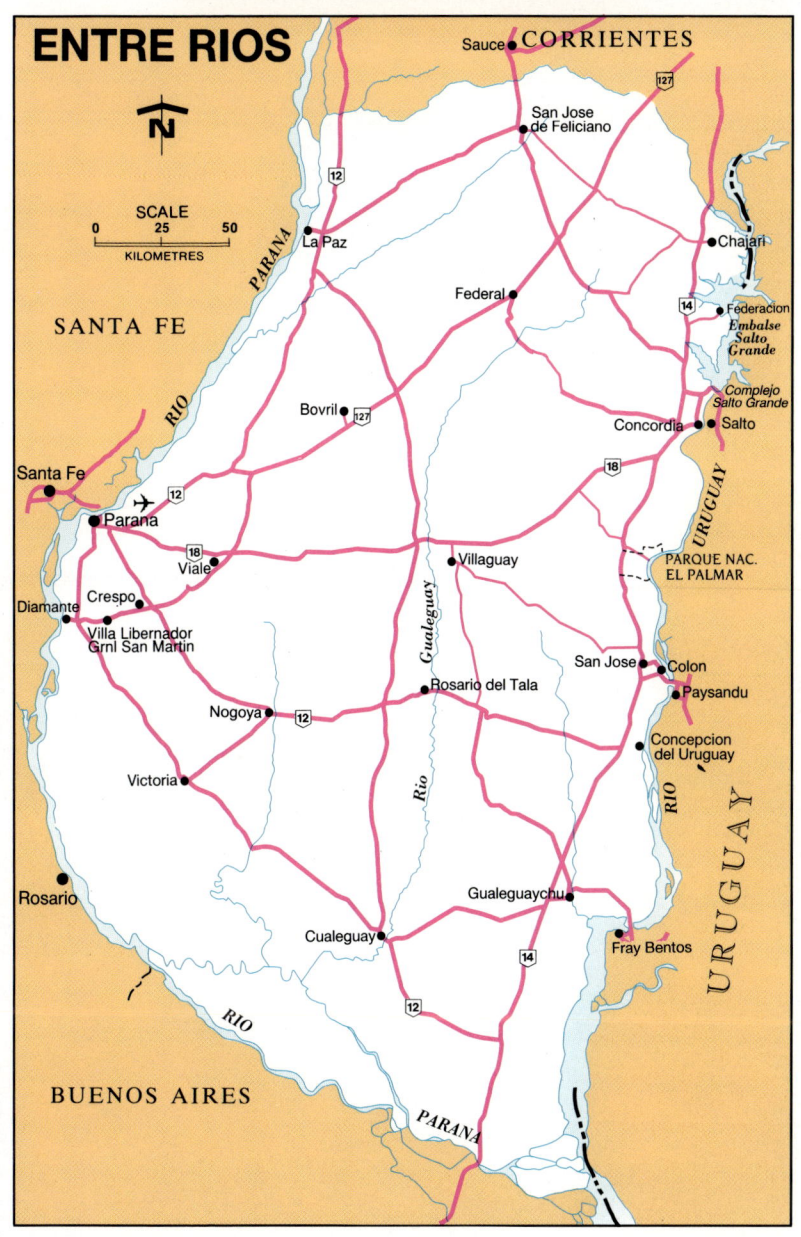

Plate 45

Map of Entre Ríos Province

Plate 46
Caranday palm, Parque Nacional El Palmar

Entre Ríos Province

Services and facilities
- Laundromat: Laverap, Congreso de Tucumán 132
- Photographic supplies: Optica Cargano, 9 de Julio 819
- Supermarket: Don José, corner of 9 de Julio and Maipú

Motoring
The roads to Paraná and Colón are both sealed.

Service stations
- ACA, corner of 9 de Julio and Ugarteche. Road maps available
- YPF, corner of 9 de Julio and San Lorenzo

Tours
- Ríoguay Tour, J J Millan 133. This company has a fleet of twelve mini-buses which it uses for tours

Shopping
The main shopping street in 9 de Julio.
- Artesanías Cherokee, 9 de Julio 772
- Artesanías Don Fabian, Eva Perón 42
- Artesanías El Charrua, Eva Perón 85
- Artesanías La Rueda, Urquiza 638

Sport
- Car racing: "Formula Entrerriana"
- Fishing: *Pejerrey, surubí, pacú,* and *bagres*. Check with the Dirrección de Recursos Naturales for details
- Golf: Golf Club Universitario, RP 39
- Horse racing
- Water sports: From October–March

Entertainment
- Disco Acapulco, corner of J D Perón and San Martín
- Disco Amarras, J D Perón 60
- Disco Le Feu Rouge, Galarza 788
- Disco La Delfina, corner of 3 de Febrero and San Martín
- Disco La Taberna, Eva Perón 130
- Disco Maximus, Galarza 850
- Disco Quijote, corner of 25 de Mayo and Rocamora
- Disco Rys, corner of Urquiza and Galarza
- Disco Sarao, Rocamora 629 (corner of Eva Perón)
- Disco Superdiscotek (also known as "Bufalo"), 25 de Mayo 130
- Whiskería Capricornio, Galarza 782

Sightseeing
- Cabildo, corner of San Martín and Moreno. This building is now the police headquarters
- Museo Delio Panizza, corner of Supremo Entrerriano and Galarza. This is supposedly the house in which Francisco Ramirez spent his early years. It is the oldest house in town and was built around 1793. Open Tues–Sun 1000–1200 and 1800–2000

Buses from Concepción del Uruguay

Destination	Fare	Depart	Services	Hours	Company
Paraná	$6.00	0100	4 services daily		Expreso San José
Buenos Aires					Central Rapido, Tata
Concordia		0430	5 services daily		Ciudad de Gualeguaychú, Empresa Itapé
Colón	$1.00	1000	2 services daily		Empresa Itapé
Gualeguaychú	$1.80				Ciudad de Gualeguaychú
Paysandú (Uruguay)		1230	2 services Mon, Sat		Copay
Posadas	$16.00	1600	2 services daily		Expreso Singer
Santa Fé	$5.50		Mon, Fri		Encon, Litoral

Concepción del Uruguay

ENTRE RÍOS PROVINCE

- Basilica de La Imaculada Concepción, built in 1859. J J de Urquiza is buried here

🍎 Excursions

- **Museo Palacio de San José**: 35 km west. Construction on this palatial home began in 1848. A mixture of Italian renaissance and colonial style, it was the private residence of General J J de Urquiza until his death in 1870. All 38 of its rooms lead onto one of three patios. The Corinthinan-style chapel is also of interest. The museum has an exhibition of lances and swords from the Battle of Caseros, as well as furniture and coins, including the only metal coin ever made in Entre Ríos, the *"Medio Entrerriano"*. The site is now a national monument. Tour companies operate half-day tours to the museum; fare $5.00
- **Salto Grande** and **Concordia**: There are full-day tours to the hydroelectric-cum-irrigation scheme of Salto Grande, a project built in conjunction with Uruguay. The tour costs $8.50
- **Parque Nacional El Palmar**: The national park extends from the main highway, RN 14, right down to the banks of the **Río Uruguay**. A half-day excursion to the park costs $6.00. Use a tour operator rather than the local bus, which will drop you off at the park, but will not pick you up for the return journey! See Parque Nacional El Palmar page 782

CONCORDIA

Postal code: 3200 • ☏ area code: (045) • Population: 93 000
Distances
- From Paraná: 262 km eastwards on RN 18
- From Colón: 105 km northwards on RN 14

Concordia is located on the east bank of the **Río Uruguay**, which forms the border between Argentina and Uruguay. It was officially founded in 1832, although people had settled here as early as 1769, at which time the river was called the Salto Chico. This early settlement was really not much more than a cluster of ranches with a chapel dedicated to San Antonio. It suffered heavi-

---

Key to Map

1	Municipalidad	11	Hotel Palmar and Residencial Argentino
2	Catedral	12	Hotel Centro
3	Post office (Encotel)	13	Hotel Concordia
4	Telephone	14	Hotel de Turismo
5	Tourist information	15	Residencial Colón
6	Hospital	16	Residencial Embajador
7	Ferry to Salto in Uruguay	17	Residencial Central
8	Cambio Tourfe	18	Residencial Colonial
9	Hotel Terminal	19	Residencial Florida
10	Hotel Salto Grande	20	Residencial Terminal

Concepción del Uruguay

Entre Ríos Province

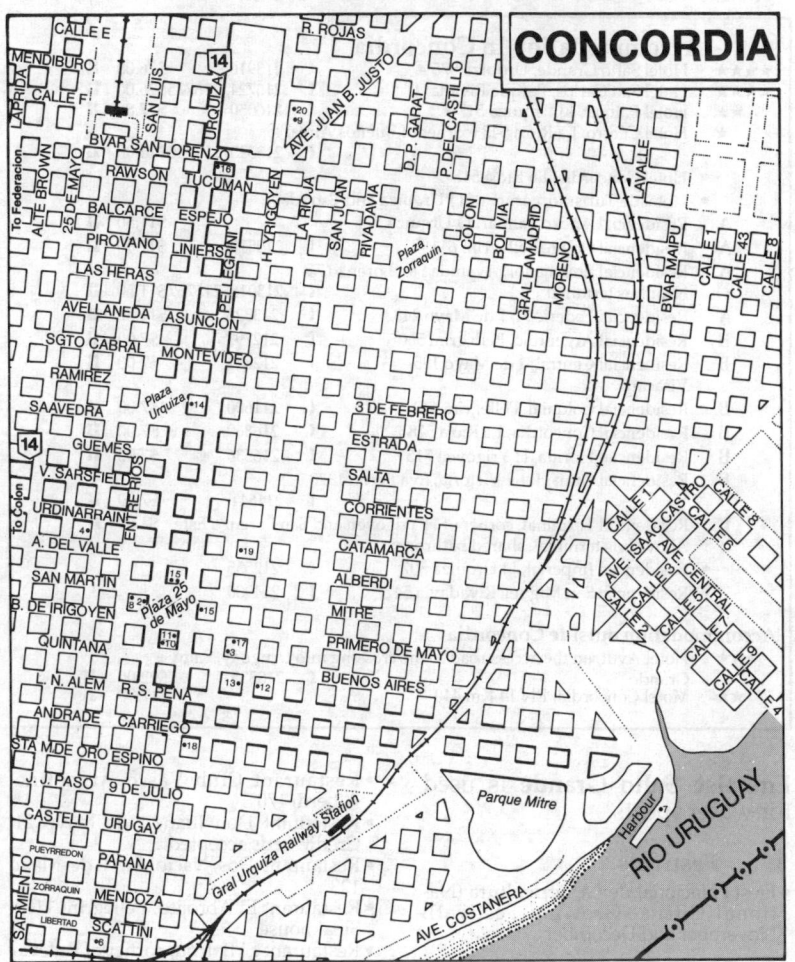

ly during the wars of independence, and finally disappeared completely in 1820.

The present city overlooks the river, and there is a ferry service over to Salto in Uruguay. The climate is pleasant all year round, with temperatures averaging 30°C in summer and 10°C in winter. Some 14 km upriver is the joint Argentine–Uruguayan hydroelectric scheme at **Salto Grande**. The huge lake created by the dam,

Entre Ríos Province

Accommodation in Concordia

★★★★	Hotel Salto Grande, Urquiza 575	(	213916	$26.00
★★★★	Hotel San Carlos, Parque Rivadavia	(	216724, 216725	$26.00
★★	Hotel Palmar, J J Urquiza 517	(	216050	$17.80
★	Hotel Centro, La Rioja 543 (corner of Buenos Aires)			
		(	213323, 217746	$14.00
•	Hotel Concordia, La Rioja 518			
•	Hotel de Turismo, corner of J J Urquiza and Estrada			
A	Residencial Anexo Palmar, J J Urquiza 521			$11.50
A	Residencial Colón, Pellegrini 611	(	215510	$11.50
A	Residencial Embajador, Avenida San Lorenzo 75 Near bus terminal	(	213018, 215767	$11.50
A	Residencial Federico I, 1 de Mayo 248	(	213323	$11.50
B	Residencial Argentino, Pellegrini 560	(	212797	$7.00
B	Residencial Central, 1 de Mayo 185 Visacard	(	212842	$7.00
B	Residencial Colonial, Pellegrini 443	(	211600	$7.00
B	Residencial Concordia, La Rioja 518	(	216869	$7.00
B	Residencial Florida, H Yrigoyen 715	(	216536	$7.00
B	Residencial Gran Hotel Victoria, Eva Perón 1320		214641	$7.00
B	Residencial Terminal, corner of H Yrigoyen and San Lorenzo Este Above bus terminal, shared bathroom			$4.00
•	Residencial Imperial, J J Urquiza 507	(	212535	
•	Residencial San Miguel, Rivadavia 547	(	214900	

Accommodation outside Concordia

★★★	Hotel Ayui, on the access road to the crossing into Uruguay, Salto Grande	(	218335	$22.00
★★	Motel Concordia, RN 14 Km 440			$17.80

Embalse Salto Grande is used for water sports.

Festivals
- Fiesta Nacional de La Citricultura (National Citrus- Growing Festival): November and December

Tourist information
- Tourist office, Bulevar Mitre 64 (corner of Plaza 25 de Mayo) (212137

Camping
- La Tortuga Alegre

Eating out
- Restaurant Cheeff, Pellegrini 576
- Restaurant Club Vasco Argentino, Alberdí 170
- Restaurant Don Juan, 1 de Mayo 21. Credit cards accepted
- Restaurant Dos Naciones, 1 de Mayo 123
- Restaurant El Abrojito, Pellegrini 1103. Steakhouse
- Restaurant El Balcón, corner of Bulevar San Lorenzo and 25 de Mayo
- Restaurant El Ciervo (Hotel San Carlos), Avenida E Perón, in the Parque Rivadavia
- Restaurant El Rey del Bife, Pellegrini 566 (corner of 1 de Mayo). Steakhouse
- Restaurant Emiliano, Catamarca 175
- Restaurant Imperio, corner of La Rioja and Buenos Aires
- Restaurant La Cabaña, 1 de Mayo 14

Entre Ríos Province

- Restaurant La Casona, Pellegrini 377 (corner of 9 de Julio)
- Restaurant La Cumbre, 1 de Mayo 65. Steakhouse
- Restaurant La Rueda, corner of Avenida Tavella and Ruta 4. Steakhouse
- Restaurant La Salida, Urquiza 1863. Steakhouse
- Restaurant La Tranquera, H Yrigoyen 1425
- Restaurant Los Sauces, Avenida Costanera
- Restaurant Papacho, corner of J B Justo and A Niez
- Restaurant Pizza, Garat 238 (corner of J B Justo)
- Restaurant Suárez, Club Viajantes, Avenida Costanera. Steakhouse
- Restaurant Terminal, corner of J B Justo and H Yrigoyen
- Pizzería Don Giuseppe, Cariego 29
- Pizzería El Reloj, corner of J B Justo and N Garat
- Pizzería La Bella, corner of Pellegrini and Buenos Aires
- Pizzería La Fontana, corner of Pellegrini and Carrilleco
- Pizzería La Recova, corner of R S Peña and Colón
- Pizzería Las Tres Ases, corner of H Yrigoyen and Alberdí. Pizza
- Pizzería Mostacho's, A del Valle 40
- Pizzería 1900, La Ríoja 524
- Cafetería Cafe de La Paz, corner of Entre Ríos and Alberdi
- Cafetería Colón, corner of 1 de Mayo and Pellegrini
- Cafetería Cristóbal, Pellegrini 607 (corner of 1 de Mayo)
- Cafetería La Cucharita, Mitre 14
- Cafetería Mafalda, corner of Entre Ríos and 3 de Febrero
- Cafetería Larrea, opposite bus terminal
- Cafetería Papacho, opposite bus terminal
- Cafetería Prestigio, Entre Ríos 471
- Chopería Ideal, corner of J J Urquiza and 1 de Mayo

Eating out outside Concordia

- Restaurant Don Giordano, Motel Concordia, RN 14
- Restaurant El Ciervo, Hotel San Carlos, Parque Rivadavia

Post and telegraph

- Telephones: San Luis 732 (corner of Urdinarrain)

Financial

- Casa de Cambio Tourfe, Bulevar Mitre 43 (corner of J J Urquiza). Travelers' checks and cash
- Casa Julio, 1 de Mayo 29

Services and facilities

- Laundromat: Laverap, San Luis 1101
- Supermarket: Masymas, Pellegrini 516

Visas, passports

- Uruguayan consulate, Entre Ríos 661. Open Mon–Fri 0730–1530

Air services

- Buenos Aires (Aeroparque Jorge Newbery): Fare $36.00; departs 1235 Mon, Tues, Thurs, Sat; 1 hour; Aerolineas Argentinas
- Paso de los Libres: Fare $19.00; departs 1100 Mon, Tues, Thurs, Sat; 1 hour; Aerolineas Argentinas

Buses

The municipal bus terminal is on the corner of Pellegrini and Alberdí; the long-distance terminal is on the corner of J B Justo and H Yrigoyen.

- Parque Nacional El Palmar: Fare $1.30
- Salto (Uruguay): Fare $1.10

Motoring

The roads to Buenos Aires, Posadas, and Paraná are all sealed.

Service stations

- ACA, corner of Corrientes and Pellegrini
- Shell, corner of J J Urquiza and Catamarca
- YPF, corner of Alberdí and J J Urquiza

Trains

"El Correntino" runs several times daily to Buenos Aires. There are also trains to Posadas and Corrientes.

Concordia

ENTRE RÍOS PROVINCE

- Buenos Aires: "El Correntino"; sleeper $22.60, Pullman $13.70, first class $9.20, tourist class $6.70; departs daily 0620; 9 hours
- Paso de los Libres: Fare $3.30

Water transport

Take bus 2, marked "Puerto", to get to the ferry terminal. Tickets are available from the small kiosk at the terminal.
- Salto (Uruguay): Fare $1.00; 5 services weekdays, 3 on Sat, 2 on Sun; 15 minutes

Shopping

- Artesanías Casa Brenner, corner of Entre Ríos and 1 de Mayo

Sport

- Camping and fishing equipment: Ferretería Bruno, 1 de Mayo 63 (corner of Urquiza)
- Race track: Club Hípico Concordia, corner of Carretera Urquiza and Salto Uruguayo
- Golf: Concordia golf club, Villa Zorraquín. This is a nine-hole course 8 km north of the city center

Entertainment

- Disco Exequiel, corner of J B Justo and Echagüe
- Disco Hostal del Río, Parque Rivadavia, below Hotel San Carlos on river
- Disco Momentos, Avenida Urquiza
- Peña La Chamarrita, San Luis 1245. Fridays only
- Whiskería La Casa de Mi Tia, Alberdí 164

Sightseeing

- Museo Regional, corner of Entre Ríos and Ramirez
- Parque Rivadavia is about 5 km out of the city, on the shores of the Río Uruguay. The circular road is occasionally used for car races. Within the grounds are the ruins of the Castilo San Carlos, a castle built last century by an eccentric Frenchman and then abandoned for unknown reasons. The Hotel San Carlos and a good nightclub are also in the park

Excursions

The Comisión de Turismo y Promoción de Asodeco, 1st floor, La Ríoja 622 (211551 organizes tours to **Salto Grande**, **Parque Nacional El Palmar**, and Termas del Daymán in Uruguay. Tours of the city are also available

- Salto in Uruguay: A short ferry trip from Concordia
- The hydroelectric scheme at **Salto Grande**: This was constructed jointly by Argentina and Uruguay and is 32 km upstream

CRESPO

Postal code: 3116 • (area code: (043)
Distance from Paraná: 45 km southwards on RN 12

Accommodation

A Residencial Holiday, corner of Moreno and Soñez $11.50

DIAMANTE

Postal code: 3105 • (area code: (043)
Distance from Paraná: 50 km southwards on RP 12

Located right on the **Río Paraná**, Diamante is well known for its fishing.

ENTRE RÍOS PROVINCE

Historically Diamante is important for several reasons. It was near here at **Punta Gorda** that Argentina installed artillery to prevent Uruguayan ships from passing. General Lavalle and General Urquiza also set out from Diamante with their armies, the latter to the Battle of Monte Caseros where he defeated the dictator Rosas.

The banks of the river are about 100 m above the water here and the area is perfect for camping, swimming, and fishing. From the banks you get sweeping views over the Río Paraná from north to south.

✗ Festivals
- Fiesta de la Jineteada y Folklore (Horse Riding and Folk Festival): *Gaucho* festival in January

⊟ Accommodation
A Residencial Mayo, San Martín 488 $11.50 ⁂

Ⓐ Camping
- Balneario Municipal. These grounds cover an area of 70 ha 🗇🍴 barbecue sites

⊕ Tours
- Diamante Turismo, Serrano 195 ℂ 9811258

FEDERACIÓN

Postal code: 3206
Distance from Paraná: 315 km south-west on RN 14, 18

Federación began as a natural outgrowth of the town of **Mandisovi** which was founded in 1810 by General Belgrano. It was founded as a city in its own right in 1847. Located on the shores **Embalse Salto Grande**, the lake created by the hydroelectric scheme at **Salto Grande**, the modern town was designed by Don Manuel Urdinarrain. The mainspring of the town's economy is tourism. It is ideally situated for water sports, and there are several boat ramps along the shores of the lake.

✗ Festivals
- Fiesta Nacional del Lago (National Lake Festival): January

ⓘ Tourist information
- Oficina de Informes, corner of San Martín and Las Rosas ℂ 81586
- Zona Portuaria, Marina Sur. Enquire here for information about launch cruises

⊟ Accommodation
★ Hotel del Lago, corner of 25 de Marzo and Irigoyen ℂ 81424 $14.00 ⁂

🍴 Eating out
- Restaurant El Tío Tom, Avenida San Martín, Local 3
- Restaurant La Biela, Los Claveles 788
- Restaurant Yan-Yul, Avenida San Martín 52
- Pizzería Cano, Las Camelias 365
- Cafetería Arce, Avenida San Martín, Local 21
- Cafetería Ideal, Avenida Entre Ríos 53
- Cafetería Keop's, Avenida Entre Ríos, Local 44

⚓ Water transport
The launch *Ciudad de Federación* does weekend trips to nearby beaches and to Termas de Arapey in Uruguay.

ENTRE RÍOS PROVINCE

The launch *Eleuteria-R* does daily trips to Santa Ana and nearby beaches.

🚘 Motoring
- Service station: Shell, corner of Avenida Entre Ríos and Avenida Salto Grande

🛒 Shopping
- Semiprecious stones: Agatas y Jaspes Pulidos, shop 18, Museo de los Asentamientos, Avenida San Martín

🎭 Entertainment
- Disco Buyeri, Avenida Río de los Pájaros, Barrio Residencial, Zona Norte
- Disco Jano's Club, Ranch Motel Federación, Antigua Ruta 14

📷 Sightseeing
- Museo de los Asentamientos, corner of Irigoyen and Las Rosas. Open Tues–Sun 0900–1200 and 1400–1800

FEDERAL

Postal code: 3180 • ☏ area code: (0454)
Distance from Paraná: 193 km northwards on RN 12 then RN 127

🛏 Accommodation
A Residencial Federal, corner of Artusi and Irigoyen $11.50 ♨
B Residencial Copacabana, Belgrano $9.50 ♨

GUALEGUAY

Postal code: 2840 • ☏ area code: (0444) •
Population: 20 000
Distances
- From Paraná: 230 km south-east on RN 12
- From Buenos Aires: 223 km north-west on RN 12

Gualeguay was founded in 1783 by Tomás de Rocamora. It is located in the southern part of the province on the **Río Gualeguay**, about 30 km north of its junction with the **Río Paraná**. The swampy area along the Río Paraná starts nearby, just south of **Puerto Ruiz**, 8 km south. Gualeguay is a quiet provincial town which offers good fishing in the Río Gualeguay and **Río Cle**.

Economically it is the center of an important cattle and sheep ranching area. The main commercial streets of the town are Calle San Antonio, Belgrano, and 25 de Mayo.

Although no longer in operation, Argentina's second oldest railroad was established in 1866 between Gualeguay and Puerto Ruiz, 8 km south. Gualeguay was so important economically last century that the main altar in the Templo de San Antonio was made from imported Carrara marble.

🎉 Festivals
- Semana de Turismo (Tourist Week): January
- Fiesta Provincial Cantando del Río (Provincial River Song Festival): In January
- Fiesta Provincial de las Comparsas: Carnival in February

ℹ Tourist information
- Oficina de Información Turística, San Antonio 203

ENTRE RÍOS PROVINCE

Accommodation
- ★★ Hotel Gran Hotel Gualeguay, Monte Caseros 217 (2985 $18.50
- B Residencial Banderin Centro, Islas Malvinas 11 (1062 $9.50
- B Residencial Italia, Alfredo Palacios 1 $9.50
- Residencial Cinco Esquinas. Next to bus stop

Camping
- Camping Municipal El Minuam

Eating out
- Restaurant Club Social, 1 de Mayo 83
- Restaurant Comedor Diez, corner of Alarcon Muñiz and Ayacucho
- Restaurant Don Pedro, corner of Reconquista and Colonel Díaz. Steakhouse
- Restaurant Jockey Club, corner of San Antonio and 1 de Mayo
- Restaurant La Negrita, Rotonda Norte. Steakhouse
- Restaurant La Norteña, corner of San Antonio and Avenida Artigas. Steakhouse
- Restaurant Los Amigos, corner of Avenida Soberania and Reconquista. Steakhouse
- Restaurant Maria Aurelia, Avenida Reconquista. Steakhouse
- Pizzería Apolito, Chacabuco 14
- Pizzería Mayo, corner of San Antonio and Pellegrini
- Cafetería Cazote, San Antonio 178
- Cafetería El Aguila, corner of San Antonio and Pellegrini

Buses
The bus terminal is on the corner of 25 de Mayo and Alberdí.
Buses run regualrly to Paraná and Buenos Aires.

Motoring
All the roads from Gualeguay to Paraná are sealed.

Tours
- Ciudad de Gualeguaychu Turismo, Avenida Del Valle 1202

Shopping
Gualeguayenses are renowned for their craftmanship.
- Centro de Artesanos, San Antonio 230

Entertainment
- Cafetería Del Gas, Belgrano 18. Dances are held here on weekends

Sightseeing
- Museo Regional "Juan B Ambrosetti", San Antonio 230. Open Mon–Sat 1300–1900
- Museo de Ciencias Naturales "Doctor Diego Echazarretta" (Dr Diego Echarratta Natural Sciences Museum), 25 de Mayo 423. Open Mon–Fri 1400–1600
- The house in which Garibaldi was tortured by the local police chief in 1837 in the time of the dictator Rosas still exists

GUALEGUAYCHÚ

Postal code: 2820 • (area code: (0446) • Population: 65 000
Distances
- From Paraná: 324 km eastwards on RP 39 then south-east on RP 20
- From Buenos Aires: 226 km north-west RN 12 then northwards on RN 14

La Villa de San José de Gualeguaychu was founded by Tomás de Rocamora in 1783. It is situated on the **Río Gualeguay**, 19 km from its junction with the **Río Uruguay**. The corner of Calle 25 de Mayo and Urquiza constitutes the center of the business district.

Entre Ríos Province

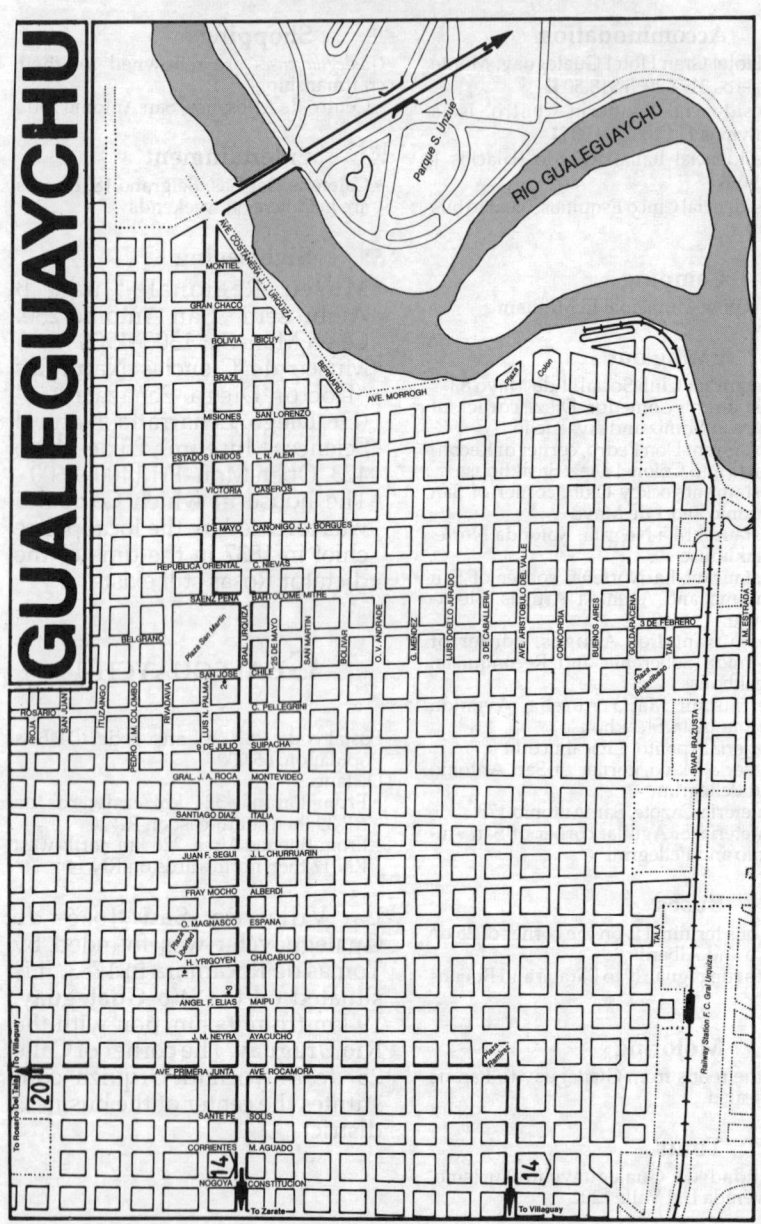

Gualeguaychú

Entre Ríos Province

Gualeguaychú's river promenade is particularly attractive.

The Puente La Balsa over the Río Gualeguaychú leads to the Parque Unzué. This 110 ha park has picnic grounds, a racecourse, and camping grounds. It is a popular place. The river here is especially pretty, with weeping willows growing profusely along its banks.

Gualeguaychú is linked by rail to Buenos Aires. There are also extensive bus services to Paraná and Posadas. The roads to these places are sealed and passable all year round. The Puente Internacional Libertador General San Martín (Liberator General Martín International Bridge) crosses the Río Uruguay at **Puerto Obligado** and leads into Fray Bentos in neighboring Uruguay. It is a toll bridge.

Festivals
- Fiesta Provincial del Carnaval Internacional del Río Uruguay (Provincial Festival of the International Río Uruguay Carnival): This exuberant festival takes place in February

Tourist information
- Dirección de Turismo, corner of Costanera and Obelisco (3668. Open daily 0800–2200

Camping
- La Delfina, Parque Unzué, in the Sector Grande

Eating out
- Restaurant Chaia, 25 de Mayo
- Restaurant Churros Ricos, Urquiza 985 (corner of H Yrigoyen)
- Restaurant Dacal, corner of Costanera and Andrade
- Restaurant Don Raúl, corner of 1ra Junta and San Juan. Steakhouse
- Restaurant El Viejo Almacén, corner of 1ra Junta and Bulevar Montana. Steakhouse
- Restaurant Grand Prix, corner of Bolívar and 3 de Febrero
- Restaurant Hotel Avenida, Rocamora 245
- Restaurant Hotel El Faro, Bolívar 565
- Restaurant Hotel Embajador, corner of San Martín and 3 de Febrero
- Restaurant Hotel Paris, corner of Bolívar and Pellegrini
- Restaurant La Cabañita, 25 de Mayo 200
- Restaurant La Tapera, corner of Costanera and Urquiza. Steakhouse
- Restaurant Los Años Locos, corner of Costanera and Doello Jurado. Steakhouse
- Restaurant Schneider, corner of Bolívar and Chile
- Restaurant Vir-Sol, Bolívar 666 (corner of Pellegrini). Steakhouse
- Pizzería Di Garda, 25 de Mayo 936
- Pizzería Pouler, corner of Urquiza and Magnasco
- Cafetería El Cerrito, Urquiza West
- Cafetería El Puente, corner of Costanera and L N Palma
- Cafetería Jeanot, corner of 25 de Mayo and Paraná
- Cafetería Schneider, corner of Bolívar and Chile

Key to Map
1. Municipalidad
2. Iglesia
3. Post office (Encotel)
4. Telephone
5. Bus terminal
6. Hotel Berlin
7. Hotel Paris
8. Hotel Yaro

ENTRE RÍOS PROVINCE

🛏 Accommodation in Gualeguaychú

★★★	Hotel Embajador, corner of San Martín and 3 de Febrero 🛗	✆ 4414, 6051	$22.50	🚻
★★	Hotel Berlin, Bolívar 733	✆ 6085, 5111	$18.50	🚻
★	Motel La Posada del Charrua, Avenida del Valle 250 (corner of San Lorenzo)	✆ 6099	$14.00	🚻
★	Hotel Paris, corner of Pellegrini and Bolívar 🛗	✆ 6260, 6260	$14.00	🚻
★	Hotel Yaro, San Martín 903	✆ 6138, 1038	$14.00	🚻
A	Residencial Alemán, Bolívar 535 ●	✆ 6153	$11.50	🚻
A	Residencial Anexo H Paris, corner of Pellegrini and Bolívar	✆ 6048	$11.50	🚻
A	Residencial Brutti, Bolívar 575 (corner of Chile)	✆ 6048	$11.50	🚻
A	Residencial El Faro, Bolívar 565 🛗	✆ 3178, 6469	$11.50	🚻
A	Residencial Entre Ríos, Andrade 1009	✆ 7214	$11.50	🚻
A	Residencial Pucará, San Martín 588	✆ 7675	$11.50	🚻
B	Residencial Avenida, Rocamora 245 🛗	✆ 6245	$9.50	🚻
B	Residencial Uruguay, Urquiza 639	✆ 6245	$9.50	🚻
B	Hospedaje Mayo, Bolívar 550	✆ 7661	$6.00	🚹
B	Hospedaje Muller, San Martín 686 Shared bathrooms	✆ 7044	$6.00	🚹
B	Hospedaje Panambi, San Martín 1243	✆ 6071	$6.00	🚹

Eating out outside Gualeguaychú

- Restaurant Pancho Ramirez, Parque Unzué. Open during summer only

📮 Post and telegraph

- Post office: Encotel, corner of Urquiza and Angel Elias
- Long distance telephone: Urquiza 910

💲 Financial

- Cambio Ayacucho, Ayacucho 114 (corner of San Martín)
- Kiosko Don Nicola, corner of Chile and San Martín. Exchanges Uruguayan *pesos* for Argentine *australes* and vice versa

🗄 Services and facilities

- Laundromat: Laverap, Perón 98
- Supermarket: Supercoop, Bolívar 683 (corner of J D Perón). Opposite the Hotel Paris

Photographic supplies

- Foto Lux, Urquiza 1037
- Foto Otto, 25 de Mayo 976

C Clubs

- French: Alliance Française, 25 de Mayo 502 (corner of Mitre)
- German: Club Alemán, Bolívar 535

🛂 Visas, passports

- Uruguayan consulate, Rivadavia 510 ✆ 4431

⇄ Border crossing

Border formalities at the Puente Internacional Libertador General San Martín crossing into Uruguay take only 10 minutes.

🚌 Buses

The bus terminal is at the corner of Bolívar and Chile. It has a restaurant, cloak room ($0.40), and a post office. Look on the noticeboard for tourist information.
- Buenos Aires: Fare $4.50; 3 hours
- Concepción del Uruguay: Fare $1.80
- Mercedes (Uruguay): Fare $2.50
- Posadas: Departs 0050; 5 services daily; Expreso Singer

Gualeguaychú

ENTRE RÍOS PROVINCE

🚗 Motoring

Service stations
- ACA, Urquiza 1000 (corner of H Yrigoyen)
- Esso, corner of Urquiza and Bulevar Daneri

The Puente Internacional Libertador General San Martín to Fray Bentos in Uruguay is a toll bridge.

🛍 Shopping
- Artesanías Entre Ríos, corner of L N Palma and Costanera

🎾 Sport
- Golf: Country Club Gualeguaychú, Urquiza West
- Tennis: Club Neptunia, Parque Unzué

🍸 Entertainment
- Disco Barbaro, corner of Bolívar and Maipú
- Disco Mi Tio Archibaldo, corner of Ituzaingó and San José
- Disco O'Barquinho, corner of Colombo and Magnasco
- Disco Reviens, corner of 25 de Mayo and Bolivia
- Pub Exequiel, 25 de Mayo 535 (corner of 3 de Febrero)

📷 Sightseeing
- Solar de los Haedo, corner of San José and Rivadavia. Built in 1783 on a piece of land originally allotted by Rocamora, this building is considered the oldest in the city. In 1845 it served as Giuseppe Garibaldi's headquarters when he invaded Entre Ríos with his Uruguayan troops

LA PAZ

Postal code: 3190 • (area code: (0437)
Distance from Paraná: 168 km north-easts on RN 12

Founded in 1835, La Paz is situated on a sandy bluff, right on the banks of the **Río Paraná**.

In 1842 the naval Battle of Costa Brava was fought here between Uruguay, under the command of Giuseppe Garibaldi, and Argentina, under the command of Admiral William Brown. When the battle began to fare badly for Garibaldi he burnt his ships, slipped across the **Río Espinillo** by boat, and returned to Uruguay via Corrientes province. The main plank of Garibaldi's ship has been preserved in the Museo Regional.

The clean sandy beaches make this a perfect spot for swimming, and the abundant *dorado* in the **Río Paraná** lure fishermen to La Paz year after year.

🎉 Festivals
- Fiesta Nacional de la Pesca Variada del Río (National Festival of Mixed River Fishing): This fishing competition is held in February

🛏 Accommodation
- ★★ Hotel Milton, Italia 1029 ▣ (1134 $18.50 ♨
- ★ Hotel La Paz, 3 de Febrero 745 ⒕ (1490 $14.00 ♨
- • Hotel Rivera, San Martín 345 ▣ (1032
- A Residencial Plaza, San Martín 862 (2208 $11.50 ♨
- B Residencial Las Dos M, Urquiza 1303 (1303 $9.50 ♨

La Paz

Entre Ríos Province

Key to Map
1. Municipalidad
2. Iglesia
3. Post office (Encotel)
4. Telephone

🍴 Eating out

Many restaurants serve seafood, especially *dorado* and *surubí*. Some cafeterias are discos at the weekend.
- Restaurant El Progreso, Moreno 1062
- Restaurant El Puerto, corner of Vieytes and Belgrano
- Restaurant El Rincón, 3 de Febrero 745
- Restaurant El Sirio, Sarmiento 745
- Restaurant J R, Galería Santa Rosa
- Restaurant La Tapera de Chiva, Vieytes 1153
- Cafetería Ideal, Moreno 910
- Cafetería Safari, Urquiza 1059
- Cafetería La Duquesita, Belgrano 780

La Paz

Entre Ríos Province

Eating out outside La Paz
- Restaurant El Arco, at the intersection of RN 12 and RP 1
- Restaurant La Cabaña del Toto, at the intersection of RN 12 and RP 1

Post and telegraph
- Post Office: Encotel, corner of 9 de Julio and España
- Telephone: Compañía Entrerriana de Telefonos, corner of San Martín and General Urquiza

Services and facilities

Fishing gear
- La Boutique del Pescador, corner of España and R S Peña
- La Comercial, San Martín 1372

Buses
Buses run regularly to both Paraná and Corrientes.

Tours
- Ciudad de La Paz, Berutti 1129 (21107 operates guided bus tours
- Agua y Sol, Vieytes 1181 (22288. Boats can be hired from this company, which also organizes guided river cruises
- Pescar, Belgrano 182 (22343. Services include guided river cruises and fishing trips

Sightseeing
- Museo Regional La Paz, Parque Beron de Astrada, corner of Berutti and 3 de Febrero. Open Tues–Sun 0900–1200 and 1700–2000

NOGOYÁ

Postal code: 3150 • (area code: (0435)
Distance from Paraná: 110 km north-west on RN 12

Accommodation
★ Hotel Luz, San Martín 640 (21232 $14.00
A Residencial Gran Hotel, 25 de Mayo 889 (21221 $11.50

Buses
Buses run regularly to Paraná and Concepción del Uruguay

PARANÁ

Postal code: 3100 • (area code: (043) •
Population: 200 000
Distance from Buenos Aires: 505 km north-west on RN 12

Paraná is the capital of Entre Ríos province, and is located on a hill which overlooks a stretch of the **Río Paraná** dotted with small islands. A provincial church was established here in 1730, although settlers had come here from Santa Fé as early as 1588. During General Urquiza's presidency from 1853 to 1862 Paraná was the capital of the Argentine confederation. Many older buildings now preserved as national monuments date from this time.

The center of town is Plaza 1 de Mayo; most of the city's administrative offices are located near here. The best views are obtained from the Parque Urquiza overlooking the river.

Temperatures average 24°C in summer and 18°C in winter.

Tourist information
- Provincial tourist information office, Corrientes 110

Entre Ríos Province

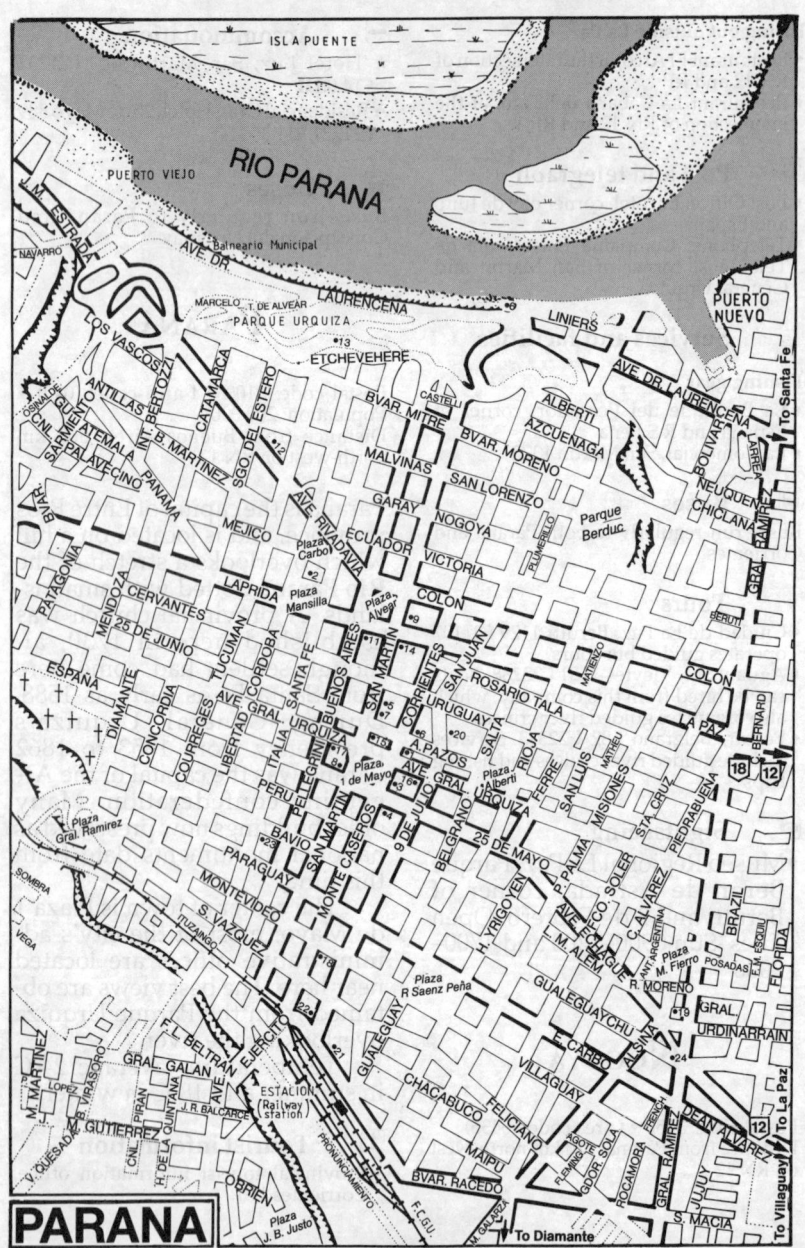

Paraná

Entre Ríos Province

- Municipal tourist office, corner of Avenida Laurencena and San Martín. This office is down by the river; it is a good place to pick up programs of cultural events taking place in Paraná

🅐 Camping

- Thompson, corner of Avenida Ramirez and Avenida Bravard (221998. These grounds are right on the river
- Toma Vieja, Blas Parrera Norte (225622. Views over the river and town

🍴 Eating out

- Restaurant Aquí Es, corner of Blas Parera and José Hernandez. Steakhouse
- Restaurant Cantina Club Echagüe, corner of Avenida Echagüe and 25 de Mayo
- Restaurant Cantina Club Estudiantes, Los Vascos 729
- Restaurant Cantina Rowing Club, Costanera Baja
- Restaurant Club de Pescadores, Puerto Viejo ("Old Harbor"). Seafood
- Restaurant Coscoino, Corrientes 377
- Restaurant Don Carlos, 25 de Mayo 215
- Restaurant Don Charras, Antonio Crespo 24. Steakhouse
- Restaurant Don Gervasio, Rotonda Parque Urquiza. Steakhouse
- Restaurant El Monchulo Viudo, corner of Antonio Crespo and Scalabrini. Seafood
- Restaurant El Reno, corner of Avenida Ramirez and Vucetich
- Restaurant Fettucini, Urquiza 1251. Pasta
- Restaurant Japón, Urquiza 1035
- Restaurant La Casona, Pellegrini 175. Steakhouse
- Restaurant La Recova, General Ramirez 2569. Opposite bus terminal
- Restaurant La Rueda, Gualeguaychú 683
- Restaurant La Taberna del Pescador, Avenida Estrada 1034. Steakhouse
- Restaurant Le Coin, Avenida Rivadavia Block 500 (corner of Santiago del Estero)
- Restaurant Los Monjes (Hotel Mayorazgo), corner of Etchevehere and Córdoba
- Restaurant Los Quinchos, Corrientes 149. Seafood
- ☞ • Restaurant Luisito, 9 de Julio 149. Credit cards accepted
- Restaurant Marimar, Avenida Ramirez 2531
- Restaurant Montecarlo, corner of Avenidade las Americas and Avenida Ramirez. Steakhouse
- Restaurant Musmon, Urquiza 843. Tearooms
- Restaurant Oasis, Urquiza 1191. Steakhouse; Arabic cuisine
- Restaurant Vera Cruz, Avenida Ramirez 2539. Opposite bus terminal; slow service
- Comedor Munich, Buenos Aires block 500 (corner of Garay)
- Pizzería Bahia General Ramirez block 1600 (corner of La Paz)
- Pizzería Don Costa, Monte Caseros 97. Also serves hamburgers
- Pizzería Don Mario, Pellegrini 280

Key to Map

1	Municipalidad
2	Casa de Gobierno
3	Catedral
4	Post office (Encotel)
5	Telephone
6	Tourist information
7	Cambio Tourfe
8	Banco de la Nación
9	Aerolineas Argentinas
11	Museo Histórico de Entre Ríos "Martiniano Leguizamón
12	Museo de Entre Ríos de Ciencias Naturales y Antropologia Antonio Serrano"
13	Hotel Mayorazgo
14	Hotel Gran Alvear
15	Hotel Gran Paraná
16	Hotel Paraná
17	Hotel Plaza
18	Hotel Superluxe
19	Residencial Bristol
20	Residencial Latino
21	Residencial City
22	Residencial 9 de Julio
23	Residencial Hotel Nuevo Florida
24	Bus terminal

Paraná

Entre Ríos Province

🛏 Accommodation in Paraná

Most cheap accommodation is near the railway station.

★★★★★	Hotel Mayorazgo, corner of Etchevehere and Miranda 🍴♿🅿 Overlooks Parque Urquiza and the river	✆ 216111		
★★★	Hotel: Gran Hotel Alvear, San Martín 637	✆ 220000	$22.50	👥
★★	Hotel: Gran Hotel Paraná, Urquiza 976	✆ 223900	$18.50	👥
★	Hotel Paraná, 9 de Julio 60 🍴	✆ 210300	$14.00	👥
★	Hotel Plaza, San Martín 918 (corner of Urquiza) 🍴	✆ 210720	$14.00	👥
★	Hotel Superluxe, Villaguay 162	✆ 212787	$14.00	👥
•	Hotel Las Colonias, Cervantes 89			
A	Residencial Bristol, Alsina 221 Near the bus terminal	✆ 213961	$11.50	👥
A	Residencial Carbo, A Carbo 850	✆ 241615	$11.50	👥
A	Residencial Latino, San Juan 158	✆ 211036	$11.50	👥
B	Residencial City, Racedo 231 Opposite the railroad terminal		$9.50	👥
B	Residencial Don Marcos, Ramirez 2681	✆ 212090	$9.50	👥
B	Residencial Hotel Nuevo Florida, Bavio 125	✆ 220517	$9.50	👥
B	Residencial Liniers, Santiago del Liniers 400		$9.50	👥
B	Residencial 9 de Julio, 9 de Julio 974 Near the railroad terminal		$9.50	👥
B	Residencial San Martín, San Martín 832	✆ 214901	$9.50	👥

Accommodation outside Paraná

★★★	Hotel Centro Autoturismo, on the access road to the Túnel Subfluvial Hernandarias	✆ 221801	$22.50	👥

- Pizzería El Gran Norman, Laprida 184
- Pizzería Gran Japon, Urquiza 1035
- Pizzería Guadaloupe, Avenida Almafuerte 240
- Pizzería Nogaro, Avenida Ramirez block 1200 (corner of Nogoya)
- Pizzería Los Tres Tigres, corner of Avenida Ramirez and Bulevar Racedo
- Pizzería Piccolino, corner of Salta and Rosario del Tala
- Pizzería Tuyú, 9 de Julio block 200 (corner of Gualeguaychú)
- Pizzería Vera Cruz, Avenida Ramirez 2539
- Pizzería Victoria 25 de Mayo 50
- Cafetería Bar o Bar, corner of Buenos Aires and Garay
- Cafetería Barajas, corner of Urquiza and Belgrano
- Cafetería Conissy, San Martín 1035. *Churros*
- Cafetería Darcy, corner of Pellegrini and Perú
- Cafetería El Timbo, Hotel Alvear, San Martín 637
- Cafetería Gran Flamingo, corner of Urquiza and San Martín
- Cafetería Honney, San Martín 865
- Cafetería JB, corner of Bulevar Mitre and Córdoba
- Cafetería Las Piedras, corner of Avenida Rivadavia and Córdoba
- Cafetería Las Piedras Centro, Urquiza 976
- Cafetería Le Coin, corner of Avenida Rivadavia and Catamarca
- Cafetería Los Alpes, corner of Avenida Rivadavia and Buenos Aires
- Cafetería Manabí, Urquiza 1055
- Chopería Bahía, Avenida Ramirez 1632
- Chopería Gambelin, corner of Alem and Gualeguay

ENTRE RÍOS PROVINCE

- Chopería La Danza de la Flecha, Rotonda Parque Urquiza
- Chopería Los Alpes, Avenida Rivadavia block 100 (corner of Buenos Aires)
- Chopería Los Vikingos, Avenida Ramirez 2017
- Chopería Victoria, 25 de Mayo 50

Eating out outside La Paz

- Restaurant Cedro Azul, Avenida de las Américas, Km 5
- Restaurant La Ruta, Avenida Almafuerte 1835. Steakhouse
- Restaurant Los Pipos, Avenida de las Américas 3611 (Ruta 11). Steakhouse

Post and telegraph

- Post Office: Encotel, corner of Monte Caseros and 25 de Mayo
- Long distance telephone: Compañía Entrerriana de Teléfonos, San Martín 735. Open 24 hours
- Public telephones, San Martín 1238

Financial

- Banco Credito, España 86. Cash advances on Visa card
- Casa de Cambio Tourfe, San Martín 777 (216429. 10% surcharge on travelers' checks

Services and facilities

- Dry cleaner: Tokyo, Pellegrini 147

Buses from Paraná

The bus terminal is on Avenida General Ramirez between Avenida Echagüe and Avenida Almafuerte. Bus 10 will take you to the railroad terminal and the budget hotels nearby.

Destination	Fare	Depart	Services	Hours	Company
Asunción (Paraguay)	$22.00		17		
Bahía Blanca		1300	2 services daily		Central Argentino, Ñandu del Sur
Buenos Aires	$8.00	2400	daily	8	Empresa San José
Concepción del Uruguay					Empresa San José
Córdoba		0217	4–5 services daily	5	El Litoral, El Serrano, Expreso Singer
Corrientes	$10.50	1200	3 services daily		T A Chevallier, TATA-Rapido
Mar del Plata		1930	Tues, Fri		Zenit Turismo
Mendoza		1930	daily		TAC, T A Villamaria
Montevideo (Uruguay)		0215	Mon–Thurs, Sat		Cora, Onda
Paso de los Libres		1640	2 services daily		El Norte Bis, Federal
Posadas		1844	daily		El Litoral, Expreso Singer
Puerto Iguazú		1640	Mon, Tues (2), Thurs, Fri		Expreso Singer, Kurtz
Rosario	$3.40	0600	9–10 services daily		El Norte Bis, El Rapido, Kurtz
San Luis		1930	2 services daily		TAC, T A Villamaria
San Miguel de Tucumán	$14.00	1930	daily	13	La Estrella
Santa Fé	$1.00	every 20 minutes			ETA
Via Túnel Subfluvial Hernandarias					
Santiago del Estero		1930	daily	10½	La Estrella
Termas de Río Hondo		1930	daily	11½	La Estrella

Entre Ríos Province

- Sauna: Gimnasio Viviana, Monte Caseros 272. Upstairs; $3.00
- Sports shop: El Surubí, San Martín block 600 (corner of Uruguay). Tents, fishing gear
- Supermarket: Spar, 25 de Mayo block 200 (corner of 9 de Julio)

Laundromats

- Laverap, 25 de Junio 395 (corner of Tucumán)
- Laverap, Cuadro 450 (corner of Monte Caseros)
- Laverap, San Juan 273
- Marva, Monte Caseros block 400 (corner of Villaguay). Open daily 0700–2200; $2.00 per load

Clubs

- German: Goethe Institut, San Martín 1314
- Italian: Sociedad Italiana, San Martín block 500 (corner of Colón)
- Spanish: Sociedad Española, San Martín 760

Visas, passports

- German consulate, Mitre 358

Air services

General Urquiza airport is 12 km from the city center.

Airlines

- Aerolineas Argentinas, San Martín 563 ℂ 210728
- Austral Lineas Aereas, Urquiza 1070 ℂ 214314

Services

- Buenos Aires (Aeroparque Jorge Newbery): Fare $37.00; departs 1700 daily except Sun; 2 hours; Austral

Trains

The F C General Urquiza terminal is on the corner of Bulevar Racedo and 9 de Julio.

Motoring

The 483 km to Paso de los Libres on RN 18 and RN 14 is sealed throughout.
The road to Santa Fé via the Túnel Subfluvial Hernandarias under the Río Paraná is a tollway; toll $1.90

Service stations

- ACA, corner of Buenos Aires and Laprida
- Isaura, corner of Avenida Dr Laurencena and Bolívar
- Shell, Almafuerte 888

Tours

- Turismo Fluvial, Avenida Costanera. This company runs one hour cruises on the Río Paraná each day at 1130, 1430, and 1600. Fare $2.00

Shopping

San Martín is a pedestrian mall from Laprida onwards.

- Provincial handicraft market, Urquiza 1239

Sport

- Golf: There is a golf course near the entrance to the Túnel Subfluvial Hernandarias
- Rowing: Paraná rowing club, corner of Avenida Dr Laurencena and M T de Alvear. Facilities include an indoor swimming pool and restaurant
- Sailing: Yacht Club, Avenida Dr Laurencena, by the river

Entertainment

- Casino, Hotel Mayorazgo, corner of Etchevehere and Córdoba
- Disco Aldea Norte, Bravard 280
- Disco Boliche, Avenida Zanni 1800
- Disco Borbolletta, Hotel Mayorazgo, corner of Etchevehere and Córdoba
- Disco Crash, corner of José Hernandez and Blas Parera
- Disco Gagacu, Almafuerte 2650
- Disco La Belle Epoque, Urquiza 1015
- Disco Lion d'Or, Avenida de Las Americas Km2
- Disco María-María, San Martín 773
- Disco Orfeo, Uruguay 174

Paraná

ENTRE RÍOS PROVINCE

- Disco Orions, Urquiza 720
- Disco Paradise, San Benito
- Disco Robertino's Club, Corrientes 645
- Shows: Café Amet, 25 de Mayo block 200 (corner of Belgrano)
- Teatro Tres de Febrero, 25 de Junio block 0 (corner of San Martín). This theater was built in 1852

Sightseeing

Museums

- Museo Histórico de Entre Ríos "Martiniano Leguizamón" (Martiniano Leguizamón Historical Museum of Entre Ríos). Located at the corner of Laprida and Buenos Aires. The main part of this museum's collection consists of newspapers from the last century. There is also a collection of other assorted memorabilia. Open Tues–Sun 0900–1200 and 1600–2000
- Museo de Entre Ríos de Ciencias Naturales y Antropologia "Antonio Serrano" (Antonio Serrano Museum of Entre Ríos, Natural Sciences, and Anthropology), Avenida Rivadavia 462. The varied collection here includes exhibits on archeology, mineralogy, botany, zoology, geology, and paleontology. Open Tues–Sun 0900–1200 and 1600–2000
- Museo Provincial de Bellas Artes (Provincial Fine Arts Museum), corner of Buenos Aires and Laprida. This modern building on the Plaza Alvear houses the Museo de Bellas Artes "Bazán" and the local history museum. It is open every day 0900–1200 and 1500–1800 except Monday

Churches

- The cathedral is located on the eastern side of Plaza 1 de Mayo. The façade is built in renaissance style, and on the main altar is a notable image of the Virgen del Rosario (Virgin of the Rosary), which was brought here in 1731. The organ was built in and imported from Germany

Public buildings and parks

- The Casa de Gobierno (Governor's Residence), which is situated on Plaza Carbo, also has a remarkable façade. The clock in the tower came from Germany in 1886 and the chime can be heard from far away
- Colegio Nuestra Señora del Huerto (School of Our Lady of the Orchard), Monte Caseros 51 (corner of Urquiza). Last century this building was the seat of the Senate of the Argentine confederation; it is now a national monument
- Parque Urquiza begins on the bank of the river and rises up a gentle slope to Bulevar Mitre. It is a showpiece of the city, and the 25 ha of gardens feature trees native to the region. There is a huge statue of General Urquiza here, and a bas relief of the Battle of Caseros, in which Urquiza defeated President Rosas. Other statues in the park worth seeing are "La Danza de Flecha" and "Mastil a la Bandera" by Perlotti. The Hotel

Paraná

Mayorazgo with its casino and nightclub is also in the park
- **Túnel Subfluvial Hernandarias** (Hernandarias River Tunnel) passes under the Río Paraná and links Entre Ríos with Santa Fé. This remarkable feat of engineering is 2400 m long and 10 m in diameter

🍀 Excursions

- **Santa Fé**: A half-hour trip by local bus from the terminal. The route passes through the 2½ km Túnel Subfluvial Hernandarias and emerges on the **Isla El Timbo**. The country here is mainly marshy. Santa Fé and Paraná are separated by several low-lying islands which move every time the river floods. See also Santa Fé on page 259
- **Reserva Provincial Parque General San Martín**, RN 12, Km 23

PARQUE NACIONAL EL PALMAR

Distances
- From Colón: 52 km northwards on RN 14
- From Concordia: 48 km southwards on RN 14

This national park is situated halfway between Colón and Concordia. The entrance is 100 m from the main highway, RN 14. The park extends from the highway right down to the **Río Uruguay**, a distance of about 14 km.

The park was created to preserve the almost extinct *yatay* palms (*Syragus yatay*), and the unique wildlife.

The solitary *yatay* palms near the entrance gradually become denser until they eventually form groves, particularly near the streams. This particular species was threatened with extinction when cattle were introduced because the cattle ate all the seeds, thereby preventing the trees from reproducing. Most of the palms are now over a hundred years old, and some of them are estimated to be over 500 years old, giving the landscape an African appearance. New protected plantatons of young palms have also been established; they are now no longer an endangered species, and grow up to 12 m high, with leaves reaching a span of two meters. These palms are the southernmost in the world.

Twelve km east of the entrance there is a large camping ground on the banks of the river, where you can hire tents. There is also a *parrilla*, or barbecue, here. The headquarters of the park rangers is nearby and has information on local flora and fauna. Several streams flow through the park.

Playful *carpinchos* (*Hydrochaeris hydrochaeris*) romp in the *lagunas* and rivulets.

Two popular walks within the park are north to **Arroyo Loro**, and to **Arroyo Palmar**.

Tour operators in both Colón and Concordia organize half-day trips to the park.

Paraná

Entre Ríos Province

ⓘ Tourist information

There is an information kiosk near the park administration building. Pamphlets are available, and one room of the kiosk features a display of the wildlife and plants in the park. Only cars are charged an entrance fee to the park; hikers can enter free of charge.

▲ Camping

It costs $2.00 per person to hire a tent, but there is no charge for camping within the park.

🍴 Eating out

There is a cafeteria at the camping ground overlooking the Río Uruguay.

🚌 Buses

Not all buses on their way to either Colón or Concordia will pick up passengers at the park. It is not an official stop and you have to flag buses down. Don't be surprised if they don't always stop. Hitchhiking to either Colón or Concordia is easy on the weekends.
- Colón: Empresa Bus Itapé
- Concordia: Departs 1345–1730; Empresa Bus Itapé

Rosario del Tala

Postal code: 3174 • ☎ area code: (0445)
Distance from Paraná: 183 km eastwards on RN 12 then RN 39

Rosario del Tala, founded in 1822, is almost at the geographic center of Entre Ríos. The upper reaches of the **Río Gualeguay** are very popular with campers and hikers.

🛏 Accommodation

A Residencial Olijnick, corner of Centenario and 3 de Febrero $11.50

▲ Camping

The Parque Balneario Dr Delio Panizza is a 50 ha recreational area with a fine sandy beachfront along the river. There is fresh water, and, in summer, a disco

🍴 Eating out

There is not a great choice of restaurants in Rosario del Tala.
- Restaurant Comedor Rancho Don Ernesto, Uruguay 20
- Restaurant Hotel Entrerriano, corner of Centenario and 3 de Febrero

🚌 Buses

The bus terminal is on Uruguay.

🚗 Motoring

- Service station: Shell, corner of Centenario and 3 de Febrero

🎭 Entertainment

- Disco El Refugio del Pirata, Balneario Municipal "Dr Delio Panizza". Open during the tourist season only
- Disco Sobremonte, Nuestra Señora del Rosario 40, Plaza Libertad

Viale

Postal code: 3109
Distance from Paraná: 58 km eastwards on RN 18

🛏 Accommodation

A Residencial Los Cedros, Santa Fé 274 $11.50

Victoria

Postal code: 3153 • ☎ area code: (0436)
Distance from Paraná: 118 km south-east on RP 11

Entre Ríos Province

Victoria is located in a flood-prone area on the **Río Victoria**, about 40 km north of its junction with the **Río Paraná**.

Until 1829 Victoria was known as Matanza, which means "killing" or "slaughter". It was an apt description of the cruel campaigns the Spanish waged against the local Indians during the colonial era. A huge cross has been erected on this site to commemorate a bloody battle which took place between the Indians and the victorious Spaniards. The town was founded during the eighteenth century, but the exact date is obscure. The oldest buildings from the "Matanza era" are located in the Quinto Cuartel section of town.

In 1899 the Benedictine order established a monastery here; it still exists and cells are available for those who want to pray or meditate. The Benedictines are renowned apiarists and produce a liqueur from their honey which is made according to old recipes.

Festivals
- Fiesta Provincial Criolla. (Provincial Rancher Festival): October
- Fiesta Provincial del Carnaval: February

Accommodation
A Residencial Plaza, Congreso 455 (1431 $11.50
A Residencial San Luis, H Yrigoyen 700 (1294 $11.50
B Residencial El Parque, Alem 222 (1315 $9.50
- Residencial Reggiardo, España 233 (1835

Camping
- Camping Municipal

Eating out
- Restaurant Comedor Jockey Club Victoria, Alem 91
- Restaurant Comedor La Tablita, Balneario Municipal
- Restaurant Comedor Rizzi, H Yrigoyen 700

Post and telegraph
- Post office: Encotel, Bulevar Mitre 473
- Telephone: Compañía Entrerriana de Teléfonos, Bartoloni 522

Water transport
Empresa de Lanchas Victoria operates a launch service to Puerto San Martín in Santa Fé province.

Buses
The bus terminal is on the corner of Junín and Alem.
- Paraná: Empresa Messina
- Buenos Aires: Empresa TATA
- Diamante: Empresa Diamante
- Gualeguay: Empresa El Inca, Empresa Messina
- Gualeguaychú: Empresa Messina
- Nogoyá: Empresa Aquino

Shopping
- Honey liqueur from the Benedictine monastery
- Centro Artesanal, Alem 87

Entertainment
- Disco Ockey, Laprida 530
- Disco Portofino, corner of Italia and Chacabuco

Sightseeing
- Monasterio Benedictino (Benedictine Monastery), 2 km outside town on RP 11. The monastery's church with its large marble-like altar is worth a visit

Victoria

ENTRE RÍOS PROVINCE

- Cerro La Matanza, north-east of the town center. This cross was erected to commemorate a bloody battle fought between Spaniards and Indians in the eighteenth century. From here there are views of the Ombues forest and the lakes created by the waters of the Río Victoria and Río Paraná
- Museo Arqueológico Indígena, corner of V Sarsfield and 25 de Mayo
- Museo de la Ciudad (City Museum), Italia 364. A small but interesting collection including pre-Columbian archeological artefacts and fossils found in the area

VILLA LIBERTADOR GENERAL SAN MARTÍN

Postal code: 3103
Distance from Paraná: 62 km south-east on RN 12, then westwards on RN 131

Accommodation
- ★ Hotel Puiggari, 9 de Julio 80 $14.00
- A Residencial Central, 25 de Mayo 150 $11.50
- A Residencial La Colina, 25 de Mayo 50 $11.50
- B Residencial Libertador, 25 de Mayo 124 $9.50

Buses
Buses run frequently to Paraná.

VILLAGUAY

Postal code: 3240 • area code: (0455)
Distance from Paraná: 155 km eastwards on RN 18

Villaguay was founded in 1833 and is located in the center of the province on the **Río Gualeguay**. It developed around a chapel made from clay and straw dedicated to Santa Rosa de Lima. The Palacio Municipal now occupies the site.

Temperatures average 28°C in summer and 15°C in winter.

Accommodation
- ★ Motel La Familia, RN 18 1048 $14.00
- A Residencial Torino, corner of Mitre and Balcarce $11.50

Eating out
- Restaurant La Delfina, corner of L Herrera and Frías. Local cuisine
- Restaurant Maximiliano, corner of L Herrera and Alem. Local cuisine

Eating out outside Villaguay
- Restaurant El Lucero (in the Shell service station), at the intersection of RN 12 and RN 18

Churches
- Lutheran church, Goyena

Motoring
- Service station: Shell, at the intersection of RN 12 and RN 18

Tours
- Empresa El Aguila, Vertiz 466 2162. This company does not operate regular tours but will organize one if requested

Entre Ríos Province

Sport
- Boat hire, at the Parque Balneario Municipal, 2 km east of town

Entertainment
- Disco L'Amour, corner of San Martín and Colón. Weekends only

Sightseeing
- Museo Histórico Regional (Regional Historical Museum), corner of Balcarce and Hermelo. Open Mon–Sat 0900–1200 and 1500–1900

Villaguay

MISIONES PROVINCE

Plate 47 Map of Misiones Province
- 790 Alba Posse
- 790 Apostóles
- 791 Aristóbulo del Valle
- 792 Bernardo de Irigoyen
- 793 Dos de Mayo
- 793 El Soberbio
- 794 Eldorado
- 795 Jardín de América
- 796 Leandro N Alem
- 796 Montecarlo
- 798 Oberá
- 799   Map
- 801 Posadas
- 802   Map
- 809 Puerto Esperanza
- 810 Puerto Iguazú
- 811   Map
- 817 Puerto Rico
- 818 San Ignacio Miní
- 820 San Javier
- 820 San Pedro
- 821 San Vicente

Misiones Province

Misiones Province

Misiones sticks out of the north-eastern corner of Argentina like a thumb. Like Corrientes and Entre Ríos, it is almost entirely surrounded by rivers. Along the north-west, the **Río Alto Paraná** forms a long border with Paraguay. To the north, east, and south-east is Brazil, the border in the south-east formed by the **Río Uruguay**, in the east and north by the **Río Pepiri Guazú** and **Río San Antonio**, and in the north by the **Río Iguazú**. The short south-eastern border with Corrientes province incorporates the **Arroyo Chimiray**.

Misiones, with its capital at Posadas, is one of the most interesting provinces for the tourist, with roaring waterfalls—the **Cataratas del Iguazú**, **Gran Salto de Moconá**, and **Salto Alegre**—rainforest, mountainous areas in the center, and the archeological remains of early Jesuit settlements.

Throughout Misiones, the Río Paraná is called the Río Alto Paraná, or "Upper Paraná".

History

As its name indicates, during the sixteenth and seventeenth centuries Misiones was the domain of Jesuit missions. Armed with a charter from the King of Spain, missionaries settled first in the area around the **Río Alto Paraná**, Río Guayra in Brazil, and **Río Guaycurú**, and made successful attempts to convert the local Guaranís to Christianity and to make the land productive. However, Brazilian slave hunters—*"Paulistas"* or *"Mamelucas"*—forced the Jesuits to abandon their settlements and to flee to the area which is now Misiones, where they established further missions, flourishing outposts of European civilization. The most important—**San José**, **Apostóles**, **Corpus**, **Santa Ana**, **La Candelaria**, **Loreto**, and **San Ignacio Miní**—are located along the Río Alto Paraná and **Río Uruguay**.

The missions were created from 1631 onwards, and managed to induce the Guaranís to adopt a European-style political, religious, and economic system. When the Jesuits were expelled from all Spanish territories their mission centers fell into disrepair, and were gradually abandoned and eventually overgrown by the jungle. The ruins of a few remain.

Economy

Misiones is one of the richest agricultural provinces in Argentina and produces almost 90 per cent of the country's total production in *maté*, tea, *tung* and *mandioca*. These products in turn have fostered ancillary industries which are located in the prosperous communities of **Apostóles**, **Montecarlo**, **Oberá**, **Puerto Rico**, and in the provincial capital **Posadas** itself. The timber industry is also very important, with one of the biggest timber mills and cellulose plants located near **Puerto Piray** on the **Río Paraná**. A vigorous reafforestation program is under way to replenish cut timber.

Tourism

Misiones is still largely untouched, with large stretches of subtropical rainforests, the home of many South American species in retreat from the advance of civilization.

The most popular tourist attraction is without doubt the **Cataratas del Iguazú** (known in English as the Iguazú Falls) located in the **Parque Nacional del Iguazú** in the northernmost corner of the province on the Brazilian border. Argentina shares the Iguazú falls with Brazil, where they are known as "Iguaçu". The flora and fauna of this national park is unsurpassed and a trip here is a must on a visit to Argentina.

Another spectacular waterfall is the **Gran Salto de Moconá**, situated on the **Río Uruguay** where the **Río Pepiri Guazú** and the **Río Pepiri Miní** join it. These rivers form the border with Brazil, and the falls are not easily accessible except by launch from El Soberbio.

Fishing for *pejerrey* and other tropical fish is good in all rivers of the province, with a major sport fishing ground in the **Reserva Nacional de Pesca de Caraguatay** on the Río Alto Paraná.

Posadas, the provincial capital, is located on the **Río Alto Paraná** opposite Encarnación in Paraguay. The road from Posadas north to **Puerto Iguazú** is virtually lined with the ruins of mission settlements, of which the best-preserved is probably **San Ignacio Miní**. Other mission settlements along this route are **Santa Ana** and **Loreto**; near **Concepción de la Sierra** near the Río Uruguay are the ruins of the **Santa María** mission.

Infrastructure

The road system, especially along the Río Paraná, is fairly good. It consists of some 3700 km of which approximately 1200 km are paved, including the full length of RN 12. Regular bus services connect the province with all parts of Argentina. Accommodation is available in all major cities, but in remote areas camping is usual.

Although most visitors will only spend enough time to visit the major tourist attractions, the province offers some remarkable spots off the beaten track, almost all of which can be reached by public transport. The interior and the area along the Brazilian border are seldom visited by tourists. The trip from Eldorado across the **Sierra de Misiones** to **Bernardo de Irigoyen** can be made with Empresa Iguazú (fare $2.50); and the trip to Bernardo de Irigoyen along the **Río San Antonio** through the **Parque**

MISIONES PROVINCE

Nacional del Iguazú can be made with Empresa Kruse (fare $4.50).

It is possible to make the trip right through the center of the province from Oberá to Puerto Iguazú with various bus companies.

The most rewarding tourist targets are:
- Don't miss : **Parque Nacional del Iguazú** with the **Cataratas del Iguazú**
- Worth a visit: **San Ignacio Miní**
- Worth a detour: **Gran Salto de Moconá** and **Posadas**
- Of interest: **Puerto Iguazú**, **Oberá**, and **Montecarlo**

ALBA POSSE

Postal code: 3363 • Population: 6000 • (area code: (0755) • Altitude: 136 m
Distances
- From Posadas 160 km eastwards on RN 12 then RN 103

Alba Posse is a border town on the **Río Uruguay**. Here the river is about 350 m wide but still fast flowing.

Accommodation outside Alba Posse

B Hotel de Turismo Correa, Ruta 8, Santa Rita (8 km north of Alba Posse) $3.50

Buses

- Aristóbulo del Valle: Departs 1130; 3 services daily; 3 hours; Empresa La Victoria. There is a connection here for buses to Puerto Rico
- Oberá: Fare $1.50; departs 0550; 5 services daily; 2 hours; Expreso Singer
- Puerto Rico: Fare $3.50; departs 1610 daily; 4 hours; Empresa La Victoria

Motoring

RN 103 to Oberá is a dirt road and delays can be experienced during wet weather. The same applies to RP 219 to Aristóbulo del Valle.

Water transport

- Launch and ferry services to Puerto Magua (Brazil): $0.30 ($0.50 on weekends); depart 0800–1700 Mon–Fri and from 0900–1600 Sat–Sun; 2 services only on Sunday

APÓSTOLES

Postal code: 3350 • Population: 17 000 (area code: (0758) • Altitude: 160 m
Distances
- From Posadas: 65 km southwards on RP 105
- From San Javier: 87 km southwards on RP 201 then eastwards on RP 2

Apóstoles was first founded as a Jesuit mission settlement in 1633 but abandoned in 1637. The modern town was founded in 1897.

Accommodation

- Hostería Apóstoles (ACA), Irigoyen (2653 $7.50
- C Residencial Misiones, Alvear 444 (2402. Dormitories
- C Residencial Rex, Avenida San Martín (2693

Buses

- Posadas: Fare $1.50; departs 0530; 12 services daily; 1 hour; Empresa Crucero del Norte
- Santo Tomé: Fare $2.60; departs 0630; 2 services daily; 2 hours; Empresa Crucero del Norte

MISIONES PROVINCE

🚗 Motoring
- Service station: YPF, town center

🞇 Excursions
- **Santa María**: Apostóles is a convenient starting point for the trip to the ruins of this mission settlement, founded by the Jesuits in the middle of the seventeenth century and now a national monument. The normal Jesuit mission layout was adhered to, with the exception of the prison block which has walls of extra thickness. Below the cell block was a corridor which led to the church. The church was adorned by huge columns. A printing press was established here in 1722. The present-day chapel was built using materials from the Jesuit mission. Take an Empresa San Javier bus going to San Javier via Concepción de la Sierra and ask the driver to let you off at the intersection leading up to the former mission. If you take the first bus (0630 in the morning) you arrive around 0800 and have ample time to catch another bus either to San Javier or back to Apostóles

ARISTÓBULO DEL VALLE

Postal code: 3364 • Population: 1900 •
(area code: (0755)
Distance from Posadas: 120 km north-east on RN 12 then eastwards on RP 7

Located in the center of the province in the **Sierra de Misiones**, Aristóbulo del Valle is the center of the local logging industry. En route to San Vicente are nearby waterfalls: **Salto Encantado**, **Salto Alegre**, and **Salto Pilaras Blancas**.

The town is on the intersection of RP 7 westwards to Jardín de América on the Río Paraná, and RN 14 running north-east to San Pedro and on to Bernardo de Irigoyen on the Brazilian border and south-west to Campo Grande, Oberá, and Leandro N Alem.

🛏 Accommodation
- Alojamiento 9 de Julio, RN 14. Shared rooms
- Alojamiento El Amigo, Avenida Las Americas 739 F40M@ 90275 $7.00 ♦♦

▲ Camping
- 18 km west on RP 7. No facilities

🍴 Eating out
- Restaurant La Cueva del Tío Cesar

🚌 Buses
Buses run regularly to Oberá and Posadas, to El Soberbio on the Río Uruguay, and to San Pedro further north in the Sierra de Misiones.

🚗 Motoring
- Service station: YPF, town center

🞇 Excursions
- Aristóbulo del Valle is in the heart of Misiones, and although logging of the primeval forest is going on unabated some of the original subtropical rainforest cover can still be seen
- Just outside town on RP 7 to Jardín de América the road descends giving some splendid views over a forested valley. There is a camping spot on the right-hand side 18 km further

Aristóbulo de Valle

on. This section of the road is a tourist area, and there are two viewing platforms. If you are traveling by bus sit on the right-hand side. After 22 km pine plantations and some cultivated land reappear, but it is still a very scenic trip

BERNARDO DE IRIGOYEN

Postal code: 3366 • Population: 7500 • (area code: (0751) • Altitude: 805 m
Distances
- From Puerto Iguazú: 157 km south-east on RP 101
- From Eldorado: 127 km eastwards on RP 17

Bernardo de Irigoyen, on the **Río Pepiri Guazú** is the easternmost town in Argentina. Across the border is the Brazilian town of Dionisio Cerqueira, and the two towns virtually merge into each other. This is a relatively relaxed land border crossing.

Accommodation
- Hotel/Motel ACA, Avenida Libertador, down from the bus terminal ⑪ (92218 $5.00 ᵢ
- C Residencial Bernardo de Irigoyen, in the main street after the turn-off to the border, on the left of the road to San Antonio

⑪ Eating out
Besides the ACA Motel there is not much choice here. However, it is only a short walk across the border to Dionisio Cerqueira where there are plenty of fairly good restaurants.
- Restaurant ACA, RN 14
- Restaurant Bella Vista, RN 14

$ Financial
Cash dollars can only be exchanged in Dionisio Cerqueira in Brazil.

Border crossing
Passport control is open 0700–1900. Argentine passport control is directly at the border. The Brazilian Policia Federal is two blocks (200 m) further up in the main street of Dionisio Cerqueira on the left hand side.

Buses
There is a bus terminal on the hill just up from the ACA Motel.
In Dionisio Cerqueira in Brazil the bus terminal ("*Rodoviaria*") is approximately seven blocks from the border, and there are services to many Brazilian destinations. There are no services to Foz do Iguaçu through Brazil, and it is better to go to Puerto Iguazú and from there to Foz do Iguaçu.
- El Dorado: Fare $2.50; departs 0515; 8 services daily; 2½ hours; Empresa Cotal, Empresa Kruse
- Puerto Iguazú: Fare $4.50; departs 1130 daily; 5 hours; Empresa Kruse

Motoring
RN 101 to Puerto Iguazú is unsealed until it reaches the entrance to the Parque Nacional Iguazú.
- Service station: YPF, RP 17

Excursions
- **Puerto Iguazú**: RN 101. Some 10 km north of Bernardo de Irigoyen is the **Salto Andresito**, but it is not visible from the road. For a while the road follows the Brazilian border; the first major settlement you reach is **San Antonio** with its twin Brazilian town, also called San Antônio. Here the **Río San Antonio** joins the **Río Iguazú**. Further down the river is the **Salto de Agua Tupa**. The whole area

Aristóbulo del Valle

Plate 47
Map of Misiones Province

Plate 48
Cataratas del Iguazú

Misiones Province

is intensively logged and most of the dense subtropical rainforest has disappeared. The bus makes a few detours to serve the small (and some not so small) new settlements which have sprung up here over the last 15 years, such as **Deseado** and **Cabure-I**. The **Parque Nacional del Igazú** starts 3 km after Cabure-I, and for the next 32 km there are no cleared patches and all is dense subtropical jungle in which abundant birdlife and the occasional monkey can be seen. This is the last vestige of the original subtropical rainforest which once covered the whole province of Misiones. At the entrance to the national park is a ranger station-cum-information kiosk

- **San Pedro** and **Oberá** via **Tobuna**: Empresa Kruse buses connect at San Pedro with buses traveling through the center of the province to **Oberá**. This is a trip through the part of Misiones unknown to most tourists. There are two services daily for the two-hour journey to San Pedro

Dos de Mayo

Postal code: 3364 • (area code: (0755)
Distance from Posadas: 180 km north-east on RN 12 then RN 7 and RN 14, via Jardín de América

Dos de Mayo is a fast-growing community located in the **Sierra de Misiones**, in the center of the province. Economic activities include logging and the production of tea and *maté*, which are locally dried.

Buses
- Alojamiento El Trebol, RN 14. Shared rooms
- Alojamiento Alex, RN 14, Km 236. Shared rooms
- Alojamiento La Cabaña, RN 14. Shared rooms

Eating out
- Restaurant Centro Comunitario

Buses
Buses run regularly to Posadas and Oberá.

Motoring
- Service station: YPF, town center

El Soberbio

Postal code: 3364 • (area code: (0755) • Altitude: 147 m
Distance from Posadas, via Oberá: 230 km north-east on RN 12, RP 4, RN 103, RN 14, and RP 212

El Soberbio is a border town located on the **Río Uruguay**.

Buses
- Oberá: Departs 1215; 2 services daily; 5 hours; Empresa Singer

Water transport
Launch services to Brazil depart 0800–1800 Mon–Fri, 1000–1600 Sat and Sun.

Excursions
- **Gran Salto de Moconá**: El Soberbio is the best place to visit

MISIONES PROVINCE

these falls. Boats can be hired to go upstream

ELDORADO

Postal code: 3380 • Population: 38 000 • (area code: (0751) • Altitude: 215 m
Distances
- From Posadas: 206 km north-east on RN 12
- From Bernardo de Irigoyen: 93 km westwards on RP 17
- From Puerto Iguazú: 101 km southwards on RN 12

Eldorado is a modern town situated near the banks of the **Río Alto Paraná**. From Puerto Eldorado Viejo, on the river, the town stretches away in east-westerly direction for 12 km, bisected by the RN 12. It is a center of *maté*, tea, and *tung* cultivation and of sawmilling. There are also citrus orchards. The town center is about 3 km up from the intersection with the RN 12. It is a suitable place for a stopover, with good restaurants and accommodation.

Tourist information
- ACA, San Martín, has information on road conditions into the interior and down to El Soberbio on the Río Uruguay

Camping
- Camping Parque Schwell, Puerto El Dorado

Eating out
- Restaurant Bella Vista, Avenida San Martín Km 9
- Restaurant El Triangulo, Avenida San Martín Km 9
- Restaurant Hotel Atlantida, Avenida San Martín Km 7
- Restaurant Hotel Los Troncos, RN 12 km 6
- Restaurant La Cueva del Tío Cesar, corner of Ríoja and Cordoba
- Pizzería Oasis, corner of Malvinas and Iguazú. Pleasant patio and decor

Eating out outside Eldorado
- Restaurant Hotel Victoria, Puerto Piray Miní

Accommodation in Eldorado

★	Hotel Eldorado ACA, Esperanza, Km 9	(21370	$8.50	
A	Residencial Atlantida, San Martín 3087	(22441	$10.00	
A	Residencial Alpa, corner of Cordoba and Ríoja Km 9			
		(21097	$9.00	
A	Residencial Buddenberg, San Martín 3275	(21415	$12.00	
B	Residencial Castellar, San Martín Km 9	(21348	$10.50	
B	Residencial Alex, corner of San Martín 3893 and Voisi			
		(22354	$12.00	
C	Residencial Parque, Triunvirato	(22279		
•	Residencial Bella Vista, RN 12 Km 9			
•	Residencial Caballito Blanco, San Martín 3811			
•	Hospedaje Italiano, corner of America and Paraguay			

Accommodation outside Eldorado

A	Residencial Los Troncos, RN 12, km 6		$3.50

MISIONES PROVINCE

💲 Financial
- Cambio Fonsecca, corner of América and San Martín

📘 Visas, passports
- Swiss consulate, corner of Cuyo and San Martín

🚌 Buses
- Bernardo de Irigoyen: Fare $2.50; departs 0800 daily; 3 hours; Empresa Iguazú
- Oberá: $6.00
- Puerto Iguazú: Fare $3.00; 2 hours

🚗 Motoring
RP 17 to Bernardo de Irigoyen on the Brazilian border is a sealed road with a good surface.

Service stations
- YPF, RN 12, Km 9
- ACA, San Martín

Excursions
- **Bernardo de Irigoyen**: RP 17. After leaving Eldorado the road runs straight for many kilometers, alongside the usual pine afforestations, tea and *maté* plantations interspersed with patches of primeval forest. Beyond these the countryside becomes undulating and very green. There is a small cafeteria at the intersection with RP 20 from San Pedro, and from here RP 20 begins a winding descent. See Bernardo de Irigoyen on page 792
- **Salto Elena**: These 10 m high falls are nearby. There is a museum, and camping is possible. RP 17 leads westwards over the **Sierra de Misiones** to **Bernardo de Irigoyen** on the **Río Uruguay**
- **Victoria**: 9 km on the RN 12. This is a small settlement. There is swimming in **Río Piray Miní** which joins the **Río Alto Paraná** nearby

JARDÍN DE AMÉRICA

Postal code: 3328 • Population: 17 000 • area code: (0752)
Distances
- From Posadas: 98 km north-east on RN 12
- From Aristóbulo del Valle: 40 km westwards on RP 7

Jardín de América is situated at the junction of RN 12 and RP 7 leading up to Aristóbulo del Valle.

ℹ️ Tourist information
- Municipalidad de Jardín de América, Belgrano 666

🛏️ Accommodation
C Residencial El Gallo de Oro, RN 12 ✆ 96199 $7.50 ⛄
C Residencial Carina, RN 12 $7.50 ⛄

Accommodation outside Jardín de América
- Municipal youth hostel, 7 km north of town, near Saltos del Tabay

⛺ Camping
- Municipal camping ground, Arroyo Tabay, 5 km north of town

🍴 Eating out
- Restaurant El Salto, on RN 12

🚌 Buses
Buses run regularly to Posadas and Puerto Iguazú.

MISIONES PROVINCE

🚗 Motoring
- Service station: YPF, RN 12

🎯 Excursions
- **Saltos del Tabay**: 8 km. A 10 m waterfall with natural swimming pool, and camping near Leoni in tropical surroundings
- **Sierra de Misiones**: A scenic drive on RP 7
- **Salto del Capioví**: 21 km north. Club Suizo, which has a dining room, is off the main road; in the village of **Capioví** is the small Hospedaje Capioví

LEANDRO N ALEM

Postal code: 3315 • Population: 18 000 •
(area code: (0755) • Altitude: 290 m
Distance from Posadas: 80 km eastwards on RN 12 then south-east on RP 4

Leandro N Alem is located in the **Sierra del Imán**, midway between the Río Paraná and the Río Uruguay, in the southern part of the province.

🛏 Accommodation
B Residencial Bambi, San Martín $9.00 ⅱ
C Residencial Avenida, corner of San Martín and San Lorenzo
- Alojamiento Carioca, San Martín 756. Shared rooms
- Alojamiento 25 de Mayo, 25 de Mayo 140. Shared rooms

🍴 Eating out
- Restaurant Tío Cesar, Avenida Vélez Sarsfield 743. *Churrasquerría*, where barbecues are served
- Restaurant Mucho Gusto, Avenida Las Heras
- Restaurant El Abuelo, corner of Avenida Los Cafetales and Alberdí

🚌 Buses
Buses run regularly to Oberá and Posadas.
- Posadas: Departs 0510 daily; 2 hours; Empresa Singer
- Oberá: Departs 0500 daily; 1 hour; Empresa Don Tito

🚗 Motoring
- Service station: YPF, Belgrano (between Corti and RP 4)

🎯 Excursions
- **San Javier** on the **Río Uruguay**: The river makes a sharp U-turn here. There is camping and fishing, and buses run regularly. See San Javier on page 820
- **Santa María**: The trip to this major Jesuit mission settlement is better made from Apostóles; see "Excursions" in Apostóles on page 791

MONTECARLO

Postal code: 3384 • Population: 15 000 •
(area code: (0751 • Altitude: 130 m
Distances
- From Posadas: 185km north-east on RN 12
- From Puerto Iguazú: 101 km south-west on RN 12

Montecarlo is situated on the **Río Alto Paraná**, halfway between Posadas and Puerto Iguazú, about 4 km off the main highway. Nearby are the **Mboibusu Zool-bal** falls on the Río Alto Paraná, and the waters around

Jardín de América

MISIONES PROVINCE

Accommodation in Montecarlo

A	Residencial Hostería ACA, Avenida Libertador, on the banks of the Río Paraná	(97023	$10.50	
A	Residencial Hostería Helvecia, Libertador 2882	(97228	$10.50	
A	Residencial Kayken, Avenida Libertador 1910			
B	Residencial Bungalow Lieselotte, Rotunda RN 12		$7.50	
B	Residencial Ideal, Poll			
B	Residencial Lieselotte, Avenida Libertador	(97262		
•	Residencial Plaza	(97356		
•	Youth hostel: "Escuela de Frontera #619" Dormitory, kitchen			

Isla Caraguatay are a haven for anglers.

Montecarlo was founded in 1920, and is the center for local reafforestation, logging, and fruit packing industries. **Puerto Piray**, some 12 km outside Montecarlo on a a turn-off to the left, is the site of the industrial complex of "Celulosa Argentina", a large paper manufacturing plant located directly on the Río Alto Paraná.

Festivals
- Fiesta Provincial de la Flor (Provincial Flower Festival): October

Tourist information
- Municipalidad de Montecarlo

Camping
- Camping Municipal Montecarlo, in the grounds of the Club de Pesca Montecarlo

Eating out
- Restaurant ACA, Avenida Libertador
- Restaurant Comedor La Esquina, RN 12
- Restaurant Comedor Montecarlo, Avenida Libertador
- Restaurant Los Paraisos, RN 12. Steakhouse

Post and telegraph
- Post office: Encotel, Libertador
- Telephone: Entel, Libertador

Buses
There are 21 services a day to Posadas (a 4-hour journey), and 17 services a day to Puerto Iguazú (a 3-hour journey).

Motoring

Service stations
- YPF, RN 12
- Shell, town center

Water transport
Launch services to Apayme in Paraguay operate only at the request of tourists.

Sport
- Fishing for *dorado* and *surubí* from the nearby Isla Caraguatay

Excursions
- **Isla Caraguatay**: A nearby national fishing reserve on the **Río Alto Paraná** at a spot where the river forms rapids

Montecarlo

MISIONES PROVINCE

OBERÁ

Postal code: 3360 • Population: 40 000 • (area code: (0755) • Altitude: 345 m
Distances
- From Posadas: 99 km eastwards on RN 12 then RN 103
- From Alba Posse on the Río Uruguay: 61 km westwards on RN 103

Oberá, founded in 1928, is located in the southern highlands of the **Sierra de Misiones**. Temperatures average 20 °C, and annual rainfall is about 1700 mm. It has a very active chamber of commerce and a college of electrical engineering. It is a center of tea, *maté*, cotton, and *tung* production and of the local logging industry.

Festivals
- San Antonio, the town's patron saint: June 13
- Feria Guazú: A fair held in October in even-numbered years, to strengthen the sense of a common heritage shared by the countries bordering the Río de la Plata basin—Brazil, Uruguay, Paraguay, and Argentina
- Fiesta Provincial del Inmigrante (Provincial Immigrants' Festival) and Fiesta Provincial de Artesanías (Provincial Crafts Festival): September. Misiones as a whole and the Oberá district in particular are a melting pot of many nations: grafted onto the local Guaraní population came Germans, Brazilians, Japanese, Italians, Spaniards, Poles, Ukrainians (particularly after the last war), Swiss, and Scandinavians. The impact of these hardworking inmigrants can be seen everywhere: attractive cities, good roads, and flourishing agriculture. Most festivities are held in the Parque de las Naciones

Tourist information
- Tourist information kiosk, corner of Avenida Libertad and Sarmiento, on Plazoleta Güemes (21808. Open daily 0700–1900
- Casa de la Cultura, corner of Buenos Aires and 9 de Julio

Eating out
- Restaurant Apolo 11, Barreyro 840
- Restaurant Club Social, Avenida Sarmiento 960
- Restaurant Copacabana, Avenida Libertad 145
- Restaurant Danubio Azul, Avenida Libertad 1100
- Restaurant Don Guillermo, Buenos Aires
- Restaurant El Cacique, corner of G Barreyro and Avenida J Ingenieros
- Restaurant El Trebol, G Barreyro 830
- Restaurant El Lapacho, 12 de Octubre
- Restaurant Gunther, Buenos Aires
- Restaurant Hotel Internacional, Avenida J Ingenieros 121
- Restaurant La Ríograndense, San Martín 1053
- Restaurant Oberá Tenis Club, San Luis 378
- Restaurant Rosales, Avenida J Ingenieros 430
- Restaurant Szewald, corner of Berutti and Chaco
- Comedor El Lapacho, corner of 12 de Octubre block 0 and Sarmiento
- Comedor Rosales, Avenida J Ingenieros 442
- Pizzería Imperial, corner of Jujuy block 100 and G Barreyro
- Pizzería Matakos, Santa Fé 76
- Pizzería Tito's, corner of Avenida J Ingenieros 197 and Larrea
- ☞ Cafetería Alemana, Salta 70. Serves good *"Kuchen"* (German cakes)
- Cafetería Capri, Santa Fé 152
- Cafetería Els Catalans, San Luis 229
- Cafetería Sweet, Avenida Sarmiento

Post and telegraph
- Post office: Encotel, corner of Santa Fé and San Martín
- Telephone: Entel, corner of Jujuy block 0 and Avenida Sarmiento

Misiones Province

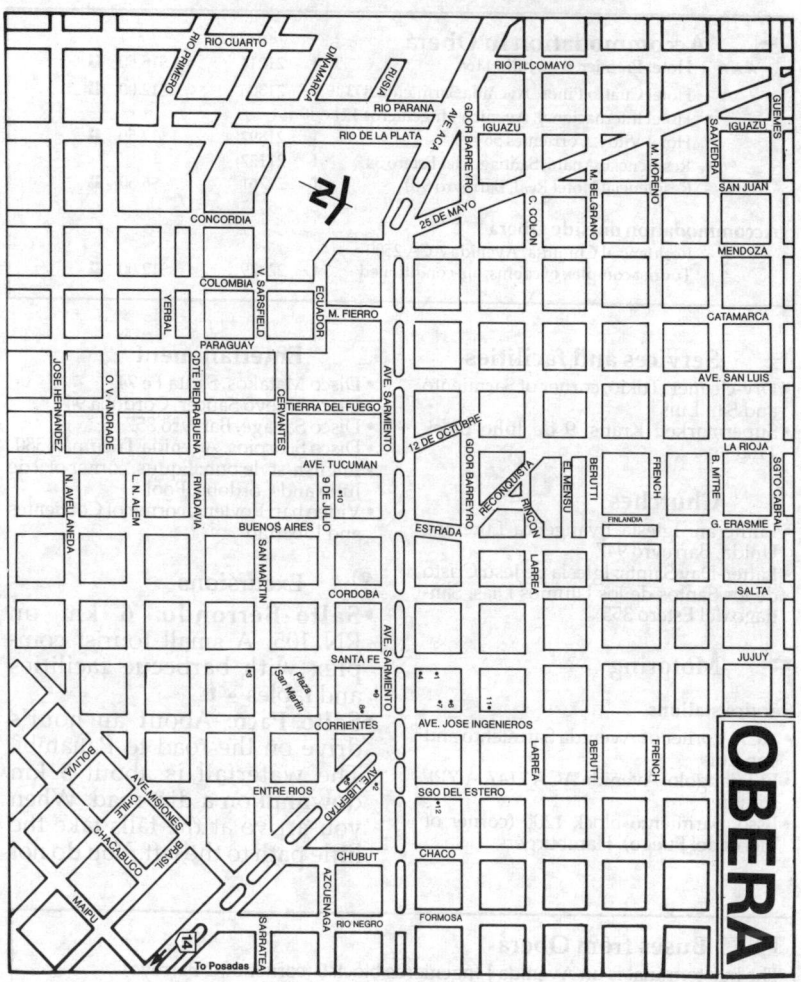

Key to Map

1. Municipalidad
2. Iglesia
3. Post office (Encotel)
4. Telephone (Entel)
5. Tourist office
6. Bus terminal
7. Museum
8. Hotel Vito I
9. Hotel Cuatro Pinos
10. Hotel Premier
11. Residencial Real Hotel
12. Residencial Anahi

Oberá

MISIONES PROVINCE

Accommodation in Oberá

★★★	Hotel Premier, 9 de Julio 1164		21214	$18.50	
A	Hotel Cuatro Pinos, Avenida Sarmiento 853		21306	$12.00	
•	Hotel Internacional, Avenida J Ingenieros 121				
•	Hotel Vito I, Corrientes 56		21892	$12.50	
•	Residencial Anahi, Santiago del Estero 34		21127		
C	Residencial Hotel Real, Barreyro 810		22761	$6.50	

Accommodation outside Oberá

★	Residencial Chiquita, Avenida ACA 2500 Tourist complex of cabins; air-conditioned		22829	$12.00	

Services and facilities

- Dry-cleaner: Tokio, corner of Sarmiento and San Luis
- Supermarket: Kraus, 9 de Julio block 1100

Churches

- Lutheran: Iglesia Evangelica Luterana Unida, Barreyro 947
- Latter-Day Saints: Iglesia de Jesú Cristo de los Santos de los Últimos Días, Santiago del Estero 355

Motoring

Service stations

- ACA, corner of Avenida Sarmiento and San Luis
- El Triangolo, Avenida ACA 2147. A YPF station
- Esso, Sarmiento block 1200 (corner of Tierra del Fuego). Hamburgers

Entertainment

- Disco Matakos, Santa Fe 74
- Disco Nuevo Saucer, Cordoba 94
- Disco Savage, Bareyro 857
- Disco Scorpios, Avenida Tucumán 580
- English-style pub: Equus, corner of 9 de Julio and Córdoba. Pool
- Video bar: Reviens, corner of Corrientes and Libertad

Excursions

- **Salto Berrondo**: 6 km on RN 105. A small tourist complex with barbecue facilities and tables
- **Salto Paco**: About an hour's drive on the road to Panambí. The waterfall is about 3 km downhill on a dirt road. When you arrive at the falls take the little path to the left. You do not

Buses from Oberá

The bus terminal is on Avenida J Ingenieros block 0 (corner of G Barreyo)

Destination	Fare	Depart	Services	Hours	Company
• Posadas		0500	19 services daily	2	Singer
• Alba Posse	$1.50	0630	5 services daily		Singer
• Buenos Aires		1130	2 services daily	18	Singer
• El Dorado	$6.00			4	Singer
• Panambí	$1.00			1	Real
• Puerto Iguazú		1045	daily	5	Singer
• Salto Paco	$0.80				
• San Javier		0530	5 services daily	3	Aguila Dorada

Oberá

MISIONES PROVINCE

have to walk far down to get a good view of the waterfall which, although not very wide, has a free fall of about 40–50 m. The area is still covered with its original subtropical forest, but heavy logging continues. The return uphill to the bus takes about 45 minutes. Empresa Real runs frequent buses (fare $1.00); ask the driver to let you off. This would be a half day excursion

- **Alba Posse** and **Santa Rita**: The road from Oberá down to the **Río Uruguay** is for the most part a dirt track, which can become difficult during the wet, season especially on the last stretch down to the Río Uruguay. The ever-decreasing rainforest alternates with tea and *maté* plantations and pine afforestations. Towards the end of the trip there are scenic views over the Río Uruguay
- **Leandro N Alem** and **San Javier** on the Río Uruguay: There are frequent bus services to Leandro N Alem; change there for the bus to San Javier. See Leandro N Alem on page 796 and San Javier on page 820
- **Aristóbulo del Valle** and back to **Eldorado** on the **Río Alto Paraná**: This inland trip north is possible using public transport. The road runs through undulating country along the top of the **Sierra de Misiones** through tea and *maté* and *tung* plantations. Isolated palm trees in the fields bear witness that not so long ago this was densely covered with subtropical rainforest. The RN 14 is sealed and in very good condition as far as **San Vicente**. It passes through pine tree plantations and occassional patches of original forest. **Campo Viera** is a center of tea production and of timber milling. See Aristóbulo del Valle on page 791 and Eldorado on page 794

POSADAS

Postal code: 3300 • Population: 180 000 • (area code: (0752) • Altitude: 82 m
Distances
- From Asunción (Paraguay): 367 km
- From Buenos Aires: 1104 km northwards on RN 14
- From Porto Alegre (Brazil): 736 km
- From Puerto Iguazú: 304 km southwards on RN 12

Posadas is located on a bluff on the **Río Paraná**, across the river from the Paraguayan town of Encarnación. It was officially founded in 1870, although the Jesuits, led by Padre Roque Gónzalez de Santa Cruz, had already established an Indian *reducción* in 1615. The Jesuit mission flourished from 1648 until 1767, when the Jesuits were expelled from all Spanish territories.

The main commercial center is on Bolívar between Azara and Junín. The oldest part of town is near the harbor, and is known as La Bajada Vieja (The Old Descent); there are some quaint old houses here worth seeing. More and more tourists are coming to Posadas each year, and informa-

Misiones Province

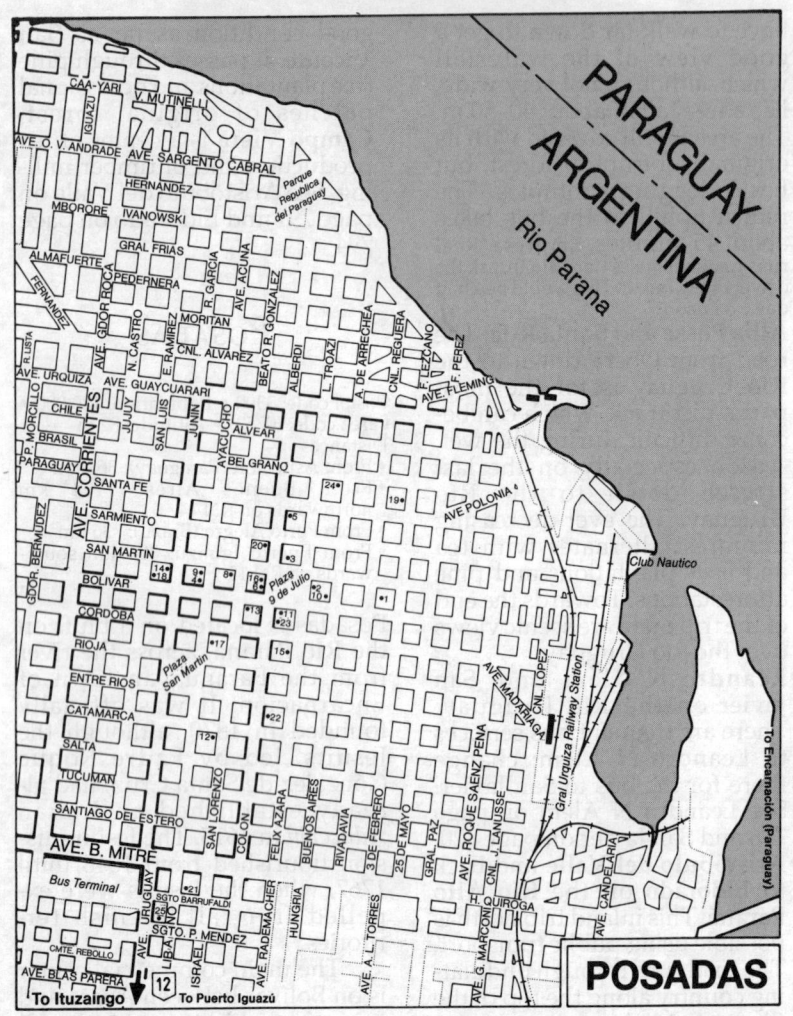

tion services are good. A new 2 km train and automobile bridge links Posadas with Encarnación in Paraguay.

During the summer months it can get very hot and humid, but winter is pleasant.

Recently the house numbering system in the center of

MISIONES PROVINCE

Key to Map
1. Municipalidad
2. Casa de Gobierno
3. Catedral
4. Post office (Encotel)
5. Telephone (Entel)
6. Tourist information
7. Cambios Mazza Turismo
8. Aerolineas Argentinas
9. Austral Lineas Aereas
10. Aerolineas Federal Argentinas
11. Hotel Continental
12. Hotel Libertador
13. Hotel Posadas
14. Hotel Canciller
15. Hotel Gran Misiones
16. Hotel City
17. Hotel Grand Hotel
18. Hotel de Turismo
19. Residencial Majestic
20. Residencial Savoy
21. Residencial Misiones
22. Residencial Colón
23. Residencial La Portuguesa
24. Residencial La Porteña
25. Residencial Nagel
26. Residencial Horianski

Posadas changed. Numbers now start from 1000, and run in the opposite direction to the previous numbers. However, the old numbers are still displayed on houses, and some street signs are missing. As a result it is not always clear whether old or new numbers are being referred to, so you need to check addresses carefully. In the addresses given in this book, the old street numbers when kown are given in parentheses; for example "San Martín 1788 (361)" means that the new number of the building in San Martín is 1788, but the old number 361 may still be displayed.

Festivals
- Festival de Litoral (Coast Festival): Held in the Anfiteatro Municipal during December

Tourist information
- Emitur, Colón 1985 (383) ☏ 24360
- Emitur Tourist Information, corner of Colón and Bolívar, opposite the park
- Public relations officer, Entitad Binacional Yacyretá, corner of Rioja block 1600 and Buenos Aires. Book here to see the huge hydroelectric scheme, the Complejo Hidroeléctrico Yacyretá Apipé, being constructed on the Río Paraná in Corrientes province

Camping
- Camping Municipal, on the Río Paraná. From the city center take buses 1, 4, or 11; from the bus terminal take bus 7. Tents can be hired for $2.00 per person

Eating out
- Restaurant Alvarez, San Lorenzo 1575
- Restaurant City Hotel, Colón 280
- Restaurant Club Tokio, Belgrano 339. Cheap meals
- Restaurant El Comedor, corner of San Lorenzo and Sarmiento. Pasta and seafood
- Restaurant El Encuentro, San Martín 1788. Credit cards accepted
- Restaurant El Mandarin, Rioja 1711 (corner of Buenos Aires). Chinese cuisine
- Restaurant El Tropezón, San Martín 2130 (185). Pasta and seafood
- Restaurant Entre Nos, San Martín block 2200 (corner of Junín). Credit cards accepted
- Restaurant Gran Tito, Córdoba 2230. Pasta and seafood
- Restaurant Hotel Continental
- Restaurant Jockey Club, San Martín 159
- Restaurant La Buena Salud, Ayacucho 602. Credit cards accepted

MISIONES PROVINCE

Accommodation in Posadas

★★★	Hotel Continental, Bolívar block 1800 (314)	ℓ	38966, 38673	$20.00	⚏
★★★	Hotel Libertador, corner of San Lorenzo 2208 and Catamarca ✉				
	10% discount for ALFA passengers	ℓ	37601, 36901	$20.00	⚏
★★★	Hotel Posadas, Bolívar block 1900 (272, 276)	ℓ	30801, 32221	$21.50	⚏
	Breakfast included; 10% discount for ALFA passengers				
★★	Hotel Canciller, Junín block 1700 (258) ✉	ℓ	31602	$15.00	⚏
★	Hotel City, Colón block 1700, opposite Plaza 9 de Julio (280)				
	10% discount for ALFA passengers	ℓ	33901, 39401	$12.00	⚏
★	Hotel Gran Hotel, Ayacucho 1967 (383)	ℓ	33305	$12.00	⚏
★	Hotel Gran Misiones, Barrufaldi 2084 (corner of Libano) ⊤				
	Near bus terminal	ℓ	22777	$12.00	⚏
•	Hotel de Turismo, Bolívar block 2200 (171)	ℓ	32711, 36501, 31801	$13.00	⚏
A	Residencial Horianski, Libano 725	ℓ	22673	$8.50	⚏
	Shared bathroom cheaper; near bus terminal				
B	Residencial Colón, Colón 2169 (485)	ℓ	25085	$8.50	⚏
B	Residencial La Portuguesa, corner of Colón 1849 and Bolívar				
	Private bath. Still being completed	ℓ	27844	$5.00	⚏
B	Residencial Majestic, Santa Fé 499	ℓ	35740	$7.00	⚏
	Shared bathroom				
B	Residencial Marlis, Avenida Corrientes 234	ℓ	25764	$8.50	⚏
B	Residencial Nagel, P Mendez 2148	ℓ	25656	$8.00	⚏
	Near bus terminal; 10% discount for ACA members				
B	Residencial Savoy, Sarmiento 296 ✉	ℓ	24430	$7.50	⚏
	Shared bathroom cheaper				
C	Residencial Argentina, Sarmiento 274	ℓ	26315	$3.50	⚏
	Shared bathroom; for budget travelers				
C	Residencial El Entrerriano, corner of General López and Madariaga				
	Near train station				
C	Residencial La Porteña, Felix de Azara block 1700 (372) ✉				
	Shared bathroom; for budget travelers	ℓ	38621	$7.50	⚏
C	Residencial Misiones, Felix de Azara	ℓ	30133		
C	Residencial Plaza, San Martín 235	ℓ	22908		
C	Residencial Uruguay, Uruguay 105	ℓ	24765	$7.50	⚏
•	Youth Hostel "Andresito Guacurari", Salta 1743	ℓ	23850		

Accommodation outside the city center

B	Residencial Carlos III, Pedernera 2136	ℓ	30301	$7.00	⚏

- Restaurant Las Cuartetas, Avenida Uruguay block 2600. Near the bus terminal
- Restaurant La Querencia, Córdoba 269, next to ACA. Steakhouse
- Restaurant La Rural, Ayacucho block 1400 (corner of Belgrano)
- ☞ Restaurant Los Troncos, Colón 1658 (corner of San Martín). A huge dome-shaped plastic tent
- Restaurant Mburucuya, Junín 1863
- Restaurant Misiones, Hotel Gran Misiones, Barrufaldi 2084. Near the bus terminal
- Restaurant Savoy, Hotel Savoy, Colón block 1600 (corner of Sarmiento)
- Cafetería ACA, corner of Córdoba and Colón. Serves early breakfast
- Cafetería Bar Español, Bolívar 2021

- Cafetería Canoa, block 1900 (corner of Colón)
- Cafetería Gaston, San Lorenzo block 1400 (corner of Belgrano)
- ☞ Cafetería Bar Ita, San Martín 2206. Coffee and sandwiches
- Cafetería La Cueva le Las Hamburguesas, Junín block 1800 (corner of Bolívar)
- Cafetería La Esquina, Bolívar block 1500 (corner of 3 de Febrero)
- Cafetería Noesigual, San Lorenzo block 2400 (corner of Santiago Del Estero). Hamburgers
- Cafetería Savoy (Hotel), Sarmiento block 1900 (corner of Colón)
- ☞ Cafetería Virage, Colón and Bolívar. Hamburgers
- Pizzería La Gran Via, Ayacucho block 1800 (corner of Córdoba)
- Pizzería La Grata Alegria, Junín block 1700. Serves breakfast from 0600
- Pizzería Los Pinos, San Lorenzo block 1700 (286)
- Pizzería Pipo, Avenida Corrientes 1711 (corner of Bolívar)
- Chopería Sibar, Bolívar block 1900 (corner of San Lorenzo)
- Pescadería Barbera, Junín block 1800 (corner of Entre Ríos). Seafood

Eating out outside Posadas

- ☞ Restaurant El Oriental, Avenida Cabred 2470. Chinese cuisine
- Restaurant La Rueda, corner of RN 12 and Rotonda

Post and telegraph

- Post office: Encotel, Bolívar block 2200 (corner of Ayacucho)
- Telephones: Entel, corner of Colón and Santa Fé

Financial

- Banco Alas, Sarmiento 1746. Cash advances on Visa card
- Cambios Mazza Tourismo, Buenos Aires 1442. Also Bolívar block 1900 (corner of San Lorenzo). Cash and checks

Services and facilities

- Bakery: Central, Ayacucho block 1500 (corner of Sarmiento)
- Pharmacy: Farmacia Bolívar, Bolívar block 1600 (442)
- Sauna: Instituto Matsumara, Tucumán 1555
- Sports equipment: El Senuelo, San Lorenzo 2476. Camping, fishing, and hunting gear

Delicatessens

- Delicatessen Alemana, 25 de Mayo block 1700 (corner of Bolívar)
- Delicatessen La Serrana, Ayacucho block 2000 (corner of Rioja)

Dry cleaners

- Colón, Colón 1254
- Executive, Junín 1637 (221) (corner of Sarmiento)
- Tokyo, Entre Ríos 2373

Photographic supplies

- Fotovision, Bolívar block 2200 (corner of San Luis). A good selection of films and photographic equipment
- Laboratorios Rolando, Bolívar 2121

Health food

- Scarsdale, San Martín 2044
- Pollen shop, Sarmiento block 1900 (corner of San Lorenzo). 1 kg $40.00

Laundromats

- La Burbuja, Buenos Aires 1654 (228). Open daily 0800–2000; $2.00
- Laverap, Ayacucho block 1400 (corner of Santa Fé). Open Mon–Sat 0800–2000
- Marval, Salta block 2100 (Ex 180) (corner of Ayacucho)

Supermarkets

- California, Santiago del Estero block 2000. A huge shop
- Supermas, Colón block 2500 (corner of Mitre)
- Tía, San Lorenzo 1942

Clubs

- British: Instituto Británico, Córdoba block 2200 (130). Translation service

Misiones Province

- French: Alliance Française, Rivadavia 136 ℓ 23519
- German: Asociación Alemán, Avenida Corrientes 666 ℓ 24187
- Italian: Sociedad Italiana, Santa Fé 2470
- Spanish: Asociación Española, Córdoba block 1600 (328)
- Chess: Club Ajedrez, Jujuy 1514 (corner of Santa Fé)
- Tango dancing: Asociación de Amigo del Tango, General Paz block 1600 (214) (corner of Sarmiento). Evening classes

Churches

- Latter Day Saints Church, R S Peña block 1900 (corner of Córdoba)
- Lutheran Evangelical Church, Entre Ríos block 2200 (130). Services are held on Sundays at 0900

Visas, passports

- Brazilian consulate, Mitre 1242
- French consulate, Sarmiento 596 ℓ 26626
- Italian consulate, Córdoba 317 ℓ 36602
- Japanese consulate ℓ 24275
- Paraguayan consulate, San Lorenzo block 1500 (179) ℓ 23858. Open Mon–Fri 0800–1200
- Spanish consulate, Córdoba 328 ℓ 26086
- West German consulate, Corrientes 564, or Avenida Ungria 141

Border crossing

The bridge across the Río Paraná linking Posadas with Encarnación in Paraguay is now finished. There is a passport checkpoint on the access road to the bridge on either side.

Air services

General San Martín airport is 12 km south of the city center, on RN 12. Tucán Turismo operates a bus to the airport for $3.00.

Airlines

- Aerolineas Argentinas, San Martín 2031 (corner of San Lorenzo)
- Austral Lineas Aereas, Ayacucho block 1700 (corner of San Martín)
- Aerolinea Federal Argentina, Buenos Aires block 1700 (292)

Services

- Buenos Aires (Aeroparque Jorge Newbery): Fare $62.00; departs 2000; 2–4 services daily; 2 hours; Aerolineas, Austral
- Córdoba: Fare $64.00; departs 2000 Mon; 2 hours; Aerolineas
- Puerto Iguazú: Fare $17.00; departs 0820 Tues; 1 hour; Federal. Fare $22.00; departs 1755 Mon; 1 hours; Aerolineas
- Resistencia: Fare $26.00; departs 0955 Tues, Thurs, Fri, Sun; 1 hour; Austral. Fare $21.00; departs 2000 Thurs; 1 hour; Federal
- Rosario: Fare $72.00; departs 1420 Tues, Thurs, Fri; 2 hours; Austral

Motoring

Service stations

- ACA, corner of Córdoba and Colón. Maps and travel information are available
- Esso, San Lorenzo block 1900 (corner of Rioja)
- Shell, San Lorenzo block 2100 (corner of Entre Ríos)

Car rental

- A-1 Rent-a-Car, San Lorenzo block 2200 (corner of Salta)
- AVIS Rent-a-Car, Colón 298 (corner of Bolívar block 1700, 179) ℓ 23483
- Liprandi Rent-a-Car, Junín 1696 (248) ℓ 32245
- Tucán Turismo. VW 1500s are available for hire; $180.00 per week, plus $0.15 per km

Trains

Trains from Posadas arrive in Buenos Aires at Lacroze station.
The F C General Urquiza station is on the corner of Coronel López and Avenida Madariaga.

- Buenos Aires: "El Gran Capitán"; sleeper $43.00, Pullman $37.00, irst class $19.00, tourist class $14.50; departs daily; 20 hours
- Concordia: First class $8.50, tourist class $6.00; 11 hours
- Paso de los Libres: First class $6.00, tourist class $4.40; 6 hours

Posadas

Misiones Province

🚌 Buses

The central municipal bus terminal is on the corner of Sarmiento and Felix de Azara. Twelve routes around the city begin here.

The long-distance bus terminal is on the corner of Avenida Mitre and Avenida Uruguay.

Destination	Fare	Depart	Services	Hours	Company
• Asunción (Paraguay)	$5.00	0830	Tues, Thurs, Sun	9	Singer
• Buenos Aires	$24.00	1255	4 services daily	15	Singer
• Colón		1255	3 services daily	11	Singer
• Concordia	$15.00	1750	2 services daily	9	Singer
• Córdoba	$27.00	1715	Tues, Thurs, Sat	20	Singer
• Corrientes	$7.80	0400	6 services daily	5	Ciudad de Posadas
• Formosa Change in Resistencia					
• Ituzaingó	$2.20	0400	6 services daily	1	Ciudad de Posadas
• La Rioja		0712	Mon, Wed, Sat		Cotal
• Mar del Plata		1730	daily	21	Tigre Iguazú
• Mendoza	$42.00	0712	Mon, Wed, Sat	33	Cotal
• Paraná	$19.00	1715	Tues, Thurs, Sat	14	Singer
• Paso de los Libres		1255	3–4 services daily	6	Kurtz, Singer
• Porto Alegre (Brazil)	$17.50	1400	Mon, Wed, Fri	14	Singer
• Puerto Iguazú	$6.50	0338	2 services daily	6	Ciudad de Posadas, Singer
• Resistencia	$8.30	0400	4 services daily	6	Ciudad de Posadas
• Rosario	$24.20	1610	daily	17	Kurtz
• San Fernando del Valle de Catamarca	$29.00	0712	Mon, Wed, Sat		Cotal
• San Ignacio	$1.50			1	Klein
• San Miguel de Tucumán	$24.50				
• Santa Fé	$19.00	1715	Tues, Thurs, Sat	15	Singer
	$20.70	1415	daily	15	Ciudad de Posadas
• Santiago del Estero	$23.00	0712	Mon, Wed, Sat		Cotal
• Santo Tomé		1255	daily	3	Singer

⚓ Water transport

At the time of writing there were still launch services running to Encarnación in Paraguay. Departure times are: Mon–Fri, every half hour from 0700–1800; 6 services on Sat, and 4 services on Sun. More services are run if there is the demand. Fares are $0.70 on weekdays and $1.50 on weekends. The ticket vendors will want to copy details from your passport when you buy tickets.

⊕ Tours

- Davina, La Rioja 2035 (25983
- Dei Castelli, Colón 1654 (28160. Two tours to the Cataratas del Iguazú (Iguazú Falls) are available: a one-day tour for $24.00 which goes to San Ignacio, Montecarlo, Wanda, and the Argentine side of the falls; a two-day tour for $48.00 which goes to San Ignacio, Montecarlo, Wanda, both the Argentine and Brazilian side of the falls, Itaipú, Puerto Presidente Stroessner in Paraguay, and Foz do Iguaçu in Brazil.

Posadas

MISIONES PROVINCE

Other tours are available to Saltos del Moconá, Encarnación in Paraguay, and the Complejo Hidroeléctrico Yaciretá Apipé (Yacyretá Hydroelectric Complex).

- Tucán Turismo, Bolívar 1620 (22436. Tours available are: to Ruinas San Ignacio, $20.00; to San Ignacio and Oberá, $28.00; to San Ignacio, Oberá and San Javier, $32.00. These fares are per person, and there is a minimum of eight persons per tour

Shopping

Misiones is an important source of gems, and topaz and amethysts in particular are found in riverbeds throughout the province. Two types of precious stones are found in this region: those which have solidified slowly and have, in the process, formed crystallized hollows inside the stone as a result of intrusions of silica, and those which have solidified suddenly and formed full, solid stones. The color of the gems depends on the chemical composition of the rock. The major area where gems are found are in the north of the province near Wanda; agates are found near the Brazilian border. In the commercial gem fields it takes 10 tonnes of rock to yield 1 kg of precious stones. Misiones is only part of a large region in which gems are found; the entire area includes southern Brazil, part of Paraguay, northern Uruguay, and Río Isla Garcia in the Paraná–Río de La Plata estuary.

- Edelsteine, 1st floor, Bolívar block 1900 (289). An amazing array of semiprecious stones, both uncut and polished
- Artesanías El Paye, Colón 1574 (190). Leather goods, wood carvings, and ceramics
- Mercado Artesanal, a craft market on Parque Republica de Paraguay

Sport

- Golf: Club Social Tacuru, on RN 12, before the police checkpoint on the way to Cataratas. This is an 18-hole course; it is also the best social club in town. Facilities include a swimming pool, tennis courts, and a restaurant
- Squash Club, Fleming 535
- Tennis Club Itapua, Avenida Corrientes 1339

Entertainment

- Casino Provincial, San Martín block 1900 (corner of San Lorenzo)
- Disco Power, corner of Bolívar and 25 de Mayo
- Disco Aliage, corner of Córdoba and Azara
- Disco Nimfas, Avenida Lavalle
- Peña Itapua, Buenos Aires block 2000 (corner of Entre Ríos)
- Piper's Club, Córdoba block 1800 (234)
- Whiskería Chicote's, San Martín block 2000

Sightseeing

- Parque Republica de Paraguay, corner of Alberdí and Cabral. To get to the park from the center of the city take a number 4 bus. The park offers a good view over the Río Paraná. From here you can see the new bridge and Encarnación over on the Paraguayan side. When the new dam at Ituzaingó is completed the lake it creates will stretch as far back as Posadas
- In the median strip of Avenida Comandante Andresito Guacurari, just before it begins its descent to the harbour, between Calle Buenos Aires and Rivadavia, you can see the ruins of the Jesuit mission. All that is left now are a few foundation stones and some pillars
- Museo de Ciencias Naturales e Histórico (Natural Sciences and History Museum), San Luis 384
- Museo Regional de Posadas (Posadas Regional Museum), Parque Republica de Paraguay. This museum consists of only one room but is good nonethe-

Posadas

less. It is a mixed collection and includes Guaraní artefacts such as canoes hewn from tree trunks, relics from the time of the Jesuits, and examples of local flora and fauna. There is also an interesting collection of butterflies and beetles, and stuffed tropical birds and jaguars. There is a small admission fee
- Museo de Arte Juan Yaparí (Juan Yaparí Art Museum), Sarmiento block 1800 (317)

Excursions
- **Garupá**: 14 km, on the **Río Garupá**. You can camp and swim at this pleasant, quiet spot
- **Candelaria**: 19 km on RN 12. This little village was the first capital of Misiones province. It is 1 km off the highway and not all buses from Posadas pass through. There are panoramic views of the surrounding area from here. Coming from the highway, the Jesuit ruins are just before the town. Facilities include an Emitur information kiosk, a YPF service station, the San Cayetano restaurant, and municipal baths
- **Santa Ana**: 40 km on RN 12. The Jesuit ruins are 2 km up from the main road (not down towards the Río Paraná!). You can camp here and there are municipal baths. The ruins themselves are overgrown and have not been restored
- **Loreto**: 46 km on RN 12. On the right is a turnoff which leads to the Jesuit ruins. It is a 3 km walk, and the ruins have not been restored
- **San Ignacio Miní**: 61 km on RN 12. The Jesuit ruins of San Ignacio Miní are the most accessible of those which have been restored. They convey a vivid picture of Jesuit culture in the sixteenth century. Here also are the steps of the **Peñón de Reina Victoria** (Queen Victoria Rock) which lead down the 150 m to the **Río Alto Paraná**. Accommodation is available in the Casa Horacio Quiroga, which is also a museum. Other accommodation is available, and there are municipal baths here as well. There are buses every half hour to and from Posadas. See also San Ignacio Miní on page 818
- **Complejo Hidroeléctrico Yacyretá Apipé**, in Corrientes province. Se Ituzaingó on page 738

Puerto Esperanza

Postal code: 3378 • area code: (0751)
Distance from Puerto Iguazú: 52 km southwards on RN 12

Although called "Puerto", Puerto Esperanza is not a port on the Río Alto Paraná, but 9 km east of the river.

Accommodation
C Residencial Las Brisas, corner of RN 12 and the access road to Río Alto Paraná (95251

MISIONES PROVINCE

🚌 Buses
Buses run regularly to Puerto Iguazú.

🚗 Motoring
- Service station: Shell, 20 de Junio

PUERTO IGUAZÚ

Postal code: 3300 • Population: 18 000 • ℂ area code: (0757) • Altitude: 160 m
Distances
- From Posadas: 303km north-east on RN 12
- From Foz do Iguaçu in Brazil: 25 km south-west
- From Puerto Presidente Stroessner in Paraguay: 31 km southwards, via Foz do Iguaçu

Puerto Iguazú is almost equidistant from Buenos Aires and Río de Janeiro in Brazil, in the northernmost corner of Argentina, on the border of Argentina, Brazil, and Paraguay. Here is situated one of South America's most popular tourist spots, the spectacular **Cataratas del Iguazú** or Iguazú Falls.

The ferry across the **Río Iguazú** to Brazil has now been replaced by the 480 m long Puente Internacional Tancred Neves (Tancred Neves International Bridge), just 3 km below the falls. The border checkpoint is open 24 hours a day and procedures are very relaxed.

The climate is very humid, and in summer the temperature ranges from 15°C to 25°C. The best time to visit is between March and June, and between August and November. It is overcrowded in July.

ℹ️ Tourist information
- Dirección Zona Internacional Iguazú, Aguirre 396 ℂ 2800

⛺ Camping
- Complejo Turistico Americano, on RN 12 at Km 5 ℂ 2820. 🍴⬛🛏🚿 Cabins are available and there is a supermarket. Fees per person: $1.80 to camp, $4.50 for cabins, $8.00 for bungalows
- Camping Pindo, almost opposite the turnoff to the Puente Internacional. Fees: $1.00 to camp, $1.00 for tent hire

🍴 Eating out
- Restaurant Camara de Comercio, Victoria Aguirre

Key to Map
1. Municipalidad
2. Iglesia
3. Post office (Encotel)
4. Telephone (Entel)
5. Tourist information
6. Cambio Viajes Dick
7. Cambio Fonsecca
8. Aerolineas Argentinas
9. Hotel Esturion Iguazú
10. Residencial Misiones
11. Residencial Arco Iris
12. Hotel Saint George
13. Residencial Los Helechos
14. Hotel Alexander
15. Residencial Tierra Colorada
16. Hotel El Libertador
17. Hotel Paraná
18. Residencial El Tucán
19. Hostería La Cabaña
20. Residencial King
21. Banco de la Nación
22. Austral Lineas Aereas
23. Residencial Iguazú

Misiones Province

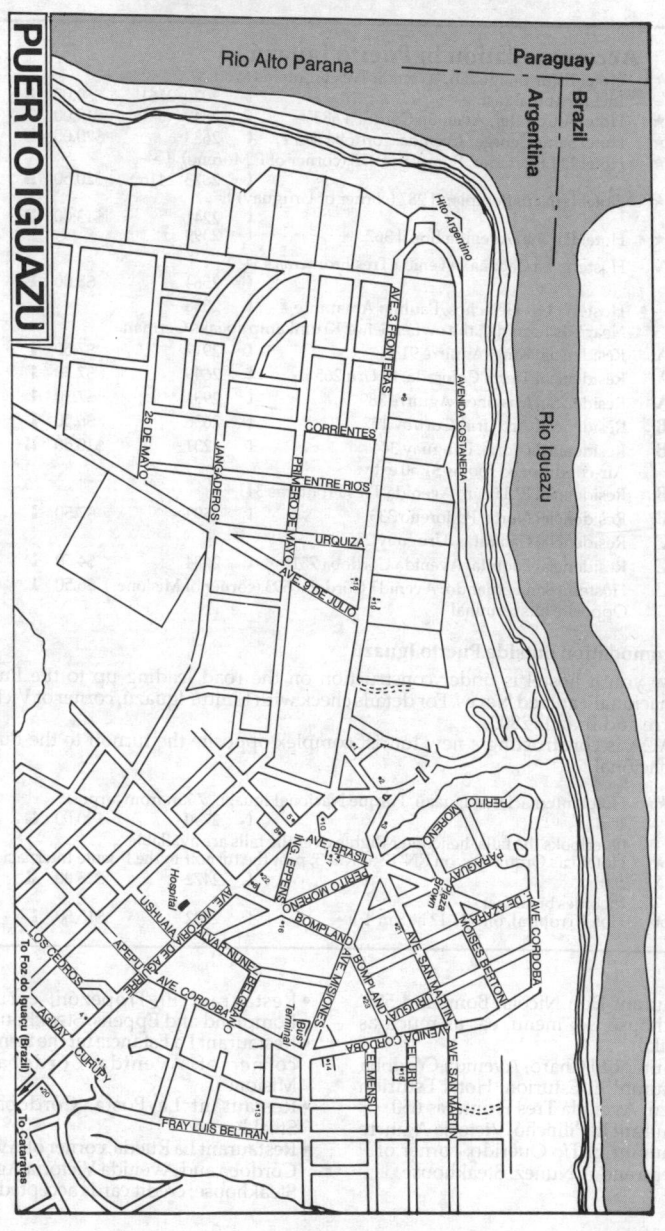

Puerto Iguazú

Misiones Province

Accommodation in Puerto Iguazú

★★★★★	Hotel Esturion Iguazú, Avenida Tres Fronteras 650 🏠				
	Includes breakfast	(	2020, 2161	$50.00	👥
★★★	Hotel Alexander, Avenida Córdoba 685	(	2249	$18.00	👥
★★★	Hotel Saint George, Avenida Córdoba 745	(	2633	$20.00	👥
★★★	Hotel El Libertador, Bompland 475 (corner of P Moreno)				
		(	2823, 2416	$20.50	👥
★★	Hotel Iguazú, Bompland 287 (corner of Uruguay)				
		(	2241	$13.00	👥
★	Hotel Paraná, Avenida Brasil 367	(	2399		
A	Hostería La Cabaña, Avenida Tres Fronteras 434				
		(	2564	$8.00	i
•	Hostería Los Helechos, Paulino Amarante	(	2338		
	Near bus terminal; the owner Señor Krumkamp speaks German				
A	Residencial King, Aguirre 915	(	2917	$7.50	i
A	Residencial Tierra Colorada, El Uru 265	(	2649	$7.50	i
A	Residencial Misiones, Aguirre 389	(	2991	$7.50	i
B	Residencial Arco Iris, Curupy 152	(	2636	$6.50	i
B	Residencial Gloria, Uruguay 344	(	2231	$10.50	👥
	Air-conditioned rooms $1.50 extra				
B	Residencial El Tucán, Avenida Tres Fronteras 341				
B	Residencial Norte, P Moreno 333	(	2592	$7.50	i
C	Residencial Cataratas, Uruguay 256				
C	Residencial Paquita, Avenida Córdoba 731	(	2434	$4.50	i
C	Hostería San Fernando, Avenida Córdoba 693 (corner of Misiones)			$6.50	i
	Opposite bus terminal				

Accommodation outside Puerto Iguazú

A new youth hostel is under construction on the road leading up to the Puente Internacional Tancred Neves. For details check with Emitur Iguazú, corner of Victoria Aguirre and Brazil (2800.

The ACA is constructing a new tourist complex opposite the turnoff to the Puente Internacional.

★★★★★	Hotel Internacional Iguazú, Parque Nacional Iguazú, 7 km from airport				
		(	2790	$90.00	👥
	Overlooks the falls; helicopter flights over the falls are available				
★★★	Hotel Las Orquídeas, on RN 12 at Km 5, past the turnoff to the Puente Internacional				
		(	2472	$25.00	👥
	Includes breakfast				
★★★	Hotel Tropical, on RN 12 at Km 4	(	2982	$15.50	i

- Restaurant Don Nicola, Bonpland 555. Steakhouse; set menu, eat as much as you like
- Restaurant El Charo, Avenida Córdoba
- Restaurant El Esturion, Hotel Esturion Iguazú, Avenida Tres Fronteras 650
- Restaurant El Pilincho, Victoria Aguirre
- Restaurant El Tío Querido, corner of P Moreno and A Nuñez. Steakhouse
- Restaurant El Tropezón, corner of Bompland and Eppens. Steakhouse
- Restaurant La Estancia (at the terminal), corner of Avenida Córdoba and Misiones
- Restaurant La Posta, Córdoba 867. Steakhouse
- Restaurant La Rueda, corner of Avenida Córdoba and Avenida Victoria Aguirre. Steakhouse; credit cards accepted

Puerto Iguazú

Misiones Province

- Restaurant Okey, Perito Moreno
- Restaurant Polo Norte, Belgrano 793. Steakhouse
- Restaurant Saint George, Hotel Saint George, Avenida Córdoba 745
- Pizzería Ser, corner of Avenida Victoria Aguirre and Bompland
- Cafetería Status, corner of Ingeniero Eppens and Brazil
- Cafetería Serafin, Avenida Victoria Aguirre
- Cafetería Timoteo, corner of Avenida Victoria Aguirre and Bompland

Eating out outside Puerto Iguazú

- Restaurant Oasis, Hotel Internacional, Parque Nacional Iguazú
- Restaurant Tropical, Hotel Tropical, RN 12
- Restaurant Las Orquídeas, Hotel Las Orquídeas, RN 12

Post and telegraph

- Post office: Encotel, corner of San Martín and Azara
- Telephone: Entel, corner of Avenida Victoria Aguirre and Los Cedros

Financial

- Cambio Argecam, Avenida Victoria Aguirre 369 (2189
- Cambio Fonseca, Avenida Brazil 353
- Casa de Cambio Dick, Avenida Victoria Aguirre 467 (2545
- Casa de Cambio Ortega, corner of Avenida Victoria Aguirre and Ingeniero Eppens (2960

Visas, passports

- Brazilian vice-consulate, corner of Avenida Victoria Aguirre and Curupy (2601. Open Mon–Fri 0830–1200 and 1500–2000

Border crossing

Procedures at the border crossing from Argentina into Brazil are relaxed, but there are some complications. If you are only making a day trip to Foz do Iguaçu in Brazil it is simple enough. There is no need to get your passport stamped; the guards at the border will just wave the bus through. These buses start at the terminal in Puerto Iguazú and end at the short distance terminal in Foz do Iguaçu. If you just want to visit the Brazilian side of the Iguazú Falls you don't even need to go all the way into Foz do Iguaçu; just get off at the intersection, about 300 m before the Brazilian border guards, and wait there for the national park bus. These buses start their journey at the short distance terminal in Foz do Iguaçu. If you are leaving Argentina, however, things are a little more complicated. Since there are no local buses from Puerto Iguazú to the border, you need to catch the international bus (fare $0.70). When you reach the border you must get your passport stamped on the Argentine side and then walk across to the Brazilian checkpoint. The international bus will not wait while you do this, but this is not a problem because there is a local bus which goes from the Brazilian checkpoint directly into Foz do Iguaçu (fare $0.10). If you wait for the next international bus you must pay the full fare again ($0.70). From the short-distance bus terminal in Foz do Iguaçu there are also international buses to Puerto Presidente Stroessner in Paraguay. The cities of Foz do Iguaçu and Puerto Presidente Stroessner almost merge into one other, more so than do Puerto Iguazú and Foz do Iguaçu. The road leading up to the Paraguayan border is lined with hotels, motels, and restaurants. There are also two long-distance bus terminals in Foz do Iguaçu.

Air services

Aeropuerto Argentino is 10 km east of town, near the Parque Nacional. Tucán Turismo operates a *colectivo* service for $4.00; or you can get a taxi for $7.50.

If you are staying at the Hotel Internacional Iguazú inside the national park, the Hotel provides free transport to the airport.

Airlines

- Austral Lineas Aereas, corner of Avenida Victoria Aguirre and Bompland
- Aerolineas Argentinas, corner of Avenida Victoria Aguirre and Eppens

Puerto Iguazú

MISIONES PROVINCE

🚌 Buses from Puerto Iguazú

The bus terminal is on the corner of Avenida Córdoba and Avenida Misiones. It has clean restrooms, a cloakroom, and a restaurant.

Destination	Fare	Depart	Services	Hours	Company
• Posadas	$5.50	1200	daily	6	El Norte Bis, Expreso Singer
Express bus	$6.50			5	Ciudad de Posadas
• Bernardo de Irigoyen	$4.50	0800	daily		Kruse
• Buenos Aires	$31.00	1200	daily	21	Singer
• San Fernando del Valle de Catamarca		0130	Wed, Sat		Cotal
• Córdoba	$34.50	1130	Tues, Wed, Fri–Sun	26	Expreso Singer, Litoral
• Corrientes	$18.00	0130	1–2 services daily	11	Ciudad de Posadas, Cotal
• Eldorado	$3.00	1000	2		
• Foz do Iguaçu (Brazil)	$0.70	0700	15 services daily	½	Tres Fronteras
• La Rioja		0130	Wed, Sat		Cotal
• Mendoza		0130	Wed, Sat		Cotal
• Paraná		1130	daily		Singer
• Parque Nacional del Iguazú	$2.80	0700	8 services daily		Cataratas
The return fare includes the ferry to the island					
• Paso de los Libres		1000	2 services daily		El Norte Bis,
• Resistencia	$18.70	0130	1–2 services daily	12	C de Posadas, Cotal
• Rosario		1000	Wed, Sat		El Norte Bis
• San Juan		0130	Wed, Sat		Cotal
• Santa Fé	$30.50	1000	2 services		El Norte Bis, Expreso Singer
• Santiago del Estero		0130	Wed, Sat		Cotal
• Wanda	$2.20	0500	17 services daily	1	various

Services

- Posadas: Fare $17.00; departs 1850 Thurs; 1 hour; Federal. Fare $22.00; departs 1900 Mon; 1 hour; Aerolineas
- Buenos Aires (Aeroparque Jorge Newbery): Fare $69.00; departs 1330; 2–5 services daily; 3 hours; Aerolineas. Fare $69.00; departs 1450 daily; 2 hours; Austral
- Córdoba: Fare $74.00; departs 1330 Mon, Fri, Sun; 2 hours; Aerolineas
- Resistencia: Fare $30.00; 0930 Tues, Thurs; 2 hours; Federal
- Rosario: Fare $67.00; departs 1330 Fri, Sun; 3 hours; Aerolineas. Fare $67.00; departs 1510 Wed, Sun; 2 hours; Austral

🚗 Motoring

- Service station: Shell service station, corner of Córdoba and Misiones

Car hire

- Avis Rent-a-Car, Avenida Tres Fronteras 650 ℂ 2020
- Liprandi Rent-a-Car, Hotel Internacional, in the Parque Nacional ℂ 2790. To hire a Fiat 147 for one week costs $350.00, including insurance and mileage
- Tucán Turismo, Avenida Brasil 339 ℂ 2425. Reservations can be made in Posadas, Bolívar 1620 ℂ 22436. To hire a VW 1500 for 1 week costs $420.00, including insurance and mileage

Puerto Iguazú

Misiones Province

Tours

Tour operators

- Privat Servis, Avenida Tres Fronteras 335 (3370. The proprietor, Señor Reinhard Foerster, speaks both English and German, and specializes in photographic safaris. He also has a large collection of local insects and butterflies
- Turismo Caracol, P Moreno 357 (2124
- Turismo Dick, Avenida Victoria Aguirre 467 (2778. Tours available are listed below

Tours

The following tours are run by Turismo Dick.

- Three-country tour: This nine-hour trip costs $18.00 and visits the Brazilian side of the Iguazú Falls, the Itaipú hydroelectric scheme, and Puerto Presidente Stroessner in Paraguay
- Cataratas del Iguazú (Iguazú Falls): A five-hour trip costing $7.00 which visits the Argentine side of the falls
- Cataratas del Iguazú (Iguazú Falls): A four-hour trip costing $9.00 which visits the Brazilian side of the falls
- Wanda: A four-hour trip costing $11.00 which visits tea plantations and gemstone mines

Shopping

- Artesanías Indígenas, corner of Avenida Victoria Aguirre and Avenida Tres Fronteras

Entertainment

- Casino Nacional. Open daily except Tuesday, from 2200
- Casino Provincial. Open daily except Monday, from 2200
- Disco Acuarela, Avenida Bonpland
- Disco Azaro, Avenida Misiones
- Disco Papette, Avenida Tres Fronteras
- Night Club Jeqiba, Hotel Internacional Iguazú
- Night Club Saudades, corner of Bompland and Misiones (in the Hotel Libertador complex)
- Whiskería Angelo, corner of Brazil and Aguirre

Sightseeing

- At the corner of Avenida Tres Fronteras and Avenida Costanera there is a lookout with panoramic views over the area where the borders of Argentina, Brazil, and Paraguay meet. The **Río Iguazú** joins the **Río Alto Paraná** at this intersection of the borders. There is a cafeteria and a picnic area. The rivers below are only about 150–200 m wide and you can easily see into Paraguay and Brazil without binoculars. There is a similiar lookout on the Brazilian side

Excursions

- **Cataratas del Iguazú**, or Iguazú Falls: 20 km eastwards. These 3½ km wide falls must be one of the most spectacular sights in South America. They are located 20 km upstream from the junction of the **Río Iguazú** with the **Río Alto Paraná**. There are two walking tracks on the Argentine side of the falls—an upper and a lower—and the flora along these paths has been labelled. The constant spray from the falls makes the air moist, and on sunny days rainbows form from many angles. It is advisable to bring or hire a raincoat if you plan to go close to any of the larger waterfalls. The lower walk leads to a ferry terminal from where it is possible to cross to the **Isla San Martín**. From the beach on the island you can climb a flight of stairs to get a closer look at the **Salto San Martín**, one of the

Puerto Iguazú

MISIONES PROVINCE

biggest falls. The roar of the water here is so loud it is impossible to hear yourself speak. There are walks in the park which pass over bridges that are only a few meters away from the sheets of water which tumble down into the mists of the gorge below. Helicopter flights over the falls are available on both sides of the border and cost $30.00 for half an hour. Be sure to bring plenty of film because the views are breathtaking. You can buy film at the falls but it is expensive. There are kiosks along the walking tracks where you can buy coffee and sandwiches, and in Puerto Canoas there is an open-air restaurant. The Argentine side is a lot larger than the Brazilian side but can be visited comfortably in one day. The bus arrives at Puerto Canoas where a catwalk (nearly 1 km long!) leads to a viewing platform overlooking the **Garganta del Diablo** ("Devil's Gorge"). There are literally thousands of people milling backwards and forwards across the catwalk, but the sight of the gorge makes it all worthwhile; this is an excellent vantage point from which to take photographs of one of the biggest waterfalls as it tumbles over the edge of the cliff. Curiously, you can see birds darting effortlessly in and out of the falling water. To really appreciate the grandeur of the falls a visit should include both the Brazilian and the Argentine side. When taking the international bus to Foz do Iguaçu in Brazil ask the driver to let you off at the intersection just after the border checkpoint, and wait there for a connecting bus to the national park. The wildlife in the park includes brightly colored parrots, toucans and tiny monkeys. Tour operators organize tours to the falls, but Empresa Cataratas also operates services every hour from the bus terminal. The return fare includes the trip to the Hotel Internacional Cataratas inside the national park, the trip from the hotel to **Puerto Canoas**, and the ferry trip to **Isla San Martín**. The $1.00 entrance fee to the park is extra. Set out early in the morning as there are literally hundreds of buses making the trip each day and the traffic is less hectic earlier in the day

- **Wanda**: To reach Wanda take RN 12 south for 48 km, until you come to a turnoff to the east. From the turnoff it is another 2 km to Wanda. Nearby is an amethyst mine which sells gemstones. This trip can be combined with a visit to the Uruga-I hydroelectric scheme currently under construction on the **Río Uruga-I**, a further 38 km southwards on RN 12. From there the site is 1 km to the west, about 3 km before the junction of the Río Uruga-I with the **Río Alto Paraná**. This is a huge project, and when it is finished the dam wall will be 665 m long. The dam itself will rise 71 m above river level and create a lake covering about 8844 ha. There is a large and developing logging industry in this region, and the electricity generated by the scheme will mainly be used to run the increasing numbers

Puerto Iguazú

Misiones Province

of papermills all over Misiones province
- **Bernardo de Irigoyen** on the **Río Uruguay**: This trip is recommended for those keen to see the "outback" of Misiones province. Empresa Kruse buses cover the entire length of the Parque Nacional Iguazú. En route you pass frontier settlements like **Cabure-I**. As the name suggests, this town was originally a Guaraní settlement. From Bernardo de Irigoyen you can make a return trip (again with Empresa Kruse) to **San Pedro**, via **Tobuna**, in the **Sierra de Misiones**. From San Pedro you can take the *sierra* road to **Oberá**, or the road back to **Eldorado**. The buses which make this trip are frequent, and Kruse, Iguazú, and Cotal all operate services. See also Bernardo de Irigoyen on page 792, San Pedro on page 820, Oberá on page 798, and Eldorado on page 794

Puerto Rico

Postal code: 3334 • Population: 12 000 • (area code: (0752) • Altitude: 205 m
Distances
- From Posadas: 129 km north-east on RN 12
- From Puerto Iguazú: 157 km south-west on RN 12

Puerto Rico is located on the **Río Alto Paraná**, and is the center of a citrus packing industry. There is a fishing club here, and some good camping spots.

Accommodation
★★ Hotel Caravan, Avenida San Martín 1527 (92346 $13.00
A Residencial Central, Avenida San Martín 2464 (92209 $7.00
A Residencial Hotel Suizo, Avenida San Martín 836(92246 $15.00
C Residencial Internacional, Reconquista 1698 (92338
C Residencial Roma, M Moreno 57 (corner of Avenida San Martín) (92382

Camping
There is a camping ground near Salto Tres de Mayo, about 15 km out of Puerto Rico. The grounds are 5 km off the main road.

Eating out
- Restaurant Matias, RN 12
- Restaurant Don Carlos, Avenida San Martín
- Restaurant Buen Comer, Avenida San Martín
- Comedor Vivi, RN 12, north of Puerto Rico

Buses
Buses run regularly to Posadas and Puerto Iguazú.

Motoring
- Service station: YPF, San Martín

Water transport
The ferry service to Puerto Triunfo in Paraguay operates daily from 0800–1730. The last ferry returns from Paraguay at 1700.

Excursions
- **Gruta India** (Indian Cave): Artefacts from pre-Columbian times have been found in this cave. The turnoff to the cave is 15 km north of Puerto Rico on RN 12. Once you have turned off RN 12 it is 7 km further on a dirt road to the cave. On the

MISIONES PROVINCE

road to the cave there is a camping ground, with natural swimming pools and the 3 de Mayo waterfall
- **Salto del Capioví**: 12 km south. This waterfall plunges down 15 m into a natural swimming pool. It is a scenic spot, and there are frequent buses to and from Puerto Rico

SAN IGNACIO MINÍ

Postal code: 3322 • Population: 8 000 • Distances
- From Posadas: 61 km south on RN 12
- From Puerto Iguazú: 249 km north on RN 12

San Ignacio Miní was initially established as a Jesuit *reducción* in 1610 in what is now the Brazilian state of Paraná. Constant attacks by the Portuguese slave-hunting *paulistas* forced the Jesuits to seek new lands further west. So in 1631 Padre Antonio Ruiz de Montoya organized the exodus of 11 000 Guaranís. Only about 3000 survived this arduous journey, rafting down the rivers, braving the rapids, and hacking their way through formidable terrain. In 1632 the second foundation of San Ignacio Miní took place on the banks of the **Arroyo Yabebiri**, near its junction with the Río Alto Paraná. This location proved unsuitable, and in 1695 the Jesuits moved the *reducción* to its present site close by.

When the Jesuits were expelled in 1767 the once-prosperous community fell into decline. The final blow came in 1816 when the Paraguayan dictator Francia ordered the destruction of all the Indian villages as part of his infamous "scorched earth policy". To prevent the destruction of San Ignacio, one of General Artigas' armies under the command of a Guaraní by the name of "Andresito" Guacurari recaptured it. After this only a small number of Guaranís remained in what had once been a flourishing town. The site was rediscovered in 1896.

Today the entrance to San Ignacio is through an archway that was originally part of the Jesuit foundations. The 100 square meter plaza is flanked by schools, cloisters, and workshops. The church was completed in 1724. This is a very interesting place, and a visit is highly recommended. Open daily from 0800–1800. There is a small charge for admission.

Strictly speaking, the name of the township is "San Ignacio", and "San Ignacio Miní" is that of the *reducción*.

ℹ️ Tourist information

Padre José Marx of the local Catholic church is an authority on the Guaranís. He has written several books on the history of the Guaranís and on the missionary work of the Jesuits. English and German translations of his books are available.

🛏 Accommodation

A Hostería ACA, Independencia 469 ▥ (3 $10.00 ⅱ

Misiones Province

A Residencial Hotel San Ignacio, San Martín 823 ⑪ ☏ 47 $6.50 ⚥
B Private accommodation: Padre José Marx, corner of Sarmiento and Rivadavia, behind the church $6.00 ⚥

⛺ Camping

- Camping Yabebiri ⑪⌂. These grounds are 8 km outside San Ignacio on the banks of the Arroyo Yabebiri, not far from Peñón Reina Victoria (Queen Victoria Rock). Accommodation is available. Check with the Dirección de Deportes y Turismo in Posadas, Córdoba 69 ☏ 26489 for permission to stay here, as it is intended to be used primarily by student groups

🍽 Eating out

Near the entrance to the San Ignacio Miní complex there are a number of *parrillas*, restaurants, and cafeterias
- Restaurant Portal del Sol, corner of Rivadavia and Medina

📞 Post and telegraph

- Telephone: Entel, corner of San Martín and Lanusse

🚌 Buses

The bus terminal is at the extreme end of Sarmiento. It has a cafeteria.
- Posadas: Fare $1.50; 18 services daily; 1 hour; Empresa Klein
- Oberá: Fare $1.80; Empresa Singer
- Puerto Iguazú: 15 services daily; 6 hours; Empresa Cotal
- Santa Ana: Fare $0.50; Empresa Klein

🚗 Motoring

- Service station: Esso, RN 12

📷 Sightseeing

- The entrance to the ruins of San Ignacio Miní is on the corner of Rivadavia and Medina. This is the best-preserved Jesuit mission center in Misiones province. Although completely destroyed by the dictator Francia 1810, they have been carefully restored and are now one of the major tourist attractions in Misiones, if not Argentina. You can explore the entire site comfortably in half a day
- The house of Horacio Quiroga. This former home of the Argentine poet has now been converted into a museum
- **Peñón de Reina Victoria** (Queen Victoria Rock). A 150 m high rock on the banks of the Río Paraná. The top of the rock has been flattened into a platform and affords panoramic views over the river below. A staircase leads up from the river to the top

🌳 Excursions

- **Santa Ana**: This is another Jesuit mission near San Ignacio which is still completely overgrown by rainforest. To get there take the local bus to Posadas, and ask the driver to let you off near the turnoff to the Ruinas de Santa Ana. From there you walk about 1½ km over a rough road; the bridge you cross on the way was built by the Jesuits. Right after the bridge there is a junction, but stay on the left-hand trail. Shortly afterwards you arrive at a clearing in the jungle and beyond this are the ruins of the former mission, the walls still overgrown with lianas and vines
- **Isla Pindo-I**: A 10 ha lush tropical island in the Río Alto

San Ignacio Miní

MISIONES PROVINCE

Paraná, which here flows quickly and forms rapids. To reach the island take RN 12 for 11 km north of San Ignacio until you come to the turnoff to **Corpus**, which is a further 7 km. This is a good fishing spot. Most buses do not go right into Corpus, and the ferry to Capitán Meza in Paraguay only operates on request

SAN JAVIER

Postal code: 3357 • Population: 11 000 • (area code: (0755)
Distance from Posadas: 123 km eastwards on RN 12 then south-east on RP 4

San Javier is located on the upper reaches of the **Río Uruguay**, right on the Brazilian border. There is a ferry service across the river to Porto Lucena in Brazil. Nearby are the ruins of a Jesuit mission settlement founded in 1629. There is good fishing in the river here. **Cerro de Monje** is a religious shrine from which you have a sweeping view of the surrounding lush country. Also nearby are the rapids of **Cumandai**.

Transport to San Javier goes via Leandro N Alem.

Accommodation

A Residencial Hostería ACA (57 $12.00

Buses

- Posadas: Departs 1045; 4 services daily; 3 hours; Empresa Aguila Dorada

- Oberá: Departs 0500; 5 services daily; 3 hours; Empresa Aguila Dorada

Motoring

- Service station: YPF, 25 de Mayo 408

Water transport

Launches and ferries to Porto Lucena in Brazil leave from Paso de la Barca. They operate Mon–Fri from 0800–1730, and Sat from 0800–1100; the fare is $0.50. There are no services on Sundays and holidays

SAN PEDRO

Postal code: 3364 • Altitude: 510 m
Distance from Posadas: 270 km north-east on RN 12 then eastwards on RP 14

San Pedro is located in the **Sierra de Misiones** at the point where RP 16 to Montecarlo meets RN 14.

Accommodation

- Residencial Paviana, 25 de Mayo and San Martín
- Residencial Americano, corner of Avenida General Güemes and 25 de Mayo. Shared rooms

Eating out

- Comedor Rotonda, Avenida General Güemes

Buses

- Posadas: Departs 0800 daily; 7 hours; Empresa Martignoni
- Bernardo de Irigoyen: Departs 0840 daily; 3 hours; Empresa Kruse
- Eldorado: Departs 0745 daily; 2 hours; Empresa Kruse
- Oberá: Departs 0300 daily; 5 hours; Empresa Singer
- Puerto Iguazú: Departs 0840 daily; 8 hours; Empresa Kruse

San Ignacio Mini

MISIONES PROVINCE

🚗 Motoring
- Service station: YPF, Avenida General Güemes

🍀 Excursions
- **Bernardo de Irigoyen** on the Brazilian border: This 70 km trip via **Tobuna** passes through little-traveled parts of Misiones province. The road is rough in places and can become unpassable in heavy rain. An overnight stop can be made in Bernardo de Irigoyen, where there is an excellent ACA *hostería*. From Bernardo de Irigoyen you can visit Dionisio Cerqueira in Brazil; from the bus terminal here buses run to various destinations, including Florianopolis and São Paulo. Or you can return to **Eldorado** on the **Río Alto Paraná** on the same day, with Empresa Kruse. See also Bernardo de Irigoyen on page 792, Puerto Iguazú on page 810, and Eldorado on page 794.

SAN VICENTE

Distance from Oberá: 92 km north-east on RN 14

San Vicente is located in the **Sierra de Misiones**, at the turnoff to El Soberbio, on the Río Uruguay. It is the center of a substantial timber industry.

🛏 Accommodation
- **B** Residencial Centro Hotel, Antigua Ruta 14
- **C** Residencial Moconá, RN 14
- **C** Residencial Portillo, Antigua Ruta 14
- Alojamiento El Entrerriano, Antigua Ruta 14. Shared rooms

🍽 Eating out
- Comedor 2 de Abril, Avenida Libertador

🚌 Buses
Buses run regularly to Oberá and El Soberbio.

🚗 Motoring
- Service station: YPF, Avenida Libertador

INDEX

This index references all place-names mentioned in the Travel Companion: cities, towns, and localities: rivers, lakes, lagunas, salters, and damns; mountains, volcanoes, and passes; and national parks and nature reserves. Each place-name referenced in the index appears in the index in bold type to enable you to access the information rapidly.

Province symbol

Each place-name is followed by a two- or three-letter code, representing the province in which the place is situated. These codes are printed opposite.

Language of entries

Spanish forms of name have been used throughout, not the English equivalent. For example, the form "Peninsula Valdés" has been used, not "Valdés Peninsula." In a few cases where the English name is particularly well-known, such as the Iguazú Falls, a cross-reference has been made from the English to the Spanish form.

Order of entries

Entries are given in the order of the English alphabet—that is to

say, Ch and Ll are treated as they are in English and not as in Spanish; and "Ñ" is treated as if it were "N". Following the practise of the maps issued by the Automóvil Club Argentina, a space within a name ("is before the letter "A", so that "La Poblacióñ" precedes "Laboulaye".

Principal references

The principal page reference for each town and city, with a separate entry in the Travel Companion, is given in bold type.

Geographic features in more than one province

When a feature such as a river or a mountain chain runs through more than one province, a separate subheading has been made for each province. For example, under the "Río Tunuyán," which runs through or forms a border of several provinces, a subheading appears for each.

Maps

The black and white street maps of the major cities and the colour maps of each province have been indexed under the subheading "Map."

INDEX

This Index references all placenames mentioned in the *Travel Companion*: cities, towns, and localities; rivers, streams, glaciers, and waterfalls; lakes, *lagunas*, *salinas*, and dams; mountains, volcanoes, and ranges; and national parks and nature reserves. Each placename referenced in the Index appears in the text in **bold type** to enable you to access the information rapidly.

Province symbol

Each placename is followed by a two- or three-letter code representing the province in which the place is situated. These codes are printed opposite.

Language of entries

Spanish forms of name have been used throughout, not the English equivalent. For example, the form "Península Valdés" has been used, not "Valdés Peninsula". In a few cases where the English name is particularly well known, such as the Iguazú Falls, a cross-reference has been made from the English to the Spanish form.

Order of entries

Entries are given in the order of the English alphabet—that is to say, "Ch" and "Ll" are treated as they are in English and not as in Spanish, and "Ñ" is treated as if it were "N". Following the practise of the maps issued by the Automóvil Club Argentina, a space within a name files before the letter A, so that "La Población" *precedes* "Laboulaye".

Principal references

The principal page reference for each town and city with a separate entry in the *Travel Companion* is given in **bold type**.

Geographic features in more than one province

When a feature such as a river or a mountain chain runs through more than one province, a separate subheading has been made for each province. For example under the "Río Paraná", which runs through or forms a border of several provinces, a subheading appears for each.

Maps

The black and white street maps of the major cities and the color maps of each province have been indexed, under the subheading "Map".

INDEX

Province codes

BA	Buenos Aires	MZA	Mendoza
CAT	Catamarca	NEU	Neuquén
CBA	Córdoba	RJA	La Rioja
CHA	Chaco	RN	Río Negro
CHU	Chubut	SAL	Salta
COR	Corrientes	SCR	Santa Cruz
ER	Entre Ríos	SDE	Santiago del Estero
FOR	Formosa	SFE	Santa Fé
JUJ	Jujuy	SJU	San Juan
LAP	La Pampa	SLU	San Luis
MIS	Misiones	TDF	Tierra del Fuego
		TUC	Tucumán

A

Abra Blanca, JUJ 662
Abra de Infiernillo, CAT 556
Abra Muñano, SAL 612, 639
Abra Pampa, JUJ 646
Abra Santa Laura, SAL 637
Achiras, CBA 143, 198
Agua Blanca, CAT 531
Agua Botada, MZA 460
Agua de Coneta, CAT 531
Agua de la Puerta, CAT 531
Agua de Oro, CBA 143
Aguada Florencia, NEU 272, 308
Aguaditas de San José, CAT 531
Aguaray, SAL 613, 624
Aguas Amarillas, CAT 534, 539
Aguas Blancas, SAL 613
Aimogasta, RJA 560, 580
Alamito, CAT 530
Alba Posse, MIS 790, 801
Albardón, SJU 493
Almafuerte, CBA 144
Alpa Corral, CBA 144, 198
Alta Gracia, CBA 144
  Map 146
Alto del Portezuelo, CAT 553
Alto Río Mayo, CHU 392
Alto Río Senguerr, CHU 359
Aluminé, NEU 272, 308
  Map 273
Alvear, COR 725

Amaicha del Valle, TUC 555, 584, 585, 602
Ambargasta, SDE 698
Ampajango, CAT 556
Añatuya, SDE 699
Ancasti, CAT 531
Ancastillo, CAT 531
Andacollo, NEU 275, 282
Andalgalá, CAT 530, 531, 539, 544, 553
Angastaco, SAL 614, 620, 640
Angastaco La Vieja, SAL 614
Angualasto, SJU 497, 498, 508
Anguinán, RJA 568
Anillaco, RJA 562, 577
Animaná, SAL 620
Anquincila, CAT 531
Anta Muerta, TUC 585, 590, 602
Antártida Argentina 448
Antofagasta de la Sierra, CAT 534, 538, 540
Apostóles, MIS 788, 790
Arauco, RJA 561
Argüello, CBA 166
Arias, CBA 149
Aristóbulo del Valle, MIS 791, 801
Arizaro, SAL 612
Arroyito, CBA 150
Arroyito, NEU 299
Arroyito Challacó, NEU 276
Arroyo Aldeco, SJU 495
Arroyo Alerce, RN 352
Arroyo Azul, BA 68
Arroyo Blanco, MZA 455
Arroyo Blanco, NEU 285, 286

Arroyo Blanco

INDEX

Arroyo Challhuaco, RN 350
Arroyo Chimiray, MIS 788
Arroyo Chorrillos, JUJ 649
Arroyo Claromecó, BA 84
Arroyo Córdoba, RN 348
Arroyo de las Cabeceras, SJU 495
Arroyo de los Paredones, CBA 148
Arroyo El Grande de la Quebrada, MZA 453
Arroyo Grande, MZA 489
Arroyo Guillermo, RN 346
Arroyo Inca Cueva, JUJ 649
Arroyo Jaguel Amarillo, MZA 460
Arroyo Las Leñas, MZA 455
Arroyo Las Mesillas, MZA 460
Arroyo Las Pircas, MZA 453
Arroyo López, RN 350
Arroyo Loro, ER 782
Arroyo Los Coihues, CHU 379
Arroyo Overo, RN 351
Arroyo Palmar, ER 782
Arroyo San Alberto, MZA 453
Arroyo Yabebiri, MIS 818
Arroyos de la Pintada, MZA 484
Arroyos Grandes, MZA 476
Ascochinga, CBA **150**, 174, 176
Atos Pampa, CBA 233
Atreuco, NEU 291
Auca Pan, NEU 291
Azul, BA **68**

B

Bahía Blanca, BA **70**
   Map 71
Bahía Encerrada, TDF 442
Bahía Lapataia, TDF 447
Bahía Lendegaia, TDF 447
Bahía Onelli, SCR 412
Bahía San Blas, BA **76**, 81
Bahía San Julián, SCR 421, 424
Bahía Uruguay, SCR 421
Bajada Rahue, NEU 308
Bajo Caracoles, SCR **403**, 415
Bajo de Gualicho, RN 329
Bajo de Santa Elena, RJA 567
Balcarce, BA **77**
Balcosna, CAT **536**
Balde, SLU **510**
Ballesteros, CBA **150**
Balneario Bahía Rosas, RN 318
Balneario Costa Bonita, BA 112
Balneario El Cóndor, RN 356
Balneario El Palmar, SLU 520
Balneario Las Grutas, RN **319**, 327, 329
Balneario Lobería, RN 356
Balneario Los Angeles, BA 112
Balneario Rada Tilly, CHU **359**, 363, 368
Balneario Utracán, LAP 240
Bañados de Añatuya, SDE 699
Baño de Higueritas, CAT 531
Baños de Capiz, MZA 480
Baños del Zapallar, SLU 520
Baños La Laja, SJU 493
Baradero, BA **77**
Bariloche, RN
   See San Carlos de Bariloche, RN
Barrancas, NEU **277**
Barranqueras, CHA 684, **685**
Barreal, MZA 491
Barreal, SJU **494**, 507
Batea Mahuida, NEU 274
Batungasta, CAT
   See Troya, CAT
Bazán, RJA 561
Belén, CAT 530, 533, **536**
Belgrano, CBA
   See Villa General Belgrano, CBA
Bell Ville, CBA **151**
Bella Vista, COR **725**
Benegas, MZA 479
Bernardo de Irigoyen, MIS 789, **792**, 795, 817, 821
Bernardo Larroude, LAP 241
Berrotarán, CBA **151**
Bialet Massé, CBA **151**, 166
Boca, Buenos Aires city 59
Boca de la Quebrada, TUC 585, 588, 603
Boca de las Sierras, BA 70
Boca del Diablo, SCR 412
Borde Alto del Payún, MZA 452
Boroa, CBA 204, 223
Bosque Alegre, CBA 149
Bosque Arrayanes, RN 349
Bosque Petrificado Carlos Darwin, MZA 486
Bosque Petrificado José Ormachea, CHU 368, 394
Bosque Petrificado Victor Szapelis, CHU 368
Bovril, ER **753**
Brazo Puerto Blest, RN 349
Buenos Aires city **31**
   Map 32
   Map of *Subte* 37
Buenos Aires province **66**
   Map Plate 5

INDEX

C

Cabo Blanco, SCR 403
Cabo Curios, SCR 424
Cabo Dos Bahías, CHU 362, 368, 399
Cabo Virgenes, SCR 431
Cabra Corral, SAL 620, 638, 639
Cabure-I, MIS 793, 817
Cacheuta, MZA 451, 452, **453**, 474, 475
Cachi, SAL 611, **614**, 620, 640
Cachipampa, SAL 612
Cafayate, SAL **616**, 638, 639
   Map 617
Calafate, SCR
   See El Calafate, SCR
Calera, CBA 166
Caleta Córdoba, CHU 363
Caleta de los Loros, RN 319
Caleta Olivia, SCR 403, **404**
Caleta Valdés, CHU 388
Calilegua, JUJ 664
Calingasta, SJU **495**, 507
Camarones, CHU 359, **360**, 368, 399
   Map 361
Campana, BA **78**
Campitos, CBA 193
Campo Arenal, CAT 539
Campo de Pulmari, NEU 274
Campo del Cielo, CHA 687
Campo Quijano, SAL 613, 639
Campo Viera, MIS 801
Campos de los Pozos, CAT 539
Cañada Honda, SLU 525
Cañada Larga, CBA 193
Cañadón de la Escarcha, RJA 582
Cañadón de las Bandurrias, SCR 421
Canal Beagle, TDF 434, 441, 442, 445, 448
Canal de Acceso, SFE 259
Canal Upsala, SCR 412
Canals, CBA **151**
Cancha Carrera, SCR 433
Candelaria, MIS 809
Candonga, CBA **152**
Cañon Águas Amarillas, CAT 534
Cañon Belén, CAT 536, 538
   See also Río Belén, CAT
Cañon Chilca, CAT 534
Cañon del Atuel, MZA 451, 452, 475, 485
   See also Río Atuel, MZA
Cañon San Rafael 451
Canota-Monument, MZA 486
Capilla Constancia, CBA 229

Capilla del Monte, CBA **152**, 170, 223
Capilla Vieja, CBA 233
Capillitas, CAT 534
Capioví, MIS 796
Capitán Solari, CHA 694
Carapari, SAL 643
Carapunco, CAT 556
Carapunco, TUC 606, 608
Carhué, BA **79**
Carmen de Patagonés, BA **80**, 352
Carolina, SLU **511**, 525, 526
Carpincho, CHA 695
Carrizal, RJA 570
Casa Bamba, CBA 174
Casa de Piedra, TUC 585
Casabindo, JUJ **647**
Cascada de la Virgen, RN 347
Cascada de la Virgen Misionera, RN 324
Cascada de los Cántaros, RN 349
Cascada Escondida, RN 324
Cascada Los Alerces, RN 326, 349
Cascada Mallín, RN 325
Cascada Olvidada, SLU 519
Cascada Río Blanco, RN 351
Cascadas de Olaen, CBA 184
Cascadas de Río Pipo, TDF 447
Casilla Negra, CBA 224
Castaño Viejo, SJU 496
Catamarca province **528**
   Map Plate 29
Catamarca, CAT
   See San Fernando del Valle de Catamarca, CAT
Cataratas del Iguazú, MIS 788, 789, 790, 810, 815
Catriel, RN **320**
Catritre, NEU 309
Caverna de las Brujas, MZA 462, 486
Caviahué, NEU **277**, 286
Cayastá, SFE 259, 267
Centenario, NEU **278**
Cerro Abanico, NEU 309
Cerro Aconcagua, MZA 451, 452, 475, 477, 494, 507
Cerro Alto de la Mina, TUC 604
Cerro Alto del Rey, TUC 591
Cerro Alumbre, SLU 513
Cerro Argentino, RN 351
Cerro Aspero, SLU 519
Cerro Bandurias, NEU 309
Cerro Barrosa, SLU 512
Cerro Bayó, NEU 272, 278
Cerro Bola, MZA 485
Cerro Bonete Chico, RJA 560
Cerro Bravard, MZA 487

INDEX

Cerro Campanario, RN 349
Cerro Catedral, RN **320**, 346, 349, 350
Cerro Champaqui, CBA 143, 188, 201, 226, 229, 235
Cerro Chañi, JUJ 662
Cerro Chapelco, NEU 271, 272, **279**, 301, 348
Cerro Chenque, CHU 362, 368
Cerro Chileno, RN 351
Cerro Ciénaga Grande, SAL 616
Cerro Colorado, CBA **153**, 201
Cerro Colorado, SJU 498
Cerro de Incahuasi, CAT 543
Cerro de la Batería, NEU 287
Cerro de la Caballada, BA 81
Cerro de la Cruz, RJA 577
Cerro de la Gloria, MZA 474, 476
Cerro de la Oveja, SLU 519
Cerro de la Ventana, BA 76
Cerro de los Siete Colores, JUJ 662
Cerro de Monje, MIS 820
Cerro del Bolsón, TUC 590
Cerro Dos Bahías, CHU 360
Cerro El Bolsón, TUC 584
Cerro El Calvario, BA 127
Cerro El Cuadrado, CBA 178, 185
Cerro El Manchao, CAT 542
Cerro El Mojón, CAT 538
Cerro El Sapo, SJU 508
Cerro El Volcán, SCR 419
Cerro Fitz Roy, SCR 403, 411, 416, 417
Cerro Hilario, SJU 496, 507
Cerro Inca Huasi, SAL 622
Cerro La Blanca, BA 125
Cerro La Movediza, BA 128
Cerro Lindero, CBA 149
Cerro López, RN 349, 350
Cerro Los Gigantes, CBA 193
Cerro Macante, SAL 612
Cerro Manchao, CAT 545, 552
Cerro Martial, TDF 442
Cerro Mercedario, SJU 494
Cerro Mogol, MZA 462
Cerro Morado, CAT 538
Cerro Moros, TUC 588
Cerro Negro, LAP 237
Cerro Negro, RJA 580
Cerro Olivia, TDF 434, 441
Cerro Otto, RN 329, 350
Cerro Pan de Azúcar, CBA 166, 168, 206, 223
Cerro Payún, MZA 452, 462
Cerro Pencales, CBA 170
Cerro Piltriquitron, RN 324
Cerro Pintado, CAT 556
Cerro Punta del Marqués, CHU 359

Cerro Punta Piedras, CHU 359
Cerro Quelli Mahuida, NEU 299
Cerro Quijada, SLU 512
Cerro San Bernardo, SAL 626, 637
Cerro San Juan, MZA 487
Cerro San Lorenzo, SCR 404
Cerro Santa Ana, CHU 359
Cerro Sosneado, MZA 486
Cerro Tiro, CAT 538
Cerro Tomolasta, SLU 510, 511
Cerro Torrecillas, CHU 381
Cerro Tres Picos, RN 323
Cerro Tronador, RN 325, 326, 345, 346, 349, 351
Cerro Tupungato, MZA 490
Cerro Uritorco, CBA 152, 153, 170
Cerro Ventisquero, RN 347
Cerro Zapaleri, JUJ 646
Cerros del Rosario, SLU 513
Cha-chin, NEU 309
Chaco province **683**
  Map   Plate 38
Chacra de los Barriales, MZA 481
Chajarí, ER **753**
Chalicán, JUJ 663
Chamical, RJA **562**
Chascomús, BA **81**
Chepes, RJA **563**
Chepes Viejo, RJA 563
Chicligasta, TUC **586**
Chicoana, SAL 616
Chilecito, RJA 560, **563**, 576, 582
  Map   564
Choele-Choel, RN **321**, 328
Cholila, CHU 347, **362**, 375
Chorrillos, SAL 612, 639
Chos Malal, NEU **281**
  Map   282
Choya Ojo Dulce, CAT 534
Chubut province **357**
  Map   Plate 18
Chumbicha, CAT **540**, 553
Chuquis, RJA 562, 577
Churriaca, NEU **283**
Cieneguillas, JUJ **648**
Cinco Dedos, BA 77
Cinco Saltos, CHU 381
Cipolletti, RN **322**
Ciudad Perico, JUJ 637
Claromecó, BA **84**, 128
Clorinda, FOR 672, **673**
Cochinoca, JUJ 647
Coctaca, JUJ 649
Colalao del Valle, TUC **586**
Colo Michi-có, NEU 275

Cerro Campanario

828

INDEX

Colón, ER 753, **754**
  Map 755
Colonia Carlos Pellegrini, COR 741
Colonia Carolina, COR 737
Colonia Caroya, CBA **154**, 173
Colonia Elisa, CHA 695
Colonia General Fotheringham, FOR 682
Colonia Sarmiento, CHU
  See Sarmiento, CHU
Colonia Suiza, RN 350
Comandante Fontana, FOR 675, **676**, 681
Comandante Luis Piedra Buena, SCR **405**
  Map 406
Comodoro Rivadavia, CHU 358, 359, **362**, 391
  Map 364
Complejo Hidroeléctrico Yacyretá Apipé, COR 738, 740, 809
Complejo Invernal Perito Moreno, RN 325
Concarán, SLU **511**
Concepción, CAT **540**
Concepción de la Ramada, TUC 584, **587**
Concepción de la Sierra, MIS 789
Concepción del Bermejo, CHA 684, 688
Concepción del Uruguay, ER **757**
  Map 759
Concordia, ER 753, **762**
  Map 763
Cóndor Huasi, CAT 530, 538
Confluencia, NEU **283**
Confluencia, RN 347, 348, 350
Copahué, NEU 277, **283**
  Map 284
Copina, CBA 224
Corcovado, CHU 375
Cordillera de Collanguil, SJU 508
Cordillera de la Totora, SJU 507
Cordillera del Viento, NEU 275, 292
Cordillera del Viento Este, NEU 276
Córdoba province **140**
  Map Plate 7
Córdoba, CBA 143, 154, 193, 707
  Map 156
Cordón de Esquel, CHU 368, 373
Cordón del Marmolejo, MZA 487
Cordón del Plata, MZA 476
Cordón del Portillo, MZA 487
Coronel Moldes, SAL **620**, 638
Corpus, MIS 788, 820
Corralito, TUC 603
Correntoso, RN 346

Corrientes province **722**
  Map Plate 43
Corrientes, COR 694, 725, **726**
  Map 729
Cosquín, CBA 143, 166, 206, 223
Crespo, ER **766**
Cruz Chica, CBA **169**, 175
Cruz de Paramillos, MZA 475
Cruz de Piedra, SLU (lake) 511, 512
Cruz de Piedra, SLU (town) **511**, 525
Cruz del Eje, CBA **169**, 171
Cruz Grande, CBA 175
Cuchi Corral, CBA 176
Cuchilla Nevada, CBA 223
Cuchillos, ER 752
Cuesta de Belén, CAT 533
Cuesta de Cerro de Oro, SLU 519
Cuesta de Escoipe, SAL 615
Cuesta de Huaco, RJA 577
Cuesta de Lipan, JUJ 662
Cuesta de los Terneros, MZA 475, 484
Cuesta de Mazán, RJA 579
Cuesta de Miranda, RJA 566, 568, 569, 576, 577, 582
Cuesta de Pasos Malos, SLU 519
Cuesta del Clavillo, TUC 585, 587, 590
Cuesta del Obispo, SAL 612, 615, 640
Cuesta del Portezuelo, CAT 553
Cuesta del Totoral, CAT 545
Cuesta El Aguay, SCR 431
Cuesta El Mogote Bayo, SLU 519
Cuesta La Rinconada, NEU 308
Cueva del Chacho, RJA 576
Cueva del Toro, BA 124
Cuevas de las Manos, SCR 419
Cuevas Maragatas, BA 81
Cumandai, MIS 820
Cumbres de Achala, CBA 149, 186, 194, 200, 224, 225, 229
Cumbres de Calchaquies, TUC 584, 604, 606
Cumbres de Gaspar, CBA 223
Cumbres de Narvaez, TUC 588
Cumbres de San Javier, TUC 609
Cumbres de Santa Ana, TUC 588
Cumbres de Santa Barbara, TUC 604
Cura Fierro, CAT 531
Curuzú Cuatiá, COR **734**
Cutral-Có, NEU **286**

Cutral-Có

INDEX

D

Déan Funes, CBA **170**
Delta, BA 64
   Map Plate 6
Desagüe de los Colorados, RJA 567, 578
Desagüe del Río Salado, RJA 579
Deseado, MIS 793
Diamante, ER **766**
Difunta Correa, SJU 496, 506, 507
Dionisio, CAT 531
Dique Agua de Toro, MZA 485
Dique Campo Alegre, SAL 637
Dique Cippolletti, MZA 457, 476
Dique Collagasta, CAT 541
Dique Cruz del Eje, CBA 153
Dique de la Viña, CBA 229
Dique del Fuerte, BA 127
Dique El Cadillal, TUC **587**, 602
Dique El Carrizal, MZA 452, 453, 458, 478, 479
Dique El Molino, TUC 587
Dique El Nihuil, MZA 452, 453, 475, 481, 485
Dique El Tigre, MZA 485
Dique Escaba, TUC **588**, 589, 603
Dique Ezequiel Ramos Mejía, RN 328
Dique Florentino Ameghino, CHU 358, 387
Dique Ibizca, CAT 531
Dique José Ignacio de la Roza, SJU
   See Gran Presa de Embalse Quebrada de Ullum, SJU
Dique La Ciénaga, SAL 637
Dique La Falda, CBA 185
Dique Las Pirquitas, CAT 553
Dique Los Cauquenes, SJU 493, 497, 499
Dique Los Molinos, CBA 178, 232
Dique Los Sauces, RJA 576, 577
Dique Río Tercero, CBA 201
Dique San Jerónimo, CBA 176
Dique San Roque, CBA 166
Dique Valle Grande, MZA 475, 485
Dolavon, CHU 358
Dolores, BA **85**
Dos de Mayo, MIS **793**
Dos Ríos, CBA 223

E

El Alisal, SAL 612
El Alto, CAT **541**
El Anfiteatro, SAL 638
El Antigal, SAL 639
El Bolsón, RN 318, **322**, 346, 349
El Cadillal, JUJ 636
El Calafate, SCR 403, 405, **407**, 431
   Map 408
El Candado, SAL 639
El Carmen, SAL 637
El Carril, SAL 639
El Carrizal, CAT 531
El Chalet, RJA 359
El Chiflón, RJA 576
El Cholar, NEU 283
El Chorrito, CBA 175
El Churcal, SAL 622
El Clavillo, CAT 534
El Cocal, COR 736
El Cocalito, COR 736
El Cóndor, CBA 149, 193, 224
El Dedal, CHU 381
El Eje, CAT 538
El Fraile, SAL 638
El Hoyo de Epuyén, CHU
   See Hoyo de Epuyén, CHU
El Huecu, NEU **287**
El Humazo, NEU 276
El Jumeal, CAT 531
El Mollar, TUC 606, 608
El Obelisco, SAL 638
El Papagayo, SLU 519
El Potrerillo, TUC 585, 587
El Potrero de Santa Lucia, CAT 534
El Pucará, CAT 534
El Quemado, JUJ 663
El Remanso, BA 105
El Rincón, SLU 519
El Rodeo, CAT **541**, 552, 553
El Rosario, CAT 531
El Shincal, CAT 546
El Soberbio, MIS **793**
El Sosneado, MZA 451, 486
El Talar, SLU 519
El Volcán, SLU **512**, 525
El Zapato, CBA 152
Eldorado, MIS **794**, 801, 817, 821
Embalse, CBA **171**
Embalse Cerro Pelado, CBA 199
Embalse del Río Tercero, CBA 199, 226, 230, 234
Embalse La Florida, SLU 526

INDEX

Embalse Los Molinos, CBA 149, 224, 225, 230
Embalse Piedras Moras, CBA 199
Embalse Ramos Mexia, NEU 299
Embalse Río Hondo
  SDE 698, 709, 718
  TUC 586
Embalse Salto Grande, ER 753, 754, 764, 767
Embarcación, SAL **620**
Empedrado, COR **734**
Enseñada, BA 89
Enseñada, TDF 447
Entre Ríos province **751**
  Map Plate 45
Epulafquen, NEU 291
Epu-Lauquen, NEU 275
Epuyén, CHU 375
Escaba de Abajo, TUC 588, 603
Escaba de Arriba, TUC 588
Esperanza, SCR **413**, 431
Esperanza, SFE 267
Esquel, CHU 346, 358, 359, **368**
  Map 370
Esquel, RN 346
Esquina, COR **735**
Estancia El Estierro, CHA 688
Estancia Facundo, CHU 391
Estancia La Malvina, LAP 243
Estancia Las Chilcas, SCR 419
Esteros del Iberá, COR 723, 725, 740, 741
Estrecho del Magallanes, TDF 434

F

Falda Ciénaga, CAT 530, 534
Famatina, RJA 568, **569**
Farellón Negro, CAT 533, 544
Federación, ER 753, **767**
Federal, ER **768**
Feria Artesanal, MZA 485
Fiambalá, CAT **542**, 553, 558
Fitz Roy, SCR **414**
Florida Blanca, SCR 424
Formosa province **672**
  Map Plate 37
Formosa, FOR 673, 674, **676**
  Map 677
Fortín Guañacos, NEU 276
Fortín Huechu Lauquen, NEU 291
Fortín Malal-Hue, MZA 462
Fortín Mamuy Malal, NEU 291
Fortín Mayo, NEU 308
Frías, SDE **699**
Fuente de Cura Fierro, CAT 539
Fuerte Cobos, SAL 637
Fuerte Fotheringham, FOR 673
Fuerte Quemado, CAT 555
Fuerte San Carlos, MZA 480
Fuerte San Rafael, MZA 481, 485
Fuerte San Serapio Martir del Arroyo Azul
  See Azul
Fuerte Santiago Sánchez, COR 734
Fundación San Roque, CBA 184

G

Gaimán, CHU 358, **375**
  Map 376
Gancedo, CHA 687
Garganta del Diablo, JUJ 668
Garganta del Diablo, MIS 816
Garganta del Diablo, MZA 475
Garganto del Diablo, RN 351
Garupá, MIS 809
General Acha, LAP **238**, 243
  Map 239
General Alvear, MZA **453**
General Belgrano, FOR 675
General Cabrera, CBA **172**
General Deheza, CBA **172**
General Güemes, SAL **621**
General Levalle, CBA **173**
General Pico, LAP 238, **241**
  Map 242
Glaciar Agassiz, SCR 413
Glaciar Alerce, RN 351
Glaciar Castaño Overo, RN 351
Glaciar Cuerno, MZA 452
Glaciar de Torre, SCR 417
Glaciar Gussfeldt, MZA 452
Glaciar Horcones, MZA 452
Glaciar Inferior, MZA 452
Glaciar Martial, TDF 447, 448
Glaciar Negro, RN 349, 351
Glaciar Onelli, SCR 413
Glaciar Perito Moreno, SCR 403, 412, 416
Glaciar Torre, SCR 412
Glaciar Torrecillas, CHU 374, 381
Glaciar Tronador, RN 326, 351
Glaciar Upsala, SCR 412, 416

Glaciar Upsala

INDEX

Glaciar Viedma, SCR 417
Gobernador Gordillo, RJA
 See Chamical, RJA
Gobernador Gregores, SCR **414**, 424
Golfo Nuevo, CHU 381, 384, 387
Golfo San Jorge
 CHU 362
 SCR 403
Golfo San José, CHU 387
Golfo San Matías, RN 317, 319, 327
Goya, COR 733, **735**
Gran Laguna Salada, CHU 358
Gran Presa de Embalse Quebrada de Ullum, SJU *(also known as* Dique José Ignacio de la Roza*)* 492, 493, 494, 500, 507
Gran Salto de Moconá, MIS 788, 789, 790, 793
Gruta de Inti Huasi, SLU 525
Gruta de la Virgen, CAT 538, 540, 553
Gruta India, MIS 817
Gruta Salamanca, CAT 535
Guadalupe, SFE 267
Gualeguay, ER **768**
Gualeguaychú, ER 753, **769**
 Map 770
Guaminí, BA **85**
Guanacoyacu, CAT 539
Guanchín, RJA 568
Guasayán, SDE **700**
Guayapa, RJA 567, 578

H

Harberton, TDF 448
Herradura, FOR 681
Hinojo, BA 113
Hipólito Yrigoyen, SLU **512**, 525
Hornaditas, JUJ 649
Hotel Las Horquetas, SCR 415
Hoyo de Epuyén, CHU 324, 377
Hua-Hum, NEU 309
Huacalera, JUJ 664
Huacle, CBA 229
Huaco, SJU **496**, 499, 507
Hualfín, CAT 538, **544**
Hualinchay, TUC 604, 605
Huaytiquina, SAL 634
Huerta Grande, CBA 184
Huinca Renancó, CBA **173**
Huingancó, NEU 275
Humahuaca, JUJ 645, **648**, 664

I

Ibatín, TUC **588**
Iglesia, SJU 492, 493
Iguazú Falls, MIS
 See Cataratas del Iguazú, MIS
Incacueva, JUJ 649
Ingeniero Guillermo N Juárez, FOR **682**
Ingeniero Jacobacci, RN 327
Ingenio Santa Rosa, TUC 603
Intendente Alvear, LAP 241
Inti Huasi, SLU 510, 511, 526
Intiyaco, CBA 233
Iruya, SAL **621**, 646, 649, 661
Ischigualasto, SJU *(also known as* Valle de la Luna*)* 493, 498, 500, 507, 508, 568, 576
Isla Caraguatay, MIS 797
Isla Centinela, RN 349
Isla Choele-Choel Grande, NEU 321
Isla de los Lobos, TDF 448
Isla de los Pájaros, CHU 386
Isla de los Pájaros, SCR 421
Isla de los Pingüinos, SCR 424
Isla del Cerrito, CHA 695, 743
Isla El Timbo, SFE 782
Isla Gable, TDF 448
Isla Jabalí, BA 76
Isla Martín Garcia, Buenos Aires city 64
Isla Monte León, SCR 425
Isla Paulina, BA 89
Isla Pindo-I, MIS 819
Isla Redonda, TDF 447
Isla San Martín, MIS 815, 816
Isla Santa Teresita, NEU 309
Isla Victoria, NEU 326, 349, 350
Islas Bridges, TDF 447
Ita Enramada, FOR 675
Itá Ibaté, COR **737**
Itatí, COR 725, 734, **737**
Itico, TUC 587
Ituzaingó, COR 725, 734, **738**
 Map 739

J

Jardín de América, MIS **795**
Jesús María, CBA 150, **173**
Juan B Alberdi, TUC 584, **589**
Juárez, FOR
 See Ingeniero Guillermo N Juárez, FOR

INDEX

Jujuy province **644**
  Map   Plate 34
Jujuy, JUJ
  See San Salvador de Jujuy, JUJ
Junín, BA **85**
Junín de los Andes, NEU **287**, 308, 309, 348
  Map   288

K

Kaiken, TDF **435**, 440

L

La Adela, LAP   327
La Aldea, CHU   392
La Angostura, CHU   377
La Angostura, NEU   274
La Angostura, TUC   602
La Arboleda, MZA   476
La Balsa, CHU   373, 375, 401
La Banda, SDE **700**
La Banderita, TUC   590
La Baquera, SAL   637
La Caldera, SAL   637
La Calera, CBA **174**
La Candelaria, MIS   788
La Carlota, CBA **174**
La Cascada, CBA   205
La Catarata, CHU   378
La Chilca, CAT   534
La Ciénaga, CAT   538, 539
La Ciénaga, JUJ   662
La Colpa, CAT   531, 539
La Cruz, CBA **174**
La Cruz, COR   725
La Cuadra, RJA   568
La Cueva, JUJ   649
La Cumbre, CBA   143, 150, 170, 174, **175**, 223
  Map   176
La Cumbrecita, CBA **178**, 224, 233
La Estanzuela, SLU   515
La Falda, CBA   143, **178**, 195, 223
  Map   180
La Florida, SLU   525, 526
La Gerónima, SCR   413
La Granja, CBA **185**
La Greda, RJA   570
La Hoya, CHU   368, 373, **378**
La Hoyada, CAT   556
La Huerta de Huachi, SJU   499
La Lobería, CHU   388
La Madrid, TUC   584
La Merced, CAT **544**
La Merced, SAL   620
La Ovejeria, TUC   605
La Paisanita, CBA   149
La Pampa province **237**
  Map   Plate 9
La Paya, CAT   530
La Paz, ER **773**
  Map   774
La Pelada, TUC   606
La Plata, BA   67, **86**
  Map   87
La Población, CBA **186**
La Poma, SAL   616
La Puerta, CAT   552
La Punta, SDE   699
La Puntilla, CAT   534
La Puntilla, RJA   580
La Quebradita, TUC   608
La Quiaca, JUJ **650**
  Map   651
La Rinconada, NEU **291**, 308, 348
La Rioja province **559**
  Map   Plate 31
La Rioja, RJA   560, 566, **570**
  Map   572
La Serranita, CBA   149
La Silleta, CAT   545
La Toma, SLU **512**, 525
La Viña, CAT   545
Laboulaye, CBA **186**
Lago Aluminé, NEU   274
Lago Argentino, SCR   403, 407, 412, 416
Lago Azul, SCR   431
Lago Bariloche, RN   349
Lago Belgrano, SCR   415
Lago Blanco, CHU   392
Lago Buenos Aires, SCR   419
Lago Cardiel, SCR   415
Lago Caviahue, NEU   286
Lago Cholila, CHU   362
Lago Cisne, CHU   381
Lago Colhué Huapi, CHU   358, 392
Lago Correntoso, NEU   326, 349
Lago Cruz de Piedra, SLU   510
Lago El Cadillal, TUC   584, 585
Lago El Mollar, TUC   602
Lago Epecuen, BA   79
Lago Epulafquen, NEU   271
Lago Epuyen, CHU   323, 324, 378

Lago Epuyen

INDEX

Lago Escaba, TUC 584, 585
Lago Escondido, RN 326
Lago Escondido, SCR 415
Lago Escondido, TDF 435, **436**, 440, 441, 448
Lago Espejo, NEU 308
Lago Fagnano, TDF 435, 440, 448
Lago Falkner
  NEU 308
  RN 326
Lago Fontana, CHU 359, 375, 392
Lago Futalaufquen, CHU 358, 371, 374, 380
Lago General Vintter, CHU 392
Lago Guillelmo, RN 346
Lago Gutierrez, RN 318, 346
Lago Hermoso, RN 326
Lago Huata Hue, RN 347
Lago Huechulafquen, NEU 272, 290
Lago Ibizca, CAT 531
Lago Ingeniero A M Allende, CBA 186, 194, 229
Lago La Angostura, TUC 606
Lago La Florida, SLU 526
Lago La Plata, CHU 359, 375
Lago Lacar, NEU 280, 301
Lago Lezama, CHU 375
Lago Los Moscos, RN 326
Lago Machonico, RN 326
Lago Mascardi, RN 318, 326, 346
Lago Melincué, SFE 249
Lago Meliquina
  NEU 308
  RN 326, 348
Lago Menéndez, CHU 374, 381
Lago Monthue, NEU 309
Lago Moquehue, NEU 274
Lago Moreno, RN 350
Lago Musters, CHU 358, 391, 392
Lago Nahuel Huapí
  NEU 271, 278, 310
  RN 318, 326, 329, 347, 349
Lago Norquinco, NEU 274
Lago Onelli, SCR 413
Lago Paimún, NEU 271, 290
Lago Pellegrini, CHU 375
Lago Piedras Moras, CBA 198
Lago Posadas, SCR 404, 415
Lago Puelo, CHU 324, 349
Lago Pulmari, NEU 274
Lago Quillén, NEU 274
Lago Rivadavia, CHU 362, 375, 380
Lago Roca, CBA 223
Lago Roca, RN 326
Lago Roca, TDF 436, 447
Lago Rucachoroi, NEU 274

Lago San Felipe, SLU 520
Lago San Roque, CBA 143, 151, 166, 193, 206, 224
Lago Situación, CHU 379
Lago Steffen, RN 347
Lago Torre, SCR 417
Lago Traful, NEU 308, 311, 349
Lago Tromen, NEU (near Chos Malal) 272, 281
Lago Tromen, NEU (near Junín de los Andes) 290
Lago Valle Grande, MZA 453, 481, 485
Lago Verde, CHU 371, 374, 380, 381
Lago Viedma, SCR 411, 416, 417
Lago Villarino, RN 326
Lago Viña, CBA 193
Laguna Achacosa, NEU 286
Laguna Adela, BA 82
Laguna Blanca, CAT 534
Laguna Blanca, FOR 675
Laguna Blanca, MZA 461
Laguna Brava, CBA 205
Laguna Brava, RJA 568, 582
Laguna Brava, SLU 512
Laguna Campos, NEU 276
Laguna Chascomús, BA 81
Laguna Chis-Chis, BA 82
Laguna Comodoro, JUJ 661
Laguna de Gómez, BA 85, 86
Laguna de la Niña Encantada, MZA 456, 462, 486
Laguna de Llancanelo, MZA 452, 461, 462
Laguna de los Cisnes, SCR 413
Laguna de los Horcones, MZA 477
Laguna de Pocho, CBA 224
Laguna de Rodeo, JUJ 661
Laguna de Volcán, JUJ 664
Laguna del Chancho, NEU 285
Laguna del Monte, BA 85
Laguna del Plesiosauro, CHU 378
Laguna del Valle Hermoso, MZA 456
Laguna del Valle, MZA 456
Laguna Desaguadero, JUJ 661
Laguna Don Tomas, LAP 243
Laguna Frías, RN 349
Laguna Frías, SCR 413
Laguna Grande, SCR 405
Laguna Guayatayoc, JUJ 646, 647
Laguna Hualcupen, NEU 286
Laguna Iberá, COR 741
Laguna La Ballena, BA 105
Laguna Lobos, BA 90
Laguna Mar Chiquita, BA 85, 86
Laguna Mar Chiquita, CBA 194
Laguna Panza de Cabra, CHA 695

INDEX

Laguna Pozuelos, JUJ 646, 647
Laguna Rincón, NEU 286
Laguna Rosario, CHU 401
Laguna Sauce Grande, BA 107
Laguna Setúbal, SFE 259
Laguna Sulfurosa, NEU 285
Laguna Tapia, NEU 276
Laguna Tonchek, RN 350
Laguna Trolope, NEU 286
Laguna Varvarco, NEU 276
Laguna Varvarco Campos, NEU 275
Laguna Verde
  NEU 285
  RN 351
Laguna Verde II, NEU 285
Laguna Vitel, BA 82
Laguna Yalca, BA 82
Lagunas de Yala, JUJ 640, 646, 660, 661
Lagunas las Mellizas, NEU 286
Laishi, FOR
  See San Francisco de Laishi, FOR
Lapachos, JUJ 636
Lapataia, TDF 436, 447
Las Aguaditas de San José, CAT 558
Las Bovedas, MZA 491
Las Cañas, SLU 519
Las Chacritas, CAT 530
Las Coloradas, NEU 308
Las Cuevas, MZA 451, 452, **454**, 475
Las Cumbrecita, CBA 230
Las Flores, SJU 508
Las Grutas, RN
  See Balneario Las Grutas, RN
Las Heras, SCR **415**
Las Higueras, MZA 486
Las Juntas, CAT **545**
Las Lajas, NEU **291**
Las Leñas, MZA 451, **454**, 456, 462, 475, 486
Las Maquinas, NEU 285
Las Maquinitas, NEU 285
Las Maravillas, CBA 193
Las Margueritas, CHU 392
Las Nalcas, RN 351
Las Olletas, NEU 276
Las Ovejas, NEU 275, **292**
Las Padrecitas, RJA 576, 577
Las Palmas, CBA 223
Las Pircas, MZA 476
Las Rabonas, CBA **186**, 229
Las Tapias, CBA 229
Leandro N Alem, MIS **796**, 801
Ledesma, JUJ 663
León, JUJ 662
Leones, CBA **186**
Libertador General San Martín, JUJ 664

Lipan, JUJ 645
Llampa, CAT 531
Llano Blanco, MZA 462, 463
Llao Llao, RN **325**, 350
Llullaillaco, SAL 611
Lobos, BA **90**
Loma Blanco, RJA 578
Loma Rica, CAT 530, 555, 556
Londres, CAT 540, **545**, 547
Loreto, MIS 788, 789, 809
Los Alazanes, CBA 153
Los Altares, CHU **379**
Los Antiguos, SCR **416**, 419
Los Arboles, MZA 489
Los Baldecitos, RJA 568
Los Baños, NEU 286
Los Bolillos, NEU 275
Los Castillos, SAL 638
Los Castillos de Pincheira, MZA 463
Los Cerillos, MZA 476
Los Cocos, CBA 153, **186**
Los Farellones, CAT 539
Los Higuerales, MZA 489
Los Hornillos, CBA **187**, 229
Los Lagos, RN 349
Los Manantiales, BA 112
Los Manzanos, RJA 568
Los Menucos, RN 327
Los Molles, MZA 452, 456, 486
Los Molles, SLU 519
Los Nacimientos, CAT 539
Los Penitentes, MZA 451, 452, **456**, 475, 477
Los Pinos, NEU 286
Los Pizarros, TUC **589**, 603
Los Pozos, CBA 229
Los Reartes, CBA 224, 233
Los Reyunos, MZA 485
Los Sarmientos, RJA 567
Los Tachos, NEU 276
Los Túneles, CBA 223
Lozano, JUJ 663
Luján, BA **90**
Luján de Cuyo, MZA **457**
Lules, TUC **589**
Lumbreras, SAL 638

M

Maimará, JUJ **653**, 668
Maipú, MZA **458**
Makallé, CHA 694

Makallé

INDEX

Mala Dormido, MZA 460
Malargüe, MZA 451, 453, **458**, 486
  Map 459
Malligasta, RJA 568
Mandisovi, ER 767
Manos Pintados, CHU 394
Manzano Histórico, MZA 476, 480, 489, 490
Mapuche, CHU 401
Mar Chiquita, BA 138
Mar Chiquita, SDE 718
Mar del Plata, BA 68, **92**
  Map 93
Mar del Sud, BA 105
Mar del Tuyú, BA **99**
  Map 101
Marcos Juárez, CBA **187**
Margarita Belén, FOR 681
Matara, SDE 698
Mboibusu Zool-bal, MIS 796
Melincué, SFE **249**
Mendoza province **450**
  Map Plate 23
Mendoza, MZA 451, **463**
  Map 464
Mercedes, BA **100**
Mercedes, COR 725, **740**
Mercedes, SLU **513**
  Map 514
Merlo, SLU 510, **515**, 525
  Map 516
Metán, SAL **621**
Metán Viejo, SAL 622
Mina Clavero, CBA **187**, 223
  Map 189
Mina La Concordia, SAL 641
Mina Uno, SCR 432, 433
Minas Capillitas, CAT 534
Mirador, RN 351
Mirador del Cerro Aconcagua, MZA 475
Miramar, BA **100**
  Map 101
Miramar, CBA 194
Misiones province **787**
  Map Plate 47
Moconá Falls, MIS
  See Gran Salto de Moconá, MIS
Mogote Los Gigantes, CBA 205, 223
Mogotes Colorados, RJA 567, 576
Molino, JUJ 645
Molinos, SAL 614, **622**, 640
Monte Caseros, COR **741**
Monte Hermoso, BA 76, **105**
Monte Pissis, RJA 560
Monte Redondo, SDE 707

Monte Susana, TDF 447
Montecarlo, MIS 788, 790, **796**
Monteros, TUC 584
Mundo Nuevo, TUC 602

N

Nacimiento del Río Alumbrera, CAT 531
Nacimientos de Hualfín, CAT 531
Nahuel Pan, CHU 374
Nahueve, NEU 276
Nant y Fall, CHU 373, 401
Necochea, BA 68, **107**
  Map 108
Neuquén province, NEU 270
  Map Plate 13
Neuquén, NEU 271, **292**, 328
  Map 293
Nevado de Queva, SAL 642
Nevado del Cachi, SAL 611, 614, 615, 616, 620, 640
Nevado del Candado, CAT 532, 553
Nevado del Chani, SAL 611
Nevado Famatina, RJA 563
Nevado Queva, SAL 611
Nevados del Aconquija
  CAT 530
  TUC 584, 590
Nogolí, SLU
  See Hipólito Yrigoyen, SLU
Nogoyá, ER 775
Nono, CBA 193, **194**, 229
Nonogasta, RJA 567, 568, 576, **577**, 582

O

Oberá, MIS 788, 790, 793, **798**, 817
  Map 799
Ojo Dulce de Choya, CAT 531, 534
Olavarría, BA **112**
Oliva, CBA **195**
Olta, RJA **577**
Oncativo, CBA **195**
Orán, SAL **622**
Ostende, BA 114

Mala Dormido

INDEX

Triana, CHU 392
Tricao Malal, NEU 276
Troya, CAT 543, 558
Tucumán province **583**
   Map Plate 33
Tucumán, TUC
   See San Miguel de Tucumán, TUC
Tucumán Viejo, TUC
   See Ibatín, TUC
Tumbaya, JUJ 662, 664, **668**
Túnel Subfluvial Hernandarias, SFE 267
Tunuyan, MZA 451, 476, **487**
   Map 488
Tupungato, MZA 451, 476, **490**

U

Ucalera, JUJ 664
Ulapes, RJA **580**
Unquillo, CBA **205**
Uquía, JUJ **668**
Ushuaia, TDF 434, 435, 439, **442**
   Map 443
Uspallata, MZA 451, 475, **490**

V

Valeria del Mar, BA 114
Valle Amanao, CAT 533, 534, 539, 544
Valle Calamuchita, CBA 201
Valle Catamarca
   CAT 553
   RJA 562
Valle Cortadera, SLU 519
Valle de Calingasta, SJU
   See Río de los Patos, SJU
Valle de la Luna, SJU
   See Ischigualasto, SJU
Valle de Siancas, SAL 637
Valle de Tartagal, SAL 624
Valle de Uco, MZA 453, 476, 480
Valle de Utracán, LAP 240
Valle del Jaurua, MZA 476
Valle Encantado, NEU 349, 350
Valle Encantado, SAL 612
Valle Fértil, SJU 493, 507
Valle Hermoso, MZA 451, 455, 486
Valle Las Leñas, MZA 462
Valle Pancanta, SLU 525

Valle Quimivil, CAT 547
Valle San Javier, TUC 602
Valle Tierra Mayor, TDF 440, 441
Valle Vuriloche, RN 351
Vallecitos, MZA 451, 476
Venado Tuerto, SFE **267**
Ventisquero Moreno, SCR 407
Veta Mina, JUJ 645
Viale, ER **783**
Victor Szapelis, CHU 394
Victoria, ER 257, **783**
Victoria, MIS 795
Vicuña Mackenna, CBA **206**
Viedma, RN 80, 317, **352**
   Map 353
Vieja Villa Río Hondo, SDE 718
Villa Alegre, CBA 166
Villa Allende, CBA 166, **206**
Villa Anizacate, CBA 149
Villa Arcadia, BA 124
Villa Atalaya, RN 346
Villa Berna, CBA 224, 230, 233
Villa Carlos Paz, CBA 143, 166, 193, **206**
   Map 208
Villa Castelli, RJA **580**
Villa Chacay, CBA 198
Villa Ciudad de América, CBA 149, **225**, 232
Villa Cura Brochero, CBA 224, **225**
Villa de la Quebrada, SLU **525**
Villa de las Rosas, CBA 229
Villa de María de Río Seco, CBA **225**
Villa de Soto, CBA **226**
Villa del Dique, CBA **226**
Villa del Sur, BA 83
Villa Dolores, CBA 143, **226**
   Map 227
Villa Elena, SLU 515, 519, 525, **526**
Villa General Belgrano, CBA **229**
   Map 230
Villa General Mitre, CBA **233**
Villa Gesell, BA **128**
Villa Giardino, CBA 178
Villa La Angostura, NEU 308, **309**, 345, 349
   Map 310
Villa La Merced, CBA 232
Villa La Serrania, CBA 149
Villa Libertador General San Martín, ER **785**
Villa Los Aromos, CBA 149
Villa María, CBA **233**
Villa Mascardi, RN 326, 346
Villa Mazán, RJA 561, 579, 580
Villa Media Agua, SJU 493

INDEX

Sierra de Misiones, MIS 789, 791, 793, 795, 796, 798, 801, 817, 820, 821
Sierra de Pastos Grandes, SAL 616
Sierra de Pocho, CBA 143, 201
Sierra de Quilmes, CAT 539, 554
Sierra de San Bernardino, CHU 391
Sierra de San Luis, SLU 510, 512, 520, 521, 526
Sierra de Sanogasta, RJA 567
Sierra de Santa Victoria, SAL 642
Sierra de Sumampa, SDE 696, 707, 708, 718
Sierra de Tandil, BA 67, 125
Sierra de Velasco, RJA 560, 563, 566, 567, 569, 570, 578, 580
Sierra del Imán, MIS 796
Sierra del Morro, SLU 513
Sierra del Valle Fértil, SJU 498
Sierra del Viento, NEU 275, 276, 282
Sierra Grande, CBA 143, 187, 193, 223, 224, 230, 233
Sierra Grande, RN 318
Sierra Iman, MIS 723
Sierra Lucio Lopez, TDF 439
Sierras de Córdoba, CBA 142, 143, 150, 153, 155, 169, 170, 171, 199, 708
Silleta de los Higueras, TUC 603
Simoca, TUC **605**
Sinsacate, CBA 173
Socompa, SAL 612
Sorcuyo, JUJ 647
Sumampa, SDE 698, **708**
Susques, JUJ 642, 645, 646, 662, **665**

T

Taco Ralo, TUC 584, **605**
Tafí del Valle, TUC 555, 584, 602, **606**
Tafí Viejo, TUC 584
Taguas, MZA 452
Talamuyuna, RJA 567
Tamal Áike, SCR 415
Tamberías, SJU 507
Tambo del Inca, RJA 568
Tandil, BA **125**
  Map 126
Taninga, CBA **204**, 223
Tanti, CBA 204, 223
Tapiales, SLU 525
Tartagal, SAL 643
Tatane, FOR 681

Termas de Agua Hedionda, SJU 493, 496, 499
Termas de Agua Negra, SJU 493, 499
Termas de Azufre, MZA 462
Termas de Cacheuta, MZA 476
Termas de Cajón Grande, MZA 462
Termas de Centenario, SJU 497, 508
Termas de Concepción, RJA 562
Termas de Copahué, NEU
  See Copahué, NEU
Termas de Fiambalá, CAT 531
Termas de Incachuli, SAL 642
Termas de Pismanta, SJU
  See Pismanta, SJU
Termas de Pompeya, SAL 641
Termas de Reyes, JUJ 640, 646, 660
Termas de Río Hondo, SDE 697, 699, **708**
  Map 711
Termas de Santa Rita, RJA 561
Termas de Talacasto, SJU 493, 508
Termas El Sosneado, MZA 486
Termas Lahuen-Có, MZA 456
Termas Lavalle, CAT 531
Termas Los Nacimientos, CAT 544
Termas Santa Teresita, RJA 560, 562, **579**
Termas Villavicencio, MZA 452, 475, **486**
Ticonte, SAL 621
Tierra del Fuego **434**
  Map Plate 21
Tigre, BA 64
Tilcara, JUJ 640, 645, 646, 664, **666**
  Map 667
Tilimuqui, RJA 568
Tilisarao, SLU **526**
Tinogasta, CAT 530, 553, **556**
Tin-Tin, SAL 612, 615, 640
Tío Mayo, CBA 153
Tiraxi, JUJ 663
Tobuna, MIS 793, 817, 821
Tolhuin, TDF 440
Tolombon, SAL 618, 619
Toquipili, SAL 638
Tornquist, BA 76
Toscas, MZA 452
Trancas, TUC 605, **608**
Trapiche, SLU **526**
Trelew, CHU 358, **394**
  Map 395
Tres Arroyos, BA **128**
Tres Cerros, SCR **433**
Tres Cruces, JUJ 645, 653
Trevelín, CHU 373, 379, **399**
  Map 400

Trevelín

INDEX

San Luis, SLU **521**
  Map 522
San Marcos Sierra, CBA 153, **201**
San Martín, MZA **480**
San Martín de los Andes, NEU 280, **301**, 347, 348, 349
  Map 302
San Miguel de Tucumán, TUC 584, **592**
  Map 594
San Miguel del Monte, BA **122**
San Nicolás, RJA 568
San Nicolás de los Arroyos, BA **122**
San Pablo, TUC 585
San Pedro, BA **123**
San Pedro, MIS 793, 817, **820**
San Pedro, SDE 699
San Pedro de Atacama, SAL 641
San Pedro de Colalao, TUC **604**
San Pedro de Jujuy, JUJ 663
San Rafael, MZA 475, **481**
  Map 482
San Ramón de la Nueva Orán, SAL
  See Orán, SAL
San Roque, CAT 558
San Salvador de Jujuy, JUJ 636, 637, 640, 645, 646, **654**
  Map 655
San Sebastián, TDF 435, **441**
San Telmo, CAP 59
San Vicente, MIS 801, **821**
Sañogasta, RJA 568
Santa Ana, MIS 788, 789, 809, 819
Santa Ana de los Guácaras, COR 733, **747**
Santa Catalina, JUJ 653
Santa Cruz province **402**
  Map Plate 20
Santa Cruz, SCR
  See Puerto Santa Cruz, SCR
Santa Elena, CBA 154
Santa Fé province **248**
  Map Plate 11
Santa Fé de la Vera Cruz, SFE 248, 249, **259**, 782
  Map 260
Santa Fé la Vieja, SFE 250
Santa Florentina, RJA 567
Santa Lucía, COR 737
Santa María, CAT 530, 538, **554**
Santa María, MIS 789, 791, 796
Santa Rita, MIS 801
Santa Rosa, LAP 238, **243**
  Map 244
Santa Rosa de Calamuchita, CBA **201**
  Map 202
Santa Rosa de Tastil, SAL 612, 639

Santa Rosa del Conlara, SLU **525**
Santa Victoria, SAL **642**, 669
Santiago del Estero province **696**
  Map Plate 41
Santiago del Estero, SDE 697, 698, 699, **701**, 718
  Map 702
Santo Tomé, COR 725, **748**
Sarmiento, CHU 391, **392**
  Map 393
Saujil, CAT 543, 553
Schaqui, RJA 579
Señor de la Peña, RJA 562, 577
Serranía Calilegua, JUJ 653
Sierra Chango Real, CAT 538
Sierra Chica
  BA 114
  CBA 143, 149, 152, 153, 154, 169, 170, 173, 178, 185, 186, 195, 199, 201, 205, 206, 230
Sierra de Achala, CBA 187, 224
Sierra de Aconquija
  CAT 529, 539, 550, 553, 554
  TUC 592, 606, 608
Sierra de Ambargasta, SDE 707
Sierra de Ambato
  CAT 540, 541, 546, 547, 550, 553
  RJA 561
Sierra de Ancasti
  CAT 531, 547
  RJA 562
Sierra de Argañaraz, RJA 563
Sierra de Belén, CAT 534
Sierra de Churriacu, NEU 283
Sierra de Comechingones
  CBA 143, 144, 178, 186, 198, 224, 226, 229
  SLU 510, 515, 519, 526
Sierra de Cuniputo, CBA 170
Sierra de Famatina, RJA 560, 563, 569
Sierra de Fiambalá, CAT 534, 558
Sierra de Graciana, CAT 544, 547
Sierra de Guasayán, SDE 696, 697, 698, 700
Sierra de la Ventana
  BA 67, 76, 124
  RN 329
Sierra de la Ventana, BA (town) **124**
Sierra de Lihuel Calel, LAP 241
Sierra de los Colorados, RJA 566, 567
Sierra de los Llanos, RJA 563
Sierra de los Quinteros, RJA 578
Sierra de Manchao, CAT 545, 553
Sierra de Mazán, RJA 561
Sierra de Michilingue, SLU 520

INDEX

Rosario de Colona, CAT 553
Rosario de la Frontera, SAL **625**
Rosario del Tala, ER **783**
Ruca Laufquen, RN 346
Ruinas de Cayparcito, CAT 535

S

Sáenz Peña, CHA
   See Presidencia Roque Sáenz Peña, CHA
Safariland, RN 348
Salada de Choya, CAT 531
Salar de Antofalla, CAT 529, 535
Salar de Pipanaco, CAT 529, 533, 536, 553
Salar del Hombre Muerto, CAT 535
Salar Pocitos, SAL 612
Salicas, RJA **578**
Salina de la Laguna Verde, CAT 529
Salina del Gualicho, RN 327
Salina Grande, CHU 386, 388
Salina Grande, JUJ 662
Salina La Antigua, RJA 560
Salinas de Ambargasta, SDE 697, 707
Salinas del Bebedero, SLU 525
Salinas Grandes
   CAT 546
   CBA 171
   RJA 560
Salinas Grandes, JUJ 645
Salsipuédes, CBA **199**
Salta province **610**
   Map Plate 34
Salta, SAL 534, 540, 611, 615, **626**, 665
   Map 627
Salto Alegre, MIS 788, 791
Salto Andresito, MIS 792
Salto Berrondo, MIS 800
Salto de Agua Tupa, MIS 792
Salto de Moconá, MIS
   See Gran Salto de Moconá, MIS
Salto del Capioví, MIS 796, 818
Salto del Tabaquillo, SLU 519
Salto Elena, MIS 795
Salto Encantado, MIS 791
Salto Grande, ER 753, 762, 763, 766, 767
Salto Paco, MIS 800
Salto Pilaras Blancas, MIS 791
Salto San Martín, MIS 815
Saltos del Apipé, COR 724
Saltos del Tabay, MIS 796

Salvador Mazza, SAL
   See Pocitos, SAL
Samay Huasi, RJA 567
Sampacho, CBA **199**
San Agustín del Valle Fértil, SJU 492, 494, **498**
San Antonio, CAT **547**
San Antonio, MIS 792
San Antonio de Areco, BA **119**
   Map 120
San Antonio de Arredondo, CBA 199
San Antonio de los Cobres, SAL 534, 540, 611, 639, **640**, 666
San Antonio Oeste, RN 318, **327**
San Blas, RJA 579
San Buenaventura del Monte Alto, CHA 685
San Carlos, COR 725
San Carlos, MZA **480**
San Carlos, SAL 640, **642**
San Carlos de Bariloche, RN 299, 308, 318, 323, 327, **329**
   Map 331
San Clemente del Tuyú, BA **121**
San Clemente, CBA 149, **200**
San Fernando del Valle de Catamarca, CAT 529, 530, **547**, 561
   Map 548
San Francisco, CBA **200**
San Francisco de Laishí, FOR 681
San Francisco del Monte de Oro, SLU **520**
San Gerónimo, SLU 510, **521**
San Ignacio Miní, MIS 788, 789, 790, 809, **818**
San Isidro, CAT **554**
San Javier, CBA 229
San Javier, MIS 796, 801, **820**
San Javier, TUC 590
San José, CAT 538, 555, 558
San José, MIS 788
San José de Jáchal, SJU 492, 493, **499**
San José de la Dormida, CBA 171, **201**
San José de los Ríos, CBA 205
San José de Morro, SLU 513
San Juan province **492**
   Map Plate 25
San Juan, SJU 491, 492, **500**
   Map 501
San Julián, SCR
   See Puerto San Julián, SCR
San Justo, SFE 267
San Lorenzo, SAL 638, **642**
San Lorenzo, SFE **259**
San Luis province **509**
   Map Plate 27

San Luis province

Index

Río Paraná—continued
  SFE 248, 249, 250, 257, 258, 259, 267
Río Paraná de las Palmas
  BA 78
  ER 752
Río Paraná Guazú, ER 752
Río Pepiri Guazú, MIS 788, 789, 792
Río Pepiri Miní, MIS 789
Río Pescado, SAL 624
Río Picheuta, MZA 453
Río Pilcomayo, FOR 672, 673, 675
Río Pincheira, MZA 463
Río Pinturas, SCR 403, 404, 419
Río Piray Miní, MIS 795
Río Poti Mallal Chico, MZA 453
Río Poti Mallal Grande, MZA 453
Río Potrero Grande, RJA 580
Río Pozo, CAT 533
Río Primero, CBA 155, 166, 174
Río Punillas, CBA 144, 151, 166, 168, 175, 185
Río Punillo, CAT 535
Río Quequén Grande, BA 111, 112, 118
Río Quillén, NEU 274
Río Quimivil, CAT 545
Río Quinto, SLU 526
Río Raco, TUC 592
Río Reyes, JUJ 660, 661, 662
Río Riachuelo, CAP 59
Río Rivadavia, CHU 380
Río Rugapampa, CBA 224
Río Saisa, SJU 507
Río Saladillo
  CAT 556
  SDE 707
Río Salado, BA 82
Río Salado, MZA 453, 461, 462
Río Salado, RJA 561, 579
  See also Desagüe del Río Salado
Río Salado, SDE 697, 698, 699
Río Salí, TUC 584, 587, 602
Río Salsacate, CBA 204
Río San Antonio, MIS 788, 789, 792
Río San Francisco
  CBA 178
  SLU 520
Río San Francisco, JUJ 663
Río San Guillermo, CBA 223
Río San Ignacio, TUC 589
Río San Javier, CBA 226
Río San Juan, SJU 492, 493, 495, 500, 507
Río San Lorenzo, SAL 642
Río Santa Lucía, COR 735
Río San Marcos, CBA 201
Río Santa Cruz, SCR 405, 417, 425
Río Santa María, CAT 539, 554

Río Santa Rosa, CBA 201
Río Santa Victoria, SAL 642
Río Sauce Grande, BA 124
Río Segundo, CBA 195
Río Senguerr, CHU 359, 368, 391
Río Siambon, TUC 592
Río Tacanas, TUC 604
Río Tafí
  CAT 556
  TUC 606, 608
Río Tapia, TUC 592, 602
Río Tercero, CBA (river) 171, 198, 199, 233, 234
Río Tercero, CBA (town) **198**
Río Tesorero, JUJ 661, 663
Río Tipas, TUC 604
Río Tiraxi, JUJ 663
Río Tordillo, MZA 453
Río Traful, NEU 283, 347, 348
Río Trocoman, NEU 283
Río Trolope, NEU 286
Río Troya, CAT 543, 558
Río Tunuyan, MZA 452, 458, 477, 479, 487
Río Tupungato, MZA 452
Río Turbio, SCR 403, 431, **432**
Río Uco, MZA 490
Río Uruga-I, MIS 816
Río Uruguay
  Buenos Aires city 64
  COR 724, 725, 741, 744
  ER 752, 753, 754, 757, 758, 762, 769, 782
  MIS 788, 789, 790, 793, 795, 796, 801, 817, 820
  SJU 507
Río Uspallata, MZA 453
Río Valenzuela, MZA 453
Río Varvarco, NEU 275
Río Vallecito, TUC 590
Río Victoria, ER 784
Río Villegas, RN 347
Río Vinchina, RJA 580, 582
Río Xibi Xibi, JUJ 654
Río Yala, JUJ 661, 662
Río Yokavil, CAT 530
Río Yuspe, CBA 205, 223
Rivadavia, MZA **477**
  Map 478
Rivadavia, SJU 493
Río Mayo, CHU (river) 391
Rocas Negras, BA 105
Rodeo, SJU **497**, 508
Roque Sáenz Peña, CHA
  See Presidencia Roque Saenz Peña, CHA
Rosario, SFE 248, **250**
  Map 251

INDEX

Río El Manzano, SLU 519
Río Empedrado, COR 734
Río Epuyén, CHU 377
Río Escorial, NEU 271
Río Espinillo
  CBA 233
  ER 773
Río Ewan, TDF 439
Río Fitz Roy, SCR 412
Río Formosa, FOR 675
Río Foyel, RN 347
Río Frías, RN 346
Río Fuego, TDF 439
Río Futalaufquén, CHU 373, 375
Río Futaleufú, CHU 379
Río Gallegos, SCR (city) 403, 406, 407, **427**
  Map 426
Río Gallegos, SCR (river) 427
Río Garupá, MIS 809
Río Gastona, TUC 586, 587
Río Grande, JUJ 648, 649, 654, 666, 668, 669
Río Grande
  MZA 462
  SLU 526
Río Grande, TDF (city) 435, **436**
  Map 438
Río Grande de Punilla, CBA 185
Río Grande del Campo, CAT 590
Río Gualeguay, ER 752, 768, 769, 783, 785
Río Gualeguaychú, ER 752
Río Guanaquitas, MZA 487
Río Guaycurú, MIS 788
Río Guerrero, JUJ 661
Río Gueuguel, SCR 419
Río Huachichocana, JUJ 662
Río Huaco
  RJA 581
  SJU 496
Río Hualcupen, NEU 286
Río Huasamayo, JUJ 666, 668
Río Icho Cruz, CBA 224
Río Iguazú, MIS 788, 792, 810, 815
Río Incamayo, SAL 639
Río Jáchal, SJU 508
Río Kalayo, JUJ 662
Río La Granja, CBA 185
Río La Leona, SCR 411
Río Las Juntas, CAT 545
Río Las Lajas, CAT 556
Río Las Salvias, CAT 545
Río Leona, SCR 417
Río Lerma, SAL 611, 616, 626, 638
Río Lileo, NEU 275

Río Limay
  NEU 271, 283, 292, 299
  RN 322, 347, 348, 349, 350
Río Lipeo, SAL 624
Río Lleretas, MZA 490
  See also Quebrada de las Lleretas, MZA
Río Los Angeles, CAT 540
Río Los Blancos, MZA 487
Río Los Chorrillos, CBA 205
Río Los Repollos, RN 347
Río Los Sauces, CBA 226
Río Los Tordillos, MZA 487
Río Lozano, JUJ 662
Río Luján, BA 90
Río Lules, TUC 590
Río Lurancato, SAL 622
Río Malargüe, MZA 463
Río Malleo, NEU 272
Río Manantiales, MZA 487, 490
Río Manso, RN 351
Río Marada, TUC 603, 605
Río Mayo, CHU (town) **391**
Río Mendoza, MZA 453, 457, 463, 475
Río Mina Clavero, CBA 188
Río Miní, COR 737
Río Mojotoro, SAL 637
Río Molino, SLU 519
Río Nahueve, NEU 276
Río Naposta, BA 70
Río Negro province **317**
  Map Plate 15
Río Negro
  BA 80
  LAP 237
Río Negro, CHA 684, 685
Río Negro, RN 319, 321, 322, 328, 352, 356
Río Neuquén, NEU 275, 282, 292
Río Olivia, TDF 441, 447
Río Olnie, SCR 415
Río Paimún, NEU 271
Río Palomares, MZA 490
Río Panaholma, CBA 188
Río Paraguay
  CHA 695
  COR 741
  FOR 672, 673, 675, 676, 681, 682
Río Paraná
  BA 77, 122, 138
  Buenos Aires city 35, 64
  CHA 685, 688, 694, 695
  COR 724, 725, 726, 734, 735, 737, 738, 741
  ER 752, 753, 766, 768, 773, 775, 784
  FOR 673
  MIS 788, 789, 794, 795, 796, 797, 801, 809, 815, 816, 817, 821

841

Río Paraná

INDEX

Resistencia, CHA 681, 684, **688**
　Map 691
Riachuelo Antequera, CHA 695
Rincón de Papagayos, SLU 515
Rincón del Este, SLU 525
Rinconada, JUJ 649
Río Abaucan
　CAT 542, 543, 556, 558
　RJA 580
Río Agrio, NEU 286, 316
Río Alerce, RN 346
Río Aluminé
　NEU 272, 274, 291
　RN 348
Río Amaicha, TUC 585
Río Areco, BA 119
Río Arias, SAL 626
Río Arrayanes, CHU 374, 381
Río Ascochinga, CBA 173
Río Atuel, MZA 451, 453, 481, 486
　See also Cañon San Rafael, MZA
Río Azul, RN 324
Río Baradero, BA 77
Río Baritú, SAL 624
Río Barrancas
　MZA 453, 463
　NEU 271
Río Barranqueras, CHA 688
Río Belén, CAT 534, 538, 539
　See also Cañon Belén, CAT
Río Bermejito, CHA 688
Río Bermejo
　CHA 684, 688
　FOR 681, 682
　SAL 624, 643
Río Bermejo, RJA 581
Río Blanco, RN 346
Río Blanco, SAL 639
Río Blanco, SJU 495
Río El Bolsón, CAT 538
Río Bonete, RJA 560
Río Bote, SCR 405, 431
Río Calamuchita, CBA 144, 229
Río Calchaqui
　CAT 530
　SAL 614, 615, 616, 620, 638, 640
　TUC 585, 586, 604
Río Calingasta, SJU 495
Río Candelaria, JUJ 663
Río Carabar, SAL 624
Río Carbon Grande, SFE 257
Río Carocas, MZA 489
Río Castaño, SJU 493
Río Castaño Viejo, SJU 495
Río Ceballos, CBA (town) **195**
Río Chango, CAT 539

Río Chango Real, CAT 539
Río Chaschuil, CAT 543, 558
Río Chico, SCR 414, 424
Río Chimehuin, NEU 272, 287, 348
Río Chubut, CHU 358, 375, 377, 381, 387, 394
Río Chunapa, SAL 638
Río Cinsel, JUJ 647
Río Claromecó, BA 128
Río Cle, ER 768
Río Cobre, MZA 453
Río Cochuna, TUC 590
Río Coctaca, JUJ 650
Río Coig, SCR 413
Río Collón Curá, NEU 348
Río Colorado
　MZA 462
　NEU 271
　RN 320, 327
Río Colorado, RJA 580
Río Colorado, RN (town) **327**
Río Concepción, CAT 540
Río Condorito, CBA 149
Río Conlara, SLU 511, 520, 526
Río Castaño, SJU 496
Río Cuanaquitas, MZA 490
Río Cuarto, CBA (river) 197
Río Cuarto, CBA (town) **197**
Río Curri Leuvu, NEU 281
Río de la Cruz, CBA 174
Río de la Plata
　BA 86, 89
　Buenos Aires city 35
Río de la Ventana, BA 76
Río de las Cuevas, MZA 452, 453, 456, 475, 477
Río de los Patos, SJU (*Also known as* Valle de Calingasta) 493, 494, 495, 507
Río de los Reartes, CBA 233
Río de los Sauces, CBA 193, 229
Río de los Sauces, RJA 580
Río de Pachón, SJU 493
Río del Cobre, MZA 456
Río del Medio, CBA 178, 233
Río del Peñon, RJA 582
Río del Portezuelo, CAT 553
Río del Valle
　CAT 554
　SJU 498
Río Desaguadero, MZA 380
Río Deseado, SCR 420
Río Diamante, MZA 475, 481, 485
Río Dulce
　CBA 194
　SDE 697, 698, 700, 701, 709, 718

Resistencia

INDEX

Punta Colorada, RN 318
Punta Cuevas, COR 725
Punta de Agua, RJA 582
Punta de Balasto, CAT 530, 539
Punta de Vacas, MZA 472, 475
Punta del Agua, SLU 520
Punta Delgada, CHU 388
Punta Este, CHU 386
Punta Gorda, ER 767
Punta Gualichu, SCR 413
Punta Lara, BA 89
Punta Loyola, SCR 427, 432
Punta María, TDF 439
Punta Marqués, CHU 360
Punta Norte, CHU 386, 387, 388
Punta Norte del Cabo de San Antonio, BA 121
Punta Pardelas, CHU 387
Punta Quilla, SCR 403, 425
Punta Tombo, CHU 387, **388**
Punto Panoramico, RN 350
Purmamarca, JUJ 662

Q

Quebrada Chica, CBA 184
Quebrada Chulca, TUC 605
Quebrada de Anta, TUC 605
Quebrada de Cafayate, SAL 638, 640
Quebrada de Escoipe, SAL 616, 640
Quebrada de Humahuaca
  JUJ 646, 662, 664, 666, 668
  SAL 640
Quebrada de las Conchas, SAL 640
Quebrada de las Llaretas, MZA 490
  See also Río Llaretas, MZA
Quebrada de López, SLU 520
Quebrada de los Árboles, CAT 543
Quebrada de los Cóndores, SLU 511, 519
Quebrada de los Condoritos, CBA 200
Quebrada de los Laureles
  SAL 640
  TUC 605
Quebrada de los Toros, SAL 612, 639
Quebrada de Lules, TUC 589
Quebrada de Salta, SAL 620
Quebrada de Talampaya, RJA 582
Quebrada de Zonda, SJU 508
Quebrada del Arroyo Grande, MZA 490
Quebrada del Condorito, CBA 149

Quebrada del León Colgado, SLU 520
Quebrada del Mal Paso, JUJ 662
Quebrada del Río de las Conchas, SAL 639
Quebrada del Toro MZA 475
Quebrada Humahuaca, JUJ 648
Quehue, LAP 240
Quequén, BA 107, 111, 112, **118**
Quila-Quina, NEU 309
Quillén, NEU **300**
Quilmes, TUC 530, 556, 584, 586, **590**, 602, 618, 619
Quimey Mahuida, RN 346
Quimilí, SDE **701**
Quines, SLU **520**

R

Raco, TUC **592**, 602
Rada Tilly, CHU
  See Balneario Rada Tilly, CHU
Rahué, NEU 274
Rawson, CHU 358, 387, **389**
  Map 390
Realico, LAP 238
Reconquista, SFE **249**
Recreo, CAT **546**
Reducción de la Cangayé, CHA 684, 685
Reducción de San Bernardo de Vértiz, CHA 684
Reducción de San Fernando del Río Negro, CHA 684, 688
Renca, SLU **520**
Reserva Nacional Copahué, NEU 283, 285, 286
Reserva Nacional de Pesca de Caraguatay, MIS 789
Reserva Natural Formosa, FOR 682
Reserva Natural Laguna Blanca, CAT 536
Reserva Natural Laguna Grande, SCR 414
Reserva Natural Sierra del Tigre, BA 127
Reserva Natural Turística, CHU 362
Reserva Provincial Laguna Azul, SCR 431
Reserva Provincial Parque General San Martín, ER 782
Reserva Provincial Tromen, NEU 281
Reserva Punta Loma, CHU 386

· 839

Reserva Punta Loma

INDEX

Paso San Francisco, CAT 543, 553
Paso Tromen, NEU (*also known as* Paso Mamuil Malal) 290, 291, 308, 309
Pasos Malos, SLU 519
Patagonés, BA
  See Carmen de Patagonés, BA
Patquía, RJA 567, 576, **578**
Payogasta, SAL 615, 640
Payún Liso, MZA 462
Payún Matrú, MZA 462
Pehuen-Có, BA 76
Pellegrini, COR
  See Colonia Carlos Pellegrini, COR
Peña, CHA
  See Presidencia Roque Sáenz Peña, CHA
Peñas Blancas, JUJ 669
Península Valdés, CHU 358, 359, 381, 384, 386, 387
Península Yuco, NEU 309
Peñón de Reina Victoria, MIS 809, 819
Perito Moreno, SCR **417**
Pico Truncado, SCR 404, **419**
Pico Turista, RN 350
Piedra Blanca, SLU 525
Piedra Buena, SCR
  See Comandante Luis Piedra Buena, SCR
Piedra del Águila, NEU **299**
Piedra del Molino, SAL 640
Piedra del Viento, RN 348
Piedra Grande 476
Piedras Moras, CBA 144
Piedras Pintadas, SDE 708
Pilar, CBA **195**
Pinamar, BA 114, 138
  Map 115
Piñihue, NEU 274
Pismanta, SJU 493, **497**, 499, 500, 507
Playa Paraná, CHU 386
Playa Unión, CHU 389, 391
Plaza General Belgrano, LAP 240
Plaza Huincul, NEU 286
Plaza Vieja, RJA 570
Poca, CBA 204
Pocitos, SAL **624**
Polco, RJA 563
Polvaredas, MZA 475
Polvarillo, SAL 634, 638, 641
Pomán, CAT **546**, 553
Pomona, RN 328
Portezuelo de Choique, MZA 463
Portezuelo del Colorado, SJU 508
Portezuelo El Tambor 507
Portillo Argentino, MZA 490
Posadas, MIS 788, 789, 790, **801**
  Map 802
Posta de Lozano, JUJ 662

Posta de Yatasto, SAL 622
Potrerillos, MZA 451, 475, **476**
Potrero de Garay, CBA 149, 232
Potrero de los Funes, SLU (lake) 519
Potrero de los Funes, SLU (town) 511, **519**
Pozo de Baez, TUC 605
Pozo de las Animas, MZA 456, 462, 486
Presidencia Roque Sáenz Peña, CHA **685**
  Map 686
Primeros Pinos, NEU 272, 274, **299**, 316
Pucará de la Alumbrera, CAT 535
Pucará de Tilcara, JUJ 668
Pucará de Yacoraite, JUJ 650
Puente Ardanaz, BA 112
Puente del Inca, MZA 452, 475, **477**
Puente Histórico Picheuta, MZA 475, 491
Puerta de Corral Quemado, CAT 534
Puerta de Talampaya, RJA 576, 582
Puerta Tastil, SAL 612
Puerto Alegre, RN 349
Puerto Almanza, TDF 448
Puerto Antequeras, CHA 695
Puerto Belgrano, BA 71
Puerto Blest, RN 326, 349
Puerto Canoas, MIS 816
Puerto Deseado, SCR 403, **420**
Puerto Esperanza, MIS **809**
Puerto Frías, RN 349
Puerto Galván, BA 71
Puerto Iguazú, MIS 789, 790, 792, **810**
  Map 811
Puerto Ingeniero White, BA 71
Puerto Limanao, CHU 371, 374, 381
Puerto Madryn, CHU 358, 359, **381**, 384
  Map 385
Puerto Obligado, ER 771
Puerto Pañuelo, RN **326**, 349, 350
Puerto Patriada, CHU 378
Puerto Pilcomayo, FOR 673, 675
Puerto Pirámides, CHU 359, 384, 386, **387**
Puerto Piray, MIS 789, 797
Puerto Rawson, CHU 389
Puerto Rico, MIS 788, **817**
Puerto Ruiz, ER 768
Puerto San Julián, SCR 403, **421**
  Map 422
Puerto Santa Cruz, SCR 405, **425**
Puerto Vélaz, FOR 681, 682
Puerto Vilelas, CHA 684
Pulares, SAL 640
Punilla, CBA 153
Punta Bermeja, RN 319

Paso San Francisco

838

INDEX

P

P R S Peña, CHA
  See Presidencia Roque Sáenz Peña, CHA
Pachaco, SJU 507
Padre Angel Buodo, LAP 240
Pagancillo, RJA 569
Pago Largo, COR 734
Palacio San José, ER 757
Palmira, COR 725
Palo Blanco, CAT 543
Palpalá, JUJ 637
Pampa Blanca, JUJ 636
Pampa de Achala, CBA 193, 199
Pampa de Gualilan, SJU 508
Pampa de Leoncito, SJU 495
Pampa de Olaen, CBA 184
Pampa de Pocho, CBA 187, 223
Pampa de San Luis, CBA 223
Pampa El Toro, RN 346
Pampa Linda, RN 351
Panaholma, CBA 193
Paraná, ER 259, 267, 752, 753, **775**
  Map 776
Parque Aconquija, TUC **590**
Parque de los Poetas, SJU 508
Parque Dunícola Florentino Ameghino, BA 104
Parque Luna Helada, RN 348
Parque Luro, LAP 247
Parque Menhir, TUC 602
Parque Nacional Baritú, SAL 611, 612, **623**
Parque Nacional Bosque Petrificado, SCR 403
Parque Nacional Calilegua, JUJ 646, **653**, 663
Parque Nacional Chaco, CHA 684, 694
Parque Nacional del Iguazú, MIS 789, 790, 793
Parque Nacional El Palmar, ER 753, 757, 762, 766, **782**
Parque Nacional El Rey, SAL 611, **624**, 638
Parque Nacional Francisco Perito Moreno, SCR 415
Parque Nacional Lago Puelo, CHU 322, 358, 359, 375, 378
Parque Nacional Laguna Blanca, NEU 271, 274, 308, 312, 316
Parque Nacional Lanín, NEU 271, 274, 290, 301, 307, 326
Parque Nacional Lapataia, TDF 435

Parque Nacional Lihuel Calel, LAP 237, 238, **241**
Parque Nacional Los Alerces, CHU 347, 358, 359, 362, 368, 374, **379**
Parque Nacional Los Cardones, SAL 611, 612
Parque Nacional Los Glaciares, SCR 403, 407, 411, **416**
Parque Nacional Nahuel Huapí, NEU 271, 278, 312, **325**
Parque Nacional Perito Moreno, SCR 403
Parque Nacional Río Pilcomayo, FOR 672, 675
Parque Nacional Tierra del Fuego, TDF 435, 436, 442, 446
Parque Provincial Aconcagua, MZA 452, 477
Parque Provincial Dunícola Miguel Lillo, BA 112
Parque Provincial El Cochuna, TUC 584, 585, **587, 590**
Parque Provincial Ernesto Tornquist, BA 67, 76, 124
Parque Provincial Luro, LAP 238
Parque Provincial Talampaya, RJA 560, 568, 576, 582
Parque Provincial Volcán Tupungato, MZA 452
Parque Rivadavia, SJU
  See Quebrada de Zonda, SJU
Parque Yacampis, RJA 577
Paso Carrenleufú, CHU 375
Paso Coihue, NEU 349
Paso Copahué, NEU 286
Paso de Córdoba, NEU 348
Paso de Jama, JUJ 645, 663
Paso de la Laguna Sico, SAL 612, 641
Paso de la Patria, COR 695, 724, 733, **741**
  Map 742
Paso de las Nubes, RN 351
Paso de los Libres, COR **744**
  Map 745
Paso del Agua Negra, SJU 493, 507
Paso del Rey, SLU 525, 526
Paso El Infiernillo, CAT 556
Paso Garibaldi, TDF 440, 441
Paso Haytaquina, SAL 641
Paso Hua-Hum, NEU 309
Paso Huemules, SCR 419
Paso Infiernillo, TUC 585
Paso Mamuil Malal, NEU
  See Paso Tromen, NEU
Paso Puyehue, NEU 309, 346
Paso Río La Leona, SCR 411, 417

INDEX

Villa Mercedes, SLU
　See Mercedes, SLU
Villa Nougués, TUC 585, 602, **609**
Villa Ojo de Agua, SDE 699, 707, **718**
Villa Río Bermejito, CHA 688
Villa Rumipal, CBA **234**
Villa Sanagasta, RJA 576, 577, **581**
Villa Santa Rosa, SJU 493
Villa Traful, NEU **311**
Villa Tulumba, CBA 171, **235**
Villa Unión, RJA 560, 566, 568, **581**, 582
Villa 25 de Mayo, MZA 481, 485
Villa Ventana, BA 124
Villa Vieja, TUC 609
Villa Vil, CAT 531
Villaguay, ER **785**
Vilú Mallín, NEU 283
Vinchina, RJA **582**
Vis-Vis, CAT 531
Vista Flores, MZA 476, 489
Volcán, JUJ 662, 664
Volcán Copahue, NEU 277, 283, 286
Volcán Domuyo, NEU 275, 276, 292
Volcán Lanín, NEU 272, 290, 301, 308
Volcán Negro, CAT 543
Volcán Tromen, NEU 281
Volcán Villarica, NEU 286

W

Wanda, MIS 816

Y

Yacanto de Calamuchita, CBA **235**
Yacyretá Apipé, COR
　See Complejo Hidroeléctrico Yacyretá Apipé, COR
Yala, JUJ 661
Yapeyú, COR 725, 747, **749**
Yaví, JUJ 646, 653, **669**
Yerba Buena, CBA 204, 223
Yerba Buena, TUC 585, 590

Z

Zapala, NEU 274, 307, **312**
　Map 313
Zárate, BA **138**